Effective Management

a multimedia approach

5th edition

Chuck Williams

BUTLER UNIVERSITY

SOUTH-WESTERN
CENGAGE Learning™

Australia • Brazil • Japan • Korea • Mexico • Singapore • Spain • United Kingdom • United States

Effective Management: A Multimedia Approach, 5e

Chuck Williams

Vice President of Editorial, Business: Jack W. Calhoun

Editor-in-Chief: Melissa S. Acuña

Executive Editor: Scott Person

Developmental Editor: Jamie Bryant, B–Books

Sr. Editorial Assistant: Ruth Belanger

Marketing Manager: Jonathan Monahan

Sr. Content Project Manager: Tamborah Moore

Media Editor: Danny Bolan

Sr. Marketing Communications Manager: Jim Overly

Sr. Print Buyer: Miranda Klapper

Production Service: S4Carlisle Publishing Services

Compositor: S4Carlisle Publishing Services

Sr. Art Director: Tippy McIntosh

Cover and Internal Designer: Ke Design; Mason, OH

Cover Image: © Heidi Kristensen, iStock

Rights Acquisitions Specialist, Text: Mardell Glinski Schultz

Text Permissions Researcher: Elaine Kosta

Rights Acquisitions Specialist, Images: Deanna Ettinger

Image Research: Scott Rosen, Bill Smith Group

Library of Congress Control Number: 2010940543

ISBN-13: 978-1-111-62695-5
ISBN-10: 1-111-52695-8

South-Western
5191 Natorp Boulevard
Mason, OH 45040
USA

Cengage Learning products are represented in Canada by Nelson Education, Ltd.

For your course and learning solutions, visit **www.cengage.com**

Purchase any of our products at your local college store or at our preferred online store **www.CengageBrain.com**

Printed in Canada
1 2 3 4 5 6 7 14 13 12 11 10

Brief Contents

Contents

Part Five Controlling 465

Preface

Different Minds Learn in Different Ways

Everyone approaches learning differently. Some learn best listening to lectures, while others learn best reading and summarizing course material on their own. Others struggle unless concepts and ideas are visually illustrated in charts, models, or graphs, while others need firsthand experience to gain understanding. Of course, many of us learn best when we combine these approaches.

In most introductory courses with most introductory textbooks, however, student learning boils down to one approach: (1) read the textbook, (2) take class notes during lecture, (3) participate in a bit of class discussion, (4) do a few assignments, and then (5) "cram" the night before each exam. Because nearly all introductory courses and nearly all introductory textbooks use this approach, students who adapt to this approach to learning tend to do well in all of their introductory courses. Yet, a surprisingly large percentage of college students struggle when using this "standard" approach. Consequently, many students work very hard in their introductory courses, but don't do very well. (Ask around. You'll be surprised by the number of students who have much higher grades in upper-level courses.) If the *Fifth Edition* of *Effective Management: A Multimedia Approach* is viewed as just another "introductory textbook," with just one approach to learning, think again. Instead of asking students to adapt their learning styles to one way of learning, *Effective Management: A Multimedia Approach* provides a variety of different learning tools to let students create and combine learning methods uniquely suited to the way in which they learn—and not the other way around. By integrating a unique organizing system in each chapter (see the following Chapter Outline, Learning Objectives and Numbering System, and Section Reviews) with the most extensive multimedia learning package available, we've put together a complete teaching and learning system designed to educate students with all kinds of learning needs in all types of classroom situations. The system is flexible enough to be used in traditional classes, in completely online classes, in combinations of those two, or in independent study. In short, the *Fifth Edition* of *Effective Management: A Multimedia Approach* taps into multiple technologies (text, graphics, video, audio, and animation) to teach management to students with all kinds of learning styles.

Using Your Book

With today's busy schedules, very few students have the opportunity to read a chapter from beginning to end in one sitting. Because of their schedules and cognitive styles, today's students take anywhere from two to five study sessions to read a chapter completely. Accordingly, a chapter outline and numbering system, learning objectives, and section reviews are used to break chapters into small, self-contained sections that can be studied separately over multiple study sessions.

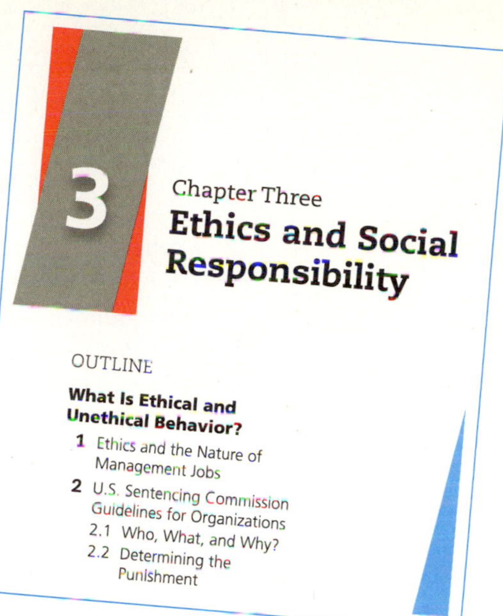

3
Chapter Three
Ethics and Social Responsibility
OUTLINE
What Is Ethical and Unethical Behavior?
1 Ethics and the Nature of Management Jobs
2 U.S. Sentencing Commission Guidelines for Organizations
2.1 Who, What, and Why?
2.2 Determining the Punishment

Chapter Outline

Each chapter begins with a detailed chapter outline in which each major part in the chapter is broken out into numbered sections and subsections. For example, the outline for the first part of Chapter 3, on Ethics and Social Responsibility, looks like this:

3 Influences on Ethical Decision Making

Although some ethical issues are easily solved, many do not have clearly right or wrong answers. So, what did IBM decide to do? Since Richard Addessi had not completed 30 full years with the company, IBM officials felt they had no choice but to give Joan Addessi and her two daughters the smaller, partial retirement benefits. Do you think IBM's decision was ethical? Probably many of you don't. You wonder how the company could be so heartless as to deny Richard Addessi's family the full benefits to which you believe they were entitled. Yet others might argue that IBM did the ethical thing by strictly following the rules laid out in its pension benefit plan. After all, being fair means applying the rules to everyone. Although the answers are rarely clear, managers do need to have a clear sense of how to arrive at an answer in order to manage this ethical ambiguity.

The ethical answers that managers choose depend on: 3.1 **the ethical intensity of the decision**, and: 3.2 **the moral development of the manager**.

3.1 Ethical Intensity of the Decision

Managers don't treat all ethical decisions the same. The manager who has to decide whether to deny or extend full benefits to Joan Addessi and her family is going to

Learning Objectives and Numbering System

The numbered information contained in the chapter outline is then repeated in the chapter as learning objectives (at the beginning of major parts of the chapter) and as numbered headings and subheadings (throughout the chapter) to help students remember precisely where they are in terms of the chapter outline.

Section Reviews

Finally, instead of a big summary at the end of the chapter, students will find a detailed review at the end of each section. Together, the chapter outline, numbering system, learning objectives, section headings (which mark the beginning of a section), and section reviews (which mark the end of a section) allow students to break the chapter into small, self-contained sections that can be read in their entirety over multiple study sessions. This format not only makes it easier for busy students to effectively spread their studying across multiple days and times, but it also adapts textbook learning to evolving student learning styles and preferences.

Finally, all student resources and instructor resources are organized by section and subsection so that students and instructors always know where they are and what they're reviewing.

.ussc.gov/training/corpover.PDF and "Sentencing Guidelines Educational Materials" at ***http://www.ussc.gov/training/educat.htm***.

REVIEW 2

U.S. Sentencing Commission Guidelines

Under the U.S. Sentencing Commission Guidelines, companies can be prosecuted and fined up to $300 million for employees' illegal actions. Fines are computed by multiplying the base fine by a culpability score, which ranges from 0.05 to 4.0. Companies that establish compliance programs to encourage ethical behavior can reduce their culpability scores and their fines. Companies without compliance programs can face much heavier fines than companies with established programs. Compliance programs must establish standards and procedures, be run by top managers, encourage hiring and promotion of honest and ethical people, encourage employees to report violations, educate employees about compliance, punish violators, and find ways to improve the program after violations occur.

Using the Student Learning Resources That Come with Your Book

To give students access to a wide variety of learning opportunities, this book is supported by an exciting set of multimedia materials on CourseMate (login .cengagebrain.com).

At CourseMate, there are materials to help you learn by reading (text), by seeing (graphics), and by doing (learning modules and self-testing). There are materials to help you learn through audio, video, and combinations of the two. The opening pages of each chapter list the key multimedia learning resources that are available with *Effective Management, 5e*. But that's not all there is. At CourseMate, you'll find study tools from PowerPoint to Podcasts.

Nearly all students quiz themselves over course material when preparing for exams. The "Self-Test" area of CourseMate allows them to do this over and over. The "Self-Test" area of Course Mate contains a short quiz comprised of true/false and multiple-choice questions and feedback covering all sections of the chapter and "Exhibit Worksheets" that allow students to test their knowledge by filling in the blank diagrams and then checking their work against the actual exhibits in the text.

Since many of today's students are used to receiving information in bullet-style lists, PowerPoint slides that list the key points of each chapter are available at CourseMate. Students can use these PowerPoint slides as a prelude to a study session, as a starting point for taking notes in class, or for creating study lists for exams and quizzes.

At CourseMate you'll also find the Pod Nod, our audio study guide in MP3 format that is similar to a condensed audio book and organized by chapter. Each chapter starts with a short lecture covering the chapter material.

For visual learners, *Effective Management* offers three kinds of videos for students to review, "Biz Flix" and "Management Workplace." "Biz Flix" videos present students with scenes from well-known feature films, such as *Friday Night Lights*, *In Bruges*, *Inside Man*, and *Failure to Launch*. Short clips from these and other films provide real-world examples of the management concepts students are learning. For example, in the clip from *Friday Night Lights*, we learn the importance of goal setting by listening to a stirring halftime speech from Coach Gary Gaines (Billy Bob Thornton), as he explains to his team what it means to be perfect. "Management Workplace" videos put management concepts in their business context. These longer segments provide a more detailed look into companies like Numi Organic Tea, Scholfield Honda, and Flight 001.

Billy Bob Thorton in *Friday Night Lights*

Amanda Shank of Flight 001

Putting It All Together

To help you see the full range of materials available in CourseMate, we have put together the following grid.

Effective Management	Chapter 1	Chapter 2	Chapter 3	Chapter 4
Self-Test	10 quiz questions, and 5 exhibit worksheets, and PowerPoints for quick review.	10 quiz questions, 3 exhibit worksheets, and PowerPoints for quick review.	10 quiz questions, 6 exhibit worksheets, and PowerPoints for quick review.	10 quiz questions, 4 exhibit worksheets, and PowerPoints for quick review.
PowerPoint	17 slides with graphics provide an outline for this chapter.	26 slides with graphics provide an outline for this chapter.	20 slides with graphics provide an outline for this chapter.	17 slides with graphics provide an outline for this chapter.
Pod Nod	Mini lecture reviews all the learning points in the chapter.	Mini lecture reviews all the learning points in the chapter.	Mini lecture reviews all the learning points in the chapter.	Mini lecture reviews all the learning points in the chapter.
Reel to Real Video	Management Workplace is a segment on Numi Organic Tea. Biz Flix is a scene from *In Good Company.*	Management Workplace is a segment on Preserve. Biz Flix is a scene from *Charlie Wilson's War.*	Management Workplace is a segment on City of Greensburg, Kansas. Biz Flix is a scene from *Emperor's Club.*	Management Workplace is a segment on Flight 001. Biz Flix is a scene from *Inside Man.*

Effective Management	Chapter 5	Chapter 6	Chapter 7	Chapter 8
Self-Test	10 quiz questions, 8 exhibit worksheets, and PowerPoints for quick review.	10 quiz questions, 6 exhibit worksheets, and PowerPoints for quick review.	10 quiz questions and PowerPoints for quick review.	10 quiz questions, 3 exhibit worksheets, and PowerPoints for quick review.
PowerPoint	20 slides with graphics provide an outline for this chapter.	22 slides with graphics provide an outline for this chapter.	21 slides with graphics provide an outline for this chapter.	28 slides with graphics provide an outline for this chapter.
Pod Nod	Mini lecture reviews all the learning points in the chapter.	Mini lecture reviews all the learning points in the chapter.	Mini lecture reviews all the learning points in the chapter.	Mini lecture reviews all the learning points in the chapter.
Reel to Real Video	Management Workplace is a segment on Numi Organic Tea. Biz Flix is a scene from *Field of Dreams.*	Management Workplace is a segment on Scholfield Honda. Biz Flix is a scene from *Field of Dreams.*	Management Workplace is a segment on Evo. Biz Flix is a scene from *Lost in Translation.*	Management Workplace is a segment on Evo. Biz Flix is a scene from *Rendition.*

Effective Management	Chapter 9	Chapter 10	Chapter 11	Chapter 12
Self-Test	10 quiz questions, 6 exhibit worksheets, and PowerPoints for quick review.	10 quiz questions, 5 exhibit worksheets, and PowerPoints for quick review.	10 quiz questions, 11 exhibit worksheets, and PowerPoints for quick review.	10 quiz questions, 6 exhibit worksheets, and PowerPoints for quick review.
PowerPoint	20 slides with graphics provide an outline for this chapter.	30 slides with graphics provide an outline for this chapter.	25 slides with graphics provide an outline for this chapter.	23 slides with graphics provide an outline for this chapter.
Pod Nod	Mini lecture reviews all the learning points in the chapter.	Mini lecture reviews all the learning points in the chapter.	Mini lecture reviews all the learning points in the chapter.	Mini lecture reviews all the learning points in the chapter.
Reel to Real Video	Management Workplace is a segment on Greensburg, Kansas. Biz Flix is a scene from *Failure to Launch*.	Management Workplace is a segment on The Maine Media Workshops. Biz Flix is a scene from *Played*.	Management Workplace is a segment on Flight 001. Biz Flix is a scene from *Friday Night Lights*.	Management Workplace is a segment on Greensburg, Kansas. Biz Flix is a scene from *Doomsday*.

Effective Management	Chapter 13	Chapter 14	Chapter 15	Chapter 16
Self-Test	10 quiz questions, 5 exhibit worksheets, and PowerPoints for quick review.	10 quiz questions, 5 exhibit worksheets, and PowerPoints for quick review.	10 quiz questions, 2 exhibit worksheets, and PowerPoints for quick review.	10 quiz questions, 3 exhibit worksheets, and PowerPoints for quick review.
PowerPoint	27 slides with graphics provide an outline for this chapter.	18 slides with graphics provide an outline for this chapter.	13 slides with graphics provide an outline for this chapter.	20 slides with graphics provide an outline for this chapter.
Pod Nod	Mini lecture reviews all the learning points in the chapter.	Mini lecture reviews all the learning points in the chapter.	Mini lecture reviews all the learning points in the chapter.	Mini lecture reviews all the learning points in the chapter.
Reel to Real Video	Management Workplace is a segment on Greensburg, Kansas. Biz Flix is a scene from *Friday Night Lights*.	Management Workplace is a segment on Numi Organic Tea. Biz Flix is a scene from *Friday Night Lights*.	Management Workplace is a segment on Numi Organic Tea. Biz Flix is a scene from *The Good Shepherd*.	Management Workplace is a segment on Preserve. Biz Flix is a scene from *In Bruges*.

Text Features

Engaging Style

Chuck's compelling writing style conveys his passion for both management and teaching. The combination of theories and current stories helps students actually relate to how text topics play out in business settings.

What Would You Do?

Chapter-opening "What Would You Do?" cases create an opportunity for students to confront the real issues that managers face before deciding on a course of action, handling a particular problem, or changing the direction of the company. Students are called upon to put themselves in the situation of the managers at companies like Caterpillar, Subaru, General Electric, Cisco, Burgerville, and Novartis.

What Really Works?

Some studies show that two drinks a day increase life expectancy by decreasing your chances of having a heart attack. Other studies show that two drinks a day decrease your life expectancy. The results of both sets of studies are presented in very definitive terms, so the conflicting information confuses and frustrates ordinary people who just want to "eat right" and "live right." Managers also have trouble figuring out what works, based on the scientific research published in scholarly business journals. But thankfully, a research tool called meta-analysis, which is a study of studies, is helping management scholars understand how well their research supports management theories. The "What Really Works?" features in *Effective Management, Fifth Edition*, present the results of various meta-analyses using an easy-to-understand statistic called the probability of success. Concrete study results presented in an accessible format give students the best estimate of what really works in the business world.

Doing the Right Thing

Because managers set the standard for others in the workplace, unethical behavior and practices quickly spread when they don't do the right thing. The *Fifth Edition* contains practical, useful advice to help you become a more ethical manager or businessperson by "Doing the Right Thing." A range of topics is explored throughout the book.

Management Facts and Trends

Management is happening every day in every company. One way to prepare for a career as a manager is by being aware of management trends today. To help students look forward to what might be happening in management tomorrow, there are short boxes titled "Management Facts" and "Management Trends" that give students a short, memorable insight into the direction management is headed.

Management Decision

These end-of-chapter assignments are tightly written and focus on a single management situation. Students must decide what to do and then answer several questions to explain their choices.

Management Team Decision

From sports to school to work to civic involvement, working in teams is increasingly part of our experience. "Management Team Decision" exercises have been designed to give students the opportunity to work as management teams to solve various workplace dilemmas.

Practice Being a Manager

These experiential exercises that give students the opportunity to role play management scenarios, discuss management dilemmas, and resolve management problems. Most are designed to be started and completed during the class session.

Self-Assessments

Self-assessments give students insights into their attitudes, beliefs, and tendencies that relate to management issues. Each PowerPoint chapter contains a special slide with an embedded spreadsheet to facilitate use of the assessments in the classroom using a simple show of hands. The slide automatically generates a distribution, which students enjoy seeing.

Reel to Real Video

The textual component to the "Biz Flix" and "Management Workplace" videos prepares students for viewing. By directing students' attention to certain chapter topics before they watch the clip or segment, students are better able to connect what they are seeing with the management concepts they have been learning.

Instructor Resources

Instructor Resource CD-ROM

Key instructor ancillaries (Instructor Manual, Test Bank, and PowerPoint) are provided on an Instructor Resource CD-ROM. The Instructor Manual is organized to get you going quickly and to minimize the time you need to prepare a superior course. Suggested plans for covering the chapter using lecture, group work, and video are included, along with a brief chapter outline, and teaching tips and solutions for all chapter assignments.

The Test Bank for *Effective Management, 5e,* is comprised of true/false, multiple-choice, scenario, short answer, and essay questions that have been reviewed by management faculty. The Test Bank contains over 2,400 questions, all of which have been tagged using AACSB categories to help collect and manage the data required for accreditation.

A comprehensive set of PowerPoint™ slides has been created for each chapter. For instructors wishing to integrate various media, we have also created a set of video PowerPoint™ in which the "Biz Flix" videos are embedded in appropriate slides.

Video

Both the "Biz Flix" and "Management Workplace" videos are available online and on DVD. CDs containing the video clips can be made on demand using the online digitized files. The Instructor Manual includes detailed teaching notes so that you can incorporate video into your class in a meaningful way.

The Business and Company Resource Center

The Business & Company Resource Center (BCRC) is a premier online business research tool that allows you to seamlessly search thousands of periodicals, journals, references, financial information, industry reports, company histories, and much more. The BCRC is a powerful and time-saving research tool for students and a wonderful tool instructors can use for building online coursepack and assigning readings and research projects. Visit *http://bcrc.swlearning.com* to learn more about how this powerful electronic tool integrates a diverse collection of resources to reflect the natural research process and contact your local representative to learn how to include the Business & Company Resource Center with your text.

ExamView

A computerized version of the Test Bank is available on your Instructor Resource CD-ROM and by special request. ExamView allows you to add or edit questions, instructions, and answers. You can create, edit, store, print, and otherwise customize all your quizzes, tests, and exams. The system is menu-driven, making it quick and easy to use.

Acknowledgments

Let's face it, writing a textbook is a long and lonely process. It's surely the most difficult (and rewarding) project I've ever tackled. And, as I sat in front of my computer with a rough outline on the left side of my desk, a two-foot stack of journal articles on the floor, and a blank screen in front of me, it was easy at times to feel isolated. But, as I found out, a book like this doesn't get done without the help of many other talented people. First, I'd like to thank the outstanding team of supplement authors: Colin Grover and John Choi (B-books Ltd.) for the superb PowerPoint slides; Joseph Champoux (University of New Mexico), for creating the engaging Biz Flix feature. I'd like to thank the world-class team at Cengage for the outstanding support (and patience) they provided while I wrote this book; Scott Person, who heads the Management group at Cengage, was calm, collected, and continuously positive through the major ups and downs of this project; and Tamborah Moore, who managed the production process, was consistently upbeat and positive with me when I deserved otherwise. Authors are prone to complain about their publishers. But that hasn't been my experience at all. Pure and simple, everyone at Cengage has been great to work with throughout the entire project. However, special thanks goes to Jamie Gleich Bryant and her team at B-books, Ltd., who maintained the high-quality standards that were set when I began writing. Their enthusiasm, professionalism, commitment, and attention to detail made me a better writer, made this a better book, and made me appreciate my good fortune to work with such an outstanding talent. Thanks, B-books, and here's to many more editions. I'd also like to thank the outstanding set of reviewers whose diligent and thoughtful comments helped shape previous editions and whose rigorous feedback improved the *Fifth Edition*.

Ali Abu-Rahma
United States International University
William Acar
Kent State University
David C. Adams
Manhattanville College
Bruce R. Barringer
University of Central Florida
Gayle Baugh
University of West Florida
James Bell
University of Texas, Austin
Greg Blundel
Kent State University, Stark
Katharine A. Bohley
University of Indianapolis
Santanu Borah
University of North Alabama
Angela Boston
University of Texas, Arlington
Michael Boyd
Owensboro Community College
Jon L. Bryan
Bridgewater State College
Victoria Mullennex
Davis & Elkins College
John J. Nader
Grand Valley State University
Charlie Nagelschmidt
Champlain College
Patrick J. Nedry
Monroe County Community College

Stephanie Newport
Austin Peay State University
Don A. Okhomina
Alcorn State University
James S. O'Rourke, IV
University of Notre Dame
Rhonda S. Palladi
Georgia State University
Lynne Patten
Clark Atlanta University
Jane Pettinger
Minnesota State University, Moorhead
Clifton Petty
Drury University
John Poirier
Bryant University
David M. Porter, Jr.
UCLA
Michael Provitera
Barry University
Abe Qastin
Lakeland College
Robert Raspberry
Southern Methodist University
Kim Rocha
Barton College
Linda Ross
Cleveland Community College
Carol Rowey
Community College of Rhode Island
Amit Shah
Frostburg State University

Thomas Shaughnessy
Illinois Central College
Penni F. Sikkila
Baker College
Michelle Slagle
University of South Alabama
James Smas
Kent State University
James O. Smith
East Carolina University
Charlotte Nix Speegle
Cisco Junior College
Gregory K. Stephens
Texas Christian University
John Striebich
Monroe Community College
Joseph Tagliaferre
Pennsylvania State University
Jennie Carter Thomas
Belmont University
Neal Thomson
Columbus State University
James Thornton
Champlain College
Mary Jo Vaughan
Mercer University
Michael Wakefield
Colorado State University, Pueblo
James Whelan
Manhattan College
Joann White
Jackson State University
Xiang Yi
Western Illinois University

Finally, my family deserves the greatest thanks of all for their love, patience, and support. Writing a textbook is an enormous project with incredible stresses and pressures on authors as well as their loved ones. However, throughout this project, my wife, Jenny, was unwavering in her support of my writing. She listened patiently, encouraged me when I was discouraged, read and commented on most of what I wrote, gave me the time to write, and took wonderful care of me and our children during this long process. My children, Benjamin, Rebecca, and Zack, also deserve special thanks for their patience and for understanding why Dad was locked away at the computer for all of this time. While writing this book has been the most rewarding professional experience of my career, it pleases me to no end that my family is as excited as I am that it's done. So, to Jenny, Benjamin, Rebecca, and Zack. The book is done. Let's play.

About the Author

Chuck Williams is Dean of the College of Business at Butler University. He received his B.A. in Psychology from Valparaiso University, and specialized in the areas of Organizational Behavior, Human Resources, and Strategic Management while earning his M.B.A and Ph.D. in Business Administration from Michigan State University. Previously, he taught at Michigan State University and was on the faculty of Oklahoma State University and Texas Christian University, where he also served as Associate Dean of the Neeley School of Business and Chair of the Management Department. He was also Dean of the Eberhardt School of Business at the University of the Pacific. His research interests include employee recruitment and turnover, performance appraisal, and employee training and goal-setting. Chuck has published research in the *Journal of Applied Psychology*, the *Academy of Management Journal, Human Resource Management Review, Personnel Psychology*, and the *Organizational Research Methods Journal*. He was a member of the *Journal of Management*'s Editorial Board, and serves as a reviewer for numerous other academic journals. He was also the webmaster for the Research Methods Division of the Academy of Management. Chuck is also a corecipient of the Society for Human Resource Management's Yoder-Heneman Research Award. Chuck has consulted for a number of organizations: General Motors, IBM, JCPenney, Tandy Corporation, Trism Trucking, Central Bank and Trust, StuartBacon, the City of Fort Worth, the American Cancer Society, and others. He has taught in executive development programs at Oklahoma State University, The University of Oklahoma, Texas Christian University, and the University of the Pacific. Chuck teaches a number of different courses, but has been privileged to teach his favorite course, Introduction to Management, for nearly 25 years. His teaching philosophy is based on four principles: (1) courses should be engaging and interesting; (2) there's nothing as practical as a good theory; (3) students learn by doing; and (4) students learn when they are challenged. Chuck has won teaching awards at several universities at the department, business school, and university levels.

Part One
Introduction to Management

Chapter 1 begins by defining management and discussing the functions of management. We look at what managers do, what it takes to be a manager, what companies look for in their managers, the most serious mistakes managers make, and what it is like to make the tough transition from being a worker to being a manager.

Chapter One
Management

Chapter 2 examines the internal and external forces that affect business, including how those forces affect the decisions and performance of a company. We cover the general environment that affects all organizations and the specific environment unique to each company.

Chapter Two
Organizational Environments and Cultures

Chapter 3 examines ethical behavior in the workplace and explains how unethical behavior can expose a business to legal penalties. You'll read about the influences on ethical decision making and learn the practical steps that managers can take to improve ethical decision making.

Chapter Three
Ethics and Social Responsibility

1 Chapter One
Management

OUTLINE

Experience Management

Experiencing Management begins in Chapter 3, after you have been introduced to the basic concepts that underpin management theories.

© ISTOCKPHOTO.COM/ ANN MARIE KURTZ

Pod Nod

Mini lecture reviews all the learning points in the chapter.

© ISTOCKPHOTO.COM/ MAGNET CREATIVE

Reel to Real Video

Biz Flix is a scene from *In Good Company*. Management Workplace is a segment on Numi Organic Tea.

© ISTOCKPHOTO.COM/ CRAFTVISION

Self Test

10 quiz questions, 5 exhibit worksheets, and PowerPoints for quick review.

© ISTOCKPHOTO.COM/ DIJITAL FILM

What Would You Do?

Starbucks Headquarters, Seattle, Washington[1]

Twenty years ago, if you had said, "Give me a venti, vanilla, nonfat latte, no room, three Splendas," people would have thought you were speaking a foreign language. And you would have been because Starbucks was just getting started. It began with 4 stores in Seattle in 1987, and today there are over 17,000 stores in 40 different countries. That means *STARBUCKS* has opened an average of 8 new stores per day! Unfortunately, with profits now a thing of the past, Starbucks has closed 800 stores and laid off 25,000 workers.

Starbucks clearly overexpanded, providing fodder for late-night TV comedians who have cracked jokes about Starbucks opening new stores inside existing stores. Customer Leslie Miller said, "Starbucks was stupid. They put them right next to each other." Because managers focused on opening new stores for new customers, they paid less attention to existing stores where same-store sales dropped by 3 percent. While that doesn't seem like much, Starbucks has to lose only six to eight customers per store per day to see a 1 percent drop in a store's sales. In other words, small changes in customer buying habits make a big difference in Starbucks' growth and profitability.

Consumers are stretching their dollars, which means Starbucks is fighting the perception—some would say reality—that Starbucks is a luxury. McDonald's coffee is undoubtedly cheaper, but Starbucks points out that half of its coffee drinks are less than $3, while one-third are less than $2. Moreover, Starbucks coffee is actually less expensive than Dunkin' Donuts coffee after adjusting for the small serving sizes at Dunkin' Donuts. Most consumers, however, don't see it that way. Graduate student Amy Osbourne has cut her monthly Starbucks budget from $60 to $30. Said Osbourne, "I haven't been going as often. I've been making my tea at home."

When Starbucks' board of directors fired CEO James Donald, it asked founder Howard Schultz to take charge again. Even though he had stepped down as CEO to become the board's chair in 2000, he stayed involved in such operational details as deciding the color of holiday cups. Schultz has always been a detail-oriented, hands-on boss, a perfectionist who demands a lot of last-minute changes. When Starbucks launched its new Pike Place Roast coffee, he selected the logo and then had it redesigned right before going to market. He even rewrote the press release. Schultz is revered at Starbucks and workers sometimes applaud when he enters meeting rooms or stores. He is such a legend within the company that "What will Howard think?" drives nearly all decisions. Not surprisingly, that creates a tremendous amount of anxiety among managers and employees. Schultz recognizes that this isn't a good thing. Said Schulz, "It's not healthy for the organization if everyone's waiting for me to tell them what to do." Still, Stanley Hainsworth, who was a vice president under Schultz, would have to tell people, "You're not meeting with the king." Said Hainsworth, "A lot of people were nervous, so if Howard asked them what they thought, they would tell him what he wanted to hear."

Schultz's return has unfortunately not yet produced a turnaround in sales or profits. Shultz, who is feeling the pressure, told employees, "We have to defend our position; we have lots of companies small and large who want to take a piece of our business away." So, what does Starbucks need to do to return to growth and profitability? Should it lower prices? Should it expand its menu? What should be its strategy? As founder, Schultz brought enormous success to Starbucks. But is he the right leader for Starbucks now? Should he continue as CEO? Is he meeting his basic responsibilities as Starbucks' top manager? What key mistakes is he making? Finally, how should Starbucks counter its new competition, McDonald's and Dunkin' Donuts?

If you were the CEO of Starbuc[ks] what would you do?

The management issues facing Starbucks are fundamental to any organization: What's our plan? What are top management's key responsibilities? How can we best position the company against key competitors? How can we get things done and put in place controls to make sure plans are followed and goals are met? Good management is basic to starting a business, growing a business, and maintaining a business once it has achieved some measure of success.

We begin this chapter by defining management and discussing the functions of management. Next, we look at what managers do by examining the four kinds of managers and reviewing the various roles that managers play. Then we investigate what it takes to be a manager by reviewing management skills, what companies look for in their managers, the most serious mistakes managers make, and what it is like to make the tough transition from being a worker to being a manager. We finish this chapter by examining the competitive advantage that companies gain from good management. In other words, we learn how to establish a competitive advantage through people.

What Is Management?

To understand how important *good* management is, think about mistakes like these: Mistake #1. A high-level bank manager reduces a marketing manager to tears by angrily criticizing her in front of others for a mistake that wasn't hers.[2] Mistake #2.

Guidant Corporation waited for 3 years, forty-five device failures, and two patient deaths before recalling 50,000 defective heart defibrillators.[3] Is it any wonder that companies pay management consultants nearly $240 billion a year for advice on basic management issues such as how to lead people effectively, organize the company efficiently, and manage large-scale projects and processes?[4] This textbook will help you understand some of the basic issues that management consultants help companies resolve. (And it won't cost you billions of dollars.)

After reading the next two sections, you should be able to:

1 describe what management is.

2 explain the four functions of management.

1 Management Is . . .

Many of today's managers got their start welding on the factory floor, clearing dishes off tables, helping customers fit a suit, or wiping up a spill in aisle 3. Similarly, lots of you will start at the bottom and work your way up. There's no better way to get to know your competition, your customers, and your business. But whether you begin your career at the entry level or as a supervisor, your job as a manager is not to do the work but to help others do theirs. **Management** is getting work done through others. Pat Carrigan, a former elementary school principal who became a manager at a General Motors plant, says, "I've never made a part in my life, and I don't really have any plans to make one. That's not my job. My job is to create an environment where people who do make them can make them right, can make them right the first time, can make them at a competitive cost, and can do so with some sense of responsibility and pride in what they're doing. I don't have to know how to make a part to do any of those things."[5]

Pat Carrigan's description of managerial responsibilities suggests that managers also have to be concerned with efficiency and effectiveness in the work process. **Efficiency** is getting work done with a minimum of effort, expense, or waste. For example, how do millions of Girl Scouts from over 200 councils across the United States sell and deliver millions of boxes of cookies each year? In other words, what makes Girl Scouts so efficient? The national organization, *GIRL SCOUTS OF AMERICA (GSA)*, licenses only two bakers, so when GSA changes or improves its cookie offerings by adding new flavors or making healthier, sugar-free options, it can do so quickly and consistently nationwide. GSA has also designed cookie packages to maximize the number of boxes that can fit in a delivery truck. The national organization optimizes its overall cookie inventory by tracking sales by type of cookie and troop. Because GSA operates efficiently, 2.9 million scouts can sell and deliver over 50 million cookies in an 8-week period.[6]

Efficiency alone, however, is not enough to ensure success. Managers must also strive for **effectiveness**, which is accomplishing tasks that help fulfill organizational objectives such as customer service and satisfaction.

REVIEW 1

Management is. . .

Good management is working through others to accomplish tasks that help fulfill organizational objectives as efficiently as possible.

management
getting work done through others

efficiency
getting work done with a minimum of effort, expense, or waste

effectiveness
accomplishing tasks that help fulfill organizational objectives

2 Management Functions

Henri Fayol, who was a managing director of a large steel company in the early 1900s, was one of the founders of the field of management. Based on his 20 years of experience, Fayol argued that "the success of an enterprise generally depends much more on the administrative ability of its leaders than on their technical ability."[7] Although Google CEO Eric Schmidt has extensive expertise and experience in computer technology, Google succeeds because of his capabilities as a manager and not because of his ability to write computer code.

According to Fayol, managers need to perform five managerial functions in order to be successful: planning, organizing, coordinating, commanding, and controlling.[8] Most management textbooks today have updated this list by dropping the coordinating function and referring to Fayol's commanding function as "leading." Fayol's management functions are thus known today in an updated form: planning, organizing, leading, and controlling. Studies indicate that managers who perform these management functions well are more successful, gaining promotions for themselves and profits for their companies. For example, the more time CEOs spend planning, the more profitable their companies are.[9] A 25-year study at AT&T found that employees with better planning and decision-making skills were more likely to be promoted into management jobs, to be successful as managers, and to be promoted into upper levels of management.[10]

The evidence is clear. Managers serve their companies well when they plan, organize, lead, and control. So we've organized this textbook based on these functions of management, as shown in Exhibit 1.1. The major sections within each chapter of this textbook are numbered using a single digit: 1, 2, 3, and so on. The subsections are consecutively numbered, beginning with the major section number. For example, "2.1" indicates the first subsection under the second major section. This numbering system should help you easily see the relationships among topics and follow the topic sequence. It will also help your instructor refer to specific topics during class discussion.

Now let's take a closer look at each of the management functions: 2.1 **planning**, 2.2 **organizing**, 2.3 **leading**, and 2.4 **controlling**.

EXHIBIT 1.1

Management Functions and Organization of the Textbook

2.1 Planning

Planning involves determining organizational goals and a means for achieving them. As you'll learn in Chapter 4, planning is one of the best ways to improve performance. It encourages people to work harder, to work hard for extended periods, to engage in behaviors directly related to goal accomplishment, and to think of better ways to do their jobs. But most importantly, companies that plan have larger profits and faster growth than companies that don't plan.

For example, the question "What business are we in?" is at the heart of strategic planning. You'll learn about this in Chapter 5. If you can answer the question "What business are you in?" in two sentences or less, chances are you have a very clear plan for your business. But getting a clear plan is not so easy. *eBAY* paid $2.6 million to acquire Skype, which makes software for free phone and video calls over the Internet. eBay is now considering selling Skype. Why? Because eBay's CEO realized it was a poor fit with its Internet auction site and its PayPal online payment service.[11] You'll learn more about planning in Chapter 4 on planning and decision making, Chapter 5 on organizational strategy, Chapter 6 on innovation and change, and Chapter 7 on global management.

2.2 Organizing

Organizing is deciding where decisions will be made, who will do what jobs and tasks, and who will work for whom in the company. On average, it costs more than $10 billion to bring a new pharmaceutical drug to market. So when *PFIZER*, the second-largest pharmaceutical firm in the world, acquired Wyeth, the eleventh largest, CEO Jeffrey Kindler decided to restructure Pfizer's research and development unit into two parts, one for small molecules or traditional pills and one for large molecules or drugs made from living cells. Kindler said, "Creating two distinct, but complementary, research organizations, led by the top scientist from each company, will provide sharper focus, less bureaucracy and clearer accountability in drug discovery."[12] In all, the new company will consist of nine businesses, including primary care, vaccines, oncology, consumer and nutritional products, and pharmaceuticals.

You'll learn more about organizing in Chapter 8 on designing organizations, Chapter 9 on managing teams, and Chapter 10 on managing human resources.

2.3 Leading

Our third management function, **leading**, involves inspiring and motivating workers to work hard to achieve organizational goals. When Anne Mulcahy became *XEROX*'s CEO, the company was on the brink of bankruptcy—it was $17.1 billion in debt and had only $154 million in cash. In addition, 3 years of steeply declining revenues and increasing losses had dropped the company's stock price from $64 a share to just $4.43. Mulcahy admitted that the responsibility of turning the company around frightened her: "Nothing spooked me as much as waking up in the middle of the night and thinking about 96,000 people and retirees and what would happen if this thing went south."[14] Still, she took the job.

Mulcahy, who traveled to two and sometimes three cities a day to talk to Xerox managers and employees, implored them to "save each dollar as if it were your own." And at each stop, she reminded them, "Remember, by my calculations, there are

planning
determining organizational goals and a means for achieving them

organizing
deciding where decisions will be made, who will do what jobs and tasks, and who will work for whom

leading
inspiring and motivating workers to work hard to achieve organizational goals

what *really* works

Meta-Analysis

Some studies show that having two drinks a day increases life expectancy by decreasing the chances of having a heart attack. Yet other studies show that having two drinks a day shortens life expectancy. For years, we've "buttered" our morning toast with margarine instead of butter because margarine was supposed to be better for our health. Now, however, studies show that the trans-fatty acids in margarine may be just as bad for our arteries as butter. Confusing scientific results like these frustrate ordinary people who want to eat right and live right. They also make many people question just how useful most scientific research really is.

Managers also find themselves questioning the conflicting scientific research published in journals like the *Academy of Management Journal,* the *Academy of Management Review,* the *Strategic Management Journal*, the *Journal of Applied Psychology*, and *Administrative Science Quarterly.* The *Wall Street Journal* may quote a management research article from one of these journals that says that total quality management is the best thing since sliced bread (without butter or margarine). Then, just 6 months later, the *Wall Street Journal* will quote a different article from the same journal that says that total quality management doesn't work. If management professors and researchers have trouble deciding what works and what doesn't, how can practicing managers know?

Thankfully, a research tool called **meta-analysis** is helping management scholars understand how well their research supports management theories. It is also useful for practicing managers because it shows what works and the conditions under which management techniques may work better or worse in the real world. Meta-analysis involves studying scientific studies themselves. It is based on a simple idea: If one study shows that a management technique doesn't work and another study shows that it does, an average of those results is probably the best estimate of how well that management practice works (or doesn't work). For example, medical researchers Richard Peto and Rory Collins averaged all of the different results from several hundred studies investigating the relationship between aspirin and heart attacks. Their analysis, based on more than 120,000 patients from numerous studies, showed that aspirin lowered the incidence of heart attacks by an average of 4 percent. Prior to this study, doctors prescribed aspirin as a preventive measure for only 38 percent of heart-attack victims. Today, because of the meta-analysis results, doctors prescribe aspirin for 72 percent of heart-attack victims.

Fortunately, you don't need a Ph.D. to understand the statistics reported in a meta-analysis. In fact, one primary advantage of meta-analysis over traditional significance tests is that you can convert meta-analysis statistics into intuitive numbers that anyone can easily understand. Each meta-analysis reported in the "What Really Works" sections of this textbook is accompanied by an easy-to-understand statistic called the *probability of success.* As its name suggests, the probability of success shows how often a management technique will work.

For example, meta-analyses suggest that the best predictor of a job applicant's on-the-job performance is a test of general mental ability. In other words, smarter people tend to be better workers. The average correlation (one of those often misunderstood statistics) between scores on general mental ability tests and job performance is .60. However, very few people understand what a correlation of .60 means. What most managers want to know is how often they will hire the right person if they choose job applicants based on general mental ability test scores. Likewise, they want to know how much difference a cognitive ability test makes when hiring new workers.

The probability of success may be high, but if the difference isn't really that large, is it worth a manager's time to have job applicants take a general mental ability test?

Well, our user-friendly statistics indicate that it's wise to have job applicants take a general mental ability test. In fact, the probability of success, shown in graphical form here, is 76 percent. This means that an employee hired on the basis of a good score on a general mental ability test stands a 76 percent chance of being a better performer than someone picked at random from the pool of all job applicants. So chances are you're going to be right much more often than wrong if you use a general mental ability test to make hiring decisions.[13]

In summary, each "What Really Works" section in this textbook is based on meta-analysis research, which provides the best scientific evidence that management professors and researchers have about what works and what doesn't work in management.

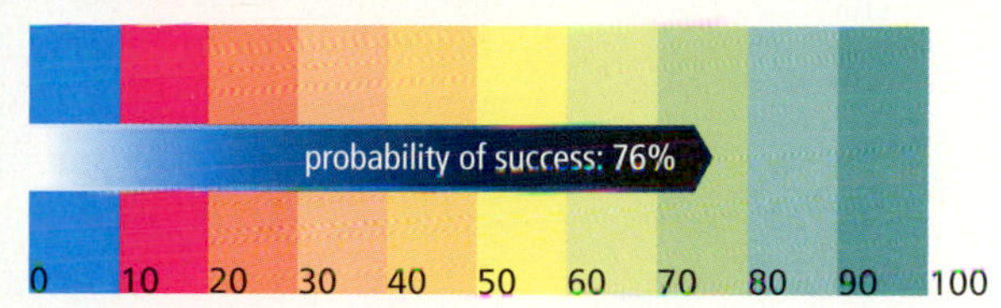

We will use the easy-to-understand index known as the *probability of success* to indicate how well a management idea or strategy is likely to work in the workplace. Of course, no idea or technique works every time and in every circumstance. Nevertheless, the management ideas and strategies discussed in the "What Really Works" sections can usually make a meaningful difference where you work. In today's competitive, fast-changing, global marketplace, few managers can afford to overlook proven management strategies like the ones discussed in "What Really Works."

[she fills in the number] selling days left in the quarter."[15] Mulcahy said, "One of the things I care most about at Xerox is the morale and motivation at the company. I think it is absolutely critical to being able to deliver results. People have to feel engaged, motivated and feel they are making a contribution to something that is important. I spend the vast majority of my time with customers and employees, and there is nothing more important for any of us to do as leaders than communicate and engage with our two most important constituencies."[16]

Today, as a result of Mulcahy's leadership and the hard work of dedicated Xerox employees, Xerox is profitable and a leading developer of color digital printing technologies.[17] Still, says Mulcahy, "The paranoia never goes away. There is a never ending journey here. You are never done. The next challenge is around the corner. You have to have an appetite for that. . . . I always find something to worry about at night."[18]

You'll learn more about leading in Chapter 11 on motivation, Chapter 12 on leadership, and Chapter 13 on managing communication.

2.4 Controlling

The last function of management, **controlling**, is monitoring progress toward goal achievement and taking corrective action when progress isn't being made. The basic control process involves setting standards to achieve goals, comparing actual performance to those standards, and then making changes to return performance to those standards. Needing to cut costs (the standard) to restore profitability (the goal), major airlines began paying *PRATT & WHITNEY* to power wash the grime

meta-analysis
a study of studies, a statistical approach that provides one of the best scientific estimates of how well management theories and practices work

controlling
monitoring progress toward goal achievement and taking corrective action when needed

from the inside of their jets' engines two to three times a year at a cost of $3,000 per wash. Why? Cleaner engines consume less fuel and can go 18 months longer before having to be rebuilt for regular maintenance—at a high cost. Johnny Holly, who manages engine maintenance and engineering for Southwest Airlines, says "A phenomenal amount of fuel can be saved doing this."[19]

You'll learn more about the control function in Chapter 14 on control, Chapter 15 on managing information, and Chapter 16 on managing service and manufacturing operations.

REVIEW 2

Management Functions

Henri Fayol's classic management functions are known today as planning, organizing, leading, and controlling. Planning is determining organizational goals and a means for achieving them. Organizing is deciding where decisions will be made, who will do what jobs and tasks, and who will work for whom. Leading is inspiring and motivating workers to work hard to achieve organizational goals. Controlling is monitoring progress toward goal achievement and taking corrective action when needed. Studies show that performing these management functions well leads to better managerial performance.

What Do Managers Do?

Not all managerial jobs are the same. The demands and requirements placed on the CEO of Sony are significantly different from those placed on the manager of your local Wendy's restaurant.

After reading the next two sections, you should be able to:

3 describe different kinds of managers.

4 explain the major roles and subroles that managers perform in their jobs.

3 Kinds of Managers

As shown in Exhibit 1.2, there are four kinds of managers, each with different jobs and responsibilities: 3.1 **top managers**, 3.2 **middle managers**, 3.3 **first-line managers**, and 3.4 **team leaders**.

3.1 Top Managers

Top managers hold positions like chief executive officer (CEO), chief operating officer (COO), chief financial officer (CFO), and chief information officer (CIO) and are responsible for the overall direction of the organization. Top managers have the following responsibilities.[20] First, they are responsible for creating a context for change. In fact, the CEOs of CitiGroup, Merrill Lynch, Home Depot, Starbucks, Motorola, and Jet Blue Airways were all fired precisely because they had not moved fast enough to bring about significant changes in their companies.[21] Thirty-five percent of all CEOs are eventually fired because of their inability to successfully change their companies.[22] Creating a context for change includes forming a long-range vision or mission for the company. As one CEO said, "The CEO has to think about the future more than anyone."[23] The second responsibility of top managers is to

top managers
executives responsible for the overall direction of the organization

EXHIBIT 1.2

Jobs and Responsibilities of Four Kinds of Managers

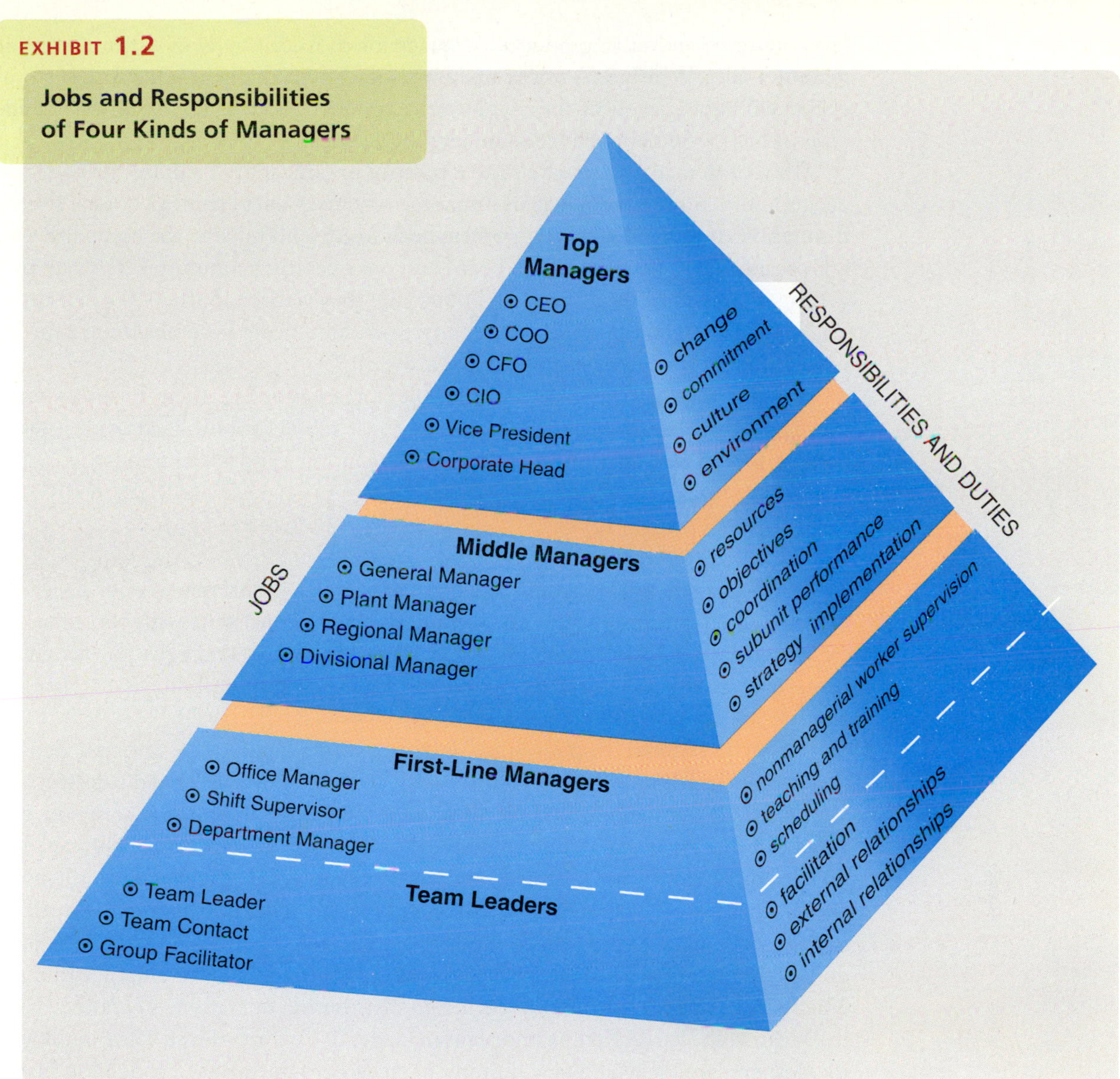

develop employees' commitment to and ownership of the company's performance. That is, top managers are responsible for creating employee buy-in. Trusting that his 61,000 employees could dramatically increase product innovation at Whirlpool, then CEO David Whitwam put $135 million directly into their hands and told them to come up with new ideas. He also encouraged them to go to their bosses with ideas. And if their bosses wouldn't listen, they were to bring their new product ideas directly to him. Employees flocked to an in-house website with a course on innovation and a list of all the new suggestions and ideas, racking up 300,000 hits on the site each month. Of the commitment displayed by his workers, Whitwam says, "I had never seen a strategy that was so energizing to so many people." Today, revenue from innovative products has quadrupled. And instead of cutting prices to maintain sales, Whirlpool's prices are now rising 5 percent per year because customers are willing to pay more for its innovative products, such as the Duet washer and dryer, which were designed based on employees' ideas.[24]

Third, top managers must create a positive organizational culture through language and action. Top managers impart company values, strategies, and lessons through what they do and say to others both inside and outside the company. One CEO said, "I write memos to the board and our operating committee. I'm sure they get the impression I dash them off, but usually they've been drafted 10 or 20 times. The bigger you get, the more your ability to communicate becomes important. So what I write, I write very carefully. I labor over it."[25]

Finally, top managers are responsible for monitoring their business environments. This means that top managers must closely monitor customer needs, competitors' moves, and long-term business, economic, and social trends.

3.2 Middle Managers

Middle managers hold positions like plant manager, regional manager, or divisional manager. They are responsible for setting objectives consistent with top management's goals and for planning and implementing subunit strategies for achieving those objectives.[26] One specific middle management responsibility is to plan and allocate resources to meet objectives.

A second major responsibility is to coordinate and link groups, departments, and divisions within a company. In February 2008, a tornado destroyed a *CATERPILLAR* plant in Oxford, Mississippi, the only plant in the company that produced a particular coupling required for many of Caterpillar's machines. The disaster threatened a worldwide production shutdown. Greg Folley, a middle manager in charge of the parts division that included the plant, gave workers 2 weeks to restore production to pretornado levels. He said, "I was betting on people to get it done." He contacted new vendors, sent engineers from other Caterpillar locations to Mississippi to check for quality, and set up distribution operations in another facility. Meanwhile, Kevin Kempa, the plant manager in Oxford, moved some employees to another plant, delivered new training to employees during the production hiatus, and oversaw reconstruction of the plant. The day before the 2-week deadline, the Oxford plant was up and running and produced 8,000 parts.[27]

A third responsibility of middle management is to monitor and manage the performance of the subunits and individual managers who report to them. Graeme Betts is the manager of the Southwest region for Lloyds Pharmacy in England. While Betts works with people at all levels, from health-care assistants to board directors, he spends most of his time with the nine area managers who report to him. In terms of monitoring and managing the performance of his area managers and, in turn, the store managers who report to them, Betts says, "We have 231 pharmacies, and as a [management] team our task is to ensure that our pharmacies are as good as they can be, and are offering a great service to our customers. To this end we are focused on providing an efficient [drug] dispensing service, and continually developing new professional services such as . . . smoking cessation and medicines-use reviews."[28] Finally, middle managers are also responsible for implementing the changes or strategies generated by top managers.

middle managers
responsible for setting objectives consistent with top management's goals and for planning and implementing subunit strategies for achieving these objectives

3.3 First-Line Managers

First-line managers hold positions like office manager, shift supervisor, or department manager. The primary responsibility of first-line managers is to manage the performance of entry-level employees who are directly responsible for producing a company's goods and services. Thus, first-line managers are the only managers who don't supervise other managers. The responsibilities of first-line managers include monitoring, teaching, and short-term planning.

First-line managers encourage, monitor, and reward the performance of their workers. For example, Jeff Dexheimer requires the waiters and waitresses he supervises at the upscale Melting Pot restaurant in St. Louis to memorize a complex menu and a 400-item wine list. To reduce turnover and keep his 65 employees motivated, Dexheimer gives out $25 nightly rewards for having the best attitude or for selling the most wine.[30]

Doing the Right Thing

Tell and Show People That Ethics Matter

Because managers set the standard for others in the workplace, unethical behavior and practices quickly spread when they don't do the right thing. One of the most important things managers can do is to tell people that ethics matter. When DuPont CEO Charles Holliday, Jr. was a young manager, he was told by DuPont's then-CEO Dick Heckert, "This company lives by the letter of its contracts and the intent of those contracts." Says Holliday, "I still remember the expression on his face when he said those words, and I've lived by that philosophy ever since." In today's business world, however, with one-third of workers reporting that they've seen their bosses lie, steal from the company, or break the law, talk clearly isn't enough. Holliday says, "Just saying you're ethical isn't very useful. You have to earn trust by what you do every day." So, tell the people whom you manage that ethics matter. Then, *show* them by doing the right thing yourself.[29]

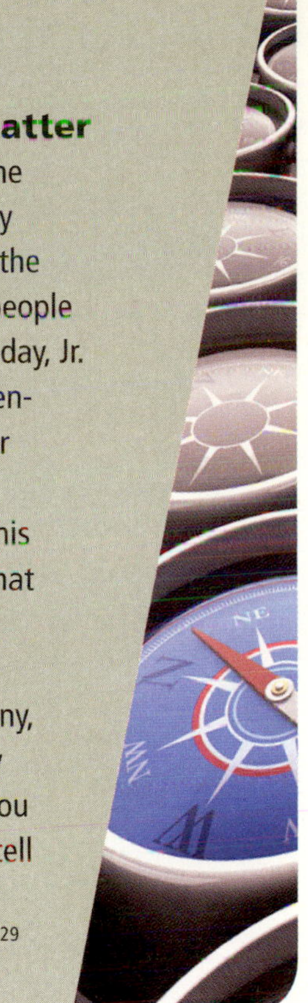

First-line managers also teach entry-level employees how to do their jobs. Damian Mogavero's company, *AVERO LLC*, helps restaurants analyze sales data for each member of the waitstaff. Restaurant managers who use these data, says Mogavero, will often take their top-selling server to lunch each week as a reward. The best managers, however, will also take their poorest-selling servers out to lunch to talk about what they can do to improve their performance.[31] Likewise, *COCA-COLA* manager Tom Mattia says, "I try to make every interaction I have with someone on my team a teaching experience. There are always specific work issues that need to get addressed, but then I try to explain my thinking behind an approach so people can get more experience."[32]

First-line managers also make detailed schedules and operating plans based on middle management's intermediate-range plans. In contrast to the long-term plans of top managers (3 to 5 years out) and the intermediate plans of middle managers (6 to 18 months out), first-line managers engage in plans and actions that typically produce results within 2 weeks.[33]

first-line managers train and supervise the performance of nonmanagerial employees who are directly responsible for producing the company's products or services

3.4 Team Leaders

The fourth kind of manager is a team leader. This relatively new kind of management job developed as companies shifted to self-managing teams, which, by definition, have no formal supervisor. In traditional management hierarchies, first-line managers are responsible for the performance of nonmanagerial employees and have the authority to hire and fire workers, make job assignments, and control resources. In this new structure, the teams themselves perform nearly all of the functions performed by first-line managers under traditional hierarchies.[34]

Team leaders have a different set of responsibilities than traditional first-line managers.[35] **Team leaders** are primarily responsible for facilitating team activities toward accomplishing a goal. This doesn't mean team leaders are responsible for team performance. They aren't. The team is. Team leaders help their team members plan and schedule work, learn to solve problems, and work effectively with each other, but the team members own the outcome. The leader is there to bring intellectual, emotional, and spiritual resources to the team. Through his or her actions, the leader should be able to show others how to think about the work that they're doing in the context of their lives.

Team leaders are responsible for fostering good relationships and addressing problematic ones within their teams. Relationships among team members are crucial to good team performance, and must be well managed. For example, studies show that it's not the surgeon but the interactions between the surgeon and all operating room team members that determine surgical outcomes. However, at 20 hospitals, 60 percent of the operating room team members—nurses, technicians, and other doctors—agreed with the statement, "In the ORs here, it is difficult to speak up if I perceive a problem with patient care."[36] And when operating room team members don't speak up, serious mistakes can occur no matter how talented the surgeon. Consequently, surgeons are using "safety pauses" to better involve members of their surgical teams. The surgeon will pause, ask if anyone has concerns or comments, and address them as needed. Studies show that safety pauses reduce mistakes, such as operating on the wrong leg or beginning surgery with key surgical instruments missing.[37]

Team leaders are also responsible for managing external relationships. Team leaders act as the bridge or liaison between their teams and other teams, departments, and divisions in a company. For example, if a member of Team A complains about the quality of Team B's work, Team A's leader is responsible for solving the problem by initiating a meeting with Team B's leader. Together, these team leaders are responsible for getting members of both teams to work together to solve the problem. If it's done right, the problem is solved without involving company management or blaming members of the other team.[38]

So the team leader's job involves a different set of skills than traditional management jobs typically do. For example, a Hewlett-Packard ad for a team leader position says, "Job seeker must enjoy coaching, working with people, and bringing about improvement through hands-off guidance and leadership."[39] Team leaders who fail to understand how their roles are different from those of traditional managers often struggle in their jobs. You will learn more about teams in Chapter 9.

team leaders
managers responsible for facilitating team activities toward goal accomplishment

REVIEW 3

Kinds of Managers

There are four different kinds of managers. Top managers are responsible for creating a context for change, developing attitudes of commitment and ownership, creating a positive organizational culture through words and actions, and monitoring their company's business environments. Middle managers are responsible for planning and allocating resources, coordinating and linking groups and departments, monitoring and managing the performance of subunits and managers, and implementing the changes or strategies generated by top managers. First-line managers are responsible for managing the performance of nonmanagerial employees, teaching employees how to do their jobs, and making detailed schedules and operating plans based on middle management's intermediate-range plans. Team leaders are responsible for facilitating team performance, managing external relationships, and facilitating internal team relationships.

Management Fact:

The study of management is just 125 years old, but management principles have been around for thousands of years. The pyramid of King Khufu, in Egypt, contains 2.3 million blocks of stone, each one carved to precise size and shape, transported by boat, and moved into a specific spot. It took 20,000 workers 23 years to complete the project, and more than 8,000 just to quarry and transport the stones. Coordinating the work of so many people for such a long time required precise planning, organizing, control, and consultation, the very same principles that are keys to effective management today.

4 Managerial Roles

Although all four types of managers engage in planning, organizing, leading, and controlling, if you were to follow them around during a typical day on the job, you would probably not use these terms to describe what they actually do. Rather, what you'd see are the various roles managers play. Professor Henry Mintzberg followed five American CEOs, shadowing each for a week and analyzing their mail, their conversations, and their actions. He concluded that managers fulfill three major roles while performing their jobs:[40]

- Interpersonal roles
- Informational roles.
- Decisional roles.

In other words, managers talk to people, gather and give information, and make decisions. Furthermore, as shown in Exhibit 1.3, these three major roles can be subdivided into ten subroles.

Let's examine each major role: 4.1 **interpersonal**, 4.2 **informational**, and 4.3 **decisional roles**—and **their ten subroles**.

4.1 Interpersonal Roles

More than anything else, management jobs are people-intensive. Estimates vary with the level of management, but most managers spend between two-thirds and four-fifths of their time in face-to-face communication with others.[41] If you're a loner, or if you consider dealing with people a pain, then you may not be cut out for management work. In fulfilling the interpersonal role of management, managers perform three subroles: figurehead, leader, and liaison.

EXHIBIT 1.3

Mintzberg's Managerial Roles and Subroles

Interpersonal Roles
- Figurehead
- Leader
- Liaison

Informational Roles
- Monitor
- Disseminator
- Spokesperson

Decisional Roles
- Entrepreneur
- Disturbance Handler
- Resource Allocator
- Negotiator

Source: Reprinted by permission of Harvard Business Review (an exhibit) from "The Manager's Job: Folklore and Fact," By Mintzberg, H. Harvard Business Review, July-August 1975. Copyright © by the President and Fellows of Harvard College. All rights reserved.

In the **figurehead role**, managers perform ceremonial duties like greeting company visitors, speaking at the opening of a new facility, or representing the company at a community luncheon to support local charities. When Wichita-based *CESSNA*, the largest manufacturer of general aviation planes in the world, opened a new 101,000-square-foot jet service facility in Mesa, Arizona, CEO Jack Pelton flew in to join Mesa's mayor, Cessna managers, and local workers and their families to celebrate the grand opening.[42]

In the **leader role**, managers motivate and encourage workers to accomplish organizational objectives. At *REDPEG MARKETING*, cofounder Brad Nierenberg motivates his employees with company perks, such as a three-bedroom beach house that is available to all 48 employees for vacations, cold beer in the refrigerator, free breakfast at staff meetings, and trophies and awards for great performance. In the **liaison role**, managers deal with people outside their units. Studies consistently indicate that managers spend as much time with outsiders as they do with their own subordinates and their own bosses.

4.2 Informational Roles

Not only do managers spend most of their time in face-to-face contact with others but they spend much of it obtaining and sharing information. Indeed, Mintzberg found that the managers in his study spent 40 percent of their time giving and getting information from others. In this regard, management can be viewed as processing information, gathering information by scanning the business environment and listening to others in face-to-face conversations, processing that information, and then sharing it with people both inside and outside the company. Mintzberg identified three informational subroles: monitor, disseminator, and spokesperson.

In the **monitor role**, managers scan their environment for information, actively contact others for information, and, because of their personal contacts, receive a great deal of unsolicited information. Besides receiving firsthand information, managers monitor their environment by reading local newspapers and the *Wall Street Journal* to keep track of customers, competitors, and technological changes that may affect their businesses. Now, managers can also take advantage of electronic monitoring and distribution services that track the news wires (Associated Press and Reuters for example) for stories related to their businesses. These services deliver customized electronic newspapers that include only stories on topics the managers specify.

Because of their numerous personal contacts and their access to subordinates, managers are often hubs for the distribution of critical information. In the **disseminator role**, managers share the information they have collected with their subordinates and others in the company. Although there will never be a complete

figurehead role
the interpersonal role managers play when they perform ceremonial duties

leader role
the interpersonal role managers play when they motivate and encourage workers to accomplish organizational objectives

liaison role
the interpersonal role managers play when they deal with people outside their units

monitor role
the informational role managers play when they scan their environment for information

substitution for face-to-face dissemination of information, *SERENA SOFTWARE*, based in Redwood City, California, uses Facebook to communicate worldwide with its 850 employees. The company relies on Facebook so much for recruiting new employees and marketing that it has become the company's de facto intranet.[43]

In contrast to the disseminator role, in which managers distribute information to employees inside the company, managers in the **spokesperson role** share information with people outside their departments and companies.

4.3 Decisional Roles

Mintzberg found that obtaining and sharing information is not an end in itself. Obtaining and sharing information with people inside and outside the company is useful to managers because it helps them make good decisions. According to Mintzberg, managers engage in four decisional subroles: entrepreneur, disturbance handler, resource allocator, and negotiator.

In the **entrepreneur role**, managers adapt themselves, their subordinates, and their units to change. Veterans Affairs (VA) hospitals long had a reputation for red tape, inefficiency, and second-class medical treatment. Today, though, independent groups rank VA hospitals as some of the best in the country. Fifteen years ago, the VA's leadership instituted a culture of accountability and change aimed at improving its entire system. Doctors, nurses, staffers, and administrators met regularly to review possible improvements. After a VA nurse in Topeka, Kansas, noticed that rental car companies used handheld bar-code scanners to check in returned cars, she suggested using bar codes on patients' ID bracelets and their bottled medicines. Today, the VA's bar-code scanners are tied to an electronic records system that prevents nurses from handing out the wrong medicines and automatically alerts the hospital pharmacy to possible harmful drug interactions or dangerous patient allergies.[44]

In the **disturbance handler role**, managers respond to pressures and problems so severe that they demand immediate attention and action. Top managers often play the role of disturbance handler, but shortly before Hurricane Katrina made landfall, *WAL-MART*'s then CEO Lee Scott realized that *all* of the company's top managers and store managers would have to be effective disturbance handlers in order to serve the company and the communities in which they worked. So Scott sent this message out: "A lot of you are going to have to make decisions above your level. Make the best decision that you can with the information that's available to you at the time, and above all, do the right thing."[45] Empowered by their CEO, employees used a forklift to crash through a warehouse door to get water, broke into a locked pharmacy to retrieve medicine for a hospital, and crashed a bulldozer through the front of a store so that supplies could be used to sustain the local community.

In the **resource allocator role**, managers decide who will get what resources and how many resources they will get. For instance, as the recession that began in the fall of 2008 deepened, companies slashed production by closing facilities, laying off workers, and cutting pay for workers and managers. But when it came to research and development (R&D) spending, the largest firms spent as much on R&D as they did before, despite revenues falling by nearly 8 percent. Why? Because in prior economic downturns, continued investments in R&D led to the development of successful products such as the iPod and fuel-efficient jet engines. Says Jim Andrew, of the Boston Consulting Group, "Companies by and large realized that

disseminator role
the informational role managers play when they share information with others in their departments or companies

spokesperson role
the informational role managers play when they share information with people outside their departments or companies

entrepreneur role
the decisional role managers play when they adapt themselves, their subordinates, and their units to change

disturbance handler role
the decisional role managers play when they respond to severe problems that demand immediate action

resource allocator role
the decisional role managers play when they decide who gets what resources

large reductions in R&D are suicidal." Therefore, companies such as Intel, which saw a 90 percent drop in its net income, still spent $5.4 billion on R&D. Likewise, 3M, which cut capital spending by 30 percent and laid off 4,700 workers, slightly increased its R&D spending so as not to sacrifice future profits from new, innovative products.[46]

In the **negotiator role**, managers negotiate schedules, projects, goals, outcomes, resources, and employee raises. After three earnings restatements in 3 years, the value of *NORTEL*'s stock had declined by $30 billion, and fed-up shareholders brought two class-action lawsuits against the company seeking $9 billion in damages. Rather than fight the lawsuit, Mike Zafirovski negotiated with the plaintiffs to partially compensate shareholders losses by paying them $2.4 billion in cash and stock. The settlement allowed Nortel to stay in business.[47]

REVIEW 4

Managerial Roles

Managers perform interpersonal, informational, and decisional roles in their jobs. In fulfilling the interpersonal role, managers act as figureheads by performing ceremonial duties, as leaders by motivating and encouraging workers, and as liaisons by dealing with people outside their units. When managers perform the informational role, they act as monitors by scanning their environment for information, as disseminators by sharing information with others in the company, and as spokespeople by sharing information with people outside their departments or companies. In decisional roles, managers act as entrepreneurs by adapting their units to incremental change, as disturbance handlers by responding to larger problems that demand immediate action, as resource allocators by deciding resource recipients and amounts, and as negotiators by bargaining with others about schedules, projects, goals, outcomes, and resources.

What Does It Take to Be a Manager?

> I didn't have the slightest idea what my job was. I walked in giggling and laughing because I had been promoted and had no idea what principles or style to be guided by. After the first day, I felt like I had run into a brick wall. (Sales Representative #1)
>
> Suddenly, I found myself saying, boy, I can't be responsible for getting all that revenue. I don't have the time. Suddenly you've got to go from [taking care of] yourself and say now I'm the manager, and what does a manager do? It takes a while thinking about it for it to really hit you . . . a manager gets things done through other people. That's a very, very hard transition to make. (Sales Representative #2)[48]

negotiator role
the decisional role managers play when they negotiate schedules, projects, goals, outcomes, resources, and employee raises

The preceding statements were made by two star sales representatives who, on the basis of their superior performance, were promoted to the position of sales manager. As their comments indicate, at first they did not feel confident about their ability to do their jobs as managers. Like most new managers, these sales managers suddenly realized that the knowledge, skills, and abilities that led to success early in their careers (and were probably responsible for their promotion into the ranks of management) would not necessarily help them succeed as managers. As sales representatives, they were responsible only for managing their own performance. But as managers, they were now directly responsible for supervising all of the sales representatives in their sales territories. Furthermore, they were now directly accountable for whether those sales representatives achieved their goals.

After reading the next three sections, you should be able to:

5 explain what companies look for in managers.
6 discuss the top mistakes that managers make in their jobs.
7 describe the transition that employees go through when they are promoted to management.

5 What Companies Look for in Managers

When companies look for employees who might be good managers, they look for individuals who have technical skills, human skills, conceptual skills, and the motivation to manage.[49] Exhibit 1.4 shows the relative importance of these four skills to the jobs of team leaders, first-line managers, middle managers, and top managers.

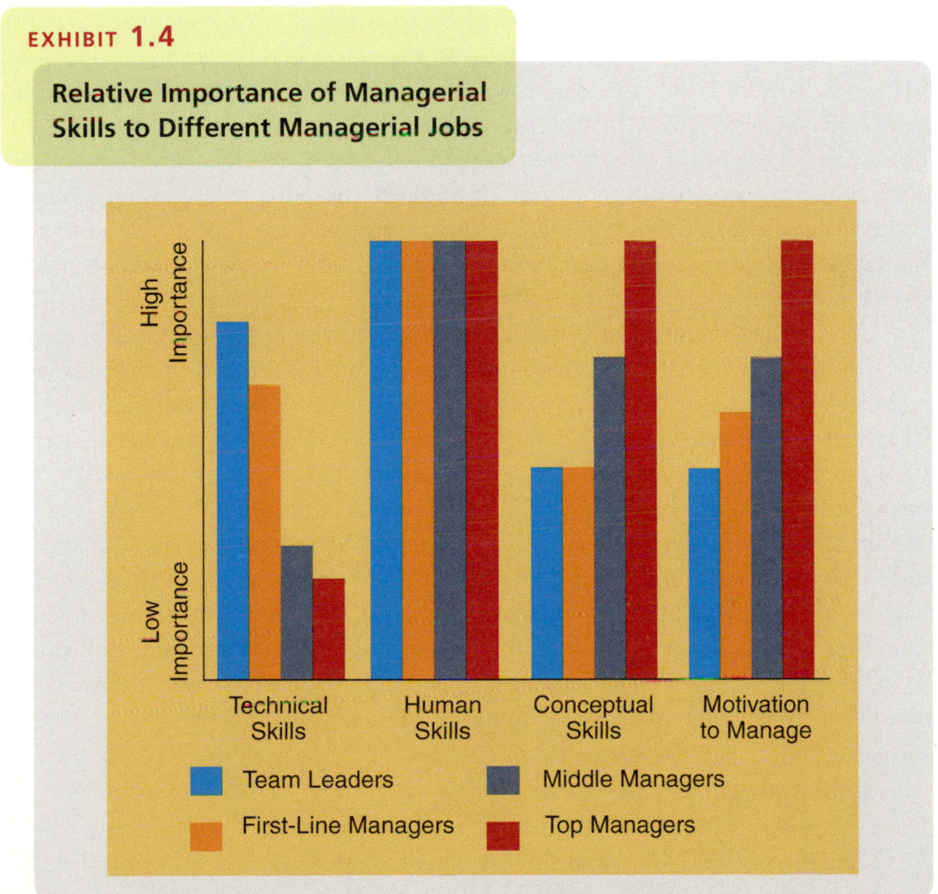

EXHIBIT 1.4

Relative Importance of Managerial Skills to Different Managerial Jobs

Technical skills are the specialized procedures, techniques, and knowledge required to get the job done. For the sales managers described above, technical skills involve the ability to find new sales prospects, develop accurate sales pitches based on customer needs, and close the sale.

Technical skills are most important for team leaders and lower-level managers because they supervise the workers who produce products or serve customers. Team leaders and first-line managers need technical knowledge and skills to train new employees and help employees solve problems. Technical knowledge and skills are also needed to troubleshoot problems that employees can't handle. Technical skills become less important as managers rise through the managerial ranks, but they are still important.

Human skills can be summarized as the ability to work well with others. Managers with human skills work effectively within groups, encourage others to express their thoughts and feelings, are sensitive to others' needs and viewpoints, and are good listeners and communicators. Human skills are equally important at all levels of management, from first-line supervisors to CEOs. However, because lower-level managers spend much of their time solving technical problems, upper-level managers may actually spend more time dealing directly with people. On average, first-line managers spend 57 percent of their time with people, but that percentage increases to 63 percent for middle managers and 78 percent for top managers.[50]

Conceptual skills are the ability to see the organization as a whole, to understand how the different parts of the company affect each other, and to recognize how the company fits into or is affected by its external environment such as the local community, social and economic forces, customers, and the competition. Good managers have to be able to recognize, understand, and reconcile multiple complex problems and perspectives. In other words, managers have to be smart! In fact, intelligence makes so much of a difference for managerial performance that managers with above-average intelligence typically outperform managers of average intelligence by approximately 48 percent.[51] Clearly, companies need to be careful to promote smart workers into management. Conceptual skills increase in importance as managers rise through the management hierarchy.

Good management involves much more than intelligence, however. For example, making the department genius a manager can be disastrous if that genius lacks technical skills, human skills, or one other factor known as the motivation to manage. **Motivation to manage** is an assessment of how motivated employees are to interact with superiors, participate in competitive situations, behave assertively toward others, tell others what to do, reward good behavior and punish poor behavior, perform actions that are highly visible to others, and handle and organize administrative tasks. Managers typically have a stronger motivation to manage than their subordinates, and managers at higher levels usually have a stronger motivation to manage than managers at lower levels. Furthermore, managers with a stronger motivation to manage are promoted faster, are rated as better managers by their employees, and earn more money than managers with a weak motivation to manage.[52]

technical skills
the ability to apply the specialized procedures, techniques, and knowledge required to get the job done

human skills
the ability to work well with others

conceptual skills
the ability to see the organization as a whole, understand how the different parts affect each other, and recognize how the company fits into or is affected by its external environment

motivation to manage
an assessment of how enthusiastic employees are about managing the work of others

REVIEW 5

What Companies Look for in Managers

Companies do not want one-dimensional managers. They want managers with a balance of skills. They want managers who know their stuff (technical skills), are equally comfortable working with blue-collar and white-collar employees (human skills), are able to assess the complexities of today's competitive marketplace and position their companies for success (conceptual skills), and want to assume positions of leadership and power (motivation to manage). Technical skills are most important for lower-level managers, human skills are equally important at all levels of management, and conceptual skills and motivation to manage increase in importance as managers rise through the managerial ranks.

6 Mistakes Managers Make

Another way to understand what it takes to be a manager is to look at the mistakes managers make. In other words, we can learn just as much from what managers shouldn't do as from what they should do. Exhibit 1.5 lists the top ten mistakes managers make.

Several studies of U.S. and British managers have compared "arrivers," or managers who make it all the way to the top of their companies, with "derailers," or managers who were successful early in their careers but were knocked off the fast track by the time they reached the middle to upper levels of management.[53] The researchers found only a few differences between arrivers and derailers. For the most part, both groups were talented and both groups had weaknesses. But what distinguished derailers from arrivers was that derailers possessed two or more fatal flaws with respect to the way they managed people. Although arrivers were by no means perfect, they usually had no more than one fatal flaw or had found ways to minimize the effects of their flaws on the people with whom they worked.

EXHIBIT 1.5

Top 10 Mistakes That Managers Make

1. Insensitive to others; abrasive, intimidating, bullying style.
2. Cold, aloof, arrogant.
3. Betrayal of trust.
4. Overly ambitious; thinking of next job, playing politics.
5. Specific performance problems with the business.
6. Overmanaging; unable to delegate or build a team.
7. Unable to staff effectively.
8. Unable to think strategically.
9. Unable to adapt to boss with different style.
10. Overdependent on advocate or mentor.

Source: M. W. McCall, Jr., & M. M. Lombardo, "What Makes a Top Executive?" *Psychology Today*, February 1983, 26–31.

The number-one mistake made by derailers was that they were insensitive to others by virtue of their abrasive, intimidating, and bullying management style. The authors of one study described a manager who walked into his subordinate's office and interrupted a meeting by saying, "I need to see you." When the subordinate tried to explain that he was not available because he was in the middle of a meeting, the manager barked, "I don't give a damn. I said I wanted to see you now."[54] Not surprisingly, only 25 percent of derailers were rated by others as being good with people, compared to 75 percent of arrivers.

The second mistake was that derailers were often cold, aloof, or arrogant. Although this sounds like insensitivity to others, it has more to do with derailed managers being so smart, so expert in their areas of knowledge, that they treated others with contempt because they weren't experts, too.

The third mistake made by derailers involved betraying a trust. Betraying a trust doesn't mean being dishonest. Instead, it means making others look bad by not doing what you said you would do when you said you would do it. That mistake, in itself, is not fatal because managers and their workers aren't machines. Tasks go undone in every company, every single business day. There's always too much to do and not enough time, people, money, or resources to do it. The fatal betrayal of trust is failing to inform others when things will not be done on time. This failure to admit mistakes, quickly inform others of the mistakes, take responsibility for the mistakes, and then fix them without blaming others clearly distinguished the behavior of derailers from arrivers. The fourth mistake was being overly political and ambitious. Managers who always have their eye on their next job rarely establish more than superficial relationships with peers and coworkers. In their haste to gain credit for successes that would be noticed by upper management, they make the fatal mistake of treating people as though they don't matter.

The fatal mistakes of being unable to delegate, build a team, and staff effectively indicate that many derailed managers were unable to make the most basic transition to managerial work: to quit being hands-on doers and get work done through others. Two things go wrong when managers make these mistakes. First, when managers meddle in decisions that their subordinates should be making—when they can't stop being doers—they alienate the people who work for them. According to Richard Kilburg of Johns Hopkins University, when managers interfere with workers decisions, "You . . . have a tendency to lose your most creative people. They're able to say, 'Screw this. I'm not staying here.'"[55] Second, because they are trying to do their subordinates' jobs in addition to their own, managers who fail to delegate will not have enough time to do much of anything well.

REVIEW 6

Mistakes Managers Make

Another way to understand what it takes to be a manager is to look at the top mistakes managers make. Five of the most important mistakes made by managers are being abrasive and intimidating; being cold, aloof, or arrogant; betraying trust; being overly ambitious; and failing to build a team and then delegate to that team.

7 The Transition to Management: The First Year

In her book *Becoming a Manager: Mastery of a New Identity*, Harvard Business School professor Linda Hill followed the development of 19 people in their first year as managers. Her study found that becoming a manager produced a profound psychological transition that changed the way these managers viewed themselves and others. As shown in Exhibit 1.6, the evolution of the managers' thoughts, expectations, and realities over the course of their first year in management reveals the magnitude of the changes they experienced.

Initially, the managers in Hill's study believed that their job was to exercise formal authority and to manage tasks—basically being the boss, telling others what to do, making decisions, and getting things done. One of the managers Hill interviewed said, "Being the manager means running my own office, using my ideas and thoughts." Another said, "[The office is] my baby. It's my job to make sure it works."[56] In fact, most of the new managers were attracted to management positions because they wanted to be in charge. Surprisingly, the new managers did not believe that their job was to manage people. The only aspects of people management mentioned by the new managers were hiring and firing.

After 6 months, most of the new managers had concluded that their initial expectations about managerial work were wrong. Management wasn't just about being the boss, making decisions, and telling others what to do. The first surprise was the fast pace and heavy workload involved. Said one of Hill's managers, "This job is much harder than you think. It is 40 to 50 percent more work than being a producer! Who would have ever guessed?" The pace of managerial work was startling, too. Another manager said, "You have eight or nine people looking for your time . . . coming into and out of your office all day long." A somewhat frustrated manager declared that management was "a job that never ended . . . a job you couldn't get your hands around."[57]

Informal descriptions like this are consistent with studies indicating that the average first-line manager spends no more than 2 minutes on a task before being interrupted by a request from a subordinate, a phone call, or an e-mail. The pace is somewhat less hurried for top managers, who spend an average of approximately 9 minutes on a task before having to switch to another. In practice, this means that supervisors may perform thirty different tasks per hour, while top managers perform seven different tasks per hour, with each task typically different from the one that preceded it. A manager described this frenetic level of activity by saying, "The only time you are in control is when you shut your door, and then I feel I am not doing the job I'm supposed to be doing, which is being with the people."[58]

The other major surprise after 6 months on the job was that the managers' expectations about what they should do were very different from their subordinates' expectations. Initially, the managers defined their jobs as helping their subordinates perform their jobs well. For the managers who still defined themselves as doers rather than managers, assisting their subordinates meant going out on sales calls or handling customer complaints. One manager said, "I like going out

EXHIBIT 1.6

The Transition to Management: Initial Expectations, after Six Months, and after a Year

MANAGERS' INITIAL EXPECTATIONS JAN FEB MAR	AFTER SIX MONTHS AS A MANAGER APR MAY JUN	AFTER A YEAR AS A MANAGER JUL AUG SEP OCT NOV DEC
Be the boss	Initial expectations were wrong	No longer "doer"
Have formal authority	Fast pace	Communicating, listening, and giving positive reinforcement
Manage tasks	Heavy workload	Learning to adapt to and control stress
Job is not managing people	Job is to be problem-solver and troubleshooter for subordinates	Job is people development

with the rep, who may need me to lend him my credibility as manager. I like the challenge, the joy in closing. I go out with the reps and we make the call and talk about the customer; it's fun."[59] But when the managers "assisted" in this way, their subordinates were resentful and viewed their help as interference. The subordinates wanted their managers to help them by solving problems that they couldn't solve. Once the managers realized this distinction, they embraced their role as problem-solver and troubleshooter. Thus, they could help without interfering with their subordinates' jobs.

After a year on the job, most of the managers thought of themselves as managers and no longer as doers. In making the transition, they finally realized that people management was the most important part of their job. One of Hill's interviewees summarized the lesson that had taken him a year to learn by saying, "As many demands as managers have on their time, I think their primary responsibility is people development. Not production, but people development."[60] Another indication of how much their views had changed was that most of the managers now regretted the rather heavy-handed approach they had used in their early attempts to manage their subordinates. "I wasn't good at managing . . . so I was bossy like a first-grade teacher." "Now I see that I started out as a drill sergeant. I was inflexible, just a lot of how-to's." By the end of the year, most of the managers had abandoned their authoritarian approach for one based on communication, listening, and positive reinforcement. One manager explained, "Last night at five I handed out an award in the boardroom. It was the first time in his career that he had [earned] $100,000, and I gave him a piece of glass [a small award] and said I'd heard a rumor that somebody here just crossed over $100,000 and I said congratulations, shook his hand, and walked away. It was not public in the sense that I gathered everybody around. But I knew and he did too."[61]

Finally, after beginning their year as managers in frustration, the managers came to feel comfortable with their subordinates, with the demands of their jobs, and with their emerging managerial styles. While being managers had made them acutely aware of their limitations and their need to develop as people, it also provided them with an unexpected reward of coaching and developing the people who worked for them. One manager said, "It gives me the best feeling to see somebody do something well after I have helped them. I get excited." Another stated, "I realize now that when I accepted the position of branch manager that it is truly an exciting vocation. It is truly awesome, even at this level; it can be terribly challenging and terribly exciting."[62]

REVIEW 7

The Transition to Management: The First Year

Managers often begin their jobs by using more formal authority and fewer people management skills. However, most find that being a manager has little to do with telling subordinates what to do. After 6 months on the job, the managers were surprised at the fast pace and heavy workload and that "helping" their subordinates was viewed as interference. After a year on the job, most of the managers had come to think of themselves not as doers, but as managers who get things done through others. And because they finally realized that people management was the most important part of their job, most of them had abandoned their authoritarian approach for one based on communication, listening, and positive reinforcement.

Why Management Matters

If you walk down the aisle of the business section in your local bookstore, you'll find hundreds of books that explain precisely what companies need to do to be successful. Unfortunately, the best-selling business books tend to be faddish, changing dramatically every few years. One thing that hasn't changed, though, is the importance of good people and good management. Companies can't succeed for long without them.

After reading the next section, you should be able to:

8 explain how and why companies can create competitive advantage through people.

8 Competitive Advantage through People

In his books *Competitive Advantage through People* and *The Human Equation: Building Profits by Putting People First*, Stanford University business professor Jeffrey Pfeffer contends that what separates top-performing companies from their competitors is the way they treat their work forces—in other words, their management style.[63]

Pfeffer found that managers in top-performing companies used ideas like employment security, selective hiring, self-managed teams and decentralization, high pay contingent on company performance, extensive training, reduced status distinctions between managers and employees, and extensive sharing of financial information to achieve financial performance that, on average, was 40 percent higher than that of other companies. These ideas, which are explained in detail in Exhibit 1.7, help organizations develop work forces that are smarter, better trained, more motivated, and more committed than their competitors' work forces. And—as indicated by the phenomenal growth and return on investment earned by these companies—smarter, better trained, and more committed work forces provide superior products and service to customers. Such customers keep buying and, by telling others about their positive experiences, bring in new customers.

According to Pfeffer, companies that invest in their people will create long-lasting competitive advantages that are difficult for other companies to duplicate. Indeed, other studies clearly demonstrate that sound management practices can produce substantial advantages in four critical areas of organizational performance: sales revenues, profits, stock market returns, and customer satisfaction.

In terms of sales revenues and profits, a study of nearly 1,000 U.S. firms found that companies that use *just some* of the ideas shown in Exhibit 1.7 had $27,044 more sales per employee and $3,814 more profit per employee than companies that didn't. For a 100-person company, these differences amount to $2.7 million more in sales and nearly $400,000 more in annual profit! For a 1,000-person company, the difference grows to $27 million more in sales and $4 million more in annual profit![64]

Another study that considers the effect of investing in people on company sales found that poorly performing companies were able to improve their average return on investment from 5.1 percent to 19.7 percent and increase sales by $94,000 per employee by adopting management techniques as simple as setting performance expectations (establishing goals, results, and schedules), coaching (informal, ongoing discussions between managers and subordinates about what is

EXHIBIT 1.7

Competitive Advantage through People: Management Practices

1. Employment Security—Employment security is the ultimate form of commitment that companies can make to their workers. Employees can innovate and increase company productivity without fearing the loss of their jobs.
2. Selective Hiring—If employees are the basis for a company's competitive advantage, and those employees have employment security, then the company needs to aggressively recruit and selectively screen applicants in order to hire the most talented employees available.
3. Self-Managed Teams and Decentralization—Self-managed teams are responsible for their own hiring, purchasing, job assignments, and production. Self-managed teams can often produce enormous increases in productivity through increased employee commitment and creativity. Decentralization allows employees who are closest to (and most knowledgeable about) problems, production, and customers to make timely decisions. Decentralization increases employee satisfaction and commitment.
4. High Wages Contingent on Organizational Performance—High wages are needed to attract and retain talented workers and to indicate that the organization values its workers. Employees, like company founders, shareholders, and managers, need to share in the financial rewards when the company is successful. Why? Because employees who have a financial stake in their companies are more likely to take a long-run view of the business and think like business owners.
5. Training and Skill Development—Like a high-tech company that spends millions of dollars to upgrade computers or research and development labs, a company whose competitive advantage is based on its people must invest in the training and skill development of its people.
6. Reduction of Status Differences—These are fancy words that indicate that the company treats everyone, no matter what the job, as equal. There are no reserved parking spaces. Everyone eats in the same cafeteria and has similar benefits. The result: much improved communication as employees focus on problems and solutions rather than on how they are less valued than managers.
7. Sharing Information—If employees are to make decisions that are good for the long-run health and success of the company, they need to be given information about costs, finances, productivity, development times, and strategies that was previously known only by company managers.

Source: J. Pfeffer, *The Human Equation: Building Profits by Putting People First* (Boston: Harvard Business School Press, 1996).

being done well and what could be done better), reviewing (annual, formal discussion about results), and rewarding employee performance (adjusting salaries and bonuses based on employee performance and results).[65] So, in addition to significantly improving the profitability of healthy companies, sound management practices can turn around failing companies.

To determine how investing in people affects stock market performance, researchers matched companies on *Fortune* magazine's list of "100 Best Companies to Work for in America" with companies that were similar in industry, size, and—this is key—operating performance. Researchers found that people who worked for the "100 Best" companies were consistently much more satisfied with their jobs and employers year after year than were employees in the matched companies. More importantly, those stable differences in employee attitudes were strongly related to differences in stock market performance. Over a 3-year period, an investment in one of the "100 Best" would have resulted in an 82 percent cumulative stock return compared with just 37 percent for the matched companies.[66] This difference is remarkable given that both sets of companies were equally good performers at the beginning of the period.

After 6 years on *Fortune*'s list of Best Companies to Work for, NetApp jumped to the top in 2009. One reason is employees' enthusiasm for the company's egalitarian culture.

Finally, research also indicates that managers have an important effect on customer satisfaction. Many people find this surprising. They don't understand how managers, who are largely responsible for what goes on inside the company, can affect what goes on outside the company. They wonder how managers, who often interact with customers under negative conditions (when customers are angry or dissatisfied), can actually improve customer satisfaction. It turns out that managers influence customer satisfaction through employee satisfaction. When employees are satisfied with their jobs, their bosses, and the companies they work for, they provide much better service to customers.[67] In turn, customers are more satisfied, too. Indeed, customers of companies on *Fortune*'s list of "100 Best," where employees are much more satisfied with their jobs and their companies, have much higher customer satisfaction scores than do customers of comparable companies who are not on *Fortune*'s list. That difference in customer satisfaction also resulted in a 1.6 percent higher return on company assets.[68] You will learn more about the service-profit chain in Chapter 16 on managing service and manufacturing operations.

REVIEW 8

Competitive Advantage through People

Why does management matter? Well-managed companies are competitive because their workforces are smarter, better trained, more motivated, and more committed. Furthermore, companies that practice good management consistently have greater sales revenues, profits, and stock market performance than companies that don't. Finally, good management matters because it leads to satisfied employees who, in turn, provide better service to customers. Because employees tend to treat customers the same way that their managers treat them, good management can improve customer satisfaction.

MANAGEMENT Decision

Making decisions is part of every manager's job. To give you practice at managerial decision making, each chapter contains a "Management Decision" or "Management Team Decision" assignment focused on a particular decision. You'll need to decide what to do in the given situation and then answer several questions to explain your choices.

Should We Try to Make More Money?

To say that the airline industry has experienced some struggles would be a huge understatement. Faced with fears over terrorist attacks and sharp rises in the price of oil, airlines have been losing money at historic rates. In 2009, only four domestic airlines were able to turn a profit, while the five largest carriers lost more than $3 billion combined.

In the midst of these struggles, the industry found an unexpected, but highly lucrative, source of revenue—baggage. For many years, passengers were allowed to travel with up to three pieces of luggage—one item to carry on the plane, and two larger items that could be checked into the storage area. But in 2008, American Airlines became the first major airline to charge passengers who wanted to check their baggage. Though this additional fee was much reviled, other airlines quickly followed suit, charging $15 to $35 per bag for each portion of a round-trip flight.

The net effects of baggage fees have been incredible. In 2009, airlines combined to collect nearly $2 billion dollars in baggage fees alone; Delta Airlines led the entire industry with $550 million. The baggage fees have also led passengers to check fewer bags. This has allowed airlines to dedicate more space to cargo, which commands a premium price. What is more, there has been a reduction in the number of mishandled bags, which led to an additional $94 million in savings. Best of all, all of this is essentially "free money"—the airlines did not lower their fares after charging for checked baggage, and they have not had to increase other expenses (such as labor).

All told, the checked bag fees have been such a success that Spirit Airlines now charges $45 for carry-on baggage that is stored in overhead bins. You are a manager of the lone holdout, Southwest Airlines, which allows passengers to check two bags with no charge. While Southwest has remained profitable during the industry's struggles, it is difficult to see competitors rake in millions of dollars in additional revenue with virtually no labor. You begin to wonder if your company shouldn't also charge for bags so that it can maintain a competitive edge. After all, as you well know, the airline industry is unpredictable, and your company could find itself in deep struggles very quickly.

Questions

1. How is this decision emblematic of your job as a manager?
2. What are the advantages and disadvantages of following competitors by charging for checked baggage?

Sources: "Airlines make a bundle through separate charges." *The Seattle Times.* April 7, 2010. Accessed at: http://seattletimes.nwsource.com/html/travel/2011539200_webtroubleshooter06.html/.

Hugo Martin, "Spirit Airlines launches $45 carry-on fee." *The Los Angeles Times.* April 7, 2010. Accessed at: http://articles.latimes.com/2010/apr/07/business/la-fi-spirit7-2010apr07.

Christine Negroni, "Less Baggage, Big Savings to Airlines" *New York Times.* April 6, 2010. Accessed at: http://www.nytimes.com/2010/04/07/business/07bags.html?src=me.

Practice being a MANAGER

Finding a Management Job

Management is a wide-ranging and exciting area of work. One way to gain a sense of the possibilities is to study the advertisements for management job openings. Companies advertise their management openings in a variety of ways, including print advertisements in such newspapers as the *Wall Street Journal* (especially its Friday career section) and online ads at job sites like Monster.com and CareerBuilder.com.

STEP 1 Find a job you'd like to have. Search through the newspaper and online ads and locate several detailed job descriptions for management positions. Select the one that you find most appealing—a job that you could picture yourself interviewing for either in the near future or later in your career. Do not be too concerned about your current qualifications in making your selection, but you should see realistic prospects of meeting the qualifications over time (if a job requires an MBA, for example, you should see yourself completing this degree sometime in the future). Print your selected detailed job description and bring it to your next class session.

STEP 2 Share your job description. In class, your professor will assign you to a group of two or three. Write your name on your selected management job description, and exchange your job description with your partner(s). Each member of the pair or triad should now have a job description other than their own.

STEP 3 Think like a hiring manager. Read the job description you received from your partner. Imagine that you are the manager responsible for hiring someone to fill this position. A human resources specialist in your company has already screened the applicants' resume and background. Thus, you may assume that your partner has met all the basic qualifications for the job. Your job as a senior manager is to ask questions that might get beyond the resume to the person—what might you ask to learn if someone is well suited to thrive in this management job and in your company?

STEP 4 Take turns interviewing. Each member of the group should be briefly interviewed (5–10 minutes) for the job he or she selected.

STEP 5 Debrief. Discuss your experiences with your partner(s). What was it like to be interviewed for your selected position? What was it like to interview someone for a management position? Now imagine the real thing. Brainstorm about how you might prepare yourself over time to become the top candidate for an attractive management position and to be a senior manager responsible for hiring the best-qualified managers for your company.

STEP 6 Discuss with the class. Share your interview experiences and brainstorming ideas with the rest of the class. Do you hear any similarities across the pairs/triads? What ideas or questions are most significant to you as you consider management job interviews?

SELF Assessment

Each chapter has a related self-assessment tool to help you consider how your own perspectives influence your management skills. Each assessment tool starts with a short description and ends with basic scoring information. (Your instructor will have interpretations of your scores.) As you advance through the book, take time to review your assessment scores together. Doing so will help you see patterns in your own perceptions and behaviors and give you insights into how those perceptions may affect your performance as a manager.

Is Management for You?

As you learned in Section 7 of this chapter, many managers begin their careers in management with specific ideas about what it means to be the boss. Although you may want to be a manager because of excitement, status, power, or rewards, knowing how to manage is not automatic; it requires specific skills and competencies, as well as desire. This assessment is meant to establish your baseline ability in the skills covered in the chapter. It will not tell you whether you should or should not be a manager, or whether you have "what it takes" to be a manager. It will, however, give you feedback on general skills that influence your overall managerial style.[69]

Be candid as you complete the assessment by circling the appropriate responses.

ML = Most like me
SL = Somewhat like me
NS = Not sure
SU = Somewhat unlike me
MU = Most unlike me

1. I can get others to do what I want them to do.
   ML SL NS SU MU
2. I frequently evaluate my job performance.
   ML SL NS SU MU
3. I prefer not to get involved in office politics.
   ML SL NS SU MU
4. I like the freedom that open-ended goals provide me.
   ML SL NS SU MU
5. I work best when things are orderly and calm.
   ML SL NS SU MU
6. I enjoy making oral presentations to groups of people.
   ML SL NS SU MU
7. I am confident in my abilities to accomplish difficult tasks.
   ML SL NS SU MU
8. I do not like to write.
   ML SL NS SU MU
9. I like solving difficult puzzles.
   ML SL NS SU MU
10. I am an organized person.
   ML SL NS SU MU
11. I have difficulty telling others they made a mistake.
   ML SL NS SU MU
12. I like to work set hours each day.
   ML SL NS SU MU
13. I view paperwork as a trivial task.
   ML SL NS SU MU
14. I like to help others learn new things.
   ML SL NS SU MU
15. I prefer to work alone.
   ML SL NS SU MU

16. I believe it is who you know, not what you know, that counts.

ML SL NS SU MU

17. I enjoy doing several things at once.

ML SL NS SU MU

18. I am good at managing money.

ML SL NS SU MU

19. I would rather back down from an argument than let it get out of hand.

ML SL NS SU MU

20. I am computer literate.

ML SL NS SU MU

SCORING

Start by reversing your scores for items 5, 8, 11, 15, and 16. For example, if you used ML, change it to MU, and vice versa; if you used SL, change it to SU, and vice versa. Now assign each answer a point value.

Number of ML answers _______ times 5 points each = _______

Number of SL answers _______ times 4 points each = _______

Number of NS answers _______ times 3 points each = _______

Number of SU answers _______ times 2 points each = _______

Number of MU answers _______ times 1 point each = _______

TOTAL = _______

You can find the interpretation for your score at: login.cengagebrain.com.

Reel to Real

Biz Flix

© GREENLIGHT

In Good Company

When a sports magazine gets taken over by a media conglomerate, a seasoned and successful ad sales executive named Dan Foreman (Dennis Quaid) is stunned by his demotion. Carter Duryea (Topher Grace)—a business school prodigy who is half Dan's age and talks a lot about "corporate synergy"—is brought in as his new boss. Dan spent years developing good relationships with his clients, but Carter thinks it's more expedient to cross-promote the magazine with the corporation's cell phone division. In this clip from the film, Carter has come to appreciate Dan's work ethic and relationship skills, but his superior, Mark Steckle (Clark Gregg), wants to fire him. Carter stands up for Dan, even though it may mean he has to follow him out the door. Carter and Dan will have to work together if they're going to find a way to save their jobs.

What to Watch for and Ask Yourself

1. Which management skills discussed in this chapter does the character Mark Steckle seem to lack?
2. The sequence shows three people who represent different hierarchical levels in the company. Based on this scene, which of the four kinds of managers do you think each of them might be?
3. Which of the characters in this clip exhibited the strongest human skills?

Management Workplace

© CENGAGE

Numi Organic Tea

When Danielle Oviedo became the manager of the Distribution Center at Numi Organic Tea in Oakland, California, her new direct reports were not happy about the change. They missed Oviedo's predecessor, who had treated them like her friends. But Numi was growing so fast that the company needed more than just a friendly face to manage its growing pains. The director of operations, Brian Durkee, hired Oviedo because her previous work experience showed she was someone who could help the company respond to the demands of rapid expansion. Oviedo says her first challenge at Numi was to get the employees to stop simply focusing on their individual tasks each day and work as a team toward common goals. In this video we see how she improved the way the company functioned to make it more efficient and competitive in a short amount of time.

What to Watch for and Ask Yourself

1. Which type of decisional role did Danielle Oviedo have to play at Numi in order to help the other employees adapt to changes she was instituting?
2. Why did Brian Durkee believe Danielle Oviedo had what it took to be an effective manager at Numi?
3. What role did Danielle Oviedo's conceptual skills play when she took over as the manager of the distribution center at Numi? How did she use these skills to make improvements in the way the company runs?

2

Chapter Two

Organizational Environments and Cultures

OUTLINE

Experience Management

Experiencing Management modules begin in Chapter 3, after you have been introduced to the basic concepts that underpin management theories.

© ISTOCKPHOTO.COM/ ANN MARIE KURTZ

Pod Nod

Mini lecture reviews all the learning points in the chapter.

© ISTOCKPHOTO.COM/ MAGNET CREATIVE

Reel to Real Video

Biz Flix is a scene from *Charlie Wilson's War*. Management Workplace is a segment on Preserve.

© ISTOCKPHOTO.COM/ CRAFTVISION

Self Test

10 quiz questions, 3 exhibit worksheets, and PowerPoints for quick review.

© ISTOCKPHOTO.COM/ DIJITAL FILM

What Would You Do?

Wal-Mart Headquarters, Bentonville, Arkansas.[1]

With annual revenue of $430 billion, 2 million employees, and 7,300 stores worldwide (and even larger numbers by the time you read this), *WAL-MART* is the largest company in the world and has held the number-one spot on the *Fortune* 500 list 6 out of the last 7 years. But, as the world's largest company, Wal-Mart is also one of the world's largest targets for anti-corporate groups and lawsuits. Indeed, to its critics, Wal-Mart has become the default symbol of corporate evil.

On the issue of employee pay, Wal-Mart has been accused of forcing employees to work off the clock (working overtime and during breaks without pay) and of paying employees wages that fall below the poverty line. In terms of health-care benefits, critics such as ***http://www.wake-upWalMart.com*** complain that Wal-Mart provides health insurance for only 43 percent of its employees compared to 66 percent for most other companies; that although managers receive health benefits their first day on the job, full-time and part-time employees must wait 6 months and 12 months, respectively, before enrolling in Wal-Mart's health insurance program; and finally, that average Wal-Mart employees must spend a disproportionate share of their income, approximately 22 to 40 percent, to cover their health insurance premiums and medical deductibles. Wal-Mart, of course, disputes these facts and allegations and argues that many of these critical organizations are financed by unions that have tried unsuccessfully for two decades to organize Wal-Mart's employees, who represent the largest work force in the world.

Environmental groups have also been highly critical of Wal-Mart. According to the Sierra Club, "Big Box" stores like Wal-Mart "threaten our landscape, our communities, and the environment by building on the fringe of town, paving vast areas for stores and parking lots, and undermining the economic health of existing downtown shopping areas." The Sierra Club also opposes new Wal-Mart stores because it believes their development destroys wetlands and increases the risk of flood-based pollution.

With the average footprint of a Wal-Mart supercenter running about 18 acres, the Sierra Club believes that Wal-Mart is a major contributor to "non-point source water pollution," which it says is the leading cause of water pollution in the U.S." According to the Sierra Club, an undeveloped acre with trees and grass and flowers and bushes produces 2,700 gallons of rainwater runoff for each inch of precipitation. In other words, most of the rainwater is absorbed into the ground. By contrast, a developed acre, one that has been paved and has buildings, produces 25,000 gallons of rainwater runoff for each inch of precipitation. Since the average Wal-Mart supercenter is 18 acres, an inch of precipitation leads to 450,000 gallons of rainwater runoff filled with oil, chemicals, and bacteria.

Unrelenting attacks have undoubtedly affected how people view Wal-Mart. Gerald Baron, founder and president of a corporate relations consulting company, says, "Wal-Mart has a reputation crisis." Ironically, though, this has had little effect on Wal-Mart's sales. Indeed, Wal-Mart's internal research shows that less than 0.1 percent of the people who are familiar with these criticisms have stopped shopping at Wal-Mart.

So, with almost no impact on its sales and little concern among its customers, should Wal-Mart take on its critics and fight back, or should it focus on its business and let its results speak for themselves? What should Wal-Mart do, if anything, in regard to highly publicized criticisms about the pay and benefits it awards to its employees? Should it ignore them or address them? Finally, should Wal-Mart view environmentalists' complaints as a threat or an opportunity for the company?

If you were the CEO of Wal-Mart, what would you do?

Anti-Wal-Mart websites, critical environmental groups, class-action lawsuits, and unions that want to unionize the largest workforce in the world create a challenging backdrop for Wal-Mart. Wherever Wal-Mart's top managers look, they see changes and forces outside the company that directly affect how they do business.

This chapter examines the internal and external forces that affect business. We begin by explaining how the changes in external organizational environments affect the decisions and performance of a company. Next, we examine the two types of external organizational environments: the general environment that affects all organizations and the specific environment unique to each company. Then, we learn how managers make sense of their changing general and specific environments. The chapter finishes with a discussion of internal organizational environments by focusing on organizational culture.

External Environments

External environments are the forces and events outside a company that have the potential to influence or affect it. From Walkmans to PlayStation video games and consoles to its top-of-the-line televisions, Sony's ability to innovate made it one of the world's top electronics companies. However, because of intense competition in its external environment from Apple (iPod and iPhone), Microsoft (Xbox 360), and Samsung and Vizio (high-definition TVs), Sony has been forced to cut costs,

external environments all events outside a company that have the potential to influence or affect it

lay off workers, and try to change its internal culture in order to restore profits (more on that later in the chapter).[2]

After reading the next four sections, you should be able to:

1 discuss how changing environments affect organizations.
2 describe the four components of the general environment.
3 explain the five components of the specific environment.
4 describe the process that companies use to make sense of their changing environments.

1 Changing Environments

Let's examine the three basic characteristics of changing external environments: 1.1 **environmental change**, 1.2 **environmental complexity**, 1.3 **resource scarcity**, and 1.4 **the uncertainty that environmental change, complexity, and resource scarcity can create for organizational managers**.

1.1 Environmental Change

Environmental change is the rate at which a company's general and specific environments change. In **stable environments**, the rate of environmental change is slow. For instance, apart from the fact that ovens are more efficient, bread is baked, wrapped, and delivered fresh to stores each day much as it was decades ago. Although some new breads have become popular, the white and wheat breads that customers bought 20 years ago are still best sellers today. In **dynamic environments**, however the rate of environmental change is fast.

Although you might think that a company's external environment would be either stable or dynamic, research suggests that companies often experience both. According to **punctuated equilibrium theory**, companies go through long periods of stability (equilibrium) during which incremental changes occur, followed by short, complex periods of dynamic, fundamental change (revolutionary periods), finishing with a return to stability (new equilibrium).[3]

Exhibit 2.1 shows one example of punctuated equilibrium—the U.S. airline industry. Three times in the last 30 years, the U.S. airline industry has experienced revolutionary periods. In the late 70's and early 80's, airlines had tremendous difficulty operating in the competitive environment created by deregulation and suffered huge losses until they were able to adjust. Then, after experiencing record growth and profits, U.S. airlines lost billions of dollars in the early 90's as the industry went through dramatic changes. Key expenses, including jet fuel and employee salaries, which had held steady for years, suddenly increased, and revenues suddenly dropped because of changes in the airlines' customer base. Leisure travelers, who wanted the cheapest flights they could get, replaced business travelers, who typically pay full-priced fares, as the largest customer base.[4] The airlines responded to these changes in their business environment by laying off 5 to 10 percent of their workers, canceling orders for new planes, and eliminating unprofitable routes. These changes helped the airline industry achieve profits far in excess of their historical levels. The industry began to stabilize, if not flourish, just as punctuated equilibrium theory predicts.[5]

The third revolutionary period for the U.S. airline industry began with the terrorist attacks of September 11, 2001, in which planes were used as missiles to bring

environmental change
the rate at which a company's general and specific environments change

stable environment
an environment in which the rate of change is slow

dynamic environment
an environment in which the rate of change is fast

punctuated equilibrium theory
the theory that companies go through long periods of stability (equilibrium)

EXHIBIT 2.1

Punctuated Equilibrium: U.S. Airline Profits since 1979

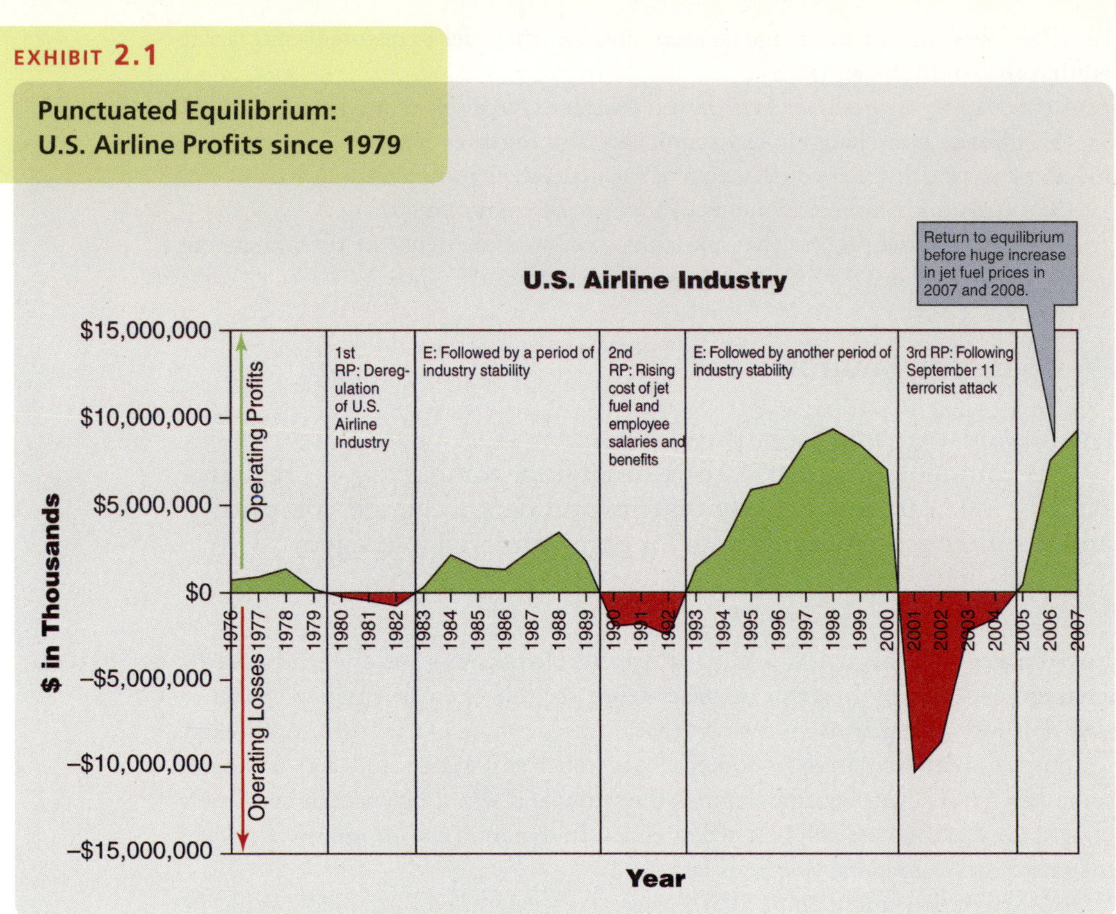

Source: "Annual Revenues and Earnings: U.S. Airlines—All Services," Air Transport Association, [Online] available at http://www.airlines.org/economics/finance/Annual + US + Financial + Results.htm, 25 April 2009.

down the World Trade Center towers and damage the Pentagon. The immediate effect was a 20 percent drop in scheduled flights, a 40 percent drop in passengers, and losses so large that the U.S. government approved a $15 billion bailout to keep the airlines in business. After losing a combined $42 billion, the airlines restructured operations to take advantage of the combined effect of increases in passenger travel, reduced costs, and a fleet reduction to return to profitability five years after the attacks.[6]

environmental complexity the number and the intensity of external factors in the environment that affect organizations

simple environment an environment with few environmental factors

complex environment an environment with many environmental factors

1.2 Environmental Complexity

Environmental complexity refers to the number and intensity of external factors in the environment that affect organizations. **Simple environments** have few environmental factors, whereas **complex environments** have many environmental factors. For example, the dairy industry has a relatively simple external environment. Even accounting for decades-old advances in processing and automatic milking machines, milk is produced the same way today as it was 100 years ago. And although food manufacturers introduce dozens of new dairy-based products each year, U.S. milk production has grown a meager 1.25 percent per year over the last decade. In short, producing milk is a highly competitive but simple business that has experienced few changes.[7]

By contrast, consider the environmental changes in the record industry. From the 1960s to the early 1980s vinyl records were the only format for music delivery. In the next few decades came new formats, including 8-track tapes, cassette tapes, and in the early 1980s, the compact disc. The record labels balanced their shipments to handle the changing desires of their customers, and in 1988 CDs outsold the vinyl-record album format for the first time. The MP3 format was patented in Germany in 1989 and over the next 10 years became the standard format for compressing high-quality digital sound to CDs or other storage devices.

But things got much more complex when, in 1999, a company called Napster created a peer-to-peer network that allowed users to easily (and, at first, illegally) share digital files with each other. Within a year, 30 percent of all PCs were running this software program, and the recording industry blamed illegal file sharing for the sharp declines in CD sales. In an effort to create a legal downloading mechanism that would support the rights of the recording industry, Sony introduced "The Store," which was quickly followed by Duet, MusicNet, Listen.com, and, of course, Apple's iTunes store. Syncing seamlessly with Apple's immensely popular iPods and iPhones, the iTunes store has sold more than 6 billion songs since inception, holds 80 percent of the digital media market, and has changed the way the recording industry distributes and profits from music.[8]

1.3 Resource Scarcity

The third characteristic of external environments is resource scarcity. **Resource scarcity** is the abundance or shortage of critical organizational resources in an organization's external environment. For example, the primary reason that flat-screen LCD (liquid crystal display) televisions with lifelike pictures were initially six times more expensive per inch than regular TVs, and 25 percent more expensive than plasma TVs, was that there weren't enough LCD screen factories to meet demand. At $2 billion to $4 billion each, LCD factories were at first a scarce resource in this industry.[9] But as sales of LCD TVs soared, more LCD factories were built to meet demand, so prices came down. So as the external environment changed, these resources became less scarce.

1.4 Uncertainty

As Exhibit 2.2 shows, environmental change, environmental complexity, and resource scarcity affect environmental **uncertainty**, which is how well managers can understand or predict the external changes and trends affecting their businesses. Starting at the left side of the figure, environmental uncertainty is lowest when environmental change and environmental complexity are at low levels and resource scarcity is small (i.e., resources are plentiful). In these environments, managers feel confident that they can understand, predict, and react to the external forces that affect their businesses. By contrast, the right side of the figure shows that environmental uncertainty is highest when environmental change and complexity are extensive and resource scarcity is a problem. In these environments, managers may not be confident that they can understand, predict, and handle the external forces affecting their businesses.

resource scarcity
the abundance or shortage of critical organizational resources in an organization's external environment

uncertainty
the extent to which managers can understand or predict which environmental changes and trends will affect their businesses

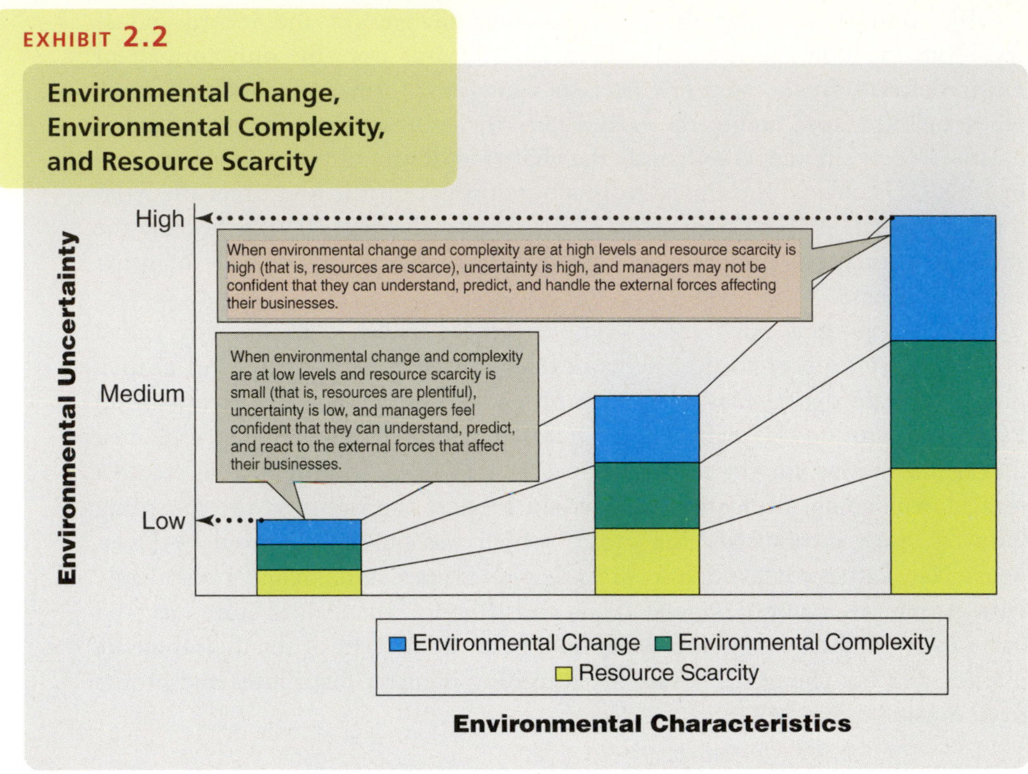
High
Medium
Low
Environmental Uncertainty
When environmental change and complexity are at high levels and resource scarcity is high (that is, resources are scarce), uncertainty is high, and managers may not be confident that they can understand, predict, and handle the external forces affecting their businesses.
When environmental change and complexity are at low levels and resource scarcity is small (that is, resources are plentiful), uncertainty is low, and managers feel confident that they can understand, predict, and react to the external forces that affect their businesses.
Environmental Change
Environmental Complexity
Resource Scarcity
Environmental Characteristics

EXHIBIT 2.2

Environmental Change, Environmental Complexity, and Resource Scarcity

REVIEW 1

Changing Environments

Environmental change, complexity, and resource scarcity are the basic components of external environments. Environmental change is the rate at which conditions or events affecting a business change. Environmental complexity is the number and intensity of external factors in an external environment. Resource scarcity is the scarcity or abundance of resources available in the external environment. The greater the degree of environmental change, environmental complexity, and resource scarcity, the less confident managers are that they can understand, predict, and effectively react to the trends affecting their businesses. According to punctuated equilibrium theory, companies experience periods of stability followed by short periods of dynamic, fundamental change, followed by a return to periods of stability.

2 General Environment

As Exhibit 2.3 shows, two kinds of external environments influence organizations: the general environment and the specific environment. The **general environment** consists of the economy and the technological, sociocultural, and political/legal trends that indirectly affect *all* organizations. Changes in any sector of the general environment eventually affect most organizations. For example, when the Federal Reserve lowers its prime lending rate, most businesses benefit because banks and credit card companies lower the interest rates they charge for loans. Consumers, who can then

general environment
the economic, technological, sociocultural, and political trends that indirectly affect all organizations

EXHIBIT 2.3

General and Specific Environments

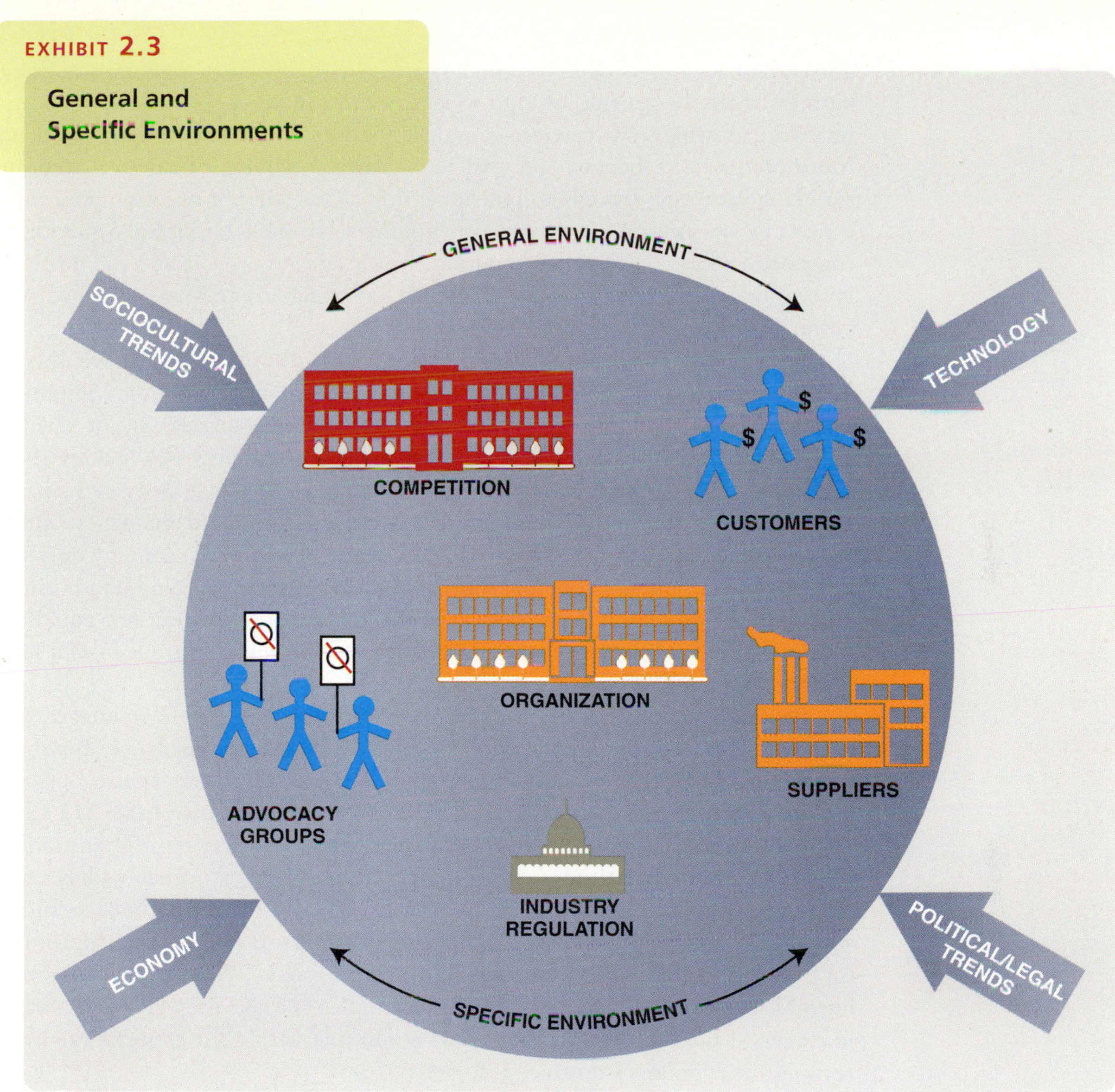

borrow money more cheaply, might borrow more to buy homes, cars, refrigerators, and large-screen TVs.

By contrast, each organization also has a **specific environment** that is unique to that firm's industry and directly affects the way it conducts day-to-day business. The specific environment, which will be discussed in detail in Section 3 of this chapter, includes customers, competitors, suppliers, industry regulation, and advocacy groups.

specific environment the customers, competitors, suppliers, industry regulations, and advocacy groups that are unique to an industry and directly affect how a company does business

First, let's take a closer look at the four components of the general environment: 2.1 **the economy**, 2.2 **the technological**, 2.3 **sociocultural**, and 2.4 **political/legal trends that indirectly affect all organizations**.

2.1 Economy

The current state of a country's economy affects virtually every organization doing business there. In general, in a growing economy, more people are working and wages are growing, and therefore consumers have relatively more money to spend. More products are bought and sold in a growing economy than in a static or shrinking economy. Though an individual firm's sales will not necessarily increase, a growing economy does provide an environment favorable for business growth. In contrast, in a shrinking economy, consumers have less money to spend and relatively fewer products are bought and sold. Thus, a shrinking economy makes growth for businesses more difficult.

Because the economy influences basic business decisions, such as whether to hire more employees, expand production, or take out loans to purchase equipment, managers scan their economic environments for signs of significant change. Unfortunately, the economic statistics that managers rely on when making these decisions are notoriously poor predictors of *future* economic activity. A manager who decides to hire ten more employees because economic data suggest future growth could very well have to lay off those workers when the economy does not in fact grow. A famous economic study found that at the beginning of a business quarter (a period of only 3 months), even the best economic forecasters could not accurately predict whether economic activity would grow or shrink *in that same quarter*![10]

Because economic statistics can be poor predictors, some managers try to predict future economic activity by tracking business confidence. **Business confidence indices** show how confident managers are about future business growth. For example, the Conference Board's CEO Confidence Index is a quarterly survey of 100 CEOs of large companies across a variety of different industries that examines attitudes regarding future growth.[11] Another widely cited measure is the Small Business Research Board's Business Confidence Index, which asks 500 small business owners and managers to express their optimism (or pessimism) about future business sales and prospects.[12] Managers often prefer business confidence indices to economic statistics because they know that other managers make business decisions that are in line with their expectations concerning the economy's future.

2.2 Technological Component

Technology is the knowledge, tools, and techniques used to transform inputs (raw materials, information, and so on) into outputs (products and services). For example, the inputs of authors, editors, and artists (knowledge) and the use of equipment like computers and printing presses (technology) transform paper, ink, and glue (raw materials) into this book (the finished product).

Changes in technology can help companies provide better products or produce their products more efficiently. For example, advances in surgical techniques and imaging equipment have made open-heart surgery much faster and safer in recent years. Although technological changes can benefit a business, they can also threaten it. Companies must embrace new technology and find effective ways to use it to improve their products and services or decrease costs. If they don't, they will lose out to those companies that do.

business confidence indices
indices that show managers' level of confidence about future business growth

technology
the knowledge, tools, and techniques used to transform input into output

For example, over-the-counter medications have traditionally been available in either pill or liquid form, but these might soon be replaced by edible films, just like quickly dissolving thin strips of breath freshener. This new technology has applications in areas where administering oral medication can be challenging, such as to children and pets. Novartis has added edible film to many of its product lines, and its Triaminic line of cold medicines now sells multiple flavors of film in children's strength. The Triaminic franchise has grown from nothing to a 20 percent share of the pediatric cough and cold market.[13] Chapter 6, on organizational change and innovation, provides a more in-depth discussion of how technology affects a company's competitive advantage.

2.3 Sociocultural Component

The sociocultural component of the general environment refers to the demographic characteristics, general behavior, attitudes, and beliefs of people in a particular society. Sociocultural changes and trends influence organizations in two important ways.

First, changes in demographic characteristics, such as the number of people with particular skills or the growth/decline in particular population segments (marital status, age, gender, ethnicity), affect how companies staff their businesses. For example, married women with children are much more likely to work today than four decades ago. In 1960, only 18.6 percent of women with children under 6 years old and 39 percent of women with children between the ages of 6 and 17 worked. By 2007, those percentages had risen to 61.5 percent and 76.2 percent, respectively.[14]

Second, sociocultural changes in behavior, attitudes, and beliefs also affect the demand for a business's products and services. Today, with more married women with children in the work force, traffic congestion creating longer commutes, and both parents working longer hours, people are much more likely to value products and services that allow them to recapture free time with their families. Thus, people—especially working mothers—use numerous services to help reduce the amount of time they spend doing chores and household management tasks.

Priscilla La Barbera, a marketing professor at New York University, says, "People are beginning to realize that their time has real value."[15] Brian Wheeler, who runs a concierge service in Washington, D.C. that performs personal tasks for busy workers says, "Many households have two adults working full time, people are working longer hours, and traffic in our region gets worse each year. When you combine these things, there isn't much time for anything outside of work and life maintenance stuff. We give them a hand and magically get things done for them during the day so that when they get home they can actually unwind or spend quality time with their family."[16]

2.4 Political/Legal Component

The political/legal component of the general environment includes the legislation, regulations, and court decisions that govern and regulate business behavior. New laws and regulations continue to impose additional responsibilities on companies. Unfortunately, many managers are unaware of these new responsibilities. For example, under the 1991 Civil Rights Act (***http://www.eeoc.gov/policy/cra91.html***), if an employee is sexually harassed by anyone at work (a supervisor, a coworker, or even a customer), the company—not just the harasser—is potentially liable for damages, attorneys' fees, and back pay.[17] Under the Family and Medical Leave Act (***http://www.dol.gov/esa/whd/fmla***), employees who have been on the job 1 year are guaranteed 12 weeks of unpaid leave per year to tend to their illnesses, elderly parents, a newborn baby, or a newly adopted child. Employees are guaranteed the same job, pay, and benefits when they return to work.[18]

Many managers are also unaware of the potential legal risks associated with traditional managerial decisions like recruiting, hiring, and firing employees. Increasingly, businesses and managers are being sued for negligent hiring and supervision, defamation, invasion of privacy, emotional distress, fraud, and misrepresentation during employee recruitment.[19] More than 14,000 suits for wrongful termination (unfairly firing employees) are filed each year.[20] In fact, wrongful termination lawsuits increased by 77 percent during the 1990s.[21] One in four employers will at some point be sued for wrongful termination. It can cost $300,000 to settle such a case once it goes to court, but employers lose 70 percent of court cases, and the former employee is awarded, on average, $1 million or more.[22] On the other hand, employers who settle before going to court typically pay just $10,000 to $100,000 per case.[23]

Not everyone agrees that companies' legal risks are too severe. Indeed, many believe that the government should do more to regulate and restrict business behavior and that it should be easier for average citizens to sue dishonest or negligent corporations. From a managerial perspective, the best medicine against legal risk is prevention. As a manager, it is your responsibility to educate yourself about the laws, regulations, and potential lawsuits that could affect your business. Failure to do so may put you and your company at risk of sizable penalties, fines, or legal charges.

REVIEW 2

General Environment

The general environment consists of economic, technological, sociocultural, and political/legal events and trends that affect all organizations. Because the economy influences basic business decisions, managers often use economic statistics and business confidence indices to predict future economic activity. Changes in technology, which transforms inputs into outputs, can be a benefit or a threat to a business. Sociocultural trends, like changing demographic characteristics, affect how companies run their businesses. Similarly, sociocultural changes in behavior, attitudes, and beliefs affect the demand for a business's products and services. Court decisions and new federal and state laws have imposed much greater political/legal responsibilities on companies. The best way to manage legal responsibilities is to educate managers and employees about laws and regulations and potential lawsuits that could affect a business.

3 Specific Environment

As you just learned, changes in any sector of the general environment (economic, technological, sociocultural, and political/legal) eventually affect most organizations. Each organization also has a specific environment that is unique to that firm's industry and directly affects the way it conducts day-to-day business. For instance, if your customers decide to use another product, your main competitor cuts prices 10 percent, your best supplier can't deliver raw materials, federal regulators mandate reductions in pollutants in your industry, or environmental groups accuse your company of selling unsafe products, the impact from the specific environment on your business is immediate.

Let's examine how the: 3.1 **customer**, 3.2 **competitor**, 3.3 **supplier**, 3.4 **industry regulation**, and 3.5 **advocacy group components of the specific environment affect businesses**.

© ISTOCKPHOTO.COM/STONE RIVER MEDIA

3.1 Customer Component

Customers purchase products and services. Companies cannot exist without customer support. Monitoring customers' changing wants and needs is critical to business success. There are two basic strategies for monitoring customers: reactive and proactive.

Reactive customer monitoring involves identifying and addressing customer trends and problems after they occur. One reactive strategy is to listen closely to customer complaints and respond to customer concerns. For example, Larry Dague, owner of Scubatoys.com, spends an hour a day reading and responding to postings in the customer forum. When a customer posts a complaint, Dague responds immediately with an apology and an explanation of how he's fixing the problem.[24]

Companies that respond quickly to customer complaints (i.e., reactive customer monitoring) are viewed much more favorably than companies that are slow to respond or never respond.[25] In particular, studies have shown that when a company thanks the customer with a follow-up letter, offers a sincere, specific response to the complaint (not a form letter, but an explanation of how the problem will be handled), and contains a small gift, coupons, or a refund to make up for the problem, customers are much more likely to purchase products or services again from that company.[26]

Proactive monitoring of customers means identifying and addressing customer needs, trends, and issues *before* they occur. Every month, *TRAVELOCITY*, one of the leading web travel sites, reviews 30,000 customer surveys, 50,000 e-mails, and notes from 500,000 phone calls! By using special software from Attensity Corporation that quickly analyzes and identifies trends in mountains of text-based data, it found that customers who purchased airline tickets on their website were blaming Travelocity when airlines canceled their flights. As a result, Travelocity's website actively prevents this problem by steering customers away from flights with small flight loads that have sold only a small portion of available tickets.[27]

3.2 Competitor Component

Competitors are companies in the same industry that sell similar products or services to customers. Ford, Toyota, Honda, Nissan, Hyundai, and Kia all compete

competitors
companies in the same industry that sell similar products or services to customers

for automobile customers. NBC, ABC, CBS, and Fox (along with hundreds of cable channels) compete for TV viewers' attention. McDonald's, Burger King, and Wendy's compete for fast-food customers' dollars. Often the difference between success and failure in business comes down to whether your company is doing a better job of satisfying customer wants and needs than the competition. Consequently, companies need to keep close track of what their competitors are doing. To do this, managers perform a **competitive analysis**, which involves identifying your competitors, anticipating competitors' moves, and determining competitors' strengths and weaknesses.

Surprisingly, managers often do a poor job of identifying potential competitors because they tend to focus on only two or three well-known competitors with similar goals and resources.[28] Historically, Coke and Pepsi spent more time keeping track of each other than they spent on other competitors until they each started losing ground to start-up energy drinks, bottled water, and fruit juices.[29] Likewise, Hoover, Dirt Devil, and more recently, Oreck competed fiercely in the market for vacuum cleaners. When Dyson entered the market with its radically different vacuum that developed and maintained significantly more suction power, the company garnered 20 percent market share within its first months on the shelves.[30] Only then did Hoover and Dirt Devil design their own bagless vacuums.

Another mistake managers may make when analyzing the competition is to underestimate potential competitors' capabilities. When this happens, managers don't take the steps they should to continue to improve their products or services. The result can be significant decreases in both market share and profits. For nearly a decade, traditional phone companies ignored the threat to their business from VoIP (Voice over Internet Protocol). Early on, for example, software products like Cool Talk, Internet Phone, and Web Phone made it possible to make inexpensive long-distance phone calls using VoIP. The sound quality was only as good as AM radio, but people who were used to poor-quality sound on their cell phones didn't care because the calls were so much cheaper.[31]

Today, because larger phone companies were slow to adopt VoIP capabilities, they're facing a rash of new, unexpected VoIP competitors, all of which have slashed prices and taken market share using high-speed Internet service. For example, *COMCAST*, a cable-TV provider that also offers high-speed Internet service, gains ten phone subscribers—at the expense of phone companies like Verizon and AT&T—for every cable TV subscriber that it loses.[42] Likewise, VoIP is threatening the phone companies' wireless services, which now account for most of their profits. Scott Mesch, of Boulder, Colorado, used to pay $3.50 a minute to call relatives in Australia. Now he uses the TruPhone Internet application on his iPhone for just a few cents a minute. Says Mesch, "A lot of times I didn't even think of using my cell phone to make calls out of the country. Now I don't hesitate . . . it's no different from any other local call."[32]

competitive analysis
a process for monitoring the competition that involves identifying competition, anticipating their moves, and determining their strengths and weaknesses

3.3 Supplier Component

Suppliers are companies that provide material, human, financial, and informational resources to other companies. U.S. Steel buys iron ore from suppliers to make steel products. When IBM sells a mainframe computer, it also provides support staff, engineers, and other technical consultants to the company that bought the computer.

suppliers
companies that provide material, human, financial, and informational resources to other companies

If you're shopping for desks, chairs, and office supplies, chances are Office Depot will be glad to help your business open a revolving charge account to pay for your purchases. When a clothing manufacturer has spent $100,000 to purchase new high-pressure "water drills" to cut shirt and pants patterns to precise sizes, the water drill manufacturer, as part of the purchase, will usually train the workers on the machinery.

A key factor influencing the impact and quality of the relationship between companies and their suppliers is how dependent they are on each other.[33] **Supplier dependence** is the degree to which a company relies on a supplier because of the importance of the supplier's product to the company and the difficulty of finding other sources for that product.

Supplier dependence is very strong in the diamond business, given that De Beers Consolidated Mines provides 66 percent of all wholesale diamonds in the world. De Beers has dominated the diamond industry for more than a century, controlling the supply, price, and quality of the best diamonds on the market. The company's 125 customers, or "sightholders," as they're known in the industry, are summoned to De Beers's London office ten times a year and given a shoebox of diamonds that they are required to buy. If they refuse, they lose the opportunity to purchase more diamonds in the future. De Beers also initiated a Supplier of Choice (SoC) program that requires sightholders to pay more of the marketing, advertising, and branding costs for De Beers diamonds. SoC sightholders sign 2-year contracts that spell out their responsibilities to develop marketing plans and advertising initiatives and to adhere to ethical guidelines. Just two-thirds of De Beers sightholders, however, qualified as SoCs. The one-third who didn't qualify as SoCs are no longer permitted to sell De Beers diamonds and must now get their diamonds from less prestigious diamond suppliers.[34]

Buyer dependence is the degree to which a supplier relies on a buyer because of the importance of that buyer to the supplier's sales and the difficulty of finding other buyers of its products. For example, when *INBEV* purchased Anheuser-Busch and renamed itself AB InBev, it became the world's largest brewer, controlling over 25 percent of global beer sales. This gave AB InBev tremendous bargaining power over its suppliers, which it leveraged by paying them for their product shipments—everything from malt to hops to yeast—120 days after being invoiced. With existing contracts providing payment 30 days after being invoiced, that meant that AB InBev's suppliers would have to wait an extra 3 months to be paid. Delaying payments gives AB InBev an additional $1.2 billion in cash flow per year, but at the expense of its suppliers.[35] There is little, however, that most AB InBev suppliers can do about this change.

As the De Beers and AB InBev examples show, a high degree of buyer or seller dependence can lead to **opportunistic behavior**, in which one party benefits at the expense of the other. Although opportunistic behavior between buyers and suppliers will never be completely eliminated, many companies believe that both buyers and suppliers can benefit by improving the buyer-supplier relationship.[36] In contrast to opportunistic behavior, **relationship behavior** focuses on establishing a mutually beneficial, long-term relationship between buyers and suppliers.[37]

supplier dependence
the degree to which a company relies on a supplier because of the importance of the supplier's product to the company and the difficulty of finding other sources of that product

buyer dependence
the degree to which a supplier relies on a buyer because of the importance of that buyer to the supplier and the difficulty of finding other buyers for its products

opportunistic behavior
a transaction in which one party in the relationship benefits at the expense of the other

relationship behavior
the establishment of mutually beneficial, long-term exchanges between buyers and suppliers

3.4 Industry Regulation Component

Whereas the political/legal component of the general environment affects all businesses, the **industry regulation** component consists of regulations and rules that govern the practices and procedures of specific industries, businesses, and professions.

industry regulation
the regulations and rules that govern the business practices and procedures of specific industries, businesses, and professions

Regulatory agencies affect businesses by creating and enforcing rules and regulations to protect consumers, workers, or society as a whole. For example, the U.S. Department of Agriculture and the Food and Drug Administration regulate the safety of seafood (as well as meat and poultry) through the science-based Hazard Analysis and Critical Control Points program. Seafood processors are required to identify hazards (toxins, chemicals, pesticides, and decomposition) that could cause the fish they process to be unsafe. They must also establish critical control points to control hazards both inside and outside their fish-processing plants and then establish monitoring, corrective action, and verification procedures to certify that the fish is safe to consume.[38]

The nearly 100 federal agencies and regulatory commissions can affect almost any kind of business. For example, the toy industry spent $200 million to increase the safety of its products after 20 million toys produced in China were recalled because of the presence of harmful chemicals. In addition to the voluntary recall by toy retailers and manufacturers, new federal regulations in the Consumer Product Safety Improvement Act of 2008 ban phthalates from children's products and now require products to be tested for them before they are sold.[39]

Overall, the number and cost of federal regulations has nearly tripled in the last 25 years. Today, for every $1 the federal government spends creating regulations, businesses spend $45 to comply with them.[40] In addition to federal regulations, businesses are also subject to state, county, and city regulations. Complying with all of these regulations costs businesses an estimated $1.1 trillion per year, or $5,633 per employee.[41] Surveys indicate that managers rank dealing with government regulation as one of the most demanding and frustrating parts of their jobs.[42]

3.5 Advocacy Groups

advocacy groups concerned citizens who band together to try to influence the business practices of specific industries, businesses, and professions

public communications an advocacy group tactic that relies on voluntary participation by the news media and the advertising industry to get the advocacy group's message out

media advocacy an advocacy group tactic that involves framing issues as public issues; exposing questionable, exploitative, or unethical practices; and forcing media coverage by buying media time or creating controversy that is likely to receive extensive news coverage

Advocacy groups are groups of concerned citizens who band together to try to influence the practices of specific industries, businesses, and professions. The members of a group generally share the same point of view on a particular issue. For example, environmental advocacy groups might try to get manufacturers to reduce smokestack pollution emissions. Unlike the industry regulation component of the specific environment, advocacy groups cannot force organizations to change their practices. Nevertheless, they can use a number of techniques to try to influence companies, including public communications, media advocacy, web pages, blogs, and product boycotts.

The **public communications** approach relies on *voluntary* participation by the news media and the advertising industry to send out an advocacy group's message. For example, a public service campaign to encourage people to quit smoking ran the following ads in newspapers and magazines throughout Europe: a photo showing the foot of a young person with a toe tag (indicating the person was dead), with the caption "Smokers die younger"; a picture showing clean lungs next to brown- and black-stained lungs, with the caption "Smoking causes fatal lung cancer"; and a photo of a baby in an intensive care unit hooked up to a respirator, with the caption "Smoking when pregnant harms your baby."[43]

Media advocacy is much more aggressive than the public communications approach. A **media advocacy** approach typically involves framing the group's concerns as a public issue (affecting everyone); exposing questionable, exploitative,

Doing the Right Thing

Dealing with Gifts and Suppliers

In hopes of getting a buyer's business or getting more business, suppliers sometimes offer buyers trips to exotic locations, dinners at expensive restaurants, or luxurious gifts. Excessive gift giving and receiving creates a conflict of interest between what's best for the company (purchasing items of the optimal quality and cost) and what's personally best for the buyer who receives the gifts. Follow these general guidelines to avoid conflicts of interest:

- Remember that there is no such thing as a free lunch.
- Make sure that business meals and entertainment (parties, outings, sporting events) have a valid business purpose and that the buyer and the supplier should take turns paying for or hosting them.
- Don't accept gifts worth more than $25. If you are offered a gift worth more than $25, ask your manager if the gift is appropriate.
- Never accept cash or cash equivalents, such as gift certificates.
- Don't accept discounts on goods and services unless the same discounts are generally available to others.
- Don't accept offers of stock in suppliers' companies.
- Don't allow personal friendships with suppliers to influence buying decisions.[46]

or unethical practices; and creating controversy that is likely to receive extensive news coverage. *PETA* (People for the Ethical Treatment of Animals), which has offices in the United States, England, Italy, and Germany, uses controversial publicity stunts and advertisements to try to change the behavior of large organizations, fashion designers, medical researchers, and anyone else it believes is hurting or mistreating animals. In one of its latest protests, called "McCruelty: I'm Hatin' It," PETA is protesting that McDonald's, which uses 290 million chickens a year, tolerates its chicken suppliers using inhumane killing methods—hanging the birds upside down, stunning them in water that has an electrical current, and then cutting their throats.[44] A McDonald's spokesperson said the company is committed to "humane treatment of animals by our suppliers in every part of the world where we do business."[45]

A **product boycott** is a tactic in which an advocacy group actively tries to persuade consumers not to purchase a company's product or service. The Rainforest Action Network (RAN) successfully influenced Citigroup's then CEO Sandy Weill to implement environmentally friendly lending policies. In 2006, the group targeted Ford Motor Company as the automobile manufacturer with the worst record of fuel efficiency. When Ford stated that RAN would have no impact on the company, RAN's executive director Michael Brune responded, "Every company says we are not having an effect—straight up to the time they make their policy change."[47]

product boycott
an advocacy group tactic that involves protesting a company's actions by persuading consumers not to purchase its product or service

REVIEW 3

Specific Environment

The specific environment is made up of five components: customers, competitors, suppliers, industry regulation, and advocacy groups. Companies can monitor customers' needs by identifying customer problems after they occur or by anticipating problems before they occur. Because they tend to focus on well-known competitors, managers often underestimate their competition or do a poor job of identifying future competitors. Suppliers and buyers are dependent on each other, and that dependence sometimes leads to opportunistic behavior, in which one benefits at the expense of the other. Regulatory agencies affect businesses by creating rules and then enforcing them. Overall, the level of industry regulation has nearly tripled in the last 25 years. Advocacy groups cannot regulate organizations' practices. Nevertheless, through public communications, media advocacy, and product boycotts, they try to convince companies to change their practices.

4 Making Sense of Changing Environments

In Chapter 1, you learned that managers are responsible for making sense of their business environments. As our discussions of the general and specific environments have indicated, however, making sense of business environments is not an easy task.

Because external environments can be dynamic, confusing, and complex, managers use a three-step process to make sense of the changes in their external environments: 4.1 **environmental scanning**, 4.2 **interpreting environmental factors**, and 4.3 **acting on threats and opportunities**.

4.1 Environmental Scanning

Environmental scanning involves searching the environment for important events or issues that might affect an organization. Managers scan the environment to stay up-to-date on important factors in their industry. The **American Hospital Association**, for instance, publishes an annual "Environmental Scan" to help hospital and health system managers understand the trends and market forces that have a "high probability of affecting the healthcare field."[48] Organizational strategies also affect environmental scanning. In other words, managers pay close attention to trends and events that are directly related to their company's ability to compete in the marketplace.[49]

Finally, environmental scanning is important because it contributes to organizational performance. Environmental scanning helps managers detect environmental changes and problems before they become organizational crises.[50] Furthermore, companies whose CEOs do more environmental scanning have higher profits.[51] CEOs in better-performing firms scan their firm's environments more frequently and scan more key factors in their environments in more depth and detail than do CEOs in poorer-performing firms.[52]

4.2 Interpreting Environmental Factors

environmental scanning searching the environment for important events or issues that might affect an organization

After scanning, managers determine what environmental events and issues mean to the organization. Typically, managers view environmental events and issues as either threats or opportunities. When managers interpret environmental events as threats, they take steps to protect the company from further harm.

For example, now that Internet phone service (VoIP) has emerged as a threat, traditional phone companies have responded by spending billions to expand their fiber-optic networks so that they too can offer VoIP, as well as Internet service and TV packages just like those the cable and satellite companies offer.

By contrast, when managers interpret environmental events as opportunities, they consider strategic alternatives for taking advantage of those events to improve company performance. To take advantage of the rapid growth of the smartphone market, Apple developed the iPhone. CEO Steve Jobs announced the release more than 6 months in advance to generate hype, stimulate demand, and dampen sales of competitors. Apple sold 21 million iPhones in its first 18 months on the market, far exceeding its goal of 10 million.[53]

4.3 Acting on Threats and Opportunities

After scanning for information on environmental events and issues and interpreting them as threats or opportunities, managers have to decide how to respond to these environmental factors. Deciding what to do under conditions of uncertainty is always difficult. Managers can never be completely confident that they have all the information they need or that they correctly understand the information they have. Nonetheless, they must make decisions and take actions that minimize threats and take advantage of opportunities.

© AP IMAGES/PAUL SAKUMA

In the end, managers must complete all three steps—environmental scanning, interpreting environmental factors, and acting on threats and opportunities—to make sense of changing external environments. Environmental scanning helps managers more accurately interpret their environments and take actions that improve company performance. Through scanning, managers keep tabs on what competitors are doing, identify market trends, and stay alert to current events that affect their company's operations. Armed with the environmental information they have gathered, managers can then minimize the impact of threats and turn opportunities into increased profits.

REVIEW 4

Making Sense of Changing Environments

Managers use a three-step process to make sense of external environments: environmental scanning, interpreting information, and acting on threats and opportunities. Managers scan their environments based on their organizational strategies, their need for up-to-date information, and their need to reduce uncertainty. When managers identify environmental events as threats, they take steps to protect the company from harm. When managers identify environmental events as opportunities, they formulate alternatives for taking advantage of them to improve company performance.

Internal Environments

We have been looking at trends and events outside of companies that have the potential to affect them. By contrast, the **internal environment** consists of trends and events *within* an organization that affect the management, employees, and organizational culture. Internal environments are important because they affect what people think, feel, and do at work.

Earlier in the chapter, you learned that innovative new products such as the iPod, iPhone, and Xbox 360, as well as aggressive cost-cutting in the booming market for high-definition TVs (i.e., the external environment), hurt Sony's market share and profitability. Sony's problems, however, were directly linked to its hypercompetitive culture where people in different parts of the company did not communicate with each other and where designing innovative, high-priced products regardless of cost was seen as the most important contribution to the company.

After reading the next section, you should be able to:

5 explain how organizational cultures are created and how they can help companies be successful.

The key component in internal environments is **organizational culture**, or the set of key values, beliefs, and attitudes shared by members of the organization.

5 Organizational Cultures: Creation, Success, and Change

Let's take a closer look at: 5.1 **how organizational cultures are created and maintained**, 5.2 **the characteristics of successful organizational cultures**, and 5.3 **how companies can accomplish the difficult task of changing organizational cultures**.

5.1 Creation and Maintenance of Organizational Cultures

A primary source of organizational culture is the company founder. Founders like Thomas J. Watson, Sr. (IBM), Sam Walton (Wal-Mart), and Bill Gates (Microsoft) create organizations in their own images and imprint them with their beliefs, attitudes, and values. Although company founders are instrumental in the creation of organizational cultures, eventually they retire, die, or choose to leave their companies. When the founders are gone, how are their values, attitudes, and beliefs sustained in the organizational culture? The answer is stories and heroes.

Organizational members tell **organizational stories** to make sense of organizational events and changes and to emphasize culturally consistent assumptions, decisions, and actions.[54] At Wal-Mart, stories abound about founder Sam Walton's thriftiness as he strove to make Wal-Mart the low-cost retailer that it is today.

> *In those days, we would go on buying trips with Sam, and we'd all stay, as much as we could, in one room or two. I remember one time in Chicago when we stayed eight of us to a room. And the room wasn't very big to begin with. You might say we were on a pretty restricted budget.* (Gary Reinboth, one of Wal-Mart's first store managers)[55]

internal environment
the events and trends inside an organization that affect management, employees, and organizational culture

organizational culture
the values, beliefs, and attitudes shared by organizational members

organizational stories
stories told by organizational members to make sense of organizational events and changes and to emphasize culturally consistent assumptions, decisions, and actions

Sam Walton's thriftiness still permeates Wal-Mart today. Everyone, including top executives and the CEO, flies coach rather than business or first class. When employees travel on business, it's still the norm to share rooms (though two to a room, not eight!) at inexpensive motels like Motel 6 and Super 8. At one of its annual meetings, former CEO Lee Scott reinforced Sam Walton's beliefs by exhorting Wal-Mart employees to bring back and use the free pencils and pens from their travels. Most people in the audience didn't think he was kidding, and he probably wasn't.[56]

Management Trend:

A change of scenery could be just what your company needs to rejuvenate creativity. Instead of renting out hotels or conference centers, managers at Duke Energy decided to hold corporate meetings at the offices of other companies. The decision was motivated, at first, by the recession, since it was thousands of dollars cheaper to meet in offices instead of hotels. But managers soon found that employees picked up ideas from other companies, were inspired by seeing different processes, learned from the expertise of others, and were energized by vibrant atmospheres. All of this led to a resurgence of innovative and creative thinking.

Source: Dana Mattioli. "New Room, New Vantage Point." *Wall Street Journal.* March 8, 2010. B7.

A second way in which organizational culture is sustained is by recognizing and celebrating heroes. By definition, **organizational heroes** are organizational people admired for their qualities and achievements within the organization. Bowa Builders is a full-service construction company in Virginia. When renovating a large auto dealership, its carpet subcontractor mistakenly scheduled the new carpet to be delivered 2 weeks *after* it was to be installed. A Bowa employee kept the project on schedule by immediately reordering the carpet, flying to the factory, renting a truck, and then driving the carpet back to the dealership, all within 48 hours. CEO and company cofounder Larry Weinberg says this story is told and retold within Bowa Builders as an example of heroic customer service. The car dealership was so delighted with this extraordinary service that it referred $10–$12 million in new business to Bowa Builders.[79]

5.2 Successful Organizational Cultures

Preliminary research shows that organizational culture is related to organizational success. As shown in Exhibit 2.4, cultures based on adaptability, involvement, a clear mission, and consistency can help companies achieve higher sales growth, return on assets, profits, quality, and employee satisfaction.[57]

Adaptability is the ability to notice and respond to changes in the organization's environment. Cultures need to reinforce important values and behaviors, but a culture becomes dysfunctional if it prevents change. One of the surest ways to do that is to discourage open discussion and disagreement. In cultures that promote higher levels of *employee involvement* in decision making, employees feel a greater sense of ownership and responsibility. For example, Genencor designs its human resources programs by regularly polling employees about which benefits they enjoy and which they would like the company to offer. Most dramatically, when Genencor built its headquarters, it gave its employees a say in the design. Scientists requested

organizational heroes people celebrated for their qualities and achievements within an organization

EXHIBIT 2.4

Successful Organizational Cultures

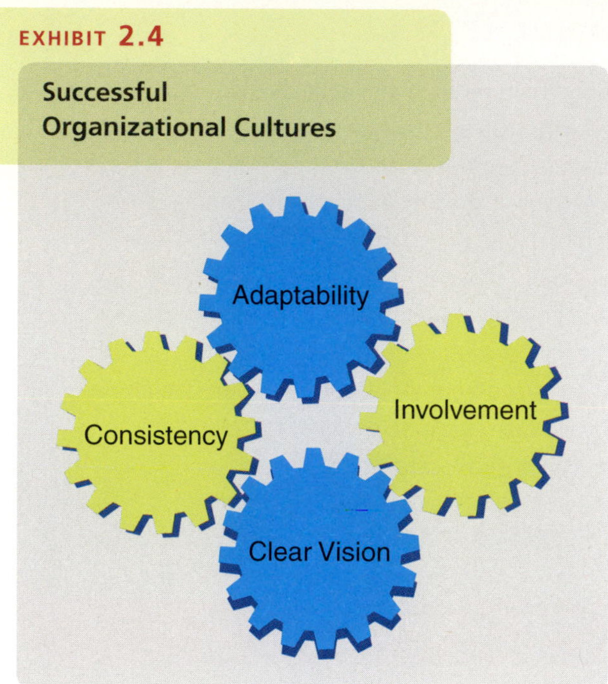

Source: D. R. Denison & A. K. Mishra, "Toward a Theory of Organizational Culture and Effectiveness," *Organization Science* 6 (1995): 204–223.

that the labs be placed along the building's exterior so they could receive natural light. The building also features a "main street," where employees congregate to collaborate and interact throughout the day. CEO Jean-Jacques Bienaime believes that these employee-driven design features lead to a more stimulating workplace. Such a commitment to employee involvement in decision making is definitely paying off for the company. Its turnover rate was less than 4 percent (the national industry average is 18.5 percent), and its employees generate approximately $60,000 more revenue per employee than its largest competitor, Novozymes.[58]

Company mission is the business's purpose or reason for existing. In organizational cultures with a clear company mission, the organization's strategic purpose and direction are apparent to everyone in the company. When managers are uncertain about their business environments, the mission helps guide the discussions, decisions, and behavior of the people in the company. For example, when Sergey Brin and Larry Page walked into Sequoia Capital seeking funding to start Google, they shared their initial vision for the company, "Google provides access to the world's information in one click."[59] Specific mission statements strengthen organizational cultures by letting everyone know why the company is in business, what really matters (i.e., the company's values), and how those values can be used to guide daily actions and behaviors.[60]

Finally, in **consistent organizational cultures**, the company actively defines and teaches organizational values, beliefs, and attitudes. McDonald's helps preserve its history and culture by having its executives work in its restaurants one day each year, on founder Ray Kroc's birthday. According to Kroc, this is to remind McDonald's executives that "if it's below [their] dignity to mop floors, clean toilets, and roll up [their] sleeves, then [they] are not going to succeed: [Their] attitude is wrong."[61]

Having a consistent or strong organizational culture doesn't guarantee good company performance. When core beliefs are widely shared and strongly held, it is very difficult to bring about needed change. Consequently, companies with strong cultures tend to perform poorly when they need to adapt to dramatic changes in their external environments.[62] Indeed, McDonald's saw its sales and profits decline in the late 1990s as customer eating patterns began to change. To rescue falling performance, the company introduced its "Plan to Win," which focused on five elements that drive its business: people, products, place, price, and promotion.

company mission
a company's purpose or reason for existing

consistent organizational culture
a company culture in which the company actively defines and teaches organizational values, beliefs, and attitudes

5.3 Changing Organizational Cultures

As shown in Exhibit 2.5, organizational cultures exist on three levels.[63] On the first, or surface, level are the reflections of an organization's culture that can be seen and observed, such as symbolic artifacts (for example, dress codes and office layouts) and workers' and managers' behaviors. Next, just below the surface, are the values and beliefs expressed by people in the company. You can't see these values and beliefs,

EXHIBIT 2.5

Three Levels of Organizational Culture

SEEN (Surface level)

- Symbolic artifacts such as dress codes
- Workers' and managers' behaviors

HEARD (Expressed values & beliefs)

- What people say
- How decisions are made and explained

BELIEVED (Unconscious assumptions & beliefs)

- Widely shared assumptions and beliefs
- Buried deep below surface
- Rarely discussed or thought about

© COMSTOCK/JUPITER IMAGES

but they become clear if you carefully listen to what people say and observe how decisions are made or explained. Finally, unconsciously held assumptions and beliefs about the company are buried deep below the surface. These are the unwritten views and rules that are so strongly held and so widely shared that they are rarely discussed or even thought about unless someone attempts to change them or unknowingly violates them. Changing such assumptions and beliefs can be very difficult. Instead, managers should focus on the parts of the organizational culture they can control. These include observable surface-level items, such as workers' behaviors and symbolic artifacts, and expressed values and beliefs, which can be influenced through employee selection. Let's see how these can be used to change organizational cultures.

One way of changing a corporate culture is to use behavioral addition or behavioral substitution to establish new patterns of behavior among managers and employees. **Behavioral addition** is the process of having managers and employees perform a new behavior, while **behavioral substitution** is having managers and employees perform a new behavior in place of another behavior. The key in both instances is to choose behaviors that are central to and symbolic of the old culture you're changing and the new culture that you want to create. When Mike Ullman became the CEO of JCPenney, he thought the company's culture was stuck in the 19th century (when the company was started). Employees called each other Mr. and Mrs. and casual attire and elaborate decoration of offices were not allowed. Ullman quickly determined that the company's stringent code of conduct was, among

behavioral addition
the process of having managers and employees perform new behaviors that are central to and symbolic of the new organizational culture that a company wants to create

behavioral substitution
the process of having managers and employees perform new behaviors central to the "new" organizational culture in place of behaviors that were central to the "old" organizational culture

other things, keeping it from recruiting the talent it needed. Mike Theilmann, the human resources officer, drafted a list of what he called "quick hits," small changes that would have a big impact on the culture. The first of Theilmann's initiatives was a campaign titled "Just Call Me Mike," which he hoped would cure employees of the entrenched practice of calling executives and managers Mr. and Mrs.[64]

Another way in which managers can begin to change corporate culture is to change the **visible artifacts** of their old culture, such as the office design and layout, company dress code, and recipients (or nonrecipients) of company benefits and perks like stock options, personal parking spaces, or the private company dining room.

Cultures can also be changed by hiring and selecting people with values and beliefs consistent with the company's desired culture. *Selection* is the process of gathering information about job applicants to decide who should be offered a job. As discussed in Chapter 10 on human resources, most selection instruments measure whether job applicants have the knowledge, skills, and abilities needed to succeed in their jobs. But companies are increasingly testing job applicants to determine how they fit with the company's desired culture (i.e., values and beliefs). Management consultant Ram Charan says, "A poor job match is not only harmful to the individual but also to the company."[65] The first step in hiring people who have values consistent with the desired culture is to define and describe that culture.

The second step is to ensure that applicants fit with the culture by using selection tests, instruments, and exercises to measure these values and beliefs in job applicants. (See Chapter 10 for a complete review of applicant and managerial selection.) At Southwest Airlines, humor and a good attitude are two of the most important requirements in its new hires. Cofounder and former CEO and board chair Herb Kelleher says, "What's important is that a customer should get off the airplane feeling: 'I didn't just get from A to B. I had one of the most pleasant experiences I ever had and I'll be back for that reason.'"[66] On one Southwest flight, Yvonne Masters jokingly introduced her fellow flight attendants as her "former husband and his new girlfriend."[67] Southwest passenger Mark Rafferty said his favorite Southwest flight attendant joke was when "they told everyone on the plane's left side, toward the terminal, to put their faces in the window and smile so our competitors can see what a full flight looks like."[68] Corny, yes, but humor is exactly what Southwest and its customers want, and the airline gets it by hiring people consistent with its hard-working, fun-loving culture. Says Kelleher, "We draft great attitudes. If you don't have a good attitude, we don't want you, no matter how skilled you are. We can change skill level through training. We can't change attitude."[69]

Corporate cultures are very difficult to change. Consequently, there is no guarantee that any one approach—changing visible cultural artifacts, using behavioral substitution, or hiring people with values consistent with a company's desired culture—will change a company's organizational culture. The best results are obtained by combining these methods. Together, these are some of the best tools managers have for changing culture because they send the clear message to managers and employees that "the accepted way of doing things" has changed.

visible artifacts
visible signs of an organization's culture, such as the office design and layout, company dress code, and company benefits and perks, like stock options, personal parking spaces, or the private company dining room

REVIEW 5

Organizational Cultures: Creation, Success, and Change

Organizational culture is the set of key values, beliefs, and attitudes shared by organizational members. Organizational cultures are often created by company founders and then sustained through the telling of organizational stories and the celebration of organizational heroes. Adaptable cultures that promote employee involvement, make clear the organization's strategic purpose and direction, and actively define and teach organizational values and beliefs can help companies achieve higher sales growth, return on assets, profits, quality, and employee satisfaction. Organizational cultures exist on three levels: the surface level, where cultural artifacts and behaviors can be observed; just below the surface, where values and beliefs are expressed; and deep below the surface, where unconsciously held assumptions and beliefs exist. Managers can begin to change company cultures by focusing on the top two levels and by using behavioral substitution and behavioral addition, changing visible artifacts, and selecting job applicants with values and beliefs consistent with the desired company culture.

Management Team Decision

Making a New Culture

Home Depot stores used to be known for customer service. A host of friendly employees would help customers navigate a huge inventory, find exactly what they needed, and even provide detailed instruction. Those days seem long gone, though. Under the leadership of the former CEO, the company shifted its focus away from customer service to reducing inventory and cutting costs. Stores that once had an employee in nearly every aisle were now being manned by just a handful, even during the busiest times. Customers looking for helpful attention could no longer find even a cashier, much less someone that could answer their questions on how to use a reciprocating saw.

Marvin Ellison, promoted to CEO in 2008, saw the disastrous results of Home Depot's lack of attention to customers. In the last three months of 2009, the company lost $54 million dollars. To make matters worse, the company's reputation took tremendous hits. For many years, it routinely ranked near the bottom of the University of Michigan's American Customer Satisfaction Index, which measures consumers' evaluations of all major retailers. Even after Home Depot recovered in these rankings slightly, it still lagged far behind competitors like Lowe's and Ace. He had to listen to countless stories of how consumers would drive an extra thirty minutes, even an hour, to avoid going to Home Depot.

To turn things around, Marvin Ellison has committed to a new company vision—a culture that is dedicated to meeting three goals—clean warehouses, stocked shelves, and top customer services. He wants employees to set aside a portion of their shift to do nothing else but take care of customers. He wants to revise evaluations so that employees' performance is reviewed primarily on the basis of customer service. He wants to give financial incentives to employees who provide great service. He wants to reduce the number of messages that stores and employees get from headquarters so that they can focus on customers. In short, he wants to restore Home Depot's reputation for providing the very best in customer service.

Ellison has appointed you to a management team in charge of setting up a training and evaluating program that will get the entire company focused on his vision of customer service. You and your team face the difficult task of changing the entire company's culture, so that everyone is focused on the customer. How will you do it?

For this Management Team Decision, form a group of three or four with other students to act as the management team, and answer the following questions.

Questions

1. What kind of training and evaluation program would you institute to change Home Depot's culture?
2. Recall from the text that there are three levels of organizational culture. What kind of changes would you make to address each level?
3. How could an analysis of the company's external environment help in establishing a new customer-based culture?

Sources: The American Customer Satisfaction Index: http://www.theacsi.org/

Jena McGregor. "Putting Home Depot's House in Order." *BusinessWeek.* May 18, 2009. p. 54.

Practice being a MANAGER

Navigating Different Organizational Cultures

Effective managers recognize that organizational culture is an important, often critical, element of organizational health and performance. But recognizing and understanding culture, especially its less visible aspects, is often quite challenging. This exercise will give you some practice in recognizing cultural differences and the challenges and opportunities that managers face as they work with diverse cultures.

Suppose that music recording company SonyBMG has announced plans to hire several college students to form a team that will invest in the "next big things in music." The selected students will be paid $50,000 per year for working part-time. SonyBMG will also allocate up to $10 million for hiring artists, producing records, and so on based on the team's recommendations.

The new team has been dubbed the Top Wave Team (TWT). If TWT's recommendations are fruitful, the company will sign each member of the team to $150,000 full-time contracts. The company also plans to keep the team together and to give members bonuses and promotions based on their group performance.

Your class has been chosen as the representative college class. The music company is now asking you to form affinity groups by musical preferences in your class (e.g., a Country Music group, an Urban/Hip-Hop group). Each group will nominate one of its members to receive the first $50,000 internship as a TWT team member at SonyBMG. The new TWT group will meet and discuss initial plans and investment recommendations, and then your class will discuss the process and outcomes.

STEP 1 Choose your musical affinity. In the class session before this exercise, your professor will ask you to submit a survey form or sheet of paper with your name and your preferred musical genre.

Identify yourself with one of the following musical genres based on (a) preference/affinity ("I prefer this music") and (b) knowledge/understanding ("Of all types of music, I know the most about _______ music/musicians"):

1. Rock
2. Country
3. Religious/Spiritual
4. Urban/Hip-Hop
5. Rap
6. Jazz/R&B
7. Pop/Mainstream
8. Classical
9. Folk/Bluegrass

Your professor will review your submitted preferences, and organize affinity groups for the next class session.

STEP 2 Organize into groups. Your professor will organize you by musical affinity. If your class is heavily concentrated in one or a few of the musical genres, you may be asked to further divide into smaller groups by subcategories (such as Rock—Heavy Metal and Rock—Popular/Top 40).

STEP 3 Prepare your recommendations. In groups, discuss what is important about your type of music and what investments should be made by the TWT team. Keep in mind that the investments made by the TWT team could have a big impact on the future of your favorite music. Recommend a dollar amount or percentage of the $10 million that your representative ought to secure for investment in your genre.

Each group should then select one of its members to receive the internship from SonyBMG and represent the group on the TWT team.

STEP 4 Discuss recommendations before the class. Nominees from the musical affinity groups should discuss their recommendations before the class. Those not on the TWT should observe the process and take notes on what happens in this meeting.

STEP 5 Hold the team meeting. Your professor will allocate a short time for the initial meeting of the TWT. It may occur before or during the class meeting. After the TWT reaches agreement on how it might allocate its investments by genre (or by some alternative approach), reaches impasse, or reaches the time limit, your professor will call an end to the TWT meeting.

STEP 6 Debrief and discuss. As a class, discuss the process and outcomes of this exercise. Consider the following questions and/or others posed by your professor:

- Did you sense some cultural affinity with others who shared your musical tastes? Why or why not?
- What expectations might be associated with choosing someone to "represent" a group on a team such as the TWT?
- What tensions and challenges might face each member of the TWT in a real-life setting of serving on a group that represents various cultures?

Check Your Tolerance for Ambiguity

Think of the difference between playing chess (where you can see all the pieces and anticipate attacks and plan counterattacks) and playing poker (where no one knows anyone else's hand, and you have to make guesses based on your interpretation of opponents' betting patterns). In chess, there is little ambiguity, whereas in poker there is tremendous ambiguity. Although many people liken business to a game of chess, probably because of the strategic aspects of the game, business is actually more like poker. The business environment is complex and uncertain, and managers never *really* know all the cards the opposition is holding. Managers must learn to adapt to environmental shifts and new developments—sometimes on a daily basis. For some managers, however, this can be a challenging task because everyone has a different comfort level when it comes to ambiguity. For some, not knowing all the details can be a source of significant stress, whereas for others uncertainty can be energizing.

As a manager, you will need to develop an appropriate tolerance for ambiguity. For example, being stressed out every time interest rates change can be counterproductive, but completely ignoring the economic environment can be detrimental to your company's performance.

Complete the following questionnaire to get a sense of your tolerance for ambiguity.[70] Indicate the extent to which you agree with the statements using the following scale:

1. Strongly disagree
2. Moderately disagree
3. Slightly disagree
4. Neutral
5. Slightly agree
6. Moderately agree
7. Strongly agree

1. I don't tolerate ambiguous situations well.
1 2 3 4 5 6 7

2. I find it difficult to respond when faced with an unexpected event.
1 2 3 4 5 6 7

3. I don't think new situations are any more threatening than familiar situations.
1 2 3 4 5 6 7

4. I am drawn to situations that can be interpreted in more than one way.
1 2 3 4 5 6 7

5. I would rather avoid solving problems that must be viewed from several different perspectives.
1 2 3 4 5 6 7

6. I try to avoid situations that are ambiguous.
1 2 3 4 5 6 7

7. I am good at managing unpredictable situations.
1 2 3 4 5 6 7

8. I prefer familiar situations to new ones.
1 2 3 4 5 6 7

9. Problems that cannot be considered from just one point of view are a little threatening.
1 2 3 4 5 6 7

10. I avoid situations that are too complicated for me to easily understand.
1 2 3 4 5 6 7

11. I am tolerant of ambiguous situations.
1 2 3 4 5 6 7

12. I enjoy tackling problems that are complex enough to be ambiguous.
1 2 3 4 5 6 7

13. I try to avoid problems that don't seem to have only one "best" solution.
1 2 3 4 5 6 7

14. I often find myself looking for something new, rather than trying to hold things constant in my life.
1 2 3 4 5 6 7

15. I generally prefer novelty over familiarity.
1 2 3 4 5 6 7

16. I dislike ambiguous situations.
1 2 3 4 5 6 7

17. Some problems are so complex that just trying to understand them is fun.
1 2 3 4 5 6 7

18. I have little trouble coping with unexpected events.
1 2 3 4 5 6 7

19. I pursue problem situations that are so complex some people call them "mind-boggling."
1 2 3 4 5 6 7

20. I find it hard to make a choice when the outcome is uncertain.
1 2 3 4 5 6 7

21. I enjoy an occasional surprise.
1 2 3 4 5 6 7

22. I prefer a situation in which there is some ambiguity.
1 2 3 4 5 6 7

SCORING

Determine your score by entering your response to each survey item below, as follows. In blanks that say *regular score*, simply enter your response for that item. If your response was a 6, place a 6 in the *regular score* blank. In blanks that say *reverse score*, subtract your response from 8 and enter the result. So if your response was a 6, place a 2 (8 − 6 = 2) in the *reverse score* blank. Add up your total score.

1. regular score ______
2. regular score ______
3. reverse score ______
4. reverse score ______
5. regular score ______
6. regular score ______
7. reverse score ______
8. regular score ______
9. regular score ______
10. regular score ______
11. regular score ______
12. reverse score ______
13. regular score ______
14. reverse score ______
15. reverse score ______
16. regular score ______
17. reverse score ______
18. reverse score ______
19. reverse score ______
20. regular score ______
21. reverse score ______
22. reverse score ______

TOTAL = _______

You can find the interpretation for your score at: login.cengagebrain.com.

Biz Flix

© GREEN LIGHT

Charlie Wilson's War

"Good-Time" Charlie Wilson (Tom Hanks) is a Democratic Congressman from East Texas with a reputation for partying, drinking, and womanizing. When Afghanistan rebels against the Soviet troop invasion in the 1980s, Wilson becomes the unlikely champion of the Afghan cause through his role in two major congressional committees that deal with foreign policy and covert operations. Julia Roberts plays the Houston socialite and conservative political activist Joanne Herring, who urges Wilson to help the rebels. Wilson's covert dealings with the rebels have some unforeseen and long-reaching effects, however. In this clip from the beginning of the movie, Charlie Wilson is at work in the Capitol Building, on his way to chambers where he's about to cast a vote.

What to Watch for and Ask Yourself

1. This chapter discussed organizational culture as having three levels of visibility. Visible artifacts are at the first level and are the easiest to see. Which visible artifacts did you observe in this sequence?
2. Values appear at the next level of organizational culture. You can infer a culture's values from the behavior of organizational members. Which values appear in this sequence?
3. Organizational members will unconsciously behave according to the basic assumptions of an organization's culture. You also infer these from observed behavior. Which basic assumptions appear in this sequence?

Management Workplace

© CENGAGE

Preserve

Eric Hudson had earned his MBA and wanted to put it to use by starting his own company when he saw an opportunity that others were missing—a "green" one. He noticed that more and more consumers were recycling and that recycled materials were plentiful, but few people ever saw what became of it. What if they were able to purchase new products made with recycled materials? Hudson broke into the natural product arena with the Preserve Toothbrush made from recycled materials in 1996, and his company was born. The product line grew to feature razors, colanders, cutting boards,

Reel to Real

tableware, and more. In this video, Hudson and his small team of employees discuss the challenges of marketing recycled products, how they practice what they preach about environmental consciousness, and ways they think the "green industry" might be different in the future.

What to Watch for and Ask Yourself

1. How would you describe the rate of Preserve's environmental change? Do you think it's more stable or more dynamic? Why?
2. How do Eric Hudson and his employees practice what they preach when it comes to environmental consciousness?
3. What aspects of the general environment are relevant to Preserve?

3 Chapter Three
Ethics and Social Responsibility

OUTLINE

Experience Management
Explore the four levels of learning by doing the simulation model on Ethics & Social Responsibility.

© ISTOCKPHOTO.COM/ ANN MARIE KURTZ

Pod Nod
Mini lecture reviews all the learning points in the chapter.

© ISTOCKPHOTO.COM/ MAGNET CREATIVE

Reel to Real Video
Biz Flix is a scene from *Emperor's Club*. Management Workplace is a segment on City of Greensburg, Kansas.

© ISTOCKPHOTO.COM/ CRAFTVISION

Self Test
10 quiz questions, 6 exhibit worksheets, and PowerPoints for quick review.

© ISTOCKPHOTO.COM/ DJJITAL FILM

What Would You Do?

San Diego Chargers Offices, San Diego, California.[1]
Say "Vick," "Stallworth," and "Burress" to any *NATIONAL FOOTBALL LEAGUE (NFL)* fan, and they'll know that Philadelphia Eagles quarterback Michael Vick pleaded guilty for dog fighting, served 18 months in prison, and was suspended by the NFL for two seasons; that after accidentally hitting and killing a pedestrian, Baltimore Ravens wide receiver Donte Stallworth pleaded guilty to drunken driving and manslaughter, served a month in jail, and was suspended for 1 year; and that former New York Giants receiver Plaxico Burress accidentally shot himself in the leg in a crowded nightclub with an unlicensed handgun, pleaded guilty, agreed to serve 2 years in prison, and was suspended for 2 years. High-profile cases like these have harmed the NFL's carefully managed reputation, but as the General Manager (GM) of the San Diego Chargers, you know that the problems go much deeper. From public intoxication, to drunken driving (29 percent of all incidents), to public urination, to assault and battery, to resisting arrest, to drug possession, approximately 10 percent of active players have been arrested, and two-thirds of those have been convicted. Indeed, the president of the NFL Players Association (NFLPA) felt that off-the-field conduct threatened the NFL's success and popularity.

As a result of these incidents, the NFL, in conjunction with the NFLPA, developed a strict personal-conduct policy where Commissioner Roger Goodell has the authority to investigate, fine, and suspend players without pay, including suspending them from league play. Teams are also fined since they must return a portion of a suspended player's salary to the league under the new policy. Although it's too early to know if the policy will work, twice as many players have been suspended under the stricter guidelines.

Not surprisingly, teams have responded to these problems with several different approaches. First, hoping that education makes a difference, all NFL teams now require their rookies to participate in an 8-hour class on "conduct-management." Second, because players are an attractive target for troublemakers, teams have hired security directors, usually former FBI agents, who do everything from running background checks on players' friends and associates to working with local police, to protecting players from scam artists. Third, following the "bad apple" theory, teams intensified the background checks they conduct on draft prospects, hoping to avoid selecting "problem" players. Dolphins GM Jeff Ireland says, "We check everything. We've got guys checking academics, guys calling the local sheriff. We've got security people and [we] talk to trainers and strength coaches." Another GM commented that background checks will "track a prospect as far back as middle school to determine patterns of behavior."

Even though many of those steps make sense to you, the Chargers' security director is pushing you to consider several more aggressive options, such as placing guards in hotel hallways (to make sure players are in their rooms the night before games), restricting where players can go in their free time (so they will stay out of bars or clubs that are known trouble spots), and even following players after practice to monitor how they behave in public (and intervene if problems occur). It's clear how those policies could reduce violations of the NFL's personal conduct policy, but you wonder if your fans would find them objectionable. Moreover, would they tolerate similar steps in their workplaces? As you decide what to do, what issues should you and the Chargers pay most attention to, economic (player and team fines), legal (charges and sentences associated with violent or illegal activities), or ethical (right versus wrong)? Which is more important and why? Finally, is it fair for the commissioner to play "judge, jury, and executioner" on personal-conduct issues that can result in lifetime banishment from the game? Should attorneys or the NFLPA be involved in this process? What's the fairest method of handling these issues?

If you were the GM of the San I Chargers, what would you do?

The dilemma facing the GM of the San Diego Chargers is an example of the tough decisions involving ethics and social responsibility that managers face. Unfortunately, no matter what you decide to do, someone or some group will be unhappy with the outcome. Managers don't have the luxury of choosing theoretically optimal, win-win solutions that are obviously desirable to everyone involved. In practice, solutions to ethics and social responsibility problems aren't optimal. Often, managers must be satisfied with a solution that just makes do or does the least harm. What is right and wrong is rarely crystal clear to managers. The business world is much messier than that.

We begin this chapter by examining ethical behavior in the workplace and explaining how unethical behavior can expose a business to penalties under the U.S. Sentencing Commission Guidelines for Organizations. Second, we examine the influences on ethical decision making and review practical steps managers can take to improve ethical decision making. We finish by considering to whom organizations are socially responsible, for what organizations are socially responsible, how organizations can respond to societal expectations for social responsibility, and whether social responsibility hurts or helps an organization's economic performance.

What Is Ethical and Unethical Workplace Behavior?

Ethics is the set of moral principles or values that defines right and wrong for a person or group. Unfortunately, numerous studies have consistently produced distressing results about the state of ethics in today's business world. A Society of Human Resources Management Survey found that only 27 percent of employees felt that their organization's leadership was ethical.[2] In a study of 1,324 randomly selected workers, managers, and executives across multiple industries, 48 percent of the respondents admitted to actually committing an unethical or illegal act! These acts included cheating on an expense account, discriminating against coworkers, forging signatures, paying or accepting kickbacks, and looking the other way when environmental laws were broken.[3]

Not all the news is bad though. When people believe their work environment is ethical, they are six times more likely to stay with that company than if they believe they work in an unethical environment.[4] One study asked 570 white-collar workers which of 28 qualities were important in company leaders. The results? Honesty (24 percent) and integrity/morals/ethics (16 percent) ranked by far the highest. (Caring/compassion was third at 7 percent.)[5] In short, much needs to be done to make workplaces more ethical, but—and this is very important—most managers and employees want this to happen.

After reading the next two sections, you should be able to:

1 discuss how the nature of management jobs creates the possibility for ethical abuses.

2 describe the U.S. Sentencing Commission Guidelines for Organizations, and explain how they both encourage ethical behavior and punish unethical behavior by businesses.

1 Ethics and the Nature of Management Jobs

Ethical behavior follows accepted principles of right and wrong. By contrast, unethical management behavior occurs when managers personally violate accepted principles of right and wrong—for example, by lying about company profits or knowingly producing an unsafe product—or encourage others to do so. Because of the nature of their jobs, managers can be tempted to engage in unethical managerial behavior in four areas: authority and power, handling information, influencing the behavior of others, and setting goals.

The *authority and power* inherent in some management positions can tempt managers to engage in unethical practices. Because they often control company resources, there is a risk that some managers will cross the line from legitimate use to personal use of these resources. For example, unless it's in an employee's job description, using an employee to do personal chores, like picking up the manager's dry cleaning, is unethical behavior. Even worse, though, is using one's managerial authority and power for direct personal gain as some managers have done by using corporate funds to pay for extravagant personal parties, lavish home decorating, jewelry, or expensive works of art.

ethics
the set of moral principles or values that defines right and wrong for a person or group

ethical behavior
behavior that conforms to a society's accepted principles of right and wrong

Handling information is another area in which managers must be careful to behave ethically. Information is a key part of management work, since managers collect it, analyze it, act on it, and disseminate it. In doing so, they are expected to be truthful and, when necessary, to keep confidential information confidential. Leaking company secrets to competitors, doctoring numbers, wrongfully withholding information, and lying are some of the ways managers may misuse information entrusted to them. *SATYAM COMPUTER* is a leading Indian outsourcing and software company that serves more than one-third of the *Fortune* 500 companies and the U.S. government. After years of "doctoring" the books, chairman and cofounder Ramalinga Raju finally admitted that he overstated profits and revenues and created a fake cash balance of $1 billion, all with the hopes of making the company appear more successful than it was so it could attract more business and investment.[6]

Managers must also be careful to behave ethically in the way they *influence the behavior of others*, especially those they supervise. Managerial work gives managers significant power to influence others. If managers tell employees to perform unethical acts (or face punishment), such as faking numbers to get results, they are abusing their managerial power. This is sometimes called the "move it or lose it" syndrome. "Move it or lose it" managers tell employees, "Do it. You're paid to do it. If you can't do it, we'll find somebody who can."[7]

Although managers can influence their employees' behavior through direct order, they can also do so indirectly through the *goals they set*. If managers set unrealistic goals, the pressure to perform and achieve those goals can influence employees to engage in unethical business behaviors, especially if they are just short of meeting their goals or a deadline.[8] When *SAFETY-KLEEN*, which provides environmentally friendly cleaning equipment, was acquired by Rollins Environmental Services, managers told investors that profits would soon be $500 million a year because of synergies and cost savings. When the company couldn't meet that aggressive goal, the chief financial officer (CFO), "made and directed other Safety-Kleen employees to make a series of false accounting entries, commonly known as 'top side adjustments,' to artificially inflate earnings for the quarter."[9]

REVIEW 1

Ethics and the Nature of Management Jobs

Ethics is the set of moral principles or values that define right and wrong. Ethical behavior occurs when managers follow those principles and values. Because they set the standard for others in the workplace, managers can model ethical behavior by using resources for company business and not for personal gain. Furthermore, managers can encourage ethical behavior by handling information in a confidential and honest fashion, by not using their authority to influence others to engage in unethical behavior, and by setting reasonable rather than unreasonable goals.

2 U.S. Sentencing Commission Guidelines for Organizations

A male supervisor is sexually harassing female coworkers. A sales representative offers a $10,000 kickback to persuade an indecisive customer to do business with his company. A company president secretly meets with the CEO of her biggest competitor, and they agree not to compete in markets where the other has already established customers. Each of these behaviors is clearly unethical (and, in these cases, also illegal). Historically, if management was unaware of such activities, the company could not be held responsible for an employee's unethical acts. Since 1991, however, when the U.S. Sentencing Commission Guidelines for Organizations were established, companies can be prosecuted and punished *even if management didn't know about the unethical behavior*. Penalties can be substantial, with maximum fines approaching a whopping $300 million.[10] An amendment made in 2004 outlines much stricter ethics training requirements and emphasizes the creation of a legal and ethical company culture.[11]

Let's examine: 2.1 **to whom the guidelines apply and what they cover**, and 2.2 **how, according to the guidelines, an organization can be punished for the unethical behavior of its managers and employees**.

2.1 Who, What, and Why?

Nearly all businesses are covered by the U.S. Sentencing Commission's guidelines. This includes nonprofits, partnerships, labor unions, unincorporated organizations and associations, incorporated organizations, and even pension funds, trusts, and joint stock companies. If your organization can be characterized as a business (remember, nonprofits count, too), then it is subject to the guidelines.[12]

The guidelines cover offenses defined by federal laws such as invasion of privacy, price fixing, fraud, customs violations, antitrust violations, civil rights violations, theft, money laundering, conflicts of interest, embezzlement, dealing in stolen goods, copyright infringements, extortion, and more. But it's not enough merely to stay within the law. The purpose of the guidelines is not just to punish companies *after* they or their employees break the law, but rather to encourage companies to take proactive steps that will discourage or prevent white-collar crime *before* it happens. The guidelines also give companies an incentive to cooperate with and disclose illegal activities to federal authorities.[13]

©ISTOCKPHOTO.COM/TERRY HANKINS PHOTOGRAPHY

2.2 Determining the Punishment

The guidelines impose smaller fines on companies that take proactive steps to encourage ethical behavior or voluntarily disclose illegal activities to federal authorities. Essentially, the law uses a carrot-and-stick approach. The stick is the threat of heavy fines that can run millions of dollars. The carrot is a greatly reduced fine, but only if the company has started an effective compliance program (discussed below) to encourage ethical behavior *before* the illegal activity occurs.[14] The method used to determine a company's punishment illustrates the importance of establishing a compliance program, as illustrated in Exhibit 3.1.

EXHIBIT 3.1

Offense Levels, Base Fines, Culpability Scores, and Possible Total Fines Under the U.S. Sentencing Commission Guidelines for Organizations

		Culpability Score					
Offense Level	Base Fine	0.05	0.5	1.0	2.0	3.0	4.0
6 or less	$ 5,000	$ 250	$ 2,500	$ 5,000	$ 10,000	$ 15,000	$ 20,000
7	7,500	375	3,750	7,500	15,000	22,500	30,000
8	10,000	500	5,000	10,000	20,000	30,000	40,000
9	15,000	750	7,500	15,000	30,000	45,000	60,000
10	20,000	1,000	10,000	20,000	40,000	60,000	80,000
11	30,000	1,500	15,000	30,000	60,000	90,000	120,000
12	40,000	2,000	20,000	40,000	80,000	120,000	160,000
13	60,000	3,000	30,000	60,000	120,000	180,000	240,000
14	85,000	4,250	42,500	85,000	170,000	255,000	340,000
15	125,000	6,250	62,500	125,000	250,000	375,000	500,000
16	175,000	8,750	87,500	175,000	350,000	525,000	700,000
17	250,000	12,500	125,000	250,000	500,000	750,000	1,000,000
18	350,000	17,500	175,000	350,000	700,000	1,050,000	1,400,000
19	500,000	25,000	250,000	500,000	1,000,000	1,500,000	2,000,000
20	650,000	32,500	325,000	650,000	1,300,000	1,950,000	2,600,000
21	910,000	45,500	455,000	910,000	1,820,000	2,730,000	3,640,000
22	1,200,000	60,000	600,000	1,200,000	2,400,000	3,600,000	4,800,000
23	1,600,000	80,000	800,000	1,600,000	3,200,000	4,800,000	6,400,000
24	2,100,000	105,000	1,050,000	2,100,000	4,200,000	6,300,000	8,400,000
25	2,800,000	140,000	1,400,000	2,800,000	5,600,000	8,400,000	11,200,000
26	3,700,000	185,000	1,850,000	3,700,000	7,400,000	11,100,000	14,800,000
27	4,800,000	240,000	2,400,000	4,800,000	9,600,000	14,400,000	19,200,000
28	6,300,000	315,000	3,150,000	6,300,000	12,600,000	18,900,000	25,200,000
29	8,100,000	405,000	4,050,000	8,100,000	16,200,000	24,300,000	32,400,000
30	10,500,000	525,000	5,250,000	10,500,000	21,000,000	31,500,000	42,000,000
31	13,500,000	675,000	6,750,000	13,500,000	27,000,000	40,500,000	54,000,000
32	17,500,000	875,000	8,750,000	17,500,000	35,000,000	52,500,000	70,000,000
34	28,500,000	1,425,000	14,250,000	28,500,000	57,000,000	85,500,000	114,000,000
35	36,000,000	1,800,000	18,000,000	36,000,000	72,000,000	108,000,000	144,000,000
36	45,500,000	2,275,000	22,750,000	45,500,000	91,000,000	136,500,000	182,000,000
37	57,500,000	2,875,000	28,750,000	57,500,000	115,000,000	172,500,000	230,000,000
38 or more	72,500,000	3,625,000	36,250,000	72,500,000	145,000,000	217,500,000	290,000,000

Source: "Chapter Eight—Part C—Fines," 2004 Federal Sentencing Guidelines, available at http://www.ussc.gov/2004guid/8c2_4.htm, 27 January 2005.

The first step is to compute the *base fine* by determining what *level of offense* has occurred. The level of the offense (i.e., its seriousness) varies depending on the kind of crime, the loss incurred by the victims, and how much planning went into the crime. For example, simple fraud is a level 6 offense (there are 38 levels in all). But if the victims of that fraud lost more than $5 million, that level 6 offense becomes a level 22 offense. Moreover, anything beyond minimal planning to commit the fraud results in an increase of two levels to a level 24 offense. How much difference would this make to the company? As Exhibit 3.1 shows, crimes at or below level 6 incur a base fine of $5,000, whereas the base fine for level 24 is $2.1 million—a difference of $2.095 million! The base fine for level 38, the top-level offense, is a hefty $72.5 million.

After assessing a *base fine*, the judge computes a culpability score, which is a way of assigning blame to the company. The culpability score can range from a minimum of 0.05 to a maximum of 4.0. The greater the corporate responsibility in conducting, encouraging, or sanctioning illegal or unethical activity, the higher the culpability score. A company that already has a compliance program and voluntarily reports the offense to authorities will incur a culpability score of 0.05. By contrast, a company whose management plans, approves, and participates in illegal or unethical activity will receive the maximum score of 4.0.

The culpability score is critical because the total fine is computed by multiplying the base fine by the culpability score. Going back to our level 24 fraud offense, the left point of the upper arrow in Exhibit 3.1 shows that a company with a compliance program that turns itself in will be fined only $105,000 ($2,100,000 × 0.05). In contrast, a company that secretly planned, approved, and participated in illegal activity will be fined $8.4 million ($2,100,000 × 4.0), as shown by the right point of the upper arrow. The difference is even greater for level 38 offenses. As shown by the left point of the bottom arrow, a company with a compliance program and a 0.05 culpability score is fined only $3.625 million, whereas a company with the maximum 4.0 culpability score is fined a whopping $290 million, as indicated by the right point of the bottom arrow. These differences clearly show the importance of having a compliance program in place. Over the last decade, 1,494 companies have been charged under the U.S. Sentencing Guidelines. Seventy-six percent of those charged were fined, with the average fine exceeding $2 million. Company fines are on average 20 times larger now than before the implementation of the guidelines in 1991.[15]

Fortunately for companies that want to avoid paying these stiff fines, the U.S. Sentencing Guidelines clearly spell out the seven necessary components of an effective compliance program.[16] Exhibit 3.2 lists those components. For more information, see "An Overview of the Organizational Sentencing Guidelines" at ***http://www.ussc.gov/training/corpover****.PDF* and "Sentencing Guidelines Educational Materials" at ***http://www.ussc.gov/training/educat.htm***.

REVIEW 2

U.S. Sentencing Commission Guidelines

Under the U.S. Sentencing Commission Guidelines, companies can be prosecuted and fined up to $300 million for employees' illegal actions. Fines are computed by multiplying the base fine by a culpability score, which ranges from 0.05 to 4.0. Companies that establish compliance programs to encourage ethical behavior can reduce their culpability scores and their fines. Companies without compliance programs can face much heavier fines than companies with established programs. Compliance programs must establish standards and procedures, be run by top managers, encourage hiring and promotion of honest and ethical people, encourage employees to report violations, educate employees about compliance, punish violators, and find ways to improve the program after violations occur.

EXHIBIT 3.2

Compliance Program Steps for the U.S. Sentencing Guidelines for Organizations

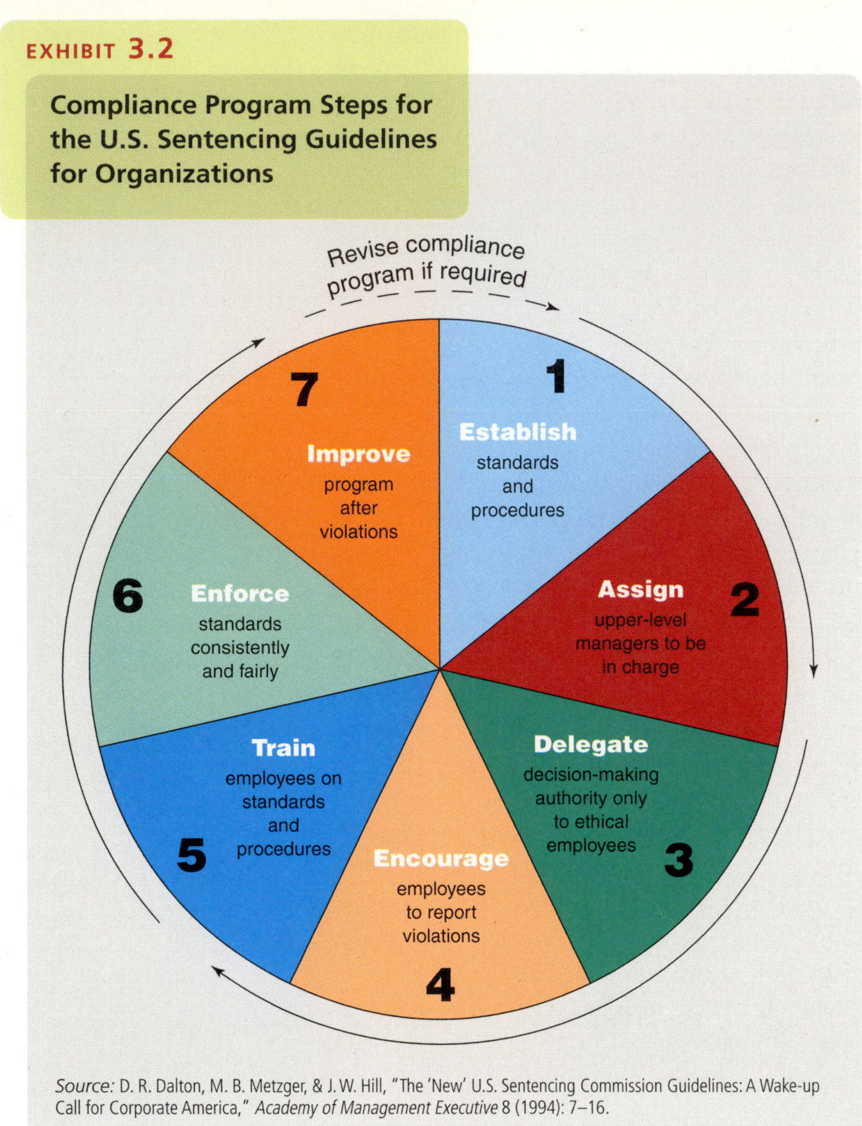

Source: D. R. Dalton, M. B. Metzger, & J. W. Hill, "The 'New' U.S. Sentencing Commission Guidelines: A Wake-up Call for Corporate America," *Academy of Management Executive* 8 (1994): 7–16.

How Do You Make Ethical Decisions?

One cold morning, in the midst of a winter storm, schools were closed and most people had decided to stay home from work. Nevertheless, Richard Addessi had already showered, shaved, and dressed for the office. He kissed his wife Joan good-bye, but before he could get to his car, he fell dead on the garage floor of a sudden heart attack. Addessi was 4 months short of his 30-year anniversary with the company. Having begun work at IBM at the age of 18, he was just 48 years old.[17]

You're the vice president in charge of benefits at IBM. Given that he was only 4 months short of full retirement, do you award full benefits to Richard Addessi's wife and daughters? If the answer is yes, they will receive $1,800 a month and free lifetime medical coverage. If you say no, his widow and two daughters will receive only $340 a month. They will also have to pay $473 a month just to continue their current medical coverage. As the VP in charge of benefits at IBM, what would be the ethical thing for you to do?

After reading the next two sections, you should be able to:

3 describe what influences ethical decision making.

4 explain what practical steps managers can take to improve ethical decision making.

3 Influences on Ethical Decision Making

Although some ethical issues are easily solved, many do not have clearly right or wrong answers. So, what did IBM decide to do? Since Richard Addessi had not completed 30 full years with the company, IBM officials felt they had no choice but to give Joan Addessi and her two daughters the smaller, partial retirement benefits. Do you think IBM's decision was ethical? Probably many of you don't. You wonder how the company could be so heartless as to deny Richard Addessi's family the full benefits to which you believe they were entitled. Yet others might argue that IBM did the ethical thing by strictly following the rules laid out in its pension benefit plan. After all, being fair means applying the rules to everyone. Although the answers are rarely clear, managers do need to have a clear sense of how to arrive at an answer in order to manage this ethical ambiguity.

The ethical answers that managers choose depend on: 3.1 **the ethical intensity of the decision**, and: 3.2 **the moral development of the manager**.

3.1 Ethical Intensity of the Decision

Managers don't treat all ethical decisions the same. The manager who has to decide whether to deny or extend full benefits to Joan Addessi and her family is going to treat that decision much more seriously than the decision of how to deal with an assistant who has been taking computer paper home for personal use. These decisions differ in their **ethical intensity**, or the degree of concern people have about an ethical issue. When addressing an issue of high ethical intensity, managers are more aware of the impact their decision will have on others. They are more likely to view the decision as an ethical or moral decision rather than as an economic decision. They are also more likely to worry about doing the right thing.

Six factors must be taken into account when determining the ethical intensity of an action. These include:

- magnitude of consequences
- social consensus
- probability of effect
- temporal immediacy
- proximity of effect
- concentration of effect.[18]

Magnitude of consequences is the total harm or benefit derived from an ethical decision. The more people who are harmed or the greater the harm to those people, the larger the consequences. **Social consensus** is agreement on whether behavior is bad or good. **Probability of effect** is the chance that something will happen and then result in harm to others. If we combine these factors, we can see the effect they can

ethical intensity
the degree of concern people have about an ethical issue

magnitude of consequences
the total harm or benefit derived from an ethical decision

social consensus
agreement on whether behavior is bad or good

probability of effect
the chance that something will happen and then harm others

have on ethical intensity. For example, if there is *clear agreement* (social consensus) that a managerial decision or action is *certain* (probability of effect) to have *large negative consequences* (magnitude of consequences) in some way, then people will be highly concerned about that managerial decision or action, and ethical intensity will be high.

Temporal immediacy is the time between an act and the consequences the act produces. Temporal immediacy is stronger if a manager has to lay off workers next week as opposed to 3 months from now. **Proximity of effect** is the social, psychological, cultural, or physical distance of a decision maker from those affected by his or her decisions. Thus, proximity of effect is greater when a manager lays off employees he knows than when he lays off employees that he doesn't know. Finally, whereas the magnitude of consequences is the total effect across all people, **concentration of effect** is how much an act affects the average person. Temporarily laying off 100 employees for 10 months without pay is a greater concentration of effect than temporarily laying off 1,000 employees for 1 month.

Which of these six factors has the most impact on ethical intensity? Studies indicate that managers are much more likely to view decisions as ethical issues when the magnitude of consequences (total harm) is high and there is a social consensus (agreement) that a behavior or action is bad.[19] Many people will likely feel IBM was wrong to deny full benefits to Joan Addessi. Why? IBM's decision met five of the six characteristics of ethical intensity. The difference in benefits, more than $23,000 per year, was likely to have serious and immediate consequences for the family, especially in terms of their monthly benefits ($1,800 and free medical coverage if full benefits were awarded versus $340 a month and medical care that costs $473 per month if they weren't). We can closely identify with Joan Addessi and her daughters as opposed to IBM's faceless, nameless corporate identity. The exception, as we will discuss below, is social consensus. Not everyone will agree that IBM's decision was unethical. The judgment also depends on your level of moral development and which ethical principles you use to decide.

3.2 Moral Development

A friend of yours has given you a copy of Microsoft Office 2010. She stuffed the software CDs in your backpack with a note saying that you should install it on your computer and get it back to her in a couple of days. You're tempted. You have papers to write, notes to take, and presentations to plan. Besides, all of your friends have the same version, and they didn't pay for it either. Copying the software to your hard drive without buying your own copy clearly violates copyright laws. But no one would find out. Even if someone does, Microsoft probably isn't going to come after you. Microsoft goes after the big fish—companies that illegally copy and distribute software to their workers and pirates that illegally sell cheap unauthorized copies.[20] Your computer has booted up, and you've got your mouse in one hand and the installation disk in the other. What are you going to do?

In part, according to psychologist Lawrence Kohlberg, your decision will be based on your level of moral development. Kohlberg identified three phases of moral development, with two stages in each phase (see Exhibit 3.3).[21] At the **preconventional level of moral development**, people make decisions based on selfish reasons. For example, if you are in Stage 1, the punishment and obedience stage, your primary concern will be to avoid trouble for yourself. So you won't copy the software because you are afraid of being caught and punished. Yet, in Stage 2, the instrumental exchange stage, you worry less about punishment and more about doing things

temporal immediacy
the time between an act and the consequences the act produces

proximity of effect
the social, psychological, cultural, or physical distance between a decision maker and those affected by his or her decisions

concentration of effect
the total harm or benefit that an act produces on the average person

preconventional level of moral development
the first level of moral development, in which people make decisions based on selfish reasons

that directly advance your wants and needs. So you copy the software.

People at the **conventional level of moral development** make decisions that conform to societal expectations. In other words, they look outside themselves to others for guidance on ethical issues. In Stage 3, the "good boy, nice girl" stage, you normally do what the other "good boys" and "nice girls" are doing. If everyone else is illegally copying software, you will, too. But if they aren't, you won't either. In the law and order stage, Stage 4, you again look for external guidance and do whatever the law permits, so you won't copy the software.

EXHIBIT 3.3

Kohlberg's Stages of Moral Development

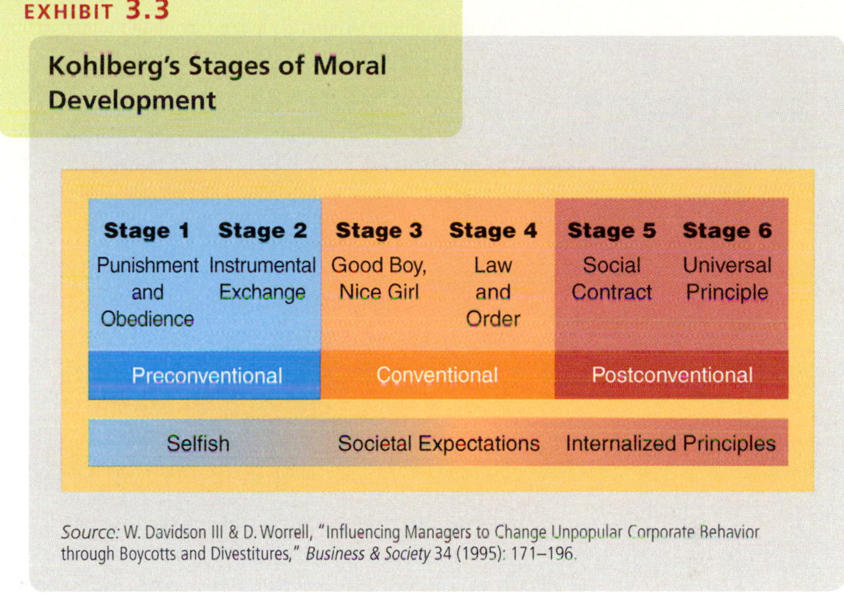

Source: W. Davidson III & D. Worrell, "Influencing Managers to Change Unpopular Corporate Behavior through Boycotts and Divestitures," *Business & Society* 34 (1995): 171–196.

People at the **postconventional level of moral development** use internalized ethical principles to solve ethical dilemmas. In Stage 5, the social contract stage, you will refuse to copy the software because, as a whole, society is better off when the rights of others—in this case, the rights of software programmers and manufacturers—are not violated. In Stage 6, the universal principle stage, you may or may not copy the software, depending on your principles of right and wrong. Moreover, you will stick to your principles even if your decision conflicts with the law (Stage 4) or what others believe is best for society (Stage 5). For example, those with socialist or communist beliefs would probably choose to copy the software because they believe goods and services should be owned by society rather than by individuals and corporations. (For information about the dos, don'ts, and legal issues concerning software piracy, see the Software & Information Industry Association's website at ***http://www.siia.net/piracy/default.asp***.)

Kohlberg believed that people would progress sequentially from earlier stages to later stages as they became more educated and mature. However, only 20 percent of adults ever reach the postconventional stage of moral development where internal principles guide their decisions. Most adults are in the conventional stage of moral development, in which they look outside themselves to others for guidance on ethical issues. This means that most people in the workplace look to and need leadership when it comes to ethical decision making.[22]

conventional level of moral development the second level of moral development, in which people make decisions that conform to societal expectations

postconventional level of moral development the third level of moral development, in which people make decisions based on internalized principles

REVIEW 3

Influences on Ethical Decision Making

Three factors influence ethical decisions: the ethical intensity of the decision, the moral development of the decision maker, and the ethical principles used to solve the problem. Ethical intensity is strong when decisions have large, certain, immediate consequences and when we are physically or psychologically close to those affected by the decision. There are three levels of moral maturity, each with two stages. At the preconventional level, decisions are made for selfish reasons. At the conventional level, decisions conform to societal expectations. At the postconventional level, internalized principles are used to make ethical decisions. Finally, managers can use a number of different principles when making ethical decisions: self-interest, personal virtue, religious injunctions, government requirements, utilitarian benefits, individual rights, and distributive justice.

4 Practical Steps to Ethical Decision Making

Managers can encourage more ethical decision making in their organizations by: 4.1 **carefully selecting and hiring ethical employees**, 4.2 **establishing a specific code of ethics**, 4.3 **training employees to make ethical decisions**, and 4.4 **creating an ethical climate**.

4.1 Selecting and Hiring Ethical Employees

As an employer, you can increase your chances of hiring an honest person if you give job applicants integrity tests. **Overt integrity tests** estimate job applicants' honesty by asking them directly what they think or feel about theft or about punishment of unethical behaviors.[23] For example, an employer might ask an applicant, "Would you ever consider buying something from somebody if you knew the person had stolen the item?" or "Don't most people steal from their companies?" Surprisingly, unethical people will usually answer "yes" to such questions because they believe that the world is basically dishonest and that dishonest behavior is normal.[24]

Personality-based integrity tests indirectly estimate job applicants' honesty by measuring psychological traits such as dependability and conscientiousness. For example, prison inmates serving time for white-collar crimes (counterfeiting, embezzlement, and fraud) scored much lower than a comparison group of middle-level managers on scales measuring reliability, dependability, honesty, conscientiousness, and abiding by rules.[25] These results show that companies can selectively hire and promote people who will be more ethical.[26] For more on integrity testing, see the "What Really Works" feature in this chapter.

4.2 Codes of Ethics

Today, almost all large corporations have an ethics code in place. Two things must still happen, however, for ethics codes to encourage ethical decision making and behavior.[27] First, a company must communicate its code to others both inside and outside the company. Second, in addition to having an ethics code with general guidelines like "do unto others as you would have others do unto you," management must also develop practical ethical standards and procedures specific to the company's line of business. Visitors to NORTEL's website at ***http://www.nortel.com/corporate/community/ethics/guide.html*** can instantly access references to very specific ethical standards on topics ranging from bribes and kickbacks to expense vouchers and illegal copying of software.

overt integrity test
a written test that estimates job applicants' honesty by directly asking them what they think or feel about theft or about punishment of unethical behaviors

personality-based integrity test
a written test that indirectly estimates job applicants' honesty by measuring psychological traits, such as dependability and conscientiousness

4.3 Ethics Training

In addition to establishing ethical standards for the company, managers must sponsor and be involved in ethics and compliance training in order to create an ethical company culture.[30] The first objective of ethics training is to develop employees' awareness

Doing the Right Thing

If You Cheat in College, Will You Cheat in the Workplace?

Studies show that college students who cheat once are likely to cheat again. Students who cheat on exams are likely to cheat on assignments and projects. Furthermore, tolerance of cheating is widespread, as 70 percent of college students don't see it as a problem. Given these relaxed attitudes toward cheating, and with on-campus cheating at all-time highs, employers want to know whether someone who cheated in college will cheat in the workplace.

Studies generally indicate that the answer is yes. Likewise, students who cheated in school were much more likely to cheat on their taxes, in politics (by committing voter fraud or accepting illegal campaign contributions), in sports, and on the job. Why is this the case? Apparently, people who cheat and then cheat again come to see their behavior as normal and rationalize it by telling themselves that cheating isn't wrong. In fact, 60 percent of the people who cheat their employers don't feel guilty about doing so. Cheating isn't situation-specific. Once you decide that cheating is acceptable, you're likely to cheat in most areas of your life.[28]

Robert Hogan, a renowned personality psychologist, says there is an intrinsic link between cheating, embezzling, marital infidelity, public drunkenness, getting traffic tickets, fighting, vandalism, and so on. "All these things involve breaking the rules, and they're all motivated by hostility toward or disregard for authority."[29] If you want to do the right thing, don't cheat in college or tolerate cheating by others. Don't slide down the slippery slope of cheating.

of ethics.[31] This means helping employees recognize which issues are ethical issues and then avoid rationalizing unethical behavior by thinking, "This isn't really illegal or immoral" or "No one will ever find out." Several companies have created board games to improve awareness of ethical issues.[32] At *WEYERHAUSER*, when employees pushed for more specific guidance on ethics, the ethics department added a series of multiple-choice answers to the scenarios that it used in its training programs.

The second objective for ethics training programs is to achieve credibility with employees. Not surprisingly, employees can be highly suspicious of management's reasons for offering ethics training. Some companies have hurt the credibility of their ethics programs by having outside instructors and consultants conduct the classes.[33] Employees often complain that outside instructors and consultants are teaching theory that has nothing to do with their jobs and the practical dilemmas they actually face on a daily basis. This is why *LOCKHEED MARTIN*, a defense and aerospace company, frequently has its top managers teach ethics classes.

Ethics training becomes even more credible when top managers teach the initial ethics classes to their subordinates who in turn teach their subordinates.[34] Michael Hoffman, executive director for the Center for Business Ethics at Bentley College, says that having managers teach ethics courses greatly reinforces the seriousness with which employees treat ethics in the workplace.[35]

The third objective of ethics training is to teach employees a practical model of ethical decision making. A basic model should help them think about the consequences

EXHIBIT 3.4

A Basic Model of Ethical Decision Making

1. **Identify the problem.** What makes it an ethical problem? Think in terms of rights, obligations, fairness, relationships, and integrity. How would you define the problem if you stood on the other side of the fence?
2. **Identify the constituents.** Who has been hurt? Who could be hurt? Who could be helped? Are they willing players, or are they victims? Can you negotiate with them?
3. **Diagnose the situation.** How did it happen in the first place? What could have prevented it? Is it going to get worse or better? Can the damage now be undone?
4. **Analyze your options.** Imagine the range of possibilities. Limit yourself to the two or three most manageable. What are the likely outcomes of each? What are the likely costs? Look to the company mission statement or code of ethics for guidance.
5. **Make your choice.** What is your intention in making this decision? How does it compare with the probable results? Can you discuss the problem with the affected parties before you act? Could you disclose without qualm your decision to your boss, the CEO, the board of directors, your family, or society as a whole?
6. **Act.** Do what you have to do. Don't be afraid to admit errors. Be as bold in confronting a problem as you were in causing it.

Source: L. A. Berger, "Train All Employees to Solve Ethical Dilemmas," *Best's Review—Life-Health Insurance Edition* 95 (1995): 70–80.

their choices will have on others and consider how they will choose between different solutions. Exhibit 3.4 presents a basic model of ethical decision making.

4.4 Ethical Climate

Organizational culture is key to fostering ethical decision making. The 2007 National Business Ethics Survey reported that only 24 percent of employees who work at companies with a strong ethical culture (where core beliefs are widely shared and strongly held) have observed others engaging in unethical behavior, whereas 98 percent of those who work in organizations with weak ethical cultures (where core beliefs are not widely shared or strongly held) have observed others engage in unethical behavior. Employees in strong ethical cultures are also more likely to report violations, because they expect that management wants them reported and won't retaliate against them for doing so.[36]

We learned in Chapter 2 that leadership is an important factor in creating an organizational culture. So, it's no surprise that in study after study, when researchers ask, "What is the most important influence on your ethical behavior at work?" the answer comes back, "My manager." The first step in establishing an ethical climate is for managers, especially top managers, to act ethically themselves.

A second step in establishing an ethical climate is for top management to be active in and committed to the company ethics program.[38] Top managers who consistently talk about the importance of ethics and back up that talk by participating in their companies' ethics programs send the clear message that ethics matter.

what *really* works

Integrity Tests

Under the 1991 and 2004 U.S. Sentencing Commission Guidelines, unethical employee behavior can lead to multimillion-dollar fines for corporations, and fraudulent behavior of executives can lead to criminal prosecution. Moreover, workplace deviance like stealing, fraud, and vandalism costs companies an estimated $660 billion a year. One way to reduce workplace deviance and the chances of a large fine for unethical employee behavior is to use overt and personality-based integrity tests to screen job applicants.

One hundred eighty-one studies, with a combined total of 576,460 study participants, examined how well integrity tests can predict job performance and various kinds of workplace deviance. These studies show that not only do integrity tests help companies reduce workplace deviance but they also help companies hire workers who are better performers in their jobs.

Workplace Deviance (Counterproductive Behaviors)

Compared with job applicants who score low, there is an 82 percent chance that job applicants who score high on overt integrity tests will participate in less illegal activity, unethical behavior, drug abuse, or workplace violence.

OVERT INTEGRITY TESTS & WORKPLACE DEVIANCES

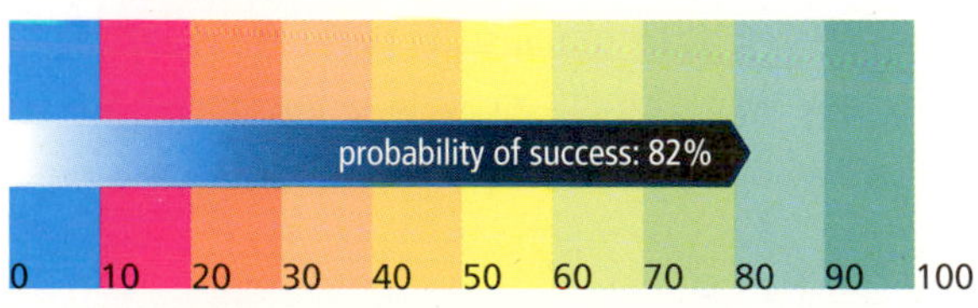

Personality-based integrity tests also do a good job of predicting who will engage in workplace deviance. Compared with job applicants who score low, there is a 68 percent chance that job applicants who score high on personality-based integrity tests will participate in less illegal activity, unethical behavior, excessive absences, drug abuse, or workplace violence.

PERSONALITY-BASED INTEGRITY TESTS & WORKPLACE DEVIANCES

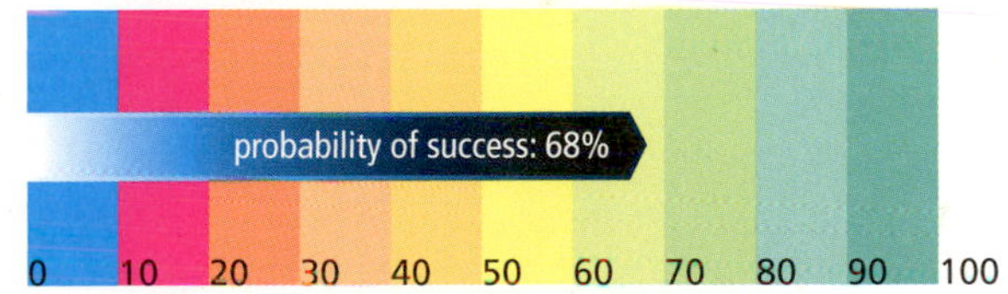

Job Performance

In addition to reducing unethical behavior and workplace deviance, integrity tests can help companies hire better performers. Compared with employees who score low, there is a 69 percent chance that employees who score high on overt integrity tests will be better performers.

OVERT INTEGRITY TESTS & JOB PERFORMANCE

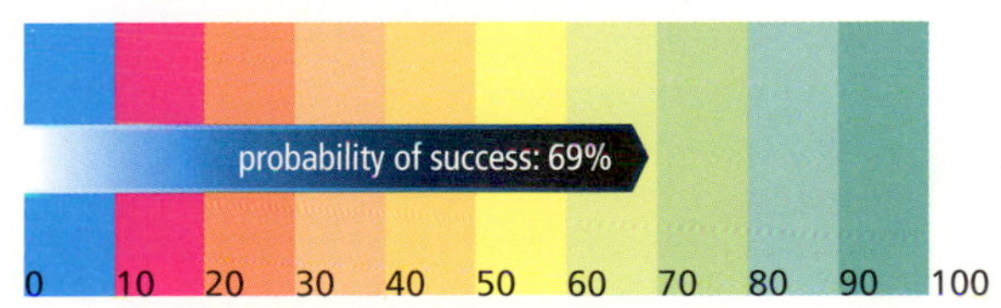

The figures are nearly identical for personality-based integrity tests. Compared with those who score low, there is a 70 percent chance that employees who score high on personality-based integrity tests will be better at their jobs.

PERSONALITY-BASED INTEGRITY TESTS & JOB PERFORMANCE

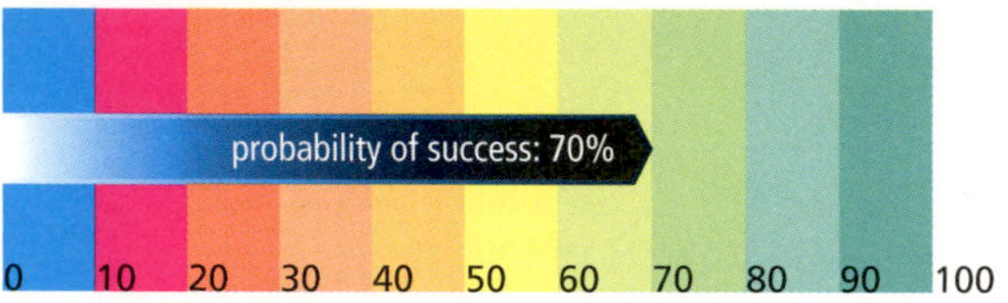

Theft

Although integrity tests can help companies decrease most kinds of workplace deviance and increase employees' job performance, they have a smaller effect on a specific kind of workplace deviance: theft. Compared with employees who score low, there is a 57 percent chance that employees who score high on overt integrity tests will be less likely to steal. No theft data were available to assess personality-based integrity tests.

OVERT INTEGRITY TESTS & THEFT

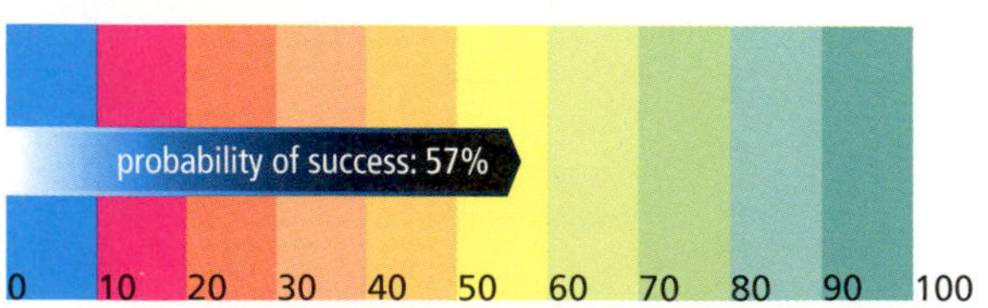

Faking and Coaching on Integrity Tests

Although overt and personality-based integrity tests do a very good job of helping companies hire people of higher integrity, it is possible to improve scores on these tests through coaching and faking. In coaching, job applicants are taught the underlying rationale of an integrity test or given specific directions for improving their integrity scores. Faking occurs when applicants simply try to "beat the test" or try to fake a good impression. Unfortunately for the companies that use integrity tests, both strategies work.

On average, coaching can improve scores on overt integrity tests by an astounding 1.5 standard deviations and on personality-based integrity tests by a statistically significant .36 standard deviation. This would be the equivalent of increasing your total SAT score by 150 and 36 points, respectively (the SAT has a mean of 500 and a standard deviation of 100). Likewise, on average, faking can improve scores on overt integrity tests by an impressive 1.02 standard deviations and on personality-based integrity tests by a statistically significant .59 standard deviation. Again, this would be the equivalent of increasing your SAT score by 102 and 59 points, respectively.

Companies that want to avoid coaching and faking effects must maintain tight security over integrity tests so that applicants have little information about them, periodically check the validity of the tests to make sure they're accurately predicting workplace deviance and job performance, or periodically switch tests if they suspect that test security has been compromised.[37]

Business writer Dayton Fandray says, "You can have ethics offices and officers and training programs and reporting systems, but if the CEO doesn't seem to care, it's all just a sham. It's not surprising to find that the companies that really do care about ethics make a point of including senior management in all of their ethics and compliance programs."[39]

A third step is to put in place a reporting system that encourages managers and employees to report potential ethics violations. **whistleblowing**, that is, reporting others' ethics violations, is a difficult action for most people to take.[40] Potential whistleblowers often fear that they, and not the ethics violators, will be punished.[41] Managers who have been interviewed about whistleblowing have said, "In every organization, someone's been screwed for standing up." "If anything, I figured that by taking a strong stand I might get myself in trouble. People might look at me as a goody two-shoes. Someone might try to force me out."

©ISTOCKPHOTO.COM/ALIJA

Today, many federal and state laws protect the rights of whistleblowers (see ***http://www.whistleblowers.org*** for more information). In particular, the Sarbanes-Oxley Act of 2002 makes it a serious crime to retaliate in any way against corporate whistleblowers in publicly owned companies. Managers who punish whistleblowers can be imprisoned for up to 10 years. Some companies, including defense contractor Northrop Grumman, have made it easier for whistleblowers to report possible violations by establishing anonymous, toll-free corporate ethics hot lines. Nortel, the telecommunications company, even publicizes which of its ethics hot lines don't have caller ID (so they can't identify the caller's phone number). The Sarbanes-Oxley Act requires all publicly held companies to establish anonymous hot lines to encourage reporting of unethical and illegal behaviors.[42]

REVIEW 4

Practical Steps to Ethical Decision Making

Employers can increase their chances of hiring ethical employees by administering overt integrity tests and personality-based integrity tests to all job applicants. Most large companies now have corporate codes of ethics. To affect ethical decision making, these codes must be known both inside and outside the organization. In addition to offering general rules, ethics codes must also provide specific, practical advice. Ethics training seeks to increase employees' awareness of ethical issues, makes ethics a serious and credible factor in organizational decisions, and teaches employees a practical model of ethical decision making. The most important factors in creating an ethical business climate are the personal examples set by company managers, involvement of management in the company ethics program, a reporting system that encourages whistleblowers to report potential ethics violations, and fair but consistent punishment of violators.

whistleblowing
reporting others' ethics violations to management or legal authorities

What Is Social Responsibility?

social responsibility
a business's obligation to pursue policies, make decisions, and take actions that benefit society

Social responsibility is a business's obligation to pursue policies, make decisions, and take actions that benefit society.[43] Unfortunately, because there are strong disagreements over to whom and for what organizations are responsible, it can be difficult for managers to know what is or will be perceived as socially responsible corporate behavior. In a recent McKinsey & Co. study of 1,144 top global executives, 79 percent predicted that at least some responsibility for dealing with future social and political issues would fall on corporations. Only 3 percent, however, said they themselves do a good job of dealing with these issues.[44] So what should managers and corporations do to be socially responsible?

After reading the next four sections, you should be able to explain:

5 to whom organizations are socially responsible.

6 for what organizations are socially responsible.

7 how organizations can choose to respond to societal demands for social responsibility.

8 whether social responsibility hurts or helps an organization's economic performance.

Some say that corporations need to give more to nonprofit organizations. In fact, corporate giving to charities has increased 22 percent to $13.7 billion in cash and in-kind gifts. Checkbook philanthropy, however, isn't enough these days, says Susan Puflea, senior vice president and director of GolinHarris Change.[45] Companies, she says, also need to be socially responsible as they conduct their businesses. Consider some examples. MB Food Processing, in South Fallsburg, New York, has stopped using chlorine-based disinfectants in its poultry processing plants. Instead, it combines salt, water, and an electrical charge to produce electrolyzed water to clean chickens and kill food-borne bacteria.[46] Wal-Mart, long assailed for its labor and global-outsourcing practices, has made a series of high-profile investments to slash overall energy use in its stores and its vast trucking fleets, and has promised to purchase more electricity derived from renewable sources.[47]

But Wal-Mart and MB Food Processing weren't socially responsible just out of the goodness of their corporate hearts. Wal-Mart took steps to reduce energy use because doing so also lowers costs. MB Food Processing switched to electrolyzed water because doing so strengthened its established reputation as a humane, environmentally friendly grower of chickens, which allows it to charge more for its products. These two examples illustrate the challenges and different motivations of acting in a socially responsible manner: balancing the needs of different groups in the face of limited resources and/or constraints.

5 To Whom Are Organizations Socially Responsible?

There are two perspectives regarding to whom organizations are socially responsible: the shareholder model and the stakeholder model. According to the late Nobel Prize–winning economist Milton Friedman, the only social responsibility that organizations have is to satisfy their owners, that is, company shareholders. This view—called the **shareholder model**—holds that the only social responsibility that businesses have is to maximize profits. By maximizing profit, the firm maximizes shareholder wealth and satisfaction. More specifically, as profits rise, the company stock owned by shareholders generally increases in value.

shareholder model
a view of social responsibility that holds that an organization's overriding goal should be profit maximization for the benefit of shareholders

Friedman argued that it is socially irresponsible for companies to divert time, money, and attention from maximizing profits to social causes and charitable organizations. The first problem, he believed, is that organizations cannot act effectively as moral agents for all company shareholders. Although shareholders are likely to agree on investment issues concerning a company, it's highly unlikely that they have common views on what social causes a company should or should not support. Rather than act as moral agents, Friedman argued, companies should maximize profits for shareholders. Shareholders can then use their time and increased wealth to contribute to the social causes, charities, or institutions they want, rather than those that companies want.

Management Trend:

Most companies are trying to make their products "green" by encouraging consumers to recycle the packaging. Frito-Lay has taken things one step further by offering the world's first 100% fully compostable bag. Its SunChips products come in a bag made from plant-based polylactic acid. According to Frito-Lay, the bag will "fully break down in just 14 weeks when placed in a hot, active compost bin or pile." So not only will this bag not take up space in a landfill, it will even help nourish farms and gardens.

Source: http://www.sunchips.com/healthier_planet.shtml?s=content_compostable_packaging

The second major problem, Friedman said, is that the time, money, and attention diverted to social causes undermine market efficiency.[48] In competitive markets, companies compete for raw materials, talented workers, customers, and investment funds. A company that spends money on social causes will have less money to purchase quality materials or to hire talented workers who can produce a valuable product at a good price. If customers find the company's product less desirable, its sales and profits will fall. If profits fall, the company's stock price will decline, and the company will have difficulty attracting investment funds that could be used to fund long-term growth. In the end, Friedman argues, diverting the firm's money, time, and resources to social causes hurts customers, suppliers, employees, and shareholders.

By contrast, under the **stakeholder model**, management's most important responsibility is the firm's long-term survival (not just maximizing profits), which is achieved by satisfying the interests of multiple corporate stakeholders (not just shareholders).[49] **Stakeholders** are persons or groups with a legitimate interest in a company.[50] Since stakeholders are interested in and affected by the organization's actions, they have a "stake" in what those actions are. Consequently, stakeholder groups may try to influence the firm to act in their own interests. Exhibit 3.5 shows the various stakeholder groups that the organization must satisfy to assure its long-term survival.

Being responsible to multiple stakeholders raises two basic questions. First, how does a company identify organizational stakeholders? Second, how does a company balance the needs of different stakeholders? Distinguishing between primary and secondary stakeholders can help answer these questions.[51]

Some stakeholders are more important to the firm's survival than others. **Primary stakeholders** are groups upon which the organization depends for its long-term survival; they include shareholders, employees, customers, suppliers, governments, and local communities. When managers are struggling to balance the needs of different stakeholders, the stakeholder model suggests that the needs of primary stakeholders take precedence over the needs of secondary stakeholders. But among primary stakeholders, are some more important than others? According to the life-cycle theory of organizations, the answer is yes.[52] Organizations' needs change

stakeholder model
a theory of corporate responsibility that holds that management's most important responsibility, long-term survival, is achieved by satisfying the interests of multiple corporate stakeholders

stakeholders
persons or groups with a "stake" or legitimate interest in a company's actions

primary stakeholder
any group on which an organization relies for its long-term survival

EXHIBIT 3.5

Stakeholder Model of Corporate Social Responsibility

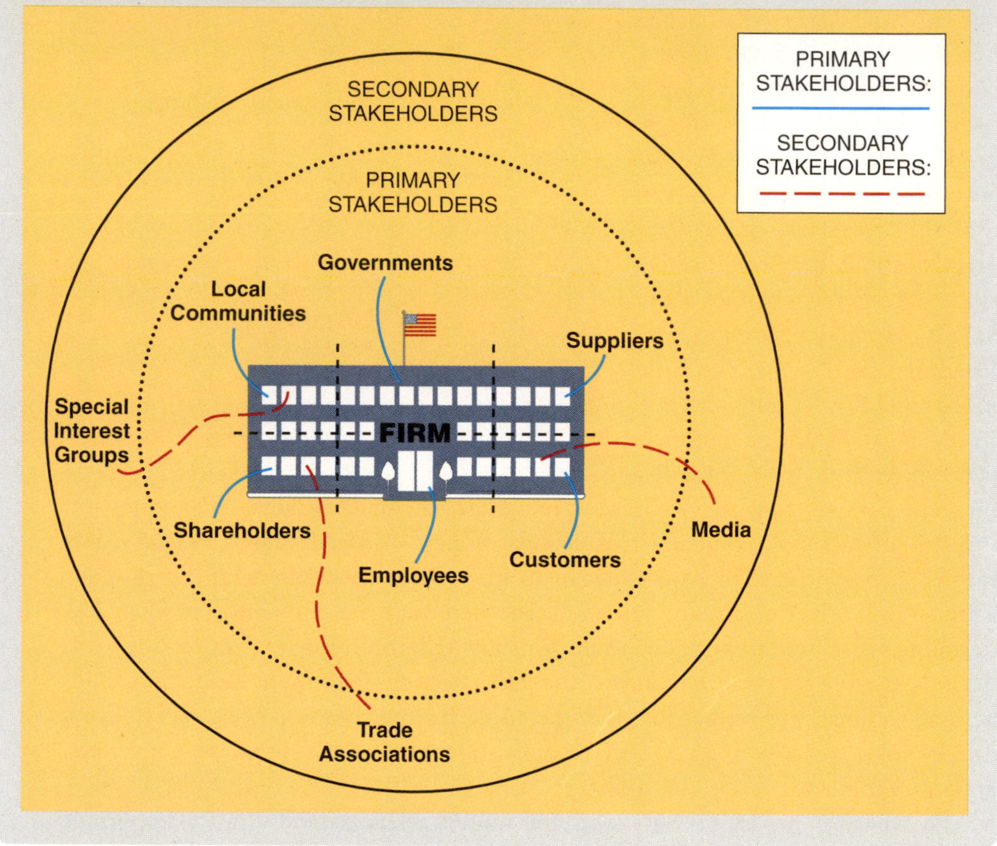

Source: Republished with permission of Academy of Management, P.O. Box 3020, Briar Cliff Manor, NY, 10510–8020. "The Stakeholder Theory of the Corporation: Concepts, Evidence and Implications" (Figure), T. Donaldson & L. E. Preston, *Academy of Management Review,* 1995, Vol. 20. Reproduced by permission of the publisher via Copyright Clearance Center, Inc.

as they go through the life-cycle stages of formation, growth, maturity, and decline. At each stage, different primary stakeholders will be critical to organizational well-being, and their concerns will take precedence over those of others primary stakeholders. In practice, though, CEOs typically give somewhat higher priority to shareholders, employees, and customers than to suppliers, governments, and local communities, no matter what stage of the life cycle a company is in.[53]

Addressing the concerns of primary stakeholders is important because if a stakeholder group becomes dissatisfied and terminates its relationship with the company, the company could be seriously harmed or go out of business. For example, *INTERPUBLIC GROUP*, one of the world's largest advertising agencies, lost a key client, Bank of America, to rival Omnicom Group. Bank of America's departure not only cost Interpublic $60 to $65 million a year in lost revenue, it also coincided with the loss of even larger clients—General Motors, Nestlé, and Unilever—who took large parts of their advertising business elsewhere.[54] Interpublic's profits and stock value have been significantly below the industry average since losing these key clients.[55]

Secondary stakeholders, such as the media and special interest groups, can influence or be influenced by the company. Unlike the primary stakeholders, however, they do not engage in regular transactions with the company and are not critical to its long-term survival. Meeting the needs of primary stakeholders is therefore usually more important than meeting the needs of secondary stakeholders. Nevertheless, secondary stakeholders are still important because they can affect public perceptions and opinions about socially responsible behavior.

So, to whom are organizations socially responsible? Many commentators, especially economists and financial analysts, continue to argue that organizations are responsible only to shareholders. Increasingly, however, top managers have come to believe that they and their companies must be socially responsible to their stakeholders. This view has gained adherents since the Great Depression, when General Electric first identified shareholders, employees, customers, and the general public as its stakeholders. In 1947, Johnson & Johnson listed customers, employees, managers, and shareholders as its stakeholders; and in 1950, Sears Roebuck announced that its most important stakeholders were "customers, employees, community, and stockholders."[56] Today, surveys show that as many as 80 percent of top-level managers believe that it is unethical to focus just on shareholders. Twenty-nine states have changed their laws to allow boards of directors to consider the needs of employees, creditors, suppliers, customers, and local communities, as well as those of shareholders.[57] Although there is not complete agreement, a majority of opinion makers would argue that companies must be socially responsible to their stakeholders.

REVIEW 5

To Whom Are Organizations Socially Responsible?

Social responsibility is a business's obligation to benefit society. To whom are organizations socially responsible? According to the shareholder model, the only social responsibility that organizations have is to maximize shareholder wealth by maximizing company profits. According to the stakeholder model, companies must satisfy the needs and interests of multiple corporate stakeholders, not just shareholders. However, the needs of primary stakeholders, on which the organization relies for its existence, take precedence over those of secondary stakeholders.

6 For What Are Organizations Socially Responsible?

If organizations are to be socially responsible to stakeholders, what are they to be socially responsible *for*? As Exhibit 3.6 illustrates, companies can best benefit their stakeholders by fulfilling their economic, legal, ethical, and discretionary responsibilities.[58] Economic and legal responsibilities are at the bottom of the pyramid because they play a larger part in a company's social responsibility than do ethical and discretionary responsibilities. However, the relative importance of these various responsibilities depends on society's expectations of corporate social responsibility at a particular point in time.[59] A century ago, society expected businesses to meet their economic and legal responsibilities and little else. Today, when society judges whether businesses are socially responsible, ethical and discretionary responsibilities are considerably more important than they used to be.

Historically, **economic responsibility**, or making a profit by producing a product or service valued by society, has been a business's most basic social responsibility.

secondary stakeholder
any group that can influence or be influenced by a company and can affect public perceptions about the company's socially responsible behavior

economic responsibility
a company's social responsibility to make a profit by producing a valued product or service

EXHIBIT 3.6

Social Responsibilities

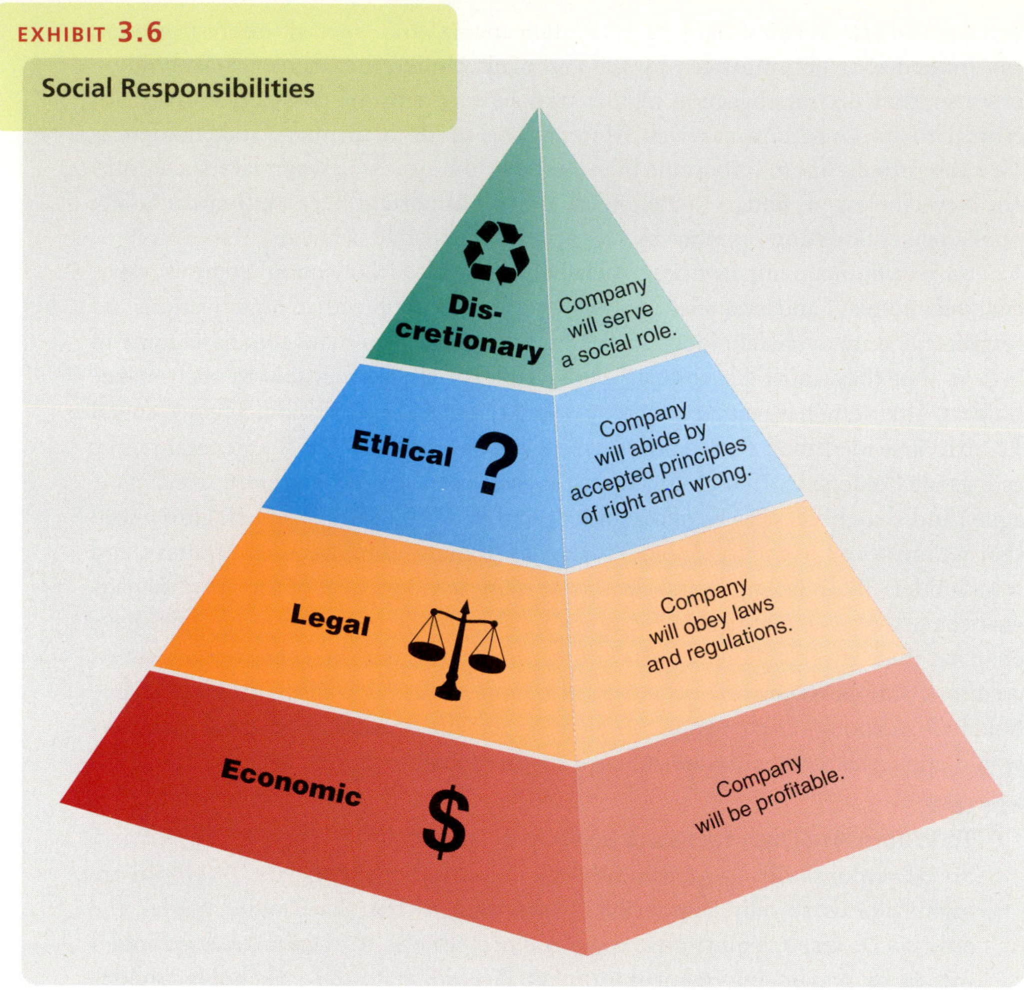

Source: Republished with permission of Academy of Management, P.O. Box 3020, Briar Cliff Manor, NY, 10510–8020. "A Three-Dimensional Conceptual Model of Corporate Performance" (Figure 3.3), A. B. Carroll, Academy of Management Review, 1979, Vol. 4. Reproduced by permission of the publisher via Copyright Clearance Center, Inc.

Organizations that don't meet their financial and economic expectations come under tremendous pressure. For example, company boards are very, very quick these days to fire CEOs. Typically, all it takes is two or three bad quarters in a row. Kevin Rollins was relieved of his duties as CEO of Dell for a single bad quarter and for allowing archrival Hewlett-Packard to increase its lead over Dell.[60] Nearly one-third of all CEOs are eventually fired because of their inability to successfully change their companies.[61] In fact, CEOs are three times more likely to be fired today than two decades ago.

legal responsibility
a company's social responsibility to obey society's laws and regulations

Legal responsibility is a company's social responsibility to obey society's laws and regulations as it tries to meet its economic responsibilities. For instance, companies award stock options so that managers and employees are rewarded when the company does well. Stock options give you the right to purchase shares of stock at a set price. Let's say that on June 1, the company awards you the right (or option) to buy 100 shares of stock, which, on that day, sells for $10 a share. If the stock price falls below $10, the options are worthless. But, if the stock price rises above $10, the options have value. Specifically, if the stock price rises to $15 a share, you can exercise your options by paying the company $1,000 (100 shares at $10 a share).

But because the stock is selling for $15, you can sell your 100 shares for $1,500 and make $500. But what if you could go back in time to, say, January 1 when the stock was selling for $5? You'd make $1,000 instead of $500. It would be unethical and illegal, however, to "backdate" your options to when the stock sold for a lower price. Doing so would illegally increase the value of your options. But, that's exactly what the president and chief operating officer did at Monster Worldwide (which runs Monster.com). By improperly backdating his options, he earned an additional $24 million.[62] At Monster, however, backdating was condoned by the CEO, who routinely backdated options for members of the management team.[63]

Ethical responsibility is a company's social responsibility not to violate accepted principles of right and wrong when conducting its business. Because different stakeholders may disagree about what is or is not ethical, meeting ethical responsibilities is more difficult than meeting economic or legal responsibilities.

Discretionary responsibilities pertain to the social roles that businesses play in society beyond their economic, legal, and ethical responsibilities. For example, dozens of companies support the fight against hunger at The Hunger Site, ***http://www.thehungersite.com***. Each time someone clicks on the "donate free food" button (only one click per day per visitor), sponsors of The Hunger Site donate money to pay for food to be sent to Bosnia, Indonesia, Mozambique, or wherever people suffer from hunger. Thanks to the corporate sponsors and the clicks of 59 million annual visitors, nearly 8 million pounds of food are distributed each year.[64] Discretionary responsibilities such as these are voluntary. Companies are not considered unethical if they don't perform them. Today, however, corporate stakeholders expect companies to do much more than in the past to meet their discretionary responsibilities.

REVIEW 6

For What Are Organizations Socially Responsible?

Companies can best benefit their stakeholders by fulfilling their economic, legal, ethical, and discretionary responsibilities. Being profitable, or meeting one's economic responsibility, is a business's most basic social responsibility. Legal responsibility consists of following a society's laws and regulations. Ethical responsibility means not violating accepted principles of right and wrong when doing business. Discretionary responsibilities are social responsibilities beyond basic economic, legal, and ethical responsibilities.

7 Responses to Demands for Social Responsibility

Social responsiveness refers to a company's strategy to respond to stakeholders' economic, legal, ethical, or discretionary expectations concerning social responsibility. A social responsibility problem exists whenever company actions do not meet stakeholder expectations. One model of social responsiveness, shown in Exhibit 3.7, identifies four strategies for responding to social responsibility problems: reactive, defensive, accommodative, and proactive. These strategies differ in the extent to which the company is willing to act to meet or exceed society's expectations.

A company using a **reactive strategy** will do less than society expects. It may deny responsibility for a problem or fight any suggestions that the company should solve a problem. The U.S. Consumer Product Safety Commission recalled 900,000 Simplicity bassinets after two infants were strangled between the product's metal bars. At the time of the recalls, Simplicity was no longer in business. It had gone

ethical responsibility
a company's social responsibility not to violate accepted principles of right and wrong when conducting its business

discretionary responsibilities
the social roles that a company fulfills beyond its economic, legal, and ethical responsibilities

social responsiveness
refers to a company's strategy to respond to stakeholders' economic, legal, ethical, or discretionary expectations concerning social responsibility

reactive strategy
a social responsiveness strategy in which a company does less than society expects

EXHIBIT 3.7

Social Responsiveness

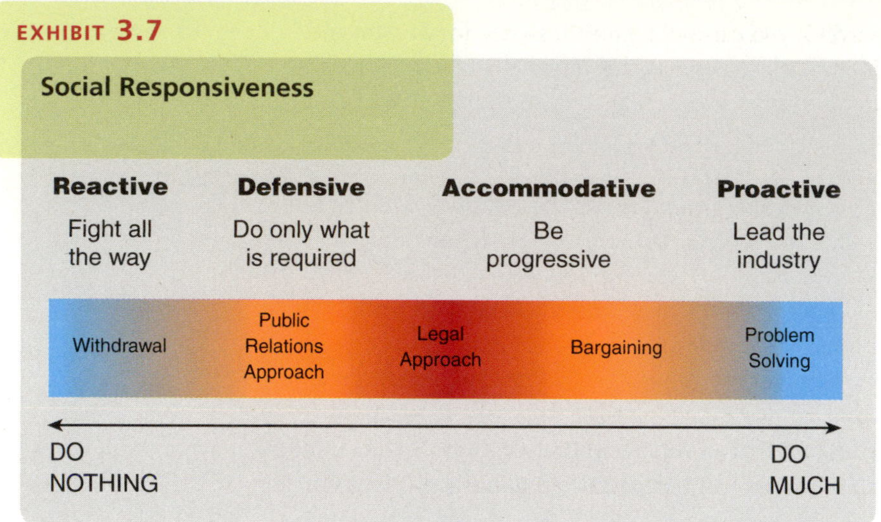

Source: Republished with permission of Academy of Management, P.O. Box 3020, Briar Cliff Manor, NY, 10510–8020. "A Three-Dimensional Conceptual Model of Corporate Performance", A. B. Carroll, Academy of Management Review, 1979, Vol. 4, 497–505. Reproduced by permission of the publisher via Copyright Clearance Center, Inc.

into bankruptcy and its assets, including the Simplicity brand name, were purchased by SFCA, Inc. SFCA, however, refused to pay for the recall, declaring, "SFCA purchased Simplicity's assets at auction after Simplicity, Inc. went out of business and has no legal liability for any products distributed previously by Simplicity."[65]

By contrast, a company using a **defensive strategy** would admit responsibility for a problem but would do the least required to meet societal expectations. Second Chance Body Armor makes bulletproof vests for police officers. Tests indicated that the protective material in its vests deteriorated quickly under high temperatures and humidity, conditions under which they're typically used. As a result, vests that were only two years old were potentially unsafe. Nevertheless, the company's executive committee would not recall the vests. Only after two vests were pierced, killing one police officer and wounding another, did Second Chance announce it would fix or replace 130,000 potentially defective vests. Although the company finally admitted responsibility for the problem, management decided to do only the minimum of what society expects (fix a defective product). Second Chance, therefore, used a defensive strategy.[66]

A company using an **accommodative strategy** will accept responsibility for a problem and take a progressive approach by doing all that could be expected to solve the problem. Finally, a company using a **proactive strategy** will anticipate responsibility for a problem before it occurs, do more than expected to address the problem, and lead the industry in its approach. Honda Motors announced that it will include side-curtain air bags (that drop from the roof and protect passengers' heads) and front-side air bags (that come out of the door to protect against side-impact collisions) as standard equipment on all of its cars. On most other cars, these were optional features for which customers had to pay extra. Brian O'Neill of the Insurance Institute for Highway Safety said, "This is a very positive development because we have been troubled by more and more manufacturers going the option route when it comes to safety equipment." Charlie Baker, Honda's vice president for U.S. research and development, says, "We are convinced this is the right direction and will save lives."[67]

defensive strategy
a social responsiveness strategy in which a company admits responsibility for a problem but does the least required to meet societal expectations

accommodative strategy
a social responsiveness strategy in which a company accepts responsibility for a problem and does all that society expects to solve that problem

proactive strategy
a social responsiveness strategy in which a company anticipates responsibility for a problem before it occurs and does more than society expects to address the problem

REVIEW 7

Responses to Demands for Social Responsibility

Social responsiveness is a company's response to stakeholders' demands for socially responsible behavior. There are four social responsiveness strategies. When a company uses a reactive strategy, it denies responsibility for a problem. When it uses a defensive strategy, it takes responsibility for a problem but does the minimum required to solve it. When a company uses an accommodative strategy, it accepts responsibility for problems and does all that society expects to solve them. Finally, when a company uses a proactive strategy, it does much more than expected to solve social responsibility problems.

8 Social Responsibility and Economic Performance

One question that managers often ask is, "Does it pay to be socially responsible?" In previous editions of this textbook, the answer was "no," as early research indicated that there was not an inherent relationship between social responsibility and economic performance.[68] Recent research, however, leads to different conclusions. There is no trade-off between being socially responsible and economic performance.[69] What is more, there is a small, positive relationship between being socially responsible and economic performance that strengthens with corporate reputation.[70] Let's explore what each of these results means.

First, there is no trade-off between social responsibility and economic performance.[71] Being socially responsible usually won't make a business less profitable. What this suggests is that the costs of being socially responsible—and those costs can be high, especially early on—can be offset by a better product or corporate reputation, which results in stronger sales or higher profit margins. For example, Unilever replaced its "All" laundry detergent with "All Small and Mighty," a triple concentrate that reduces the amount needed to wash a load of clothes by two-thirds. Changing to All Small and Mighty required Unilever to change its packaging, its advertising, and its distribution methods. But while Unilever incurred significant upfront costs to be more socially responsible, in the long run, those costs won't necessarily prevent it from making a profit with this product.

Second, it usually *does* pay to be socially responsible, and that relationship becomes stronger when a company or its products have a strong reputation for social responsibility.[72] For example, *GE*, long one of the most admired and profitable corporations in the world, was one of the first and largest *Fortune* 500 companies to make a strategic commitment to providing environmentally friendly products and service. CEO Jeffrey Immelt wants GE to "develop and drive the technologies of the future that will protect and clean our environment."[73] Is Immelt doing this because of personal beliefs? He says no. "It's no great thrill for me to do this stuff . . . I never put it in right versus wrong terms." GE calls its strategy "ecoimagination," which it says is "helping to solve the world's biggest environmental challenges while driving profitable growth for GE." Says Immelt, "We invest in the basic strategies that we think are going to fit into [ecoimagination], but make money for our investors at the same time."[74] And, in just 5 years, GE has increased the number of ecoimagination products from 17 to 80. As a result, it now sells more than $17 billion of such products and services each year, with annual revenue growth increasing by double digits.[75]

Finally, even if there is generally a small positive relationship between social responsibility and economic performance that becomes stronger when a company or its products have a positive reputation for social responsibility, and even if there is no trade-off between social responsibility and economic performance, there is no guarantee that socially responsible companies will be profitable. Simply put, socially responsible companies experience the same ups and downs in economic performance that traditional businesses do. A good example is Ben & Jerry's, the ice cream people. Ben & Jerry's started in 1978 when founders Ben Cohen and Jerry Greenfield sent away for a $5 course on how to make ice cream. Ben & Jerry's is as famous for its commitment to social responsibility as for its super premium ice cream. The company donates 7.5 percent of its pretax profits to support AIDS patients, homeless people, and the environment.[76] Moreover, customers buy Ben & Jerry's ice cream because it tastes great *and* because they want to support a socially responsible company. As Ben Cohen says, "We see ourselves as somewhat of a social service agency and somewhat of an ice cream company."[77] But—and this is a big "but"—despite its outstanding reputation as a socially responsible company, Ben & Jerry's consistently had financial troubles after going public (selling shares of stock to the public) 15 years ago. In fact, its financial problems became so severe that Ben and Jerry sold the company to British-based Unilever.[78] Being socially responsible may be the right thing to do, and is usually associated with increased profits, but it doesn't guarantee business success.

REVIEW 8

Social Responsibility and Economic Performance

Does it pay to be socially responsible? Studies show that there is generally no trade-off between social responsibility and economic performance. In most circumstances, there is generally a small positive relationship between social responsibility and economic performance that becomes stronger when a company or its products have a positive reputation. Social responsibility, however, does not guarantee profitability, as socially responsible companies experience the same ups and downs as other companies.

Responding to Tragedy

On April 5, 2010, an explosion at the Upper Big Branch coal mine in Montcoal, West Virginia killed 29 workers. Over the next several weeks and days, as nationwide attention turned to this tragedy, it was discovered that the mine's operating company, Massey Energy, was cited for numerous safety and regulatory violations. One month prior to the accident, the mine was written up more than 50 times, with 12 of those notices relating to an excessive buildup of coal dust and methane, conditions that can cause explosions like the one that occurred. The very day of the explosion, federal regulators identified two more safety violations, a failure to have updated maps of escape routes in case of an accident and a failure to outfit miners with required communication and tracking equipment that would help them stay in contact with aboveground employees. All told, officials found 1,342 safety violations at Upper Big Branch from 2005 to April 2009. And according to these investigators, miners at Upper Big Branch lost more time to work-site accidents than any other mine in the country.

In spite of the large number of violations, Massey continues to insist that they are committed to safety. On its website, the company proclaims "Safety is the top priority for every Massey member. . . . We work hard to instill a zero-tolerance policy and commitment from all members, whether they work at corporate headquarters or in the mines, to make safety the number one priority—every day." However, the company's reactions to regulators' citations have generally been resistant and confrontational. According to government records, Massey has contested or appealed a good portion of the violations it has received since 2005. By doing so, it has been able to avoid paying the fines and making the safety changes required by regulators.

The question for you, as a manager at Massey Energy is this: How will you address your company's ethical responsibility? Will you continue to insist that the company is doing everything it can for safety, even as the number of violations skyrockets? Will you insist that all safety violations be addressed immediately, and that unsafe mines be closed until they pass inspections, at the cost of hundreds of millions of dollars? What steps could you take to insure that your company is an industry leader in safety, while also remaining profitable?

Questions

1. How would you describe Massey's current approach to its ethical and social responsibility?
2. Which approach to social responsibility would you recommend that Massey take in the future?
3. How might the temporary closure of dangerous mines and the investment of funds into new safety systems, be an economic stimulus for Massey?

Sources: Michael Cooper and Ian Urbina. "Mine Operator Escapes Extra Oversight after Warning." *New York Times*. April 9, 2010. Accessed at http://www.nytimes.com/2010/04/10/us/10westvirginia.html?hp

Steven Mufson, Jerry Markon, and Ed O'Keefe. "West Virginia Mine Has Been Cited for Myriad Safety Violations." *The Washington Post*. April 7, 2010. Accessed at http://www.washingtonpost.com/wp-dyn/content/article/2010/04/05/AR2010040503877.html

"Safety." Massey Energy Company. http://www.masseyenergyco.com/safety/index.shtml

Ian Urbina and Bernie Becker. "As Rescue Efforts Continue for Miners, Officials Press for Answers." *New York Times*. April 8–7, 2010. Accessed at http://www.nytimes.com/2010/04/08/us/08westvirginia.html

Practice being a Manager

Discerning Unethical Behavior

Applying ethical judgment in an organizational setting can be challenging. This exercise offers you the opportunity to consider how you might approach such a situation as a manager in an investment firm.

Read the scenario and prepare your responses to the individual (homework) questions in advance of discussing this exercise in class.

Scenario

Imagine that you are a newly hired portfolio manager at Excalibur Funds. Although you're new to this job, you have 8 years' experience in the mutual fund business. You left a larger and more established mutual fund company to join Excalibur because of its reputation as a bright, up-and-coming investment company, a place where someone like yourself could participate in building a new and dynamic company.

Your new fund, the Pioneer Fund, is a growth-oriented fund investing in small companies. The majority of the fund's stock investments is in high-technology companies. Pioneer is moving up fast in its peer group, and if the fund continues to perform well, you stand a good chance of being the manager recognized when it breaks into the top tier of performance.

One of the features that attracted you to this job is the opportunity to work with a seasoned group of traders, analysts, and staff professionals. The Pioneer Fund staff has averaged 10 percent turnover over the past 5 years, unusual in an industry where turnover typically reaches 60 to 80 percent. After a month of working with your new team, however, you have noticed some troubling patterns. First, you felt that some of your staff were delaying or stonewalling you on several occasions when you requested more detailed information on particular trades. It took too long to get the information, and when you did receive it, the information looked a little *too* neat and well organized. Second, the analysts have seemed guarded in their interaction with some of the technology companies in which the Pioneer Fund invests. On more than one occasion you've noticed analysts quickly ending phone calls when you entered the office or minimizing computer screens when you walk by their desks. Finally, the group just seems a bit too *nice* when you are around. The investment business is often hectic and stressful. Shouting matches over investment decisions are not uncommon, and grumbling is a second language. But all you get are smiles and charm.

So here you are at your desk on a Saturday evening, finishing off the last of a pot of coffee and planning for Monday morning. One thing is clear—you must begin to scratch below the surface of the Pioneer Fund team. Your gut tells you that something is wrong here, perhaps very wrong. For all you know, you may be sitting on the next big investment scandal. Your head tells you that you have no hard evidence of unethical or illegal behavior and that you'd better tread carefully. If your gut is wrong and you run around making hasty accusations, you may lose what appears to be a very talented investment team.

What steps should you take starting Monday morning?

Preparing for Class Discussion

Complete the following steps individually in preparation for class discussion. Write your responses to the questions in each step.

STEP 1 Understand the situation and key considerations. What considerations would be important to you in developing a plan of action in this situation? What resources might you draw upon to determine whether or not particular actions are unethical and/or illegal?

STEP 2 Develop a plan of action. What steps would you follow in this scenario? What factors should you consider in planning your timing of these steps?

STEP 3 Anticipate response(s). How might the Pioneer Fund employees respond to your plan of action? Develop a few scenarios.

Small Group and Class Discussion

Your professor will assign you to a small discussion group. Your group should discuss the following questions and be prepared to share your thoughts with the class:

1. What are the most difficult aspects of responding to a murky situation—those situations in which you sense the presence of unethical and/or illegal behavior but haven't seen unequivocal proof of wrongdoing?
2. What are the risks of waiting for unequivocal proof before beginning to take action? What are the risks of acting decisively based on your "gut" sense of a situation?
3. What is different about acting ethically within an organizational environment like that of the Pioneer Fund versus acting ethically as an individual? What are the particular challenges and dynamics associated with ethical and responsible behavior in an organization?

An Ethical Baseline

Most people think they are ethical, particularly when the right thing to do appears to be obvious. But as you read in the chapter, 75 percent of respondents in a nationwide survey indicated that they had witnessed unethical behavior at work. In another study across multiple industries, 48 percent of the respondents admitted to actually committing an unethical or illegal act in the past year! And recall that with so many ways to approach ethical decision making, ethical choices are not always cut-and-dried. To give you an idea of your ethical perspective, take this assessment.[79]

Answer each of the questions using the following scale:

1. Strongly agree
2. Agree
3. Not sure
4. Disagree
5. Strongly disagree

1. Did you ever think about taking money from where you worked, but didn't go through with it?
   1 2 3 4 5
2. Have you ever borrowed something from work without telling anyone?
   1 2 3 4 5
3. There are times I've been provoked into a fistfight.
   1 2 3 4 5
4. Is it okay to get around the law if you don't break it?
   1 2 3 4 5
5. I've had fellow employees show me how to take things from where I work.
   1 2 3 4 5
6. I will usually take someone up on a dare.
   1 2 3 4 5

7. I've always driven insured vehicles.
   1 2 3 4 5
8. If you were sent an extra item with an order, would you send it back?
   1 2 3 4 5
9. Would you say everyone is a little dishonest?
   1 2 3 4 5
10. Most supervisors treat their employees fairly.
    1 2 3 4 5
11. I worry about getting hurt at work.
    1 2 3 4 5
12. People say that I'm a workaholic.
    1 2 3 4 5
13. I like to plan things carefully ahead of time.
    1 2 3 4 5
14. Have you found a way a dishonest person in your job could take things from work?
    1 2 3 4 5
15. I often act quickly without stopping to think things through.
    1 2 3 4 5
16. It doesn't bother me what other people think.
    1 2 3 4 5
17. I have friends who are a little dishonest.
    1 2 3 4 5
18. I am not a thrill seeker.
    1 2 3 4 5
19. I have had my driver's license revoked.
    1 2 3 4 5
20. Are you too honest to steal?
    1 2 3 4 5
21. Do most employees take small items from work?
    1 2 3 4 5
22. Do most employees get along well with their supervisors?
    1 2 3 4 5
23. I'm lucky to avoid having accidents.
    1 2 3 4 5
24. I always finish what I start.
    1 2 3 4 5
25. I make sure everything is in its place before leaving home.
    1 2 3 4 5

SCORING

Determine your average score for each category by entering your response to each survey item below, as follows. In blanks that say *regular score*, simply enter your response for that item. If your response was a 4, place a 4 in the *regular score* blank. In blanks that say *reverse score*, subtract your response from 6 and enter the result. So if your response was a 4, place a 2 ($6 - 4 = 2$) in the *reverse score* blank. Total your scores; then compute your average score for each section.

Antisocial Behavior

1. regular score ______
2. regular score ______
3. regular score ______
4. regular score ______
5. regular score ______
6. regular score ______
7. reverse score ______
8. reverse score ______
14. regular score ______
15. regular score ______
16. regular score ______
17. regular score ______
18. reverse score ______
19. regular score ______
20. reverse score ______

TOTAL = ___ ÷15 = ___ (your average for Antisocial Behavior)

Orderliness/Diligence

12. regular score ______
13. regular score ______
24. regular score ______
25. regular score ______

TOTAL = ___ ÷ 4 = ___ (your average for Orderliness/Diligence)

Positive Outlook

9. reverse score ______
10. regular score ______
11. reverse score ______
21. reverse score ______
22. regular score ______
23. regular score ______

TOTAL = ___ ÷ 6 = ___ (your average for Positive Outlook)

You can find the interpretation for your scores at: login.cengagebrain.com.

Reel to Real

Biz Flix

Emperor's Club

William Hundert (Kevin Kline), a professor at Saint Benedict's preparatory school, believes in teaching his students about living a principled life as well as teaching them his beloved classical literature. Hundert's principled ways are challenged, however, by a new student, Sedgewick Bell (Emile Hirsch). Bell's behavior during the 73rd annual Julius Caesar competition causes Hundert to suspect that Bell leads a less than principled life.

Years later, Hundert is the honored guest of his former student Sedgewick Bell (Joel Gretsch) at Bell's estate and competes in a reenactment of the Julius Caesar competition. Bell nearly wins the competition, but when Hundert notices that Bell is wearing an earpiece and is cheating with an assistant's help, he gives him a question he knows he cannot answer.

This scene is an edited portion of the competition reenactment.

What to Watch for and Ask Yourself

1. Based on the clip, what ethical principles do you think most inform William Hundert's thinking?
2. Describe Sedgewick Bell's level of moral development.

Management Workplace

City of Greensburg, Kansas

On May 4, the city of Greensburg, Kansas, was leveled by violent storms and tornadoes. Steve Hewitt, the city administrator, and Mayor Lonnie McCollum rallied the people and vowed to rebuild a new and improved Greensburg—as a "green town." In this video, the townspeople explain what they initially thought about this unusual idea when it was presented to them, why they decided to rebuild in a socially responsible way, and what they're now doing to make it a reality.

What to Watch for and Ask Yourself

1. If you lived in Greensburg and your home was destroyed by the tornado along with 95 percent of the town, how would you feel about the mayor's proposal to rebuild in an environmentally friendly way? What about the plan would appeal to you? What reservations would you have?
2. How do you think Greensburg is demonstrating social responsibility?
3. At what stage of moral development would you say Hewitt and McCollum are preconventional, conventional, or postconventional? Please explain.

Part Two
Planning

This chapter examines the benefits and pitfalls of planning, making plans work, and the different plans used in organizations. You'll also learn the steps and limitations of rational decision making and review various group decision techniques.

This chapter examines how managers use strategies to obtain a sustainable competitive advantage. Then you learn the strategy-making process and how companies answer these questions: What business should we be in? How should we compete in this industry? How should we compete against a particular firm?

This chapter reviews the issues associated with organizational innovation. The first part of this chapter shows you why innovation matters and how to manage innovation to create and sustain a competitive advantage. In the second part of the chapter, you will learn about organizational change and about the risk of not changing.

In this chapter, we examine the impact of global business on U.S. firms and review the basic rules and agreements that govern global trade. You'll learn how and when companies go global. And you'll read how companies decide where to expand globally and confront issues like business climates and cultural differences.

4 Chapter Four
Planning and Decision Making

OUTLINE

Experience Management

Explore the four levels of learning by doing the simulations modules on Planning & Strategic Processes, Organizational Control, and Decision Making.

© ISTOCKPHOTO.COM/ ANN MARIE KURTZ

Pod Nod

Mini lecture reviews all the learning points in the chapter.

© ISTOCKPHOTO.COM/ MAGNET CREATIVE

Reel to Real Video

Biz Flix is a scene from *Inside Man.* Management Workplace is a segment on Flight 001.

© ISTOCKPHOTO.COM/ CRAFTVISION

Self Test

10 quiz questions, 4 exhibit worksheets, and PowerPoints for quick review.

© ISTOCKPHOTO.COM/ DIJITAL FILM

What Would You Do?

Ford Motor Company Dearborn, Michigan.[1]

You turned Boeing around from billion-dollar losses to huge profits and increased market share. But when you became *FORD MOTOR COMPANY'S* CEO, people asked, "What does an airplane guy know about the car business?" Well, on your first day as CEO, you reviewed the product lineup and discovered something missing, the Ford Taurus, the best-selling car in company history. "Where was it?" you asked. "We killed it. After a while, they didn't sell very well, so we stopped." Incredulous, you replied, "You stopped? How many billions of dollars did it cost to build brand loyalty around the Taurus name? Well, you've got until tomorrow to find a vehicle to put the Taurus name on. Then, you have two years to make a new Taurus which had better be the coolest vehicle that you can possibly make." So, in less than 4 hours, you made your first billion-dollar decision. It wouldn't be your last. With billions of dollars in losses, you eliminated 46,000 jobs, sold off Aston Martin, Jaguar, Volvo, and Land Rover, discontinued the underperforming Mercury brand, and cut truck and SUV production by 40 percent. Despite these drastic moves, Ford still lost $12.6 billion your second year and $2.7 billion your third.

With losses still mounting, the first major issue you need to address is vehicle customization, that is, maximizing consumer choice by producing different cars with different parts for different world markets. Vehicle customization originated in 1967 when Ford's European operations were created to design and manufacture cars just for Europe. Consequently, when Ford attempted to cut costs by creating a common "world car" to be sold in Europe and the United States, it failed. The resulting cars (yes, "cars"), one designed in Detroit and the other in Germany, were completely different except for two shared parts.

The second major issue is that Ford's management teams have had difficulty staying on target and tracking company performance. Even with downsizing, Ford is a complex company with 205,000 employees, multiple product lines, and international operations on four continents. Surprisingly, Ford's managers only stay in their jobs a few years. And, if you're off to your next job and don't have to live with the consequences of your decisions, why care about whether you meet your department's or division's goals?

The final issue is that contentious relationships between Ford's divisions have produced dysfunctional decision making. Different geographic regions and functional divisions, such as engineering, production, and sales, are more interested in doing what they want than what is best for Ford as a whole. Feelings on this issue are so strong that your management team pleaded with you to remove Ford's blue logo from one of your PowerPoint presentations so as not to "alienate" those who worked for Ford's Volvo, Jaguar, and Lincoln divisions. At the time you agreed, but now realize it was a mistake.

Three years ago, you arranged for $23 billion in loans to get the company through tough times. And with Chrysler and GM in bankruptcy, and industry sales off 35 percent, you've needed every dime. But, you're 65 percent through those funds, so you've got to address these key issues. Ford's survival depends on it. Should Ford continue to make different cars for Europe and the United States? If so, how do you lower expenses? If not, then how do you get the company to produce "world cars," when it has failed to do so before? What should Ford's strategic objective be here? Beyond making managers stay longer in their jobs, which won't be popular, how will you change Ford's culture so that managers pay attention to company plans and feel accountable for meeting performance targets? Finally, what will you do to address the dysfunctional way in which decisions are made, where different departments and units care more about their issues than the company's issues?

If you were the new CEO of For what would you do?

Even inexperienced managers know that planning and decision making are central parts of their jobs. Figure out what the problem is. Generate potential solutions or plans. Pick the best one. Make it work. Experienced managers, however, know how hard it really is to make good plans and decisions. One seasoned manager says: "I think the biggest surprises are the problems. Maybe I had never seen it before. Maybe I was protected by my management when I was in sales. Maybe I had delusions of grandeur, I don't know. I just know how disillusioning and frustrating it is to be hit with problems and conflicts all day and not be able to solve them very cleanly."[2]

This chapter begins by examining the benefits and pitfalls of planning. Next, you will learn how to make a plan that works. Then you will look at the different kinds of plans that are used from the top to the bottom in most companies. In the second part of the chapter, we discuss the steps of rational decision making and consider its limitations. We finish the chapter by discussing how managers can use groups and group decision techniques to improve decisions.

Planning

planning
choosing a goal and developing a strategy to achieve that goal

Planning is choosing a goal and developing a method or strategy to achieve that goal. In the face of tougher regulations and an industry-wide reputation for selling junk food, *GENERAL MILLS* decided that 20 percent of its products would meet more rigorous nutrition standards. Managers had to adapt old products and develop new ones that were higher in whole grains, lower in sugar and salt, and would encourage people to eat their vegetables. Some products, like single-serving vegetables, were successful. Others, like Go-Gurt yogurt in a plastic tube, were flops. But setting clear standards for nutritional value and tying annual executive bonuses to achievement of those standards helped General Mills meet its goal. The company is now well on its way to its next goal: having 40 percent of its products meeting rigorous nutrition standards by 2010.[3]

After reading the next three sections, you should be able to:

1 discuss the benefits and pitfalls of planning.
2 describe how to make a plan that works.
3 discuss how companies can use plans at all management levels, from top to bottom.

1 Benefits and Pitfalls of Planning

Are you one of those naturally organized people who always make a daily to-do list, write everything down so you won't forget, and never miss a deadline because you keep track of everything with your handy time management notebook or iPhone or PC? Or are you one of those flexible, creative, go-with-the-flow people who dislike planning and organizing because it restricts your freedom, energy, and performance? Some people are natural planners. They love it and can see only its benefits. Others dislike planning and can see only its disadvantages. It turns out that *both* views have real value. Planning has advantages and disadvantages.

Let's learn about 1.1 **the benefits**, and 1.2 **the pitfalls of planning**.

1.1 Benefits of Planning

Planning offers several important benefits: intensified effort, persistence, direction, and creation of task strategies.[4] First, managers and employees put forth greater effort when following a plan. Take two workers. Instruct one to "do your best" to increase production, and instruct the other to achieve a 2 percent increase in production each month. Research shows that the one with the specific plan will work harder.[5] Second, planning leads to persistence, that is, working hard for long periods. In fact, planning encourages persistence even when there may be little chance of short-term success.[6] The third benefit of planning is direction. Plans encourage managers and employees to direct their persistent efforts *toward* activities that help accomplish their goals and *away* from activities that don't.[7]

The fourth benefit of planning is that it encourages the development of task strategies. In other words, planning not only encourages people to work hard for extended periods and to engage in behaviors directly related to goal accomplishment, it also encourages them to think of better ways to do their jobs. Finally, perhaps the most compelling benefit of planning is that it has been proved to work for both companies and individuals. On average, companies with plans have larger profits and grow much faster than companies that don't.[8] The same holds true for individual managers and employees: There is no better way to improve the performance of the people who work in a company than to have them set goals and develop strategies for achieving those goals.

1.2 Pitfalls of Planning

Despite the significant benefits associated with planning, it is not a cure-all. Plans won't fix all organizational problems. In fact, many management authors and consultants believe that planning can harm companies in several ways.[9] The first pitfall of planning is that it can impede change and prevent or slow needed adaptation. Sometimes companies become so committed to achieving the goals set forth in their plans, or on following the strategies and tactics spelled out in them, that they fail to see that their plans aren't working or that their goals need to change. When it comes to environmentally sound cars, *GENERAL MOTORS* missed its initial opportunity to innovate because its culture was "wedded to big cars and horsepower." While Toyota formed its "green group" in the mid-1990s, which led to the development of the Prius, its popular hybrid, GM didn't begin developing experimental technology for an electric car until 2003. And then, it killed the project after deciding to continue selling highly profitable SUVs (sport utility vehicles). GM restarted its work on hybrid cars in 2006, but its Chevy Volt won't be ready until 2011.[10]

The second pitfall is that planning can create a false sense of certainty. Planners sometimes feel that they know exactly what the future holds for their competitors, their suppliers, and their companies. However, all plans are based on assumptions: "The price of gasoline will increase by 4 percent per year"; "Exports will continue to rise." For plans to work, the assumptions on which they are based must hold true. If the assumptions turn out to be false, then the plans based on them are likely to fail.

The third potential pitfall of planning is the detachment of planners. In theory, strategic planners and top-level managers are supposed to focus on the big picture and not concern themselves with the details of implementation (i.e., carrying out the plan). According to management professor Henry Mintzberg, detachment leads planners to plan for things they don't understand.[11] Plans are meant to be guidelines for action, not abstract theories. Consequently, planners need to be familiar with the daily details of their businesses if they are to produce plans that can work.

REVIEW 1

Benefits and Pitfalls of Planning

Planning involves choosing a goal and developing a method to achieve that goal. Planning is one of the best ways to improve organizational and individual performance. It encourages people to work harder (intensified effort), to work hard for extended periods (persistence), to engage in behaviors directly related to goal accomplishment (directed behavior), and to think of better ways to do their jobs (task strategies). Most importantly, companies that plan have larger profits and faster growth than companies that don't plan. However, planning also has three potential pitfalls. Companies that are overly committed to their plans may be slow to adapt to changes in their environment. Planning is based on assumptions about the future, and when those assumptions are wrong, the plans are likely to fail. Finally, planning can fail when planners are detached from the implementation of plans.

2 How to Make a Plan That Works

Planning is a double-edged sword. If done right, planning brings about tremendous increases in individual and organizational performance. If planning is done wrong, however, it can have just the opposite effect and harm individual and organizational performance. In this section, you will learn how to make a plan that works.

As depicted in Exhibit 4.1, planning consists of 2.1 **setting goals**, 2.2 **developing commitment to the goals**, 2.3 **developing effective action plans**, 2.4 **tracking progress toward goal achievement**, and 2.5 **maintaining flexibility in planning**.

2.1 Setting Goals

The first step in planning is to set goals. To direct behavior and increase effort, goals need to be specific and challenging.[12] For example, deciding to "increase sales this year" won't direct and energize workers as much as deciding to "increase North American sales by 4 percent in the next 6 months." Likewise, deciding to "drop a few pounds" won't motivate you as much as deciding to "lose 15 pounds." Specific, challenging goals provide a target for which to aim and a standard against which to measure success.

One way of writing effective goals for yourself, your job, or your company is to use the S.M.A.R.T. guidelines. **S.M.A.R.T. goals** are **S**pecific, **M**easurable, **A**ttainable, **R**ealistic, and **T**imely.[13] Let's see how a heating, ventilation, and air-conditioning (HVAC) company might use S.M.A.R.T. goals in its business.

EXHIBIT 4.1

How to Make a Plan That Works

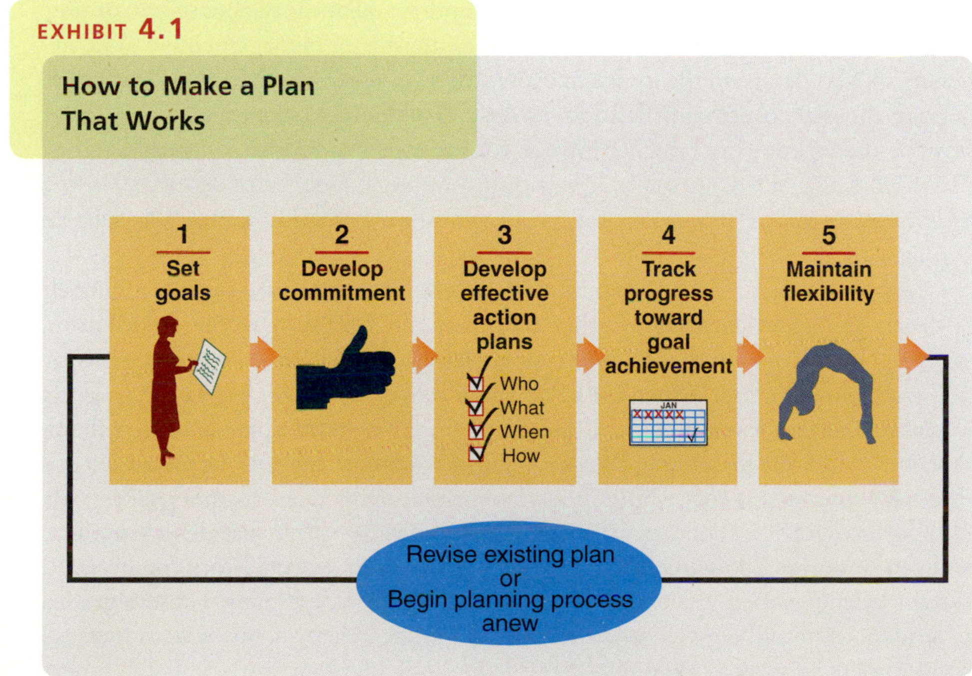

S.M.A.R.T. Goals goals that are specific, measurable, attainable, realistic, and timely

The HVAC business is cyclical. It's extremely busy at the beginning of summer, when homeowners find that their air-conditioning isn't working, and at the beginning of winter, when furnaces and heat pumps need repair. During these times, most HVAC companies have more business than they can handle, while at other times of year their business can be very slow. So a *specific* goal would be to increase sales by 50 percent during the fall and spring, when business is slower. This goal could be *measured* by keeping track of the number of annual maintenance contracts sold to customers. This goal of increasing sales during the off-seasons is *attainable* because maintenance contracts typically include spring tune-ups (air-conditioning systems) and fall tune-ups (furnace or heating systems). Moreover, a 50 percent increase in sales during the slow seasons appears to be *realistic*. Because customers want their furnaces and air conditioners to work the first time it gets cold or hot each year, a well-designed pitch may make them very open to buying service contracts that ensure their equipment is in working order. Tune-up work can then be scheduled during the slow seasons, increasing sales at those times. Finally, this goal can be made *timely* by asking the staff to push sales of maintenance contracts before Labor Day, the traditional end of summer, when people start thinking about the cold days ahead, and in March, when winter-weary people start longing for hot days in air-conditioned comfort. The result should be more work during the slow fall and spring seasons.

2.2 Developing Commitment to Goals

Just because a company sets a goal doesn't mean that people will try to accomplish it. If workers don't care about a goal, that goal won't encourage them to work harder or smarter. Thus, the second step in planning is to develop commitment to goals.[14]

Goal commitment is the determination to achieve a goal. Commitment to achieve a goal is not automatic. Managers and workers must choose to commit themselves to a goal. Edwin Locke, professor emeritus of management at the University of Maryland and the foremost expert on how, why, and when goals work, tells a story about an overweight friend who lost 75 pounds. Locke says, "I asked him how he did it, knowing how hard it was for most people to lose so much weight." His friend responded, "Actually, it was quite simple. I simply decided that I *really wanted* to do it."[15] Put another way, goal commitment is really wanting to achieve a goal.

So how can managers bring about goal commitment? The most popular approach is to set goals participatively. Rather than assigning goals to workers ("Johnson, you've got till Tuesday of next week to redesign the flux capacitor so it gives us 10 percent more output"), managers and employees choose goals together. The goals are more likely to be realistic and attainable if employees participate in setting them. Another technique for gaining commitment to a goal is to make the goal public. For example, college students who publicly communicated their semester grade goals ("This semester, I'm shooting for a 3.5") to significant others (usually a parent or sibling) were much more committed to achieving their grades. More importantly, those students earned grades that were nearly a half-grade higher than the grades of students who did not tell others about their grade goals. So, one way to increase commitment to goals is to go public by having individuals or work units tell others about their goals. Still another way to increase goal commitment is to obtain top management's support. Top management can show support for a plan or program by

goal commitment
the determination to achieve a goal

providing funds, speaking publicly about the plan, or participating in the plan itself.

2.3 Developing Effective Action Plans

The third step in planning is to develop effective action plans. An **action plan** lists the specific steps (how), people (who), resources (what), and time period (when) for accomplishing a goal. Unlike most CEOs, Randy Papadellis has a unique goal that requires an extraordinary action plan. As the CEO of Ocean Spray, Papadellis has to buy all of the cranberries that his farmers produce (Ocean Spray is a farmer cooperative) and buy the crop at the highest possible price. Then, it's Papadellis's job to figure out how to sell the entire crop of high-cost berries. Under Papadellis's direction, Ocean Spray began looking for alternative uses for cranberries beyond the traditional juice and canned products, uses that would involve new methods, people, and resources. The company invented dried-fruit Craisins by reinfusing juice into husks that used to be thrown away. Craisins have grown into a $100 million product line. Ocean Spray also developed a set of light drinks that had just 40 calories, mock berries that could be infused with other flavors (such as blueberry and strawberry) and used in muffins and cereals, and was the first company to introduce juice boxes. Because of these actions, Ocean Spray has been able to increase the price it pays its farmers over 100 percent in the past three years.[17]

Doing the Right Thing

Stretch Goals: Avoid the "15 Percent Delusion"

Stretch goals are extremely ambitious goals that you don't know how to reach. They are so demanding that they force managers and workers to throw away old, comfortable solutions and adopt radical, never-used solutions. Setting stretch goals can help companies and individuals achieve extraordinary improvements in performance. Though stretch goals may encourage large improvements, they may also pressure people to do anything to meet "the numbers." The most common stretch goal CEOs set is "15 percent annual growth," the magical number that doubles corporate earnings every 5 years. But with earnings growth averaging just 8 percent over the last 40 years, the chances of achieving 15 percent growth every year are extremely low. So instead of promising generally unobtainable results, managers should set more realistic stretch goals. When Bob Eckert became CEO of Mattel, he dumped the company's stated goals of 15 percent annual earnings growth and 10 percent revenue growth. Says Eckert, "They were not realistic. We were not going to play that game anymore."[16]

2.4 Tracking Progress

The fourth step in planning is to track progress toward goal achievement. There are two accepted methods of tracking progress. The first is to set proximal goals and distal goals. **Proximal goals** are short-term goals or subgoals, whereas **distal goals** are long-term or primary goals.[18] The idea behind setting proximal goals is that achieving them may be more motivating and rewarding than waiting to reach far-off distal goals.

action plan
the specific steps, people, and resources needed to accomplish a goal

proximal goals
short-term goals or subgoals

distal goals
long-term or primary goals

Management Fact:

If you want people to do a better job of tracking the quality and timeliness of their work, use proximal goals to set multiple deadlines. In a study at MIT, students were given a proofreading assignment—they would be paid 10 cents for each error they found, but penalized $1 per day for submitting their work late. One group of students was given a single deadline—a distal goal, while another was given weekly deadlines—proximal goals. The single-deadline group turned in their work 12 days late and found only 70 errors, while the multiple-deadline group was only half a day late and found 136 errors.

Source: D. Ariely and K. Wertenboch. "Procrastination, Deadlines, and Performance: Self-Control by Precommitment." *Psychological Science* 13 (2002): 219–224.

The second method of tracking progress is to gather and provide performance feedback. Regular, frequent performance feedback allows workers and managers to track their progress toward goal achievement and make adjustments in effort, direction, and strategies.[19] Exhibit 4.2 shows the impact of feedback on safety behavior at a large bakery company with a worker safety record that was two-and-a-half times worse than the industry average. During the baseline period, workers in the wrapping department, who measure and mix ingredients, roll the bread dough, and put it into baking pans, performed their jobs safely about 70 percent of the time (see 1 in Exhibit 4.2). The baseline safety record for workers in the makeup department, who bag and seal baked bread and assemble, pack, and tape cardboard cartons for shipping, was somewhat better at 78 percent (see 2). The company then gave workers 30 minutes of safety training, set a goal of 90 percent safe behavior, and then provided daily feedback (such as a chart similar to Exhibit 4.2). Performance improved dramatically. During the intervention period, safely performed behaviors rose to an average of 95.8 percent for wrapping workers (see 3) and 99.3 percent for workers in the makeup department (see 4), and never fell below 83 percent. Thus, the combination of training, a challenging goal, and feedback led to a dramatic increase in performance. The importance of feedback alone can be seen in the reversal stage, when the company quit posting daily feedback on safe behavior. Without daily feedback, the percentage of safely performed behavior returned to baseline levels—70.8 percent for the wrapping department (see 5) and 72.3 percent for the makeup department (see 6). For planning to be effective, workers need both a specific, challenging goal and regular feedback to track their progress. Indeed, additional research indicates that the effectiveness of goal setting can be doubled by the addition of feedback.[20]

2.5 Maintaining Flexibility

Because action plans are sometimes poorly conceived and goals sometimes turn out not to be achievable, the last step in developing an effective plan is to maintain flexibility. One method of maintaining flexibility while planning is to adopt an options-based approach.[21] The goal of **options-based planning** is to keep options open by making small, simultaneous investments in many alternative plans. Then, when one or a few of these plans emerge as likely winners, you invest even more in these plans while discontinuing or reducing investment in the others.

options-based planning maintaining planning flexibility by making small, simultaneous investments in many alternative plans

EXHIBIT 4.2

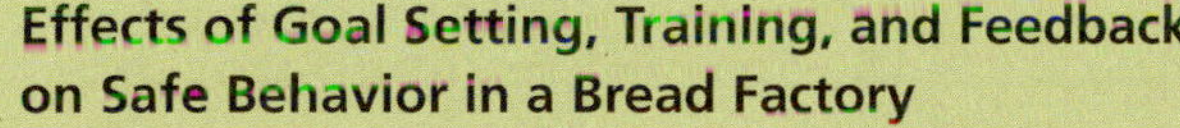

Effects of Goal Setting, Training, and Feedback on Safe Behavior in a Bread Factory

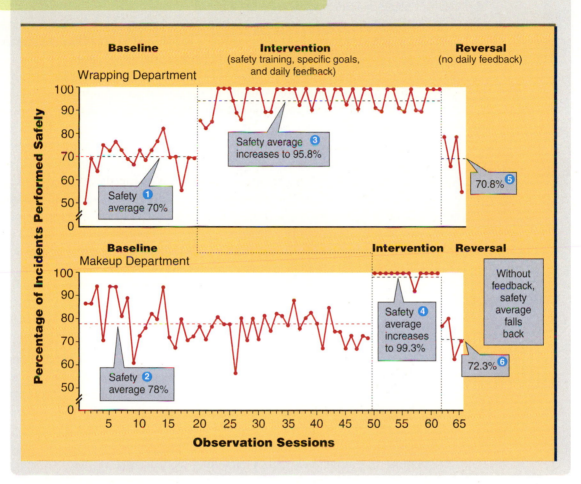

In part, options-based planning is the opposite of traditional planning. Whereas the purpose of an action plan is to commit people and resources to a particular course of action, the purpose of options-based planning is to leave those commitments open by maintaining **slack resources**, that is, a cushion of resources, such as extra time, people, money, or production capacity, that can be used to address and adapt to unanticipated changes, problems, or opportunities.[22] Holding options open gives you choices. And choices, combined with slack resources, give you flexibility.

Facing steep declines in circulation, many newspaper publishers are turning to options-based planning by making small, simultaneous investments in a number of alternatives.[23] One example is E. W. Scripps's *Naples Daily News*, which has aggressively tried to counter the national decline in print subscriptions as the audience turns to the Internet for its news. To increase readership, the *Naples Daily News* offers content via TV, radio, magazines, cell phones, PlayStations, and iPhones. The

slack resources
a cushion of extra resources that can be used with options-based planning to adapt to unanticipated changes, problems, or opportunities

newspaper posts a 15-minute video newscast on its website each day and offers services like calling readers at the end of each quarter in a football game to update the score. Publisher John Fish says profits are "a good bit higher than our print margins. It's just going to grow in the future. And if we don't provide the services, someone else will come up under us."[24]

Another method of maintaining flexibility while planning is to take a learning-based approach. Traditional planning assumes that initial action plans are correct and will lead to success. By contrast, **learning-based planning** assumes that action plans need to be continually tested, changed, and improved as companies learn better ways of achieving goals.[25] For example, Joe Ferry's design team at Virgin Atlantic Airways was charged with coming up with a new reclining sleeper seat for use in both the first- and business-class sections. But the year Virgin started design and development, chief competitor British Airways launched a truly flat bed (not just a reclining seat) in business class, making Virgin's plan all but useless. Moreover, customers complained about discomfort when using the seat in the reclined position. So Virgin changed the plan from designing a seat to designing a suite and allocated an additional $127 million to the project. Different from the first attempt, the seats in Virgin's so-called upper-class suite have been a hit with customers, using two types of foam so that passengers are comfortable in both sleeping and sitting positions. Virgin expected the change in plans to increase market share by 1 percent, but after only 2 years, the new seats have allowed the company to exceed that goal.[26]

REVIEW 2

How to Make a Plan That Works

There are five steps to making a plan that works: (1) Set S.M.A.R.T. goals, or goals that are **S**pecific, **M**easurable, **A**ttainable, **R**ealistic, and **T**imely. (2) Develop commitment to the goals from the people who contribute to goal achievement. Managers can increase workers' goal commitment by encouraging worker participation in goal setting, making goals public, and getting top management to show support for workers' goals. (3) Develop action plans for goal accomplishment. (4) Track progress toward goal achievement by setting both proximal and distal goals and by providing workers with regular performance feedback. (5) Maintain flexibility. Keeping options open through options-based planning and seeking continuous improvement through learning-based planning help organizations maintain flexibility as they plan.

3 Planning from Top to Bottom

Planning works best when the goals and action plans at the bottom and middle of the organization support the goals and action plans at the top of the organization. In other words, planning works best when everybody pulls in the same direction. Exhibit 4.3 illustrates this planning continuity, beginning at the top with a clear definition of the company purpose and ending at the bottom with the execution of operational plans.

learning-based planning learning better ways of achieving goals by continually testing, changing, and improving plans and strategies

Let's see how 3.1 **top managers create the organization's purpose statement and strategic objective**, 3.2 **middle managers develop tactical plans and use management by objectives to motivate employee efforts toward the overall purpose and strategic objective**, and 3.3 **first-level managers**

EXHIBIT 4.3

Planning from Top to Bottom

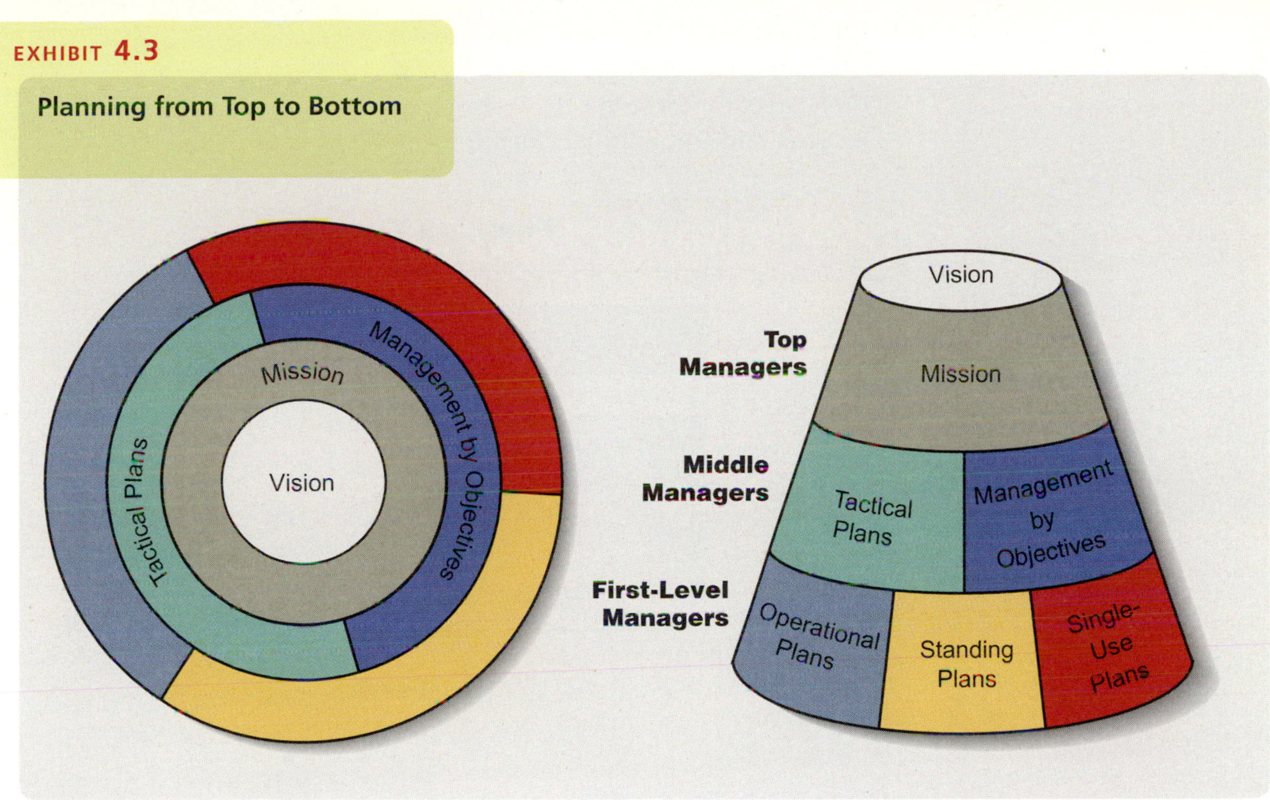

use operational, single-use, and standing plans to implement the tactical plans.

3.1 Starting at the Top

As shown in Exhibit 4.4, top management is responsible for developing long-term **strategic plans** that make clear how the company will serve customers and position itself against competitors in the next 2 to 5 years. (The strategic planning and management process is examined in its entirety in Chapter 5.) Strategic planning begins with the creation of an organizational purpose.

A **purpose statement**, which is often referred to as an organizational mission or vision, is a statement of a company's purpose or reason for existing.[27] Purpose statements should be brief—no more than two sentences. They should also be enduring, inspirational, clear, and consistent with widely shared company beliefs and values. An excellent example of a well-crafted purpose statement is that of Avon, the cosmetics company: "to be the company that best understands and satisfies the product service and self-fulfillment needs of women globally." This statement guides everyone in the organization and provides a focal point for the delivery of beauty products and services to the customer, women around the world. The purpose is the same whether Avon is selling lipstick to women in India, shampoo packets to women in the Amazon, or jewelry to women in the United States. Despite regional differences in specific strategy, the overall goal—understanding the needs of women

strategic plans overall company plans that clarify how the company will serve customers and position itself against competitors over the next two to five years

purpose statement a statement of a company's purpose or reason for existing

EXHIBIT 4.4

Time Lines for Strategic, Tactical, and Operational Plans

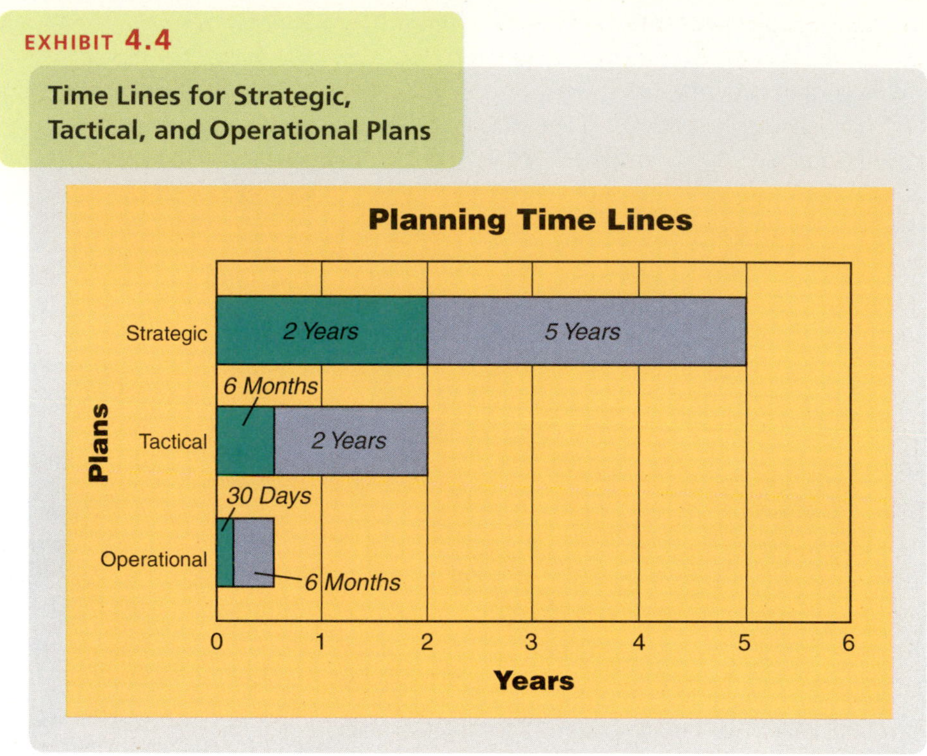

globally—does not change. Other examples of organizational purposes that have been particularly effective include Walt Disney Company's "to make people happy" and Schlage Lock Company's "to make the world more secure."[28]

The **strategic objective**, which flows from the purpose, is a more specific goal that unifies company-wide efforts, stretches and challenges the organization, and possesses a finish line and a time frame.[29] For example, in 1961, President John F. Kennedy established a strategic objective for *NASA* with this simple statement: "Achieving the goal, before this decade is out, of landing a man on the moon and returning him safely to earth."[30] NASA achieved this strategic objective on July 20, 1969, when astronaut Neil Armstrong walked on the moon. Once the strategic objective has been accomplished, a new one should be chosen. The new strategic objective must grow out of the organization's purpose, which does not change significantly over time. For example, NASA hopes to accomplish its latest strategic goal, or what it calls its "exploration systems mission directorate," between 2015 and 2020. NASA's strategic goal is to "return to the moon where we will build a sustainable long term human presence." NASA further explains its strategic goal by saying, "As the space shuttle approaches retirement and the International Space Station nears completion, NASA is building the next fleet of vehicles to bring astronauts back to the moon, and possibly to Mars and beyond."[31]

strategic objective
a more specific goal that unifies company-wide efforts, stretches and challenges the organization, and possesses a finish line and a time frame

tactical plans
plans created and implemented by middle managers that specify how the company will use resources, budgets, and people over the next six months to two years to accomplish specific goals within its mission

3.2 Bending in the Middle

Middle management is responsible for developing and carrying out tactical plans to accomplish the organization's strategic objective. **Tactical plans** specify how a company will use resources, budgets, and people to accomplish specific goals related to its strategic objective for the next 5 years. Whereas strategic plans and objectives are used to focus company efforts over the next 2 to 5 years, tactical plans and objectives are used to direct behavior, efforts, and attention over the next 6 months to 2 years. Several years ago, *CLOROX*, a $4 billion global consumer products company, was not meeting sales goals for 30 percent of its products. So it developed a simple, but powerful, tactical plan where the chief financial officer, director of supply chain, and vice presidents of sales, marketing, and operations met monthly to identify products that were performing below sales and profit goals. Products exceeding targets were graded green. Those within 5 percent were graded yellow. But products more than 5 percent below goal targets were graded red, and the managers responsible for those product lines were required to develop plans to improve sales or to identify whether and how to eliminate product lines whose sales were unlikely to improve. Two years after implementing this tactical plan, over 90 percent of Clorox's products met sales and profit goals, and the average sales per product increased by 25 percent, giving Clorox the highest sales per product in its industry.[32]

Management by objectives is a management technique often used to develop and carry out tactical plans. **Management by objectives (MBO)** is a four-step process in which managers and their employees (1) discuss possible goals; (2) collectively select goals that are challenging, attainable, and consistent with the company's overall goals; (3) jointly develop tactical plans that lead to the accomplishment of tactical goals and objectives; and (4) meet regularly to review progress toward accomplishment of those goals. At *KINDERMUSIK INTERNATIONAL*, a music education publisher, all 50 employees attend weekly 1-hour meetings to review the company's weekly goals and financial results. Half-day review sessions are held each quarter to review results and to discuss how to cut costs and increase revenues. Because they regularly reviewed and discussed goal progress, employees were sensitive to reducing costs, so they proposed replacing the company's 5-day sales convention, which costs about $50,000, with a series of meetings. CEO Michael Dougherty said, "If you'd asked me, I would have said, 'We've always done the convention.' But the folks who are closer to the event and closer to the customers know that there were other and better ways to achieve the same goal."[33]

management by objectives (MBO)
a four-step process in which managers and employees discuss and select goals, develop tactical plans, and meet regularly to review progress toward goal accomplishment

3.3 Finishing at the Bottom

Lower-level managers are responsible for developing and carrying out **operational plans**, which are the day-to-day plans for producing or delivering the organization's products and services. Operational plans direct the behavior, efforts, and priorities of operative employees for periods ranging from 30 days to 6 months. There are three kinds of operational plans: single-use plans, standing plans, and budgets.

Single-use plans deal with unique, one-time-only events. When Industrial Motion, Inc., an international procurement service, moved from California to North Carolina, it needed a single-use plan for everything from managing business data, relocating key employees, and buying furniture.[36]

Unlike single-use plans that are created, carried out, and then never used again, **standing plans** save managers time because once the plans are created, they can be used repeatedly to handle frequently recurring events. If you encounter a problem that you've seen before, someone in your company has probably written a standing plan that explains how to address it. Using this plan rather than reinventing the

operational plans
day-to-day plans, developed and implemented by lower-level managers, for producing or delivering the organization's products and services over a 30-day to six-month period

single-use plans
plans that cover unique, one-time-only events

standing plans
plans used repeatedly to handle frequently recurring events

what *really* works

Management by Objectives

For years, both managers and management researchers have wondered how much of an effect planning has on organizational performance, or if it has any effect at all. While proponents argued that planning encourages workers to work hard, persist in their efforts, engage in behaviors directly related to goal accomplishment, and develop better strategies for achieving goals, opponents argued that planning impedes organizational change and adaptation, creates the illusion of managerial control, and artificially separates thinkers and doers. Now, however, the results from 70 different organizations strongly support the effectiveness of management by objectives (i.e., short-term planning).

Management by Objectives (MBO)

Management by objectives is a process in which managers and subordinates at all levels of a company sit down together to set goals jointly, share information and discuss strategies that could lead to goal achievement, and regularly meet to review progress toward accomplishing those goals. Thus, MBO is based on goals, participation, and feedback. On average, companies that effectively use MBO outproduce those that don't by an incredible 44.6 percent. And in companies where top management is committed to MBO, that is, where objective setting begins at the top, the average increase in performance is an even more astounding 56.5 percent. By contrast, when top management does not participate in or support MBO, the average increase in productivity is only 6.1 percent. In all, there is a 97 percent chance that companies that use MBO will outperform those that don't! Thus, MBO can make a very big difference to the companies that use it.[34]

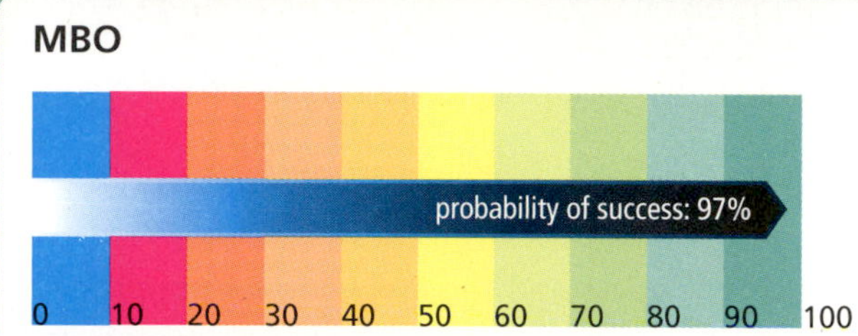

When done right, MBO is an extremely effective method of tactical planning. Still, MBO is not without disadvantages. Some MBO programs involve excessive paperwork, requiring managers to file annual statements of plans and objectives, plus quarterly or semiannual written reviews assessing goal progress. Today, however, electronic and web-based management systems and software make it easier for managers and employees to set goals, link them to the organization's strategic direction, and continuously track and evaluate their progress.[35] Another difficulty is that managers are frequently reluctant to give employees feedback about their performance. A third disadvantage is that managers and employees sometimes have difficulty agreeing on goals. And when employees are forced to accept goals that they don't want, goal commitment and employee effort suffer. Last, because MBO focuses on quantitative, easily measured goals, employees may neglect important but unmeasured parts of their jobs. In other words, if your job performance is judged only by whether you reduce costs by 3 percent or raise revenues by 5 percent, then you are unlikely to give high priority to the unmeasured but still important parts of your job, such as mentoring new employees or sharing knowledge and skills with coworkers.

wheel will save you time. There are three kinds of standing plans: policies, procedures, and rules and regulations.

Policies indicate the general course of action that company managers should take in response to a particular event or situation. A well-written policy will also specify why the policy exists and what outcome the policy is intended to produce. At *AMERICAN HONDA* travel expense tracking software sends e-mails to employees and their bosses pointing out that a $1,000 ticket purchased by the employee could have been purchased for $800 a week earlier. This system helps employees adhere to the company's travel policies and expense guidelines.[37]

Procedures are more specific than policies because they indicate the series of steps that should be taken in response to a particular event. A manufacturer's procedure for handling defective products might include the following steps. Step 1: Rejected material is locked in a secure area with "reject" documentation attached. Step 2: Material Review Board (MRB) identifies the defect and how far outside the standard the rejected products are. Step 3: MRB determines the disposition of the defective product as either scrap or as rework. Step 4: Scrap is either discarded or recycled, and rework is sent back through the production line to be fixed. Step 5: If delays in delivery will result, MRB member notifies customer.[38]

Rules and regulations are even more specific than procedures because they specify what must happen or not happen. They describe precisely how a particular action should be performed. For instance, many companies have rules and regulations forbidding managers from writing job reference letters for employees who have worked at their firms because a negative reference may prompt a former employee to sue for defamation of character.[39]

After single-use plans and standing plans, budgets are the third kind of operational plan. **Budgeting** is quantitative planning because it forces managers to decide how to allocate available money to best accomplish company goals. According to Jan King, author of *Business Plans to Game Plans*, "Money sends a clear message about your priorities. Budgets act as a language for communicating your goals to others." Exhibit 4.5 shows the operating budget outlays for the U.S. federal government. Together, social programs (Social Security and income security, or welfare) and health-care programs (Medicare and health) account for nearly 60 percent of the federal budget.

REVIEW 3

Planning from Top to Bottom

Proper planning requires that the goals at the bottom and middle of the organization support the objectives at the top of the organization. Top management develops strategic plans that indicate how a company will serve customers and position itself against competitors over a period of 2 to 5 years. Middle managers use techniques like management by objectives to develop tactical plans that direct behavior, efforts, and priorities over the next 6 months to 2 years. Finally, lower-level managers develop operational plans that guide daily activities in producing or delivering an organization's products and services. Operational plans typically span periods ranging from 30 days to 6 months. There are three kinds of operational plans: single-use plans, standing plans (policies, procedures, and rules and regulations), and budgets.

policies
a standing plan that indicates the general course of action that should be taken in response to a particular event or situation

procedures
a standing plan that indicates the specific steps that should be taken in response to a particular event

rules and regulations
standing plans that describe how a particular action should be performed, or what must happen or not happen in response to a particular event

budgeting
quantitative planning through which managers decide how to allocate available money to best accomplish company goals

EXHIBIT 4.5

2009 U.S. Federal Government Budget Outlays

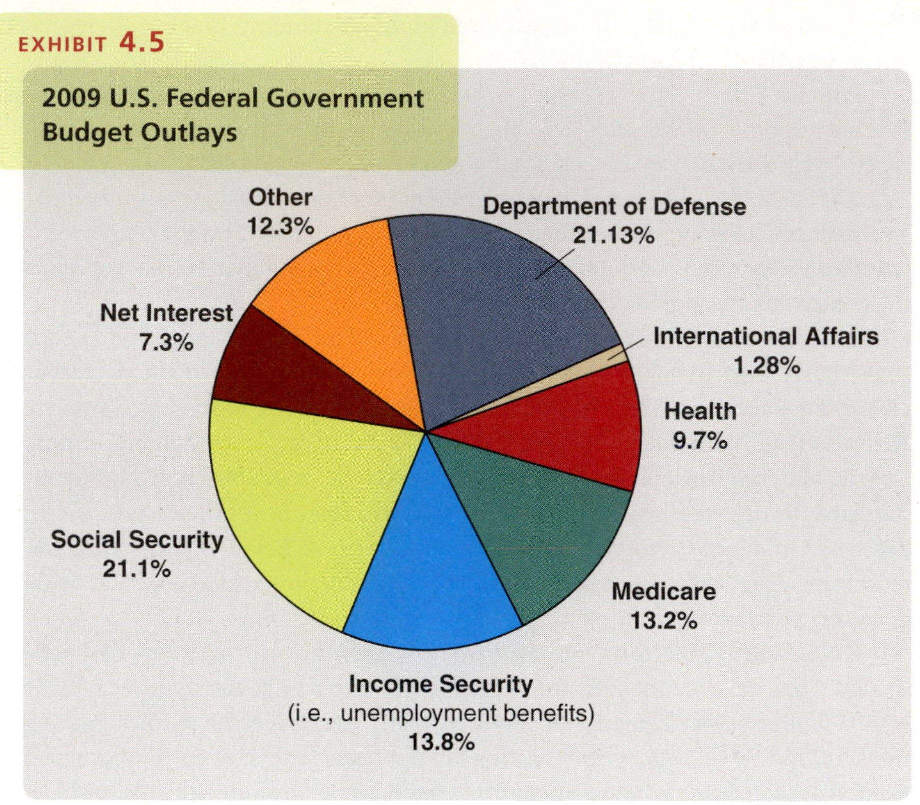

 What Is Rational Decision Making?

Imagine that your boss asks you for a recommendation on outfitting the sales force, many of whom travel regularly, with new computers. She asks you to prepare a report that details the problems the sales team has been having with its current computers and summarizes both current and future computer needs. You need to come up with at least five plans or options for getting computers to help members of the sales team do their job as efficiently as possible no matter where they are. When your boss delegates this "computer problem," what she really wants from you is a rational decision. **Decision making** is the process of choosing a solution from available alternatives.[40] **Rational decision making** is a systematic process in which managers define problems, evaluate alternatives, and choose optimal solutions that provide maximum benefits to their organizations. Thus, your boss expects you to define and analyze the computer problem and explore alternatives. Furthermore, your solution has to be optimal, because the department is going to live with the computer equipment you recommend for the next 3 years.

decision making
the process of choosing a solution from available alternatives

rational decision making
a systematic process of defining problems, evaluating alternatives, and choosing optimal solutions

After reading the next two sections, you should be able to:

4 explain the steps and limits to rational decision making.

5 explain how group decisions and group decision-making techniques can improve decision making.

4 Steps and Limits to Rational Decision Making

Exhibit 4.6 shows the six steps of the rational decision-making process.

Let's learn more about each of these steps: 4.1 **define the problem**, 4.2 **identify decision criteria**, 4.3 **weight the criteria**, 4.4 **generate alternative courses of action**, 4.5 **evaluate each alternative**, and 4.6 **compute the optimal decision**. Then we'll consider 4.7 **limits to rational decision making**.

EXHIBIT 4.6

Steps of the Rational Decision-Making Process

1. Define the Problem
2. Identify Decision Criteria
3. Weight the Criteria
4. Generate Alternative Courses of Action
5. Evaluate Each Alternative
6. Compute the Optimal Decision

4.1 Define the Problem

The first step in decision making is identifying and defining the problem. A **problem** exists when there is a gap between a desired state (what is wanted) and an existing state (the situation you are actually facing). For instance, women want to look good and be comfortable in properly fitted clothes. But since the garment industry's size standards were collected 60 years ago on a small group of Caucasian women in their 20s, fit varies tremendously. A size 8 in one brand will be a size 10 in another. As a result, women who can't find good-fitting clothes leave without purchasing or are forced to buy poorly fitting clothes that are returned to the store or discarded after several wearings. Either way, the result is the same—Clothing manufacturers have a problem because dissatisfied customers won't buy their brands in the future.[41]

The presence of a gap between an existing state and a desired state (such as selling clothes that should fit, but don't) is no guarantee that managers will make decisions to solve problems. Three things must occur for this to happen.[42] First, managers have to be aware of the gap. They have to know there is a problem before they can begin solving it. For example, after noticing that people were spending more money on their pets, a new dog food company created an expensive, high-quality dog food. To emphasize its quality, the dog food was sold in cans and bags with gold labels, red letters, and detailed information about its benefits and nutrients. Yet the product did not sell very well, and the company went out of business in less than a year. Its founders didn't understand why. When they asked a manager at a competing dog food company what their biggest mistake had been, the answer was, "Simple. You didn't have a picture of a dog on the package."[43] This problem would have been easy to solve, if management had only been aware of it.

Being aware of a problem isn't enough to begin the decision-making process. Managers also have to be motivated to reduce the gap between a desired and an existing state. To reverse its struggles, Starbucks has closed nearly a 1,000 stores and laid off over 25,000 employees to cut expenses by $100 million. But, it wasn't until McDonald's rolled out a national advertising campaign for its lower-priced

problem
a gap between a desired state and an existing state

McCafé mochas, lattes, and cappuccinos that Starbucks was finally motivated to cut product prices. CEO Howard Schultz said, "We know customers are looking for meaningful value, not just a lower price. In the coming days we're going to arm our consumers and partners with the facts about Starbucks coffee."[44] Those facts include lowering the price of basic drinks, such as a "grande" iced coffee, by 45 cents to less than $2. With profits down 77 percent and same-store sales down 8 percent, and with McDonald's now selling specialty coffee drinks for $3 or less, Starbucks was motivated to take steps to keep customers who might be tempted by McDonald's lower prices.

Finally, it's not enough to be aware of a problem and be motivated to solve it. Managers must also have the knowledge, skills, abilities, and resources to fix the problem. Product designer Cricket Lee tried to solve the sizing problem in the women's clothing industry by developing Fitlogic, a sizing standard that takes account of body types and is not intimidating for larger women.[45] Although relatively unknown, Lee has convinced QVC (a home shopping TV network), Nordstroms, Macy's, and Jones Apparel to license Fitlogic to help women with different body shapes buy better-fitting clothes.[46]

4.2 Identify Decision Criteria

Decision criteria are the standards used to guide judgments and decisions. Typically, the more criteria a potential solution meets, the better that solution will be. Let's return to the employee who was given the responsibility for making a rational decision about the office computer setup. What general factors would be important when purchasing computers for the office? Reliability, price, warranty, on-site service, and compatibility with existing software, printers, and computers would all be important, but you must also consider the technical details. What specific factors would you want the office computers to have? Well, with technology changing so quickly, you'll probably want to buy computers with as much capability and flexibility as you can afford.

Today, for the first time, laptops now account for over 50 percent of the market.[47] Business laptops come in four distinct model types. There are budget models that are good for routine office work but are usually saddled with a slower processor; workhorse models that are not lightweight, but have everything included; slim models for traveling that usually require an external drive to read/write to a DVD/CD; and tablet models that include such items as handwriting recognition software.[48] So, will users need to burn CDs and DVDs, or just read them? How much memory and hard drive space will the users need? Should you pay extra for durability, file encryption, and extra-large batteries? Answering questions like these will help you identify the criteria that will guide the purchase of the new equipment.

decision criteria
the standards used to guide judgments and decisions

absolute comparisons
a process in which each decision criterion is compared to a standard or ranked on its own merits

4.3 Weight the Criteria

After identifying decision criteria, the next step is deciding which criteria are more or less important. Although there are numerous mathematical models for weighting decision criteria, all require the decision maker to provide an initial ranking of the criteria. Some use **absolute comparisons**, in which each criterion is compared

EXHIBIT 4.7

Absolute Weighting of Decision Criteria for a Car Purchase

Highlighted numbers indicate how important the particular criterion is to a hypothetical car buyer. Your rankings might be very different.

	CI	NVI	SI	I	CI
1. Predicted reliability	1	2	3	4	5
2. Owner satisfaction	1	2	3	4	5
3. Predicted depreciation	1	2	3	4	5
4. Avoiding accidents	1	2	3	4	5
5. Fuel economy	1	2	3	4	5
6. Crash protection	1	2	3	4	5
7. Acceleration	1	2	3	4	5
8. Ride	1	2	3	4	5
9. Front seat comfort	1	2	3	4	5

Note: CI: completely unimportant; NVI: not very important; SI: somewhat important; I: important; CI: critically important.

with a standard or ranked on its own merits. For example, *Consumer Reports* uses this checklist when it rates and recommends new cars: predicted reliability, previous owners' satisfaction, predicted depreciation (the price you could expect if you sold the car), ability to avoid an accident, fuel economy, crash protection, acceleration, ride, and front seat comfort.[49]

Different individuals will rank these criteria differently, depending on what they value or require in a car. Exhibit 4.7 shows the absolute weights that someone buying a car might use. Because these weights are absolute, each criterion is judged on its own importance, using a five-point scale, with "5" representing "critically important" and "1" representing "completely unimportant." In this instance, predicted reliability, fuel economy, and front seat comfort were rated most important, and acceleration and predicted depreciation were rated least important.

Another method uses **relative comparisons**, in which each criterion is compared directly with every other criterion.[50] Exhibit 4.8 shows six criteria that someone might use when buying a house. Moving down the first column of Exhibit 4.8, we see that the time of the daily commute has been rated less important (−1) than school system quality; more important (+1) than having an inground pool, sun room, or a quiet street; and just as important as the house being brand new (0). Total weights, which are obtained by adding the scores in each column, indicate that the daily commute and school system quality are the most important factors to this home buyer, while an inground pool, sun room, and a quiet street are the least important.

relative comparisons a process in which each decision criterion is compared directly with every other criterion

EXHIBIT 4.8

Relative Comparison of Home Characteristics

Home Characteristics	DC	SSQ	IP	SR	QS	NBH
Daily commute (DC)		+1	−1	−1	−1	0
School system quality (SSQ)	−1		−1	−1	−1	−1
Inground pool (IP)	+1	+1		0	0	+1
Sun room (SR)	+1	+1	0		0	0
Quiet street (QS)	+1	+1	0	0		0
Newly built house (NBH)	0	+1	−1	0	0	
Total weight	+2	+5	−3	−2	−2	0

4.4 Generate Alternative Courses of Action

After identifying and weighting the criteria that will guide the decision-making process, the next step is to identify possible courses of action that could solve the problem. In general, at this step, the idea is to generate as many alternatives as possible. Let's assume that you're trying to select a city in Europe for the location of a major office. After meeting with your staff, you generate a list of possible alternatives: Amsterdam, the Netherlands; Barcelona or Madrid, Spain; Berlin or Frankfurt, Germany; Brussels, Belgium; London, England; Milan, Italy; Paris, France; and Zurich, Switzerland.

4.5 Evaluate Each Alternative

The next step is to systematically evaluate each alternative against each criterion. Because of the amount of information that must be collected, this step can take much longer and be much more expensive than other steps in the decision-making process. When selecting a European city for your office, you could contact economic development offices in each city, systematically interview businesspeople or executives who operate there, retrieve and use published government data on each location, or rely on published studies such as Cushman & Wakefield's *European Cities Monitor*, which conducts an annual survey of more than 500 senior European executives who rate thirty-four European cities on twelve business-related criteria.[51]

No matter how you gather the information, once you have it, the key is to systematically use that information to evaluate each alternative against each criterion. Exhibit 4.9 shows how each of the ten cities on your staff's list fared on each of the 12 criteria (higher scores are better), from qualified staff to freedom from pollution. Although London has the most qualified staff, the best access to markets and telecommunications, and is the easiest city to travel to and from, it is also one of the most polluted and expensive cities on the list. Paris offers excellent access to markets and clients, but if your staff is multilingual, Amsterdam may be a better choice.

EXHIBIT 4.9

Criteria Ratings Used to Determine the Best Locations in Europe for a New Office

	WEIGHTS	Amsterdam	Barcelona	Berlin	Brussels	Frankfurt	London	Madrid	Munich	Paris	Zurich
QUALIFIED STAFF	57%	.42	.35	.30	.40	.63	1.55	.36	.59	.75	.25
ACCESS TO MARKETS	60%	.39	.34	.26	.44	.68	1.32	.40	.42	1.15	.19
TRAVEL TO/ FROM CITY	51%	.61	.24	.23	.53	1.29	1.76	.51	.45	1.51	.26
TELE-COMMUNI-CATIONS	54%	.35	.23	.32	.36	.63	1.28	.34	.38	.80	.17
BUSINESS CLIMATE	26%	.45	.44	.35	.45	.21	.53	.34	.28	.26	.40
COST OF STAFF	35%	.17	.63	.38	.20	.16	.12	.53	.10	.12	.01
COST & VALUE OF OFFICE SPACE	34%	.33	.61	.70	.43	.37	.65	.62	.30	.35	.10
AVAILABLE OFFICE SPACE	25%	.13	.61	.70	.43	.37	.65	.62	.30	.35	.10
TRAVEL WITHIN CITY	23%	.42	.51	.67	.38	.39	1.23	.56	.44	1.14	.41
LANGUAGES SPOKEN	24%	.97	.27	.49	1.00	.50	1.42	.28	.34	.47	.62
QUALITY OF LIFE	21%	.46	1.13	.29	.37	.79	.47	.63	.68	.57	.54
FREEDOM FROM POLLUTION	17%	.46	.41	.21	.32	.19	.10	.14	.67	.15	.91
WEIGHTED AVERAGE SCORE		1.67	1.44	1.39	1.67	2.24	4.31	1.59	1.53	2.95	1.02
RANKING		7	6	9	5	3	1	4	8	2	10

Source: "European Cities Monitor," Cushman & Wakefield Healy & Baker, available at http://www.cushmanwakefield.com/cwglobal/docviewer/European%20Cities%20Monitor.pdf?id=ca1500006&repositoryKey=CoreRepository&itemDesc=document.

4.6 Compute the Optimal Decision

The final step in the decision-making process is to compute the optimal decision by determining the optimal value of each alternative. This is done by multiplying the rating for each criterion (Step 4.5) by the weight for that criterion (Step 4.3), and then summing those scores for each alternative course of action that you generated (Step 4.4). For example, the 500 executives participating in Cushman & Wakefield's survey of the best European cities for business rated the twelve decision criteria in terms of importance as shown in the first column of Exhibit 4.9. Access to quality staff, markets, telecommunication, and easy travel to and from the city were the four most important factors, while quality of life and freedom from pollution were the least important factors. To calculate the optimal value for Paris, its score in each category is multiplied by the weight for each category (.57 × .75 in the qualified staff category, for example). Then all of these scores are added together to produce the optimal value, as follows:

$$
\begin{aligned}
&(.57 \times .75) \pm (.60 \times 1.15) \pm (.51 \times 1.51) \\
&\pm (.54 \times .80) \pm (.26 \times .26) \pm (.35 \times .12) \\
&\pm (.34 \times .35) \pm (.25 \times .35) \pm (.23 \times 1.14) \\
&\pm (.24 \times .47) \pm (.21 \times .57) \pm (.17 \times .15) = -2.95
\end{aligned}
$$

Since London has a weighted average of 4.57 compared to 2.95 for Paris and 2.24 for Frankfurt, London clearly ranks as the best location for your company's new European office because of its large number of qualified staff; easy access to markets; outstanding ease of travel to, from, and within the city; excellent telecommunications; and top-notch business climate.

4.7 Limits to Rational Decision Making

In general, managers who diligently complete all six steps of the rational decision-making model will make better decisions than those who don't. So whenever possible, managers should try to follow the steps in the rational decision-making model, especially for big decisions with long-range consequences.

It's highly doubtful, however, that rational decision making can always help managers choose *optimal* solutions that provide *maximum* benefits to their organizations. The terms *optimal* and *maximum* suggest that rational decision making leads to perfect or near-perfect decisions. Of course, for managers to make perfect decisions, they have to operate in perfect worlds with no real-world constraints. In an optimal world, the manager who asked you to develop a computer strategy for the sales team would be able to define clearly which salespeople needed budget laptops, slim laptops, workhorse laptops, or tablet laptops and simply ensure that all team members received exactly what they needed to do their jobs effectively. You would not be constrained by price or time as you developed solutions. Furthermore, without any constraints, the manager could identify and weigh an extensive list of decision criteria, generate a complete list of possible solutions, and then test and evaluate each computer against each decision criterion. Finally, the manager would have the necessary experience and knowledge with computers to easily make sense of all the sophisticated information. Of course, it never works like that in the real world. Managers face time and money constraints. They often don't have time to make extensive lists of decision criteria. And they often don't have the resources to test all possible solutions against all possible criteria.

The rational decision-making model describes the way decisions *should* be made. In other words, decision makers wanting to make optimal decisions *should not* have to face time and cost constraints. They *should* have unlimited resources and time to generate and test all alternative solutions against all decision criteria. And they *should* be willing to recommend any decision that produces optimal benefits for the company, even if that decision would harm their own jobs or departments. Of course, very few managers actually make rational decisions the way they *should*. The way in which managers actually make decisions is more accurately described as bounded (or limited) rationality. **Bounded rationality** means that managers try to take a rational approach to decision making but are restricted by real-world constraints, incomplete and imperfect information, and their own limited decision-making capabilities.

Doing the Right Thing

PLUS—A Process for Ethical Decision Making

People are often unsure how to include ethics in their decision-making processes. To help them, the Ethics Resource Center recommends using the following PLUS guidelines throughout the various steps of the rational decision-making model:

- P is for policies. Is your decision consistent with your organization's policies, procedures, and guidelines?
- L is for legal. Is your decision acceptable under applicable laws and regulations?
- U is for universal. Is your decision consistent with your organization's values and principles?
- S is for self. Does your decision satisfy your personal sense of right, good, and fair?

The PLUS guidelines can't guarantee ethical decisions, but they can help employees be more attentive to ethical issues as they define problems, evaluate alternatives, and choose solutions.[52]

In theory, fully rational decision makers **maximize** decisions by choosing the optimal solution. In practice, however, limited resources along with attention, memory, and expertise problems make it nearly impossible for managers to maximize decisions. Consequently, most managers don't maximize—they satisfice. Whereas maximizing is choosing the best alternative, **satisficing** is choosing a "good-enough" alternative. With 24 decision criteria, 50 computers to choose from, two computer labs with hundreds of thousands of dollars of equipment, and unlimited time and money, the manager could test all alternatives against all decision criteria and choose the perfect PC. In reality, however, the manager's limited time, money, and expertise mean that only a few alternatives will be assessed against a few decision criteria. In practice, the manager will visit two or three computer or electronic stores, read a couple of recent computer reviews, and get bids from Dell, Lenovo, and Hewlett-Packard as well as some online superstores like CDW or PC Connection. The decision will be complete when the manager finds a good-enough laptop that meets a few decision criteria.

bounded rationality
a decision-making process restricted in the real world by limited resources, incomplete and imperfect information, and managers' limited decision-making capabilities

maximize
choosing the best alternative

satisficing
choosing a "good enough" alternative

REVIEW 4

Steps and Limits to Rational Decision Making

Rational decision making is a six-step process in which managers define problems, evaluate alternatives, and compute optimal solutions. The first step is identifying and defining the problem. Problems exist where there is a gap between desired and existing states. Managers won't begin the decision-making process unless they are aware of the gap, motivated to reduce it, and possess the necessary resources to fix it. The second step is defining the decision criteria that are used when judging alternatives. In Step 3, an absolute or relative comparison process is used to rate the importance of the decision criteria. Step 4 involves generating as many alternative courses of action (i.e., solutions) as possible. Potential solutions are assessed in Step 5 by systematically gathering information and evaluating each alternative against each criterion. In Step 6, criterion ratings and weights are used to compute the optimal value for each alternative course of action. Rational managers then choose the alternative with the highest optimal value.

The rational decision-making model describes how decisions should be made in an ideal world without limits. However, bounded rationality recognizes that in the real world, managers' limited resources, incomplete and imperfect information, and limited decision-making capabilities restrict their decision-making processes. These limitations often prevent managers from being rational decision makers.

5 Using Groups to Improve Decision Making

According to a study reported in *Fortune* magazine, 91 percent of U.S. companies use teams and groups to solve specific problems (i.e., make decisions).[53] Why so many? Because when done properly, group decision making can lead to much better decisions than those typically made by individuals. In fact, numerous studies show that groups consistently outperform individuals on complex tasks.

Let's explore the 5.1 **advantages and pitfalls of group decision making and see how the following group decision-making methods**, 5.2 **structured conflict**, 5.3 **the nominal group technique**, 5.4 **the Delphi technique**, 5.5 **the stepladder technique**, and 5.6 **electronic brainstorming—can be used to improve decision making**.

5.1 Advantages and Pitfalls of Group Decision Making

Groups can do a much better job than individuals in two important steps of the decision-making process: defining the problem and generating alternative solutions. There are four reasons for this. First, groups are able to view problems from multiple perspectives because group members usually possess different knowledge, skills, abilities, and experiences. Being able to view problems from different perspectives, in turn, can help groups perform better on complex tasks and make better decisions than individuals.[54]

Second, groups can find and access much more information than individuals alone. At 1-800-GOT-JUNK?, a national chain of over 200 locations that provides efficient, timely junk removal, applicants are not interviewed by one person. Instead, each applicant is interviewed by eight people with eight different areas of expertise. Together they assess the candidate immediately following the interview. CEO Brian Scudamore believes there is wisdom in crowds, and relying on groups to conduct interviews has helped his company maintain a remarkably low employee turnover rate of only 1.4 percent.[55]

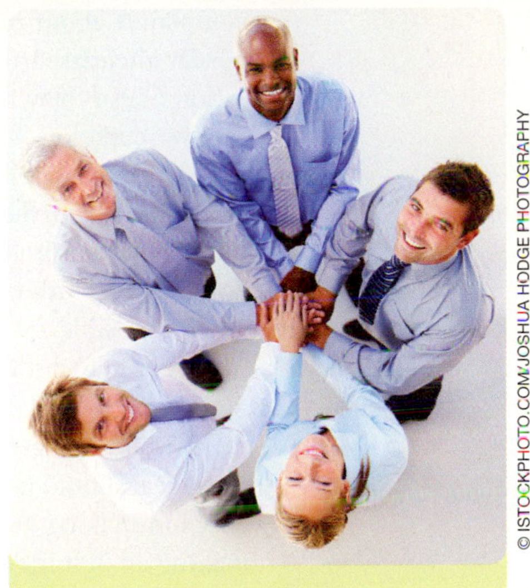

Third, the increased knowledge and information available to groups make it easier for them to generate more alternative solutions. Studies show that generating lots of alternative solutions is critical to improving the quality of decisions. Finally, if groups are involved in the decision-making process, group members will be more committed to making chosen solutions work.

Although groups can do a better job of defining problems and generating alternative solutions, group decision making is subject to some pitfalls that can quickly erase these gains. One possible pitfall is groupthink. **Groupthink** occurs in highly cohesive groups when group members feel intense pressure to agree with each other so that the group can approve a proposed solution.[56] Because groupthink leads to consideration of a limited number of solutions and restricts discussion of any considered solutions, it usually results in poor decisions. Groupthink is most likely to occur under the following conditions:

- The group is insulated from others with different perspectives.
- The group leader begins by expressing a strong preference for a particular decision.
- The group has no established procedure for systematically defining problems and exploring alternatives.
- Group members have similar backgrounds and experiences.[57]

Groupthink may be one of the reasons that Merck's prescription drug Vioxx stayed on the market for over 5 years despite fatal side effects. Merck, one of the largest drug makers in the world, viewed Vioxx as a miracle pain reliever, and over 100 million prescriptions for the drug were written in the 5 years it was available. The *New England Journal of Medicine*, however, had reported that Vioxx users suffered from significant heart problems almost from the beginning. Court documents revealed that Merck's internal studies showed an association between Vioxx usage and an elevated incidence of heart attacks. Litigants allege that because the drug generated a substantial profit, managers chose to listen to positive feedback about how well the drug worked as a painkiller rather than act on the information about the drug's risky side effects. After several years in court, Merck agreed to a $4.85 billion settlement with 45,000 eligible claimants.[58]

groupthink
a barrier to good decision making caused by pressure within the group for members to agree with each other

A second potential problem with group decision making is that it takes considerable time. Reconciling schedules so that group members can meet takes time. Furthermore, it's a rare group that consistently holds productive task-oriented meetings to work effectively through the decision process. Some of the most common complaints about meetings (and thus decision making) are that the meeting's purpose is unclear, participants are unprepared, critical people are absent or late, conversation doesn't stay focused on the problem, and no one follows up on the decisions that were made.

A third possible pitfall to group decision making is that sometimes one or two people, perhaps the boss or a strong-willed, vocal group member, can dominate discussion and limit the group's consideration of different problem definitions and alternative solutions. And, unlike individual decisions where people feel personally responsible for making a good choice, another potential problem is that group members may not feel accountable for the decisions made and actions taken by the group.

Although these pitfalls can lead to poor decision making, this doesn't mean that managers should avoid using groups to make decisions. When done properly, group decision making can lead to much better decisions. The pitfalls of group decision making are not inevitable. Managers can overcome most of them by using the various techniques described next.

5.2 Structured Conflict

Most people view conflict negatively. Yet the right kind of conflict can lead to much better group decision making. **c-type conflict**, or "cognitive conflict," focuses on problem – and issue-related differences of opinion.[59] In c-type conflict, group members disagree because their different experiences and expertise lead them to view the problem and its potential solutions differently. C-type conflict is also characterized by a willingness to examine, compare, and reconcile those differences to produce the best possible solution.

By contrast, **a-type conflict**, meaning "affective conflict," refers to the emotional reactions that can occur when disagreements become personal rather than professional. A-type conflict often results in hostility, anger, resentment, distrust, cynicism, and apathy. Unlike c-type conflict, a-type conflict undermines team effectiveness by preventing teams from engaging in the activities characteristic of c-type conflict that are critical to team effectiveness. Examples of a-type conflict statements are "your idea," "our idea," "my department," "you don't know what you are talking about," or "you don't understand our situation." Rather than focusing on issues and ideas, these statements focus on individuals.[60]

c-type conflict (Cognitive Conflict)
disagreement that focuses on problem- and issue-related differences of opinion

a-type conflict (Affective Conflict)
disagreement that focuses on individuals or personal issues

devil's advocacy
a decision-making method in which an individual or a subgroup is assigned the role of a critic

dialectical inquiry
a decision making method in which decision makers state the assumptions of a proposed solution (a thesis) and generate a solution that is the opposite (antithesis) of that solution

Two methods of introducing structured c-type conflict into the group decision-making process are devil's advocacy and dialectical inquiry. The **devil's advocacy** approach can be used to create c-type conflict by assigning an individual or a subgroup to the role of critic. The following five steps establish a devil's advocacy program:

1. Generate a potential solution.
2. Assign a devil's advocate to criticize and question the solution.
3. Present the critique of the potential solution to key decision makers.
4. Gather additional relevant information.
5. Decide whether to use, change, or not use the originally proposed solution.[61]

Dialectical inquiry creates c-type conflict by forcing decision makers to state the assumptions of a proposed solution (a thesis) and then generate a solution that is the opposite (antithesis) of the proposed solution. The following are the five steps of the dialectical inquiry process:

1. Generate a potential solution.
2. Identify the assumptions underlying the potential solution.
3. Generate a conflicting counterproposal based on the opposite assumptions.
4. Have advocates of each position present their arguments and engage in a debate in front of key decision makers.
5. Decide whether to use, change, or not use the originally proposed solution.[62]

BMW uses dialectical inquiry in its design process, typically creating six internal design teams to compete against each other to design a new car. After a front-runner or leading design emerges from one of the teams, another team is assigned to design a car that is diametrically opposed to the leading design (Step 3 of the dialectical inquiry method).[63]

When properly used, both the devil's advocacy and dialectical inquiry approaches introduce c-type conflict into the decision-making process. Contrary to the common belief that conflict is bad, studies show that these methods lead not only to less a-type conflict but also improved decision quality and greater acceptance of decisions once they have been made.[64] See the "What Really Works" feature for more information on both techniques.

5.3 Nominal Group Technique

Nominal means "in name only." Accordingly, the **nominal group technique** received its name because it begins with a quiet time in which group members independently write down as many problem definitions and alternative solutions as possible. In other words, the nominal group technique begins by having group members act as individuals. After the quiet time, the group leader asks each group member to share one idea at a time with the group. As they are read aloud, ideas are posted on flipcharts or wallboards for all to see. This step continues until all ideas have been shared. In the next step, the group discusses the advantages and disadvantages of the ideas. The nominal group technique closes with a second quiet time in which group members independently rank the ideas presented. Group members then read their rankings aloud, and the idea with the highest average rank is selected.[65]

The nominal group technique improves group decision making by decreasing a-type conflict. But it also restricts c-type conflict. Consequently, the nominal group technique typically produces poorer decisions than do the devil's advocacy and dialectical inquiry approaches. Nonetheless, more than 80 studies have found that nominal groups produce better ideas than those produced by traditional groups.[66]

nominal group technique
a decision-making method that begins and ends by having group members quietly write down and evaluate ideas to be shared with the group

5.4 Delphi Technique

In the **delphi technique**, the members of a panel of experts respond to questions from each other until reaching agreement on an issue. The first step is to assemble a panel of experts. Unlike other approaches to group decision making, however, it isn't necessary to bring the panel members together in one place. Because the Delphi technique does not require the experts to leave their offices or disrupt their schedules, they are more likely to participate. For example, a colleague and I were asked by a local government agency to use a Delphi technique to assess the

delphi technique
a decision making method in which members of a panel of experts respond to questions and to each other until reaching agreement on an issue

what *really* works

Devil's Advocacy, Dialectical Inquiry, and Considering Negative Consequences

Ninety percent of the decisions managers face are well-structured problems that recur frequently under conditions of certainty. For example, for most retailers, a customer's request for a refund on a returned item without a receipt is a well-structured problem. It happens every day (recurs frequently), and it's easy to determine if a customer has a receipt (condition of certainty).

Well-structured problems are solved with programmed decisions, in which a policy, procedure, or rule clearly specifies how to solve the problem. Thus, there's no mystery about what to do when someone shows up without a receipt: Allow the item to be exchanged for one of similar value, but don't give a refund.

In some sense, programmed decisions really aren't decisions because anyone with experience knows what to do. No thought is required. What keeps managers up at night is the other 10 percent of problems. Ill-structured problems that are novel (no one's seen them before) and exist under conditions of uncertainty are solved with nonprogrammed decisions. Nonprogrammed decisions do not involve standard methods of resolution. Every time managers make a nonprogrammed decision, they have to figure out a new way of handling a new problem. That's what makes the decisions so tough.

Both the devil's advocacy and dialectical inquiry approaches to decision making, along with a related approach, considering negative consequences, can be used to improve nonprogrammed decision making. All three work because they force decision makers to identify and criticize the assumptions underlying the nonprogrammed decisions that they hope will solve ill-structured problems.

Devil's Advocacy

There is a 58 percent chance that decision makers who use the devil's advocacy approach to criticize and question their solutions will produce decisions that are better than decisions based on the advice of experts.

Dialectical Inquiry

There is a 55 percent chance that decision makers who use the dialectical inquiry approach to criticize and question their solutions will produce decisions that are better than decisions based on the advice of experts.

Note that each technique has been compared with decisions obtained by following experts' advice. So, although these probabilities of success, 55 percent and 58 percent, seem small, they very likely understate the effects of both techniques. In other words, the probabilities of better decisions would have been much larger if both techniques had been compared with unstructured decision-making processes.

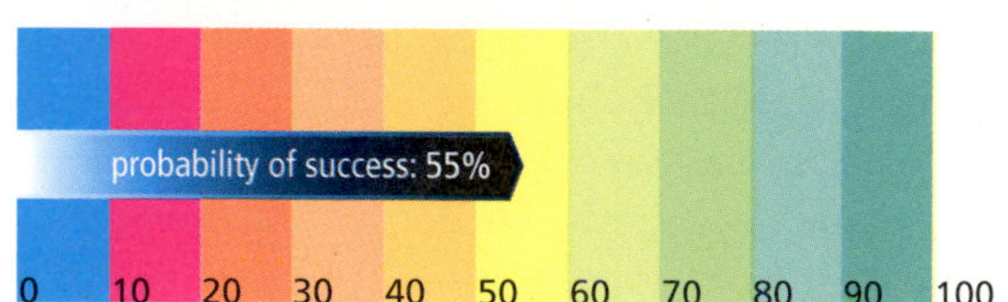

Group Decision Making and Considering Negative Consequences
Considering negative consequences, such as with a devil's advocate or via critical inquiry, means pointing out the potential disadvantages of proposed solutions. There is an 86 percent chance that groups that consider negative consequences will produce better decisions than those that don't.[67]

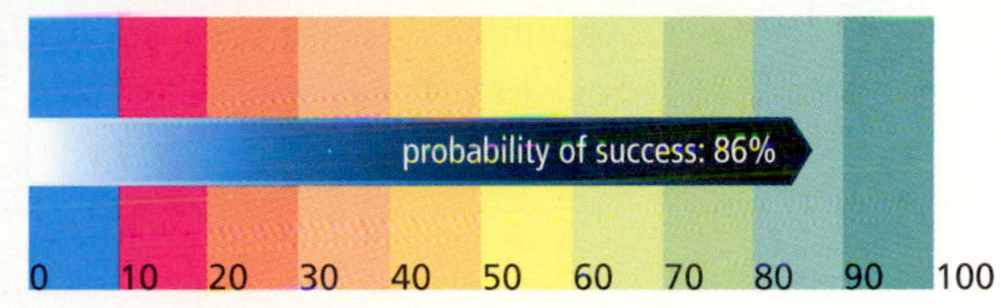

"10 most important steps for small businesses." The first step is to assemble the group. We assembled a panel of local top-level managers and CEOs.

The second step is to create a questionnaire consisting of a series of open-ended questions for the group. We asked our panel of experts questions like: "What is the most common mistake made by small-business persons?" "Right now, what do you think is the biggest threat to the survival of most small businesses?" "If you had one piece of advice to give to the owner of a small business, what would it be?"

In Step 3, the group members' written responses are analyzed, summarized, and fed back to the group for reactions until the members reach agreement. In our Delphi study, it took about a month to get the panel members' written responses to the first three questions. Then we summarized their responses in a brief report (no more than two pages). We sent the summary to the panel members and asked them to explain why they agreed or disagreed with these conclusions from the first round of questions. Asking group members why they agree or disagree is important because it helps uncover their unstated assumptions and beliefs. Again, this process of summarizing panel feedback and obtaining reactions to that feedback continues until the panel members reach agreement. For our study, it took just one more round for the panel members to reach a consensus. In all, it took approximately 3 1/2 months to complete our Delphi study.

5.5 Stepladder Technique

The stepladder technique improves group decision making by ensuring that each member's contributions are independent and are considered and discussed by the group. As shown in Exhibit 4.10, the **stepladder technique** begins with discussion between two group members who share their thoughts, ideas, and recommendations before jointly making a tentative decision. Other group members are added to the discussion one at a time at each step, like a stepladder. The existing group members take the time to listen to and understand each new member's thoughts, ideas, and recommendations. Then they share the ideas and suggestions they had already considered. The group discusses the new and old ideas together and makes a tentative decision. This process (new member's ideas are heard, group shares previous ideas and suggestions, discussion is held, tentative group decision is made) continues until each group member's ideas have been discussed.

stepladder technique a decision making method In which group members are added to a group discussion one at a time (like a stepladder). The existing group members listen to each new member's thoughts, ideas, and recommendations; then the group shares the ideas and suggestions that it had already considered, discusses the new and old ideas, and makes a decision

EXHIBIT 4.10

Stepladder Technique for Group Decision Making

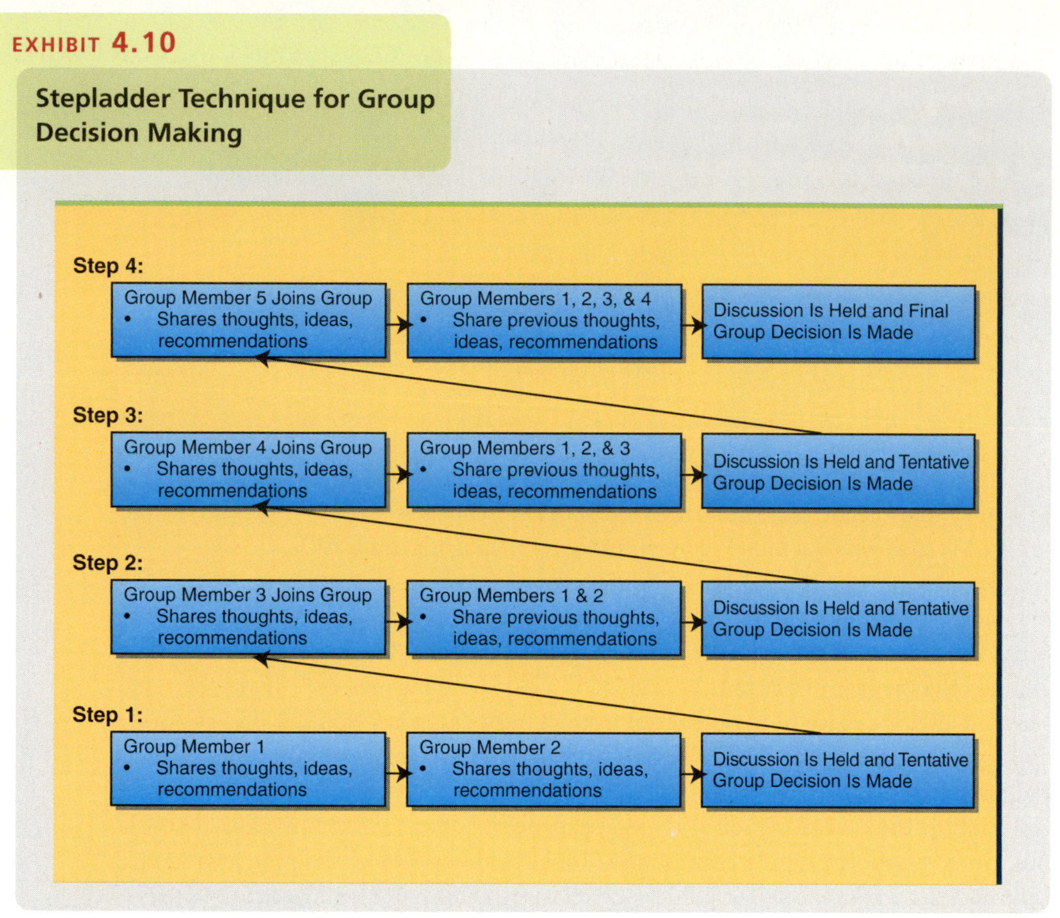

For the stepladder technique to work, group members must have enough time to consider the problem or decision on their own, to present their ideas to the group, and to thoroughly discuss all ideas and alternatives with the group at each step. Rushing through a step destroys the advantages of this technique. Also, groups must make sure that subsequent group members are completely unaware of previous discussions and suggestions. This will ensure that each member who joins the group brings truly independent thoughts and suggestions, thus greatly increasing the chances of making better decisions. All members must be present before a final decision is made.

One study found that groups using the stepladder technique produced significantly better decisions than did traditional groups in which all group members are present for the entire discussion. Moreover, the stepladder groups performed better than the best individual member of their group 56 percent of the time, whereas traditional groups outperformed the best individual member of their group only 13 percent of the time.[68] Besides better performance, groups using the stepladder technique also generated more ideas and were more satisfied with the decision-making process. This technique also works particularly well with audio conferencing, in which geographically dispersed group members make decisions via a telephone conference call.[69]

5.6 Electronic Brainstorming

Brainstorming, in which group members build on others' ideas, is a technique for generating a large number of alternative solutions. Brainstorming has four rules:

1. The more ideas, the better.
2. All ideas are acceptable, no matter how wild or crazy they might seem.
3. Other group members' ideas should be used to come up with even more ideas.
4. Criticism or evaluation of ideas is not allowed.

Although brainstorming is great fun and can help managers generate a large number of alternative solutions, it does have a number of disadvantages. Fortunately, **electronic brainstorming**, in which group members use computers to communicate and generate alternative solutions, overcomes the disadvantages associated with face-to-face brainstorming.[70]

brainstorming
a decision-making method in which group members build on each others' ideas to generate as many alternative solutions as possible

electronic brainstorming
a decision-making method in which group members use computers to build on each others' ideas and generate as many alternative solutions as possible

production blocking
a disadvantage of face-to-face brainstorming in which a group member must wait to share an idea because another member is presenting an idea

evaluation apprehension
fear of what others will think of your ideas

The first disadvantage that electronic brainstorming overcomes is **production blocking**, which occurs when you have an idea but have to wait to share it because someone else is already presenting an idea to the group. During this short delay, you may forget your idea or decide that it really wasn't worth sharing. Production blocking doesn't happen with electronic brainstorming. All group members are seated at computers, so everyone can type in ideas whenever they occur. There's no waiting your turn to be heard by the group.

The second disadvantage that electronic brainstorming overcomes is **evaluation apprehension**, that is, being afraid of what others will think of your ideas. With electronic brainstorming, all ideas are anonymous. When you type in an idea and hit the Enter key to share it with the group, group members see only the idea. Furthermore, many brainstorming software programs also protect anonymity by displaying ideas in random order. So if you laugh maniacally when you type "Cut top management's pay by 50 percent!" and then hit the Enter key, it won't show up immediately on everyone's screen. This makes it doubly difficult to determine who is responsible for which comments.

In the typical layout for electronic brainstorming, all participants sit in front of computers around a U-shaped table. This configuration allows them to see their computer screens, the other participants, a large main screen, and a meeting leader or facilitator. Exhibit 4.11 shows what the typical electronic brainstorming group member will see on his or her computer screen. Step 1 in electronic brainstorming is to generate as many ideas as possible anonymously. Groups commonly generate 100 ideas in a half-hour period. Step 2 is to edit the generated ideas, categorize them, and eliminate redundancies. Step 3 is to rank the categorized ideas in terms of quality. Step 4, the last step, has three parts: generate a series of action steps, decide the best order

EXHIBIT 4.11

What You See on the Computer During Electronic Brainstorming

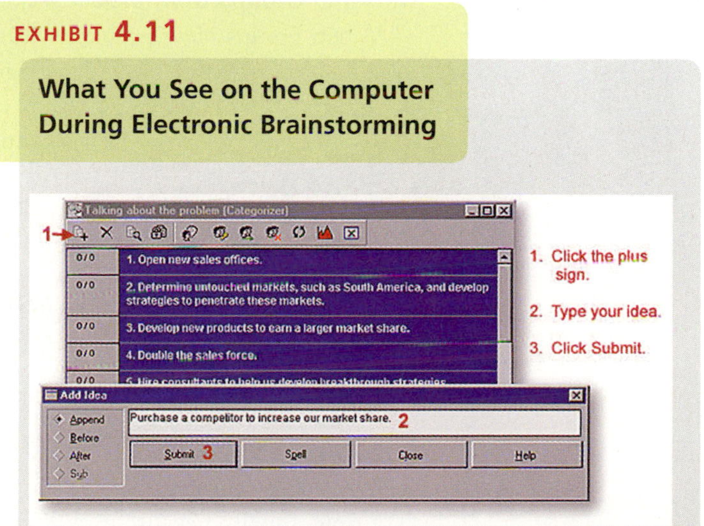

Source: Developing Consensus with GroupSystems. © 2002 GroupSystems.com

for accomplishing these steps, and identify who is responsible for each step. All four steps are accomplished with computers and electronic brainstorming software.[71]

Studies show that electronic brainstorming is much more productive than face-to-face brainstorming. Four-person electronic brainstorming groups produce 25 to 50 percent more ideas than four-person regular brainstorming groups, and 12-person electronic brainstorming groups produce 200 percent more ideas than regular groups of the same size! In fact, because production blocking (having to wait your turn) is not a problem for electronic brainstorming, the number and quality of ideas generally increase with group size.[72]

Even though it works much better than traditional brainstorming, electronic brainstorming has disadvantages, too. An obvious problem is the expense of computers, networks, software, and other equipment. As these costs continue to drop, however, electronic brainstorming will become cheaper.

Another problem is that the anonymity of ideas may bother people who are used to having their ideas accepted by virtue of their position (i.e., the boss). On the other hand, one CEO said, "Because the process is anonymous, the sky's the limit in terms of what you can say, and as a result it is more thought-provoking. As a CEO, you'll probably discover things you might not want to hear but need to be aware of."[73]

A third disadvantage is that outgoing individuals who are more comfortable expressing themselves verbally may find it difficult to express themselves in writing. Finally, the most obvious problem is that participants have to be able to type. Those who can't type, or who type slowly, may be easily frustrated and find themselves at a disadvantage to experienced typists. For example, one meeting facilitator was informed that an especially fast typist was pretending to be more than one person. Says the facilitator, "He'd type 'Oh, I agree' and then 'Ditto, ditto' or 'What a great idea,' all in quick succession, using different variations of uppercase and lowercase letters and punctuation. He tried to make it seem like a lot of people were concurring, but it was just him." Eventually, the person sitting next to him got suspicious and began watching his screen.[74]

REVIEW 5

Using Groups to Improve Decision Making

When groups view problems from multiple perspectives, use more information, have a diversity of knowledge and experience, and become committed to solutions they help choose, they can produce better solutions than individual decision makers. However, group decisions can suffer from these disadvantages: groupthink, slowness, discussions dominated by just a few individuals, and unfelt responsibility for decisions. Group decisions work best when group members encourage c-type conflict. However, group decisions don't work as well when groups become mired in a-type conflict. The devil's advocacy and dialectical inquiry approaches improve group decisions because they bring structured c-type conflict into the decision-making process. By contrast, the nominal group technique and the Delphi technique both improve decision making by reducing a-type conflict through limited interactions between group members. The stepladder technique improves group decision making by adding each group member's independent contributions to the discussion one at a time. Finally, because it overcomes the problems of production blocking and evaluation apprehension, electronic brainstorming is a more effective method of generating alternatives than face-to-face brainstorming.

Management Team Decision

To Pay or Not to Pay

Toyota used to sit on top of the world. It basked in the reputation of building high-quality cars efficiently. It enjoyed unprecedented growth, even surpassing General Motors as the largest car manufacturer in the world. But all of that came tumbling down with reports that cars were accelerating out of control, careening down highways, and putting everyone's lives in danger. There was even a recording of a 911 call from an off-duty policeman who lost control of his car and died in the ensuing crash. Toyota responded with a recall of historic proportions—nearly 8 million cars in the United States and 1.8 million in Europe. It even suspended sales of brand new models, including the best-selling Camry and Corolla, until the vehicles could be repaired. But still, there was confusion about what was causing the problems—was it the floor mats, the braking system, the software controlling the engine, or something else? Conspiracy theorists argued that Toyota had no clue what was causing the sudden acceleration, and that their recall was basically worthless.

By early 2009, your company was in a situation it had not faced for decades—it's sales had dropped by 16 percent. Even General Motors, the bankrupt General Motors, which looked like it could do nothing right for many years, grew 8 percent during the same time. According to some journalists, the recall cost Toyota more than $2 billion. But by March 2010, things seemed to be on the rebound. Sales picked up dramatically, 35 percent from the previous year, and 88 percent from the previous month. Customers were once again buying Toyotas, and putting their confidence in its ability to produce reliable cars.

But just as things seemed to be rosy again, Transportation Secretary Ray LaHood announced plans to levy a fine of $16.4 million against your company. The money itself isn't necessarily a problem. Even with sales losses, Toyota still made $1.8 billion in the fourth quarter of 2009. The fine would be less than 1 percent of what you earned in just 3 months. So why not just "take the medicine" as it were, pay the fine, and move on from the whole mess? Because the fine comes attached with a statement that Toyota "knowingly hid" safety problems in order to avoid a costly recall. According to LaHood, "We now have proof that Toyota failed to live up to its legal obligations. Worse yet, they knowingly hid a dangerous defect for months from U.S. officials and did not take action to protect millions of drivers and their families."

So what will you choose to do? You could just pay the fine and admit fault, but if you do, the company's reputation for quality will take a perhaps fatal blow. You wouldn't just be admitting that you made a mistake, but that you deliberately lied about it in order to keep making money. What's more, an admission of covering up would give great support to the hundreds of lawsuits that claim Toyota committed consumer fraud. How much money would those settlements cost? You could, of course, just contest the fine and the admission. But, your company's reputation is already fragile, and fighting the government (and potentially losing) may make things even worse.

Form a group with three or four other students and discuss what decision you would make as a Toyota management team by answering the questions below.

Questions

1. What is your recommendation for how Toyota should approach this situation?
2. What are the decision criteria that should be used in this situation, and how should they be weighted?
3. Under what conditions do you think it is acceptable for Toyota to settle for a "good enough" decision?

Sources: Ashby Jones. "The Toyota Fine: The $16M might not be Toyota's Biggest Problem." *Wall Street Journal.* April 7, 2010. Accessed at http://blogs.wsj.com/law/2010/04/07/the-toyota-fine-the-16m-might-not-be-toyotas-biggest-problem/

Micheline Maynard and Hiroko Tabuchi. "Toyota sees sales rebounding." *New York Times.* March 30, 2010. Accessed at http://www.nytimes.com/2010/03/31/business/global/31toyota.html

"Sizing up the damage." *Marketwatch.* January 29, 2010. Accessed at http://www.marketwatch.com/story/toyota-faces-grim-january-sales-2010-01-29

"Toyota car recall may cost $2bn." *BBC.* Accessed at http://news.bbc.co.uk/2/hi/business/8493414.stm

Practice being a Manager

Effective planning and decision making are crucial to the success of organizations. Your success as a manager will be determined in large part by your planning and decision-making capabilities. This exercise highlights some well-tested tools for strengthening your planning and decision-making skills.

Individual Preparation

STEP 1 Identify your "best company." Suppose that you are going to develop a plan that will result in your being hired to work for the single BEST COMPANY possible. "Best company" has not been defined for you, so you must determine what this might mean. Identify your "best company," and make your plan. You need to consider such aspects as building the right academic and work profile, marketing yourself to the company, and interviewing effectively. Carefully record both your plan and the steps that you took to develop it. In class you will be asked to share this information with a small discussion group.

Small Group Discussion

STEP 2 Discuss your plan. Taking turns, individually share your plan with the members of your discussion group. Members should listen carefully, ask questions, and make notes regarding the similarities and differences of individual plans.

STEP 3 Create a brochure. Now suppose that your group has been asked to develop a brochure for distribution in college career centers. The brochure will be titled "Getting a Job with Your Dream Company."

Using what you have learned from sharing your individual plans, work as a group to develop a sketch/outline of this brochure.

Class Discussion

STEP 4 As a class, discuss the following questions:

- Did you follow the rational decision-making process in identifying your best company and creating your plan for landing a job with this company? Why or why not?
- What role might bounded rationality have played in your individual and/or team decision-making process?
- Does planning increase the likelihood of success in being hired by a great company? Why or why not?
- If you were an editor assigned the project of developing the brochure "Getting a Job with Your Dream Company," would you be more likely to give the assignment to (1) a qualified individual or (2) a qualified group? Considering your recent experiences in this exercise, what are the trade-offs of each approach (individual versus group decision making)?

Self Assessment

Self-Management

A key part of planning is setting goals and tracking progress toward their achievement. As a manager, you will be involved in some type of planning in an organization. But the planning process is also used in a personal context, where it is called self-management. Self-management involves setting goals for yourself, developing a method or strategy to achieve them, and then carrying it out. For some people, self-management comes naturally. Everyone seems to know someone who is highly organized, self-motivated, and disciplined. That someone may even be you. If that someone is not you, however, then you will need to develop your self-management skills as a means to becoming a better manager.

A part of planning, and therefore management, is setting goals and tracking progress toward goal achievement.[75] Answer each of the questions using the following scale:

1. Strongly disagree
2. Disagree
3. Not sure
4. Agree
5. Strongly agree

1. I regularly set goals for myself.
   1 2 3 4 5
2. I keep track of how well I've been doing.
   1 2 3 4 5
3. I generally keep the resolutions that I make.
   1 2 3 4 5
4. I often seek feedback about my performance.
   1 2 3 4 5
5. I am able to focus on positive aspects of my work.
   1 2 3 4 5
6. I'll sometimes deny myself something until I've set my goals.
   1 2 3 4 5
7. I use a to-do list to plan my activities.
   1 2 3 4 5
8. I have trouble working without supervision.
   1 2 3 4 5
9. When I set my mind on some goal, I persevere until it's accomplished.
   1 2 3 4 5
10. I'm a self-starter.
   1 2 3 4 5
11. I make lists of things I need to do.
   1 2 3 4 5
12. I'm good at time management.
   1 2 3 4 5
13. I'm usually confident that I can reach my goals.
   1 2 3 4 5
14. I am careful about how I manage my time.
   1 2 3 4 5
15. I always plan my day.
   1 2 3 4 5
16. I often find I spend my time on trivial things and put off doing what's really important.
   1 2 3 4 5
17. Unless someone pushes me a bit, I have trouble getting motivated.
   1 2 3 4 5

18. I reward myself when I meet my goals.
1 2 3 4 5

19. I tend to dwell on unpleasant aspects of the things I need to do.
1 2 3 4 5

20. I tend to deal with life as it comes rather than to try to plan things.
1 2 3 4 5

21. I generally try to find a place to work where I'll be free from interruptions.
1 2 3 4 5

22. I'm pretty disorganized.
1 2 3 4 5

23. The goals I set are quite specific.
1 2 3 4 5

24. Distractions often interfere with my performance.
1 2 3 4 5

25. I sometimes give myself a treat if I've done something well.
1 2 3 4 5

26. I am able to focus on positive aspects of my activities.
1 2 3 4 5

27. I use notes or other prompts to remind myself of schedules and deadlines.
1 2 3 4 5

28. I seem to waste a lot of time.
1 2 3 4 5

29. I use a day planner or other aids to keep track of schedules and deadlines.
1 2 3 4 5

30. I often think about how I can improve my performance.
1 2 3 4 5

31. I tend to lose track of the goals I've set for myself.
1 2 3 4 5

32. I tend to set difficult goals for myself.
1 2 3 4 5

33. I plan things for weeks in advance.
1 2 3 4 5

34. I try to make a visible commitment to my goals.
1 2 3 4 5

35. I set aside blocks of time for important activities.
1 2 3 4 5

SCORING

Determine your score by entering your response to each survey item below, as follows. In blanks that say *regular score*, simply enter your response for that item. If your response was a 4, place a 4 in the *regular score* blank. In blanks that say *reverse score*, subtract your response from 6 and enter the result. So if your response was a 4, place a 2 (6 − 4 = 2) in the *reverse score* blank. Add up your total score.

1. regular score ________
2. regular score ________

3. regular score ________
4. regular score ________
5. regular score ________
6. regular score ________
7. regular score ________
8. reverse score ________
9. regular score ________
10. regular score ________
11. regular score ________
12. regular score ________
13. regular score ________
14. regular score ________
15. regular score ________
16. reverse score ________
17. reverse score ________
18. regular score ________
19. reverse score ________
20. reverse score ________
21. regular score ________
22. reverse score ________
23. regular score ________
24. reverse score ________
25. regular score ________
26. regular score ________
27. regular score ________
28. reverse score ________
29. regular score ________
30. regular score ________
31. reverse score ________
32. regular score ________
33. regular score ________
34. regular score ________
35. regular score ________

TOTAL = ________

You can find the interpretation for your score at: login.cengagebrain.com.

Reel to Real

Biz Flix

© GREENLIGHT

Inside Man

The 2006 crime thriller *Inside Man* features Denzel Washington as a tough NYPD hostage negotiator. He finds himself in a high-stakes cat-and-mouse game with a clever bank robber (Clive Owen), who confuses and outwits the police at every turn. Bank robber Dalton Russell is holding 50 people hostage in the vault of the Manhattan Trust Bank building, and Detective Frazier is determined to get them out alive, but the movie's tagline—"It looked like the perfect bank robbery. But you can't judge a crime by its cover"—tells us that there is more going on than it seems. In this scene, Captain John Darius (Willem Dafoe) updates Detective Frazier on what is happening inside the bank.

What to Watch for and Ask Yourself

1. Does this scene show strategic or tactical planning?
2. What pieces of the planning type does it specifically show? Give examples from the scene.
3. Do you expect this plan to succeed? Why or why not?

Management Workplace

© CENGAGE

Flight 001

Brad John and John Sencion, cofounders of Flight 001, traveled often between the United States, Europe, and Japan during their careers in the fashion industry. Before each trip, they found themselves shopping all over town for last-minute essentials. Then, on a 1998 flight from New York to Paris, the weary travelers came up with a solution: a one-stop travel shop for globe-trotters like themselves. Now in business for over 10 years, Flight 001 sells guidebooks, cosmetics, laptop bags, luggage, electronics and gadgets, passport covers, and other personal consumer products. Sencion summed up their mission: "We're trying to bring a little fun and glamor back in to travel." In this video, they discuss the challenges of business planning when the economy doesn't always cooperate and their hopes to expand into every major city in the United States, Europe, and Asia.

What to Watch for and Ask Yourself

1. What plans need to be in place before they can meet their expansion goals?
2. In what ways might the introduction of the Flight 001 brand of products be considered a stretch goal?
3. How did the change in the economy affect Flight 001's plans for the year?

5

Chapter Five

Organizational Strategy

OUTLINE

Experience Management

Experience the four levels of learning by doing the simulation module on Planning & Strategic Processes.

© ISTOCKPHOTO.COM/ ANN MARIE KURTZ

Pod Nod

Mini lecture reviews all the learning points in the chapter.

© ISTOCKPHOTO.COM/ MAGNET CREATIVE

Reel to Real

Biz Flix is a scene from *Field of Dreams*. Management workplace is a segment on Numi Organic Tea.

© ISTOCKPHOTO.COM/ CRAFTVISION

Self Test

10 quiz questions, 8 exhibit worksheets, and PowerPoints for quick review.

© ISTOCKPHOTO.COM/ DIJITAL FILM

What Would You Do?

Cisco Headquarters, Palo Alto, California.[1]

Your board of directors wants to know: How should *CISCO* grow? Your response was, "Well, the way we've grown in the past is..." "No. That's not the question. Looking backward is easy. How should we grow in the future? Should we build or buy?" With the next board meeting in only 3 months, you don't have much time to come up with the answer. Cisco started in 1984 as cyber-plumbers, making the switches and routers that direct data traffic over corporate networks and then later, the Internet. Its products weren't sexy, but every company with an expanding network needed them. So Cisco became the fastest-growing and most valuable company in the world (on the basis of its stock price and total market capitalization), that is, until the technology crash of 2001, which resulted in a $2.5 billion charge for unsold inventory and a stock price that dropped by 83 percent. However, by laying off 10,000 employees, redesigning routers and switches to have fewer and more interchangeable parts, and reducing its 50 product lines to 40, Cisco cut expenses 17 percent and became profitable again.

Nearly a decade later, things are much different. Cisco's revenues are six times larger than the combined revenues of its top 11 competitors. Cisco has nearly 60,000 employees who work in 450 offices in 96 countries. And, the company pulls in $40 billion a year in revenue, three-quarters of which comes from routers and switches (i.e., "plumbing") with 65 percent gross profit margins. But as you and your board know from experience, there's no guarantee that this success will last, especially in high-tech, where competitors catch up with and replace the leading firms in their industries on a regular basis.

How should Cisco grow? Build or buy? Well, 75 percent of our revenues already come from routers and switches, and it's unlikely that we could become more dominant in this area. So if we were to build, in other words, to come up with new products in new areas, what might those be? Should we focus on products that businesses buy? After all, that's who we sell to now. Or, should we take our expertise in routers and switches and focus on consumer products? Finally, while Cisco is growing 15 percent per year, that's down significantly from the 40 percent growth that we've had since inception, save for 2001. So we need to identify high-growth markets and products that we could design and build.

If we grow by purchasing technology firms with already established products or services, should we stick to our knitting by buying firms with products and services closely related to our existing business? Or should we diversify by buying firms that are very different from our basic business, routers, and switches? For instance, Cisco has the opportunity to acquire a firm that specializes in technology security (spam, viruses, malware, and other Internet threats), an area in which it has no experience. What's more likely to work and be less risky, buying firms with similar products or services or buying firms with different products or services? Basically, should Cisco move beyond its core business?

Finally, if we do decide to buy firms with already established products or services, how can we make sure those acquisitions work? Study after study shows that most mergers and acquisitions have no better than a 50–50 shot of success. Those are lousy odds. If we buy existing firms, what could we do to increase the odds that our acquisitions would be successful?

If you were the CEO of Cisco, what would you do?

In Chapter 4, you learned that *strategic plans* are overall plans that clarify how a company intends to serve customers and position itself against competitors over the next 2 to 5 years. While Cisco dominates the market for network routers and switches, what made Cisco successful in the past won't necessarily make it successful in the future. That's why Cisco has to decide on a strategy, build or buy, for future growth.

This chapter begins with an in-depth look at how managers create and use strategies to obtain a sustainable competitive advantage like Cisco's. Then you will learn the three steps of the strategy-making process. Next, you will learn about corporate-level strategies that help managers answer the question, "What business or businesses should we be in?" You will then examine the industry-level competitive strategies that help managers determine how to compete successfully within a particular line of business. The chapter finishes with a review of the firm-level strategies of direct competition and entrepreneurship.

Basics of Organizational Strategy

With the release of its iPod in October 2001, Apple Computers quickly set the standard for all other music devices. Using existing and readily available technology, the iPod boasted low battery consumption and enough storage to hold thousands of songs, all with a stylish and compact design. Competitors like Sony, Samsung, and Dell soon released their own devices, trying to steal, or at least minimize, Apple's competitive advantage. Sony's new Walkman includes software that examines the user's musical taste and, at push of a button, suggests new artists that the user might like. SanDisk's Sansa e280 offers twice the storage space of an iPod at roughly the same price. Microsoft's Zune can store almost 100 hours of video, more than double the 40-hour capacity of a video iPod. Plus, the Zune allows users to share music wirelessly. Despite the efforts of its competitors, however, Apple still holds a commanding 75 percent of the market for digital music players. SanDisk, its nearest competitors, has less than 10 percent of the market.[2]

How can a company like Apple, which dominates a particular industry, maintain its competitive advantage as strong, well-financed competitors enter the market? What steps can Apple and other companies take to better manage their strategy-making process?

After reading the next two sections, you should be able to:

1 specify the components of sustainable competitive advantage, and explain why it is important.

2 describe the steps involved in the strategy-making process.

1 Sustainable Competitive Advantage

Resources are the assets, capabilities, processes, employee time, information, and knowledge that an organization controls. Firms use their resources to improve organizational effectiveness and efficiency. Resources are critical to organizational strategy because they can help companies create and sustain an advantage over competitors.[3]

Organizations can achieve a **competitive advantage** by using their resources to provide greater value for customers than competitors can. For example, the iPod's competitive advantage came from its simple, attractive design relative to its price. But Apple's most important advantage was iTunes, which made buying and downloading music simple and convenient for users. Apple negotiated agreements with nearly all of the major record labels to distribute their songs from a central online library, and iTunes quickly became the premier platform for music downloading. The easy-to-understand site came with free downloadable software customers could use to organize and manage their digital music libraries.[4]

The goal of most organizational strategies is to create and then sustain a competitive advantage. A competitive advantage becomes a **sustainable competitive advantage** when other companies cannot duplicate the value a firm is providing to customers. Sustainable competitive advantage is *not* the same as a long-lasting competitive advantage, though companies obviously want a competitive advantage to last a long time. Instead, a competitive advantage is *sustained* if competitors have tried unsuccessfully to duplicate the advantage and have, for the moment, stopped trying to duplicate it. It's the corporate equivalent of your competitors saying, "We give up. You win. We can't do what you do, and we're not even going to try to do it anymore." As Exhibit 5.1 shows, four conditions must be met if a firm's resources are to be used to achieve a sustainable competitive advantage. The resources must be valuable, rare, imperfectly imitable, *and* nonsubstitutable.

Valuable resources allow companies to improve their efficiency and effectiveness. Unfortunately, changes in customer demand and preferences, competitors' actions, and technology can make once-valuable resources much less valuable. For sustained competitive advantage, valuable resources must also be rare resources. Think about it: How can a company sustain a competitive advantage if all of its competitors have similar resources and capabilities? Consequently, **rare resources**, those that are

resources
the assets, capabilities, processes, employee time, information, and knowledge that an organization uses to improve its effectiveness and efficiency, create and sustain competitive advantage, and fulfill a need or solve a problem

competitive advantage
providing greater value for customers than competitors can

sustainable competitive advantage
a competitive advantage that other companies have tried unsuccessfully to duplicate and have, for the moment, stopped trying to duplicate

valuable resource
a resource that allows companies to improve efficiency and effectiveness

rare resource
a resource that is not controlled or possessed by many competing firms

EXHIBIT 5.1

Four Requirements for Sustainable Competitive Advantage

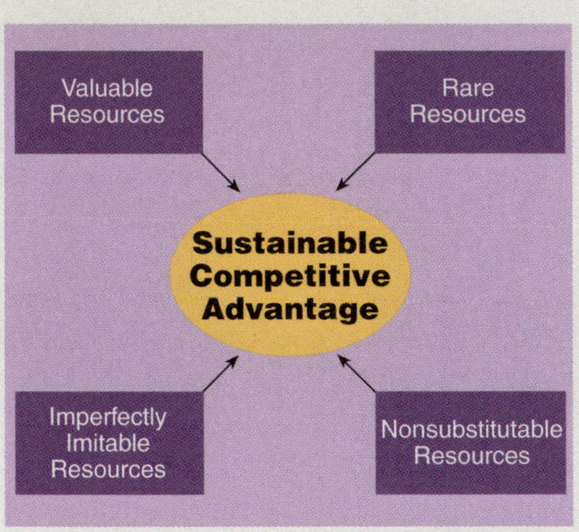

not controlled or possessed by competing firms, are necessary to sustain a competitive advantage. When Apple introduced the iPod, no other portable music players on the market used existing hard-drive technology in their design. The iPod gained an immediate advantage over competitors because it was able to satisfy the desire of consumers to carry large numbers of songs in a portable device, something other MP3 systems and older CD players could not do. One of Apple's truly rare resources is its ability to reconfigure existing technology into a package that is easy to use, elegantly designed, and therefore highly desired by customers. Another example of this capability is the iPod Touch, of which Apple has sold 16 million. The iPod Touch can do nearly everything an iPhone can—run apps, browse the web, and use touch-screen controls—save for making phone calls. But, with apps like Skype, iPod Touch owners will even be able to make phone calls as long as they have a Wi-Fi connection.[5]

As this example shows, valuable and rare resources can create temporary competitive advantage. For sustained competitive advantage, however, other firms must be unable to imitate or find substitutes for those valuable, rare resources. **Imperfectly imitable resources** are those resources that are impossible or extremely costly or difficult to duplicate. For example, despite numerous attempts by competitors to imitate it, iTunes has retained its competitive lock on the music download business. In addition to its customer-friendly interface and its extensive media library, Apple has developed a relatively closed system that makes it seamless to download music, podcasts, and videos from iTunes to iPods. By contrast, many more steps are required when using other download sites or other MP3 players. As a result, many iPod and iTunes users wouldn't even consider using another brand. Kelly Moore, a sales representative for a Texas software company, takes her pink iPod everywhere she goes and keeps it synchronized with her iBook laptop. She says, "Once I find something I like, I don't switch brands."[6] She's not alone. As of this writing, sales at the iTunes store total over 6 billion songs, 200 million TV shows, and 1 billion applications.[7] No other competitor comes close to those numbers.

Valuable, rare, imperfectly imitable resources can produce sustainable competitive advantage only if they are also **nonsubstitutable resources**, meaning that no other resources can replace them and produce similar value or competitive advantage. The industry has tried to produce equivalent substitutes for iTunes, but competitors have had to experiment with different business models in order to get customers to accept them. Napster founders Shawn Fanning and Wayne Rosso have created a subscription-based service called Mashboxx, which charges $15 a month for unlimited downloads. Zune Marketplace has established a similar system with over 3 million songs, downloadable videos, podcasts, and audiobooks.[8] In addition to straight subscription models, some companies experimented with price. At Amie Street, a newly posted track can be downloaded for

imperfectly imitable resource
a resource that is impossible or extremely costly or difficult for other firms to duplicate

nonsubstitutable resource
a resource that produces value or competitive advantage and has no equivalent substitutes or replacements

free, but as the number of downloads increases, so does the song's price, until it reaches the maximum of 98 cents.[9] In response to competitors' experimentation, Apple went to variable pricing: 69 cents, 99 cents, or $1.29 per song, and also removed digital rights management, which restricted the extent to which users could copy their music from one device to another.[10]

© FRANCISCO MARTINEZ/ALAMY

In summary, Apple has reaped the rewards of a first-mover advantage from its interdependent iPod and iTunes. The company's history of developing customer-friendly software, the innovative capabilities of the iPod, the simple pay-as-you-go sales model of iTunes, and the unmatched list of music and movies available for download provided customers with a service that has been valuable, rare, relatively nonsubstitutable, and, in the past, imperfectly imitable. Past success is, however, no guarantee of future success: Apple needs to continually change and develop its offerings or risk being unseated by a more nimble competitor whose products are more relevant and have higher perceived value to the consumer.

REVIEW 1

Sustainable Competitive Advantage

Firms can use their resources to create and sustain a competitive advantage, that is, to provide greater value for customers than competitors can. A competitive advantage becomes sustainable when other companies cannot duplicate the benefits it provides and have, for now, stopped trying. To provide a sustainable competitive advantage, the firm's resources must be valuable (capable of improving efficiency and effectiveness), rare (not possessed by many competing firms), imperfectly imitable (extremely costly or difficult to duplicate), and nonsubstitutable (competitors cannot substitute other resources to produce similar value).

2 Strategy-Making Process

In order to create a sustainable competitive advantage, a company must have a strategy.[11]

Exhibit 5.2 displays the three steps of the strategy-making process: 2.1 **assess the need for strategic change**, 2.2 **conduct a situational analysis**, and then 2.3 **choose strategic alternatives. Let's examine each of these steps in more detail**.

2.1 Assessing the Need for Strategic Change

The external business environment is much more turbulent than it used to be. With customers' needs constantly growing and changing, and with competitors working harder, faster, and smarter to meet those needs, the first step in creating a strategy is determining the need for strategic change. In other words, the company should determine whether it needs to change its strategy to sustain a competitive advantage.[12]

"There's a great deal of uncertainty in strategic business environments."

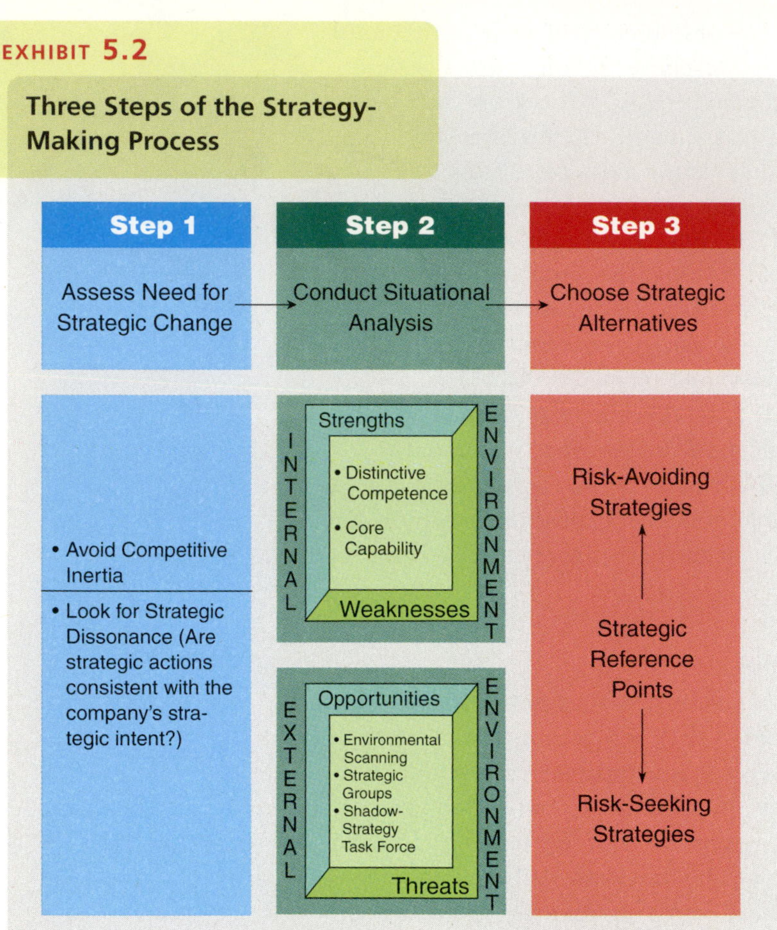

Determining the need for strategic change might seem easy to do, but it's really not. There's a great deal of uncertainty in strategic business environments. Furthermore, top-level managers are often slow to recognize the need for strategic change, especially at successful companies that have created and sustained competitive advantages. Because they are acutely aware of the strategies that made their companies successful, they continue to rely on those strategies, even as the competition changes. In other words, success often leads to **competitive inertia**—a reluctance to change strategies or competitive practices that have been successful in the past.

Sheraton Hotels, which are a unit of *STARWOOD HOTELS AND RESORTS WORLDWIDE INC.*, are a prime example of competitive inertia. Sheraton, once one of the largest and best recognized hotel chains in the world, is now viewed by many as having convenient locations, but old decor, variable quality, and unexceptional service. Those problems show up in prices that people are willing to pay. For example, the average Sheraton room goes for $100.72 compared to $112.62 at Marriott. Hoyt Harper, who is in charge of strategy, said "Sheraton for eight years has been the ugly stepchild…" Realizing that what worked in the past won't work anymore, Harper has developed an aggressive plan to close 33 poor-performing Sheraton hotels, and then spend $4 billion to update remaining hotels' lobbies, workout facilities, and rooms, all the way down to the coffee in the rooms and the sheets on the bed.[13]

Besides being aware of the dangers of competitive inertia, what can managers do to improve the speed and accuracy with which they determine the need for strategic change? One method is to actively look for signs of strategic dissonance. **Strategic dissonance** is a discrepancy between a company's intended strategy and the strategic actions managers take when actually implementing that strategy.[14] For example, when Edgar Bronfman, Jr., bought the struggling Warner Music Group, his intended strategy was to cut costs and stop excessive spending. He laid off 1,200 employees to save $250 million and cut remaining salaries by as much as 50 percent. Bronfman justified the cuts by stating that managers, lawyers, accountants, and salespeople shouldn't be earning double or triple their normal salaries just because they worked for a music company. A few weeks later, however, Bronfman quietly restored some executives' salaries after complaints.[15]

competitive inertia
a reluctance to change strategies or competitive practices that have been successful in the past

strategic dissonance
a discrepancy between a company's intended strategy and the strategic actions managers take when implementing that strategy

Note, however, that strategic dissonance is not the same thing as when a strategy does not produce the results that it's supposed to. It can also mean that the intended strategy is out of date and needs to be changed.

2.2 Situational Analysis

A situational analysis can also help managers determine the need for strategic change. A **situational analysis**, also called a **SWOT analysis** for *strengths*, *weaknesses*, *opportunities*, and *threats*, is an assessment of the strengths and weaknesses in an organization's internal environment and the opportunities and threats in its external environment.[16] Ideally, as shown in Step 2 of Exhibit 5.2, a SWOT analysis helps a company determine how to increase internal strengths and minimize internal weaknesses while maximizing external opportunities and minimizing external threats.

When Memorial Hospital of Fremont, Ohio, decided that the process it used to order all the necessary medical and administrative supplies was out of control, managers asked all the departments to work together to conduct a SWOT analysis. The process helped the hospital identify its strengths, such as the experience of the materials management group, and its weaknesses, which included allowing anyone in the organization to order anything he or she wanted from any vendor. Departments outlined opportunities to dramatically improve the quality and flow of supplies while controlling costs. The hospital began requiring all vendors to register when they entered the building, and processed all orders through the central purchasing department. Soon, the hospital staff developed the right mix of products and product inventories required for each area of the hospital and, at the same time, dramatically reduced the number of staff involved in purchasing and stocking supplies. Over the next 2 years, the hospital saved more than $1 million.[17]

As this example illustrates, a SWOT analysis can be used to evaluate entire companies or individual operations within an organization. All companies' competitive advantages can erode over time if internal strengths eventually become weaknesses. Consequently, an analysis of an organization's internal environment, that is, a company's strengths and weaknesses, often begins with an assessment of its distinctive competencies and core capabilities. A **distinctive competence** is something that a company can make, do, or perform better than its competitors. For example, *Consumer Reports* magazine consistently ranks Honda and Toyota cars either number one or two in quality and reliability.[18] Similarly, *PC Magazine* readers ranked Apple's desktop and laptop computers best in terms of service and reliability.[19]

Whereas distinctive competencies are tangible—for example, a product or service is faster, cheaper, or better—the core capabilities that produce distinctive competencies are not. **Core capabilities** are the less visible, internal decision-making routines, problem-solving processes, and organizational cultures that determine how efficiently inputs can be turned into outputs. Distinctive competencies cannot be sustained for long without superior core capabilities. Offering gourmet, environmentally conscious food products at a low cost is the distinctive competence at *TRADER JOE'S*. One can find ten kinds of hummus and every kind of dried fruit imaginable. Most of the products sold at Trader Joe's have no artificial colors, artificial flavors, or preservatives. The core capability the company uses to execute this strategy is its ability to buy in large quantities and bargain directly with producers. Trader Joe's also offers 80 percent of its products as house brands, compared to 16 percent industry-wide, and does

situational (SWOT) analysis
an assessment of the strengths and weaknesses in an organization's internal environment and the opportunities and threats in its external environment

distinctive competence
what a company can make, do, or perform better than its competitors

core capabilities
the internal decision-making routines, problem-solving processes, and organizational cultures that determine how efficiently inputs can be turned into outputs

Doing the Right Thing

Is Ethics an Overlooked Source of Competitive Advantage?

Volvo's reputation for selling safe cars has been a source of competitive advantage for years. You didn't buy a boxy Volvo for its looks; you bought it because your family would be well protected in an accident. If safety can be a source of competitive advantage, could ethics be one, too?

Though competitive advantage usually comes from physical capital (plant, equipment, finances), organizational capital (structure, planning, systems), and human capital (skills, judgment, adaptability of your work force), Johnson & Johnson is still widely admired, two decades afterward, for its response when several people died after someone put cyanide in Tylenol capsules. The company quickly pulled Tylenol from store shelves and introduced tamper-proof packaging. The move cost Johnson & Johnson half a billion dollars, but protected consumers from further harm. The company's market share was back to number 1 within a year of the reintroduction.

Should ethics be your first source of competitive advantage? Probably not. It makes more sense to start with low costs, good service, or unique product capabilities. But when you're looking for another way to create or sustain a competitive advantage, consider that a reputation as an ethical corporation may be an additional way to differentiate your company from the competition.[20]

not carry any mass-market brands like Crest or Pepsi. These capabilities allow Trader Joe's to offer similar products at lower prices than competitors like Whole Foods Market. One customer said, "I love Trader Joe's because they let me eat like a yuppie without taking all my money." Stores also feature fifteen or more new products each week, bringing the curious customer back to find out what's new.[21]

After examining internal strengths and weaknesses, the second part of a situational analysis is to look outside the company and assess opportunities and threats in the external environment. In Chapter 2, you learned that *environmental scanning* involves searching the environment for important events or issues that might affect the organization, such as pricing trends or new products and technology. In a situational analysis, however, managers use environmental scanning to identify specific opportunities and threats that can either improve or harm the company's ability to sustain its competitive advantage. Identification of strategic groups and formation of shadow-strategy task forces are two ways to do this.

Strategic groups are not groups that actually work together. They are companies—usually competitors—that managers closely follow. More specifically, a **strategic group** is a group of companies within an industry against which top managers compare, evaluate, and benchmark their company's strategic threats and opportunities.[23] (*Benchmarking* involves identifying outstanding practices, processes, and standards at other companies and adapting them to your own company.) Typically, managers include companies as part of their strategic group if they compete directly with those companies for customers or if those companies use strategies similar to theirs. The U.S. home improvement industry has annual sales in excess of $290 billion.[24]

strategic group
a group of companies within an industry against which top managers compare, evaluate, and benchmark strategic threats and opportunities

what *really* works

Strategy Making for Firms, Big and Small

Companies create strategies that produce sustainable competitive advantage by using the strategy-making process (assessing the need for strategic change, conducting a situational analysis, and choosing strategic alternatives). For years, it had been thought that strategy making was something that only large firms could do well. It was believed that small firms did not have the time, knowledge, or staff to do a good job of strategy making. However, two meta-analyses indicate that strategy making can improve the profits, sales growth, and return on investment of both big *and* small firms.

Strategy Making for Big Firms

There is a 72 percent chance that big companies that engage in the strategy-making process will be more profitable than big companies that don't. Not only does strategy making improve profits but it also helps companies grow. Specifically, there is a 75 percent chance that big companies that engage in the strategy-making process will have greater sales and earnings growth than big companies that don't. Thus, in practical terms, the strategy-making process can make a significant difference in a big company's profits and growth.

STATEGIC PLANNING & PROFITS FOR BIG COMPANIES

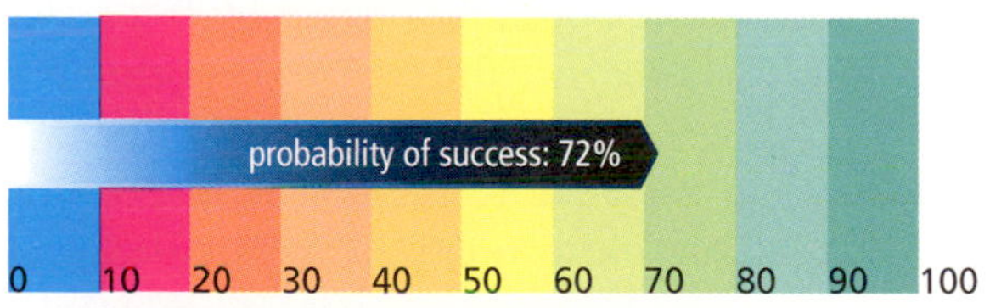

STATEGIC PLANNING & GROWTH FOR BIG COMPANIES

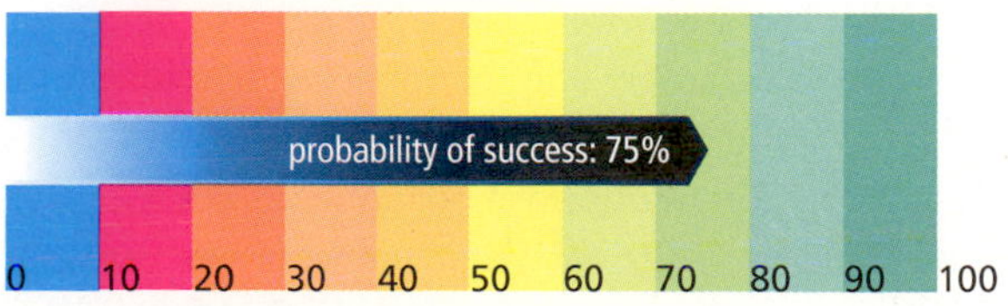

Strategy Making for Small Firms

Strategy making can also improve the performance of small firms. There is a 61 percent chance that small firms that engage in the strategy-making process will have more sales growth than small firms that don't. Likewise, there is a 62 percent chance that small firms that engage in the strategy-making process will have a larger return on investment than small companies that don't. Thus, in practical terms, the strategy-making process can make a significant difference in a small company's profits and growth, too.

STRATEGIC PLANNING & SALES GROWTH FOR SMALL COMPANIES

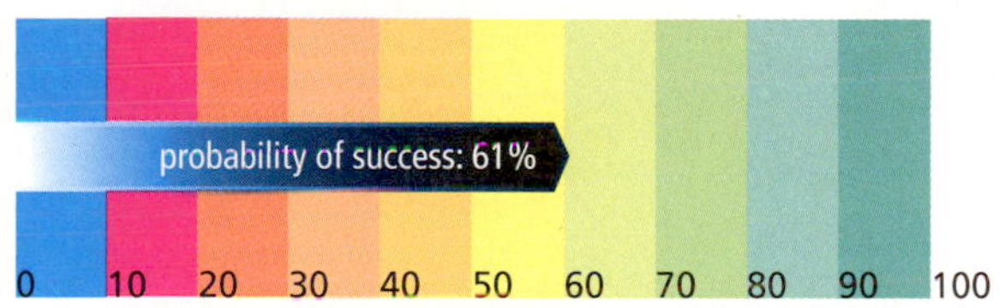

STRATEGIC PLANNING & RETURN ON INVESTMENT FOR SMALL COMPANIES

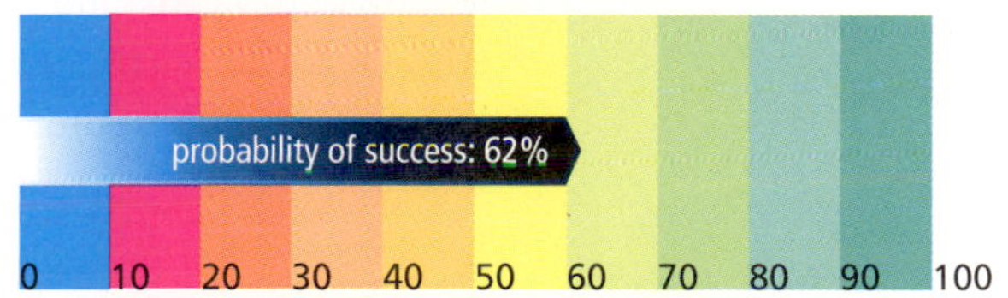

External Growth Through Acquisitions

One way to grow a company is through external growth, or buying other companies (see Section 3.1 on portfolio strategy). However, researchers have long debated whether buying other companies actually adds value to the acquiring company or not. A meta-analysis based on 103 studies and a sample of 25,205 companies indicates that, on average, acquiring other companies actually *hurts* the value of the acquiring firm. In other words, there is only a 45 percent chance that growing a company through external acquisitions will work![22]

STRATEGIC PLANNING & EXTERNAL GROWTH ACQUISITIONS

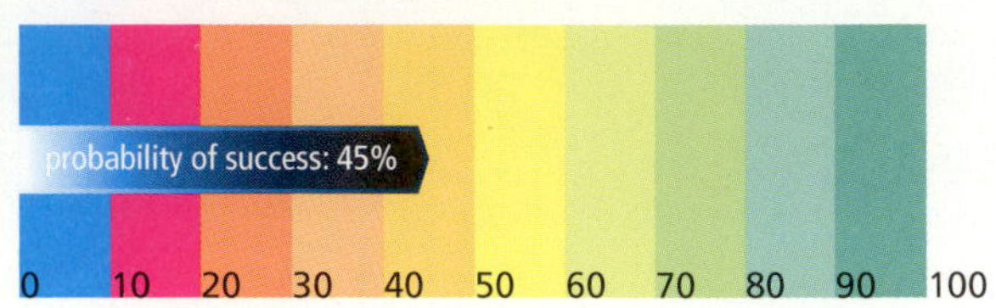

It's likely that the managers at Home Depot, the largest U.S. home improvement and hardware retailer, assess strategic threats and opportunities by comparing their company to a strategic group consisting of the other major home improvement supply companies.

In fact, when scanning the environment for strategic threats and opportunities, managers tend to categorize the different companies in their industries as core, secondary, and transient firms.[25] **Core firms** are the central companies in a strategic group. Among home improvement supply stores, Lowe's is closest in terms of the number of stores, store size, and revenues, and would be classified as the core firm in Home Depot's strategic group.[26] When most managers scan their environments for strategic threats and opportunities, they concentrate on the strategic actions of core firms, not unrelated firms.[27] For example, unlike Lowe's, Home Depot's management probably doesn't include Aubuchon Hardware in its core strategic group, because it has only 130 stores in New England and upstate New York.

Secondary firms are firms that use strategies related to but somewhat different from those of core firms. 84 Lumber has 320 stores in 35 states, but even though its stores are open to the public, the company focuses on supplying professional contractors, to which it sells 95 percent of its products. Home Depot would most likely classify 84 Lumber as a secondary firm in its strategic group analysis.[28] Managers need to be aware of the potential threats and opportunities posed by secondary firms, but they usually spend more time assessing the threats and opportunities associated with core firms.

In short, a situational analysis has two basic parts. The first is to examine internal strengths and weaknesses by focusing on distinctive competencies and core capabilities. The second is to examine external opportunities and threats by focusing on environmental scanning, strategic groups, and shadow-strategy task forces.

core firms
the central companies in a strategic group

secondary firms
the firms in a strategic group that follow strategies related to but somewhat different from those of the core firms

2.3 Choosing Strategic Alternatives

After determining the need for strategic change and conducting a situational analysis, the last step in the strategy-making process is to choose strategic alternatives that will help the company create or maintain a sustainable competitive advantage. According to strategic reference point theory, managers choose between two basic alternative strategies. They can choose a conservative, *risk-avoiding strategy* that aims to protect an existing competitive advantage. Or they can choose an aggressive, *risk-seeking strategy* that aims to extend or create a sustainable competitive advantage. Menards is a hardware store chain with 40,000 employees and 210 locations throughout the Midwest.[29] When hardware giant Home Depot entered the Midwest, Menards faced a choice: Avoid risk by continuing with the strategy it had in place before Home Depot's arrival or seek risk by trying to establish a competitive advantage against Home Depot, which is six times its size. Some of its competitors decided to fold. Kmart closed all of its Builders Square hardware stores when Home Depot came to Minneapolis. Handy Andy liquidated its 74 stores when Home Depot came to the Midwest. But Menards decided to fight, spending millions to open 35 new stores at the same time that Home Depot was opening 44 of its own.[30]

The choice to seek or avoid risk typically depends on whether top management views the company as falling above or below strategic reference points. **Strategic reference points** are the targets that managers use to measure whether their firm has developed the core competencies that it needs to achieve a sustainable competitive advantage. If a hotel chain decides to compete by providing superior quality and service, then top management will track the success of this strategy through customer surveys or published hotel ratings such as those provided by the prestigious Forbes Travel Guide. If a hotel chain decides to compete on price, it will regularly conduct market surveys to check the prices of other hotels. The competitors' prices are the hotel managers' strategic reference points against which to compare their own pricing strategy. If competitors can consistently underprice them, then the managers need to determine whether their staff and resources have the core competencies to compete on price.

As shown in Exhibit 5.3, when a company is performing above or better than its strategic reference points, top management will typically be satisfied with the company's strategy. Ironically, this satisfaction tends to make top management conservative and risk-averse. Since the company already has a sustainable competitive advantage, the worst thing that could happen would be to lose it, so new issues or changes in the company's external environments are viewed as threats. By contrast, when a company is performing below or worse than its strategic reference points, top management will typically be dissatisfied with the company's strategy. In this instance, managers are much more likely to choose a daring, risk-taking strategy. If the current strategy is producing substandard results, the company has nothing to lose by switching to risky new strategies in the hopes that it can create a sustainable competitive advantage. Managers of companies in this situation view new issues or changes in external environments as opportunities for potential gain.

Strategic reference point theory is not deterministic, however. Managers are not predestined to choose risk-averse or risk-seeking strategies for their companies. Indeed, one of the most important elements of the theory is that managers *can* influence the strategies chosen by their company by *actively changing and adjusting* the strategic reference points they use to judge strategic performance. If a company has become complacent after consistently surpassing its strategic reference points, then top management can change from a risk-averse to a risk-taking orientation by raising the standards of performance (i.e., the strategic reference points). This is just what happened at Menards.

strategic reference points
the strategic targets managers use to measure whether a firm has developed the core competencies it needs to achieve a sustainable competitive advantage

EXHIBIT 5.3

Strategic Reference Points

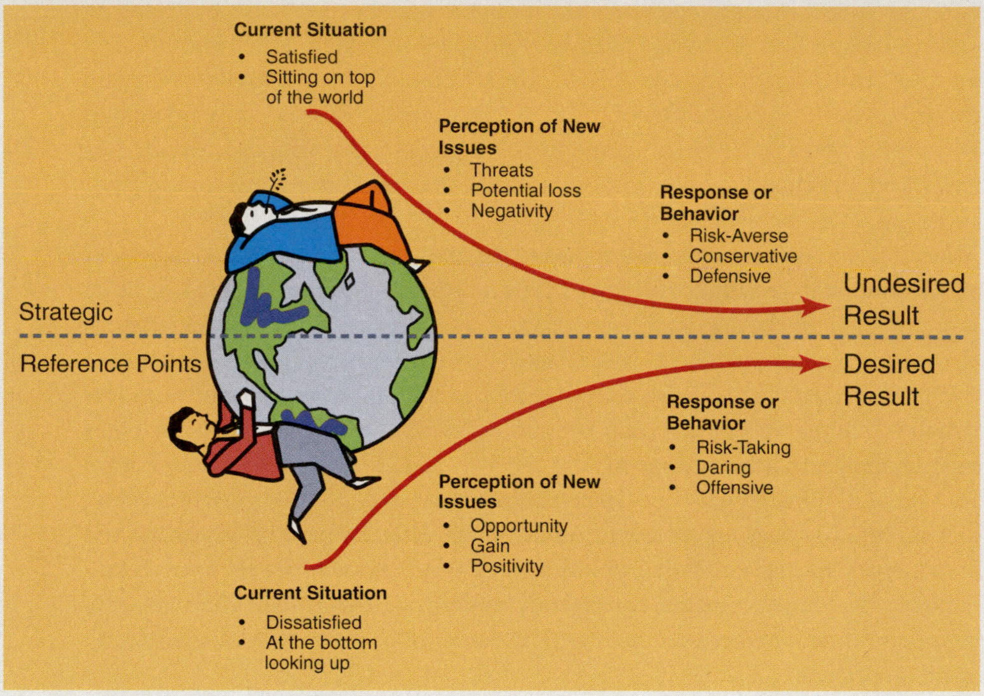

Source: A. Fiegenbaum, S. Hart, & D. Schendel, "Strategic Reference Point Theory," *Strategic Management Journal* 17 (1996): 219–235.

Instead of being satisfied with merely protecting its existing stores (a risk-averse strategy), founder John Menard changed the strategic reference points the company had been using to assess strategic performance. To encourage a daring, offensive-minded strategy that would allow the company to open nearly as many new stores as Home Depot, he determined that Menards would have to beat Home Depot on not one or two, but four strategic reference points: price, products, sales per square foot, and "friendly accessibility." The strategy appears to be succeeding. In terms of price, market research indicates that a 100-item shopping cart of goods is consistently cheaper at Menards. In terms of products, Menards sells 50,000 products per store, the same as Home Depot. In terms of sales per square foot, Menards ($407 per square foot) outsells Home Depot ($300 per square foot).[31] Finally, unlike Home Depot's warehouse-like stores, Menards' stores are built to resemble grocery stores. Shiny tiled floors, wide aisles, and easy-to-reach products all make Menards a "friendlier" place for shoppers. And now with Lowe's, the second-largest hardware store chain in the nation, also entering its markets, Menards has added a fifth strategic reference point: store size. At 225,000 square feet, most new Menards stores are more than double the size of Home Depot's stores and 100,000 square feet larger than Lowe's biggest stores.[32]

So even when (perhaps *especially* when) companies have achieved a sustainable competitive advantage, top managers must adjust or change strategic reference points to challenge themselves and their employees to develop new core competencies for the future. In the long run, effective organizations will frequently revise their strategic reference points to focus managers' attention on the new challenges and opportunities that occur in their ever-changing business environments.

REVIEW 2

Strategy-Making Process

The first step in the strategy-making process is determining whether a strategy needs to be changed to sustain a competitive advantage. Because uncertainty and competitive inertia make this difficult to determine, managers can improve the speed and accuracy of this step by looking for differences between top management's intended strategy and the strategy actually implemented by lower-level managers (i.e., looking for strategic dissonance). The second step is to conduct a situational analysis that examines internal strengths and weaknesses (distinctive competencies and core capabilities), as well as external threats and opportunities (environmental scanning, strategic groups, and shadow-strategy task forces). In the third step of the strategy-making process, strategic reference point theory suggests that when companies are performing better than their strategic reference points, top management will typically choose a risk-averse strategy. When performance is below strategic reference points, it is more likely to choose risk-seeking strategies. Importantly, however, managers can influence the choice of strategic alternatives by actively changing and adjusting the strategic reference points they use to judge strategic performance.

Corporate-, Industry-, and Firm-Level Strategies

To formulate effective strategies, companies must be able to answer these three basic questions:

What business are we in?

How should we compete in this industry?

Who are our competitors, and how should we respond to them?

These simple but powerful questions are at the heart of corporate-, industry-, and firm-level strategies.

After reading the next three sections, you should be able to:

3 explain the different kinds of corporate-level strategies.
4 describe the different kinds of industry-level strategies.
5 explain the components and kinds of firm-level strategies.

3 Corporate-Level Strategies

Corporate-level strategy is the overall organizational strategy that addresses the question "What business or businesses are we in or should we be in?"

Exhibit 5.4 shows the two major approaches to corporate-level strategy that companies use to decide which businesses they should be in: 3.1 **portfolio strategy**, and 3.2 **grand strategies**.

3.1 Portfolio Strategy

One of the standard strategies for stock market investors is **diversification**, or owning stocks in a variety of companies in different industries. The purpose of this strategy is to reduce risk in the overall portfolio (the entire collection of stocks). The basic idea is simple: If you invest in ten companies in ten different industries, you won't lose your entire investment if one company performs poorly. Furthermore, because they're in different industries, one company's losses are likely to be offset by another company's gains. Portfolio strategy is based on these same ideas. We'll start by taking a look at the theory and ideas behind portfolio strategy and then proceed with a critical review that suggests that some of the key ideas behind portfolio strategy are *not* supported.

corporate-level strategy the overall organizational strategy that addresses the question "What business or businesses are we in or should we be in?"

diversification a strategy for reducing risk by buying a variety of items (stocks or, in the case of a corporation, types of businesses) so that the failure of one stock or one business does not doom the entire portfolio

portfolio strategy a corporate-level strategy that minimizes risk by diversifying investment among various businesses or product lines

Portfolio strategy is a corporate-level strategy that minimizes risk by diversifying investments among various businesses or product lines.[33] Just as a diversification strategy guides an investor who invests in a variety of stocks, portfolio strategy guides the strategic decisions of corporations that compete in a variety of businesses. For example, portfolio strategy could be used to guide the strategy of a company like 3M, which makes 55,000 products for six different businesses.[34] Just as investors consider the mix of stocks in their portfolio when deciding what to buy or sell, managers following portfolio strategy try to acquire companies that fit well with the rest of their corporate portfolio and to sell those that don't. Portfolio strategy provides the following guidelines to help companies make these difficult decisions.

EXHIBIT 5.4

Corporate-Level Strategies

Part 2 Planning

Portfolio Strategy	Grand Strategies
• Acquisitions, unrelated diversification, related diversification, single businesses	• Growth
• Boston Consulting Group matrix	• Stability
• Stars	• Retrenchment/recovery
• Question marks	
• Cash cows	
• Dogs	

First, according to portfolio strategy, the more businesses in which a corporation competes, the smaller its overall chances of failing. Think of a corporation as a stool and its businesses as the legs. The more legs or businesses added to the stool, the less likely it is to tip over. Using this analogy, portfolio strategy reduces 3M's risk of failing because the corporation's survival depends on essentially six different business sectors. Managers employing portfolio strategy can either develop new businesses internally or look for **acquisitions**, that is, other companies to buy. Either way, the goal is to add legs to the stool.

Second, beyond adding new businesses to the corporate portfolio, portfolio strategy predicts that companies can reduce risk even more through **unrelated diversification**—creating or acquiring companies in completely unrelated businesses (more on the accuracy of this prediction later). According to portfolio strategy, when businesses are unrelated, losses in one business or industry should have minimal effect on the performance of other companies in the corporate portfolio. One of the best examples of unrelated diversification is Samsung of Korea. Samsung has five businesses in electronics, five in machinery and heavy industry, two in chemicals, three in financial services, and other businesses in areas ranging from automobiles to hotels and entertainment.[35] Because most internally grown businesses tend to be related to existing products or services, portfolio strategy suggests that acquiring new businesses is the preferred method of unrelated diversification.

Third, investing the profits and cash flows from mature, slow-growth businesses into newer, faster-growing businesses can reduce long-term risk. The best-known portfolio strategy for guiding investment in a corporation's businesses is the Boston Consulting Group (BCG) matrix.[36] The **BCG matrix** is a portfolio strategy that managers use to categorize their corporation's businesses by growth rate and relative market share, helping them decide how to invest corporate funds. The matrix, shown in Exhibit 5.5, separates businesses into four categories based on how fast the market is growing (high-growth or low-growth) and the size of the business's share of that market (small or large). **Stars** are companies that have a large share of a fast-growing market. To take advantage of a star's fast-growing market and its strength in that market (large share), the corporation must invest substantially in it. The investment is usually worthwhile, however, because many stars produce sizable future profits. **Question marks** are companies that have a small share of a fast-growing market. If the corporation invests in these companies, they may eventually become stars, but their relative weakness in the market (small share) makes investing in question marks more risky than investing in stars. **Cash cows** are companies that have a large share of a slow-growing market. Companies in this situation are often highly profitable, hence the name "cash cow." Finally, **dogs** are companies that have a small share of a slow-growing market. As the name suggests, having a small share of a slow-growth market is often not profitable.

Since the idea is to redirect investment from slow-growing to fast-growing companies, the BCG matrix starts by recommending that while the substantial cash flows from cash cows last, they should be reinvested in stars (see 1 in Exhibit 5.5) to help them grow even faster and obtain even more market share. Using this strategy, current profits help produce future profits. Over time, as their market growth slows, some stars may turn into cash cows (see 2). Cash flows should also be directed to some question marks (see 3). Though riskier than stars, question marks have great potential because of their fast-growing market. Managers must decide which question

acquisition
the purchase of a company by another company

unrelated diversification
creating or acquiring companies in completely unrelated businesses

BCG matrix
a portfolio strategy, developed by the Boston Consulting Group, that categorizes a corporation's businesses by growth rate and relative market share, and helps managers decide how to invest corporate funds

star
a company with a large share of a fast-growing market

question mark
a company with a small share of a fast-growing market

cash cow
a company with a large share of a slow-growing market

dog
a company with a small share of a slow-growing market

EXHIBIT 5.5

Boston Consulting Group Matrix

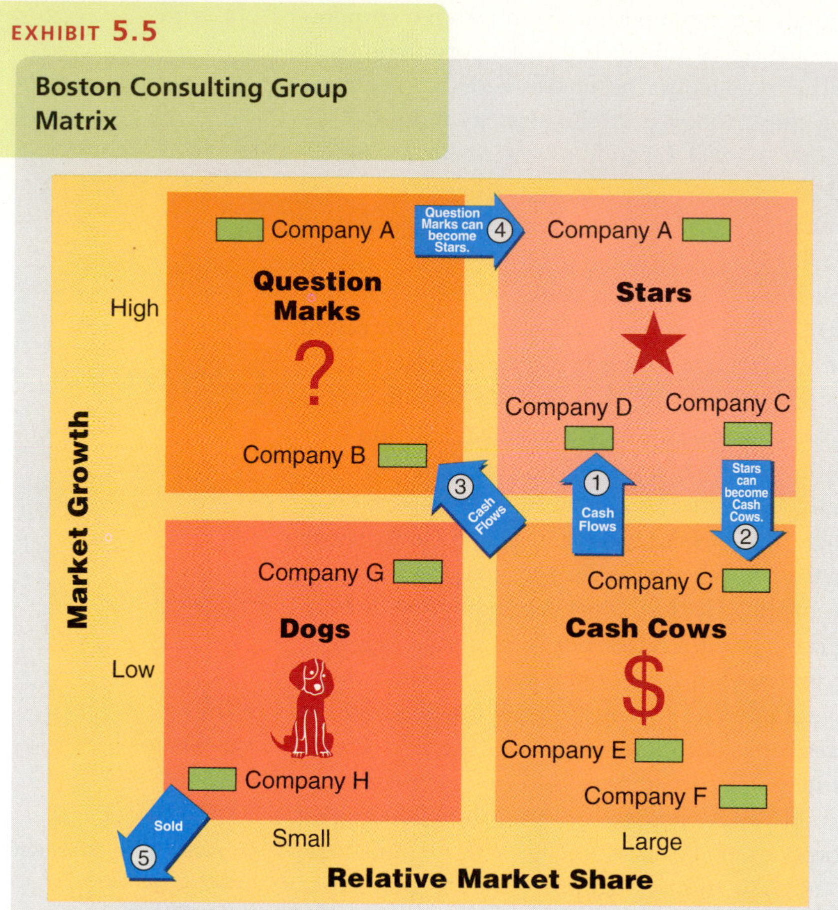

marks are most likely to turn into stars (and therefore warrant further investment) and which ones are too risky and should be sold. Over time, managers hope some question marks will become stars as their small markets become large ones (see 4). Finally, because dogs lose money, the corporation should "find them new owners" or "take them to the pound." In other words, dogs should either be sold to other companies or closed down and liquidated for their assets (see 5).

Although the BCG matrix and other forms of portfolio strategy are relatively popular among managers, it does have some drawbacks. The most significant? Contrary to the predictions of portfolio strategy, evidence suggests that acquiring unrelated businesses is *not* useful. As shown in Exhibit 5.6, there is a U-shaped relationship between diversification and risk. The left side of the curve shows that single businesses with no diversification are extremely risky (if the single business fails, the entire business fails). So, in part, the portfolio strategy of diversifying is correct—competing in a variety of different businesses can lower risk. However, portfolio strategy is partly wrong, too—the right side of the curve shows that conglomerates composed of completely unrelated businesses are even riskier than single, undiversified businesses.[37]

A second set of problems with portfolio strategy has to do with the dysfunctional consequences that can occur when companies are categorized as stars, cash cows, question marks, or dogs. Contrary to expectations, the BCG matrix often yields incorrect judgments about a company's potential. In other words, managers using the BCG matrix aren't very good at accurately determining which companies should be categorized as stars, cash cows, questions marks, or dogs. The most common mistake is simply miscategorizing highly profitable companies as dogs.[38] In part, this is because the BCG relies on past performance, which is a notoriously poor predictor of future company performance. More worrisome, however, is research which indicates that the BCG matrix actually makes managers worse at judging the future profitability of a business. A study, conducted in six countries over 5 years, gave managers and business students clear information about the current and future profits of three companies and asked them to select the one that would be most successful in the future. Although not labeled this way, one company was clearly a star, another was a dog, and the last was a cash cow. Just exposing people to the ideas in the BCG matrix led them to incorrectly categorize less profitable businesses as the most successful businesses 64 percent of the time, while actually *using* the BCG matrix led to making the same mistake 87 percent of the time.[39]

Furthermore, using the BCG matrix can also weaken the strongest performer in the corporate portfolio, the cash cow. As funds are redirected from cash cows to stars, corporate managers essentially take away the resources needed to take advantage of the cash cow's new business opportunities. As a result, the cash cow becomes less aggressive in seeking new business or in defending its present business. Finally, labeling a top performer as a cash cow can harm employee morale. Cash-cow employees realize that they have inferior status and that instead of working for themselves, they are now working to fund the growth of stars and question marks.

EXHIBIT 5.6

U-Shaped Relationship Between Diversification and Risk

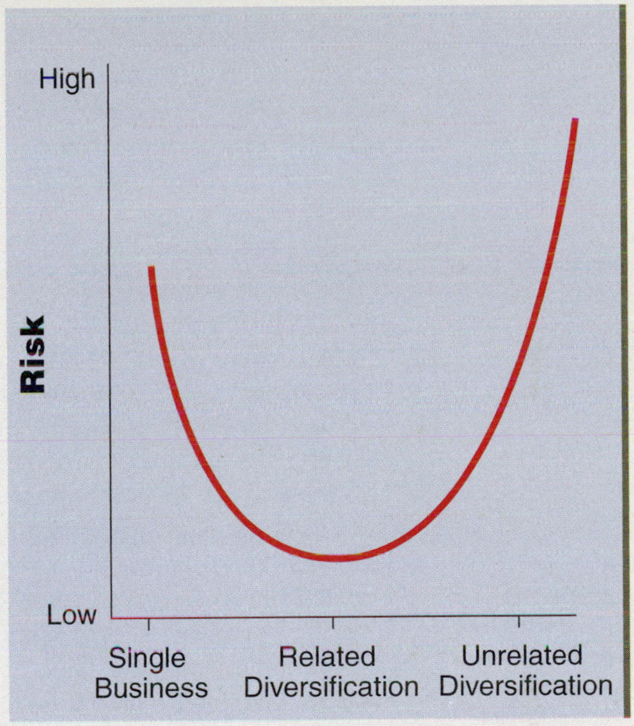

Source: Republished with permission of Academy of Management, P.O. Box 3020, Briar Cliff, NY, 10510–8020. M. Lubatkin & P.J. Lane, "Psst The Merger Mavins Still Have It Wrong," Academy of Management Executive 10 (1996) 21-39. Reproduced by permission of the publisher via Copyright Clearance Center, Inc.

So, what kind of portfolio strategy does the best job of helping managers decide which companies to buy or sell? The U-shaped curve in Exhibit 5.6 indicates that, contrary to the predictions of portfolio strategy, the best approach is probably **related diversification**, in which different business units share similar products, manufacturing, marketing, technology, or cultures. The key to related diversification is to acquire or create new companies with core capabilities that complement the core capabilities of businesses already in the corporate portfolio. Hormel Foods is an example of related diversification in the food business. The company both manufactures and markets a variety of foods, from deli meats to salsa to the infamous SPAM.

We began this section with the example of 3M and its 55,000 products sold in over seven different business sectors. While seemingly different, most of 3M's product divisions are based in some fashion on its distinctive competencies in adhesives and tapes (e.g., wet or dry sandpaper, Post-it notes, Scotchgard fabric protector, transdermal skin patches, and reflective material used in traffic signs). Furthermore, all of 3M's divisions share its strong corporate culture that promotes and encourages

related diversification creating or acquiring companies that share similar products, manufacturing, marketing, technology, or cultures

risk taking and innovation. In sum, in contrast to a single, undiversified business or unrelated diversification, related diversification reduces risk because the different businesses can work as a team, relying on each other for needed experience, expertise, and support.

3.2 Grand Strategies

A **grand strategy** is a broad strategic plan used to help an organization achieve its strategic goals.[40] Grand strategies guide the strategic alternatives that managers of individual businesses or subunits may use in deciding what businesses they should be in. There are three kinds of grand strategies: growth, stability, and retrenchment/recovery.

The purpose of a **growth strategy** is to increase profits, revenues, market share, or the number of places (stores, offices, locations) in which the company does business. Companies can grow in several ways. They can grow externally by merging with or acquiring other companies in the same or different businesses. Some of the largest mergers and acquisitions of recent years include Roche acquiring Genentech (pharmaceuticals), Pfizer acquiring Wyeth (pharmaceuticals), and InBev acquiring Anheuser-Busch (beer and alcoholic beverages).

Another way to grow is internally, directly expanding the company's existing business or creating and growing new businesses. Nestlé, the global food company with well-known brands like Nesquik chocolate milk, KitKat chocolate bars, and Gerber baby food, typically aims for and achieves internal growth rates of 7 to 8 percent by growing sales of existing products or developing new products.

The purpose of a **stability strategy** is to continue doing what the company has been doing, but doing it better. Companies following a stability strategy try to improve the way in which they sell the same products or services to the same customers. Since its inception in 1938, *REI* has never strayed from its focus on the outdoors. Its Mountain Safety Research division designs and makes mountaineering equipment, clothing, and camping products. REI Adventures offers adventure travel packages (e.g., kayaking, climbing, and backpacking) with hand-picked local guides on all seven continents. Finally, in addition to its website, REI has 80 stores in 27 states selling high-quality outdoor gear, clothing, and footwear.[41] And today, with 3.5 million members whose membership entitles them to discounts and expert advice, REI is one of the largest retail co-ops in the world. Companies often choose a stability strategy when their external environment doesn't change much or after they have struggled with periods of explosive growth.

The purpose of a **retrenchment strategy** is to turn around poor company performance by shrinking the size or scope of the business or, if a company is in multiple businesses, by closing or shutting down different lines of the business. The first steps of a typical retrenchment strategy might include making significant cost reductions; laying off employees; closing poorly performing stores, offices, or manufacturing plants; or closing or selling entire lines of products or services.[42]

After cutting costs and reducing a business's size or scope, the second step in a retrenchment strategy is recovery. **Recovery** consists of the strategic actions that a company takes to return to a growth strategy. This two-step process of cutting and recovery is analogous to pruning roses. Prior to each

grand strategy
a broad corporate-level strategic plan used to achieve strategic goals and guide the strategic alternatives that managers of individual businesses or subunits may use

growth strategy
a strategy that focuses on increasing profits, revenues, market share, or the number of places in which the company does business

stability strategy
a strategy that focuses on improving the way in which the company sells the same products or services to the same customers

retrenchment strategy
a strategy that focuses on turning around very poor company performance by shrinking the size or scope of the business

recovery
the strategic actions taken after retrenchment to return to a growth strategy

growing season, roses should be cut back to two-thirds their normal size. Pruning doesn't damage the roses; it makes them stronger and more likely to produce beautiful, fragrant flowers. The retrenchment-and-recovery process is similar. Cost reductions, layoffs, and plant closings are sometimes necessary to restore companies to good health. When company performance drops significantly, a strategy of retrenchment and recovery may help the company return to a successful growth strategy.

REVIEW 3

Corporate-Level Strategies

Corporate-level strategies such as portfolio strategy and grand strategies help managers determine what businesses they should be in. Portfolio strategy focuses on lowering business risk by being in multiple, unrelated businesses and by investing the cash flows from slow-growth businesses into faster-growing businesses. One portfolio strategy, the BCG matrix, suggests that cash flows from cash cows should be reinvested in stars and in carefully chosen question marks. Dogs should be sold or liquidated. Portfolio strategy has several problems, however. Acquiring unrelated businesses actually increases risk rather than lowering it. The BCG matrix is often wrong when predicting companies' futures (as dogs or cash cows, for example). And redirecting cash flows can seriously weaken cash cows. The most successful way to use the portfolio approach to corporate strategy is to reduce risk through related diversification.

The three kinds of grand strategies are growth, stability, and retrenchment/recovery. Companies can grow externally by merging with or acquiring other companies, or they can grow internally through direct expansion or creating new businesses. Companies choose a stability strategy—selling the same products or services to the same customers—when their external environment changes very little or after they have dealt with periods of explosive growth. Retrenchment strategy, shrinking the size or scope of a business, is used to turn around poor performance. If retrenchment works, it is often followed by a recovery strategy that focuses on growing the business again.

4 Industry-Level Strategies

Industry-level strategy addresses the question "How should we compete in this industry?"

Let's find out more about industry-level strategies by discussing 4.1 **the five industry forces that determine overall levels of competition in an industry as well as,** 4.2 **the positioning strategies**, and 4.3 **adaptive strategies that companies can use to achieve sustained competitive advantage and above-average profits**.

4.1 Five Industry Forces

industry-level strategy a corporate strategy that addresses the question "How should we compete in this industry?"

According to Harvard professor Michael Porter, five industry forces determine an industry's overall attractiveness and potential for long-term profitability. These include the character of the rivalry, the threat of new entrants, the threat of substitute products or services, the bargaining power of suppliers, and the bargaining power

EXHIBIT 5.7

Porter's Five Industry Forces

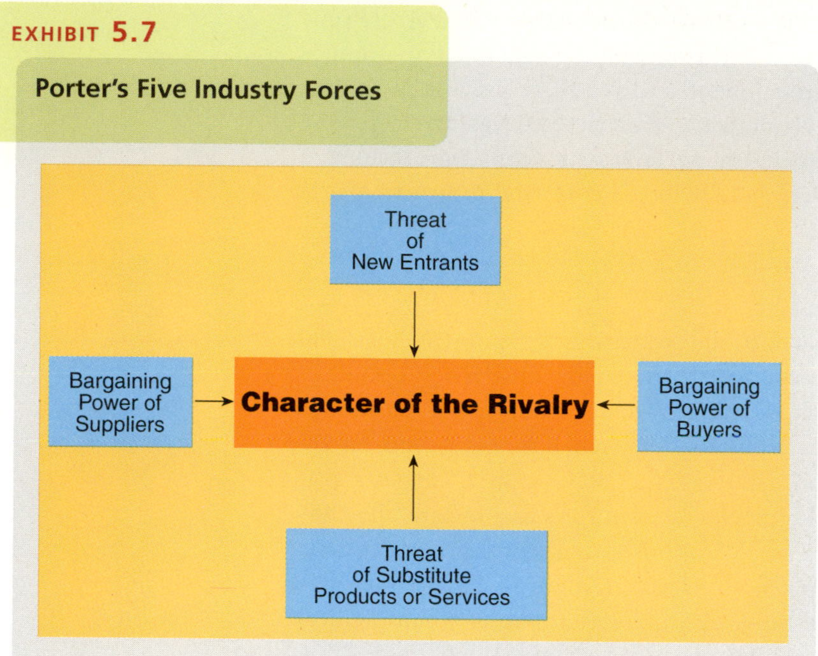

Source: Adapted and reprinted by permission of Harvard Business Review. From "How Competitive Forces Shape Strategy," by Michael E. Porter, *Harvard Business Review,* March/April 1979, copyright © 1979 by the President and Fellows of Harvard College. All rights reserved.

of buyers. The stronger these forces, the less attractive the industry becomes to corporate investors because it is more difficult for companies to be profitable. Porter's industry forces are illustrated in Exhibit 5.7. Let's examine how these forces are bringing changes to several kinds of industries.

Character of the rivalry is a measure of the intensity of competitive behavior among companies in an industry. Is the competition among firms aggressive and cutthroat, or do competitors focus more on serving customers than on attacking each other? Both industry attractiveness and profitability decrease when rivalry is cutthroat. For example, selling cars is a highly competitive business. Pick up a local newspaper on Friday, Saturday, or Sunday morning, and you'll find dozens of pages of car advertising. In fact, competition in new car sales is so intense that if it weren't for used-car sales, repair work, and replacement parts, many auto dealers would actually lose money.

The **threat of new entrants** is a measure of the degree to which barriers to entry make it easy or difficult for new companies to get started in an industry. If new companies can easily enter the industry, then competition will increase and prices and profits will fall. On the other hand, if there are sufficient barriers to entry, such as large capital requirements to buy expensive equipment or plant facilities or the need for specialized knowledge, then competition will be weaker and prices and profits will generally be higher. For instance, high costs and intense competition make it very difficult to enter the video-game business. The barriers to entry for this business are extremely high given that today's average video game takes 12 to 36 months to create, $10 to $20 million to develop, and teams of highly paid creative workers to develop realistic graphics, captivating story lines, and innovative game capabilities, who must also be disciplined enough to meet budgets and very strict deadlines and still produce efficient, reliable, bug-free code.[43] These barriers to entry are also in place for online video games, like *ACTIVISION BLIZZARD'S World of Warcraft*, which are growing even faster than traditional video games. Regarding online gaming, industry analyst Arvind Bhatia says, "This is a very hard and expensive market to enter, let alone be successful."[44]

character of the rivalry
a measure of the intensity of competitive behavior between companies in an industry

threat of new entrants
a measure of the degree to which barriers to entry make it easy or difficult for new companies to get started in an industry

threat of substitute products or services
a measure of the ease with which customers can find substitutes for an industry's products or services

The **threat of substitute products or services** is a measure of the ease with which customers can find substitutes for an industry's products or services. If customers can easily find substitute products or services, the competition will be greater and profits will be lower. If there are few or no substitutes, competition will be weaker and profits will be higher. Generic medicines are some of the best-known examples of substitute products.

Bargaining power of suppliers is a measure of the influence that suppliers of parts, materials, and services to firms in an industry have on the prices of these inputs. When companies can buy parts, materials, and services from numerous suppliers, the companies will be able to bargain with the suppliers to keep prices low. On the other hand, if there are few suppliers, or if a company is dependent on a supplier with specialized skills and knowledge, then the suppliers will have the bargaining power to dictate price levels. Today, there are so many suppliers of inexpensive, standardized parts, computer chips, and video screens that dozens of new companies are beginning to manufacture flat-screen TVs. One of those companies is *XOCECO* (ZO-say-co), a Chinese company that has made inexpensive, low-quality TVs for two decades. But with dozens of companies able to supply the high-tech parts it needs, Xoceco was able to enter the flat-screen TV market without having to spend millions of dollars on research and development. Instead, it is simply buying the parts and software it needs directly from suppliers, assembling the TVs in its factories, and then undercutting the prices of now-struggling market leaders like Sony.[45]

Bargaining power of buyers is a measure of the influence that customers have on a firm's prices. If a company sells a popular product or service to multiple buyers, then the company has more power to set prices. By contrast, if a company is dependent on just a few high-volume buyers, those buyers will typically have enough bargaining power to dictate prices. For example, Wal-Mart is the largest single buyer in the history of retailing. The company buys 30 percent of all toothpaste, shampoo, and paper towels made by retail suppliers; 15 to 20 percent of all CDs, videos, and DVDs; 15 percent of all magazines; 14 percent of all groceries; and 20 percent of all toys. And, of course, Wal-Mart uses its purchasing power as a buyer to push down prices.

bargaining power of suppliers
a measure of the influence that suppliers of parts, materials, and services to firms in an industry have on the prices of these inputs

bargaining power of buyers
a measure of the influence that customers have on a firm's prices

4.2 Positioning Strategies

After analyzing industry forces, the next step in industry-level strategy is to protect your company from the negative effects of industry-wide competition and to create a sustainable competitive advantage. According to Michael Porter, there are three positioning strategies: cost leadership, differentiation, and focus.

Cost leadership means producing a product or service of acceptable quality at consistently lower production costs than competitors so that the firm can offer the product or service at the lowest price in the industry. Cost leadership protects companies from industry forces by deterring new entrants, who will have to match low costs and prices. Cost leadership also forces down the prices of substitute products and services, attracts bargain-seeking buyers, and increases bargaining power with suppliers, who have to keep their prices low if they want to do business with the cost leader.

Differentiation means making your product or service sufficiently different from competitors' offerings so that customers are willing to pay a premium price for the extra value or performance that it provides. Differentiation protects companies from industry forces by reducing the threat of substitute products. It also protects companies by making it easier to retain customers and more difficult for new entrants trying

cost leadership
the positioning strategy of producing a product or service of acceptable quality at consistently lower production costs than competitors can, so that the firm can offer the product or service at the lowest price in the industry

differentiation
the positioning strategy of providing a product or service that is sufficiently different from competitors' offerings that customers are willing to pay a premium price for it

Management Fact:

When looking for threats and opportunities, many managers focus on competitors in the external environment. Others, however, prefer to examine the internal environment through a shadow-strategy task force. This strategy involves a company actively seeking out its own weaknesses, and then, thinking like a competitors, trying to determine how they can be exploited for competitive advantage. To make sure that the task force challenges conventional thinking, its members should be independent-minded, come from a variety of company functions and levels, and have the access and authority to question the company's current strategic actions and intent.

Source: W. B. Werther, Jr., and J. L. Kerr. "The Shifting Sands of Competitive Advantage." *Business Horizons* (May–June 1995): 11–17.

to attract new customers. For example, why would anyone pay $2,000 for a washing machine when they could purchase a regular washer for $350? The answer is that the Whirlpool Duet does huge loads, nearly twice that of a regular washer, while using half as much water. Most importantly, the Duet saves time by allowing people to do fewer, larger loads.

With a **focus strategy**, a company uses either cost leadership or differentiation to produce a specialized product or service for a limited, specially targeted group of customers in a particular geographic region or market segment. Focus strategies typically work in market niches that competitors have overlooked or have difficulty serving. While eBay dominates the online auction business, smaller, more-focused auction sites serve select groups of online buyers and sellers. Artists who sell jewelry and handmade goods are attracted to Silkfair because it has larger pictures (which is important when you sell small items like jewelry) and lets sellers use video, customer forums, and blogs to promote their products and interact with customers. Cathleen McLain, who sells her jewelry on Silkfair, said, "I don't need a million people to see my things, just the right people who have hopefully good taste to buy my things."[46] Likewise, *ETSY* sells only handmade goods and has a focused mission: "to enable people to make a living making things, and to reconnect makers with buyers." Since inception, 100,000 different sellers have used Etsy to sell their handmade products.[47]

focus strategy
the positioning strategy of using cost leadership or differentiation to produce a specialized product or service for a limited, specially targeted group of customers in a particular geographic region or market segment

defenders
companies using an adaptive strategy aimed at defending strategic positions by seeking moderate, steady growth and by offering a limited range of high-quality products and services to a well-defined set of customers

4.3 Adaptive Strategies

Adaptive strategies are another set of industry-level strategies. Whereas the aim of positioning strategies is to minimize the effects of industry competition and build a sustainable competitive advantage, the purpose of adaptive strategies is to choose an industry-level strategy that is best suited to changes in the organization's external environment. There are four kinds of adaptive strategies: defenders, prospectors, analyzers, and reactors.[48]

Defenders seek moderate, steady growth by offering a limited range of products and services to a well-defined set of customers. In other words, defenders aggressively "defend" their current strategic position by doing the best job they can to hold on to customers in a particular market segment. Nestlé's KitKat, chocolate-covered, two-fingered wafers, are so popular in the United Kingdom (UK) that one is eaten every 47 seconds. For years, Nestlé used a defender strategy, producing only slight changes to the original. Wanting to jump-start the slow, but steady growth, Nestlé abandoned its defender strategy and introduced a huge variety of new flavors. While sales increased at first, traditional customers soon complained. Within 2 years, Nestlé killed the new flavors. Sales, which had dropped, are now up thanks to increased advertising and a return to giving customers what they want, the basic KitKat bar and just a few variants.[49]

Prospectors seek fast growth by searching for new market opportunities, encouraging risk taking, and being the first to bring innovative new products to market. Prospectors are analogous to gold miners who "prospect" for gold nuggets (i.e., new products) in hopes that the nuggets will lead them to a rich deposit of gold (i.e., fast growth).

prospectors
companies using an adaptive strategy that seeks fast growth by searching for new market opportunities, encouraging risk taking, and being the first to bring innovative new products to market

Analyzers are a blend of the defender and prospector strategies. They seek moderate, steady growth *and* limited opportunities for fast growth. Analyzers are rarely first to market with new products or services. Instead, they try to minimize risk and maximize profits simultaneously by following or imitating the proven successes of prospectors.

analyzers
companies using an adaptive strategy that seeks to minimize risk and maximize profits by following or imitating the proven successes of prospectors

Finally, unlike defenders, prospectors, or analyzers, **reactors** do not follow a consistent strategy. Rather than anticipating and preparing for external opportunities and threats, reactors tend to "react" to changes in their external environment after they occur. Not surprisingly, reactors tend to be poorer performers than defenders, prospectors, or analyzers. A reactor approach is inherently unstable, and firms that fall into this mode of operation must change their approach or face almost certain failure. *HARD ROCK CAFÉ INTERNATIONAL* has 125 restaurants and 10 hotels around the world. When it spent $400 million in Myrtle Beach, South Carolina, to create the Hard Rock Café Park, a rock and roll–based theme park with monster rides, there was every expectation that success would follow. But, bankruptcy occurred after just one season because the park's managers did not anticipate or prepare for the basic challenges they would face. In a town famous for its beautiful and *free* beach, admission was $50 per customer. Moreover, park managers didn't coordinate their limited promotions with nearby hotels or local tourism officials.[50]

reactors
companies using an adaptive strategy of not following a consistent strategy, but instead reacting to changes in the external environment after they occur

© HANS MARTENS/ISTOCKPHOTO.COM

Smaller, more-focused auction sites serve select groups of online buyers and sellers, such as artists and handicrafters. Silkfair and Etsy are two sites that focus on these special target markets.

REVIEW 4

Industry-Level Strategies

Industry-level strategies focus on how companies choose to compete in their industry. Five industry forces determine an industry's overall attractiveness to corporate investors and its potential for long-term profitability. Together, a high level of new entrants, substitute products or services, bargaining power of suppliers, bargaining power of buyers, and rivalry among competitors combine to increase competition and decrease profits. Three positioning strategies can help companies protect themselves from the negative effects of industry-wide competition. Under a cost leadership strategy, firms try to keep production costs low so that they can sell products at prices lower than competitors can. Differentiation is a strategy aimed at making a product or service sufficiently different from competitors' products that it can command a premium price. Using a focus strategy, firms seek to produce a specialized product or service for a limited, specially targeted group of customers. The four adaptive strategies help companies adapt to changes in the external environment. Defenders want to "defend" their current strategic positions. Prospectors look for new market opportunities by bringing innovative new products to market. Analyzers minimize risk by following the proven successes of prospectors. Reactors do not follow a consistent strategy, but instead react to changes in their external environment after they occur.

5 Firm-Level Strategies

Microsoft brings out its Xbox 360 video-game console; Sony counters with its PlayStation 3. Sprint Nextel drops prices and increases monthly cell phone minutes; Verizon strikes back with a faster network and even lower prices and more minutes. Starbucks Coffee opens a store, and nearby locally-run coffeehouses respond by improving service, increasing portions, and holding the line on prices. Attack and respond, respond and attack. **Firm-level strategy** addresses the question "How should we compete against a particular firm?"

Let's find out more about firm-level strategies (direct competition between companies) by reading about 5.1 **the basics of direct competition**, and 5.2 **the strategic moves involved in direct competition between companies**.

5.1 Direct Competition

Although Porter's five industry forces indicate the overall level of competition in an industry, most companies do not compete directly with all the firms in their industry. For example, McDonald's and Red Lobster are both in the restaurant business, but no one would characterize them as competitors. McDonald's offers low-cost, convenient fast food in a seat-yourself restaurant, while Red Lobster offers mid-priced, sit-down seafood dinners complete with servers and a bar.

Instead of competing with an industry, most firms compete directly with just a few companies within it. **Direct competition** is the rivalry between two companies offering similar products and services that acknowledge each other as rivals and take offensive and defensive positions as they act and react to each other's strategic actions.[51] Two factors determine the extent to which firms will be in direct competition with each other: market commonality and resource similarity. **Market commonality** is the degree to which two companies have overlapping products, services, or customers in multiple markets. The more markets in which there is product, service, or customer overlap, the more intense the direct competition between the two companies. **Resource similarity** is the extent to which a competitor has similar amounts and kinds of resources, that is, similar assets, capabilities, processes, information, and knowledge used to create and sustain an advantage over competitors. From a competitive standpoint, resource similarity means that your direct competitors can probably match the strategic actions that your company takes.

Exhibit 5.8 shows how market commonality and resource similarity interact to determine when and where companies are in direct competition.[52] The overlapping area in each quadrant (between the triangle and the rectangle, or between

firm-level strategy
a corporate strategy that addresses the question "How should we compete against a particular firm?"

direct competition
the rivalry between two companies that offer similar products and services, acknowledge each other as rivals, and act and react to each other's strategic actions

market commonality
the degree to which two companies have overlapping products, services, or customers in multiple markets

resource similarity
the extent to which a competitor has similar amounts and kinds of resources

the differently colored rectangles) depicts market commonality; the larger the overlap, the greater the market commonality. Shapes depict resource similarity, with rectangles representing one set of competitive resources and triangles representing another. Quadrant I shows two companies in direct competition because they have similar resources at their disposal and a high degree of market commonality. These companies try to sell similar products and services to similar customers. McDonald's and Burger King would clearly fit here as direct competitors.

EXHIBIT 5.8

A Framework of Direct Competition

Source: Republished with permission of Academy of Management, P.O. Box 3020, Briar Cliff, NY, 10510–8020. M. Chen, "Competitor Analysis and InterFirm Rivalry: Toward a Theoretical Integration," *Academy of Management Review* 21. Reproduced by permission of the publisher via Copyright Clearance Center, Inc.

In Quadrant II, the overlapping parts of the triangle and rectangle show two companies going after similar customers with some similar products or services but with different competitive resources. McDonald's and Wendy's restaurants would fit here. Wendy's is after the same lunchtime and dinner crowds that McDonald's is. Nevertheless, with its more expensive hamburgers, fries, shakes, and salads, Wendy's is less of a direct competitor to McDonald's than is Burger King. Wendy's Garden Sensation salads (using fancy lettuce varieties, grape tomatoes, and mandarin oranges) bring in customers who would have eaten at more expensive casual dining restaurants like Applebee's.[53]

In Quadrant III, the very small overlap shows two companies with different competitive resources and little market commonality. McDonald's and Luby's Cafeterias fit here. Although both are in the fast-food business, there's almost no overlap in terms of products and customers. Luby's sells baked chicken, turkey, roasts, meat loaf, and vegetables, none of which are available at McDonald's. Furthermore, Luby's customers aren't likely to eat at McDonald's. In fact, Luby's is not really competing with other fast-food restaurants at all, but with eating at home.

Finally, in Quadrant IV, the small overlap between the two rectangles shows that McDonald's and Subway compete with similar resources but with little market commonality. In terms of resources, sales at McDonald's are much larger, but Subway has grown substantially in the last decade and now has 33,048 stores worldwide, compared to 32,000 worldwide at McDonald's (just 13,000 in the United States).[54] Though Subway and McDonald's compete, they aren't direct competitors in terms of market commonality in the way that McDonald's and Burger King are because Subway, unlike McDonald's, sells itself as a provider of healthy fast food.

5.2 Strategic Moves of Direct Competition

While corporate-level strategies help managers decide what business to be in and industry-level strategies help them determine how to compete within an industry, firm-level strategies help managers determine when, where, and what strategic actions should be taken against a direct competitor. Firms in direct competition can make two basic strategic moves: attacks and responses.

An **attack** is a competitive move designed to reduce a rival's market share or profits. Hoping to increase its market share at Burger King's expense, McDonald's began a brutal price war by putting eight items on a $1 value menu, including two sandwiches, the Big N' Tasty quarter-pounder and the McChicken sandwich, that usually sold for $1.99.[55] Sales of those sandwiches doubled within weeks.[56] The attack worked very well at first, putting a lot of pressure on Burger King. A **response** is a countermove, prompted by a rival's attack, that is designed to defend or improve a company's market share or profit. There are two kinds of responses.[57] The first is to match or mirror your competitor's move. This is what Burger King did to McDonald's by selling 11 menu items at 99 cents each, including its popular double cheeseburgers. The second kind of response, however, is to respond along a different dimension from your competitor's move or attack. For example, instead of cutting prices, Burger King could have introduced a new menu item to attract customers away from McDonald's.

Market commonality and resource similarity determine the likelihood of an attack or response, that is, whether a company is likely to attack a direct competitor or to strike back with a strong response when attacked. When market commonality is strong and companies have overlapping products, services, or customers in multiple markets, there is less motivation to attack and more motivation to respond to an attack. The reason for this is straightforward: When firms are direct competitors in a large number of markets, they have a great deal at stake. So when McDonald's launched an aggressive price war with its value menu, Burger King had no choice but to respond by cutting its own prices.

Whereas market commonality affects the likelihood of an attack or a response to an attack, resource similarity largely affects response capability, that is, how quickly and forcefully a company can respond to an attack. When resource similarity is strong, the responding firm will generally be able to match the strategic moves of the attacking firm. Consequently, a firm is less likely to attack firms with similar levels of resources because it is unlikely to gain any sustained advantage when the responding firms strike back. On the other hand, if one firm is substantially stronger than another (i.e., there is low resource similarity), then a competitive attack is more likely to produce sustained competitive advantage.

With over 32,000 stores to Burger King's 11,565, and much greater financial resources, McDonald's hoped its price war would inflict serious financial damage on Burger King while suffering minimal financial damage itself. This strategy worked to some extent. Although Burger King sold 11 menu items for 99 cents, it admitted that it couldn't afford to match McDonald's price cuts on more expensive sandwiches. Thanks to its much larger financial resources, McDonald's had the funds to outlast Burger King in the price war. As often happens, though, the price war ended up hurting both companies' profits.[58] McDonald's ended the price war when it became clear that lower prices didn't draw more customers to its restaurants.

attack
a competitive move designed to reduce a rival's market share or profits

response
a competitive countermove, prompted by a rival's attack, to defend or improve a company's market share or profit

In general, the more moves (i.e., attacks) a company initiates against direct competitors, and the greater a company's tendency to respond when attacked, the better its performance. More specifically, attackers and early responders (companies that are quick to launch a retaliatory attack) tend to gain market share and profits at the expense of late responders. This is not to suggest that a full-attack strategy always works best. In fact, attacks can provoke harsh retaliatory responses. When it first came on the market, Sony's PlayStation 3 (PS3) cost $599, but it came with an 80-GB hard drive and a then-rare Blu-ray drive. Sales lagged. However, Nintendo's Wii game console cost $249 and Microsoft's Xbox 360 game console cost $400. So Sony cut the price of the 80-GB PS3 to $499 and introduced a 40-GB PS3 for $399.[59] Microsoft responded over the next 4 years with a combination of price cuts from which Sony has yet to recover, cutting the Xbox 360 with a 20-GB hard drive from $349 to $299, cutting the price of an Xbox 360 with a 60-GB hard drive from $349 to $299, and cutting a 120-GB Xbox 360 from $399 to $299.[60] Sony's PS3 sales have continued to slow, running at about 20 percent of Wii sales and 40 percent of Xbox 360 sales.[61] Consequently, when deciding when, where, and what strategic actions to take against a direct competitor, managers should always consider the possibility of retaliation.

REVIEW 5

Firm-Level Strategies

Firm-level strategies are concerned with direct competition between firms. Market commonality and resource similarity determine whether firms are in direct competition and thus likely to attack each other or respond to each other's attacks. In general, the more markets in which there is product, service, or customer overlap, and the greater the resource similarity between two firms, the more intense the direct competition between them. When firms are direct competitors in a large number of markets, attacks are less likely because responding firms are highly motivated to defend their profits and market share quickly and forcefully. By contrast, resource similarity affects response capability, meaning how quickly and forcefully a company responds to an attack. When resource similarity is strong, attacks are much less likely to produce a sustained advantage because the responding firm is capable of striking back with equal force.

Market entries and exits are the most important kinds of attacks and responses. Entering a new market is a clear offensive signal, while exiting a market is a clear signal that a company is retreating. Market entry is perhaps the most forceful attack or response because it sends a clear signal that the company is committed to gaining or defending market share and profits at a direct competitor's expense. In general, attackers and early responders gain market share and profits at the expense of late responders. Attacks must be carefully planned and carried out, however, because they can provoke harsh retaliatory responses.

Finally, the basic strategic act of entrepreneurship is new entry. To carry out an entrepreneurial strategy, a company must create an entrepreneurial orientation by encouraging risk taking, autonomy, innovativeness, proactiveness, and competitive aggressiveness.

Management Decision

Dealing with Competition

You are an executive at Pepsi, and you've just made what feels like a great decision. For many years, various health and children's groups have been calling for reductions of high-calorie and high-fat foods in U.S. schools. Even if schools provided nutritious, fresh, and healthy food, they argued, it was no competition for the salty and sugary treats available in vending machines. These groups even had the first lady, Michelle Obama, lead a nationwide campaign.

In response, you've made a monumental decision, the first by any soft drink producer—to remove full-calorie beverages from all schools in over 200 countries by 2012. Your decision is being hailed by numerous organizations, from the World Heart Federation and the American Heart Association to the William J. Clinton Foundation. Not only do they credit your company for taking an important first step in the fight against childhood obesity, but they also celebrate your willingness to take initiative instead of waiting for government regulations.

Some of your colleagues, however, are not in a celebratory mood. Though your company has received some great publicity, they've read numerous reports that Coca-Cola will take a different course. While all soft-drink producers agreed not to sell full-calorie products in primary/elementary schools, Coca-Cola recently revised its sales policy to allow sales in schools if parents or school officials request it. What is more, Coca-Cola has decided that it will continue to sell full-calorie beverage to secondary schools, as they argue that parents and school officials "should have the right to choose what is best for their schools."

Your colleagues worry that Coca-Cola's policy could give them a huge competitive advantage. Even though Pepsi will still have a presence in primary and secondary schools, their offerings will be limited to low-calorie diet drinks, bottled water, low-fat milk, and juice with no added sugar. These products may have to compete with Coca-Cola's lineup of full-calorie, sugar-loaded drinks. There doesn't seem to be much doubt about what the students will choose. After all, if students opted for diet drinks or water in the first place, the sale of full-calorie drinks would not have turned into a public health issue.

Your colleagues fear that Pepsi's commitment to public health will give Coca-Cola an insurmountable competitive edge. So late in one business day, a group of colleagues come to your office. "You're the one that came up with this great plan," they say, "how are we going to respond?"

Questions

1. Using Porter's Five Industry Forces, map the soft-drink industry.
2. What are the risks and opportunities of the strategies followed by Pepsi? Of Coca-Cola?
3. How would you respond to Coca-Cola's change in sales policy? How would you ensure Pepsi's board that this response will allow you to remain competitive and profitable?

Sources: Betsy McKay. "Soft-Drink Sales Drop in Schools, Group Says." *Wall Street Journal.* March 8, 2010. B3.

"Pepsi Says No to Soda Sales at Schools." *Wall Street Journal.* March 17, 2010. D3.

Practice being a MANAGER

Most Likely to Succeed

Organizational strategy is aimed at achieving sustainable competitive advantage over rivals in a particular market. This exercise will offer you the opportunity to consider how companies in the restaurant industry might develop a strategy and attempt to gain sustainable competitive advantage.

For purposes of this exercise, your professor will organize your class into small teams. Each team will be competing for the title of "Most Likely to Succeed." One team will be designated as judges for this competition.

STEP 1 (15 MINUTES) Develop a concept for a new restaurant business. You may choose to develop your concept as a local, regional, or national company—but in all cases, you must plan to open a restaurant in your local area. Your concept should include the following: (a) name for your restaurant/chain; (b) description of your menu, layout, and any other distinguishing features; and (c) likely direct competitors of your new concept. Prepare an informal presentation of not more than 2 minutes.

STEP 2 (20 MINUTES) Present the concepts. Each team will make an informal 2-minute presentation of the restaurant concepts.

STEP 3 (5 MINUTES) Judge the presentations. Judges will confer and reach a decision regarding the top concepts on the basis of "Most Likely to Succeed." Judges should apply sustainable competitive advantage concept/factors in making their selections. While the judges are conferring, each team should discuss and evaluate the concepts presented by the competing teams. Teams should apply the tools and concepts in this chapter in evaluating these concepts.

STEP 4 Discuss as a class.

- What are the challenges of achieving sustainable competitive advantage in the restaurant business? Consider cases of failure and success in your local market—what factors seemed to play a role in determining success or failure?
- What *strategic groups*, or clusters of direct competitors (for example, fast-food burgers), were identified in the team presentations? Which strategic groups might be tougher to enter in your local area? Which might be easier to enter?
- Do major restaurant chains have a built-in sustainable competitive advantage over local competition in your area? If you think so, what is the source of this advantage, and is it more pronounced in some strategic groups than in others (e.g., greater in tacos than in fine dining)? If not, what strategies have the "locals" used to successfully compete with larger restaurant chains?

Strategy Questionnaire

Generally speaking, a strategy is a plan of action that is designed to help you achieve a goal. Strategies are not limited to grand plans that help you accomplish grand goals. You probably use strategies every day in simple ways. For example, think of a route you regularly drive. Do you know how fast (or slow) you need to go to catch all the lights on green? Or where to swerve to avoid a pothole? Or even when to take a side street to shave a few minutes off your commute? Speeding up for one block in order to catch the green lights at the next five intersections is a strategy. Strategy, then, involves thinking about how you are going to accomplish what you set out (i.e., have planned) to do.

This assessment will provide some baseline information on attitudes you might have that will relate to your management skills.[62] Answer each of the questions either true or false. Try not to spend too much time on any one item, and be sure to answer all the questions.

1. I get satisfaction from competing with others.
2. It's usually not important to me to be the best.
3. Competition destroys friendships.
4. Games with no clear-cut winners are boring.
5. I am a competitive individual.
6. I will do almost anything to avoid an argument.
7. I try to avoid competing with others.
8. I would like to be on a debating team.
9. I often remain quiet rather than risk hurting another person.
10. I find competitive situations unpleasant.
11. I try to avoid arguments.
12. In general, I will go along with the group rather than create conflict.
13. I don't like competing against other people.
14. I don't like games that are winner-take-all.
15. I dread competing against other people.
16. I enjoy competing against an opponent.
17. When I play a game, I like to keep score.
18. I often try to outperform others.
19. I like competition.
20. I don't enjoy challenging others even when I think they are wrong.

To determine your score, count the number of responses marked "True" and enter it here ____. You can find the interpretation for your score at: login.cengagebrain.com.

Biz Flix

© GREEN LIGHT

Field of Dreams

In the classic 1989 film *Field of Dreams*, Ray Kinsella (Kevin Costner) hears a voice while working in his Iowa cornfield that says, "If you build it, he will come." Ray concludes that "he" is legendary "Shoeless Joe" Jackson (Ray Liotta), a 1919 Chicago White Sox player suspended for rigging the 1919 World Series. With the support of his wife Annie (Amy Madigan), Ray jeopardizes his farm by plowing under a cornfield and creating a modern baseball diamond in its place. Shoeless Joe soon arrives, followed by the rest of the suspended players. This charming fantasy film, based on W. P. Kinsellas's novel *Shoeless Joe,* shows the rewards of pursuing a dream. In this clip, Ray's brother-in-law Mark (Timothy Busfield) insists that they will have to start farming on the field again if they're going to make enough money to avoid foreclosure on their property, but Ray's daughter Karin (Gaby Hoffman) suggests another idea.

What to Watch For and Ask Yourself

1. If you were Ray, what would you do in this situation? Would you be more likely to take Mark's advice or Karin's?
2. If Ray decides to do what his daughter Karin suggests with the field, could you call that an example of entrepreneurship? Intrapreneurship?
3. What are the risks Ray faces if he acts on Karin's suggestion?

Management Workplace

© CENGAGE

Numi Organic Tea

Ahmed Rahim, the cofounder and CEO of Numi Organic Tea, doesn't hire new employees lightly. He still interviews nearly every serious prospect—and most are interviewed at least three times before getting a job offer. Employees must have more than just a willingness to work hard; Numi is looking for people with passion. Rahim explained the philosophy this way: "People are everything for a company. You can have a great product and great mission, but without the right people, you don't have the right formula." Fifty people currently work for this progressive, Oakland-based company. Given the pace of growth, Numi can't afford to lose the time and energy resulting from hasty hiring decisions and the inevitable turnover. As you'll see in this video, the company would rather make sure each person it hires has the desired skills

Reel to Real

and experience, fits well with the culture, and can serve as a Numi ambassador everywhere he or she goes.

What to Watch For and Ask Yourself

1. What are some of the company's resources that are discussed in this video?
2. How important is the hiring process at Numi to the company's success? Can hiring the right people create a competitive advantage for Numi?
3. Do you think you could get hired at Numi? How well do you think you would fit into its work environment?

6

Chapter Six

Innovation and Change

OUTLINE

Experience Management

Explore the four levels of learning by doing the simulation module on Innovation & Change.

© ISTOCKPHOTO.COM/ ANN MARIE KURTZ

Pod Nod

Mini lecture reviews all the learning points in the chapter.

© ISTOCKPHOTO.COM/ MAGNET CREATIVE

Reel to Real Video

Biz Flix is a scene from *Field of Dreams*. Management Workplace is a segment on Scholfield Honda.

© ISTOCKPHOTO.COM/ CRAFTVISION

Self Test

10 quiz questions, 6 exhibit worksheets, and PowerPoints for quick review.

© ISTOCKPHOTO.COM/ DIJITAL FILM

What Would You Do?

Novartis AG Headquarters, Basel, Switzerland.[1]

In Hollywood, a "blockbuster" movie often represents the difference between a profitable and unprofitable year for a movie studio. The same holds true in the pharmaceutical industry. The more "blockbuster" drugs a pharmaceutical company has, the more money it makes. Like Hollywood studios, pharmaceutical companies have to keep coming up with "blockbusters" in order to sustain profitability and market share. A patent on a drug lasts for 20 years, during which time only the patent holder can sell that drug. Patents on many "old" blockbuster drugs are about to expire, and pharmaceutical companies could lose $140 billion in sales over the next 5 years to generic drug manufacturers, who sell low-cost versions of those same drugs as soon as they're no longer patent protected. How bad is the threat? *MERCK* estimates that its sales of Zocor, a cholesterol reducing drug, dropped 82 percent the first year off of its patent. So, unless they come up with new blockbuster drugs to replace lost sales, pharmaceutical companies will shrink dramatically or go out of business. The problem, however, is that drug companies are struggling to develop new drugs. Eli Lilly's former CEO Sidney Taurel said, "I think the industry is doomed if we don't change."

The question, of course, is how? One area that needs to change is how pharmaceutical companies develop their drugs and their drug pipeline. Because of the need for blockbuster drugs with blockbuster revenues, most pharmaceutical firms have focused on finding treatments for large-market diseases like cancer, heart disease, or depression. Under this approach, company researchers would identify as many different chemical treatments as possible, and then rapidly test them hoping, often through sheer numbers, to discover treatments with potential. Swinging for the fences, however, has led to many strikeouts. For example, Richard Pasternak, Merck's vice president of Cardiovascular Clinical Research, says, "There haven't been any new therapies that are proven to reduce death and disability for atherosclerosis since the introduction of [cholesterol-lowering] statins in the 1980s." Indeed, over the last 5 years, pharmaceutical companies spent $65.2 billion on research and development, but brought 57 percent fewer new drugs to market compared to the previous 5-year period.

NOVARTIS is not immune to the threats to the pharmaceutical industry. Like its competitors, it is struggling to bring new drugs to market. For example, Galvus, its promising diabetes drug, which the company hoped would provide blockbuster sales, failed in late-stage testing. Profits are down 45 percent, by nearly a billion dollars in the last quarter. As a result, the company is eliminating 2,500 jobs, closing research centers in Vienna and Japan, cutting management layers, and restructuring into four divisions. Those are only short-term moves, however. If Novartis is to be successful in the long run, it must find a way to fundamentally change the way it researches new drugs. But, if it doesn't follow the blockbuster model, what should it do instead? Innovation comes from great ideas, so how can Novartis do a better job of managing the sources of innovation within the company?

As a manager at Novartis, you're not happy with the research leadership within the company, particularly in the key labs near headquarters in Basel. You know a change needs to be made, but you're not sure if you should promote a talented person from within or go for an outsider. And, you're not sure if the new leader should have stronger research skills or stronger business skills. Finally, for two decades, pharmaceutical companies have relied on multifunctional teams, comprised of researchers, doctors, market analysts, and managers, to bring new drugs to market. With change and innovation desperately needed, should you continue to use these multifunctional teams?

If you were in charge at Novartis AG, what would you do?

We begin this chapter by reviewing the issues associated with organizational innovation, the problem facing Novartis. **Organizational innovation** is the successful implementation of creative ideas in an organization.[2] **Creativity**, which is a form of organizational innovation, is the production of novel and useful ideas.[3] In the first part of this chapter, you will learn why innovation matters and how to manage innovation to create and sustain a competitive advantage. In the second part, you will learn about **organizational change**, which is a difference in the form, quality, or condition of an organization over time.[4] You will also learn about the risk of not changing and the ways in which companies can manage change.

organizational innovation
the successful implementation of creative ideas in organizations

creativity
the production of novel and useful ideas

organizational change
a difference in the form, quality, or condition of an organization over time

Organizational Innovation

Sometimes the solution to a problem causes another problem. *JERNHUSEN AB*, a Swedish property-administration firm, is building a new 13-story office and retail building near Stockholm's Central Station. How should the company heat it? Problem number two: How should it get rid of excess heat in the train station, generated by the 250,000 people who pass through it every day? As Karl Sundholm, representative of Jernhusen, puts it, "All people produce heat, and that heat is in fact fairly difficult to get rid of. Instead of opening windows and letting all that heat go to waste we want to harness it through the ventilation system."[5] The innovative solution to both problems? Convert the heat in the station to hot water and pump it through the heating system of the new building using pipes that connect the building to the station. Sundholm estimates the system will cost about 300,000 *kronor* ($47,000) to install, and it is likely to reduce energy consumption by 15 percent. Per Berggren, Jernhusen's managing director, notes, "It's more like thinking out of the box, being environmentally smart."[6]

Organizational innovation is the successful implementation of creative ideas, like using the heat generated by train terminal passengers to heat the train terminal.[7]

After reading the next two sections, you should be able to:

1 explain why innovation matters to companies.
2 discuss the different methods that managers can use to effectively manage innovation in their organizations.

1 Why Innovation Matters

When was the last time you used a record player to listen to music, tuned up your car, baked cookies from scratch, or used a dial to change the channel on your TV? Because of product innovations and advances in technology, it's hard to remember, isn't it? We can only guess what changes technological innovations will bring in the next 20 years. Will we carry computers in our pockets? Today's iPhones, Blackberries, and Android phones are a step in that direction. Will solar power and wind power get cheap and efficient enough so that your home has a stand-alone power source off the main electrical grid? And will HDTVs, now the standard, be replaced by lifelike 3-D holographic images (think of R2D2 projecting Princess Leia in *Star Wars*)?[8] Who knows? The only thing we do know about the next 20 years is that innovation will continue to change our lives.

Let's begin our discussion of innovation by learning about 1.1 **technology cycles**, and 1.2 **innovation streams**.

1.1 Technology Cycles

In Chapter 2, you learned that technology consists of the knowledge, tools, and techniques used to transform inputs (raw materials and information) into outputs (products and services). A **technology cycle** begins with the birth of a new technology and ends when that technology reaches its limits and dies as it is replaced by a newer, substantially better technology.[9] For example, technology cycles occurred when air-conditioning supplanted fans, when Henry Ford's Model T replaced horse-drawn carriages, when planes replaced trains as a means of cross-country travel, when vaccines that prevented diseases replaced medicines designed to treat them, and when battery-powered wristwatches replaced mechanically powered, stem-wound wristwatches.

technology cycle
a cycle that begins with the "birth" of a new technology and ends when that technology reaches its limits and is replaced by a newer, substantially better technology

From Gutenberg's invention of the printing press in the 1400s to the rapid advance of the Internet, studies of hundreds of technological innovations have shown that nearly all technology cycles follow the **s-curve pattern of innovation** shown in Exhibit 6.1.[10] Early in a technology cycle, there is still much to learn, so progress is slow, as depicted by point A on the S-curve. The flat slope indicates that

s-curve pattern of innovation
a pattern of technological innovation characterized by slow initial progress, then rapid progress, and then slow progress again as a technology matures and reaches its limits

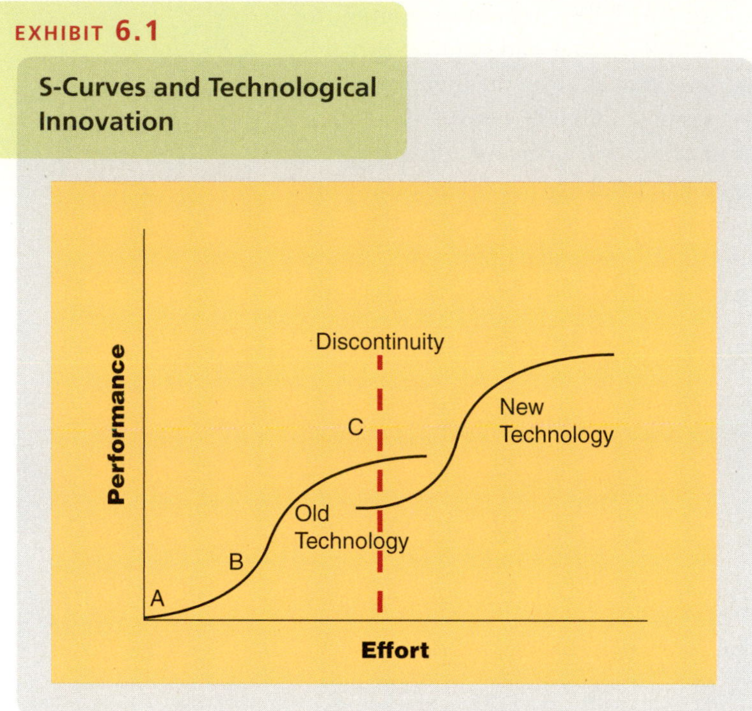

Source: R. N. Foster, *Innovation: The Attacker's Advantage* (New York: Summit, 1986).

increased effort (in terms of money or research and development) brings only small improvements in technological performance.

INTEL'S technology cycles have followed this pattern. Intel spends billions to develop new computer chips and to build new production facilities. Intel has found that the technology cycle for its integrated circuits is about 3 years. In each 3-year cycle, Intel introduces a new chip, improves the chip by making it a little bit faster each year, and then replaces that chip at the end of the cycle with a brand-new, substantially faster chip. At first, though, the billions Intel spends typically produce only small improvements in performance. For instance, Intel's first 60-megahertz (MHz) Pentium processors ran at a speed of 51 based on the iComp Index, as shown in Exhibit 6.2. (The iComp Index is a benchmark test for measuring relative computer speed. For example, a computer with an iComp score of 200 is twice as fast as a computer with an iComp score of 100.) Six months later, Intel's new 75-MHz Pentium was only slightly faster, with an iComp speed of 67.

Fortunately, as the new technology matures, researchers figure out how to get better performance from it. This is represented by point B of the S-curve in Exhibit 6.1. The steeper slope indicates that small amounts of effort will result in significant increases in performance. Again, Intel's technology cycles have followed this pattern. After 6 months to a year with a new chip design, Intel's engineering and production people typically figure out how to make the new chips much faster. Despite slow progress at point A in the first 6 months, Intel soon rolled out 100-MHz, 120-MHz, 133-MHz, 150-MHz, and 166-MHz Pentium chips that, based on the iComp Index, were 76 percent, 96 percent, 117 percent, 124 percent, and 149 percent faster than the original 60-MHz speed (see Exhibit 6.2).

At point C in Exhibit 6.1, the flat slope again indicates that further efforts to develop this particular technology will result in only small increases in performance. More importantly, however, point C indicates that the performance limits of that particular technology are being reached. In other words, additional significant improvements in performance are highly unlikely. Exhibit 6.2 shows that with iComp speeds of 127 and 142, Intel's 166-MHz and 200-MHz Pentiums were 2.49 and 2.78 times as fast as its original 60-MHz Pentiums. Yet, despite these impressive gains in performance, Intel was unable to make its Pentium chips run any faster because the basic design had reached its limits.

After a technology has reached its limits at the top of the S-curve, significant improvements in performance usually come from radical new designs or new performance-enhancing materials. In Exhibit 6.1, that new technology is represented by the second S-curve. The changeover or discontinuity between the old and new technologies is represented by the dotted line. At first, the old and new technologies will likely coexist. Eventually, however, the new technology will replace the old technology. When that happens, the old technology cycle will be complete, and a new one will have started.

The changeover between Intel's Pentium processors, the old technology, and its Pentium II processors, the new technology (despite their similar names, these chips used significantly different technologies), took approximately 1 year. Exhibit 6.2 shows the changeover or discontinuity between the two technologies. With an iComp speed of 267, the first Pentium II (233 MHz) was 88 percent faster than the last Pentium processor. And because their design and performance were significantly different from (and faster than) Pentium II chips, Intel's Pentium III chips represented the beginning of yet another S-curve technology cycle—a 450-MHz Pentium III chip was 21 percent faster than a 450-MHz Pentium II chip. Over time, improving existing technology (tweaking the performance of the current technology cycle), combined with replacing old technology with new technology cycles (the Pentium 4 replacing the Pentium III replacing the Pentium II replacing the Pentium), has increased the speed of Pentium computer processors by a factor of 58 in just 17 years and all computer processors by a factor of 300!

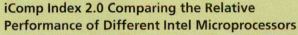

EXHIBIT 6.2

iComp Index 2.0 Comparing the Relative Performance of Different Intel Microprocessors

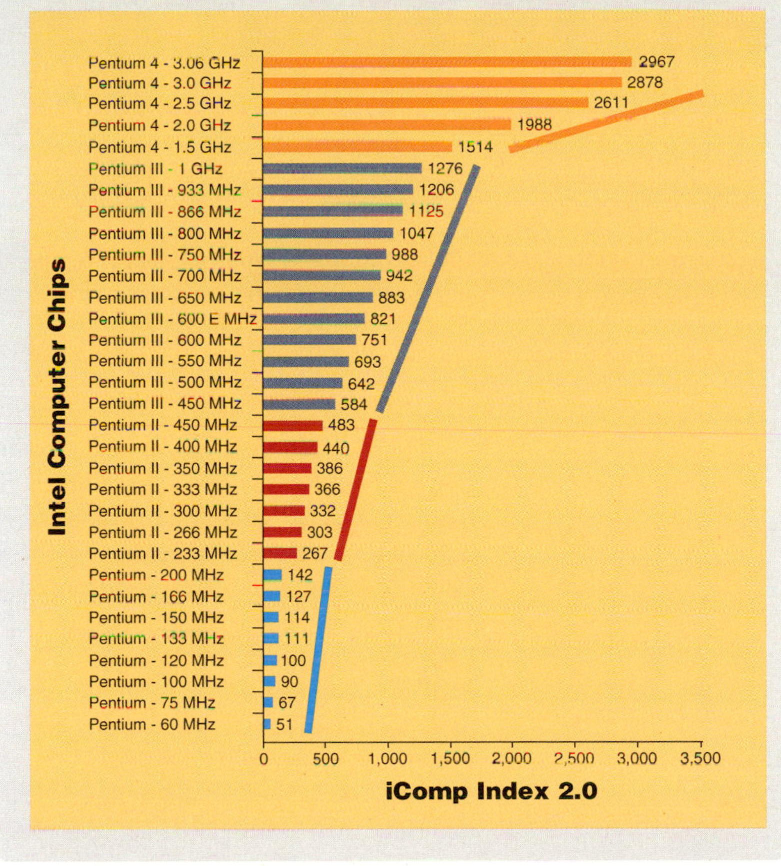

Sources: "Intel iComp (Full List)," Ideas International, available at http://www.ideasinternational.com, 16 May 2002; "Benchmark Resources: iComp Index3.0," Intel, available at http://developer.intel.com, 13 October 2001; "PC CPU Benchmarks, News, Prices and Reviews," *CPU Scorecard*, available at http://www.cpuscorecard.com, 17 March 2003.

Though the evolution of Intel's Pentium chips has been used to illustrate S-curves and technology cycles, it's important to note that technology cycles and technological innovation don't necessarily involve faster computer chips or cleaner-burning automobile engines. Remember, *technology* is simply the knowledge, tools, and techniques used to transform inputs into outputs. So a technology cycle occurs whenever there are major advances or changes in the *knowledge, tools*, and *techniques* of a field or discipline, whatever they may be.

Because US Railcar's DMUs (diesel multiple units) are self-propelled by two built-in diesel engines and can pull up to two other passenger cars, they don't require expensive electrical rail systems or locomotive engines.

For example, most modern cities could benefit from commuter rail transportation systems, but the cost is prohibitive relative to the benefits except in the most highly populated cities, like Boston, New York, or Chicago. Even above-ground light rail systems, which are supposed to be less expensive, cost $5 million a mile. This is why the self-powered rail cars made by *US RAIL CAR* are so innovative. Unlike typical passenger trains that are pulled by a locomotive, US Rail's single-deck (94 passengers) and double-deck (188 passengers) cars are self-propelled by two built-in diesel engines and can pull up to two other passenger cars. As a result, passenger loads are 18 percent higher, fuel costs are half of normal passenger car systems, and pollution is reduced by 72 percent. And, because they are engineered to use existing rail lines, no new rail has to be laid. Furthermore, they're 75 percent less expensive than light rail because the self-propelled cars avoid the cost of electrifying each mile of track to run the system. The only cost is new stations and parking lots. Finally, initial capital outlays are small because cities don't have to buy an entire fleet of locomotives and passenger cars. If initial ridership is light, simply buy one or two self-propelled cars and have them pull one or two passenger cars. As ridership slowly grows, add more self-propelled cars.[11]

So, when you think about technology cycles, don't automatically think "high technology." Instead, broaden your perspective by considering advances or changes in any kind of knowledge, tools, and techniques.

1.2 Innovation Streams

In Chapter 5, you learned that organizations can create *competitive advantage* for themselves if they have a *distinctive competence* that allows them to make, do, or perform something better than their competitors. A competitive advantage becomes sustainable if other companies cannot duplicate the benefits obtained from that distinctive competence. Technological innovation, however, can enable competitors to duplicate the benefits obtained from a company's distinctive advantage. It can also quickly turn a company's competitive advantage into a competitive disadvantage.

EXHIBIT 6.3

Innovation Streams: Technology Cycles over Time

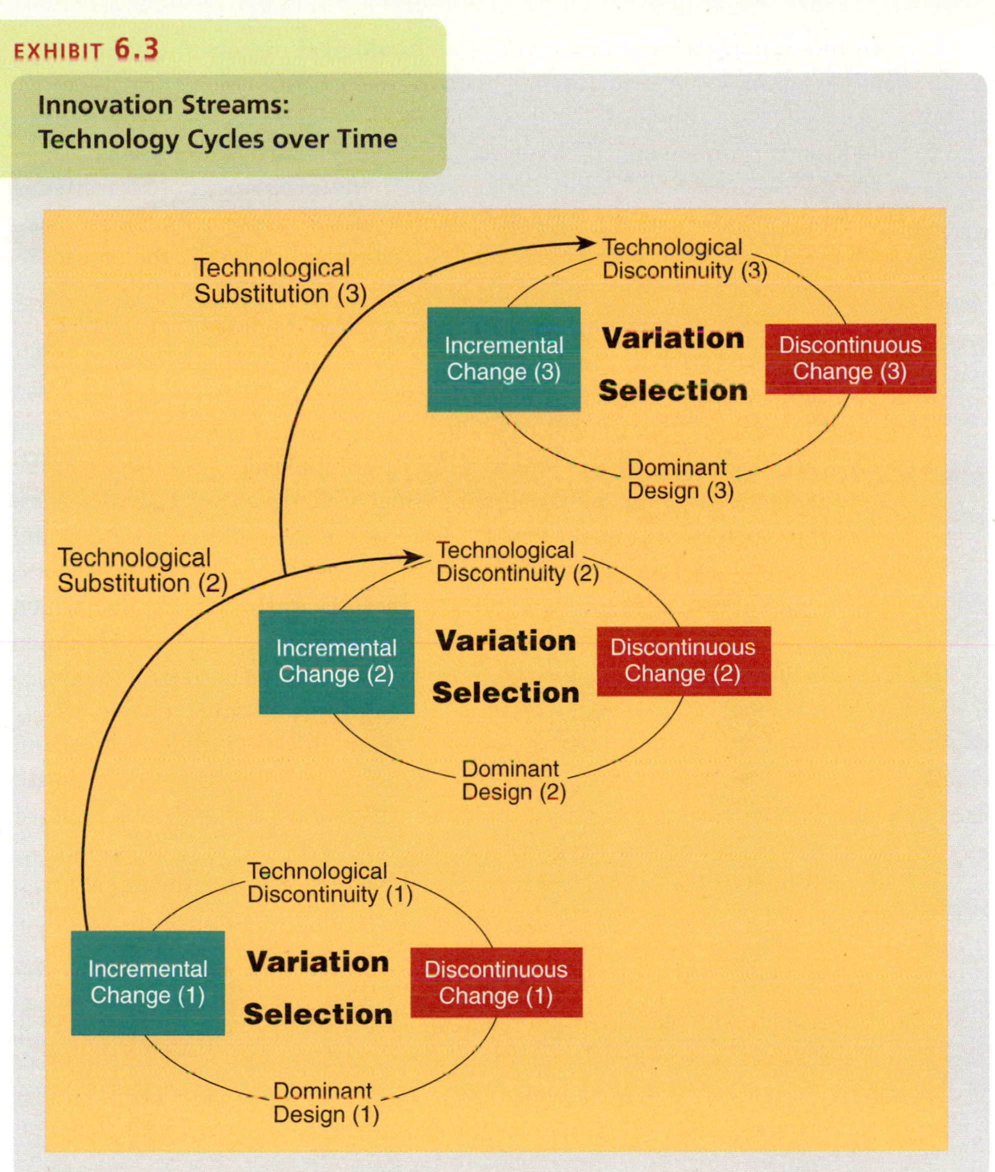

Source: Adapted from M.L. Tushman, P.C. Anderson, & C. Oreilly, "Technology Cycles, Innovation Streams and Ambidextrous Organizations: Organization Renewal Through Innovation Streams and Strategic Change," On *Managing Strategic Innovation and Change*, eds. M.L. Tushman & P. Anderson (1997). 3–23, New Oxford Press (c) by Oxford University Press, Inc. Used by permission of Oxford University Press, Inc.

Companies that want to sustain a competitive advantage must understand and protect themselves from the strategic threats of innovation. Over the long run, the best way for a company to do that is to create a stream of its own innovative ideas and products year after year. Consequently, we define **innovation streams** as patterns of innovation over time that can create sustainable competitive advantage.[12] Exhibit 6.3 shows a typical innovation consisting of a series of technology cycles. Recall that a technology cycle begins with a new technology and ends when it is replaced by a newer, substantially better technology. The innovation stream in Exhibit 6.3 shows three such technology cycles.

innovation streams patterns of innovation over time that can create sustainable competitive advantage

An innovation stream begins with a **technological discontinuity**, in which a scientific advance or a unique combination of existing technologies creates a significant breakthrough in performance or function. For example, minimally invasive techniques are revolutionizing brain surgery. When Douglas Baptist had a golf ball–sized tumor, his surgeon cut a tiny opening through his eyebrow, removed the tumor, and sewed up the opening, leaving practically no trace of the operation. Previously, his skull would have been sawed open. Dr. John Mangiardi, who did the procedure, says, "We used to have to shave off half the head. We don't do that anymore."[13] Today, surgeons use endoscopes (tiny cameras with lights attached to mini surgical tools) and MRI and CT scans (which create 3-D maps of the brain) to remove brain tumors with precision and little physical trauma. Further advances in technology are now being used to remove brain tumors via an endoscope inserted through the patient's nose. Dr. Carl Snyderman, of the University of Pittsburgh Medical Center, says, "We go into the center of a tumor and take it out in small little pieces and take these little pieces out through the nose one at a time."[14] As a result of these advances, the cost and length of hospital stays associated with these surgeries have been cut in half.

Technological discontinuities are followed by a **discontinuous change**, which is characterized by technological substitution and design competition. **Technological substitution** occurs when customers purchase new technologies to replace older technologies. For example, when the telegraph was invented, people used it instead of the Pony Express for cross-country communication. Indeed, telegraph companies were so successful that the Pony Express went out of business almost immediately after the completion of the transcontinental telegraph, which linked telegraph systems from coast to coast.

Discontinuous change is also characterized by **design competition**, in which the old technology and several different new technologies compete to establish a new technological standard. Because of large investments in old technology, and because the new and old technologies are often incompatible with each other, companies and consumers are reluctant to switch to a different technology during a design competition. In addition, during design competition, the older technology usually improves significantly in response to the competitive threat from new technologies; this response also slows the changeover from older to newer technologies.

Discontinuous change is followed by the emergence of a **dominant design**, which becomes the new accepted market standard for technology.[15] Dominant designs emerge in several ways. One is critical mass, meaning that a particular technology can become the dominant design simply because most people use it. This happened in the design competition between Toshiba's HD DVD and Sony's Blu-ray for dominance in establishing a new standard format for high-definition home video. Toshiba lost the design competition because Warner Bros., which had been using both technologies, decided to go exclusively with Blu-ray. At the time of Warner's announcement, Blu-ray held 64 percent of the market, compared to 36 percent for HD DVD.[16] Retailers soon joined Warner Bros. in announcing their intentions to sell only Blu-ray equipment and movies.

The best technology doesn't always become the dominant design because a number of other factors come into play. For instance, a design can become dominant if it solves a practical problem. The QWERTY keyboard (named for the top left line of letters) became the dominant design for typewriters because it slowed

technological discontinuity
the phase of an innovation stream in which a scientific advance or unique combination of existing technologies creates a significant breakthrough in performance or function

discontinuous change
the phase of a technology cycle characterized by technological substitution and design competition

technological substitution
the purchase of new technologies to replace older ones

design competition
competition between old and new technologies to establish a new technological standard or dominant design

dominant design
a new technological design or process that becomes the accepted market standard

typists who, by typing too fast, caused mechanical typewriter keys to jam. Though computers can easily be switched to the DVORAK keyboard layout, which doubles typing speed and cuts typing errors by half, QWERTY lives on as the standard keyboard. In this instance, the QWERTY keyboard solved a problem that, with computers, is no longer relevant. Yet it remains the dominant design not because it is the best technology, but because most people learned to type that way and continue to use it.

Dominant designs can also emerge through independent standards bodies. The International Telecommunication Union (ITU; ***http://www.itu.ch***) is an independent organization that establishes standards for the communications industry. Various standards are proposed, discussed, negotiated, and changed until agreement is reached on a final set of standards that communication industries (Internet, telephony, satellites, radio) will follow worldwide.

No matter how it happens, the emergence of a dominant design is a key event in an innovation stream. First, the emergence of a dominant design indicates that there are winners and losers. Technological innovation is both competence-enhancing and competence-destroying. Companies that bet on the now-dominant design usually prosper. By contrast, when companies bet on the wrong design or the old technology, they may experience **technological lockout**, which occurs when a new dominant design (i.e., a significantly better technology) makes it difficult for a company from competitively selling its products.[17] Second, the emergence of a dominant design signals a shift from design experimentation and competition to **incremental change**, a phase in which companies innovate by lowering the cost and improving the functioning and performance of the dominant design. For example, manufacturing efficiencies enable Intel to cut the cost of its chips by one-half to two-thirds during a technology cycle, while doubling or tripling their speed. This focus on improving the dominant design continues until the next technological discontinuity occurs.

REVIEW 1

Why Innovation Matters

Technology cycles typically follow an S-curve pattern of innovation. Early in the cycle, technological progress is slow and improvements in technological performance are small. As a technology matures, however, performance improves quickly. Finally, as the limits of a technology are reached, only small improvements occur. At this point, significant improvements in performance must come from new technologies.

The best way to protect a competitive advantage is to create a stream of innovative ideas and products. Innovation streams begin with technological discontinuities that create significant breakthroughs in performance or function. Technological discontinuities are followed by discontinuous change, in which customers purchase new technologies (technological substitution) and companies compete to establish the new dominant design (design competition). Dominant designs emerge because of critical mass, because they solve a practical problem, or because of the negotiations of independent standards bodies. Because technological innovation is both competence-enhancing and competence-destroying, companies that bet on the wrong design often struggle (technological lockout), while companies that bet on the eventual dominant

technological lockout the inability of a company to competitively sell its products because it relied on old technology or a nondominant design

incremental change the phase of a technology cycle in which companies innovate by lowering costs and improving the functioning and performance of the dominant technological design

design usually prosper. Emergence of a dominant design leads to a focus on incremental change, lowering costs, and making small, but steady improvements in the dominant design. This focus continues until the next technological discontinuity occurs.

2 Managing Innovation

One consequence of technology cycles and innovation streams is that managers must be equally good at managing innovation in two very different circumstances. First, during discontinuous change, companies must find a way to anticipate and survive the technological changes that can suddenly transform industry leaders into losers and industry unknowns into powerhouses. Companies that can't manage innovation following technological discontinuities risk quick organizational decline and dissolution. Second, after a new dominant design emerges following discontinuous change, companies must manage the very different process of incremental improvement and innovation. Companies that can't manage incremental innovation slowly deteriorate as they fall farther behind industry leaders.

Unfortunately, what works well when managing innovation during discontinuous change doesn't work well when managing innovation during periods of incremental change (and vice versa).

Consequently, to successfully manage innovation streams, companies need to be good at three things: 2.1 **managing sources of innovation**, 2.2 **managing innovation during discontinuous change**, and 2.3 **managing innovation during incremental change**.

2.1 Managing Sources of Innovation

Innovation comes from great ideas. So a starting point for managing innovation is to manage the sources of innovation, that is, where new ideas come from. One place that new ideas originate is with brilliant inventors. Do you know who invented the telephone, the lightbulb, a way to collect and store electricity, air-conditioning, radio, television, automobiles, the jet engine, computers, and the Internet? These innovations were created by Alexander Graham Bell, Thomas Edison, Pieter van Musschenbroek, Willis Carrier, Guglielmo Marconi, John Baird and Philo T. Farnsworth, Gottlieb Daimler and Wilhelm Maybach, Sir Frank Whittle, Charles Babbage, and Vint Cerf and Robert Kahn, respectively. These innovators and their innovations forever changed the course of modern life. But only a few companies have the likes of an Edison, Marconi, or Bell working for them. Given that great thinkers and inventors are in short supply, what might companies do to ensure a steady flow of good ideas?

Well, when we say that innovation begins with great ideas, we're really saying that innovation begins with creativity. As we defined it at the beginning of this chapter, creativity is the production of novel and useful ideas.[18] Although companies can't command employees to be creative ("You *will* be more creative!"), they can jump-start innovation by building **creative work environments** in which workers perceive that creative thoughts and ideas are welcomed and valued. As Exhibit 6.4 shows, creative work environments have six components that encourage creativity: challenging work, organizational encouragement, supervisory encouragement, work group encouragement, freedom, and a lack of organizational impediments.[19]

creative work environments
workplace cultures in which workers perceive that new ideas are welcomed, valued, and encouraged

EXHIBIT 6.4

Components of Creative Work Environments

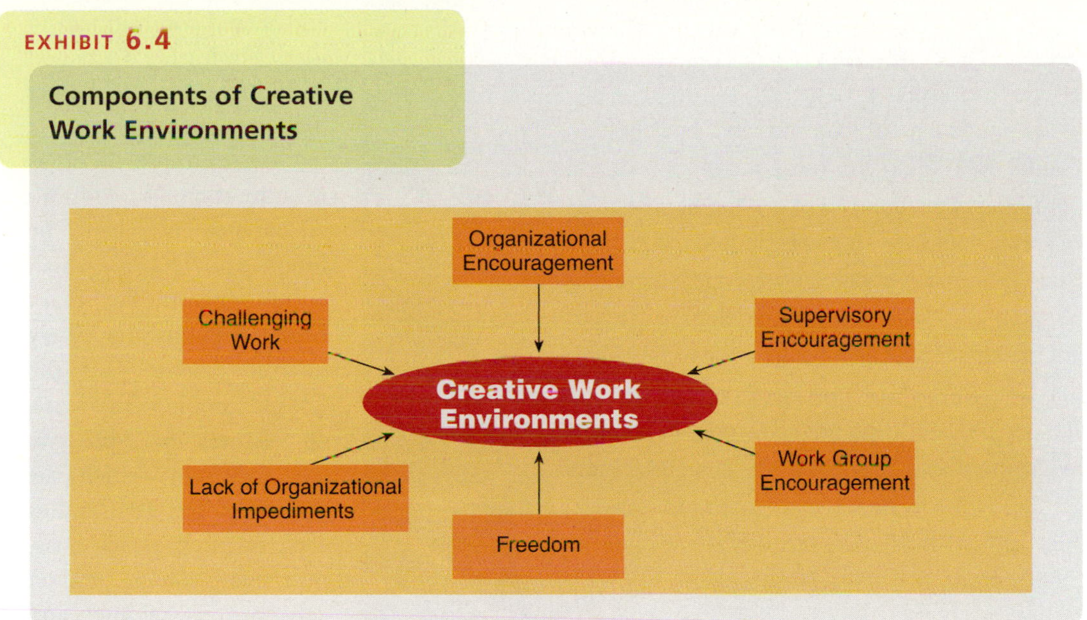

Sources: T. M. Amabile, R. Conti, H. Coon, J. Lazenby, & M. Herron, "Assessing the Work Environment for Creativity," *Academy of Management Journal* 39 (1996): 1154–1184.

Work is *challenging* when it requires effort, demands attention and focus, and is perceived as important to others in the organization. According to researcher Mihaly Csikszentmihalyi (pronounced ME-high-ee CHICK-sent-me-high-ee), challenging work promotes creativity because it creates a rewarding psychological experience known as "flow." **Flow** is a psychological state of effortlessness, in which you become completely absorbed in what you're doing and time seems to fly. When flow occurs, who you are and what you're doing become one. Csikszentmihalyi first encountered flow when studying artists: "What struck me by looking at artists at work was their tremendous focus on the work, this enormous involvement, this forgetting of time and body. It wasn't justified by expectation of rewards, like, 'Aha, I'm going to sell this painting.'"[20] Csikszentmihalyi has found that chess players, rock climbers, dancers, surgeons, and athletes regularly experience flow, too. A key part of creating flow experiences, and thus creative work environments, is to achieve a balance between skills and task challenge. Workers become bored when they can do more than is required of them and anxious when their skills aren't sufficient to accomplish a task. When skills and task challenge are balanced, however, flow and creativity can occur.

A creative work environment requires three kinds of encouragement: organizational, supervisory, and work group encouragement. *Organizational encouragement* of creativity occurs when management encourages risk taking and new ideas, supports and fairly evaluates new ideas, rewards and recognizes creativity, and encourages the sharing of new ideas throughout different parts of the company. *Supervisory encouragement* of creativity occurs when supervisors provide clear goals, encourage open interaction with subordinates, and actively support development teams' work and ideas. *Work group encouragement* occurs when group members have diverse experience, education, and backgrounds and the group fosters mutual openness to ideas; positive, constructive challenge to ideas;

flow
a psychological state of effortlessness, in which you become completely absorbed in what you're doing and time seems to pass quickly

Doing the Right Thing

Give Credit, Don't Take It

You came up with a great idea and ran it by your boss, who loved it. Next thing you know, the office is buzzing about this "next best thing." But instead of giving you the credit, your boss shamelessly sold the idea as his own. Not only is stealing others' ideas wrong, but nothing kills a creative work environment faster than not giving people credit for their ideas. If you're the boss, no matter who comes up with "the" idea, give that person credit. Spread the recognition and acknowledgment around so that their coworkers and your boss's boss know about your employees' great ideas. Do the right thing. Give credit where it's due. You'll be rewarded with more great ideas.[22]

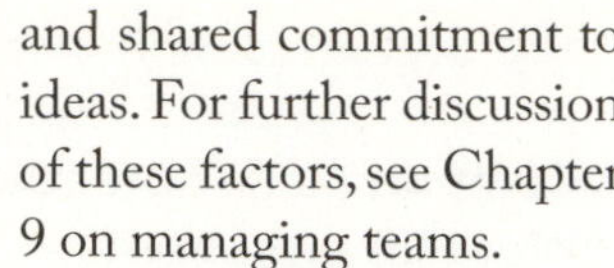

and shared commitment to ideas. For further discussion of these factors, see Chapter 9 on managing teams.

An example of organizational and supervisory encouragement can be found at *ADOBE*, which builds software for business and publishing. Every quarter, Adobe hosts the Idea Champion Showcase, an American Idol-style "ideathon" in which six presenters get 10 minutes each to pitch a new business idea involving product concept, packaging, and technology. Top executives are not invited to the showcase because their cautiousness caused them to "hurl rocks" at new ideas before they have a chance to develop. Rick Bess, an idea mentor at Adobe who developed the showcase, said, "If you had an idea that needed [management approval for] a new sales channel, a new business model, or new packaging, well, good luck. It was hard for ideas to get through the hierarchy."[21] So Bess developed the showcase after an internal study showed that too many roadblocks were being thrown in front of new ideas.

Freedom means having autonomy over one's day-to-day work and a sense of ownership and control over one's ideas. Numerous studies have indicated that creative ideas thrive under conditions of freedom. To foster creativity, companies may also have to *remove impediments* to creativity from their work environments. Internal conflict and power struggles, rigid management structures, and a conservative bias toward the status quo can all discourage creativity. They create the perception that others in the organization will decide which ideas are acceptable and deserve support. *BEST BUY* developed a unique, somewhat risky program called ROWE (results-only work environment). At the company's headquarters in Minneapolis there are no office hours, no set meetings, and no need to come into the office at all—provided you get your work done. Employees are strictly evaluated on output measures that are determined by the management of the company. Since its inception, productivity has risen 35 percent, turnover has dropped dramatically, and employee satisfaction has skyrocketed.

2.2 Experiential Approach: Managing Innovation During Discontinuous Change

A study of 72 product-development projects (i.e., innovation) in 36 computer companies across the United States, Europe, and Asia sheds light on how to manage innovation. Companies that succeeded in periods of discontinuous change (characterized by technological substitution and design competition, as described earlier) typically followed an experiential approach to innovation.[23] The **experiential approach to innovation** assumes that innovation occurs within a highly uncertain environment and that the key to fast product innovation is to use intuition, flexible options, and hands-on experience to reduce uncertainty and accelerate learning and understanding. The experiential approach to innovation has five aspects: design iterations, testing, milestones, multifunctional teams, and powerful leaders.[24]

An iteration is a repetition. So a **design iteration** is a cycle of repetition in which a company tests a prototype of a new product or service, improves on the design, and then builds and tests the improved product or service prototype. A **product prototype** is a full-scale working model that is tested for design, function, and reliability. **Testing** is a systematic comparison of different product designs or design iterations. Companies that want to create a new dominant design following a technological discontinuity quickly build, test, improve, and retest a series of different product prototypes. *RICKSTER POWELL* has jumped from an airplane 20,000 times in order to test parachute designs for sporting and military uses.[25] Powell explains how it works: "When . . . the chief parachute designer . . . comes up with a new design and we're going to test it for the first time [and are] not sure whether it will fly or not, I put on a skydiving rig which is composed of an emergency backup parachute as well as a main parachute, and then the parachute to be tested will go on the front. So that's in case there's a real problem with it, [such as] it doesn't fly, [or] it's unstable, then I can get rid of that parachute and still be in a normal skydiving situation with a main parachute and a reserve parachute."[26] He and a partner strap cameras to their bodies to film the chute's deployment, which enables the manufacturers to look for problems. Not all of the parachute design iterations end up working as planned. In fact, only 9 out of 50 designs he's tested have actually been produced.

By trying a number of very different designs or making successive improvements and changes in the same design, frequent design iterations reduce uncertainty and improve understanding. Simply put, the more prototypes you build, the more likely you are to learn what works and what doesn't. Also, when designers and engineers build a number of prototypes, they are less likely to fall in love with a particular prototype. Instead, they'll be more concerned with improving the product or technology as much as they can. Testing speeds up and improves the innovation process, too. When two very different design prototypes are tested against each other, or the new design iteration is tested against the previous iteration, product design strengths and weaknesses quickly become apparent. Likewise, testing uncovers errors early in the design process when they are easiest to correct. Finally, testing accelerates learning and understanding by forcing engineers and product designers to examine hard data about product performance. When there's hard evidence that prototypes are testing well, the confidence of the design team grows. Also, personal conflict between design team members is less likely when testing focuses on hard measurements and facts rather than personal hunches and preferences.

Milestones are formal project review points used to assess progress and performance. For example, a company that has put itself on a 12-month schedule to complete a project might schedule milestones at the 3-month, 6-month, and 9-month points on the schedule. By making people regularly assess what they're doing, how well they're performing, and whether they need to take corrective action, milestones

experiential approach to innovation
an approach to innovation that assumes a highly uncertain environment and uses intuition, flexible options, and hands-on experience to reduce uncertainty and accelerate learning and understanding

design iteration
a cycle of repetition in which a company tests a prototype of a new product or service, improves on that design, and then builds and tests the improved prototype

product prototype
a full-scale working model that is being tested for design, function, and reliability

testing
the systematic comparison of different product designs or design iterations

milestones
formal project review points used to assess progress and performance

provide structure to the general chaos that follows technological discontinuities. Milestones also shorten the innovation process by creating a sense of urgency that keeps everyone on task. When Florida Power & Light was building its first nuclear power facility, the company's construction manager passed out 2,000 desk calendars to company employees, construction contractors, vendors, and suppliers to ensure that everyone involved in the project was aware of the construction timeline. Contractors that regularly missed deadlines were replaced.[27] Finally, milestones are beneficial for innovation because meeting regular milestones builds momentum by giving people a sense of accomplishment.

Multifunctional teams are work teams composed of people from different departments. Multifunctional teams accelerate learning and understanding by mixing and integrating technical, marketing, and manufacturing activities. By involving all key departments in development from the start, multifunctional teams speed innovation through early identification of new ideas or problems that would typically not have been generated or addressed until much later.

At Ford, researchers, who dream up and test ideas, and product engineers, who find ways to get them to work, usually work in separate buildings. But to design the hybrid Escape, they worked side by side in cubicles for over 3 years. Team member Tom Gee says, "Before, it might have been a half mile apart, but even one building away is a barrier compared with what we have now. It makes a huge difference."[28]

Powerful leaders provide the vision, discipline, and motivation to keep the innovation process focused, on time, and on target. Powerful leaders are able to get resources when they are needed, are typically more experienced, have high status in the company, and are held directly responsible for the products' success or failure. On average, powerful leaders can get innovation-related projects done 9 months faster than leaders with little power or influence.

2.3 Compression Approach: Managing Innovation During Incremental Change

Whereas the experiential approach is used to manage innovation in highly uncertain environments during periods of discontinuous change, the compression approach is used to manage innovation in more certain environments during periods of incremental change. Whereas the goals of the experiential approach are significant improvements in performance and the establishment of a *new* dominant design, the goals of the compression approach are lower costs and incremental improvements in the performance and function of the *existing* dominant design.

The general strategies in each approach are different, too. With the experiential approach, the general strategy is to build something new, different, and substantially better. Because there's so much uncertainty—no one knows which technology will become the market leader—companies adopt a winner-take-all approach by trying to create the market-leading, dominant design. With the compression approach, the general strategy is to compress the time and steps needed to bring about small, consistent improvements in performance and functionality. Because a dominant technology design already exists, the general strategy is to continue improving the existing technology as rapidly as possible.

In short, a **compression approach to innovation** assumes that innovation is a predictable process, that incremental innovation can be planned using a series of steps, and that compressing the time it takes to complete those steps can speed up innovation.

multifunctional teams
work teams composed of people from different departments

compression approach to innovation
an approach to innovation that assumes that incremental innovation can be planned using a series of steps and that compressing those steps can speed innovation

Management Trend:

Everyone is looking for a clean, sustainable energy source. How about the human body? Researchers at Texas A&M University developed a method of powering cell phones with the human voice. It uses a device that is 5,000 times thinner than a human hair that produces electricity from voice vibrations. Engineers in Toulouse, France, have literally taken things one step further by installing power-generating modules into sidewalks. Every time pedestrians walk over these modules, a small amount of electricity is generated from the vibrations, enough to power the streetlamps along the sidewalk.

Sources: Adam Aston. "Your Motormouth May Power Your Mobile." *BusinessWeek*. January 12, 2009. 50.

Lizzy Davies. "Pavement Power Lights Up Toulouse." *guardian.co.uk*. April 13, 2010. Accessed at http://www.guardian.co.uk/world/2010/apr/13/pavement-power-toulouse-streets

The compression approach to innovation has five aspects: planning, supplier involvement, shortening the time of individual steps, overlapping steps, and multifunctional teams.[29]

In Chapter 4, *planning* was defined as choosing a goal and a method or strategy to achieve that goal. When *planning for incremental innovation*, the goal is to squeeze or compress development time as much as possible, and the general strategy is to create a series of planned steps to accomplish that goal. Planning for incremental innovation helps avoid unnecessary steps and enables developers to sequence steps in the right order to avoid wasted time and delays between steps. Planning also reduces misunderstandings and improves coordination.

Most planning for incremental innovation is based on the idea of generational change. **Generational change** occurs when incremental improvements are made to a dominant technological design such that the improved version of the technology is fully backward compatible with the older version.[30] Software is backward compatible if a new version of the software will work with files created by older versions. One of the expected and important features of gaming machines like PlayStation 3, Xbox 360, and the Nintendo Wii is their ability to play games purchased for earlier machines. In fact, the latest Game Boy can play games released more than 20 years ago. By contrast, when developing its PlayStation 3 (PS3), Sony decided to reduce the game machine's backward compatibility with its predecessor, the PlayStation 2 (PS2), because of production costs.

Because the compression approach assumes that innovation can follow a series of preplanned steps, one of the ways to shorten development time is *supplier involvement*. Delegating some of the preplanned steps in the innovation process to outside suppliers reduces the amount of work that internal development teams must do. Plus, suppliers provide an alternative source of ideas and expertise that can lead to better designs. *ROWMARK* produces thin plastic sheets that can be engraved or shaped by a thermoforming process. In an effort to improve the performance of its product, lower raw material costs, and avoid supply disruptions, it recruits the companies who supply its resin and additives to participate in the product design and manufacturing processes.

Another way to shorten development time is simply to *shorten the time of individual steps* in the innovation process. A common way to do that is through computer-aided design (CAD). CAD speeds up the design process by allowing

generational change change based on incremental improvements to a dominant technological design such that the improved technology is fully backward compatible with the older technology

designers and engineers to make and test design changes using computer models rather than physically testing expensive prototypes. CAD also speeds innovation by making it easy to see how design changes affect engineering, purchasing, and production. Karenann Terrell, director of e-business strategy at Chrysler, explains how the company's CAD system, FASTCAR, works: "FastCar takes a virtual CAD/CAM design and teams it with all the other information that we already have on hand about the part or vehicle. So, no longer do we change a part and then ask: 'How much do those new components cost? What are the quality implications?' As we make changes, all that information is integrated into the new designs."[31]

In a sequential design process, each step must be completed before the next step begins. But sometimes multiple development steps can be performed at the same time. *Overlapping steps* shorten the development process by reducing delays or waiting time between steps. For example, Warner Bros. is using overlapping steps to reduce the time it will take to make the entire series of seven *Harry Potter* films—one for each of the seven books in J. K. Rowling's series chronicling the seven years the title character spends at Hogwarts School of Witchcraft and Wizardry. Unfortunately, it was taking Warner Bros. more than 2 years to write, shoot, and produce each movie. All the actors were aging and would soon resemble adults more than high school students. So Warner Bros. decided to use new directors and new production teams for each of the movies in the *Harry Potter* series. That way, the company could begin shooting the next film while the previous one was in postproduction and the one prior to that was in the theaters. While *Harry Potter and the Half Blood Prince* was released in July 2009, the seventh book, *Harry Potter and the Deathly Hallows*, was already in production so that it could be released in two parts, the first in 2010 and the second in 2011.[32] Without this effort, young Harry Potter might have been in his early 30s by the time of the seventh and final movie.[33]

REVIEW 2

Managing Innovation

To successfully manage innovation streams, companies must manage the sources of innovation and learn to manage innovation during both discontinuous and incremental change. Since innovation begins with creativity, companies can manage the sources of innovation by supporting a creative work environment in which creative thoughts and ideas are encouraged. Creative work environments provide challenging work; offer organizational, supervisory, and work group encouragement; allow significant freedom; and remove organizational impediments to creativity.

Companies that succeed in periods of discontinuous change typically follow an experiential approach to innovation. The experiential approach assumes that intuition, flexible options, and hands-on experience can reduce uncertainty and accelerate learning and understanding. This approach involves frequent design iterations, frequent testing, regular milestones, creation of multifunctional teams, and use of powerful leaders to guide the innovation process. A compression approach to innovation works best during periods of incremental change. This approach assumes that innovation can be planned using a series of steps and that compressing the time it takes to complete those steps can speed up innovation. The five aspects of the compression approach are planning (generational change), supplier involvement, shortening the time of individual steps (computer-aided design), overlapping steps, and multifunctional teams.

Organizational Change

Four years ago, *EMI*, the fourth-largest music publisher in the world, invited some of its teenage customers to its London headquarter to talk to managers about their music preferences. At the end of the discussion, the EMI managers thanked them by telling them to please take whatever CDs they wanted from a nearby table. But, even though they were free, not one CD was taken. That, said someone from EMI, "Was the moment we realized the game was completely up."[34] While CD sales still account for over 85 percent of music sales in the United States, those sales are dropping sharply, from 449.2 million CDs in 2007 to 360.6 million CDs in 2008, the last years for which full data were available. Similar declines occurred in Britain, Japan, France, Spain, Italy, Australia, and Canada.[35] The decline in CD sales will be incredibly difficult for music companies to overcome. With CD sales down, retailers like Wal-Mart are now dedicating 30 percent less floor space to CDs. Publishers like EMI, which are losing hundreds of millions of dollars each year, no longer have the marketing budgets and resources to publicize bands and their music. Finally, advances in recording and publishing technology have made it easy for major artists like Madonna, the Eagles, or Radiohead to sell or release their music directly to consumers without record companies.[36]

It's no surprise the music companies are struggling. CD sales have been declining ever since Naptser made it possible to download digital music without paying for it, and even more since iTunes made it possible to download one song at a time for just 99 cents. Yet the music companies have been unable to change their business quickly enough to stop the bleeding. Indeed, all businesses operate in a constantly changing environment. Recognizing and adapting to internal and external changes can mean the difference between continued success and going out of business. Companies that fail to change run the risk of **organizational decline**. Music companies' inability to change may eventually lead to their demise.

After reading the next section, you should be able to:

3 discuss the different methods that managers can use to better manage change as it occurs.

organizational decline
a large decrease in organizational performance that occurs when companies don't anticipate, recognize, neutralize, or adapt to the internal or external pressures that threaten their survival

3 Managing Change

According to social psychologist Kurt Lewin, change is a function of the forces that promote change and the opposing forces that slow or resist change.[37] **Change forces** lead to differences in the form, quality, or condition of an organization over time. By contrast, **resistance forces** support the status quo, that is, the existing conditions in an organization. Change is difficult under any circumstances. In a study of heart bypass patients, doctors told participants straightforwardly to change their eating and health habits or they would die. Unbelievably, a full 90 percent of participants did *not* change their habits at all![38] This fierce resistance to change also applies to organizations.

change forces
forces that produce differences in the form, quality, or condition of an organization over time

resistance forces
forces that support the existing state of conditions in organizations

Resistance to change is caused by self-interest, misunderstanding and distrust, and a general intolerance for change.[39] People resist change out of *self-interest* because they fear that change will cost or deprive them of something they value. For example, resistance might stem from a fear that changes in the workplace will result in a loss of pay, power, responsibility, or even perhaps one's job. People also resist change because of *misunderstanding and distrust*; they don't understand the change or the reasons for

resistance to change
opposition to change resulting from self-interest, misunderstanding and distrust, or a general intolerance for change

it, or they distrust the people—typically management—behind the change. Resistance isn't always visible at first. In fact, some of the strongest resisters may initially support the changes in public, nodding and smiling their agreement, but then ignore the changes in private and do their jobs as they always have. Management consultant Michael Hammer calls this deadly form of resistance the "Kiss of Yes."[40]

Resistance may also come from a generally low tolerance for change. Some people are simply less capable of handling change than others. People with a *low tolerance for change* feel threatened by the uncertainty associated with change and worry that they won't be able to learn the new skills and behaviors needed to successfully negotiate change in their companies.

Because resistance to change is inevitable, successful change efforts require careful management. In this section, you will learn about 3.1 **managing resistance to change**, 3.2 **what not to do when leading organizational change**, and 3.3 **different change tools and techniques**.

3.1 Managing Resistance to Change

According to Kurt Lewin, managing organizational change is a basic process of unfreezing, change intervention, and refreezing. **Unfreezing** is getting the people affected by change to believe that change is needed. During the **change intervention** itself, workers and managers change their behavior and work practices. **Refreezing** is supporting and reinforcing the new changes so that they stick.

Resistance to change is an example of frozen behavior. Given the choice between changing and not changing, most people would rather not change. Because resistance to change is natural and inevitable, managers need to unfreeze resistance to change to create successful change programs. The following methods can be used to manage resistance to change: education and communication, participation, negotiation, top-management support, and coercion.[41]

When resistance to change is based on insufficient, incorrect, or misleading information, managers should *educate* employees about the need for change and *communicate* change-related information to them. Managers must also supply the information and funding or other support employees need to make changes. For example, resistance to change can be particularly strong when one company buys another company. This is because one company in the merger usually has a higher status due to its size, or higher profitability, or the fact that it is the acquiring company. These status differences are important to managers and employees, particularly if they're in the lower-status company, because they may worry about retaining their jobs or influence after the merger. That fear or concern can greatly increase resistance to change.[42] To avoid such a scenario, *NEW YORK–PRESBYTERIAN HEALTHCARE SYSTEM* reduced resistance to change by designating mentors to coach individuals, groups, and departments in newly acquired companies about its procedures and practices. New York–Presbyterian's Diane Iorfida said at the time, "Keeping employees informed every step of the way is so important. It's also important to tell the truth, whatever you do."

Another way to reduce resistance to change is to have those affected by the change *participate in planning and implementing the change process*. Employees who participate have a better understanding of the change and the need for it. Furthermore, employee concerns about change can be addressed as they occur if employees participate in the planning and implementation process. *THE SAN DIEGO ZOO*

unfreezing
getting the people affected by change to believe that change is needed

change intervention
the process used to get workers and managers to change their behavior and work practices

refreezing
supporting and reinforcing new changes so that they "stick"

AND WILD ANIMAL PARK took innovative steps in order to reposition itself as a leader in conservation. A core element of the planning was input from the zoo's staff, as the strategy team invited employees from all departments to provide insights on what they felt the zoo did well and what it could do better. Through this process, the zoo enacted a plan that would highlight its internal resources and capabilities through an expansion of its consulting business, the use of facilities to display sustainable technology and products, and hosting events that would highlight the knowledge of zoo scientists.[43]

Employees are also less likely to resist change if they are allowed *to discuss and agree on who will do what* after change occurs. When Best Buy, the electronics superstore chain, started ***http://www.blueshirtnation.com***—its retail associates all wear short-sleeved blue shirts—it was simply trying to get employees to share good advertising ideas. But Steve Bendt, who helped start the website, said, "We found out real fast that employees didn't want to play that game. Instead, they gave us new rules and told us what they wanted on the site and at the company. We shut up pretty quickly and realized we needed to just listen."[44] What happened on the website is that the employees who were into photography communicated and shared ideas, as did those who were into computers, home networking, video games, or high-definition TVs and entertainment systems. And, because they, not management, controlled the conversations, they began discussing how to solve store problems. For example, after an employee put together a floor display case for a digital camera that was much too large, he posted a picture to see if other stores had the same problem. When others agreed it was an issue, display designers at headquarters realized their mistake and sent out a smaller display. Similar discussions in which employees complained that not having Best Buy e-mail accounts made it difficult for them to communicate with each other or follow up with customers led the company to give all full-time employees company e-mail accounts.

Resistance to change also decreases when change efforts receive *significant managerial support*. Managers must do more than talk about the importance of change, though. They must provide the training, resources, and autonomy needed to make change happen. For example, animators at *WALT DISNEY*, who traditionally drew their films by hand, were concerned that computer-generated animation (CG) would render their art and talents obsolete. Disney supported the difficult change by putting all of its animators through a 6-month "CG Boot Camp," where they learned how to "draw" animated characters with computers.[45]

Finally, resistance to change can be managed through **coercion**, or the use of formal power and authority to force others to change. Because of the intense negative reactions it can create (e.g., fear, stress, resentment, sabotage of company products), coercion should be used only when a crisis exists or when all other attempts to reduce resistance to change have failed. Exhibit 6.5 summarizes some additional suggestions for what managers can do when employees resist change.

3.2 What Not to Do When Leading Change

So far, you've learned about the basic change process (unfreezing, change, refreezing) and managing resistance to change. Harvard Business School professor John Kotter argues that knowing what *not* to do is just as important as knowing what to do when it comes to achieving successful organizational change.[46]

coercion
the use of formal power and authority to force others to change

EXHIBIT 6.5

What to Do When Employees Resist Change

UNFREEZING	
• Share reasons	Share the reasons for change with employees.
• Empathize	Be empathetic to the difficulties that change will create for managers and employees.
• Communicate	Communicate the details simply, clearly, extensively, verbally, and in writing.
CHANGE	
• Explain benefits	Explain the benefits, "what's in it for them."
• Champion	Identify a highly respected manager to manage the change effort.
• Seek input	Allow the people who will be affected by change to express their needs and offer their input.
• Choose timing	Don't begin change at a bad time, for example, during the busiest part of the year or month.
• Maintain security	If possible, maintain employees' job security to minimize fear of change.
• Offer training	Offer training to ensure that employees are both confident and competent to handle new requirements.
• Pace yourself	Change at a manageable pace. Don't rush.

Source: G. J. Iskat & J. Liebowitz, "What to Do When Employees Resist Change," *Supervision*, 1 August 1996.

Exhibit 6.6 shows the most common errors that managers make when they lead change. The first two errors occur during the unfreezing phase, when managers try to get the people affected by change to believe that change is really needed. The first and potentially most serious error is *not establishing a great enough sense of urgency*. Indeed, Kotter estimates that more than half of all change efforts fail because the people affected are not convinced that change is necessary. People will feel a greater sense of urgency if a leader in the company makes a public, candid assessment of the company's problems and weaknesses. *CELESTICA, INC.*, located in Toronto, Canada, is an electronics manufacturing services company that produces complex printed circuit assemblies for use in PC motherboards, networking cards, flat-screen TVs, and Xbox video game systems. When Craig Muhlhauser took over as president and CEO, Celestica, Inc., was losing money and market share. Muhlhauser went to work right away. He informed employees that the company couldn't survive if it didn't change. Within his first 30 days as CEO, he reduced staff by 35 percent, moved new people into important positions, and had everyone in the company's attention.[47]

The second mistake that occurs in the unfreezing process is *not creating a powerful enough coalition*. Change often starts with one or two people, but it has to be supported by a critical and growing group of people if an entire department, division, or company is to be affected. Besides top management, Kotter recommends that key employees, managers, board members, customers, and even union leaders be members of a *core change coalition* that guides and supports organizational change. "In a turnaround, there are three kinds of employees," said Celestica's CEO Craig Muhlhauser—those on your side, those on the fence, and those who will never buy in. The latter have to be let go and those on the fence should be persuaded to contribute or leave. Says Muhlhauser, "We have to make change, change is difficult and as we make change, it is important to realize that there are people who are going to resist that change. In talking to those people, the objective is to move everybody into the column of supporters. But that is probably unachievable."[48] It's also important to strengthen this core change coalition's resolve by periodically bringing its members together for off-site retreats.

EXHIBIT 6.6

Errors Managers Make When Leading Change

UNFREEZING	
1.	Not establishing a great enough sense of urgency.
2.	Not creating a powerful enough guiding coalition.
CHANGE	
3.	Lacking a vision.
4.	Undercommunicating the vision by a factor of 10.
5.	Not removing obstacles to the new vision.
6.	Not systematically planning for and creating short-term wins.
REFREEZING	
7.	Declaring victory too soon.
8.	Not anchoring changes in the corporation's culture.

Source: J. P. Kotter, "Leading Change: Why Transformation Efforts Fail," *Harvard Business Review* 73, no. 2 (March–April 1995): 59.

The next four errors that managers make occur during the change phase, when a change intervention is used to try to get workers and managers to change their behavior and work practices. *Lacking a vision* for change is a significant error at this point. A *vision* (defined as a *purpose statement* in Chapter 4) is a statement of a company's purpose or reason for existence. A vision for change makes clear where a company or department is headed and why the change is occurring. Change efforts that lack vision tend to be confused, chaotic, and contradictory. By contrast, change efforts guided by visions are clear and easy to understand and can be explained in 5 minutes or less.

Undercommunicating the vision by a factor of 10 is another mistake in the change phase. According to Kotter, companies mistakenly hold just one meeting to announce the vision. Or, if the new vision receives heavy emphasis in executive speeches or company newsletters, senior management undercuts the vision by behaving in ways contrary to it. Successful communication of the vision requires that top managers link everything the company does to the new vision and that they "walk the talk" by behaving in ways consistent with the vision. Furthermore, even companies that begin change with a clear vision sometimes make the mistake of *not removing obstacles to the new vision*. They leave formidable barriers to change in place by failing to redesign jobs, pay plans, and technology to support the new way of doing things. One of Celestica's key obstacles was efficiently and effectively managing a complex supply chain network. CEO Craig Muhlhauser and his management team reduced shipping speeds and kept costs low by implementing Liveshare, an information system that gave it and its suppliers real-time data on sales, production, inventory, and shipping for all of its products. With Liveshare, it can see live, up-to-date numbers indicating how many video games are rolling off Celestica's production lines or are now on trucks in route to Best Buy trucking depots.[49]

Another error in the change phase is *not systematically planning for and creating short-term wins*. Most people don't have the discipline and patience to wait 2 years to see if the new change effort works. Change is threatening and uncomfortable, so people need to see an immediate payoff if they are to continue to support it. Kotter recommends that managers create short-term wins by actively picking people and projects that are likely to work extremely well early in the change process. Celestica's Craig Muhlhauser understood the important of short-term wins. Said Muhlhauser, "My approach was to look at the first 30 days, then at the first 3 months, then at the first 12 months and then I took a look at the 3 years. In a turnaround, you have to take hold very quickly. You have to show relatively quick hits [i.e., short-term wins] to show your turnaround strategy is working—and then you deal with a multitude of issues in a very focused way that will allow you to continue to show improvement."[50]

The last two errors that managers make occur during the refreezing phase, when attempts are made to support and reinforce changes so that they stick. *Declaring victory too soon* is a tempting mistake in the refreezing phase. Managers typically declare victory right after the first large-scale success in the change process. Declaring success too early has the same effect as draining the gasoline out of a car: It stops change efforts dead in their tracks. With success declared, supporters of the change process stop pushing to make change happen. After all, why push when success has been achieved? Rather than declaring victory, managers should use the momentum from short-term wins to push for even bigger or faster changes. This maintains urgency and prevents change supporters from slacking off before the changes are frozen into the company's culture.

The last mistake that managers make is *not anchoring changes in the organization's culture*. An *organization's culture* is the set of key values, beliefs, and attitudes shared by organizational members that determines the accepted way of doing things in a company. As you learned in Chapter 2, changing cultures is extremely difficult and time-consuming. According to Kotter, two things help anchor changes in a corporation's culture. The first is showing people directly that changes have actually improved performance. At Celestica, this was demonstrated by the quick increase in quarterly profits, which led to a 60 percent increase in its stock price.[51] The second is to make sure that the people who get promoted fit the new culture. If they don't, it's a clear sign that the changes were only temporary. To anchor this change, Muhlhauser created a culture of meritocracy that rewarded managers and employees for their contributions. The rewards came in the form of promotions, pay increases, and huge bonuses. Customer satisfaction has improved. With the increasing demand for consumer products, such as smart phones, employees are excited about the prospects for Celestica. "We've got some new programs in the pipeline so we're optimistic about our ability to compete in and win in that market," said CEO Craig Muhlhauser.[52]

3.3 Change Tools and Techniques

Imagine that your boss came to you and said, "All right, genius, you wanted it. You're in charge of turning around the division." Where would you begin? How would you encourage change-resistant managers to change? What would you do to include others in the change process? How would you get the change process off to a quick start? Finally, what approach would you use to promote long-term effectiveness and performance? Results-driven change, the General Electric workout, transition management teams, and organizational development are different change tools and techniques that can be used to address these issues.

One of the reasons that organizational change efforts fail is that they are activity-oriented rather than results-oriented. In other words, they focus primarily on changing company procedures, management philosophy, or employee behavior. Typically, there is much buildup and preparation as consultants are brought in, presentations are made, books are read, and employees and managers are trained. There's a tremendous emphasis on doing things the new way. But, with all the focus on "doing," almost no attention is paid to *results*, to seeing if all this activity has actually made a difference.

By contrast, **results-driven change** supplants the emphasis on activity with a laserlike focus on quickly measuring and improving results.[53] Top managers at *HYUNDAI* knew that if they were to compete successfully against the likes of Honda and Toyota, they would have to substantially improve the quality of their cars. So top managers guided the company's results-driven change process by first increasing the number of quality teams from 100 to 865. Then, all employees were required to attend seminars on quality improvement and use the results of industry quality studies, like those published annually by J. D. Power and Associates, as their benchmark. Hyundai then measured the effects of the focus on quality. Before the change, a new Hyundai averaged 23.4 initial quality problems; after the results-driven change efforts, that number dropped to 9.6.[54] Today, Hyundai ranks fourth, according to J. D. Power, in initial car quality behind luxury brands Lexus, Porsche, and Cadillac.[55]

An advantage of results-driven change is that quick, visible improvements motivate employees to continue to make additional changes to improve measured performance. A few years into Hyundai's change process, Chrysler and Mitsubishi Motors announced that they would use Hyundai-designed four-cylinder engines in their small and mid-sized cars, reinforcing that all the changes Hyundai had made to the way it measured and improved car quality had been worth the effort.[56] As at Hyundai, quick successes associated with results-driven change can be particularly effective at reducing resistance to change. Exhibit 6.7 describes the basic steps of results-driven change.

The **General Electric workout** is a special kind of results-driven change. The "workout" involves a 3-day meeting that brings together managers and employees from different levels of an organization to generate quickly and act on solutions to specific business problems.[57] On the first morning, the boss discusses the agenda and targets specific business problems that the group will solve. Then, the boss leaves and an outside facilitator breaks the group (typically 30 to 40 people) into five or six teams and helps them spend the next day and a half discussing and debating solutions.

On day three, in what GE calls a "town meeting," the teams present solutions to their boss, who has been gone since day one. As each team's spokesperson makes specific suggestions, the boss has only three options: agree on the spot, say no, or ask for more information so that a decision can be made by an agreed-on date. GE boss Armand Lauzon sweated his way through a town meeting. To encourage him to say yes, his workers set up the meeting room to put pressure on Lauzon. He says, "I was wringing wet within half an hour. They had 108 proposals, I had about a minute to say yes or no to each one, and I couldn't make eye contact with my boss without turning around, which would show everyone in the room that I was chicken."[58] In the end, Lauzon agreed to all but eight suggestions. Furthermore, once those decisions were made, no one at GE was allowed to overrule them.

results-driven change change created quickly by focusing on the measurement and improvement of results

General Electric workout a three-day meeting in which managers and employees from different levels and parts of an organization quickly generate and act on solutions to specific business problems

EXHIBIT 6.7

Results-Driven Change Programs

- Management should create measurable, short-term goals to improve performance.
- Management should use action steps only if they are likely to improve measured performance.
- Management should stress the importance of immediate improvements.
- Consultants and staffers should help managers and employees achieve quick improvements in performance.
- Managers and employees should test action steps to see if they actually yield improvements. Action steps that don't should be discarded.
- It takes few resources to get results-driven change started.

Source: R. H. Schaffer & H. A. Thomson, J.D, "Successful Change Programs Begin with Results," *Harvard Business Review on Change* (Boston: Harvard Business School Press, 1998): 189–213.

While the GE workout clearly speeds up change, it may also fragment change if different managers approve conflicting suggestions in separate town meetings across a company. By contrast, a transition management team provides a way to coordinate change throughout an organization. A **transition management team (TMT)** is a group of 8 to 12 people whose full-time job is to manage and coordinate a company's change process.[59] One member of the TMT is assigned to anticipate and manage the emotions and behaviors related to resistance to change. Despite their importance, many companies overlook the impact that negative emotions and resistant behaviors can have on the change process. TMT members report to the CEO every day, decide which change projects to approve and fund, select and evaluate the people in charge of different change projects, and make sure that different change projects complement one another.

For example, when FleetBoston Financial merged with Bank of America (BoA), a TMT was used to implement Six Sigma quality programs quickly (see Chapter 16 for an explanation of Six Sigma) throughout the entire merged organization. Since BoA had been using Six Sigma for 4 years and FleetBoston for just 2, the goal of the TMT was to ensure that the Six Sigma programs for FleetBoston's half of the merged company would catch up as quickly as possible.[60]

It is also important to say what a TMT is *not*. A TMT is not an extra layer of management further separating upper management from lower managers and employees. A TMT is not a steering committee that creates plans for others to carry out. Instead, the members of the TMT are fully involved with making change happen on a daily basis. Furthermore, it's not the TMT's job to determine how and why the company will change. That responsibility belongs to the CEO and upper management. Finally, a TMT is not permanent. Once the company has successfully changed, the TMT is disbanded. Indeed, Bank of America won't need a TMT anymore once everyone in the merged companies has been trained in Six Sigma practices. Exhibit 6.8 lists the primary responsibilities of TMTs.

transition management team (TMT)
a team of 8 to 12 people whose full-time job is to manage and coordinate a company's change process

organizational development
a philosophy and collection of planned change interventions designed to improve an organization's long-term health and performance

change agent
the person formally in charge of guiding a change effort

Organizational development is a philosophy and collection of planned change interventions designed to improve an organization's long-term health and performance. Organizational development takes a long-range approach to change; assumes that top-management support is necessary for change to succeed; creates change by educating workers and managers to change ideas, beliefs, and behaviors so that problems can be solved in new ways; and emphasizes employee participation in diagnosing, solving, and evaluating problems.[61] As shown in Exhibit 6.9, organizational development interventions begin with the recognition of a problem. Then, the company designates a **change agent** to be formally in charge of guiding

EXHIBIT 6.8

Primary Responsibilities of Transition Management Teams

1. Establish a context for change and provide guidance.
2. Stimulate conversation.
3. Provide appropriate resources.
4. Coordinate and align projects.
5. Ensure congruence of messages, activities, policies, and behaviors.
6. Provide opportunities for joint creation.
7. Anticipate, identify, and address people problems.
8. Prepare the critical mass.

Source: J. D. Duck, "Managing Change: The Art of Balancing," *Harvard Business Review on Change* (Boston: Harvard Business School Press, 1998): 55–81.

EXHIBIT 6.9

General Steps for Organizational Development Interventions

1. **Entry**	A problem is discovered and the need for change becomes apparent. A search begins for someone to deal with the problem and facilitate change.
2. **Startup**	A change agent enters the picture and works to clarify the problem and gain commitment to a change effort.
3. **Assessment & feedback**	The change agent gathers information about the problem and provides feedback about it to decision makers and those affected by it.
4. **Action planning**	The change agent works with decision makers to develop an action plan.
5. **Intervention**	The action plan, or organizational development intervention, is carried out.
6. **Evaluation**	The change agent helps decision makers assess the effectiveness of the intervention.
7. **Adoption**	Organizational members accept ownership and responsibility for the change, which is then carried out through the entire organization.
8. **Separation**	The change agent leaves the organization after first ensuring that the change intervention will continue to work.

Source: W. J. Rothwell, R. Sullivan, & G. M. McLean, *Practicing Organizational Development: A Guide for Consultants* (San Diego: Pfeiffer & Co., 1995).

what *really* works

Change the Work Setting or Change the People? Do Both!

Let's assume that you believe that your company needs to change. Congratulations! Just recognizing the need for change puts you ahead of 80 percent of the companies in your industry. But now that you've recognized the need for change, how do you make change happen? Should you focus on changing the work setting or the behavior of the people who work in that setting? It's a classic chicken-or-egg type of question. What would you do?

A recent meta-analysis based on 52 studies and a combined total of 29,611 study participants indicated that it's probably best to do both!

Changing the Work Setting

An organizational work setting has four parts: organizing arrangements (control and reward systems, organizational structure), social factors (people, culture, patterns of interaction), technology (how inputs are transformed into outputs), and the physical setting (the actual physical space in which people work). Overall, there is a 55 percent chance that organizational change efforts will successfully bring changes to a company's work setting. Although the odds are 55–45 in your favor, this is a much lower probability of success than you've seen with the management techniques discussed in other chapters. This simply reflects how strong resistance to change is in most companies.

CHANGING THE WORK SETTING

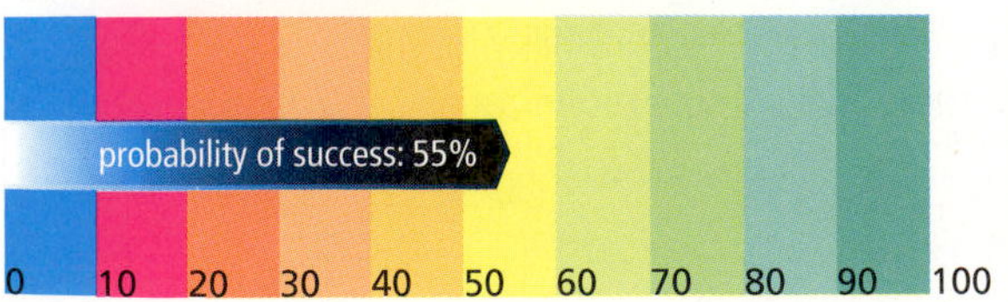

Changing the People

Changing people means changing individual work behavior. The idea is powerful. Change the decisions people make. Change the activities they perform. Change the information they share with others. And change the initiatives they take on their own. Change these individual behaviors and collectively you change the entire company. Overall, there is a 57 percent chance that organizational change efforts will successfully change people's individual work behavior. If you're wondering why the odds aren't higher, consider how difficult it is to change personal behavior. It's incredibly difficult to quit smoking, change your diet, or maintain a daily exercise program. Not surprisingly, changing personal behavior at work is also difficult. Viewed in this context, a 57 percent chance of success is quite high.

CHANGING PEOPLE

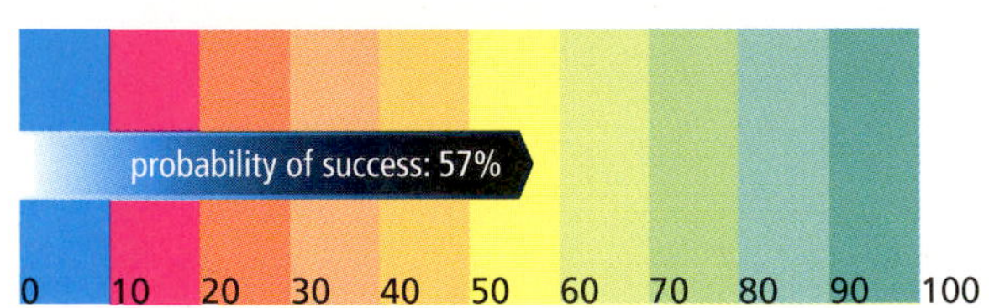

Changing Individual Behavior and Organizational Performance

The point of changing individual behavior is to improve organizational performance (increase profits, market

CHANGING INDIVIDUAL BEHAVIOR

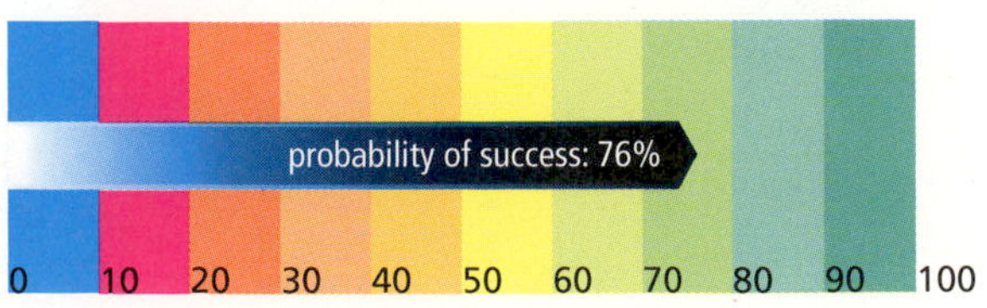

share, and productivity, and lower costs). Overall, there is a 76 percent chance that changes in individual behavior will produce changes in organizational outcomes. So, if you want to improve your company's profits, market share, or productivity, focus on changing the way that your people behave at work.[64]

the change effort. This person can be someone from the company or a professional consultant. The change agent clarifies the problem, gathers information, works with decision makers to create and implement an action plan, helps to evaluate the plan's effectiveness, implements the plan throughout the company, and then leaves (if from outside the company) after making sure the change intervention will continue to work.

Change agent Hajime Oba is one of the key reasons that *TOYOTA* has had such a great reputation for quality (before, of course, its recent troubles with recalls). Oba's job is to work closely with suppliers, showing them how to increase quality and decrease costs. For example, *MICHIGAN SUMMIT POLYMERS* installed a $280,000 paint system with robots and an oven to bake paint onto the dashboard vents that went into Toyota cars, but Oba showed that a $12 hair dryer did the job better and faster (3 minutes versus 90 minutes for the robots and paint oven). Because of Oba's demonstration, Summit replaced the robots with simple but effective $150 spray guns and the paint oven with intense light bulbs. Overall, Oba has helped Summit cut its defects from 3,000 parts per million to less than 60 parts per million.[62] Oba's efforts as a change agent have significantly improved the quality of parts at Toyota's other suppliers as well. That, in turn, has helped Toyota reach the top of the quality rankings issued by J. D. Power and Associates and *Consumer Reports* magazine.[63]

REVIEW 3

Managing Change

The basic change process involves unfreezing, change, and refreezing. Resistance to change, which stems from self-interest, misunderstanding and distrust, and a general intolerance for change, can be managed through education and communication, participation, negotiation, top-management support, and coercion. Knowing what not to do is as important as knowing what to do to achieve successful change. Managers should avoid these errors when leading change: not establishing urgency, not creating a guiding coalition, lacking a vision, undercommunicating the vision, not removing obstacles to the vision, not creating short-term wins, declaring victory too soon, and not anchoring changes in the corporation's culture.

Finally, managers can use a number of change techniques. Results-driven change and the GE workout reduce resistance by getting change efforts off to a fast start. Transition management teams, which manage a company's change process, coordinate change efforts throughout an organization. Organizational development is a collection of planned change interventions (large system, small group, person-focused), guided by a change agent, that are designed to improve an organization's long-term health and performance.

Management Team Decision

Coming Soon to Netflix

When Reed Hastings started Netflix in 1997, he already knew that his fledgling business was doomed. True, his company brought fundamental changes to the movie rental business, crippling once-mighty competitors like Blockbuster, and spawning a number of imitators. But Hastings always knew that the idea that a customer would need to obtain a physical object to watch a movie would quickly fade.

For this reason, Hastings is guiding Netflix into what he hopes will be the next innovation in movie rentals—Internet streaming. Instead of picking up a DVD from a brick-and-mortar store, or waiting for it in the mail, streaming allows customers to select a movie from an on-line database and watch it in just a few minutes. No more hassle of driving to the video store. No more wondering when the next movie in your cue will show up in the mail. All the consumer needs to do is go on-line, pick a movie or TV show, and sit back and enjoy.

Netflix's streaming service began rather humbly in 2007, with a selection of older films and TV shows that could only be watched on a computer. But even with the limited selections, nearly 20 percent of Netflix subscribers have used the service, confirming Hastings' suspicions that future prosperity lies in streaming. For this reason, Netflix has set plans for the expansion of its streaming service. The company is looking to increase the number of movies that it can offer through the Internet by obtaining licenses from film studios. It is also looking to expand streaming beyond the computer. By partnering with TV and audiovisual manufacturers such as Samsung, Nintendo, and Tivo, Netflix aims to deliver movies instantly to a family's TV, not just its desktop computer.

As ambitious as these plans are, however, Netflix faces some significant challenges. First, by focusing all of its innovative energies on Internet streaming, Netflix may be missing out on other lucrative opportunities. For example, the company has made no significant plans on international expansion, even though most analysts agree that it would lead to huge profits. Second, there is the issue of equipment. Netflix has decided that it will not produce the hardware required for its streaming service, instead relying on other consumer-electronic companies. While this will help the company avoid getting into an unfamiliar market, it will limit the number of consumers it can reach. That is, Netflix may only be able to reach people who buy a Samsung TV but not a Sony or Sharp.

Finally, there is the issue of licensing. Even if Netflix develops the best streaming infrastructure, it is useless without the studios' permissions to show movies. But herein lies the problem—Netflix must compete with cable channels such as HBO and Showtime, which have bigger audiences and can pay higher fees, for the right to broadcast movies. Netflix could be forced to wait years before obtaining Internet streaming rights. Further, movie studios are hesitant to support Internet streaming because they want to preserve the lucrative DVD market for as long as they can. Consider, the recent film *Twilight: New Moon* brought in $296 million dollars in theaters for Summit Entertainment. In just over two weeks, however, the DVD of the movie brought in an additional $132 million dollars. The question is, naturally, why would any movie studio jeopardize their DVD-sales profits by granting Netflix a license to stream movies over the Internet?

These are the challenges that you face as a part of Netflix's management team. How will you negotiate the various challenges that Netflix faces in its efforts to bring yet another innovation to the movie rental industry? Form a group with three or four other students and consider the following questions.

Questions

1. Do you agree or disagree with Netflix's decision to not enter into foreign markets? Why?
2. What arguments would you make to persuade film studios to grant Netflix exclusive rights to their newly released DVDs? How would you

demonstrate to them that your business model will lead to their long-term benefit?

3. What are the advantages and disadvantages of Netflix not entering into hardware/equipment production? Do you think that the company should produce its own "box top" sets that allow Netflix access?

Sources: "US DVD Sales Chart for Week Ending Apr 4, 2010." Accessed at http://www.the-numbers.com/dvd/charts/weekly/thisweek.php; "The Twilight Saga: New Moon." Accessed at: http://boxofficemojo.com/movies/?id=newmoon.htm; Nick Wingfield. "Netflix Boss Plots Life after the DVD." *Wall Street Journal.* June 23, 2009. A1, 12.

Practice being a MANAGER

Supporting Creativity

Successfully managing innovation is challenging. Companies must find ways to support creativity and invention, while at the same time screening their investments in support of innovation. This exercise will give you an opportunity to experience a bit of the organizational dynamic regarding innovation and investment.

STEP 1 Assign roles. Your professor will assign you to a small group and give your team a role as either "Inventors" or "Investors." Regardless of role, assume that you work for a large clothing and accessories company that targets college students. Your company makes some traditional clothing and gear (such as backpacks and folios) but also prides itself on developing new and innovative products. And recently there has been some interest in considering new services that the company might offer to the college market, things like event or trip planning.

STEP 2 Work with your partner(s) on the following tasks depending on your assigned role.

Inventors: Brainstorm and work to develop a new product or service concept. Be prepared to explain your concept to those inside the company who screen ideas and recommend investments.

Investors: Discuss and agree upon some criteria that your company should use to screen new-product and service concepts and to identify which ones to recommend to senior management. Be prepared to listen to one or more concept presentations, ask questions, and then use your criteria to evaluate the concept(s).

STEP 3 Pair up. As instructed by your professor, Inventor and Investor groups should pair up. Inventors will now present their new concept, and investors will ask questions and then use their criteria to rate the concept.

STEP 4 Change roles. As time allows, your professor will rotate Inventor and Investor pairings through a few rounds of concept presentation and investor evaluation.

STEP 5 Debrief. Return to your original Inventor or Investor pair/group, and discuss your experiences in this role play. What are some of the challenges of playing this role? What was it like to interact with the "other side" of the presentation/evaluation process?

STEP 6 Discuss challenges. As a class, discuss the challenges likely faced by companies as they try to successfully manage innovation. Some items for discussion might include:

1. What is the impact of an "evaluation/rating" on the creative process?
2. Do you think that "inventor units" (such as product development and R&D) and "investor units" (finance) often clash over new-product investment decisions? Why or why not?
3. What role might organizational culture (and subculture) play in the innovation and investment processes?
4. How might managers support healthy innovation and wise investment?

Mind Benders

Innovation is a key to corporate success. Companies that innovate and embrace the changes in their business environment tend to outperform those that stand still. Even so, innovative companies don't simply rely on the creativity of their own workforce. They often contract with outside providers to generate new ideas for everything from operations to new products. In other words, innovative companies fill gaps in their own creativity by looking outside the organization.

As a manager, you will benefit from understanding how you are creative (not *if* you are creative). And just as important as your own creativity is your attitude toward creative endeavors.

This assessment will provide some baseline information you can use as you develop your managerial skills.[65] Indicate the extent to which each of the following statements is true of either your actual behavior or your intentions at work. That is, describe the way you are or the way you intend to be on the job. Use this scale for your responses:

1. Almost never true
2. Seldom true
3. Not applicable
4. Often true
5. Almost always true

1. I openly discuss with my supervisor how to get ahead.
   1 2 3 4 5
2. I try new ideas and approaches to problems.
   1 2 3 4 5
3. I take things or situations apart to find out how they work.
   1 2 3 4 5
4. I welcome uncertainty and unusual circumstances related to my tasks.
   1 2 3 4 5
5. I negotiate my salary openly with my supervisor.
   1 2 3 4 5
6. I can be counted on to find a new use for existing methods or equipment.
   1 2 3 4 5
7. Among my colleagues and coworkers, I will be the first or nearly the first to try out a new idea or method.
   1 2 3 4 5
8. I take the opportunity to translate communications from other departments for my work group.
   1 2 3 4 5
9. I demonstrate originality.
   1 2 3 4 5
10. I will work on a problem that has caused others great difficulty.
   1 2 3 4 5
11. I provide critical input toward a new solution.
   1 2 3 4 5

12. I provide written evaluations of proposed ideas.
    1 2 3 4 5

13. I develop contacts with experts outside my firm.
    1 2 3 4 5

14. I use personal contacts to maneuver into choice work assignments.
    1 2 3 4 5

15. I make time to pursue my own pet ideas or projects.
    1 2 3 4 5

16. I set aside resources for the pursuit of a risky project.
    1 2 3 4 5

17. I tolerate people who depart from organizational routine.
    1 2 3 4 5

18. I speak out in staff meetings.
    1 2 3 4 5

19. I work in teams to try to solve complex problems.
    1 2 3 4 5

20. If my coworkers are asked, they will say I am a wit.
    1 2 3 4 5

TOTAL = _______

You can find an interpretation of your score at: login.cengagebrain.com.

Reel to Real

BIZ FLIX

© GREENLIGHT

Field of Dreams

In the classic 1989 film *Field of Dreams*, Ray Kinsella (Kevin Costner), while working in his Iowa cornfield, hears a voice that says, "If you build it, he will come." Ray concludes that "he" is legendary "Shoeless Joe" Jackson (Ray Liotta), a Chicago White Sox player suspended for rigging the 1919 World Series. With the support of his wife Annie (Amy Madigan), Ray jeopardizes his farm by plowing under a cornfield and creating a modern baseball diamond in its place. Shoeless Joe soon arrives, followed by the rest of the suspended players. This charming fantasy film, based on W. P. Kinsellas' novel *Shoeless Joe,* shows the rewards of pursuing a dream. In this clip, Ray's brother-in-law Mark (Timothy Busfield) insists that they will have to start farming on the field again if they're going to make enough money to avoid foreclosure on their property, but Ray's daughter Karin (Gaby Hoffman) suggests another idea.

What to Watch for and Ask Yourself

1. When someone suggests an idea to you that you don't completely understand, how open are you to considering it?
2. Which character is the most resistant to the idea of changing the farm into a ball field? Why?
3. Which characters demonstrate the most creativity and vision?

MANAGEMENT WORKPLACE

© CENGAGE

Scholfield Honda

Roger Scholfield, general manager of Scholfield Honda in Wichita, Kansas, says, "The world and the marketplace are constantly changing, so if you're not a person comfortable with change, then this business is not for you." As gas prices soar and concerns about the environment grow, many people are looking for innovative solutions to energy problems. Lee Lindquist, alternative fuels specialist at Scholfield Honda, learned Honda had been selling a natural gas vehicle in New York and California since 1998, where it was marketed as a way for municipalities and fleet customers to address air quality issues. Lindquist convinced Scholfield that they should sell the Civic GX at their dealership in Wichita, too. In this video, Scholfield and Lindquist discuss the challenges of selling natural gas vehicles in Kansas, who the early adopters have been, and why they believe the cars are good for both customers and the environment.

What to Watch for and Ask Yourself

1. What might explain dealers' failure to promote the Civic GX, beyond fueling issues?
2. How might Scholfield Honda expand on the changes put into motion by Lindquist?
3. How could the Honda Corporation capitalize on innovation at the dealership level?

Chapter Seven
Global Management

OUTLINE

Experience Management

Explore the four levels of learning by doing the simulation module on International Management.

© ISTOCKPHOTO.COM/ ANN MARIE KURTZ

Pod Nod

Mini lecture reviews all the learning points in the chapter.

© ISTOCKPHOTO.COM/ MAGNET CREATIVE

Reel to Real

Biz Flix is a scene from *Lost in Translation.* Management Workplace is a segment on Evo.

© ISTOCKPHOTO.COM/ CRAFTVISION

Self Test

10 quiz questions and PowerPoints for quick review.

© ISTOCKPHOTO.COM/ DUITAL FILM

What Would You Do?

Caterpillar Headquarters, Peoria, Illinois.[1]

One of General Motors' and Chrysler's key mistakes, which eventually led to their bankruptcies, was not recognizing in the 1970s that the automobile industry had gone global. With 50+ percent market share in the United States, GM was so dominant that it ignored Toyota, Nissan (then called Datsun), and Honda when they entered the U.S. market. *CATERPILLAR* has not and will not make that mistake as long as you are in charge. Your global view is simple, but powerful: Since the United States has only 5 percent of the world's population, 95 percent of your customers are located abroad. For example, combine India's and China's populations with 8 to 10 percent annual growth in their economies and huge infrastructure investments by their governments, and it's clear that Caterpillar's future opportunities will be strongest in Asia. But there are also big opportunities in the Middle East and in developing economies, particularly in Latin America. So the question is not whether Caterpillar will be global, but how?

Indeed, while global opportunities abound, they don't come easily. Aggressive competitors like Komatsu have already sold or leased 23,000 heavy-duty construction, earth-moving, and mining machines in China. Komatsu dominates the Chinese market for the gigantic dump trucks used at mines, selling two of every three that are bought there. Ironically, many of the products that Komatsu sells globally are made at its U.S.-based plant in Peoria, Illinois, just a few miles from Caterpillar's world headquarters. But that is just one of Komatsu's many production facilities throughout the world. Kunio Noji, Komatsu's CEO, believes that being American-based is a disadvantage for Caterpillar. Said Noji, "Caterpillar is suffering because of being centered in the U.S." Why? Because Caterpillar gets 40 percent of its sales in the U.S. market and doesn't think or act like a global company. Caterpillar will also have to match the combined reliability and innovation in Komatsu's products. For instance, each Komatsu truck or excavator is outfitted with a satellite antenna that transmits a continuous stream of data to headquarters that tells Komatsu where the machines are, what they are doing, how well they are running, and when they will need maintenance. (Another benefit is that Komatsu can shut the machines down if companies are late with their payments.)

So how should Caterpillar go global? Should you manufacture in the United States and export? It took years to build relationships with suppliers and distributors in the United States. Will you be able to replicate that abroad? Should you look for a partner and consider a joint venture? Or should you build or buy manufacturing plants overseas so that your factories are closer to your customers? Another key question is whether the company should be run the same way abroad as it is in Peoria? Will the sales and marketing approaches that worked in North America also work in China and India?

Finally, when companies go abroad, they search for locations with the best business climates. With so much growth potential in China, India, the Middle East, and Latin America, that won't be difficult for Caterpillar. Instead, the challenge will be finding the right mix of products and services to position the company against the boom-and-bust cycle inherent in the industry. When the heavy machinery industry booms, no one can keep up with demand and everyone builds new factories and hires tens of thousands of new employees. But when the industry goes bust, factories are closed and tens of thousands of employees are laid off. How can Caterpillar position itself to handle this challenging aspect of its global business?

If you were the CEO of Caterpillar, what would you do?

Caterpillar's struggle with international expansion is an example of the key issue in global business: How can you be sure that the way you run your business in one country is the right way to run that business in another? This chapter discusses how organizations answer that question. We start by examining global business in two ways—first by exploring its impact on U.S. businesses and then by reviewing the basic rules and agreements that govern global trade. Next, we examine how and when companies go global by examining the trade-off between consistency and adaptation and by discussing how to organize a global company. Finally, we look at how companies decide where to expand globally. Here, we consider how to find the best business climate, how to adapt to cultural differences, and how to prepare employees for international assignments.

What Is Global Business?

Business is the buying and selling of goods or services. Buying this textbook was a business transaction. So was selling your first car. So was getting paid for babysitting or for mowing lawns. **Global business** is the buying and selling of goods and services by people from different countries. The Timex watch I wore as I wrote this chapter was purchased at a Wal-Mart in Texas. But since it was made in the Philippines, I participated in global business when I wrote Wal-Mart a check. Wal-Mart, for its part, had already paid Timex, which had paid the company that employs the Filipino managers and workers who made my watch. Of course, there is more to global business than buying imported products at Wal-Mart.

global business
the buying and selling of goods and services by people from different countries

After reading the next section, you should be able to:

1 discuss the impact of global business and the trade rules and agreements that govern it.

1 Global Business, Trade Rules, and Trade Agreements

If you want a simple demonstration of the impact of global business, look at the label on your shirt, the inside of your shoes, and the inside of your cell phone (take out your battery). Chances are, all of these items were made in different places around the world. As I write this, my shirt, shoes, and cell phone were made in Thailand, China, and Korea. Where were yours made?

Let's learn more about 1.1 **the impact of global business**, 1.2 **how tariff and nontariff trade barriers have historically restricted global business**, and 1.3 **how consumers are responding to those changes in trade rules and agreements**.

1.1 The Impact of Global Business

Thomas Friedman, author and columnist for the *New York Times*, observed global business in action when he visited Infosys, a consulting and information technology company, in India:

> Nandan Nilekani, the Infosys CEO, was showing me his global videoconference room, pointing with pride to a wall-size flat-screen TV, which he said was the biggest in Asia. Infosys, he explained, could hold a virtual meeting of the key players from its entire global supply chain for any project at any time on that supersize screen. Above the screen there were eight clocks that pretty well summed up the Infosys workday: 24/7/365. The clocks were labeled United States West, United States East, G.M.T., India, Singapore, Hong Kong, Japan, Australia.[2]

Infosys does global business by selling products and services worldwide with managers and employees from different continents working together as seamlessly as if they were next door to each other. But Infosys isn't unique. There are thousands of other multinational companies just like it.

Multinational corporations are corporations that own businesses in two or more countries. In 1970, more than half of the world's 7,000 multinational corporations were headquartered in just two countries: the United States and the United Kingdom. Today, there are 79,000 multinational corporations, more than 11 times as many as in 1970, and only 2,418, or 3.1 percent, are based in the United States.[3] Today, 56,448 multinationals, or 71.5 percent, are based in other developed countries (e.g., Germany, Italy, Canada, and Japan), while 20,586, or 26.1 percent, are based in developing countries (e.g., Colombia, South Africa, and others). So, today, multinational companies can be found by the thousands all over the world!

multinational corporation
a corporation that owns businesses in two or more countries

Another way to appreciate the impact of global business is by considering direct foreign investment. **Direct foreign investment** occurs when a company builds a new business or buys an existing business in a foreign country. *LUFTHANSA*, the German-based airline, made direct foreign investments when it paid $300 million for U.S.-based JetBlue Airways, $91 million for a 45 percent stake in Brussels Airlines, and increased its ownership of British Midland Airways to 80 percent.[4] Of course, companies from many other countries also own businesses in the United States. As Exhibit 7.1 shows, companies from the United Kingdom, Japan, Canada,

direct foreign investment
a method of investment in which a company builds a new business or buys an existing business in a foreign country

EXHIBIT 7.1

Direct Foreign Investment in the United States

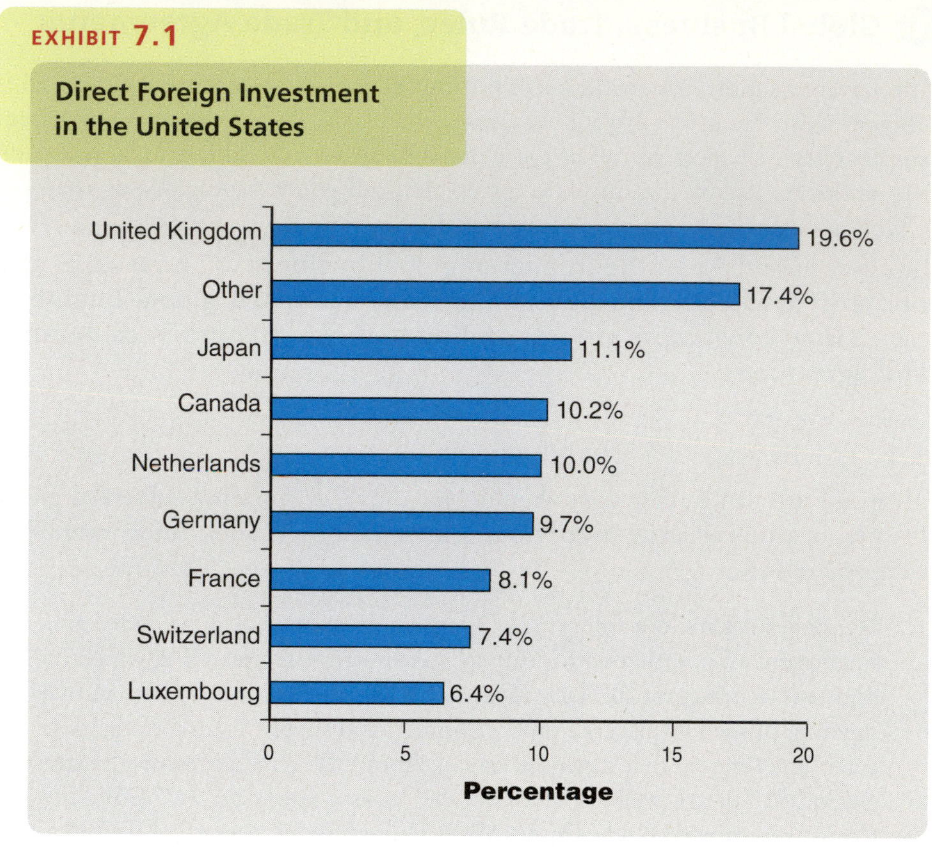

the Netherlands, Germany, France, Switzerland, and Luxembourg have the largest direct foreign investment in the United States. Overall, foreign companies invest more than $2.1 trillion a year to do business in the United States.

But direct foreign investment in the United States is only half the picture. U.S. companies also have made large direct foreign investments in countries throughout the world. For example, *HERSHEY CO.*, a Pennsylvania-based candy company, purchased Barry Callebaut AG's Van Houten consumer chocolate business in Asia, allowing Hershey, which gets most of its growth from North America, to expand internationally.[5] As Exhibit 7.2 shows, U.S. companies have made their largest direct foreign investments in the United Kingdom, the Netherlands, and Canada. Overall, U.S. companies invest more than $2.8 trillion a year to do business in other countries.

So, whether foreign companies invest in the United States or U.S. companies invest abroad, direct foreign investment is an increasingly important and common method of conducting global business.

1.2 Trade Barriers

Although today's consumers usually don't care where the products they buy come from (more on this in Section 1.4), national governments have traditionally preferred that consumers buy domestically made products in hopes that such purchases would increase the number of domestic businesses and workers. Indeed, governments have done much more than hope that you will buy from domestic companies. Historically,

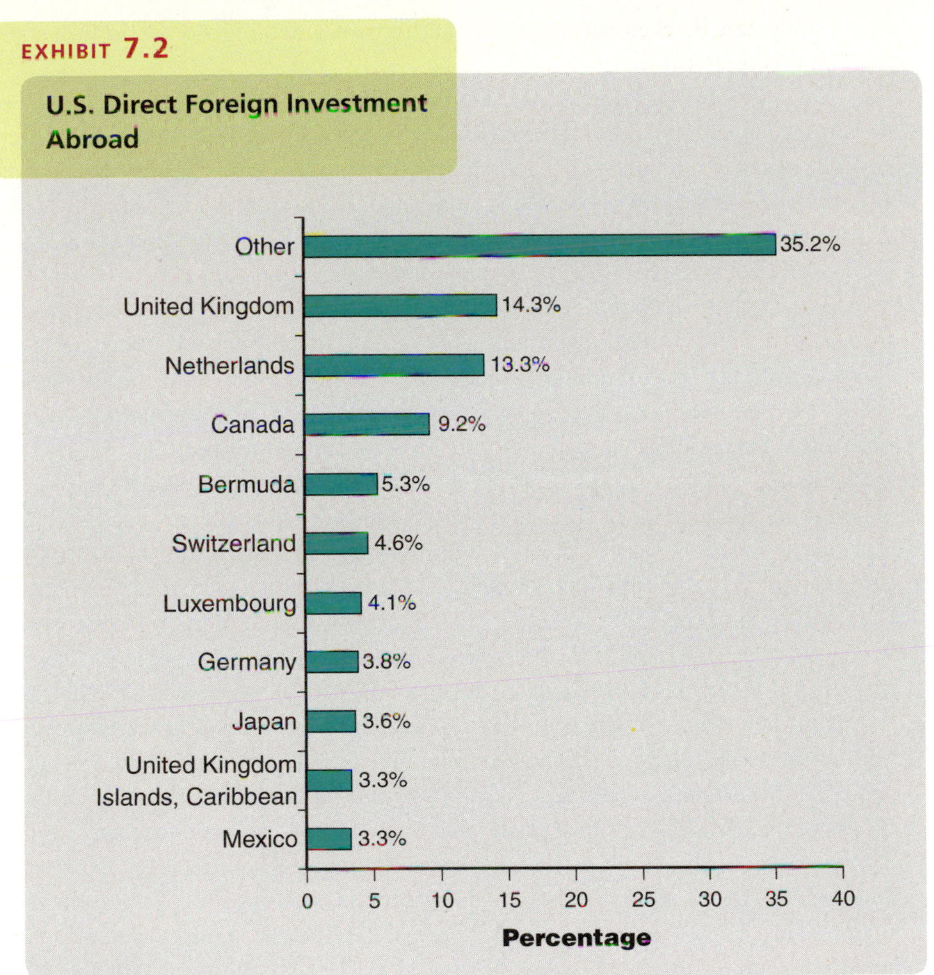

governments have actively used **trade barriers** to make it much more expensive or difficult (or sometimes impossible) for consumers to buy or consume imported goods. For example, the European Union places a 34 percent tax on frozen strawberries imported from China.[6] The U.S. government imposes a tariff of 54 cents a gallon on imported ethanol, which is blended with gasoline for use in automobiles.[7] By establishing these restrictions and taxes, the governments of the European Union and the United States are engaging in **protectionism**, which is the use of trade barriers to protect local companies and their workers from foreign competition.

Governments have used two general kinds of trade barriers—tariff and nontariff barriers. A **tariff** is a direct tax on imported goods. Like the U.S. government's 54-cents-per-gallon tax on imported ethanol, tariffs increase the cost of imported goods relative to that of domestic goods. For example, the U.S. import tax on trucks is 25 percent. This means that U.S. buyers must pay $25,000 for an imported truck valued at $20,000, with $5,000 going to the U.S. government. As a result, fewer than 10,000 pickup trucks are imported by the United States each year.[8] **Nontariff barriers** are nontax methods of increasing the cost or reducing the volume of imported goods. There are five types of nontariff barriers: quotas, voluntary export restraints, government import standards, government subsidies, and customs valuation/classification. Because there are so many different kinds of nontariff

trade barriers
government-imposed regulations that increase the cost and restrict the number of imported goods

protectionism
a government's use of trade barriers to shield domestic companies and their workers from foreign competition

tariff
a direct tax on imported goods

nontariff barriers
nontax methods of increasing the cost or reducing the volume of imported goods

barriers, they can be even more potent methods of shielding domestic industries from foreign competition.

Quotas are specific limits on the number or volume of imported products. For example, raw sugarcane imports into the United States are limited to approximately 1.1 million metric tons per year because of strict import quotas.[9] Since this is well below the demand for sugar in the United States, domestic U.S. sugar prices are twice as high as sugar prices in the rest of the world.[10] Like quotas, **voluntary export restraints** limit the amount of a product that can be imported annually. The difference is that the exporting country rather than the importing country imposes restraints. Usually, however, the "voluntary" offer to limit exports occurs because the importing country has implicitly threatened to impose quotas. According to the World Trade Organization (see the discussion in Section 1.3), however, voluntary export restraints are illegal and should not be used to restrict imports.[11]

In theory, **government import standards** are established to protect the health and safety of citizens. In reality, such standards are often used to restrict or ban imported goods. For example, Japan used to ban the importation of nearly all U.S. apples, which are one-third the cost of Japanese apples. Ostensibly, the ban was to prevent transmission of fire blight bacteria to Japanese apple orchards, but research conducted *jointly* by U.S. and Japanese scientists "does not support Japan's assertion that mature, symptomless apples can transmit" the fire blight bacteria.[12] The Japanese government was actually using this government import standard to protect the economic health of its apple farmers rather than the biological health of its apple orchards. Only after the World Trade Organization ruled that there was no scientific basis for the ban did Japan allow U.S. apples to be imported without restrictions.[13]

Many nations also use **subsidies**, such as long-term, low-interest loans, cash grants, and tax deferments, to develop and protect companies in special industries. European and Japanese governments have invested billions of dollars to develop airplane manufacturers and steel companies, while the United States has provided subsidies for manufacturers of computer chips. Not surprisingly, businesses complain about unfair trade practices when foreign companies receive government subsidies.

The last type of nontariff barrier is **customs classification**. As products are imported into a country, they are examined by customs agents, who must decide into which of nearly 9,000 categories they should classify a product. Classification is important because the category assigned by customs agents can greatly affect the size of the tariff and whether the item is subject to import quotas. For example, the U.S. Customs Service has several customs classifications for imported shoes. Tariffs on imported leather or "nonrubber" shoes are about 10 percent, whereas tariffs on imported rubber shoes, such as athletic footwear or waterproof shoes, range from 20 to 84 percent. (See ***http://www.usitc.gov*** for full information on tariffs.) The difference is large enough that some importers try to make their rubber shoes look like leather in hopes of receiving the nonrubber customs classification and lower tariff.

quotas
a limit on the number or volume of imported products

voluntary export restraints
voluntarily imposed limits on the number or volume of products exported to a particular country

government import standard
a standard ostensibly established to protect the health and safety of citizens but, in reality, often used to restrict imports

subsidies
government loans, grants, and tax deferments given to domestic companies to protect them from foreign competition

customs classification
a classification assigned to imported products by government officials that affects the size of the tariff and imposition of import quotas

General Agreement on Tariffs and Trade (GATT)
a worldwide trade agreement that reduced and eliminated tariffs, limited government subsidies, and established protections for intellectual property

1.3 Trade Agreements

Thanks to the trade barriers described above, buying imported goods has often been much more expensive and difficult than buying domestic goods. During the 1990s, however, the regulations governing global trade were transformed. The most significant change was that 124 countries agreed to adopt the Uruguay Round of the **General Agreement on Tariffs and Trade (GATT)**. GATT, which existed from

1947 to 1995, was an agreement to regulate trade among (eventually) 120+ countries, the purpose of which was "substantial reduction of tariffs and other trade barriers and the elimination of preferences."[14] GATT members engaged in eight rounds of trade negotiations, with the Uruguay Round signed in 1994 and going into effect in 1995. Although GATT itself was replaced by the **World Trade Organization (WTO)** in 1995, the changes that it made continue to encourage international trade.

As shown in Exhibit 7.3, the WTO headquartered in Geneva, Switzerland, administers trade agreements, provides a forum for trade negotiations, handles trade disputes, monitors national trade policies, and offers technical assistance and training for developing countries. Through tremendous decreases in tariff and nontariff barriers, the Uruguay round of GATT made it much easier and cheaper for consumers in all countries to buy foreign products. GATT also established stricter limits on government subsidies. For example, the Uruguay round of GATT put limits on how much national governments can subsidize company research in electronic and high-technology industries. The Uruguay round of GATT also established protections for intellectual property, such as trademarks, patents, and copyrights.

Finally, trade disputes between countries are fully settled by arbitration panels from the WTO. In the past, countries could use their veto power to cancel a panel's decision. Now, however, countries that are members of the WTO (every country that agreed to GATT is a member) no longer have veto power. Thus, WTO rulings are complete and final.

The second major development that has reduced trade barriers has been the creation of **regional trading zones**, or zones in which tariff and nontariff barriers are

World Trade Organization (WTO) the successor to GATT; the only international organization dealing with the global rules of trade between nations. Its main function is to ensure that trade flows as smoothly, predictably, and freely as possible

regional trading zones areas in which tariff and nontariff barriers on trade between countries are reduced or eliminated

EXHIBIT 7.3

World Trade Organization

FACT FILE

WORLD TRADE ORGANIZATION

Location: Geneva, Switzerland
Established: 1 January 1995
Created by: Uruguay Round negotiations (1986–1994)
Membership: 150 countries (as of 11 October 2007)
Budget: 175 million Swiss francs for 2006
Secretariat staff: 635
Head: Pascal Lamy (director-general)

Functions:

- Administering WTO trade agreements
- Providing a forum for trade negotiations.
- Handling trade disputes
- Monitoring national trade policies
- Providing technical assistance and training for developing countries.
- Cooperating with other international organizations.

Source: "WTO: About the Organization," World Trade Organization, available at http://www.wto.org/english/thewto_e/whatis_e/whatis_e.htm, 7 February 2007.

reduced or eliminated for countries within the trading zone (see Exhibit 7.4). The largest and most important trading zones are in Europe (the Maastricht Treaty), North America (the North American Free Trade Agreement, or NAFTA), Central America (Central America Free Trade Agreement, or CAFTA-DR), South America (Union of South American Nations, or UNASUR), and Asia (the Association of Southeast Asian Nations, or ASEAN, and Asia-Pacific Economic Cooperation, or APEC).

In 1992, Belgium, Denmark, France, Germany, Greece, Ireland, Italy, Luxembourg, the Netherlands, Portugal, Spain, and the United Kingdom implemented the **Maastricht Treaty** of Europe. The purpose of this treaty was to transform their twelve different economies and twelve currencies into one common economic market, called the European Union (EU), with one common currency. Austria, Finland, and Sweden joined the EU in 1995, followed by Cyprus, the Czech Republic, Estonia, Hungary, Latvia, Lithuania, Malta, Poland, Slovakia, and Slovenia in 2004, and Bulgaria and Romania joined in 2007, bringing the total membership to 27 countries. Croatia, Macedonia, and Turkey have applied and are being considered for membership. On 1 January 2002, a single common currency, the euro, went into circulation in twelve of the EU's members (Austria, Belgium, Finland, France, Germany, Greece, Ireland, Italy, Luxembourg, the Netherlands, Portugal, and Spain).

NAFTA, the **North American Free Trade Agreement** between the United States, Canada, and Mexico, went into effect on 1 January 1994. More than any other regional trade agreement, NAFTA has liberalized trade between countries so that businesses can plan for one market (North America) rather than for three separate markets (the United States, Canada, and Mexico). One of NAFTA's most important achievements was to eliminate most product tariffs *and* prevent the three countries from increasing existing tariffs or introducing new ones. Before NAFTA, Wal-Mart used expensive intermediaries to distribute goods to its stores, and Mexican officials often pressured managers for bribes. Because of burdensome paperwork, deliveries sometimes took months to clear customs. Before NAFTA, a Sony TV imported from Japan was sold in Mexico for $1,600 after a 23% tariff. This all changed with NAFTA. Sony built a new factory in Mexico, enabling it to ship the TVs duty-free anywhere in the United States, Canada, or Mexico. With minimal shipping costs and the 23 percent tariff eliminated, Wal-Mart was able to sell the same flat-screen TVs for $600 in Mexico, about what they sold for in the United States at that time.[16] Overall, Mexican and Canadian exports to the United States are up 247 percent since NAFTA went into effect. U.S. exports to Mexico and Canada are up 171 percent, too, growing twice as fast as U.S. exports to any other part of the world.[17] In fact, Mexico and Canada now account for one-third of all U.S. exports.[18] For more information about NAFTA, see the Office of NAFTA & Inter-American Affairs at ***http://www.ustr.gov/Trade_Agreements/Regional/NAFTA/Section_Index.html.***

CAFTA-DR, the new **Central America Free Trade Agreement** between the United States, the Dominican Republic, and the Central American countries of Costa Rica, El Salvador, Guatemala, Honduras, Nicaragua, and the Dominican Republic went into effect in August 2005. With a combined population of 347.6 million (compared to 302.3 million in the United States), the CAFTA-DR countries together are the tenth-largest U.S. export market in the world and the third-largest U.S. export market in Latin America, after Mexico and Brazil. For more information about CAFTA-DR, see ***http://www.fas.usda.gov/itp/CAFTA/cafta.asp.***

Maastricht Treaty
a regional trade agreement between most European countries

North American Free Trade Agreement (NAFTA)
a regional trade agreement between the United States, Canada, and Mexico

Central America Free Trade Agreement (CAFTA-DR)
a regional trade agreement between Costa Rica, the Dominican Republic, El Salvador, Guatemala, Honduras, Nicaragua, and the United States

On 23 May 2008, twelve South American countries signed the **Union of South American Nations (UNASUR)** Constitutive Treaty, which united the former Mercosur (Argentina, Brazil, Paraguay, Uruguay, and Venezuela) and Andean Community (Bolivia, Colombia, Ecuador, and Peru) alliances along with Guyana, Suriname, and Chile. UNASUR aims to create a unified South America by permitting free movement between nations, creating a common infrastructure that includes an interoceanic highway, and establishing the region as a single market by eliminating tariffs by 2019.[19] For more about UNASUR see ***http://www.comunidadandina.org/ingles/sudamerican.htm***.

ASEAN, the **Association of Southeast Asian Nations**, and **APEC**, the **Asia-Pacific Economic Cooperation**, are the two largest and most important regional trading groups in Asia. ASEAN is a trade agreement between Brunei Darussalam, Cambodia, Indonesia, Lao PDR, Malaysia, Myanmar, the Philippines, Singapore, Thailand, and Vietnam, which form a market of more than 575 million people.[20] An ASEAN free trade area will begin in 2015 for the six original countries (Brunei Darussalam, Indonesia, Malaysia, the Philippines, Singapore, and Thailand) and in 2018 for the newer member countries (Cambodia, Lao PDR, Myanmar, and Vietnam).[21] For more information about ASEAN, see ***http://www.aseansec.org***.

APEC is a broader agreement that includes Australia, Canada, Chile, China, Japan, Mexico, New Zealand, Papua New Guinea, Peru, Russia, South Korea, Taiwan, the United States, and all the members of ASEAN except Cambodia, Lao PDR, and Myanmar. APEC's 21 member countries contain 2.6 billion people, account for 47 percent of all global trade, and have a combined gross domestic product of over $19 trillion. APEC countries began reducing trade barriers in 2000, though all the reductions will not be completely phased in until 2020.[22] For more information about APEC, see ***http://www.apec.org***.

South American Nations (UNASUR)
(UNASUR) a regional trade agreement between Argentina, Bolivia, Brazil, Chile, Columbia, Ecuador, Guyana, Paraguay, Peru, Suriname, Uruguay, and Venezuela

Association of Southeast Asian Nations (ASEAN)
a regional trade agreement between Brunei Darussalam, Cambodia, Indonesia, Laos, Malaysia, Myanmar, the Philippines, Singapore, Thailand, and Vietnam

Asia-Pacific Economic Cooperation (APEC)
a regional trade agreement between Australia, Canada, Chile, the People's Republic of China, Hong Kong, Japan, Mexico, New Zealand, Papua New Guinea, Peru, Russia, South Korea, Taiwan, the United States, and all the members of ASEAN, except Cambodia, Laos, and Myanmar

1.4 Consumers, Trade Barriers, and Trade Agreements

In Tokyo, a 12-ounce Coke costs about $1.38.[23] A cup of regular coffee costs $10.19 in Moscow, $6.77 in Paris, and $6.62 in Athens.[24] In the United States, each of these items costs about a dollar. A McDonald's Big Mac sandwich costs an average of $3.54 in the United States, $3.30 in the United Kingdom, and $5.60 in Switzerland.[25] Although not all products are more expensive in other countries (in some, they are cheaper; for example, a Big Mac costs $1.83 in China and $2.30 in Mexico), international studies find that American consumers get much more for their money than most other consumers in the world. For example, the average worker earns nearly $60,820 a year in Switzerland, $77,370 in Norway, $37,790 in Japan, and $46,040 in America.[26] Yet, after adjusting these incomes for how much they can buy, the Swiss income is equivalent to just $44,410, the Norwegian income to $53,650, and the Japanese income to $34,750![27] This is the same as saying that $1 of income can buy you only 73 cents worth of goods in Switzerland, 69 cents in Norway, and 92 cents' worth in Japan. In other words, Americans can buy much more with their incomes than those in other countries can.

One reason that Americans get more for their money is that the U.S. marketplace is the most competitive in the world and has been one of the easiest for foreign companies to enter.[28] Although some U.S. industries, such as textiles, have been heavily protected from foreign competition by trade barriers, for the most part,

EXHIBIT 7.4

Global Map of Regional Trade Agreements

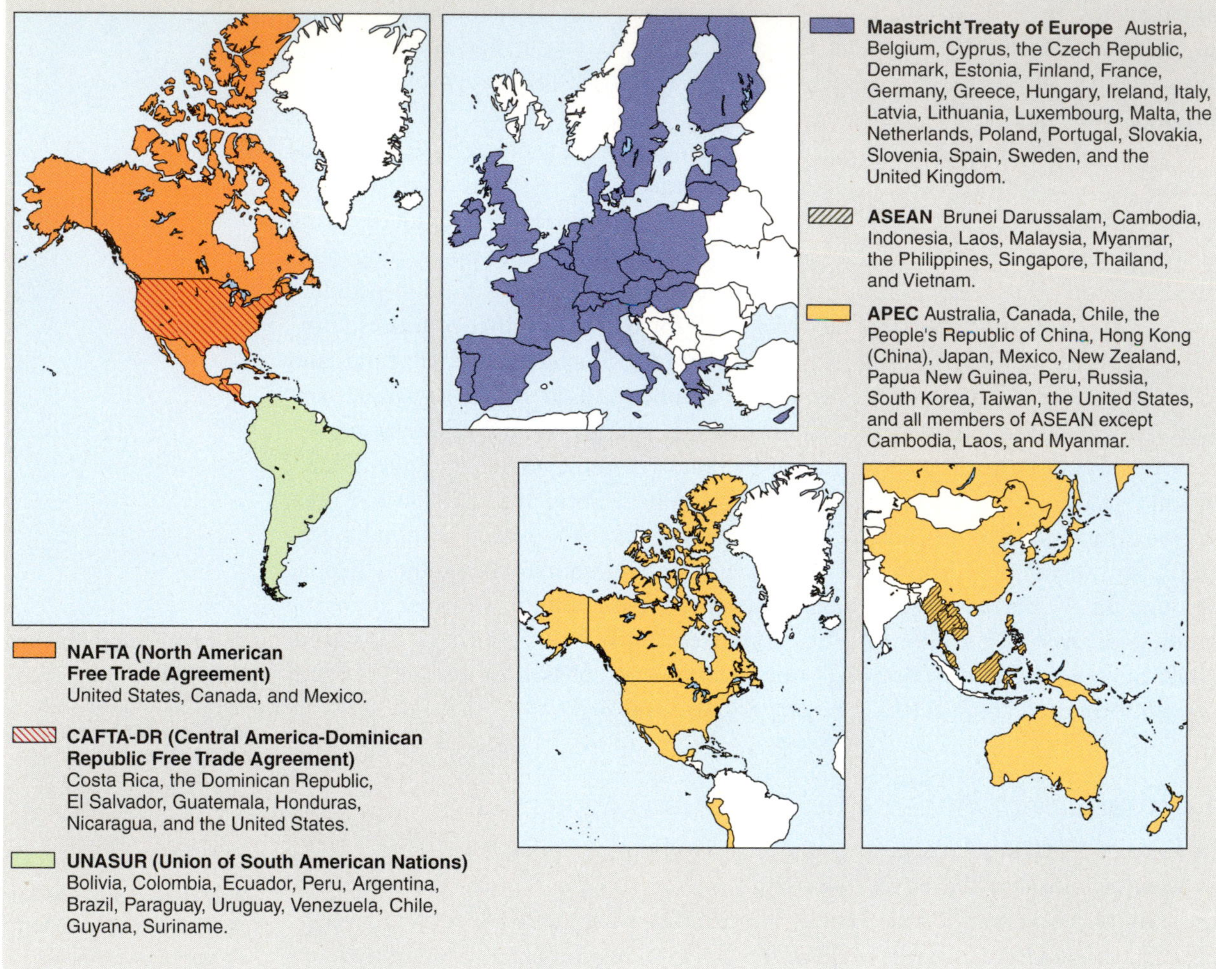

American consumers (and businesses) have had plentiful choices among American-made and foreign-made products. More important, the high level of competition between foreign and domestic companies that creates these choices helps keep prices low in the United States. Furthermore, it is precisely the lack of choice and the low level of competition that keep prices higher in countries that have not been as open to foreign companies and products. For example, Japanese trade barriers are estimated to cost Japanese consumers more than $100 billion a year. In fact, Japanese trade barriers amount to a 51 percent tax on food for the average Japanese family.[29]

So why do trade barriers and free trade agreements matter to consumers? They're important because free trade agreements increase choices, competition, and purchasing power and thus decrease what people pay for food, clothing, necessities, and luxuries. Accordingly, today's consumers rarely care where their products and services come from.

REVIEW 1

Global Business, Trade Rules, and Trade Agreements

Today, there are more than 79,000 multinational corporations worldwide; just 3.1 percent are based in the United States. Global business affects the United States in two ways—through direct foreign investment in the United States by foreign companies, and through U.S. companies' investment in business in other countries. United States direct foreign investment throughout the world amounts to about $2.8 trillion per year, whereas direct foreign investment by foreign companies in the United States amounts to $2.1 trillion per year. Historically, tariffs and nontariff trade barriers, such as quotas, voluntary export restraints, government import standards, government subsidies, and customs classifications, can make buying foreign goods much harder or more expensive than buying domestically produced products. In recent years, however, worldwide trade agreements such as GATT, along with regional trading agreements like the Maastricht Treaty, NAFTA, CAFTA-DR, USAN, ASEAN, and APEC, have substantially reduced tariff and nontariff barriers to international trade. Companies have responded by investing in growing markets in Asia, Eastern Europe, and Latin America.

How to Go Global?

Once a company has decided that it *will* go global, it must decide *how* to go global. For example, if you decide to sell in Singapore, should you try to find a local business partner who speaks the language, knows the laws, and understands the customs and norms of Singapore's culture? Or should you simply export your products from your home country? What do you do if you are also entering Eastern Europe, perhaps starting in Hungary? Should you use the same approach in Hungary that you used in Singapore?

Although there is no magic formula for answering these questions, after reading the next two sections, you should be able to:

2 explain why companies choose to standardize or adapt their business procedures.

3 explain the different ways that companies can organize to do business globally.

2 Consistency or Adaptation?

In this section, we turn to a key issue: How can you be sure that the way you run your business in one country is the right way to run that business in another? In other words, how can you strike the right balance between global consistency and local adaptation?

Global consistency means that when a multinational company has offices, manufacturing plants, and distribution facilities in different countries, it will use the same rules, guidelines, policies, and procedures to run those offices, plants, and facilities. Managers at company headquarters value global consistency because it

global consistency when a multinational company has offices, manufacturing plants, and distribution facilities in different countries and runs them all using the same rules, guidelines, policies, and procedures simplifies decisions. In contrast, a company with a **local adaptation** policy modifies its standard operating procedures to adapt to differences in foreign customers, governments, and regulatory agencies. Local adaptation is typically more important to local managers who are charged with making the international business successful in their countries.

If companies lean too much toward global consistency, they run the risk of using management procedures poorly suited to particular countries' markets, cultures, and employees (i.e., a lack of local adaptation). Unlike the United States, which has widely shared tastes in fashion from state to state, in Europe Tommy *HILFIGER* found highly fragmented consumer tastes that differed significantly across countries. Consequently, while Hilfiger sells most of its products via the same large department and discount stores throughout the United States, in Europe it has taken the opposite strategy by signing sales agreements with 4,500 small boutique stores in 15 countries.

If companies focus too much on local adaptation, however, they run the risk of losing the cost efficiencies and productivity that result from using standardized rules and procedures throughout the world. For example, to keep these 4,500 small retailers happy and wanting to sell more Hilfiger products, the company opened 21 regional showrooms, each featuring at least 25 clothing lines, many of which are adapted to particular markets. While this leads to much higher costs for Hilfiger, those higher costs also produce larger sales. And with profit margins 50 percent to 100 percent higher in Europe, those higher costs still produce much higher profits.[30]

REVIEW 2

Consistency or Adaptation?

Global business requires a balance between global consistency and local adaptation. Global consistency means using the same rules, guidelines, policies, and procedures in each location. Managers at company headquarters like global consistency because it simplifies decisions. Local adaptation means adapting standard procedures to individual markets. Local managers prefer a policy of local adaptation because it gives them more control. Not all businesses need the same combinations of global consistency and local adaptation. Some thrive by emphasizing global consistency and ignoring local adaptation. Others succeed by ignoring global consistency and emphasizing local adaptation.

3 Forms for Global Business

Besides determining whether to adapt organizational policies and procedures, a company must also determine how to organize itself for successful entry into foreign markets.

Historically, companies have generally followed the *phase model of globalization*, in which a company makes the transition from a domestic company to a global company in the following sequential phases: 3.1 **exporting**, 3.2 **cooperative contracts**, 3.3 **strategic alliances**, and 3.4 **wholly owned affiliates**.

local adaptation
modifying rules, guidelines, policies, and procedures to adapt to differences in foreign customers, governments, and regulatory agencies

At each step, the company grows much larger, uses resources to enter more global markets, is less dependent on home country sales, and is more committed in its orientation to global business. Some companies, however, do not follow the phase model of globalization.[31] Some skip phases on their way to becoming more global and less domestic. Others don't follow the phase model at all.

These are known as 3.5 **global new ventures**. This section reviews these forms of global business.[32]

3.1 Exporting

When companies produce products in their home countries and sell those products to customers in foreign countries, they are **exporting**. Located about 90 minutes from Shanghai, the city of Honghe is one of China's largest sweater producers. Half of its 100,000 citizens work in over 100 factories that generate $650 million a year by producing and exporting 200 million sweaters annually.[33]

Exporting as a form of global business offers many advantages. It makes the company less dependent on sales in its home market and provides a greater degree of control over research, design, and production decisions. *American Idol* has been America's number-one television show for nearly a decade. But did you know that there are 38 other versions of *American Idol* around the world? And did you know that *FREMANTLE MEDIA*, which owns and exports those different versions of *American Idol*, produces global versions of *The Apprentice* (16 countries), *Family Feud* (47 countries), *The Price Is Right* (38 countries), and *America's Got Talent* (22 countries)?[34] What makes this work in so many different countries is Fremantle Media's tight control of production. CEO Tony Cohen says, "It's not just about the licensing of formats but the brilliance with which you execute it. You've got to do it well. These things have been through evolution and are pretty well perfect. You can't tamper with it, we're very possessive about that."[35]

Though advantageous in a number of ways, exporting also has its disadvantages. The primary disadvantage is that many exported goods are subject to tariff and nontariff barriers that can substantially increase their final cost to consumers. A second disadvantage is that transportation costs can significantly increase the price of an exported product. There is yet a third disadvantage: Companies that export depend on foreign importers for product distribution. If, for example, the foreign importer makes a mistake on the paperwork that accompanies a shipment of imported goods, those goods can be returned to the foreign manufacturer at the manufacturer's expense.

exporting
selling domestically produced products to customers in foreign countries

3.2 Cooperative Contracts

When an organization wants to expand its business globally without making a large financial commitment to do so, it may sign a **cooperative contract** with a foreign business owner who pays the company a fee for the right to conduct that business in his or her country. There are two kinds of cooperative contracts—licensing and franchising.

cooperative contract
an agreement in which a foreign business owner pays a company a fee for the right to conduct that business in his or her country

Under a **licensing** agreement, a domestic company, the *licensor*, receives royalty payments for allowing another company, the *licensee*, to produce its product, sell its service, or use its brand name in a particular foreign market. In India, the *MURJANI GROUP* licenses Tommy Hilfiger products. In the last 3 years, Murjani has built ten new Hilfiger retail stores in India that produce between $20 and $25 million in annual revenues.

licensing
an agreement in which a domestic company, the licensor, receives royalty payments for allowing another company, the licensee, to produce the licensor's product, sell its service, or use its brand name in a specified foreign market

One of the most important advantages of licensing is that it allows companies to earn additional profits without investing more money. As foreign sales increase, the royalties paid to the licensor by the foreign licensee increase. Moreover, the licensee,

Doing the Right Thing

Fair and Safe Working Conditions in Foreign Factories

Requiring workers to work 15-hour days or to work 7 days a week with no overtime pay, beating them for arriving late, requiring them to apply toxic materials with their bare hands, charging them excessive fees for food and lodging—these are just a few of the workplace violations found in the overseas factories that make shoes, clothes, bicycles, and other goods for large U.S. and multinational companies. The Fair Labor Association, which inspects overseas factories for Adidas-Salomon, Levi Strauss, Liz Claiborne, Nike, Reebok, Ralph Lauren, and others, recommends the following workplace standards for foreign factories.

- Make sure there is no forced labor or child labor; no physical, sexual, psychological, or verbal abuse or harassment; and no discrimination.
- Provide a safe and healthy working environment to prevent accidents.
- Respect the rights of employees to freedom of association and collective bargaining. Compensate employees fairly by paying the legally required minimum wage or the prevailing industry wage, whichever is higher.
- Provide legally required benefits. Employees should not be required to work more than 48 hours per week and 12 hours of overtime (for which they should receive additional pay), and they should have at least 1 day off per week.

Do the right thing. Investigate and monitor the working conditions of overseas factories where the goods sold by your company are made. Insist that improvements be made. Find another supplier if they aren't.[36]

not the licensor, invests in production equipment and facilities to produce the licensed product. Licensing also helps companies avoid tariff and nontariff barriers. Since the licensee manufactures the product within the foreign country, tariff and nontariff barriers don't apply. For example, Britvic Corona is licensed to bottle and distribute Pepsi-Cola within the United Kingdom. Because it bottles the soft drink in Britain, tariff and nontariff barriers do not apply.

The biggest disadvantage associated with licensing is that the licensor gives up control over the quality of the product or service sold by the foreign licensee. Unless the licensing agreement contains specific restrictions, the licensee controls the entire business from production to marketing to final sales. Many licensors include inspection clauses in their license contracts, but closely monitoring product or service quality from thousands of miles away can be difficult. An additional disadvantage is that licensees can eventually become competitors, especially when a licensing agreement includes access to important technology or proprietary business knowledge.

A **franchise** is a collection of networked firms in which the manufacturer or marketer of a product or service, the *franchisor*, licenses the entire business to another person or organization, the *franchisee*. For the price of an initial franchise fee plus royalties, franchisors provide franchisees with training, assistance with marketing and advertising, and an exclusive right to conduct business in a particular location. Most franchise fees run between $5,000 and $35,000. Franchisees pay McDonald's, one of the largest franchisors in the world, an initial fee of $45,000. Another $950,900 to $1,797,700 is needed beyond that to pay for food inventory, kitchen equipment, construction, landscaping, and other expenses (the cost varies per country). While they typically borrow part of this cost from a bank, McDonald's requires franchisees to put down 40 percent in cash for the initial investment.[37] Since typical royalties range from 2.0 to 12.5 percent of gross sales, franchisors are well rewarded for the help they provide to franchisees. More than 400 U.S. companies franchise their businesses to foreign franchise partners.

Overall, franchising is a fast way to enter foreign markets. Over the last 20 years, U.S. franchisors have more than doubled their global franchises, for a total of more than 100,000 global franchise units. Because it gives the franchisor additional cash flows from franchisee fees and royalties, franchising can be a good strategy when a company's domestic sales have slowed. Despite the many advantages of franchising, franchisors face a loss of control when they sell businesses to franchisees who are thousands of miles away.

Although there are exceptions, franchising success may be somewhat culture-bound. Because most global franchisors begin by franchising their businesses in similar countries or regions, and because 65 percent of franchisors make absolutely no change in their business for overseas franchisees, that success may not generalize to cultures with different lifestyles, values, preferences, and technological infrastructures. When Jim Bryant began opening *SUBWAY* sandwich shops in China 10 years ago, Americans living there were elated (one kissed the floor), but Chinese customers didn't know how to order (he had to make signs explaining how) or how to eat a sandwich (they peeled the wrapper like a banana because they didn't want to touch their food). Likewise, because the tuna in the tuna salad didn't have a visible head or a tail, they didn't believe it was actually fish.[38] Management consultant Dennis Custage says, "The number one mistake companies make is trying to run everything the way it was in their home country, with a bunch of expatriates."[39] Furthermore, unlike McDonald's, which added a new spicy chicken burger, and KFC, which replaced coleslaw with shredded carrots, fungus, or bamboo shoots, Subway didn't change its menu for Chinese tastes. Luo Bing Ling, who runs a Subway store in Beijing, says, "Subway should have at least one item tailored to Chinese tastes to show they are respecting the local culture."[40]

franchise
a collection of networked firms in which the manufacturer or marketer of a product or service, the franchisor, licenses the entire business to another person or organization, the franchisee

3.3 Strategic Alliances

Companies forming **strategic alliances** combine key resources, costs, risks, technology, and people. The most common strategic alliance is a **joint venture**, which occurs when two existing companies collaborate to form a third company. The two founding companies remain intact and unchanged, except that together they now own the newly created joint venture. One of the oldest and most successful global joint ventures is *FUJI XEROX*, a joint venture between Fuji Film of Japan and U.S.-based Xerox Corporation, which makes copiers and automated office systems. More than 45 years after its creation, Fuji Xerox employs 42,000 employees and has close to $12 billion in revenues. Fuji Xerox is largely responsible for copier sales in Asia, whereas Xerox is responsible for North American sales.[41]

strategic alliance
an agreement in which companies combine key resources, costs, risk, technology, and people

joint venture
a strategic alliance in which two existing companies collaborate to form a third, independent company

Management Fact:

Protection of intellectual property has become an increasingly important issue in global trade because of widespread piracy. For example, 90 percent of all computer software and 95 percent of all videogames sold in China are illegal copies. Likewise, Chinese bootleggers regularly sell copies of movies that are still running in theaters, months before studios release official copies to stores. Here in the United States, file sharing software such as Bit Torrent and Gnutella make it easy for computer users to download music, movies, and software. All told, product piracy costs movie studios, distributors, theaters, and software companies nearly $18 billion in lost revenue each year.

Sources: H. Blodget. "How to Solve China's Piracy Problem: A Dozen Ideas. Maybe One Will Work." *Slate*, 12 April 2005, available online at http://www.slate.com/id/2116629 [accessed 18 March 2009].

G. Fowler. "Estimates of Copyright Piracy Losses Vary Widely." *Wall Street Journal*, 2 June 2006, A13.

One of the advantages of global joint ventures is that, like licensing and franchising, they help companies avoid tariff and nontariff barriers to entry. Another advantage is that companies participating in a joint venture bear only part of the costs and the risks of that business. Many companies find this attractive because of the expense of entering foreign markets or developing new products.

Global joint ventures can be especially advantageous to smaller local partners who link up with larger, more experienced foreign firms that can bring advanced management, resources, and business skills to the joint venture. For example, *ARROW ENERGY, LTD.* is an oil and natural gas exploration and production company based in Calgary, Canada. Arrow is partnering with Royal *DUTCH SHELL PLC* in a global joint venture to mine and export natural gas from coal seams in Australia.[42] Global joint ventures are not without problems, though. Because companies share costs and risks with their joint venture partners, they must also share profits. At one time, sharing of profits created some tension between Fuji Film and Xerox. In fact, until Xerox's recent turnaround, the company struggled for so long that business experts joked that Fuji Xerox, which has been highly profitable, should purchase Xerox.

Managing global joint ventures can also be difficult because they represent a merging of four cultures: the country and the organizational cultures of the first partner, and the country and the organizational cultures of the second partner. Because of these problems, companies forming global joint ventures should carefully develop detailed contracts that specify the obligations of each party. The joint venture contract specifies how much each company will invest, what its rights and responsibilities are, and what it is entitled to if the joint venture does not work out. These steps are important because for the failure rate of global joint ventures is estimated to be as high as 70 percent.[43]

3.4 Wholly Owned Affiliates (Build or Buy)

wholly owned affiliates foreign offices, facilities, and manufacturing plants that are 100 percent owned by the parent company

Approximately one-third of multinational companies enter foreign markets through wholly owned affiliates. Unlike licensing arrangements, franchises, or joint ventures, **wholly owned affiliates** are 100 percent owned by the parent company. For example, Honda Motors of America in Marysville, Ohio, is 100 percent owned by Honda Motors of Japan. Likewise, Ford Motor of Germany in Cologne is 100 percent owned by the Ford Motor Company in Detroit, Michigan.[44]

The primary advantage of wholly owned businesses is that the parent company receives all of the profits and has complete control over the foreign facilities. The biggest disadvantage is the expense of building new operations or buying existing businesses. Although the payoff can be enormous if wholly owned affiliates succeed, the losses can be immense if they fail because the parent company assumes all of the risk. *VALUE CITY*, which is a wholly owned subsidiary of Retail Ventures Inc., has 113 stores in the Midwest and the Southeast. Value City, which sells discount merchandise, has struggled against Wal-Mart and Target in recent years and is losing over $50 million a year. As a result of those losses, Retail Ventures is selling Value City so it can focus on DSW, which is a discount shoe retailer with 250 stores in 36 states.[45]

3.5 Global New Ventures

Companies used to evolve slowly from small operations selling in their home markets to large businesses selling to foreign markets. Furthermore, as companies went global, they usually followed the phase model of globalization. Recently, however, three trends have combined to allow companies to skip the phase model when going global. First, quick, reliable air travel can transport people to nearly any point in the world within one day. Second, low-cost communication technologies such as e-mail, teleconferencing, and phone conferencing, make it easier to communicate with global customers, suppliers, managers, and employees. Third, there is now a critical mass of businesspeople with extensive personal experience in all aspects of global business.[46] This combination of developments has made it possible to start companies that are global from inception. With sales, employees, and financing in different countries, **global new ventures** are companies that are founded with an active global strategy.[47]

Although there are several different kinds of global new ventures, all share two factors. First, the company founders successfully develop and communicate the company's global vision from inception. Second, rather than going global one country at a time, new global ventures bring a product or service to market in several foreign markets at the same time. Companies like VistaPrint, which prints business cards, brochures, and invitations for a worldwide clientele, bring a product or service to several foreign markets at the same time. VistaPrint receives 15,000 orders a day from customers in 120 different countries who design their business cards, brochures, and invitations online using 17 different VistaPrint websites, each representing a different language or location. Printing happens at two automated production facilities, one in the Netherlands and the other in Canada. Once printed, the products are cut and sized by robots and then packaged and delivered just 3 days after ordering.[48]

global new ventures
new companies that are founded with an active global strategy and have sales, employees, and financing in different countries

REVIEW 3

Forms for Global Business

The phase model of globalization says that as companies move from a domestic to a global orientation, they use these organizational forms in sequence: exporting, cooperative contracts (licensing and franchising), strategic alliances, and wholly owned affiliates. Yet not all companies follow the phase model. For example, global new ventures are global from their inception.

Where to Go Global?

Deciding where to go global is just as important as deciding how your company will go global.

After reading the next three sections, you should be able to:

4 explain how to find a favorable business climate.
5 discuss the importance of identifying and adapting to cultural differences.
6 explain how to prepare workers for international assignments.

4 Finding the Best Business Climate

An attractive global business climate 4.1 **positions the company for easy access to growing markets**, 4.2 **is an effective but cost-efficient place to build an office or manufacturing facility**, and 4.3 **minimizes the political risk to the company**.

4.1 Growing Markets

The most important factor in an attractive business climate is access to a growing market. For example, no product is known and purchased by as many people throughout the world as Coca-Cola. Yet even Coke, which is available in over 200 countries, still has tremendous potential for further global growth. Coca-Cola gets 76 percent of its sales outside of North America. And emerging markets, where it has seen its fastest growth, now account for half of Coke's sales worldwide.[49]

Two factors help companies determine the growth potential of foreign markets: purchasing power and foreign competitors. **Purchasing power** is measured by comparing the relative cost of a standard set of goods and services in different countries. Earlier in the chapter we noted that a Coke averages $1.38 in Tokyo. Because a 12-ounce Coke costs less than $1 in the United States, the average American would have more purchasing power than the average Japanese. Purchasing power is strong in countries like Mexico, India, and China, which have low average levels of income. This is because basic living expenses such as food, shelter, and transportation are very inexpensive in those countries, so consumers still have money to spend after paying for necessities.

Consequently, countries with high and growing levels of purchasing power are good choices for companies looking for attractive global markets. Coke has found that the per capita consumption of Coca-Cola, or the number of Cokes a person drinks per year, rises directly with purchasing power. For example, in China, Brazil, and Spain, where the average person earns, respectively, $7,600, $8,600, and $27,000 annually, the number of Coca-Cola soft drinks consumed per year increases, respectively, from 18 to 156 to 305. The more purchasing power people have, the more likely they are to purchase (among other things) soft drinks.

The second part of assessing the growth potential of global markets involves analyzing the degree of global competition, which is determined by the number and quality of companies that already compete in a foreign market. *INTEL* has been in China for 20 years not only because of the size of the potential market (China has 1.3 billion people and 95 percent of Chinese homes still don't have a computer)

purchasing power
the relative cost of a standard set of goods and services in different countries

but also because there was almost no competition. But now that China is the third-largest computer chip market in the world, Intel faces significant competition. Intel's 20-year head start, however, has given it a dominating 75 percent share of the Chinese market.[50]

Doing the Right Thing

Foreign Corrupt Business Practices Act

The Foreign Corrupt Business Practices Act (FCPA) prohibits company managers, employees, or agents from offering money or anything else of value to bribe officials of foreign governments or political parties to use their influence to help that firm acquire new business or keep existing business in that country. Individuals violating the FCPA can be fined up to $100,000 and imprisoned for up to 10 years. Companies that violate the FCPA can be fined up to $2 million, suspended from government contracts, denied export licensing privileges, and investigated by the Securities and Exchange Commission. U.S. businesspeople often worry that the FCPA puts them at a disadvantage because other countries have permitted bribes to be deducted as business expenses. Recently, however, 33 major trading partners of the United States agreed to enact laws similar to the FCPA.[53]

4.2 Choosing an Office/Manufacturing Location

Companies do not have to establish an office or manufacturing location in each country they enter. They can license, franchise, or export to foreign markets, or they can serve a larger region from one country. But there are many reasons why a company might choose to establish a location in a foreign country.

The criteria for choosing an office/manufacturing location are different from the criteria for entering a foreign market. Rather than focusing on costs alone, companies should consider both qualitative and quantitative factors. Two key qualitative factors are workforce quality and company strategy. Workforce quality is important because it is often difficult to find workers with the specific skills, abilities, and experience that a company needs to run its business. Workforce quality is one reason that many companies doing business in Europe locate their customer call centers in the Netherlands. Workers in the Netherlands are the most linguistically gifted in Europe, with 73 percent speaking two languages, 44 percent speaking three languages, and 12 percent speaking more than three. Of course, with employees who speak several languages, call centers located in the Netherlands can handle calls from more countries and generally employ 30 to 50 percent fewer employees than those located in other parts of Europe.[51]

A company's strategy is also important when choosing a location. For example, a company pursuing a low-cost strategy may need plentiful raw materials, low-cost transportation, and low-cost labor. A company pursuing a differentiation strategy (typically a higher-priced, better product or service) may need access to high-quality materials and a highly skilled and educated work force. Quantitative factors such as the kind of facility being built, tariff and nontariff barriers, exchange rates, and transportation and labor costs should also be considered when choosing an office/manufacturing location.

4.3 Minimizing Political Risk

When managers think about political risk in global business, they envision burning factories and riots in the streets. Although events such as these receive dramatic and extended coverage from the media, the political risks that most companies face usually are not covered as breaking stories on Fox News and CNN. Nonetheless, the negative consequences of ordinary political risk can be just as devastating to companies that fail to identify and minimize that risk.[52]

When conducting global business, companies should attempt to identify two types of political risk: political uncertainty and policy uncertainty.[54] **Political uncertainty** is associated with the risk of major changes in political regimes that can result from war, revolution, death of political leaders, social unrest, or other influential events. **Policy uncertainty** refers to the risk associated with changes in laws and government policies that directly affect the way foreign companies conduct business.

Policy uncertainty is the most common—and perhaps most frustrating—form of political risk in global business, especially when changes in laws and government policies directly undercut sizable investments made by foreign companies. Royal Dutch Shell joined with Russia-based Gazprom, a state-owned company, to develop Sakhalin-2, one of the world's largest liquefied natural gas fields. Shell and its partners took the lead role with 55 percent ownership and a $20 billion investment. However, after years of development and billions invested, the Russian government banned foreign companies from owning more than 49 percent of any energy development project. This forced Royal Dutch Shell to relinquish majority ownership to Gazprom in return for $7.45 billion and greatly reduced its access to other Russian gas fields.[55]

Several strategies can be used to minimize or adapt to the political risk inherent in global business. An *avoidance strategy* is used when the political risks associated with a foreign country or region are viewed as too great. If firms are already invested in high-risk areas, they may divest or sell their businesses. If they have not yet invested, they will likely postpone their investment until the risk shrinks.

Control is an active strategy to prevent or reduce political risks. Firms using a control strategy lobby foreign governments or international trade agencies to change laws, regulations, or trade barriers that hurt their business in that country. Another method for dealing with political risk is *cooperation*, which involves using joint ventures and collaborative contracts, such as franchising and licensing. Although cooperation does not eliminate the political risk of doing business in a country, it can limit the risk associated with foreign ownership of a business. For example, a German company forming a joint venture with a Chinese company to do business in China may structure the joint venture contract so that the Chinese company owns 51 percent or more of the joint venture. Doing so qualifies the joint venture as a Chinese company and exempts it from Chinese laws that apply to foreign-owned businesses.

political uncertainty
the risk of major changes in political regimes that can result from war, revolution, death of political leaders, social unrest, or other influential events

policy uncertainty
the risk associated with changes in laws and government policies that directly affect the way foreign companies conduct business

REVIEW 4

Finding the Best Business Climate

The first step in deciding where to take your company global is finding an attractive business climate. Look for a growing market where consumers have strong purchasing power and foreign competitors are weak. When locating an office or manufacturing facility, consider both qualitative and quantitative factors. In assessing political risk, be sure to examine political uncertainty and policy uncertainty. If the location you choose has considerable political risk, you can avoid it, try to control the risk, or use a cooperation strategy.

5 Becoming Aware of Cultural Differences

Some of the more interesting and amusing aspects of global business are the unexpected confrontations that people have with cultural differences, "the way they do things over there." *Wall Street Journal* columnist Geoffrey Fowler wrote of an incident in Hong Kong where a Chinese colleague casually observed that he had gained weight.[56] Uttered in the United States, such comments would be considered rude. Fowler indicates that in China, where people openly talk about people's weight, body shapes, and salaries, such comments are probably just friendliness. So what does Fowler say when his friendly Chinese colleagues tell him he's fat? "There's so much good food here."

National culture is the set of shared values and beliefs that affects the perceptions, decisions, and behavior of the people from a particular country. The first step in dealing with culture is to recognize that there are meaningful differences. Professor Geert Hofstede spent 20 years studying cultural differences in 53 different countries. His research shows that there are five consistent cultural dimensions across countries: power distance, individualism, masculinity/feminity, uncertainty avoidance, and short-term versus long-term orientation.[57]

Power distance is the extent to which people in a country accept that power is distributed unequally in society and organizations. In countries where power distance is weak, such as Denmark and Sweden, employees don't like their organization or their boss to have power over them or tell them what to do. They want to have a say in decisions that affect them.

Individualism is the degree to which societies believe that individuals should be self-sufficient. In individualistic societies, employees put loyalty to themselves first and loyalty to their company and work group second.

Masculinity and *femininity* capture the difference between highly assertive and highly nurturing cultures. Masculine cultures emphasize assertiveness, competition, material success, and achievement, whereas feminine cultures emphasize the importance of relationships, modesty, caring for the weak, and quality of life.

The cultural difference of *uncertainty avoidance* is the degree to which people in a country are uncomfortable with unstructured, ambiguous, unpredictable situations. In countries with strong uncertainty avoidance, like Greece and Portugal, people tend to be aggressive and emotional and seek security rather than uncertainty.

Short-term/long-term orientation addresses whether cultures are oriented to the present and seek immediate gratification or to the future and defer gratification. Not surprisingly, countries with short-term orientations are consumer-driven, whereas countries with long-term orientations are savings-driven.

Cultural differences affect perceptions, understanding, and behavior. Recognizing cultural differences is critical to succeeding in global business. Nevertheless, as Hofstede pointed out, descriptions of cultural differences are based on averages—the average level of uncertainty avoidance in Portugal, the average level of power distance in Argentina, and so forth. Accordingly, says Hofstede, "If you are going

national culture
the set of shared values and beliefs that affects the perceptions, decisions, and behavior of the people from a particular country

to spend time with a Japanese colleague, you shouldn't assume that all cultural statements about Japanese society automatically apply to this person."[58] Similarly, cultural beliefs may differ significantly from one part of a country to another.

After becoming aware of cultural differences, the second step is deciding how to adapt your company to those differences. Unfortunately, studies investigating the effects of cultural differences on management practice point more to difficulties than to easy solutions. One problem is that different cultures will probably perceive management policies and practices differently.

Another difficulty is that cultural values are changing, albeit slowly, in many parts of the world. The fall of communism in Eastern Europe and the former Soviet Union and the broad economic reforms in China have produced sweeping changes on two continents in the last decade. Thanks to increased global trade resulting from GATT and other regional free trade agreements, major economic transformations are also under way in India, Mexico, Central America, and South America. Consequently, when trying to adapt management practices to cultural differences, companies must ensure that they are not basing their adaptations on outdated and incorrect assumptions about a country's culture.

REVIEW 5

Becoming Aware of Cultural Differences

National culture is the set of shared values and beliefs that affects the perceptions, decisions, and behavior of the people from a particular country. The first step in dealing with culture is to recognize meaningful differences such as power distance, individualism, masculinity, uncertainty avoidance, and short-term/long-term orientation. Cultural differences should be carefully interpreted because they are based on averages, not individuals. Adapting managerial practices to cultural differences is difficult because policies and practices can be perceived differently in different cultures. Another difficulty is that cultural values may be changing in many parts of the world. Consequently, when companies try to adapt management practices to cultural differences, they need to be sure that they are not using outdated assumptions about a country's culture.

6 Preparing for an International Assignment

Around a conference table in a large office tower, three American executives sat with their new boss, Akiro Kusumoto, the newly appointed head of a Japanese firm's American subsidiary, and two of his Japanese lieutenants. The meeting was called to discuss ideas for reducing operating costs. Kusumoto began by outlining his company's aspirations for its long-term U.S. presence. He then turned to budgetary matters. A Japanese manager politely offered one suggestion, and an American then proposed another. After gingerly discussing the alternatives for quite some time, the exasperated American blurted out: "Look, that idea is just not going to have much impact. Look at the numbers!" In the face of such bluntness, uncommon and unacceptable in Japan, Kusumoto fell silent. He leaned back, drew air between his teeth, and felt a deep longing to return home. He realized his life in this country would be filled with many such jarring encounters and lamented his posting to a land of such rudeness.[59]

Akiro Kusumoto is a Japanese **expatriate**, someone who lives and works outside his or her native country. The cultural shock that he was experiencing is common. The difficulty of adjusting to language, cultural, and social differences is the primary reason for expatriate failure in overseas assignments. For example, although there have recently been disagreements among researchers about these numbers, it is probably safe to say that 5 to 20 percent of American expatriates sent abroad by their companies will return to the United States before they have successfully completed their assignments.[60] Of those who do complete their international assignments, about one-third are judged by their companies to be no better than marginally effective.[61] Since the average cost of sending an employee on a 3-year international assignment is $1 million, failure in those assignments can be extraordinarily expensive.[62]

The chances for a successful international assignment can be increased through 6.1 **language and cross-cultural training**, and 6.2 **consideration of spouse, family, and dual-career issues**.

6.1 Language and Cross-Cultural Training

Predeparture language and cross-cultural training can reduce the uncertainty that expatriates feel, the misunderstandings that take place between expatriates and natives, and the inappropriate behaviors that expatriates unknowingly commit when they travel to a foreign country. Indeed, simple things like using a phone, locating a public toilet, asking for directions, finding out how much things cost, exchanging greetings, or understanding what people want can become tremendously complex when expatriates don't know a foreign language or a country's customs and cultures. In his book *Blunders in International Business*, David Ricks tells the story of an American manager working in the South Pacific who, by hiring too many local workers from one native group, unknowingly upset the balance of power in the island's traditional status system. The islanders met on their own and quickly worked out a solution to the problem. After concluding their meeting at 3 A.M., they calmly went to the manager's home to discuss their solution with him (time was not important in their culture). But since the American didn't speak their language and didn't understand why they had shown up en masse outside his home at 3 A.M, he called in the Marines, who were stationed nearby, to disperse what he thought was a riot.

Expatriates who receive predeparture language and cross-cultural training make faster adjustments to foreign cultures and perform better on their international assignments.[63] Unfortunately, only a third of the managers who go on international assignments are offered any kind of predeparture training, and only half of those actually participate in the training![64] This is somewhat surprising given the failure rates for expatriates and the high cost of those failures. Furthermore, with the exception of some language courses, predeparture training is not particularly expensive or difficult to provide. Three methods can be used to prepare workers for international assignments—documentary training, cultural simulations, and field experiences.

Documentary training focuses on identifying specific critical differences between cultures. For example, when 60 workers at *AXCELIS TECHNOLOGIES* in Beverly, Massachusetts, were preparing to do business in India, they learned that while Americans make eye contact and shake hands firmly when greeting others, Indians, as a sign of respect, do just the opposite, avoiding eye contact and shaking hands limply.[65]

expatriate
someone who lives and works outside his or her native country

After learning specific critical differences through documentary training, trainees can then participate in *cultural simulations*, in which they practice adapting to cultural differences. After the workers at Axcelis Technologies learned about key differences between their culture and India's, they practiced adapting to those differences by role playing. Some Axcelis workers would take the roles of Indian workers, while others would play themselves and try to behave in a way consistent with Indian culture.

Finally, *field simulation* training, a technique made popular by the U.S. Peace Corps, places trainees in an ethnic neighborhood for 3 to 4 hours to talk to residents about cultural differences. For example, a U.S. electronics manufacturer prepared workers for assignments in South Korea by having trainees explore a nearby South Korean neighborhood and talk to shopkeepers and people on the street about South Korean politics, family orientation, and day-to-day living practices.

6.2 Spouse, Family, and Dual-Career Issues

Not all international assignments are as difficult for expatriates and their families, but the evidence clearly shows that how well an expatriate's spouse and family adjust to the foreign culture is the most important factor in determining the success or failure of an international assignment.[66] A number of companies have found that adaptability screening and intercultural training for families can lead to more successful overseas adjustment.

Adaptability screening is used to assess how well managers and their families are likely to adjust to foreign cultures. For example, *PRUDENTIAL RELOCATION MANAGEMENT'S* international division has developed an "Overseas Assignment Inventory" to assess a spouse and family's open-mindedness, respect for others' beliefs, sense of humor, and marital communication. But adaptability screening does not just involve a company assessing an employee; it can also involve an employee screening international assignments for desirability. Since more employees are becoming aware of the costs of international assignments (spouses having to give up or change jobs, children having to change schools, everyone having to learn a new language), some companies are willing to pay for a preassignment trip so the employee and his or her spouse can investigate the country *before* accepting the international assignment.[67]

what *really* works

Cross-Cultural Training

Most expatriates will tell you that cross-cultural training helped them adjust to foreign cultures. Such anecdotal data, however, are not as convincing as systematic studies. Twenty-one studies, with a combined total of 1,611 participants, examined whether cross-cultural training affects the self-development, relationships, perceptions, adjustment, and job performance of expatriates. Overall, they show that cross-cultural training works extremely well in most instances.

Self-Development

When you first arrive in another country, you must learn how to make decisions that you took for granted in your home country: how to get to work, how to get to the grocery, how to pay your bills, and so on. If you've generally been confident about yourself and your abilities, an overseas assignment can challenge that sense of self. Cross-cultural training helps expatriates deal with these and other challenges. Expatriates who receive cross-cultural training are 79 percent more likely to report healthy psychological well-being and self-development than those who don't receive training.

PSYCHOLOGICAL WELL-BEING & SELF-DEVELOPMENT

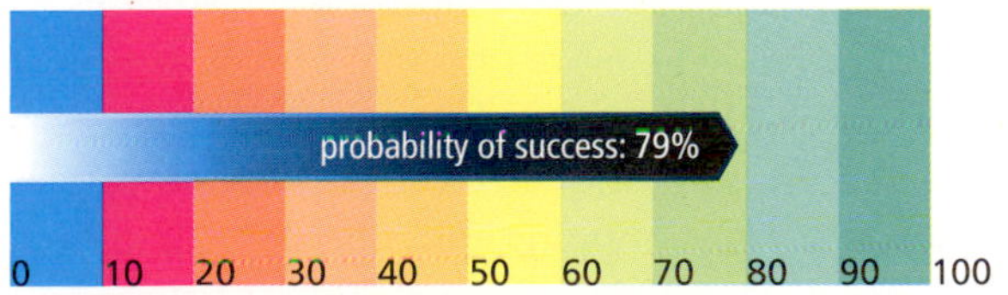

Fostering Relationships

One of the most important aspects of an overseas assignment is establishing and maintaining relationships with host nationals. If you're in Brazil, you need to make friends with Brazilians. Many expatriates, however, make the mistake of making friends only with other expatriates from their home country. In effect, they become social isolates in a foreign country. They work and live there, but as much as they can, they speak their native language, eat their native foods, and socialize with other expatriates from their home country. Cross-cultural training makes a big difference in whether expatriates establish relationships with host nationals. Expatriates who receive cross-cultural training are 74 percent more likely to establish such relationships.

FOSTERING RELATIONSHIPS WITH NATIVE CITIZENS

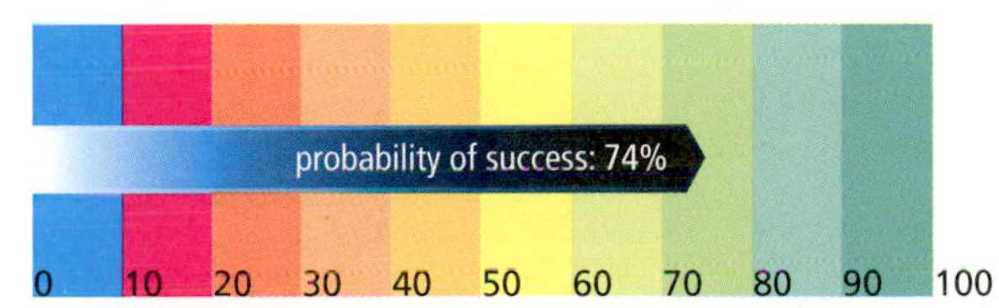

Accurate Perceptions of Culture

Another characteristic of successful expatriates is that they understand the cultural norms and practices of the host country. For example, many Americans do not understand the famous pictures of Japanese troops turning their backs to American military commanders on V-J Day, when Japan surrendered to the United States to end World War II. Americans viewed this as a lack of respect, when, in fact, in Japan turning one's

ACCURATE CULTURAL PERCEPTIONS

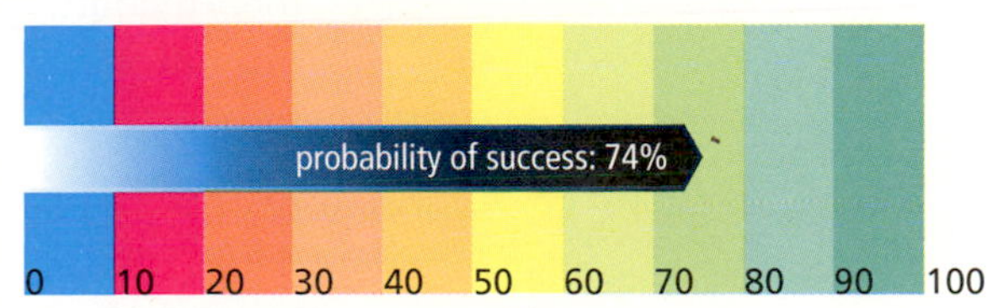

back in this way is a sign of respect. Cross-cultural training makes a big difference in the accuracy of perceptions concerning host country norms and practices. Expatriates who receive cross-cultural training are 74 percent more likely to have accurate perceptions.

Rapid Adjustment

New employees are most likely to quit in the first 6 months because this initial period requires the most adjustment: learning new names, new faces, new procedures, and new information. It's tough. Of course, expatriates have a much harder time adjusting to their new jobs because they are also learning new languages, new foods, new customs, and often new lifestyles. Expatriates who receive cross-cultural training are 74 percent more likely to make a rapid adjustment to a foreign country.

RAPID ADJUSTMENT TO FOREIGN CULTURES AND COUNTRIES

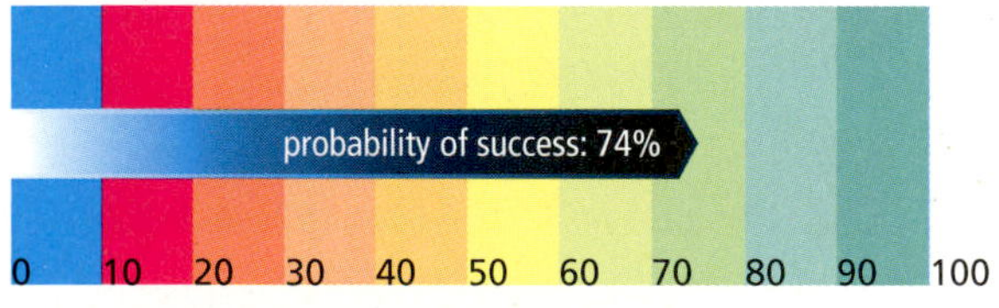

Job Performance

It's good that cross-cultural training improves self-development, fosters relationships, improves the accuracy of perceptions, and helps expatriates make rapid adjustments to foreign cultures. From an organizational standpoint, however, the ultimate test of cross-cultural training is whether it improves expatriates' job performance. The evidence shows that cross-cultural training makes a significant difference in expatriates' job performance, although the difference is not quite as large as for the other factors. Nonetheless, it is estimated that cross-cultural training for 100 managers could bring about $390,000 worth of benefits to a company, or nearly $4,000 per manager. This is an outstanding return on investment, especially when you consider the high rate of failure for expatriates. Expatriates who have received cross-cultural training are 71 percent more likely to have better on-the-job performance than those who did not receive cross-cultural training.[68]

ON-THE-JOB PERFORMANCE

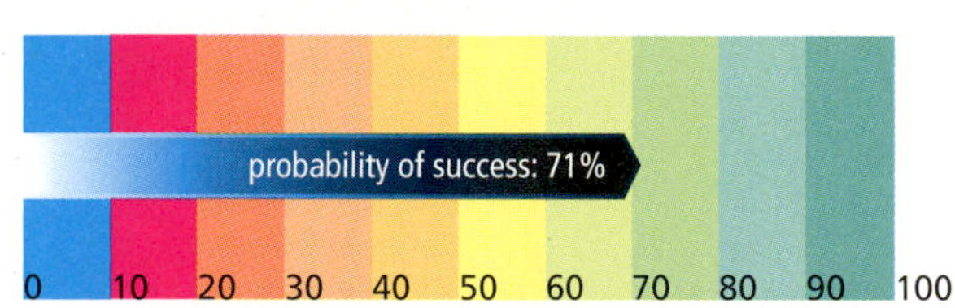

Only 40 percent of expatriates' families receive language and cross-cultural training, yet such training is just as important for the families of expatriates as for the expatriates themselves.[69] In fact, it may be more important because, unlike expatriates, whose professional jobs often shield them from the full force of a country's culture, spouses and children are fully immersed in foreign neighborhoods and schools. Households must be run, shopping must be done, and bills must be paid. Expatriates' children must deal with different cultural beliefs and practices, too. In addition to helping families prepare for the cultural differences they will encounter, language and cross-cultural training can help reduce uncertainty about how to act and decrease misunderstandings between expatriates and their families and locals.

REVIEW 6

Preparing for an International Assignment

Many expatriates return prematurely from international assignments because of poor performance. However, premature return is much less likely to happen if employees receive language and cross-cultural training, such as documentary training, cultural simulations, or field experiences, before going on assignment. Adjustment of expatriates' spouses and families, which is the most important determinant of success in international assignments, can be improved through adaptability screening and intercultural training.

Management Decision

Back in the U.S.?

For years now, U.S.-based companies have saved an unbelievable amount of money by outsourcing—moving groups, divisions, and even entire operations overseas to take advantage of lower labor costs, looser regulations, and significant tax incentives. Most of Nike's shoes are manufactured in Asia. Many of the cars that GM sells in the United States are made in Mexico. Vizio's LCD televisions are produced in China. But outsourcing isn't limited to manufacturing. A good portion of Ford's IT and engineering services are now located in India. And as almost anyone who has had to call a customer service center has experienced, many companies operate call centers in English-speaking foreign countries.

Five years ago, your company, which makes leather accessories, decided to move all manufacturing to Guatemala. It was, admittedly, an unpopular move. Employees were shocked. Community leaders were angry. There were lots of demonstrations and near-riots. But you always told yourself that the move overseas was a necessary step for your company to stay in business.

In recent days, however, you've heard a lot of reports about companies that are saving money by "onshoring." Reversing a decades-old trend, these companies are closing overseas manufacturing facilities and bringing those jobs back to the United States. General Electric recently closed a water heater plant in China and replaced it with a facility in Louisville, Kentucky. U.S. Block Windows shifted production from China to Pensacola, Florida. And Caterpillar, a heavy-machinery manufacturer, announced plans to open a new U.S.-based plant that would consolidate production from factories located in Japan and Chicago.

There are a number of reasons why companies are choosing to return to the United States. For one, the weakening of the U.S. dollar in the global market has made it more expensive to import products from overseas. Second, various federal and state agencies, trying to bring a quick end to the recession, have offered great incentives to businesses that stay in the United States. Third, it appears that globalization has lost some of its appeal. True, outsourcing does allow a company to take advantage of lower labor costs. But is also brings increased shipping costs, complications of logistics, quality control issues, language and cultural barriers, political unrest, and the potential for theft of intellectual property. Just in the past year, most of the money that you saved from cheap labor went straight into paying for higher fuel costs, bribing corrupt local officials, and competing against a group of former employees who are now manufacturing cheaper imitations of your entire product line.

All of this makes you wonder whether it's worth it to stay in Guatemala. Maybe your company would be better served by bringing production back to the United States. You might even be celebrated for bringing jobs back to the community.

Questions

1. What are the advantages and disadvantages of outsourcing? Of "inshoring"?
2. How would you convince your board of directors that paying higher labor costs in the United States would be better for the long-term health of the company?
3. Whether it's in the United States or a foreign country, what conditions would you look for when selecting the ideal business climate?

Source: Kris Maher and Bob Tata. "Caterpillar Joins 'Onshoring' Trend." *Wall Street Journal.* March 12, 2010. B1, 7.

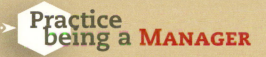

Practice being a MANAGER

Hometown Culture

One of the major dilemmas in global management concerns the degree to which a multinational firm should adapt its business practices to particular locations and cultures versus the degree to which it should maintain consistency across all its operations. In general, firms prefer consistency because it streamlines operations and may result in global economies of scale. At the same time, multinational firms cannot gloss over differences without running the risk of losing a particular market to more responsive (local) competition. In this exercise, you will interpret your "hometown" culture for a large multinational company.

Suppose that a large multinational equipment company (based outside your country of origin) is planning to open a major production facility and retail dealership in your hometown. This company has hired you as a consultant to help it successfully establish operations in your hometown.

STEP 1 **Describe your hometown.** Write a brief sketch (one to two pages, using bullet points will suffice) in which you describe the important cultural features of your hometown, including such aspects as language, dress, courtesy/customs, and attitudes toward "foreignness" and newcomers. Try as much as possible to capture aspects of the location and culture of your hometown that would be important for newcomers to recognize and respect.

STEP 2 **Form a team.** Your professor will assign you to small discussion groups of three to five students.

STEP 3 **Share your description.** Take turns in your discussion groups introducing yourselves, identifying your hometown, and sharing the highlights of your brief sketch of your hometown. Listen for similarities and differences across your hometowns.

STEP 4 **Make recommendations.** As a group, agree on some recommendations to the multinational company. Assume that the company is planning to enter all of your hometowns simultaneously. To what degree might the company use a consistent (same) approach in entering your hometowns? Is one or more of your hometowns likely to require a foreign multinational to make more particular adaptations?

STEP 5 **Share findings with class.** Each group should share its list of hometowns and its recommendations with the class.

STEP 6 **Consider challenges.** As a class discuss the challenges of entering global markets, particularly in regard to achieving the appropriate mix of consistency and adaptation.

Are You Nation-Minded or World-Minded?

Attitudes about global business are as varied as managers are numerous. It seems that the business press can always find someone who is for globalization and someone who is against it. But regardless of your opinion on the subject, managers will increasingly confront issues related to the globalization of the business environment. It is probable that, as a manager, you will need to develop global sensibilities (if you don't already have them). Understanding your own cultural perspective is the first step in doing so.

This assessment has three parts: Step 1, complete the questionnaire shown below; Step 2, determine your score; Step 3, develop a plan to increase your global managerial potential.[70]

STEP 1 Use the 6-point rating scale to complete the 32-question inventory shown below.

Rating Scale

1 Strongly disagree
2. Disagree
3. Mildly disagree
4. Mildly agree
5. Agree
6. Strongly agree

1. Our country should have the right to prohibit certain racial and religious groups from entering.
   1 2 3 4 5 6
2. Immigrants should not be permitted to come into our country if they compete with our own workers.
   1 2 3 4 5 6
3. It would set a dangerous precedent if every person in the world had equal rights that were guaranteed by an international charter.
   1 2 3 4 5 6
4. All prices for exported food and manufactured goods should be set by an international trade committee.
   1 2 3 4 5 6
5. Our country is probably no better than many others.
   1 2 3 4 5 6
6. Race prejudice may be a good thing for us because it keeps many undesirable foreigners from coming into this country.
   1 2 3 4 5 6
7. It would be a mistake for us to encourage certain racial groups to become well educated because they might use their knowledge against us.
   1 2 3 4 5 6
8. We should be willing to fight for our country without questioning whether it is right or wrong.
   1 2 3 4 5 6
9. Foreigners are particularly obnoxious because of their religious beliefs.
   1 2 3 4 5 6
10. Immigration should be controlled by a global organization rather than by each country on its own.
    1 2 3 4 5 6
11. We ought to have a world government to guarantee the welfare of all nations irrespective of the rights of any one.
    1 2 3 4 5 6
12. Our country should not cooperate in any global trade agreements that attempt to improve world economic conditions at our expense.
    1 2 3 4 5 6
13. It would be better to be a citizen of the world than of any particular country.
    1 2 3 4 5 6
14. Our responsibility to people of other races ought to be as great as our responsibility to people of our own race.
    1 2 3 4 5 6
15. A global committee on education should have full control over what is taught in all countries about history and politics.
    1 2 3 4 5 6

16. Our country should refuse to cooperate in a total disarmament program even if some other nations agree to it.
1 2 3 4 5 6

17. It would be dangerous for our country to make international agreements with nations whose religious beliefs are antagonistic to ours.
1 2 3 4 5 6

18. Any healthy individual, regardless of race or religion, should be allowed to live wherever he or she wants to in the world.
1 2 3 4 5 6

19. Our country should not participate in any global organization that requires that we give up any of our national rights or freedom of action.
1 2 3 4 5 6

20. If necessary, we ought to be willing to lower our standard of living to cooperate with other countries in getting an equal standard for every person in the world.
1 2 3 4 5 6

21. We should strive for loyalty to our country before we can afford to consider world brotherhood.
1 2 3 4 5 6

22. Some races ought to be considered naturally less intelligent than ours.
1 2 3 4 5 6

23. Our schools should teach the history of the whole world rather than of our own country.
1 2 3 4 5 6

24. A global police force ought to be the only group in the world allowed to have arms.
1 2 3 4 5 6

25. It would be dangerous for us to guarantee by international agreement that every person in the world should have complete religious freedom.
1 2 3 4 5 6

26. Our country should permit the immigration of foreign peoples, even if it lowers our standard of living.
1 2 3 4 5 6

27. All national governments ought to be abolished and replaced by one central world government.
1 2 3 4 5 6

28. It would not be wise for us to agree that working conditions in all countries should be subject to international control.
1 2 3 4 5 6

29. Patriotism should be a primary aim of education so that our children will believe our country is the best in the world.
1 2 3 4 5 6

30. It would be a good idea if all the races were to intermarry until there was only one race in the world.
1 2 3 4 5 6

31. We should teach our children to uphold the welfare of all people everywhere, even though it may be against the best interests of our own country.
1 2 3 4 5 6

32. War should never be justifiable, even if it is the only way to protect our national rights and honor.
1 2 3 4 5 6

STEP 2 Determine your score by entering your response to each survey item below, as follows. In blanks that say *regular score*, simply enter your response for that item. If your response was a 4, place a 4 in the *regular score* blank. In blanks that say *reverse score*, subtract your response from 7 and enter the result. So if your response was a 4, place a 3 (7 − 4 = 3) in the *reverse score* blank.

1. reverse score ______
2. reverse score ______
3. reverse score ______
4. regular score ______
5. regular score ______
6. reverse score ______
7. reverse score ______
8. reverse score ______
9. reverse score ______
10. regular score ______
11. regular score ______
12. reverse score ______
13. regular score ______
14. regular score ______
15. regular score ______
16. reverse score ______
17. reverse score ______
18. regular score ______
19. reverse score ______
20. regular score ______
21. reverse score ______
22. reverse score ______
23. regular score ______
24. regular score ______
25. reverse score ______
26. regular score ______
27. regular score ______
28. reverse score ______
29. reverse score ______
30. regular score ______
31. regular score ______
32. regular score ______

SCORING

Total your scores from items 1–16 ______

Total your scores from items 17–32 ______

Add together to compute TOTAL ______

You can find an interpretation of your score at: login.cengagebrain.com.

Biz Flix

© GREENLIGHT

Lost in Translation

The 2003 film *Lost in Translation,* based on Sofia Coppola's Academy Award–winning screenplay, stars Scarlett Johansson as a recent college graduate and newlywed named Charlotte. She visits Tokyo with her husband, a photographer on assignment in the city, who leaves her alone to navigate her way through a country whose culture and language she doesn't understand. When she meets Bob Harris (Bill Murray), an actor who is there to shoot a whiskey commercial and pocket a quick $2 million for it, they forge an unlikely friendship. This clip is an edited composite taken from different scenes in the movie. It shows us what Japan looks like through Charlotte's eyes as she explores it on her own and tries to make sense of what she sees.

What to Watch for and Ask Yourself

1. Imagine you have just arrived in Japan, and you are experiencing what Charlotte is for the first time. Do you understand everything you see?
2. If you were managing a company that had operations in foreign countries, how important do you think it would be to experience new places and learn about different cultures the way Charlotte does?
3. How might it change the way you did business in those countries if you had actually been to them?
4. Does Charlotte seem to be culturally sensitive or insensitive?

Reel to Real

Management Workplace

© CENGAGE

Evo

Evo is a Seattle-based online retailer of all ski-, snowboard-, wake-, and skate-related items, but the company has loyal customers who live in places as far away as Bahrain and Bali. Their website, ***http://www.evogear.com***, is quickly establishing them as a global brand. Founder Bryce Phillips recently added evoTRIP to the website, a program that offers extreme ski, snowboarding, and surf expeditions to places like South America and Switzerland. In this video, Phillips explains the difficulties facing his company, such as licensing and distribution agreements with manufacturers. The majority of Evo's international transactions are relatively seamless, but day-to-day operations can still be affected by global events. He is confident,

however, that his company will be able to expand its global reach as licensing practices change to reflect the boundary-free world of e-commerce, and as Evo becomes more established as a global brand.

What to Watch for and Ask Yourself

1. What are some of the obstacles Evo has encountered in global e-commerce?
2. What cultural differences should Evo and evoTRIP participants pay attention to when traveling abroad?
3. Do you think the management at Evo benefits more from practicing global consistency or local adaptation?

Part Three
Organizing

This chapter shows you the traditional organizational structure approach to organizational design (the vertical and horizontal configuration of departments, authority, and jobs within a company), as well as how contemporary organizations are redesigning their processes to better transform inputs into outputs.

Chapter Eight
Designing Adaptive Organizations

Chapter 9 reviews the advantages and disadvantages of teams and explores when companies should use them. You'll also read about the different types of work teams and the characteristics common to all teams and learn practical steps to managing teams—team goals and priorities, and organizing, training, and compensating teams.

Chapter Nine
Managing Teams

This chapter covers the key aspects of human resource systems: determining your human resource needs; finding qualified employees; developing the knowledge, skills, and abilities of the workforce; implementing effective compensation practices; and effectively managing separation.

Chapter Ten
Managing Human Resources

8 Chapter Eight
Designing Adaptive Organizations

OUTLINE

Experience Management

Explore the four levels of learning by doing the simulation module on Organizational Design.

© ISTOCKPHOTO.COM/ ANN MARIE KURTZ

Pod Nod

Mini lecture reviews all the learning points in the chapter.

© ISTOCKPHOTO.COM/ MAGNET CREATIVE

Reel to Real

Biz Flix is a scene from *Rendition*. Management Workplace is a segment on Evo.

© ISTOCKPHOTO.COM/ CRAFTVISION

Self Test

10 quiz questions, 3 exhibit worksheets, and PowerPoints for quick review.

© ISTOCKPHOTO.COM/ DIJITAL FILM

What Would You Do?

Yahoo! Headquarters, Sunnyvale, California.[1]

When *YAHOO!* co-founder Jerry Yang invited you to his house, you said, "I'm not taking the CEO job, so I hope you have good wine." When Yang started talking about Yahoo!, it was a bit confusing, so you asked him to draw an organizational chart so you could follow along. As he drew, you thought, "That's really the organization?" So you asked who makes key decisions about, for example, Yahoo!'s search function and engine. Yang started drawing arrows, lines crisscrossed all over, and you thought, "This is just like a Dilbert cartoon." You couldn't figure out who was in charge of what. "I got it," you told him, "What Yahoo! needs is a manager."

But, you weren't the first to figure that out. Several years earlier, Yahoo! senior executive Brad Garlinghouse wrote what came to be known as the "Peanut Butter Manifesto," in which he said, "I've heard our strategy described as spreading peanut butter across the myriad opportunities that continue to evolve in the online world. The result: a thin layer of investment spread across everything we do and thus we focus on nothing in particular. I hate peanut butter. We all should." Garlinghouse went on to say that Yahoo! lacked "a focused, cohesive vision," "clarity of ownership and accountability," and "decisiveness." He attributed many of those problems to the company's structure, saying, "We are separated into silos that far too frequently don't talk to each other. And when we do talk, it isn't to collaborate on a clearly focused strategy, but rather to argue and fight about ownership, strategies and tactics. We now operate in an organizational structure—admittedly created with the best of intentions—that has become overly bureaucratic. For far too many employees, there is another person with dramatically similar and overlapping responsibilities. This slows us down and burdens the company with unnecessary costs." In the end, Garlinghouse concluded, "The current business unit structure must go away," and that "the smoothly spread peanut butter needs to turn into a deliberately sculpted strategy—that is narrowly focused."

This is not the first time that Yahoo! has had problems finding the right organizational structure. At one time, Yahoo! didn't even have a direct sales unit! Speedy growth, organizational complexity, and the fast-paced change of online business have made it difficult to structure the company properly. Indeed, Yahoo! recently went through a reorganization in which the heads of international markets were given more autonomy so their units could do a better job of appealing to customer preferences in different parts of the world. But complaints started immediately, as few in the company really understood who was responsible for what. Clay Moran, senior vice president and market research analyst for an investment firm, summed up skeptics' views by saying, "We have seen no noticeable impact from recent restructurings."

With profits down 78 percent and a recent layoff of 5 percent of the company workforce, you wonder where you should start. Clearly, with so many different business units and widespread confusion under the current matrix structure, a new structure is inevitable. But, as you look at Yahoo!'s website, you wonder if a functional, customer, product, or geographic structure would work best, and why. Next, what steps can you take to instill ownership, accountability, and decisiveness throughout the company, but still give the techies enough freedom to innovate and create? In other words, what trade-offs and balance do you need to make in terms of centralization and decentralization? Finally, the lack of a cohesive vision appears to be at the center of Yahoo!'s organizational structure issues. Is Yahoo!, like Google, a search and web advertising company? Is it a media company that draws 600 million visitors a year to its rich sources of news, financial information, and online communities? Or, is it a technology conglomerate that builds and delivers web applications and services? What should be Yahoo!'s cohesive vision, and what's the right way to structure the company to support that vision?

If you were the new CEO at Yahoo!, what would you do?

No one builds a house without first looking at the design. Put a window there. Take out a wall here. Soon you've got the design you want. Only then do you start building. These days, the design of a company is just as important as the design of a house. Even successful companies, such as Yahoo!, must constantly examine their organizational design.

This chapter begins by reviewing the traditional organizational structure approach to organizational design. **Organizational structure** is the vertical and horizontal configuration of departments, authority, and jobs within a company. Organizational structure is concerned with questions such as "Who reports to whom?" and "Who does what?" and "Where is the work done?" For example, *SONY CORPORATION OF AMERICA* is headed by Chairman and CEO Howard Stringer, who is based in New York City. But Sony has a number of divisions to handle different sectors of the company's business, each headed by its own president or CEO. PlayStations are developed and managed in Foster City, California, by Sony Computer Entertainment. Sony camcorders, home theater equipment, LCD TVs, VAIO computers, Blu-ray disc players, and the Walkman are handled in San Diego by Sony Electronics. The Spider-Man films and *Seinfeld* were brought to you by Sony Pictures, a division of Sony Entertainment in Culver City, California, while the

organizational structure
the vertical and horizontal configuration of departments, authority, and jobs within a company

EXHIBIT 8.1

Sony Corporation's Organizational Chart

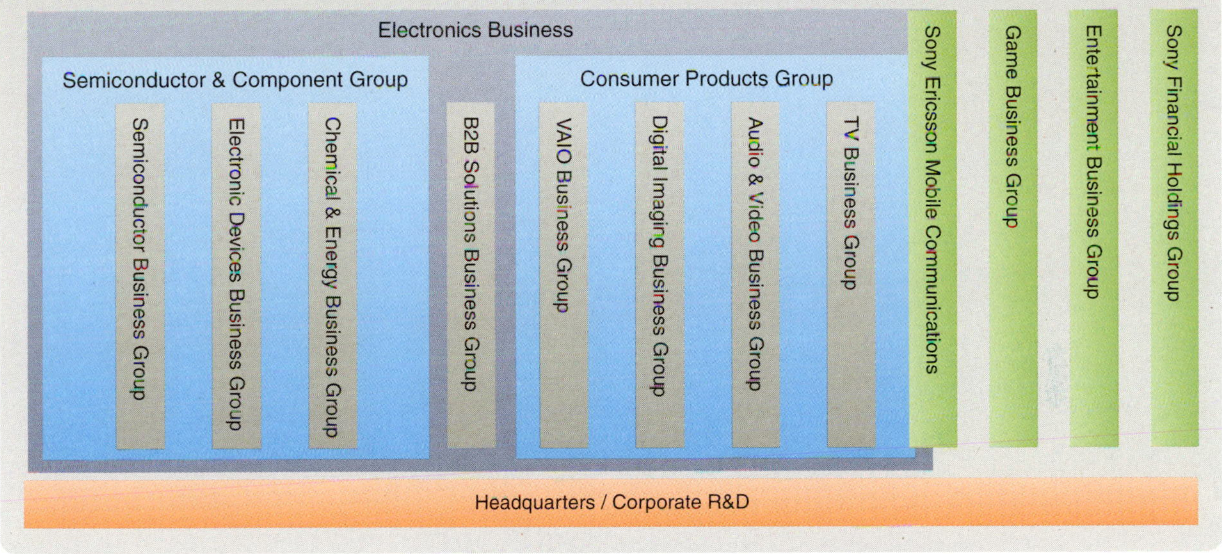

Source: Sony Organizational Chart available online at http://www.sony.net/SonyInfo/CorporateInfo/Data/organization.html, [accessed 10 September 2008].

music of Justin Timberlake and Avril Lavigne comes courtesy of Sony/BMG in New York City.[2] Companies like Sony use organizational structure to set up departments and relationships among employees in order to make business happen. You can see Sony's organizational structure in Exhibit 8.1. In the first half of the chapter, you will learn about the traditional vertical and horizontal approaches to organizational structure, including departmentalization, organizational authority, and job design.

In the second half of the chapter, you will learn how contemporary organizations are becoming more adaptive by redesigning their internal and external processes. An **organizational process** is the collection of activities that transform inputs into outputs that customers value.[3] Organizational process asks "How do things get done?" For example, *MICROSOFT* uses basic internal and external processes to write computer software, as shown in Exhibit 8.2. The process starts when Microsoft gets feedback from customers through Internet newsgroups, e-mail, phone calls, or letters. This information helps Microsoft understand customers' needs and problems and identify important software issues and needed changes and functions. Microsoft then rewrites the software, testing it internally at the company and then externally through its beta testing process, in which customers who volunteer or are selected by Microsoft give the company extensive feedback, which is then used to make improvements. The beta testing process may take as long as a year and involve thousands of knowledgeable people. After final corrections are made to the software, the company distributes and sells it to customers. They start the process again by giving Microsoft more feedback. Indeed, Microsoft's advertising campaign for the kickoff of Windows 7, which was developed through extensive beta testing, was "I'm a PC, and Windows 7 was my idea."

organizational process
the collection of activities that transform inputs into outputs that customers value

EXHIBIT 8.2

Process View of Microsoft's Organization

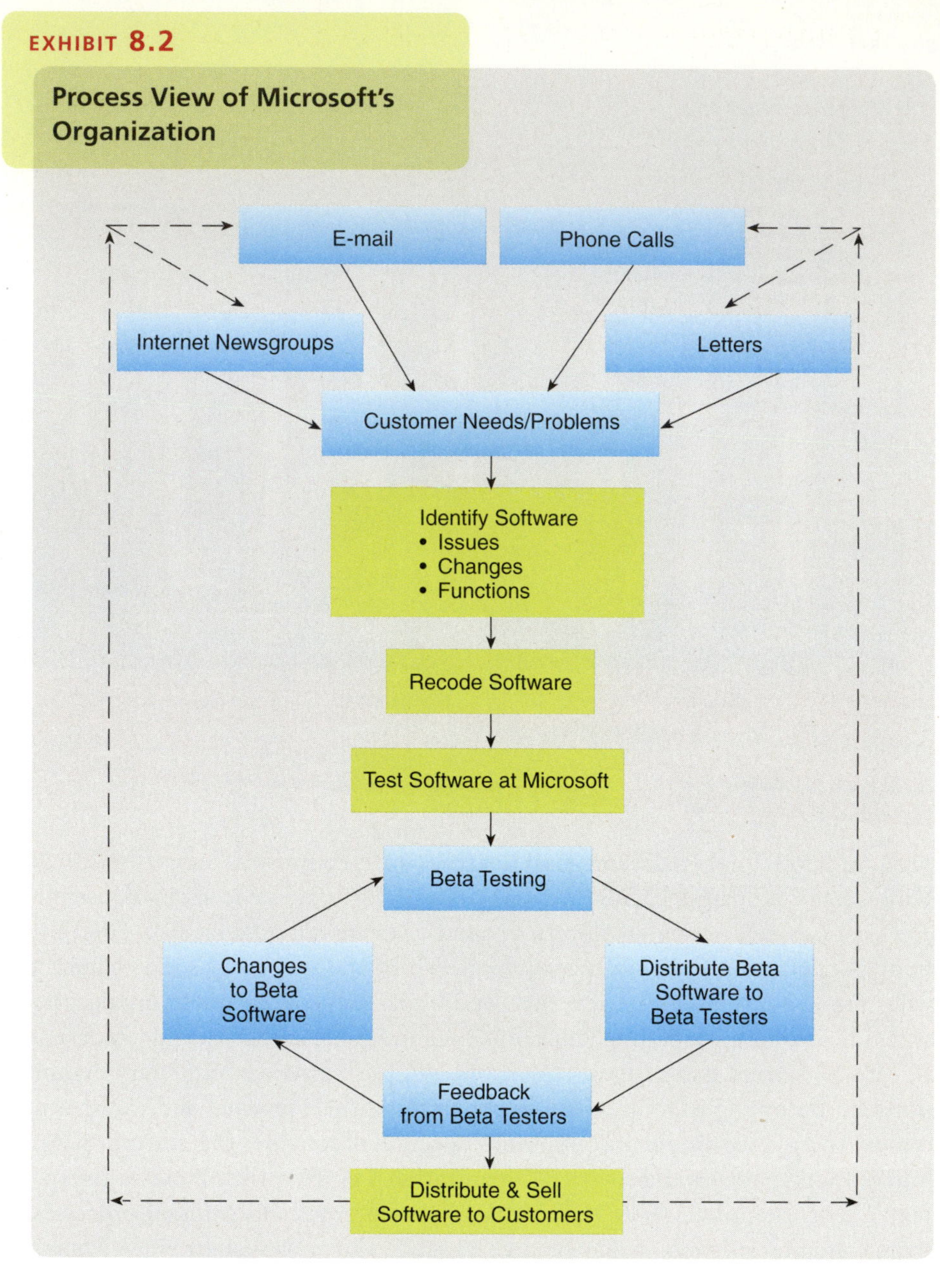

This process view of Microsoft, which focuses on how things get done, is very different from the hierarchical view of Sony, which focuses on accountability, responsibility, and positions within the chain of command. In the second half of the chapter, you will learn how companies use reengineering, empowerment, and behavioral informality to redesign their internal organizational processes. The chapter ends with a discussion about the ways in which companies are redesigning their external processes, that is, how they are changing to improve their interactions with those outside the company. In that discussion, you will explore the basics of modular and virtual organizations.

Designing Organizational Structures

With offices and operations in 58 countries, products in over 200, and more than 150,000 employees worldwide, *SARA LEE CORPORATION* owns some of the best-known brands in the world (Sara Lee, Hillshire Farm, Ball Park, and Jimmy Dean). To improve company performance, Sara Lee changed its organizational structure to focus on several key customer/geographic markets: North American Retail (packaged meats such as Hillshire Farm, Ballpark or Jimmy Dean brands, and Senseo coffee), North American Fresh Bakery (bakery goods to retail and institutional customers), North American Foodservice (meat, bakery, and beverages to foodservice distributors, restaurants, and hospitals in North America), International Beverage (coffee and tea products in Europe, Australia, and Brazil), International Bakery (bakery and dough products to retail and foodservice customers in Europe and Australia), and International Household and Body Care (body care, air care, shoe care, and insecticide products sold in Europe, Africa, Australia, and Asia).

Why would a large company like Sara Lee with 41,000 employees and $12 billion in annual revenues completely restructure its organizational design? What does it expect to gain from this change?

After reading the next three sections, you'll have a better understanding of the importance of organizational structure because you should be able to:

1 describe the departmentalization approach to organizational structure.
2 explain organizational authority.
3 discuss the different methods for job design.

1 Departmentalization

Traditionally, organizational structures have been based on some form of departmentalization. **Departmentalization** is a method of subdividing work and workers into separate organizational units that take responsibility for completing particular tasks.[4] Bayer, a German-based company, has separate departments or divisions for health care, crop science, material science, and services.[5]

Traditionally, organizational structures have been created by departmentalizing work according to five methods: 1.1 **functional**, 1.2 **product**, 1.3 **customer**, 1.4 **geographic**, and 1.5 **matrix**.

1.1 Functional Departmentalization

The most common organizational structure is functional departmentalization. Companies tend to use this structure when they are small or just starting out. **Functional departmentalization** organizes work and workers into separate units responsible for particular business functions or areas of expertise. A common functional structure might have individuals organized into accounting, sales, marketing, production, and human resources departments.

Not all functionally departmentalized companies have the same functions. The insurance company and the advertising agency shown in Exhibit 8.3 both have sales, accounting, human resources, and information systems departments, as indicated by the green boxes. The blue and khaki boxes indicate the functions that are different. As would be expected, the insurance company has separate departments for life,

departmentalization
subdividing work and workers into separate organizational units responsible for completing particular tasks

functional departmentalization
organizing work and workers into separate units responsible for particular business functions or areas of expertise

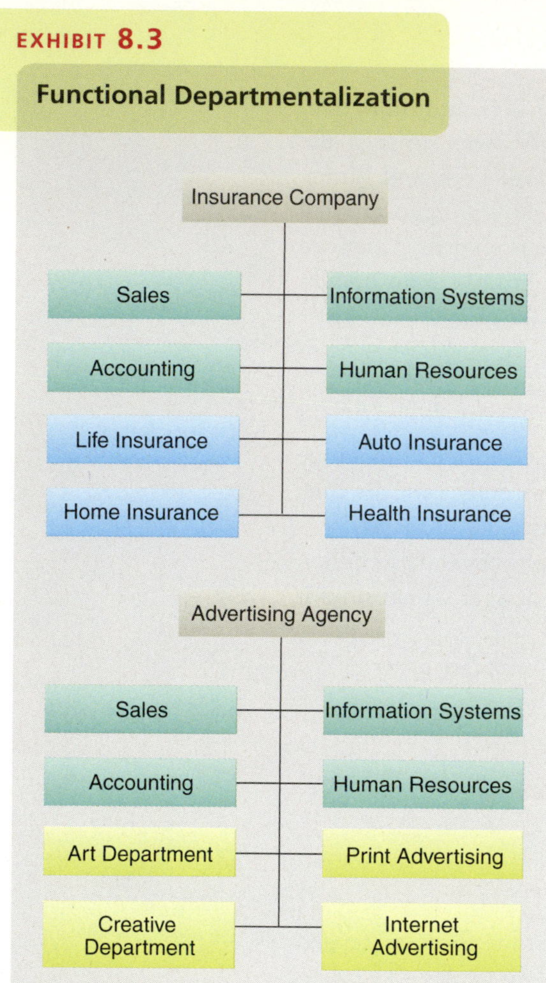

auto, home, and health insurance. The advertising agency has departments for artwork, creative work, print advertising, and Internet advertising. So the departments in a company that uses functional structure depend in part on the business or industry a company is in.

Functional departmentalization has some advantages. First, it allows work to be done by highly qualified specialists. While the accountants in the accounting department take responsibility for producing accurate revenue and expense figures, the engineers in research and development can focus their efforts on designing a product that is reliable and simple to manufacture. Second, it lowers costs by reducing duplication. When the engineers in research and development come up with that fantastic new product, they don't have to worry about creating an aggressive advertising campaign to sell it. That task belongs to the advertising experts and sales representatives in marketing. Third, with everyone in the same department having similar work experience or training, communication and coordination are less problematic for departmental managers.

At the same time, functional departmentalization has a number of disadvantages. To start, cross-department coordination can be difficult. Managers and employees are often more interested in doing what's right for their function than in doing what's right for the entire organization. A good example is the traditional conflict between marketing and manufacturing. Marketing typically pushes for spending more money to make more products with more accessories and capabilities to meet customer needs. By contrast, manufacturing pushes for fewer products with simpler designs so that manufacturing facilities can ship finished products on time and keep costs within expense budgets. As companies grow, functional departmentalization may also lead to slower decision making and produce managers and workers with narrow experience and expertise.

1.2 Product Departmentalization

Product departmentalization organizes work and workers into separate units responsible for producing particular products or services. Exhibit 8.4 shows the product departmentalization structure used by *UNITED TECHNOLOGIES CORPORATION (UTC)*, which is organized along seven different product lines: Carrier (heating, ventilating, and air-conditioning), Hamilton Sundstrand (aircraft electrical power generation and distribution systems), Otis (design, manufacture, installation, maintenance, and servicing of elevators and escalators), Pratt & Whitney (commercial and military jet aircraft engines), Sikorsky (military and commercial helicopters), Chubb (fire safety and security products and services), and UTC Power (fuel cells and power systems).[6]

product departmentalization organizing work and workers into separate units responsible for producing particular products or services

One of the advantages of product departmentalization is that, like functional departmentalization, it allows managers and workers to specialize in one area of expertise. Unlike the narrow expertise and experiences in functional departmentalization, however, managers and workers develop a broader set of experiences and expertise related to an entire product line. Likewise, product departmentalization makes it easier for top managers to assess work-unit performance. Because of the clear separation of their seven different product divisions, United Technologies' top managers can easily compare the performance of its Otis elevators to its Pratt & Whitney aircraft engines. The divisions had similar revenues—almost $12.9 billion for Otis and $13 billion for Pratt & Whitney—but Otis had a profit of $2.5 billion (a 19.4 percent profit margin) compared with just $2.1 billion (a 16.2 percent profit margin) for Pratt & Whitney.[7] Finally, decision making should be faster because managers and workers are responsible for the entire product line rather than for separate functional departments; in other words, there are fewer conflicts compared to functional departmentalization.

EXHIBIT 8.4

Product Departmentalization: United Technologies

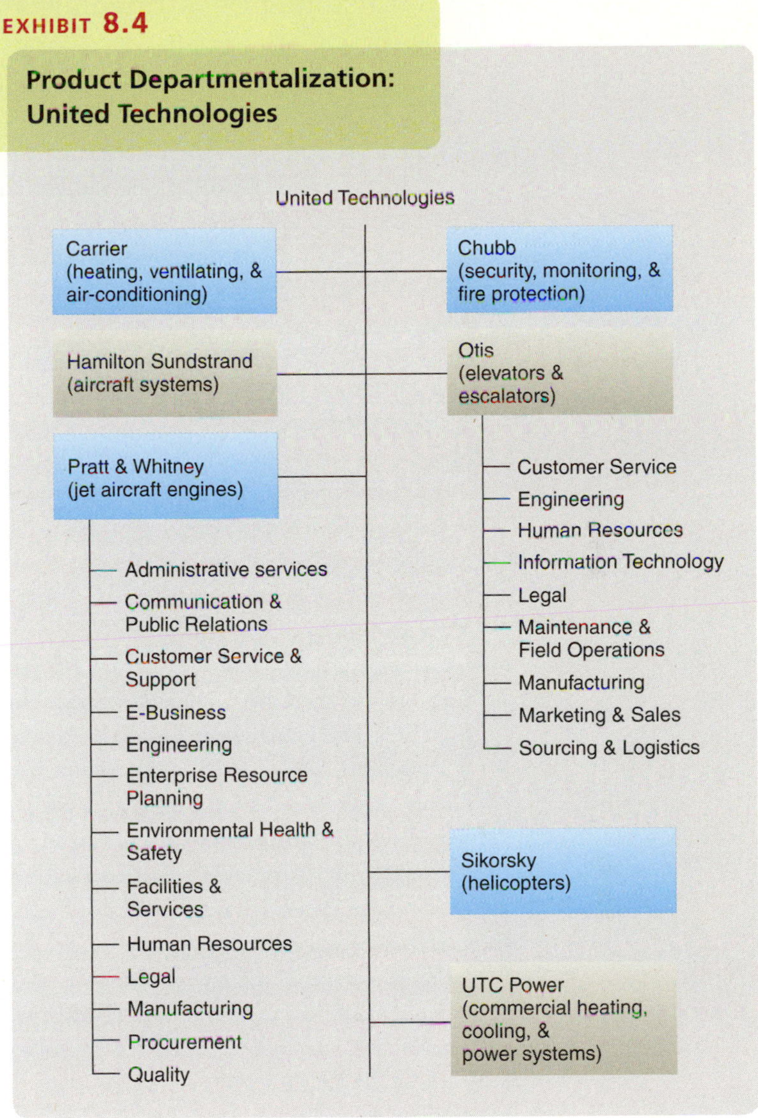

Source: United Technologies Corporation 2004 Annual Report, United Technologies, available at http://www.utc.com/annual_reports/2004/2004_ar.pdf, 1 May 2005.

The primary disadvantage of product departmentalization is duplication. You can see in Exhibit 8.4 that UTC's Otis elevators and Pratt & Whitney divisions both have customer service, engineering, human resources, legal, manufacturing, and procurement (similar to sourcing and logistics) departments. Duplication like this often results in higher costs. If United Technologies were instead organized by function, one lawyer could handle matters related to both elevators and aircraft engines rather than working on only one or the other.

A second disadvantage is the challenge of coordinating across the different product departments. United Technologies would probably have difficulty standardizing its policies and procedures in product departments as different as the Carrier (heating, ventilating, and air-conditioning) and Sikorsky (military and commercial helicopters) divisions.

1.3 Customer Departmentalization

Customer departmentalization organizes work and workers into separate units responsible for particular kinds of customers. For example, as Exhibit 8.5 shows, *SWISSCOM AG*, Switzerland's leading telecommunications provider, is organized into departments by type of customer: residential, small- and medium-sized businesses, larger corporations, and network and IT customers.[8]

The primary advantage of customer departmentalization is that it focuses the organization on customer needs rather than on products or business functions. Furthermore, creating separate departments to serve specific kinds of customers allows companies to specialize and adapt their products and services to customer needs and problems. The primary disadvantage of customer departmentalization is that, like product departmentalization, it leads to duplication of resources. It can be difficult to achieve coordination across different customer departments, as is also the case with product departmentalization. Finally, the emphasis on meeting customers' needs may lead workers to make decisions that please customers but hurt the business.

1.4 Geographic Departmentalization

Geographic departmentalization organizes work and workers into separate units responsible for doing business in particular geographic areas. Exhibit 8.6 shows the geographic departmentalization used by *COCA-COLA ENTERPRISES (CCE)*, the largest bottler and distributor of Coca-Cola products in the world. (The Coca-Cola Company develops and advertises soft drinks. CCE, which is a separate company with its own stock, buys the soft-drink concentrate from the Coca-Cola Company, combines it with other ingredients, and then distributes the final product in cans, bottles, or fountain containers.) As shown in Exhibit 8.6, CCE has two regional groups: North America and Europe. As the table in the exhibit shows, each of these regions would be a sizable company by itself. The European Group serves people in Belgium, Great Britain, France, Luxembourg, Monaco, and the Netherlands, sells half a billion cases of soft drinks a year, employs 10,500 people, and runs 46 bottling facilities.

The primary advantage of geographic departmentalization is that it helps companies respond to the demands of different markets. This can be especially important when the company sells in different countries. CCE's geographic divisions sell products suited to taste preferences in different countries. For example, CCE bottles and distributes the following products in Europe but not in the United States: Aquarius, Bonaqua, Burn, Coca-Cola Light (which is somewhat different from Diet Coke), Cresta, Five Alive, Kia-Ora, Kinley, Lilt, Malvern, and Oasis.[9] Another advantage is that geographic departmentalization can reduce costs by locating unique organizational resources closer to customers. For instance, it is cheaper in the long run for CCE to build bottling plants in Belgium than to bottle Coke in England and then transport it across the English Channel to Belgium.

The primary disadvantage of geographic departmentalization is that it can lead to duplication of resources. For example, while it may be necessary to adapt products and marketing to different geographic locations, it's doubtful that CCE needs significantly different inventory tracking systems from location to location. Also, even more than with the other forms of departmentalization, it can be difficult to

customer departmentalization organizing work and workers into separate units responsible for particular kinds of customers

geographic departmentalization organizing work and workers into separate units responsible for doing business in particular geographic areas

EXHIBIT 8.5

Customer Departmentalization: Swisscom AG

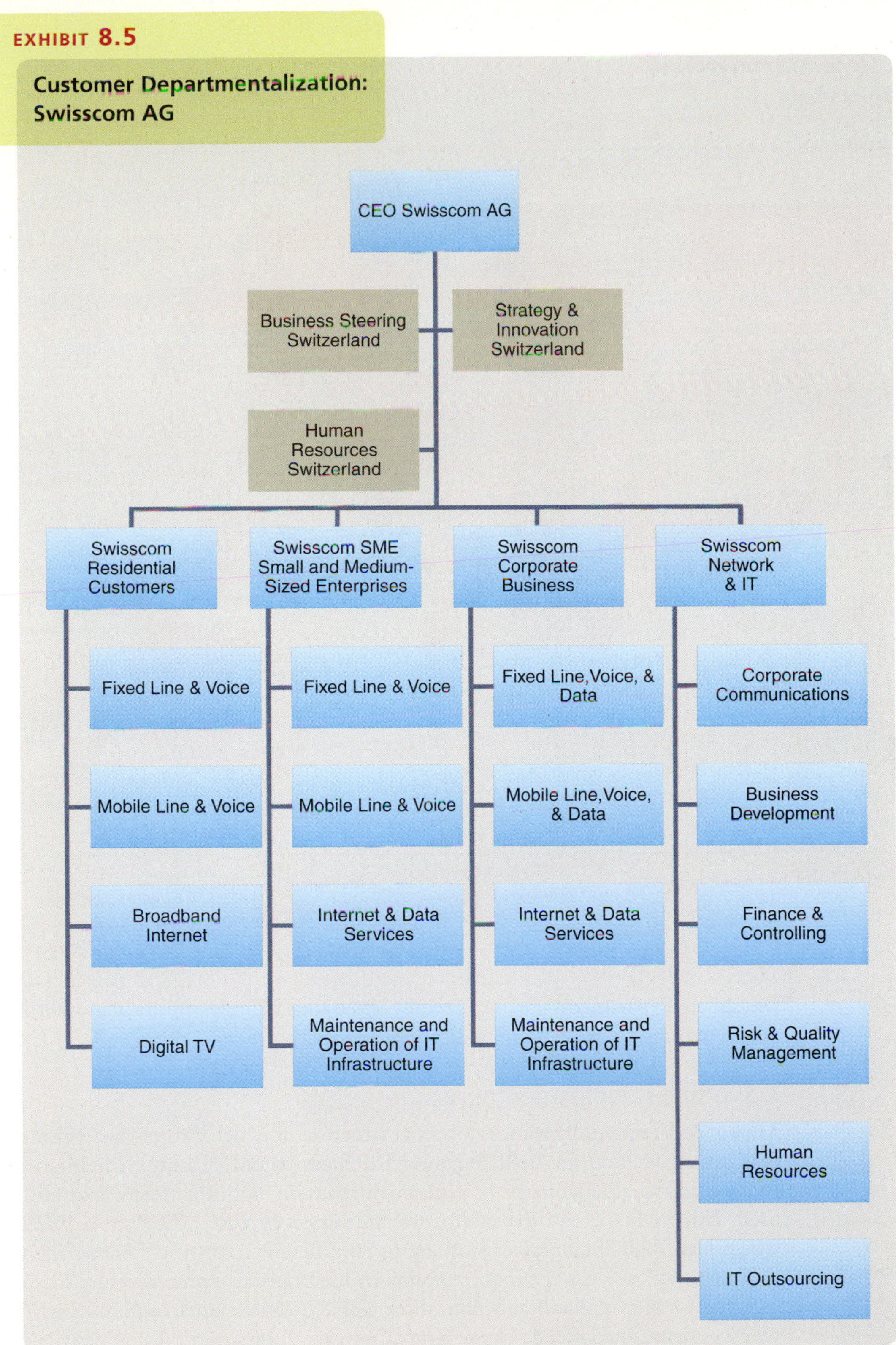

Source: http://www.swisscom.ch/GHQ/content/Portraet/Unternehmen/Unternehmensstruktur/Swisscom_Schweiz/Unternehmensstruktur/Unternehmensstruktur.htm.

EXHIBIT 8.6

Geographic Departmentalization: Coca-Cola Enterprises

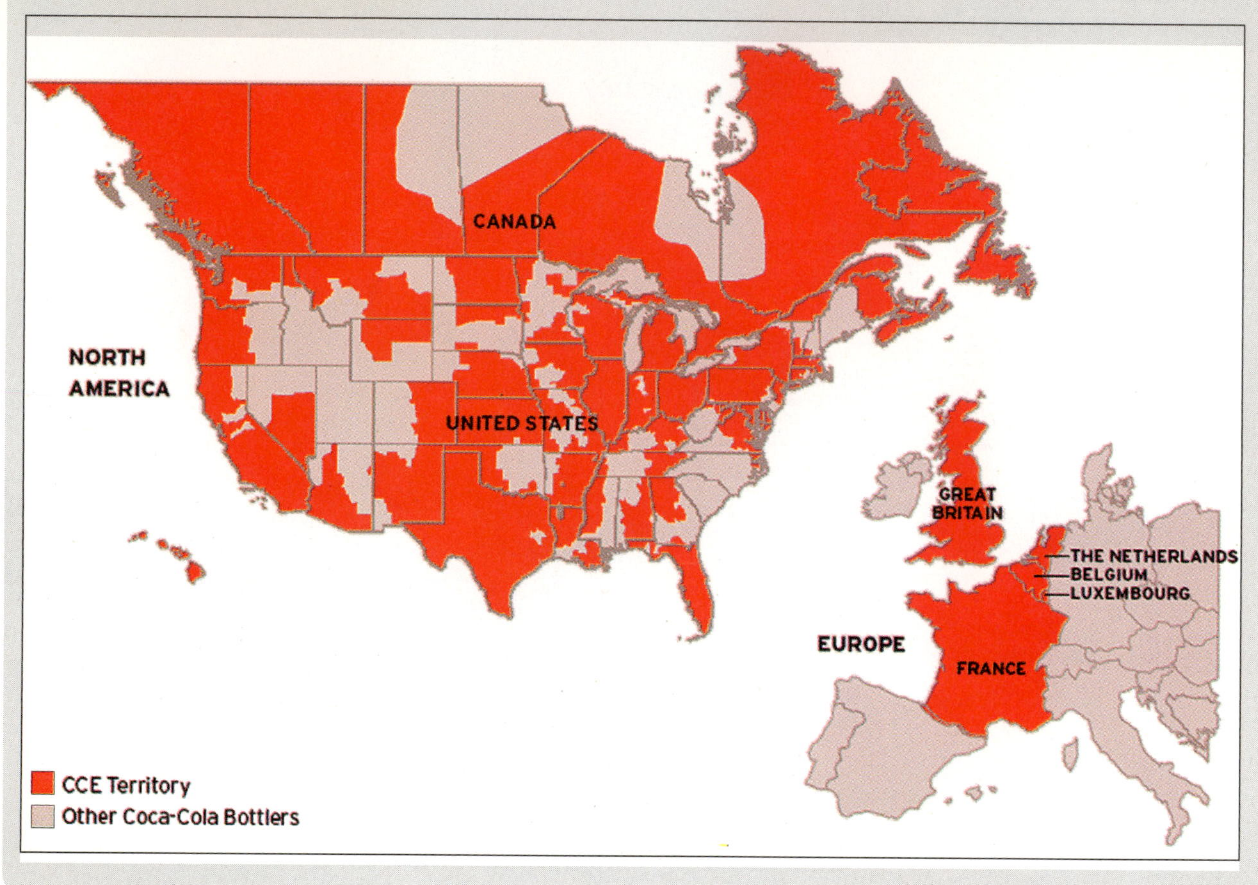

Source: "Our Business at a Glance," Coca-Cola Enterprises, available online at http://www.cokecce.com [accessed 14 November 2009.]

coordinate departments that are literally thousands of miles from each other and whose managers have very limited contact with each other.

1.5 Matrix Departmentalization

Matrix departmentalization is a hybrid structure in which two or more forms of departmentalization are used together. The most common matrix combines the product and functional forms of departmentalization, but other forms may also be used. Exhibit 8.7 shows the matrix structure used by *PROCTER & GAMBLE*, which has 138,000 employees working in 80 different countries.[10] Across the top of Exhibit 8.7, you can see that the company uses a product unit structure where it groups its billion-dollar brands into three global business units, each of which has two segments. The left side of the figure, however, shows that the company is also using a functional structure based on three functions: market development, global business services, and corporate functions.[11]

matrix departmentalization a hybrid organizational structure in which two or more forms of departmentalization, most often product and functional, are used together

EXHIBIT 8.7

Matrix Departmentalization: Procter & Gamble

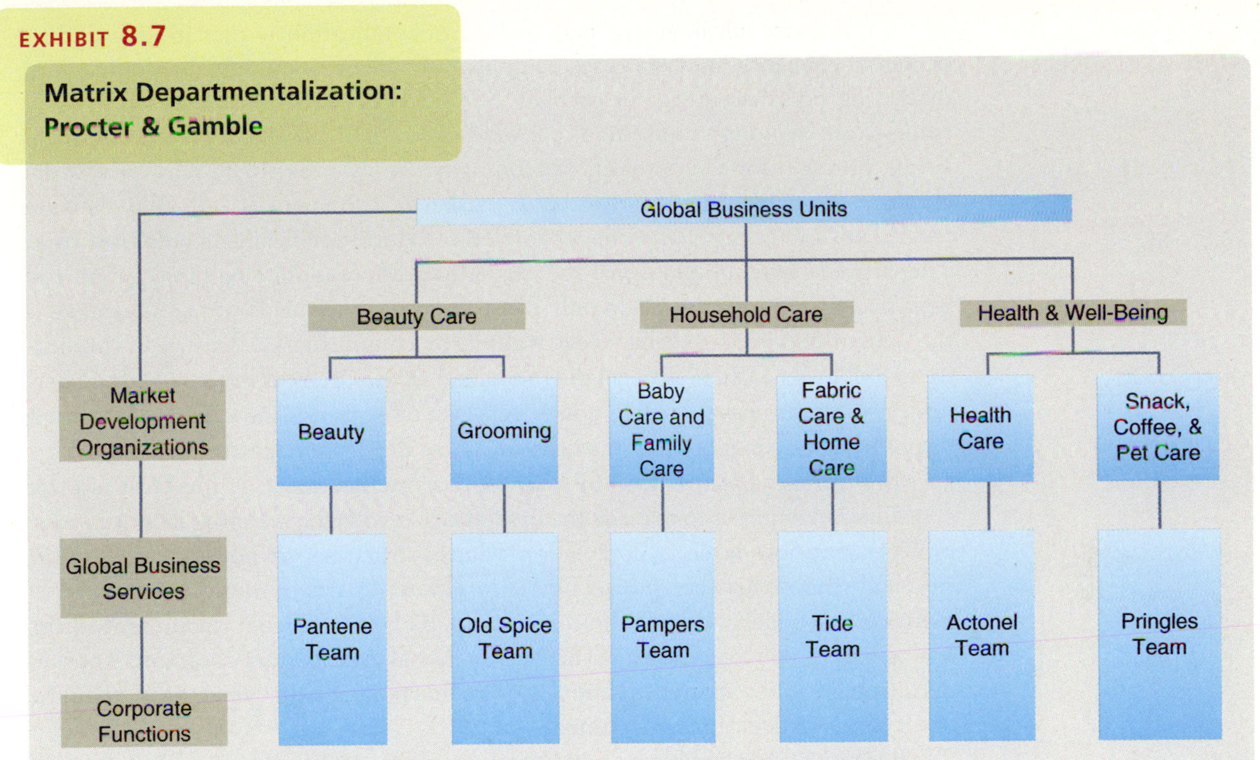

Sources: "Corporate Info: Corporate Structure—Four Pillars," Procter & Gamble, http://www.pg.com/jobs/corporate_structure/four_pillars.jhtml; "P&G Management," Procter & Gamble, http://www.pg.com/news/management/bios_photos.jhtml.

The boxes in the figure represent the matrix structure, created by the combination of the product and functional structures. For example, the Pantene Team (Pantene is a set of haircare products within the beauty segment of the beauty care global business unit) would work with market development to adapt and sell Pantene products worldwide, use global business services to work with suppliers and keep costs down, and then rely on corporate functions for assistance in hiring employees, billing customers, and paying suppliers.

Several things distinguish matrix departmentalization from the other traditional forms of departmentalization.[12] First, most employees report to two bosses, one from each core part of the matrix. For example, as shown in Exhibit 8.7, a manager on the Pampers team responsible for marketing would report to a boss in the baby care and family care segment of the household care global business unit as well as to a boss in the market development unit. Second, by virtue of their hybrid design, matrix structures lead to much more cross-functional interaction than other forms of departmentalization. In fact, while matrix workers are typically members of only one functional department (based on their work experience and expertise), they are also commonly members of several ongoing project, product, or customer groups. Third, because of the high level of cross-functional interaction, matrix departmentalization requires significant coordination between managers in the different parts of the matrix. In particular, managers have the complex job of tracking and managing multiple demands (project, product, customer, or functional) on employees' time.

The primary advantage of matrix departmentalization is that it allows companies to efficiently manage large, complex tasks like researching, developing, and marketing pharmaceuticals or carrying out complex global businesses. Efficiency comes from avoiding duplication. For example, rather than having an entire marketing function for each project, the company simply assigns and reassigns workers from the marketing department (or market development at P&G) as they are needed at various stages of product completion. More specifically, an employee from a department may simultaneously be part of five different ongoing projects but may be actively completing work on only a few projects at a time. Another advantage is the pool of resources available to carry out large, complex tasks. Because of the ability to pull in expert help from all the functional areas of the company quickly, matrix project managers have a much more diverse set of expertise and experience at their disposal than do managers in the other forms of departmentalization.

The primary disadvantage of matrix departmentalization is the high level of coordination required to manage the complexity involved in running large, ongoing projects at various levels of completion. Matrix structures are notorious for confusion and conflict between project bosses in different parts of the matrix. Disagreements or misunderstandings about schedules, budgets, available resources, and the availability of employees with particular functional expertise are common. Another disadvantage is that matrix structures require much more management skill than the other forms of departmentalization.

Because of these problems, many matrix structures evolve from a **simple matrix**, in which managers in different parts of the matrix negotiate conflicts and resources directly, to a **complex matrix**, in which specialized matrix managers and departments are added to the organizational structure. In a complex matrix, managers from different parts of the matrix might report to the same matrix manager, who helps them sort out conflicts and problems.

Sometimes, however, even these steps aren't enough to alleviate the problems that can occur in matrix structures. Europe-based *UNILEVER* is the maker and marketer of such well-known products as Dove soap, Lipton teas, and Lawry's seasonings. Unilever was run using a complex matrix with dual headquarters in Rotterdam, the Netherlands, and London, England. The confusion and conflict associated with having two sets of management were so great that Unilever has now switched to just one CEO and one headquarters, and has moved to a simpler organizational structure.[13]

simple matrix
a form of matrix departmentalization in which managers in different parts of the matrix negotiate conflicts and resources

complex matrix
a form of matrix departmentalization in which managers in different parts of the matrix report to matrix managers, who help them sort out conflicts and problems

REVIEW 1

Departmentalization

The five traditional departmental structures are functional, product, customer, geographic, and matrix. Functional departmentalization is based on the different business functions or expertise used to run a business. Product departmentalization is organized according to the different products or services a company sells. Customer departmentalization focuses its divisions on the different kinds of customers a company has. Geographic departmentalization is based on the different geographic areas or markets in which the company does business. Matrix departmentalization is a hybrid form that combines two or more forms of departmentalization, the most common being the product and functional forms. There is no single best departmental structure. Each structure has advantages and disadvantages.

2 Organizational Authority

The second part of traditional organizational structures is authority. **Authority** is the right to give commands, take action, and make decisions to achieve organizational objectives.[14]

Traditionally, organizational authority has been characterized by the following dimensions: 2.1 **chain of command**, 2.2 **line versus staff authority**, 2.3 **delegation of authority**, and 2.4 **degree of centralization**.

2.1 Chain of Command

Turn back a few pages to Sony's organizational chart in Exhibit 8.1. If you place your finger on any position in the chart, say, VAIO Business Group (under Electronic Business), you can trace a line upward to the company's CEO, Howard Stringer. This line, which vertically connects every job in the company to higher levels of management, represents the chain of command. The **chain of command** is the vertical line of authority that clarifies who reports to whom throughout the organization. People higher in the chain of command have the right, *if they so choose*, to give commands, take action, and make decisions concerning activities occurring anywhere below them in the chain. In the following discussion about delegation and decentralization, you will learn that managers don't always choose to exercise their authority directly.[15]

One of the key assumptions underlying the chain of command is **unity of command**, which means that workers should report to just one boss.[16] In practical terms, this means that only one person can be in charge at a time. Matrix organizations, in which employees have two bosses automatically violate this principle. This is one of the primary reasons that matrix organizations are difficult to manage. Unity of command serves an important purpose: to prevent the confusion that might arise when an employee receives conflicting commands from two different bosses. When Bill Gates became chair of Microsoft (after being CEO) and Steve Ballmer became CEO, there was confusion about the chain of command at Microsoft. In one meeting, Gates approved a budget increase for a project. Ballmer then denied the increase, shouting at Gates, "You put me in charge of the company. Let me run it."[17]

2.2 Line Versus Staff Authority

A second dimension of authority is the distinction between line and staff authority. **Line authority** is the right to command immediate subordinates in the chain of command. For example, Sony CEO Howard Stringer has line authority over the head of Sony Entertainment Business Group, which includes Sony Pictures. Stringer can issue orders to that division president and expect them to be carried out. In turn, the head of Sony Entertainment Business Group can issue orders to his subordinates and expect them to be carried out. **Staff authority** is the right to *advise* but not command others who are not subordinates in the chain of command. For example, a manager in human resources at Sony might advise the manager in charge of Sony's TV Business Group on a hiring decision but cannot giver orders to hire a certain applicant.

The terms *line* and *staff* are also used to describe different functions within the organization. A **line function** is an activity that contributes directly to creating or

authority
the right to give commands, take action, and make decisions to achieve organizational objectives

chain of command
the vertical line of authority that clarifies who reports to whom throughout the organization

unity of command
a management principle that workers should report to just one boss

line authority
the right to command immediate subordinates in the chain of command

staff authority
the right to advise, but not command, others who are not subordinates in the chain of command

line function
an activity that contributes directly to creating or selling the company's products

selling the company's products. So, for example, activities that take place within the manufacturing and marketing departments would be considered line functions. A **staff function**, such as accounting, human resources, or legal services, does not contribute directly to creating or selling the company's products, but instead supports line activities. For example, marketing managers might consult with the legal staff to make sure the wording of a particular advertisement is legal.

2.3 Delegation of Authority

Managers can exercise their authority directly by completing the tasks themselves, or they can choose to pass on some of their authority to subordinates. **Delegation of authority** is the assignment of direct authority and responsibility to a subordinate to complete tasks for which the manager is normally responsible.

staff function an activity that does not contribute directly to creating or selling the company's products, but instead supports line activities

delegation of authority the assignment of direct authority and responsibility to a subordinate to complete tasks for which the manager is normally responsible

centralization of authority the location of most authority at the upper levels of the organization

When a manager delegates work, three transfers occur, as illustrated in Exhibit 8.8. First, the manager transfers full responsibility for the assignment to the subordinate. Many managers find giving up full responsibility somewhat difficult and often fear that the task won't be done as well as if they did it themselves. However, one CEO says, "If you can delegate a task to somebody who can do it 75 percent to 80 percent as well as you can today, you delegate it immediately." Why? The reason is that many tasks don't need to be done perfectly; they just need to be *done*. And delegating tasks that someone else can do frees managers to assume other important responsibilities. Delegating authority can generate a related problem: micromanaging. Sometimes managers delegate only to later interfere with how the employee is performing the task. But delegating full responsibility means that the employee—not the manager—is now completely responsible for task completion.

The second transfer that occurs with delegation is that the manager gives the subordinate full authority over the budget, resources, and personnel needed to do the job. To do the job effectively, subordinates must have the same tools and information at their disposal that managers had when they were responsible for the same task. In other words, for delegation to work, delegated authority must be commensurate with delegated responsibility.

EXHIBIT 8.8

Delegation: Responsibility, Authority, and Accountability

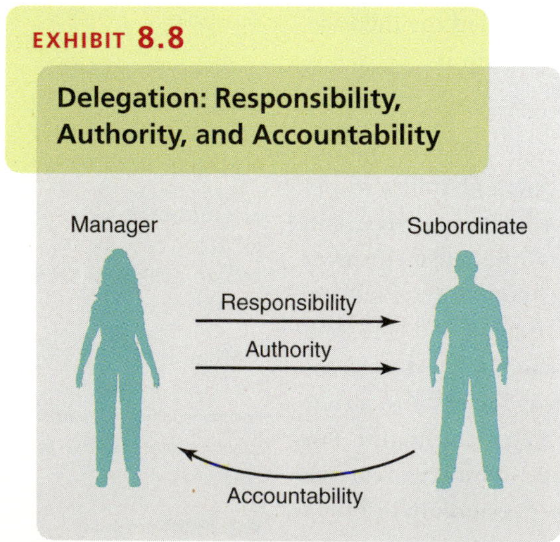

Source: C. D. Pringle, D. F. Jennings, & J. G. Longenecker, *Managing Organizations: Functions and Behaviors* © 1990. Adapted by permission of Pearson Education, Inc., Upper Saddle River, NJ.

The third transfer that occurs with delegation is the transfer of accountability. The subordinate now has the authority and responsibility to do the job and in return is accountable for getting the job done. In other words, managers delegate their managerial authority and responsibility to subordinates in exchange for results. Exhibit 8.9 gives some tips on how to be an effective delegator.

2.4 Degree of Centralization

If you've ever called a company's toll-free number with a complaint or a special request and been told by the customer-service representative, "I'll have to ask my manager" or "I'm not authorized to do that," you know that centralization of authority exists in that company. **Centralization of authority** is the location of most authority at the upper levels of the organization. In a centralized organization, managers make most decisions,

EXHIBIT 8.9

How to Be a More Effective Delegator

1. Trust your staff to do a good job. Recognize that others have the talent and ability to complete projects.
2. Avoid seeking perfection. Establish a standard of quality and provide a time frame for reaching it.
3. Give effective job instructions. Make sure employees have enough information to complete the job successfully.
4. Know your true interests. Delegation is difficult for some people who actually prefer doing the work themselves rather than managing it.
5. Follow up on progress. Build in checkpoints to help identify potential problems.
6. Praise the efforts of your staff.
7. Don't wait until the last minute to delegate. Avoid crisis management by routinely delegating work.
8. Ask questions, expect answers, and assist employees to help them complete the work assignments as expected.
9. Provide the resources you would expect if you were doing an assignment yourself.
10. Delegate to the lowest possible level to make the best possible use of organizational resources, energy, and knowledge.

Source: S. B. Wilson, "Are You an Effective Delegator?" *Female Executive*, 1 November 1994, 19.

even the relatively small ones. That's why the customer-service representative you called couldn't make a decision without first asking the manager.

If you are lucky, however, you may have talked to a customer-service representative at another company who said, "I can take care of that for you right now." In other words, the person was able to handle your problem without any input from or consultation with management. **Decentralization** is the location of a significant amount of authority in the lower levels of the organization. An organization is decentralized if it has a high degree of delegation at all levels. In a decentralized organization, workers closest to problems are authorized to make the decisions necessary to solve the problems on their own.

Decentralization has a number of advantages. It develops employee capabilities throughout the company and leads to faster decision making and more satisfied customers and employees. Furthermore, a study of 1,000 large companies found that companies with a high degree of decentralization outperformed those with a low degree of decentralization in terms of return on assets (6.9 percent versus 4.7 percent), return on investment (14.6 percent versus 9.0 percent), return on equity

decentralization
the location of a significant amount of authority in the lower levels of the organization

(22.8 percent versus 16.6 percent), and return on sales (10.3 percent versus 6.3 percent). Surprisingly, the same study found that few large companies actually are decentralized. Specifically, only 31 percent of employees in these 1,000 companies were responsible for recommending improvements to management. Overall, just 10 percent of employees received the training and information needed to support a truly decentralized approach to management.[18]

With results like these, the key question is no longer *whether* companies should decentralize, but *where* they should decentralize. One rule of thumb is to stay centralized where standardization is important and to decentralize where standardization is unimportant. **Standardization** is solving problems by consistently applying the same rules, procedures, and processes.

REVIEW 2

Organizational Authority

Organizational authority is determined by the chain of command, line versus staff authority, delegation, and the degree of centralization in a company. The chain of command vertically connects every job in the company to higher levels of management and makes clear who reports to whom. Managers have line authority to command employees below them in the chain of command but have only staff, or advisory, authority over employees not below them in the chain of command. Managers delegate authority by transferring to subordinates the authority and responsibility needed to do a task; in exchange, subordinates become accountable for task completion. In centralized companies, most authority to make decisions lies with managers in the upper levels of the company. In decentralized companies, much of the authority is delegated to the workers closest to problems, those who can make the decisions necessary for solving the problems themselves. Centralization works best for tasks that require standardized decision making. When standardization isn't important, decentralization can lead to faster decisions, greater employee and customer satisfaction, and significantly better financial performance.

3 Job Design

Imagine that McDonald's decided to pay $75,000 a year to its drive-through window cashiers. That's $75,000 for saying, "Welcome to McDonald's. May I have your order please?" Would you take the job? Sure you would. Work a couple of years. Make one hundred and fifty grand. Why not? Let's assume, however, that to get this salary, you have to be a full-time McDonald's drive-through window cashier for the next 10 years. Would you still take the job? Just imagine, 40 to 60 times an hour, you'd repeat the same basic process:

1. "Welcome to McDonald's. May I have your order please?"
2. Listen to the order. Repeat it for accuracy. State the total cost. "Please drive to the second window."
3. Take the money. Make change.
4. Give customers drinks, straws, and napkins.
5. Give customers food.
6. "Thank you for coming to McDonald's."

standardization
solving problems by consistently applying the same rules, procedures, and processes

Could you stand to do the same simple tasks an average of 50 times per hour, 400 times per day, 2,000 times per week, 8,000 times per month? Few can. Fast-food workers rarely stay on the job more than 6 months. Indeed, McDonald's and other fast-food restaurants have well over 100 percent employee turnover each year.[19]

In this next section, you will learn about **job design**—the number, kind, and variety of tasks that individual workers perform in doing their jobs.

You will learn 3.1 **why companies continue to use specialized jobs like the McDonald's drive-through position**, 3.2 **how job rotation, job enlargement, job enrichment**, and 3.3 **the job characteristics model are being used to overcome the problems associated with job specialization**.

3.1 Job Specialization

Job specialization occurs when a job comprises a small part of a larger task or process. Specialized jobs are characterized by simple, easy-to-learn steps, low variety, and high repetition, like the *MCDONALD*'s drive-through window job just described. One of the clear disadvantages of specialized jobs is that, being so easy to learn, they quickly become boring. This, in turn, can lead to low job satisfaction and high absenteeism and employee turnover, all of which are very costly to organizations.

Why, then, do companies continue to create and use specialized jobs? The primary reason is that specialized jobs are very economical. Once a job has been specialized, it takes little time to learn and master. Consequently, when experienced workers quit or are absent, the company can replace them with new employees and lose little productivity. For example, next time you're at McDonald's, notice the pictures of the food on the cash registers. These pictures make it easy for McDonald's trainees to quickly learn to take orders. Likewise, to simplify and speed operations, the drink dispensers behind the counter are set to automatically fill drink cups. Put a medium cup below the dispenser. Punch the medium drink button. The soft-drink machine then fills the cup to within a half-inch of the top, while that same worker goes to get your fries. At McDonald's, every task has been simplified in this way. Because the work is designed to be simple, wages can remain low since it isn't necessary to pay high salaries to attract highly experienced, educated, or trained workers.

3.2 Job Rotation, Enlargement, and Enrichment

Because of the efficiency of specialized jobs, companies are often reluctant to eliminate them. Consequently, job redesign efforts have focused on modifying jobs to keep the benefits of specialized jobs while reducing their obvious costs and disadvantages. Three methods—job rotation, job enlargement, and job enrichment—have been used to try to improve specialized jobs.[20]

In factory work or even some office jobs, many workers perform the same task all day long. If you attach side mirrors in an auto factory, you probably complete this task 45 to 60 times an hour. If you work as the cashier at a grocery store, you check out a different customer every 2 to 3 minutes. And if you work as an office receptionist, you may answer and direct phone calls up to 200 times an hour. **Job rotation** attempts to overcome the disadvantages of job specialization by periodically moving workers from one specialized job to another to give them more variety and the opportunity to use different skills. For example, an office receptionist who

job design
the number, kind, and variety of tasks that individual workers perform in doing their jobs

job specialization
a job composed of a small part of a larger task or process

job rotation
periodically moving workers from one specialized job to another to give them more variety and the opportunity to use different skills

Management Trend:

Telecommuting is great for employees, since it gives them lots of flexibility to deal with their personal lives. And it's great for companies, since it boosts employee morale and productivity. It could change very quickly, though. Recently, the Tax Court of New Jersey ruled that Telebright, a software company headquartered in Maryland, would have to pay New Jersey business taxes because one of its telecommuting employees lived in that state. As precedent, the court's decision would be disastrous, since companies would face an increased tax burden for allowing employees to work at home.

Source: William P. Barrett. "Bad News for Telecommuters." Forbes.com March 30, 2010. Accessed at http://www.forbes.com/2010/03/30/state-corporate-tax-telecommuters-amazon-personal-finance-new-jersey-tax-grab.html?boxes=financechannellatest.

does nothing but answer phones could be systematically rotated to a different job, such as typing, filing, or data entry, every day or two. Because employees simply switch from one specialized job to another, job rotation allows companies to retain the economic benefits of specialized work. At the same time, the greater variety of tasks makes the work less boring and more satisfying for workers.

Another way to counter the disadvantages of specialization is to enlarge the job. **Job enlargement** increases the number of different tasks that a worker performs within one particular job. Instead of being assigned just one task, workers with enlarged jobs are given several tasks to perform. For example, an enlarged "mirror attacher" job might include attaching the mirror, checking to see that the mirror's power adjustment controls work, and then cleaning the mirror's surface. Though job enlargement increases variety, many workers report feeling more stress when their jobs are enlarged. Consequently, many workers view enlarged jobs as simply more work, especially if they are not given additional time to complete the additional tasks.

Job enrichment attempts to overcome the deficiencies in specialized work by increasing the number of tasks *and* by giving workers the authority and control to make meaningful decisions about their work.[21] At *AES*, an independent power company that sells electricity to public utilities and steam (for power) to industrial organizations, workers have been given an extraordinary level of authority and control. For example, with his hands still blackened after unloading coal from a barge, employee Jeff Hatch calls a broker to determine which Treasury bills the company should buy to maximize the short-term return on its available cash. Hatch asks his broker, "What kind of rate can you give me for $10 million at 30 days?" When the broker tells him, "6.09 percent," he responds, "But I just got a 6.13 percent quote from Chase."[22] Indeed, ordinary plant technicians at AES are given budgets worth several million dollars and are trusted to purchase everything from mops to gas turbines.

job enlargement
increasing the number of different tasks that a worker performs within one particular job

job enrichment
increasing the number of tasks in a particular job and giving workers the authority and control to make meaningful decisions about their work

job characteristics model (JCM)
an approach to job redesign that seeks to formulate jobs in ways that motivate workers and lead to positive work outcomes

3.3 Job Characteristics Model

In contrast to job rotation, job enlargement, and job enrichment, which focus on providing variety in job tasks, the **job characteristics model (JCM)** is an approach to job redesign that seeks to formulate jobs in ways that motivate workers and lead to positive work outcomes.[23]

As shown in Exhibit 8.10, the primary goal of the model is to create jobs that result in positive personal and work outcomes, such as internal work motivation, satisfaction with one's job, and work effectiveness. Of these, the central

EXHIBIT 8.10

Job Characteristics Model

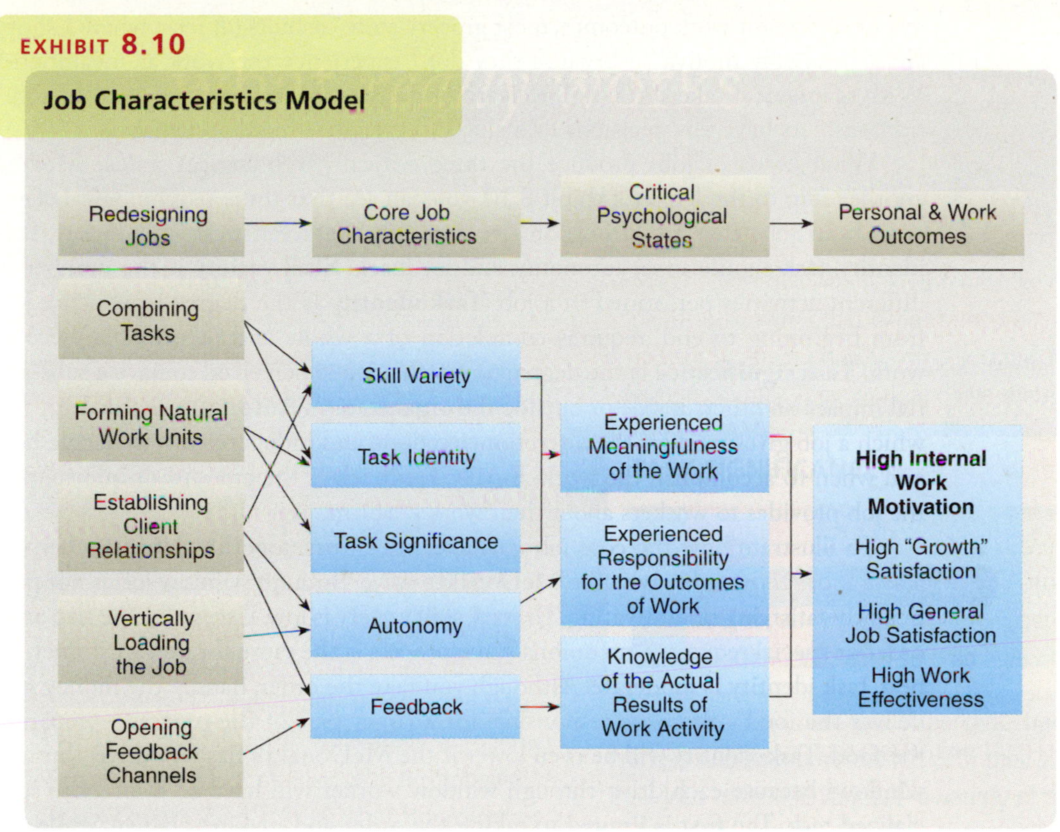

Source: J. R. Hackman & G. R. Oldham, *Work Redesign* (Reading, MA: Addison-Wesley, 1980). Reprinted by permission of Addison-Wesley Longman.

concern of the JCM is internal motivation. **Internal motivation** is motivation that comes from the job itself rather than from outside rewards such as a raise or praise from the boss. If workers feel that performing the job well is itself rewarding, then the job has internal motivation. Statements such as "I get a nice sense of accomplishment" or "I feel good about myself and what I'm producing" are examples of internal motivation.

Moving to the left in Exhibit 8.10, you can see that the JCM specifies three critical psychological states that must occur for work to be internally motivating. First, workers must *experience the work as meaningful*; that is, they must view their job as being important. Second, they must *experience responsibility for work outcomes*—they must feel personally responsible for the work being done well. Third, workers must have *knowledge of results*; that is, they must know how well they are performing their jobs. All three critical psychological states must occur for work to be internally motivating.

Let's return to our grocery store cashier. Cashiers usually have knowledge of results. When you're slow, your checkout line grows long. If you make a mistake, customers point it out. Likewise, cashiers experience responsibility for work outcomes. At the end of the day, the register is totaled and the money is counted. If the money in the till is less than what's recorded in the register, most stores make the cashier pay the difference. Nonetheless, despite knowing the results and experiencing

internal motivation motivation that comes from the job itself rather than from outside rewards

These statistics indicate that, on average, the JCM has at worst a 66 percent chance of improving workers' job satisfaction. In all, this is impressive evidence that the model works. In general, you can expect these results when redesigning jobs based on the model.

We can be more accurate about the effects of the JCM, however, if we split workers into two groups: those with high growth need strength and those with low growth need strength. *Growth need strength* is the need or desire to achieve personal growth and development through one's job. Workers high in growth need strength respond well to jobs designed according to the JCM because they enjoy work that challenges them and allows them to learn new skills and knowledge. In fact, there is an 84 percent chance that workers with high growth need strength will be more satisfied with their work when their jobs are redesigned according to the JCM.

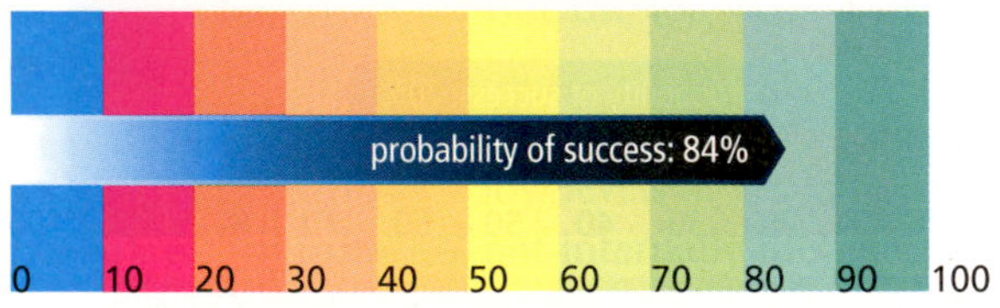

By comparison, because they aren't as interested in being challenged or learning new things at work, there is only a 69 percent chance that workers low in growth need strength will be satisfied with jobs that have been redesigned according to the principles of the JCM. This is still a favorable percentage, but it is weaker than the 84 percent chance of job satisfaction that occurs for workers high in growth need strength.

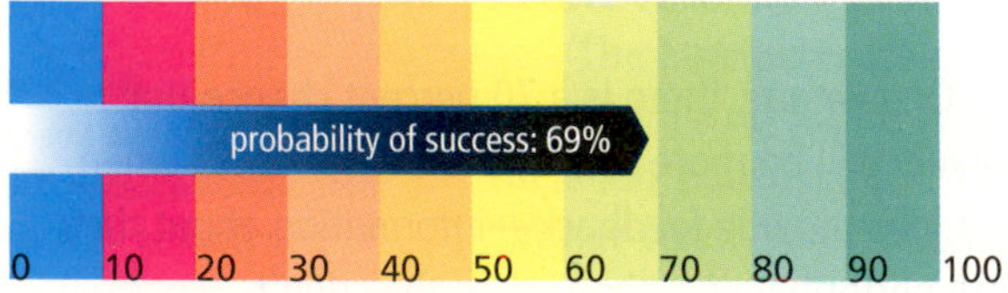

Workplace Absenteeism

Although not shown in the job characteristics model displayed in Exhibit 8.10, workplace absenteeism is an important personal or work outcome affected by a job's core characteristics. In general, the "richer" your job is with task identity, task significance, skill variety, autonomy, and feedback, the more likely you are to show up for work every day.

Workers are 63 percent more likely to attend work when their jobs have task identity than when they don't.

Workers are 68 percent more likely to attend work when their jobs have task significance than when they don't.

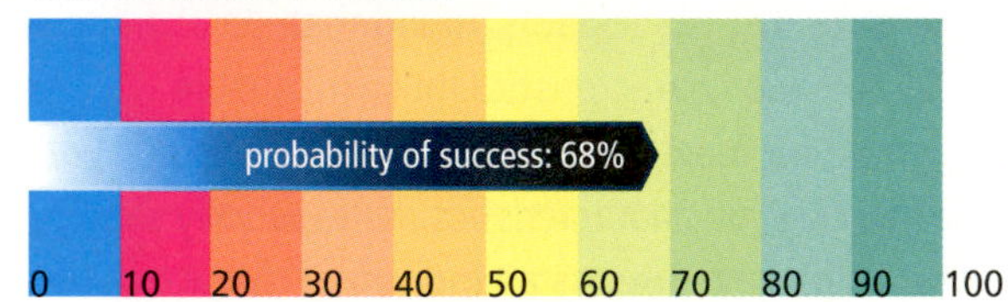

Workers are 72 percent more likely to attend work when their jobs have skill variety than when they don't.

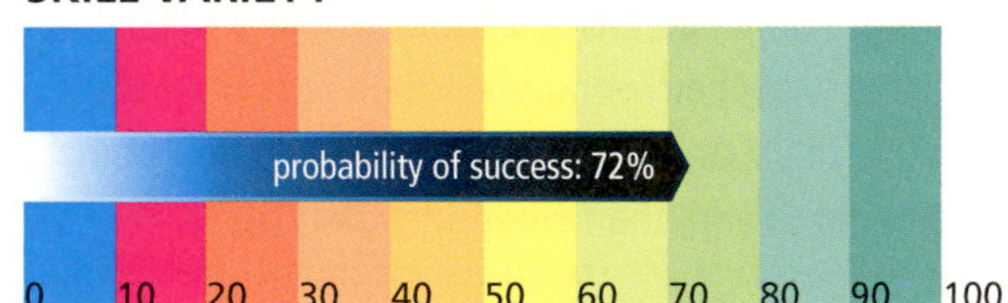

Workers are 74 percent more likely to attend work when their jobs have autonomy than when they don't.

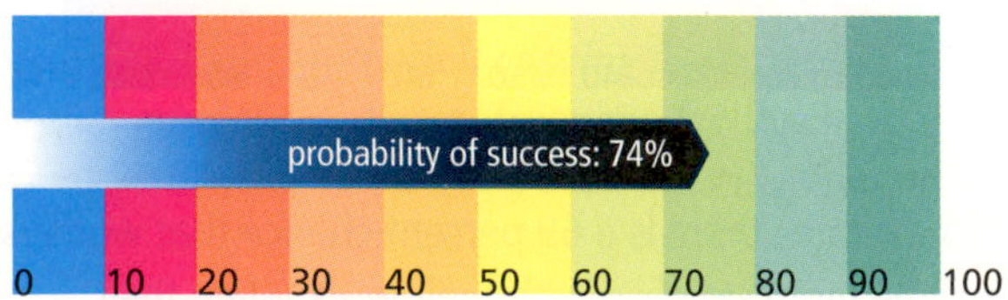

Workers are 72 percent more likely to attend work when their jobs provide feedback than when they don't.[24]

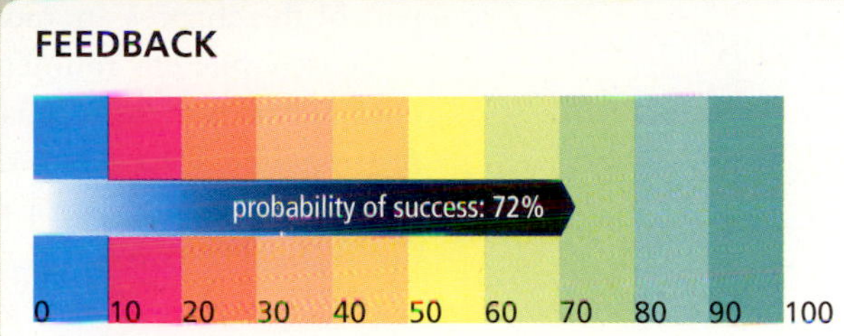

REVIEW 3

Job Design

Companies use specialized jobs because they are economical and easy to learn and don't require highly paid workers. But specialized jobs aren't motivating or particularly satisfying for employees. Companies have used job rotation, job enlargement, job enrichment, and the job characteristics model to make specialized jobs more interesting and motivating. With job rotation, workers move from one specialized job to another. Job enlargement simply increases the number of different tasks within a particular job. Job enrichment increases the number of tasks in a job and gives workers authority and control over their work. The goal of the job characteristics model is to make jobs intrinsically motivating. For this to happen, jobs must be strong on five core job characteristics (skill variety, task identity, task significance, autonomy, and feedback), and workers must experience three critical psychological states (knowledge of results, responsibility for work outcomes, and meaningful work). If jobs aren't internally motivating, they can be redesigned by combining tasks, forming natural work units, establishing client relationships, vertical loading, and opening feedback channels.

Designing Organizational Processes

More than 40 years ago, Tom Burns and G. M. Stalker described how two kinds of organizational design, mechanistic and organic, are appropriate for different kinds of organizational environments.[25] **Mechanistic organizations** are characterized by specialized jobs and responsibilities, precisely defined, unchanging roles, and a rigid chain of command based on centralized authority and vertical communication. This type of organization works best in stable, unchanging business environments. By contrast, **organic organizations** are characterized by broadly defined jobs and responsibility, loosely defined, frequently changing roles, and decentralized authority and horizontal communication based on task knowledge. This type of organization works best in dynamic, changing business environments.

mechanistic organization
an organization characterized by specialized jobs and responsibilities; precisely defined, unchanging roles; and a rigid chain of command based on centralized authority and vertical communication

organic organization
an organization characterized by broadly defined jobs and responsibility; loosely defined, frequently changing roles; and decentralized authority and horizontal communication based on task knowledge

The organizational design techniques described in the first half of this chapter—departmentalization, authority, and job design—are better suited for mechanistic organizations and the stable business environments that were more prevalent before 1980. By contrast, the organizational design techniques discussed in the second part of the chapter, are more appropriate for organic organizations and the increasingly dynamic environments in which today's businesses compete. The key difference between these approaches is that mechanistic organizational designs focus on organizational structure, whereas organic organizational designs are concerned with organizational process, or the collection of activities that transform inputs into outputs valued by customers.

After reading the next two sections, you should be able to:

4 explain the methods that companies are using to redesign internal organizational processes (i.e., intraorganizational processes).

5 describe the methods that companies are using to redesign external organizational processes (i.e., interorganizational processes).

4 Intraorganizational Processes

An **intraorganizational process** is the collection of activities that take place within an organization to transform inputs into outputs that customers value. The steps involved in an automobile insurance claim are a good example of an intraorganizational process:

1. Document the loss (the accident).
2. Assign an appraiser to determine the dollar amount of damage.
3. Make an appointment to inspect the vehicle.
4. Inspect the vehicle.
5. Write an appraisal and get the repair shop to agree to the damage estimate.
6. Pay for the repair work.
7. Return the repaired car to the customer.

Let's take a look at how companies are using 4.1 **reengineering**, 4.2 **empowerment**, and 4.3 **behavioral informality to redesign intraorganizational processes like these**.

4.1 Reengineering

In their best-selling book *Reengineering the Corporation*, Michael Hammer and James Champy define **reengineering** as "the *fundamental* rethinking and *radical* redesign of business *processes* to achieve *dramatic* improvements in critical, contemporary measures of performance, such as cost, quality, service and speed."[26] Hammer and Champy further explained the four key words shown in italics in this definition. The first key word is *fundamental*. When reengineering organizational designs, managers must ask themselves, "Why do we do what we do?" and "Why do we do it the way we do?" The usual answer is "Because that's the way we've always done it." The second key word is *radical*. Reengineering is about significant change, about starting over by throwing out the old ways of getting work done. The third key word is *processes*. Hammer and Champy noted that "most business people are not process oriented; they are focused on tasks, on jobs, on people, on structures, but not on processes." The fourth key word is *dramatic*. Reengineering is about achieving quantum improvements in company performance.

intraorganizational process
the collection of activities that take place within an organization to transform inputs into outputs that customers value

reengineering
fundamental rethinking and radical redesign of business processes to achieve dramatic improvements in critical measures of performance, such as cost, quality, service, and speed

An example from IBM Credit's operation illustrates how work can be reengineered.[27] *IBM CREDIT* lent businesses money to buy IBM computers. Previously, the loan application bounced around five departments over 6 days before being approved or denied. Of course, this delay cost IBM business. Some customers got loans elsewhere. Others, frustrated by the wait, simply canceled their orders.

Finally, two IBM managers decided to walk a loan straight through each of the departments involved in the process. At each step, they asked the workers to stop what they were doing and immediately process their loan application. They were shocked by what they found. From start to finish, the entire process took just 90 minutes! The 6-day turnaround time was almost entirely due to delays in handing off the work from one department to another. The solution: IBM redesigned the process so that one person, not five people in five separate departments, would handle the entire loan approval process without any handoffs. The results were indeed dramatic. Reengineering the credit process reduced approval time from 6 days to 4 hours and allowed IBM Credit to increase the number of loans it handled by a factor of 100![28]

Reengineering changes an organization's orientation from vertical to horizontal. Instead of taking orders from upper management, lower- and middle-level managers and workers take orders from a customer who is at the beginning and end of each process. Instead of running independent functional departments, managers and workers in different departments take ownership of cross-functional processes. Instead of simplifying work so that it becomes increasingly specialized, reengineering complicates work by giving workers increased autonomy and responsibility for complete processes.

task interdependence the extent to which collective action is required to complete an entire piece of work

pooled interdependence work completed by having each job or department independently contribute to the whole

sequential interdependence work completed in succession, with one group's or job's outputs becoming the inputs for the next group or job

reciprocal interdependence work completed by different jobs or groups working together in a back-and-forth manner

In essence, reengineering changes work by changing **task interdependence**, the extent to which collective action is required to complete an entire piece of work. As shown in Exhibit 8.11, there are three kinds of task interdependence.[29] In **pooled interdependence**, each job or department independently contributes to the whole. In **sequential interdependence**, work must be performed in succession, as one group's or job's outputs become the inputs for the next group or job. Finally, in **reciprocal interdependence**, different jobs or groups work together in a back-and-forth manner to complete the process. By reducing the handoffs between different jobs or groups, reengineering decreases sequential interdependence. Likewise, reengineering decreases pooled interdependence by redesigning work so that formerly independent jobs or departments now work together to complete processes. Finally, reengineering increases reciprocal interdependence by making groups or individuals responsible for larger, more complete processes in which several steps may be accomplished at the same time.

EXHIBIT 8.11

Reengineering and Task Interdependence

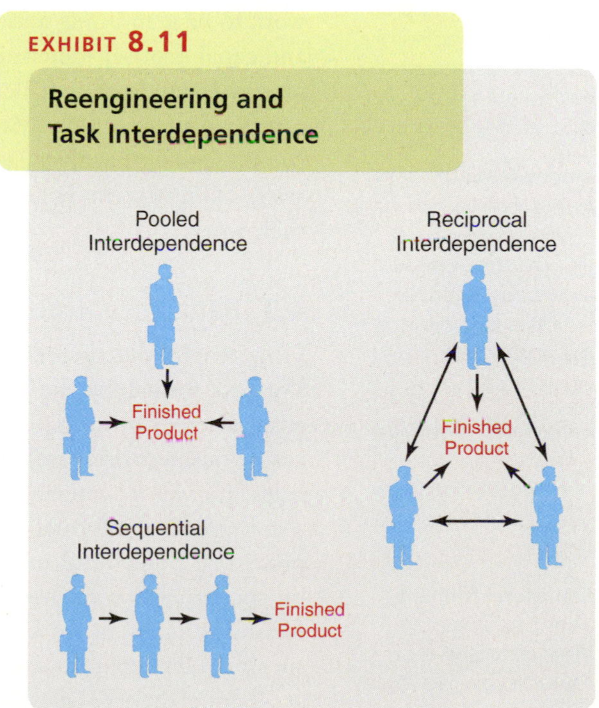

As an organizational design tool, reengineering promises big rewards, but it has also come under severe criticism. The most serious complaint is that because it allows a few workers to do the work formerly done by many, reengineering is simply a corporate code word for cost cutting and worker layoffs.[30] For this reason, detractors claim that reengineering hurts morale and performance. Even though ordering times were reduced from 3 weeks to 3 days, *LEVI STRAUSS* ended an $850 million reengineering project because of the fear and turmoil it created in the company's workforce. One low point occurred when Levi management, encouraged by its reengineering consultants, told 4,000 workers that they would have to "reapply for their jobs" as the company shifted from its traditional vertical structure to a process-based form of organizing. Today, even reengineering gurus Hammer and Champy admit that roughly 70 percent of all reengineering projects fail because of how they affect people in the workplace. Says Hammer, "I wasn't smart enough about [the people issues]. I was reflecting my engineering background and was insufficiently appreciative of the human dimension. I've [now] learned that's critical."[31]

4.2 Empowerment

Another way of redesigning intraorganizational processes is through empowerment. **Empowering workers** means permanently passing decision-making authority and responsibility from managers to workers. For workers to be fully empowered, companies must give them the information and resources they need to make and carry out good decisions and then reward them for taking individual initiative.[32] Unfortunately, this doesn't happen often enough.

When workers are given the proper information and resources and are allowed to make good decisions, they experience strong feelings of empowerment. **Empowerment** is a feeling of intrinsic motivation, in which workers perceive their work to have meaning and perceive themselves to be competent, having an impact, and capable of self-determination.[33] Work has meaning when it is consistent with personal standards and beliefs. Workers feel competent when they believe they can perform an activity with skill. The belief that they are having an impact comes from a feeling that they can affect work outcomes. A feeling of self-determination arises from workers' belief that they have the autonomy to choose how best to do their work.

empowering workers
permanently passing decision-making authority and responsibility from managers to workers by giving them the information and resources they need to make and carry out good decisions

empowerment
feelings of intrinsic motivation, in which workers perceive their work to have impact and meaning and perceive themselves to be competent and capable of self-determination

behavioral informality
a workplace atmosphere characterized by spontaneity, casualness, and interpersonal familiarity

behavioral formality
a workplace atmosphere characterized by routine and regimen, specific rules about how to behave, and impersonal detachment

4.3 Behavioral Informality

How would you describe the atmosphere in the office where you last worked? Was it a formal, by-the-book, follow-the-rules, address-each-other-by-last-names atmosphere? Or was it more informal, with an emphasis on results rather than rules, casual business dress rather than suits, and first names rather than last names and titles? Or was it somewhere in between?

Behavioral informality (or formality) is a third influence on intraorganizational processes. **Behavioral informality** refers to workplace atmospheres characterized by spontaneity, casualness, and interpersonal familiarity. By contrast, **behavioral formality** refers to workplace atmospheres characterized by routine and regimen, specific rules about how to behave, and impersonal detachment.

Casual dress policies and open office systems are two of the most popular methods for increasing behavioral informality. In fact, a survey conducted by the Society for Human Resource Management indicates that casual dress policies (no suits, ties, jackets, dresses, or formal clothing required) are extremely popular.[34] Today, 84 percent of companies have some form of casual dress code, up from 63 percent 9 years ago and 24 percent 14 years ago.[35] Similarly, 42 percent of all companies permit casual dress at least one day a week, compared with 17 percent 5 years ago. Moreover, 33 percent of companies permit casual dress every day of the week, up from 20 percent 7 years ago.

Indeed, casual dress appears to improve employee attitudes. Colin Stanbridge, the chief executive of London's Chamber of Commerce, says, "People tend to work at their best when they feel most comfortable. And today I think the vast majority of people feel at their most comfortable when wearing casual dress."[36] In fact, 85 percent of human resources directors believe that casual dress can improve office morale, and 79 percent say that employees are very satisfied with casual dress codes.[37] Moreover, nearly two-thirds of the human resources directors believe that casual dress policies are an important tool for attracting qualified employees in tight labor markets. Michael Losey, president of the Society for Human Resource Management, concludes that "for the majority of corporations and industries, allowing casual dress can have clear advantages at virtually no cost."[38]

While casual dress increases behavioral informality by having managers and workers at all levels dress in a more relaxed manner, open office systems increase behavioral informality by significantly increasing the level of communication and interaction among employees. By definition, **open office systems** try to increase interaction by removing physical barriers that separate workers. One characteristic of open office systems is that they have much more shared space than private space. **Shared spaces** are areas used by and open to all employees. Cubicles with low-to-the-ground partitions (used by 75 percent of office workers), offices with no doors or with glass walls, collections of comfortable furniture that encourage people to congregate, and common areas with tables and chairs that encourage people to meet, work, or eat together are examples of shared space.[39] In contrast, **private spaces**, such as private offices with doors, are used by and open to just one employee.

The advantage of an open office with extensive shared space is that it dramatically increases the amount of unplanned, spontaneous, and chance communication among employees.[40] People are much more likely to plan meetings and work together when numerous collaboration spaces with conference tables, white boards, and computers are readily available. With no office walls, inviting common areas, and different departments mixed together in large open spaces, spontaneous communication occurs more often.

After *RADIO SHACK* moved from two traditional, 19-story office towers into a new headquarters with open offices, cubicles, and immense amounts of shared space, the volume of corporate e-mail dropped by 37 percent because people were much more likely to run into and actually talk to each other. Also, open office systems increase chance encounters by making it much more likely that people from different departments or areas will run into each other. *SIGMA-ALDRICH*, a biotechnology firm, built a new office with a three-story, open staircase. The open staircase is complemented by benches and expansive landings on each story so people could sit and talk. Indeed, soon after the move to the new office, two scientists from opposite sides of the building ran into each other on the stairs, stopped to talk, and ended up generating a significant new reagent for scientific testing.[41]

open office systems
offices in which the physical barriers that separate workers have been removed in order to increase communication and interaction

shared spaces
spaces used by and open to all employees

private spaces
spaces used by and open to just one employee

Doing the Right Thing

Don't Scavenge That Office if Somebody Is Still in It

It's like roadkill in the animal kingdom. As soon as the word gets out that someone is leaving the company, coworkers start scheming to scavenge the office leftovers—chairs, computer monitors, filing cabinets, even staplers. "This issue is practically everywhere," says Mary Wong, president of a human resources consulting company. "Professionals—anyone you and I would normally consider to be very adult—turn into children" over the prospect of picking an empty office clean of its "goodies." Sometimes—and this is where it gets disrespectful—office scavengers move in even before the employee, who's often been laid off, has left. Ethics consultant Steve Lawler tells the story of a laid-off manager who, just hours after hearing the bad news, was already getting requests for the expensive Herman Miller Aeron chair in which he was still sitting. Office scavenging is a strange and predictable aspect of office life. It happens everywhere. But if you're going to scavenge, and you probably will, do the right thing by maintaining the dignity of departing coworkers: Wait until the office is empty before you strike.[44]

Not everyone is enthusiastic about open offices, however. For example, Ingrid Tischer, who sits in a cubicle next to the kitchen in her office, says she can't help being distracted by others' conversations and frequently joins in. Because of the location of her cubicle, "I know things about my colleagues' lives, and they know things about mine."[42] In fact, cubicle dwellers are interrupted by "noise, visual distractions, and chatty visitors" up to 21 times a day. And, since it takes about 3 minutes each time to refocus on what they were doing, cubicle workers can lose an hour a day to these interruptions. For this reason, Sun Microsystems and Microsoft give their employees private offices. William Agnello, Sun's vice president of real estate and the workplace, says, "We have researched the heck out of this. Our studies show that, for our engineers, there are just too many distractions and interruptions."[43]

REVIEW 4

Intraorganizational Processes

Today, companies are using reengineering, empowerment, and behavioral informality to change their intraorganizational processes. Through fundamental rethinking and radical redesign of business processes, reengineering changes an organization's orientation from vertical to horizontal. Reengineering changes work processes by decreasing sequential and pooled interdependence and by increasing reciprocal interdependence. Reengineering promises dramatic increases in productivity and customer satisfaction, but it has been criticized as simply an excuse to cut costs and lay off workers.

Empowering workers means taking decision-making authority and responsibility from managers and giving it to workers. Empowered workers develop feelings of competence and self-determination and believe that their work has meaning and impact. Workplaces characterized by behavioral informality are spontaneous and casual. Casual dress policies and open office systems are two of the most popular methods for increasing behavioral informality.

5 Interorganizational Processes

An **interorganizational process** is a collection of activities that occur *among companies* to transform inputs into outputs that customers value. In other words, many companies work together to create a product or service that keeps customers happy. For example, when you purchase a *LIZ CLAIBORNE* outfit, you're not just buying from Liz Claiborne; you're also buying from a network of 250 suppliers in 35 countries from Saipan, to Mexico, to Cambodia, to China that make those clothes for Liz Claiborne. After Liz Claiborne's New York–based designers come up with a concept, it is shipped to a sourcing team in Hong Kong, which changes the design as needed to keep costs low and then finds companies that can produce the right fabrics and the entire line of clothing. Those companies then manufacture the first product prototypes and send them back to the New York designers for final inspection and possibly last-minute changes.[45]

interorganizational process a collection of activities that take place among companies to transform inputs into outputs that customers value

modular organization an organization that outsources noncore business activities to outside companies, suppliers, specialists, or consultants

In this section, you'll explore interorganizational processes by learning about 5.1 **modular organizations**, and 5.2 **virtual organizations**.[46]

5.1 Modular Organizations

Except for core business activities that they can perform better, faster, and cheaper than others, **modular organizations** outsource all remaining business activities to outside companies, suppliers, specialists, or consultants. The term *modular* is used because the business activities purchased from outside companies can be added and dropped as needed, much like adding pieces to a three-dimensional puzzle. Exhibit 8.12 depicts a modular organization in which the company has chosen to keep training, human resources, sales, product design, manufacturing, customer service, research and development, and information technology as core business activities but has outsourced the noncore activities of product distribution, web page design, advertising, payroll, accounting, and packaging.

EXHIBIT 8.12

Modular Organization

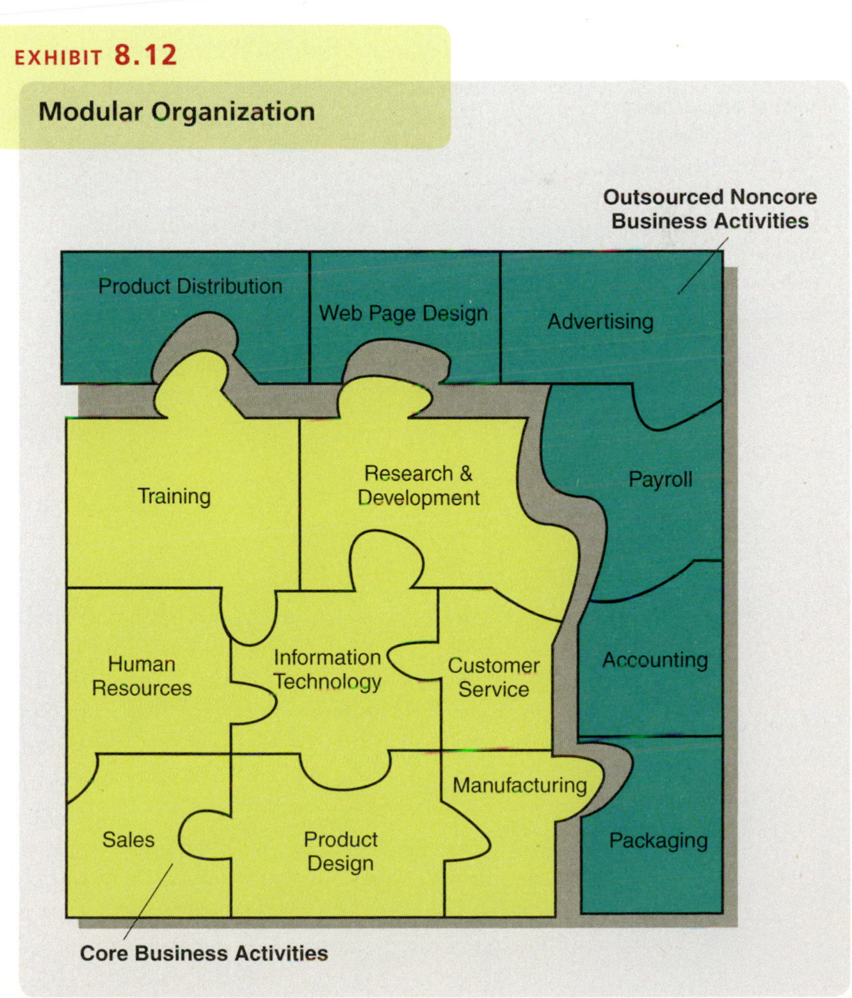

Modular organizations have several advantages. First, because modular organizations pay for

outsourced labor, expertise, or manufacturing capabilities only when needed, they can cost significantly less to run than traditional organizations. For example, when Apple came up with its iPod digital music player, it outsourced the audio chip design and manufacture to SigmaTel in Austin, Texas, and final assembly to Asutek Computers in Taiwan. Doing so not only reduced costs and sped up production (beating Sony's Network Walkman to market) but also allowed Apple to do what it does best—design innovative products with easy-to-use software.[47]

Modular organizations have disadvantages, too. The primary disadvantage is the loss of control that occurs when key business activities are outsourced to other companies. Also, companies may reduce their competitive advantage in two ways if they mistakenly outsource a core business activity. First, as a result of competitive and technological change, the noncore business activities a company has outsourced may suddenly become the basis for competitive advantage. Second, related to that point, suppliers to whom work is outsourced can sometimes become competitors.

5.2 Virtual Organizations

In contrast to modular organizations in which the interorganizational process revolves around a central company, a **virtual organization** is part of a network in which many companies share skills, costs, capabilities, markets, and customers with each other. Exhibit 8.13 shows a virtual organization in which, for "today," the parts of a virtual company consist of product design, purchasing, manufacturing, advertising, and information technology. Unlike modular organizations, in which the outside organizations are tightly linked to one central company, virtual organizations work with some companies in the network alliance, but not with all. So, whereas a puzzle with various pieces is a fitting metaphor for a modular organization, a potluck dinner is an appropriate metaphor for a virtual organization. All participants bring their finest food dish but eat only what they want.

virtual organization
an organization that is part of a network in which many companies share skills, costs, capabilities, markets, and customers to collectively solve customer problems or provide specific products or services

Another difference is that the working relationships between modular organizations and outside companies tend to be more stable and longer lasting than the shorter, often temporary relationships found among the virtual companies in a network alliance. The composition of a virtual organization is always changing. The combination of network partners that a virtual corporation has at any one time depends on the expertise needed to solve a particular problem or provide a specific product or service. This is why the businessperson in the network organization shown in Exhibit 8.13 is saying, "Today, I'll have. . . ." Tomorrow, the business could want something completely different. In this sense, the term *virtual organization* means the organization that exists "at the moment."

EXHIBIT 8.13
Virtual Organization

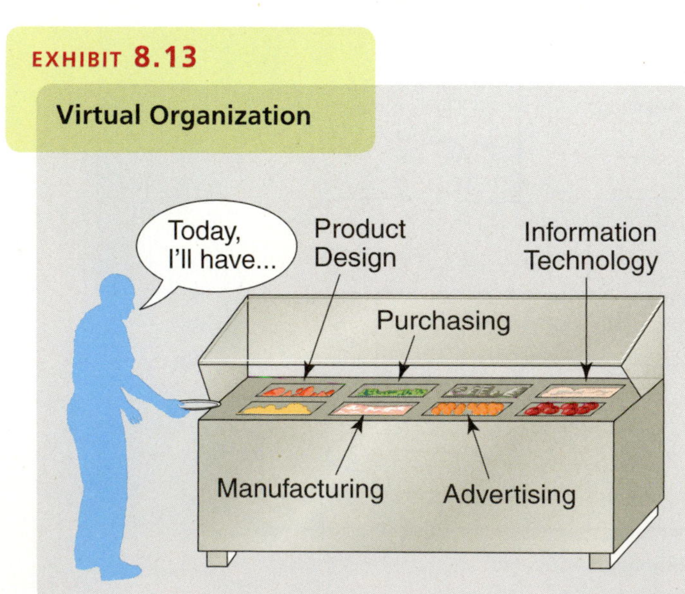

For example, 21 carton manufacturers have formed a network of virtual organizations called the *INDEPENDENT CARTON GROUP (ICG)*.[48] The original network, which brought five independent carton companies together, was designed so that each of the five companies could help each other in case a catastrophe occurred at one of their production facilities. For instance, if an ICG company ever experienced a disaster at a production facility, the other four members of the ICG would be there to temporarily provide alternative production arrangements so the affected company wouldn't lose its customers. However, as the group grew, they realized they could trade off manufacturing capacities with each other to better serve customers' needs, so they combined their efforts to provide carton packaging in 16 different industries, from automotive to biotech to food to electronics. ICG customers benefit from competitive pricing, uninterrupted supplies, and group purchasing power.

Virtual organizations have a number of advantages. They let companies share costs. And, because members of virtual organizations can quickly combine their efforts to meet customers' needs, they are fast and flexible. Finally, because each member of the network alliance is the best at what it does, virtual organizations should, in theory, provide better products and services in all respects.

As with modular organizations, a disadvantage of virtual organizations is that once work has been outsourced, it can be difficult to control the quality of work done by network partners. The greatest disadvantage, however, is that tremendous managerial skills are required to make a network of independent organizations work well together, especially since their relationships tend to be short and based on a single task or project.

Virtual organizations are using two methods to solve this problem. The first is to use a *broker*, whose job is to create and assemble the knowledge, skills, and resources from different companies for outside parties, such as customers.[49] The second way to make networks of virtual organizations more manageable is to use a *virtual organization agreement* that, somewhat like a contract, specifies the schedules, responsibilities, costs, payouts, and liabilities for participating organizations.[50] For more information on how a virtual organizations works, see ***http://www.independentcartongroup.com***.

REVIEW 5

Interorganizational Processes

Organizations use modular and virtual organizations to change interorganizational processes. Because modular organizations outsource all noncore activities to other businesses, they are less expensive to run than traditional companies. However, modular organizations require extremely close relationships with suppliers, may result in a loss of control, and could create new competitors if the wrong business activities are outsourced. Virtual organizations participate in a network in which they share skills, costs, capabilities, markets, and customers. As customer problems, products, or services change, the combination of virtual organizations that work together changes. Virtual organizations can reduce costs, respond quickly, and, if they can successfully coordinate their efforts, produce outstanding products and service.

Management Team Decision

China—The Future of General Motors?

It's been a rough ride for General Motors. In 2008, GM's remarkable run of 77 years as the world's largest automaker came to a crashing halt. In 2009, after a decade of mismanagement and declining sales, the company declared bankruptcy and needed a massive government bailout and thorough reorganization to stay afloat. During that time, more than 2,000 dealers were closed for good, and almost 23,000 employees were laid off. There is some hope that the new, streamlined GM, featuring new models, will regain its once-dominant position in the U.S. auto market. However, it is becoming increasingly clear that GM's future may lie in China.

In 2009, there were 13.6 million cars sold in China, an increase of 46 percent from 2008, and nearly 3 million more cars than were sold in the United States at the same time. In 1977, there were just 1 million cars in China; as of 2008, there were 51 million, and it's conservatively expected that the Chinese auto market will grow 10 to 15 percent every year. Unlike in the United States, GM hasn't been stuck on the sidelines in China. It sold 1.83 million cars in 2009, an increase of 67 percent over the previous year, and has a solid record of 15 consecutive months in which its sales have grown by double digits. By 2015, GM hopes to sell 3 million cars per year in China. This would not only make GM the largest auto seller in China, but it would make China GM's largest and most lucrative market.

Currently, GM operates in China as part of a joint venture with the SAIC Motor Corporation. Through the partnership, GM owns a minority stake in two companies, SAIC-GM-Wuling and Shanghai General Motors. Increasingly, however, you've heard your GM colleagues argue that a new organizational design is needed, one that will give the company a stronger presence in China, and decrease its dependence on the U.S. market. A group of these managers has come to you to seek out your opinion on how GM can organize to best take advantage of shifting conditions in the global auto market.

Questions

1. The text describes a number of different approaches concerning organizational structure. Which do you think would be ideal for GM's success in China? Which of the structures would help GM expand to other foreign markets?
2. What are the advantages and disadvantages of promoting decentralization in GM's operations in China?

Sources: "China Ends U.S's Reign as Largest Auto Market." *Bloomberg News.* Accessed at http://www.bloomberg.com/apps/news?pid=20601087&sid=aE.x_r_l9NZE

"GM's China Sales Exceed U.S. for Third Straight Month." *BusinessWeek.* April 2, 2010. Accessed at http://www.businessweek.com/news/2010-04-02/gm-sales-gain-in-china-on-government-stimulus-update1-.html

Ester Fung. "GM Sees Chain Sales Exceeding 3 Mln Units in 2015." *Wall Street Journal.* April 12, 2010. Accessed at http://online.wsj.com/article/BT-CO-20100412-701317.html?mod=WSJ_World_MIDDLEHeadlinesAsia

Practice being a Manager

Work Dynamics

Effective organization is vital to the accomplishment of company objectives. Two critical aspects of effective organization are departmentalization and the design of jobs. In this role-play exercise you will have the opportunity to experience some of the work dynamics surrounding the grouping of workers and the design of jobs.

STEP 1 Form work groups. Your professor will form groups and give you a role assignment.

STEP 2 **Review your role.** Read your role assignment carefully, and prepare to begin working per your role assignment.

STEP 3 (10–20 MINUTES) **Begin acting.** When your professor directs you to begin, you should start working as assigned by your role.

STEP 4 **Compile your results.** Total your results by work group, and compare across the teams.

STEP 5 **Debrief as a class.** Discuss the results as a class. What factors seemed to play a role in the efficiency and effectiveness of the work groups? What role did organization and job design play? If this were an actual organizational work group, what might you do to improve performance and worker satisfaction?

Flexibility and Structure

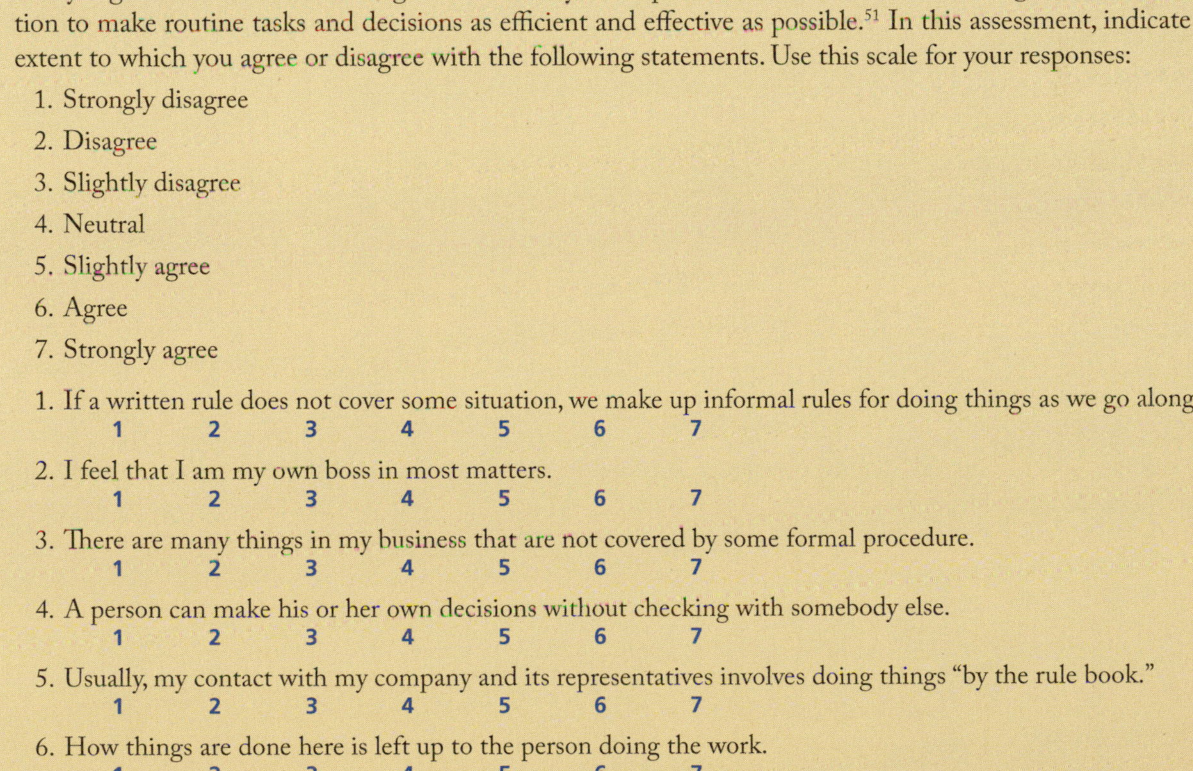

Every organization needs some degree of flexibility and standardization. In other words, companies need to have enough flexibility in their organizations to respond to changes in their business environment, but firms also must have certain structures in place to ensure smooth operations. For example, if someone gets hurt on company property, clear procedures about what to do in the case of an accident help managers respond quickly and confidently. But being overly committed to following rules can hamstring an organization and keep it from growing. As a manager, you will probably encounter both types of situations, and to respond appropriately you will need to have an idea of how comfortable you are in a formal environment versus a more loosely structured workplace. Every organization needs some degree of flexibility to adapt to new situations and some degree of standardization to make routine tasks and decisions as efficient and effective as possible.[51] In this assessment, indicate the extent to which you agree or disagree with the following statements. Use this scale for your responses:

1. Strongly disagree
2. Disagree
3. Slightly disagree
4. Neutral
5. Slightly agree
6. Agree
7. Strongly agree

1. If a written rule does not cover some situation, we make up informal rules for doing things as we go along.
   1 2 3 4 5 6 7
2. I feel that I am my own boss in most matters.
   1 2 3 4 5 6 7
3. There are many things in my business that are not covered by some formal procedure.
   1 2 3 4 5 6 7
4. A person can make his or her own decisions without checking with somebody else.
   1 2 3 4 5 6 7
5. Usually, my contact with my company and its representatives involves doing things "by the rule book."
   1 2 3 4 5 6 7
6. How things are done here is left up to the person doing the work.
   1 2 3 4 5 6 7

7. Contacts with my company and its representatives are on a formal, preplanned basis.
   1 2 3 4 5 6 7

8. People here are allowed to do almost anything as they please.
   1 2 3 4 5 6 7

9. I ignore the rules and reach informal agreements to handle some situations.
   1 2 3 4 5 6 7

10. Most people here make their own rules on the job.
    1 2 3 4 5 6 7

11. When rules and procedures exist in my company, they are usually written agreements.
    1 2 3 4 5 6 7

12. The employees are constantly being checked on for rule violations.
    1 2 3 4 5 6 7

13. People here feel as though they are constantly being watched, to see that they obey all the rules.
    1 2 3 4 5 6 7

SCORING

Determine your score by entering your response to each survey item below, as follows. In blanks that say *regular score*, simply enter your response for that item. If your response was a 6, place a 6 in the *regular* score blank. In blanks that say *reverse score*, subtract your response from 8 and enter the result. So if your response was a 6, place a 2 (8 − 6 = 2) in the *reverse score* blank.

1. reverse score ______
2. reverse score ______
3. reverse score ______
4. reverse score ______
5. regular score ______
6. reverse score ______
7. regular score ______
8. reverse score ______
9. reverse score ______
10. reverse score ______
11. regular score ______
12. regular score ______
13. regular score ______

TOTAL = ______

You can see where you fall on the formality continuum and find the interpretation of your score at: login.cengagebrain.com.

Biz Flix

© CENGAGE

Rendition

"What if someone you love . . . just disappeared?" This is the question posed by the 2007 dramatic thriller *Rendition*. Anwar El-Ibrahimi (Omar Metwally) boards a flight in South Africa but never arrives home to his family in the States. His pregnant wife Isabella (Reese Witherspoon) doesn't know that he has been named as a suspected terrorist and sent to a secret detention facility in North Africa, where he is tortured and interrogated. Eventually, CIA analyst Douglas Freeman (Jake Gyllenhaal), who has overseen the interrogation, becomes convinced of El-Ibrahimi's innocence, but he is ordered to continue with the detention. In this scene, Senator Hawkins (Alan Arkin) is talking to congressional aide Alan Smith (Peter Sarsgaard) about the situation and explaining why they think there may be a connection between the terrorists and El-Ibrahimi.

What to Watch for and Ask Yourself

1. How would you describe the workplace atmosphere in this scene? Would you say it demonstrates behavioral informality or formality?
2. Do you think the scene shows line authority or staff authority between these two men?
3. What kind of feedback is Alan Smith getting from Senator Hawkins? Is it primarily positive or negative?

Management Workplace

© CENGAGE

Evo

When Bryce Phillips started selling ski and snow-board equipment on eBay, he managed everything—customer care, supply chain, technology, buying, and finance—all from his own apartment. Eight years later, Phillips runs a hugely successful e-commerce site, employs more than 60 people, manages its Seattle flagship store, and operates a 40,000-square-foot distribution center. His company, called Evo, has grown at least 70 percent every year and recently hit $10 million in sales. To effectively lead this rapidly expanding venture, Phillips continually looks for ways to delegate responsibilities to the capable managers around him. In this video, you'll learn about some of the challenges Evo has faced as the company has grown and hear why Phillips believes employee empowerment is so important.

What to Watch for and Ask Yourself

1. Given Evo's current structure and pace of growth, what organizational challenges might arise in the future?
2. Is Evo a centralized or decentralized company? Explain.
3. Imagine it is 20 years from now and Evo is organized into divisions. What are they?

9

Chapter Nine

Managing Teams

OUTLINE

Experience Management

Explore the four levels of learning by doing the simulation module on Teams.

© ISTOCKPHOTO.COM/ ANN MARIE KURTZ

Pod Nod

Mini lecture reviews all the learning points in the chapter.

© ISTOCKPHOTO.COM/ MAGNET CREATIVE

Reel to Real

Biz Flix is a scene from *Failure to Launch*. Management Workplace is a segment on Greensburg, Kansas.

© ISTOCKPHOTO.COM/ CRAFTVISION

Self Test

10 quiz questions, 7 exhibit worksheets, and PowerPoints for quick review.

© ISTOCKPHOTO.COM/ DIJITAL FILM

What Would You Do?

GE Aircraft Engines, Durham, N.C.[1]
In 1917, when the United States entered World War I, the government was looking for a company that could develop the first airplane engine "booster" or turbo supercharger. Under wartime secrecy, *GE* began testing and developing various engine designs. Months later, at Pike's Peak, 14,000 ft. above sea level, GE demonstrated a 350 horsepower, turbo supercharged Liberty aircraft engine. GE landed the federal contract and went full-time into the aircraft engine business. Today, GE Aircraft Engines, with revenues of nearly $11 billion, develops and manufactures jet engines for military and commercial aircraft. Indeed, nearly half of the aircraft flown by the U.S. military, as well as half of the aircraft flown by commercial airlines, are powered by GE jet engines. GE's jet engines are so reliable that its CF6-80C2 jet engine was selected to power Air Force One, the Boeing 747 used to fly the President of the United States.

Today, you and your management team are responsible for planning a new factory to build the GE 90, one of GE's most popular commercial jet engines. The location has already been decided, an empty GE manufacturing plant in Durham, North Carolina. However, all other decisions are up to you and your managers. Fortunately, you have designed and started a new plant from the ground up before, what management consultants call a greenfield site. You think to yourself, "This is a great opportunity. But, we're going to have to be very careful, because whatever we establish from the start is what will get perpetuated in the end. Fortunately, though, starting a culture is so much easier than changing a culture." The question, of course, is what to create.

Well, one way to answer that is to hit the road and visit well-run factories at other companies. You're bound to come up with good ideas that way. One of your managers has an interesting suggestion, too. He thinks that everyone who is hired to work in the plant should have an FAA mechanic's license. In other words, the people who are building GE's jet engines should be capable of repairing any kind of jet engine. He said, "That would mean we'd start with a better caliber of employee and we wouldn't have to spend time in basic training." And you say, thinking out loud, "We might just want to consider using teams to run everything." As you look around the room, you can sense mixed reactions. One of your managers says, "Boy, I just don't know. At the GE plant where I used to work, we switched to teams and the employee turnover rate, which was near zero, jumped to double digits." Another manager says, "Levi's tried teams, too, and had a horrible results."

You respond, "I understand your reluctance. Teams can be tricky. But, they hold a lot of promise, too. If we do teams properly, productivity, quality, and employee satisfaction should rise, while costs decrease." "Well, we don't have to decide today. As we travel and visit other factories, let's see if we can't answer these questions. First, when does it make sense to use teams and when does it make sense to not? Second, if we determine that teams would be appropriate for our factory, what kind of teams should we use and why? Third, how should people who work on teams be paid? We've got to find a way to encourage individual initiative, while at the same time getting people to work together on teams. OK, that's set. Get your airline tickets and we'll be back here in two weeks to make our decision."

If you were the manager at GE Aircraft Engines new Durham, North Carolina, plant, what would you do?

Ninety-one percent of all organizations are significantly improving their effectiveness by using work teams.[2] Procter & Gamble and Cummins Engine began using teams in 1962 and 1973, respectively. Boeing, Caterpillar, Champion International, Ford Motor Company, 3M, and General Electric established work teams in the mid- to late-1980s. Today, most companies use teams to tackle a variety of issues.[3] "Teams are ubiquitous. Whether we are talking about software development, Olympic hockey, disease outbreak response, or urban warfare, teams represent the critical unit that 'gets things done' in today's world."[4]

We begin this chapter by reviewing the advantages and disadvantages of teams and exploring when companies should use teams instead of more traditional approaches. Next, we discuss the different types of work teams and the characteristics that all teams share. The chapter ends by focusing on the practical steps to managing teams: team goals and priorities and organizing, training, and compensating teams.

Why Work Teams?

work team
a small number of people with complementary skills who hold themselves mutually accountable for pursuing a common purpose, achieving performance goals, and improving interdependent work processes

Work teams consist of a small number of people with complementary skills who hold themselves mutually accountable for pursuing a common purpose, achieving performance goals, and improving interdependent work processes.[5] By this definition, computer programmers working on separate projects in the same department of a company would not be considered a team. To be a team, the programmers would have to be interdependent and share responsibility and accountability for the quality and amount of computer code they produced.[6] Teams are becoming more important in many industries because they help organizations respond to specific problems and challenges. Though work teams are not the answer for every situation or organization, if the right teams are used properly and in the right settings, teams can dramatically improve company performance over more traditional management approaches and instill a sense of vitality in the workplace that is otherwise difficult to achieve.

After reading the next two sections, you should be able to:

1. explain the good and bad of using teams.
2. recognize and understand the different kinds of teams.

1 The Good and Bad of Using Teams

Let's begin our discussion of teams by learning about 1.1 **the advantages of teams**, 1.2 **the disadvantages of teams**, and 1.3 **when to use and not use teams**.

1.1 The Advantages of Teams

Companies are making greater use of teams because teams have been shown to improve customer satisfaction, product and service quality, speed and efficiency in product development, employee job satisfaction, and decision making.[7] Teams help businesses increase *customer satisfaction* in several ways. One way is to create work teams that are trained to meet the needs of specific customers. *HEWITT ASSOCIATES*, a consulting firm, manages benefits administration for hundreds of multinational client firms. To ensure customer satisfaction, Hewitt reengineered its customer service center and created specific teams to handle benefits-related questions posed by employees of specific client organizations.[8]

Businesses also create problem-solving teams and employee involvement teams to study ways to improve overall customer satisfaction and make recommendations for improvements. Teams like these typically meet on a weekly or monthly basis.

Teams also help firms improve *product and service quality* in several ways.[9] In contrast to traditional organizational structures where management is responsible for organizational outcomes and performance, teams take direct responsibility for the quality of the products and service they produce. At *WHOLE FOODS*, a supermarket chain, the ten teams that manage each store are responsible for store quality and performance. They are also directly accountable because the size of their team bonus depends on the store's performance. Productive teams get an extra $1.50 to $2.00 per hour in every other paycheck.[10] Making teams directly responsible for service and product quality pays off. At Whole Foods, comparable store sales (meaning a particular store's sales this year compared with its sales last year) are increasing between 7.7 and 10 percent per year on average!

As you learned in Chapter 6, companies that are slow

to innovate or integrate new features and technologies into their products are at a competitive disadvantage. Therefore, a third reason that teams are increasingly popular is that they can increase *speed and efficiency when designing and manufacturing products*.[11] *LOUIS VUITTON*, the French-based world-renowned fashion house, designs and makes some of the most expensive, best-selling purses, shoulder bags, tote bags, and luggage in the world. With many bags costing $1,000 or more, it might surprise you to learn that it used to take 30 craftspeople eight days to produce just one Louis Vuitton bag! This was because each worker completed just one task, such as cutting leather, gluing, sewing, or stitching the lining, and bottlenecks would form as the slower workers forced faster workers to wait for the next purse to come to them for work. Louis Vuitton fixed the problem by switching to teams of six to twelve workers who learned to complete four different production steps. Teams were then positioned in U-shaped workstations with sewing machines and assembly tables so that team members could pass bags back and forth without waiting. The result? It takes just one day and six to twelve workers to produce a Louis Vuitton bag. Furthermore, since team members complete multiple tasks, teams can now work on different kinds of bags, which allows the company to quickly switch production to its best-selling items. Finally, with quality up significantly, returns of defective bags have dropped by two-thirds.[12]

Another reason for using teams is that teamwork often leads to increased *job satisfaction*.[13] One reason that teamwork can be more satisfying than traditional work is that it gives workers a chance to improve their skills. This is often accomplished through **cross-training**, in which team members are taught how to do all or most of the jobs performed by the other team members. The advantage for the organization is that cross-training allows a team to function normally when one member is absent, quits, or is transferred.

A second reason that teamwork is satisfying is that work teams often receive proprietary business information that is available only to managers at most companies. For example, Whole Foods has an "open books, open door, open people" philosophy. Team members are given full access to their store's financial information and everyone's salaries, including those of the store manager and the CEO.[14] Each day, next to the time clock, Whole Foods employees can see the previous day's sales for each team as well as the sales on the same day from the previous year. Each week, team members can examine the same information, broken down by team, for all of the Whole Foods stores in their region. And each month, store managers review information on profitability, including sales, product costs, wages, and operating profits, with each team in the store. Since team members decide how much to spend, what to order, what things should cost, and how many team members should work each day, this information is critical to creating effective teams at Whole Foods.[15]

Team members also gain job satisfaction from unique leadership responsibilities that are not typically available in traditional organizations. Orchestras are led by a conductor who is clearly in charge. Can you imagine an orchestra without a conductor? The award-winning, New York City–based *ORPHEUS CHAMBER ORCHESTRA* does not have a conductor. Instead, it has a concertmaster who is responsible for a performance. What is most interesting is that the concertmaster's role is rotated among different members of the orchestra. While a typical concertmaster is a violinist, the position even rotates around the various instruments of the orchestra. Flutist Susan Palma-Nidel says that assuming the concertmaster's role "has allowed me to discover strengths that I didn't

cross-training
training team members to do all or most of the jobs performed by the other team members

know I had."[16] Furthermore, rotating leadership among team members can lead to more participation and cooperation in team decision making and improved team performance.[17]

Finally, teams share many of the advantages of group decision making discussed in Chapter 4. For instance, because team members possess different knowledge, skills, abilities, and experiences, a team is able to view problems from multiple perspectives. This diversity of viewpoints increases the odds that team decisions will solve the underlying causes of problems and not just address the symptoms. The increased knowledge and information available to teams also make it easier for them to generate more alternative solutions, a critical part of improving the quality of decisions. Because team members are involved in decision-making processes, they are also likely to be more committed to making those decisions work. In short, teams can do a much better job than individuals in two important steps of the decision-making process: defining the problem and generating alternative solutions.

Doing the Right Thing

Don't Be a Team Slacker—Do Your Share

Given the amount of teamwork required in business classes, most of you have encountered slackers in student groups. Perhaps you've even slacked yourself from time to time. From an ethical perspective, though, slacking is clearly wrong. In reality, it's no different from cheating on an exam. When you slack, you're relying on others to do your work. You benefit without putting forth effort. And your team's project, paper, or presentation hasn't benefited from your contributions. In fact, it's very likely that your slacking may have significantly hurt your team's performance. Furthermore, in the real world, the consequences of team slacking, such as lost sales, poor decisions, lower-quality service or products, or lower productivity, are much larger. So, do the right thing. Whether it's in class or in business, don't be a slacker. Don't cheat your teammates. Pull your share of the "rope."

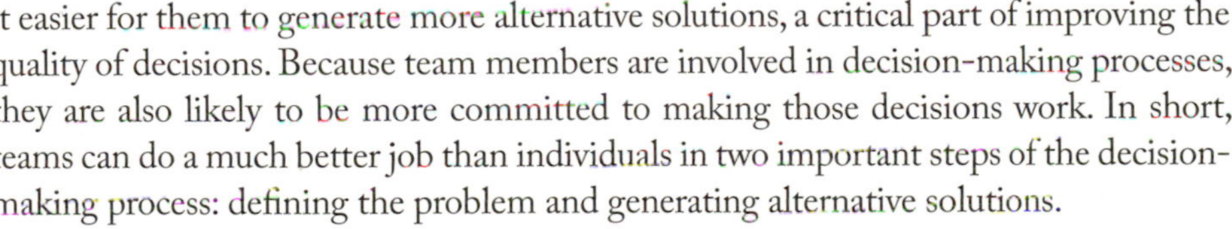

1.2 The Disadvantages of Teams

Although teams can significantly improve customer satisfaction, product and service quality, speed and efficiency in product development, employee job satisfaction, and decision making, using teams does not guarantee these positive outcomes. In fact, if you've ever participated in team projects in your classes, you're probably already aware of some of the problems inherent in work teams. Despite all of their promise, teams and teamwork are also prone to these significant disadvantages: initially high turnover, social loafing, and the problems associated with group decision making.

The first disadvantage of work teams is *initially high turnover*. Teams aren't for everyone, and some workers balk at the responsibility, effort, and learning required in team settings. When General Electric's Salisbury plant switched to teams, the turnover rate jumped from near zero to 14 percent.[18] Other people may quit because they object to the way team members closely scrutinize each other's job performance, particularly when teams are small. Randy Savage, who works for *EATON CORPORATION*, a manufacturer of car and truck parts, said, "They say there are no bosses here, but if you screw up, you find one pretty fast." Beverly Reynolds, who quit Eaton's team-based system after 9 months, says her coworkers "weren't standing watching me, but from afar, they were watching me." And even though her teammates were willing to help her improve her job performance, she concludes, "As it turns out, it just wasn't for me at all."[19]

Social loafing is another disadvantage of work teams. **Social loafing** occurs when workers withhold their efforts and fail to perform their share of the work.[20] A 19th-century French engineer named Maximilian Ringlemann first documented social loafing when he found that one person pulling on a rope alone exerted an average of 139 pounds of force. In groups of three, the average force dropped to 117 pounds per person. In groups of eight, the average dropped to just 68 pounds per person. Ringlemann concluded that the larger the team, the smaller the individual effort. In fact, social loafing is more likely to occur in larger groups where identifying and monitoring the efforts of individual team members can be difficult.[21] In other words, social loafers count on being able to blend into the background where their lack of effort isn't easily spotted. From team-based class projects, most students already know about social loafers or "slackers," who contribute poor, little, or no work whatsoever. Not surprisingly, a study of 250 student teams found that the most talented students are typically the least satisfied with teamwork because of having to carry slackers and do a disproportionate share of their team's work.[22] Perceptions of fairness are negatively related to the extent of social loafing within teams.[23]

How prevalent is social loafing on teams? One study found that when team activities were not mandatory, only 25 percent of manufacturing workers volunteered to join problem-solving teams; 70 percent were quiet, passive supporters (that is, they didn't put forth effort); and 5 percent were actively opposed to these activities.[24] Another study found that on management teams, 56 percent of managers withheld their effort in one way or another. Exhibit 9.1 lists the factors that encourage people to withhold effort in teams.

social loafing
behavior in which team members withhold their efforts and fail to perform their share of the work

EXHIBIT 9.1

Factors That Encourage People to Withhold Effort in Teams

1. **The presence of someone with expertise.** Team members will withhold effort when another team members is highly qualified to make a decision or comment on an issue.
2. **The presentation of a compelling argument.** Team members will withhold effort if the arguments for a course of action are very persuasive or similar to their own thinking.
3. **The lack of confidence in one's ability to contribute.** Team members will withhold effort if they are unsure about their ability to contribute to discussions, activity, or decisions. This is especially so for high-profile decisions.
4. **An unimportant or meaningless decision.** Team members will withhold effort by mentally withdrawing or adopting a "who cares" attitude if decisions don't affect them or their units, or if they don't see a connection between their efforts and their team's successes or failures.
5. **A dysfunctional decision-making climate.** Team members will withhold effort if other team members are frustrated or indifferent or if a team is floundering or disorganized.

Source: P.W. Mullvey, J.F. Veiga, & P.M. Elsass, "When Teammates Raise a Write Flag," *Academy of Management Executive* 10, no. 1 (1996): 40–49.

Finally, teams share many of the *disadvantages of group decision making* discussed in Chapter 4, such as groupthink. In *groupthink*, members of highly cohesive groups feel intense pressure not to disagree with each other so that the group can approve a proposed solution. Because groupthink restricts discussion and leads to consideration of a limited number of alternative solutions, it usually results in poor decisions. Also, team decision making takes considerable time, and team meetings can often be unproductive and inefficient. Another possible pitfall is *minority domination*, where just one or two people dominate team discussions, restricting consideration of different problem definitions and alternative solutions. Finally, team members may not feel accountable for the decisions and actions taken by the team.

1.3 When to Use Teams

As the two previous subsections made clear, teams have significant advantages *and* disadvantages. Therefore, the question is not whether to use teams, but *when* and *where* to use teams for maximum benefit and minimum cost. As Doug Johnson, associate director at the Center for Collaborative Organizations at the University of North Texas, puts it, "Teams are a means to an end, not an end in themselves. You have to ask yourself questions first. Does the work require interdependence? Will the team philosophy fit company strategy? Will management make a long-term commitment to this process?"[25] Exhibit 9.2 provides some additional guidelines on when to use or not use teams.[26]

First, teams should be used when there is a clear, engaging reason or purpose for using them. Too many companies use teams because they're popular or because the companies assume that teams can fix all problems. Teams are much more likely to succeed if they know why they exist and what they are supposed to accomplish, and more likely to fail if they don't. Johan Bruyneel has won the Tour de France nine times as team director, seven with Lance Armstrong and two with Alberto Contador. No other team director has even come close. What accounts for his teams'

EXHIBIT 9.2

When to Use or Not Use Teams

USE TEAMS WHEN . . .	DON'T USE TEAMS WHEN . . .
✓ there is a clear, engaging reason or purpose.	✗ there isn't a clear, engaging reason or purpose.
✓ the job can't be done unless people work together.	✗ the job can be done by people working independently.
✓ rewards can be provided for teamwork and team performance.	✗ rewards are provided for individual effort and performance.
✓ ample resources are available.	✗ the necessary resources are not available.
✓ teams will have clear authority to manage and change how work gets done.	✗ management will continue to monitor and influence how work gets done.

Source: R. Wageman, "Critical Success Factors for Creating Superb Self-Managing Teams," *Organizational Dynamics* 26, no. 1 (1997): 49–61.

successes? Clear purposes and goals. Bruyneel plans out the entire year before the race, mixing in the right combination of training, racing, and rest. Then, for each team member he develops daily, week, monthly, and annual goals to prepare them to fulfill their roles.[27]

Second, teams should be used when the job can't be done unless people work together. This typically means that teams are needed when tasks are complex, require multiple perspectives, or require repeated interaction with others to complete. For example, contrary to stories of legendary programmers who write software programs by themselves, *MICROSOFT* uses teams to write computer code because of the enormous complexity of today's software, and because writing good software requires repeated interaction with others. When developing and testing Windows 7, Microsoft development teams shared their plans with each other, and spent time listening and collaborating with engineers at computer manufacturers like HP and Dell. The collaboration among teams and with computer manufacturers paid off in Windows 7 being faster, more reliable, and flexible than the much criticized Vista.[28]

If tasks are simple and don't require multiple perspectives or repeated interaction with others, however, teams should not be used.[29] For instance, production levels dropped by 23 percent when *LEVI STRAUSS* introduced teams in its factories. Levi Strauss' mistake was assuming that teams were appropriate for garment work, where workers perform single, specialized tasks, like sewing zippers or belt loops. Because this kind of work does not require interaction with others, Levi Strauss unwittingly pitted the faster workers against the slower workers on each team. Arguments, infighting, insults, and threats were common between faster workers and the slower workers who held back team performance. One seamstress even had to physically restrain an angry coworker who was about to throw a chair at a faster worker who constantly nagged her about her slow pace.[30]

Third, teams should be used when rewards can be provided for teamwork and team performance. Rewards that depend on team performance rather than individual performance are the key to rewarding team behaviors and efforts. You'll read more about team rewards later in the chapter, but for now it's enough to know that if the type of reward (individual versus team) is not matched to the type of performance (individual versus team), teams won't work. This was the case with Levi Strauss, where a team structure was superimposed on individual jobs that didn't require interaction between workers. After the switch to teams, faster workers placed tremendous pressure on slower workers to increase their production speed. And since pay was determined by team performance, top individual performers saw their pay drop by several dollars an hour, while slower workers saw their pay increase by several dollars an hour—all while overall productivity dropped in the plant.[31]

REVIEW 1

The Good and Bad of Using Teams

In many industries, teams are growing in importance because they help organizations respond to specific problems and challenges. Teams have been shown to increase customer satisfaction (specific customer teams), product and service quality (direct responsibility), speed and efficiency in product development (overlapping development phases), and employee job satisfaction (cross-training, unique opportunities, and leadership responsibilities). Although teams can produce significant improvements in these areas, using teams does not guarantee these positive outcomes. Teams and teamwork have the disadvantages of initially high turnover and social loafing (especially in large groups). Teams also share many of the advantages (multiple perspectives, generation of more alternatives, and more commitment) and disadvantages (groupthink, time-consuming, poorly run meetings, domination by a few team members, and weak accountability) of group decision making. Finally, teams should be used for a clear purpose, when the work requires that people work together, when rewards can be provided for both teamwork and team performance, when ample resources can be provided, and when teams can be given clear authority over their work.

2 Kinds of Teams

Companies use different kinds of teams for different purposes. Google uses teams to innovate and develop new products as well as tweak and improve its search algorithms and functions.[32] At *CHILDREN'S HOSPITAL BOSTON*, the use of teams and team-based rewards helped shorten the billing cycle by reducing the average number of days a bill spent in the accounts receivable department from 100 to just 65 days.[33] At Federal Express, teams were able to cut service errors by 13 percent.[34]

Let's continue our discussion of teams by learning about the different kinds of teams that companies like Google and Children's Hospital Boston use to make themselves more competitive. We look first at 2.1 **how teams differ in terms of autonomy, which is the key dimension that makes one team different from another**, and then at 2.2 **some special kinds of teams**.

2.1 Autonomy, the Key Dimension

Teams can be classified in a number of ways, such as permanent or temporary, or functional or cross-functional. However, studies indicate that the amount of autonomy possessed by a team is the key difference among teams.[35] *Autonomy* is the degree to which workers have the discretion, freedom, and independence to decide how and when to accomplish their jobs. Exhibit 9.3 shows how five kinds of teams differ in terms of autonomy. Moving left to right across the autonomy continuum at the top of the exhibit, traditional work groups and employee involvement groups have the least autonomy, semiautonomous work groups have more autonomy, and, finally, self-managing teams and self-designing teams have the most autonomy. Moving from bottom to top along the left side of the exhibit, note that the number of responsibilities given to each kind of team increases directly with its autonomy. Let's review each of these kinds of teams and their autonomy and responsibilities in more detail.

The smallest amount of autonomy is found in **traditional work groups**, where two or more people work together to achieve a shared goal. In these groups, workers are responsible for doing the work or "executing the task," but they do not have direct responsibility or control over their work. Workers report to managers, who are responsible for their performance and have the authority to hire and fire them, make job assignments, and control resources.

traditional work group
a group composed of two or more people who work together to achieve a shared goal

Employee involvement teams, which have somewhat more autonomy, meet on company time on a weekly or monthly basis to provide advice or make suggestions to management concerning specific issues such as plant safety, customer relations, or product quality.[36] Though they offer advice and suggestions, they do not have the authority to make decisions. Membership on these teams is often voluntary,

employee involvement team
team that provides advice or makes suggestions to management concerning specific issues

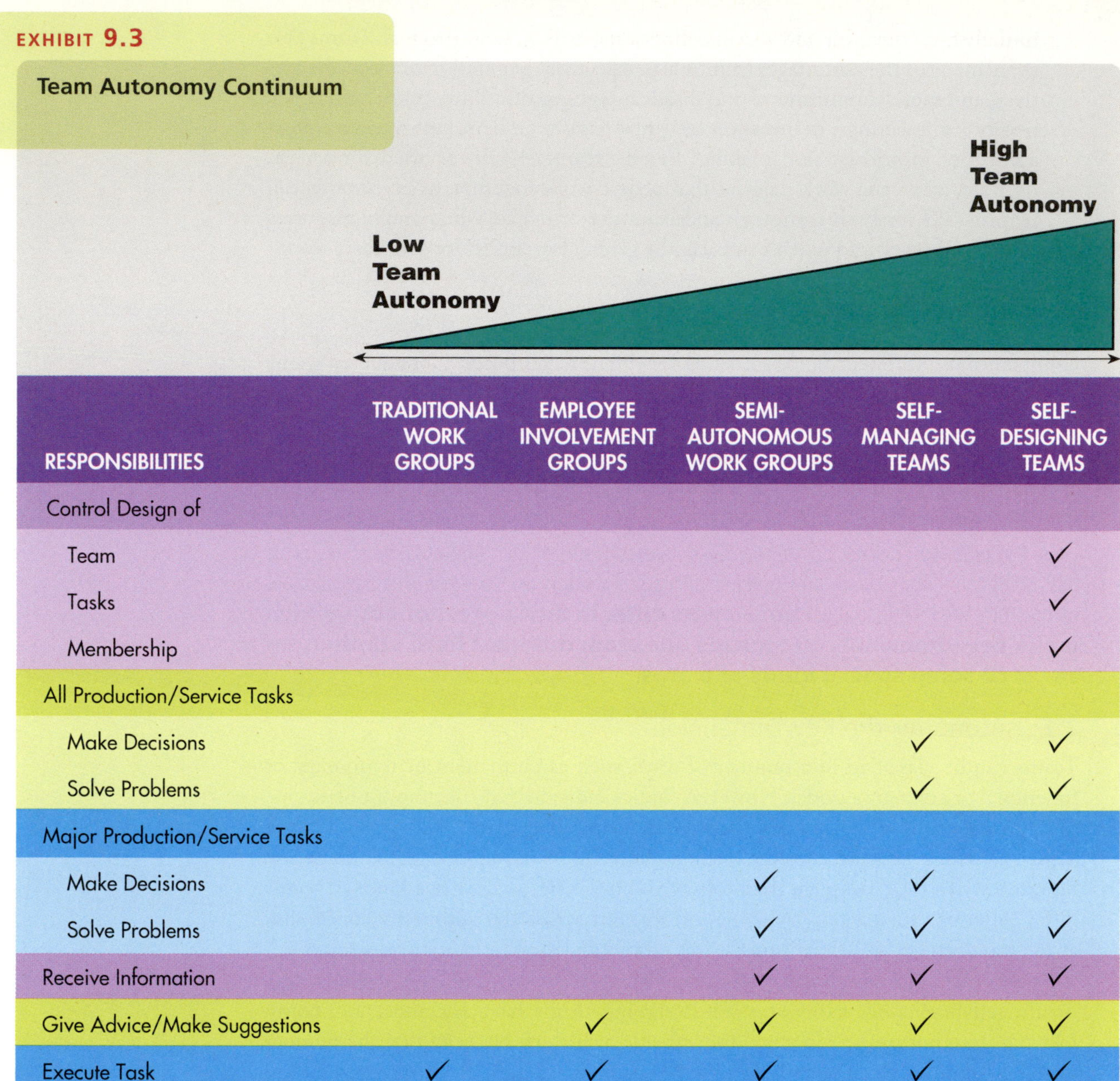

RESPONSIBILITIES	TRADITIONAL WORK GROUPS	EMPLOYEE INVOLVEMENT GROUPS	SEMI-AUTONOMOUS WORK GROUPS	SELF-MANAGING TEAMS	SELF-DESIGNING TEAMS
Control Design of					
Team					✓
Tasks					✓
Membership					✓
All Production/Service Tasks					
Make Decisions				✓	✓
Solve Problems				✓	✓
Major Production/Service Tasks					
Make Decisions			✓	✓	✓
Solve Problems			✓	✓	✓
Receive Information			✓	✓	✓
Give Advice/Make Suggestions		✓	✓	✓	✓
Execute Task	✓	✓	✓	✓	✓

Source: R. D. Banker, J. M. Field, R. G. Schroeder, & K. K. Sinha, "Impact of Work Teams on Manufacturing Performance: A Longitudinal Field Study," *Academy of Management Journal 39* (1996): 867–890; J. R. Hackman, "The Psychology of Self-Management in Organizations," in *Psychology and Work: Productivity, Change, and Employment,* ed. M. S. Pallak & R. Perlof (Washington, DC: American Psychological Association), 85–136.

but members may be selected because of their expertise. The idea behind employee involvement teams is that the people closest to the problem or situation are best able to recommend solutions.

semiautonomous work group
a group that has the authority to make decisions and solve problems related to the major tasks of producing a product or service

Semiautonomous work groups not only provide advice and suggestions to management but also have the authority to make decisions and solve problems related to the major tasks required to produce a product or service. Semiautonomous groups regularly receive information about budgets, work quality and performance, and competitors' products. Furthermore, members of semiautonomous work groups are typically cross-trained in a number of different skills and tasks. In short, semiautonomous work groups give employees the authority to make decisions that are typically made by supervisors and managers.

That authority is not complete, however. Managers still play a role, though much reduced compared with traditional work groups, in supporting the work of semiautonomous work groups. The role a manager plays on a team usually evolves over time. "It may start with helping to transition problem-solving responsibilities to the team, filling miscellaneous requests for the team, and doing ad hoc tasks," says Steven Hitchcock, president of *AXIS PERFORMANCE ADVISORS* in Portland, Oregon. Later, the team may develop into a mini-enterprise and the former manager becomes externally focused—sort of an account manager for the customer. Managers have to adjust what they do based on the sophistication of the team.[37] A lot of what managers of semiautonomous work groups do is ask good questions, provide resources, and facilitate performance of group goals.

Self-managing teams differ from semiautonomous work groups in that team members manage and control *all* of the major tasks *directly related* to production of a product or service without first getting approval from management. This includes managing and controlling the acquisition of materials, making a product or providing a service, and ensuring timely delivery. **Self-designing teams** have all the characteristics of self-managing teams, but they can also control and change the design of the teams themselves, the tasks they do and how and when they do them, and the membership of the teams. *ICU MEDICAL* in San Clemente, California, is organized around self-designing teams; any worker can form any team to address any problem. The teams set meetings, assign tasks, and determine deadlines.

2.2 Special Kinds of Teams

Cross-functional teams are intentionally composed of employees from different functional areas of the organization.[38] Because their members have different functional backgrounds, education, and experience, cross-functional teams usually attack problems from multiple perspectives and generate more ideas and alternative solutions, all of which are especially important when trying to innovate or do creative problem solving.[39] Cross-functional teams can be used almost anywhere in an organization and are often used in conjunction with matrix and product organizational structures (see Chapter 8). They can also be used either with part-time or temporary team assignments or with full-time, long-term teams.

Virtual teams are groups of geographically and/or organizationally dispersed coworkers who use a combination of telecommunications and information technologies to accomplish an organizational task.[40] Christopher Rice, CEO of Blessing White, a global consulting firm indicates that virtual teams are common. Said Rice, "In three-quarters of large organizations, team members are dispersed across different locations and time zones."[41] Members of virtual teams rarely meet face-to-face; instead, they use e-mail, videoconferencing, and group communication software. For example, *MYSQL*, an open source database software developer, has 320 workers in 25 countries, located from Tennessee to the Ukraine. They communicate with each other using a company chat room (or Skype when live voice conversations are necessary) and are accountable for completing tasks using a program called Worklog.[42] Virtual teams can be employee involvement teams, self-managing teams, or nearly any kind of team discussed in this chapter.

self-managing team
a team that manages and controls all of the major tasks of producing a product or service

self-designing team
a team that has the characteristics of self-managing teams but also controls team design, work tasks, and team membership

cross-functional team
a team composed of employees from different functional areas of the organization

virtual team
a team composed of geographically and/or organizationally dispersed coworkers who use telecommunication and information technologies to accomplish an organizational task

The principal advantage of virtual teams is their flexibility. Employees can work with each other, regardless of physical location, time zone, or organizational affiliation.[43] Because the team members don't meet in a physical location, virtual teams also find it much easier to include other key stakeholders such as suppliers and customers. Plus, virtual teams have certain efficiency advantages over traditional team structures. Because the teammates do not meet face-to-face, a virtual team typically requires a smaller time commitment than a traditional team does. Moreover, employees can fulfill the responsibilities of their virtual team membership from the comfort of their own offices without the travel time or downtime typically required for face-to-face meetings.[44]

A drawback of virtual teams is that the team members must learn to express themselves in new contexts.[45] The give-and-take that naturally occurs in face-to-face meetings is more difficult to achieve through video conferencing or other methods of virtual teaming. Similarly, several studies have shown that physical proximity enhances information processing.[46] Therefore, some companies bring virtual team members together on a regular basis to try to minimize these problems. Exhibit 9.4 provides a number of tips for successfully managing virtual teams.

EXHIBIT 9.4

Tips for Managing Successful Virtual Teams

- Select people who are self-starters and strong communicators.
- Keep the team focused by establishing clear, specific goals and by explaining the consequences and importance of meeting these goals.
- Provide frequent feedback so that team members can measure their progress.
- Keep team interactions upbeat and action-oriented by expressing appreciation for good work and completed tasks.
- "Personalize" the virtual team by periodically bringing team members together and by encouraging team members to share information with each other about their personal lives. This is especially important when the virtual team first forms.
- Improve communication through increased telephone calls, e-mails, and Internet messaging and videoconference sessions.
- Periodically ask team members how well the team is working and what can be done to improve performance.
- Empower virtual teams so they have the discretion, freedom, and independence to decide how and when to accomplish their jobs.

Source: W. F. Cascio, "Managing a Virtual Workplace," *Academy of Management Executive* 14 (2000): 81–90; B. Kirkman, B. Rosen, P. Tesluk, & C. Gibson, "The Impact of Team Empowerment on Virtual Team Performance: The Moderating Role of Face-to-Face Interaction," *Academy of Management Journal* 47 (2004): 175–192; S. Furst, M. Reeves, B. Rosen, & R. Blackburn, "Managing the Life Cycle of Virtual Teams," *Academy of Management Executive* (May 2004): 6–20; C. Solomon, "Managing Virtual Teams," *Workforce* 80 (June 2001): 60.

Project teams are created to complete specific, one-time projects or tasks within a limited time.[47] Project teams are often used to develop new products, significantly improve existing products, roll out new information systems, or build new factories or offices. The project team is typically led by a project manager who has the overall responsibility for planning, staffing, and managing the team, which usually includes employees from different functional areas. One advantage of project teams is that drawing employees from different functional areas can reduce or eliminate communication barriers. In turn, as long as team members feel free to express their ideas, thoughts, and concerns, free-flowing communication encourages cooperation among separate departments and typically speeds up the design process.[48] Another advantage of project teams is their flexibility. When projects are finished, project team members either move on to the next project or return to their functional units. For example, publication of this book required designers, editors, page compositors, and web designers, among others. When the task was finished, these people applied their skills to other textbook projects. Because of this flexibility, project teams are often used with the matrix organizational designs discussed in Chapter 8.

project team
a team created to complete specific, one-time projects or tasks within a limited time

REVIEW 2

Kinds of Teams

Companies use different kinds of teams to make themselves more competitive. Autonomy is the key dimension that makes teams different. Traditional work groups (which execute tasks) and employee involvement groups (which make suggestions) have the lowest levels of autonomy. Semiautonomous work groups (which control major direct tasks) have more autonomy, while self-managing teams (which control all direct tasks) and self-designing teams (which control membership and how tasks are done) have the highest levels of autonomy. Cross-functional, virtual, and project teams are common but are not easily categorized in terms of autonomy. Cross-functional teams combine employees from different functional areas to help teams attack problems from multiple perspectives and generate more ideas and solutions. Virtual teams use telecommunications and information technologies to bring coworkers together, regardless of physical location or time zone. Virtual teams reduce travel and work time, but communication may suffer since team members don't work face-to-face. Finally, project teams are used for specific, one-time projects or tasks that must be completed within a limited time. Project teams reduce communication barriers and promote flexibility; teams and team members are reassigned to their department or new projects as old projects are completed.

Managing Work Teams

"Why did I ever let you talk me into teams? They're nothing but trouble."[49] Lots of managers have this reaction after making the move to teams. Many don't realize that this reaction is normal, both for them and for workers. In fact, such a reaction is characteristic of the *storming* stage of team development (discussed in Section 3.5). Managers who are familiar with these stages and with the other important characteristics of teams will be better prepared to manage the predictable changes that occur when companies make the switch to team-based structures.

After reading the next two sections, you should be able to:

3 understand the general characteristics of work teams.

4 explain how to enhance work team effectiveness.

3 Work Team Characteristics

Understanding the characteristics of work teams is essential for making teams an effective part of an organization.

Therefore, in this section you'll learn about 3.1 **team norms**, 3.2 **team cohesiveness**, 3.3 **team size**, 3.4 **team conflict**, and 3.5 **the stages of team development**.

3.1 Team Norms

Over time, teams develop **norms**, which are informally agreed-on standards that regulate team behavior.[50] Norms are valuable because they let team members know what is expected of them. Studies indicate that norms are one of the most powerful influences on work behavior because they regulate the everyday actions that allow teams to function effectively. Team norms are often associated with positive outcomes such as stronger organizational commitment, more trust in management, and stronger job and organizational satisfaction.[51] Effective work teams develop norms about the quality and timeliness of job performance, absenteeism, safety, and honest expression of ideas and opinions. To encourage the development of team norms, trainer Tom Ruddy created a deck of 35 playing cards describing problems that Xerox's customer service teams usually encounter. Ruddy has teams discuss each card/problem. When they agree what to do, they write their solution on the card along with the word *norm*. Everyone then gets a copy of the deck with the team's norms on them. When a team norm is broken, such as one teammate cutting off another's point, the card with the violated norm is played—in this case "everyone's opinion will be heard." It's a little corny at first, but, says Ruddy, "After a while, team members internalize the proper behavior. That's when the team really starts to click."[52]

Norms can also influence team behavior in negative ways. For example, most people would agree that damaging organizational property, saying or doing something to hurt someone at work, intentionally doing one's work badly, incorrectly, or slowly, griping about coworkers, deliberately bending or breaking rules, or doing something to harm the company or boss are negative behaviors. A study of workers from 34 teams in 20 different organizations found that teams with negative norms strongly influenced their team members to engage in these negative behaviors. In fact, the longer individuals were members of a team with negative norms and the more frequently they interacted with their teammates, the more likely they were to perform negative behaviors. Since team norms typically develop early in the life of a team, these results indicate how important it is for teams to establish positive norms from the outset.[53]

norms
informally agreed-on standards that regulate team behavior

cohesiveness
the extent to which team members are attracted to a team and motivated to remain in it

3.2 Team Cohesiveness

Cohesiveness is another important characteristic of work teams. **Cohesiveness** is the extent to which team members are attracted to a team and motivated to remain in it.[54] The level of cohesiveness in a group is important for several reasons.

what *really* works

Cohesion and Team Performance

Have you ever worked in a really cohesive group where everyone liked and enjoyed each other and was glad to be part of the group? It's great. By contrast, have you ever worked in a group where everyone really disliked each other and was unhappy to be part of the group? It's terrible. Anyone who has had either of these experiences can appreciate how important group cohesion is and the effect it can have on team performance. Indeed, 46 studies based on 1,279 groups confirm that cohesion does matter.

Team Performance

On average, there is a 66 percent chance that cohesive teams will outperform less cohesive teams.

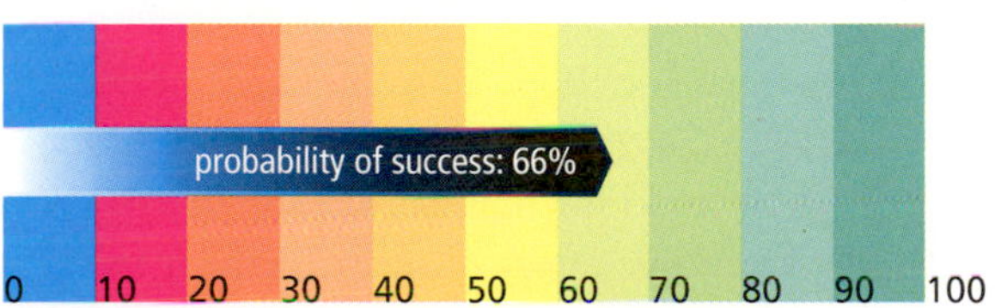

Team Performance with Interdependent Tasks

Teams work best for interdependent tasks that require people to work together to get the job done. When teams perform interdependent tasks, there is a 73 percent chance that cohesive teams will outperform less cohesive teams.

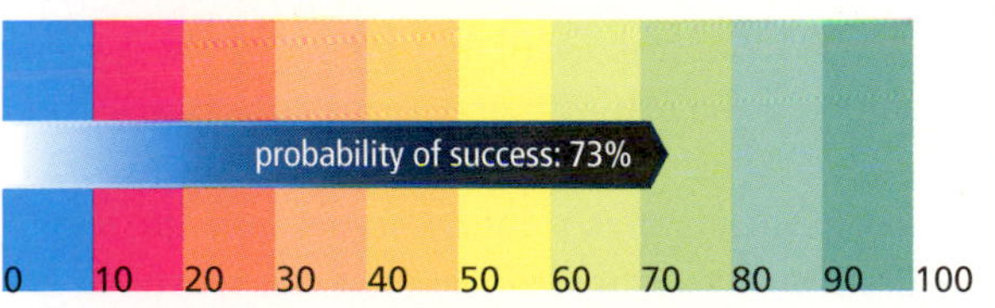

Team Performance with Independent Tasks

Teams generally are not suited for independent tasks that people can accomplish by themselves. When teams perform independent tasks, there is only a 60 percent chance that cohesive teams will outperform less cohesive teams.

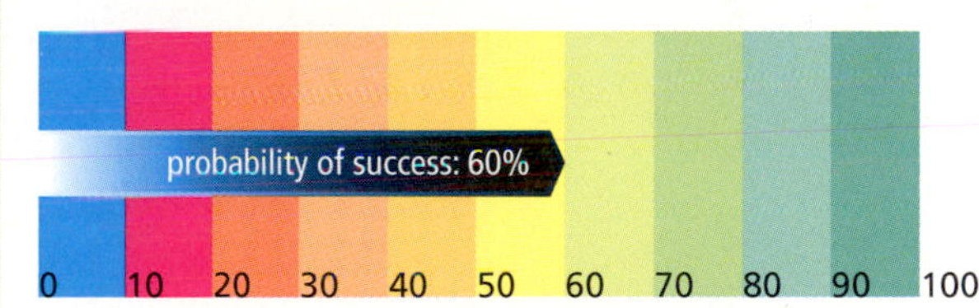

Some caution is warranted in interpreting these results. For example, there is always the possibility that a team could become so cohesive that its team goals become more important than organizational goals. Also, teams sometimes unite around negative goals and norms that are harmful rather than helpful to organizations. Nonetheless, there is also room for even more optimism about cohesive teams. Teams that are cohesive *and* committed to the goals they are asked to achieve should have an even higher probability of success than the numbers shown here.[62]

To start, cohesive groups have a better chance of retaining their members. As a result, cohesive groups typically experience lower turnover.[55] In addition, team cohesiveness promotes cooperative behavior, generosity, and a willingness on the part of team members to assist each other.[56] When team cohesiveness is high, team members are more motivated to contribute to the team because they want to gain the approval of other team members. For these reasons and others, studies have clearly established that cohesive teams consistently perform better.[57] Furthermore, cohesive teams quickly achieve high levels of performance. By contrast, teams low in cohesiveness take much longer to reach the same levels of performance.[58]

What can be done to promote team cohesiveness? First, make sure that all team members are present at team meetings and activities. Team cohesiveness suffers when members are allowed to withdraw from the team and miss team meetings and events.[59] Second, create additional opportunities for teammates to work together by rearranging work schedules and creating common workspaces. When task interdependence is high and team members have lots of chances to work together, team cohesiveness tends to increase.[60] Third, engaging in nonwork activities as a team can help build cohesion. At a company where teams put in extraordinarily long hours coding software, the teams maintained cohesion by doing "fun stuff" together. Team leader Tammy Urban says, "Teams work best when you get to know each other outside of work—what people's interests are, who they are. Personal connections go a long way when you're developing complex applications in our kind of time frames."[61] Finally, companies build team cohesiveness by making employees feel that they are part of an organization.

3.3 Team Size

The relationship between team size and performance appears to be curvilinear. Very small or very large teams may not perform as well as moderately sized teams. For most teams, the right size is somewhere between six and nine members.[63] This size is conducive to high team cohesion, which has a positive effect on team performance, as discussed above. A team of this size is small enough for the team members to get to know each other and for each member to have an opportunity to contribute in a meaningful way to the success of the team. At the same time, the team is also large enough to take advantage of team members' diverse skills, knowledge, and perspectives. It is also easier to instill a sense of responsibility and mutual accountability in teams of this size.[64]

By contrast, when teams get too large, team members find it difficult to get to know one another, and the team may splinter into smaller subgroups. When this occurs, subgroups sometimes argue and disagree, weakening overall team cohesion. As teams grow, there is also a greater chance of *minority domination*, where just a few team members dominate team discussions. Even if minority domination doesn't occur, larger groups may not have time for all team members to share their input. And when team members feel that their contributions are unimportant or not needed, the result is less involvement, effort, and accountability to the team.[65] Large teams also face logistical problems such as finding an appropriate time or place to meet. Finally, the incidence of social loafing, discussed earlier in the chapter, is much higher in large teams.

Just as team performance can suffer when a team is too large, it can also be negatively affected when a team is too small. Teams with just a few people may lack the diversity of skills and knowledge found in larger teams. Also, teams that are too small are unlikely to gain the advantages of team decision making (multiple perspectives, generating more ideas and alternative solutions, and stronger commitment) found in larger teams.

What signs indicate that a team's size needs to be changed? If decisions are taking too long, if the team has difficulty making decisions or taking action, if a few members dominate the team, or if the commitment or efforts of team members are weak, chances are the team is too big. In contrast, if a team is having difficulty coming up with ideas or generating solutions, or if the team does not have the expertise to address a specific problem, chances are the team is too small.

Management Fact:

The level of autonomy that a team possesses determines how it will respond to an uncooperative member. Suppose that an experienced worker blatantly refuses to do his share of the work. In a team with low autonomy, such as a traditional work group, the responsibility of getting that employee to put forth effort belongs to the supervisor. In a team with a high level of autonomy, such as a self-designing team or self-managing team, it is the entire team's responsibility to get that team member to do his work well.

3.4 Team Conflict

Conflict and disagreement are inevitable in most teams. But this shouldn't surprise anyone. From time to time, people who work together are going to disagree about what and how things get done. What causes conflict in teams? Although almost anything can lead to conflict—casual remarks that unintentionally offend a team member or fighting over scarce resources—the primary cause of team conflict is disagreement over team goals and priorities.[66] Other common causes of team conflict include disagreements over task-related issues, interpersonal incompatibilities, and simple fatigue.

Though most people view conflict negatively, the key to dealing with team conflict is not avoiding it, but rather making sure that the team experiences the right kind of conflict. In Chapter 4, you learned about *c-type conflict*, or *cognitive conflict*, which focuses on problem-related differences of opinion, and *a-type conflict*, or *affective conflict*, which refers to the emotional reactions that can occur when disagreements become personal rather than professional.[67] Cognitive conflict is strongly associated with improvements in team performance, whereas affective conflict is strongly associated with decreases in team performance.[68] Why does this happen? With cognitive conflict, team members disagree because their different experiences and expertise lead them to different views of the problem and solutions. Indeed, managers who participated on teams that emphasized cognitive conflict described their teammates as "smart," "team players," and "best in the business." They described their teams as "open," "fun," and "productive." One manager summed up the positive attitude that team members had about cognitive conflict by saying, "We scream a lot, then laugh, and then resolve the issue."[69] Thus, cognitive conflict is also characterized by a willingness to examine, compare, and reconcile differences to produce the best possible solution.

By contrast, affective conflict often results in hostility, anger, resentment, distrust, cynicism, and apathy. Managers who participated on teams that emphasized affective conflict described their teammates as "manipulative," "secretive," "burned out," and "political."[70] Not surprisingly, affective conflict can make people uncomfortable and cause them to withdraw and decrease their commitment to a team.[71] Affective conflict also lowers the satisfaction of team members, may lead to personal hostility between coworkers, and can decrease team cohesiveness.[72] So, unlike cognitive conflict, affective conflict undermines team performance by preventing teams from engaging in the kinds of activities that are critical to team effectiveness.

So, what can managers do to manage team conflict? First, they need to realize that emphasizing cognitive conflict alone won't be enough. Studies show that cognitive and affective conflicts often occur together in a given team activity! Sincere attempts to reach agreement on a difficult issue can quickly deteriorate from cognitive to affective conflict if the discussion turns personal and tempers and emotions flare. While cognitive conflict is clearly the better approach to take, efforts to engage in cognitive conflict should be managed well and checked before they deteriorate and the team becomes unproductive.

Can teams disagree and still get along? Fortunately, they can. In an attempt to study this issue, researchers examined team conflict in twelve high-tech companies. In four of the companies, work teams used cognitive conflict to address work problems but did so in a way that minimized the occurrence of affective conflict.

forming
the first stage of team development, in which team members meet each other, form initial impressions, and begin to establish team norms

3.5 Stages of Team Development

As teams develop and grow, they pass through four stages of development. As shown in Exhibit 9.5, those stages are forming, storming, norming, and performing.[73] Although not every team passes through each of these stages, teams that do tend to be better performers.[74] This holds true even for teams composed of seasoned executives. After a period of time, however, if a team is not managed well, its performance may start to deteriorate as the team begins a process of decline and progresses through the stages of de-norming, de-storming, and de-forming.[75]

EXHIBIT 9.5

Stages of Team Development

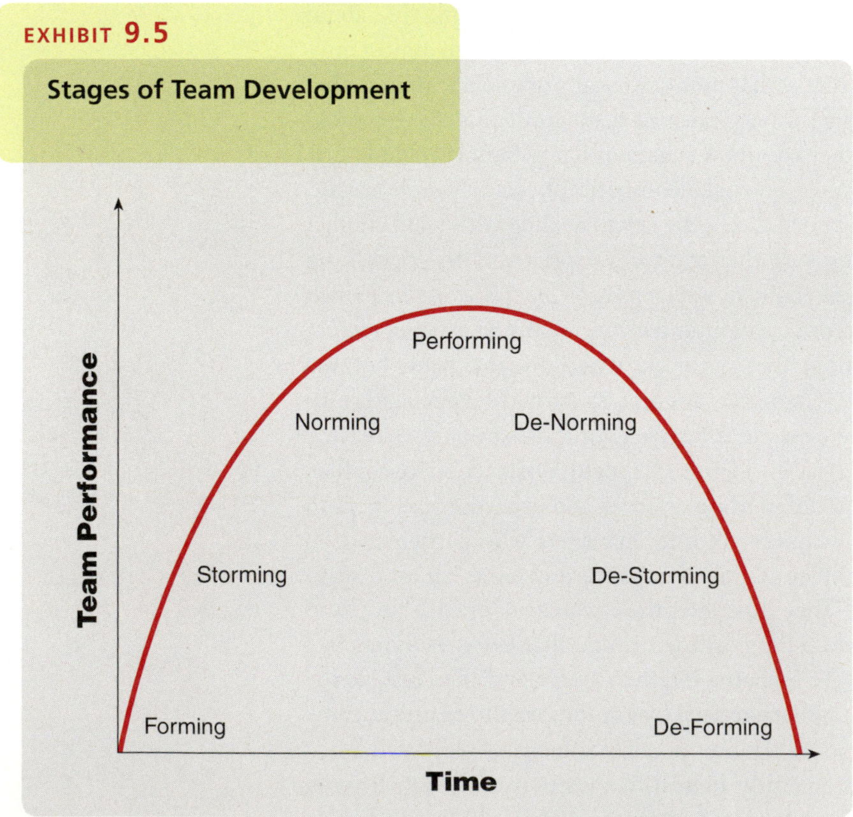

Sources: J. F. McGrew, J. G. Bilotta, & J. M. Deeney, "Software Team Formation and Decay: Extending the Standard Model for Small Groups," *Small Group Research 30*, no. 2 (1999): 209–234; B. W. Tuckman, "Development Sequence in Small Groups," *Psychological Bulletin 63*, no. 6 (1965): 384–399.

Forming is the initial stage of team development. This is the getting-acquainted stage in which team members first meet each other, form initial impressions, and try to get a sense of what it will be like to be part of the team. Some of the first team norms will be established during this stage as team members begin to find out what behaviors will and won't be accepted by the team.

During this stage, team leaders should allow time for team members to get to know each other, set early ground rules, and begin to set up a preliminary team structure.

Conflicts and disagreements often characterize the second stage of team development, **storming**. As team members begin working together, different personalities and work styles may clash. Team members become more assertive at this stage and more willing to state opinions. This is also the stage when team members jockey for position and try to establish a favorable role for themselves on the team. In addition, team members are likely to disagree about what the group should do and how it should do it. Team performance is still relatively low, given that team cohesion is weak and team members are still reluctant to support each other. Since teams that get stuck in the storming stage are almost always ineffective, it is important for team leaders to focus the team on team goals and on improving team performance. Team members need to be particularly patient and tolerant with each other in this stage.

During **norming**, the third stage of team development, team members begin to settle into their roles as team members. Positive team norms will have developed by this stage, and teammates should know what to expect from each other. Petty differences should have been resolved, friendships will have developed, and group cohesion will be relatively strong. At this point, team members will have accepted team goals, be operating as a unit, and, as indicated by the increase in performance, be working together effectively. This stage can be very short and is often characterized by someone on the team saying, "I think things are finally coming together." Note, however, that teams may also cycle back and forth between storming and norming several times before finally settling into norming.

In the last stage of team development, **performing**, performance improves because the team has finally matured into an effective, fully functioning team. At this point, members should be fully committed to the team and think of themselves as members of a team and not just employees. Team members often become intensely loyal to one another at this stage and feel mutual accountability for team successes and failures. Trivial disagreements, which can take time and energy away from the work of the team, should be rare. At this stage, teams get a lot of work done, and it is fun to be a team member.

The team should not become complacent, however. Without effective management, its performance may begin to decline as the team passes through the stages of de-norming, de-storming, and de-forming.[76] Indeed, John Puckett, manufacturing vice president for circuit-board manufacturer *XEL COMMUNICATIONS,* says, "The books all say you start in this state of chaos and march through these various stages, and you end up in this state of ultimate self-direction, where everything is going just great. They never tell you it can go back in the other direction, sometimes just as quickly."[77]

In **de-norming**, which is a reversal of the norming stage, team performance begins to decline as the size, scope, goal, or members of the team change. With new members joining the group, older members may become defensive as established ways of doing things are questioned and challenged. Expression of ideas and opinions becomes less open. New members change team norms by actively rejecting or passively neglecting previously established team roles and behaviors.

In **de-storming**, which is a reversal of the storming phase, the team's comfort level decreases. Team cohesion weakens as more group members resist conforming

storming
the second stage of development, characterized by conflict and disagreement, in which team members disagree over what the team should do and how it should do it

norming
the third stage of team development, in which team members begin to settle into their roles, group cohesion grows, and positive team norms develop

performing
the fourth and final stage of team development, in which performance improves because the team has matured into an effective, fully functioning team

de-norming
a reversal of the norming stage, in which team performance begins to decline as the size, scope, goal, or members of the team change

de-storming
a reversal of the storming phase, in which the team's comfort level decreases, team cohesion weakens, and angry emotions and conflict may flare

to team norms and quit participating in team activities. Angry emotions flare as the group explodes in conflict and moves into the final stage of de-forming.

In **de-forming**, which is a reversal of the forming stage, team members position themselves to gain control of pieces of the team. Team members begin to avoid each other and isolate themselves from team leaders. Team performance rapidly declines as the members quit caring about even minimal requirements of team performance.

If teams are actively managed, decline is not inevitable. However, managers need to recognize that the forces at work in the de-norming, de-storming, and de-forming stages represent a powerful, disruptive, and real threat to teams that have finally made it to the performing stage. Getting to the performing stage is half the battle. Staying there is the second half.

REVIEW 3

Work Team Characteristics

The most important characteristics of work teams are team norms, cohesiveness, size, conflict, and development. Norms let team members know what is expected of them and can influence team behavior in positive and negative ways. Positive team norms are associated with organizational commitment, trust, and job satisfaction. Team cohesiveness helps teams retain members, promotes cooperative behavior, increases motivation, and facilitates team performance. Attending team meetings and activities, creating opportunities to work together, and engaging in non-work activities can increase cohesiveness. Team size has a curvilinear relationship with team performance. Teams that are very small or very large do not perform as well as moderate-sized teams of six to nine members. Teams of this size are cohesive and small enough for team members to get to know each other and contribute in a meaningful way but are large enough to take advantage of team members' diverse skills, knowledge, and perspectives. Conflict and disagreement are inevitable in most teams. The key to dealing with team conflict is to maximize cognitive conflict, which focuses on issue-related differences, and minimize affective conflict, the emotional reactions that occur when disagreements become personal rather than professional. As teams develop and grow, they pass through four stages of development: forming, storming, norming, and performing. After a period of time, however, if a team is not managed well, its performance may decline as the team regresses through the stages of de-norming, de-storming, and de-forming.

4 Enhancing Work Team Effectiveness

Making teams work is a challenging and difficult process.

Nonetheless, companies can increase the likelihood that teams will succeed by carefully managing 4.1 **the setting of team goals and priorities**, and 4.2 **how work team members are selected**, 4.3 **trained**, and 4.4 **compensated**.[78]

de-forming
a reversal of the forming stage, in which team members position themselves to control pieces of the team, avoid each other, and isolate themselves from team leaders

4.1 Setting Team Goals and Priorities

In Chapter 4, you learned that having specific, measurable, attainable, realistic, and timely (S.M.A.R.T.) goals is one of the most effective means for improving individual job performance. Fortunately, team goals also improve team performance. In fact, team goals lead to much higher team performance 93 percent of the time.[79] For example, Nucor Corporation sets specific, challenging *hourly* goals for each of its production teams, which consist of first-line supervisors and production and maintenance workers. The average rate of production in the steel industry is 10 tons of steel per hour. Nucor production teams have an hourly goal of 8 tons per hour, but get a 5 percent bonus for every ton over 8 tons that they produce. With no limit on the bonuses they can receive, Nucor's production teams produce an average of 35 to 40 tons of steel per hour![80]

Why is setting *specific* team goals so critical to team success? One reason is that increasing a team's performance is inherently more complex than just increasing one individual's job performance. For instance, consider that any team is likely to involve at least four different kinds of goals: each member's goal for the team, each member's goal for himself or herself on the team, the team's goal for each member, and the team's goal for itself.[81] In other words, without a specific goal for the team itself (the last of the four goals listed), team members may head off in all directions at once pursuing these other goals. Consequently, setting a specific goal *for the team* clarifies team priorities by providing a clear focus and purpose.

Challenging team goals affect how hard team members work. In particular, they greatly reduce the incidence of social loafing. When faced with difficult goals, team members necessarily expect everyone to contribute. Consequently, they are much more likely to notice and complain if a teammate isn't doing his or her share. In fact, when teammates know each other well, when team goals are specific, when team communication is good, and when teams are rewarded for team performance (discussed below), there is only a 1 in 16 chance that teammates will be social loafers.[82]

What can companies and teams do to ensure that team goals lead to superior team performance? One increasingly popular approach is to give teams stretch goals. *Stretch goals* are extremely ambitious goals that workers don't know how to reach.[83] For example, *SUBARU'S* manufacturing plant in Lafayette, Indiana, has the stretch goal of producing zero landfill waste. That's right—an automobile assembly plant with the goal of producing no waste—zero, zip, nada. Denise Coogan, the plant's environmental compliance manager, said, "We didn't redefine 'zero.' Zero means zero. Nothing from our manufacturing process goes to the landfill."[84] The purpose of stretch goals is to achieve extraordinary improvements in performance by forcing managers and workers to throw away old, comfortable solutions and adopt radical, never-used-before solutions.[85]

Four things must occur for stretch goals to effectively motivate teams.[86] First, teams must have a high degree of autonomy or control over how they achieve their goals. At *CSX's* railroad division, top management challenged one of its new management teams to ship the same amount of coal each month, but do it with 4,200 railcars instead of 5,000. The local team quickly figured out that trains were spending too much time sitting idly in the rail yards. Headquarters wouldn't let the trains run until they had 160 full railcars to pull, but amassing that many cars could take nearly a week. Since the local management team had the autonomy to pay for the extra crews to run the trains more frequently, it started running trains with as few as 78 cars. Now, coal cars never wait more than a day to be transported to customers, and productivity has skyrocketed.[87]

Second, teams must be empowered with control resources, such as budgets, workspaces, computers, or whatever else they need to do their jobs. Steve Kerr,

Goldman Sachs' chief learning officer, says, "We have a moral obligation to try to give people the tools to meet tough goals. I think it's totally wrong if you don't give employees the tools to succeed, then punish them when they fail."[88]

Third, teams need structural accommodation. **Structural accommodation** means giving teams the ability to change organizational structures, policies, and practices if doing so helps them meet their stretch goals. Finally, teams need bureaucratic immunity. **Bureaucratic immunity** means that teams no longer have to go through the frustratingly slow process of multilevel reviews and sign-offs to get management approval before making changes. Once granted bureaucratic immunity, teams are immune from the influence of various organizational groups and are accountable only to top management. Therefore, teams can act quickly and even experiment with little fear of failure.

4.2 Selecting People for Teamwork

University of Southern California management professor Edward Lawler says, "People are very naive about how easy it is to create a team. Teams are the Ferraris of work design. They're high performance but high maintenance and expensive."[89] It's almost impossible to have an effective work team without carefully selecting people who are suited for teamwork or for working on a particular team. A focus on teamwork (individualism-collectivism), team level, and team diversity can help companies choose the right team members.[90]

Are you more comfortable working alone or with others? If you strongly prefer to work alone, you may not be well suited for teamwork. Indeed, studies show that job satisfaction is higher in teams when team members prefer working with others.[91] An indirect way to measure someone's *preference for teamwork* is to assess the person's degree of individualism or collectivism. **Individualism-collectivism** is the degree to which a person believes that people should be self-sufficient and that loyalty to one's self is more important than loyalty to one's team or company.[92] *Individualists*, who put their own welfare and interests first, generally prefer independent tasks in which they work alone. In contrast, *collectivists*, who put group or team interests ahead of self-interests, generally prefer interdependent tasks in which they work with others. Collectivists would also rather cooperate than compete and are fearful of disappointing team members or of being ostracized from teams. Given these differences, it makes sense to select team members who are collectivists rather than individualists. Indeed, many companies use individualism-collectivism as an initial screening device for team members. While many people think of golf as the ultimate individual game, for eight decades, European and American golfers have squared off against each other in the Ryder Cup, a team-based competition. Instead of selecting players based on their golf records alone (i.e., individualism), U.S. coach Paul Azinger and assistasnt Olin Browne selected players based on their ability to fit into the overall team of 12 players and into smaller "pods" of 4 players (i.e., collectivism).[93] If team diversity is desired, however, individualists may also be appropriate, as discussed below. To determine your preference for teamwork, take the Team Player Inventory shown in Exhibit 9.6.

Team level is the average level of ability, experience, personality, or any other factor on a team. For example, a high level of team experience means that a team has

structural accommodation
the ability to change organizational structures, policies, and practices in order to meet stretch goals

bureaucratic immunity
the ability to make changes without first getting approval from managers or other parts of an organization

individualism-collectivism
the degree to which a person believes that people should be self-sufficient and that loyalty to one's self is more important than loyalty to team or company

team level
the average level of ability, experience, personality, or any other factor on a team

EXHIBIT 9.6

The Team Player Inventory

	STRONGLY DISAGREE				STRONGLY AGREE
1. I enjoy working on team/group projects.	1	2	3	4	5
2. Team/group project work easily allows others to not pull their weight.	1	2	3	4	5
3. Work that is done as a team/group is better than the work done individually.	1	2	3	4	5
4. I do my best work alone rather than in a team/group.	1	2	3	4	5
5. Team/group work is overrated in terms of the actual results produced.	1	2	3	4	5
6. Working in a team/group gets me to think more creatively.	1	2	3	4	5
7. Teams/groups are used too often, when individual work would be more effective.	1	2	3	4	5
8. My own work is enhanced when I am in a team/group situation.	1	2	3	4	5
9. My experiences working in team/group situations have been primarily negative.	1	2	3	4	5
10. More solutions/ideas are generated when working in a team/group situation than when working alone.	1	2	3	4	5

Reverse score items 2, 4, 5, 7, and 9. Then add the scores for items 1 to 10. Higher scores indicate a preference for teamwork, whereas lower total scores indicate a preference for individual work.

Source: T. J. B. Kline, "The Team Player Inventory: Reliability and Validity of a Measure of Predisposition Toward Organizational Team-Working Environments," *Journal for Specialists in Group Work* 24, no. 1 (1999): 102–112.

particularly experienced team members. This does not mean that every member of the team has considerable experience, but that enough team members do to significantly raise the average level of experience on the team. Team level is used to guide selection of teammates when teams need a particular set of skills or capabilities to do their jobs well.

Whereas team level represents the average level or capability on a team, **team diversity** represents the variances or differences in ability, experience, personality, or any other factor on a team.[94] From a practical perspective, why is team diversity important? Professor John Hollenbeck explains, "Imagine if you put all the extroverts together. Everyone is talking, but nobody is listening. [By contrast,] with a team of [nothing but] introverts, you can hear the clock ticking on the wall."[95] Not only do strong teams have talented members (that is, a high team level), but those talented members are also different in terms of ability, experience, or personality. Team diversity is often used to guide the selection of team members when teams must complete a wide range of different tasks or when tasks are particularly complex.

team diversity the variances or differences in ability, experience, personality, or any other factor on a team

Once the right team has been put together in terms of individualism-collectivism, team level, and team diversity, it's important to keep the team together as long as practically possible. Interesting research by the National Transportation Safety Board shows that 73 percent of serious mistakes made by jet cockpit crews are made the very first day that a crew flies together as a team and that 44 percent of serious mistakes occur on their very first flight together that day (pilot teams fly two to three flights per day). Moreover, research has shown that fatigued pilot crews who have worked together before make significantly fewer errors than rested crews who have never worked together.[96] Their experience working together helps them overcome their fatigue and outperform new teams that have not worked together before. So, once you've created effective teams, keep them together as long as possible.

4.3 Team Training

After selecting the right people for teamwork, you need to train them. To be successful, teams need significant training, particularly in interpersonal skills, decision-making and problem-solving skills, conflict resolution skills, and technical training. Organizations that create work teams *often underestimate the amount of training* required to make teams effective. This mistake occurs frequently in successful organizations where managers assume that if employees can work effectively on their own, they can work effectively in teams. In reality, companies that use teams successfully provide thousands of hours of training to make sure that teams work.

Most commonly, members of work teams receive training in interpersonal skills. **Interpersonal skills** such as listening, communicating, questioning, and providing feedback enable people to have effective working relationships with others.

Because of teams' autonomy and responsibility, many companies also give team members training in *decision-making* and *problem-solving skills* to help them do a better job of cutting costs and improving quality and customer service. Many organizations also teach *conflict resolution skills*. "Teams at *DELTA FAUCET* have specific protocols for addressing conflict. For example, if an employee's behavior is creating a problem within a team, the team is expected to work it out without involving the team leader. Two team members will meet with the problem team member and work toward a resolution. If this is unsuccessful, the whole team meets and confronts the issue. If necessary, the team leader can be brought in to make a decision, but . . . it is a rare occurrence for a team to reach that stage."[97]

Firms must also provide team members with the *technical training* they need to do their jobs, particularly if they are being cross-trained to perform all of the different jobs on the team. Before teams were created at *MILWAUKEE MUTUAL INSURANCE*, separate employees performed the tasks of rating, underwriting, and processing insurance policies. After extensive cross-training, however, each team member can now do all three jobs.[98] Cross-training is less appropriate for teams of highly skilled workers. For instance, it is unlikely that a group of engineers, computer programmers, and systems analysts would be cross-trained for each other's jobs.

interpersonal skills
skills, such as listening, communicating, questioning, and providing feedback, that enable people to have effective working relationships with others

Team leaders need training, too, as they often feel unprepared for their new duties. Exhibit 9.7 lists the top ten problems team leaders face. The solution to these problems is extensive training. Overall, does team training work? One recent study found that across a wide variety of settings, tasks, team types, and 2,650 teams in different organizations, team training was positively related to team performance outcomes.[99]

Management Decision

Should I Hit the Recruiting Trail?

Your life as a college basketball coach used to be fairly easy, since it was based on just one principle—get the most talented players. A few months every year, you and your army of assistants and scouts would comb the country, looking high and low for the best players, and convincing them that your program was where they belonged. And even if recruiting didn't go your way one year, you could expect that that the players you got before would be a part of your program for 3 or 4 years.

Well, times have certainly changed. You still have to go recruiting, but the allure of playing big-time college basketball for 4 years has faded. At first, your players started leaving for the NBA before they graduated, some as early as their sophomore years. And then, elite high school players decided that they didn't need to go to college at all, going straight into the pros. To try and revitalize the college game, the NBA passed the "one and done" rule in 2005, requiring that its players be 1 year removed from high school graduation. But this made your job even tougher—even though the best high school players came to play for you, they only stayed one season. Some committed to your program, but then decided that playing professionally in Europe would be better than spending a year at college. This left your program with little continuity and stability. What's worse, you were left with little margin of error—if you didn't recruit well each and every year, your team would be quickly passed by the competition.

There have been a number of basketball programs that have found success using a completely different approach to team building. Rather than aiming for top talent that might be at school for 2 years, if lucky, coaches at smaller, lesser-known schools, often called "mid-majors," recruit lesser-known, complementary role-players who have little ambitions for the pros and will likely be a part of the team for 4 years. And even though these coaches won't be working with the next Michael Jordan, many have created cohesive teams that have had great success. Gonzaga University has made the NCAA tournament every year since 1999, while Xavier University has reached the "dance" every year since 2001. George Mason reached the "Final Four" in 2006, while Butler University made it all the way to the championship game in 2010. It's not just that these teams are lucky. They're the product of an approach to team building that emphasizes cohesion, cooperation, and commitment to the team, rather than individual glory.

So, which approach to team building do you think would be the best for your program, and more importantly, your sanity? Will you continue to look for as many superstars as you can, knowing that they may not stay around too long? Or, are you willing to pay more attention to complementary role players?

Questions

1. What are advantages and disadvantages of each type of team?
2. If you were to decide on the superstar-player approach, how would you deal with the instability within your organization?
3. If you were to take the team/role-player approach, what steps would you take to help the team, its members, and outsiders deal with the perceived lack of talent?

4.4 Team Compensation and Recognition

Compensating teams fairly is very difficult. For instance, one survey found that only 37 percent of companies were satisfied with their team compensation plans and even fewer, just 10 percent, reported being "very positive."[100] One of the problems, according to Susan Mohrman of the Center for Effective Organizations at the University of Southern California is that "there is a very strong set of beliefs in most organizations that people should be paid for how well they do. So when people first get put into team-based organizations, they really balk at being paid for how well the team does. It sounds illogical to them. It sounds like their individuality and their sense of self-worth are being threatened."[101] Consequently, companies need to carefully choose a team compensation plan and then fully explain how teams will be rewarded. One basic requirement for team compensation to work is that the level of rewards (individual versus team) must match the level of performance (individual versus team).

Exhibit 9.7

Top Ten Problems Reported by Team Leaders

1. Confusion about their new roles and about what they should be doing differently.
2. Feeling they've lost control.
3. Not knowing what it means to coach or empower.
4. Having personal doubts about whether the team concept will really work.
5. Uncertainty about how to deal with employees' doubts about the team concept.
6. Confusion about when a team is ready for more responsibility.
7. Confusion about how to share responsibility and accountability with the team.
8. Concern about promotional opportunities, especially about whether the "team leader" title carries any prestige.
9. Uncertainty about the strategic aspects of the leader's role as the team matures.
10. Not knowing where to turn for help with team problems, as few, if any, of their organization's leaders have led teams.

Source: B. Filipczak, M. Hequet, C. Lee, M. Picard, & D. Stamps, "More Trouble with Teams," *Training*, October 1996, 21.

Employees can be compensated for team participation and accomplishments in three ways: skill-based pay, gainsharing, and nonfinancial rewards. **Skill-based pay** programs pay employees for learning additional skills or knowledge.[102] These programs encourage employees to acquire the additional skills they will need to perform multiple jobs within a team and to share knowledge with others within their work groups.[103] For example, at XEL Communications, the circuit-board manufacturer, the number of skills each employee has mastered determines his or her individual pay. An employee who takes a class and on-the-job training in advanced soldering will earn 30 cents more per hour. Passing a written test or satisfactorily performing a skill or job for a supervisor or trainer certifies mastery of new skills and results in increased pay.

skill-based pay compensation system that pays employees for learning additional skills or knowledge

gainsharing a compensation system in which companies share the financial value of performance gains, such as productivity, cost savings, or quality, with their workers

In **gainsharing** programs, companies share the financial value of performance gains, such as productivity increases, cost savings, or quality improvements, with their workers.[104] Walk into any Nucor Corporation plant and nearly every production worker can tell you within a tenth of a percent what his team's weekly bonus will be at that point. Team size ranges from 12 to 20 and each team includes production workers, maintenance workers, and supervisors. "People expect a complicated [incentive] plan, but our plan is really simple: quality tons out the door and pay weekly," says Dan Krug, manager of HR and organizational development at Nucor.

With bonuses included, the typical Nucor steel mill worker makes $72,000 a year.[105] *Nonfinancial rewards* are another way to reward teams for their performance. These rewards, which can range from vacation trips to T-shirts, plaques, and coffee mugs, are especially effective when coupled with management recognition, such as awards, certificates, and praise.[106] Nonfinancial awards tend to be most effective when teams or team-based interventions, such as total quality management (see Chapter 16), are first introduced.[107]

Which team compensation plan should your company use? In general, skill-based pay is most effective for self-managing and self-directing teams performing complex tasks. In these situations, the more each team member knows and can do, the better the whole team performs. By contrast, gainsharing works best in relatively stable environments where employees can focus on improving the productivity, cost savings, or quality of their current work system.

Finally, given the level of dissatisfaction with most team compensation systems, what compensation plans would today's managers like to use with the teams in their companies? Among managers, 40.5 percent would directly link merit-pay increases to team performance but allow adjustments within teams for differences in individual performance. By contrast, 13.7 percent would also link merit-based increases directly to team performance but give each team member an equal share of the team's merit-based reward. In addition, 19.1 percent would use gainsharing plans based on quality, delivery, productivity, or cost reduction and then provide equal payouts to all teams and team members. Another 14.5 percent would also use gainsharing, but they would vary the team gainsharing award depending on how much money the team saved the company. Payouts would still be equally distributed within teams. Finally, 12.2 percent of managers would opt for plant-wide profit-sharing plans tied to overall company or division performance.[108] In this case, there would be no payout distinctions between or within teams.

REVIEW 4

Enhancing Work Team Effectiveness

Companies can make teams more effective by setting team goals and managing how team members are selected, trained, and compensated. Team goals provide a clear focus and purpose, reduce the incidence of social loafing, and lead to higher team performance 93 percent of the time. Extremely difficult stretch goals can be used to motivate teams as long as teams have autonomy, control over resources, structural accommodation, and bureaucratic immunity. Not everyone is suited for teamwork. When selecting team members, companies should select people who have a preference for teamwork (individualism-collectivism) and should consider team level (average ability on a team) and team diversity (different abilities on a team). Organizations that successfully use teams provide thousands of hours of training to make sure that teams work. The most common types of team training are for interpersonal skills, decision-making and problem-solving skills, conflict resolution, technical training to help team members learn multiple jobs (that is, cross-training), and training for team leaders. Employees can be compensated for team participation and accomplishments in three ways: skill-based pay, gainsharing, and nonfinancial rewards.

Practice being a MANAGER

Campus Improvement

Teamwork is vital to the success of organizations. And this makes creating high-performance teams an important management challenge. In this exercise, you will work with fellow students to brainstorm the creation of a high-performing team. Pay particular attention to the assumptions that you and your peers bring to this process regarding what works, and what doesn't work, in relation to creating a high-performance team. At the conclusion of the exercise, you will have an opportunity to discuss the theory and common assumptions regarding effective team building.

STEP 1 Get into groups. Your professor will organize small groups.

STEP 2 Review the situation. Assume that your group has been hand-picked by the president of your college or university to work for one semester as a "campus improvement" team. At the end of the year, you will submit your recommendations to the president and the board of your institution. These leaders have assured you that they will make every effort to implement your recommendations.

STEP 3 Develop a plan. Brainstorm and develop a plan for working as a team to achieve the objective of delivering a set of quality recommendations to the president and the board. You should consider the following in developing your plan:

- Working well together as a team
- Establishing criteria for "quality recommendations" (such as representing the various important constituencies and interests on campus)
- Outlining steps, areas and types of work, and assignments for each member that are most likely to take full advantage of the capabilities and resources in your team

STEP 4 Discuss your plans as a class. Is this the sort of project that is well suited to using a work team? Why or why not? How might work team characteristics such as norms, cohesiveness, and team size play a role in this team effort? What conflicts might be likely down the road, and at what stage of the process are these conflicts most likely to occur?

SELF Assessment

Working in Groups

From sports to school to work to civic involvement, working in teams is increasingly part of our experience. Even though teams are frequently used to get work done, people still have widely varying opinions of their value. Think of your own situation. When a professor divides the class into groups to complete a project, do you respond with an inward smile or a heavy sigh? Do you enjoy team projects, or would you rather just do your own work? The following 20-question survey assesses your thoughts about working in teams.[109] Indicate the extent to which you agree with each of the following statements. Try not to spend too much time on any one item, and be sure to answer all the questions. Use this scale for your responses:

1. Strongly disagree
2. Disagree
3. Slightly disagree

4. Neutral
5. Slightly agree
6. Agree
7. Strongly agree

1. Only those who depend on themselves get ahead in life.
   1 2 3 4 5 6 7
2. To be superior, a person must stand alone.
   1 2 3 4 5 6 7
3. If you want something done right, you've got to do it yourself.
   1 2 3 4 5 6 7
4. What happens to me is my own doing.
   1 2 3 4 5 6 7
5. In the long run, the only person you can count on is yourself.
   1 2 3 4 5 6 7
6. Winning is everything.
   1 2 3 4 5 6 7
7. I feel that winning is important in both work and games.
   1 2 3 4 5 6 7
8. Success is the most important thing in life.
   1 2 3 4 5 6 7
9. It annoys me when other people perform better than I do.
   1 2 3 4 5 6 7
10. Doing your best isn't enough; it is important to win.
    1 2 3 4 5 6 7
11. I prefer to work with others in a group rather than working alone.
    1 2 3 4 5 6 7
12. Given the choice, I would rather do a job where I can work alone rather than doing a job where I have to work with others in a group.
    1 2 3 4 5 6 7
13. Working with a group is better than working alone.
    1 2 3 4 5 6 7
14. People should be made aware that if they are going to be part of a group, then sometimes they are going to have to do things they don't want to do.
    1 2 3 4 5 6 7
15. People who belong to a group should realize that they're not always going to get what they want.
    1 2 3 4 5 6 7
16. People in a group should realize that they sometimes are going to have to make sacrifices for the sake of the group as a whole.
    1 2 3 4 5 6 7
17. People in a group should be willing to make sacrifices for the sake of the group's well-being.
    1 2 3 4 5 6 7
18. A group is more productive when its members do what they want to do rather than what the group wants them to do.
    1 2 3 4 5 6 7

19. A group is most efficient when its members do what they think is best rather than doing what the group wants them to do.

1 2 3 4 5 6 7

20. A group is more productive when its members follow their own interests and desires.

1 2 3 4 5 6 7

SCORING

Determine your score by entering your response to each survey item below, as follows. In blanks that say *regular score*, simply enter your response for that item. If your response was a 3, place a 3 in the *regular score* blank. In blanks that say *reverse score*, subtract your response from 8 and enter the result. So if your response was a 3, place a 5 (8 − 3 = 5) in the *reverse score* blank.

1. reverse score ______
2. reverse score ______
3. reverse score ______
4. reverse score ______
5. reverse score ______
6. reverse score ______
7. reverse score ______
8. reverse score ______
9. reverse score ______
10. reverse score ______
11. regular score ______
12. reverse score ______
13. regular score ______
14. regular score ______
15. regular score ______
16. regular score ______
17. regular score ______
18. reverse score ______
19. reverse score ______
20. reverse score ______

TOTAL = ______

You can find the interpretation of your score at: login.cengagebrain.com.

Biz Flix

© GREENLIGHT

Failure to Launch

In the 2006 romantic comedy *Failure to Launch*, Matthew McConaughey plays Tripp, a thirty-five-year-old confirmed bachelor who lives a great life in a nice house—his parents'. Whenever a woman starts getting too serious about him, Tripp brings them home to see his childhood bedroom. It's his surefire way of getting rid of clingy girlfriends without ever having to break up with them. His mother Sue (Kathy Bates) and father Al (Terry Bradshaw) are desperate to get Tripp out of the house, so they hire Paula (Sarah Jessica Parker), who specializes in detaching grown children from their families. In this scene, Paula's quirky roommate Kit (Zooey Deschanel) enlists Tripp's friend Ace (Justin Bartha) in getting rid of a bird that has been making too much noise outside her window.

What to Watch for and Ask Yourself

1. Do you think Kit and Ace make a good team? How well do they work together to first shoot the bird and then save it?
2. Is there a clear leader? Who is making most of the decisions in this scene?
3. Is there any evidence of team conflict?

Management Workplace

© CENGAGE

Greensburg, Kansas

It's hard to assign credit to only one person for Greensburg's decision to rebuild the small Kansas town as a model green community after a tornado destroyed most of its buildings. Lonnie McCollum, the mayor at the time, expressed interest in exploring the possibilities of running Greensburg's municipal buildings on solar and wind power well before the EF5 tornado hit in May 2004. After the storm, he saw an opportunity to reinvent the dying town and put it back on the map. But McCollum was not the sole decision maker. He had an ally in Steve Hewitt, Greensburg's city administrator, who took McCollum's vision and expanded it. As this video shows, the real work was convincing Greensburg's residents and city council members to implement the proposed plan.

What to Watch for and Ask Yourself

1. What were the criticisms that Greensburg resident Janice Haney had about the community leaders and the decisions they made on the town's behalf?
2. Who was part of the "work team" that made decisions for the town?
3. If you lived in Greensburg, how would you feel about the way decisions were made?

Reel to Real

10 Chapter Ten
Managing Human Resources

OUTLINE

Experience Management

Explore the four levels of learning by doing the simulation modules on Human Resources.

© ISTOCKPHOTO.COM/ ANN MARIE KURTZ

Pod Nod

Mini lecture reviews all the learning points in the chapter.

© ISTOCKPHOTO.COM/ MAGNET CREATIVE

Reel to Real

Biz Flix is a scene from *Played*. Management Workplace is a segment on The Maine Media Workshops.

© ISTOCKPHOTO.COM/ CRAFTVISION

Self Test

10 quiz questions, 5 exhibit worksheets, and PowerPoints for quick review.

© ISTOCKPHOTO.COM/ DIJITAL FILM

What Would You Do?

Burgerville Headquarters, Vancouver, Washington.[1] "Hey boss, where's the drive-through cook? Customers' cars are backed up to the street and are waiting 7 minutes for their orders, way over our goal of 3 minutes!" Well, the drive-through cook never showed up, and with employee turnover running 128 percent per year, a cook isn't coming until you hire a new one.

The problem with that much turnover is you can't consistently produce a quality product. Making hamburgers and fries may seem simple, but a Burgerville customer spends about $2 more on average than a McDonald's customer, which is reflected in the complexity of your menu. For example, because you source all ingredients locally, hamburgers are not frozen, but made fresh from grass-fed beef. That means more steps are involved than just throwing a frozen hamburger patty onto a hot grill. Each summer, fresh Oregon blackberries and raspberries are hand processed by your employees to make smoothies and milk shakes. Your vice president of marketing and menu development explains the extra work involved, "Each year we train our staff to quickly clean, hull, and chop these berries to ensure freshness," and each restaurant goes through an average of eight flats a day of fresh berries! Likewise, each summer, employees hand cut 250,000 pounds of fresh onions from Walla Walla, Washington to make Burgerville's famous (and huge!) onion rings. Again, your vice president of marketing and menu development explains, "To ensure consistent quality, each year we have a training session at one of our supplier partners to teach trainers the best ways to slice the onions, coat them in batter, [and] season and fry them." Finally, salads are made with wild Coho salmon, hazelnuts, shell-smoked blue cheese, baby brunia arugula, organic cranberries and apples, and cheeseburgers are made with locally produced Tillamook cheddar cheese.

Burgerville turned to local sourcing and fresh ingredients in the 1990s because it couldn't compete with McDonald's, Burger King, or Wendy's. Guest counts had dropped significantly, so it looked for a way to differentiate itself from the burger giants. Higher costs usually prevent fast-food restaurants from using fresh, locally grown ingredients, but with an aggressive supply chain effort, you found ways to work successfully with local suppliers and keep costs down. But now, your high turnover rates are threatening the company's strategy. Indeed, a quit rate of 128 percent means the company has to recruit, hire, and train 1,920 workers a year just to maintain its workforce of 1,500 employees across 39 restaurants. The restaurant industry estimates that it costs $3,000 to replace each hourly worker, so employee turnover is costing Burgerville $5.76 million a year in replacement costs alone, not to mention the lost revenue from decreases in quality (which hurt sales and customer retention) and lost productivity (it takes 30–90 days for most of your employees to learn their jobs). The question, of course, is what to do about it.

Most of your jobs pay minimum wage. So, should you increase pay like Starbucks has, or are there other things on which you should focus to recruit more qualified applicants? After all, the company mission is to "Serve with Love." Again, what's the best way to make that happen? One thing you have to quit doing is simply hiring the next warm body that walks through the door. But, how do you select or screen people for preparing food, handling the cash register, and taking orders? Are interviews enough? Finally, what might you do to make working at Burgerville more satisfying? That is, once people have taken the job, how do you get them to stay more than a few months? You're realistic about this, as nobody stays in these jobs forever. But, if you can get people to stay 3 months, they'll often stay a year or two.

If you were in charge at Burgerv what would you do?

Human resource management (HRM), or the process of finding, developing, and keeping the right people to form a qualified workforce, is one of the most difficult and important of all management tasks. The chapter begins by reviewing the major federal laws that affect human resource practice. Next, we explore how companies use recruiting and selection techniques to attract and hire qualified employees to fulfill those needs. The third part of the chapter discusses how training and performance appraisal can develop the knowledge, skills, and abilities of the workforce. The chapter concludes with a review of compensation and employee separation; that is, how companies can keep their best workers through effective compensation practices and how they can manage the separation process when employees leave the organization.

Understanding Human Resource Legislation

Understanding how employment legislation affects business is a critical first step in human resource planning and management. This is because there are employment laws that govern each stage of the human resource process, from how employees are recruited and selected, to how employees are terminated, and nearly every stage in between.

human resource management (HRM) the process of finding, developing, and keeping the right people to form a qualified workforce

After reading the next section, you should be able to:

1 explain how different employment laws affect human resource practice.

1 Employment Legislation

Since their inception, *HOOTERS* restaurants have hired only female servers. Moreover, consistent with the company's marketing theme, the servers wear short nylon shorts and cutoff T-shirts that show their midriffs. The Equal Employment Opportunity Commission (EEOC) began an investigation of Hooters when a Chicago man filed a sex-based discrimination charge. The man alleged that he had applied for a server's job at a Hooters restaurant and was rejected because of his sex. The dispute between Hooters and the EEOC quickly gained national attention. One sarcastic letter to the EEOC printed in *Fortune* magazine read as follows:

> Dear EEOC:
>
> Hi! I just wanted to thank you for investigating those Hooters restaurants, where the waitresses wear those shorty shorts and midriffy T-shirts. I think it's a great idea that you have decided to make Hooters hire men as—how do you say it?—waitpersons. Gee, I never knew so many men wanted to be waitpersons at Hooters. No reason to let them sue on their own either. You're right, the government needs to take the lead on this one.[2]

This letter characterized public sentiment at the time. Given its backlog of 100,000 job discrimination cases, many wondered if the EEOC didn't have better things to do with its scarce resources.

Three years after the initial complaint, the EEOC ruled that Hooters had violated antidiscrimination laws and offered to settle the case if the company would agree to pay $22 million to the EEOC for distribution to male victims of the "Hooters Girl" hiring policy, establish a scholarship fund to enhance opportunities or education for men, and provide sensitivity training to teach Hooters' employees how to be more sensitive to men's needs. Hooters responded with a $1 million publicity campaign criticizing the EEOC's investigation. Billboards featuring "Vince," a man dressed in a Hooters Girl uniform and blond wig, sprang up all over the country. Hooters customers were given postcards to send complaints to the EEOC. Of course, Hooters paid the postage. As a result of the publicity campaign, restaurant sales increased by 10 percent. Soon thereafter, the EEOC announced that it would not pursue discriminatory hiring charges against Hooters.[3] Nonetheless, the company ended up paying $3.75 million to settle a class-action suit brought by seven men who claimed that their inability to get a job at Hooters violated federal law.[4] Under the settlement, Hooters maintained its women-only policy for server jobs but had to create additional support jobs, such as hosts and bartenders, which would also be open to men. The story doesn't end there, however, as another male applicant has sued Hooters, seeking to overturn the settlement, which would allow him only to be a host or bartender.[5]

As the Hooters example illustrates, the human resource planning process occurs in a very complicated legal environment.

Let's explore employment legislation by reviewing 1.1 **the major federal employment laws that affect human resource practice**, 1.2 **how the concept of adverse impact is related to employment discrimination**, and 1.3 **the laws regarding sexual harassment in the workplace**.

EXHIBIT 10.1

Summary of Major Federal Employment Laws

Law	Website	Description
Equal Pay Act of 1963	http://www.eeoc.gov/policy/epa.html	Prohibits unequal pay for males and females doing substantially similar work.
Civil Rights Act of 1964	http://www.eeoc.gov/policy/vii.html	Prohibits discrimination on the basis of race, color, religion, sex, or national origin.
Age Discrimination in Employment Act of 1967	http://www.eeoc.gov/policy/adea.html	Prohibits discrimination in employment decisions against persons age 40 and over.
Pregnancy Discrimination Act of 1978	http://www.eeoc.gov/facts/fs-preg.html	Prohibits discrimination in employment against pregnant women.
Americans with Disabilities Act of 1990	http://www.eeoc.gov/policy/ada.html	Prohibits discrimination on the basis of physical or mental disabilities.
Civil Rights Act of 1991	http://www.eeoc.gov/policy/cra91.html	Strengthened the provisions of the Civil Rights Act of 1964 by providing for jury trials and punitive damages.
Family and Medical Leave Act of 1993	http://www.dol.gov/whd/fmla/index.html	Permits workers to take up to 12 weeks of unpaid leave for pregnancy and/or birth of a new child, adoption or foster care of a new child, illness of an immediate family member, or personal medical leave.
Uniformed Services Employment and Reemployment Rights Act of 1994	http://www.osc.gov/userra.htm	Prohibits discrimination against those serving in the Armed Forces Reserve, the National Guard, or other uniformed services; guarantees that civilian employers will hold and then restore civilian jobs and benefits for those who have completed uniformed service.

1.1 Federal Employment Laws

Exhibit 10.1 lists the major federal employment laws and websites where you can find more detailed information about them. Except for the Family and Medical Leave Act and the Uniformed Services Employment and Reemployment Rights Act, hich are administrated by the Department of Labor (***http://www.dol.gov***), all of these laws are administered by the EEOC (***http://www.eeoc.gov***). The general effect of this body of law, which is still evolving through court decisions, is that employers may not discriminate in employment decisions on the basis of sex, age, religion, color, national origin, race, or disability. The intent is to make these factors irrelevant in employment decisions. Stated another way, employment decisions should be based on factors that are "job related," "reasonably necessary," or a "business necessity" for successful job performance. The only time that sex, age, religion, and the like can be used to make employment decisions is when they are considered a bona fide occupational qualification.[6] Title VII of the 1964 Civil Rights Act says that it is lawful to hire and employ someone on the basis of sex, religion, or national origin when there is a **bona fide occupational qualification (BFOQ)** that is "reasonably necessary to the normal operation of that particular business." A Baptist church hiring a new minister can reasonably specify that being a Baptist rather than

bona fide occupational qualification (BFOQ) an exception in employment law that permits sex, age, religion, and the like to be used when making employment decisions, but only if they are "reasonably necessary to the normal operation of that particular business." BFOQs are strictly monitored by the Equal Employment Opportunity Commission.

a Catholic or Presbyterian is a BFOQ for the position. However, it's unlikely that the church could specify race or national origin as a BFOQ. In general, the courts and the EEOC take a hard look when a business claims that sex, age, religion, color, national origin, race, or disability is a BFOQ. For instance, the EEOC disagreed with Hooters' claim that it was "in the business of providing vicarious sexual recreation" and that "female sexuality is a bona fide occupational qualification."[7]

Employers who use sex, age, race, or religion to make employment-related decisions when those factors are unrelated to an applicant's or employee's ability to perform a job may face charges of discrimination from employee lawsuits or the EEOC. For example, Morgan Stanley, an investment bank, agreed to pay $54 million in damages after the EEOC filed a sex discrimination suit on behalf of 300 of the firm's female employees. The women were paid less and promoted less often than comparable male employees with whom they worked.[8]

In addition to the laws presented in Exhibit 10.1, there are two other important sets of federal laws: labor laws and laws and regulations governing safety standards. Labor laws regulate the interaction between management and labor unions that represent groups of employees. These laws guarantee employees the right to form and join unions of their own choosing. For more information about labor laws, see the National Labor Relations Board at ***http://www.nlrb.gov***. The Occupational Safety and Health Act (OSHA) requires that employers provide employees with a workplace that is "free from recognized hazards that are causing or are likely to cause death or serious physical harm." This law is administered by the Occupational Safety and Health Administration (which, like the act, is referred to as OSHA). OSHA sets safety and health standards for employers and conducts inspections to determine whether those standards are being met. Employers who do not meet OSHA standards may be fined.[9] For example, OSHA fined British Petroleum $23.8 million for "egregious, willful violations" of safety standards after a refinery explosion in Texas City, Texas, killed 15 workers and injured 180 employees.[10] The U.S. Chemical Safety and Hazard Investigation Board, a government agency that investigates major workplace accidents, accused BP of knowing about "widespread safety problems" prior to the accident, which it said was the result of "drastic cost-cutting at the Texas refinery, where maintenance and infrastructure deteriorated over time, setting the stage for the disaster."[11] For more information about OSHA, see ***http://www.osha.gov***.

1.2 Adverse Impact and Employment Discrimination

The EEOC has investigatory, enforcement, and informational responsibilities. Therefore, it investigates charges of discrimination, enforces the employment discrimination laws in federal court, and publishes guidelines that organizations can use to ensure they are in compliance with the law. One of the most important guidelines jointly issued by the EEOC, the Department of Labor, the U.S. Justice Department, and the federal Office of Personnel Management is the *Uniform Guidelines on Employee Selection Procedures*, which can be read in their entirety at ***http://www.ipacweb.org/files/ug.pdf***. These guidelines define two important criteria, disparate treatment and adverse impact, that are used in determining whether companies have engaged in discriminatory hiring and promotion practices.

Disparate treatment, which is *intentional* discrimination, occurs when people, despite being qualified, are *intentionally* not given the same hiring, promotion, or membership opportunities as other employees because of their race, color, age, sex,

disparate treatment intentional discrimination that occurs when people are purposely not given the same hiring, promotion, or membership opportunities because of their race, color, sex, age, ethnic group, national origin, or religious beliefs

ethnic group, national origin, or religious beliefs.[12] *ABERCROMBIE & FITCH* paid $50 million to settle a lawsuit that alleged systematic discrimination against Hispanic, African American, Asian American, and female applicants and employees in its employment practices.[13] Legally, a key element of discrimination lawsuits is establishing motive, meaning that the employer intended to discriminate. If no motive can be established, then a claim of disparate treatment may actually be a case of adverse impact. **Adverse impact**, which is *unintentional* discrimination, occurs when members of a particular race, sex, or ethnic group are *unintentionally* harmed or disadvantaged because they are hired, promoted, or trained (or any other employment decision) at substantially lower rates than others. The courts and federal agencies use the **four-fifths (or 80 percent) rule** to determine if adverse impact has occurred. Adverse impact occurs if the decision rate for a protected group of people is less than four-fifths (or 80 percent) of the decision rate for a nonprotected group (usually white males). So, if 100 white applicants and 100 black applicants apply for entry-level jobs, and 60 white applicants are hired (60/100 = 60%), but only 20 black applicants are hired (20/100 = 20%), adverse impact has occurred (0.20/0.60 = 0.33). The criterion for the four-fifths rule in this situation is 0.48 (0.60 × 0.80 = 0.48). Since 0.33 is less than 0.48, the four-fifths rule has been violated.

adverse impact
unintentional discrimination that occurs when members of a particular race, sex, or ethnic group are unintentionally harmed or disadvantaged because they are hired, promoted, or trained (or any other employment decision) at substantially lower rates than others

four-fifths (or 80 percent) rule
a rule of thumb used by the courts and the EEOC to determine whether there is evidence of adverse impact. A violation of this rule occurs when the selection rate for a protected group is less than 80 percent or four-fifths of the selection rate for a nonprotected group.

Violation of the four-fifths rule is not an automatic indication of discrimination, however. If an employer can demonstrate that a selection procedure or test is valid, meaning that the test accurately predicts job performance or that the test is job related because it assesses applicants on specific tasks actually used in the job, then the organization may continue to use the test. If validity cannot be established, however, then a violation of the four-fifths rule may likely result in a lawsuit brought by employees, job applicants, or the EEOC itself.

1.3 Sexual Harassment

According to the EEOC, **sexual harassment** is a form of discrimination in which unwelcome sexual advances, requests for sexual favors, or other verbal or physical conduct of a sexual nature occurs. From a legal perspective, there are two kinds of sexual harassment, quid pro quo and hostile work environment.[14]

sexual harassment
a form of discrimination in which unwelcome sexual advances, requests for sexual favors, or other verbal or physical conduct of a sexual nature occurs while performing one's job

Quid pro quo sexual harassment occurs when employment outcomes, such as hiring, promotion, or simply keeping one's job, depend on whether an individual submits to being sexually harassed. For example, in a quid pro quo sexual harassment lawsuit against *COSTCO*, a female employee alleged that her boss groped her and bumped into her from behind to simulate sex. "He would tell her: 'You work with me and I'll work with you,' motioning to his private area."[15] The supervisor also allegedly told her that he would fire her if she reported his activities to upper management. In quid pro quo cases requests for sexual acts are linked to economic outcomes such as keeping a job. By contrast, a **hostile work environment** occurs when unwelcome and demeaning sexually related behavior creates an intimidating, hostile, and offensive work environment. In contrast to quid pro quo cases, a hostile work environment may not result in economic injury. However, it can lead to psychological injury from a stressful work environment. An Illinois-based trucking company, *CUSTOM COMPANIES*, was fined in excess of $1.1 million by a federal judge for creating a sexually hostile work environment. The EEOC had charged that three female sales representatives were subjected to unwelcome groping, lewd sexual language, sexual propositions, and pornography. The judge overseeing the case concluded, "Defendants' actions were reprehensible," and wrote that "There

quid pro quo sexual harassment
a form of sexual harassment in which employment outcomes, such as hiring, promotion, or simply keeping one's job, depend on whether an individual submits to sexual harassment

hostile work environment
a form of sexual harassment in which unwelcome and demeaning sexually related behavior creates an intimidating and offensive work environment

was evidence of repeated touching . . . sexually explicit comments and jokes, sexual advances, and a sexually charged atmosphere. . . . The harassment came from employees in positions of power."[16]

What common mistakes do managers make when it comes to sexual harassment laws?[17] First, many assume that the victim and harasser must be of opposite sexes. According to the courts, they do not. Sexual harassment can also occur between people of the same sex. Second, managers often assume that sexual harassment can occur only between coworkers or between supervisors and subordinates. Not so. Agents of employers, such as consultants, and even nonemployees can be sexual harassers. The key is not employee status but whether the harassment takes place while company business is being conducted. Third, it is often assumed that only people who have themselves been harassed can file complaints or lawsuits. In fact, especially in hostile work environments, anyone affected by offensive conduct can file a complaint or lawsuit.

Finally, what should companies do to make sure that sexual harassment laws are followed and not violated?[18] First, respond immediately when sexual harassment is reported. A quick response encourages victims of sexual harassment to report problems to management rather than to lawyers or the EEOC. Furthermore, a quick and fair investigation may serve as a deterrent to future harassment. A lawyer for the EEOC says, "Worse than having no sexual harassment policy is a policy that is not followed. It's merely window dressing. You wind up with destroyed morale when people who come forward are ignored, ridiculed, retaliated against, or nothing happens to the harasser."[19] Next, take the time to write a clear, understandable sexual harassment policy that is strongly worded, gives specific examples of what constitutes sexual harassment, spells outs sanctions and punishments, and is widely publicized within the company. This lets potential harassers and victims know what will not be tolerated and how the firm will deal with harassment should it occur.

Next, establish clear reporting procedures that indicate how, where, and to whom incidents of sexual harassment can be reported. The best procedures ensure that a complaint will receive a quick response, that impartial parties will handle the complaint, and that the privacy of the accused and accuser will be protected. At *DUPONT, AVON*, and *TEXAS INDUSTRIES*, employees can call a confidential hotline 24 hours a day, 365 days a year.[20]

Finally, managers should also be aware that most states and many cities or local governments have their own employment-related laws and enforcement agencies. So compliance with federal law is often not enough. In fact, organizations can be in full compliance with federal law and at the same time be in violation of state or local sexual harassment laws.

REVIEW 1

Employment Legislation

Human resource management is subject to the following major federal employment laws: Equal Pay Act, Civil Rights Acts of 1964 and 1991, Age Discrimination in Employment Act, Pregnancy Discrimination Act, Americans with Disabilities Act, Family and Medical Leave Act, and Uniformed Services Employment and Reemployment Rights Act. Human resource management is also subject to review by these federal agencies: Equal Employment Opportunity Commission, Department of Labor, Occupational Safety and Health Administration, and National Labor Relations Board. In general, these laws state that sex, age, religion, color, national origin, race, disability, and pregnancy may not be considered in employment decisions unless these factors reasonably qualify as BFOQs. Two important criteria, disparate treatment (intentional discrimination) and adverse impact (unintentional discrimination), are used to decide whether companies have wrongly discriminated against someone. Motive is a key part of determining disparate treatment; the courts and federal enforcement agencies use the four-fifths rule to determine if adverse impact has occurred. The two kinds of sexual harassment are quid pro quo and hostile work environment. Managers often wrongly assume that the victim and harasser must be of the opposite sex, that sexual harassment can occur only between coworkers or between supervisors and their employees, and that only people who have themselves been harassed can file complaints or lawsuits. To ensure compliance with sexual harassment laws, companies should respond immediately when harassment is reported; write a clear, understandable sexual harassment policy; establish clear reporting procedures; and be aware of and follow city and state laws concerning sexual harassment.

Finding Qualified Workers

Despite record-high unemployment levels, , and the highest average wages in Australia, Australia's mining companies are finding it nearly impossible to find the workers they need. David Knox, CEO of Santos, Ltd., an oil and gas exploration and production company, said, "One of the real challenges in Australia is continuing to get a really high-quality, high-skilled labor force."[21] With some estimating that the industry needs as many as 70,000 to 100,000 more skilled workers, Australian mining companies have had to go as far as London, Berlin, Amsterdam, and India to find and recruit applicants. Similar shortages occur in dairy farming. Ed Schoen, who runs a 180-cow farm and is on the board of the Dairy Farmers of America, said, "We need a stable supply of labor. The dairy industry's survival depends on it . . . worrying about workers is another level of stress we don't need."[22]

As these examples illustrate, finding qualified workers can be an increasingly difficult task. But it is just the first step. Deciding which applicants to hire is the second. Gail Hyland-Savage, CEO of real estate and marketing firm Michaelson, Connor & Boul, says, "Staffing is absolutely critical to the success of every company. To be competitive in today's economy, companies need the best people to create ideas and execute them for the organization. Without a competent and talented workforce, organizations will stagnate and eventually perish. The right employees are the most important resources of companies today."[23]

After reading the next two sections, you should be able to:

2 explain how companies use recruiting to find qualified job applicants.

3 describe the selection techniques and procedures that companies use when deciding which applicants should receive job offers.

2 Recruiting

Recruiting is the process of developing a pool of qualified job applicants.

recruiting
the process of developing a pool of qualified job applicants

Let's examine 2.1 **what job analysis is and how it is used in recruiting**, and 2.2 **how companies use internal recruiting and external recruiting to find qualified job applicants**.

2.1 Job Analysis and Recruiting

Job analysis is a "purposeful, systematic process for collecting information on the important work-related aspects of a job."[24] A job analysis typically collects four kinds of information:

- Work activities such as what workers do and how, when, and why they do it.
- The tools and equipment used to do the job.
- The context in which the job is performed, such as the actual working conditions or schedule.
- The personnel requirements for performing the job, meaning the knowledge, skills, and abilities needed to do a job well.[25]

job analysis
a purposeful, systematic process for collecting information on the important work-related aspects of a job

job description
a written description of the basic tasks, duties, and responsibilities required of an employee holding a particular job

job specifications
a written summary of the qualifications needed to successfully perform a particular job

Job analysis information can be collected by having job incumbents and/or supervisors complete questionnaires about their jobs, by direct observation, by interviews, or by filming employees as they perform their jobs.

Job descriptions and job specifications are two of the most important results of a job analysis. A **job description** is a written description of the basic tasks, duties, and responsibilities required of an employee holding a particular job. **Job specifications**, which are often included as a separate section of a job description, are a summary of the qualifications needed to successfully perform the job. Exhibit 10.2 shows a job

EXHIBIT **10.2**

Job Description and Job Specifications for a Helicopter Pilot for the City of Little Rock, Arkansas

Job Description for Helicopter Pilot

To provide assistance for air searches, river rescues, high-rise building rescues, and other assignments, by providing air survey and aviation response. Pilots a rotary-wing aircraft, serving as pilot or copilot, to assist in air searches, river rescues, high-rise building rescues, and other assignments. Ensures that aircraft is properly outfitted for each assignment (equipment, rigging tools, supplies, etc.). Performs preflight inspection of aircraft; checks rotors, fuel, lubricants, controls, etc. Prepares written reports on assignments; maintains flight logs. Obtains weather reports; determines to proceed with assignments given forecasted weather conditions. Operates a radio to maintain contact with and to report information to airport personnel and police department personnel.

Job Specifications for Helicopter Pilot

Must possess a valid Commercial Pilot's License for rotary-wing aircraft before employment and maintain licensure for the duration of employment in this position. Must have considerable knowledge of Federal Aviation Administration (FAA) laws and regulations, rotary-wing aircraft operating procedures, air traffic safety, flying procedures and navigational techniques, and FAA and police radio operation and procedures. Must have some knowledge of preventive maintenance methods, repair practices, safety requirements, and inspection procedures. Must have skill in the operation of a rotary-wing aircraft and radio equipment and the ability to conduct safety inspections of aircraft, to maintain aircraft maintenance logs and prepare reports, to detect and identify aircraft malfunction symptoms, to detect and recognize ground conditions and characteristics (utility line breaks, river currents, etc.), to read maps and air navigation charts, and to communicate effectively, both orally and in writing. Must have completed high school; at least one thousand hours of flight time experience in piloting rotary-wing aircraft; OR any equivalent combination of experience and training that provides the required knowledge, skills, and abilities.

Source: "Job Description: Helicopter Pilot," City of Little Rock, Arkansas, http://www.littlerock.org, 31 May 2003.

EXHIBIT 10.3

Importance of Job Analysis to Human Resource Management

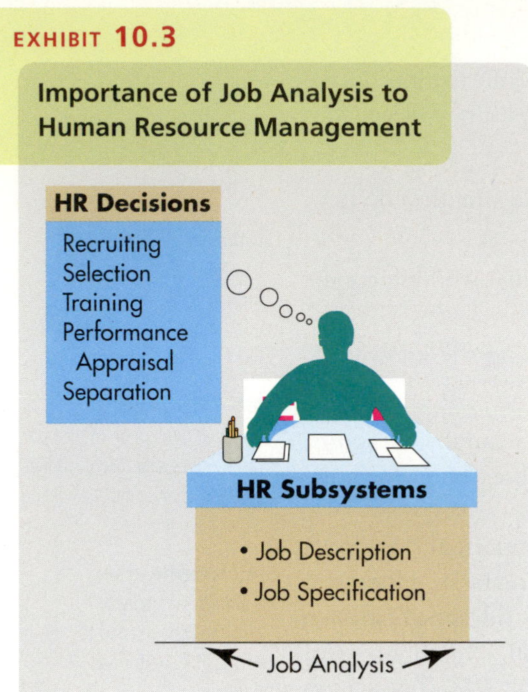

description and the job specifications for a helicopter pilot for the city of Little Rock, Arkansas.

Because a job analysis specifies what a job entails as well as the knowledge, skills, and abilities that are needed to do the job well, companies must complete a job analysis *before* beginning to recruit job applicants. Exhibit 10.3 shows that job analysis, job descriptions, and job specifications are the foundation on which all critical human resource activities are built. They are used during recruiting and selection to match applicant qualifications with the requirements of the job. Therefore, it is critically important that job descriptions be accurate. Job descriptions are also used throughout the staffing process to ensure that selection devices and the decisions based on these devices are job related. For example, the questions asked in an interview should be based on the most important work activities identified by a job analysis. Likewise, during performance appraisals, employees should be evaluated in areas that a job analysis has identified as the most important in a job.

Job analyses, job descriptions, and job specifications also help companies meet the legal requirement that their human resource decisions be job related. To be judged *job related*, recruitment, selection, training, performance appraisals, and employee separations must be valid and be directly related to the important aspects of the job as identified by a careful job analysis. In fact, in *Griggs v. Duke Power Co.* and *Albemarle Paper Co. v. Moody*, the U.S. Supreme Court stated that companies should use job analyses to help establish the job relatedness of their human resource procedures.[26] The EEOC's *Uniform Guidelines on Employee Selection Procedures* also recommend that companies base their human resource procedures on job analysis.

2.2 Internal Recruiting and External Recruiting

Internal recruiting is the process of developing a pool of qualified job applicants from people who already work in the company. Internal recruiting, sometimes called "promotion from within," improves employee commitment, morale, and motivation. Recruiting current employees also reduces recruitment startup time and costs, and because employees are already familiar with the company's culture and procedures, they are more likely to succeed in new jobs.

Job posting is a procedure for advertising job openings within the company to existing employees. A job description and requirements are typically posted on a bulletin board, in a company newsletter, or in an internal computerized job bank that is accessible only to employees. Job posting helps organizations discover hidden talent, allows employees to take responsibility for career planning, and makes it easier for companies to retain talented workers who are dissatisfied in their current jobs and would otherwise leave the company.[27] A *career path* is a planned sequence of jobs through which employees may advance within an organization. For example, a person who starts as a sales representative may move up to sales manager and then to district or regional sales manager. Career paths help employees focus on long-term goals and development while also helping companies increase employee retention.

internal recruiting
the process of developing a pool of qualified job applicants from people who already work in the company

External recruiting is the process of developing a pool of qualified job applicants from outside the company. External recruitment methods include advertising (newspapers, magazines, direct mail, radio, or television), employee referrals (asking current employees to recommend possible job applicants), walk-ins (people who apply on their own), outside organizations (universities, technical/trade schools, professional societies), employment services (state or private employment agencies, temporary help agencies, and professional search firms), special events (career conferences or job fairs), and Internet job sites. Which external recruiting method should you use? Studies show that employee referrals, walk-ins, newspaper advertisements, and state employment agencies tend to be used most frequently for office/clerical and production/service employees. By contrast, newspaper advertisements and college/university recruiting are used most frequently for professional/technical employees. When recruiting managers, organizations tend to rely most heavily on newspaper advertisements, employee referrals, and search firms.[28]

In the last decade, the biggest change in external recruiting has been the increased use of the Internet, which provides an inexpensive way to post very detailed openings. Because these sites attract so many applicants and offer so many services, companies save by finding qualified applicants without having to use more expensive recruitment and search firms, which typically charge one-third or more of a new hire's salary.[29]

Despite their many benefits, however, job websites have a significant drawback: Companies may receive hundreds, if not thousands, of applications from *unqualified* applicants. The sheer volume increases the importance of proper screening and selection. Many organizations avoid this problem by advertising job openings directly on their websites, assuming that the most qualified applicants will learn something about the company before applying. In fact, 60 percent of the people hired via the Internet have applied at a company website.

REVIEW 2

Recruiting

Recruiting is the process of finding qualified job applicants. The first step in recruiting is to conduct a job analysis to collect information about the important work-related aspects of the job. The job analysis is then used to write a job description of basic tasks, duties, and responsibilities and to write job specifications indicating the knowledge, skills, and abilities needed to perform the job. Job analyses, descriptions, and specifications help companies meet the legal requirement that their human resource decisions be job related. Internal recruiting, or finding qualified job applicants from inside the company, can be done through job posting and career paths. External recruiting, or finding qualified job applicants from outside the company, is done through advertising, employee referrals, walk-ins, outside organizations, employment services, special events, and Internet job sites. The Internet is a particularly promising method of external recruiting because of its low cost, wide reach, and ability to communicate and receive unlimited information.

3 Selection

Once the recruitment process has produced a pool of qualified applicants, the selection process is used to determine which applicants have the best chance of performing well on the job. When the East Providence, Rhode Island, Police Department

external recruiting
the process of developing a pool of qualified job applicants from outside the company

has job openings, it follows a "rule of three," meaning that no matter how many candidates it has for an opening, it looks at only the top three applicants as determined by a standardized written test. Those top three applicants for every position must then pass a physical fitness test and a background check. Every applicant who makes it that far is then put on a list of official candidates for police jobs for 2 years. Only the best candidates on that list participate in group interviews with the city manager, police chief, deputy chief, a police captain, and the department's personnel director and affirmative action officer, each of whom privately ranks the candidates after each interview. Applicants with the highest rankings from the group interviews are offered positions in the Police Academy. The remaining applicants from the group interviews may be considered two more times before being rejected.[30]

As this example illustrates, **selection** is the process of gathering information about job applicants to decide who should be offered a job. To make sure that selection decisions are accurate and legally defendable, the EEOC's *Uniform Guidelines on Employee Selection Procedures* recommend that all selection procedures be validated. **Validation** is the process of determining how well a selection test or procedure predicts future job performance. The better or more accurate the prediction of future job performance, the more valid a test is said to be. See the "What Really Works" feature later in this chapter for more on the validity of common selection tests and procedures.

Let's examine common selection procedures such as 3.1 **application forms and résumés**, 3.2 **references and background checks**, 3.3 **selection tests**, and 3.4 **interviews**.

3.1 Application Forms and Résumés

The first selection devices that most job applicants encounter when they seek a job are application forms and résumés. Both contain similar information about an applicant, such as name, address, job and educational history, and so forth. Though an organization's application form often asks for information already provided by the applicant's résumé, most organizations prefer to collect this information in their own format for entry into a human resource information system.

Employment laws apply to application forms just as they do to all selection devices. Application forms may ask applicants for only valid, job-related information. Nonetheless, application forms commonly ask applicants for non-job-related information such as marital status, maiden name, age, or date of high school graduation. Indeed, one study found that 73 percent of organizations had application forms that violated at least one federal or state law.[31] Exhibit 10.4 lists the kinds of information that companies may *not* request in application forms, during job interviews, or in any other part of the selection process. Courts will assume that you consider all of the information you request of applicants even if you don't. Be sure to ask only those questions that directly relate to the candidate's ability and motivation to perform the job.

Companies should also be aware that employment laws in other countries may differ from U.S. laws. For instance, employers in France may ask applicants for non-job-related personal information such as their age or the number of children. And most French employers expect applicants to include a picture with their résumé.[32] Consequently, companies should closely examine their application forms, interview questions, and other selection procedures for compliance with the law wherever they do business.

selection
the process of gathering information about job applicants to decide who should be offered a job

validation
the process of determining how well a selection test or procedure predicts future job performance. The better or more accurate the prediction of future job performance, the more valid a test is said to be

EXHIBIT 10.4

Topics That Employers Should Avoid in Application Forms, Interviews, or Other Parts of the Selection Process

1. *Children.* Don't ask applicants if they have children, plan to have them, or have or need child care. Questions about children can unintentionally single out women.
2. *Age.* Because of the Age Discrimination in Employment Act, employers cannot ask job applicants their age during the hiring process. Since most people graduate high school at the age of 18, even asking for high school graduation dates could violate the law.
3. *Disabilities.* Don't ask if applicants have physical or mental disabilities. According to the Americans with Disabilities Act, disabilities (and reasonable accommodations for them) cannot be discussed until a job offer has been made.
4. *Physical characteristics.* Don't ask for information about height, weight, or other physical characteristics. Questions about weight could be construed as leading to discrimination toward overweight people, who studies show are less likely to be hired in general.
5. *Name.* Yes, you can ask an applicant's name, but you cannot ask a female applicant for her maiden name because it indicates marital status. Asking for a maiden name could also lead to charges that the organization was trying to establish a candidate's ethnic background.
6. *Citizenship.* Asking applicants about citizenship could lead to claims of discrimination on the basis of national origin. However, according to the Immigration Reform and Control Act, companies may ask applicants if they have a legal right to work in the United States.
7. *Lawsuits.* Applicants may not be asked if they have ever filed a lawsuit against an employer. Federal and state laws prevent this to protect whistleblowers from retaliation by future employers.
8. *Arrest records.* Applicants cannot be asked about their arrest records. Arrests don't have legal standing. However, applicants can be asked whether they have been convicted of a crime.
9. *Smoking.* Applicants cannot be asked if they smoke. Smokers might be able to claim that they weren't hired because of fears of higher absenteeism and medical costs. However, they can be asked if they are aware of company policies that restrict smoking at work.
10. *AIDS/HIV.* Applicants can't be asked about AIDS, HIV, or any other medical condition. Questions of this nature would violate the Americans with Disabilities Act, as well as federal and state civil rights laws.

Source: J. S. Pouliot, "Topics to Avoid with Applicants," *Nation's Business* 80, no. 7 (1992): 57.

Résumés also pose problems for companies, but in a different way. Accu-Screen Inc. has kept records for 14 years on résumé falsification data and reports that approximately 43 percent of résumés and job applications contain false information. According to a study conducted by J.J. Keller & Associates, Inc., the nation's leading provider of risk and regulatory management solutions, 55 percent of human resource professionals have discovered lies on résumés or applications when conducting pre-employment background or reference checks.[33] Therefore, managers should verify

Doing the Right Thing

Don't Embellish Your Résumé

Your résumé is supposed to help you get the interview that can get you a job. So where do you draw the line between making yourself look attractive to a potential employer and lying? Despite the strong temptation to improve your odds of getting a job, embellishing your résumé is wrong. Moreover, the information on your résumé is legally binding. If you misrepresent information or lie on your résumé—and many people do—you're breaking the law and can be fired. But where should you draw the line? In general, if what you put on your résumé feels wrong, don't do it. More specifically, don't embellish job titles, responsibilities, employment dates, college degrees, certifications, general qualifications, or previous experience in any way. Do the right thing. Tell the truth on your résumé.[34]

the information collected via résumés and application forms by comparing it with additional information collected during interviews and other stages of the selection process, such as references and background checks, which are discussed next.

3.2 References and Background Checks

Nearly all companies ask an applicant to provide **employment references**, such as previous employers or coworkers, whom they can contact to learn more about the candidate. **Background checks** are used to verify the truthfulness and accuracy of information that applicants provide about themselves and to uncover negative, job-related background information not provided by applicants. Background checks are conducted by contacting "educational institutions, prior employers, court records, police and governmental agencies, and other informational sources, either by telephone, mail, remote computer access, or through in-person investigations."[35]

Unfortunately, employers are increasingly reluctant to provide references or background information for fear of being sued by previous employees for defamation.[36] If former employers provide potential employers with unsubstantiated information that damages applicants' chances of being hired, applicants can (and do) sue for defamation. As a result, 54 percent of employers will not provide information about previous employees.[37] Many provide only dates of employment, positions held, and date of separation.

employment references
sources such as previous employers or coworkers who can provide job-related information about job candidates

background checks
procedures used to verify the truthfulness and accuracy of information that applicants provide about themselves and to uncover negative, job-related background information not provided by applicants

specific ability tests (aptitude tests)
tests that measure the extent to which an applicant possesses the particular kind of ability needed to do a job well

3.3 Selection Tests

We're all aware that some people do well in jobs while other people do poorly, but how do you determine which category an applicant falls into? Selection tests give organizational decision makers a chance to know who will likely do well in a job and who won't. The basic idea behind selection testing is to have applicants take a test that measures something directly or indirectly related to doing well on the job. The selection tests discussed here are specific ability tests, cognitive ability tests, biographical data, personality tests, work sample tests, and assessment centers.

Specific ability tests measure the extent to which an applicant possesses the particular kind of ability needed to do a job well. Specific ability tests are also called

aptitude tests because they measure aptitude for doing a particular task well. For example, if you took the SAT to get into college, then you've taken the aptly named Scholastic Aptitude Test, which is one of the best predictors of how well students will do in college (i.e., scholastic performance). Specific ability tests also exist for mechanical, clerical, sales, and physical work. For example, clerical workers have to be good at accurately reading and scanning numbers as they type or enter data.

Cognitive ability tests measure the extent to which applicants have abilities in perceptual speed, verbal comprehension, numerical aptitude, general reasoning, and spatial aptitude. In other words, these tests indicate how quickly and how well people understand words, numbers, logic, and spatial dimensions. Whereas specific ability tests predict job performance in only particular types of jobs, cognitive ability tests accurately predict job performance in almost all kinds of jobs.[38] Why is this so? The reason is that people with strong cognitive or mental abilities are usually good at learning new things, processing complex information, solving problems, and making decisions, and these abilities are important in almost all jobs.[39] In fact, cognitive ability tests are almost always the best predictors of job performance. Consequently, if you were allowed to use just one selection test, a cognitive ability test would be the one to use (In practice, though, companies use a battery of different tests because doing so leads to much more accurate selection decisions.).[40]

Biographical data, or **biodata**, are extensive surveys that ask applicants questions about their personal backgrounds and life experiences. The basic idea behind biodata is that past behavior (personal background and life experience) is the best predictor of future behavior. For example, during World War II, the *U.S. AIR FORCE* had to test tens of thousands of men without flying experience, and do it quickly, to determine who was likely to be a good pilot. Since flight training took several months and was very expensive, selecting the right people for training was important. After examining extensive biodata, it found that one of the best predictors of success in flight school was whether students had ever built model airplanes that actually flew. This one biodata item was almost as good a predictor as the entire set of selection tests that the Air Force was using at the time.[41]

Most biodata questionnaires have over 100 items that gather information about habits and attitudes, health, interpersonal relations, money, what it was like growing up in your family (parents, siblings, childhood years, teen years), personal habits, current home (spouse, children), hobbies, education and training, values, preferences, and work.[42] In general, biodata are very good predictors of future job performance, especially in entry-level jobs.

You may have noticed that some of the information requested in biodata surveys also appears in Exhibit 10.4 as topics employers should avoid in applications, interviews, or other parts of the selection process. This information can be requested in biodata questionnaires provided the company can demonstrate that the information is job related (i.e., valid) and does not result in adverse impact against protected groups of job applicants. Biodata surveys should be validated and tested for adverse impact before they are used to make selection decisions.[43]

Personality is the relatively stable set of behaviors, attitudes, and emotions displayed over time that makes people different from each other. **Personality tests** measure the extent to which applicants possess different kinds of job-related personality dimensions. Of these, only conscientiousness, the degree to which someone

cognitive ability tests
tests that measure the extent to which applicants have abilities in perceptual speed, verbal comprehension, numerical aptitude, general reasoning, and spatial aptitude

biographical data (biodata)
extensive surveys that ask applicants questions about their personal backgrounds and life experiences

personality tests
tests that measure the extent to which applicants possess different kinds of job-related personality dimensions

Doing the Right Thing

Don't Use Psychics, Lie Detectors, or Handwriting Analysis to Make HR Decisions

The Coronado Bay Resort in San Diego hired a psychic to work with its 18-member management team as a way of "moving the managers to the next step." Seventy-five percent of the organizations in France and Switzerland use handwriting analysis for hiring and promotion decisions. In the past, employers in the United States regularly used polygraphs (lie detectors) for preemployment screening. What do these methods have in common? They don't work. For example, there is no scientific evidence that handwriting analysis works, yet managers continue to use it. Lie detectors are no more accurate than a coin flip in screening out unethical employees. Fortunately, the Employee Polygraph Protection Act now prevents organizations from using polygraphs for hiring and promotion decisions. As for psychics at work—well, enough said. So, when you're hiring and promoting people, do the right thing. Stay away from fads. Use the reliable, valid, scientifically proven selection and assessment procedures discussed here to hire the right workers and promote the right people into management.[45]

is organized, hardworking, responsible, persevering, thorough, and achievement oriented, predicts job performance across a wide variety of jobs.[44] Conscientiousness works especially well in combination with cognitive ability tests, allowing companies to select applicants who are organized, hardworking, responsible, and smart!

Work sample tests, also called *performance tests*, require applicants to perform tasks that are actually done on the job. So, unlike specific ability, cognitive ability, biographical data, and personality tests, which are indirect predictors of job performance, work sample tests directly measure job applicants' capability to do the job. For example, a computer-based work sample test has applicants assume the role of a real estate agent who must decide how to interact with virtual clients in a game-like scenario. As in real life, the clients can be frustrating, confusing, demanding, or indecisive. In one situation, the wife loves the virtual house but the husband hates it. The applicants, just like actual real estate agents, must demonstrate what they would do in these realistic situations.[46] This work sample simulation gives real estate companies direct evidence of whether applicants can do the job if they are hired. Work sample tests are generally very good at predicting future job performance; however, they can be expensive to administer and can be used for only one kind of job. For example, an auto dealership could not use a work sample test for mechanics as a selection test for sales representatives.

work sample tests tests that require applicants to perform tasks that are actually done on the job

Are tests perfect predictors of job performance? No, they aren't. Some people who do well on selection tests will do poorly in their jobs. Likewise, some people who do poorly on selection tests (and therefore weren't hired) would have been very good performers. Nonetheless, valid tests will minimize these selection errors (hiring people who should not have been hired and not hiring people who should have been hired) while maximizing correct selection decisions (hiring people who should have been hired and not hiring people who should not have been hired). In short, tests increase the chances that you'll hire the right person for the job, that is, someone who turns out to be a good performer. So, although tests aren't perfect, almost nothing predicts future job performance as well as the selection tests discussed here. For more on how well selection tests increase the odds of hiring the right person for the job, see the "What Really Works" feature.

3.4 Interviews

In **interviews**, company representatives ask applicants job-related questions to determine whether they are qualified for the job. Interviews are probably the most frequently used selection device. There are several basic kinds of interviews: unstructured, structured, and semistructured. In **unstructured interviews**, interviewers are free to ask applicants anything they want, and studies show that they do. Because interviewers often disagree about which questions should be asked during interviews, different interviewers tend to ask applicants very different questions.[47] Furthermore, individual interviewers even seem to have a tough time asking the same questions from one interview to the next. This high level of inconsistency lowers the validity of unstructured interviews as a selection device because comparing applicant responses can be difficult. As a result, while unstructured interviews do predict job performance with some success, they are about half as accurate as structured interviews at predicting which job applicants should be hired.[48]

By contrast, in **structured interviews**, standardized interview questions are prepared ahead of time so that all applicants are asked the same job-related questions.[49] Four kinds of questions are typically asked in structured interviews:

- Situational questions ask applicants how they would respond in a hypothetical situation ("What would you do if . . . ?"). These questions are more appropriate for hiring new graduates, who are unlikely to have encountered real-work situations because of their limited work experience.
- Behavioral questions ask applicants what they did in previous jobs that were similar to the job for which they are applying ("In your previous jobs, tell me about . . ."). These questions are more appropriate for hiring experienced individuals.
- Background questions ask applicants about their work experience, education, and other qualifications ("Tell me about the training you received at . . .").
- Job-knowledge questions ask applicants to demonstrate their job knowledge (e.g., nurses might be asked, "Give me an example of a time when one of your patients had a severe reaction to a medication. How did you handle it?").[50]

The primary advantage of structured interviews is that comparing applicants is much easier because they are all asked the same questions. Structuring interviews also ensures that interviewers ask only for important, job-related information. Not only are the accuracy, usefulness, and validity of the interview improved but the chances that interviewers will ask questions about topics that violate employment laws are reduced (go back to Exhibit 10.4 for a list of these topics).

interviews
a selection tool in which company representatives ask job applicants job-related questions to determine whether they are qualified for the job

unstructured interviews
interviews in which interviewers are free to ask the applicants anything they want

structured interviews
interviews in which all applicants are asked the same set of standardized questions, usually including situational, behavioral, background, and job-knowledge questions

what *really* works

Using Selection Tests to Hire Good Workers

Hiring new employees is always something of a gamble. When you say, "We'd like to offer you the job," you never know how it's going to turn out. Nonetheless, the selection tests discussed in this chapter can go a long way toward taking the gambling aspect out of the hiring process. Indeed, more than 1,000 studies based on over 100,000 study participants strongly indicate that selection tests can give employers a much better than average (50–50) chance of hiring the right workers. If you had odds like these working for you in Las Vegas, you'd make so much money the casinos wouldn't let you in the door.

Cognitive Ability Tests

There is a 76 percent chance that applicants who do well on cognitive ability tests will be much better performers in their jobs than applicants who do not do well on such tests.

COGNITIVE ABILITY TESTS

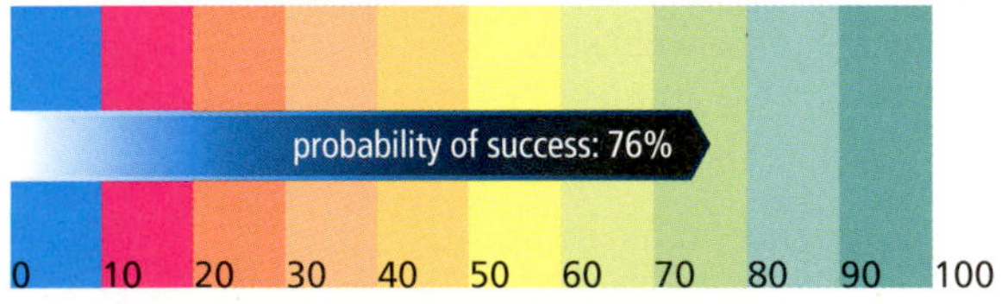

Work Sample Tests

There is a 77 percent chance that applicants who do well on work sample tests will be much better performers in their jobs than applicants who do not do well on such tests.

WORK SAMPLE TESTS

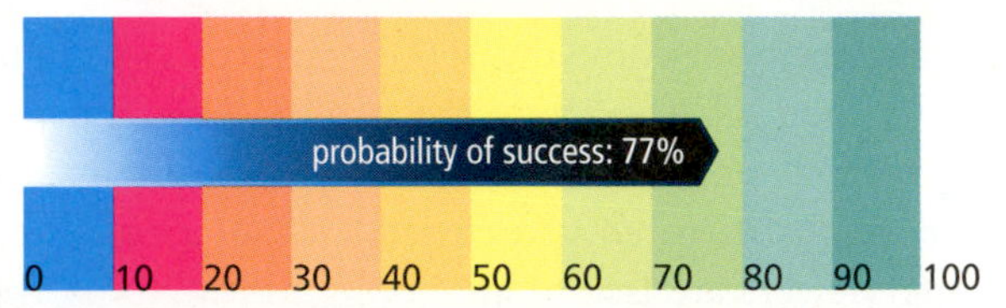

Assessment Centers

There is a 69 percent chance that applicants who do well on assessment center exercises will be much better managers than applicants who do not do well on such exercises.

ASSESSMENT CENTER TESTS

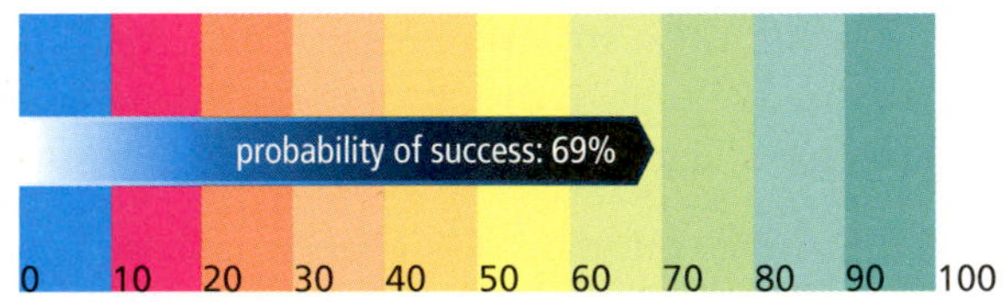

Structured Interviews

There is a 76 percent chance that applicants who do well in structured interviews will be much better performers in their jobs than applicants who do not do well in such interviews.

STRUCTURED INTERVIEWS

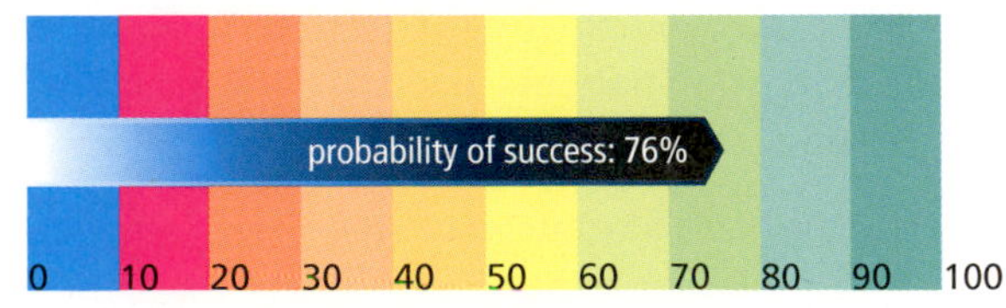

Cognitive Ability—Work Sample Tests

When deciding whom to hire, most companies use a number of tests to make even more accurate selection decisions. There is an 82 percent chance that applicants who do well on a combination of cognitive ability tests and work sample tests will be much better performers in their jobs than applicants who do not do well on both tests.

COGNITIVE ABILITY TESTS—WORK SAMPLE TESTS

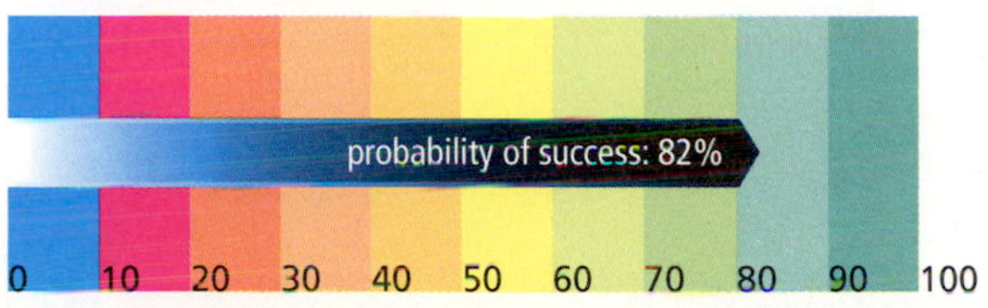

Cognitive Ability—Integrity Tests

There is an 83 percent chance that applicants who do well on a combination of cognitive ability tests and integrity tests (see Chapter 3 for a discussion of integrity tests) will be much better performers in their jobs than applicants who do not do well on both tests.

COGNITIVE ABILITY—INTEGRITY TESTS

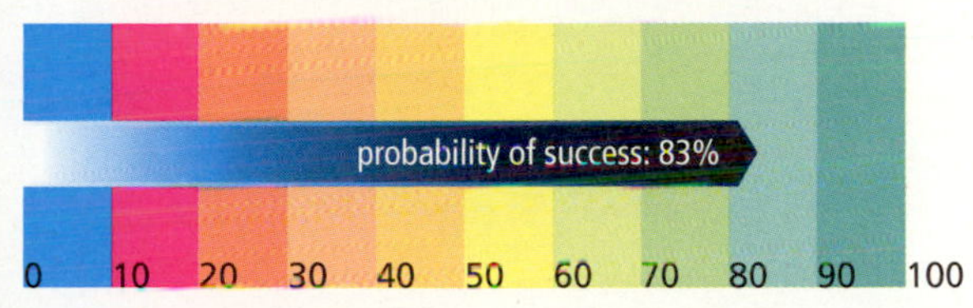

Cognitive Ability—Structured Interviews

There is an 82 percent chance that applicants who do well on a combination of cognitive ability tests and structured interviews will be much better performers in their jobs than applicants who do not do well on both tests.[51]

COGNITIVE ABILITY—STRUCTURED INTERVIEWS

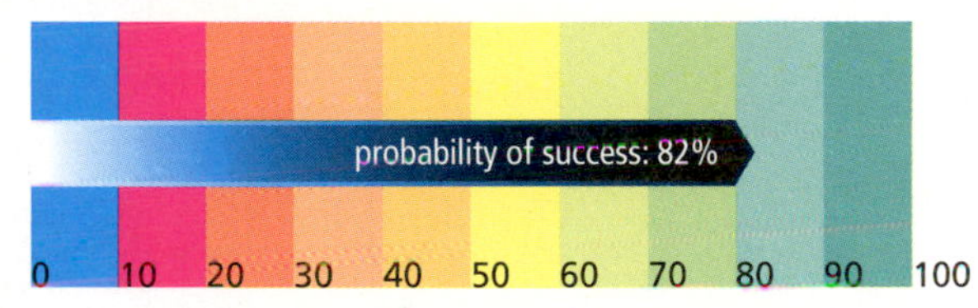

Semistructured interviews are in between structured and unstructured interviews. A major part of the semistructured interview (perhaps as much as 80 percent) is based on structured questions, but some time is set aside for unstructured interviewing to allow the interviewer to probe into ambiguous or missing information uncovered during the structured portion of the interview.

How well do interviews predict future job performance? Contrary to what you've probably heard, recent evidence indicates that even unstructured interviews do a fairly good job.[52] When conducted properly, however, structured interviews can lead to much more accurate hiring decisions than unstructured interviews. In some cases, the validity of structured interviews can rival that of cognitive ability tests. But even more important, because interviews are especially good at assessing applicants' interpersonal skills, they work particularly well with cognitive ability tests. Combining the two—using structured interviews together with cognitive ability tests to identify smart people who work well in conjunction with others—leads to even better selection decisions than using either alone.[53] Exhibit 10.5 provides a set of guidelines for conducting effective structured employment interviews.

EXHIBIT 10.5

Guidelines for Conducting Effective Structured Interviews

Interview Stage	What to Do
 **Planning the Interview**	• Identify and define the knowledge, skills, abilities, and other (KSAO) characteristics needed for successful job performance. • For each essential KSAO, develop key behavioral questions that will elicit examples of past accomplishments, activities, and performance. • For each KSAO, develop a list of things to look for in the applicant's responses to key questions.
 **Conducting the Interview**	• Create a relaxed, nonstressful interview atmosphere. • Review the applicant's application form, résumé, and other information. • Allocate enough time to complete the interview without interruption. • Put the applicant at ease; don't jump right into heavy questioning. • Tell the applicant what to expect. Explain the interview process. • Obtain job-related information from the applicant by asking those questions prepared for each KSAO. • Describe the job and the organization to the applicant. Applicants need adequate information to make a selection decision about the organization.
 **After the Interview**	• Immediately after the interview, review your notes and make sure they are complete. • Evaluate the applicant on each essential KSAO. • Determine each applicant's probability of success and make a hiring decision.

Source: B. M. Farrel, "The Art and Science of Employment Interviews," *Personnel Journal* 65 (1986): 91–94.

REVIEW 3

Selection

Selection is the process of gathering information about job applicants to decide who should be offered a job. Accurate selection procedures are valid, are legally defendable, and improve organizational performance. Application forms and résumés are the most common selection devices. Because many application forms request illegal, non-job-related information, and as many as one-third of job applicants falsify information on résumés, these procedures are often of little value in making hiring decisions. References and background checks can also be problematic, given that previous employers are reluctant to provide such information for fear of being sued for defamation. Unfortunately, without this information, other employers are at risk of negligent hiring lawsuits. Selection tests generally do the best job of predicting applicants' future job performance. In general, cognitive ability tests, work sample tests, biographical data, and assessment centers are the most valid tests, followed by personality tests and specific ability tests, which are still good predictors. Selection tests aren't perfect predictors of job performance, but almost nothing predicts future job performance as well as selection tests. The three kinds of job interviews are unstructured, structured, and semistructured interviews. Of these, structured interviews work best because they ensure that all applicants are consistently asked the same situational, behavioral, background, or job-knowledge questions, in the same order.

Developing Qualified Workers

According to a recent survey by Mercer Human Resource Consulting, 49 percent of companies are increasing their training budgets. For instance, *HEWLETT-PACKARD* recently increased its training budget to a whopping $300 million.[54] What is driving the infusion of dollars into training and development budgets of companies? Companies like HP recognize that it is more cost-efficient and competitive to develop talent from within rather than compete for talent on the open market.[55] In addition, according to the American Society for Training and Development, a typical investment in training increases productivity by an average of 17 percent, reduces employee turnover, and makes companies more profitable.[56]

Giving employees the knowledge and skills they need to improve their performance is just the first step in developing employees, however. The second step—and not enough companies do this—is giving employees formal feedback about their actual job performance. A CEO of a large telecommunications company hired an outside consultant to assess and coach (provide feedback to) the company's top 50 managers. To the CEO's surprise, 75 percent of those managers indicated that the feedback they received from the consultant regarding their strengths and weaknesses was the only substantial feedback they had received about their performance in the last 5 years. On a more positive note, as a result of that feedback, two-thirds of the managers then took positive steps to improve their skills, knowledge, and job performance and expressed a clear desire for more feedback, especially from their boss, the CEO.[57] So in today's competitive business environment, even top managers understand the importance of formal performance feedback to their growth and development.

After reading the next two sections, you should be able to:

4 describe how to determine training needs and select the appropriate training methods.

5 discuss how to use performance appraisal to give meaningful performance feedback.

4 Training

Training means providing opportunities for employees to develop the job-specific skills, experience, and knowledge they need to do their jobs or improve their performance. American companies spend more than $60 billion a year on training.

training
developing the skills, experience, and knowledge employees need to perform their jobs or improve their performance

To make sure those training dollars are well spent, companies need to 4.1 **select appropriate training methods**, and 4.2 **evaluate training**.

4.1 Training Methods

Assume that you're a training director for a major oil company and that you're in charge of making sure all employees know how to respond effectively in case of an oil spill.[58] Exhibit 10.6 lists a number of training methods you could use: films and videos, lectures, planned readings, case studies, coaching and mentoring, group discussions, on-the-job training, role-playing, simulations and games, vestibule training, and computer-based learning. Which method would be best?

To choose the best method, you should consider a number of factors, such as the number of people to be trained, the cost of training, and the objectives of the training. For instance, if the training objective is to impart information or knowledge to trainees, then you should use films and videos, lectures, and planned readings. In our example, trainees might read a manual or attend a lecture about how to protect a shoreline to keep it from being affected by the spill.

If developing analytical and problem-solving skills is the objective, then use case studies, coaching and mentoring, and group discussions. In our example, trainees might view a video documenting how a team handled exposure to hazardous substances, talk with first responders, and discuss what they would do in a similar situation.

If practicing, learning, or changing job behaviors is the objective, then use on-the-job training, role-playing, simulations and games, and vestibule training. In our example, trainees might participate in a mock shoreline cleanup to learn what to do in the event oil comes to shore. This simulation could take place on an actual shoreline or on a video-game-like virtual shoreline.

If training is supposed to meet more than one of these objectives, then your best choice may be to combine one of the previous methods with computer-based training. *CDW* (Computer Discount Warehouse) now uses avatar-based training. If you've ever played a video game, you've encountered an avatar, which is a computerized depiction of a person. In CDW's sales course, an avatar describes a situation, such as an unhappy customer whose computer won't connect to the office network. Next, a picture of the customer appears on the screen, accompanied by audio of the customer speaking. Finally, with help from the avatar (just double click if you need it), the employee taking the training decides what to do and then receive feedback from the avatar and another response from his customer.[59]

These days, many companies are adopting Internet training, or "e-learning." E-learning can offer several advantages. Because employees don't need to leave their jobs, travel costs are greatly reduced. Also, because employees can take training modules when it is convenient (i.e., they don't have to fall behind at their jobs to attend week-long training courses), workplace productivity should increase and employee stress should decrease.

There are, however, several disadvantages to e-learning. First, despite its increasing popularity, it's not always the appropriate training method. E-learning can be a good way to impart information, but it isn't always as effective for changing job behaviors or developing problem-solving and analytical skills. Second, e-learning requires a significant investment in computers and high-speed Internet connections for all employees. Finally, though e-learning can be faster, many employees find it so

EXHIBIT 10.6

Training Objectives and Methods

Training Objective	Training Method
Impart Information and Knowledge	• **Films and videos.** Films and videos share information, illustrate problems and solutions, and effectively hold trainees' attention. • **Lectures.** Trainees listen to instructors' oral presentations. • **Planned readings.** Trainees read about concepts or ideas before attending training.
Develop Analytical and Problem-Solving Skills	• **Case studies.** Cases are analyzed and discussed in small groups. The cases present a specific problem or decision, and trainees develop methods for solving the problem or making the decision. • **Coaching and mentoring.** Coaching and mentoring of trainees by managers involves informal advice, suggestions, and guidance. This method is helpful for reinforcing other kinds of training and for trainees who benefit from support and personal encouragement. • **Group discussions.** Small groups of trainees actively discuss specific topics. The instructor may perform the role of discussion leader.
Practice, Learn, or Change Job Behaviors	• **On-the-job training (OJT).** New employees are assigned to experienced employees. The trainee learns by watching the experienced employee perform the job and eventually by working alongside the experienced employee. Gradually, the trainee is left on his or her own to perform the job. • **Role-playing.** Trainees assume job-related roles and practice new behaviors by acting out what they would do in job-related situations. • **Simulations and games.** Experiential exercises place trainees in realistic job-related situations and give them the opportunity to experience a job-related condition in a relatively low-cost setting. The trainee benefits from "hands-on experience" before actually performing the job where mistakes may be more costly. • **Vestibule training.** Procedures and equipment similar to those used in the actual job are set up in a special area called a vestibule. The trainee is then taught how to perform the job at his or her own pace without disrupting the actual flow of work, making costly mistakes, or exposing the trainee and others to dangerous conditions.
Impart Information and Knowledge; Develop Analytical and Problem-Solving Skills; and Practice, Learn, or Change Job Behaviors	• **Computer-based learning.** Interactive videos, software, CD-ROMs, personal computers, teleconferencing, and the Internet may be combined to present multimedia-based training.

Source: A. Fowler, "How to Decide on Training Methods," *People Management* 25, no. 1 (1995): 36.

boring and unengaging that they may choose to do their jobs rather than complete e-learning courses when sitting alone at their desks. E-learning may become more interesting, however, as more companies incorporate game-like features such as avatars and competition into their e-learning courses.

4.2 Evaluating Training

After selecting a training method and conducting the training, the last step is to evaluate the training. Training can be evaluated in four ways: on *reactions* (how satisfied trainees were with the program), on *learning* (how much employees improved their knowledge or skills), on *behavior* (how much employees actually changed their on-the-job behavior because of training), or on *results* (how much training improved job performance, such as increased sales or quality, or decreased costs).[60] In general, training provides meaningful benefits for most companies if it is done well. For example, a study by the American Society for Training and Development shows that a training budget as small as $680 per employee can increase a company's total return on investment by 6 percent.[61]

REVIEW 4

Training

Training is used to give employees the job-specific skills, experience, and knowledge they need to do their jobs or improve their job performance. To make sure training dollars are well spent, companies need to determine specific training needs, select appropriate training methods, and then evaluate the training. Selection of an appropriate training method depends on a number of factors, including the number of people to be trained, the cost of training, and the objectives of the training. If training is supposed to meet more than one of these objectives, then it may be best to combine one of the previous methods with computer-based training. Training can be evaluated on reactions, learning, behavior, or results.

5 Performance Appraisal

Performance appraisal is the process of assessing how well employees are doing their jobs. Most employees and managers intensely dislike the performance appraisal process. One manager says, "I hate annual performance reviews. I hated them when I used to get them, and I hate them now that I give them. If I had to choose between performance reviews and paper cuts, I'd take paper cuts every time. I'd even take razor burns and the sound of fingernails on a blackboard."[62] Unfortunately, attitudes like this are all too common. In fact, 70 percent of employees are dissatisfied with the performance appraisal process in their companies. Likewise, according to the Society for Human Resource Management, 90 percent of human resource managers are dissatisfied with the performance appraisal systems used by their companies.[63]

Performance appraisals are used for four broad purposes: making administrative decisions (e.g., pay increase, promotion, retention), providing feedback for employee development (e.g., performance feedback, developing career plans), evaluating human resource programs (e.g., validating selection systems), and for documentation purposes (e.g., documenting performance ratings and decisions based on those ratings).[64]

performance appraisal
the process of assessing how well employees are doing their jobs

Let's explore how companies can avoid some of these problems with performance appraisals by 5.1 **accurately measuring job performance**, and 5.2 **effectively sharing performance feedback with employees**.

5.1 Accurately Measuring Job Performance

Workers often have strong doubts about the accuracy of their performance appraisals—and they may be right. For example, it's widely known that assessors are prone to errors when rating worker performance. Three of the most common rating errors are central tendency, halo, and leniency. *Central tendency error* occurs when assessors rate all workers as average or in the middle of the scale. *Halo error* occurs when assessors rate all workers as performing at the same level (good, bad, or average) in all parts of their jobs. *Leniency error* occurs when assessors rate all workers as performing particularly well. One of the reasons managers make these errors is that they often don't spend enough time gathering or reviewing performance data.

One of the ways companies try to improve performance appraisal measures is to use as many objective performance measures as possible. **Objective performance measures** are measures of performance that are easily and directly counted or quantified. Common objective performance measures include output, scrap, waste, sales, customer complaints, and rejection rates. But when objective performance measures aren't available (and frequently they aren't), subjective performance measures have to be used instead. **Subjective performance measures** require that someone judge or assess a worker's performance. The most common kind of subjective performance measure is the graphic rating scale (GRS) shown in Exhibit 10.7. Graphic rating scales are most widely used because they are easy to construct, but they are very susceptible to rating errors.

A popular alternative to graphic rating scales is the **behavior observation scale (BOS)**. BOS requires raters to rate the frequency with which workers perform specific behaviors representative of the job dimensions that are critical to successful job performance. Exhibit 10.7 shows a BOS for two important job dimensions for a retail salesperson: customer service and money handling. Notice that each dimension lists several specific behaviors characteristic of a worker who excels in that dimension of job performance. (Normally, the scale would list 7 to 12 items per dimension, not 3, as in the exhibit.) Not only do BOSs work well for rating critical dimensions of performance, but studies also show that managers strongly prefer BOSs for giving performance feedback; accurately differentiating between poor, average, and good workers; identifying training needs; and accurately measuring performance.

The second approach to improving the measurement of workers' job performance is **rater training**. The most effective is frame-of-reference training, in which a group of trainees learn how to do performance appraisals by watching a videotape of an employee at work. Next, they evaluate the performance of the person in the videotape. A trainer (an expert in the subject matter) then shares his or her evaluations, and trainees' evaluations are compared with the expert's. The expert then explains the rationales behind his or her evaluations. This process is repeated until the difference in evaluations given by trainees and evaluations by the expert are minimized. The underlying logic behind the frame-of-reference training is that by adopting the frame of reference used by an expert, trainees will be able to accurately observe, judge, and use the scale to evaluate performance of others.[65]

objective performance measures
measures of job performance that are easily and directly counted or quantified

subjective performance measures
measures of job performance that require someone to judge or assess a worker's performance

behavior observation scales (BOSs)
rating scales that indicate the frequency with which workers perform specific behaviors that are representative of the job dimensions critical to successful job performance

rater training
training performance appraisal raters in how to avoid rating errors and increase rating accuracy

EXHIBIT 10.7

Subjective Performance Appraisal Scales

Graphic Rating Scale

Example 1:

	Very Poor	Poor	Average	Good	Very Good
1. Quality of work performed is........	1	2	3	4	5

Example 2:

	Very Poor (20% errors)	Poor (15% errors)	Average (10% errors)	Good (5% errors)	Very Good (less than 5% errors)
2. Quality of work performed is........	1	2	3	4	5

Behavioral Observation Scale

Dimension: Customer Service

	Almost Never				Almost Always
1. Greets customers with a smile and a "hello."............................	1	2	3	4	5
2. Calls other stores to help customers find merchandise that is not in stock.	1	2	3	4	5
3. Promptly handles customer concerns and complaints.	1	2	3	4	5

Dimension: Money Handling

	Almost Never				Almost Always
1. Accurately makes change from customer transactions.	1	2	3	4	5
2. Accounts balance at the end of the day, no shortages or surpluses.	1	2	3	4	5
3. Accurately records transactions in computer system.	1	2	3	4	5

5.2 Sharing Performance Feedback

After gathering accurate performance data, the next step is to share performance feedback with employees. Unfortunately, even when performance appraisal ratings are accurate, the appraisal process often breaks down at the feedback stage.

Employees become defensive and dislike hearing any negative assessments of their work, no matter how small. Managers become defensive, too, and dislike giving appraisal feedback as much as employees dislike receiving it. One manager says, "I myself don't go as far as those who say performance reviews are inherently destructive and ought to be abolished, but I agree that the typical annual-review process does nothing but harm. It creates divisions. It undermines morale. It makes people angry, jealous, and cynical. It unleashes a whole lot of negative energy, and the organization gets nothing in return."[66]

What can be done to overcome the inherent difficulties in performance appraisal feedback sessions? Since performance appraisal ratings have traditionally been the judgments of just one person, the boss, one possibility is to use **360-degree feedback**. In this approach, feedback comes from four sources: the boss, subordinates, peers and coworkers, and the employees themselves. The data, which are obtained anonymously (except for the boss's), are compiled into a feedback report comparing the employee's self-ratings with those of the boss, subordinates, and peers and coworkers. Usually, a consultant or human resource specialist discusses the results with the employee. The advantage of 360-degree programs is that negative feedback ("You don't listen") is often more credible when it comes from several people.

A word of caution, though: About half of the companies using 360-degree feedback for performance appraisal now use the feedback only for developmental purposes. They found that sometimes when raises and promotions were on the line, peers and subordinates would give high ratings in order to get high ratings from others. Ed Smiley, a manager who works for a manufacturer, says they stopped using 360-degree feedback at his company because of too much "mutual back-scratching." Said Smiley, "What you don't get is true feedback."[67] Conversely, in some situations employees distorted ratings to harm competitors or help people they liked. A senior manager at a New York City marketing company agrees, saying that 360-degree feedback "also allows people to vent their frustrations and anger on bosses and colleagues in an insensitive way."[68] On the other hand, studies clearly show that ratees prefer to receive feedback from multiple raters, so 360-degree feedback is likely to continue to grow in popularity.[69]

Herbert Meyer, who has been studying performance appraisal feedback for more than 30 years, recommends a list of topics to discuss in performance appraisal feedback sessions.[70] Furthermore, managers can do three different things to make performance reviews more comfortable and productive. First, they should separate developmental feedback, which is designed to improve future performance, from administrative feedback, which is used as a reward for past performance, such as for raises. When managers give developmental feedback, they're acting as coaches, but when they give administrative feedback, they're acting as judges. These roles, coaches and judges, are clearly incompatible. As coaches, managers are encouraging, pointing out opportunities for growth and improvement, and employees are typically open and receptive to feedback. But as judges, managers are evaluative, and employees are typically defensive and closed to feedback.

360-degree feedback
a performance appraisal process in which feedback is obtained from the boss, subordinates, peers and coworkers, and the employees themselves

Second, Meyer suggests that performance appraisal feedback sessions be based on self-appraisals, in which employees carefully assess their own strengths, weaknesses, successes, and failures in writing. Because employees play an active role in the review of their performance, managers can be coaches rather than judges. Also, because the focus is on future goals and development, both employees and managers are likely to be more satisfied with the process and more committed to future plans and changes. And, because the focus is on development and not administrative assessment, studies show that self-appraisals lead to more candid self-assessments than traditional supervisory reviews.[71] Finally, what people do with the performance feedback they receive really matters. A study of 1,361 senior managers found that managers who reviewed their 360-degree feedback with an executive coach (hired by the company) were more likely to set specific goals for improvement, ask their bosses for ways to improve, and subsequently improve their performance.[72]

REVIEW 5

Performance Appraisal

Most employees and managers intensely dislike the performance appraisal process. Some of the problems associated with appraisals can be avoided, however, by accurately measuring job performance and effectively sharing performance feedback with employees. Organizations should develop good performance appraisal scales and preferably use behavior observation scales (BOSs). They should train raters to accurately evaluate performance, perhaps by providing frame-of-reference training. They should impress upon managers the value of providing feedback in a clear, consistent, and fair manner and of setting goals and monitoring progress toward those goals.

One way to overcome the inherent difficulties in performance appraisal feedback is to provide 360-degree feedback, in which feedback is obtained from four sources: the boss, subordinates, peers and coworkers, and the employees themselves. Feedback tends to be more credible if it is heard from several sources. Finally, especially for managers, it's helpful to have people discuss the feedback they received with executive coaches or the people who provided it.

Keeping Qualified Workers

At *PENSKE AUTOMOTIVE GROUP*, which has 300 car dealerships worldwide, 8 percent of CEO Roger Penske's bonus is tied to keeping employee turnover below 31 percent. Pep Boys, a car parts retail chain, does the same, making 10 percent of its middle managers' pay contingent on low employee turnover. Likewise, ExlService Holdings, an Indian-based outsourcing company, links 30 percent of its lower-level managers' pay to employee turnover. Why link managers' pay to employee turnover? According to Tony Pordon, senior vice president at Penske Automotive, "We believe that employee turnover is a symptom of bigger problems at the dealership level."[73] Mark Royal, a consultant for the Hay Group, which specializes in employee compensation, further explains that linking managers' pay to turnover, "is a recognition, on the one hand, of people as a driver of business success. It also reflects a recognition that turnover is costly."[74]

After reading the next two sections, you should be able to:

6 describe basic compensation strategies and explain how they affect human resource practice.

7 discuss the four kinds of employee separations: termination, downsizing, retirements, and turnover.

6 Compensation

Compensation includes both the financial and the nonfinancial rewards that organizations give employees in exchange for their work.

Let's learn more about compensation by examining the 6.1 **compensation decisions that managers must make**, and 6.2 **the role that employment benefits play in compensating today's employees**.

6.1 Compensation Decisions

There are four basic kinds of compensation decisions: pay level, pay variability, pay structure, and employment benefits. We'll discuss employment benefits in the next subsection.[75]

Pay-level decisions are decisions about whether to pay workers at a level that is below, above, or at current market wages. Companies use job evaluation to set their pay structures. **Job evaluation** determines the worth of each job by determining the market value of the knowledge, skills, and requirements needed to perform it. After conducting a job evaluation, most companies try to pay the going rate, meaning the current market wage. There are always companies, however, whose financial situation causes them to pay considerably less than current market wages. While a director of a child-care center in Vermont may make up to $25 an hour, teachers make only $9–11 an hour.[76] According to the American Federation of Teachers, the average annual wage for early child-care workers is $18,820, and hourly wages have increased only 39 cents in the last 25 years.[77] Some companies choose to pay above-average wages to attract and keep employees. *Above-market wages* can attract a larger, more qualified pool of job applicants, increase the rate of job acceptance, decrease the time it takes to fill positions, and increase the time that employees stay.[78]

Pay-variability decisions concern the extent to which employees' pay varies with individual and organizational performance. Linking pay to performance is intended to increase employee motivation, effort, and job performance. Piecework, sales commissions, profit sharing, employee stock ownership plans, and stock options are common pay-variability options. For instance, under **piecework** pay plans, employees are paid a set rate for each item produced up to some standard (e.g., 35 cents per item produced for output up to 100 units per day). Once productivity exceeds the standard, employees are paid a set amount for each unit of output over the standard (e.g., 45 cents for each unit above 100 units). Under a sales **commission** plan, salespeople are paid a percentage of the purchase price of items they sell. The more they sell, the more they earn.

Because pay plans such as piecework and commissions are based on individual performance, they can reduce the incentive that people have to work together. Therefore, companies also use group incentives (discussed in Chapter 9) and organizational incentives, such as profit sharing, employee stock ownership plans, and stock options, to encourage teamwork and cooperation.

With **profit sharing**, employees receive a portion of the organization's profits over and above their regular compensation. The more profitable the company, the more profit is shared. Employees of *DELTA AIRLINES* share profits on 5.5 percent of eligible earnings. In a good year, Delta pays $158 million in profit sharing to its employees.[79]

Employee stock ownership plans (ESOPs) compensate employees by awarding them shares of company stock in addition to their regular compensation. Joe

compensation
the financial and nonfinancial rewards that organizations give employees in exchange for their work

job evaluation
a process that determines the worth of each job in a company by evaluating the market value of the knowledge, skills, and requirements needed to perform it

piecework
a compensation system in which employees are paid a set rate for each item they produce

commission
a compensation system in which employees earn a percentage of each sale they make

profit sharing
a compensation system in which a company pays a percentage of its profits to employees in addition to their regular compensation

employee stock ownership plan (ESOP)
a compensation system that awards employees shares of company stock in addition to their regular compensation

© BIG CHEESE PHOTO/JUPITER IMAGES

Hernandez, a 41-year-old migrant worker at *MCKAY NURSERY* in Waterloo, Wisconsin, makes $20,000 a year working from April to November. But Joe also gets an additional 20 to 25 percent in company stock. So far, he's accumulated more than $80,000 through the company ESOP.[80]

Stock options give employees the right to purchase shares of stock at a set price. Options work like this. Let's say you are awarded the right (or option) to buy 100 shares of stock from the company for $5 a share. If the company's stock price rises to $15 a share, you can exercise your options and make $1,000. When you exercise your options, you pay the company $500 (100 shares at $5 a share), but, because the stock is selling for $15 in the stock market, you can sell your 100 shares for $1,500 and make $1,000. Of course, as the company's profits and share values increase, stock options become even more valuable to employees. Stock options have no value, however, if the company's stock falls below the option "grant price," the price at which the options have been issued to you. To learn more about ESOPs and stock options, see the National Center for Employee Ownership (***http://www.nceo.org***).

Pay-structure decisions are concerned with internal pay distributions, meaning the extent to which people in the company receive very different levels of pay.[81] *Hierarchical pay structures* involve big differences from one pay level to another. The highest pay levels are for people near the top of the pay distribution. The basic idea behind hierarchical pay structures is that large differences in pay between jobs or organizational levels should motivate people to work harder to obtain those higher-paying jobs. Many publicly owned companies have hierarchical pay structures by virtue of the huge amounts they pay their top managers and CEOs. For example, the average CEO now makes 364 times as much as the average worker, down from 525 times the pay of average workers just 8 years ago. But with CEO pay packages averaging $18.8 million per year and average workers earning just $36,140, the difference is still incredible and can have a significant effect on employee morale.[82]

By contrast, *compressed pay structures* typically have fewer pay levels and smaller differences in pay between levels. Pay is less dispersed and more similar across jobs in the company. The basic idea behind compressed pay structures is that similar pay levels should lead to higher levels of cooperation, feelings of fairness and a common purpose, and better group and team performance.

stock options
a compensation system that gives employees the right to purchase shares of stock at a set price, even if the value of the stock increases above that price

So should companies choose hierarchical or compressed pay structures? The evidence isn't straightforward, but studies seem to indicate that there are significant problems with the hierarchical approach. The most damaging finding is that there appears to be little link between organizational performance and the pay of top managers.[83] Furthermore, studies of professional athletes indicate that hierarchical pay structures (e.g., paying superstars 40 to 50 times as much as the lowest-paid athlete on the team) hurt the performance of teams and individual players.[84] For now, it seems that hierarchical pay structures work best for independent work, where it's easy to determine the contributions of individual performers and little coordination with others is needed to get the job done. In other words, hierarchical pay structures work best when clear links can be drawn between individual performance and individual rewards. By contrast, compressed pay structures, in which everyone receives similar pay, seem to work best for interdependent work, which requires employees to work together. Some companies are pursuing a middle ground: combining hierarchical and compressed pay structures by giving ordinary workers the chance to earn more through ESOPs, stock options, and profit sharing.

6.2 Employment Benefits

Employment benefits include virtually any kind of compensation other than direct wages paid to employees.[85] Three employee benefits are mandated by law: Social Security, workers' compensation insurance, and unemployment insurance. To attract and retain a good workforce, however, most organizations offer a wide variety of benefits, including retirement plans and pensions, paid holidays, paid vacations, sick leave, health insurance, life insurance, dental care, eye care, day-care facilities, paid personal days, legal assistance, physical fitness facilities, educational assistance, and discounts on company products and services. While the cost of employee benefits varies by company and by industry, according to the Bureau of Labor Statistics, on average, benefits cost organizations about 29.3 percent of their payroll.[86] Managers should understand that although benefits are unlikely to improve employee motivation and performance, they do affect job satisfaction, employee decisions about staying with or leaving the company, and the company's attractiveness to job applicants.[87] One way that organizations make their benefit plans more attractive is by offering **cafeteria benefit plans** or **flexible benefit plans**, which allow employees to choose which benefits they receive, up to a certain dollar value.[88] Many cafeteria or flexible benefit plans start with a core of benefits, such as health insurance and life insurance, which are available to all employees. Then employees are allowed to select the other benefits that best fit their needs, up to a predetermined dollar amount. Some organizations allow employees to choose from several packages of benefits. The packages are of equivalent value but offer a different mix of benefits. For example, older employees may prefer more benefit dollars spent on retirement plans, while younger employees may prefer additional vacation days. The drawback to flexible benefit plans has been the high cost of administering them. With advances in information processing technology and HRISs (Human Resource Information Systems), however, the cost has begun to drop in recent years.

employment benefits
a method of rewarding employees that includes virtually any kind of compensation other than wages or salaries

cafeteria benefit plans (flexible benefit plans)
plans that allow employees to choose which benefits they receive, up to a certain dollar value

REVIEW 6

Compensation

Compensation includes both the financial and the nonfinancial rewards that organizations give employees in exchange for their work. There are four basic kinds of compensation decisions: pay level, pay variability, pay structure, and employment benefits. Pay-level decisions determine whether workers will receive wages below, above, or at current market levels. Pay-variability decisions concern the extent to which pay varies with individual and organizational performance. Piecework, sales commissions, profit sharing, employee stock ownership plans, and stock options are common pay-variability options. Pay-structure decisions concern the extent to which people in the company receive very different levels of pay. Hierarchical pay structures work best for independent work, while compressed pay structures work best for interdependent work.

Employee benefits include virtually any kind of compensation other than direct wages paid to employees. Flexible or cafeteria benefit plans offer employees a wide variety of benefits, improve job satisfaction, increase the chances that employees will stay with companies, and make organizations more attractive to job applicants. The cost of administering flexible benefit plans has begun to drop in recent years.

7 Employee Separations

Employee separation is a broad term covering the loss of an employee for any reason. *Involuntary separation* occurs when employers terminate or lay off employees. *Voluntary separation* occurs when employees quit or retire. Because employee separations affect recruiting, selection, training, and compensation, organizations should forecast the number of employees they expect to lose through terminations, layoffs, turnover, or retirements when doing human resource planning.

Let's explore employee separation by examining 7.1 **terminations**, 7.2 **downsizing**, and 7.3 **turnover**.

7.1 Terminating Employees

The words "You're fired!" may have never been directed at you, but lots of people hear them, as more than 400,000 people get fired from their jobs every year. Getting fired is a terrible thing, but many managers make it even worse by bungling the firing process, needlessly provoking the person who was fired and unintentionally inviting lawsuits. Manager Craig Silverman had to fire the head of a company that his organization had just acquired. He was specifically instructed to invite her to a meeting, which would require her to travel halfway across the country and then fire her immediately on arrival. He said, "I literally had to tell the car service to wait. I don't think it ever entered [her] mind that [she] would be terminated."[89] A computer systems engineer was fired on "Take Your Daughter to Work Day," with his eight-year-old daughter sitting next to him in the human resource manager's office. He and his daughter were both escorted from the building.[90] How would you feel if you had been fired in one of these ways? Though firing is never pleasant (and managers hate firings nearly as much as employees do), managers can do several things to minimize the problems inherent in firing employees.

First, in most situations, firing should not be the first option. Instead, employees should be given a chance to change their behavior. When problems arise, employees should have ample warning and must be specifically informed as to the nature and seriousness of the trouble they're in. After being notified, they should be given sufficient time to change. If the problems continue, the employees should again be counseled about their job performance, what could be done to improve it, and the possible consequences if things don't change (such as a written reprimand, suspension without pay, or firing). Sometimes this is enough to solve the problem. If the problem isn't corrected after several rounds of warnings and discussions, however, the employee may be terminated.[91]

employee separation the voluntary or involuntary loss of an employee

Second, employees should be fired only for a good reason. Employers used to hire and fire employees under the legal principle of employment at will, which allowed them to fire employees for a good reason, a bad reason, or no reason at all. (Employees could also quit for a good reason, a bad reason, or no reason whenever they desired.) As employees began contesting their firings in court, however, the principle of wrongful discharge emerged. **Wrongful discharge** is a legal doctrine that requires employers to have a job-related reason to terminate employees. In other words, like other major human resource decisions, termination decisions should be made on the basis of job-related factors such as violating company rules or consistently poor performance. And with former employees winning 68 percent of wrongful discharge cases and the average wrongful termination award at $532,000 and climbing, managers should record the job-related reasons for termination, document specific instances of rule violations or continued poor performance, and keep notes and documents from the counseling sessions held with employees.[92]

Management Trend:

Social media is useful for findings new friends, keeping in touch with old ones, and now as IBM, Microsoft, and others are showing, establishing an "alumni" network. The recession has forced many companies to let go of highly skilled employees. But rather than severing all connections with them, companies are viewing them as "alumni," and encouraging them to maintain ties with the company, and with each other, through social media sites. These networks allow the recently unemployed to establish contacts, get the latest industry updates and job leads. The company, meanwhile, benefits by keeping in touch with people who could become business partners later, or even return to work for the company.

Source: Stephen Baker. "You're Fired—But Stay in Touch." *BusinessWeek.* May 4, 2009. 54–55.

Finally, to reduce the chances of a wrongful discharge suit, employees should always be fired in private. State the reason for discharge, but don't go into detail or engage in a lengthy discussion with the employee. Make every attempt to be as kind and respectful as possible when informing someone that he or she is being fired. It is permissible and sometimes a good idea to have a witness present. This person should be from human resources or part of the employee's chain of command, such as the supervisor's boss. Company security may be nearby but should not be in the room unless the employee has made direct threats toward others. Finally, managers should be careful not to publicly criticize the employee who has just been fired, as this can also lead to a wrongful discharge lawsuit. In general, unless someone has a "business reason to know" why an employee was fired, the reasons and details related to the firing should remain confidential.[93]

7.2 Downsizing

Downsizing is the planned elimination of jobs in a company. Whether it's because of cost cutting, declining market share, previous overaggressive hiring and growth, or outsourcing, companies typically eliminate 1 million to 1.9 million jobs a year.[94] Two-thirds of companies that downsize will downsize a second time within a year. Does downsizing work? In theory, downsizing is supposed to lead to higher productivity

wrongful discharge
a legal doctrine that requires employers to have a job-related reason to terminate employees

downsizing
the planned elimination of jobs in a company

EXHIBIT 10.8

Guidelines for Conducting Layoffs

1. Provide clear reasons and explanations for the layoffs.
2. To avoid laying off employees with critical or irreplaceable skills, knowledge, and expertise, get input from human resources, the legal department, and several levels of management.
3. Train managers in how to tell employees that they are being laid of (stay calm; make the meeting short; explain why, but don't be personal; and provide information about immediate concerns, such as benefits, job search, and collecting personal goods).
4. Give employees the bad news early in the day, and try to avoid laying off employees just before holidays.
5. Provide outplacement services and counseling to help laid-off employees find new jobs.
6. Communicate with survivors to explain how the company and their jobs will change.

Source: M. Boyle, "The Not-So-Fine Art of the Layoff," *Fortune,* 19 March 2001, 209.

and profits, better stock performance, and increased organizational flexibility. However, numerous studies demonstrate that it doesn't. For instance, a 15-year study found that downsizing 10 percent of a company's workforce produced only a 1.5 percent decrease in costs, that firms that downsized increased their stock price by only 4.7 percent over 3 years, compared with 34.3 percent for firms that didn't, and that profitability and productivity were generally not improved.[95] Downsizing can also result in the loss of skilled workers who would be expensive to replace when the company grows again.[96] These results make it clear that the best strategy is to conduct effective human resource planning and avoid downsizing altogether. Indeed, downsizing should always be a last resort.

If companies do find themselves in financial or strategic situations where downsizing is required for survival, however, they should train managers in how to break the news to downsized employees, have senior managers explain in detail why downsizing is necessary, and time the announcement so that employees hear it from the company and not from other sources, such as TV or newspaper reports.[97] Finally, companies should do everything they can to help downsized employees find other jobs. One of the best ways to do this is to use **outplacement services** that provide employment counseling for people faced with downsizing. Outplacement services often include advice and training in preparing résumés, getting ready for job interviews, and even identifying job opportunities in other companies. Fifty-five percent of companies provide outplacement services for laid-off employees, 76 percent provide extended health coverage, and 45 percent offer extended access to employee assistance programs.[98] Exhibit 10.8 provides additional guidelines for conducting layoffs.

Companies also need to pay attention to the survivors, the employees remaining after layoffs have occurred. University of Pennsylvania management professor Peter Cappelli says that survivors "may feel like they could just as easily be the next person laid off."[99] Lori Stewart Coletti, director of client services at Elaine Construction, a Newton, Massachusetts-based firm, said, "The general feeling is, 'Could I be next?' That's the level of uncertainty that you really have to combat."[100]

outplacement services employment-counseling services offered to employees who are losing their jobs because of downsizing

employee turnover loss of employees who voluntarily choose to leave the company

7.3 Employee Turnover

Employee turnover is the loss of employees who voluntarily choose to leave the company. In general, most companies try to keep the rate of employee turnover low to reduce recruiting, hiring, training, and replacement costs. Not all kinds of employee turnover are bad for organizations, however. In fact, some turnover can actually be good. **Functional turnover** is the loss of poor-performing employees who choose to leave the organization.[101] Functional turnover gives the organization a chance to replace poor performers with better workers. In fact, one study found that simply replacing poor-performing leavers with average workers would increase the revenues produced by retail salespeople in an upscale department store by $112,000 per person per year.[102] By contrast, **dysfunctional turnover**, the loss of high performers who choose to leave, is a costly loss to the organization.

Employee turnover should be carefully analyzed to determine whether good or poor performers are choosing to leave the organization. If the company is losing too many high performers, managers should determine the reasons and find ways to reduce the loss of valuable employees. The company may have to raise salary levels, offer enhanced benefits, or improve working conditions to retain skilled workers. One of the best ways to influence functional and dysfunctional turnover is to link pay directly to performance. A study of four salesforces found that when pay was strongly linked to performance via sales commissions and bonuses, poor performers were much more likely to leave (that is, functional turnover). By contrast, poor performers were much more likely to stay when paid large, guaranteed monthly salaries and small sales commissions and bonuses.[103]

REVIEW 7

Employee Separations

Employee separation is the loss of an employee; separation can occur voluntarily or involuntarily. Before firing or terminating employees, managers should give employees a chance to improve. If firing becomes necessary, it should be done because of job-related factors, such as violating company rules or consistently performing poorly. Downsizing is supposed to lead to higher productivity and profits, better stock performance, and increased organizational flexibility, but studies show that it doesn't. The best strategy is to downsize only as a last resort. Companies that do downsize should offer outplacement services to help employees find other jobs. Companies generally try to keep the rate of employee turnover low to reduce costs. Functional turnover can be good for organizations, however, because it offers the chance to replace poor performers with better workers. Managers should analyze employee turnover to determine who is resigning and take steps to reduce the loss of good performers.

functional turnover
loss of poor-performing employees who voluntarily choose to leave a company

dysfunctional turnover
loss of high-performing employees who voluntarily choose to leave a company

MANAGEMENT Team Decision

Training for Great Service

At one time or another, almost every retailer claims that their first and only priority is to make the customer happy. Few, however, can duplicate what Nordstrom does. For the Seattle-based upscale retailer, "the customer is always right" is not just a promotional motto but a way of life that guides the organization. The entire company is directed toward one goal—catering to the needs of customers. Sales associates are given incredible freedom to do what is needed to make customers happy—refunding a purchase made years ago, personally delivering items to airports and hotels for busy customers, and even lending out jewelry for a customer who was attending a party. The importance of making a customer happy even extends into store inventory, as managers try to stock every conceivable size, color, and variant of an item so that customers will always find what they are looking for. And in the rare instance that they can't, employees will call other Nordstrom stores, or even competitor stores, to track it down.

This emphasis on customer service has even spawned an urban legend. The story goes that many years ago, a man walked into a Nordstrom store in Alaska (or Seattle) with two snow tires. Nordstrom, of course, doesn't sell tires (snow or otherwise); the man had bought them from a tire store that had recently closed, the site of which was taken over by Nordstrom. Nonetheless, the man took the tires to a counter, said that he was unhappy with them, and asked for a full refund. The sales associate, eager to please, gave it to him.

As the HR team of Nordstrom, you face a particular challenge—you need to create a team that is not only skilled for the job, but has the personality, attitude, and motivation to provide the kind of superior customer service that spawns urban legends. Form a group with three or four other students and discuss how you would approach staffing and training issues at Nordstrom by answering the following questions.

Questions

1. Can a friendly, customer-oriented attitude be developed in a person? Can Nordstrom "train" employees to prioritize making customers happy, or is it purely a matter of personality?
2. What kind of selection tools would you use to find people who would fit Nordstrom's culture of customer service?

Practice being a MANAGER

Legal Recruiting

Managing human resources in today's complex business and legal environment is not easy. Not only must companies hire the creative and hard-working employees who will fuel growth and competitive advantage but they must be careful to do so legally and ethically. Unfair discrimination in any HR process will result in poor placement, turnover, and legal woes. This exercise will give you some practice in navigating the challenges of legal and effective recruitment and selection of employees.

STEP 1 Get into groups. Your professor will assign you to groups of four or five students. One student will be given the role of HR attorney for the applicants, two students the role of nursing shift (day/night) managers at Montclair Hospital, and the remaining student(s) will be assigned the role of senior hospital administrator at Montclair Hospital.

Scenario: Montclair Hospital needs to hire new nurses. In fact, the hospital is in a bit of a crisis. Three nurses were recently fired for using drugs while on duty. In the following days, a journalist uncovered that two of these nurses were convicted felons. As if these problems were not enough, nurse turnover is up 20 percent this year over last, and productivity of the remaining staff is substandard. Absences are also up lately, particularly those related to child-care or elder-care issues.

Both the day and the night nursing shift managers need to hire some quality nurses—and fast. Hospital administrators have made it abundantly clear that they do not want a repeat of the headline "Felons and Drug Users among Montclair Nursing Staff." Your compensation and benefits are competitive, and, with the exception of the recent news coverage, your hospital enjoys a strong reputation. The nursing labor market is tight (there are fewer nurses than openings), and most new hires are recent nursing school graduates.

Nursing shift managers need to work together to develop a plan to achieve the following:

1. Hire top-flight nurses to fill vacancies left by recent firings and resignations.
2. Stem the turnover of quality nurses already employed by Montclair.
3. Reduce absenteeism, especially unplanned "emergency" absences that wreak havoc with planning the work of an upcoming shift.

STEP 2A Outline a plan. The day and the night nursing shift managers should work together to sketch out a plan for making progress on the three concerns of Montclair Hospital administration (hiring, turnover, absenteeism). Some elements of this plan might include

- Deciding where and how to recruit top nursing candidates
- Screening applicants to reduce risks of turnover, criminal/behavioral problems, and disruptive absenteeism
- Dealing with the turnover, absenteeism, and productivity problems of existing nursing staff

STEP 2B Review the plan. Students in the roles of hospital administrator and HR attorney should listen to the nursing managers as they sketch out their plans. Do not offer comments unless one of the managers asks you for your input. Take careful notes regarding what you hear, paying particular attention to concerns and questions. Those in the HR attorney role should consider what you hear from the perspective of both potential applicants (and litigants) and Montclair Hospital (defense of HR practices).

Are the nursing managers developing a plan likely to successfully address the three concerns related to hiring, turnover, and absenteeism? Why or why not? Do you hear anything that might raise a legal concern (such as inappropriate interview questions, possible discrimination)?

STEP 3 Debrief as a class. Students should open with comments from each perspective: (1) HR attorneys, (2) hospital administrators, and (3) nursing shift managers. What are some of the specific concerns or questions that arose in your mind as you played your particular role? What are some of the tensions that face the managers and administrators in this situation? How might the HR system of a hospital be improved? Why might nurses represent a particularly challenging set of HR concerns?

Interview Anxiety

How would you feel if you got a call to interview for your dream job? Excited? Nervous? Or downright panicked? It's not uncommon to get butterflies in your stomach at the prospect of a job interview, but some candidates have more than weak knees and sweaty palms. Complete the assessment below by indicating the extent to which you agree with each of the following statements.[104] Your score will be a baseline as you begin working on the skills you'll need during your job hunt. Try not to spend too much time on any one item, and be sure to answer all the questions. Use this scale for your responses:

1. Strongly disagree
2. Disagree
3. Neutral
4. Agree
5. Strongly agree

1. I become so apprehensive in job interviews that I am unable to express my thoughts clearly.
   1 2 3 4 5
2. I often feel uneasy about my appearance when I am being interviewed for a job.
   1 2 3 4 5
3. While taking a job interview, I become concerned that the interviewer will perceive me as socially awkward.
   1 2 3 4 5
4. In job interviews, I get very nervous about whether my performance is good enough.
   1 2 3 4 5
5. During job interviews, my hands shake.
   1 2 3 4 5
6. I get so anxious while taking job interviews that I have trouble answering questions that I know.
   1 2 3 4 5
7. Before a job interview I am so nervous that I spend an excessive amount of time on my appearance.
   1 2 3 4 5
8. I become very uptight about having to socially interact with a job interviewer.
   1 2 3 4 5
9. I am overwhelmed by thoughts of doing poorly when I am in job interview situations.
   1 2 3 4 5
10. My heartbeat is faster than usual during job interviews.
    1 2 3 4 5
11. During job interviews, I often can't think of a thing to say.
    1 2 3 4 5
12. In job interviews, I worry that the interviewer will focus on what I consider to be my least attractive physical features.
    1 2 3 4 5
13. I get afraid about what kind of personal impression I am making on job interviews.
    1 2 3 4 5
14. I worry that my job interview performance will be lower than that of other applicants.
    1 2 3 4 5

15. It is hard for me to avoid fidgeting during a job interview.
1 2 3 4 5

16. I feel that my verbal communication skills are strong.
1 2 3 4 5

17. If I do not look my absolute best in a job interview, I find it very hard to be relaxed.
1 2 3 4 5

18. During a job interview, I worry that my actions will not be considered socially appropriate.
1 2 3 4 5

19. During a job interview, I am so troubled by thoughts of failing that my performance is reduced.
1 2 3 4 5

20. Job interviews often make me perspire (e.g., sweaty palms and underarms).
1 2 3 4 5

21. During job interviews, I find it hard to understand what the interviewer is asking me.
1 2 3 4 5

22. I feel uneasy if my hair is not perfect when I walk into a job interview.
1 2 3 4 5

23. I worry about whether job interviewers will like me as a person.
1 2 3 4 5

24. During a job interview, I worry about what will happen if I don't get the job.
1 2 3 4 5

25. My mouth gets very dry during job interviews.
1 2 3 4 5

26. I find it easy to communicate my personal accomplishments during a job interview.
1 2 3 4 5

27. During a job interview, I worry about whether I have dressed appropriately.
1 2 3 4 5

28. When meeting a job interviewer, I worry that my handshake will not be correct.
1 2 3 4 5

29. While taking a job interview, I worry about whether I am a good candidate for the job.
1 2 3 4 5

30. I often feel sick to my stomach when I am interviewed for a job.
1 2 3 4 5

SCORING

Reverse your score on items 16 and 26. That is, if you wrote in a "5," change it to a "1" and vice versa; if you wrote in a "4," change it to a "2" and vice versa.

TOTAL = ______

You can find the interpretation of your score at: login.cengagebrain.com.

Reel to Real

Biz Flix

© GREENLIGHT

Played

Thief-for-hire Ray Burns (Mick Rossi) just served 8 years of prison time thanks to a crooked cop (Vinnie Jones). Now he's back on the streets and plans to settle the score. *Played* is a fast-moving crime thriller from 2006. The film is a gritty look inside London's criminal underground. In this clip from the movie, a shipment of heroin is arriving from Amsterdam, and they're making plans to pick it up. But first they need to assemble a team.

What to Watch for and Ask Yourself

1. How would you write the job description for the recruits who will carry out the task discussed in this scene?
2. Would you say this is an example of internal or external recruiting?
3. Is compensation discussed?

Management Workplace

© CENGAGE

The Maine Media Workshops

The Maine Media Workshops began in 1973 as a kind of summer camp for both amateurs and professionals who wanted to hone their filmmaking, photography, and writing skills. Over the years, students have had the opportunity to work with and learn from some of Hollywood's heavy hitters, such as the Oscar-winning cinematographer Vilmos Zsigmond and the Emmy-winning director Alan Myerson. In this video, the MMW staff members talk about one of the biggest challenges they face now that the program hosts hundreds of courses throughout the year: hiring part-time instructors to teach them. The director of education, Elizabeth Greenburg, explains, "Just because somebody is good at making images doesn't make him or her a good teacher. What makes a good teacher is someone who is generous enough and open enough to share her life, her experience, her career and her knowledge 24/7 with students."

What to Watch for and Ask Yourself

1. What are some of the unique challenges the Maine Media Workshops staff members face when hiring instructors?
2. What kind of training would you suggest for part-time instructors, if any?
3. What kinds of information would be included in a job analysis for part-time instructors at MMW?

Part Four
Leading

This chapter covers the basics of motivation—effort, needs, and intrinsic and extrinsic rewards. As we progress through the chapter, we build on that basic model of motivation by adding equity, expectancy, reinforcement, and goal-setting theories. There's also a summary of practical, theory-based actions that managers can take to motivate their workers.

© AP IMAGES/PRNEWSFOTO/ANNTAYLOR

Chapter Eleven
Motivation

This chapter discusses what leadership is, what characteristics are common of leaders, and what leaders do that makes them different from people who aren't leaders. We examine major contingency theories of leadership and review strategic leadership issues, such as charismatic and transformational leadership.

© GEORGE ROSE/GETTY IMAGES

Chapter Twelve
Leadership

This chapter examines perception in communication, the communication process, and the different kinds of organizational communication. You'll also learn about effective one-on-one communication as well as techniques for organization-wide communication.

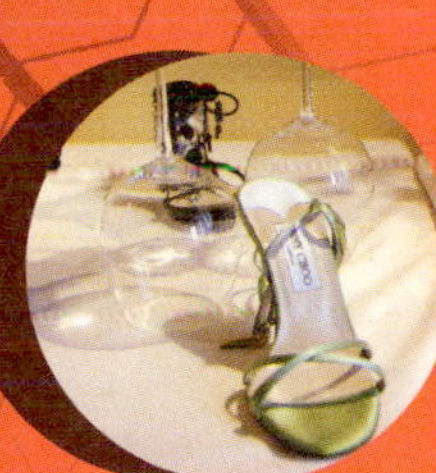

© AMANDA EDWARDS/GETTYIMAGES

Chapter Thirteen
Communication

Chapter Eleven
Motivation

OUTLINE

Experience Management
Explore the four levels of learning by doing the simulation module on motivation.

© ISTOCKPHOTO.COM/ ANN MARIE KURTZ

Pod Nod
Mini lecture reviews all the learning points in the chapter.

© ISTOCKPHOTO.COM/ MAGNET CREATIVE

Reel to Real
Biz Flix is a scene from *Friday Night Lights*. Management Workplace is a segment on Flight 001.

© ISTOCKPHOTO.COM/ CRAFTVISION

Self Test
10 quiz questions, 11 exhibit worksheets, and PowerPoints for quick review.

© ISTOCKPHOTO.COM/ DIJITAL FILM

What Would You Do?

Ann Taylor Headquarters, New York, New York.[1]

It's been a tough 18 months for *ANN TAYLOR*. When the recession blew in like a hurricane, the subsequent 19 percent drop in sales resulted in thousands of job cuts and 117 store closings. Six months and an additional 56 store closings later, you finished the year with a $334 million loss, telling investors, "While this economic crisis was felt across all demographics, the aspirational luxury consumer was particularly hard hit, including the professional working woman, the core client of our Ann Taylor division." Six months later, you made what you hoped were your last cuts, eliminating more jobs, mostly at headquarters, and closing 30 more stores. Sales are now 43 percent below a year ago, which were already off considerably because of the recession. But this time, using the term "self-inflicted," you don't blame the economy to account for these latest results—you blame yourself and your management team.

With this last set of closings and cuts, you believe that costs are finally in line. The key to recovery, therefore, is increasing Ann Taylor's top line revenues by growing same-store sales, the most common measure of retail performance in which each store's sales are compared to its sales from a year ago, with the results averaged across stores to produce an overall measure of increasing or decreasing same-store sales. So, you turn to your stores to figure out why sales have dropped so drastically. One problem is simply the line of clothes offered in your stores. Sales data indicated that customers were snapping up higher priced and higher quality items whenever you stocked them, so the company debuted its Ann Taylor Collection, a line of 50 upscale items that are about 40 percent more expensive than the typical clothing sold in your stores. The timing, just 6 months before the recession, however, was terrible. Now you've hired a new designer and asked her to trim prices but deliver greater value.

You also suspect that there might be issues with the effort being put forth in your stores. For example, it wasn't uncommon for employees to come in 2 hours before opening and then spend 1 hour drinking coffee and discussing the latest TV shows or movies. There are also problems with staffing not matching up with sales. For decades, your managers have done their store schedules by hand, balancing associates' work preferences against trends in daily sales from the previous year. Scheduling this way left you with way too many associates on the floor during the slow part of the day and too few when things got busy. Other retailers, like Gap and The Limited, have addressed this issue through customer counting and workforce management. Rather than daily sales figures, customer counting tracks the number of customers in terms of walk-ins and purchases in 15-minute increments throughout the day, thus helping determine when stores are busiest, how long customers spend in the store, whether staffing is optimum (too few, too many, or just right), and the conversion rates, the percentage of visitors who actually purchase something. Workforce management, in turn, uses those data to schedule the highest performing employees during stores' busiest times. If you're not a top performer, you're scheduled during slower sales periods.

What steps might you take to increase efficiency in your stores, that is, to have staff associates be more productive so you can increase sales without increasing costs? How would you measure efficiency gains and what would you ask associates to do differently to increase their efforts? Second, should Ann Taylor adopt customer counting and workforce management? What advantages and disadvantages do you see for the company, its managers, and its sales associates? Finally, what effect might workforce management have on employee turnover and on your ability to attract top-notch sales associates? Likewise, what effects will it have on customer satisfaction? Overall would it work?

If you were the CEO of Ann Taylor, what would you do?

What makes people happiest and most productive at work? Is it money, benefits, opportunities for growth, interesting work, or something else altogether? And if people desire different things, how can a company keep everyone motivated? It takes insight and hard work to motivate workers to join the company, perform well, and then stay with the company.

This chapter begins by reviewing the basics of motivation—effort, needs, and intrinsic and extrinsic rewards. We will start with a basic model of motivation and add to it as we progress through each section in the chapter. Next, we will explore how employees' equity perceptions and reward expectations affect their motivation. If you're familiar with the phrase "perception is reality," you're off to a good start in understanding the importance of perceptions and expectations in motivation. The third part of the chapter reviews the role that rewards and goals play in motivating employees. You'll see that finding the right combination of goals and rewards is much harder in practice than it looks. The chapter finishes with a summary of practical, theory-based actions that managers can take to motivate their workers.

What Is Motivation?

motivation
the set of forces that initiates, directs, and makes people persist in their efforts to accomplish a goal

Motivation is the set of forces that initiates, directs, and makes people persist in their efforts to accomplish a goal.[2] *Initiation of effort* is concerned with the choices that people make about how much effort to put forth in their jobs ("Do I really knock myself out for these performance appraisals or just do a decent job?"). *Direction of effort* is concerned with the choices that people make in deciding where to put forth effort in their jobs ("I should be spending time with my high-dollar accounts instead of learning this new computer system!"). *Persistence of effort* is concerned with the choices that people make about how long they will put forth effort in their jobs before reducing or eliminating those efforts ("I'm only halfway through the project, and I'm exhausted. Do I plow through to the end, or just call it quits?"). As Exhibit 11.1 shows, initiation, direction, and persistence are at the heart of motivation.

EXHIBIT 11.1

The Components of Motivation

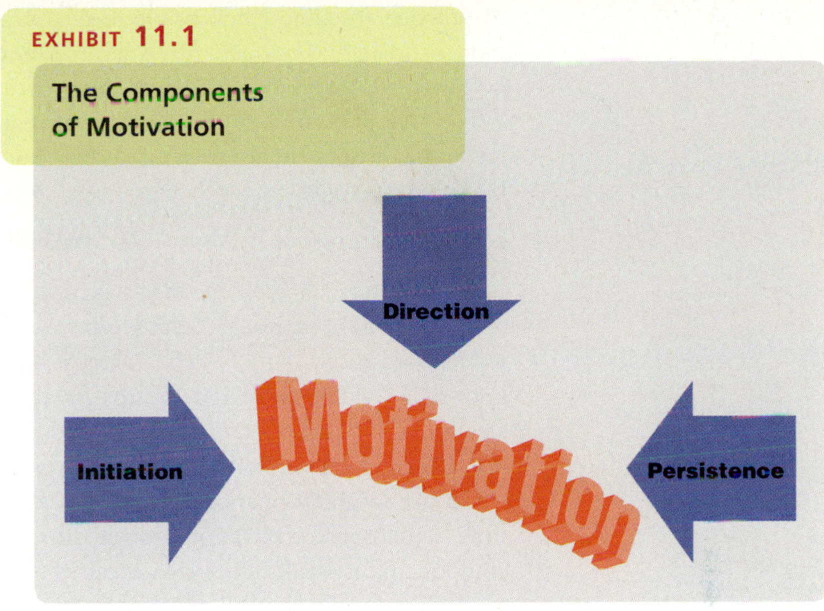

After reading the next section, you should be able to:

1 explain the basics of motivation.

1 Basics of Motivation

Nobody picks their salary and their bonus, right? But what if your boss let you do just that? At San Francisco-based *SKYLINE CONSTRUCTION*, Vice President Mark Trento and Senior Project Manager Adam Chelini were allowed, along with 13 others, to choose their salaries, which had to be between $125,000 and $150,000. Choosing a higher salary meant Trento and Chelini would get a smaller bonus and less overall compensation. By contrast, choosing a smaller salary would give them the opportunity—but no guarantee—to earn a larger bonus and higher overall compensation.[3] If you were in their shoes, which would you choose? A lower bonus but the security of a higher salary, or the smaller salary with potential for a larger bonus and higher overall compensation? Which would motivate you more? Why? What motivates people to take one option versus the other? Answering questions like these is at the heart of figuring out how best to motivate people at work.

Let's learn more about motivation by building a basic model of motivation out of 1.1 **effort and performance**, 1.2 **need satisfaction**, and 1.3 **extrinsic and intrinsic rewards** and then discussing 1.4 **how to motivate people with this basic model of motivation**.

1.1 Effort and Performance

When most people think of work motivation, they think that working hard (effort) should lead to a good job (performance). Exhibit 11.2 shows a basic model of work motivation and performance, displaying this process. The first thing to notice about Exhibit 11.2 is that this is a basic model of work motivation *and* performance.

In practice, it's almost impossible to talk about one without mentioning the other. Not surprisingly, managers often assume motivation to be the only determinant of performance, saying things such as "Your performance was really terrible last quarter. What's the matter? Aren't you as motivated as you used to be?" In fact, motivation is just one of three primary determinants of job performance. In industrial psychology, job performance is frequently represented by this equation:

Job Performance = Motivation × Ability × Situational Constraints

In this formula, *job performance* is how well someone performs the requirements of the job. *Motivation*, as defined above, is effort, the degree to which someone works hard to do the job well. *Ability* is the degree to which workers possess the knowledge, skills, and talent needed to do a job well. And *situational constraints* are factors beyond the control of individual employees, such as tools, policies, and resources that have an effect on job performance.

Since job performance is a multiplicative function of motivation times ability times situational constraints, job performance will suffer if any one of these components is weak. Does this mean that motivation doesn't matter? No, not at all. It just means that all the motivation in the world won't translate into high performance when you have little ability and high situational constraints.

1.2 Need Satisfaction

In Exhibit 11.2, we started with a very basic model of motivation in which effort leads to job performance. But managers want to know, "What leads to effort?" and they will try almost anything they can to find the answer. For example, at *SAS*, the leading maker of statistical software, employees can earn "SAS bucks" for free on-site haircuts, drop their cars off to be washed and detailed and their clothes to be altered or dry-cleaned, use the free fitness center, or drop their children off at the on-campus daycare center.[4] At Seattle-based *ZILLOW*, an online real-estate valuation service, teams had to work overtime to add new features to the company's website. So the company added foosball, Ping-Pong, and air-hockey tables and free all-you-can-drink soft drinks, juice, and milk to its downtown offices.[5] *ENVISION TECHNOLOGY*, a Seattle software company, offers a variety of health-oriented perks, including on-site massages and "Business Boxes" of fresh fruit and healthy snacks.[6]

needs
the physical or psychological requirements that must be met to ensure survival and well-being

EXHIBIT 11.2

A Basic Model of Work Motivation and Performance

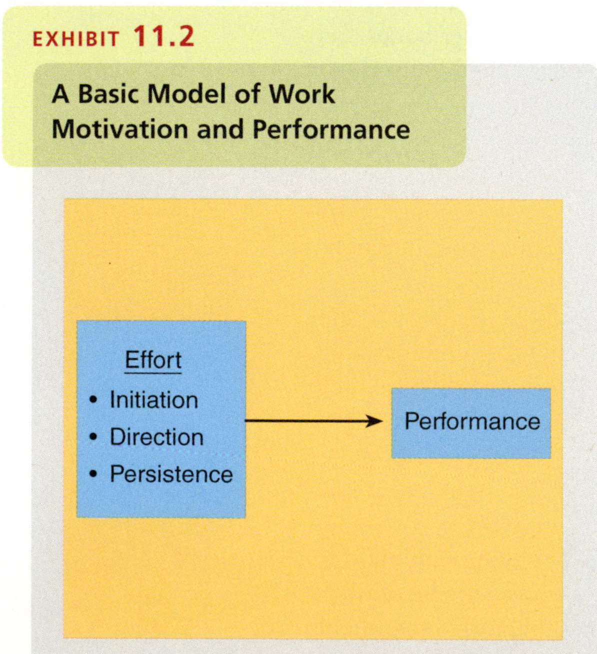

Needs are the physical or psychological requirements that must be met to ensure survival and well-being.[7] As shown on the left side of Exhibit 11.3, a person's unmet need creates an uncomfortable, internal state of tension that must be resolved. For example, if you normally skip breakfast, but then have to work through lunch, chances are you'll be so hungry by late afternoon that the only thing you'll be motivated to do is find something to eat. So, according to needs theories, people are motivated by unmet needs. But once a need is met, it no longer motivates. When this occurs, people become satisfied, as shown on the right side of Exhibit 11.3.

EXHIBIT **11.3**

Adding Need Satisfaction to the Model

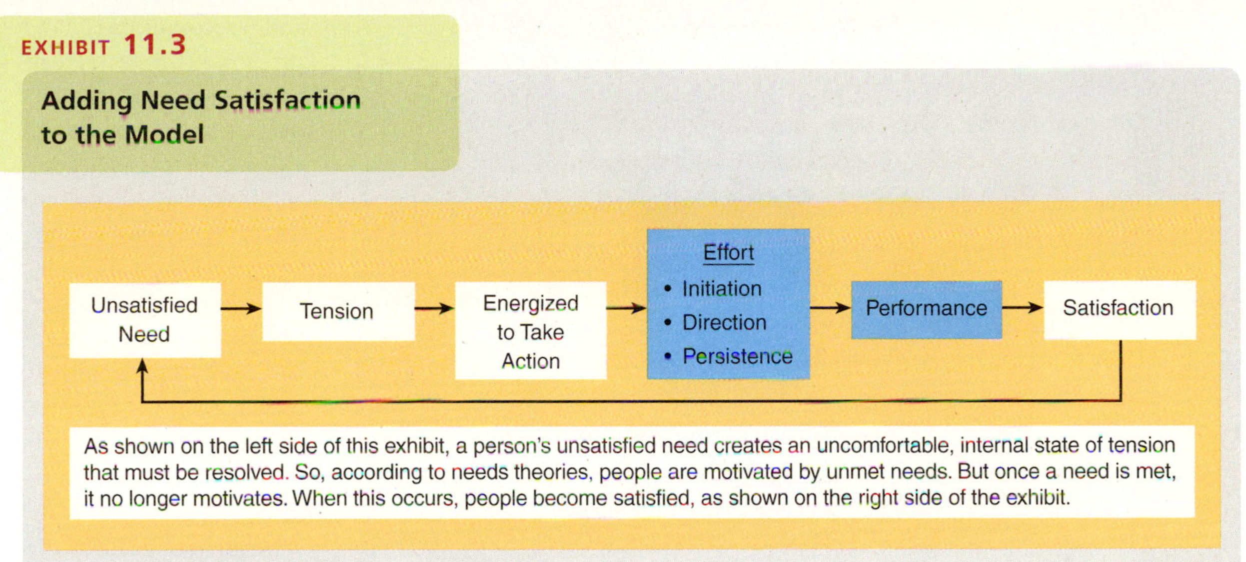
Unsatisfied Need
Tension
Energized to Take Action
Effort
• Initiation
• Direction
• Persistence
Performance
Satisfaction
As shown on the left side of this exhibit, a person's unsatisfied need creates an uncomfortable, internal state of tension that must be resolved. So, according to needs theories, people are motivated by unmet needs. But once a need is met, it no longer motivates. When this occurs, people become satisfied, as shown on the right side of the exhibit.

Note: Throughout the chapter, as we build on the basic model, the parts of the model that we've already discussed will appear in blue boxes. For example, since we've already discussed the effort → performance part of the model, those components are shown with a blue background. When we add new parts to the model, they will have a white background. Since we're adding need satisfaction to the model at this step, the need-satisfaction components of unsatisfied need, tension, energized to take action, and satisfaction are shown with a white background. This shading convention should make it easier to understand the work motivation model as we add to it in each section of the chapter.

Since people are motivated by unmet needs, managers must learn what those unmet needs are and address them. This is not always a straightforward task, however, because different needs theories suggest different categories of needs. Exhibit 11.4 shows needs from three well-known theories. Maslow's Hierarchy of Needs suggests that people are motivated by *physiological* (food and water), *safety* (physical and economic), *belongingness* (friendship, love, social interaction), *esteem* (achievement

EXHIBIT **11.4**

Needs Classification of Different Theoriess

	Maslow's Hierarchy	Alderfer's Erg	McClelland Learned Needs
Higher-Order Needs	Self-Actualization Esteem Belongingness	Growth Relatedness	Power Achievement Affiliation
Lower-Order Needs	Safety Physiological	Existence	

Doing the Right Thing

Faking it, Not Making It

With technological assistance, you may be tempted to engage in "impression management" to try to convince your boss and coworkers that you're working hard when you're really not. For instance, a tech support worker who enjoyed 3-hour lunches used a program on his PDA to remotely control his office computer. He would open, close, and move files so it would look as if he had just stepped away from his desk. Other employees write e-mail before they go home and then "send" them after midnight (we won't tell you how this is done) to make it look as though they are still at work. Some people leave early and, on their way home, send e-mails via their Blackberry so it will appear they are still at the office. You may be thinking that these ruses are harmless, but 59 percent of human resources managers and 53 percent of supervisors have caught employees lying about the hours they work. Furthermore, if you're using technology to fake it, you're usually leaving high-tech tracks and footprints along the way. That tech worker who controlled his office computer with his PDA was fired for habitual lateness. Motivation is all about effort. So, do the right thing. Work hard for your company, your customers, and yourself.[14]

and recognition), and *self-actualization* (realizing your full potential) needs.[8] Alderfer's ERG Theory collapses Maslow's five needs into three: *existence* (safety and physiological needs), *relatedness* (belongingness), and *growth* (esteem and self-actualization).[9] McClelland's Learned Needs Theory suggests that people are motivated by the need for *affiliation* (to be liked and accepted), the need for *achievement* (to accomplish challenging goals), or the need for *power* (to influence others).[10]

Things become even more complicated when we consider the different predictions made by these theories. According to Maslow, needs are arranged in a hierarchy from low (physiological) to high (self-actualization). Within this hierarchy, people are motivated by their lowest unsatisfied need. As each need is met, they work their way up the hierarchy from physiological to self-actualization needs. By contrast, Alderfer says that people can be motivated by more than one need at a time. Furthermore, he suggests that people are just as likely to move down the needs hierarchy as up, particularly when they are unable to achieve satisfaction at the next higher need level. McClelland argues that the degree to which particular needs motivate varies tremendously from person to person. Some people are motivated primarily by achievement and others by power or affiliation. Moreover, McClelland says that needs are learned, not innate. For instance, studies show that children whose parents own a small business or hold a managerial position are much more likely to have a high need for achievement.[11]

So, with three different sets of needs and three very different ideas about how needs motivate, how do we provide a practical answer to managers who just want to know "What leads to effort?" Fortunately, the research evidence simplifies things a bit. To start, studies indicate that there are two basic kinds of needs categories.[12] As shown in Exhibit 11.4, *lower-order needs* are concerned with safety and with physiological and existence requirements, whereas *higher-order needs* are concerned with relationships (belongingness, relatedness, and affiliation); challenges and accomplishments (esteem, self-actualization, growth, and achievement); and influence (power). Studies generally show that higher-order needs will not motivate people as long as lower-order needs remain unsatisfied.[13] So, what leads to effort? In part, needs do. After we discuss rewards in subsection 1.3, in subsection 1.4 we discuss how managers can use what we know from need-satisfaction theories to motivate workers.

1.3 Extrinsic and Intrinsic Rewards

No discussion of motivation would be complete without considering rewards. Let's add two kinds of rewards, extrinsic and intrinsic, to the model in Exhibit 11.5.[15]

Extrinsic rewards are tangible and visible to others and are given to employees contingent on the performance of specific tasks or behaviors.[16] External agents (managers, for example) determine and control the distribution, frequency, and amount of extrinsic rewards, such as pay, company stock, benefits, and promotions. Why do companies need extrinsic rewards? To get people to do things they wouldn't otherwise do. Companies use extrinsic rewards to motivate people to perform four basic behaviors: join the organization, regularly attend their jobs, perform their jobs well, and stay with the organization.[17] Think about it. Would you show up at work every day to do the best possible job that you could just out of the goodness of your heart? Very few people would. This is why *COGNEX*, a maker of industrial vision systems (robots that "see"), rewards its employees for perseverance, or staying with the company. The longer an employee stays, the greater the rewards. Says founder and CEO Dr. Robert Shillman, "After three years of service, you get a very nice-looking watch engraved on the back with the date you started. At five years, you get a gold pin and extra weekend vacation someplace. The 15-year perseverance award is a trip for you and your spouse to one of the wonders of the world, like the Great Wall of China. All you do is show up. You get $1,000 in spending money and an extra week vacation. After 20 years, it's the same thing with eight of your best friends plus your spouse and $1,500 in spending money."[18]

Intrinsic rewards are the natural rewards associated with performing a task or activity for its own sake. For example, aside from the external rewards management offers for doing something well, employees often find the activities or tasks they perform interesting and enjoyable. Examples of intrinsic rewards include a sense of accomplishment or achievement, a feeling of responsibility, the chance to learn something new or interact with others, or simply the fun that comes from performing an interesting, challenging, and engaging task.

Which types of rewards are most important to workers in general? A number of surveys suggest that both extrinsic and intrinsic rewards are important. One survey found that the most important rewards were good benefits and health insurance, job security, a week or more of vacation (all extrinsic rewards), interesting work, the opportunity to learn new skills, and independent work situations (all intrinsic rewards). And employee preferences for intrinsic and extrinsic rewards appear to be relatively stable. Studies conducted over the last three decades have consistently found that employees are twice as likely to report that important and meaningful work is more important than the amount they are paid.[19] Indeed, when asked, "If you were to get enough money to live as comfortably as you would like for the rest of your life, would you continue to work or would you stop working?" 69 percent of American workers said they would keep working. Clearly, intrinsic rewards matter.[20]

extrinsic reward
a reward that is tangible, visible to others, and given to employees contingent on the performance of specific tasks or behaviors

intrinsic reward
a natural reward associated with performing a task or activity for its own sake

EXHIBIT 11.5

Adding Rewards to the Model

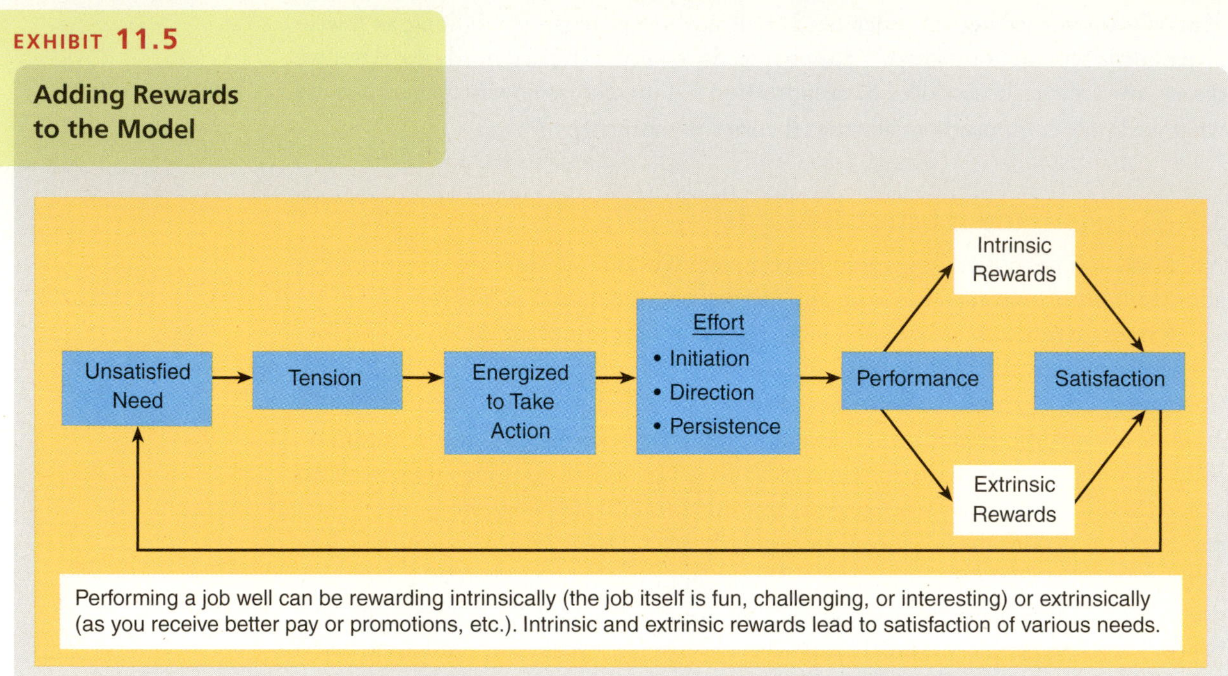

Performing a job well can be rewarding intrinsically (the job itself is fun, challenging, or interesting) or extrinsically (as you receive better pay or promotions, etc.). Intrinsic and extrinsic rewards lead to satisfaction of various needs.

1.4 Motivating with the Basics

So, given the basic model of work motivation in Exhibit 11.5, what practical steps can managers take to motivate employees to increase their effort?

Start by asking people what their needs are. Tommy Lee Hayes-Brown, who is in charge of recognition programs at *METLIFE*, one of the largest insurance companies, puts it this way: "Let's say you decide to reward an employee's great performance with a ham. If he doesn't eat ham, it's not going to be all that meaningful."[21] In other words, if managers don't know what workers' needs are, they won't be able to provide them the opportunities and rewards that can satisfy those needs.

Next, *satisfy lower-order needs first.* Since higher-order needs will not motivate people as long as lower-order needs remain unsatisfied, companies should satisfy lower-order needs first. In practice, this means providing the equipment, training, and knowledge necessary to create a safe workplace free of physical risks, paying employees well enough to provide financial security, and offering a benefits package that will protect employees and their families through good medical coverage and health and disability insurance. Indeed, a survey based on a representative sample of Americans found that when people choose jobs or organizations, three of the four most important factors—starting pay/salary (62 percent), employee benefits (57 percent), and job security (47 percent)—are lower-order needs.[22] Consistent with the idea of satisfying lower-order needs first, a survey of 12,000 employees found that inadequate compensation is the number-one reason employees leave organizations.[23]

Third, managers should *expect people's needs to change.* As some needs are satisfied or situations change, what motivated people before may not motivate them now. Likewise, what motivates people to accept a job may not necessarily motivate them once they have it. For instance, David Stum, president of the Loyalty Institute, says,

"The [attractive] power of pay and benefits is only [strong] during the recruitment stage. After employees take the job, pay and benefits become entitlements to them. They think, 'Now that I work here, you owe me that.'"[24]

Managers should also expect needs to change as people mature.[25] For older employees, benefits are as important as pay, which is always ranked as more important by younger employees. Older employees also rank job security as more important than personal and family time, which is more important to younger employees.[26]

Finally, *as needs change and lower-order needs are satisfied, create opportunities for employees to satisfy higher-order needs*. Recall that intrinsic rewards such as accomplishment, achievement, learning something new, and interacting with others are the natural rewards associated with performing a task or activity for its own sake. And, with the exception of influence (power), intrinsic rewards correspond very closely to higher-order needs that are concerned with relationships (belongingness, relatedness, and affiliation) and challenges and accomplishments (esteem, self-actualization, growth, and achievement). Therefore, one way for managers to meet employees' higher-order needs is to create opportunities for employees to experience intrinsic rewards by providing challenging work, encouraging employees to take greater responsibility for their work, and giving employees the freedom to pursue tasks and projects they find naturally interesting.

We began this section by asking what you would do if your company allowed you to choose your salary. At Skyline Construction, Vice President Mark Trento chose the added certainty of a higher salary. By contrast, Senior Project Manager Adam Chelini chose a smaller salary and larger bonus because he wanted the chance to increase his total compensation. In the end, both were happy. And allowing top managers to choose how they want to be compensated appears to be working, as Skyline's revenues increased $42 to $76 million in just 3 years.[27]

Management Trend:

For managers who fear destroying morale with layoffs, cutting pay is a valuable alternative—no one gets fired and no one worries about job security. Even so, companies have shown that there is a right way and a wrong way to handle pay cuts. First, nearly all agree that across-the-board pay cuts should be avoided at all costs. Second, employees should be given something in exchange for their lost pay, such as time off. Third, there should be clear and honest communication. Some companies, such as Hewlett-Packard, have even instituted tiered pay cuts, which reflect how people's jobs have changed during the recession.

Source: Michelle Conlin. "Pay Cuts Made Palatable." *BloombergBusinessweek*. May 4, 2009. 67.

REVIEW 1

Basics of Motivation

Motivation is the set of forces that initiates, directs, and makes people persist in their efforts over time to accomplish a goal. Managers often assume motivation to be the only determinant of performance, but job performance is a multiplicative function of motivation times ability times situational constraints. If any one of these components is weak, job performance will suffer. Needs are the physical or psychological requirements that must be met to ensure survival and well-being. When needs are not met, people experience an internal state of tension. But once a particular need is met, it no longer motivates. When this occurs, people become satisfied and are then motivated by other unmet needs.

Different motivational theories, such as Maslow's Hierarchy of Needs (physiological, safety, belongingness, esteem, and self-actualization), Alderfer's ERG Theory (existence, relatedness, and growth), and McClelland's Learned Needs Theory (affiliation, achievement, and power), specify a number of different needs. However, studies show that there are only two general kinds of needs, lower-order needs and higher-order needs, and that higher-order needs will not motivate people as long as lower-order needs remain unsatisfied.

Both extrinsic and intrinsic rewards motivate people. Extrinsic rewards, which include pay, company stock, benefits, and promotions, are used to motivate people to join organizations and attend and perform their jobs. The basic model of motivation suggests that managers can motivate employees by asking them what their needs are, satisfying lower-order needs first, expecting people's needs to change, and satisfying higher-order needs through intrinsic rewards.

How Perceptions and Expectations Affect Motivation

When employees perceive that they will be unable to perform at a level necessary to obtain rewards, whether extrinsic or intrinsic, they are likely to be *demotivated.* Reward systems at many organizations are geared toward top performers and ignore mid-level performers. Most banks, for instance, reward the top 10 percent of the sales force; other sales representatives, who don't believe they can generate enough sales to end up in the top category, simply give up. Stephen O'Malley, an independent consultant, says that one way to avoid this scenario is to create an open-ended incentive program that keeps the top-performer programs intact while offering awards for mid-level performers who surpass their annual sales goals by 10 percent. This system, implemented at a large U.S.-based financial services institution, was successful in influencing perceptions and expectations of mid-level performers, resulted in better performance from all employees, and increased revenue for the company. Specifically, two-thirds of the company's mid-level performers qualified for rewards by collectively contributing almost 80 percent of the total sales growth and creating $14 million in incremental profit. The contributions of these mid-level performers as a group outpaced the growth of top performers by 16 percent. By influencing perceptions and expectations of the entire sales force, the company was able to achieve a 47 percent overall increase in sales growth, three times the industry average.[28]

After reading the next two sections, you should be able to:

2 use equity theory to explain how employees' perceptions of fairness affect motivation.

3 use expectancy theory to describe how workers' expectations about rewards, effort, and the link between rewards and performance influence motivation.

2 Equity Theory

Finnish businessman Jaako Rytsola was out driving in his car one evening. "The road was wide and I was feeling good. It was nice to be driving when there was no one in sight." Unfortunately for Rytsola, he wasn't alone. A police officer pulled him over and issued him a speeding ticket for driving 43 mph in a 25 mph zone. The cost of the ticket: $71,400! Janne Rajala, a college student, was also pulled over for driving 18 mph over the speed limit. However, Rajala's ticket cost him only $106. The $71,294 difference occurred because Finland bases traffic fines on the severity of the offense, which was identical in this case, *and* the income of the driver, which clearly wasn't.

Is Finland's method of determining speeding fines fair or unfair? Most Americans would argue that Finland's approach is unfair, that fairness requires that fines be proportional to the offense and that everyone who breaks the law to the same degree should pay the same fine. By contrast, most Finns believe that fines proportional to income are fair. Erkki Wuouma of Finland's Ministry of the Interior says, "This is a Nordic tradition. We have progressive taxation and progressive punishments. So the more you earn, the more you pay." Rytsola pays more because he is a high-earning Internet entrepreneur. Rajala pays less because he's a low-earning college student.[29]

Fairness, or what people perceive to be fair, is also a critical issue in organizations. **Equity theory** says that people will be motivated at work when they *perceive* that they are being treated fairly. In particular, equity theory stresses the importance of perceptions. So, regardless of the actual level of rewards people receive, they must also perceive that, relative to others, they are being treated fairly. As explained below, equity theory doesn't focus on objective equity (that is, where all employees make about the same amount of money). Instead, equity theory says that equity, like beauty, is in the eye of the beholder.

Let's learn more about equity theory by examining 2.1 **the components of equity theory**, 2.2 **how people react to perceived inequities**, and 2.3 **how to motivate people using equity theory**.

equity theory
a theory that states that people will be motivated when they perceive that they are being treated fairly

2.1 Components of Equity Theory

The basic components of equity theory are inputs, outcomes, and referents. **Inputs** are the contributions employees make to the organization. They include education and training, intelligence, experience, effort, number of hours worked, and ability. **Outcomes** are what employees receive in exchange for their contributions to the organization. Outcomes include pay, fringe benefits, status symbols, and job titles and assignments. And, since perceptions of equity depend on comparisons, **referents** are others with whom people compare themselves to determine if they have been treated fairly. Usually, people choose to compare themselves with referents who hold the same or similar jobs or who are otherwise similar in gender, race, age, tenure, or other characteristics.[30]

According to the equity theory process shown in Exhibit 11.6, employees compare their outcomes (the rewards they receive from the organization) with their inputs (their contributions to the organization). This comparison of outcomes with inputs is called the **outcome/input (O/I) ratio**. After an internal comparison in which they compare their outcomes with their inputs, employees then make an external comparison in which they compare their O/I ratio with the O/I ratio of a referent.[31] When people perceive that their O/I ratio is equal to the referent's O/I ratio, they conclude that they are being treated fairly. But when people perceive that their O/I ratio is different from their referent's O/I ratio, they conclude that they have been treated inequitably or unfairly.

inputs
in equity theory, the contributions employees make to the organization

outcomes
in equity theory, the rewards employees receive for their contributions to the organization

referents
in equity theory, others with whom people compare themselves to determine if they have been treated fairly

outcome/input (O/I) ratio
in equity theory, an employee's perception of how the rewards received from an organization compare with the employee's contributions to that organization

EXHIBIT 11.6

Motivating to Increase Effort

$$\frac{\text{OUTCOMES}_{\text{SELF}}}{\text{INPUTS}_{\text{SELF}}} = \frac{\text{OUTCOMES}_{\text{REFERENT}}}{\text{INPUTS}_{\text{REFERENT}}}$$

Inequity can take two forms, underreward and overreward. **Underreward** occurs when a referent's O/I ratio is better than your O/I ratio. In other words, you are getting fewer outcomes relative to your inputs than the referent you compare yourself with is getting. When people perceive that they have been underrewarded, they tend to experience anger or frustration. For example, when a manufacturing company received notice that some important contracts had been canceled, management cut employees' pay by 15 percent in one plant but not in another. Just as equity theory predicts, theft doubled in the plant that received the pay cut. Likewise, employee turnover increased from 5 percent to 23 percent.[32]

By contrast, **overreward** occurs when a referent's O/I ratio is worse than your O/I ratio. In this case, you are getting more outcomes relative to your inputs than your referent is. In theory, when people perceive that they have been overrewarded, they experience guilt. But, not surprisingly, people have a very high tolerance for overreward. It takes a tremendous amount of overpayment before people decide that their pay or benefits are more than they deserve.

2.2 How People React to Perceived Inequity

As a child do you ever remember calling for a do-over? Even as children, we have a strong desire for fairness, for being treated equitably. When this need isn't met, we are strongly motivated to find a way to restore equity and be fair, hence the do-over. Not surprisingly, equity is just as important at the office as it is on the playground.

So what happens when people perceive that they have been treated inequitably at work? Exhibit 11.7 shows that perceived inequity affects satisfaction. In the case of underreward, this usually translates into frustration or anger; with overreward, the reaction is guilt. These reactions lead to tension and a strong need to take action to restore equity in some way. At first, a slight inequity may not be strong enough to motivate an employee to take immediate action. If the inequity continues or there are multiple inequities, however, tension may build over time until a point of intolerance is reached, and the person is energized to take action.[33]

When people perceive that they have been treated unfairly, they may try to restore equity by reducing inputs, increasing outcomes, rationalizing inputs or outcomes, changing the referent, or simply leaving. We will discuss these possible responses in terms of the inequity associated with underreward, which is much more common than the inequity associated with overreward.

People who perceive that they have been underrewarded may try to restore equity by *decreasing or withholding their inputs (that is, effort)*. Pilots at *AMERICAN AIRLINES* took a 23 percent pay cut after 9/11 to help keep the airline out of bankruptcy. When American began doing well again, top managers collectively received a quarter-billion dollars in stock, whereas pilots and other employees received only small pay raises.[34] During a previous confrontation over salary and benefits, 2,400 American pilots reported in "sick," resulting in the cancellation of 1,100 flights.[35]

Increasing outcomes is another way people try to restore equity. This might include asking for a raise or pointing out the inequity to the boss and hoping that he or she takes care of it. Sometimes, however, employees may go to external organizations

underreward
a form of inequity in which you are getting fewer outcomes relative to inputs than your referent is getting

overreward
a form of inequity in which you are getting more outcomes relative to inputs than your referent

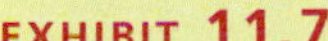
EXHIBIT 11.7

Adding Equity Theory to the Model

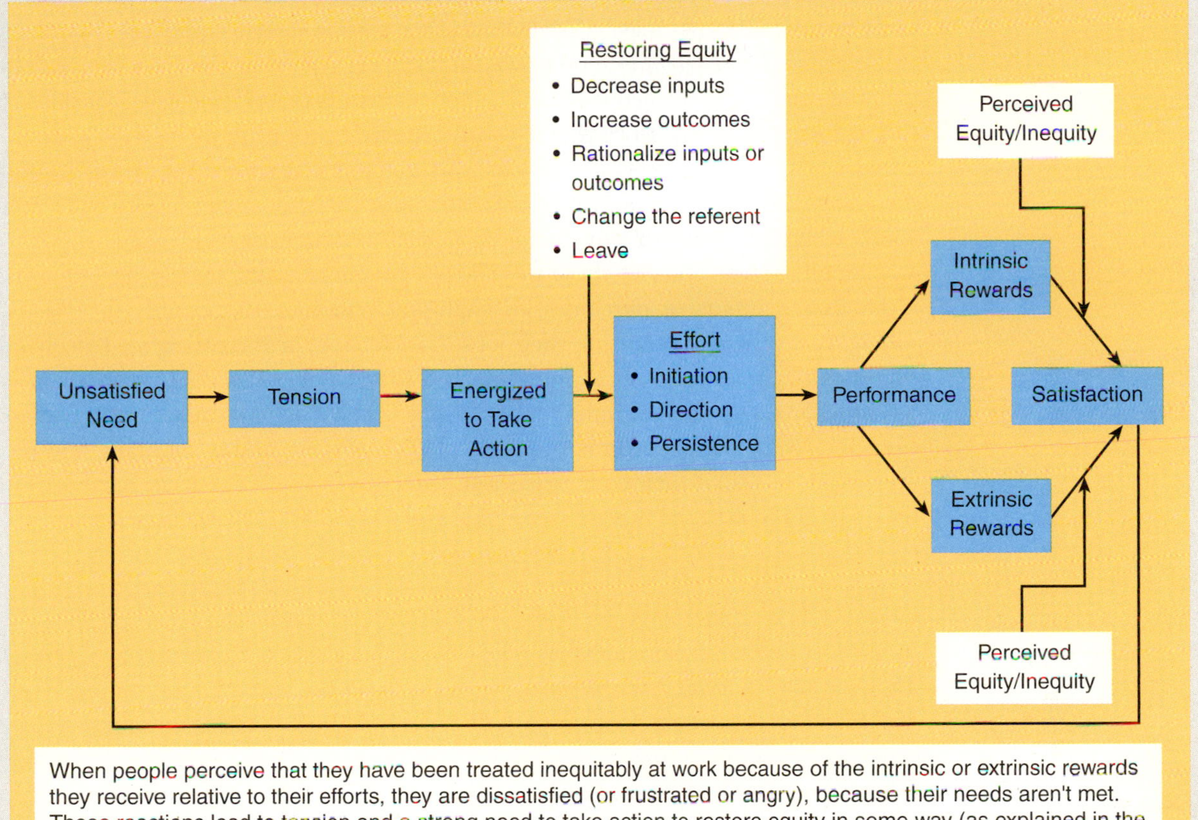

When people perceive that they have been treated inequitably at work because of the intrinsic or extrinsic rewards they receive relative to their efforts, they are dissatisfied (or frustrated or angry), because their needs aren't met. Those reactions lead to tension and a strong need to take action to restore equity in some way (as explained in the "Restoring Equity" box).

such as labor unions, federal agencies, or the courts for help in increasing outcomes to restore equity. For instance, the U.S. Department of Labor estimates that 10 percent of workers are not getting the extra overtime pay they deserve when they work more than 40 hours a week.[36] These are known as Fair Labor Standards Act violations. In fact, more than 30,000 such cases are brought each year, and employees win two-thirds of them.[37] Edward Harold, a partner with the law firm of Fisher & Phillips in New Orleans, says, "There has been an explosion of Fair Labor Standards Act litigation since 2002."[38] For example, the managers of *WAFFLE HOUSE* restaurants sued the company because they were working an average of 89 hours a week without any overtime pay.[39] The company contended that as managers, they were exempt from the Fair Labor Standards Act (FLSA), which mandates that only workers, that is, nonexempt employees, be paid time and a half for any work beyond 40 hours a week.

Another method of restoring equity is to *rationalize or distort inputs or outcomes*. Instead of decreasing inputs or increasing outcomes, employees restore equity by making mental or emotional adjustments in their O/I ratios or the O/I ratios of their referents. For example, suppose that a company downsizes 10 percent of its workforce. It's likely that the survivors (the people who still have jobs) will be angry or frustrated with company management because of the layoffs. If alternative jobs are difficult to find, however, these survivors may rationalize or distort their O/I ratios and conclude, "Well, things could be worse. At least I still have my job." Rationalizing or distorting outcomes may be used when other ways to restore equity aren't available.

Changing the referent is another way of restoring equity. In this case, people compare themselves with someone other than the referent they had been using for previous O/I ratio comparisons. Since people usually choose to compare themselves with others who hold the same or similar jobs or who are otherwise similar (i.e., friends, family members, neighbors who work at other companies), they may change referents to restore equity when their personal situations change, such as a decrease in job status or pay.[40]

Finally, when none of these methods—reducing inputs, increasing outcomes, rationalizing inputs or outcomes, or changing referents—is possible or effective, *employees may leave* by quitting their jobs, transferring, or increasing absenteeism.[41] For example, attorneys and accountants at the *SECURITIES AND EXCHANGE COMMISSION (SEC)* quit their jobs at twice the rate of employees in other federal agencies. Why? One reason is that the SEC's attorneys and accountants are paid 40 percent less than their counterparts at other government agencies. Furthermore, they can get jobs in the private sector that pay $180,000 to $250,000 per year.[42]

2.3 Motivating with Equity Theory

What practical steps can managers take to use equity theory to motivate employees? They can *start by looking for and correcting major inequities*. Among other things, equity theory makes us aware that an employee's sense of fairness is based on subjective perceptions. What one employee considers grossly unfair may not affect another employee's perceptions of equity at all. Although these different perceptions make it difficult for managers to create conditions that satisfy all employees, it's critical that they do their best to take care of major inequities that can energize employees to take disruptive, costly, or harmful actions such as decreasing inputs or leaving. So, whenever possible, managers should look for and correct major inequities. At *BURGERVILLE*, a 39-restaurant fast-food chain based in Vancouver, Washington, annual employee turnover was 128 percent per year. The key inequity? Employees making $9 an hour couldn't afford health insurance for themselves and their families. While Burgerville's health plan was cheap at $42 a month for employees and $105 a month for families, it provided limited benefits and came with a $1,000 deductible. As a result, only 3 percent of employees were enrolled in it. Under Burgerville's revised health plan, employees who work at least 20 hours a week get full health insurance at a cost of just $15 a month for themselves and $90 a month for their families—in both instances, there's no deductible. Although the new plan was expensive, nearly doubling health-care costs from $2.1 million to $4.1 million, the cost was easily offset by lower employee turnover, which dropped from 128 percent per year to 54 percent per year, and higher sales, which were up 11 percent.[43]

© ISTOCKPHOTO.COM/JOHN PEACOCK

Second, managers can *reduce employees' inputs*. Increasing outcomes is often the first and only strategy that companies use to restore equity, yet reducing employee inputs is just as viable a strategy. In fact, with dual-career couples working 50-hour weeks, more and more employees are looking for ways to reduce stress and restore a balance between work and family. Consequently, it may make sense to ask employees to do less, not more; to have them identify and eliminate 20 percent of their jobs that doesn't increase productivity or add value for customers; and to eliminate company-imposed requirements that really aren't critical to the performance of managers, employees, or the company (for example, unnecessary meetings and reports).

Finally, managers should *make sure decision-making processes are fair*. Equity theory focuses on **distributive justice**, the degree to which outcomes and rewards are fairly distributed or allocated. However, **procedural justice**, the fairness of the procedures used to make reward allocation decisions, is just as important.[44] Procedural justice matters because even when employees are unhappy with their outcomes (that is, low pay), they're much less likely to be unhappy with company management if they believe that the procedures used to allocate outcomes are fair. For example, employees who are laid off tend to be hostile toward their employer when they perceive that the procedures leading to the layoffs were unfair. By contrast, employees who perceive layoff procedures to be fair tend to continue to support and trust their employers.[45] Also, if employees perceive that their outcomes are unfair (that is, distributive injustice), but that the decisions and procedures leading to those outcomes were fair (that is, procedural justice), they are much more likely to seek constructive ways of restoring equity, such as discussing these matters with their manager. By contrast, if employees perceive both distributive and procedural injustice, they may resort to more destructive tactics, such as withholding effort, absenteeism, tardiness, or even sabotage and theft.[46]

REVIEW 2

Equity Theory

The basic components of equity theory are inputs, outcomes, and referents. After an internal comparison in which employees compare their outcomes with their inputs, they then make an external comparison in which they compare their O/I ratio with the O/I ratio of a referent, a person who works in a similar job or is otherwise similar. When their O/I ratio is equal to the referent's O/I ratio, employees perceive that they are being treated fairly. But when their O/I ratio is different from their referent's O/I ratio, they perceive that they have been treated inequitably or unfairly.

There are two kinds of inequity, underreward and overreward. Underreward occurs when a referent's O/I ratio is better than the employee's O/I ratio and leads to anger or frustration. Overreward occurs when a referent's O/I ratio is worse than the employee's O/I ratio and can lead to guilt, but only when the level of overreward is extreme. When employees perceive that they have been treated inequitably (underrewarded), they may try to restore equity by reducing inputs, increasing outcomes, rationalizing inputs or outcomes, changing the referent, or simply leaving.

Managers can use equity theory to motivate workers by looking for and correcting major inequities, reducing employees' inputs, and emphasizing procedural as well as distributive justice.

distributive justice
the perceived degree to which outcomes and rewards are fairly distributed or allocated

procedural justice
the perceived fairness of the process used to make reward allocation decisions

3 Expectancy Theory

How attractive do you find each of the following rewards? A company concierge service that will pick up your car from the mechanic and send someone to be at your house when the cable guy or repair person shows up. A "7 to 7" travel policy stipulating that no one has to leave home for business travel before 7 am on Mondays and that everyone should be home from business travel by 7 pm on Fridays. The opportunity to telecommute so that you can feed your kids breakfast, pick them up after school, and tuck them into bed at night.[47]

If you have kids, you might love the chance to telecommute; but if you don't, you may not be interested. If you don't travel much on business, you won't be interested in the "7 to 7" travel policy; but if you do, you'll probably love it. One of the hardest things about motivating people is that not everyone is attracted to the same rewards. **Expectancy theory** says that people will be motivated to the extent to which they believe that their efforts will lead to good performance, that good performance will be rewarded, and that they will be offered attractive rewards.[48]

Let's learn more about expectancy theory by examining 3.1 **the components of expectancy theory**, and 3.2 **how to use expectancy theory as a motivational tool.**

3.1 Components of Expectancy Theory

Expectancy theory holds that people make conscious choices about their motivation. The three factors that affect those choices are valence, expectancy, and instrumentality.

Valence is simply the attractiveness or desirability of various rewards or outcomes. Expectancy theory recognizes that the same reward or outcome—say, a promotion—will be highly attractive to some people, will be highly disliked by others, and will not make much difference one way or the other to still others. Accordingly, when people are deciding how much effort to put forth, expectancy theory says that they will consider the valence of all possible rewards and outcomes that they can receive from their jobs. The greater the sum of those valences, each of which can be positive, negative, or neutral, the more effort people will choose to put forth on the job.

Expectancy is the perceived relationship between effort and performance. When expectancies are strong, employees believe that their hard work and efforts will result in good performance, so they work harder. By contrast, when expectancies are weak, employees figure that no matter what they do or how hard they work, they won't be able to perform their jobs successfully, so they don't work as hard.

Instrumentality is the perceived relationship between performance and rewards. When instrumentality is strong, employees believe that improved performance will lead to better and more rewards, so they choose to work harder. When instrumentality is weak, employees don't believe that better performance will result in more or better rewards, so they choose not to work as hard.

Expectancy theory holds that for people to be highly motivated, all three variables—valence, expectancy, and instrumentality—must be high. Thus, expectancy theory can be represented by the following simple equation:

$$\text{Motivation} = \text{Valence} \times \text{Expectancy} \times \text{Instrumentality}$$

expectancy theory
the theory that people will be motivated to the extent to which they believe that their efforts will lead to good performance, that good performance will be rewarded, and that they will be offered attractive rewards.

valence
the attractiveness or desirability of a reward or outcome

expectancy
the perceived relationship between effort and performance

instrumentality
the perceived relationship between performance and rewards

EXHIBIT 11.8

Adding Expectancy Theory to the Model

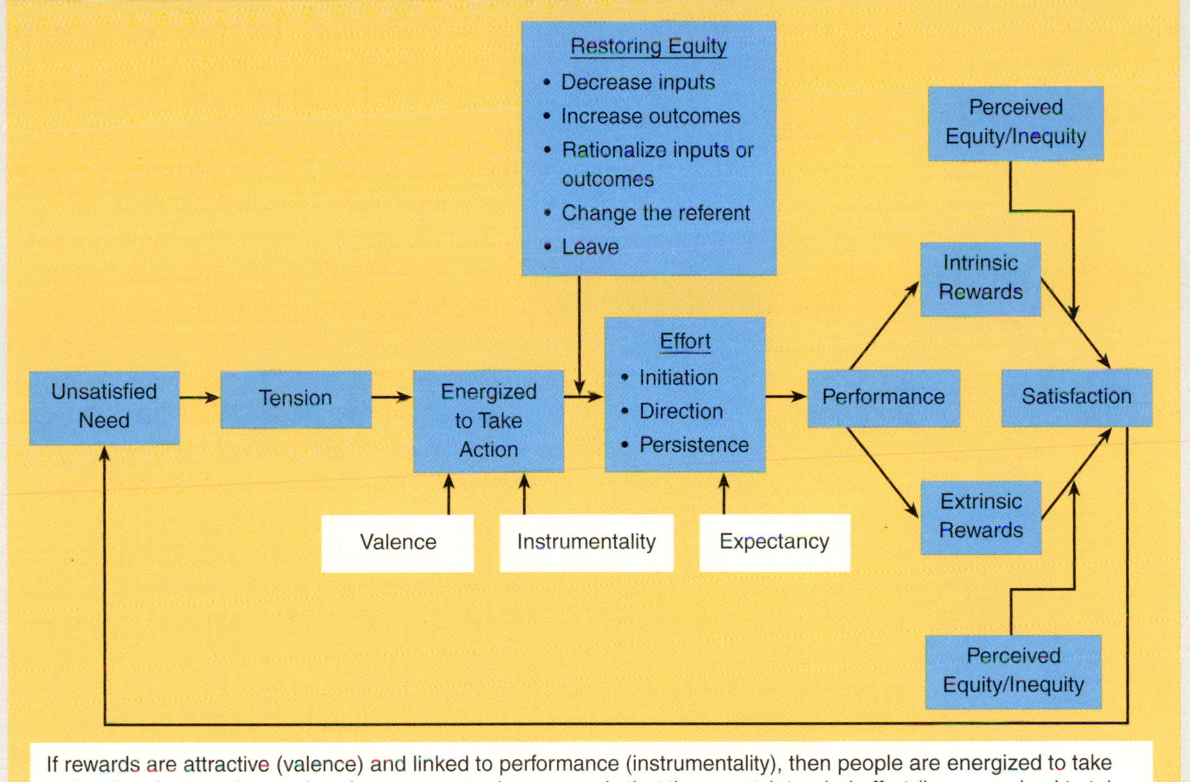

Restoring Equity
• Decrease inputs
• Increase outcomes
• Rationalize inputs or outcomes
• Change the referent
• Leave
Perceived Equity/Inequity
Intrinsic Rewards
Unsatisfied Need
Tension
Energized to Take Action
Effort
• Initiation
• Direction
• Persistence
Performance
Satisfaction
Extrinsic Rewards
Valence
Instrumentality
Expectancy
Perceived Equity/Inequity
If rewards are attractive (valence) and linked to performance (instrumentality), then people are energized to take action. In other words, good performance gets them rewards that they want. Intended effort (i.e., energized to take action) turns into actual effort when people believe that their hard work and efforts will result in good performance. After all, why work hard if that hard work is wasted?

If any one of these variables (valence, expectancy, or instrumentality) declines, overall motivation will decline, too.

Exhibit 11.8 incorporates the expectancy theory variables into our motivation model. Valence and instrumentality combine to affect employees' willingness to put forth effort (i.e., the degree to which they are energized to take action), while expectancy transforms intended effort ("I'm really going to work hard in this job") into actual effort. If you're offered rewards that you desire and you believe that you will in fact receive these rewards for good performance, you're highly likely to be energized to take action. However, you're not likely to actually exert effort unless you also believe that you can do the job (i.e., that your efforts will lead to successful performance).

3.2 Motivating with Expectancy Theory

What practical steps can managers take to use expectancy theory to motivate employees? First, they can *systematically gather information to find out what employees want from their jobs.* In addition to individual managers directly asking employees what they want from their jobs (see Subsection 1.4, "Motivating with the Basics"), companies need to survey their employees regularly to determine their wants, needs, and dissatisfactions. Since people consider the valence of all the possible rewards and outcomes that they can receive from their jobs, regular identification of wants, needs, and dissatisfactions gives companies the chance to turn negatively valent rewards and outcomes into positively valent rewards and outcomes, thus raising overall motivation and effort.

Second, managers can *take specific steps to link rewards to individual performance in a way that is clear and understandable to employees.* Unfortunately, most employees are extremely dissatisfied with the link between pay and performance in their organizations. In one study, based on a representative sample, 80 percent of the employees surveyed wanted to be paid according to a different kind of pay system! Moreover, only 32 percent of employees were satisfied with how their annual pay raises were determined, and only 22 percent were happy with the way the starting salaries for their jobs were determined.[49]

One way to make sure that employees see the connection between pay and performance (see Chapter 10 for a discussion of compensation strategies) is for managers to publicize the way in which pay decisions are made. This is especially important given that only 41 percent of employees know how their pay increases are determined.[50] HR executive Kerry Solomon of Atlanta-based Internet security services provider *SECUREWORKS* believe that communicating how pay rates and increases are determined is important because it allows employees to gain an accurate sense of where they stand—and to appreciate their employer's generosity.[51]

Finally, managers should *empower employees to make decisions if management really wants them to believe that their hard work and effort will lead to good performance.* If valent rewards are linked to good performance, people should be energized to take action. However, this works only if they also believe that their efforts will lead to good performance. One of the ways that managers destroy the expectancy that hard work and effort will lead to good performance is by restricting what employees can do or by ignoring employees' ideas. In Chapter 8, you learned that *empowerment* is a feeling of intrinsic motivation, in which workers perceive their work to have meaning and perceive themselves to be competent, to have an impact, and to be capable of self-determination.[52] So, if managers want workers to have strong expectancies, they should empower them to make decisions. Doing so will motivate employees to take active rather than passive roles in their work.

REVIEW 3

Expectancy Theory

Expectancy theory holds that three factors affect the conscious choices people make about their motivation: valence, expectancy, and instrumentality. Valence is simply the attractiveness or desirability of various rewards or outcomes. Expectancy is the perceived relationship between effort and performance. Instrumentality is the perceived relationship between performance and rewards. Expectancy theory holds that all three factors must be high in order for people to be highly motivated. If any one of these factors declines, overall motivation will decline, too. Managers can use expectancy theory to motivate workers by systematically gathering information to find out what employees want from their jobs, by linking rewards to individual performance in a way that is clear and understandable to employees, and by empowering employees to make decisions, which will increase their expectancies that hard work and effort will lead to good performance.

How Rewards and Goals Affect Motivation

When used properly, rewards motivate and energize employees. But when used incorrectly, they can demotivate, baffle, and even anger them.

Goals are supposed to motivate employees. But leaders who focus blindly on meeting goals at all costs often find that they destroy motivation. For instance, a president of a technology company calls his vice president of sales *daily* and asks, "Did you make your numbers *today*?" Consultant Richard Hapburg, who works with the vice president who receives these daily calls, says that the VP should be focusing on long-term solutions that increase sales, but "he's under enormous pressure to meet certain sales and profit targets on a *daily basis* now." The clear danger to using goals in this way, says Hapburg, is "that it's hard to capture employees' hearts, and best efforts, with numbers alone."[53]

After reading the next three sections, you should be able to:

4 explain how reinforcement theory works and how it can be used to motivate.

5 describe the components of goal-setting theory and how managers can use them to motivate workers.

6 discuss how the entire motivation model can be used to motivate workers.

4 Reinforcement Theory

Reinforcement theory says that behavior is a function of its consequences, that behaviors followed by positive consequences (i.e., reinforced) will occur more frequently, and that behaviors either followed by negative consequences or not followed by positive consequences will occur less frequently.[54] For example, more and more hotels with "100% smoke-free policies" have increased fines (i.e., negative consequences) for customers who smoke in their rooms. *SHERATON HOTELS* charges a $200 fine, *WALT DISNEY WORLD* charges $500, and *SWISSOTEL CHICAGO* raised its fine from $175 to $250. Swissotel's marketing director, Nicole Jachimiak, says, "$175 wasn't quite enough to get people to stop."[55] More specifically, **reinforcement** is the process of changing behavior by changing the consequences that follow behavior.[56]

Reinforcement has two parts: reinforcement contingencies and schedules of reinforcement. **Reinforcement contingencies** are the cause-and-effect relationships between the performance of specific behaviors and specific consequences. For example, if you get docked an hour's pay for being late to work, then a reinforcement contingency exists between a behavior (being late to work) and a consequence (losing an hour's pay). A **schedule of reinforcement** is the set of rules regarding reinforcement contingencies such as which behaviors will be reinforced, which consequences will follow those behaviors, and the schedule by which those consequences will be delivered.[57]

reinforcement theory the theory that behavior is a function of its consequences, that behaviors followed by positive consequences will occur more frequently, and that behaviors followed by negative consequences, or not followed by positive consequences, will occur less frequently

reinforcement the process of changing behavior by changing the consequences that follow behavior

reinforcement contingencies cause-and-effect relationships between the performance of specific behaviors and specific consequences

schedule of reinforcement rules that specify which behaviors will be reinforced, which consequences will follow those behaviors, and the schedule by which those consequences will be delivered

EXHIBIT 11.9

Adding Reinforcement Theory to the Model

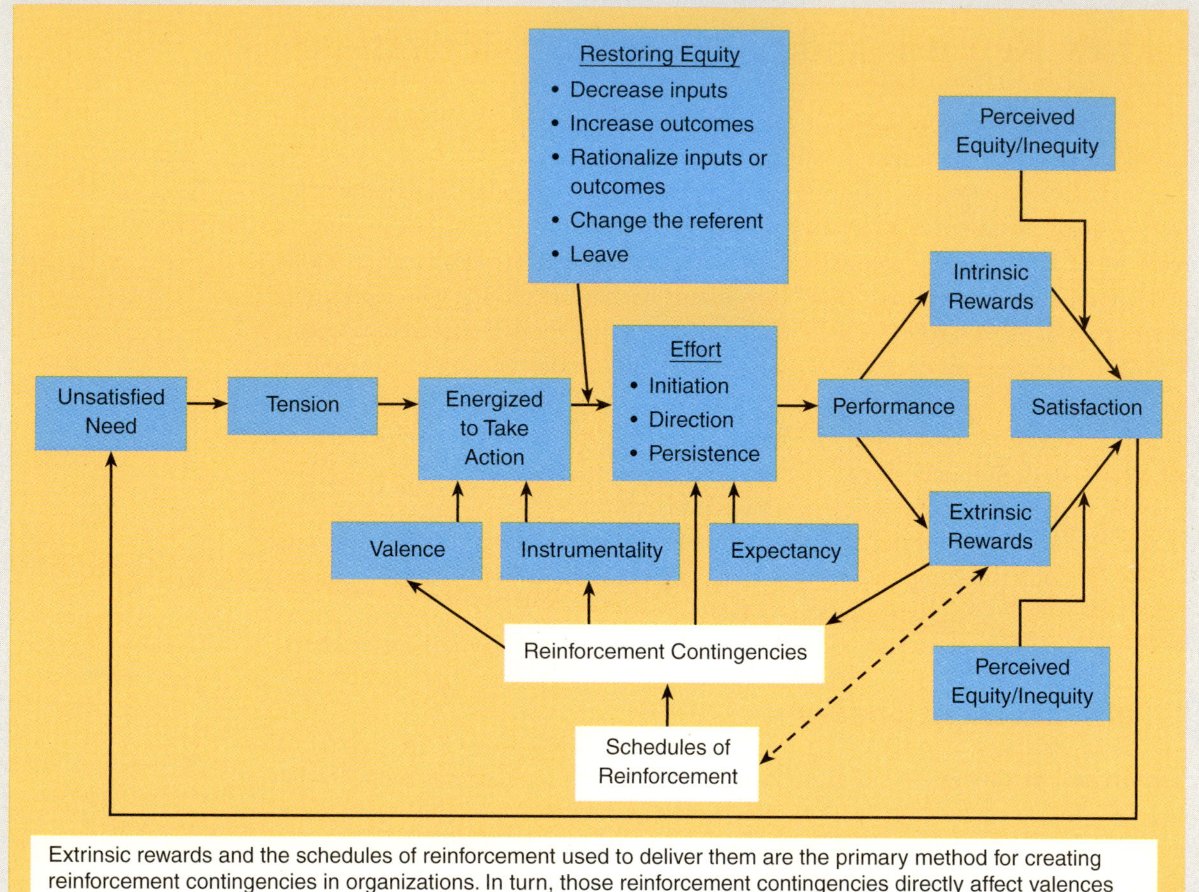

Extrinsic rewards and the schedules of reinforcement used to deliver them are the primary method for creating reinforcement contingencies in organizations. In turn, those reinforcement contingencies directly affect valences (the attractiveness of rewards), instrumentality (the perceived link between rewards and performance), and effort (how hard employees will work).

Exhibit 11.9 incorporates reinforcement contingencies and reinforcement schedules into our motivation model. First, notice that extrinsic rewards and the schedules of reinforcement used to deliver them are the primary method for creating reinforcement contingencies in organizations. In turn, those reinforcement contingencies directly affect valences (the attractiveness of rewards), instrumentality (the perceived link between rewards and performance), and effort (how hard employees will work).

Let's learn more about reinforcement theory by examining 4.1 **the components of reinforcement theory**, 4.2 **the different schedules for delivering reinforcement**, and 4.3 **how to motivate with reinforcement theory**.

4.1 Components of Reinforcement Theory

As just described, *reinforcement contingencies* are the cause-and-effect relationships between the performance of specific behaviors and specific consequences. There are four kinds of reinforcement contingencies: positive reinforcement, negative reinforcement, punishment, and extinction.

Positive reinforcement strengthens behavior (i.e., increases its frequency) by following behaviors with desirable consequences. **Negative reinforcement** strengthens behavior by withholding an unpleasant consequence when employees perform a specific behavior. Negative reinforcement is also called avoidance learning because workers perform a behavior to avoid a negative consequence. For example, at the Florist Network, a small business in Buffalo, New York, company management instituted a policy of requiring good attendance for employees to receive their annual bonuses. Employee attendance has improved significantly now that excessive absenteeism can result in the loss of $1,500 or more.[58]

By contrast, **punishment** weakens behavior (i.e., decreases its frequency) by following behaviors with undesirable consequences. The standard disciplinary or punishment process in most companies is an oral warning ("Don't ever do that again"), followed by a written warning ("This letter is to discuss the serious problem you're having with . . ."), followed by 3 days off without pay ("While you're at home not being paid, we want you to think hard about . . ."), followed by being fired ("That was your last chance"). Though punishment can weaken behavior, managers have to be careful to avoid the backlash that sometimes occurs when employees are punished at work. For example, *FRITO-LAY* began getting complaints from customers that they were finding potato chips with obscene messages written on them. Frito-Lay eventually traced the problem to a potato chip plant where supervisors had fired 58 out of the 210 workers for disciplinary reasons over a 9-month period. The remaining employees were so angry over what they saw as unfair treatment from management that they began writing the phrases on potato chips with felt-tip pens.[59]

Extinction is a reinforcement strategy in which a positive consequence is no longer allowed to follow a previously reinforced behavior. By removing the positive consequence, extinction weakens the behavior, making it less likely to occur. Based on the idea of positive reinforcement, most companies give company leaders and managers substantial financial rewards when the company performs well. Based on the idea of extinction, you would then expect that leaders and managers would not be rewarded (i.e., the positive consequence would be removed) when companies perform poorly. If companies really want pay to reinforce the right kinds of behaviors, then rewards have to be removed when company management doesn't produce successful performance. For example, with a $1 billion loss, and stock price down 35 percent, Agilent's board of directors cut CEO Ned Barnholt's base pay by 10 percent and didn't award him a cash or stock bonus.

positive reinforcement
reinforcement that strengthens behavior by following behaviors with desirable consequences

negative reinforcement
reinforcement that strengthens behavior by withholding an unpleasant consequence when employees perform a specific behavior

punishment
reinforcement that weakens behavior by following behaviors with undesirable consequences

extinction
reinforcement in which a positive consequence is no longer allowed to follow a previously reinforced behavior, thus weakening the behavior

4.2 Schedules for Delivering Reinforcement

As mentioned earlier, a *schedule of reinforcement* is the set of rules regarding reinforcement contingencies such as which behaviors will be reinforced, which consequences will follow those behaviors, and the schedule by which those consequences will be delivered. There are two categories of reinforcement schedules: continuous and intermittent.

EXHIBIT 11.10

Intermittent Reinforcement Schedules

	Intermittent Reinforcement Schedules Fixed	**Variables**
INTERVAL (TIME)	Consequences follow behavior after a fixed time has elapsed.	Consequences follow behavior after different times, some shorter and some longer, that vary around a specific average time.
RATIO (BEHAVIOR)	Consequences follow a specific number of behaviors.	Consequences follow a different number of behaviors, sometimes more and sometimes less, that vary around a specified average number of behaviors.

continuous reinforcement schedule a schedule that requires a consequence to be administered following every instance of a behavior

intermittent reinforcement schedule a schedule in which consequences are delivered after a specified or average time has elapsed or after a specified or average number of behaviors has occurred

fixed Interval reinforcement schedule an intermittent schedule in which consequences follow a behavior only after a fixed time has elapsed

variable interval reinforcement schedules an intermittent schedule in which the time between a behavior and the following consequences varies around a specified average

fixed ratio reinforcement schedule an intermittent schedule in which consequences are delivered following a specific number of behaviors

variable ratio reinforcement schedule an intermittent schedule in which consequences are delivered following a different number of behaviors, sometimes more and sometimes less, that vary around a specified average number of behaviors

With **continuous reinforcement schedules**, a consequence follows every instance of a behavior. For example, employees working on a piece-rate pay system earn money (consequence) for every part they manufacture (behavior). The more they produce, the more they earn. By contrast, with **intermittent reinforcement schedules**, consequences are delivered after a specified or average time has elapsed or after a specified or average number of behaviors has occurred. As Exhibit 11.10 shows, there are four types of intermittent reinforcement schedules. Two of these are based on time and are called *interval reinforcement schedules*; the other two, known as *ratio schedules*, are based on behaviors.

With **fixed interval reinforcement schedules**, consequences follow a behavior only after a fixed time has elapsed. For example, most people receive their paychecks on a fixed interval schedule (e.g., once or twice per month). As long as they work (behavior) during a specified pay period (interval), they get a paycheck (consequence). With **variable interval reinforcement schedules**, consequences follow a behavior after different times, some shorter and some longer, that vary around a specified average time. On a 90-day variable interval reinforcement schedule, you might receive a bonus after 80 days or perhaps after 100 days, but the average interval between performing your job well (behavior) and receiving your bonus (consequence) would be 90 days.

With **fixed ratio reinforcement schedules**, consequences are delivered following a specific number of behaviors. For example, a car salesperson might receive a $1,000 bonus after every 10 sales. Therefore, a salesperson with only 9 sales would not receive the bonus until he or she finally sold a 10th car.

With **variable ratio reinforcement schedules**, consequences are delivered following a different number of behaviors, sometimes more and sometimes less, that vary around a specified average number of behaviors. With a 10-car variable ratio reinforcement schedule, a salesperson might receive the bonus after 7 car sales, or after 12, 11, or 9 sales, but the average number of cars sold before receiving the bonus would be 10 cars.

Which reinforcement schedules work best? In the past, the standard advice was to use continuous reinforcement when employees were learning new behaviors because reinforcement after each success leads to faster learning. Likewise, the standard advice was to use intermittent reinforcement schedules to maintain behavior after it is learned because intermittent rewards are supposed to make behavior much less subject to extinction.[60] Research shows, however, that except for interval-based systems, which usually produce weak results, the effectiveness of continuous reinforcement, fixed ratio, and variable ratio schedules differs very little.[61] In organizational settings, all three produce consistently large increases over noncontingent reward schedules. So managers should choose whichever of these three is easiest to use in their companies.

4.3 Motivating with Reinforcement Theory

What practical steps can managers take to use reinforcement theory to motivate employees? University of Nebraska business professor Fred Luthans, who has been studying the effects of reinforcement theory in organizations for more than a quarter of a century, says that there are five steps to motivating workers with reinforcement theory: identify, measure, analyze, intervene, and evaluate critical performance-related behaviors.[62]

Identify means singling out critical, observable, performance-related behaviors. These are the behaviors that are most important to successful job performance. In addition, they must also be easily observed so that they can be accurately measured. *Measure* means determining the baseline frequencies of these behaviors. In other words, find out how often workers perform them. *Analyze* means studying the causes and consequences of these behaviors. Analyzing the causes helps managers create the conditions that produce these critical behaviors, and analyzing the consequences helps them determine if these behaviors produce the results that they want. *Intervene* means changing the organization by using positive and negative reinforcement to increase the frequency of these critical behaviors. *Evaluate* means assessing the extent to which the intervention actually changed workers' behavior. This is done by comparing behavior after the intervention to the original baseline of behavior before the intervention. For more on the effectiveness of reinforcement theory, see the "What Really Works?" feature in this chapter.

In addition to these five steps, managers should remember three other key things when motivating with reinforcement theory. First, *don't reinforce the wrong behaviors*. Although reinforcement theory sounds simple, it's actually very difficult to put into practice. One of the most common mistakes is accidentally reinforcing the wrong behaviors. Sometimes managers reinforce behaviors that they don't want!

Managers should also *correctly administer punishment at the appropriate time*. Many managers believe that punishment can change workers' behavior and help them improve their job performance. Furthermore, managers believe that fairly punishing workers also lets other workers know what is or isn't acceptable.[63] A danger of using punishment is that it can produce a backlash against managers and companies. But, if administered properly, punishment can weaken the frequency of undesirable behaviors without creating a backlash.[64] To be effective, the punishment must be strong enough to stop the undesired behavior and must be administered objectively (same rules applied to everyone), impersonally (without emotion or anger), consistently and contingently (each time improper behavior occurs), and quickly (as soon as possible following the undesirable behavior). In addition, managers should clearly explain what the appropriate behavior is and why the employee is being punished. Employees typically respond well when punishment is administered this way.[65]

Finally, managers should *choose the simplest and most effective schedule of reinforcement*. When choosing a schedule of reinforcement, managers need to balance effectiveness against simplicity. In fact, the more complex the schedule of reinforcement, the more likely it is to be misunderstood and resisted by managers and employees. Since continuous reinforcement, fixed ratio, and variable ratio schedules are about equally effective, continuous reinforcement schedules may be the best choice in many instances by virtue of their simplicity.

REVIEW 4

Reinforcement Theory

Reinforcement theory says that behavior is a function of its consequences. Reinforcement has two parts: reinforcement contingencies and schedules of reinforcement. The four kinds of reinforcement contingencies are positive reinforcement and negative reinforcement (which strengthen behavior), and punishment and extinction (which weaken behavior). There are two kinds of reinforcement schedules, continuous and intermittent; intermittent schedules, in turn, can be divided into fixed and variable interval schedules and fixed and variable ratio schedules. Managers can use reinforcement theory to motivate workers by following five steps (identify, measure, analyze, intervene, and evaluate critical performance-related behaviors); not reinforcing the wrong behaviors; correctly administering punishment at the appropriate time; and choosing a reinforcement schedule, such as continuous reinforcement, that balances simplicity and effectiveness.

5 Goal-Setting Theory

The basic model of motivation with which we began this chapter showed that individuals feel tension after becoming aware of an unfulfilled need. Once they experience tension, they search for and select courses of action that they believe will eliminate this tension. In other words, they direct their behavior toward something. This something is a **goal**, a target, objective, or result that someone tries to accomplish. *US AIRWAYS* had one of the worst on-time records in the airline industry. Many employees actually thought that as long as a flight pushed back from the gate no more than 30 minutes after its scheduled departure it was still scored as "on time."[67] That's when Robert Isom, the company's chief operating officer, established a new company-wide goal, "D-zero," which meant that every flight had to take off before or at its scheduled time. In addition to cash bonuses, US Airways added 100 more mechanics to fix problems quickly, took bags directly to connecting flights instead of to a central sorting area, and authorized managers to make hiring, spending, and operational decisions without approval from headquarters. The result? In less than a year, US Airways went from worst in on-time performance to first.

goal
a target, objective, or result that someone tries to accomplish

goal-setting theory
the theory that people will be motivated to the extent to which they accept specific, challenging goals and receive feedback that indicates their progress toward goal achievement

Goal-setting theory says that people will be motivated to the extent to which they accept specific, challenging goals and receive feedback that indicates their progress toward goal achievement.

what *really* works

Financial, Nonfinancial, and Social Rewards

Throughout this chapter, we have been making the point that there is more to motivating people than money. But we haven't yet examined how well financial (money or prizes), nonfinancial (performance feedback), and social (recognition and attention) rewards motivate workers by themselves or in combination. However, the results of two meta-analyses, one with 19 studies based on more than 2,800 people (study 1) and another based on 72 studies and 13,301 people (study 2), clearly indicate that rewarding and reinforcing employees greatly improve motivation and performance, especially when combined.

Financial Rewards

On average, there is a 68 percent chance that employees whose behavior is reinforced with financial rewards will outperform employees whose behavior is not reinforced. This increases to 84 percent in manufacturing organizations but drops to 61 percent in service organizations.

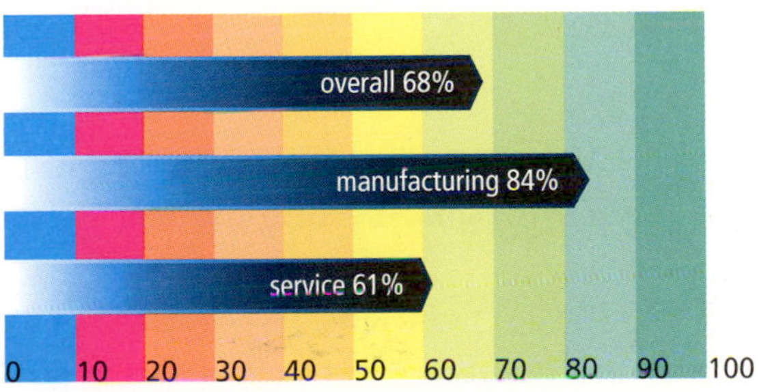

Nonfinancial Rewards

On average, there is a 58 percent chance that employees whose behavior is reinforced with nonfinancial rewards will outperform employees whose behavior is not reinforced. This increases to 87 percent in manufacturing organizations but drops to 54 percent in service organizations.

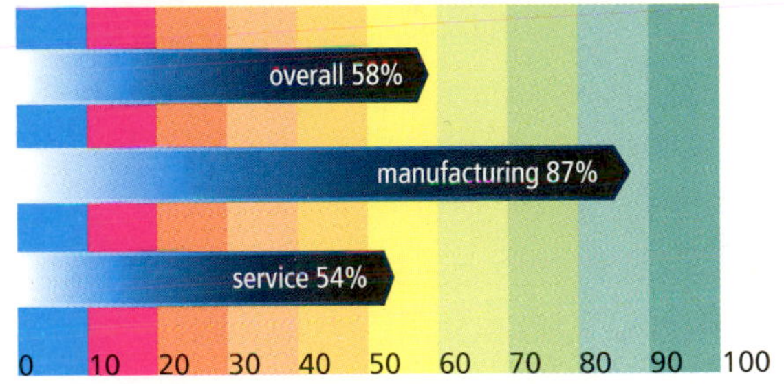

Social Rewards

On average, there is a 63 percent chance that employees whose behavior is reinforced with social rewards will outperform employees whose behavior is not reinforced.

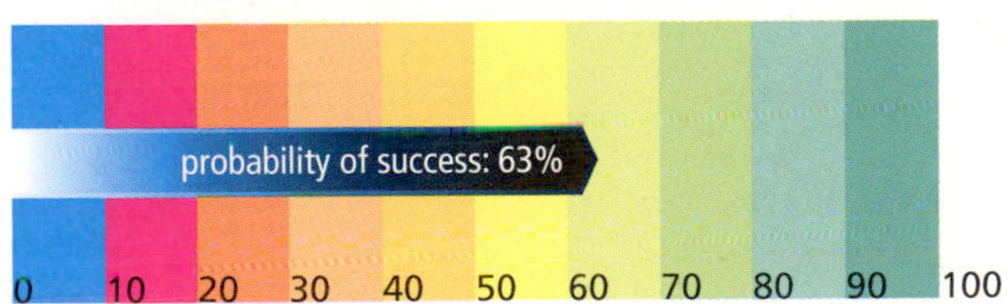

Financial and Nonfinancial Rewards
On average, there is a 62 percent chance that employees whose behavior is reinforced with a combination of financial and nonfinancial rewards will outperform employees whose behavior is not reinforced.

Nonfinancial and Social Rewards
On average, there is a 61 percent chance that employees whose behavior is reinforced with a combination of nonfinancial and social rewards will outperform employees whose behavior is not reinforced.

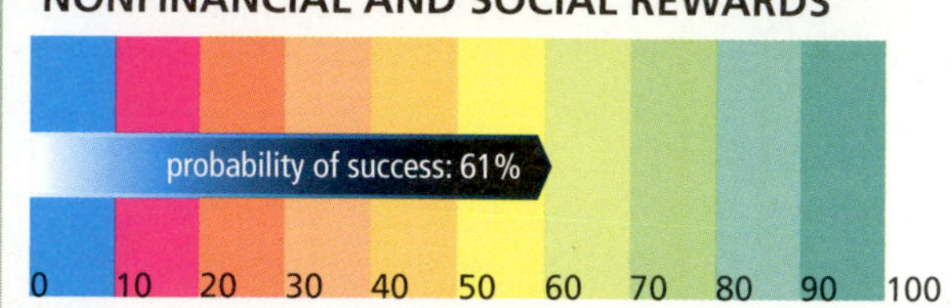

Financial and Social Rewards
On average, there is only a 52 percent chance that employees whose behavior is reinforced with a combination of financial and social rewards will outperform employees whose behavior is not reinforced.

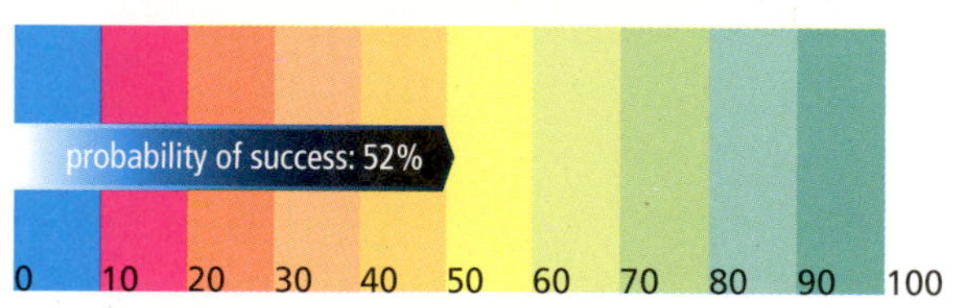

Financial, Nonfinancial, and Social Rewards
On average, there is a 90 percent chance that employees whose behavior is reinforced with a combination of financial, nonfinancial, and social rewards will outperform employees whose behavior is not reinforced.[66]

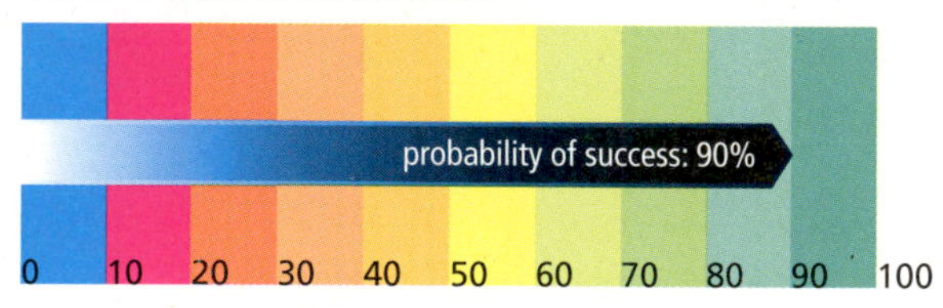

Let's learn more about goal setting by examining 5.1 **the components of goal-setting theory**, and 5.2 **how to motivate with goal-setting theory**.

5.1 Components of Goal-Setting Theory

goal specificity the extent to which goals are detailed, exact, and unambiguous

goal difficulty the extent to which a goal is hard or challenging to accomplish

The basic components of goal-setting theory are goal specificity, goal difficulty, goal acceptance, and performance feedback.[68] **Goal specificity** is the extent to which goals are detailed, exact, and unambiguous. Specific goals, such as "I'm going to have a 3.0 average this semester," are more motivating than general goals, such as "I'm going to get better grades this semester." **Goal difficulty** is the extent to which a goal is hard or challenging to accomplish. Difficult goals, such as "I'm going to have a 3.5 average and make the Dean's List this semester," are more motivating than easy goals, such as "I'm going to have a 2.0 average this semester."

Goal acceptance, which is similar to the idea of goal commitment discussed in Chapter 4, is the extent to which people consciously understand and agree to goals. Accepted goals, such as "I really want to get a 3.5 average this semester to show my parents how much I've improved," are more motivating than unaccepted goals, such as "My parents really want me to get a 3.5 average this semester, but there's so much more I'd rather do than study!"

Performance feedback is information about the quality or quantity of past performance and indicates whether progress is being made toward the accomplishment of a goal. Performance feedback, such as "My prof said I need a 92 on the final to get an 'A' in his class," is more motivating than no feedback ("I have no idea what my grade is in that class)". In short, goal-setting theory says that people will be motivated to the extent to which they accept specific, challenging goals and receive feedback that indicates their progress toward goal achievement.

How does goal setting work? To start, challenging goals focus employees' attention (i.e., direction of effort) on the critical aspects of their jobs and away from unimportant areas. Goals also energize behavior. When faced with unaccomplished goals, employees typically develop plans and strategies to reach those goals. Goals also create tension between the goal, which is the desired future state of affairs, and where the employee or company is now, meaning the current state of affairs. This tension can be satisfied only by achieving or abandoning the goal. Finally, goals influence persistence. Since goals only go away when they are accomplished, employees are more likely to persist in their efforts in the presence of goals. Exhibit 11.11 incorporates goals into the motivation model by showing how goals directly affect tension, effort, and the extent to which employees are energized to take action.

5.2 Motivating with Goal-Setting Theory

What practical steps can managers take to use goal-setting theory to motivate employees? One of the simplest, most effective ways to motivate workers is to give them specific, challenging goals. For example, *VALPAK DIRECT MARKETING SYSTEMS* is a direct-mailing company that awards regional franchises to people with enough business experience and cash. However, if you work for Valpak and meet the goal of $1.1 million in sales over 3 years, the company lets you choose your reward: $50,000 toward the purchase of a small regional territory, or $10,000 toward getting your MBA. Joe Bourdow, Valpak's president, said, "Sharp people coming out of school have choices, and so we're trying to give them a reason to at least consider us."[69] For more information on assigning specific, challenging goals, see the discussion in Chapter 4 on S.M.A.R.T. goals.

Second, managers should *make sure workers truly accept organizational goals.* Specific, challenging goals won't motivate workers unless they really accept, understand, and agree to the organization's goals. For this to occur, people must see the goals as fair and reasonable. Plus, they must trust management and believe that managers are using goals to clarify what is expected from them rather than to exploit or threaten them ("If you don't achieve these goals . . ."). Participative goal setting, in

goal acceptance
the extent to which people consciously understand and agree to goals

performance feedback
information about the quality or quantity of past performance that indicates whether progress is being made toward the accomplishment of a goal

EXHIBIT 11.11

Adding Goal-Setting Theory to the Model

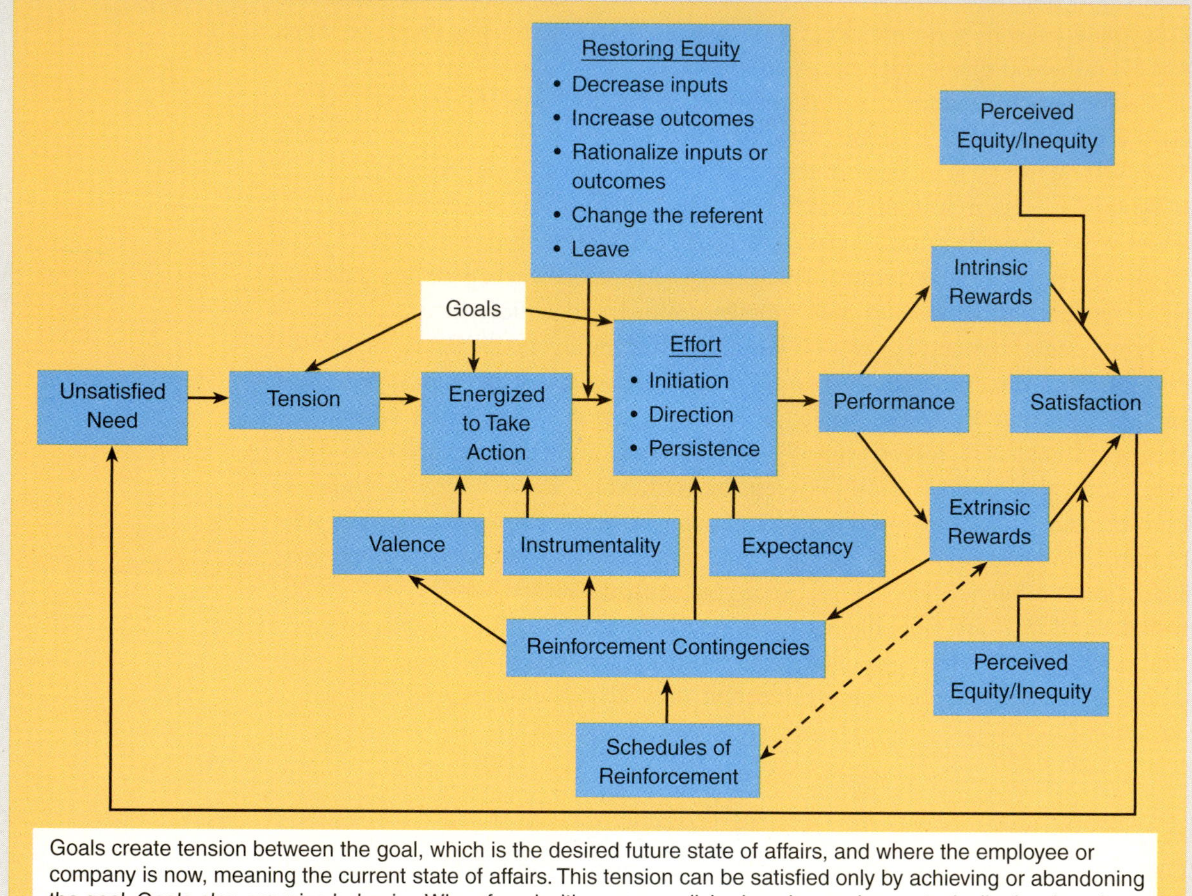

Goals create tension between the goal, which is the desired future state of affairs, and where the employee or company is now, meaning the current state of affairs. This tension can be satisfied only by achieving or abandoning the goal. Goals also energize behavior. When faced with unaccomplished goals, employees typically develop plans and strategies to reach those goals. Finally, goals influence persistence.

which managers and employees generate goals together, can help increase trust and understanding and thus acceptance of goals. Furthermore, providing workers with training can help increase goal acceptance, particularly when workers don't believe they are capable of reaching the organization's goals.[70]

Finally, managers should *provide frequent, specific, performance-related feedback*. Once employees have accepted specific, challenging goals, they should receive frequent performance-related feedback so that they can track their progress toward goal completion. Feedback leads to stronger motivation and effort in three ways.[71] Receiving specific feedback about the quality of their performance can encourage employees who don't have specific, challenging goals to set goals to improve their performance. Once people meet goals, performance feedback often encourages them to set higher, more difficult goals. And feedback lets people know whether they need to increase their efforts or change strategies in order to accomplish their goals.

For example, in an effort to improve worker safety on offshore oil-drilling platforms, an oil company generated a list of dangerous work behaviors by analyzing previous accident reports, reviewing industry safety manuals, and interviewing and observing workers. Following detailed safety training, each work crew set goals to engage in safe behaviors 100 percent of the time on each shift. Management posted a weekly safety record in the galley of each rig, so workers could see it when they gathered for meals and coffee breaks. Previously, employees were engaging in safe work behaviors just 76 percent of the time. After a year of goal setting (100 percent safe behavior on each shift) and weekly performance feedback at two oil rigs, however, workers behaved safely over 90 percent of the time. So, to motivate employees with goal-setting theory, make sure they receive frequent performance-related feedback so that they can track their progress toward goal completion.

REVIEW 5

Goal-Setting Theory

A goal is a target, objective, or result that someone tries to accomplish. Goal-setting theory says that people will be motivated to the extent to which they accept specific, challenging goals and receive feedback that indicates their progress toward goal achievement. The basic components of goal-setting theory are goal specificity, goal difficulty, goal acceptance, and performance feedback. Goal specificity is the extent to which goals are detailed, exact, and unambiguous. Goal difficulty is the extent to which a goal is hard or challenging to accomplish. Goal acceptance is the extent to which people consciously understand and agree to goals. Performance feedback is information about the quality or quantity of past performance and indicates whether progress is being made toward the accomplishment of a goal. Managers can use goal-setting theory to motivate workers by assigning specific, challenging goals, making sure workers truly accept organizational goals, and providing frequent, specific, performance-related feedback.

6 Motivating with the Integrated Model

We began this chapter by defining motivation as the set of forces that initiates, directs, and makes people persist in their efforts to accomplish a goal. We also asked the basic question that managers ask when they try to figure out how to motivate their workers—"What leads to effort?" Though the answer to that question is likely to be somewhat different for each employee, Exhibit 11.12 helps you begin to answer it by consolidating the practical advice from the theories reviewed in this chapter in one convenient location. So, if you're having difficulty figuring out why people aren't motivated where you work, Exhibit 11.12 provides a useful, theory-based starting point.

EXHIBIT 11.12

Motivating with the Integrated Model

MOTIVATING WITH. . .	MANAGERS SHOULD. . .
THE BASICS	• Ask people what their needs are. • Satisfy lower-order needs first. • Expect people's needs to change. • As needs change and lower-order needs are satisfied, create opportunities for employees to satisfy higher-order needs.
EQUITY THEORY	• Look for and correct major inequities. • Reduce employees' inputs. • Make sure decision-making processes are fair.
EXPECTANCY THEORY	• Systematically gather information to find out what employees want from their jobs. • Take specific steps to link rewards to individual performance in a way that is clear and understandable to employees. • Empower employees to make decisions if management really wants them to believe that their hard work and efforts will lead to good performance.
REINFORCEMENT THEORY	• Identify, measure, analyze, intervene, and evaluate critical performance-related behaviors. • Don't reinforce the wrong behaviors. • Correctly administer punishment at the appropriate time. • Choose the simplest and most effective schedule of reinforcement.
GOAL-SETTING THEORY	• Assign specific, challenging goals. • Make sure workers truly accept organizational goals. • Provide frequent, specific, performance-related feedback.

Why Won't They Take a Break?

Five years ago, your company assigned you to a management position in its new research facility in South Korea. You were thrilled with the promotion, and grateful to your bosses, who recognized your skills and talents. At the same time, there was a lot to be nervous about—adjusting to a new culture and language, finding a school for your kids and a job for your wife, figuring out where to buy familiar groceries. But even with all the struggles, you've thoroughly enjoyed your time in Korea, as you got to learn new things from your employees and teach them new things from your experiences. In fact, you're quite surprised that you've had such little conflict with your Korean associates.

There is, however, one area that you could never quite get a handle on—vacation time. Like every other employee in the company, your employees were given 3 weeks of paid vacation per year. But, other than the occasional 3-day weekend, they never took any time off. At first, you wondered if this was just unique to your company. But then, you saw statistics that showed that Koreans, on average, worked 600 more hours per year than the average American. While these long hours show great organizational commitment, they have extremely negative effects. Overworked employees are more prone to stress and physical illness, and are less likely to be efficient or productive. Indeed, according to the Organization of Economic Cooperation and Development, an international group comprised of 30 of the world's largest economies, South Korea ranks near the bottom in terms of productivity.

Even the South Korean government has taken notice of the dangers of overwork. A few months ago, President Myung Bak Lee announced that all state employees would be required to take 16 days of vacation per year. You were quite happy to hear about this policy, and hopeful that it would influence the private sector. But, you also wonder if there aren't other changes needed. From your conversations with Korean managers, you've learned that there is one big reason why Korean employees don't take vacation time—because their supervisors don't take vacation time. Even while requiring government employees to take 16 days off, President Lee himself has taken off only 4 days since his 2008 election. Even you, the "enlightened" American, remember working through Lunar New Year's Day, one of the biggest holidays in Korea.

You desperately want your employees to take more time off. It's what's best for them, their families, and for the company's productivity and efficiency. What is the best way to motivate them to take a break?

Questions

1. Which motivation theory(s) do you think would help communicate the importance of vacation time to your employees?
2. How would you convince your employees that working less hours, not more, is more beneficial for them and the company?

Source: Evan Ramstad and Jaeyeon. Woo "South Korea Works Overtime to Tackle Vacation Shortage." *Wall Street Journal.* March 1, 2010. A1, 22.

Practice being a MANAGER

The Makings of Motivation

Motivation is an invisible and powerful force. Strong motivation can drive individuals and organizations to remarkable heights of achievement. A loss of motivation can leave us dispirited and ineffective. One of the fundamental responsibilities of managers is to support healthy worker motivation. This exercise will allow you to practice designing support for worker motivation.

STEP 1 Divide into groups. Your professor will organize you in pairs or groups of three.

STEP 2 Prepare interviews. Between this class session and the target date set by your professor, you and your partner(s) will each interview two individuals about motivation at work. You should brainstorm about possible types of work, interesting individuals, and so on, and then agree on each partner's list of interviewees/jobholders.

Some considerations for brainstorming include jobs or types of work that you consider particularly interesting, appealing, or mysterious; jobs or types of work that you consider particularly uninteresting, dull, or monotonous (how does a person do that work day after day?); and self-employed or creative work (how do such workers manage their own motivation without a boss or supervisor?)

STEP 3 Conduct interviews. Outside of class each student should complete their assigned interviews. Inform the potential interviewee that you are interested in talking about workplace motivation. Set a time that is convenient and ensure that you arrive on time and prepared. Make the interview brief, with 15–20 minutes a good target. Go beyond 20 minutes only if the interviewee gives permission and the discussion is lively. Be sure to thank the interviewee for taking the time to visit with you.

Your instructor may give additional instructions for these interviews, and you should carefully follow these guidelines in conducting the interview.

Interview questions might include the following:

1. How would you describe your work? What are some of the things that you particularly like about your work?
2. We are currently studying the topic of motivation in one of my classes. What boosts your motivation at work? If you have ever experienced a period of low motivation, can you identify things that might have contributed to your losing steam in your work?
3. What kinds of rewards or incentives work best to motivate individuals and/or teams who do your type of work? What kinds of rewards or incentives don't work so well?

STEP 4 Summarize your findings. Write a one-page paper summarizing your interview findings. Be prepared to compare notes with your partners and to contribute to class discussion.

STEP 5 Debrief as a class. Pairs/small groups report their findings and discuss as a class. What did you learn from your interviews? Did you notice common themes or issues across the interviews you conducted? Did you notice any striking differences across individuals or types of work? What are some possible implications of these interview findings for managers who are responsible for cultivating healthy motivation in a particular work setting?

What Do You Need?

What people want out of their jobs is as varied as the jobs themselves.[72] And as you would expect, need theories show why not everyone wants to be CEO. Take the example of the woman who is extremely organized and efficient in her job as an assistant. She is so effective that she is offered a promotion to management, but she turns it down flatly, saying that she has no interest in moving up the ladder, that she is happy doing what she does. What she needs from work clearly differs from the needs of the person who jumps at every opportunity to move up the corporate hierarchy. Not everyone needs or wants the same things from their jobs.[73] Indicate the extent to which you agree with each of the following statements. Try not to spend too much time on any one item, and be sure to answer all the questions. Use this scale for your responses:

1. Strongly disagree
2. Disagree
3. Slightly disagree
4. Neutral
5. Slightly agree
6. Agree
7. Strongly agree

1. I get enough money from my job to live comfortably.
   1 2 3 4 5 6 7
2. Our benefits cover many of the areas they should.
   1 2 3 4 5 6 7
3. My boss encourages people to make suggestions.
   1 2 3 4 5 6 7
4. I can count on my coworkers to give me a hand when I need it.
   1 2 3 4 5 6 7
5. I always get the feeling that I learn new things from my work.
   1 2 3 4 5 6 7
6. I often think about how to improve my job performance.
   1 2 3 4 5 6 7
7. My pay is adequate to provide for the basic things in life.
   1 2 3 4 5 6 7
8. The benefits program of my job gives nearly all the security I want.
   1 2 3 4 5 6 7
9. My boss takes account of my wishes and desires.
   1 2 3 4 5 6 7
10. My coworkers will speak out in my favor if justified.
   1 2 3 4 5 6 7
11. My job requires that a person use a wide range of abilities.
   1 2 3 4 5 6 7

12. I will actively try to improve my job performance in the future.
1 2 3 4 5 6 7

13. Considering the work required, the pay is what it should be.
1 2 3 4 5 6 7

14. Compared to other places, our benefits are excellent.
1 2 3 4 5 6 7

15. My boss keeps me informed about what is happening in the company.
1 2 3 4 5 6 7

16. I can tell my coworkers how I honestly feel.
1 2 3 4 5 6 7

17. My job requires making one (or more) important decision(s) every day.
1 2 3 4 5 6 7

18. I intend to do a lot more at work in the future.
1 2 3 4 5 6 7

19. Compared to the rates for similar work, my pay is good.
1 2 3 4 5 6 7

20. The benefit program at my job is adequate.
1 2 3 4 5 6 7

21. My boss lets me know when I could improve my performance.
1 2 3 4 5 6 7

22. My coworkers welcome opinions different from their own.
1 2 3 4 5 6 7

23. I have the opportunity to do challenging things at work.
1 2 3 4 5 6 7

24. I will probably do my best to perform well on the job in the future.
1 2 3 4 5 6 7

SCORING

(A) Add together your scores for items 1, 2, 7, 8, 13, 14, 19, and 20: _____

(B) Add together your scores for items 3, 4, 9, 10, 15, 16, 21, and 22: _____

(C) Add together your scores for items 5, 6, 11, 12, 17, 18, 23, and 24: _____

You can find the interpretation for your score at: login.cengagebrain.com.

Reel to Real

Biz Flix

© GREENLIGHT

Friday Night Lights

In the small town of Odessa, Texas, everyone lives for Friday nights when the high school football team, the Permian Panthers, takes the field. The town is proud of their Panthers, led by quarterback Mike Winchell (Lucas Black) and superstar tailback Boobie Miles (Derek Luke), and they're used to winning. They expect a state championship, and nothing less. When Boobie suffers a career-ending injury in the first game of the season, the team isn't sure they can win without him. But Coach Gary Gaines (Billy Bob Thornton) isn't ready to give up yet. In this scene, Coach visits the home of his QB Mike Winchell and tries to motivate him, even though it seems like all hope for the Panthers is lost.

What to Watch for and Ask Yourself

1. This chapter defines motivation as "the set of forces that initiates, directs, and makes people persist in their efforts to accomplish a goal." Does Mike Winchell show the characteristics of this definition early in the sequence? Do you expect him to show any of the characteristics after the sequence ends and he returns to the team?
2. How does Coach Gaines try to motivate his QB? Do you think his approach is effective?
3. Apply the various parts of goal-setting theory to this sequence. Which parts of that theory appear in the sequence?

Management Workplace

© CENGAGE

Flight 001

In this video we meet Amanda Shank, who works at Flight 001, a store for seasoned travelers. She says that the respect and encouragement she receives from the store owners motivates her to do her best work. She wants her ideas to be taken seriously, and at Flight 001, they are. At her last job, her boss told her, "You're just a number. You can be replaced at any time." Shank says, "When you're told something like that, why would you want to put any effort in?" Store leader Claire Rainwater echoes Shank's sentiments, adding that while pay is important, she also wants to feel supported and valued for the work she does. Shank says she is happy to have found a place where she can make a contribution and be challenged. "At this company they make an effort to show you you're appreciated; you have a say in what goes on. You're given compliments and feedback about what you could be better at."

What to Watch for and Ask Yourself

1. According to Maslow's hierarchy, which basic needs did Shank's old boss fail to meet?
2. What do you think would motivate you most if you were working in a retail position?
3. What types of intrinsic and extrinsic rewards does Flight 001 offer its employees?

Chapter Twelve

Leadership

OUTLINE

What Is Leadership?

1 Leadership
- 1.1 Leaders Versus Managers

2 Who Leaders Are and What Leaders Do
- 2.1 Leadership Traits
- 2.2 Leadership Behaviors

Situational Approaches to Leadership

3 Putting Leaders in the Right Situation: Fiedler's Contingency Theory
- 3.1 Leadership Style: Least Preferred Coworker
- 3.2 Situational Favorableness
- 3.3 Matching Leadership Styles to Situations

4 Adapting Leader Behavior: Path-Goal Theory
- 4.1 Leadership Styles
- 4.2 Subordinate and Environmental Contingencies
- 4.3 Outcomes

5 Adapting Leader Behavior: Hersey and Blanchard's Situational Leadership Theory
- 5.1 Worker Readiness
- 5.2 Leadership Styles

6 Adapting Leader Behavior: Normative Decision Theory
- 6.1 Decision Styles
- 6.2 Decision Quality and Acceptance

Strategic Leadership

7 Visionary Leadership
- 7.1 Charismatic Leadership
- 7.2 Transformational Leadership

Management Team Decision

Practice Being a Manager

Self Assessment

Reel to Real

Experience Management
Explore the four levels of learning by doing the simulations module on Leadership.

© ISTOCKPHOTO.COM/ ANN MARIE KURTZ

Pod Nod
Mini lecture reviews all the learning points in the chapter.

© ISTOCKPHOTO.COM/ MAGNET CREATIVE

Reel to Real
Biz Flix is a scene from *Doomsday*. Management Workplace is a segment on Greensburg, Kansas.

© ISTOCKPHOTO.COM/ CRAFTVISION

Self Test
10 quiz questions, 6 exhibit worksheets, and PowerPoints for quick review.

© ISTOCKPHOTO.COM/ DIJITAL FILM

What Would You Do?

PepsiCo Headquarters, Purchase, New York.[1]

Growing up in India, the city water supply was only on between 3 am and 5 am, so that's when you got up to fill every bucket in the house. Two buckets were for cooking, and there were two each for you, your sister, and your brother. Because water was scarce, "you learned to live your life off those two buckets." Well, it's a long way from those buckets to being CEO of *PEPSICO*, one of the leading beverage and snack companies in the world. Fourteen years ago, in your first job as Pepsi's chief of strategy and head of mergers and acquisitions, the CEO asked you to create a strategy that would make Pepsi the "defining corporation for the 21st century." You responded with a bold plan to sell PepsiCo's restaurants, Kentucky Fried Chicken, Pizza Hut, and Taco Bell. With the billions of dollars made from that sale, you then recommended acquiring Tropicana (the juice company) for $3 billion and Quaker (Quaker Oats and Gatorade) for $14 billion.

These were huge, but very successful, changes for PepsiCo, and helped it address significant competitive issues. Now, as Pepsi's CEO, the challenges that you face are no less daunting. Commodity prices have soared worldwide, so PepsiCo is paying more for everything from corn, to oats, to cooking oil—the main ingredients in many of its products. The Coca-Cola Company, your primary worldwide competitor in beverages, is thriving again under new leadership and is taking away market share. Coke moved aggressively into healthy, noncarbonated beverages, recently acquiring Energy Brands and its fast-growing Vitaminwater and Smartwater product lines. In carbonated beverages, PepsiCo sales are down 3 to 4 percent. As a significant source of profits and cash flows, that must not continue. Even Frito-Lay, Pepsi's bulletproof cash cow, which controls 60 percent of the U.S. snack food market and provides 50 percent of company profits, faces significant challenges. With public-health experts and the medical profession drawing attention to widespread obesity, activists, the media, and government are turning their focus to fast-food restaurants and snack food companies that sell cheap, calorie-dense foods. Schools are eliminating soft drinks and "unhealthy" snacks from vending machines. Soccer moms, who bring treats for their children's teams, are under pressure to buy healthy snacks—but because of allergies and other medical restrictions, they can't bring nuts or products with wheat. The challenge for Frito-Lay is to adapt its best-selling brands, such as Lay's, Doritos, Tostitos,

Cheetos, and Fritos—none of which are thought of as healthy products—to this changing consumer market.

Of course, as CEO, you won't do any of these things yourself. Your job is to lead, inspire, and influence PepsiCo's people to address these challenges. Your first leadership issue is to find a way to motivate and challenge PepsiCo's hard-working managers and employees to make significant changes once again to keep the company competitive. What will you do to get them to be creative and innovative, to question assumptions, and to look at problems and situations in new ways? Your second leadership issue is to choose a strategic direction for Pepsi's future that will address the challenges to its business. How should PepsiCo position itself to compete with Coca-Cola, address rising commodity prices, and produce healthier products without sacrificing profits and market share? Finally, you need to build a management team to help lead the company. With these challenges, should your top executives have stronger leadership or management skills? Which are more important? And, you have to find a way to keep the top manager who lost out to you when PepsiCo made you CEO. How are you going to do that?

If you were the CEO of PepsiCo what would you do?

If you've ever been in charge, or even just thought about it, chances are you've considered questions like: Do I have what it takes to lead? What are the most important things leaders do? How can I transform a poorly performing department, division, or company? Do I need to adjust my leadership depending on the situation and the employee? Why doesn't my leadership inspire people? If you feel overwhelmed at the prospect of being a leader, you're not alone—millions of leaders in organizations across the world struggle with these fundamental leadership issues on a daily basis.

We begin this chapter by discussing what leadership is, who leaders are (meaning their traits and characteristics), and what leaders do that makes them different from people who aren't leaders. Next we examine four major contingency theories of leadership that specify which leaders are best suited for which situations or how leaders should change their behavior to lead different people in different circumstances. The chapter ends with a review of strategic leadership issues, such as charismatic and transformational leadership, which address how to work with others to meet long-term goals and how to create a viable future for an organization.

What Is Leadership?

How does an ensemble of 100 or more musicians, all playing different parts at different times on different instruments, manage to produce something as beautiful as Beethoven's Fifth Symphony? (Or, if Gustav Mahler's "Symphony of a Thousand" is on the program, a lot more people might be involved!) The conductor, like a CEO, is responsible for managing all of this complexity and ensuring a great performance. But conductors do much more than just keep the beat with a baton. According to Ramona Wis, author of *The Conductor as Leader: Principles of Leadership Applied to Life on the Podium*, conductors must also build connections between people, inspire them with vision, command their trust, and persuade them to participate in the ensemble at their very best.

After reading the next two sections, you should be able to:

1 explain what leadership is.
2 describe who leaders are and what effective leaders do.

Whether the end result is a stirring musical performance, innovation of new products, or increased profits, **leadership** is the process of influencing others to achieve group or organizational goals. The knowledge and skills you'll learn in this chapter won't make the task of leadership less daunting, but they will help you navigate it.

1 Leadership

In Chapter 1, we defined *management* as getting work done through others. In other words, managers don't do the work themselves. Managers help others do their jobs better. By contrast, *leadership* is the process of influencing others to achieve group or organizational goals. What then are the key differences between leaders and managers? Let's learn more about leadership by exploring 1.1 **the differences between leaders and managers**:

1.1 Leaders Versus Managers

leadership
the process of influencing others to achieve group or organizational goals

According to University of Southern California business professor Warren Bennis, the primary difference between leaders and managers, as shown in Exhibit 12.1, is that leaders are concerned with doing the right thing, while managers are concerned with doing things right.[2] In other words, leaders begin with the question, "What should we be doing?" while managers start with "How can we do what we're already doing better?" Leaders focus on vision, mission, goals, and objectives, while managers focus on productivity and efficiency. Managers see themselves as preservers of the status quo, while leaders see themselves as promoters of change and challengers of the status quo in that they encourage creativity and risk taking.

EXHIBIT 12.1
Managers Versus Leaders

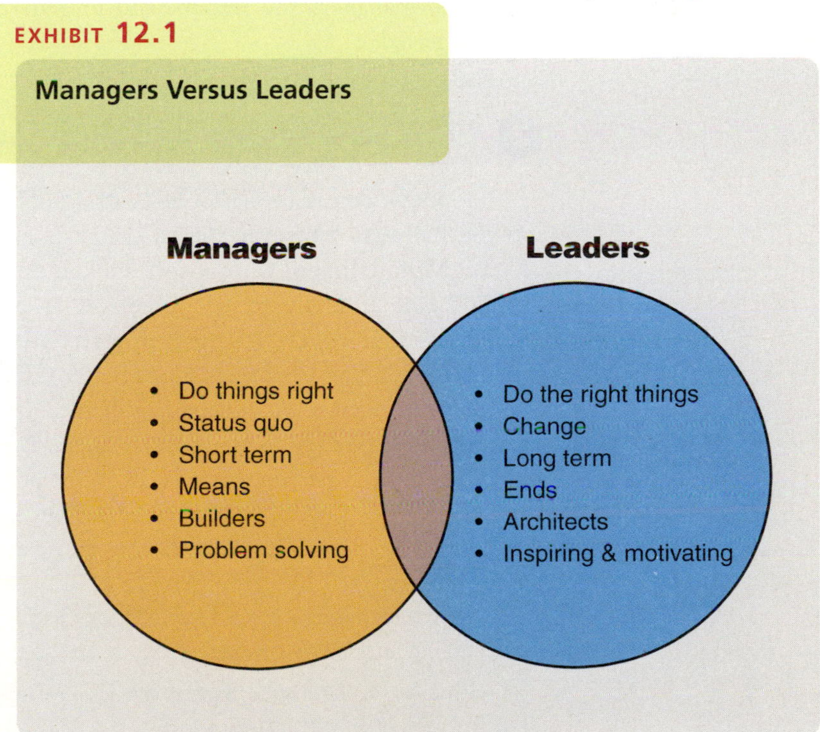

Another difference is that managers have a relatively short-term perspective, while leaders take a long-term view. Managers are concerned with control and limiting the choices of others, while leaders are more concerned with expanding people's choices and options.[3] Managers also solve problems so that others can do their work, while leaders inspire and motivate others to find their own solutions.

Finally, managers are also more concerned with *means*, how to get things done, while leaders are more concerned with *ends*, what gets done. Although leaders are different from managers, organizations need them both. Managers are critical to getting out the day-to-day work, and leaders are critical to inspiring employees and setting the organization's long-term direction. The key issue for any organization is the extent to which it is properly led and properly managed. As Warren Bennis said in summing up the difference between leaders and managers, "American organizations (and probably those in much of the rest of the industrialized world) are underled and overmanaged. They do not pay enough attention to doing the right thing, while they pay too much attention to doing things right."[4]

REVIEW 1

Leadership

Leadership is the process of influencing others to achieve group or organizational goals. Leaders are different from managers. The primary difference is that leaders are concerned with doing the right thing, while managers are concerned with doing things right. Furthermore, managers have a short-term focus and are concerned with the status quo, with means rather than ends, and with solving others' problems. By contrast, leaders have a long-term focus and are concerned with change, with ends rather than means, and with inspiring and motivating others to solve their own problems. Organizations need both managers and leaders. But in general, companies are overmanaged and underled.

2 Who Leaders Are and What Leaders Do

Indra Nooyi, PepsiCo's CEO, talks straight, has a sharp sense of humor, and sings in the hallways wherever she is. Nooyi is an extrovert. By contrast, JCPenney's CEO, Mike Ullman, who is soft-spoken and easy to approach, is an introvert.[6] Which one is likely to be successful as a CEO? According to a survey of 1,542 senior managers, it's the extrovert. Forty-seven percent of those 1,542 senior managers felt that extroverts make better CEOs, while 65 percent said that being an introvert hurts a CEO's chances of success.[7] So clearly, senior managers believe that extroverted CEOs are better leaders. But are they? Not necessarily. In fact, a relatively high percentage of CEOs, 40 percent, are introverts. Sara Lee CEO Brenda Barnes says, "I've always been shy. . . . People wouldn't call me that [an introvert], but I am."[8] Indeed, Barnes turns down all speaking requests and rarely gives interviews.

So, what makes a good leader? Does leadership success depend on who leaders are, such as introverts or extroverts, or on what leaders do and how they behave?

Let's learn more about who leaders are by investigating 2.1 **leadership traits**, and 2.2 **leadership behaviors**.

2.1 Leadership Traits

Trait theory is one way to describe who leaders are. **Trait theory** says that effective leaders possess a similar set of traits or characteristics. **Traits** are relatively stable characteristics such as abilities, psychological motives, or consistent patterns of behavior. Trait theory is also known as the "great person" theory because early versions of the theory stated that leaders are born, not made. In other words, you either have the right stuff to be a leader, or you don't. And if you don't, there is no way to get it.

For some time, it was thought that trait theory was wrong and that there are no consistent trait differences between leaders and nonleaders, or between effective and ineffective leaders. However, more recent evidence shows that "successful leaders are not like other people," that successful leaders are indeed different from the rest of us.[9] More specifically, as shown in Exhibit 12.2, leaders are different from nonleaders in the following traits: drive, the desire to lead, honesty/integrity, self-confidence, emotional stability, cognitive ability, and knowledge of the business.[10]

Drive refers to high levels of effort and is characterized by achievement, motivation, initiative, energy, and tenacity. In terms of achievement and ambition, leaders always try to make improvements or achieve success in what they're doing. Because of their initiative, they have strong desires to promote change or solve problems. Leaders typically have more energy—they have to, given the long hours they put in and followers' expectations that they be positive and upbeat. Thus, leaders must have physical, mental, and emotional vitality. Leaders are also more tenacious than

Doing the Right Thing

The Three M's: Mission, Mentor, and Mirror

Doctors take the Hippocratic oath. Lawyers swear to protect and enforce the law. Leaders . . . well, there's no equivalent for business leaders. That's why Harvard professor Howard Gardner says that business leaders can develop personal ethics by focusing on their mission, a mentor, and the mirror.

First, leaders need to develop a personal mission statement by asking themselves these questions: Why am I doing what I'm doing? What do I want from my work? What are my personal goals? Let your personal mission statement, and not the company's, guide your ethical behavior. Second, take care in choosing a mentor. An interesting study compared 20 business leaders selected at random with 20 "good" business leaders nominated by businesspeople, business school professors, and deans. The randomly selected business leaders focused on short-term goals exclusively, worrying only about next quarter's results. By contrast, 18 of the 20 "good" executives focused on the long term, what was right for the company in the long run. So, if you want to be a good leader, choose a "good" mentor. Third, periodically stand in front of the mirror to assess your ethical performance as a business leader. Are you proud or ashamed of what you accomplished and how you accomplished it? Are you proud or ashamed of your company? What needs to change to make you proud? So, do the right thing. Develop a personal mission statement. Choose the right mentor. And look hard at yourself in the mirror.[5]

trait theory
a leadership theory that holds that effective leaders possess a similar set of traits or characteristics

traits
relatively stable characteristics, such as abilities, psychological motives, or consistent patterns of behavior

EXHIBIT 12.2

Leadership Traits

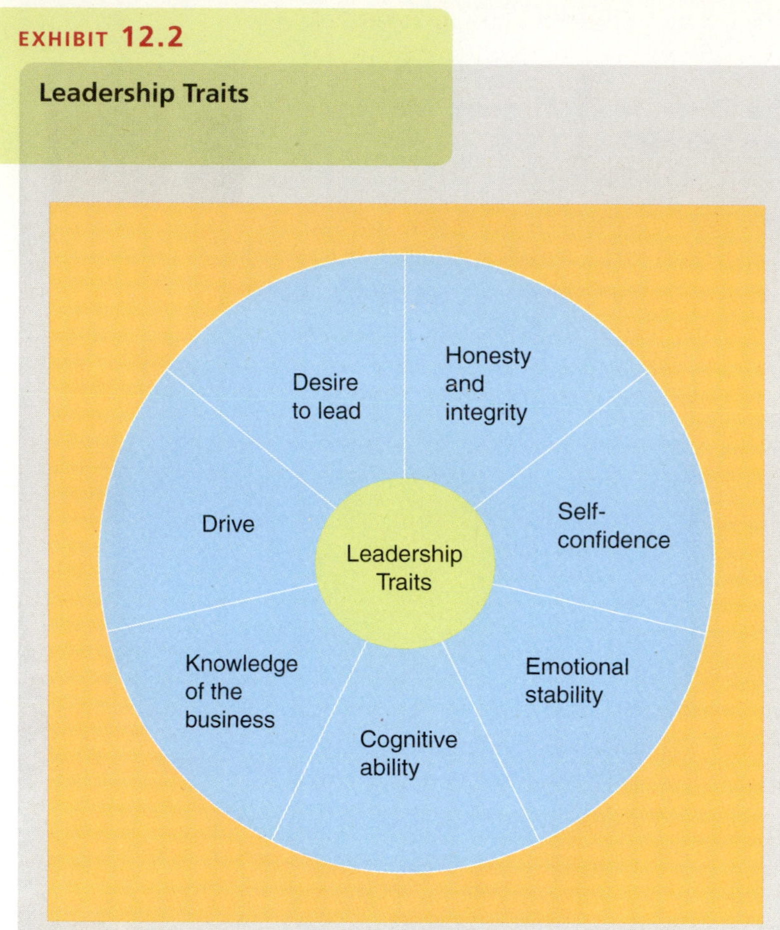

nonleaders and are better at overcoming obstacles and problems that would deter most of us.

Successful leaders also have a stronger *desire to lead.* They want to be in charge and think about ways to influence or convince others about what should or shouldn't be done. *Honesty/integrity* is also important to leaders. *Honesty*, being truthful with others, is a cornerstone of leadership. Without it, leaders won't be trusted. When leaders are honest, subordinates are willing to overlook other flaws. *Integrity* is the extent to which leaders do what they say they will do. Leaders may be honest and have good intentions, but if they don't consistently deliver on what they promise, they won't be trusted.

Self-confidence, or believing in one's abilities, also distinguishes leaders from nonleaders. Self-confident leaders are more decisive and assertive and are more likely to gain others' confidence. Moreover, self-confident leaders will admit mistakes because they view them as learning opportunities rather than a refutation of their leadership capabilities. This also means that leaders have *emotional stability*. Even when things go wrong, they remain even-tempered and consistent in their outlook and in the way they treat others. Leaders who can't control their emotions, who become angry quickly or attack and blame others for mistakes, are unlikely to be trusted.

Leaders are also smart. Leaders typically have strong *cognitive abilities*. This doesn't mean that leaders are necessarily geniuses—far from it. But it does mean that leaders have the capacity to analyze large amounts of seemingly unrelated, complex information and see patterns, opportunities, or threats where others might not see them. Finally, leaders also know their stuff, which means they have superior technical knowledge about the businesses they run. Leaders who have a good *knowledge of the business* understand the key technological decisions and concerns facing their companies. More often than not, studies indicate that effective leaders have long, extensive experience in their industries.

2.2 Leadership Behaviors

Thus far, you've read about who leaders *are*. But traits alone are not enough to make a successful leader. They are, however, a precondition for success. After all, it's hard to imagine a truly successful leader who lacks most of these qualities. Leaders who have these traits (or many of them) must then take actions that encourage people to achieve group or organizational goals.[11] Accordingly, we now examine what leaders *do*, meaning the behaviors they perform or the actions they take to influence others to achieve group or organizational goals.

Researchers at the University of Michigan, Ohio State University, and the University of Texas examined the specific behaviors that leaders use to improve subordinate satisfaction and performance. Hundreds of studies were conducted and hundreds of leader behaviors were examined. At all three universities, two basic leader behaviors emerged as central to successful leadership: initiating structure (called *job-centered leadership* at the University of Michigan and *concern for production* at the University of Texas) and considerate leader behavior (called *employee-centered leadership* at the University of Michigan and *concern for people* at the University of Texas).[12] These two leader behaviors form the basis for many of the leadership theories discussed in this chapter.

Initiating structure is the degree to which a leader structures the roles of followers by setting goals, giving directions, setting deadlines, and assigning tasks. A leader's ability to initiate structure primarily affects subordinates' job performance. When Jamie Dimon became CEO of *JPMORGAN CHASE*, the financial services company had four different computer systems from previously acquired companies, making it difficult to access information on account histories, credit cards, and mortgages. Dimon told his executives to put one system in place, and, "If you don't do it in six weeks, I'll make all the choices myself."[13] The deadline was met. Now, with just one software system, the annual cost of processing credit card statements has dropped from $80 to $52 per customer and Morgan has increased its open credit card accounts by 55 percent.

Consideration is the extent to which a leader is friendly, approachable, and supportive and shows concern for employees. Consideration primarily affects subordinates' job satisfaction. Specific leader consideration behaviors include listening to employees' problems and concerns, consulting with employees before making decisions, and treating employees as equals. Former *HP* CEO Mark Hurd was very focused on "execution," that is, initiating structure. Hurd, however, was also a considerate leader. The managers and employers who worked for him appreciated that he listened and was willing to help them with their problems and concerns. Dave Booth, senior vice president for sales, says, "If I pick up the phone and tell Mark's office I have an urgent customer request, if he isn't already with a customer, he'll stop what he's doing and call me to find out what he can do. The fact that I pick up the phone and call his office directly and not go through channels is new."[14]

Although researchers at all three universities generally agreed that initiating structure and consideration were basic leader behaviors, their interpretation differed on how these two behaviors are related to one another and which are necessary for effective leadership. The University of Michigan studies indicated that initiating structure and consideration were mutually exclusive behaviors on opposite ends of the same continuum. In other words, leaders who wanted to be more considerate would have to do less initiating of structure (and vice versa). The University of Michigan studies also indicated that only considerate leader behaviors (i.e., employee-centered behaviors) were associated with successful leadership. By contrast, researchers at Ohio State University and the University of Texas found that initiating structure and consideration were independent behaviors, meaning

initiating structure
the degree to which a leader structures the roles of followers by setting goals, giving directions, setting deadlines, and assigning tasks

consideration
the extent to which a leader is friendly, approachable, and supportive and shows concern for employees

what *really* works

Leadership Traits That Do Make a Difference

For decades, researchers assumed that leadership traits such as drive, emotional stability, cognitive ability, and charisma were *not* related to effective leadership. More recent evidence, however, shows that there are reliable trait differences between leaders and nonleaders. In fact, 54 studies based on more than 6,000 people clearly indicate that in terms of leadership traits, "successful leaders are not like other people."

Traits and Perceptions of Leadership Effectiveness

Several leadership models argue that in order to be successful, leaders must be viewed as good leaders by their followers. (This is completely different from determining whether leaders actually improve organizational performance.) Consequently, one test of trait theory is whether leaders with particular traits are viewed as more or less effective leaders by their followers.

Intelligence. On average, there is a 75 percent chance that intelligent leaders will be seen as better leaders than less intelligent leaders.

INTELLIGENCE

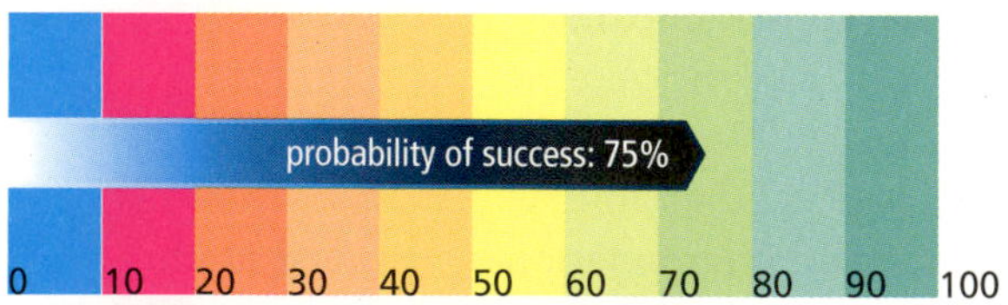

Dominance. On average, there is only a 57 percent chance that leaders with highly dominant personalities will be seen as better leaders than those with less dominant personalities.

DOMINANCE

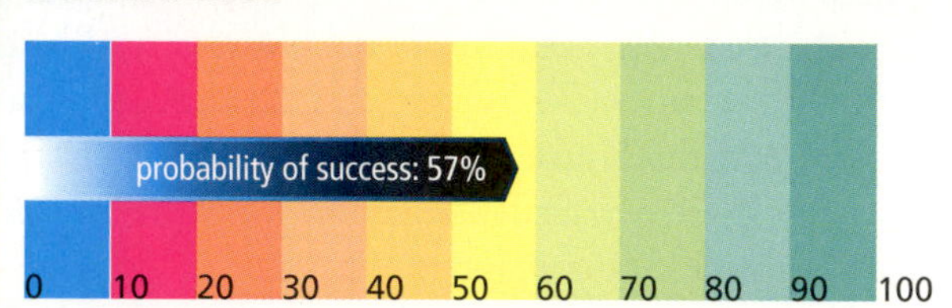

Extroversion. On average, there is a 63 percent chance that extroverts will be seen as better leaders than introverts.

EXTROVERSION

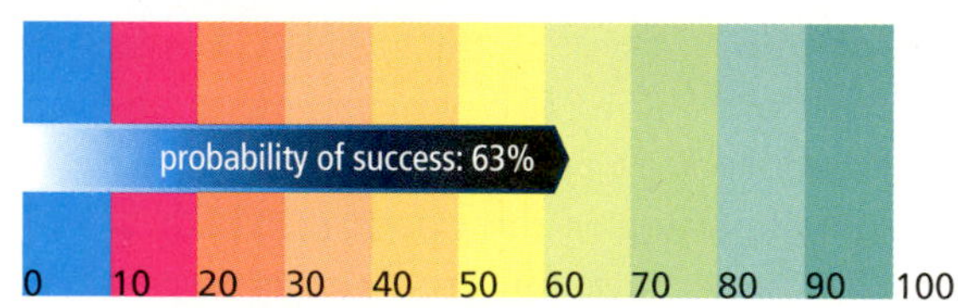

Charisma and Leadership Effectiveness

As discussed at the end of the chapter, *charismatic leadership* is the set of behavioral tendencies and personal characteristics of leaders that creates an exceptionally strong relationship between leaders and their followers. More specifically, charismatic leaders articulate a clear vision for the future that is based on strongly held values or morals; model those values by acting in a way consistent with the company's vision; communicate high performance expectations to followers; and display confidence in followers' abilities to achieve the vision.

Charisma and Performance. On average, there is a 72 percent chance that charismatic leaders will have better-performing followers and organizations than less charismatic leaders.

CHARISMA AND PERFORMANCE

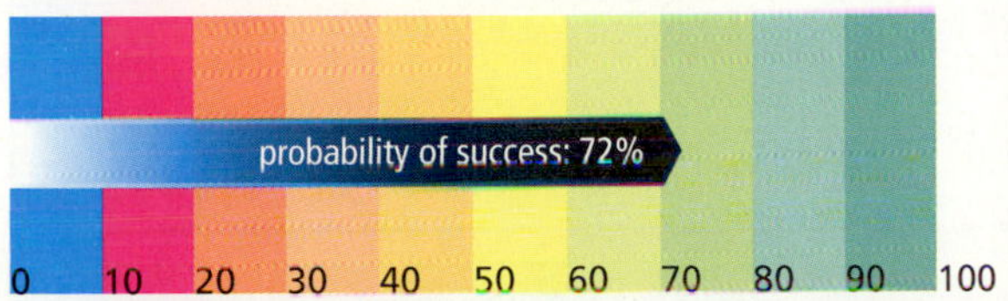

Charisma and Perceived Leader Effectiveness. On average, there is an 89 percent chance that charismatic leaders will be perceived as more effective leaders than less charismatic leaders.

CHARISMA AND PERCEIVED LEADER EFFECTIVENESS

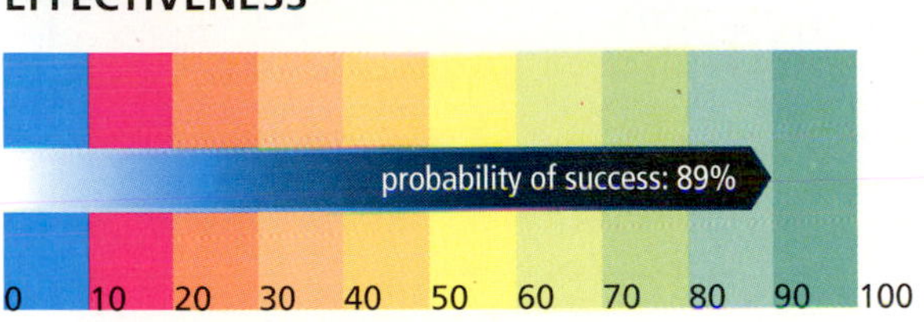

Charisma and Leader Satisfaction. On average, there is a 90 percent chance that the followers of charismatic leaders will be more satisfied with their leaders than the followers of less charismatic leaders.[15]

CHARISMA AND LEADER SATISFACTION

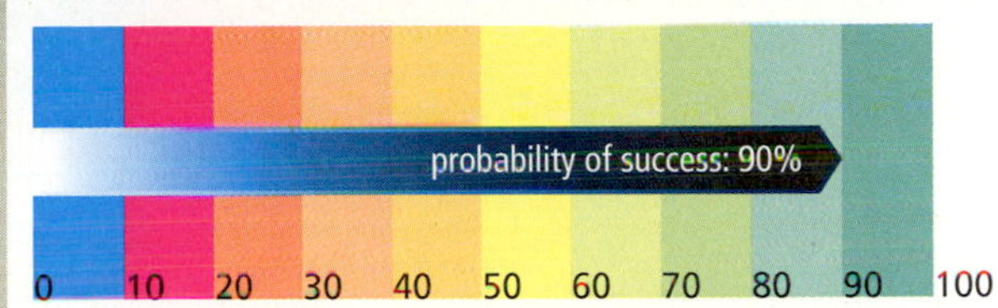

that leaders can be considerate and initiate structure at the same time. Additional evidence confirms this finding.[16] The same researchers also concluded that the most effective leaders were strong on both initiating structure and considerate leader behaviors.

This "high-high" approach can be seen in the upper right corner of the Blake/Mouton leadership grid, shown in Exhibit 12.3. Blake and Mouton used two leadership behaviors, concern for people (i.e., consideration) and concern for production (i.e., initiating structure), to categorize five different leadership styles. Both behaviors are rated on a 9-point scale, with 1 representing "low" and 9 representing "high." Blake and Mouton suggest that a "high-high," or 9, 9 leadership style is the best. They call this style *team management* because leaders who use it display a high concern for people (9) and a high concern for production (9).

By contrast, leaders use a 9, 1 *authority-compliance* leadership style when they have a high concern for production and a low concern for people. A 1, 9 *country club* style occurs when leaders care about having a friendly, enjoyable work environment but don't really pay much attention to production or performance. The worst leadership style, according to the grid, is the 1, 1 *impoverished* leader, who shows little concern for people or production and does the bare minimum needed to keep his or her job. Finally, the 5, 5 *middle-of-the-road* style occurs when leaders show a moderate amount of concern for both people and production.

Is the team management style, with a high concern for production and a high concern for people, the best leadership style? Logically, it would seem so. Why

EXHIBIT 12.3

Blake/Mouton Leadership Grid

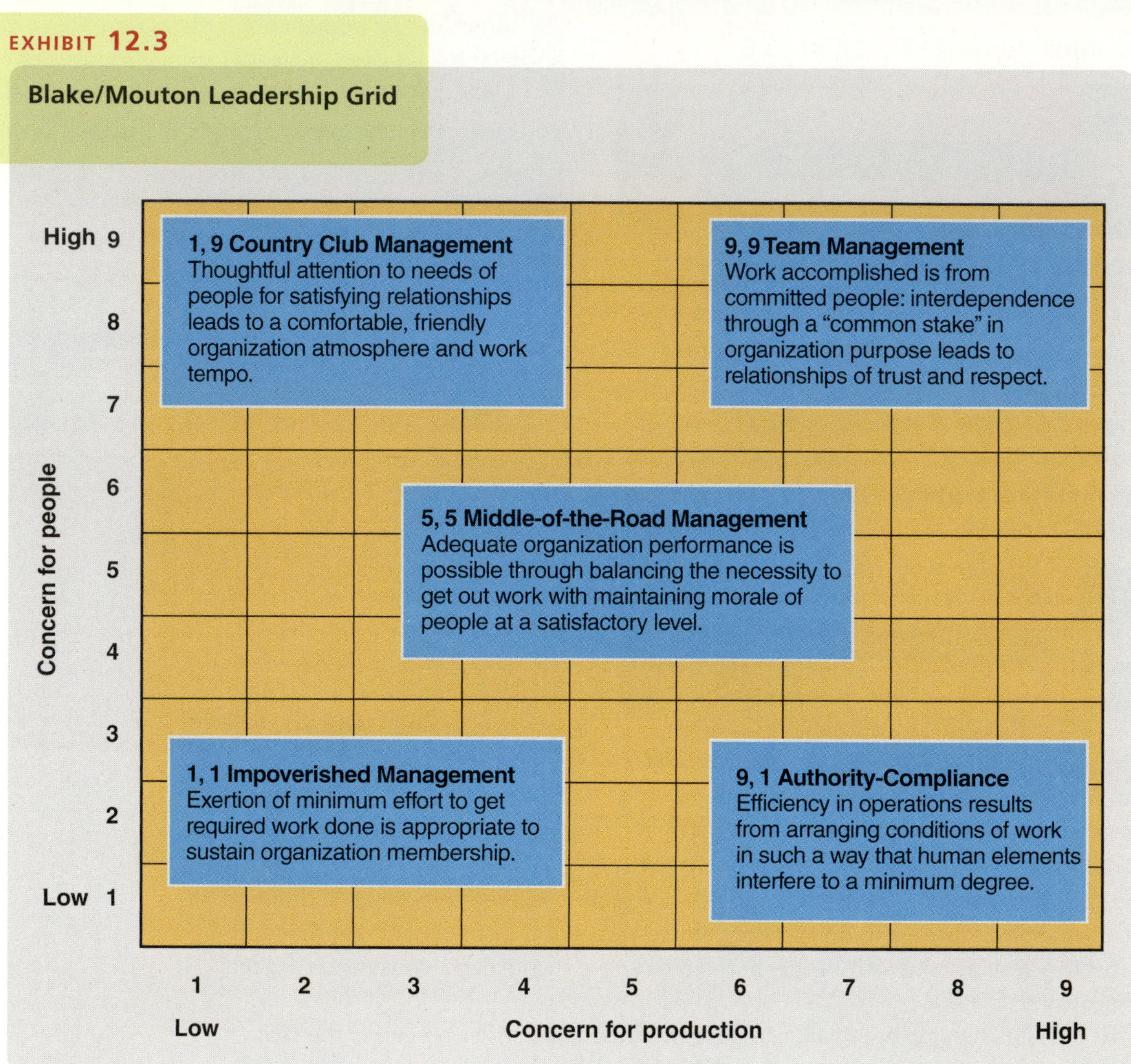

Source: R. R. Blake & A. A. McCanse, "The Leadership Grid®," *Leadership Dilemmas—Grid Solutions* (Houston: Gulf Publishing Company), 21. Copyright © 1991, by Scientific Methods, Inc. Reproduced by permission of the owners.

wouldn't you want to show high concern for both people and production? Nonetheless, nearly 50 years of research indicates that there isn't one best leadership style. The best leadership style depends on the situation. In other words, no one leadership behavior by itself and no one combination of leadership behaviors works well across all situations and employees.

REVIEW 2

Who Leaders Are and What Leaders Do

Trait theory says that effective leaders possess traits or characteristics that differentiate them from nonleaders. Those traits are drive, the desire to lead, honesty/integrity, self-confidence, emotional stability, cognitive ability, and knowledge of the business. Traits alone aren't enough for successful leadership, however; leaders who have these traits (or many of them) must also behave in ways that encourage people to achieve group or organizational goals. Two key leader behaviors are initiating structure, which improves subordinate performance, and consideration, which improves subordinate satisfaction. There is no single best combination of these behaviors. The best leadership style depends on the situation.

Situational Approaches to Leadership

After leader traits and behaviors, the situational approach to leadership is the third major method used in the study of leadership. We'll review four major situational approaches to leadership—Fiedler's contingency theory, path-goal theory, Hersey and Blanchard's Situational Leadership theory, and Vroom and Yetton's normative decision model. All assume that the effectiveness of any **leadership style**, the way a leader generally behaves toward followers, depends on the situation.[17] Nonetheless, these theories differ in one significant way. Accordingly, there is no one "best" leadership style. According to situational leadership theories, there is no one best leadership style. But one of these situational theories differs from the other three in one significant way. Fiedler's contingency theory assumes that leadership styles are consistent and difficult to change. Therefore, leaders must be placed in or matched to a situation that fits their leadership style. By contrast, the other three situational theories all assume that leaders are capable of adapting and adjusting their leadership styles to fit the demands of different situations.

After reading the next four sections, you should be able to:

3 explain Fiedler's contingency theory.
4 describe how path-goal theory works.
5 discuss Hersey and Blanchard's Situational Leadership theory.
6 explain the normative decision theory.

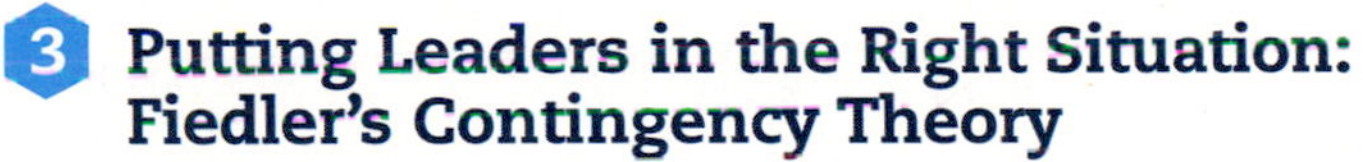

3 Putting Leaders in the Right Situation: Fiedler's Contingency Theory

Fiedler's **contingency theory** states that, in order to maximize work group performance, leaders must be matched to the right leadership situation.[18] More specifically, as shown in Exhibit 12.4, the first basic assumption of Fiedler's theory is that leaders are effective when the work groups they lead perform well. So, instead of judging leaders' effectiveness by what they do (i.e., initiating structure and consideration) or who they are (i.e., trait theory), Fiedler assesses leaders by the conduct and performance of the people they supervise. Second, Fiedler assumes that leaders are generally unable to change their leadership styles and that they will be more effective when their styles are matched to the proper situation. Third, Fiedler assumes that the favorableness of a situation for a leader depends on the degree to which the situation permits the leader to influence the behavior of group members. Fiedler's third assumption is consistent with our definition of leadership as the process of influencing others to achieve group or organizational goals. In other words, in addition to traits, behaviors, and a favorable situation to match, leaders have to be allowed to lead.

leadership style
the way a leader generally behaves toward followers

contingency theory
a leadership theory that states that in order to maximize work group performance, leaders must be matched to the situation that best fits their leadership style

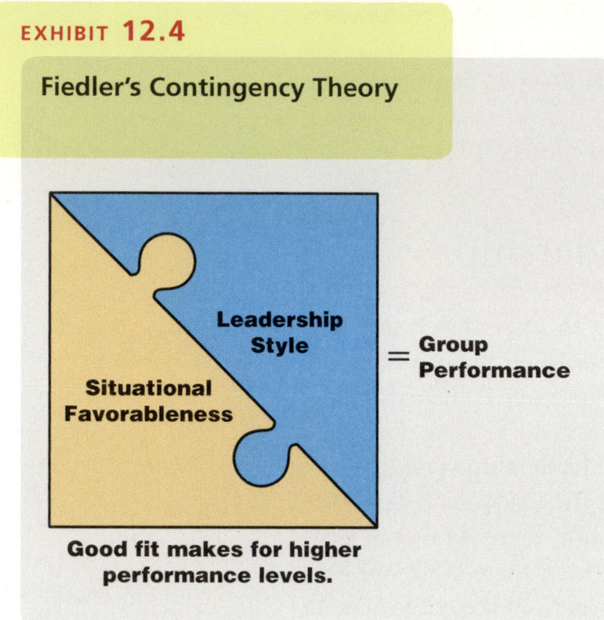

Let's learn more about Fiedler's contingency theory by examining 3.1 **the least preferred coworker and leadership styles**, 3.2 **situational favorableness**, and 3.3 **how to match leadership styles to situations**.

3.1 Leadership Style: Least Preferred Coworker

When Fiedler refers to *leadership style*, he means the way that leaders generally behave toward their followers. However, Fiedler also assumes that leadership styles are tied to leaders' underlying needs and personalities. Since personality and needs are relatively stable, he assumes that leaders are generally incapable of changing their leadership styles. In other words, the way that leaders treat people now is probably the way they've always treated others. So, according to Fiedler, if your boss's first instinct is to yell and scream and blame others, chances are he or she has always done that.

Fiedler uses a questionnaire called the Least Preferred Coworker (LPC) scale to measure leadership style; a sample of the scale is shown in Exhibit 12.5 (see the Self-Assessment at the end of this chapter for the full LPC scale). When completing the LPC scale, people are instructed to consider all of the people with whom they have ever worked and then to choose the one person with whom they have worked *least* well. Fiedler explains, "This does not have to be the person you liked least well, but should be the one person with whom you have the most trouble getting the job done."[19]

Would you describe your LPC as pleasant, friendly, supportive, interesting, cheerful, and sincere? Or would you describe the person as unpleasant, unfriendly, hostile, boring, gloomy, and insincere? People who describe their LPC in a positive way (scoring 64 and above) have *relationship-oriented* leadership styles. After all, if they can still be positive about their least preferred coworker, they must be people-oriented. By contrast, people who describe their LPC in a negative way (scoring 57 or below) have *task-oriented* leadership styles. Given a choice, they'll focus first on getting the job done and second on making sure everyone gets along. Finally, those with moderate scores (from 58 to 63) have a more flexible leadership style and can be somewhat relationship-oriented or somewhat task-oriented.

3.2 Situational Favorableness

Fiedler assumes that leaders will be more effective when their leadership styles are matched to the proper situation. More specifically, Fiedler defines **situational favorableness** as the degree to which a particular situation either permits or denies a leader the chance to influence the behavior of group members.[20] In highly favorable situations, leaders find that their actions influence followers. But in highly unfavorable situations, leaders have little or no success influencing the people they are trying to lead.

situational favorableness
the degree to which a particular situation either permits or denies a leader the chance to influence the behavior of group members

EXHIBIT 12.5

Sample from Fiedler's Least Preferred Coworker Scale

Pleasant	8	7	6	5	4	3	2	1	Unpleasant
Friendly	8	7	6	5	4	3	2	1	Unfriendly
Supportive	8	7	6	5	4	3	2	1	Hostile
Boring	1	2	3	4	5	6	7	8	Interesting
Gloomy	1	2	3	4	5	6	7	8	Cheerful
Insincere	1	2	3	4	5	6	7	8	Sincere

Source: F. E. Fiedler & M. M. Chemers, *Improving Leadership Effectiveness: The Leader Match Concept*, 2nd ed. (New York: Wiley, 1984). Available at http://depts.washington.edu/psych/faculty/*cw/fiedler_cv.pdf, 23 March 2002. Reprinted by permission of the authors.

Three situational factors determine the favorability of a situation: leader-member relations, task structure, and position power. The most important situational factor is **leader-member relations**, which refers to how well followers respect, trust, and like their leaders. When leader-member relations are good, followers trust the leader and there is a friendly work atmosphere. **Task structure** is the degree to which the requirements of a subordinate's tasks are clearly specified. With highly structured tasks, employees have clear job responsibilities, goals, and procedures. **Position power** is the degree to which leaders are able to hire, fire, reward, and punish workers. The more influence leaders have over hiring, firing, rewards, and punishments, the greater their power.

Leader-member relations, task structure, and position power can be combined into eight situations that differ in their favorability to leaders. In general, the most favorable situations for leaders occur when followers like and trust their leaders, when followers know what to do because their tasks are highly structured, and when leaders have the power to hire, fire, reward, and punish workers. In this situation, it's relatively easy for a leader to influence followers. By contrast, the least favorable situations for leaders occur when followers don't like or trust their leaders, when followers are not sure what they're supposed to be doing because their tasks or jobs are highly unstructured, and when leaders don't have the ability to hire, fire, reward, or punish the people who work for them. In short, it's very difficult to influence followers under these conditions.

leader-member relations
the degree to which followers respect, trust, and like their leaders

task structure
the degree to which the requirements of a subordinate's tasks are clearly specified

position power
the degree to which leaders are able to hire, fire, reward, and punish workers

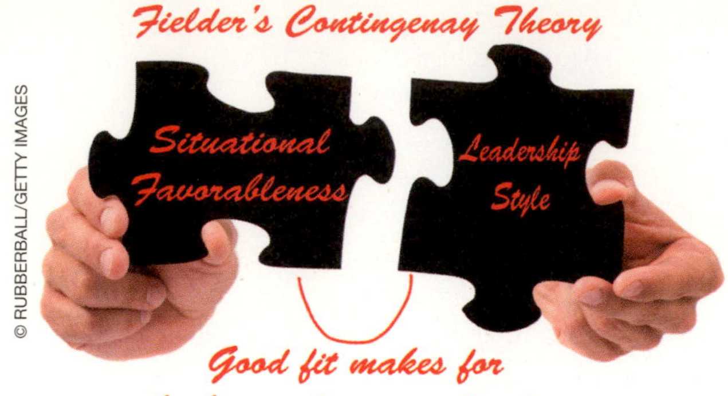

Good fit makes for higher performance levels

3.3 Matching Leadership Styles to Situations

After studying thousands of leaders and followers in hundreds of different situations, Fiedler found that the performance of relationship- and task-oriented leaders followed the pattern displayed in Exhibit 12.6.

Relationship-oriented leaders with high LPC scores were better leaders (i.e., their groups performed more effectively) under moderately favorable situations. In moderately favorable situations, the leader may be liked somewhat, tasks may be somewhat structured, and the leader may have some position power. In this situation, a relationship-oriented leader improves leader-member relations, which is the most important of the three situational factors. In turn, morale and performance improve. How did Gordon Bethune turn around *CONTINENTAL AIRLINES* and its previously poisonous labor-management relations? He explains it this way: "When I was a mechanic, I knew how much faster I could fix an airplane when I wanted to fix it than when I didn't. I've tried to make it so our guys want to do it."[21]

By contrast, as Exhibit 12.6 shows, task-oriented leaders with low LPC scores are better leaders in highly favorable and unfavorable situations. Task-oriented leaders do well in favorable situations where leaders are liked, tasks are structured, and the leader has the power to hire, fire, reward, and punish. In these favorable situations, task-oriented leaders effectively step on the gas of a well-tuned car. Their focus on performance sets the goal for the group, which then charges forward to meet it. But task-oriented leaders also do well in unfavorable situations where leaders are disliked, tasks are unstructured, and the leader doesn't have the power to hire, fire, reward, and punish. In these unfavorable situations, the task-oriented leader sets goals, which focus attention on performance and clarify what needs to be done, thus overcoming low task structure. This is enough to jump-start performance even if workers don't like or trust the leader.

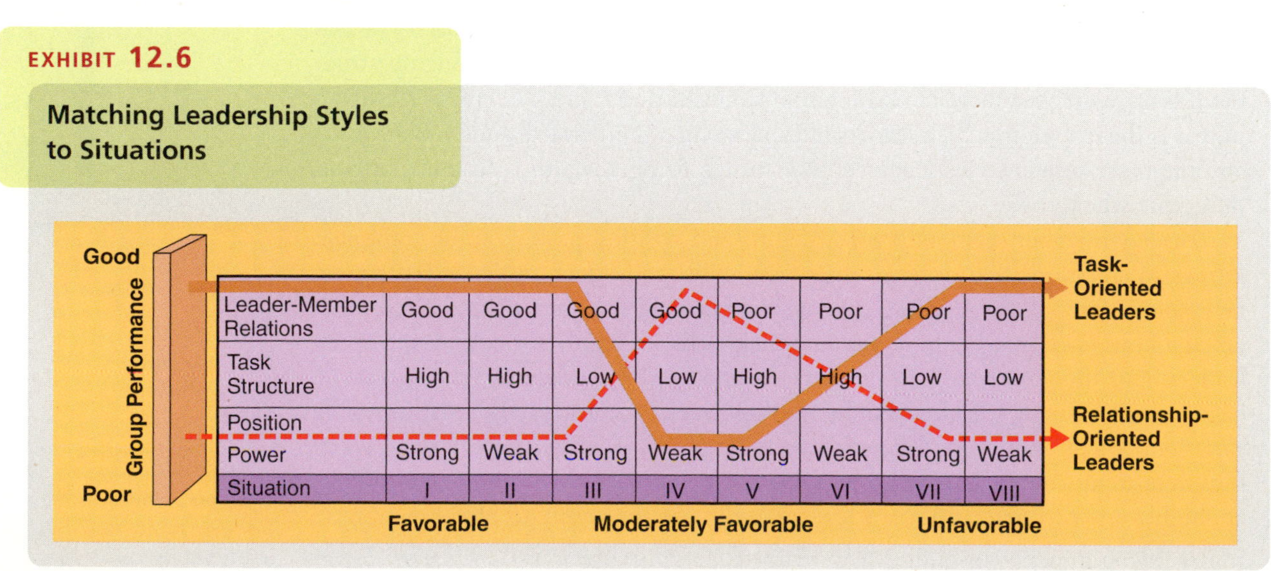

EXHIBIT 12.6
Matching Leadership Styles to Situations
Good
Group Performance
Poor
Leader-Member Relations | Good | Good | Good | Good | Poor | Poor | Poor | Poor
Task Structure | High | High | Low | Low | High | High | Low | Low
Position Power | Strong | Weak | Strong | Weak | Strong | Weak | Strong | Weak
Situation | I | II | III | IV | V | VI | VII | VIII
Favorable
Moderately Favorable
Unfavorable
Task-Oriented Leaders
Relationship-Oriented Leaders

Finally, though not shown in Exhibit 12.6, people with moderate LPC scores, who can be somewhat relationship-oriented or somewhat task-oriented, tend to do fairly well in all situations because they can adapt their behavior. Typically, though, they don't perform quite as well as relationship-oriented or task-oriented leaders whose leadership styles are well matched to the situation.

Recall, however, that Fiedler assumes leaders to be incapable of changing their leadership styles. Accordingly, the key to applying Fiedler's contingency theory in the workplace is to accurately measure and match leaders to situations or to teach leaders how to change situational favorableness by changing leader-member relations, task structure, or position power. Though matching or placing leaders in appropriate situations works particularly well, practicing managers have had little luck reengineering situations to fit their leadership styles. The primary problem, as you've no doubt realized, is the complexity of the theory.

In a study designed to teach leaders how to reengineer their situations to fit their leadership styles, Fiedler found that most of the leaders simply did not understand what they were supposed to do to change their situations. Furthermore, if they didn't like their LPC profile (perhaps they felt they were more relationship-oriented than their scores indicated), they arbitrarily changed it to better suit their view of themselves. Of course, the theory won't work as well if leaders are attempting to change situational factors to fit their perceived leadership style rather than their real leadership style.[22]

REVIEW 3

Putting Leaders in the Right Situation: Fiedler's Contingency Theory

Fiedler's theory assumes that leaders are effective when their work groups perform well, that leaders are unable to change their leadership styles, that leadership styles must be matched to the proper situation, and that favorable situations permit leaders to influence group members. According to the Least Preferred Coworker (LPC) scale, there are two basic leadership styles. People who describe their LPC in a positive way have relationship-oriented leadership styles. People who describe their LPC in a negative way have task-oriented leadership styles. Situational favorableness occurs when leaders can influence followers and is determined by leader-member relations, task structure, and position power. In general, relationship-oriented leaders with high LPC scores are better leaders under moderately favorable situations, whereas task-oriented leaders with low LPC scores are better leaders in highly favorable and unfavorable situations. Since Fiedler assumes that leaders are incapable of changing their leadership styles, the key is to accurately measure and match leaders to situations or to teach leaders how to change situational factors. Although matching or placing leaders in appropriate situations works well, reengineering situations to fit leadership styles doesn't because the model is complex and difficult for people to understand.

4 Adapting Leader Behavior: Path-Goal Theory

Just as its name suggests, **path-goal theory** states that leaders can increase subordinate satisfaction and performance by clarifying and clearing the paths to goals and by increasing the number and kinds of rewards available for goal attainment.

path-goal theory
a leadership theory that states that leaders can increase subordinate satisfaction and performance by clarifying and clearing the paths to goals and by increasing the number and kinds of rewards available for goal attainment

EXHIBIT 12.7

Path-Goal Theory

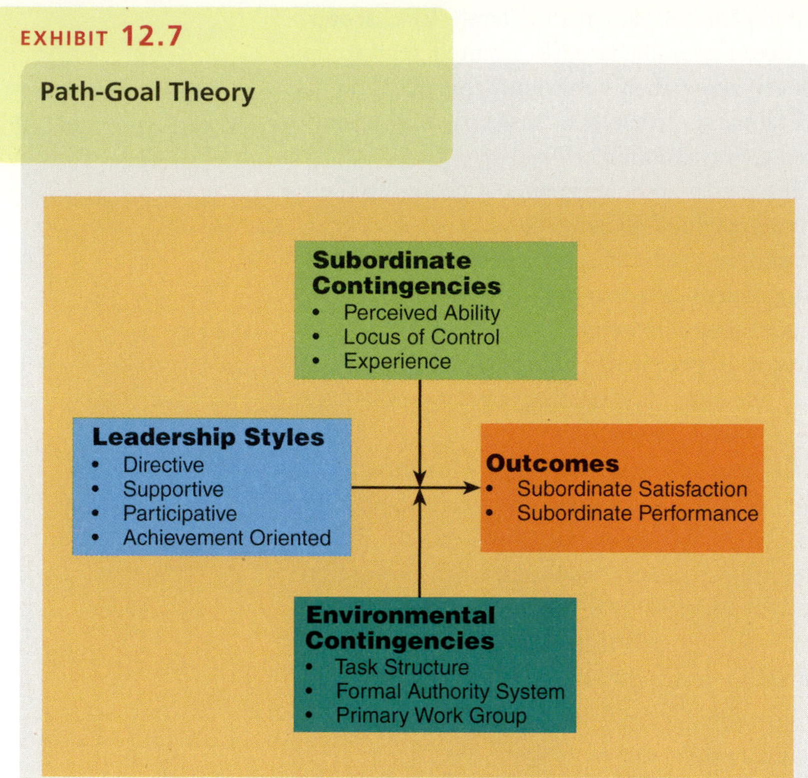

Said another way, leaders need to clarify how followers can achieve organizational goals, take care of problems that prevent followers from achieving goals, and then find more and varied rewards to motivate followers to achieve those goals.[23]

Leaders must meet two conditions for path clarification, path clearing, and rewards to increase followers' motivation and effort. First, leader behavior must be a source of immediate or future satisfaction for followers. The things you do as a leader must either please your followers today or lead to activities or rewards that will satisfy them in the future. Second, while providing the coaching, guidance, support, and rewards necessary for effective work performance, leader behaviors must complement and not duplicate the characteristics of followers' work environments. Thus, leader behaviors must offer something unique and valuable to followers beyond what they're already experiencing as they do their jobs or what they can already do for themselves. In contrast to Fiedler's contingency theory, path-goal theory assumes that leaders *can* change and adapt their leadership styles. Exhibit 12.7 illustrates this process, showing that leaders change and adapt their leadership styles contingent on their subordinates or the environment in which those subordinates work.

Let's learn more about path-goal theory by examining 4.1 **the four kinds of leadership styles that leaders use**, 4.2 **the subordinate and environmental contingency factors that determine when different leader styles are effective**, and 4.3 **the outcomes of path-goal theory in improving employee satisfaction and performance**.

4.1 Leadership Styles

directive leadership
a leadership style in which the leader lets employees know precisely what is expected of them, gives them specific guidelines for performing tasks, schedules work, sets standards of performance, and makes sure that people follow standard rules and regulations

As illustrated in Exhibit 12.7, the four leadership styles in path-goal theory are directive, supportive, participative, and achievement oriented.[24] **Directive leadership** involves letting employees know precisely what is expected of them, giving them specific guidelines for performing tasks, scheduling work, setting standards of performance, and making sure that people follow standard rules and regulations. For example, "each month, *AUDI*'s chief executive, Martin Winterkorn, rolls up his sleeves and leads a trouble-shooting session with managers and engineers at the company's electronics center, zeroing in on faulty systems and problem parts. Winterkorn's rules: no shifting the blame to anyone else, such as suppliers; no phone calls to subordinates—the brains to remedy the defects better be in the room; and no one leaves until a fix is found."[25] Why is Winterkorn so demanding (i.e., directive)? As he explains, "We want [Audi] to be the No. 1 premium [car] brand."

Supportive leadership involves being approachable and friendly to employees, showing concern for them and their welfare, treating them as equals, and creating a friendly climate. Supportive leadership is very similar to considerate leader behavior. Supportive leadership often results in employee satisfaction with the job and with leaders. This leadership style may also result in improved performance when it increases employee confidence, lowers employee job stress, or improves relations and trust between employees and leaders.[26] **Participative leadership** involves consulting employees for their suggestions and input before making decisions. Participation in decision making should help followers understand which goals are most important and clarify the paths to accomplish them. Furthermore, when people participate in decisions, they become more committed to making them work.

Achievement-oriented leadership means setting challenging goals, having high expectations of employees, and displaying confidence that employees will assume responsibility and put forth extraordinary effort. Simon Cooper, president and COO of the Ritz-Carlton luxury hotel chain, uses the phrase "He who says it, does" to describe achievement-oriented leadership. Cooper explains, "I use this phrase whenever someone convinces me that they can achieve something I consider to be un-achievable. In the past I've been known to add focus to a goal by making a bet to see if they can make it—sometimes with amusing consequences. I remember being at a mountain resort in Canada and proposing an incredible goal for the season. The team convinced me that they could achieve it, and I offered to jump into the lake if they did. It's a long story, but they made it. There's a great scene of a hole being cut in the ice and an ambulance on standby while I gave a whole new meaning to the term 'dunking.' The cognac [afterward] was very welcome."[27]

4.2 Subordinate and Environmental Contingencies

As shown in Exhibit 12.7, path-goal theory specifies that leader behaviors should be adapted to subordinate characteristics. The theory identifies three kinds of subordinate contingencies: perceived ability, experience, and locus of control. *Perceived ability* is simply how much ability subordinates believe they have for doing their jobs well. Subordinates who perceive that they have a great deal of ability will be dissatisfied with directive leader behaviors. Experienced employees are likely to react in a similar way. Since they already know how to do their jobs (or perceive that they do), they don't need or want close supervision. By contrast, subordinates with little experience or little perceived ability will welcome directive leadership.

Locus of control is a personality measure that indicates the extent to which people believe that they have control over what happens to them in life. *Internals* believe that what happens to them, good or bad, is largely a result of their choices and actions. *Externals*, on the other hand, believe that what happens to them is caused by external forces beyond their control. Accordingly, externals are much more comfortable with a directive leadership style, whereas internals greatly prefer a participative leadership style because they like to have a say in what goes on at work.

Path-goal theory specifies that leader behaviors should complement rather than duplicate the characteristics of followers' work environments. There are three kinds

supportive leadership
a leadership style in which the leader is friendly and approachable to employees, shows concern for employees and their welfare, treats them as equals, and creates a friendly climate

participative leadership
a leadership style in which the leader consults employees for their suggestions and input before making decisions

achievement-oriented leadership
a leadership style in which the leader sets challenging goals, has high expectations of employees, and displays confidence that employees will assume responsibility and put forth extraordinary effort

of environmental contingencies: task structure, the formal authority system, and the primary work group. As in Fiedler's contingency theory, *task structure* is the degree to which the requirements of a subordinate's tasks are clearly specified. When task structure is low and tasks are unclear, directive leadership should be used because it complements the work environment. When task structure is high and tasks are clear, however, directive leadership is not needed because it duplicates what task structure provides. Alternatively, when tasks are stressful, frustrating, or dissatisfying, leaders should respond with supportive leadership.

The *formal authority system* is an organization's set of procedures, rules, and policies. When the formal authority system is unclear, directive leadership complements the situation by reducing uncertainty and increasing clarity. But when the formal authority system is clear, directive leadership is redundant and should not be used.

Primary work group refers to the amount of work-oriented participation or emotional support that is provided by an employee's immediate work group. Participative leadership should be used when tasks are complex and there is little existing work-oriented participation in the primary work group. When tasks are stressful, frustrating, or repetitive, supportive leadership is called for.

Finally, since keeping track of all of these subordinate and environmental contingencies can get a bit confusing, Exhibit 12.8 provides a summary of when directive, supportive, participative, and achievement-oriented leadership styles should be used.

4.3 Outcomes

Does following path-goal theory improve subordinate satisfaction and performance? Preliminary evidence suggests that it does.[28] In particular, people who work for supportive leaders are much more satisfied with their jobs and their bosses. Likewise,

EXHIBIT 12.8

Path-Goal Theory: When to Use Directive, Supportive, Participative, or Achievement-Oriented Leadership

Directive Leadership	Supportive Leadership	Participative Leadership	Achievement-Oriented Leadership
Unstructured tasks	Structured, simple, repetitive tasks	Experienced workers	Unchallenging tasks
Inexperienced workers	Stressful, frustrating tasks	Workers with high perceived ability	
Workers with low perceived ability	When workers lack confidence	Workers with internal locus of control	
Workers with external locus of control	Clear formal authority system	Workers not satisfied with rewards	
Unclear formal authority system		Complex tasks	

people who work for directive leaders are more satisfied with their jobs and bosses (but not quite as much as when their bosses are supportive) and perform their jobs better, too. Does adapting one's leadership style to subordinate and environmental characteristics improve subordinate satisfaction and performance? At this point, because it is difficult to test this complex theory completely, it's too early to tell.[29] However, since the data clearly show that it makes sense for leaders to be both supportive *and* directive, it also makes sense that leaders can improve subordinate satisfaction and performance by adding participative and achievement-oriented leadership styles to their leadership capabilities.

REVIEW 4

Adapting Leader Behavior: Path-Goal Theory

Path-goal theory states that leaders can increase subordinate satisfaction and performance by clarifying and clearing the paths to goals and by increasing the number and kinds of rewards available for goal attainment. For this to work, however, leader behavior must be a source of immediate or future satisfaction for followers and must complement rather than duplicate the characteristics of followers' work environments. In contrast to Fiedler's contingency theory, path-goal theory assumes that leaders can and do change and adapt their leadership styles (directive, supportive, participative, and achievement-oriented), depending on their subordinates (experience, perceived ability, internal or external) or the environment in which those subordinates work (task structure, formal authority system, or primary work group).

5 Adapting Leader Behavior: Hersey and Blanchard's Situational Leadership® Theory

Have you ever had a new job that you didn't know how to do and your boss was not around to help you learn it? Conversely, have you ever known exactly how to do your job but your boss kept treating you as though you didn't? Hersey and Blanchard's Situational Leadership theory is based on the idea of follower readiness. Hersey and Blanchard argue that employees have different levels of readiness for handling different jobs, responsibilities, and work assignments. Accordingly, Hersey and Blanchard's **situational theory** states that leaders need to adjust their leadership styles to match followers' readiness.[30]

Let's learn more about Hersey and Blanchard's situational theory by examining 5.1 **worker readiness**, and 5.2 **different leadership styles**.

5.1 Worker Readiness

Worker readiness is the ability and willingness to take responsibility for directing one's behavior at work. Readiness is composed of two components. *Job readiness* consists of the amount of knowledge, skill, ability, and experience people have to perform their jobs. As you would expect, people with greater skill, ability, and experience do a better job of supervising their own work. *Psychological readiness*, on the other hand, is a feeling of self-confidence or self-respect. Confident people are better at guiding their own work than insecure people are. Hersey and Blanchard combine job readiness and psychological readiness to produce four different levels of readiness in their situational leadership theory. The lowest level, R1, represents

situational theory
a leadership theory that states that leaders need to adjust their leadership styles to match their followers' readiness

worker readiness
the ability and willingness to take responsibility for directing one's behavior at work

insecure people who are neither willing nor able to take responsibility for guiding their own work. R2 represents people who are confident and willing but not able to take responsibility for guiding their own work. R3 represents people who are insecure and able but not willing to take responsibility for guiding their own work. And R4 represents people who are confident, willing, and able to take responsibility for guiding their own work. It's important to note that a follower's readiness is usually task-specific. For example, you may be highly confident and capable when it comes to personal computers but know nothing about setting up budgets for planning purposes. You would possess readiness (R4) with respect to computers but not with respect to budgets.

5.2 Leadership Styles

Similar to Blake and Mouton's managerial grid, situational theory defines leadership styles in terms of task behavior (i.e., concern for production) and relationship behavior (i.e., concern for people). These two behaviors can be combined to form four different leadership styles: telling, selling, participating, and delegating. Leaders choose one of these styles depending on the readiness a follower has for a specific task.

A *telling* leadership style (high task behavior and low relationship behavior) is based on one-way communication in which followers are told what, how, when, and where to do particular tasks. Telling is used when people are at the R1 stage. For instance, someone using a telling leadership style would identify all the steps in a project and give explicit instructions on exactly how to execute each one.

A *selling* leadership style (high task behavior and high relationship behavior) involves two-way communication and psychological support to encourage followers to own, or buy into, particular ways of doing things. Selling is used most appropriately at the R2 stage. For instance, someone using a selling leadership style might say, "We're going to start a company newsletter. I really think that's a great idea, don't you? We're going to need some cost estimates from printers and some comments from each manager. But that's pretty straightforward. Oh, don't forget that we need the CEO's comments, too. She's expecting you to call. I know that you'll do a great job on this. We'll meet next Tuesday to see if you have any questions once you've dug into this. By the way, we need to have this done by next Friday."

A *participating* style (low task behavior and high relationship behavior) is based on two-way communication and shared decision making. Participating is used with employees at R3. Since the problem is with motivation rather than ability, someone using a participating leadership style might solicit ideas from a subordinate about a project and let the subordinate get started but ask to review progress along the way.

A *delegating* style (low task behavior and low relationship behavior) is used when leaders basically let workers run their own show and make their own decisions. Delegating is used for people at R4. For instance, someone using a delegating leadership style might say, "We're going to start a company newsletter. You've got 10 days to do it. Run with it. Let me know when you've got it done. I'll e-mail you a couple of ideas, but other than that, do what you think is best. Thanks."

In general, as people become more ready and thus more willing and able to guide their own behavior, leaders should become less task-oriented and more relationship-oriented. As people become even more ready, leaders should become less task-oriented *and* less relationship-oriented until people eventually manage their own work with little input from their leaders.

How well does Hersey and Blanchard's situational theory work? Despite its intuitive appeal (managers and consultants tend to prefer it over Fiedler's contingency theory because of its underlying logic and simplicity), most studies don't support situational theory.[31] While managers generally do a good job of judging followers' readiness levels, the theory doesn't seem to work well except at lower levels, where a telling style is recommended for people who are insecure and neither willing nor able to take responsibility for guiding their own work.[32]

REVIEW 5

Adapting Leader Behavior: Hersey and Blanchard's Situational Leadership® Theory

According to situational theory, leaders need to adjust their leadership styles to match their followers' readiness, which is the ability (job readiness) and willingness (psychological readiness) to take responsibility for directing one's work. Job readiness and psychological readiness combine to produce four different levels of readiness (R1–R4). The levels vary based on people's confidence, ability, and willingness to guide their own work. Situational theory combines task and relationship behavior to create four leadership styles—telling (R1), selling (R2), participating (R3), and delegating (R4)—that are used with employees at different readiness levels.

6 Adapting Leader Behavior: Normative Decision Theory

Many people believe that making tough decisions is at the heart of leadership. Yet experienced leaders will tell you that deciding *how* to make decisions is just as important. The **normative decision theory** (also known as the *Vroom-Yetton-Jago model*) helps leaders decide how much employee participation (from none to letting employees make the entire decision) should be used when making decisions.[33]

Let's learn more about normative decision theory by investigating 6.1 **decision styles**, and 6.2 **decision quality and acceptance**.

6.1 Decision Styles

Unlike nearly all of the other leadership theories discussed in this chapter, which have specified *leadership* styles, that is, the way a leader generally behaves toward followers, the normative decision theory specifies five different *decision* styles, or ways of making decisions. (See Chapter 4 for a more complete review of decision making in organizations.) As shown in Exhibit 12.9, those styles vary from *autocratic decisions* (AI or AII) on the left, in which leaders make the decisions by themselves, to *consultative decisions* (CI or CII), in which leaders share problems with subordinates but still make the decisions themselves, to *group decisions* (GII) on the right, in which leaders share the problems with subordinates and then have the group make the decisions.

normative decision theory
a theory that suggests how leaders can determine an appropriate amount of employee participation when making decisions

GE Aircraft Engines in Durham, North Carolina, uses a similar approach when making decisions. According to *Fast Company* magazine, "At GE/Durham, every decision is either an 'A' decision, a 'B' decision, or a 'C' decision. An 'A' decision

EXHIBIT 12.9

Decision Styles and Levels of Employee Participation

Leader solves the problem or makes the decision

Leader is willing to accept any decision supported by the entire group

AI
Using information available at the time, the leader solves the problem or makes the decision.

AII
The leader obtains necessary information from employees, and then selects a solution to the problem. When asked to share information, employees may or may not be told what the problem is.

CI
The leader shares the problem and gets ideas and suggestions from relevant employees on an individual basis. Individuals are not brought together as a group. Then the leader makes the decision, which may or may not reflect their input.

CII
The leader shares the problem with employees as a group, obtains their ideas and suggestions, and then makes the decision, which may or may not reflect their input.

GII
The leader shares the problem with employees as a group. Together, the leader and employees generate and evaluate alternatives and try to reach an agreement on a solution. The leader acts as a facilitator and does not try to influence the group. The leader is willing to accept and implement any solution that has the support of the entire group.

Source: Adapted from Table 2.1 Decision Methods for Group and Individual Problems and Figure 9.3 Decision-Process Flow Chart for Both Individual and Group Problems, from *Leadership and Decision Making*, by Victor H. Vroom and Philip W. Yetton, (c) 1973. Reprinted by permission of the University of Pittsburg Press.

is one that the plant manager makes herself, without consulting anyone."[34] Plant manager Paula Sims says, "I don't make very many of those, and when I do make one, everyone at the plant knows it. I make maybe 10 or 12 a year."[35] "B" decisions are also made by the plant manager but with input from the people affected. "C" decisions, the most common type, are made by consensus, by the people directly involved, with plenty of discussion. With "C" decisions, the view of the plant manager doesn't necessarily carry more weight than the views of those affected."[36]

6.2 Decision Quality and Acceptance

According to the normative decision theory, using the right degree of employee participation improves the quality of decisions and the extent to which employees accept and are committed to decisions. Exhibit 12.10 lists the decision rules that normative decision theory uses to increase the quality of a decision and the degree to which employees accept and commit to it. The quality, leader information, subordinate information, goal congruence, and problem structure rules are used to increase decision quality. For example, the leader information rule states that if a leader doesn't have enough information to make a decision on his or her own, then the leader should not use an autocratic style.

The commitment probability, subordinate conflict, and commitment requirement rules shown in Exhibit 12.10 are used to increase employee acceptance and

EXHIBIT **12.10**

Normative Theory Decision Rules

Decision Rules to Increase Decision Quality
Quality Rule. If the quality of the decision is important, then don't use an autocratic decision style.
Leader Information Rule. If the quality of the decision is important, and if the leader doesn't have enough information to make the decision on his or her own, then don't use an autocratic decision style.
Subordinate Information Rule. If the quality of the decision is important, and if the subordinates don't have enough information to make the decision themselves, then don't use a group decision style.
Goal Congruence Rule. If the quality of the decision is important, and subordinates' goals are different from the organization's goals, then don't use a group decision style.
Problem Structure Rule. If the quality of the decision is important, the leader doesn't have enough information to make the decision on his or her own, and the problem is unstructured, then don't use an autocratic decision style.
Decision Rules to Increase Decision Acceptance
Commitment Probability Rule. If having subordinates accept and commit to the decision is important, then don't use an autocratic decision style.
Subordinate Conflict Rule. If having subordinates accept the decision is important and critical to successful implementation and subordinates are likely to disagree or end up in conflict over the decision, then don't use an autocratic or consultative decision style.
Commitment Requirement Rule. If having subordinates accept the decision is absolutely required for successful implementation and subordinates share the organization's goals, then don't use an autocratic or consultative style.

Sources: Adapted from V. H. Vroom, "Leadership," in *Handbook of Industrial and Organizational Psychology,* ed. M. D. Dunnette (Chicago: Rand McNally, 1976); V. H. Vroom & A. G. Jago, *The New Leadership: Managing Participation in Organizations* (Englewood Cliffs, NJ: Prentice Hall, 1988).

commitment to decisions. For example, the commitment requirement rule says that if decision acceptance and commitment are important, and subordinates share the organization's goals, then you shouldn't use an autocratic or consultative style. In other words, if followers want to do what's best for the company and you need their acceptance and commitment to make a decision work, then use a group decision style and let them make the decision.

As you can see, these decision rules help leaders improve decision quality and follower acceptance and commitment by eliminating decision styles that don't fit the particular decision or situation they're facing. Normative decision theory then operationalizes these decision rules in the form of yes/no questions, which are shown in the decision tree displayed in Exhibit 12.11. You start at the left side of the model and answer the first question, "How important is the technical quality of this decision?" by choosing "high" or "low." Then you continue by answering each question as you proceed along the decision tree until you get to a recommended decision style.

Let's use the model to make the decision of whether to change from a formal business attire policy to a casual wear policy. The problem sounds simple, but it is

EXHIBIT 12.11

Normative Decision Theory Tree for Determining the Level of Participation in Decision Making

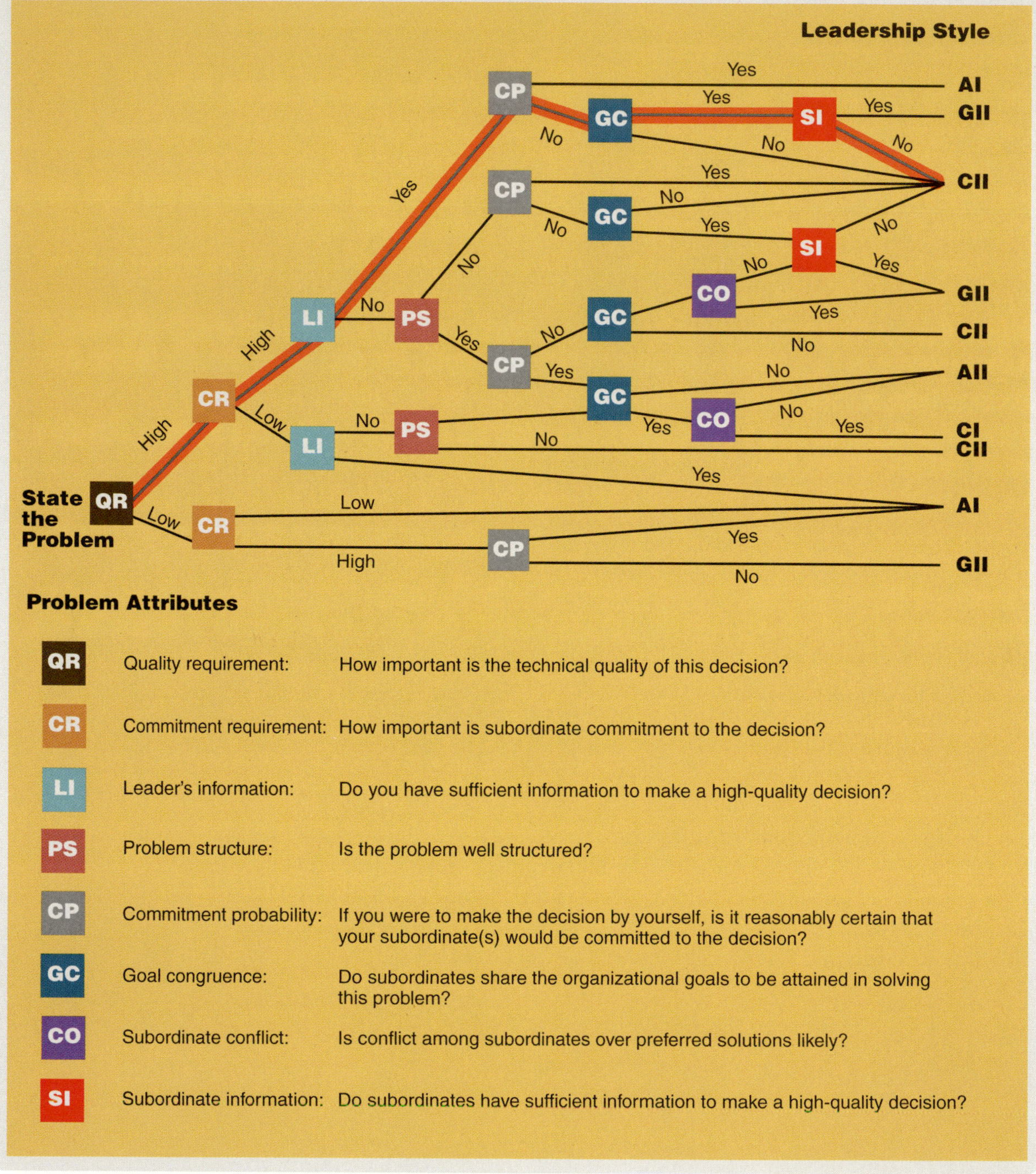

Leadership Style
State the Problem
QR
High
Low
CR
High
Low
LI
No
Yes
PS
CP
GC
SI
CO
Yes
No
AI
GII
CII
AII
CI
Problem Attributes
QR Quality requirement: How important is the technical quality of this decision?
CR Commitment requirement: How important is subordinate commitment to the decision?
LI Leader's information: Do you have sufficient information to make a high-quality decision?
PS Problem structure: Is the problem well structured?
CP Commitment probability: If you were to make the decision by yourself, is it reasonably certain that your subordinate(s) would be committed to the decision?
GC Goal congruence: Do subordinates share the organizational goals to be attained in solving this problem?
CO Subordinate conflict: Is conflict among subordinates over preferred solutions likely?
SI Subordinate information: Do subordinates have sufficient information to make a high-quality decision?

Source: Excerpt from Table 2.1 Decision Methods for Group and Individual Problems, and the Normative Decision Theory Tree for Determining the Level of Participation in Decision Making from Figure 9.3 Decision-Process Flow Chart for Both Individual and Group Problems, from *Leadership and Decision Making* by Victor H. Vroom & Philip W. Yetton, (c) 1973. Reprinted by permission of the University of Pittsburgh Press.

actually more complex than you might think. Follow the orange line in Exhibit 12.11 as we work through the decision in the following discussion.

Problem: Change to Casual Wear?

1. *Quality requirement: How important is the technical quality of this decision?* High. This question has to do with whether there are quality differences in the alternatives and whether those quality differences matter. In other words, is there a lot at stake in this decision? Although most people would assume that quality isn't an issue here, it really is, given the overall positive changes that generally accompany changes to casual wear.
2. *Commitment requirement: How important is subordinate commitment to the decision?* High. Changes in culture, like dress codes, require subordinate commitment or they fail.
3. *Leader's information: Do you have sufficient information to make a high-quality decision?* Yes. Let's assume that you've done your homework. Much has been written about casual wear, from how to make the change to the effects it has in companies (almost all positive).
4. *Commitment probability: If you were to make the decision by yourself, is it reasonably certain that your subordinate(s) would be committed to the decision?* No. Studies of casual wear find that employees' reactions are almost uniformly positive. Nonetheless, employees are likely to be angry if you change something as personal as clothing policies without consulting them.
5. *Goal congruence: Do subordinates share the organizational goals to be attained in solving this problem?* Yes. The goals that usually accompany a change to casual dress policies are a more informal culture, better communication, and less money spent on business attire.
6. *Subordinate information: Do subordinates have sufficient information to make a high-quality decision?* No. Most employees know little about casual wear policies or even what constitutes casual wear in most companies. Consequently, most companies have to educate employees about casual wear practices and policies before making a decision.
7. *CII is the answer:* With a CII, or consultative decision process, the leader shares the problem with employees as a group, obtains their ideas and suggestions, and then makes the decision, which may or may not reflect their input. So, given the answers to these questions (remember, different managers won't necessarily answer these questions the same way), the normative decision theory recommends that leaders consult with their subordinates before deciding whether to change to a casual wear policy.

How well does the normative decision theory work? A prominent leadership scholar has described it as the best supported of all leadership theories.[37] In general, the more managers violate the decision rules in Exhibit 12.10, the less effective their decisions are, especially with respect to subordinate acceptance and commitment.[38]

REVIEW 6

Adapting Leader Behavior: Normative Decision Theory

The normative decision theory helps leaders decide how much employee participation should be used when making decisions. Using the right degree of employee participation improves the quality of decisions and the extent to which employees accept and are committed to decisions. The theory specifies five different decision styles or ways of making decisions: autocratic decisions (AI or AII), consultative decisions (CI or CII), and group decisions (GII). The theory improves decision quality via the quality, leader information, subordinate information, goal congruence, and unstructured problem decision rules. The theory improves employee commitment and acceptance via the commitment probability, subordinate conflict, and commitment requirement decision rules. These decision rules help leaders improve decision quality and follower acceptance and commitment by eliminating decision styles that don't fit the decision or situation they're facing. Normative decision theory then makes these decision rules more concrete by framing them as yes/no questions, as shown in the decision tree displayed in Exhibit 12.11.

Strategic Leadership

Thus far, you have read about three major leadership ideas: traits, behaviors, and situational theories. Leader *traits* are relatively stable characteristics such as abilities or psychological motives. Traits capture who effective leaders are. Leader *behaviors* are the actions leaders take to influence others to achieve group or organizational goals. Behaviors capture what effective leaders do (i.e., initiate structure and consideration). And *situational theories* indicate that the effectiveness of a leadership style, the way a leader generally behaves toward followers, depends on the situation. Situational theories capture what leaders need to do or not do in particular situations or circumstances. This final part of the chapter introduces a fourth major leadership idea—strategic leadership—and its components, visionary, charismatic, and transformational leadership.

Strategic leadership is the ability to anticipate, envision, maintain flexibility, think strategically, and work with others to initiate changes that will create a positive future for an organization.[39] General Electric was one of the best run and most profitable companies in the world. Yet, since taking charge 9 years ago, CEO Jeffrey Immelt has led GE through a series of strategic changes that have made the company more global, more customer-oriented, and more focused on developing new technology for new markets.[40] Immelt explains his strategic leadership this way: "In my case, I was taking over a well-known company that had been led by a famous and excellent CEO [Jack Welch]. But I never wanted to run *that* company, and I never wanted to be *that* CEO. [But] I knew the company had to change. I would say most of us were trained to have a pretty healthy disrespect for history. We respect performance, respect integrity, but everybody was trained to have a look-forward attitude instead of look-backward. I inherited a company that had great strengths for a long time—good risk management, good cost control, good productivity—and I viewed the mission for my generation as not to lose those things but to build capability around growth, which we didn't have."[41] Thus, strategic leadership captures how leaders inspire their companies to change and their followers to give extraordinary effort to accomplish organizational goals.

strategic leadership the ability to anticipate, envision, maintain flexibility, think strategically, and work with others to initiate changes that will create a positive future for an organization

After reading the next section, you should be able to:

7 explain how visionary leadership (i.e., charismatic and transformational leadership) helps leaders achieve strategic leadership.

7 Visionary Leadership

In Chapter 4, we defined a purpose statement, which is often referred to as an organizational mission or vision, as a statement of a company's purpose or reason for existing. Similarly, **visionary leadership** creates a positive image of the future that motivates organizational members and provides direction for future planning and goal setting.[42]

The two kinds of visionary leadership are 7.1 **charismatic leadership**, and 7.2 **transformational leadership**.

7.1 Charismatic Leadership

Charisma is a Greek word meaning "divine gift." The ancient Greeks saw people with charisma as inspired by the gods and capable of incredible accomplishments. German sociologist Max Weber viewed charisma as a special bond between leaders and followers.[43] Weber wrote that the special qualities of charismatic leaders enable them to strongly influence followers. Weber also noted that charismatic leaders tend to emerge in times of crisis and that the radical solutions they propose enhance the admiration that followers feel for them. Indeed, charismatic leaders tend to have incredible influence over followers who may be inspired by their leaders and become fanatically devoted to them. From this perspective, charismatic leaders are often seen as larger-than-life or more special than other employees of the company.

Charismatic leaders have strong, confident, dynamic personalities that attract followers and enable the leaders to create strong bonds with their followers. Followers trust charismatic leaders, are loyal to them, and are inspired to work toward the accomplishment of the leader's vision. Followers who become devoted to charismatic leaders may go to extraordinary lengths to please them. Therefore, we can define **charismatic leadership** as the behavioral tendencies and personal characteristics of leaders that create an exceptionally strong relationship between them and their followers. Charismatic leaders also

- Articulate a clear vision for the future that is based on strongly held values or morals,
- Model those values by acting in a way consistent with the vision,
- Communicate high performance expectations to followers, and
- Display confidence in followers' abilities to achieve the vision.[44]

Does charismatic leadership work? Studies indicate that it often does. In general, the followers of charismatic leaders are more committed and satisfied, are better performers, are more likely to trust their leaders, and simply work harder.[45] Nonetheless, charismatic leadership also has risks that are at least as large as its benefits. The problems are likely to occur with ego-driven charismatic leaders who take advantage of fanatical followers.

In general, there are two kinds of charismatic leaders, ethical charismatics and unethical charismatics.[46] **Ethical charismatics** provide developmental opportunities for followers, are open to positive and negative feedback, recognize others' contributions, share information, and have moral standards that emphasize the larger interests of the group, organization, or society. By contrast, **unethical charismatics** control and manipulate followers, do what is best for themselves instead of their

visionary leadership leadership that creates a positive image of the future that motivates organizational members and provides direction for future planning and goal setting

charismatic leadership the behavioral tendencies and personal characteristics of leaders that create an exceptionally strong relationship between them and their followers

ethical charismatics charismatic leaders who provide developmental opportunities for followers, are open to positive and negative feedback, recognize others' contributions, share information, and have moral standards that emphasize the larger interests of the group, organization, or society

unethical charismatics charismatic leaders who control and manipulate followers, do what is best for themselves instead of their organizations, want to hear only positive feedback, share only information that is beneficial to themselves, and have moral standards that put their interests before everyone else's

organizations, want to hear only positive feedback, share information that is only beneficial to themselves, and have moral standards that put their interests before everyone else's. Because followers can become just as committed to unethical charismatics as to ethical characteristics, unethical characteristics pose a tremendous risk for companies. According to *Fast Company*, "We're worshipful of top executives who seem charismatic, visionary, and tough. So long as they're lifting profits and stock prices, we're willing to overlook that they can also be callous, cunning, manipulative, deceitful, verbally and psychologically abusive, remorseless, exploitative, self-delusional, irresponsible, and megalomaniacal."[47]

There are stark differences between ethical and unethical charismatics on several leader behaviors: exercising power, creating the vision, communicating with followers, accepting feedback, stimulating followers intellectually, developing followers, and living by moral standards. For example, ethical charismatics account for the concerns and wishes of their followers when creating a vision by having followers participate in the development of the company vision. By contrast, unethical charismatics develop a vision by themselves solely to meet their personal agendas. One unethical charismatic said, "The key thing is that it is my idea; and I am going to win with it at all costs."[48]

What can companies do to reduce the risks associated with unethical charismatics? To start, they need a clearly written code of conduct that is fairly and consistently enforced for all managers. Next, companies should recruit, select, and promote managers with high ethical standards. Also, companies need to train leaders to value, seek, and use diverse points of view. Both leaders and subordinates need training regarding ethical leader behaviors so that abuses can be recognized and corrected. Finally, companies should celebrate and reward people who exhibit ethical behaviors, especially ethical leader behaviors.[49]

7.2 Transformational Leadership

While charismatic leadership involves articulating a clear vision, modeling values consistent with that vision, communicating high performance expectations, and establishing very strong relationships with followers, **transformational leadership** goes further by generating awareness and acceptance of a group's purpose and mission and by getting employees to see beyond their own needs and self-interest for the good of the group.[50] Like charismatic leaders, transformational leaders are visionary, but they transform their organizations by getting their followers to accomplish more than they intended and even more than they thought possible.

Transformational leaders are able to make their followers feel that they are a vital part of the organization and help them see how their jobs fit with the organization's vision. By linking individual and organizational interests, transformational leaders encourage followers to make sacrifices for the organization because they know that they will prosper when the organization prospers. As Exhibit 12.12 shows, transformational leadership has four components: charismatic leadership or idealized influence, inspirational motivation, intellectual stimulation, and individualized consideration.[51]

transformational leadership
leadership that generates awareness and acceptance of a group's purpose and mission and gets employees to see beyond their own needs and self-interests for the good of the group

Charismatic leadership or idealized influence means that transformational leaders act as role models for their followers. Because transformational leaders put others' needs ahead of their own and share risks with their followers, they are admired, respected, and trusted, and followers want to emulate them. Thus, in contrast to purely charismatic leaders (especially unethical charismatics), transformational leaders can be counted on to do the right thing and maintain high standards for ethical and personal conduct. After Jim McNerney became Boeing's third CEO in 3 years, he pushed company lawyers to settle ethics violations that occurred under his predecessors. Under a settlement with the U.S. Justice Department, Boeing agreed to pay a $615 million penalty. But that wasn't enough for McNerney. He apologized before a Senate committee and refused to take a $200 million tax deduction to which Boeing was entitled for its costs in obtaining the settlement. McNerney also instituted a new organization-wide ethics program and has linked bonuses and promotion to ethical behavior.

EXHIBIT 12.12

Components of Transformational Leadership

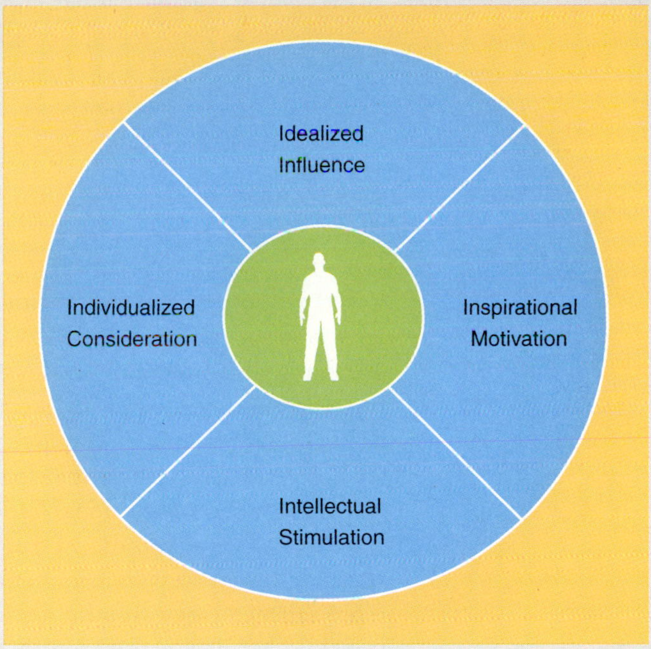

Idealized Influence
Individualized Consideration
Inspirational Motivation
Intellectual Stimulation

Inspirational motivation means that transformational leaders motivate and inspire followers by providing meaning and challenge to their work. By clearly communicating expectations and demonstrating commitment to goals, transformational leaders help followers envision future states, such as the organizational vision or mission. In turn, this leads to greater enthusiasm and optimism about the future.

Intellectual stimulation means that transformational leaders encourage followers to be creative and innovative, to question assumptions, and to look at problems and situations in new ways even if their ideas are different from the leaders. Carol Bartz, former CEO of *AUTODESK*, the industry leader in computer-aided design software, and now CEO of *YAHOO*!, pushes the people who work for her to think beyond their original assumptions by asking questions. Says Bartz, "all you have to do is ask questions. You just have to keep asking questions. You ask questions and guess what, they go, 'Oh, I never thought of that.' Because it unleashes so much power in people by just asking. Why do I [as the CEO] have to be the know-it-all? My God, I'm not that smart. But I'm smart enough to just keep asking questions and say, 'Is that the best you can do? Does that excite you? Will that excite the customer? Does this really have to work this way?'"[52]

Individualized consideration means that transformational leaders pay special attention to followers' individual needs by creating learning opportunities, accepting and tolerating individual differences, encouraging two-way communication, and being good listeners. At *CORPORATE INK PUBLIC RELATIONS*, a small public relations firm in Newton, Massachusetts, company president and founder Amy Bermar says, "Junior people have a lot of opportunities to influence some really significant activities at our firm."[53] For example, any PR representative who snags a high-profile interview for a client gets to handle it from beginning to end, even less experienced PR representatives. Adam Parken, a 29-year-old account manager with Corporate Ink says "Here at Corporate Ink, no matter what position you're in, you're expected to help strategize."[54]

Management Fact:

One of the basic assumptions about leadership is that organizations are sure to fail without good leadership. But, there are some circumstances when leadership is not likely to make much of a difference. When subordinates have ability, expertise, training, and knowledge about their jobs, their performance is unlikely to improve under a task-related leader. In other circumstances, there are subordinate, task, or organizational characteristics that can make it impossible for a leader to influence followers. This could occur when subordinates are indifferent toward organizational rewards, or are forced to deal with inflexible rewards.

Finally, a distinction needs to be drawn between transformational leadership and transactional leadership. While transformational leaders use visionary and inspirational appeals to influence followers, **transactional leadership** is based on an exchange process in which followers are rewarded for good performance and punished for poor performance. When leaders administer rewards fairly and offer followers the rewards that they want, followers will often reciprocate with effort. A problem, however, is that transactional leaders often rely too heavily on discipline or threats to bring performance up to standards. This may work in the short run, but it's much less effective in the long run. Also, as discussed in Chapters 10 and 11, many leaders and organizations have difficulty successfully linking pay practices to individual performance. As a result, studies consistently show that transformational leadership is much more effective on average than transactional leadership. In the United States, Canada, Japan, and India and at all organizational levels, from first-level supervisors to upper-level executives, followers view transformational leaders as much better leaders and are much more satisfied when working for them. Furthermore, companies with transformational leaders have significantly better financial performance.[55]

transactional leadership leadership based on an exchange process, in which followers are rewarded for good performance and punished for poor performance

REVIEW 7

Visionary Leadership

Strategic leadership requires visionary, charismatic, and transformational leadership. Visionary leadership creates a positive image of the future that motivates organizational members and provides direction for future planning and goal setting. Charismatic leaders have strong, confident, dynamic personalities that attract followers, enable the leader to create strong bonds, and inspire followers to accomplish the leader's vision. Followers of ethical charismatic leaders work harder, are more committed and satisfied, are better performers, and are more likely to trust their leaders. Followers can be just as supportive and committed to unethical charismatics, but these leaders can pose a tremendous risk for companies. Unethical charismatics control and manipulate followers and do what is best for themselves instead of their organizations. To reduce the risks associated with unethical charismatics, companies need to enforce a clearly written code of conduct; recruit, select, and promote managers with high ethical standards; train leaders to value, seek, and use diverse points of view; teach everyone in the company to recognize unethical leader behaviors; and celebrate and reward people who exhibit ethical behaviors. Transformational leadership goes beyond charismatic leadership by generating awareness and acceptance of a group's purpose and mission and by getting employees to see beyond their own needs and self-interest for the good of the group. The four components of transformational leadership are charisma or idealized influence, inspirational motivation, intellectual stimulation, and individualized consideration.

MANAGEMENT Team Decision

Setting Executive Salaries

You are a member of the Board of Directors of a large, multinational bank that is looking to hire a new CEO. The previous CEO did as well as he could to guide your company through the recession, but everyone agrees that a new leader, with a fresh vision, is needed to lead the bank back to profitability.

You have been assigned to a committee that will create the new CEO's compensation package. Five years ago, this would have been a cakewalk assignment—put together a multi-million-dollar deal with cash, stock options, and tons of perks. But these are different times. You don't want to give out a lucrative package in the middle of the worst recession in 70 years—what would your employees think? What would the public think? At the same time, you're worried that if you don't offer extraordinary compensation, you'll never find the right person for the job.

One of the committee members shows up to a meeting with some recent research on CEO salaries. She reports that there are many CEOs who have taken drastic cuts in their pay during the past year. David Cote, the CEO of Honeywell, took a 57% salary cut. Vikram Pandit, the CEO of Citigroup, receives just $1 per year, and has publicly vowed not to take any additional compensation until the company returns to profitability. In fact, it appears that CEOs (and companies) across the country have lowered their expectations. A recent survey shows that CEO pay decreased by 8.6% from the previous year, and since 2000, CEO pay is down nearly 40%. This includes decreases in perks like private planes, security details, and country club memberships. While you certainly don't expect your next CEO to work for nothing, this does give you some hope that he or she would be willing to lower their demands a bit.

But as the committee member continues her report, she points out a disturbing trend. While the total package that CEOs receive is down, the amount that they receive in cash is up and the amount they receive in stock options is down. What does all of this mean? It means that more companies are placing less emphasis on long-term incentives. Instead of using stocks to link CEO pay to a company's performance, many companies are emphasizing short-term thinking by giving CEOs lots of cash. Even if the company does not perform well, their executives will still benefit financially.

You and the rest of the committee are left to wonder what the right approach is. Can you find the right CEO with a reduced salary package? Do you ask your new CEO to accept more stock options, so that his financial well-being is tied to the company's? Or, do you offer as much cash as possible, with the hopes of attracting top-flight talent? Form a group with three or four other students and consider these issues as you discuss the questions below?

Questions

1. What are the advantages and disadvantages of tying an executive's pay to the company's performance?
2. How would you explain to concerned shareholders and employees why it is so important that the CEO receive a multi-million-dollar salary package?
3. How much input would you give company employees in making a decision on executive pay?

Source: Jessica Silver-Greenberg, Tara Kawalski, and Alexis Leondis. "CEO Pay Drops, But . . . Cash Is King." *Bloomberg BusinessWeek.* April 5, 2010. 50–56.

Practice being a MANAGER

Changing Directions

Leadership is a highly prized process and capability. Organizations invest billions of dollars each year in recruiting and developing leadership talent. As more companies compete primarily on the basis of how well they employ their human capabilities, the importance of leadership continues to grow. This exercise will provide you with an opportunity to play coach to a leader entering a challenging situation.

STEP 1 Get into groups. Your professor will assign you to pairs or small groups.

Scenario: The opening "What would you do?" segment in this chapter focused on the challenges facing the new CEO of PepsiCo. PepsiCo is a company with a remarkable tradition of product and management innovations, but as the opening segment makes clear, over the past several years PepsiCo is facing increased competition from its archrival Coca-Cola and struggling to navigate the challenges of an ever-changing marketplace. As the new CEO scans the situation, it is difficult to know how to prioritize. Where to begin?

Assume that the members of your small team are a group of consultants working with Pepsi's new CEO. Your job is behind the scenes—you are simply helping the CEO brainstorm and think carefully about how to lead this company, improve performance, and restore the once-vibrant culture of creativity that made PepsiCo a leader in its industry.

STEP 2 Outline leadership criteria. Work as a team to develop a set of leadership recommendations that are well matched to the PepsiCo situation. What do you think employees need most from their new leader? Should the CEO help employees look back and learn from the company's past, or should the CEO encourage employees to move on and focus on the future? What are the trade-offs in each approach? The opening segment highlights some key areas of concern: (a) increased competition; (b) rising cost structures; (c) declining financial and marketing performance; (d) declining brand image (e.g., as a contributor to unhealthy eating habits and childhood obesity). So how would you recommend that the CEO prioritize these issues? Are there creative possibilities for tackling some of these concerns simultaneously?

STEP 3 Determine a coaching plan. Prepare to coach the CEO during the process of transforming PepsiCo. How might path-goal thinking help the CEO guide PepsiCo employees through the transition? What should the CEO keep in mind regarding such situational factors as worker readiness, situation favorableness, and environmental contingencies? Assuming the CEO possesses charismatic capabilities, would you recommend relying on a charismatic leadership style in this situation? Why or why not?

STEP 4 Debrief as a class. Share some of the highlights of your recommendations, and discuss what leadership consultants/coaches need to know to effectively advise their clients.

SELF Assessment

Leadership Orientation

Think of everyone you have ever worked with in jobs, clubs, volunteer positions, student projects—everything. Now that you have all those situations in mind, try to identify the one person with whom you least liked to work. Who was the most difficult person to work with to get a job done? For whatever reason, you had trouble working with this person. The person can be a peer, boss, or subordinate. Once you have that person in mind, think of how you would describe him or her to another person. The Least Preferred Coworker scale uses 18 oppositional adjective pairs to help you build your description.[56] For each pair, choose the number closest to the word that best describes your LPC.

Pleasant	8	7	6	5	4	3	2	1	Unpleasant
Friendly	8	7	6	5	4	3	2	1	Unfriendly
Rejecting	1	2	3	4	5	6	7	8	Accepting
Tense	1	2	3	4	5	6	7	8	Relaxed
Distant	1	2	3	4	5	6	7	8	Close
Cold	1	2	3	4	5	6	7	8	Warm
Supportive	8	7	6	5	4	3	2	1	Hostile
Boring	1	2	3	4	5	6	7	8	Interesting
Quarrelsome	1	2	3	4	5	6	7	8	Harmonious
Gloomy	1	2	3	4	5	6	7	8	Cheerful
Open	8	7	6	5	4	3	2	1	Guarded
Backbiting	1	2	3	4	5	6	7	8	Loyal
Untrustworthy	1	2	3	4	5	6	7	8	Trustworthy
Considerate	8	7	6	5	4	3	2	1	Inconsiderate
Nasty	1	2	3	4	5	6	7	8	Nice
Agreeable	8	7	6	5	4	3	2	1	Disagreeable
Insincere	1	2	3	4	5	6	7	8	Sincere
Kind	8	7	6	5	4	3	2	1	Unkind

TOTAL = ______

SCORING

Determine your leadership style by totaling all the numbers you selected into a single sum. Your score will fall between 18 and 96. You can find the interpretation for your score at: login.cengagebrain.com

Reel to Real

BIZ FLIX

© GREENLIGHT

Doomsday

In the futuristic action thriller *Doomsday*, the "Reaper Virus" strikes the British Isles in 2007 and devastates the population in Scotland. Authorities go to desperate lengths to quarantine it, sealing off the borders and not allowing anyone to enter or leave the country. Social decay spreads, and cannibalistic behavior develops among the few remaining survivors. When the Reaper Virus reemerges in 2032, this time in London, England, classified satellite images show signs of life in Glasgow and Edinburgh. In this scene, Major Eden Sinclair (Rhona Mitra) is given the task of going into the city to find the scientist who they hope may have the cure for the virus. If she can't find him in time, she is told, "then you needn't bother coming back."

What to Watch for and Ask Yourself

1. Assess the behavior of both Major Sinclair and Michael Canaris. Which leadership traits does their behavior show?
2. Does this film sequence show any aspects of charismatic and transformational leadership? Draw some examples from the sequence.

MANAGEMENT WORKPLACE

© CENGAGE

City of Greensburg, Kansas

After working in Oklahoma City as a parks director, Steve Hewitt wanted to run an entire town. A smaller community seemed the perfect place to get hands-on leadership experience before tackling a bigger city, so Hewitt took the city administrator position in his hometown of Greensburg, Kansas (population: 1,500). Standing in the remains of his kitchen, looking up at the dark sky on May 4, 2007, after a tornado destroyed his town, he realized that he got more than he'd bargained for. When Mayor Lonnie McCollum resigned, he said, "They didn't need me; they had good leadership," referring to the younger, tougher-skinned Hewitt. This video focuses on City Administrator Steve Hewitt and his efforts to transform Greensburg in the wake of the storm.

What to Watch for and Ask Yourself

1. Based on this video, which leadership traits would you say Hewitt displays?
2. How does having two distinct leadership roles, mayor and city administrator, create a challenging environment for effective leadership?
3. How would you characterize Hewitt's leadership style?

13

Chapter Thirteen

Managing Communication

OUTLINE

What Is Communication?

1 Perception and Communication Problems
- 1.1 Basic Perception Process
- 1.2 Perception Problems
- 1.3 Perceptions of Others
- 1.4 Self-Perception

2 Kinds of Communication
- 2.1 The Communication Process
- 2.2 Communication Channels
- 2.3 Coaching and Counseling: One-on-One Communication
- 2.4 Nonverbal Communication

How to Improve Communication

3 Managing One-on-One Communication
- 3.1 Choosing the Right Communication Medium
- 3.2 Listening
- 3.3 Giving Feedback
- 3.4 Improving Cross-Cultural Communication

4 Managing Organization-Wide Communication
- 4.1 Improving Transmission: Getting the Message Out
- 4.2 Improving Reception: Hearing What Others Feel and Think

Management Decision

Practice Being a Manager

Self Assessment

Reel to Real

Experience Management

Explore the four levels of learning by doing the simulation model on Communication.

© ISTOCKPHOTO.COM/ ANN MARIE KURTZ

Pod Nod

Mini lecture reviews all the learning points in the chapter.

© ISTOCKPHOTO.COM/ MAGNET CREATIVE

Reel to Real

Biz Flix is a scene from *Friday Night Lights*. Management Workplace is a segment on Greensburg, Kansas.

© ISTOCKPHOTO.COM/ CRAFTVISION

Self Test

10 quiz questions, 5 exhibit worksheets, and PowerPoints for quick review.

© ISTOCKPHOTO.COM/ DIJITAL FILM

What Would You Do?

Zappos Headquarters and Call Center, Las Vegas, Nevada.[1]

"Shoes? You sell shoes online? Who buys shoes online?" That was your reaction when the founder of Shoesite.com suggested you invest in his company. With $265 million from the sale of your first Internet business, you could invest in or start any company you wanted. And you did, starting 27 different businesses. But, something was missing. You weren't having any fun. You were depressed. As you told your friends, "the easiest way to explain it was that going into the office started to feel like work." The problem was that the people working in your first company weren't committed to long-term success. "The Silicon Valley culture is, 'I'm going to work hard for years and make millions of dollars and then retire.'" So you vowed that if you ever ran another Internet business, you would create a company where employees were happy, satisfied, and committed to providing great service to customers.

You never realized that opportunity would come through Shoesite.com. Sure, selling shoes online sounded silly at first. But that was before you knew the U.S. shoe market was $40 billion a year and that $2 billion in sales came through mail order catalogs. If people bought shoes through mail order catalogs, they would buy via the Internet. So you not only bought a share of the company, which changed its name to *ZAPPOS.COM* ("Zappos" is derived from *zapatos*, the Spanish word for shoes), you helped run it. Six years after joining, the founder left, and you were Zappos's CEO.

Your first major challenge was how to get people to buy from you instead of your competitors. JCPenney took its mail order catalog shoe business and flipped it online. Then came new competitors, such as Piperlime.com, a division of Gap Inc., which carries 100 brands; Shoemall .com, which was started by a company with 100 years in the shoe business; Shoebuy.com, which, with 800 brands, bills itself as "The World's Largest Site for Shoes"; and Endless.com, which was started by Amazon.com, to sell shoes and handbags. Figuring that there was no other way to get consumers to choose Zappos over your competition, you instituted free shipping and free returns. The allure of this policy was simple. Choose the wrong size or wrong style and you can send the shoes back at no cost. However, "free" shipping and "free" returns cost you $100 million a year. While that has helped you build market share, Shoebuy.com now offers the same thing, so free shipping and free returns may not be enough to sustain your competitive advantage.

Your long-term goal is to combine free shipping and free returns with the best customer service in the business so that most of your profits come from repeat customers. What would that customer service look like? What would customers expect? How can you make sure that every new person hired in the company "gap it" as you build your corporate culture around great service? While you don't intend to compete on price, competition will make you keep costs down. Given Zappos's emphasis on culture and customer service, it doesn't make sense, like many companies have done, to outsource the call center to India. So, to keep costs down, you need to find a way to improve the communication between headquarters, the call center, and the distribution warehouse, all of which are in different locations. Finally, market research indicates that new shoppers don't see many differences between you and your competition. The websites are similar and your message of great customer service hasn't sunk in yet. This isn't a marketing issue. It's a communication issue. What steps can you personally take as the CEO to effectively and frequently talk about Zappos so that employees and customers have a deeper, more meaningful connection to the company?

If you were in charge at Zappos, what would you do?

It's estimated that managers spend over 80 percent of their day communicating with others.[2] Indeed, much of the basic management process—planning, organizing, leading, and controlling—cannot be performed without effective communication. If this weren't reason enough to study communication, consider that effective oral communication—achieved by listening, following instructions, conversing, and giving feedback—is the most important skill for college graduates who are entering the workforce.[3] Furthermore, across all industries, poor communication skills rank as the single most important reason that people do not advance in their careers.[4] Communication is especially important for top managers like the CEO of Zappos. As Mark DeMichele, former CEO of Arizona Public Service Company, puts it, "Communication is the key to success. CEOs can have good ideas, a vision, and a plan. But they also have to be able to communicate those plans to people who work for them."[5]

This chapter begins by examining the role of perception in communication and how perception can make it difficult for managers to communicate effectively. Next, you'll read about the communication process and the various kinds of communication found in most organizations. In the last half of the chapter, the focus is on improving communication in organizations. You'll learn about one-on-one communication and then about how to communicate effectively and listen to others organization-wide.

What Is Communication?

Many bosses try to make bad news sound good with phrases like "rightsizing" for layoffs, "merger of equals" for acquisition by another company, "pursuing other interests" for employees who were fired, and "cost efficiencies" for outsourced jobs. Why do managers sugarcoat bad news? Because, says Dartmouth management professor Paul Argenti, they think "they'll get less flak."

Communication is the process of transmitting information from one person or place to another. While some bosses sugarcoat bad news, smart managers understand that effective, straightforward communication between managers and employees is essential for success.

After reading the next two sections, you should be able to:

1 explain the role that perception plays in communication and communication problems.

2 describe the communication process and the various kinds of communication in organizations.

1 Perception and Communication Problems

One study found that when *employees* were asked whether their supervisor gave recognition for good work, only 13 percent said their supervisor gave a pat on the back, and a mere 14 percent said their supervisor gave sincere and thorough praise. But when the *supervisors* of these employees were asked if they gave recognition for good work, 82 percent said they gave pats on the back, while 80 percent said that they gave sincere and thorough praise.[6] Given that these managers and employees worked closely together, how could they have had such different perceptions of something as simple as praise?

Let's learn more about perception and communication problems by examining 1.1 **the basic perception process**, 1.2 **perception problems**, 1.3 **how we perceive others**, and 1.4 **how we perceive ourselves**. We'll also consider how all of these factors make it difficult for managers to communicate effectively.

1.1 Basic Perception Process

As shown in Exhibit 13.1, **perception** is the process by which individuals attend to, organize, interpret, and retain information from their environments. And since communication is the process of transmitting information from one person or place to another, perception is obviously a key part of communication. Yet perception can also be a key obstacle to communication.

As people perform their jobs, they are exposed to a wide variety of informational stimuli such as e-mail, direct conversations with the boss or coworkers, rumors heard over lunch, stories about the company in the press, or a video broadcast of a speech from the CEO. Just being exposed to an informational stimulus, however, is no guarantee that an individual will pay attention or attend to that stimulus. People experience stimuli through their own **perceptual filters**—the personality-, psychology-, or experience-based differences that influence them to ignore or pay attention to particular stimuli. Because of filtering, people exposed to the same information will often disagree about what they saw or heard.

communication
the process of transmitting information from one person or place to another

perception
the process by which individuals attend to, organize, interpret, and retain information from their environments

perceptual filters
the personality-, psychology-, or experience-based differences that influence people to ignore or pay attention to particular stimuli

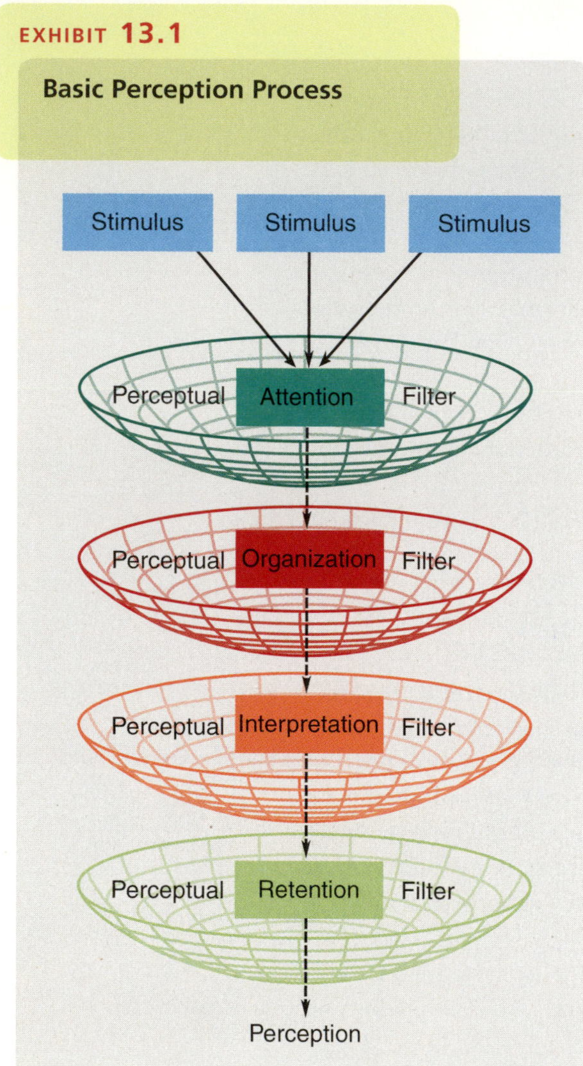

EXHIBIT 13.1

Basic Perception Process

For example, almost every stadium in the National Football League has a huge TV monitor on which fans can watch replays. As the slow-motion video is replayed on the monitor, you can often hear cheers *and* boos, as fans of competing teams perceive the same replay in completely different ways. This happens because the fans' perceptual filters predispose them to attend to stimuli that support their team and not their opponents.[7] The same perceptual filters that affect whether we believe our favorite team was "robbed" by the referees also affect communication, that is, the transmitting of information from one person or place to another. As shown in Exhibit 13.1, perceptual filters affect each part of the *perception process*: attention, organization, interpretation, and retention.

Attention is the process of noticing, or becoming aware of, particular stimuli. Because of perceptual filters, we attend to some stimuli and not others. For instance, a study at the University of Illinois asked viewers to watch people in black shirts and white shirts toss a basketball back and forth and to count the number of times someone in a black shirt tossed the basketball. Because their perceptual filters had narrowed to track the activities of people in black shirts, half of the viewers did not notice when the experimenters had someone in a gorilla suit walk through the midst of the people tossing the basketball back and forth.[8] *Organization* is the process of incorporating new information (from the stimuli that you notice) into your existing knowledge. Because of perceptual filters, we are more likely to incorporate new knowledge that is consistent with what we already know or believe. *Interpretation* is the process of attaching meaning to new knowledge. Because of perceptual filters, our preferences and beliefs strongly influence the meaning we attach to new information (e.g., "This decision must mean that top management supports our project."). Finally, *retention* is the process of remembering interpreted information. Retention affects what we recall and commit to memory after we have perceived something. Of course, perceptual filters affect retention as much as they do organization and interpretation.

In short, because of perception and perceptual filters, people are likely to pay attention to different things, organize and interpret what they pay attention to differently, and, finally, remember things differently. Consequently, even when people are exposed to the same communications (e.g., organizational memos, discussions with managers or customers), they can end up with very different perceptions and understandings. This is why communication can be so difficult and frustrating for managers. Let's review some of the communication problems created by perception and perceptual filters.

1.2 Perception Problems

Perception creates communication problems for organizations because people exposed to the same information can end up with completely different ideas and understandings. Two of the most common perception problems in organizations are selective perception and closure.

At work, we are constantly bombarded with sensory stimuli: phones ringing, people talking in the background, computers dinging as new e-mail arrives, people calling our names, and so forth. As limited processors of information, we cannot possibly notice, receive, and interpret all of this information. As a result, we attend to and accept some stimuli but screen out and reject others. This isn't a random process.

Selective perception is the tendency to notice and accept objects and information consistent with our values, beliefs, and expectations while ignoring or screening out inconsistent information. For example, when Jack Smith, the former CEO of General Motors, was a junior-level executive, he traveled to Japan to learn why Toyota's cars were so reliable and why Toyota was so productive. When he learned that Toyota could build a car with half as many people as GM, he wrote a report and shared his findings with GM's all-powerful executive committee. But no one on the committee believed what he told them. The executives just couldn't accept that a Japanese company was so much more effective than GM. Says Smith, "Never in my life have I been so quickly and unceremoniously blown out of the water."[9]

Once we have initial information about a person, event, or process, **closure** is the tendency to fill in the gaps where information is missing, that is, to assume that what we don't know is consistent with what we already do know. If employees are told that budgets must be cut by 10 percent, they may automatically assume that 10 percent of employees will lose their jobs, too, even if that isn't the case. Not surprisingly, when closure occurs, people sometimes fill in the gaps with inaccurate information, which can create problems for organizations.

selective perception
the tendency to notice and accept objects and information consistent with our values, beliefs, and expectations, while ignoring or screening out or not accepting inconsistent information

closure
the tendency to fill in gaps of missing information by assuming that what we don't know is consistent with what we already know

1.3 Perceptions of Others

Attribution theory says that we all have a basic need to understand and explain the causes of other people's behavior.[10] In other words, we need to know why people do what they do. According to attribution theory, we use two general reasons or attributions to explain people's behavior: an *internal attribution*, in which behavior is thought to be voluntary or under the control of the individual; and an *external attribution*[11] in which behavior is thought to be involuntary and outside of the control of the individual.

Have you ever seen someone changing a flat tire on the side of the road and thought to yourself, "What rotten luck—somebody's having a bad day"? If you did, you perceived the person through an external attribution known as the defensive bias. The **defensive bias** is the tendency for people to perceive themselves as personally and situationally similar to someone who is having difficulty or trouble.[12] When we identify with the person in a situation, we tend to use external attributions (i.e., features related to the situation) to explain the person's behavior. For instance, since flat tires are common, it's easy to perceive ourselves in that same situation and put the blame on external causes such as running over a nail.

attribution theory
the theory that we all have a basic need to understand and explain the causes of other people's behavior

defensive bias
the tendency for people to perceive themselves as personally and situationally similar to someone who is having difficulty or trouble

Now, let's assume a different situation, this time in the workplace: A utility company worker puts a ladder on a utility pole and then climbs up to do his work. As he's working, he falls from the ladder and seriously injures himself.[13] Answer this question: Who or what caused the accident? If you thought, "It's not the worker's fault. Anybody could fall from a tall ladder," then you interpreted the incident with a defensive bias in which you saw yourself as personally and situationally similar to someone who is having difficulty or trouble. In other words, you made an external attribution by attributing the accident to an external cause, or some feature of the situation.

Most accident investigations, however, initially blame the worker (i.e., an internal attribution) and not the situation (i.e., an external attribution). Typically, 60 to 80 percent of workplace accidents each year are blamed on "operator error," that is, the employees themselves. In reality, more complete investigations usually show that workers are responsible for only 30 to 40 percent of all workplace accidents.[14] Why are accident investigators so quick to blame workers? The reason is that they are committing the **fundamental attribution error**, which is the tendency to ignore external causes of behavior and to attribute other people's actions to internal causes.[15] In other words, when investigators examine the possible causes of an accident, they're much more likely to assume that the accident is a function of the person and not the situation.

Which attribution—the defensive bias or the fundamental attribution error—are workers likely to make when something goes wrong? In general, employees and coworkers are more likely to perceive events and explain behavior from a defensive bias. Because they do the work themselves and see themselves as similar to others who make mistakes, have accidents, or are otherwise held responsible for things that go wrong at work, employees and coworkers are likely to attribute problems to external causes such as failed machinery, poor support, or inadequate training. By contrast, because they are typically observers (who don't do the work themselves) and see themselves as situationally and personally different from workers, managers (i.e., the boss) tend to commit the fundamental attribution error and blame mistakes, accidents, and other things that go wrong on workers (i.e., an internal attribution).

Consequently, workers and managers in most workplaces can be expected to take opposite views when things go wrong. Therefore, the defensive bias, which is typically used by workers, and the fundamental attribution error, which is typically made by managers, together present a significant challenge to effective communication and understanding in organizations.

fundamental attribution error
the tendency to ignore external causes of behavior and to attribute other people's actions to internal causes

self-serving bias
the tendency to overestimate our value by attributing successes to ourselves (internal causes) and attributing failures to others or the environment (external causes)

1.4 Self-Perception

The **self-serving bias** is the tendency to overestimate our value by attributing successes to ourselves (internal causes) and attributing failures to others or the environment (external causes).[16] The self-serving bias can make it especially difficult for managers to talk to employees about performance problems. In general, people have a need to maintain a positive self-image. This need is so strong that when people seek feedback at work, they typically want verification of their worth (rather than information about performance deficiencies) or assurance that mistakes or problems weren't their fault.[17] People can become defensive and emotional when managerial communication threatens their positive self-image. They quit listening, and communication becomes ineffective. In the second half of the chapter, which focuses on improving communication, we'll explain ways in which managers can minimize this self-serving bias and improve effective one-on-one communication with employees.

Management Fact:

One of the most frequent causes of communication problems is jargon, vocabulary that is particular to a group. Any idea what "rightsizing," "delayering," and "unsiloing," mean? Rightsizing means laying off workers. Delayering means firing managers. Unsiloing means getting workers in different parts of the company to work with people in other areas. And because there is always new jargon being developed, it is important that managers not assume that other people, even their own employees, are familiar with their meaning.

REVIEW 1

Perception and Communication Problems

Perception is the process by which people attend to, organize, interpret, and retain information from their environments. Perception is not a straightforward process. Because of perceptual filters such as selective perception and closure, people exposed to the same information stimuli often end up with very different perceptions and understandings. Perception-based differences can also lead to differences in the attributions (internal or external) that managers and workers make when explaining workplace behavior. In general, workers are more likely to explain behavior from a defensive bias, in which they attribute problems to external causes (the situation). Managers, on the other hand, tend to commit the fundamental attribution error, attributing problems to internal causes (the worker associated with a mistake or error). Consequently, when things go wrong, it's common for managers to blame workers and for workers to blame the situation or context in which they do their jobs. Finally, this problem is compounded by a self-serving bias that leads people to attribute successes to internal causes and failures to external causes. So workers may become defensive and emotional and not hear what managers have to say when they receive negative feedback from managers. In short, perceptions and attributions represent a significant challenge to effective communication and understanding in organizations.

2 Kinds of Communication

Each year, on the anniversary of your hiring date, you receive a written assessment of your performance from your boss. This year, after receiving your performance appraisal, you gripe about it to your best friend, a coworker in a cubicle down the hall. Despite your griping, however, you appreciate that your boss cut you some slack, giving you extra days off when you went through a divorce earlier this year. How did your boss know you were having personal problems? He knew something was wrong from your nonverbal communication—your rounded shoulders, the bags under your eyes, and your overall lack of energy. There are many kinds of communication—formal, informal, coaching/counseling, and nonverbal—but they all follow the same fundamental process.

Let's learn more about the different kinds of communication by examining 2.1 **the communication process**, 2.2 **communication channels**, 2.3 **coaching and counseling, or one-on-one communication**, and 2.4 **nonverbal communication**.

2.1 The Communication Process

Earlier in the chapter, we defined *communication* as the process of transmitting information from one person or place to another. Exhibit 13.2 displays a model of the communication process and its major components: the sender (message to be conveyed, encoding the message, transmitting the message); the receiver (receiving message, decoding the message, and the message that was understood); and noise, which interferes with the communication process.

encoding
putting a message into a written, verbal, or symbolic form that can be recognized and understood by the receiver

decoding
the process by which the receiver translates the written, verbal, or symbolic form of a message into an understood message

feedback to sender
in the communication process, a return message to the sender that indicates the receiver's understanding of the message

The communication process begins when a *sender* thinks of a message he or she wants to convey to another person. For example, a few years ago, the CEO of a phone company turned a corner near his house, saw a pay phone booth sitting there, and thought, "That's an odd location for a phone booth. I wonder how much money it earns us."[18] The next step is to encode the message. **Encoding** means putting a message into a verbal (written or spoken) or symbolic form that can be recognized and understood by the receiver. The sender then *transmits the message* via *communication channels*. With some communication channels such as the telephone and face-to-face communication, the sender receives immediate feedback, whereas with others such as e-mail (or text messages and file attachments), fax, voice mail, memos, and letters, the sender must wait for the receiver to respond.

After the message is transmitted and received, the next step is for the receiver to decode it. **Decoding** is the process by which the receiver translates the written, verbal, or symbolic form of the message into an understood message. However, the message as understood by the receiver isn't always the same message that was intended by the sender. Because of different experiences or perceptual filters, receivers may attach a completely different meaning to a message than was intended. The last step of the communication process occurs when the receiver gives the sender feedback. **Feedback to sender** is a return message to the sender that indicates the receiver's understanding of the message (of what the receiver was supposed to know, to do, or not to do). Feedback makes senders aware of possible miscommunications and

EXHIBIT 13.2
The Interpersonal Communication Process

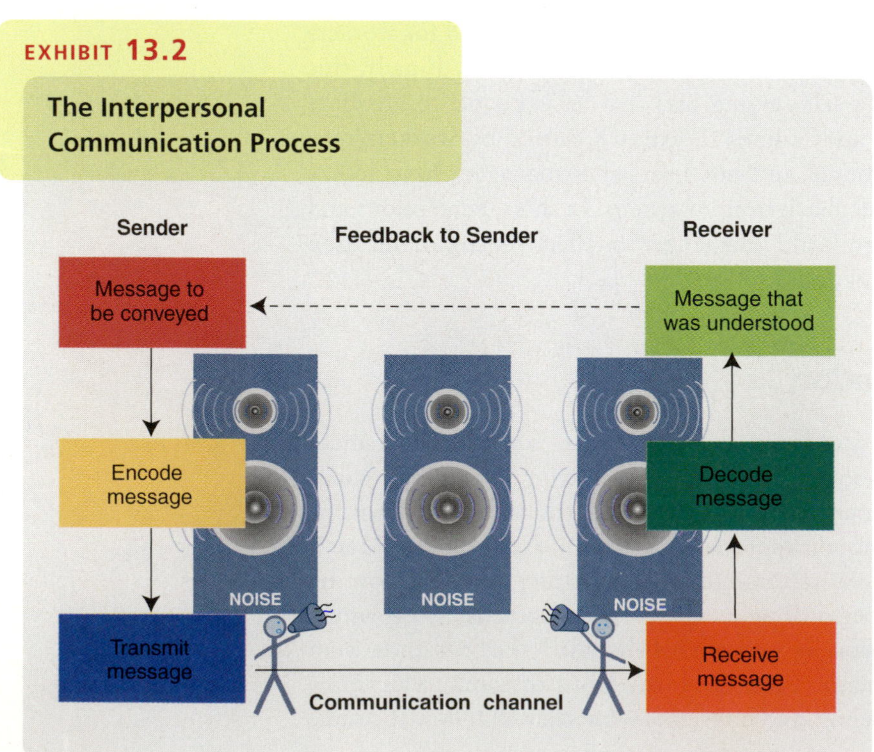

enables them to continue communicating until the receiver understands the intended message. Unfortunately, feedback doesn't always occur in the communication process.

Complacency and overconfidence about the ease and simplicity of communication can lead senders and receivers to simply assume that they share a common understanding of the message and, consequently, to not use feedback to improve the effectiveness of their communication. This is a serious mistake, especially since messages and feedback are always transmitted with and against a background of noise. **Noise** is anything that interferes with the transmission of the intended message. Noise can occur in any of the following situations:

- The sender isn't sure what message to communicate.
- The message is not clearly encoded.
- The wrong communication channel is chosen.
- The message is not received or decoded properly.
- The receiver doesn't have the experience or time to understand the message.

When managers wrongly assume that communication is easy, they reduce communication to something called the conduit metaphor.[19] Strictly speaking, a conduit is a pipe or tube that protects electrical wire. The **conduit metaphor** refers to the mistaken assumption that senders can pipe their intended messages directly into the heads of receivers with perfect clarity and without noise or perceptual filters interfering with the receivers' understanding of the message. However, this just isn't possible. Even if managers could telepathically direct their thoughts straight into receivers' heads, misunderstandings and communication problems would still occur because words and symbols typically have multiple meanings, depending on how they're used. Consider the common word, *fine*. Depending on how you use it, *fine* can mean a penalty; a good job; that something is delicate, small, pure, or flimsy; or that something is okay.

In summary, the conduit metaphor causes problems in communication by making managers too complacent and confident in their ability to easily and accurately transfer messages to receivers. Managers who want to be effective communicators need to carefully choose words and symbols that will help receivers derive the intended meaning of a message. Furthermore, they need to be aware of all steps in the communication process, beginning with the sender (message to be conveyed, encoding the message, transmitting the message) and ending with the receiver (receiving the message, decoding the message, understanding the message, and using feedback to communicate what was understood).

2.2 Communication Channels

Communication channels can be formal or informal. An organization's **formal communication channel** is the system of official channels that carry organizationally approved messages and information. Organizational objectives, rules, policies, procedures, instructions, commands, and requests for information are all transmitted via the formal communication system or channel. There are three formal communication channels: downward communication, upward communication, and horizontal communication.[20] **Downward communication** flows from higher to lower levels in an organization. Downward communication is used to issue orders down the organizational hierarchy, to give organizational members

noise
anything that interferes with the transmission of the intended message

conduit metaphor
the mistaken assumption that senders can pipe their intended messages directly into the heads of receivers with perfect clarity and without noise or perceptual filters interfering with the receivers' understanding of the message

formal communication channel
the system of official channels that carry organizationally approved messages and information

downward communication
communication that flows from higher to lower levels in an organization

job-related information, to give managers and workers performance reviews from upper managers, and to clarify organizational objectives and goals.[21]

Upward communication flows from lower levels to higher levels in an organization. Upward communication is used to give higher-level managers feedback about operations, issues, and problems; to help higher-level managers assess organizational performance and effectiveness; to encourage lower-level managers and employees to participate in organizational decision making; and to give those at lower levels the chance to share their concerns with higher-level authorities.

upward communication communication that flows from lower to higher levels in an organization

horizontal communication communication that flows among managers and workers who are at the same organizational level

informal communication channel ("grapevine") the transmission of messages from employee to employee outside of formal communication channels

SONY executive Ken Kutaragi was known for not communicating with his bosses or other Sony units. That wasn't a problem when he was in charge of Sony's successful rollouts of the PlayStation 1 and PlayStation 2. But it became a problem during the development of the PlayStation 3 when he went over his budget by several hundred million dollars without telling the CEO.[22]

Horizontal communication flows among managers and workers who are at the same organizational level, such as when a day shift nurse comes in at 7:30 am for a half-hour discussion with the midnight nurse supervisor who leaves at 8:00 am. Horizontal communication helps facilitate coordination and cooperation between different parts of a company and allows coworkers to share relevant information. It also helps people at the same level resolve conflicts and solve problems without involving high levels of management.

In general, what can managers do to improve formal communication? First, decrease reliance on downward communication. Second, increase chances for upward communication by increasing personal contact with lower-level managers and workers. Third, encourage much better use of horizontal communication. Finally, be aware of the problems associated with downward, upward, and horizontal communication.

EXHIBIT 13.3

Grapevine Communication Networks

Gossip Chain

Cluster Chain

Source: K. Davis & J. W. Newstrom, *Human Behavior at Work: Organizational Behavior,* 8th ed. (New York: McGraw-Hill, 1989).

An organization's **informal communication channel**, sometimes called the **grapevine**, is the transmission of messages from employee to employee outside of formal communication channels. The grapevine arises out of curiosity, that is, the need to know what is going on in an organization and how it might affect you or others. To satisfy this curiosity, employees need a consistent supply of relevant, accurate, in-depth information about "who is doing what and what changes are occurring within the organization."[23]

Grapevines arise out of informal communication networks such as the gossip or cluster chains shown in Exhibit 13.3. In a *gossip chain*, one highly connected individual shares information with many other managers and workers. By contrast, in a *cluster chain*, numerous people simply tell a few of their friends. The result in both cases is that information flows freely and quickly through the organization. Some believe that grapevines are a waste of employees' time, that they promote gossip and rumors that fuel political speculation, and that they are sources of highly unreliable, inaccurate information. Yet studies clearly show that grapevines are highly accurate sources of information for a number of reasons.[24] First, because grapevines typically carry "juicy" information that is interesting and timely, information spreads rapidly. Second, since information is typically spread by face-to-face conversation, receivers can send feedback to make sure they understand the message that is being communicated. This reduces misunderstandings and increases accuracy. Third, since most of the information in a company moves along the grapevine rather than formal communication channels, people can usually verify the accuracy of information by checking it out with others.

What can managers do to manage organizational grapevines? The very worst thing they can do is withhold information or try to punish those who share information with others. The grapevine abhors a vacuum, so rumors and anxiety will flourish in the absence of information from company management. A better strategy is to embrace the grapevine and keep employees informed about possible changes and strategies. Failure to do so will just make things worse. An employee who works in a company where management maintains a culture of silence says, "They [management] think that not communicating the tough stuff will keep employees unaware of it. Of course, it doesn't work. It just fuels the grapevine."[25] Finally, in addition to using the grapevine to communicate with others, managers should not overlook the grapevine as a tremendous source of valuable information and feedback. In fact, information flowing through organizational grapevines is estimated to be 75 to 95 percent accurate.[26]

2.3 Coaching and Counseling: One-on-One Communication

Coaching and counseling are two kinds of one-on-one communication. **Coaching** is communicating with someone for the direct purpose of improving the person's on-the-job performance or behavior.[27] Managers tend to make several mistakes when coaching employees. First, they wait for a problem before coaching. Jim Concelman, manager for leadership development at Development Dimensions International, says, "Of course, a boss has to coach an employee if a mistake has been made, but they shouldn't be waiting for the error. While it is a lot easier to see a mistake and correct it, people learn more through success than through failure, so bosses should ensure that employees are experiencing as many successes as possible. Successful employees lead to a more successful organization."[28] Second, when mistakes *are* made, managers wait much too long before talking to the employee about the problem. Management professor Ray Hilgert says, "A manager must respond as soon as possible after an incident of poor performance. Don't bury your head. . . . When employees are told nothing, they assume everything is okay."[29] When Jay Whitehead, now president of Outsourcing Today, was a manager at a previous company, one of his employees accidentally copied an e-mail to a customer that insulted the customer. Whitehead immediately talked to the employee, who offered to quit. Whitehead told him, "No, instead you're going to do something much harder. You're going to apologize." He did, and, according to White, "all was forgiven."[30] The key to this successful result was that Whitehead acted immediately to coach the employee on his mistake. In Section 3, you'll learn a number of specific steps for effective one-on-one communication and coaching.

In contrast to coaching, **counseling** is communicating with someone about non-job-related issues such as stress, child care, health issues, retirement planning,

coaching
communicating with someone for the direct purpose of improving the person's on-the-job performance or behavior

counseling
communicating with someone about non-job-related issues that may be affecting or interfering with the person's performance

or legal issues that may be affecting or interfering with the person's performance. But counseling does not mean that managers should try to be clinicians, even though an estimated 20 percent of employees are dealing with personal problems at any one time. Dana Kiel, who works for Cigna Behavioral Health, says, "We call it the quicksand. If you're a good supervisor, you do care about your employees, but it's not your job to be a therapist."[31] Instead, managers should discuss specific performance problems, listen if the employee chooses to share personal issues, and then recommend that the employee call the company's *Employee Assistance Program (EAP)*. EAPs are typically free when provided as part of a company's benefit package. In emergencies or times of crisis, EAPs can offer immediate counseling and support; they can also provide referrals to organizations and professionals that can help employees and their family members address personal issues.

2.4 Nonverbal Communication

When people talk, they send both verbal and nonverbal messages. Verbal messages are sent and received through the words we speak, as when we congratulate a speaker by saying "That was a great presentation." By contrast, nonverbal messages are sent through body language, facial expressions, or tone of voice. Hearing "*That* was a *great* presentation!" is very different from hearing "ahem [clearing throat], that was, ahem, ahem, a great presentation."

More generally, **nonverbal communication** is any communication that doesn't involve words. Nonverbal communication almost always accompanies verbal communication and may either support and reinforce the verbal message or contradict it. The importance of nonverbal communication is well established. Researchers have estimated that as much as 93 percent of any message is transmitted nonverbally, with 55 percent coming from body language and facial expressions and 38 percent coming from the tone and pitch of the voice.[32] Since many nonverbal cues are unintentional, receivers often consider nonverbal communication to be a more accurate representation of what senders are thinking and feeling than the words they use. If you have ever asked someone out on a date and been told "yes," but realized that the real answer was "no," then you understand the importance of paying attention to nonverbal communication.

Kinesics and paralanguage are two kinds of nonverbal communication.[33] **Kinesics** (from the Greek word *kinesis*, meaning "movement") are movements of the body and face.[34] These movements include arm and hand gestures, facial expressions, eye contact, folding arms, crossing legs, and leaning toward or away from another person. For example, people tend to avoid eye contact when they are embarrassed or unsure of the message they are sending. Crossed arms or legs usually indicate defensiveness or that the person is not receptive to the message or the sender. Also, people tend to smile frequently when they are seeking someone's approval. It turns out that kinesics play an incredibly important role in communication.

Paralanguage includes the pitch, rate, tone, volume, and speaking pattern (use of silences, pauses, or hesitations) of one's voice. For example, when people are unsure of what to say, they tend to decrease their communication effectiveness by speaking softly. When people are nervous, they tend to talk faster and louder. These characteristics have a tremendous influence on whether listeners are receptive to what speakers are saying. For example, Vinya Lynch believes that her "timid and

nonverbal communication
any communication that doesn't involve words

kinesics
movements of the body and face

paralanguage
the pitch, rate, tone, volume, and speaking pattern (i.e., use of silences, pauses, or hesitations) of one's voice

© BLEND IMAGES/JUPITERIMAGES

sing-songy" voice is why others don't take her seriously and cut her off when she makes presentations. Lynch says, "When I listen to myself, it doesn't sound intelligent." She began working with a speech coach ($2,250 for 10 sessions) because, as she says, "I want my voice to be charismatic and confident all at the same time."[35]

In short, because nonverbal communication is so informative, especially when it contradicts verbal communication, managers need to learn how to monitor and control their nonverbal behavior.

REVIEW 2

Kinds of Communication

Communication within an organization depends on the communication process, formal and informal communication channels, one-on-one communication, and nonverbal communication. The major components of the communication process are the sender, the receiver, noise, and feedback. The conduit metaphor refers to the mistaken assumption that senders can pipe their intended messages directly into receivers' heads with perfect clarity. With noise, perceptual filters, and little feedback, however, this just isn't possible. Formal communication channels such as downward, upward, and horizontal communication carry organizationally approved messages and information. By contrast, the informal communication channel, called the grapevine, arises out of curiosity and is carried out through gossip or cluster chains. Managers should use the grapevine to keep employees informed and to obtain better, clearer information for themselves. There are two kinds of one-on-one communication. Coaching is used to improve on-the-job performance while counseling is used to communicate about non-job-related issues affecting job performance. Nonverbal communication such as kinesics and paralanguage accounts for as much as 93 percent of a message's content and interpretation. Since nonverbal communication is so informative, managers need to learn how to monitor and control their nonverbal behavior.

 How to Improve Communication

An employee comes in late every day, takes long lunches, and leaves early. His coworkers resent his tardiness and having to do his share of the work. Another employee makes as many as ten personal phone calls a day on company time. Another employee's job performance has dropped significantly in the last 3 months. How do you communicate with these employees to begin solving these problems? Or suppose that you supervise a division of 50, 100, or even 1,000 people. How can you communicate effectively with everyone in that division? Moreover, how can top managers communicate effectively with everyone in the company when employees work in different offices, states, countries, and time zones? Turning that around, how can managers make themselves accessible so that they can hear what employees feel and think throughout the organization?

When it comes to improving communication, managers face two primary tasks, managing one-on-one communication and managing organization-wide communication.

After reading the next two sections, you should be able to:

3 explain how managers can manage effective one-on-one communication.

4 describe how managers can manage effective organization-wide communication.

3 Managing One-on-One Communication

You learned in Chapter 1 that, on average, first-line managers spend 57 percent of their time with people, middle managers spend 63 percent of their time directly with people, and top managers spend as much as 78 percent of their time dealing with people.[36] These numbers make it clear that managers spend a great deal of time in one-on-one communication with others.

Learn more about managing one-on-one communication by reading how to 3.1 **choose the right communication medium**, 3.2 **be a good listener**, 3.3 **give effective feedback**, and 3.4 **improve cross-cultural communication**.

3.1 Choosing the Right Communication Medium

Sometimes messages are poorly communicated simply because they are delivered using the wrong **communication medium**, which is the method used to deliver a message. For example, the wrong communication medium is being used when an employee returns from lunch, picks up the note left on her office chair, and learns she has been fired. The wrong communication medium is also being used when an employee pops into your office every 10 minutes with a simple request (an e-mail would be better).

There are two general kinds of communication media: oral and written communication. *Oral communication* includes face-to-face and group meetings through telephone calls, videoconferencing, or any other means of sending and receiving spoken messages. Studies show that managers generally prefer oral communication over written because it provides the opportunity to ask questions about parts of the message that they don't understand. Oral communication is also a rich

communication medium the method used to deliver an oral or written message

communication medium because it allows managers to receive and assess the nonverbal communication that accompanies spoken messages (i.e., body language, facial expressions, and the voice characteristics associated with paralanguage).

Furthermore, you don't need a personal computer and an Internet connection to conduct oral communication. Simply schedule an appointment, track someone down in the hall, or catch someone on the phone. But the oral medium should not be used for *all* communication. In general, when the message is simple, such as a quick request or a presentation of straightforward information, a memo or e-mail is often the better communication medium.

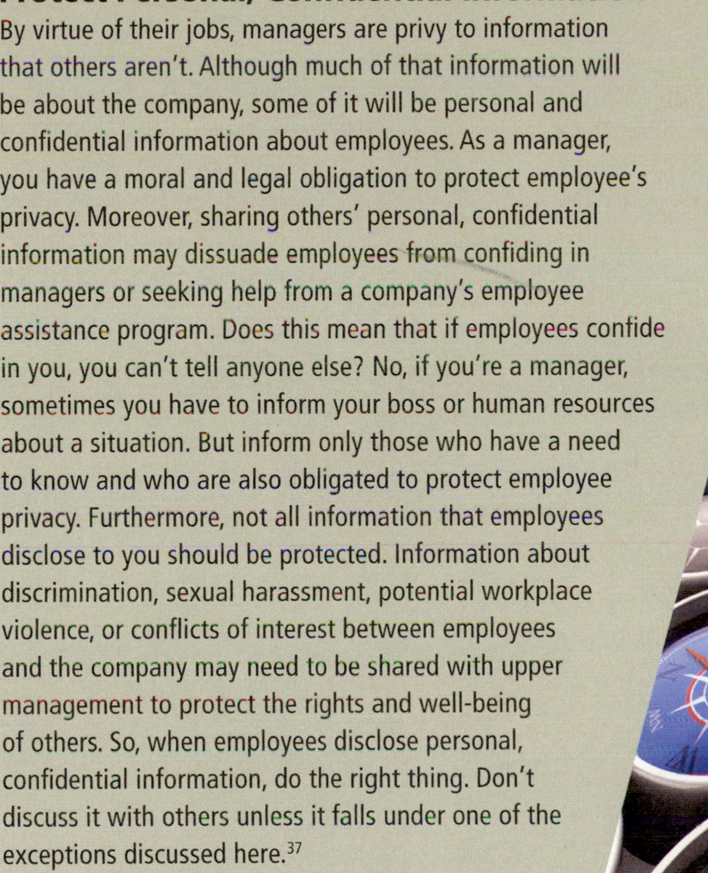

Doing the Right Thing

Protect Personal, Confidential Information

By virtue of their jobs, managers are privy to information that others aren't. Although much of that information will be about the company, some of it will be personal and confidential information about employees. As a manager, you have a moral and legal obligation to protect employee's privacy. Moreover, sharing others' personal, confidential information may dissuade employees from confiding in managers or seeking help from a company's employee assistance program. Does this mean that if employees confide in you, you can't tell anyone else? No, if you're a manager, sometimes you have to inform your boss or human resources about a situation. But inform only those who have a need to know and who are also obligated to protect employee privacy. Furthermore, not all information that employees disclose to you should be protected. Information about discrimination, sexual harassment, potential workplace violence, or conflicts of interest between employees and the company may need to be shared with upper management to protect the rights and well-being of others. So, when employees disclose personal, confidential information, do the right thing. Don't discuss it with others unless it falls under one of the exceptions discussed here.[37]

Written communication includes letters, e-mail, and memos. Although most managers still like and use oral communication, e-mail in particular is changing how they communicate with workers, customers, and each other. E-mail is the fastest-growing form of communication in organizations primarily because of its convenience and speed. For instance, because people read six times faster than they can listen, they usually can read 30 e-mail messages in 10 to 15 minutes.[38] By contrast, dealing with voice messages can take a considerable amount of time. Fred DeLuca, founder of the Subway sandwich shop franchise, says, "I get about 60 messages a day from employees and franchisees, and I listen to all of them. For my sanity, I set a time limit of 75 seconds, because people can be long-winded when they're excited. When I hear, 'You have 30 messages,' I know right away that I'll spend 60 minutes on voice mail. I take two minutes per message, listening and returning or forwarding."[39]

Written communication such as e-mail is well suited for delivering straightforward messages and information. Furthermore, with e-mail accessible at the office, at home, and on the road, managers can use e-mail to stay in touch from anywhere at almost any time. And, since e-mail and other written communications don't have to be sent and received simultaneously, messages can be sent and stored for reading at any time. Consequently, managers can send and receive many more messages using e-mail than by using oral communication, which requires people to get together in person or by phone or video conference.

E-mail has its own drawbacks, however. One is that it lacks the formality of paper memos and letters. It is easy to fire off a rushed e-mail that is not well written or fully thought through. Another drawback to e-mail is that it lacks nonverbal cues, making e-mails very easy to misinterpret.

3.2 Listening

Are you a good listener? You probably think so. In fact, most people, including managers, are terrible listeners, retaining only about 25 percent of what they hear.[40] You qualify as a poor listener if you frequently interrupt others, jump to conclusions about what people will say before they've said it, hurry the speaker to finish his or her point, are a passive listener (not actively working at your listening), or simply don't pay attention to what people are saying.[41] On this last point—attentiveness—college students were periodically asked to record their thoughts during a psychology course. On average, 20 percent of the students were paying attention (only 12 percent were actively working at being good listeners), 20 percent were thinking about sex, 20 percent were thinking about things they had done before, and the remaining 40 percent were thinking about other things unrelated to the class (e.g., worries, religion, lunch, daydreaming).[42]

How important is it to be a good listener? In general, about 45 percent of the total time you spend communicating with others is spent listening. Furthermore, listening is important for managerial and business success, even for those at the top of an organization. As Feargal Quinn, CEO of Irish grocery chain *SUPERQUINN*'s, points out, "If you expect to learn from your customers and employees, don't rely on market research or a suggestion box. Host customer panels, solicit complaints, step into your customer's shoes, plant your people at the front lines, and learn a dozen customer names a week. Listening is not an activity you can delegate—no matter who you are."[43] Quinn continues, "Genuine listening ability is one of the true forms of competitive advantage."[44] Which is why company meetings with suppliers, managers, and employees take place in the stores as customers are shopping. Superquinn's managers are also expected to "jump the counter," or, spend time "in the customer's shoes" by shopping, waiting in line, asking questions, and so on.

hearing
the act or process of perceiving sounds

listening
making a conscious effort to hear

active listening
assuming half the responsibility for successful communication by actively giving the speaker nonjudgmental feedback that shows you've accurately heard what he or she said

So, what can you do to improve your listening ability? First, understand the difference between hearing and listening. According to *Webster's New World Dictionary*, **hearing** is the "act or process of perceiving sounds," whereas **listening** is "making a conscious effort to hear." In other words, we react to sounds, such as bottles breaking or music being played too loud, because hearing is an involuntary physiological process. By contrast, listening is a voluntary behavior. So, if you want to be a good listener, you have to choose to be a good listener. Typically, that means choosing to be an active, empathetic listener.[45]

Active listening means assuming half the responsibility for successful communication by actively giving the speaker nonjudgmental feedback that shows you've accurately heard what he or she said. Active listeners make it clear from

EXHIBIT 13.4

Clarifying, Paraphrasing, and Summarizing Responses for Active Listeners

Clarifying Responses	Paraphrasing Responses	Summarizing Responses
Could you explain that again?	What you're really saying is . . .	Let me summarize . . .
I don't understand what you mean.	If I understand you correctly . . .	Okay, your main concerns are . . .
I'm not sure how . . .	In other words . . .	To recap what you've said . . .
I'm confused. Would you run through that again?	So your perspective is that . . .	Thus far, you've discussed . . .
	Tell me if I'm wrong, but what you're saying is . . .	

Source: E. Atwater, *I Hear You*, revised ed. (New York: Walker, 1992).

their behavior that they are listening carefully to what the speaker has to say. Active listeners put the speaker at ease, maintain eye contact, and show the speaker that they are attentively listening by nodding and making short statements.

Several specific strategies can help you be a better active listener. First, *clarify responses* by asking the speaker to explain confusing or ambiguous statements. Second, when there are natural breaks in the speaker's delivery, use this time to paraphrase or summarize what has been said. *Paraphrasing* is restating what has been said in your own words. *Summarizing* is reviewing the speaker's main points or emotions. Paraphrasing and summarizing give the speaker the chance to correct the message if the active listener has attached the wrong meaning to it. Paraphrasing and summarizing also show the speaker that the active listener is interested in the speaker's message. Exhibit 13.4 lists specific statements that listeners can use to clarify responses, paraphrase, or summarize what has been said.

Active listeners also avoid evaluating the message or being critical until the message is complete. They recognize that their only responsibility during the transmission of a message is to receive it accurately and derive the intended meaning from it. Evaluation and criticism can take place after the message is accurately received. Finally, active listeners also recognize that a large portion of any message is transmitted nonverbally and thus pay very careful attention to the nonverbal cues transmitted by the speaker.

Empathetic listening means understanding the speaker's perspective and personal frame of reference and giving feedback that conveys that understanding to the speaker. Empathetic listening goes beyond active listening because it depends on our ability to set aside our own attitudes or relationships to be able to see and understand things through someone else's eyes. Empathetic listening is just as important as active listening, especially for managers, because it helps build rapport and trust with others.

empathetic listening understanding the speaker's perspective and personal frame of reference and giving feedback that conveys that understanding to the speaker

The key to being a more empathetic listener is to show your desire to understand and to reflect people's feelings. You can *show your desire to understand* by listening, that is, asking people to talk about what's most important to them and then by giving them sufficient time to talk before responding or interrupting. Reflecting feelings is also an important part of empathetic listening because it demonstrates that you understand the speaker's emotions. Unlike active listening, in which you restate or summarize the informational content of what has been said, the focus is on the affective part of the message. As an empathetic listener, you can use the following statements to *reflect the speaker's emotions*:

- So, right now it sounds like you're feeling . . .
- You seem as if you're . . .
- Do you feel a bit . . .?
- I could be wrong, but I'm sensing that you're feeling . . .

In the end, says management consultant Terry Pearce, empathetic listening can be boiled down to these three steps. First, wait 10 seconds before you respond. It will seem an eternity, but waiting prevents you from interrupting others and rushing your response. Second, to be sure you understand what the speaker wants, ask questions to clarify the speaker's intent. Third, only then should you respond first with feelings and then facts (notice that facts *follow* feelings).[46]

3.3 Giving Feedback

In Chapter 10, you learned that performance appraisal feedback (i.e., judging) should be separated from developmental feedback (i.e., coaching).[47] We can now focus on the steps needed to communicate feedback one-on-one to employees.

To start, managers need to recognize that feedback can be constructive or destructive. **Destructive feedback** is disapproving without any intention of being helpful and almost always causes a negative or defensive reaction in the recipient. In fact, one study found that 98 percent of employees responded to destructive feedback from their bosses with either verbal aggression (two-thirds) or physical aggression (one-third).[48] By contrast, **constructive feedback** is intended to be helpful, corrective, and/or encouraging. It is aimed at correcting performance deficiencies and motivating employees.

For feedback to be constructive rather than destructive, it must be immediate, focused on specific behaviors, and problem-oriented. *Immediate feedback* is much more effective than delayed feedback because manager and worker can recall the mistake or incident more accurately and discuss it in detail. For example, if a worker is rude to a customer and the customer immediately reports the incident to management, and if the manager, in turn, immediately discusses the incident with the employee, there should be little disagreement over what was said or done. By contrast, it's unlikely that either the manager or the worker will be able to accurately remember the specifics of what occurred if the manager waits several weeks to discuss the incident. When that happens, it's usually too late to have a meaningful conversation.

Specific feedback focuses on particular acts or incidents that are clearly under the control of the employee. For instance, instead of telling an employee that he or she is "always late for work," it's much more constructive to say, "In the last 3 weeks, you have been 30 minutes late on four occasions and more than an hour late on two others." Furthermore, specific feedback isn't very helpful unless employees have control over the problems that the feedback addresses. Giving negative feedback about behaviors beyond someone's control is likely to be seen as unfair. Similarly,

destructive feedback
feedback that disapproves without any intention of being helpful and almost always causes a negative or defensive reaction in the recipient

constructive feedback
feedback intended to be helpful, corrective, and/or encouraging

giving positive feedback about behaviors beyond someone's control may be viewed as insincere.

Last, *problem-oriented feedback* focuses on the problems or incidents associated with the poor performance rather than on the worker or the worker's personality. Giving feedback does not give managers the right to personally attack workers. Although managers may be frustrated by a worker's poor performance, the point of problem-oriented feedback is to draw attention to the problem in a nonjudgmental way so that the employee has enough information to correct it. For example, if an employee has body odor, a surprisingly common workplace problem, don't leave deodorant, soap, or shampoo on the person's desk (for all to see) or say, "You stink." *HR Magazine* advises handling the problem this way: "Because this is a sensitive issue and the employee will likely be uncomfortable and embarrassed in discussing it, keep the meeting private and confidential. Be compassionate but direct. Treat it as you would handle any other job-related performance issue. Explain the problem and the need to correct it. Be specific about expectations. . . . If the employer has a dress and grooming policy, refer to the policy and provide the employee with a copy."[49]

3.4 Improving Cross-Cultural Communication

As you know by now, effective communication is very difficult to accomplish. **Cross-cultural communication**, which involves transmitting information from a person in one culture to a person from another culture, is even more difficult.

You can do a number of things to increase your chances for successful cross-cultural communication:

- Familiarize yourself with a culture's general work norms.
- Determine whether a culture is emotionally affective or neutral.
- Develop respect for other cultures.
- Understand how address terms and attitudes toward time differ from culture to culture.

In Chapter 7, you learned that expatriates who receive predeparture language and cross-cultural training make faster adjustments to foreign cultures and perform better on their international assignments.[50] Therefore, the first step for successful cross-cultural communication is *familiarizing yourself with a culture's general work norms*, that is, the shared values, beliefs, and perceptions toward work and how it should be done. (See Chapter 7 for a more complete discussion of international cultures.) Don't assume that it will be easy; but no matter how difficult, you should work hard to learn different cultures and languages.

Determining whether a culture is emotionally affective or neutral is also important to cross-cultural communication. People in **affective cultures** tend to display their emotions and feelings openly when communicating, whereas people in **neutral cultures** do not.[51] While Italians are prone to strong bursts of emotion (positive and negative), Chinese don't show strong emotions because doing so is thought to disrupt harmony and lead to conflict. Likewise, a smiling American is displaying happiness, but a smiling Japanese may be trying to hide another emotion or avoid answering a question.[52] The mistake most managers make is misunderstanding the differences between affective and neutral cultures. People from neutral cultures aren't by definition cold and unfeeling. They just don't show their emotions in the

cross-cultural communication
transmitting information from a person in one country or culture to a person from another country or culture

affective cultures
cultures in which people display emotions and feelings when communicating

neutral cultures
cultures in which people do not display emotions and feelings when communicating

EXHIBIT **13.5**

Affective and Neutral Cultures

In Affective Cultures, People	In Neutral Cultures, People
1. Reveal thoughts and feelings through verbal and nonverbal communication	1. Don't reveal what they are thinking or feeling
2. Express and show feelings of tension	2. Hide tension and only show it accidentally in face or posture
3. Let their emotions show easily, intensely, and without inhibition	3. Suppress emotions, leading to occasional "explosions"
4. Admire heated, animated, and intense expression of emotion	4. Admire remaining cool, calm, and relaxed
5. Are used to touching, gesturing, and showing strong emotions through facial expressions (all are common)	5. Resist touching, gesturing, and showing strong emotions through facial expressions
6. Make statements with emotion	6. Often make statements in an unexpressive manner

Source: F. Trompenaars, *Riding the Waves of Culture: Understanding Diversity in Global Business* (London: Economist Books, 1994).

same way or with the same intensity as people from affective cultures. The key is to recognize the differences and then make sure your judgments are not based on the lack or presence of emotional reactions. Exhibit 13.5 provides a more detailed explanation of the differences between affective and neutral cultures.

Respecting other cultures is also an important part of improving cross-cultural communication. Because we use our own culture as the standard of comparison, it's very easy to make the common mistake of assuming that "different" means "inferior."[53]

According to Nancy Adler, "Evaluating others' behavior rarely helps in trying to understand, communicate with, or conduct business with people from another culture."[54] The key, she says, is taking a step back and realizing that you don't know or understand everything that is going on and that your assumptions and interpretations of others' behavior and motives may be wrong.

So, instead of judging or evaluating your international business colleagues, observe what they do. Also, delay your judgments until you have more experience with your colleagues and their culture. Last, treat any judgments or conclusions you do make as guesses and then double-check those judgments or conclusions with others.[55] The more patient you are in forming opinions and drawing conclusions, the better you'll be at cross-cultural communication.

You can also improve cross-cultural communication by *knowing the address terms* that different cultures use to address each other in the workplace.[56] **Address terms** are the cultural norms that establish whether you address businesspeople by their first names, family names, or titles. When meeting for the first time, Americans and Australians tend to be informal and address each other by first names, even nicknames. Such immediate informality is not accepted in many cultures. For instance, an American manager working in one of his company's British subsidiaries introduced himself as "Chuck" to his British employees and

address terms
cultural norms that establish whether you should address businesspeople by their first names, family names, or titles

coworkers. Nonetheless, even after 6 months on the job, his British counterparts still referred to him as "Charles." And the more he insisted they call him "Chuck," the more they seemed to dig in their heels and call him "Charles."[57] So, to decrease defensiveness, know your address terms before addressing your international business counterparts.

Understanding different cultural attitudes toward time is another major consideration for effective cross-cultural communication. Cultures tend to be either monochronic or polychronic in their orientation toward time.[58] In **monochronic cultures**, people tend to do one thing at a time and view time as linear, meaning that time is the passage of sequential events. You may have heard the saying, "There are three stages in people's lives: when they believe in Santa Claus, when they don't believe in Santa Claus, and when they are Santa Claus." The progression from childhood, to young adulthood, to parenthood (when they are Santa Claus) reflects a linear view of time. Schedules are important in monochronic cultures because you schedule time to get a particular thing done. By contrast, in **polychronic cultures**, people tend to do more than one thing at a time and view time as circular, meaning that it is a combination of the past, present, and future.

As you can easily imagine, businesspeople from monochronic cultures are driven to distraction by what they perceive as the laxness of polychronic cultures, while people from polychronic cultures chafe under what they perceive as the strict regimentation of monochronic cultures. Exhibit 13.6 provides a more detailed explanation of the differences between monochronic and polychronic cultures.

monochronic cultures cultures in which people tend to do one thing at a time and view time as linear

polychronic cultures cultures in which people tend to do more than one thing at a time and view times as circular

EXHIBIT **13.6**

Monochronic Versus Polychronic Cultures

People in Monochronic Cultures	People in Polychronic Cultures
• Do one thing at a time	• Do many things at once
• Concentrate on the job	• Are highly distractible and subject to interruptions
• Take time commitments (deadlines, schedules) seriously	• Meet time commitments only if possible without extreme measures
• Are committed to the job	• Are committed to people
• Adhere scrupulously to plans	• Change plans easily and often
• Are concerned about not disturbing others (privacy is to be respected)	• Are more concerned with relationships (family, friends, business associates) than with privacy
• Show respect for private property (rarely lend or borrow things)	• Frequently borrow and lend things
• Emphasize promptness	• Vary their promptness by the relationship
• Are accustomed to short-term relationships	• Tend to build lifetime relationships

Source: E. T. Hall & M. R. Hall, *Understanding Cultural Differences* (Yarmouth, ME: Intercultural Press, 1990).

Differences in monochronic and polychronic time show up in four important temporal concepts that affect cross-cultural communication: appointment time, schedule time, discussion time, and acquaintance time.[59] **Appointment time** refers to how punctual you must be when showing up for scheduled appointments or meetings. In the United States, you are considered late if you arrive more than 5 minutes after the appointed time. Swedes don't even allow 5 minutes, expecting others to arrive on the dot. By contrast, in Latin American countries people can arrive 20 to 30 minutes after a scheduled appointment and still not be considered late.

Schedule time is the time by which scheduled projects or jobs should actually be completed. In the United States and other Anglo cultures, a premium is placed on completing things on time. By contrast, more relaxed attitudes toward schedule time can be found throughout Asia and Latin America.

Discussion time concerns how much time should be spent in discussion with others. In the United States, we carefully manage discussion time to avoid wasting time on nonbusiness topics. In Brazil, though, because of the emphasis on building relationships, as much as 2 hours of general discussion on nonbusiness topics can take place before moving on to business issues.

Finally, **acquaintance time** is how much time you must spend getting to know someone before the person is prepared to do business with you. Again, in the United States, people get down to business quickly and are willing to strike a deal on the same day if the terms are good and initial impressions are positive. In the Middle East, however, it may take 2 or 3 weeks of meetings before reaching this comfort level. The French also have a different attitude toward acquaintance time. Polly Platt, author of *French or Foe*, a book that explains French culture and people for travelers and businesspeople, says, "Know that things are going to take longer and don't resent it. Realize that the time system is different. Time is not a quantity for them. We save time, we spend time, we waste time; all this comes from money. The French don't. They pass time. It's a totally different concept."[60]

appointment time
a cultural norm for how punctual you must be when showing up for scheduled appointments or meetings

schedule time
a cultural norm for the time by which scheduled projects or jobs should actually be completed

discussion time
a cultural norm for how much time should be spent in discussion with others

acquaintance time
a cultural norm for how much time you must spend getting to know someone before the person is prepared to do business with you

REVIEW 3

Managing One-on-One Communication

One-on-one communication can be managed by choosing the right communication medium, being a good listener, giving effective feedback, and understanding cross-cultural communication. Managers generally prefer oral communication because it provides the opportunity to ask questions and assess nonverbal communication. Oral communication is best suited to complex, ambiguous, or emotionally laden topics. Written communication is best suited for delivering straightforward messages and information. Listening is important for managerial success, but most people are terrible listeners. To improve your listening skills, choose to be an active listener (clarify responses, paraphrase, and summarize) and an empathetic listener (show your desire to understand, reflect feelings). Feedback can be constructive or destructive. To be constructive, feedback must be immediate, focused on specific behaviors, and problem-oriented. Finally, to increase the chances for successful cross-cultural communication, familiarize yourself with a culture's general work norms, determine whether a culture is emotionally affective or neutral, develop respect for other cultures, and understand how address terms and attitudes toward time (polychronic versus monochronic time; appointment, schedule, discussion, and acquaintance time) differ from culture to culture.

4 Managing Organization-Wide Communication

Although managing one-on-one communication is important, managers must also know how to communicate effectively with a larger number of people throughout an organization. When Bill Zollars became CEO of Yellow Corporation, a trucking company, he decided that he needed to communicate directly with all 25,000 of the company's employees, most of whom did not work at company headquarters in Overland Park, Kansas. For a year and a half, he traveled across the country conducting small, town hall meetings. Zollars says, "When I first got to Yellow, we were in a bad state. So I spent 85 percent of my time on the road talking to people one-on-one or in small groups. I would start off in the morning with the sales force, then talk to drivers, and then the people on the docks. At the end of the day I would have a customer dinner. I would say the same thing to every group and repeat it ad nauseam. The people traveling with me were ready to shoot me. But you have to be relentless in terms of your message."[61] Effective leaders, however, don't just communicate to others. They also make themselves accessible so they can hear what employees throughout their organizations are thinking and feeling.

Learn more about organization-wide communication by reading the following sections about 4.1 **improving transmission by getting the message out**, and 4.2 **improving reception by finding ways to hear what others feel and think**.

4.1 Improving Transmission: Getting the Message Out

Several methods of electronic communication—e-mail, collaborative discussion sites, televised/videotaped speeches and conferences, and broadcast voice mail—now make it easier for managers to communicate with people throughout the organization and get the message out.

Although we normally think of *e-mail*, the transmission of messages via computers, as a means of one-on-one communication, it also plays an important role in organization-wide communication. With the click of a button, managers can send e-mail to everyone in the company via distribution lists. Many CEOs now use this capability regularly to keep employees up-to-date on changes and developments. Many CEOs and top executives also make their e-mail addresses public and encourage employees to contact them directly.

Collaborative websites are another means of electronically promoting organization-wide communication. **Online discussion forums** use web- or software-based discussion tools to allow employees across the company to easily ask questions and share knowledge with each other. The point is to share expertise and not duplicate solutions already discovered by others in the company. Furthermore, because collaborative discussion sites remain online, they provide a historical database for people who are dealing with particular problems for the first time. Collaborative discussion sites are typically organized by topic, project, or person and can take the shape of blogs that allow readers to post comments, wikis to allow collaborative discussions, document sharing and editing, or traditional discussion forums (see Chapter 15 on managing information for further explanation).

Televised/videotaped speeches and meetings are a third electronic method of organization-wide communication. **Televised/videotaped speeches and meetings** are simply speeches and meetings originally made to a small audience that are

online discussion forums
the in-house equivalent of Internet newsgroups. By using web- or software-based discussion tools that are available across the company, employees can easily ask questions and share knowledge with each other

televised/videotaped speeches and meetings
speeches and meetings originally made to a smaller audience that are either simultaneously broadcast to other locations in the company or videotaped for subsequent distribution and viewing

either simultaneously broadcast to other locations in the company or videotaped for subsequent distribution and viewing by a broader audience.

Voice messaging, or voice mail, is a telephone answering system that records audio messages. In one survey, 89 percent of respondents said that voice messaging is critical to business communication, 78 percent said that it improves productivity, and 58 percent said they would rather leave a message on a voice messaging system than with a receptionist.[62] Nonetheless, most people are unfamiliar with the ability to *broadcast voice mail* by sending a recorded message to everyone in the company. Broadcast voice mail gives top managers a quick, convenient way to address their workforces via oral communication. Harry Kraemer, former CEO of pharmaceutical giant Baxter International, described Baxter's broadcast voice mail system: "We have more than 30,000 Baxter team members hooked onto the same voice-mail system. That includes everybody but the folks on the factory line. This is hooked up in over 50 countries."[63] At Ernst & Young, the company-wide broadcast voice mails of former chairman Phil Laskawy were so well known and well liked that E & Y employees called them "Travels with Phil." No matter where he was traveling on business for the company—and he traveled all over the world—Phil would begin his voice mails, most of which lasted 5 to 10 minutes, with a weather report, a couple of bad jokes, and an update on his beloved New York Yankees baseball team. Then came the core part of his message.[64]

4.2 Improving Reception: Hearing What Others Feel and Think

When people think of "organization-wide" communication, they think of the CEO and top managers getting their message out to people in the company. But organization-wide communication also means finding ways to hear what people throughout the organization are thinking and feeling. This is important because most employees and managers are reluctant to share their thoughts and feelings with top managers. Surveys indicate that only 29 percent of first-level managers feel that their companies encourage employees to express their opinions openly. Another study of 22 companies found that 70 percent of the people surveyed were afraid to speak up about problems they knew existed at work.

Withholding information about organizational problems or issues is called **organizational silence**. Organizational silence occurs when employees believe that telling management about problems won't make a difference or that they'll be punished or hurt in some way for sharing such information.[65] For example, the norm in most operating rooms is that the surgeon is clearly in charge. At first look, there doesn't seem to be anything wrong with that. After all, if the surgeon wasn't in charge, who would be? However, a survey of 20 hospitals showed that 60 percent of operating room staffers—nurses, technicians, and other doctors—agreed with the statement "In the ORs [Operating Rooms] here, it is difficult to speak up if I perceive a problem with patient care."[66] This is a problem because serious mistakes can occur when nurses and other operating room staffers don't speak up. *VHA INC.*, which helps 2,400 hospitals coordinate best practices, has a new program called "Transformation of the Operating Room," in which operating teams use safety pauses and time-outs. The surgical team pauses for a moment, asks if anyone has concerns or comments, and then addresses them if need be. Studies show that programs such as this are not only changing the norms in operating rooms but also reducing mistakes such as operating on the wrong leg or noticing that key surgical instruments are missing prior to beginning surgery.

organizational silence
when employees withhold information about organizational problems or issues

Company hotlines are phone numbers that anyone in the company can call anonymously to leave information for upper management. Hotlines are particularly important because 44 percent of employees will not report misconduct. Why not? The reason is twofold: They don't believe anything will be done, *and* they "fear that the report will not be kept confidential."[67] David Childers, CEO of EthicsPoint, which runs hotlines for corporations, says that companies can expect 1 to 1.5 percent of their employees to call their hotlines.[68] Company hotlines are incredibly useful, as 47 percent of the calls placed to them result in an investigation and some form of corrective action within the organization. Anonymity is critical, too, because as those investigations proceed, 54 percent of the callers did not want their identities revealed.[69]

Survey feedback is information that is collected by survey from organization members and then compiled, disseminated, and used to develop action plans for improvement. Many organizations make use of survey feedback by surveying their managers and employees several times a year. FedEx, for example, runs its own Survey Feedback Action program. The survey, which is administered online and is completely anonymous, includes sections for employees to evaluate their managers and the overall environment at FedEx, including benefits, incentives, and working conditions.

Frequent *informal meetings* between top managers and lower-level employees are one of the best ways for top managers to hear what others think and feel. Many people assume that top managers are at the center of everything that goes on in organizations, but top managers commonly feel isolated from most of their lower-level managers and employees.[70] Consequently, more and more top managers are scheduling frequent informal meetings with people throughout their companies. Yogesh Gupta, CEO of *FATWIRE*, which makes software to manage business websites, says that managers must not get defensive during informal meetings. Says Gupta, "I've heard so many executives tell employees to be candid and then jump down their throats if they bring up a problem or ask a critical question."[71] Gupta has spent hundreds of hours in informal meetings with his 200 managers and 9 executives. He meets with each privately because he believes that it encourages people to be candid. And, he asks each these questions:

- What am I doing wrong?
- What would you do differently if you were running the company?
- What's the biggest thing getting in the way of you doing your job well?

As a result of these meetings, Gupta learned that Fatwire was understaffed in marketing and product development.

Have you ever been around when a supervisor learns that upper management is going to be paying a visit? First, there's shock. Next, there's anxiety. And then there's panic, as everyone is told to drop what he or she is doing to polish, shine, and spruce up the workplace so that it looks perfect for the visit. Of course, when visits are conducted under these conditions, top managers don't get a realistic look at what's going on in the company. Consequently, one of the ways to get an accurate picture is to pay *surprise visits* to various parts of the organization. These visits should not just be surprise inspections, but should also be used as an opportunity to encourage meaningful upward communication from those who normally don't get a chance to communicate with upper management.

company hotlines
phone numbers that anyone in the company can call anonymously to leave information for upper management

survey feedback
information that is collected by surveys from organizational members and then compiled, disseminated, and used to develop action plans for improvement

Blogs are another way to hear what people are thinking and saying, both inside and outside the organization. A **blog** is a personal website that provides personal opinions or recommendations, news summaries, and reader comments. At Google, which owns the blog-hosting service Blogger, hundreds of employees are writing *internal blogs*. One employee even wrote a blog, posting all the notes from the brainstorming sessions used to redesign the search page used by millions each day. Marissa Mayer, Vice President, Search Products & User Experience, says "Our legal department loves the blogs, because it basically is a written-down, backed-up, permanent time-stamped version of the scientist's notebook. When you want to file a patent, you can now show in blogs where this idea happened."[72]

External blogs and *twitter feeds* (micro blogs where entries are limited to 140 characters), written by people outside the company, can be a good way to find out what others are saying or thinking about your organization or its products or actions. But it means that someone in the firm has to actively monitor what is being said on web, blog, and twitter feed. Some companies have created the new position of chief blogging officer to manage internal company blogs and to monitor what is said about the company and its products on external blogs.[73]

blog
a personal website that provides personal opinions or recommendations, news summaries, and reader comments

REVIEW 4

Managing Organization-Wide Communication

Managers need methods for managing organization-wide communication and for making themselves accessible so they can hear what employees throughout their organizations are thinking and feeling. E-mail, collaborative discussion sites, televised/videotaped speeches and conferences, and broadcast voice mail make it much easier for managers to improve message transmission and get the message out. By contrast, anonymous company hotlines, survey feedback, frequent informal meetings, and surprise visits help managers avoid organizational silence and improve reception by hearing what others in the organization feel and think. Monitoring internal blogs and external blogs and twitter sites is another way to find out what people are saying and thinking about your organization.

A Communication Policy for the Internet Generation

In your short tenure as the manager of a restaurant chain, you've come up with some brilliant ideas—the Super Bowl parties, unlimited wings night, and who could forget 80's Karaoke Flashdance Fever? But one of your best ideas came a few months ago, when you decided that your company needed to be on Twitter. You've used it to announce promotions, concerts, special menu items, and even offer discounts. One day, you tweeted that the first 1,000 people to follow your Twitter feed would get a free meal for four; about 2,700 people joined up in 1 hour. Your loyal Twitter followers have even spread word of your restaurants overseas. Just the other day, a huge tourist group from Hong Kong stopped at one of your eateries (and spent a ton of money) because they heard about it on Twitter.

Your venture into social media has been such a success that you want to use it for communication within the organization. Instead of phone calls, faxes, and memos, you envision sending a company-wide Tweet announcing policy changes, identifying employees-of-the-month on the Facebook wall, or using text messages to alert chefs of menu changes. As you begin a trial run within the warehouse division, the possibilities seem endless. You get a sharp dose of reality, however, when some senior managers start calling you, frantically asking "What does FTW mean? Someone sent me a performance review that said KUTGW—what is that? Who the heck is @jimbo? One of my employees asked me to give them a 'tweet'—does that violate our sexual harassment policy?" One even told you about how she thought LOL meant "lots of love" and sent it as a text message to an employee whose grandfather had passed away.

All these questions made you aware of how much work was involved in integrating social media into the rest of your company. It would not be as easy as giving people new computers or phones; they would have to learn a whole new language. All of the shorthand, abbreviations, and symbols that seemed so obvious to a generation raised on the Internet are a dark and mysterious code to a generation raised on phone calls, newspapers, and handwritten letters. These managers aren't ready to give up yet—they certainly see the vast potential for social media. But, they are asking—demanding—that you provide them with training so that they can tell the difference between FTW and WTF.

Questions

1. In your opinion, what is the most ideal way to train people who are unfamiliar with social media on how to use it for organization-wide communication?
2. Do you think it is appropriate to use tweets or text messages for organization-wide communication? Why or why not?

Source: Stephanie Raposo. "Quick! Tells Us What KUTGW Means." *Wall Street Journal*. August 5, 2009. D1, 3.

Practice being a MANAGER

Avoiding Communication Breakdown

When problems occur in organizations, they are frequently attributed to a breakdown in communication. The communication process may get more than its share of the blame for some breakdowns that result from organizational or leadership problems. But there is some truth to the common perception that communication is problematic. In this exercise, you will have the opportunity to consider how you might improve your own communication from two sides of the table—coaching/disciplining an employee and receiving coaching/disciplining from a manager.

STEP 1 Get into groups and read the scenario. Your professor will organize you in small groups of three or four students.

Scenario: Chalet is a fine-dining restaurant in a ski resort setting. The restaurant is well known for its gourmet cuisine, fine wine selection, and outstanding service. Dinner for two at Chalet easily runs $100 or more. A key management responsibility at Chalet is the training and development of waitstaff. Service quality is carefully monitored and standards are rigorously maintained. In exchange for meeting these demanding standards, Chalet waitstaff are well compensated and enjoy good benefits. As time permits, you should complete conversations in which you play each of the following roles: Dennis/Denise (new waitstaff member with 3 months of experience at Chalet); Christy/Chris (service manager); and D.J./R.J. (communication consultant to Chalet).

Here are some basic facts of the situation:

- The service manager has not directly observed any problems with Dennis/Denise interacting with customers of the restaurant.
- This past busy weekend, three tables of customers reported problems with the service they received from Dennis/Denise. Only one other table received any negative feedback at all during the weekend, and that concerned the quality of a particular dessert item.
- The reports about Dennis/Denise were rather vague—"server seemed distant, unresponsive" and "acted aloof, like we were a bother."
- Christy/Chris, the service manager, did catch the tail end of what seemed like an argument between Dennis/Denise and one of the cooks on Friday night. When the cook was asked about the incident, she said, "It was nothing . . . usual cook versus server stuff."
- Dennis/Denise needs this job to pay for college and is taking a full load of classes.

The role play should involve a brief conversation (5 to 7 minutes) initiated by Christy/Chris on Monday afternoon prior to opening. The focus of this conversation should be to coach and/or discipline regarding the concerns of the previous weekend. Those playing the role of communication consultant should take notes and provide feedback on the communication in this conversation (strengths and areas for improvement). As time allows, rotate roles after completing a conversation and hearing consultant feedback.

STEP 2 Do the role play. Complete a role-play conversation with one person playing the role of the service manager (Christy/Chris) and another person playing the role of the waitstaffer (Dennis/Denise). Communication consultant(s) should listen and take notes in order to provide feedback to the two individuals who are role-playing the coaching/discipline conversation.

STEP 3 Give feedback. Communication consultant(s) should give feedback to the role-players at the conclusion of the conversation, considering key aspects of communication discussed in this chapter.

STEP 4 Switch roles. Switch roles and repeat the role-play conversation and post-conversation feedback as time allows.

STEP 5 Debrief as a class. What challenges face the communicators in this scenario? Which role was most difficult for you, and why? Why is it important for managers to coach and discipline effectively? Why might managers avoid (or underutilize) this form of communication?

How Do You Listen?

Have you ever been eager to tell someone a funny story, only to have that person interrupt you repeatedly to ask for details or clarification? And have you ever said in exasperation, "Will you just listen?" Some people prefer an inquisitive listening style, whereas others prefer a contemplative listening style. What listening style best describes you? This listening styles inventory will help you establish a baseline to use as a foundation for developing your listening skills.

The following items relate to listening style.[74] Circle the appropriate responses. Please be candid.

	Almost always	Often	Sometimes	Seldom	Almost never
1. I want to listen to what others have to say when they are talking.	5	4	3	2	1
2. I do not listen at full capacity when others are talking.	1	2	3	4	5
3. By listening, I can guess a speaker's intent or purpose without being told.	5	4	3	2	1
4. I have a purpose for listening when others are talking.	5	4	3	2	1
5. I keep control of my biases and attitudes when listening to others speak so that these factors won't affect my interpretation of the message.	5	4	3	2	1
6. I analyze my listening errors so as not to make them again.	5	4	3	2	1
7. I listen to the entire message before making judgments about what the speaker has said.	5	4	3	2	1
8. I cannot tell when a speaker's biases or attitudes are affecting his or her message.	1	2	3	4	5
9. I ask questions when I don't fully understand a speaker's message.	5	4	3	2	1
10. I am aware of whether or not a speaker's meaning of words and concepts is the same as mine.	5	4	3	2	1

SUBTOTAL = ___ + ___ + ___ + ___ + ___ =

GRAND TOTAL = ___

You can find the interpretation of your score at: login.cengagebrain.com.

Reel to Real

Biz Flix

© GREENLIGHT

Friday Night Lights

In the small town of Odessa, Texas, everyone lives for Friday nights when the high school football team, the Permian Panthers, takes the field. The town is proud of their Panthers, led by quarterback Mike Winchell (Lucas Black) and superstar tailback Boobie Miles (Derek Luke), and they're used to winning. They expect a state championship, and nothing less. When Boobie suffers a career-ending injury in the first game of the season, the team isn't sure they can win without him. But Coach Gary Gaines (Billy Bob Thornton) isn't ready to give up yet. In this clip from the film, Coach Gaines gathers the team around during the half-time break to talk about what success really means and how he wants them to achieve it.

What to Watch for and Ask Yourself

1. Both the speaker and the listener(s) are necessary components in the communication process. Coach Gaines is the speaker and each team member and the assistant coaches are listeners. Only Gaines spoke. Did he still meet the basic requirements of effective communication? Draw examples from his speech to support your conclusions.
2. How well do the members of the team and the assistant coaches seem to be listening to the message the coach is communicating to them? How can you tell?
3. Assess the effectiveness of the coach's communication to the team. How do you expect the team to play in the second half of the game as a result?

Management Workplace

© CENGAGE

Greensburg Public Schools

Greensburg superintendent Darrin Headrick was driving home the night the tornado hit town. He stopped at a friend's house to take cover. After the storm passed, he discovered that the entire school system was wiped out. Every building was gone. Textbooks were scattered all over town, and the computers had been destroyed. Only the bleachers behind the football field remained. Headrick had some tough decisions to make. If families were going to feel like it was worth coming back to Greensburg, then he had to reassure them school would be back in session by fall. In this video, he states that the biggest challenge in the days after the tornado was probably communication and he explains why. He also talks about why communication in the town is actually better now than it was before the disaster.

What to Watch for and Ask Yourself

1. Why was communication so difficult in the days following the tornado?
2. Describe the advantages and disadvantages of text messaging as the preferred communication channel in Greensburg after the tornado.
3. In what ways has communication in Greensburg improved since then?

Part Five
Controlling

This chapter examines the basic and in-depth methods that companies use to achieve control, as well as those things that companies choose to control (finances, customer retention, and product quality, among others).

Chapter Fourteen
Control

This chapter explains why information matters, the value of strategic information to companies, and the cost and characteristics of good information. We investigate how companies capture, process, and protect information, and how information, knowledge, and expertise are shared.

Chapter Fifteen
Managing Information

This chapter discusses the daily production of goods and services, starting with the basics of productivity and quality. Next, you will read about managing service and manufacturing operations, and the measures, costs, and methods for managing inventory.

Chapter Sixteen
Managing Service and Manufacturing Operations

14

Chapter Fourteen

Control

OUTLINE

Experience Management

Explore the four levels of learning by doing the simulation module on Organizational Control.

© ISTOCKPHOTO.COM/ ANN MARIE KURTZ

Pod Nod

Mini lecture reviews all the learning points in the chapter.

© ISTOCKPHOTO.COM/ MAGNET CREATIVE

Reel to Real

Biz Flix is a scene from *Friday Night Lights*. Management Workplace is a segment on Numi Organic Tea.

© ISTOCKPHOTO.COM/ CRAFTVISION

Self Test

10 quiz questions, 5 exhibit worksheets, and PowerPoints for quick review.

© ISTOCKPHOTO.COM/ DIJITAL FILM

What Would You Do?

Subaru of Indiana Automotive, Lafayette, Indiana.[1]

With gas prices rising and more drivers desiring ecologically friendly vehicles, auto manufacturers turned to hybrid gas/electric cars, like the Toyota Prius and the Ford Fusion, to significantly improve gas mileage and reduce auto emissions. In the next few years, thanks to advances in battery technology, environmentally minded consumers will be able to shop for plug-in cars, like the Nissan Leaf, which have a range of about 40 miles per charge. So, instead of filling up with gas on your way home, you'll plug in your Leaf in your garage at the end of the day. Business/environment consultant Gary List is not surprised at these trends. Says List, "Green has become a hot commodity. It's something customers are asking about. Employees want to work for companies that are green and politicians are struggling to be greener than the next politician." While auto manufacturers are making progress on emissions and gas mileage, most pay little attention to the environmental impact of their manufacturing facilities, which send hundreds of millions of tons of waste to landfills each year. That waste, in turn, contributes to increases in the methane gas emitted from landfills, which some estimate to be more than 20 times as damaging to the environment as carbon dioxide emissions.

Your *SUBARU* manufacturing facility has an outstanding record on environmental issues. It was the first smoke-free auto assembly plant in the United States, the first to be ISO 14001 certified (indicating that you have taken steps to identify and control the environmental impact of your plant's activities, product, and services), and the first to have an on-site solvent recovery system (typically, solvents are some of the worst pollutants in manufacturing). Yet, despite this progress, your Subaru plant sends nearly 500 pounds of waste per car to landfills each year. And with annual production nearing 200,000 cars, that means 100 million pounds of waste were going to landfills each year (including 26 million pounds of steel and 3 million pounds of cardboard and paper). With Subaru's long commitment to being a green manufacturer, no one is happy with the current situation. While it sounds impossible, you've heard about leading-edge companies that are taking steps to become zero-landfill manufacturers. That's right, zero, zip, nada. Despite producing hundreds of thousands of products, they send no waste to landfills—nothing. You wonder if your production facility could do this too.

Before you even start, you and your management team must answer some key questions. First, should you become a zero waste plant even if it costs you money to do so? What if only breaks even? Or should you do it only if it saves you money? Sure, the company's got a long-standing commitment to the environment, but you're running a business, not the Sierra Club. What trade-offs, if any, is the company willing to make in terms of costs and profits to become a zero-landfill manufacturing facility? Second, when environmental consultants work with companies, they help them address four levels of waste minimization, but you'll only focus on three, since the fourth deals with safely preparing materials for landfills. The first level is to prevent waste and pollution before they occur, or to reduce them when they do occur. At the second level, called recycle and reuse, wastes are reduced by reusing materials as long as possible or by collecting materials for on- or off-site recycling. From steel, to cardboard and paper, to plastics and foam, what steps could you take to minimize waste on these two levels? Finally, at the third level of waste minimization, consultants work with companies to treat waste via biological, chemical, or other processes to turn potentially harmful waste into harmless compounds or useful by-products. What steps might you take at this level to again avoid sending any materials to landfills?

If you were in charge of this Sub manufacturing plant, what wou you do?

As Subaru's situation shows, past success is no guarantee of future success. Even successful companies fall short, face challenges, and have to make changes. **Control** is a regulatory process of establishing standards to achieve organizational goals, comparing actual performance against the standards, and taking corrective action when necessary to restore performance to those standards. Control is achieved when behavior and work procedures conform to standards and when company goals are accomplished.[2] Control is not just an after-the-fact process, however. Preventive measures are also a form of control.

We begin this chapter by examining the basic control process used in organizations. In the second part of the chapter, we go beyond the basics to an in-depth examination of the different methods that companies use to achieve control. We conclude the chapter by looking at the things that companies choose to control (finances, customer retention, and product quality, among others).

control
a regulatory process of establishing standards to achieve organizational goals, comparing actual performance against the standards, and taking corrective action, when necessary

Basics of Control

If you're at home and it's too warm, you turn down your thermostat to kick on the air-conditioning. But if it's too warm in a *WAL-MART* store, then the store manager has to contact a team of energy control specialists at the company's Bentonville,

Arkansas, headquarters. Wal-Mart's Charles Zimmerman says, "It's not like a store manager can turn down a thermostat two degrees. He has to call us to make that happen."[3] In addition to monitoring a store's heating and cooling, Wal-Mart's energy control processes are so sophisticated that if a freezer door is accidentally left open for 45 minutes, a sensor alerts someone at headquarters to contact the store manager. Wal-Mart spokesperson Dave Tovar says, the "monitoring team saves the company millions of dollars by detecting and responding to situations that could cause Wal-Mart to lose money on wasted energy or spoiled food."[4]

After reading the next section, you should be able to:

1 describe the basic control process.

1 The Control Process

The basic control process 1.1 **begins with the establishment of clear standards of performance**, 1.2 **involves a comparison of performance to those standards**, 1.3 **takes corrective action, if needed, to repair performance deficiencies**; 1.4 **is a dynamic, cybernetic process**, and 1.5 **consists of three basic methods: feedback control, concurrent control, and feedforward control**. However, as much as managers would like, 1.6 **control isn't always worthwhile or possible**.

1.1 Standards

The control process begins when managers set goals such as satisfying 90 percent of customers or increasing sales by 5 percent. Companies then specify the performance standards that must be met to accomplish those goals. **Standards** are a basis of comparison for measuring the extent to which organizational performance is satisfactory or unsatisfactory. For example, many pizzerias use 30–40 minutes as the standard for delivery times. Since anything longer is viewed as unsatisfactory, they'll typically reduce the price if they can't deliver a hot pizza to you within that time period.

So how do managers set standards? How do they decide which levels of performance are satisfactory and which are unsatisfactory? The first criterion for a good standard is that it must enable goal achievement. If you're meeting the standard but still not achieving company goals, then the standard may have to be changed. In the salmon industry, to maximize productivity, it was standard procedure to grow as many fish as possible in fish farms and then deal with diseases (that spread from the fish being in such close proximity) through liberal use of antibiotics in fish food. This was effective until a few years ago, when the new ISA (infectious salmon anemia) virus, which is resistant to antibiotics, developed. Norwegian salmon farms, the largest in the world, sharply reduced the incidence of ISA by developing new production standards that involved the use of antiviral vaccines and no longer allowing overcrowded fish pens.[5]

Companies also determine standards by listening to customers' comments, complaints, and suggestions or by observing competitors. Standards can also be determined by benchmarking other companies. **Benchmarking** is the process of determining how well other companies (though not just competitors) perform business functions or tasks. In other words, benchmarking is the process of determining other companies' standards.

standards
a basis of comparison for measuring the extent to which various kinds of organizational performance are satisfactory or unsatisfactory

benchmarking
the process of identifying outstanding practices, processes, and standards in other companies and adapting them to your company

Next, identify the companies against which to benchmark your standards and then collect data to determine other companies' performance standards. *INTEL*, the leading manufacturer of microprocessors, used benchmarking to assess every aspect of its multi-billion-dollar fabrication plants. CEO Paul Otellini said, ". . . we used external benchmarks—best-of-class benchmarks—for every element of the operation and then weighed that against what we were doing."[6] As a result of benchmarking, Otellini says that Intel has cuts its factory throughput from 90 to 45 days, significantly increasing speed and reducing costs and inventory.

1.2 Comparison to Standards

The next step in the control process is to compare actual performance to performance standards. Although this sounds straightforward, the quality of the comparison depends largely on the measurement and information systems a company uses to keep track of performance. The better the system, the easier it is for companies to track their progress and identify problems that need to be fixed. One way for retailers to verify that performance standards are being met is to use secret shoppers. Retail stores spend $600 million a year to hire these consultants, who visit stores pretending to be customers but are really there to determine whether employees provide helpful customer service.

1.3 Corrective Action

The next step in the control process is to identify performance deviations, analyze those deviations, and then develop and implement programs to correct them. This is similar to the planning process discussed in Chapter 4. Regular, frequent performance feedback allows workers and managers to track their performance and make adjustments in effort, direction, and strategies.

1.4 Dynamic, Cybernetic Process

As shown in Exhibit 14.1, control is a continuous, dynamic, cybernetic process. Control begins by setting standards, measuring performance, and then comparing performance to the standards. If the performance deviates from the standards, then managers and employees analyze the deviations and develop and implement corrective programs that (they hope) achieve the desired performance by meeting the standards. Managers must repeat the entire process again and again in an endless feedback loop (a continuous process). Thus, control is not a one-time achievement or result. It continues over time (i.e., it is dynamic) and requires daily, weekly, and monthly attention from managers to maintain performance levels at the standard (i.e., it is cybernetic).

EXHIBIT 14.1

Cybernetic Control Process

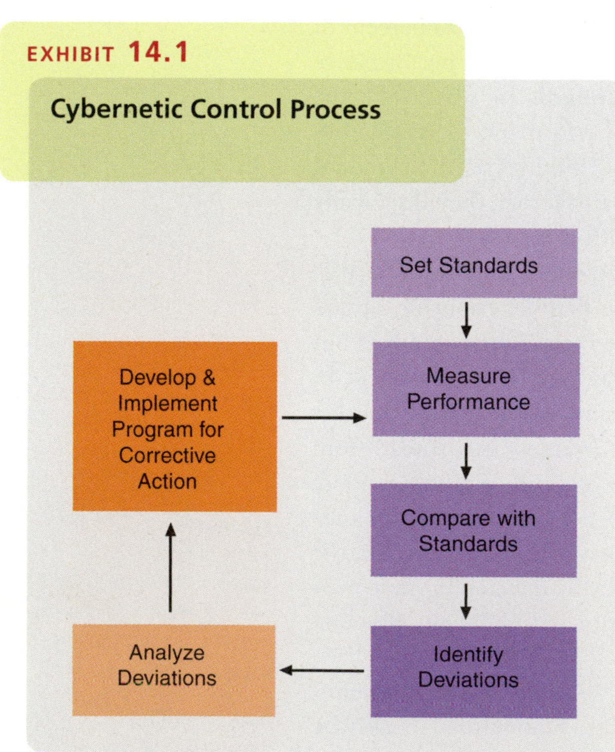

Source: Reprinted from *Business Horizons*, June 1972, H. Koontz & R. W. Bradspies, "Managing Through Feedforward Control: A Future Directed View," 25–36, Copyright (c) 1972, with permission from Elsevier.

Cybernetic derives from the Greek word *kubernetes*, meaning "steersman," that is, one who steers or keeps on course. Wiener, N. *Cybernetics; Or Control and Communication in the Animal and the Machine*. New York: Wiley, 1948.

Keeping control of business expenses is an example of a continuous, dynamic, cybernetic process. A company that doesn't closely monitor expenses usually finds that they quickly get out of control, even for the smallest things. When Eddie Lampert became the chairman of KMart, he saw expenses that could be cut everywhere he looked. He demanded that everyone stop looking at sales and instead focus on profitability. He told all of his store managers that he was willing to spend money but only when they could assure the company of a big return. He didn't approve a proposal to improve lighting in stores that would have cost more than $2 million. Declaring, "It doesn't matter what Target and Wal-Mart do," Lampert wanted to know the positive value of every investment. He quickly eliminated what he referred to as "crazy promotions" that were designed to clear out inventory. KMart stopped pricing DVDs at Wal-Mart levels (i.e., heavily discounted) and began selling them only at full price. Lampert knew the stores would sell less in terms of volume but make more profit on each sale; he said, "For the first year or so, we had declining same-store sales, but more stores made a profit." Sure, it's a cliché, but it's just as true in business as in sports: If you take your eye off the ball, you're going to strike out. Control is an ongoing, dynamic, cybernetic process.

1.5 Feedback, Concurrent, and Feedforward Control

The three basic control methods are feedback control, concurrent control, and feedforward control. **Feedback control** is a mechanism for gathering information about performance deficiencies *after* they occur. This information is then used to correct or prevent performance deficiencies. Study after study has clearly shown that feedback improves both individual and organizational performance. In most instances, any feedback is better than no feedback. But, if feedback has a downside, it's that feedback always comes after the fact.

That's why **concurrent control** addresses the problems inherent in feedback control by gathering information about performance deficiencies *as* they occur. Thus, it is an improvement over feedback because it attempts to eliminate or shorten the delay between performance and feedback about the performance. Apple and Nike teamed up to create a real-time exercise feedback system called Nike + iPod. After a runner installs the system in her shoes, it transmits concurrent information to her iPod. The system measures time, distance, calories burned, and pace. Runners can actually track their efforts every moment of their run and make changes on the fly. Greg Joswiak, Apple's vice president of worldwide iPod marketing, says, "We've enabled people to have a much better running experience than ever before."[7]

Feedforward control is a mechanism for gathering information about performance deficiencies *before* they occur. In contrast to feedback and concurrent control, which provide feedback on the basis of outcomes and results, feedforward control provides information about performance deficiencies by monitoring inputs rather than outputs. Thus, feedforward control seeks to prevent or minimize performance deficiencies before they happen. Exhibit 14.2 lists guidelines that companies can follow to get the most out of feedforward control.

feedback control
a mechanism for gathering information about performance deficiencies after they occur

concurrent control
a mechanism for gathering information about performance deficiencies as they occur, thereby eliminating or shortening the delay between performance and feedback

feedforward control
a mechanism for monitoring performance inputs rather than outputs to prevent or minimize performance deficiencies before they occur

EXHIBIT 14.2

Guidelines for Using Feedforward Control

1. Thorough planning and analysis are required.
2. Careful discrimination must be applied in selecting input variables.
3. The feedforward system must be kept dynamic.
4. A model of the control system should be developed.
5. Data on input variables must be regularly collected.
6. Data on input variables must be regularly assessed.
7. Feedforward control requires action.

Source: Reprinted from *Business Horizons*, June 1972, H. Koontz & R. W. Bradspies, "Managing Through Feedforward Control: A Future Directed View," 25–36, Copyright (c) 1972, with permission from Elsevier.

1.6 Control Isn't Always Worthwhile or Possible

Control is achieved when behavior and work procedures conform to standards and goals are accomplished. By contrast, **control loss** occurs when behavior and work procedures do not conform to standards.[8] After *AMERICAN AIRLINES* missed a deadline to conduct wiring inspections of its planes, the U.S. Federal Aviation Administration grounded each American plane that had not yet been inspected and certified. With nearly 1,500 flights canceled and thousands of customers stranded, American's CEO Gerard Arpey promised that the company would spend "tens of millions of dollars" to cover the overtime pay and costs of the inspections and, if needed, repairs. American also promised to refund and rebook customers' flights.[9] Clearly, however, control loss occurred, because American should never have missed the deadline for completing these routine inspections.

Maintaining control is important because control loss prevents organizations from achieving their goals. When control loss occurs, managers need to find out what, if anything, they could have done to prevent it. Usually, that means identifying deviations from standard performance, analyzing the causes of those deviations, and taking corrective action. Even so, implementing controls isn't always worthwhile or possible. Let's look at regulation costs and cybernetic feasibility to see why this is so.

To determine whether control is worthwhile, managers need to carefully assess **regulation costs**, that is, whether the costs and unintended consequences of control exceed its benefits. If a control process costs more than it benefits, it may not be worthwhile. For example, the European Union uses the metric system—kilograms and centimeters—to ensure standard pricing throughout its 27 member states. But, since the United Kingdom uses the British imperial system (pounds, ounces, inches, miles, etc.), the EU regulation allows businesses to use both metric *and* imperial measures. So when Janet Devers, who runs a vegetable stall at the Ridley Road market in East London, sold vegetables only by the pound and the ounce, she faced 13 criminal charges and fines totaling $130,000 for not also posting prices using the metric system.[10] Since everyone in Britain buys fruits and vegetables by the pound or ounce, the British public was outraged by the charges because the regulatory costs clearly outweighed their benefits.

An often overlooked factor in determining the cost of control is that *unintended consequences* sometimes accompany increased control. Control systems help companies, managers, and workers accomplish their goals. But, while they help solve some problems, they can create others. For example, Motorola's focus on

control loss
the situation in which behavior and work procedures do not conform to standards

regulation costs
the costs associated with implementing or maintaining control

achieving near-perfect production (99.9997 percent error-free) was stifling the company's creativity and innovation, both of which are critical for organizations to grow. In the late 1990s, Motorola lost its lead in mobile phones to Nokia, in part because tight manufacturing control systems were crushing efforts to develop new products.[11]

Management Trend:

Facebook, YouTube, ESPN.com, personal e-mail, even news sites—all of these represent a challenge to companies that are trying to maintain employee productivity. To decrease the amount of time lost, many companies have banned non-work-related Internet usage. A recent study in Australia suggests, however, that such bans actually reduce productivity. The study argues that giving employees time to visit websites of personal interest gives them a mental break and raises productivity by 9%. Further, many technology experts argue that if employees are blocked from visiting certain sites, they will actually spend more time trying to get around the block instead of getting back to work. An Internet ban may even hurt a company's staffing. A recent study in England showed that 39% of 18- to 24-year-olds would quit their jobs if social media access was restricted.

Sources: http://www.readwriteweb.com/archives/shocking_news_scientists_say_workplace_social_netw.php

http://www.v3.co.uk/vnunet/news/2218385/workers-consider-quitting

http://mashable.com/2010/04/13/social-media-ban-backfire/

Another factor to consider is **cybernetic feasibility**, the extent to which it is possible to implement each step of the control process: clear standards of performance, comparison of performance against standards, and corrective action. If one or more steps cannot be implemented, then maintaining effective control may be difficult or impossible. For example, retail stores are struggling to find successful ways to provide discounts via the web or social media. When Indianapolis-based *MARSH GROCERIES* used its Facebook site to give 3,100 customers who had signed up as its Facebook "friends" a $10 coupon and then encouraged them to share that coupon with their friends, the number of people who tried to redeem the downloadable coupons exploded and spiraled out of control, so that Marsh had to halt the offer after 4 days.

cybernetic feasibility the extent to which it is possible to implement each step in the control process

REVIEW 1

The Control Process

The control process begins by setting standards, measuring performance, and then comparing performance against the standards. The better a company's information and measurement systems, the easier it is to make these comparisons. The control process continues by identifying and analyzing performance deviations and then developing and implementing programs for corrective action. Control is a continuous, dynamic, cybernetic process, not a onetime achievement or result. Control requires frequent managerial attention. The three basic control methods are feedback control (after-the-fact performance information), concurrent control (simultaneous performance information), and feedforward control (preventive performance information). Control has regulation costs and unanticipated consequences and therefore isn't always worthwhile or possible.

How and What to Control

Skiers and snowboarders who love the thrill of racing down steep mountain slopes may have to start tying a radar detector onto their ski passes. In response to the more than 70,000 accidents each year on Swiss ski slopes, *SWISS ACCIDENT INSURANCE (SUVA)*, the country's biggest provider of compulsory skiing insurance, will now be using radar guns on the slopes to track and "pull over" skiers and snowboarders who go faster than 19 mph. Studies using crash test dummies on skis show that going faster than 19 mph is not safe, and that going faster than 30 mph can be potentially fatal. Although speeders will only be warned at first, they could eventually be fined and have their ski passes taken away.[12]

If you managed a ski resort, would you use radar guns to "pull over" skiers and snowboarders who were going too fast? Would skiers and snowboarders see this as something your resort was doing for their safety or something the company was doing to lower its costs and legal risks? Is this a reasonable policy that you should pursue, or is this something that you shouldn't even consider? Should you also require all skiers and snowboarders to where helmets on your slopes? If you were running a ski slope, what would you do?

After reading the next two sections, you should be able to:

2 discuss the various methods that managers can use to maintain control.

3 describe the behaviors, processes, and outcomes that today's managers are choosing to control in their organizations.

2 Control Methods

Managers can use five different methods to achieve control in their organizations: 2.1 **bureaucratic**, 2.2 **objective**, 2.3 **normative**, 2.4 **concertive**, and 2.5 **self-control**.

2.1 Bureaucratic Control

When most people think of managerial control, what they have in mind is bureaucratic control. **Bureaucratic control** is top-down control, in which managers try to influence employee behavior by rewarding or punishing employees for compliance or noncompliance with organizational policies, rules, and procedures. Most employees, however, would argue that bureaucratic managers emphasize punishment for noncompliance much more than rewards for compliance.

For instance, one manager gave an employee a written reprimand for "leaving work without permission"—after she passed out in the bathroom and was whisked by ambulance to a nearby hospital. Another manager, a school principal, forced a teacher to work through the day even after the teacher said her arm was throbbing after slipping on ice outside the school. "He decided there was no way I could have broken my arm, probably just bruised it." The teacher said, "During first period, my arm hurt horribly, but I continued teaching. But when I reached for chalk, and my fingers would not move, I did go [to the hospital] where my broken arm was set."[13]

bureaucratic control the use of hierarchical authority to influence employee behavior by rewarding or punishing employees for compliance or noncompliance with organizational policies, rules, and procedures

As you learned in Chapter 1, bureaucratic management and control were created to prevent just this type of managerial behavior. By encouraging managers to apply well-thought-out rules, policies, and procedures in an impartial, consistent manner to everyone in the organization, bureaucratic control is supposed to make companies more efficient, effective, and fair. Ironically, it frequently has just the opposite effect. Managers who use bureaucratic control often emphasize following rules above all else.

Another characteristic of bureaucratically controlled companies is that, due to their rule- and policy-driven decision making, they are highly resistant to change and slow to respond to customers and competitors. Even Max Weber, the German philosopher who is largely credited with popularizing bureaucratic ideals in the late 19th century, referred to bureaucracy as the "iron cage." He said, "Once fully established, bureaucracy is among those social structures which are the hardest to destroy."[14]

2.2 Objective Control

In many companies, bureaucratic control has evolved into **objective control**, which is the use of observable measures of employee behavior or output to assess performance and influence behavior. Whereas bureaucratic control focuses on whether policies and rules are followed, objective control focuses on observing and measuring worker behavior or output. Three employees at Kwik Trip Convenience stores were fired for postings they made about the company on the social networking website Facebook. Because the employees' postings were complaints about rude customers and their jobs in general, the company determined that their behavior was not appropriate, especially given that an employee can be let go for treating customers badly in the store.[15]

There are two kinds of objective control: behavior control and output control. **Behavior control** is regulating behaviors and actions that workers perform on the job. The basic assumption of behavior control is that if you do the right things (i.e., the right behaviors) every day, then those things should lead to goal achievement. Behavior control is still management-based, however, which means that managers are responsible for monitoring and rewarding or punishing workers for exhibiting desired or undesired behaviors.

For example, companies that use global positioning satellite (GPS) technology to track where workers are and what they're doing are using behavior control. After getting complaints that his Clinton Township, New Jersey, police officers weren't always on the job, Sergeant John Kuczynski quietly put GPS tracking devices in his officers' cars. Contrary to the officers' reports indicating that they were patrolling streets or using radar to catch speeding drivers, the GPS tracking software soon showed that five officers were sitting for long periods in parking lots or taking long breaks for meals. All five are now barred from law enforcement jobs.[16]

Instead of measuring what managers and workers do, **output control** measures the results of their efforts. Whereas behavior control regulates, guides, and measures how workers behave on the job, output control gives managers and workers the freedom to behave as they see fit as long as they accomplish prespecified, measurable results. Output control is often coupled with rewards and incentives. Three things must occur for output control and rewards to lead to improved business results. First, output control measures must be reliable, fair, and accurate. Second, employees and managers must believe that they can produce the desired results. If they don't, then the output controls won't affect their behavior. Third, the rewards or incentives tied

objective control the use of observable measures of worker behavior or outputs to assess performance and influence behavior

behavior control the regulation of the behaviors and actions that workers perform on the job

output control the regulation of workers' results or outputs through rewards and incentives

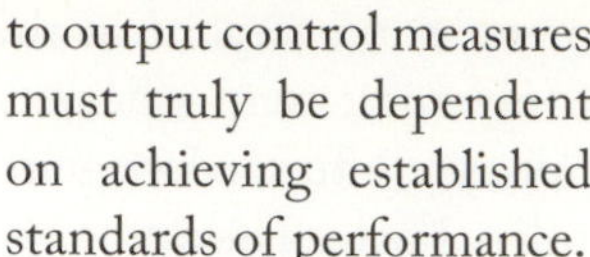

Doing the Right Thing

Don't Cheat on Travel Expense Reports

Workers are often tempted to pad their travel expense reports. As one puts it, "After a while, you feel that they owe it to ya, so the hell with 'em. I'm going to expense it." Frank Navran of the Ethics Resource Center says that people justify this by telling themselves, "I'm not really stealing from the company—I'm just getting back what I feel I'm entitled to." However, Joel Richards, executive vice president and chief administrative officer of El Paso Corporation, says, "You learn a lot about people from their expense reports. If you can't trust an employee to be truthful on an expense report, if you can't trust them with small dollars, how can you trust them with making decisions involving millions of dollars?" So, do the right thing. Don't cheat on your travel expense reports."[17]

to output control measures must truly be dependent on achieving established standards of performance.

For example, Smithfield Foods CEO Joseph Luter doesn't earn a bonus unless pretax profits exceed $100 million. Ray Goldberg, chairman of the company's compensation committee, explains, "We were trying to make sure [Luter's] rewards are based on the ups and downs of the company."[18] So, with pretax profits of $227.1 million, Luter's bonus, based on 2 percent of earnings between $100 million and $300 million, and 3 percent of profits over $300 million, would total just over $2.5 million. For output control to work with rewards, the rewards must truly be at risk if performance doesn't measure up.

2.3 Normative Control

Rather than monitoring rules, behavior, or output, another way to control what goes on in organizations is to use normative control to shape the beliefs and values of the people who work there. With **normative controls**, a company's widely shared values and beliefs guide workers' behavior and decisions. For example, at Nordstrom, a Seattle-based department store chain, one value permeates the entire workforce from top to bottom: extraordinary customer service. On the first day of work at Nordstrom, trainees begin their transformation to the "Nordstrom way" by reading the employee handbook. Sounds boring, doesn't it? But Nordstrom's handbook is printed on one side of a 3-by-5-inch note card. In its entirety, it reads:

> Welcome to Nordstrom's. We're glad to have you with our company. Our Number One goal is to provide outstanding customer service. Set both your personal and professional goals high. We have great confidence in your ability to achieve them. Nordstrom Rules: Rule #1: Use your good judgment in all situations. There will be no additional rules. Please feel free to ask your department manager, store manager, or division general manager any question at any time.[19]

normative control
the regulation of workers' behavior and decisions through widely shared organizational values and beliefs

According to its website (***http://about.nordstrom.com***), the company's philosophy has remained unchanged for more than 100 years: Offer the best possible service, selection, quality, and value. That's it. No lengthy rules. No specifics about what behavior is or is not appropriate. Use your judgment.[20]

Normative controls are created in two ways. First, companies that use normative controls are very careful about who they hire. While many companies screen potential applicants on the basis of their abilities, normatively controlled companies are just as likely to screen potential applicants based on their attitudes and values. For example, before building stores in a new city, Nordstrom sends its human resource team into town to interview prospective applicants. In a few cities, the company canceled its expansion plans when it could not find enough qualified applicants who embodied the service attitudes and values for which Nordstrom is known. Nordstrom would rather give up potential sales in lucrative markets than do business using people who cannot provide Nordstrom's level of service.[21]

Second, with normative controls, managers and employees learn what they should and should not do by observing experienced employees and by listening to the stories they tell about the company. At Nordstrom, many of these stories, which employees call "heroics," have been inspired by the company motto, "Respond to Unreasonable Customer Requests!"[22] "Nordies," as Nordstrom employees call themselves, like to tell the story about a customer who just had to have a pair of burgundy Donna Karan slacks that had gone on sale but could not find her size. The sales associate who was helping her contacted five nearby Nordstrom stores, but none had the customer's size. So rather than leave the customer dissatisfied with her shopping experience, the sales associate went to her manager for petty cash and then went across the street and paid full price for the slacks at a competitor's store. She then resold them to the customer at Nordstrom's lower sale price.[23] Obviously, Nordstrom would quickly go out of business if this were the norm. Nevertheless, this story makes clear the attitude that drives employee performance at Nordstrom in ways that rules, behavioral guidelines, or output controls could not.

2.4 Concertive Control

Whereas normative controls are based on beliefs that are strongly held and widely shared throughout a company, **concertive controls** are based on beliefs that are shaped and negotiated by work groups.[24] Whereas normative controls are driven by strong organizational cultures, concertive controls usually arise when companies give work groups complete autonomy and responsibility for task completion (see Chapter 9, "Managing Teams," for a complete discussion of the role of autonomy in teams and groups). The most autonomous groups operate without managers and are completely responsible for controlling work group processes, outputs, and behavior. Such groups do their own hiring, firing, worker discipline, work schedules, materials ordering, budget making and meeting, and decision making.

Concertive control is not established overnight. Highly autonomous work groups evolve through two phases as they develop concertive control. In phase one, group members learn to work with each other, supervise each other's work, and develop the values and beliefs that will guide and control their behavior. And because they develop these values and beliefs themselves, work group members feel strongly about following them.

Nucor has a unique culture that gives real power to employees on the line and fosters teamwork throughout the organization. This type of teamwork can be a difficult thing for a newly acquired group of employees to get used to. For example, at Nucor's first big acquisition in Auburn, New York, if the steelworkers doing the cutting got backed up, then the workers doing the rolling would just take a break.

concertive control the regulation of workers' behavior and decisions through work group values and beliefs

Now, frontline supervisor David Hutchins says, "Wherever the bottleneck is, we go there, and everyone works on it."[25]

The second phase in the development of concertive control is the emergence and formalization of objective rules to guide and control behavior. The beliefs and values developed in phase one usually develop into more objective rules as new members join teams. The clearer those rules, the easier it becomes for new members to figure out how and how not to behave.

Ironically, concertive control may lead to even more stress for workers to conform to expectations than bureaucratic control. Under bureaucratic control, most workers only have to worry about pleasing the boss. But with concertive control, their behavior has to satisfy the rest of their team members. For example, one team member says, "I don't have to sit there and look for the boss to be around; and if the boss is not around, I can sit there and talk to my neighbor or do what I want. Now the whole team is around me and the whole team is observing what I'm doing."[26] Plus, with concertive control, team members have a second, much more stressful role to perform: that of making sure that their team members adhere to team values and rules.

2.5 Self-Control

Self-control, also known as **self-management**, is a control system in which managers and workers control their own behavior.[27] Self-control does not result in anarchy, in which everyone gets to do whatever he or she wants. In self-control or self-management, leaders and managers provide workers with clear boundaries within which they may guide and control their own goals and behaviors.[28] Leaders and managers also contribute to self-control by teaching others the skills they need to maximize and monitor their own work effectiveness. In turn, individuals who manage and lead themselves establish self-control by setting their own goals, monitoring their own progress, rewarding or punishing themselves for achieving or for not achieving their self-set goals, and constructing positive thought patterns that remind them of the importance of their goals and their ability to accomplish them.[29]

For example, let's assume you need to do a better job of praising and recognizing the good work that your staff does for you. You can use goal setting, self-observation, and self-reward to manage this behavior on your own. For self-observation, write "praise/recognition" on a 3-by-5-inch card. Put the card in your pocket. Put a check on the card each time you praise or recognize someone. (Wait until the person has left before you do this.) Keep track for a week. This serves as your baseline or starting point. Simply keeping track will probably increase how often you do this. After a week, assess your baseline or starting point and then set a specific goal. For instance, if your baseline was praising employees' work twice a day, you might set a specific goal of dong so five times a day. Continue monitoring your performance with your cards. Once you've achieved your goal every day for a week, give yourself a reward (perhaps a CD, a movie, lunch with a friend at a new restaurant) for achieving your goal.[30]

self-control (self-management)
a control system in which managers and workers control their own behavior by setting their own goals, monitoring their own progress, and rewarding themselves for goal achievement

As you can see, the components of self-management, self-set goals, self-observation, and self-reward have their roots in the motivation theories you read about in Chapter 11. The key difference, though, is that the goals, feedback, and rewards originate from employees themselves and not from their managers or organizations.

REVIEW 2

Control Methods

The five methods of control are bureaucratic, objective, normative, concertive, and self-control (self-management). Bureaucratic and objective controls are top-down, management-based, and measurement-based. Normative and concertive controls represent shared forms of control because they evolve from company-wide or team-based beliefs and values. Self-control, or self-management, is a control system in which managers turn over much, but not all, control to the individuals themselves.

Bureaucratic control is based on organizational policies, rules, and procedures. Objective controls are based on reliable measures of behavior or outputs. Normative control is based on strong corporate beliefs and careful hiring practices. Concertive control is based on the development of values, beliefs, and rules in autonomous work groups. Self-control is based on individuals' setting their own goals, monitoring themselves, and rewarding or punishing themselves with respect to goal achievement.

Each of these control methods may be more or less appropriate depending on the circumstances. Examine Exhibit 14.3 to find out when each of these five control methods should be used.

3 What to Control?

In the first section of this chapter, we discussed the basics of the control process and the fact that control isn't always worthwhile or possible. In the second section, we looked at the various ways in which control can be obtained. In this third and final section, we address an equally important issue: What should managers control? Costs? Quality? Customer satisfaction? The way managers answer this question has critical implications for most businesses.

After reading this section, you should be able to explain 3.1 **the balanced scorecard approach to control and how companies can achieve balanced control of company performance by choosing to control**, 3.2 **budgets, cash flows, and economic value added**, 3.3 **customer defections**, 3.4 **quality**, and 3.5 **waste and pollution**.

3.1 The Balanced Scorecard

Most companies measure performance using standard financial and accounting measures such as return on capital, return on assets, return on investments, cash flow, net income, and net margins. The **balanced scorecard** encourages managers to look beyond such traditional financial measures to four different perspectives on company performance. How do customers see us (the customer perspective)? At what must we excel (the internal perspective)? Can we continue to improve and create value (the innovation and learning perspective)? How do we look to shareholders (the financial perspective)?[31]

The balanced scorecard has several advantages over traditional control processes that rely solely on financial measures. First, it forces managers at each level of the company to set specific goals and measure performance in each of the four areas. For example, Exhibit 14.4 shows that Southwest Airlines uses nine different measures in its balanced scorecard in order to determine whether it is meeting the standards

balanced scorecard measurement of organizational performance in four equally important areas: finances, customers, internal operations, and innovation and learning

EXHIBIT 14.3

When to Use Different Methods of Control

BUREAUCRATIC CONTROL	• When it is necessary to standardize operating procedures • When it is necessary to establish limits
BEHAVIOR CONTROL	• When it is easier to measure what workers do on the job than what they accomplish on the job • When "cause-effect" relationships are clear, that is, when companies know which behaviors will lead to success and which won't • When good measures of worker behavior can be created
OUTPUT CONTROL	• When it is easier to measure what workers accomplish on the job than what they do on the job • When good measures of worker output can be created • When it is possible to set clear goals and standards for worker output • When "cause-effect" relationships are unclear
NORMATIVE CONTROL	• When organizational culture, values, and beliefs are strong • When it is difficult to create good measures of worker behavior • When it is difficult to create good measures of worker output
CONCERTIVE CONTROL	• When responsibility for task accomplishment is given to autonomous work groups • When management wants workers to take "ownership" of their behavior and outputs • When management desires a strong form of worker-based control
SELF-CONTROL	• When workers are intrinsically motivated to do their jobs well • When it is difficult to create good measures of worker behavior • When it is difficult to create good measures of worker output • When workers have or are taught self-control and self-leadership skills

Sources: L. J. Kirsch, "The Management of Complex Tasks in Organizations: Controlling the Systems Development Process," *Organization Science* 7 (1996): 1–21; S. A. Snell, "Control Theory in Strategic Human Resource Management: The Mediating Effect of Administrative Information," *Academy of Management Journal* 35 (1992): 292–327.

it has set for itself in the control process. Of those, only three—market value, seat revenue, and plane lease costs (at various compounded annual growth rates, or CAGR)—are standard financial measures of performance. In addition, Southwest measures its Federal Aviation Administration (FAA) on-time arrival rating and the cost of its airfares compared with those of competitors (customer perspective); how much time each plane spends on the ground after landing and the percentage of planes that depart on time (internal business perspective); and the percentage of its ground crew workers, such as mechanics and luggage handlers, who own company stock and have received job training (learning perspective).

EXHIBIT 14.4

Southwest Airlines' Balanced Scorecard

	OBJECTIVES	MEASURES	TARGETS	INITIATIVES
FINANCIAL	Profitability	Market Value	30% CAGR	
	Increased Revenue	Seat Revenue	20% CAGR	
	Lower Costs	Plane Lease Cost	5% CAGR	
CUSTOMER	On-Time Flights	FAA On-Time Arrival Rating	#1	Quality Management, Customer Loyalty Program
	Lowest Prices	Customer Ranking (Market Survey)	#1	
INTERNAL	Fast Ground Turnaround	Time on Ground	30 Minutes	Cycle Time Optimization Program
		On-Time Departure	90%	
LEARNING	Ground Crew Alignment with Company Goals	% Ground Crew Shareholders	Year 1: 70% Year 3: 90% Year 5: 100%	Employee Stock Option Plan Ground Crew Training
		% Ground Crew Trained		

Sources: G. Anthes, "ROI Guide: Balanced Scorecard," *Computer World* available at http://www.computerworld.com/managementtopics/roi/story/0,10801,78512,00.html, 5 May 2003.

The second major advantage of the balanced scorecard approach to control is that it minimizes the chances of **suboptimization**, which occurs when performance improves in one area at the expense of decreased performance in others. Jon Meliones, chief medical director at Duke Children's Hospital, says, "We explained the [balanced scorecard] theory to clinicians and administrators like this—if you sacrifice too much in one quadrant to satisfy another, your organization as a whole is thrown out of balance. We could, for example, cut costs to improve the financial quadrant by firing half the staff, but that would hurt quality of service, and the customer quadrant would fall out of balance. Or we could increase productivity in the internal business quadrant by assigning more patients to a nurse, but doing so would raise the likelihood of errors—an unacceptable trade-off."[32] Likewise, Toyota's president, Akio Toyoda, admits that the company's all-out-push to become the world's largest car maker might have come at the expense of product quality, bloated inventories, and huge financial losses. As a result, he has vowed to rebalance Toyota's priorities.[33]

suboptimization performance improvement in one part of an organization but only at the expense of decreased performance in another part

Let's examine some of the ways in which companies are controlling the four basic parts of the balanced scorecard: the financial perspective (budgets, cash flows, and economic value added), the customer perspective (customer defections), the internal perspective (total quality management), and the innovation and learning perspective (waste and pollution).

3.2 The Financial Perspective: Controlling Budgets, Cash Flows, and Economic Value Added

The traditional approach to controlling financial performance focuses on accounting tools such as cash flow analysis, balance sheets, income statements, financial ratios, and budgets.

Though no one would dispute their importance for determining the financial health of a business, accounting research also indicates that the complexity and sheer amount of information contained in these accounting tools can shut down the brain and glaze over the eyes of even the most experienced manager.[34] Sometimes there's simply too much information to make sense of. The balanced scorecard simplifies things by focusing on one simple question when it comes to finances: How do we look to shareholders? One way to answer that question is through something called economic value added.

Conceptually, **economic value added (EVA)** is not the same thing as profits. It is the amount by which profits exceed the cost of capital in a given year. It is based on the simple idea that capital is necessary to run a business and that capital comes at a cost. Although most people think of capital as cash, once it is invested (i.e., spent), capital is more likely to be found in a business in the form of computers, manufacturing plants, employees, raw materials, and so forth. And just like the interest that a homeowner pays on a mortgage or that a college student pays on a student loan, there is a cost to that capital.

The most common costs of capital are the interest paid on long-term bank loans used to buy resources, the interest paid to bondholders (who lend organizations their money), and the dividends (cash payments) and growth in stock value that accrue to shareholders. EVA is positive when company profits (revenues minus expenses minus taxes) exceed the cost of capital in a given year. In other words, if a business is to grow, its revenues must be large enough to cover both short-term costs (annual expenses and taxes) and long-term costs (the cost of borrowing capital from bondholders and shareholders). If you're a bit confused, the late Roberto Goizueta, the former CEO of Coca-Cola, explained it this way: "You borrow money at a certain rate and invest it at a higher rate and pocket the difference. It is simple. It is the essence of banking."[35]

Why is EVA so important? First and most importantly, because it includes the cost of capital, it shows whether a business, division, department, profit center, or product is really paying for itself. The key is to make sure that managers and employees can see how their choices and behavior affect the company's EVA. For example, because of EVA training and information systems, factory workers at Herman Miller, a leading office furniture manufacturer, understand that using more efficient materials, such as less expensive wood-dust board instead of real wood sheeting, contributes an extra dollar of EVA from each desk the company makes.[36]

economic value added (EVA)
the amount by which company profits (revenues, minus expenses, minus taxes) exceed the cost of capital in a given year

Second, because EVA can easily be determined for subsets of a company such as divisions, regional offices, manufacturing plants, and sometimes even departments, it makes managers and workers at all levels pay much closer attention to their segment of the business. When company offices were being refurbished at Genesco, a shoe company, a worker who had EVA training handed CEO Ben Harris $4,000 in cash. The worker explained that he now understood the effect his job had on the company's ability to survive and prosper. Since the company was struggling, he sold the old doors that had been removed during remodeling so that the company could have the cash.[37] In other words, EVA motivates managers and workers to think like small-business owners who must scramble to contain costs and generate enough business to meet their bills each month. And, unlike many kinds of financial controls, EVA doesn't specify what should or should not be done to improve performance. Thus, it encourages managers and workers to be creative in looking for ways to improve EVA performance.

Exhibit 14.5 shows the top ten U.S. companies in terms of EVA and market value added (MVA), as measured by the EVA Dimensions EVA/MVA Annual Rankings. Remember that EVA is the amount by which profits exceed the cost of capital in a given year. So the more that EVA exceeds the total dollar cost of capital, the better a company has used investors' money that year. MVA is simply the cumulative EVA created by a company over time. Thus, MVA indicates how much value or wealth a company has created or destroyed in total during its existence. As indicated by the MVA figures in Exhibit 14.5, over time the top ten companies have created considerable wealth, ranging from almost $101 billion at Cisco to $207 billion at Microsoft; thus, they have returned substantially more than they took in. All of the top ten in MVA had positive EVAs in the most recent year. However, this doesn't always happen. Good businesses sometimes have years with negative EVAs.

EXHIBIT 14.5

Leading Companies by Market Value Added and Economic Value Added

MVA RANKING IN 2004	MVA RANKING IN 2009	COMPANY	MARKET VALUE ADDED ($ MILLIONS)	ECONOMIC VALUE ADDED/ [LOST] ($ MILLIONS)
1	1	General Electric	$299,810	$5,288
2	9	ExxonMobil	197,782	14,456
3	3	Microsoft	178,032	6,426
4	2	Wal-Mart	161,693	4,972
5	10	Johnson & Johnson	138,199	5,655
6	15	United Health Group	112,755	1,897
7	7	Procter & Gamble	105,858	3,951
8	4	CitiGroup	99,485	4,536
9	5	Intel	97,468	1,720
10	13	Dell	88,086	1,891

Source: R. Grizzetti, "U.S. Performance 1000," Stern Stewart & Co, available by request, http://www.sternstewart.com, 20 June 2005.

3.3 The Customer Perspective: Controlling Customer Defections

The second aspect of organizational performance that the balanced scorecard helps managers monitor is customers. It does so by forcing managers to address the question, "How do customers see us?" Unfortunately, most companies try to answer this question through customer satisfaction surveys, but these are often misleadingly positive. Most customers are reluctant to talk about their problems because they don't know who to complain to or think that complaining will not do any good. Indeed, a study by the federal Office of Consumer Affairs found that 96 percent of unhappy customers never complain to anyone in the company.[38]

One reason that customer satisfaction surveys can be misleading is that sometimes even very satisfied customers will leave to do business with competitors. Another challenge is getting effective feedback when there is a problem. Jon Piot, cofounder of Impact Innovations Group, an IT solutions provider, sent a team of 20 employees to work with a client. All of the feedback from the client's CIO (chief information officer) was positive. So Piot was shocked when the client did not renew Impact's contract. As it turned out, the rest of the client's organization was very dissatisfied with the performance of Impact's employees.[39]

Rather than poring over customer satisfaction surveys from current customers, studies indicate that companies may do a better job of answering the question "How do customers see us?" by closely monitoring **customer defections**, that is, by identifying which customers are leaving the company and measuring the rate at which they are leaving. Unlike the results of customer satisfaction surveys, customer defections and retention do have a great effect on profits.

For example, very few managers realize that obtaining a new customer costs ten times as much as keeping a current one. In fact, the cost of replacing old customers with new ones is so great that most companies could double their profits by increasing the rate of customer retention by just 5 to 10 percent per year.[40] Retaining customers obviously means having more customers, but how much more?

Consider two companies starting with a customer base of 100,000 customers and an acquisition rate of 20 percent (i.e., each company's customer base grows by 20 percent every year). Assuming company B has a retention rate just 5 percent higher than company A (90 percent retention rate for company B versus an 85 percent retention rate for company A), company B will double its customer base around the 9th year, while it will take company A slightly more than 15 years to double its customer base. On average, this means company B also profits by a higher percentage.[41] And if a company can keep a customer for life, the benefits are even larger. According to Stew Leonard, owner of the Connecticut-based Stew Leonard's grocery store chain: "The lifetime value of a customer in a supermarket is about $246,000. Every time a customer comes through our front door I see, stamped on their forehead in big red numbers, '$246,000.' I'm never going to make that person unhappy with me. Or lose her to the competition."[42]

customer defections
a performance assessment in which companies identify which customers are leaving and measure the rate at which they are leaving

Beyond the clear benefits to the bottom line, the second reason to study customer defections is that customers who have left are much more likely than current customers to tell you what you are doing wrong. Perhaps the best way to tap into this good source of feedback is to have top-level managers from various departments talk directly to customers who have left. It's also worthwhile to have top managers talk to dissatisfied customers who are still with the company. At Vanguard, a leading investment fund company, CEO Jack Brennan visits the customer call center and, working alongside call representatives, answers customer questions and addresses customer complaints.[43] Some might argue that it's a waste of valuable executive time to have upper-level managers make or listen to these calls, but there's no faster way for the people in charge to learn what needs to be done than to hear it directly from customers who are unhappy with the company's performance.

Finally, companies that understand why customers leave can not only take steps to fix ongoing problems but can also identify which customers are likely to leave and can make changes to prevent them from leaving.

3.4 The Internal Perspective: Controlling Quality

The third part of the balanced scorecard, the internal perspective, consists of the processes, decisions, and actions that managers and workers make within the organization. In contrast to the financial perspective of EVA and the outward-looking customer perspective, the internal perspective focuses on internal processes and systems that add value to the organization. For McDonald's, it could be processes and systems that enable the company to provide consistent, quick, low-cost food. For Toyota, it could be reliability—when you turn on your car it starts, no matter whether the car has 20,000 or 200,000 miles on it. Yet no matter what area a company chooses, the key is to excel in that area. Consequently, the internal perspective of the balanced scorecard usually leads managers to a focus on quality.

Quality is typically defined and measured in three ways: excellence, value, and conformance to expectations.[44] When the company defines its quality goal as *excellence*, managers must try to produce a product or service of unsurpassed performance and features. **Value** is the customer perception that the product quality is excellent for the price offered. At a higher price, for example, customers may perceive the product to be less of a value. When a company emphasizes value as its quality goal, managers must simultaneously control excellence, price, durability, or other features of a product or service that customers strongly associate with value. Aldi, a grocery store company with 7,500 stores worldwide, stocks only 3 percent of the products that a typical grocery store carries, and most of its products are store brands. Yet Aldi's store brands have consistently beaten the name-brand rivals in taste and quality, and Aldi was voted the most trusted name in the grocery business in Germany.[45]

When a company defines its quality goal as conformance to specifications, employees must base decisions and actions on whether services and products measure up to the standard. In contrast to excellence and value-based definitions of quality that can be somewhat ambiguous, measuring whether products and services are "in spec" is relatively easy. Furthermore, while conformance to specifications (e.g., precise tolerances for a part's weight or thickness) is usually associated with manufacturing, it can be used equally well to control quality in nonmanufacturing jobs. Exhibit 14.6 shows a checklist that a cook or restaurant owner would use to ensure quality when buying fresh fish.

The way in which a company defines quality affects the methods and measures that workers use to control quality. Accordingly, Exhibit 14.7 shows the advantages and disadvantages associated with the excellence, value, and conformance to specification definitions of quality.

value
customer perception that the product quality is excellent for the price offered

EXHIBIT 14.6

Conformance to Specifications Checklist for Buying Fresh Fish

QUALITY CHECKLIST FOR BUYING FRESH FISH

FRESH WHOLE FISH	ACCEPTABLE	NOT ACCEPTABLE
Gills	• bright red; free of slime; clear mucus	• brown to grayish; thick, yellow mucus
Eyes	• clear, bright, bulging, black pupils	• dull, sunken, cloudy, gray pupils
Smell	• inoffensive, slight ocean smell	• ammonia or putrid smell
Skin	• opalescent sheen; scales adhere tightly to skin	• dull or faded color; scales missing or easily removed
Flesh	• firm and elastic to touch, tight to the bone	• soft and flabby, separating from the bone
Belly cavity	• no viscera or blood visible; lining intact; no bone protruding	• incomplete evisceration; cuts or protruding bones; off-odor

Sources: "A Closer Look: Buy It Fresh, Keep It Fresh," *Consumer Reports Online*, available at *http://www.seagrant.sunysb.edu/SeafoodTechnology/SeafoodMedia/CR02-2001/CR-SeafoodII020101.htm*, 20 June 2005; National Fisheries Institute, "How to Purchase: Buying Fish," *http://www.aboutseafood.com*, 20 June 2005.

3.5 The Innovation and Learning Perspective: Controlling Waste and Pollution

The last part of the balanced scorecard, the innovation and learning perspective, addresses the question "Can we continue to improve and create value?" Thus, the innovation and learning perspective involves continuous improvement in ongoing products and services (discussed in Chapter 16), as well as relearning and redesigning the processes by which products and services are created (discussed in Chapter 6). Since these are discussed in more detail elsewhere in the text, this section reviews an increasingly important topic, waste and pollution minimization. Exhibit 14.8 shows the four levels of waste minimization, ranging from waste disposal, which produces the smallest minimization of waste, to waste prevention and reduction, which produces the greatest minimization.[46]

The goals of the top level, *waste prevention and reduction*, are to prevent waste and pollution before they occur or to reduce them when they do occur. There are three strategies for waste prevention and reduction:

1. *Good housekeeping*—performing regularly scheduled preventive maintenance for offices, plants, and equipment. Examples of good housekeeping include fixing leaky valves quickly to prevent wasted water and making sure machines are running properly so that they don't use more fuel than necessary.
2. *Material/product substitution*—replacing toxic or hazardous materials with less harmful materials.
3. *Process modification*—changing steps or procedures to eliminate or reduce waste.

EXHIBIT 14.7

Advantages and Disadvantages of Different Measures of Quality

QUALITY MEASURE	ADVANTAGES	DISADVANTAGES
Excellence	Promotes clear organizational vision.	Provides little practical guidance for managers.
	Being/providing the "best" motivates and inspires managers and employees.	Excellence is ambiguous. What is it? Who defines it?
Value	Appeals to customers, who "know excellence when they see it."	Difficult to measure and control.
	Customers recognize differences in value.	Can be difficult to determine what factors influence whether a product/service is seen as having value.
	Easier to measure and compare whether products/services differ in value.	Controlling the balance between excellence and cost (i.e., affordable excellence) can be difficult.
Conformance to Specifications	If specifications can be written, conformance to specifications is usually measurable.	Many products/services cannot be easily evaluated in terms of conformance to specifications.
	Should lead to increased efficiency.	Promotes standardization, so may hurt performance when adapting to changes is more important.
	Promotes consistency in quality.	May be less appropriate for services, which are dependent on a high degree of human contact.

Source: Republished with permission of Academy of Management, PO Box 3020, Briar Cliff Manor, NY, 10510-8020. C. A. Reeves & D. A. Bednar, " Defining Quality: Alternatives and Implications," *Academy of Management Review* 19 (1994): 419–445. Reproduced by permission of the publisher via Copyright Clearance Center, Inc.

At the second level of waste minimization, *recycle and reuse*, wastes are reduced by reusing materials as long as possible or by collecting materials for on- or off-site recycling.

A growing trend in recycling is *design for disassembly*, where products are designed from the start for easy disassembly, recycling, and reuse once they are no longer usable. For example, the European Union (EU) is moving toward prohibiting companies from selling products unless most of the product and its packaging can be recycled.[47] Since companies, not consumers, will be held responsible for recycling the products they manufacture, they must design their products from the start with recycling in mind.[48] At reclamation centers throughout Europe, companies will have to be able to recover and recycle 80 percent of the parts that go into their original products.[49] Under the EU's end-of-life vehicle program, all cars built in Europe since June 2002 are subject to the 80 percent requirement, which rose to 85 percent in 2006 and will be 95 percent by 2015 for autos. Moreover, the EU requires

EXHIBIT 14.8

Four Levels of Waste Minimization

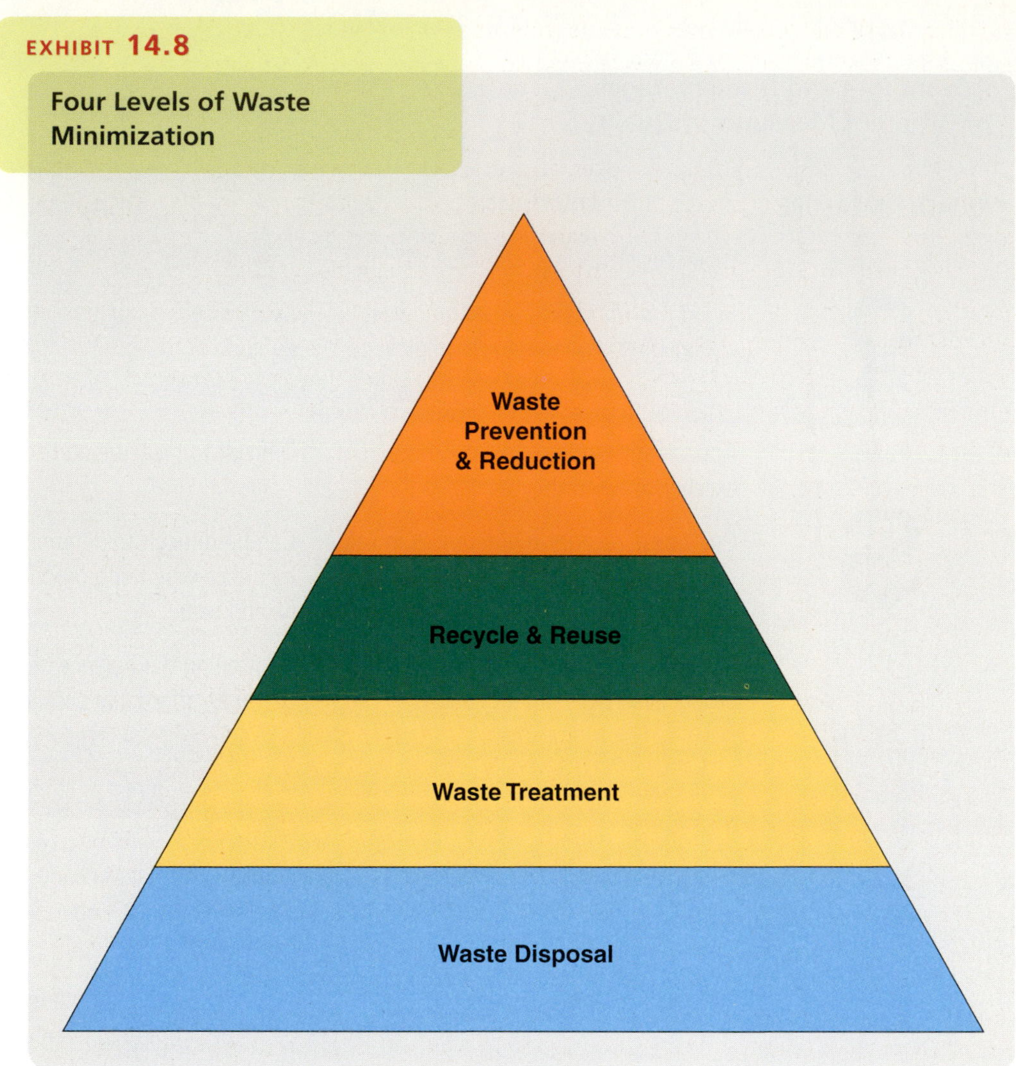

Source: Reprinted from *Business Horizons*, September-October 1995, D.R. May & B.L. Flannery, "Cutting Waste with Employee Involvement Teams," 28–38, Copyright © 1995, with permission from Elsevier.

auto manufacturers to pay to recycle all the cars they made between 1989 and 2002.[50] Roughly 160 million cars in Europe are covered by these strict end-of-life regulations.

At the third level of waste minimization, *waste treatment*, companies use biological, chemical, or other processes to turn potentially harmful waste into harmless compounds or useful by-products. In Africa, animal slaughterhouses often dump untreated animal waste into rivers and lakes. This spreads disease and generates methane and carbon dioxide—greenhouse gases that contribute to global warming. Unlike traditional treatment processes, *COWS TO KILOWATTS PARTNERSHIP LIMITED* uses an advanced anaerobic reactor to turn animal blood and waste into bio-gas, which is then processed and compressed into cooking gas or fuel to run household generators. Even the leftover sludge can be reused as environmentally friendly fertilizer.[51]

The fourth and lowest level of waste minimization is *waste disposal*. Wastes that cannot be prevented, reduced, recycled, reused, or treated should be safely disposed of in processing plants or in environmentally secure landfills that prevent leakage and contamination of soil and underground water supplies. Contrary to common belief, all businesses, not just manufacturing firms, have waste disposal problems. For example, with the average computer lasting just 3 years, approximately 60 million computers come out of service each year, creating disposal problems for offices all over the world. But organizations can't just throw old computers away, since they have toxic metals in the circuit boards, paint-coated plastic, and metal coatings that can contaminate groundwater.[52] Many companies give old computers and computer equipment to local computer recycling centers that distribute usable computers to nonprofit organizations or safely dispose of lead and other toxic materials.

REVIEW 3

What to Control?

Deciding what to control is just as important as deciding whether or how to control. In most companies, performance is measured using financial measures alone. However, the balanced scorecard encourages managers to measure and control company performance from four perspectives: financial, customers, internal operations, and innovation and learning. Traditionally, financial control has been achieved through cash flow analysis, balance sheets, income statements, financial ratios, and budgets. Another way to measure and control financial performance is through economic value added (EVA). Unlike traditional financial measures, EVA helps managers assess whether they are performing well enough to pay the cost of the capital needed to run the business. Instead of using customer satisfaction surveys to measure performance, companies should pay attention to customer defectors, who are more likely to speak up about what the company is doing wrong. Performance of internal operations is often measured in terms of quality, which is defined in three ways: excellence, value, and conformance to expectations. Minimization of waste has become an important part of innovation and learning in companies. The four levels of waste minimization are waste prevention and reduction, recycling and reuse, waste treatment, and waste disposal.

Management Team Decision

Making Airports More Secure

Everything you do as an official at the Department of Homeland Security is about control. Your task is to maintain strict security standards at all U.S. airports, while also trying to keep things running smoothly and efficiently. As the training program you created repeats emphatically, and as recent events have demonstrated, just one slip, one small mistake, can quickly escalate into a disaster. It is your responsibility to make sure that tragedy does not occur again.

The security measures that DHS has put in place have created a complex system of checks designed around past threats. Passengers are now required to show a valid photo ID and a boarding pass to proceed to the terminal. They cannot take knives or other sharp objects on board the plane, as a reaction to the events of 9/11. They need to take off their shoes at the x-ray machines, as a reaction against the shoe bomb plot of 2001. There are strict limits to how much liquid they can take on board, as a reaction against the liquid bomb plot of 2006. And at many major airports, they are subject to full body scans, as a reaction to the underwear bomb plot of Christmas 2009. In addition, the DHS maintains several lists of people who are either subjected to additional security or prevented from flying at all.

There are, however, many critics to these measures. They argue that scanning shoes or limiting liquids is only a reactionary step against tactics that future terrorists wouldn't think of using. They argue, further, that DHS's control methods are not refined enough. Mikey Hicks, an 8-year-old boy from New Jersey, is included on a "selectee" list maintained by the government that subjects him to a high level of security every time he flies. Even when he was 2 years old, he was subject to pat downs, a thorough frisking, and even an interview with DHS screeners. There are many other stories about people who, because they have the same name as a suspected terrorist, are subjected to extraordinary delays. Even the late Senator Ted Kennedy found himself on a suspected-persons list! As congressmen William J. Pascrell comments "We can't just throw a bunch of names on these lists and call it security. If we can't get an 8-year-old off the list, the whole list becomes suspect."

Other critics argue that the primary effect of federal control methods is to heighten the sense of paranoia in the skies. In January of 2009, a US Airways flight heading to Louisville, Kentucky, was diverted to Philadelphia because passengers saw a Jewish passenger wearing phylacteries, leather straps that Jews wrap around their heads and arms as part of a prayer ritual. After the underwear bomb plot of 2009, some airlines prohibited passengers from using blankets or toilet facilities for the last hour of the flight.

You have been assigned to a DHS team charged with refining the agency's control methods. How can you maintain security in the nation's airports while also providing passengers with an efficient and smooth experience? Is there a way you can prevent 8-year-old boys from ending up on a suspected terrorist list? Form a group with three or four other students and discuss the questions below.

Questions

1. In your opinion, is there a way to you can maintain airport security without sacrificing efficiency? What would such a system look like?
2. How could you incorporate feedforward control (gathering information about performance deficiencies before they occur) into airport security measure?

Sources: Lizette Alvarez. "Meet Mikey, 8: U.S. Has Him on Watch List." *New York Times*. January 14, 2010. Accessed at http://www.nytimes.com/2010/01/14/nyregion/14watchlist.html

"Religious Item Led to False Bomb Scare on US Plane." January 21, 2010. Accessed at http://www.reuters.com/article/idUSN2122260520100121

Practice being a MANAGER

In Control or Control Freak?

Control is one of the most controversial aspects of management. Exercising too much control can foster employee resentment and bureaucratic delays. Exercising too little control can raise employee stress and breed organizational chaos. And not only must managers work to achieve a healthy *level* of control but they must also strive to set controls around the *right targets*. The control process is about more than charts and feedback loops—it is about focusing personal and organizational efforts toward desired outcomes. This exercise will allow you an opportunity to try your hand at developing a control system that is tailored to a particular company and type of work.

STEP 1 Get into groups. Your professor will organize your class into teams of three or four students per team. One team will be designated as Company Leadership.

Scenario: Razor's Edge (RE) is a young and growing company that serves the needs of those who engage in extreme sports, adventure/exploration, and guiding services. Some examples of RE's core market include expert/professional mountain climbers, white-water rafting guides, and polar explorers. The founders of RE are the husband and wife team of Dan and Alice Connors, world-famous mountain climbers and explorers. Dan and Alice have both reached the summit of Mount Everest and each is well respected in the rather small and close-knit community of adventurers and explorers. RE is an eclectic company of employees who, like Dan and Alice, share a passion for adventure and extreme sports. The company not only designs and sells its own lines of specialized products such as mountain-climbing shoes and ropes but also develops software designed to support expedition planning, communication and navigation, and simulation and scenario response (i.e., training tools for guides and newer expedition members).

For the first 5 years of its development, RE did not worry too much about organizational policies or controls. Employees were encouraged to climb, trek, and guide, and attendance issues were addressed on a case-by-case basis. Although officially all employees are given 2 weeks of paid vacation, many employees were allowed to take up to 2 months off at half-pay so that they could complete an expedition. Sick days were jokingly referred to as "mountain flu" days, and it was not unusual for the small company to be thinly staffed on Mondays and Fridays. But in the past 3 years, RE has grown from 25 employees to 85. The company is too big, and the jobs too diverse, for Dan and Alice to deal with each employee request for "expedition time" away from work. And the "mountain flu" has occasionally weakened the company's response to customers. Dan and Alice have also become victims of their own success as they attracted other climbers to join their company—most climbers want time off in the peak climbing seasons. But this also happens to be a peak time for RE orders and service requests.

The company has organized all employees into teams and announced a contest. Each team should come up with an approach for controlling staffing levels to meet or exceed customer expectations for responsiveness, while at the same time preserving RE's tradition as a company of active adventurers and explorers. The company has announced that each member of the employee team that develops the winning solution will receive $2,500 worth of RE gear of their choice.

STEP 2 Determine staffing levels. You are a team of workers at RE. Design an approach to controlling daily staffing levels so that RE is able to meet or exceed customer expectations for responsiveness without sacrificing its own identity as a company of adventurers and explorers. Keep in mind that RE is somewhat unusual in that even its accounting staff members (five full-time employees) are experienced adventurers and explorers and are expected to answer customer questions and handle their service needs. You should consider the following elements:

- Paid vacation
- Expedition time
- Sick days and "mountain flu" (Monday/Friday absences)

- Dealing with peak times, and/or most desirable times for vacation or expedition
- Knowing whether customers are pleased with RE's responsiveness to their needs

STEP 3 Outline a proposal. Submit a one-page handwritten outline of your proposal to the Company Leadership team.

STEP 4 Present the proposal. Each team will briefly present its proposal to the Company Leadership team, and members of the Company Leadership team may ask questions.

STEP 5 Vote. The Company Leadership will confer, vote, and announce the winning proposal.

STEP 6 Debrief as a class. What tensions confronted you as you worked to design an approach to staffing control for Razor's Edge? What trade-offs and challenges might you anticipate for the company when it implements the winning proposal? In what ways is control related to employee motivation? In what ways is control related to organizational culture? Do you think that the winning RE proposal would be well suited for use by a major outdoor and casual clothing company such as Lands' End? Why or why not?

SELF Assessment

Too Much Information?

Imagine that your professor handed back term papers, and the only mark on yours was the grade. Would you be content, or would you feel frustrated? People have different comfort levels about receiving feedback: Some thrive on it; others are ambivalent. What about you? Would you rather see comments in the margins of your term paper or not? This self-assessment will give you insights into your perceptions of feedback. Understanding your preferences in this area will help you develop the skills you'll need as a manager.[53]

As you complete this feedback inventory, be candid as you circle the appropriate responses. 1 is "Extremely Untrue" and 6 is "Extremely True."

1. It is important for me to obtain useful information about my performance.
   1 2 3 4 5 6
2. If I receive negative feedback, I would have a negative attitude toward myself, so I try to avoid criticism.
   1 2 3 4 5 6
3. I am not really worried about what people will think of me if I ask for feedback about my performance.
   1 2 3 4 5 6
4. I like people to hear about my good performance at work (or at college).
   1 2 3 4 5 6
5. Receiving feedback about my performance helps me to improve my skills.
   1 2 3 4 5 6
6. Negative feedback doesn't really lower my self-worth, so I don't go out of my way to avoid it.
   1 2 3 4 5 6
7. I'm concerned about what people would think of me if I were to ask for feedback.
   1 2 3 4 5 6
8. Seeking feedback from my supervisor (instructor) is one way to show that I want to improve my performance.
   1 2 3 4 5 6

9. I would like to obtain more information to let me know how I am performing.
   1 2 3 4 5 6

10. Receiving negative feedback wouldn't really change the way I feel about myself.
   1 2 3 4 5 6

11. I am worried about the impression I would make if I were to ask for feedback.
   1 2 3 4 5 6

12. I want people to know when I ask for feedback so I can show my responsible nature.
   1 2 3 4 5 6

13. I would like to receive more useful information about my performance.
   1 2 3 4 5 6

14. It's hard to feel good about myself when I receive negative feedback.
   1 2 3 4 5 6

15. I don't really worry about what others would think of me if I asked for feedback.
   1 2 3 4 5 6

16. I don't really care if people hear the good feedback that is given to me.
   1 2 3 4 5 6

17. I'm not really concerned about whether I receive useful information about my performance.
   1 2 3 4 5 6

18. I don't really worry about getting negative feedback because I still feel I am a person of worth.
   1 2 3 4 5 6

19. I don't really care if people know the type of feedback I get.
   1 2 3 4 5 6

20. When I receive praise, I don't really want others to hear it.
   1 2 3 4 5 6

21. Feedback is not really useful to help me improve my performance.
   1 2 3 4 5 6

22. I try to avoid negative feedback because it makes me feel bad about myself.
   1 2 3 4 5 6

23. If I sought feedback about my performance, I wouldn't want other people to know what type of feedback I received.
   1 2 3 4 5 6

24. I don't care either way if people see me asking my supervisor (instructor) for feedback.
   1 2 3 4 5 6

25. Obtaining useful feedback information is not very important to me.
   1 2 3 4 5 6

26. I worry about receiving feedback that is likely to be negative because it hurts to be criticized.
   1 2 3 4 5 6

27. I am usually concerned about other people hearing the content of the individual feedback I receive.
   1 2 3 4 5 6

28. I hope positive feedback about my performance will make a good impression on others.
   1 2 3 4 5 6

29. I don't really require more feedback to let me know how I am performing.
   1 2 3 4 5 6

30. Negative feedback doesn't really worry me because I still have a positive attitude about myself.
   1 2 3 4 5 6

31. It doesn't worry me if people know how I've performed at something.
    1 2 3 4 5 6

32. I don't really need to impress others by letting them know about the positive feedback I receive regarding my performance.
    1 2 3 4 5 6

SCORING

Determine your average score for each category by entering your response to each survey item below, as follows. In blanks that say *regular score*, simply enter your response for that item. If your response was a 4, place a 4 in the *regular score* blank. In blanks that say *reverse score*, subtract your response from 7 and enter the result. So if your response was a 4, place a 3 ($7 - 4 = 3$) in the *reverse score* blank. Total your scores, then compute each average score.

Desire for Useful Information

1. regular score ____________________
5. regular score ____________________
9. regular score ____________________
13. reverse score ____________________
17. reverse score ____________________
21. reverse score ____________________
25. reverse score ____________________
29. reverse score ____________________

TOTAL = _______

Ego Defense

2. regular score ____________________
6. reverse score ____________________
10. regular score ____________________
14. regular score ____________________
18. reverse score ____________________
22. reverse score ____________________
26. regular score ____________________
30. regular score ____________________

TOTAL = _______

Defensive Impression Management

3. reverse score ____________________
7. reverse score ____________________
11. reverse score ____________________
15. reverse score ____________________
19. reverse score ____________________

23. reverse score ____________________

27. reverse score ____________________

31. reverse score ____________________

TOTAL = _______

Assertive Impression Management

4. reverse score ____________________

8. reverse score ____________________

12. reverse score ____________________

16. reverse score ____________________

20. reverse score ____________________

24. reverse score ____________________

28. reverse score ____________________

32. reverse score ____________________

TOTAL = _______

You can find the interpretation for your score at: login.cengagebrain.com

Reel to Real

Biz Flix

© GREENLIGHT

Friday Night Lights

In the small town of Odessa, Texas, everyone lives for Friday nights when the high school football team, the Permian Panthers, takes the field. The town is proud of their Panthers, led by quarterback Mike Winchell (Lucas Black) and superstar tailback Boobie Miles (Derek Luke), and they're used to winning. They expect a state championship, and nothing less. When Boobie suffers a career-ending injury in the first game of the season, the team isn't sure they can win without him. But Coach Gary Gaines (Billy Bob Thornton) isn't ready to give up yet. In this clip from the film, Coach Gaines gathers the team around during the half-time break to talk about what success really means and how he wants them to achieve it.

What to Watch for and Ask Yourself

1. The control process begins when managers set goals and create standards. In this scene, what does Coach Gaines state that he expects from the members of his team?
2. Based on the topics discussed in this chapter, what similarities could you draw between what a coach and the manager of a company must do to ensure success for their team?
3. Which method of control do you think most football coaches exert over their teams: bureaucratic, objective, normative, or concertive? Why?

Management Workplace

© CENGAGE

Numi Organic Tea

When Brian Durkee shows up at Numi Organic Tea every day to work as the director of operations, he's on a mission to make his company a worldwide leader in sustainable supply chain management. Setting up and maintaining an efficient enterprise resource planning (ERP) system turned out to be much easier than converting Chinese suppliers to profoundly different farming methods and ways of doing business. Numi had just begun to implement an ERP system with integrated inventory management and accounting when Durkee joined the company. In this video, he explains how Numi is dedicated to sustainable supply chain management, eliminating waste, and using recycled materials.

What to Watch for and Ask Yourself

1. The control process begins when managers decide what is most important to the company. What are the main three things that Durkee says that Numi focuses on?
2. What are some of Numi's practices that aim to minimize waste?
3. What are some of the challenges that Numi faces when trying to maintain product standards?

Chapter Fifteen
Managing Information

OUTLINE

Experience Management

Explore the four levels of learning by doing the simulation module on Communication.

© ISTOCKPHOTO.COM/ ANN MARIE KURTZ

Pod Nod

Mini lecture reviews all the learning points in the chapter.

© ISTOCKPHOTO.COM/ MAGNET CREATIVE

Reel to Real

Biz Flix is a scene from *The Good Shepherd.* Management Workplace is a segment on Numi Organic Tea.

© ISTOCKPHOTO.COM/ CRAFTVISION

Self Test

10 quiz questions, 2 exhibit worksheets, and PowerPoints for quick review.

© ISTOCKPHOTO.COM/ DIJITAL FILM

What Would You Do?

Starbucks Headquarters, Seattle, Washington.[1]

In its first 20 years, *STARBUCKS* grew from 4 to 17,000 stores. But, in the last 2 years, Starbucks closed 800 stores and laid off 25,000 workers. In the middle of an economic downturn, consumers bought less because they perceived Starbucks as more expensive than McDonald's or Dunkin' Donuts. After founder Howard Schultz returned as CEO, Starbucks introduced its $3.95 breakfast pairings (a drink and a breakfast sandwich), offered the "gold card" (which costs $25 per year, but comes with a 10 percent discount on all food and drinks), and began selling a $2 cup of coffee to fend off McDonald's, which had introduced new, cheaper lattes and cappuccinos. Schultz also ousted the chief information officer (CIO) and hired you as the replacement. Your assignment as Starbucks' new CIO is to "craft a digital strategy" that creates a digital aspect to the Starbucks experience and increases how much people spend every time they visit a Starbucks.

In addition to crafting a digital strategy, several key issues have come up in your discussions with Schultz. First, should Starbucks offer free Wi-Fi? The fact that you're even considering this question tells you how much things have changed. Starbucks has always charged for wireless Internet access because it didn't want people camping out all day and taking up tables and chairs that new customers might use. It's the same philosophy that restaurants use: keep "turning over" the tables. In other words, the more customers who sit at a table every day, the more money you make. Historically, to make sure that Wi-Fi didn't encourage people to "camp out," Starbucks charged $6 an hour for the first hour and then $.10 for every additional minute of wireless access. At roughly 15,000 of its 30,000 restaurants, however, McDonald's charges just $2.95 for 2 hours of wireless Internet access. Panera Bread bakery-cafés, by contrast, charge nothing. Paula Rosenblum, of Retail Systems Research, says, "It's a part of Panera's value proposition because I think that they like to increase average transaction value and get loyalty at the same time." Panera's CIO, Tom Kish, said, "We were the first major concept to offer it free and have established one of the largest free Wi-Fi networks in the U.S. with approximately 1,200 cafés providing the service." He goes on to say, "We see it as another amenity for our customers. Free Internet access is one of a series of Panera's innovations designed to engage, connect and support our customers."

How can Starbucks use technology to do a better job of connecting with its customers? As you told Shultz, "When you look at our customers and what's happening in our stores, you see wireless devices, iPhones, converged networks, laptops. You see a generation of customers who are entering our stores and engaging [with us] in new ways. We have to understand our customers in ways that we've never had to in the past."

Finally, now that Starbucks is a global chain, the security of its food chain is at risk. Someone wanting to harm Starbucks' reputation could do so by tampering with the food that gets delivered and sold at Starbucks stores around the world. Starbucks has 40,000 suppliers who drop off sandwiches, pastries, milk, coffee beans, and other supplies every night. A further complication is that not only do all of Starbucks food products have to be fresh every day, many of them have to be refrigerated while being transported. Furthermore, since many of the deliveries have to be made after store hours, and you need to keep costs down by not keeping staff on hand to receive them, how can you give those 40,000 suppliers access to Starbucks stores so they can make those deliveries and not walk out with as much stuff as they dropped off?

If you were the new CIO at Starbucks, what would you do?

A generation ago, computer hardware and software had little to do with managing business information. Rather than storing information on hard drives, managers stored it in filing cabinets. Instead of uploading daily sales and inventory levels by satellite to corporate headquarters, they mailed hard-copy summaries to headquarters at the end of each month. Instead of word processing, reports were completed on a typewriter. Instead of spreadsheets, calculations were made on adding machines. Managers communicated by sticky notes, not e-mail. Phone messages were written down by assistants and coworkers, not left on voice mail. Workers did not use desktop or laptop computers as a daily tool to get work done. Instead, they scheduled limited access time to run batch jobs on the mainframe computer (and prayed that the code they wrote would work).

Today, a generation later, computer hardware and software are an integral part of managing business information. This is due mainly to something called **Moore's law**. Gordon Moore is one of the founders of Intel Corporation, which makes 75 percent of the integrated processors used in personal computers. In 1965, Moore predicted that computer-processing power would double and that its cost would drop by 50 percent every 2 years.[2] As Exhibit 15.1 shows, Moore was right. Computer power, as measured by the number of transistors per computer chip, *has* more than doubled every few years. Consequently, the computer sitting in your lap or on your desk is not only smaller but also much cheaper and more powerful than the large mainframe computers used by *Fortune* 500 companies 15 years ago. In fact, if car manufacturers had achieved the same power increases and cost decreases attained by computer manufacturers, a fully outfitted Lexus or Mercedes sedan would cost less than $1,000!

Moore's law
the prediction that about every 2 years, computer processing power would double and its cost would drop by 50 percent

EXHIBIT 15.1

Moore's Law

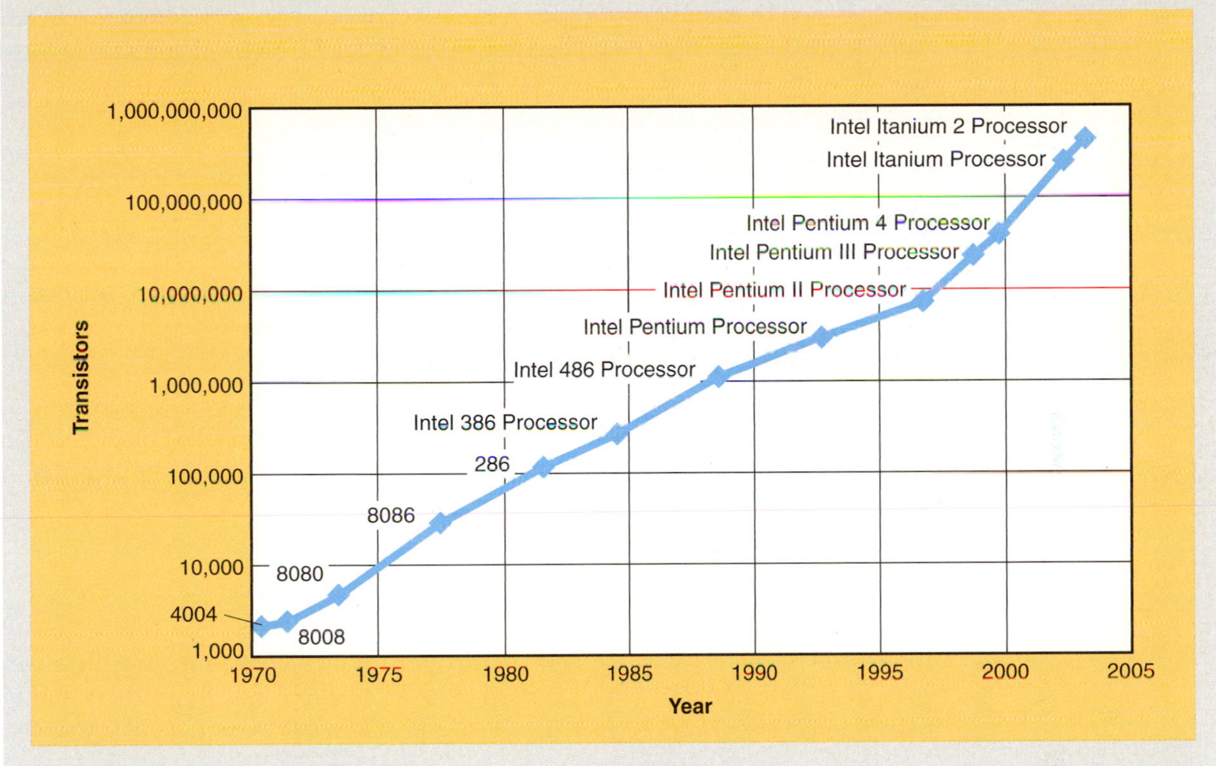

Source: "Moore's Law: Overviews," © Intel Corporation, available at http://www.intel.com/technology/mooreslaw, 27 June 2005.

We begin this chapter by explaining why information matters. In particular, you will learn the value of strategic information to companies as well as the cost and characteristics of good information. Next, you will investigate how companies capture, process, and protect information. Finally, you'll learn how information is accessed and shared with those both inside and outside the company and how knowledge and expertise (not just information or data) are shared, too.

Why Information Matters

Raw data are facts and figures. For example, 11, $452, 16, and 26,100 are some data that I used the day I wrote this section of the chapter. However, facts and figures aren't particularly useful unless they have meaning. For example, you probably can't guess what these four pieces of raw data represent, can you? If you can't, these data are useless. That's why researchers make the distinction between raw data and information. Whereas raw data consist of facts and figures, **information** is useful data that can influence someone's

raw data
facts and figures

information
useful data that can influence people's choices and behavior

choices and behavior. One way to think about the difference between data and information is that information has context.

So what did those four pieces of data mean to me? Well, 11 stands for Channel 11, the local CBS affiliate on which I watched part of the men's PGA golf tournament; $452 is how much it would cost me to rent a minivan for a week if I go skiing over spring break; 16 is for the 16-gigabyte storage card that I want to add to my digital camera (prices are low, so I'll probably buy it); and 26,100 means that it's time to get the oil changed in my car.

After reading the next two sections, you should be able to:

1 explain the strategic importance of information.

1 Strategic Importance of Information

In today's hypercompetitive business environments, information is as important as capital (i.e., money) for business success, whether it's about furniture delivery, product inventory, pricing, or costs.

It takes money to get businesses started, but businesses can't survive and grow without the right information. Information has strategic importance for organizations because it can be used to 1.1 **obtain first-mover advantage**, and 1.2 **sustain competitive advantage once it has been created**.

1.1 First-Mover Advantage

First-mover advantage is the strategic advantage that companies earn by being the first in an industry to use new information technology to substantially lower costs or to differentiate a product or service from that of competitors. By investing $90 billion over the last decade to replace copper coaxial lines with digital lines that feed high-speed cable modems and digital TV cable channels, cable companies convinced two out of every three high-speed Internet subscribers to choose cable over the DSL service provided by phone companies.[3] The phone companies are beginning to catch up. They now sign up more new high-speed Internet subscribers than do cable providers. But does that mean that cable companies' first-mover advantage is slipping away? Well, not yet, as 57 percent of high-speed Internet subscribers still choose cable.[4] And with a growing subscriber base for residential phone service, the cable companies are now going after the phone companies' business customers, offering them high-speed Internet and business phone service.[5]

First-mover advantages like those established by high-speed Internet cable companies can be sizable. On average, first movers earn a 30 percent market share compared to 19 percent for the companies that follow.[6] Likewise, over 70 percent of market leaders started as first movers.[7]

first-mover advantage
the strategic advantage that companies earn by being the first to use new information technology to substantially lower costs or to make a product or service different from that of competitors

1.2 Sustaining Competitive Advantage

As described, companies that use information technology to establish first-mover advantage usually have higher market shares and profits. According to the resource-based view of information technology shown in Exhibit 15.2, companies need to address three critical questions in order to sustain a competitive advantage through information technology. First, does the information technology create value for the firm by lowering costs or providing a better product or service? If an information

EXHIBIT 15.2

Using Information Technology to Sustain a Competitive Advantage

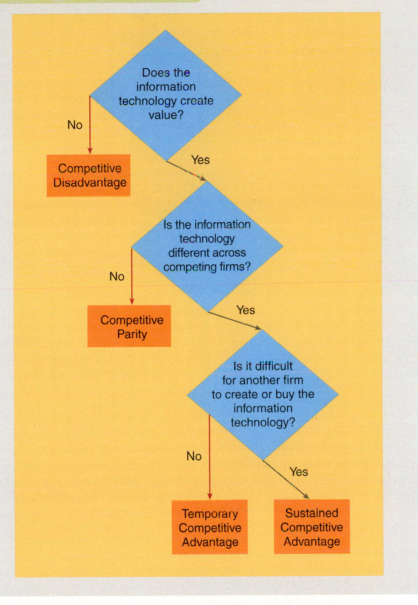

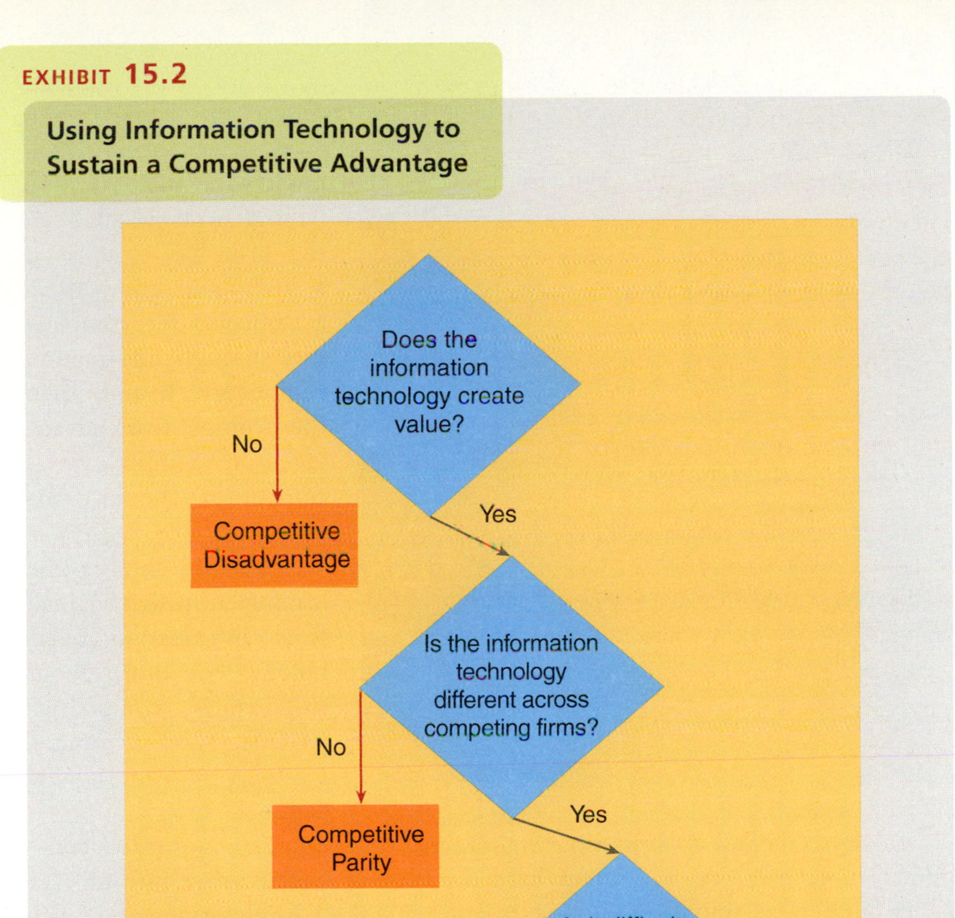

Source: Permission to reprint figure from F.J. Mata, W.L. Fuerst, & J.B. Barney, "Information Technology and Sustained Competitive Advantage: A Resource-Based Analysis," *MIS Quarterly* 19:4, 4, December 1995; pp. 487–505. Copyright © 1995, Regents of the University of Minnesota. Reprinted by permission.

technology doesn't add value, then investing in it would put the firm at a competitive disadvantage to companies that choose information technologies that do add value.

Second, is the information technology the same or different across competing firms? If all the firms have access to the same information technology and use it in the same way, then no firm has an advantage over another (i.e., there is competitive parity).

Doing the Right Thing

Recycling and Disposing of Computer Equipment

With most companies replacing computers every 4 years, an estimated 250 million computers will be discarded over the next 5 years. Computers and computer monitors contains hazardous materials, however, so you can't just toss them in the trash. Doing that is not just wrong—it's against the law. Instead, contact your state's department of environmental protection for help in finding a recycling company. Or donate your old computers to deserving individuals or charitable organizations. Or sell the computers at a steep discount to your employees. And when you buy your new corporate computers, bargain with the vendor to make it responsible for recycling those computers the next time around.[11]

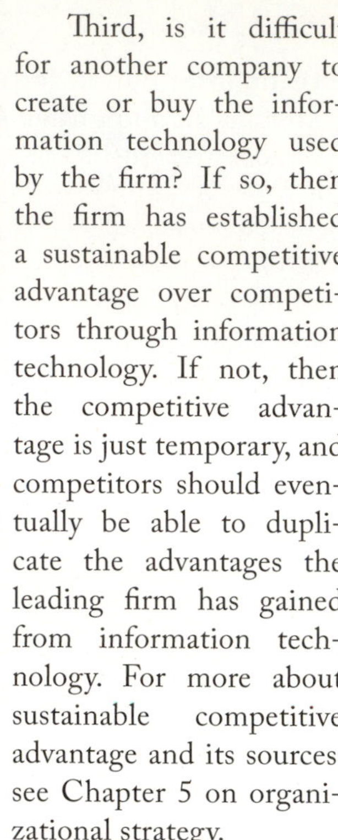

Third, is it difficult for another company to create or buy the information technology used by the firm? If so, then the firm has established a sustainable competitive advantage over competitors through information technology. If not, then the competitive advantage is just temporary, and competitors should eventually be able to duplicate the advantages the leading firm has gained from information technology. For more about sustainable competitive advantage and its sources, see Chapter 5 on organizational strategy.

In short, the key to sustaining a competitive advantage is not faster computers, more memory, and larger hard drives. The key is using information technology to continuously improve and support the core functions of a business. Ron Ireland, a former Wal-Mart manager, says, "Wal-Mart has always considered information technology as a competitive advantage, never as a business expense."[8] Thanks to innovative use of information technology and the largest private satellite network and database system in the world, Wal-Mart's costs are 10 percent lower than its competitors'.[9] Wal-Mart was one of the first retailers to use computers and bar codes to track sales and inventory data and then share those data with suppliers. Today, Wal-Mart's supplier network, Retail Link, allows vendors like Ted Haedicke of Coca-Cola to "look at how much [and what kind of] Coke [has] sold . . . and at what prices at any store in the Wal-Mart system." He went on to say, "You can't do that with any other retailer today."[10]

Companies like Wal-Mart that achieve first-mover advantage with information technology and then sustain it with continued investment create a moving target that competitors have difficulty hitting.

REVIEW 1

Strategic Importance of Information

The first company to use new information technology to substantially lower costs or differentiate products or services often gains first-mover advantage, which can lead to higher profits and larger market share. Creating a first-mover advantage can be difficult, expensive, and risky. According to the resource-based view of information technology, sustainable competitive advantage occurs when information technology adds value, is different across firms, and is difficult to create or acquire.

Getting and Sharing Information

In 1907, Metropolitan Life Insurance built a huge office building in New York City for its brand-new, state-of-the-art information technology system. What was this great breakthrough in information management? Card files. That's right, the same card file system that every library in America used before computers. Metropolitan Life's information technology consisted of 20,000 separate file drawers that sat in hundreds of file cabinets more than 15 feet tall. This filing system held 20 million insurance applications, 700,000 accounting books, and 500,000 death certificates. Metropolitan Life employed 61 workers who did nothing but sort, file, and climb ladders to pull files as needed.[12]

How we get and share information has clearly changed. The cost, inefficiency, and ineffectiveness of using this formerly state-of-the-art system would put an insurance company out of business within months. Today, if storms, fire, or accidents damage policyholders' property, insurance companies write checks on the spot to cover the losses. When policyholders buy a car, they call their insurance agent from the dealership to activate their insurance before driving off in their new car. And now, insurance companies are marketing their products and services to customers directly from the Internet. From card files to Internet files in just under a century, the rate of change in information technology is spectacular.

After reading the next two sections, you should be able to:

2 explain the basics of capturing, processing, and protecting information.

3 describe how companies can access and share information and knowledge.

2 Capturing, Processing, and Protecting Information

When you go to your local Rite Aid pharmacy to pick up a prescription, the pharmacist reviews an electronic file that shows all of the medications you're taking. That same system automatically checks to make sure that your new prescription won't create adverse side effects by interacting with your other medications. When you pay for your prescription, Rite Aid's point-of-sale information system determines whether you've written any bad checks lately (to Rite Aid or other stores), records your payment, and then checks with the computer of the pharmaceutical company that makes your prescription drugs to see if it's time to reorder. Throughout the process, Rite Aid protects your information to make sure that your data are readily available only to you, your physician, and your pharmacist.

In this section, you will learn about the information technologies that companies like Rite Aid use to 2.1 **capture**, 2.2 **process**, and 2.3 **protect information**.

2.1 Capturing Information

There are two basic methods of capturing information: manual and electronic. Manual capture of information is a slow, costly, labor-intensive, and often inaccurate process, which entails recording and entering data by hand into a data storage device. For example, when you applied for a driver's license, you probably recorded personal information about yourself by filling out a form. Then, after you passed your driver's test, someone typed your handwritten information into the department of motor vehicles' computer database so that local and state police could access it from their patrol cars in the event they pulled you over for speeding. (Isn't information great?) Consequently, companies are relying more on electronic capture. They use electronic storage devices such as bar codes, radio frequency identification tags, and document scanners to capture and record data electronically.

bar code
a visual pattern that represents numerical data by varying the thickness and pattern of vertical bars

radio frequency identification (RFID) tags
tags containing minuscule microchips that transmit information via radio waves and can be used to track the number and location of the objects into which the tags have been inserted

electronic scanner
an electronic device that converts printed text and pictures into digital images

optical character recognition
the ability of software to convert digitized documents into ASCII text (American Standard Code for Information Interchange) that can be searched, read, and edited by word processing and other kinds of software

Bar codes represent numerical data by varying the thickness and pattern of vertical bars. The primary advantage of bar codes is that the data they represent can be read and recorded in an instant with a handheld or pen-type scanner. One pass of the scanner (okay, sometimes several) and "beep!" the information has been captured. Bar codes cut checkout times in half, reduce data entry errors by 75 percent, and save stores money because stockers don't have to go through the labor-intensive process of putting a price tag on each item in the store.[13] Consumer product companies, like Unilever, are now partnering with grocery stores and technology companies to test bar code-based coupons that can be scanned directly from consumers' cell phones.[14]

Radio frequency identification (RFID) tags contain minuscule microchips and antennas that transmit information via radio waves.[15] Unlike bar codes, which require direct line-of-sight scanning, RFID tags are read by turning on an RFID reader that, like a radio, tunes into a specific frequency to determine the number *and* location of products, parts, or anything else to which the RFID tags are attached. Turn on an RFID reader, and every RFID tag within the reader's range (from several hundred to several thousand feet) is accounted for.

Because they are now so inexpensive, RFID tags and readers are being put to thousands of uses in all kinds of businesses. For example, **Blue C Sushi** has five restaurants in Seattle where RFID tags are used to make sure that food is fresh. With RFID tags on all of its plates, plates are scanned as they leave each chef's workstation and then are periodically scanned on the conveyor belt to determine if they are still fresh. If a plate of food is still on the belt after 90 minutes, the system issues an alert to remove it. The system also keeps track of which plates are selling the fastest and when sales begin to slow. This has helped each of the company's five restaurants, which would typically throw out 80 to 100 plates of food each night, cut waste by about 45 percent.[16]

Electronic scanners, which convert printed text and pictures into digital images, have become an increasingly popular method of capturing data electronically because they are inexpensive and easy to use. The first requirement for a good scanner is a *document feeder* that automatically feeds document pages into the scanner or turns the pages (often with a puff of air) when scanning books or bound documents.[17] Text that has been digitized cannot be searched or edited like the regular text in your word processing software, however, so the second requirement for a good scanner is **optical character recognition** software to scan and convert original or digitized documents into ASCII text (American Standard Code for Information Interchange) or Adobe PDF documents.

2.2 Processing Information

Processing information means transforming raw data into meaningful information that can be applied to business decision making. Evaluating sales data to determine the best- and worst-selling products, examining repair records to determine product reliability, and monitoring the cost of long-distance phone calls are all examples of processing raw data into meaningful information. And with automated, electronic capture of data, increased processing power, and cheaper and more plentiful ways to store data, managers no longer worry about getting data. Instead, they scratch their heads about how to use the overwhelming amount of data that pours into their businesses every day. Furthermore, most managers know little about statistics and have neither the time nor the inclination to learn how to use them to analyze data.

One promising tool to help managers dig out from under the avalanche of data is data mining. **Data mining** is the process of discovering patterns and relationships in large amounts of data.[18] Data mining works by using complex algorithms such as neural networks, rule induction, and decision trees. If you don't know what those are, that's okay. With data mining, you don't have to. Most managers only need to know that data mining looks for patterns that are already in the data but are too complex for them to spot on their own. For example, when Yahoo! decided to redesign its front page, it was faced with analyzing 10 terabytes (a terabyte is the same as 500 million pages of single-spaced text) of data per day generated by users' clicks! Yahoo! bought DMX Group, a company that provides simple data mining tools to employees who pose simple questions, such as "Are users more likely to click on an ad placed in the middle of the page or at the top of the page?" Bassel Ojjeh, vice president of DMX, says that Yahoo! is now using data and not wild guesses to make changes to its websites.[19]

Data mining typically splits a data set in half, finds patterns in one half, and then tests the validity of those patterns by trying to find them again in the second half of the data set. The data typically come from a **data warehouse** that stores huge amounts of data that have been prepared for data mining analysis by being cleaned of errors and redundancy. The data in a data warehouse can then be analyzed using two kinds of data mining. **Supervised data mining** usually begins with the user telling the data mining software to look and test for specific patterns and relationships in a data set. Typically, this is done through a series of "what-if?" questions or statements. For instance, a grocery store manager might instruct the data mining software to determine if coupons placed in the Sunday paper increase or decrease sales. By contrast, with **unsupervised data mining,** the user simply tells the data mining software to uncover whatever patterns and relationships it can find in a data set. For example, State Farm Insurance used to have three pricing categories for car insurance depending on your driving record: preferred for the best drivers, standard for typical drivers, and nonstandard for the worst drivers. Now, however, it has moved to tiered pricing based on the 300 different kinds of driving records that its data mining software was able to discover. This allows State Farm to be much more precise in matching 300 different price levels to 300 different kinds of driving records.[20]

Unsupervised data mining is particularly good at identifying association or affinity patterns, sequence patterns, and predictive patterns. It can also identify what data mining technicians call data clusters.[21] **Association or affinity patterns** occur when

processing information
transforming raw data into meaningful information

data mining
the process of discovering unknown patterns and relationships in large amounts of data

data warehouse
stores huge amounts of data that have been prepared for data mining analysis by being cleaned of errors and redundancy

supervised data mining
the process when the user tells the data mining software to look and test for specific patterns and relationships in a data set

unsupervised data mining
the process when the user simply tells the data mining software to uncover whatever patterns and relationships it can find in a data set

association or affinity patterns
when two or more database elements tend to occur together in a significant way

©ISTOCKPHOTO/ERIC ISSELÉE
©ISTOCKPHOTO/NICOLE WARING

two or more database elements tend to occur together in a significant way. Surprisingly, Osco Drugs, based in Chicago, found that beer and diapers tended to be bought together between 5 and 7 pm. The question, of course, was: Why? The answer, on further review, was fairly straightforward. Fathers, who were told by their wives to buy some diapers on their way home, decided to pick up a six-pack for themselves, too.[22]

Sequence patterns occur when two or more database elements occur together in a significant pattern in which one of the elements precedes the other. StratBridge provides data mining capability to professional sports teams like basketball's Boston Celtics so they can analyze their ticket sales in real time. One season, after the Celtics had been eliminated from playoff eligibility, StratBridge's data mining analysis revealed that families typically bought tickets behind the basket just a few hours before tipoff. When the Celtics noticed that sales were lagging for those seats, they bundled them together in a family four-pack, dropped the prices, added food coupons, and then e-mailed a list of local families who had previously purchased tickets to the game. As a result, all of those unsold seats sold.[23]

Predictive patterns are just the opposite of association or affinity patterns. Whereas association or affinity patterns look for database elements that seem to go together, **predictive patterns** help identify database elements that are different. Banks and credit card companies use predictive data mining to distinguish customers who are good credit risks from those who are poor credit risks and less likely to pay their loans and monthly bills. Insurance companies use it to determine which insurance claims are likely to be legitimate or fraudulent. At *HIGHMARK BLUE CROSS BLUE SHIELD* of Pennsylvania, which ensures 4.6 million people, it used to take weeks to sift through potential fraud cases one variable at a time. But according to Tom Brennan, director of special investigations, with predictive data mining software, "Now we can do our analysis in minutes, rather than days."[24] Since 2002, data mining has helped Highmark recover $23 million in fraudulent payouts.

Data clusters are the last kind of pattern found by data mining. **Data clusters** occur when three or more database elements occur together (i.e., cluster) in a significant way. For example, after analyzing several years' worth of repair and warranty claims, Ford Motor Company might find that, compared with cars built in its Chicago plant, the cars it builds in Kansas City (first element) are more likely to have problems with overtightened fan belts (second element) that break (third element) and result in overheated engines (fourth element), ruined radiators (fifth element), and payments for tow trucks (sixth element), which are paid for by Ford's 5-year, 60,000-mile power train warranty.

Traditionally, data mining has been very expensive and very complex. Today, however, data mining and analysis services are much more affordable and within reach of most companies' budgets. And, if it follows the path of most technologies, it will become even easier and cheaper to use in the future.

sequence patterns
when two or more database elements occur together in a significant pattern, but one of the elements precedes the other

predictive patterns
patterns that help identify database elements that are different

data clusters
when three or more database elements occur together (i.e., cluster) in a significant way

2.3 Protecting Information

Protecting information is the process of ensuring that data are reliably and consistently retrievable in a usable format for authorized users but no one else. For instance, when customers purchase prescription medicine at Drugstore.com, an online drugstore and health-aid retailer, they want to be confident that their medical information is available only to them, the pharmacists at Drugstore.com, and their doctors. So Drugstore.com has an extensive privacy policy.[25]

Companies like Drugstore.com find it necessary to protect information because of numerous security threats to data and data security. People inside and outside companies can steal or destroy company data in various ways, including denial-of-service web server attacks that can bring down some of the busiest and best-run sites on the Internet; viruses and spyware/adware that spread quickly and can result in data loss and business disruption; keystroke monitoring in which every mouse click and keystroke you make is monitored, stored, and sent to unauthorized users; password-cracking software that steals supposedly secure passwords; and phishing, where fake but real-looking e-mails and websites trick users into sharing personal information (user names, passwords, account numbers) leading to unauthorized account access. There are numerous steps that can be taken to secure data and data networks. Some of the most important are authentication and authorization, firewalls, antivirus software for PCs and e-mail servers, data encryption, and virtual private networks.[26] We will review those steps and then finish this section with a brief review of the dangers of wireless networks, which are exploding in popularity.

Two critical steps are required to make sure that data can be accessed by authorized users and no one else. One is **authentication**, that is, making sure users are who they claim to be.[27] The other is **authorization**, that is, granting authenticated users approved access to data, software, and systems.[28] When an ATM prompts you to enter your personal identification number (PIN), the bank is authenticating that you are you. Once you've been authenticated, you are authorized to access your funds and no one else's. Of course, as anyone who has lost a PIN or password or had one stolen knows, user authentication systems are not foolproof. In particular, users create security risks by not changing their default account passwords (such as birth dates) or by using weak passwords such as names ("Larry") or complete words ("football") that are quickly guessed by password-cracker software.[29] (See "Doing the Right Thing" on password do's and don'ts to learn how to prevent this.)

This is why many companies are now turning to **two-factor authentication**, which is based on what users know, such as a password, and what they have, such as a secure ID card.[30] In order to log on to their computer accounts, employees at Bloomberg, a global provider of business news, data, and analysis, must enter a password, such as a four-digit personal identification number, plus a secure number that changes every 60 seconds and is displayed on the tiny screen of the secure electronic ID (about the size of a pack of gum) they carry. For these same reasons, some companies are turning to biometrics for two-factor authentication. With **biometrics** such as fingerprint recognition or iris scanning, users are identified by unique, measurable body features.[31] Of course, since some fingerprint scanners can be fooled by fingerprint molds, some companies take security measures even further by requiring users to simultaneously scan their fingerprint *and* insert a secure, smart card

protecting information
the process of ensuring that data are reliably and consistently retrievable in a usable format for authorized users, but no one else

authentication
making sure potential users are who they claim to be

authorization
granting authenticated users approved access to data, software, and systems

two-factor authentication
authentication based on what users know, such as a password, and what they have in their possession, such as a secure ID card or key

biometrics
identifying users by unique, measurable body features, such as fingerprint recognition or iris scanning

containing a digital file of their fingerprint. This is another form of two-factor authentication.

Unfortunately, stolen or cracked passwords are not the only way for hackers and electronic thieves to gain access to an organization's computer resources. Unless special safeguards are put in place, every time corporate users are online there's literally nothing between their personal computers and the Internet (home users with high-speed DSL or cable Internet access face the same risks). Hackers can access files, run programs, and control key parts of computers if precautions aren't taken. To reduce these risks, companies use **firewalls**, hardware or software devices that sit between the computers in an internal organizational network and outside networks such as the Internet. Firewalls filter and check incoming and outgoing data. They prevent company insiders from accessing unauthorized sites or from sending confidential company information to people outside the company. Firewalls also prevent outsiders from identifying and gaining access to company computers and data. Indeed, if a firewall is working properly, the computers behind the company firewall cannot be seen or accessed by outsiders.

firewall
a protective hardware or software device that sits between the computers in an internal organizational network and outside networks, such as the Internet

virus
a program or piece of code that, without your knowledge, attaches itself to other programs on your computer and can trigger anything from a harmless flashing message to the reformatting of your hard drive to a systemwide network shutdown

data encryption
the transformation of data into complex, scrambled digital codes that can be unencrypted only by authorized users who possess unique decryption keys

virtual private network (VPN)
software that securely encrypts data sent by employees outside the company network, decrypts the data when they arrive within the company computer network, and does the same when data are sent back to employees outside the network

A **virus** is a program or piece of code that, without your knowledge, attaches itself to other programs on your computer and can trigger anything from a harmless flashing message to the reformatting of your hard drive to a system-wide network shutdown. Today's viruses are very sophisticated. In fact, with some viruses, just being connected to a network can infect your computer. *Antivirus software for personal computers* scans e-mail, downloaded files, and computer hard drives, disk drives, and memory to detect and stop computer viruses from doing damage. However, this software is effective only to the extent that users of individual computers have and use up-to-date versions. With new viruses appearing all the time, users should update their antivirus software weekly or, even better, configure their virus software to automatically check for, download, and install updates. By contrast, *corporate antivirus software* automatically scans e-mail attachments such as Microsoft Word documents, graphics, or text files as they come across the company e-mail server. It also monitors and scans all file downloads across company databases and network servers. So, while antivirus software for personal computers prevents individual computers from being infected, corporate antivirus software for e-mail servers, databases, and network servers adds another layer of protection by preventing infected files from multiplying and being sent to others.

Another way of protecting information is to encrypt sensitive data. **Data encryption** transforms data into complex, scrambled digital codes that can be unencrypted only by authorized users who possess unique decryption keys. One method of data encryption is to use products by PGP (Pretty Good Privacy; ***http://www.pgp.com***) to encrypt the files stored on personal computers or network servers and databases. This is especially important with laptop computers, which are easily stolen.[33] With people increasingly gaining unauthorized access to e-mail messages—e-mail snooping—it's also important to encrypt sensitive e-mail messages and file attachments.

Although firewalls can protect personal computers and network servers connected to the corporate network, people away from their offices (e.g., salespeople, business travelers, telecommuters) who interact with their company networks via the

Internet face a security risk. Because Internet data are not encrypted, packet sniffer software easily allows hackers to read everything sent or received except files that have been encrypted before sending. Previously, the only practical solution was to have employees dial in to secure company phone lines for direct access to the company network. Of course, with international and long-distance phone calls, the costs quickly added up. Now, **virtual private networks (VPNs)** have solved this problem by using software to encrypt all Internet data at both ends of the transmission process. Instead of making long-distance calls, employees connect to the Internet. But, unlike typical Internet connections in which data packets are unencrypted, the VPN encrypts the data sent by employees outside the company computer network, decrypts the data when they arrive within the company network, and does the same when data are sent back to the computer outside the network.

Alternatively, many companies are now adopting web-based **secure sockets layer (SSL) encryption** to provide secure off-site access to data and programs. If you've ever entered your credit card in a web browser to make an online purchase, you've used SSL technology to encrypt and protect that information. You can tell if SSL encryption is being used if you see a gold padlock icon in Internet Explorer or Mozilla Firefox, or if the URL begins with https. SSL encryption works

Doing the Right Thing

Password Do's and Don'ts

Anyone with access to sensitive personal (personnel or medical files), customer (credit cards), or corporate data (costs) has a clear responsibility to protect those data from unauthorized access. Use the following do's and don'ts to maintain a "strong" password system and protect your data.

- Don't use any public information such as part of your name, address, or birthdate to create a password.
- Don't use complete words, English or foreign, that are easily guessed by password software using "dictionary attacks."
- Use eight or more characters and include some unique characters such as !@#$ to create passwords like cow@#boy.
- The longer the password and the more unique characters, the more difficult it is to guess.
- Consider using "passphrases," such as "My European vacation starts July 8th," instead of shorter passwords. The longer password, including upper- and lower-case letters, spaces, numbers, is easy to remember and much more difficult to guess using password-cracking software.
- Remember your password and don't write it down on a sticky note attached to your computer.
- Change your password every 6 weeks. Better yet, specify that your computer system force all users to change their passwords this often.
- Don't reused old passwords.

Together, these basic steps can make it much more difficult to gain unauthorized access to sensitive data.[32]

secure sockets layer (SSL) encryption
Internet browser–based encryption that provides secure off-site web access to some data and programs

the same way in the workplace. Managers and employees who aren't at the office simply connect to the Internet, open a web browser, and then enter a user name and password to gain access to SSL-encrypted data and programs. For example, the Catholic Health System of Buffalo, New York, uses an SSL system to allow radiologists to access and review medical images like X-rays from their homes. Likewise, lawyers at Sonnenschein, Nath & Rosenthal, a Chicago law firm, use the Internet and their SSL-encrypted system to securely access case records from anywhere in the world.[34] SSL encryption is cheaper than VPN, but it typically provides only limited access to data and files. By contrast, VPN connections provide complete, secure access to everything on a company's network.

Finally, many companies now have wireless networks, which make it possible for anybody with a laptop to access the company network from anywhere in the office. Though wireless networks come equipped with security and encryption capabilities that, in theory, permit only authorized users to access the wireless network, those capabilities are easily bypassed with the right tools. Compounding the problem, many wireless networks are shipped with their security and encryption capabilities turned off for ease of installation.[35] Caution is important even when encryption is turned on because the WEP (Wired Equivalent Privacy) security protocol is easily compromised. If you work at home or are working on the go, extra care is critical because Wi-Fi networks in homes and public places like hotel lobbies are among the most targeted by hackers.[36] See the Wi-Fi Alliance site at ***http://www.wi-fi.org*** for the latest information on wireless security and encryption protocols that provide much stronger protection for your company's wireless network.

REVIEW 2

Capturing, Processing, and Protecting Information

Electronic data capture (bar codes, radio frequency identification [RFID] tags, scanners, and optical character recognition) is much faster, easier, and cheaper than manual data capture. Processing information means transforming raw data into meaningful information that can be applied to business decision making. Data mining helps managers with this transformation by discovering unknown patterns and relationships in data. Supervised data mining looks for patterns specified by managers; unsupervised data mining looks for four general kinds of data patterns: association/affinity patterns, sequence patterns, predictive patterns, and data clusters. Protecting information ensures that data are reliably and consistently retrievable in a usable format by authorized users but no one else. Authentication and authorization, firewalls, antivirus software for PCs and corporate e-mail and network servers, data encryption, virtual private networks, and web-based secure sockets layer (SSL) encryption are some of the best ways to protect information. Be careful with wireless networks, which are easily compromised even when security and encryption protocols are in place.

3 Accessing and Sharing Information and Knowledge

After reading this section, you should be able to explain how companies use information technology to improve 3.1 **internal access and sharing of information**, 3.2 **external access and sharing of information**, and 3.3 **the sharing of knowledge and expertise**.

3.1 Internal Access and Sharing

Executives, managers, and workers inside the company use three kinds of information technology to access and share information: executive information systems, intranets, and portals. An **executive information system (EIS)** uses internal and external sources of data to provide managers and executives the information they need to monitor and analyze organizational performance.[37] The goal of an EIS is to provide accurate, complete, relevant, and timely information to managers.

Managers at Lands' End, the web/mail-order company, use their EIS, which they call their "dashboard," to see how well the company is running. With just a few mouse clicks and basic commands such as *find, compare*, and *show*, the EIS displays costs, sales revenues, and other kinds of data in color-coded charts and graphs. Managers can drill down to view and compare data by region, state, time period, and product. Lands' End CIO Frank Giannantonio says, "Our dashboards include an early alert system that utilizes key performance metrics to target items selling faster than expected and gives our managers the ability to adjust product levels far earlier than they were able to do in the past."[38]

Intranets are private company networks that allow employees to easily access, share, and publish information using Internet software. Intranet websites are just like external websites, but the firewall separating the internal company network from the Internet permits only authorized internal access.[39] Companies typically use intranets to share information (e.g., about benefits) and to replace paper forms with online forms. Many company intranets are built on the web model as it existed a decade ago. Companies like Motorola, however, are building new systems based on the web 2.0 model. The new intranet is collaborative like social media sites, allowing employees to network with one another beyond departmental boundaries and share their own information rather than just access company-published documents. Ninety-two percent of the company's employees use Motorola's Intranet 2.0 and collectively contribute about 100,000 documents per day.[40] Exhibit 15.3 further explains why companies use intranets.

executive information system (EIS)
a data processing system that uses internal and external data sources to provide the information needed to monitor and analyze organizational performance

intranets
private company networks that allow employees to easily access, share, and publish information using Internet software

EXHIBIT 15.3

Why Companies Use Intranets

- Intranets are inexpensive.
- Intranets increase efficiencies and reduce costs.
- Intranets are intuitive and easy to use and web-based.
- Intranets work across all computer systems and platforms (web-based).
- Intranets can be built on top of an existing computer network.
- Intranets work with software programs that easily convert electronic documents to HTML files for intranet use.
- Much of the software required to set up an intranet is either freeware (no cost) or shareware (try before you buy, usually less expensive than commercial software).

Finally, **corporate portals** are a hybrid of executive information systems and intranets. While an EIS provides managers and executives with the information they need to monitor and analyze organizational performance, and intranets help companies distribute and publish information and forms within the company, corporate portals allow managers and employees to access customized information *and* complete specialized transactions using a web browser. Hilman Group is a company that sells the nuts, bolts, fasteners, keys, and key cutting machines that you find in Home Depot, Lowes, Ace, and nearly every other hardware store. To manage information related to all this work, Hillman's CIO created a corporate portal that contains a real-time report for each product that continuously updates sales and production numbers. The portal and report are so useful that CEO Mick Hillman began using them on a daily basis. Today, Hillman's portal contains 75 specialized reports that are accessed by 800 managers and employees.[41]

3.2 External Access and Sharing

Historically, companies have been unable or reluctant to let outside groups have access to corporate information. Now, however, a number of information technologies—electronic data interchange, extranets, web services, and the Internet—are making it easier to share company data with external groups like suppliers and customers. They're also reducing costs, increasing productivity by eliminating manual information processing (70 percent of the data output from one company, like a purchase order, ends up as data input at another company, such as a sales invoice or shipping order), reducing data entry errors, improving customer service, and speeding communications. As a result, managers are scrambling to adopt these technologies.

With **electronic data interchange,** or **EDI**, two companies convert purchase and ordering information to a standardized format to enable direct electronic transmission of that information from one company's computer system to the other company's system. For example, when a Wal-Mart checkout clerk drags an Apple iPod across the checkout scanner, Wal-Mart's computerized inventory system automatically reorders another iPod through the direct EDI connection that its computer has with Apple's manufacturing and shipping computer. No one at Wal-Mart or Apple fills out paperwork. No one makes phone calls. There are no delays to wait to find out whether Apple has the iPod in stock. The transaction takes place instantly and automatically because the data from both companies were translated into a standardized, shareable, compatible format.

Web services are another way for companies to directly and automatically transmit purchase and ordering information from one company's computer system to another company's computer system. **Web services** use standardized protocols to describe and transfer data from one company in such a way that those data can automatically be read, understood, transcribed, and processed by different computer systems in another company.[42] Route One was started by the financing companies of DaimlerChrysler, Ford, General Motors, and Toyota. Not surprisingly, each auto company had a different computer system with different operating systems, different programs, and different data structures. Route One relies on web services to connect these different computer systems to the wide variety of different databases and software used by various auto dealers, credit bureaus, banks, and other auto financing companies. Without web services, there's no way these different companies and systems could share information.[43]

corporate portal
a hybrid of executive information systems and intranets that allows managers and employees to use a web browser to gain access to customized company information and to complete specialized transactions

electronic data interchange (EDI)
when two companies convert their purchase and ordering information to a standardized format to enable the direct electronic transmission of that information from one company's computer system to the other company's computer system

web services
using standardized protocols to describe data from one company in such a way that those data can automatically be read, understood, transcribed, and processed by different computer systems in another company

In EDI and web services, the different purchasing and ordering applications in each company interact automatically without any human input. No one has to lift a finger to click a mouse, enter data, or hit the return key. An **extranet**, by contrast, allows companies to exchange information and conduct transactions by purposely providing outsiders with direct, web–based access to authorized parts of a company's intranet or information system. Typically, user names and passwords are required to access an extranet.[44] General Mills uses an extranet to provide web-based access to its trucking database to 20 other companies that ship their products over similar distribution routes to make sure that its distribution trucks don't waste money by running half empty (or make late deliveries to customers because it waited to ship until the trucks were full). When other companies are ready to ship products, they log on to General Mills' trucking database, check availability, and then enter the shipping load, place, and pickup time. By sharing shipping capacity on its trucks, General Mills can run them fully loaded all the time. In several test areas, General Mills saved 7 percent on shipping costs (nearly $2 million) in the first year. Expanding the program company-wide is producing even larger cost savings.[45]

Finally, companies are reducing paperwork and manual information processing by using the Internet to automate transactions with customers; this is similar to the way in which extranets are used to handle transactions with suppliers and distributors. For example, most airlines have automated the ticketing process by eliminating paper tickets altogether. Simply buy an e-ticket via the Internet, and then check yourself in online by printing your boarding pass from your personal computer or from a kiosk at the airport. Internet purchases, ticketless travel, and automated check-ins have together fully automated the purchase of airline tickets. Use of self-service kiosks is expanding, too. For example, Alamo Rent-a-Car has introduced kiosks that print rental agreements, permit upgrades to nicer cars, and allow customers to add additional drivers or buy rental insurance. Jerry Dow, Alamo's chief marketing officer, says, "Customers are already comfortable using the check-in kiosk for flights. Using a self-service kiosk for car rental is a natural progression."[64] Alamo has found that kiosks reduce check-in times by 50 percent.

In the long run, the goal is to link customer Internet sites with company intranets (or EDI) and extranets so that everyone—all the employees and managers within a company as well as the suppliers and distributors outside the company—involved in providing a service or making a product for a customer is automatically notified when a purchase is made. Companies that use EDI, web services, extranets, and the Internet to share data with customers and suppliers achieve increases in productivity 2.7 times larger than those that don't.[46]

3.3 Sharing Knowledge and Expertise

At the beginning of the chapter, we distinguished between raw data, which consist of facts and figures, and information, which consists of useful data that influence someone's choices and behavior. One more important distinction needs to be made, namely, that data and information are not the same as knowledge. **Knowledge** is the understanding that one gains from information. Importantly, knowledge does not reside in information. Knowledge resides in people. That's why companies hire consultants and why family doctors refer patients to specialists. Unfortunately, it can be quite expensive to employ consultants, specialists, and experts. So companies have begun using two information technologies to capture and share the knowledge

extranets
networks that allow companies to exchange information and conduct transactions with outsiders by providing them direct, web-based access to authorized parts of a company's intranet or information system

knowledge
the understanding that one gains from information

Management Trend:

While it is best known for its Internet search engine—"to google" is even in the Oxford English Dictionary—Google is trying to change the ways people work with information. The Google Docs software suite offers inexpensive, easy access to cloud computing. Rather than a single machine, cloud computing allows files to be stored and edited on the Internet, allowing easy and efficient file-sharing. A new update to Google Docs even allows for multi-author collaboration; up to 50 people can work on the same file at the same time. All of this allows users of Google Docs to build a collaborative work environment in an online setting.

Source: http://bits.blogs.nytimes.com/2010/04/12/new-collaborative-google-docs-unveiled/

of consultants, specialists, and experts with other managers and workers: decision support systems and expert systems.

Whereas an executive information system speeds up and simplifies the acquisition of information, a **decision support system (DSS)** helps managers understand problems and potential solutions by acquiring and analyzing information with sophisticated models and tools.[47] Furthermore, whereas EIS programs are broad in scope and permit managers to retrieve all kinds of information about a company, DSS programs are usually narrow in scope and targeted toward helping managers solve specific kinds of problems. DSS programs have been developed to help managers pick the shortest and most efficient routes for delivery trucks, select the best combination of stocks for investors, and schedule the flow of inventory through complex manufacturing facilities. It's important to understand that DSS programs don't replace managerial decision making—they *improve* it by furthering managers' and workers' understanding of the problems they face and the solutions that might work.

Expert systems are created by capturing the specialized knowledge and decision rules used by experts and experienced decision makers. They permit nonexpert employees to draw on expert knowledge base to make decisions. Most expert systems work by using a collection of "if–then" rules to sort through information and recommend a course of action. For example, let's say that you're using your American Express card to help your spouse celebrate a promotion. After dinner and a movie, the two of you stroll by a travel office with a Las Vegas poster in its window. Thirty minutes later, caught up in the moment, you find yourselves at the airport ticket counter trying to purchase last-minute tickets to Vegas. But there's just one problem. American Express didn't approve your purchase. In fact, the ticket counter agent is now on the phone with an American Express customer service agent.

So what put a temporary halt to your weekend escape to Vegas? An expert system that American Express calls "Authorizer's Assistant."[48] The first "if–then" rule that prevented your purchase was the rule "*if* a purchase is much larger than the cardholder's regular spending habits, *then* deny approval of the purchase." This if–then rule, just one of 3,000, is built into American Express's transaction-processing system that handles thousands of purchase requests per second. Now that the American Express customer service agent is on the line, he or she is prompted by the Authorizer's Assistant to ask the ticket counter agent to examine your identification. You hand over your driver's license and another credit card to prove you're you.

decision support system (DSS) an information system that helps managers understand specific kinds of problems and potential solutions and analyze the impact of different decision options using "what if" scenarios

expert system an information system that contains the specialized knowledge and decision rules used by experts and experienced decision makers so that nonexperts can draw on this knowledge base to make decisions

Then the ticket agent asks for your address, phone number, Social Security number, and your mother's maiden name and relays the information to American Express. Finally, your ticket purchase is approved. Why? Because you met the last series of "if–then" rules. *If* the purchaser can provide proof of identity and *if* the purchaser can provide personal information that isn't common knowledge, *then* approve the purchase.

REVIEW 3

Accessing and Sharing Information and Knowledge

Executive information systems, intranets, and corporate portals facilitate internal sharing and access to company information and transactions. Electronic data interchange, web services, and the Internet allow external groups like suppliers and customers to easily access company information. All three decrease costs by reducing or eliminating data entry, data errors, and paperwork and by speeding up communication. Organizations use decision support systems and expert systems to capture and share specialized knowledge with nonexpert employees.

Management Decision

Switching to the iPad

As part of the antirecession stimulus bill, the federal government allocated $19 billion dollars to subsidize the modernization of medical records. You've been considering making the switch to computer-based records for some time now, and the stimulus funds will certainly make that decision a little easier. But, which system will you buy? You've visited a number of other practices and hospitals to see what they're using, and you've found a dizzying variety—desktops, laptops, PDAs, smartphones, all running different software.

You've heard, though, that Apple's iPad might trump them all. Released in April 2010, Apple's tablet has an elegant design and an operating system that is so easy to use that a widespread YouTube video shows a 2-year-old figuring out how to use it in just 5 minutes. With its great battery life, light weight, and sharp display, many in the medical industry are practically giddy about how the iPad can revolutionize medical records. Already, insurance giant Kaiser Permanente, Harvard Medical Schools, and the prestigious Cedars-Sinai Hospital have conducted trial programs to test the iPad's functionality in medical facilities. Best of all, it's relatively cheap compared to other laptop computers, and it has a low learning curve, since most of the doctors in your practice already use the iPhone.

In addition to getting federal funding, then, the iPad can bring several first-mover advantages for your practice. Your medical records will be consolidated and more efficient than competitors, which will make your entire operation run more smoothly. Patients will have to spend less time waiting for you and your staff to retrieve their charts and review their history. And, it never hurts to have a reputation for being a practice that uses cutting edge technology. But just as you're about to order iPads for everyone in the office, one of your colleagues has some warnings. Do you think that flimsy thing can handle the rigors of a medical setting, he asks? He doesn't think it would last more than a month in a pediatrician's office, much less a hectic emergency room. And what about security? What kind of features does it have that will protect patient confidentiality? And then, he drops this bomb on you: "You know, people who buy first-generation Apple products are suckers. . . ." He reminds you that the first iPhone sold for $600, but had a minimal number of applications. Just 2 months later, the price was cut to $400, and 10 months after that, they sold the iPhone 3G, with faster network access and thousands of more apps, for just $300. Hundreds and thousands of people lined up to buy the new iPhone 4, which they soon discovered had a critical error—it had to be held just right, or the phone would lose its signal. You could buy the iPad now, he says, but why not wait until Apple releases a cheaper, faster iPad with better features? And then, he reminds you that HP, Google, and other competitors will soon be releasing their own tablet computers. What if those are even better for medical records and they become the industry standard? Do we want to be left behind?

Questions

1. Considering the various first-mover and second-mover advantages, would you switch to the iPad or wait?
2. How important is it that the medical records system you select for your practice reflects the industry standard?
3. Do the benefits of having a computerized medical records system outweigh the costs involved in setting that system up?

Sources: Dana Blankenhorn. "Medicine Is The Apple iPad Sweet Spot." *ZDNet*. January 28, 2010. Accessed at http://healthcare.zdnet.com/?p=3257

Martha C. White. "An Apple a Day." *The Big Money.com*. April 7, 2010. Accessed at http://www.thebigmoney.com/articles/0s-1s-and-s/2010/04/07/apple-day

Practice being a Manager

Information Pipeline

Information is the lifeblood of organizations and one of the keys to sustaining a competitive advantage. The tools for processing and sharing information have improved and proliferated rapidly over the past few decades. But growing sophistication has also meant growing challenges in maintaining quality and security across far-flung corporate information systems. And managers increasingly feel deluged by the rising flow of e-mail, text messages, and near-instantaneous reports. To thrive in the information-rich environment of modern business, managers must effectively utilize the various tools available. This exercise will give you an opportunity to consider which tools might work best for a given need.

STEP 1 Get into groups and read the scenario. Your professor will organize you into pairs or groups of three.

Scenario: Suppose that you and your partner(s) are going into business together. Brainstorm about some new ventures that might interest you. Select one of the ideas that seems appealing, and then talk about how you might build a sustainable competitive advantage for your new business. (*Hint:* You may want to review the first few sections of the chapter.) With this initial sketch of your business plan in mind, discuss how you might use information systems and tools to accomplish the following tasks:

- Researching the likely competition that you will face
- Finding out what steps will be required to get the necessary permits, licenses, and/or regulatory approvals to open and maintain your business
- Determining what price you should charge for your product(s) or service(s)
- Deciding what computer and communication equipment you will need to buy to support your new venture
- Recruiting and hiring the best people for available jobs in your new company

STEP 2 Discuss the issues. Discuss how you might develop the information system that your company needs to successfully launch and grow. Be sure to include security issues/concerns in your discussion.

STEP 3 Debrief as a class. What are the major challenges in creating and maintaining a sustainable competitive advantage? What role does information and information technology play in successfully competing with other companies in a given market? Is it possible to secure sensitive information and at the same share information with employees and/or other key stakeholders (suppliers, customers)?

Self Assessment

Computer Comfort

Computers are ubiquitous in modern society, but that does not mean that everyone embraces them. As with any innovation, some people are reluctant to adopt computer technology for whatever reason. How comfortable are you with computer technology?[49] Be candid as you complete the assessment by circling the appropriate responses from 1, strongly disagree, to 5, strongly agree.

1. I hesitate to use a computer for fear of making mistakes that I cannot correct.

   1 2 3 4 5

2. The challenge of learning about computers is exciting.
   1 2 3 4 5
3. I feel apprehensive about using computers.
   1 2 3 4 5
4. I am confident that I can learn computer skills.
   1 2 3 4 5
5. I feel insecure about my ability to interpret a computer printout.
   1 2 3 4 5
6. I look forward to using a computer on my job.
   1 2 3 4 5
7. I have avoided computers because they are unfamiliar and somewhat intimidating to me.
   1 2 3 4 5
8. Learning to operate computers is like learning any new skill—the more you practice, the better you become.
   1 2 3 4 5
9. It scares me to think that I could cause the computer to destroy a large amount of information by hitting the wrong key.
   1 2 3 4 5
10. If given the opportunity, I would like to learn about and use computers.
   1 2 3 4 5
11. I have difficulty in understanding the technical aspects of computers.
   1 2 3 4 5
12. I am sure that with time and practice, I will be as comfortable working with computers as I am working with a typewriter.
   1 2 3 4 5
13. You have to be a genius to understand all the special keys contained on most computer terminals.
   1 2 3 4 5
14. Anyone can learn to use a computer if he or she is patient and motivated.
   1 2 3 4 5
15. I do not think I would be able to learn a computer programming language.
   1 2 3 4 5
16. I feel computers are necessary tools in both educational and work settings.
   1 2 3 4 5
17. I dislike working with machines that are smarter than I am.
   1 2 3 4 5
18. I feel that I will be able to keep up with the advances happening in the computer field.
   1 2 3 4 5
19. I am afraid that if I begin using computers, I will become dependent on them and lose some of my reasoning skills.
   1 2 3 4 5

   TOTAL = ______

SCORING

Reverse scores on even-numbered items. Reverse means, for instance, a 1 becomes a 5; a 4 becomes a 2, and so on. Using the reversed scores and the remaining scores, compute your score for the 19 items by adding up the scores. You can find the interpretation for your score at: logain.cengagebrain.com.

Biz Flix

© GREENLIGHT

The Good Shepherd

In the 2006 film *The Good Shepherd*, Edward Wilson (Matt Damon) is an idealistic young man who values honor, morality, and discretion. As the head of the CIA counterintelligence, Wilson is in charge of covert operations during the Bay of Pigs. The agency suspects that Castro was tipped off about the invasion, and Wilson is looking for the mole. As he investigates, his idealism gives way to something else: distrust of everyone in his office, fueled by Cold War paranoia. In this clip from the movie, Wilson is being briefed in the Technical Services Division on the clues found in a photograph and in a recording of a woman's voice.

What to Watch for and Ask Yourself

1. Which parts of this scene show data?
2. Which parts of this scene show information?
3. These film scenes show the information technology used during the 1960s at the CIA. In what ways do you think this investigation might progress differently with modern technology?

Management Workplace

© CENGAGE LEARNING

Numi Organic Tea

When Brian Durkee shows up at Numi Organic Tea every day to work as the director of operations, he's on a mission to make Numi a worldwide leader in sustainable supply chain management. Setting up and maintaining an efficient enterprise resource planning (ERP) system turned out to be much easier than converting Chinese suppliers to profoundly different farming methods and ways of doing business. Numi had just begun to implement an ERP system with integrated inventory management and accounting when Durkee joined the company. In this video, Durkee explains how Numi is dedicated to sustainable supply chain management, eliminating waste, and using recycled materials.

What to Watch for and Ask Yourself

1. What kinds of challenges does Numi face in managing information?
2. Why was it no longer sufficient for Numi to use programs like Excel and QuickBooks to manage its information?
3. What are some of the advantages Durkee mentions that have come with using the ERP system?

Reel to Real

16

Chapter Sixteen

Managing Service and Manufacturing Operations

OUTLINE

Experience Management

Explore the four levels of learning by doing the simulation module on Operations Management.

© ISTOCKPHOTO.COM/ ANN MARIE KURTZ

Pod Nod

Mini lecture reviews all the learning points in the chapter.

© ISTOCKPHOTO.COM/ MAGNET CREATIVE

Reel to Real

Biz Flix is *In Bruges* and Management Workplace is at Preserve.

© ISTOCKPHOTO.COM/ CRAFTVISION

Self Test

10 quiz questions, 3 exhibit worksheets, and PowerPoints for quick review.

© ISTOCKPHOTO.COM/ DIJITAL FILM

What Would You Do?

JCPenney, Plano, Texas.[1]

The retail sector has been hard hit by the downturn in the economy. Seventy-three thousand retail store sites have closed in the first six months of this year, roughly the same as the 148,000 store sites that closed last year. Not surprisingly, sales at JCPenney, as measured by same-store sales (comparing each store to its sales one year before) have dropped seven quarters in a row. So instead of spending $1 billion to open 50 new stores and renovate 65 existing stores this year, JCPenney will spend $650 million to open 20 new stores and renovate 10 to 15 existing stores.

One of those new stores, however, will be in the Manhattan Mall in midtown New York City, which sits directly over the 33rd Street PATH train station (from New Jersey) and the 34th Street Herald Square subway station, through which 250,000 commuters pass each day. The store site was "dark and menacing" when you first examined it, but after an investment of $84 million it should look great. You were delighted to have been handpicked by the CEO to open and run what should be Penney's highest grossing store, but you're increasingly concerned about the challenges you face. It doesn't help that New York City real estate experts believe that the Manhattan Mall is a "loser." Indeed, despite the prime location, its retailers have struggled. JCPenney will be the mall's new store anchor (or largest store). The first two anchor stores, however, closed. It's your job to make sure that JCPenney is not the third.

Founded in Wyoming in 1902, but now headquartered in Plano, Texas, JCPenney has always emphasized value and conservative fashions. The company expanded aggressively in the 1980s and 1990s and now reports $18.5 billion in revenues, 1,106 stores, and 150,000 employees. Over time, the company's traditional image has proven difficult to change. Recent market research found that while consumers still went to JCPenney for quality and value, they viewed it as a place where their mothers and grandmothers shop. Since most of Manhattan's boutiques and department stores cater to upscale, brand-conscious consumers, it will be difficult to attract and keep customers without high-end brands. As a store manager, you can't fix that on your own. But, you do have upper management's ear. How, you wonder, is management going to persuade popular, upscale brands to begin selling their high-quality products at a traditional store like JCPenney? You need the right inventory in order to succeed.

JCPenney already has stores in New York City's Bronx, Queens, and Staten Island boroughs, but Manhattan presents special challenges that have kept out retailers like Wal-Mart and Target. Storage space is expensive and complicated, as is transporting merchandise from distribution centers to stores. With New York City traffic, you can't just park 18-wheeler semi-trucks on the street and unload them like you do at other locations. Yet, you need to make sure you have the right merchandise in the right quantities in the store at all times while also keeping inventory costs to a minimum. So what can you do to make that work?

Finally, your store sits on some of the most expensive retail space in the United States, which means that you're going to have to generate more sales per square foot than any other JCPenney store. Also, New Yorkers are not known for their patience, and with a potentially heavy flow of customers, you're going to have to make sure that checkout flows smoothly and lines are short—anything over 90 seconds will have customers heading out the door forever. That means more cashiers and cash registers, but that also means higher labor costs, which, per employee, are already much higher in New York City than at other stores. All of these add to the cost of doing business and will lower store profits unless you can offset the additional expenses with higher productivity. You wonder how to do just that.

If you were the manager of JCPenney's new Manhattan sto[r]e in New York, what would you d[o]

As you read in the opening vignette, JCPenney is opening a new store in Midtown Manhattan and faces the challenges of adapting its operations, managing inventory, and improving productivity. In this chapter, you will learn about **operations management**—managing the daily production of goods and services. You will begin by learning about the basics of operations management: productivity and quality. Next, you will read about managing operations, beginning with service operations, turning next to manufacturing operations, and finishing with an examination of the types, measures, costs, and methods for managing inventory.

Managing for Productivity and Quality

Modeled after U.S.-based Southwest Airlines, Ryanair (based in Ireland) achieves dramatically lower prices through aggressive price cutting and much higher productivity. Want a frequent-flier plan? You won't find one at Ryanair. It's too expensive. Want a meal on your flight? Pack a lunch. Ryanair doesn't even serve peanuts because it takes too much time (i.e., expense) to get them out of the seat cushions. Passengers enter and exit the planes using old-fashioned rolling stairs because they're quicker and cheaper than extendable boarding gates. As a result of such cost-cutting moves, Ryanair does more with less and thus has higher productivity. Most airlines break even on their flights when they're 75 percent full, but Ryanair's

operations management managing the daily production of goods and services

productivity allows it to break even when its planes are only half full, even with its incredibly low prices. With this low break-even point, Ryanair attracts plenty of customers who enable it to fill most of its seats (84 percent) and earn 20 percent net profit margins. Finally, because of its extremely low prices (and its competitors' much higher prices), Ryanair has increased passenger traffic and profits for 19 straight years. Ryanair is the third-largest airline in Europe in terms of passenger numbers and the world's largest in terms of international passenger numbers.[2]

After reading the next two sections, you should be able to:

1 discuss the kinds of productivity and their importance in managing operations.

2 explain the role that quality plays in managing operations.

1 Productivity

At their core, organizations are production systems. Companies combine inputs such as labor, raw materials, capital, and knowledge to produce outputs in the form of finished products or services. **Productivity** is a measure of performance that indicates how many inputs it takes to produce or create an output.

$$\text{Productivity} = \frac{\text{Outputs}}{\text{Inputs}}$$

The fewer inputs it takes to create an output (or the greater the output from one input), the higher the productivity. For example, a car's gas mileage is a common measure of productivity. A car that gets 35 miles (output) per gallon (input) is more productive and fuel efficient than a car that gets 18 miles per gallon.

Let's examine 1.1 **why productivity matters**, and 1.2 **the different kinds of productivity**.

1.1 Why Productivity Matters

Why does productivity matter? For companies, higher productivity—that is, doing more with less—results in lower costs for the company, lower prices for consumers, faster service, higher market share, and higher profits. For example, every second saved in the drive-through lane at a fast-food restaurant increases sales by 1 percent. Furthermore, increasing the efficiency of drive-through service by 10 percent adds nearly 10 percent to a fast-food restaurant's sales. And with up to 75 percent of all fast-food restaurant sales coming from the drive-through window, it's no wonder that Wendy's (average drive-through time of 131 seconds per vehicle), Burger King (average time of 153 seconds per vehicle), and McDonald's (average time of 167.1 seconds per vehicle) continue to look for ways to shorten the time it takes to process a drive-through order.[3]

The productivity of businesses within a country matters to that country because it results in a higher standard of living. One way productivity leads to a higher standard of living is through increased wages. When companies can do more with less, they can raise employee wages without increasing prices or sacrificing normal profits. Thanks to long-term increases in business productivity, the average American family today earns 37 percent more than the average family in 1980 and 65 percent more than the average family in 1967—and that's after accounting for inflation.[4]

productivity
a measure of performance that indicates how many inputs it takes to produce or create an output

Rising income stemming from increased productivity creates other benefits as well. Productivity increased an average of 2.7 percent between 1995 and 2002, and then slowed to an average of 1.4 percent from 2005 to 2007.[5] And, from 1996 to 2006, the U.S. economy created nearly 17.5 million new jobs.[6] And when more people have jobs that pay more, they give more to charity. For example, in 2007 Americans donated over $306 billion to charities, 3.9 percent more than they gave in 2006.

Another benefit of productivity is that it makes products more affordable or better. For example, while inflation has pushed the average cost of a car to about $28,929 (after incentives and discounts), increases in productivity have actually made cars cheaper.[7] In 1960, the average family needed 26 weeks of income to pay for the average car. Today, the average family needs only 24.1 weeks of income—and today's car is loaded with accessories that weren't even available in 1960, including air bags, power steering and brakes, power windows, cruise control, stereo/CD/DVD players, seat warmers, air-conditioning, and satellite navigation.[8] So, in terms of real purchasing power, productivity gains have actually made today's $28,929 car cheaper than a $2,000 car in 1960.[9]

1.2 Kinds of Productivity

Two common measures of productivity are partial productivity and multifactor productivity. **Partial productivity** indicates how much of a particular kind of input it takes to produce an output.

$$\text{Partial Productivity} = \frac{\text{Outputs}}{\text{Single Kind of Input}}$$

Labor is one kind of input that is frequently used when determining partial productivity. *Labor productivity* typically indicates the cost or number of hours of labor it takes to produce an output. In other words, the lower the cost of the labor to produce a unit of output, or the less time it takes to produce a unit of output, the higher the labor productivity. For example, the automobile industry often measures labor productivity by determining the average number of hours of labor needed to completely assemble a car. According to the most recent Harbour Report, the three Detroit-based automakers have reached near parity with their Japanese rivals in manufacturing efficiency. Toyota and Chrysler assemble a car in 30.37 hours, Honda in 31.33 hours, GM in 32.29 hours, Nissan in 32.96 hours, and Ford in 33.88 hours. The gap between the most and least productive automakers has narrowed from 10.51 labor hours in 2003 to just 3.5 labor hours in 2008.[10] Partial productivity assesses how efficiently companies use only one input, such as labor, when creating outputs. Multifactor productivity is an overall measure of productivity that assesses how efficiently companies use all the inputs it takes to make outputs. More specifically, **multifactor productivity** indicates how much labor, capital, materials, and energy it takes to produce an output.[11]

partial productivity
a measure of performance that indicates how much of a particular kind of input it takes to produce an output

multifactor productivity
an overall measure of performance that indicates how much labor, capital, materials, and energy it takes to produce an output

$$\text{Multifactor Productivity} = \frac{\text{Outputs}}{\text{Labor} + \text{Capital} + \text{Materials} + \text{Energy}}$$

Exhibit 16.1 shows the trends in multifactor productivity across a number of U.S. industries from 1987 to 2007. With a 182 percent increase between 1997 (scaled at 100) and 2006 (when it reached a level of 282) and a tenfold increase since 1987, the growth in multifactor productivity in the computer and electronic products industry far exceeded the productivity growth in retail stores, auto manufacturing, mining,

EXHIBIT 16.1

Multifactor Productivity Growth Across Industries

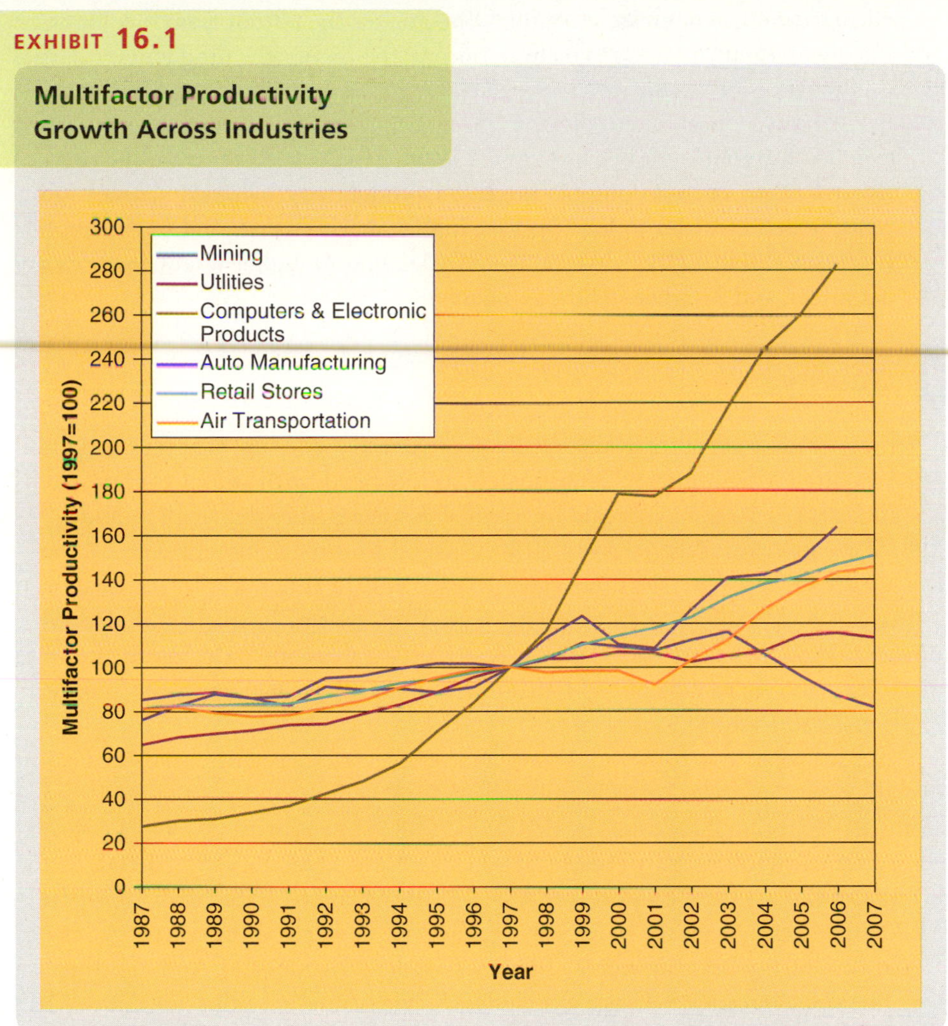

Source: "Productivity and Costs," Bureau of Labor Statistics, available at http://data.bls.gov/cgi-bin/surveymost?ip, 1 July 2005.

utilities, and air transportation as well as most other industries tracked by the U.S. government.

Should managers use multiple or partial productivity measures? In general, they should use both. Multifactor productivity indicates a company's overall level of productivity relative to its competitors. In the end, that's what counts most. However, multifactor productivity measures don't indicate the specific contributions that labor, capital, materials, or energy make to overall productivity. To analyze the contributions of these individual components, managers need to use partial productivity measures. Doing so can help them determine what factors need to be adjusted or in what areas adjustment can make the most difference in overall productivity.

REVIEW 1

Productivity

At their core, companies are production systems that combine inputs (such as labor), raw materials, capital, and knowledge to produce outputs (such as finished products or services). Productivity is a measure of how many inputs it takes to produce or create an output. The greater the output from one input, or the fewer inputs it takes to create an output, the higher the productivity. Partial productivity measures how much of a single kind of input (such as labor) is needed to produce an output. Multifactor productivity is an overall measure of productivity that indicates how much labor, capital, materials, and energy are needed to produce an output. Increased productivity helps companies lower costs, which can lead to lower prices, higher market share, and higher profits. Increased productivity helps countries by leading to higher wages, lower product prices, and a higher standard of living.

2 Quality

With the average car costing $28,929, buyers want to make sure that they're getting good quality for their money.[12] Fortunately, as indicated by the number of problems per 100 cars (PP100), today's cars are of much higher quality than earlier models. In 1981, Japanese cars averaged 240 PP100, General Motors' cars averaged 670, Ford's averaged 740, and Chrysler's averaged 870 PP100! In other words, the quality of American cars was two to three times worse than that of Japanese cars. By 1992, however, U.S. carmakers had made great strides, significantly reducing the number of problems to an average of 155 PP100. Japanese vehicles had improved, too, averaging just 125 PP100.

According to the 2009 J.D. Power and Associates survey of initial car quality, overall quality improved to 108 problems per 100 vehicles (PP100) in 2009, down from 125 PP100 in 2007 and 118 PP100 in 2008.[13] Lexus, with just 84 PP100, had the best quality, followed by Porsche at 90 PP100 and Hyundai at 95 PP100. At the bottom of the list were Land Rover, with 150 PPM, and Cooper, with 165 PP100. In 2009, however, even the worst cars on the J.D. Power and Associates Survey of Initial Car quality beat the scores of Japanese cars of decades ago. And high-quality cars like the Mercedes S-Class and Audi A8 even came in with scores under 100 (72 to be exact). That means there's less than one problem per car![14] The American Society for Quality gives two meanings for **quality**. It can mean a product or service free of deficiencies, such as the number of problems per 100 cars, or it can mean the characteristics of a product or service that satisfy customer needs.[15] Today's cars are of higher quality than those produced 20 years ago in both senses. Not only do they have fewer problems per 100 cars, they also have a number of additional standard features that were not available in the past (power brakes and steering, stereo/CD/MP3 player, power windows and locks, air bags, cruise control).

In this part of the chapter, you will learn about 2.1 **quality-related characteristics for products and services**, 2.2 **ISO 9000 and 14000**, 2.3 **the Baldrige National Quality Award**, and 2.4 **total quality management**.

2.1 Quality-Related Characteristics for Products and Services

quality
a product or service free of deficiencies, or the characteristics of a product or service that satisfy customer needs

Quality products usually possess three characteristics: reliability, serviceability, and durability.[16] A breakdown occurs when a product quits working or doesn't do what it was designed to do. The longer it takes for a product to break down, or the longer the time between breakdowns, the more reliable the product. Consequently, many companies define *product reliability* in terms of the average time between breakdowns.

Serviceability refers to how easy or difficult it is to fix a product. The easier it is to maintain a working product or fix a broken product, the more serviceable that product is. The REVA is an electric two-seater car built in India for city use. It goes 50 miles on a single battery charge (a recharge takes just 5 hours), and its operating costs per mile are one-third those of a typical gasoline-powered car. The REVA has high serviceability by virtue of a computerized diagnostic system that plugs into a portable electronic tool (PET) about the size of a smartphone that assesses how well the car is running. Because the PET can be linked to a phone, customers can easily transmit their REVA's operational history to instantly find out if their car needs work and, if so, what kind.[17]

A product breakdown assumes that a product can be repaired. However, some products don't break down; they fail. *Product failure* means products can't be repaired. They can only be replaced. *Durability* is defined as the mean time to failure. Typically, for example, when an LCD screen quits working, it "dies" and can't be repaired. Consequently, durability, or the average time before failure, is a key part of LCD quality. Why buy a great-looking LCD if it's only going to last a few years? Indeed, Toshiba is now producing thin-film transistor LCDs with a mean time between failures of 100,000 hours, or 11.4 years.[18]

While high-quality products are characterized by reliability, serviceability, and durability, services are different. There's no point in assessing the durability of a service because services don't last but are consumed the minute they're performed. For example, once a lawn service has mowed your lawn, the job is done until the mowers come back next week to do it again. Services also don't have serviceability. You can't maintain or fix a service. If a service wasn't performed correctly the first time, all you can do is perform it again. Rather than serviceability and durability, the quality of service interactions often depends on how the service provider interacts with the customer. Was the service provider friendly, rude, or helpful?

Five characteristics typically distinguish a quality service: reliability, tangibles, responsiveness, assurance, and empathy.[19] *Service reliability* is the ability to consistently perform a service well. Studies clearly show that reliability matters more to customers than anything else when buying services. When you take your clothes to the dry cleaner, you don't want them returned with cracked buttons or wrinkles down the front. If your dry cleaner gives you back perfectly clean and pressed clothes every time, it's providing a reliable service.

Although services themselves are not tangible (you can't see or touch them), they are provided in tangible places. Thus, *tangibles* refer to the appearance of the offices, equipment, and personnel involved with the delivery of a service. One of the best examples of the effect of tangibles on the perception of quality is the restroom. When you eat at a fancy restaurant, you expect clean, if not upscale, restrooms. How different is your perception of a business, say a gas station, if it has clean restrooms rather than filthy ones?

Responsiveness is the promptness and willingness with which service providers give good service (your dry cleaner returning your laundry perfectly clean and pressed in a day or an hour). *Assurance* is the confidence that service providers are knowledgeable, courteous, and trustworthy. *Empathy* is the extent to which service providers give individual attention and care to customers' concerns and problems.

EMC Corporation makes highly reliable computers that are used by some of the largest companies in the world, including banks, phone companies, and auto

Management Trend:

There are several elements that constitute good internal service quality. For employees to do a good job serving customers, management must implement policies and procedures that support good customer service; provide workers the tools and training they need to do their jobs; reward, recognize, and support good customer service; facilitate communication; and encourage people and departments to work together as teams to accomplish company goals with respect to internal service quality and customer service. For example, companies that reward employees for low rates of customer complaints unwittingly encourage those employees to ignore dissatisfied customers so that their problems aren't acknowledged and counted (which would endanger employee bonuses).

manufacturers. If EMC's equipment goes down for even a few minutes, its customers can lose millions from vanished sales. Although its equipment is incredibly reliable, what distinguishes EMC from its competition is the level of service it provides when problems do occur. In other words, EMC is a standout performer in *service reliability*, the ability to consistently perform a service well. Because of its excellent service, EMC retains an amazing 99 percent of its customers from year to year.

EMC also excels in *responsiveness*, the promptness and willingness with which service providers give good service. When a Wisconsin bank lost access to all its data (no account numbers, no deposits, no withdrawals—nada!), which were stored on an EMC machine, EMC service engineers were on the problem within minutes. (EMC's computers "call home" automatically whenever a problem arises.) In 4 hours, EMC created a setup identical to the bank's in a $1 billion facility designed for such purposes. There, EMC engineers identified the problem and put together a software patch that had the bank up and running by the end of the day.[20]

EMC also provides quality service by virtue of clear *assurance* that it can be trusted. Every customer knows that the company follows a disciplined procedure for addressing customer problems.[21] Finally, EMC provides quality service because of the *empathy* it has for its customers' problems. Early in the company's history, its customers' businesses were suffering because EMC could not figure out why one of its best-selling systems had unexpectedly become unreliable. Rather than make excuses or empty promises, EMC gave its customers the choice between a brand-new EMC computer system or a similar system, made by EMC's competitor, IBM. At the height of its problems, EMC installed more of IBM's machines than its own.[22]

Consistent with its dedication to service reliability, *Fortune* magazine ranks EMC as the only technology company among the World's 10 Most Admired Companies for Product and Service Quality and was named "Industry Champion" as the most admired company in the technology industry for two straight years.[23]

ISO 9000
a series of five international standards, from ISO 9000 to ISO 9004, for achieving consistency in quality management and quality assurance in companies throughout the world

2.2 ISO 9000 and 14000

ISO, pronounced *eye-so*, comes from the Greek word *isos*, meaning "equal, similar, alike, or identical" and is also an acronym for the *INTERNATIONAL ORGANIZATION FOR STANDARDIZATION*, which helps set standards for 162 countries. The purpose of this agency is to develop and publish standards that facilitate the international exchange of goods and services.[24] **ISO 9000** is a series of five international standards, from ISO 9000 to ISO 9004, for achieving consistency in quality management and quality assurance in companies throughout the world. **ISO 14000** is a series of international standards for managing, monitoring, and minimizing an organization's harmful effects on the environment.[25] (For more on environmental quality and issues, see Section 3.5 of Chapter 14 on controlling waste and pollution.)

The ISO 9000 and 14000 standards publications, which are available from the American National Standards Institute (see the end of this section), are general and can be used for manufacturing any kind of product or delivering any kind of service. Importantly, the ISO 9000 standards don't describe how to make a better-quality car, computer, or widget. Instead, they describe how companies can extensively document (and thus standardize) the steps they take to create and improve the quality of their products. Studies show that customers clearly prefer to buy from companies that are ISO 9000 certified.[26]

To become ISO certified, a process that can take months, a company must show that it is following its own procedures for improving production, updating design plans and specifications, keeping machinery in top condition, educating and training workers, and satisfactorily dealing with customer complaints.[27] An accredited third party oversees the ISO certification process, just as a certified public accountant verifies that a company's financial accounts are up-to-date and accurate. Once a company has been certified as ISO 9000 compliant, the accredited third party will issue an ISO 9000 certificate that the company can use in its advertising and publications. This is the quality equivalent of the *Good Housekeeping* Seal of Approval. But continued ISO 9000 certification is not guaranteed. Accredited third parties typically conduct periodic audits to make sure the company is still following quality procedures. If it is not, its certification is suspended or canceled.

To get additional information on ISO 9000 guidelines and procedures, see the American National Standards Institute (***http://www.webstoreansi.org***; the ISO 9000 and ISO 14000 standards publications are available here for about $400 and $300, respectively), the American Society for Quality (***http://www.asq.org***), and the International Organization for Standardization (***http://www.iso.org***).

2.3 Baldrige National Quality Award

The Baldrige National Quality Award, which is administered by the U.S. government's National Institute for Standards and Technology, is given "to recognize U.S. companies for their achievements in quality and business performance and to raise awareness about the importance of quality and performance excellence as a competitive edge."[28] Each year, up to three awards may be given in these categories: manufacturing, service, small business, education, and health care.

The cost of applying for the Baldrige Award includes a $150 eligibility fee, an application fee of $7,000 for manufacturing firms and $3,500 for small businesses, and a site visitation fee of $20,000 to $35,000 for manufacturing firms and $10,000 to $17,000 for small businesses.[29] Why does it cost so much? Because you get a great deal of useful information about your business even if you don't win. At minimum, each company that applies receives an extensive report based on 300 hours of assessment from at least eight business and quality experts. At $10 an hour for small businesses and about $20 an hour for manufacturing and service businesses, the *Journal for Quality and Participation* called the Baldrige feedback report "the best bargain in consulting in America."[30]

ISO 14000
a series of international standards for managing, monitoring, and minimizing an organization's harmful effects on the environment

Businesses that apply for the Baldrige Award are judged on a 1,000-point scale based on the seven criteria shown in Exhibit 16.2.[31] The most important category is "Results," as it takes up 450 out of 1,000 points. In other words, in addition to the six other criteria, companies must show that they have achieved superior quality when it comes to products and services, customers, financial performance and market share, treatment of employees, work systems and processes, and leadership

EXHIBIT 16.2

Criteria for the Baldrige National Quality Award

	2009 Categories/Items	Point Values
1	**Leadership**	120
	Senior Leadership	70
	Governance and Societal Responsibilities	50
2	**Strategic Planning**	85
	Strategy Development	40
	Strategy Deployment	45
3	**Customer Focus**	85
	Customer Engagement	40
	Voice of the Customer	45
4	**Measurement, Analysis, and Knowledge Management**	90
	Measurement, Analysis, and Improvement of Organizational Performance	45
	Management of Information, Knowledge, and Information Technology	45
5	**Workforce Focus**	85
	Workforce Engagement	45
	Workforce Environment	40
6	**Process Management**	85
	Work Systems	35
	Work Processes	50
7	**Results**	450
	Product Outcomes	100
	Customer-Focused Outcomes	70
	Financial and Market Outcomes	70
	Workforce-Focused Outcomes	70
	Process Effectiveness Outcomes	70
	Leadership Outcomes	70
	TOTAL POINTS	1,000

Source: "Criteria for Performance Excellence," 2009–2010 Baldrige National Quality Program available online at http://www.quality.nist.gov/PDF_files/2009–2010_Business_Nonprofit_Criteria.pdf [accessed 12 September 2009].

and social responsibility. This emphasis on results is what differentiates the Baldrige Award from the ISO 9000 standards. The Baldrige Award indicates the extent to which companies have actually achieved world-class quality. The ISO 9000 standards simply indicate whether a company is following the management system it put into place to improve quality. In fact, ISO 9000 certification covers less than 10 percent of the requirements for the Baldridge Award.[32] Most companies that apply for the Baldridge Award do so to grow, prosper, and stay competitive. Furthermore, the companies that have won the Baldrige Award have achieved superior financial returns. Since 1988, an investment in Baldrige Award winners would have outperformed the Standard & Poor's 500 stock index 80 percent of the time.[33] For additional information about the Baldrige Award, see the National Institute of Standards and Technology website at ***http://www.quality.nist.gov***.

2.4 Total Quality Management

Total quality management (TQM) is an integrated, organization-wide strategy for improving product and service quality.[34] TQM is not a specific tool or technique. Rather, TQM is a philosophy or overall approach to management that is characterized by three principles: customer focus and satisfaction, continuous improvement, and teamwork.[35]

Although most economists, accountants, and financiers argue that companies exist to earn profits for shareholders, TQM suggests that customer focus and customer satisfaction should be a company's primary goals. **Customer focus** means that the entire organization, from top to bottom, should be focused on meeting customers' needs. The result of that customer focus should be **customer satisfaction**, which occurs when the company's products or services meet or exceed customers' expectations.

At companies where TQM is taken seriously, such as Enterprise Rent-A-Car, paychecks and promotions depend on keeping customers satisfied.[36] Enterprise measures customer satisfaction with a detailed survey called the Enterprise Service Quality index. Enterprise not only ranks each branch office by operating profits and customer satisfaction but also makes promotions to higher-paying jobs contingent on above-average customer satisfaction scores.

Continuous improvement is an ongoing commitment to increase product and service quality by constantly assessing and improving the processes and procedures used to create those products and services. How do companies know whether they're achieving continuous improvement? Besides higher customer satisfaction, continuous improvement is usually associated with a reduction in variation. **Variation** is a deviation in the form, condition, or appearance of a product from the quality standard for that product. The less a product varies from the quality standard, or the more consistently a company's products meet a quality standard, the higher the quality.

At Freudenberg-NOK, a manufacturer of seals and gaskets for the automotive industry, continuous improvement means shooting for a goal of Six Sigma quality, meaning just 3.4 defective or nonstandard parts per million (PPM). Achieving this goal would eliminate almost all product variation. In a recent year, Freudenberg-NOK made over 200 million seals and gaskets with a defect rate of 9 PPM.[37] This figure represents a significant improvement from just 7 years ago, when Freudenberg-NOK was averaging 650 defective PPM.

The third principle of TQM is teamwork. **Teamwork** means collaboration between managers and nonmanagers, across business functions, and between the company and its customers and suppliers. In short, quality improves when everyone

total quality management (TQM)
an integrated, principle-based, organization-wide strategy for improving product and service quality

customer focus
an organizational goal to concentrate on meeting customers' needs at all levels of the organization

customer satisfaction
an organizational goal to provide products or services that meet or exceed customers' expectations

continuous improvement
an organization's ongoing commitment to constantly assess and improve the processes and procedures used to create products and services

variation
a deviation in the form, condition, or appearance of a product from the quality standard for that product

teamwork
collaboration between managers and nonmanagers, across business functions, and between companies, customers, and suppliers

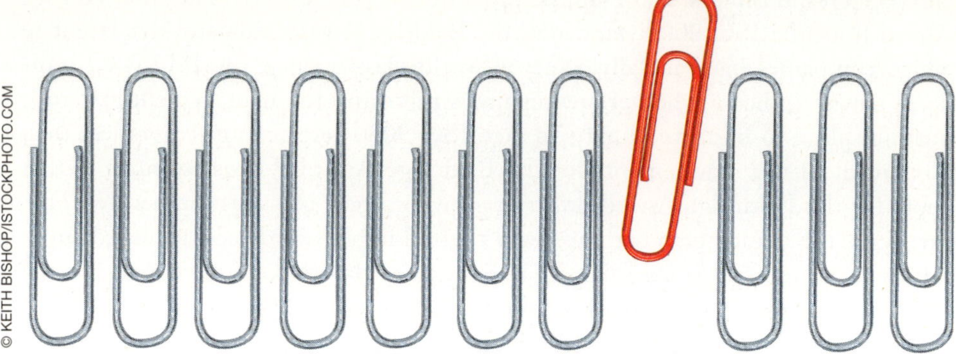

© KEITH BISHOP/ISTOCKPHOTO.COM

Reduction in variation is typically associated with even (and higher) quality. The pinnacle is achieving only 3.4 nonconforming parts per million which indicates attainment of Six Sigma.

in the company is given the incentive to work together and the responsibility and authority to make improvements and solve problems. At Valassis, a printing company long famous for its use of teams, management turned to employees for suggestions when business fell during a recession. Teams offered so many ideas to cut costs and raise quality that the company was able to avoid layoffs.[38]

Customer focus and satisfaction, continuous improvement, and teamwork mutually reinforce each other to improve quality throughout a company. Customer-focused continuous improvement is necessary to increase customer satisfaction. At the same time, continuous improvement depends on teamwork from different functional and hierarchical parts of the company.

REVIEW 2

Quality

Quality can refer to a product or service free of deficiencies or the characteristics of a product or service that satisfy customer needs. Quality products usually possess three characteristics: reliability, serviceability, and durability. Quality service involves reliability, tangibles, responsiveness, assurance, and empathy. ISO 9000 is a series of five international standards for achieving consistency in quality management and quality assurance; ISO 14000 is a set of standards for minimizing an organization's harmful effects on the environment. The ISO 9000 standards can be used for any product or service because they ensure that companies carefully document the steps they take to create and improve quality. ISO 9000 certification is awarded following a quality audit from an accredited third party. The Baldrige National Quality Award recognizes U.S. companies for their achievements in quality and business performance. Each year, up to three Baldrige Awards may be given for manufacturing, service, small business, education, and health care. Companies that apply for the Baldrige Award are judged on a 1,000-point scale based on leadership, strategic planning, customer focus, measurement, analysis, and knowledge management, work force focus, process management, and results. Total quality management (TQM) is an integrated, organization-wide strategy for improving product and service quality. TQM is based on three mutually reinforcing principles: customer focus and satisfaction, continuous improvement, and teamwork.

Managing Operations

At the start of this chapter, you learned that operations management means managing the daily production of goods and services. Then you learned that, to manage production, you must oversee the factors that affect productivity and quality. In this half of the chapter, you will learn about managing operations in service and manufacturing businesses. The chapter ends with a discussion of inventory management, a key factor in a company's profitability.

After reading the next three sections, you should be able to:

3 explain the essentials of managing a service business.

4 describe the different kinds of manufacturing operations.

3 Service Operations

Imagine that your trusty TIVO digital video recorder (DVR) breaks down as you try to record your favorite TV show. You've got two choices. You can run to Wal-Mart and spend $250 to purchase a new DVR, or you can spend less (you hope) to have it fixed at a repair shop. Either way, you end up with the same thing, a working DVR. However, the first choice, getting a new DVR, involves buying a physical product (a good), while the second, dealing with a repair shop, involves buying a service.

Services differ from goods in several ways. First, goods are produced or made, but services are performed. In other words, services are almost always labor-intensive; someone typically has to perform the service for you. A repair shop could give you the parts needed to repair your old DVR, but you're still going to have a broken DVR. Second, goods are tangible, but services are intangible. You can touch and see that new DVR, but you can't touch or see the service provided by the technician who fixed your old DVR. All you can "see" is that the DVR works. Third, services are perishable and unstorable. If you don't use them when they're available, they're wasted. For example, if your DVR repair shop is backlogged on repair jobs, then you'll just have to wait until next week to get your DVR repaired. You can't store an unused service and use it when you like. By contrast, you can purchase a good, such as motor oil, and store it until you're ready to use it. Finally, services account for 59 percent of gross national product, whereas manufacturing accounts for only 30.8 percent.[39]

Because services are different from goods, managing a service operation is different from managing a manufacturing or production operation.

Let's look at 3.1 **the service-profit chain**, and 3.2 **service recovery and empowerment**.

3.1 The Service-Profit Chain

One of the key assumptions in the service business is that success depends on how well employees—that is, service providers—deliver their services to customers. But success actually begins with how well management treats service employees, as the service-profit chain, depicted in Exhibit 16.3, demonstrates.[40]

The key concept behind the service-profit chain is *internal service quality*, meaning the quality of treatment that employees receive from a company's internal service providers, such as management, payroll and benefits, human resources, and so forth. For example, *HCL TECHNOLOGIES*, an India-based technology services company,

EXHIBIT 16.3

Service-Profit Chain

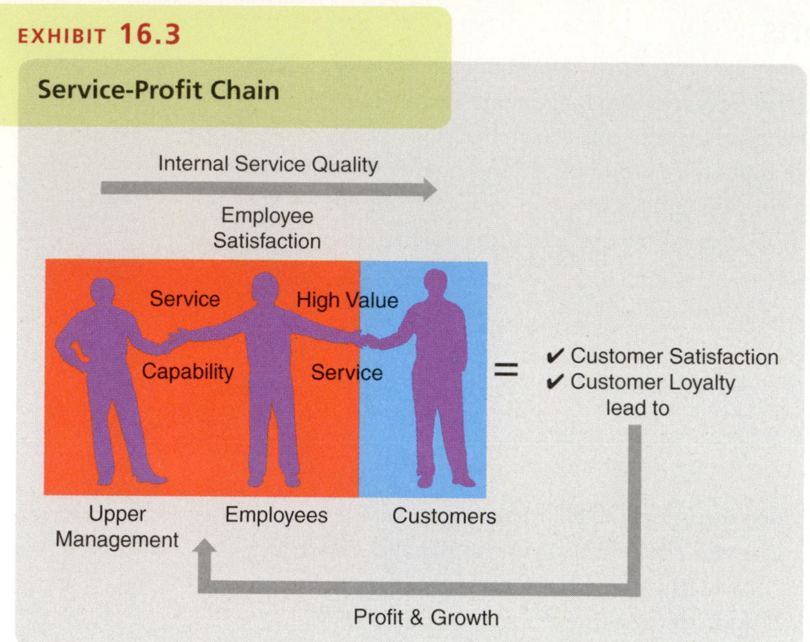

Sources: R. Hallowell, L. A. Schlesinger, & J. Zornitsky, "Internal Service Quality, Customer and Job Satisfaction: Linkages and Implications for Management," *Human Resource Planning* 19 (1996): 20–31; J. L. Heskett, T. O. Jones, G. W. Loveman, W. E. Sasser, Jr., & L. A. Schlesinger, "Putting the Service-Profit Chain to Work," *Harvard Business Review*, March–April 1994, 164–174.

created an "Employee First" strategy to increase employee satisfaction with internal service quality, meaning the way they are treated by others in the company. One way in which HCL encourages better treatment of its employees is its online "smart service desk," where employees file "tickets" or complaints about any issue in the company, from overly cold air-conditioning to food sold in the cafeteria. And, to make sure the "smart service desk" matters, only employees who have filed the "tickets" can close them, and tickets remain open until employees feel that their problems and issues have been fairly addressed.

As depicted in Exhibit 16.3, good internal service leads to employee satisfaction and service capability. *Employee satisfaction* occurs when companies treat employees in a way that meets or exceeds their expectations. In other words, the better employees are treated, the more satisfied they are, and the more likely they are to give high-value service that satisfies customers. How employers treat employees is important because it affects service capability. *Service capability* is an employee's perception of his or her ability to serve customers well. When an organization serves its employees in ways that help them to do their jobs well, employees, in turn, are more likely to believe that they can and ought to provide high-value service to customers.

Finally, according to the service-profit chain shown in Exhibit 16.3, *high-value service* leads to *customer satisfaction* and *customer loyalty*, which, in turn, lead to *long-term profits and growth*.[41] What's the link between customer satisfaction and loyalty and profits? To start, the average business keeps only 70 to 90 percent of its existing customers each year. No big deal, you say? Just replace leaving customers with new customers. Well, there's one significant problem with that solution. It costs ten times as much to find a new customer as it does to keep an existing customer. Also, new customers typically buy only 20 percent as much as established customers. In fact, keeping existing customers is so cost-effective that most businesses could double their profits by simply keeping 5 percent more customers per year![42] How does this work? Imagine that keeping more of your customers turns some of those customers into customers for life? How much of a difference would that make to company profits? Consider that just one lifetime customer spends $8,000 on pizza and over $330,000 on luxury cars![43]

3.2 Service Recovery and Empowerment

service recovery
restoring customer satisfaction to strongly dissatisfied customers

When mistakes are made, when problems occur, and when customers become dissatisfied with the service they've received, service businesses must switch from the process of service delivery to the process of **service recovery**, or restoring customer satisfaction to strongly dissatisfied customers.[44] Service recovery sometimes requires service employees not only to fix whatever mistake was made but also perform heroic service acts that delight highly dissatisfied customers by surpassing their expectations of fair treatment. When accountant Tom Taylor checked into his room at a Hampton Inn in Greenville, South Carolina, he wasn't happy. The company website had given him incorrect directions. The lights in his room weren't plugged in. The shower controls were backward—"hot" was cold and "cold" was hot—and the air-conditioning was malfunctioning, so his room was freezing cold. When he complained, the employee at the front desk immediately offered him two free nights of lodging.[45]

Doing the Right Thing

Protect Your Frontline Staff: The Customer Isn't Always Right

In 1909, Harry Gordon Selfridge, an American who founded London's famous Selfridge department store, coined the phrase "The customer is always right." But, even though managers and employees should do what they can to provide great service and make up for mistakes with great service recovery, the customer isn't always right. Companies should "fire" customers who use foul language, make threats against employees or other customers, demand unethical or illegal service, try to bully frontline employees into granting special favors, or are just generally belligerent. Management consultant John Curtis says, "If you don't [fire those customers], you're telling your employees and your other customers that you care more about money than the safety of the people in the business." So, do the right thing. Protect your frontline staff by telling bad customers that you won't tolerate these kinds of behavior. Ask them to leave. Close their accounts. Inform them that they'll need to go elsewhere.[46]

Unfortunately, when mistakes occur, service employees often don't have the discretion to resolve customer complaints. Customers who want service employees to correct or make up for poor service are frequently told, "I'm not allowed to do that," "I'm just following company rules," or "I'm sorry, only managers are allowed to make changes of any kind." In other words, company rules prevent them from engaging in acts of service recovery meant to turn dissatisfied customers back into satisfied customers. The result is frustration for customers and service employees and lost customers for the company.

Now, however, many companies are empowering their service employees.[47] In Chapter 8, you learned that *empowering workers* means permanently passing decision-making authority and responsibility from managers to workers. With respect to service recovery, empowering workers means giving service employees the authority and responsibility to make decisions that immediately solve customer problems.[48] At Hampton Inn, all employees are empowered to solve customer problems. Senior vice president Phil Cordell says, "You don't have to call an 800 number. Just mention it at the front desk or to any employee—a housekeeper, maintenance person or breakfast hostess—and, on the spot, your stay is free."[49] Similarly, all of the front-desk employees at Ritz-Carlton Hotels are authorized to credit up to $2,000 to a dissatisfied customer's account. Empowering service workers does entail some costs, although they are usually less than the company's savings from retaining customers.

REVIEW 3

Service Operations

Services are different from goods. Goods are produced, tangible, and storable. Services are performed, intangible, and perishable. Likewise, managing service operations is different from managing production operations. The service-profit chain indicates that success begins with internal service quality, or how well management treats service employees. Internal service quality leads to employee satisfaction and service capability, which, in turn, lead to high-value service to customers, customer satisfaction, customer loyalty, and long-term profits and growth. Keeping existing customers is far more cost-effective than finding new ones. Consequently, to prevent disgruntled customers from leaving, some companies are empowering service employees to perform service recovery—restoring customer satisfaction to strongly dissatisfied customers—by giving them the authority and responsibility to immediately solve customer problems. The hope is that empowered service recovery will prevent customer defections.

4 Manufacturing Operations

Ford makes cars and Dell makes computers. BP produces gasoline, whereas Sherwin-Williams makes paint. Boeing makes jet planes, but Budweiser makes beer. Maxtor makes hard drives, and Maytag makes appliances. The *manufacturing operations* of these companies all produce physical goods, but not all manufacturing operations, especially these, are the same.

Let's learn how various manufacturing operations differ in terms of 4.1 **the amount of processing that is done to produce and assemble a product**, 4.2 **the different types of inventory**, 4.3 **how to measure inventory levels**, 4.4 **the costs of maintaining an inventory**, and 4.5 **the different systems for managing inventory**.

4.1 Amount of Processing in Manufacturing Operations

As Exhibit 16.4 shows, manufacturing operations can be classified according to the amount of processing or assembly that occurs after a customer order is received. The highest degree of processing occurs in **make-to-order operations**. A make-to-order operation does not start processing or assembling products until it receives a customer order. In fact, some make-to-order operations may not even order parts until a customer order is received. Not surprisingly, make-to-order operations produce or assemble highly specialized or customized products for customers.

For example, *DELL* has one of the most advanced make-to-order operations in the computer business. Because Dell has no finished goods inventory and no component parts inventory, its computers always have the latest, most advanced components, and Dell can pass on price cuts to customers. Plus, Dell can customize all of its orders, big and small. So whether you're ordering 5,000 personal computers for your company or just 1 personal computer for your home, Dell doesn't make the computers until you order them.

make-to-order operation
a manufacturing operation that does not start processing or assembling products until a customer order is received

A moderate degree of processing occurs in **assemble-to-order operations**. A company using an assemble-to-order operation divides its manufacturing or assembly process into separate parts or modules. The company orders parts and assembles modules ahead of customer orders. Then, based on actual customer orders or research forecasting what customers will want, those modules are combined to create semicustomized products. For example, when a customer orders a new car, General Motors may have already ordered the basic parts or modules it needs from suppliers. In other words, based on sales forecasts, GM may already have ordered enough tires, air-conditioning compressors, brake systems, and seats from suppliers to accommodate nearly all customer orders on a particular day. Special orders from customers and car dealers are then used to determine the final assembly checklist for particular cars as they move down the assembly line.

EXHIBIT **16.4**

Processing in Manufacturing Operations

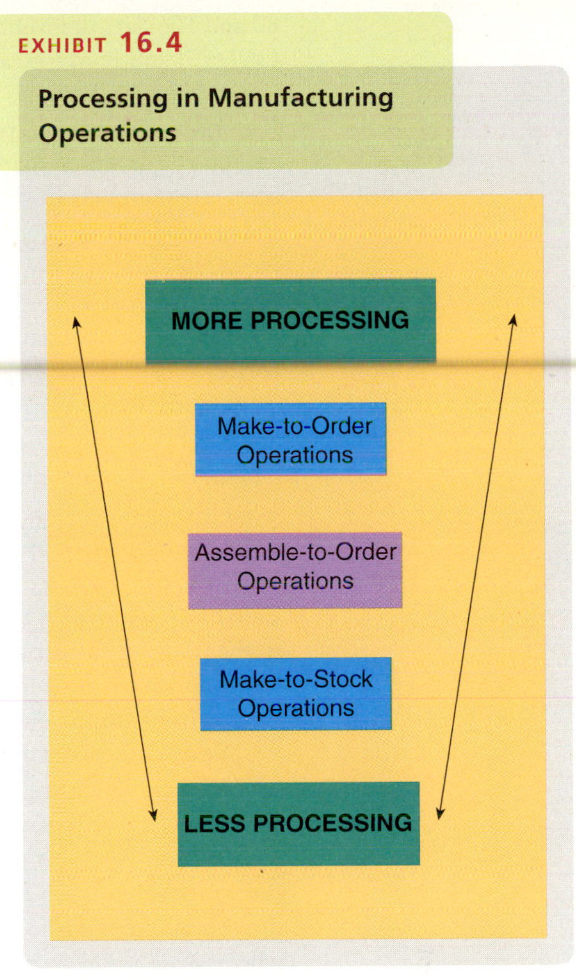

The lowest degree of processing occurs in **make-to-stock operations** (also called build-to-stock). Because the products are standardized, meaning each product is exactly the same as the next, a company using a make-to-stock operation starts ordering parts and assembling finished products before receiving customer orders. Customers then purchase these standardized products—such as storage containers, microwave ovens, and vacuum cleaners—at retail stores or directly from the manufacturer. Because parts are ordered and products are assembled before customers order the products, make-to-stock operations are highly dependent on the accuracy of sales forecasts. If sales forecasts are incorrect, make-to-stock operations may end up building too many or too few products, or they may make products with the wrong features or without the features that customers want.

assemble-to-order operation
a manufacturing operation that divides manufacturing processes into separate parts or modules that are combined to create semicustomized products

make-to-stock operation
a manufacturing operation that orders parts and assembles standardized products before receiving customer orders

inventory
the amount and number of raw materials, parts, and finished products that a company has in its possession

4.2 Types of Inventory

With SUVs and pickup trucks accounting for nearly 80 percent of its sales, Chrysler was reluctant to stop making them even when consumer demand dried up. Despite a lack of orders, Chrysler kept building SUVs and pickups and ended up with nearly a 4-month supply of inventory. In addition to what was already on dealer lots, the automaker had 50,000 vehicles sitting on random storage lots around the midwestern United States. Ultimately, Chrysler had to significantly reduce production for 6 months to sell off its unsold vehicles.[50]

Inventory is the amount and number of raw materials, parts, and finished products that a company has in its possession. Like Chrysler, General Motors made the mistake of having too much inventory on hand; GM had to reduce production by over 10 percent at its plants to let existing sales draw down inventory levels to an acceptable and affordable level. Industry experts estimate Chrysler has somewhere between

80 and 126 days of inventory on hand, and it has more SUV inventory (82 days) than GM (77) and Ford (74) and almost three times as much as Toyota (28).[51]

Exhibit 16.5 shows the four kinds of inventory a manufacturer stores: raw materials, component parts, work-in-process, and finished goods. The flow of inventory through a manufacturing plant begins when the purchasing department buys raw materials from vendors. **Raw material inventories** are the basic inputs in the manufacturing process. For example, to begin making a car, automobile manufacturers purchase raw materials like steel, iron, aluminum, copper, rubber, and unprocessed plastic.

Next, raw materials are fabricated or processed into **component parts inventories**, meaning the basic parts used in manufacturing a product. For example, in an automobile plant, steel is fabricated or processed into a car's body panels, and steel and iron are melted and shaped into engine parts like pistons or engine blocks. Some component parts are purchased from vendors rather than fabricated in-house.

The component parts are then assembled to make unfinished **work-in-process inventories**, which are also known as partially finished goods. This process is also called *initial assembly*. For example, steel body panels are welded to each other and to the frame of the car to make a "unibody," which comprises the unpainted interior frame and exterior structure of the car. Likewise, pistons, camshafts, and other parts are inserted into the engine block to create a working engine.

Next, all the work-in-process inventories are assembled to create **finished goods inventories**, which are the final outputs of the manufacturing process. This process is also called *final assembly*. For a car, the engine, wheels, brake system, suspension, interior, and electrical system are assembled into a car's painted unibody to make the working automobile, which is the factory's finished product. In the last step in the process, the finished goods are sent to field warehouses, distribution centers, or wholesalers, and then to retailers for final sale to customers.

raw material inventories
the basic inputs in a manufacturing process

component parts inventories
the basic parts used in manufacturing that are fabricated from raw materials

work-in-process inventories
partially finished goods consisting of assembled component parts

finished goods inventories
the final outputs of manufacturing operations

average aggregate inventory
average overall inventory during a particular time period

4.3 Measuring Inventory

As you'll learn next, uncontrolled inventory can lead to huge costs for a manufacturing operation. Consequently, managers need good measures of inventory to prevent costs from becoming too large. Three basic measures of inventory are average aggregate inventory, weeks of supply, and inventory turnover.

If you've ever worked in a retail store and had to take inventory, you probably weren't too excited about the process of counting every item in the store and storeroom. It's an extensive task that's a bit easier today because of bar codes that mark items and computers that can count and track them. Nonetheless, inventories still differ from day to day. An inventory count taken at the beginning of the month will likely be different from a count taken at the end of the month. Similarly, an inventory count taken on a Friday will differ from a count taken on a Monday. Because of such differences, companies often measure **average aggregate inventory**, which is the average overall inventory during a particular time period. Average aggregate inventory for a month can be determined by simply averaging the inventory counts at the end of each business day for that month. One way companies know whether they're carrying too much or too little inventory is to compare their average aggregate inventory with the industry average for aggregate inventory. For example, 72 days of inventory is the average for the automobile industry.

Most industries measure inventory in terms of *weeks of supply*, meaning the number of weeks it would take for a company to run out of its current supply of inventory. In general, there is an acceptable number of weeks of inventory for a particular kind of business. Too few weeks of inventory on hand, and a company risks a **stockout**—running out of inventory. For example, when Apple introduced the iPhone 3GS its retail and online stores ran out of inventory in 44 states.[52] On the other hand, a business that has too many weeks of inventory on hand incurs high costs.

Another common inventory measure, **inventory turnover**, is the number of times per year that a company sells or "turns over" its average inventory. For example, if a company keeps an average of 100 finished widgets in inventory each month, and it sold 1,000 widgets this year, then it turned its inventory ten times this year.

EXHIBIT 16.5

Types of Inventory

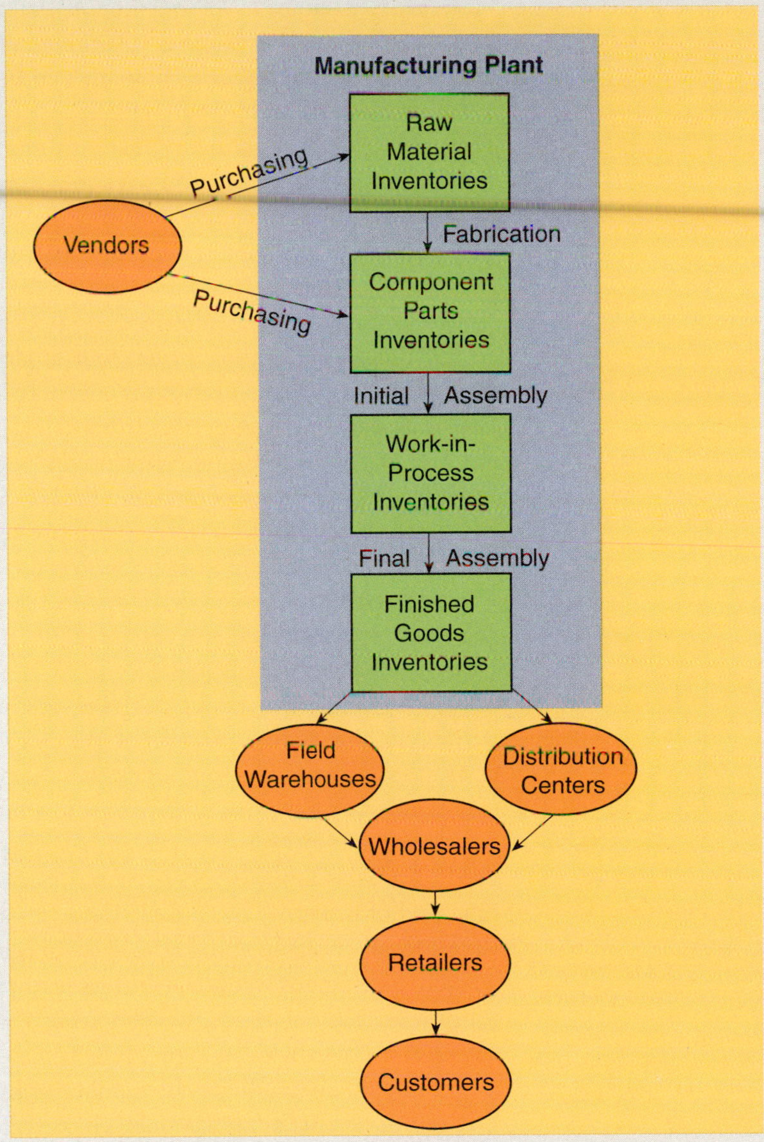

Source: R. E. Markland, S. K. Vickery, & R. A. Davis, *Operations Management*, 2nd ed. (Mason, OH: South-Western, 1998).

In general, the higher the number of inventory turns, the better. In practice, a high turnover means that a company can continue its daily operations with just a small amount of inventory on hand. For example, let's take two companies, A and B, which have identical inventory levels (520,000 widget parts and raw materials) over the course of a year. If company A turns its inventories 26 times a year, it will completely replenish its inventory every 2 weeks and have an average inventory of 20,000 widget parts and raw materials. By contrast, if company B turns its inventories only two times a year, it will completely replenish its inventory every 26 weeks and have an average inventory of 260,000 widget parts and raw materials. So, by turning its inventory more often, company A has 92 percent less inventory on hand at any one time than company B.

stockout
the point when a company runs out of finished product

inventory turnover
the number of times per year that a company sells or "turns over" its average inventory

The average number of inventory turns across all kinds of manufacturing plants is approximately eight per year.[53] The inventory turn rates for some of the best companies in each industry may differ considerably from the average turn rates. Whereas the average auto company turns its entire inventory 13 times per year, some of the best auto companies more than double that rate, turning their inventory 27.8 times per year, or once every 2 weeks.[54] Turning inventory more frequently than the industry average can cut an auto company's costs by several hundred million dollars per year. Finally, it should be pointed out that even make-to-order companies like Dell turn their inventory. In theory, make-to-order companies have no inventory. In fact, they've got inventory, but you have to measure it in hours. For example, Dell turns the inventory in its faculties 500 times a year, which means that on average it has 17 hours—that's *hours* and not days—of inventory on hand in its factories.[55]

4.4 Costs of Maintaining an Inventory

Maintaining an inventory incurs four kinds of costs: ordering, setup, holding, and stockout. **Ordering cost** is not the cost of the inventory itself but the costs associated with ordering the inventory. It includes the costs of completing paperwork, manually entering data into a computer, making phone calls, getting competing bids, correcting mistakes, and simply determining when and how much new inventory should be reordered. For example, ordering costs are relatively high in the restaurant business because 80 percent of foodservice orders are processed manually. A report, *Enabling Profitable Growth in the Food-Prepared-Away-from-Home Industries*, estimated that the food industry could save $14.3 billion if all restaurants converted to electronic data interchange (see Chapter 15).

Setup cost is the cost of changing or adjusting a machine so that it can produce a different kind of inventory.[56] For example, 3M uses the same production machinery to make several kinds of industrial tape, but it must adjust the machines whenever it switches from one kind of tape to another. There are two kinds of setup costs, downtime and lost efficiency. *Downtime* occurs whenever a machine is not being used to process inventory. If it takes 5 hours to switch a machine from processing one kind of inventory to another, then 5 hours of downtime have occurred. Downtime is costly because companies earn an economic return only when machines are actively turning raw materials into parts or parts into finished products. The second setup cost is *lost efficiency*. Recalibrating a machine to its optimal settings after a switchover typically takes some time. It may take several days of fine-tuning before a machine finally produces the number of high-quality parts that it is supposed to. So each time a machine has to be changed to handle a different kind of inventory, setup costs (downtime and lost efficiency) rise.

ordering cost
the costs associated with ordering inventory, including the cost of data entry, phone calls, obtaining bids, correcting mistakes, and determining when and how much inventory to order

setup cost
the costs of downtime and lost efficiency that occur when a machine is changed or adjusted to produce a different kind of inventory

holding cost
the cost of keeping inventory until it is used or sold, including storage, insurance, taxes, obsolescence, and opportunity costs

Holding cost, also known as *carrying* or *storage cost*, is the cost of keeping inventory until it is used or sold. Holding cost includes the cost of storage facilities, insurance to protect inventory from damage or theft, inventory taxes, the cost of obsolescence (holding inventory that is no longer useful to the company), and the opportunity cost of spending money on inventory that could have been spent elsewhere in the company. For example, it's estimated that U.S. airlines have a total of $44 billion worth of airplane parts in stock at any one time for maintenance, repair, and overhauling their planes. The holding cost for managing, storing, and purchasing these parts is nearly $11 billion—or one-fourth of the cost of the parts themselves.[57]

Stockout costs are the costs incurred when a company runs out of a product, as happened to Apple when it failed to have enough iPods during the holiday shopping season. There are two basic kinds of stockout costs. First, the company incurs the transaction costs of overtime work, shipping, and the like in trying to replace quickly out-of-stock inventories with new inventories. The second and perhaps more damaging cost is the loss of customers' goodwill when a company cannot deliver the products it promised. Stockouts occur more often than you might think. In the United States, the supermarket industry's average out-of-stock rate (the percentage of items that are unavailable at a given time) is 7.9 percent, according to research firm Market6. Most importantly, retailers can increase sales by 4 percent if they never run out of stock.[50]

© LUIS CARLOS TORRES/ISTOCKPHOTO.COM

4.5 Managing Inventory

Inventory management has two basic goals. The first is to avoid running out of stock and thus angering and dissatisfying customers. This goal seeks to increase inventory to a safe level that won't risk stockouts. The second is to reduce inventory levels and costs as much as possible without impairing daily operations. This goal seeks a minimum level of inventory. The following inventory management techniques—economic order quantity (EOQ), just-in-time inventory (JIT), and materials requirement planning (MRP)—are different ways of balancing these competing goals.

Economic order quantity (EOQ) is a system of formulas that helps determine how much and how often inventory should be ordered. EOQ takes into account the overall demand (D) for a product while trying to minimize ordering costs (O) and holding costs (H). The formula for EOQ is:

$$\text{EOQ} = \sqrt{\frac{2\text{DO}}{\text{H}}}$$

For example, if a factory uses 40,000 gallons of paint a year (D), ordering costs (O) are $75 per order, and holding costs (H) are $4 per gallon, then the optimal quantity to order is 1,225 gallons:

$$\text{EOQ} = \sqrt{\frac{2(40{,}000)(75)}{4}} = 1{,}225$$

With 40,000 gallons of paint being used per year, the factory uses approximately 110 gallons per day:

$$\frac{40{,}000 \text{ gallons}}{365 \text{ days}} = 110$$

Consequently, the factory would order 1,225 new gallons of paint approximately every 11 days:

$$\frac{1{,}225 \text{ gallons}}{110 \text{ gallons per day}} = 11.1 \text{ days}$$

stockout costs
the costs incurred when a company runs out of a product, including transaction costs to replace inventory and the loss of customers' goodwill

economic order quantity (EOQ)
a system of formulas that minimizes ordering and holding costs and helps determine how much and how often inventory should be ordered

While EOQ formulas try to minimize holding and ordering costs, the just-in-time (JIT) approach to inventory management attempts to eliminate holding costs by reducing inventory levels to near zero. With a **just-in-time (JIT) inventory system**, component parts arrive from suppliers just as they are needed at each stage of production. By having parts arrive just in time, the manufacturer has little inventory on hand and thus avoids the costs associated with holding inventory. By combining a JIT inventory system with its make-to-order production system, Dell turns its inventory more than 500 times a year, as mentioned above.

To have just the right amount of inventory arrive at just the right time requires a tremendous amount of coordination between manufacturing operations and suppliers. One way to promote tight coordination under JIT is close proximity. Most parts suppliers for Toyota's JIT system at its Georgetown, Kentucky, plant are located within 200 miles. Furthermore, parts are picked up from suppliers and delivered to Toyota as often as 16 times a day.[59] A second way to promote close coordination under JIT is to have a shared information system that allows a manufacturer and its suppliers to know the quantity and kinds of parts the other has in stock. Generally, factories and suppliers facilitate information sharing by using the same part numbers and names. Ford's seat supplier accomplishes this by sticking a bar code on each seat, which Ford uses to route the seat through its factory.

Manufacturing operations and their parts suppliers can also facilitate close coordination by using the system of kanban. **Kanban**, which is Japanese for "sign," is a simple ticket-based system that indicates when it is time to reorder inventory. Suppliers attach kanban cards to batches of parts. Then, when an assembly-line worker uses the first part out of a batch, the kanban card is removed. The cards are then collected, sorted, and quickly returned to the supplier, who begins resupplying the factory with parts that match the order information on the kanban cards. Because prices and batch sizes are typically agreed to ahead of time, kanban tickets greatly reduce paperwork and ordering costs.[60]

just-in-time (JIT) inventory system
an inventory system in which component parts arrive from suppliers just as they are needed at each stage of production

kanban
a ticket-based JIT system that indicates when to reorder inventory

materials requirement planning (MRP)
a production and inventory system that determines the production schedule, production batch sizes, and inventory needed to complete final products

independent demand system
an inventory system in which the level of one kind of inventory does not depend on another

A third method for managing inventory is **materials requirement planning (MRP)**. MRP is a production and inventory system that, from beginning to end, precisely determines the production schedule, production batch sizes, and inventories needed to complete final products. The three key parts of MRP systems are the master production schedule, the bill of materials, and inventory records. The *master production schedule* is a detailed schedule that indicates the quantity of each item to be produced, the planned delivery dates for those items, and the time by which each step of the production process must be completed in order to meet those delivery dates. Based on the quantity and kind of products set forth in the master production schedule, the *bill of materials* identifies all the necessary parts and inventory, the quantity or volume of inventory to be ordered, and the order in which the parts and inventory should be assembled. *Inventory records* indicate the kind, quantity, and location of inventory that is on hand or that has been ordered. When inventory records are combined with the bill of materials, the resulting report indicates what to buy, when to buy it, and what it will cost to order. Today, nearly all MRP systems are available in the form of powerful, flexible computer software.[61]

Which inventory management system should you use? Economic order quantity (EOQ) formulas are intended for use with **independent demand systems**, in which the level of one kind of inventory does not depend on another. For example, because inventory levels for automobile tires are unrelated to the inventory levels of women's dresses, Sears could use EOQ formulas to calculate separate optimal order quantities for dresses and tires. By contrast, JIT and MRP are used with **dependent demand systems**, in which the level of inventory depends on the number of finished units to be produced. For example, if Yamaha makes 1,000 motorcycles a day, then it will need 1,000 seats, 1,000 gas tanks, and 2,000 wheels and tires each day. So, when optimal inventory levels depend on the number of products to be produced, use a JIT or MRP management system.

REVIEW 4

Manufacturing Operations

Manufacturing operations produce physical goods. Manufacturing operations can be classified according to the amount of processing or assembly that occurs after receiving an order from customers. Make-to-order operations, in which assembly doesn't begin until products are ordered, involve the most processing. The next-highest degree of processing occurs in assemble-to-order operations, in which preassembled modules are combined after orders are received to produce semicustomized products. The least processing occurs in make-to-stock operations, in which standard parts are ordered on the basis of sales forecasts and assembled before orders are received.

There are four kinds of inventory: raw materials, component parts, work-in-process, and finished goods. Because companies incur ordering, setup, holding, and sometimes stockout costs when handling inventory, inventory costs can be enormous. To control those costs, companies measure and track inventory in three ways: average aggregate inventory, weeks of supply, and turnover. Companies meet the basic goals of inventory management (avoiding stockouts and reducing inventory without hurting daily operations) through economic order quantity (EOQ) formulas, just-in-time (JIT) inventory systems, and materials requirement planning (MRP).

EOQ formulas minimize holding and ordering costs by determining how much and how often inventory should be ordered. By having parts arrive just when they are needed at each stage of production, JIT systems attempt to minimize inventory levels and holding costs. JIT systems often depend on proximity, shared information, and the system of kanban made popular by Japanese manufacturers. MRP precisely determines the production schedule, production batch sizes, and the ordering of inventories needed to complete final products. The three key parts of MRP systems are the master production schedule, the bill of materials, and inventory records. Use EOQ formulas when inventory levels are independent, and use JIT and MRP when inventory levels are dependent on the number of products to be produced.

dependent demand system
an inventory system in which the level of inventory depends on the number of finished units to be produced

Management Team Decision

Going Lean at Starbucks

It started off as a day basically like any other. You went into the Starbucks that you manage, helped employees open, and thought about making a dent in the mountain of paperwork left over from the previous week. But then, you got an unexpected visit from a team at the corporate office. They started talking about the need to lower labor costs, improve efficiency, and increase productivity. When you asked them how they planned on doing all that, they responded, "lean production."

They informed you that lean production is a management philosophy derived from Toyota that is focused on reducing waste. Whether it's wasted motion, wasted time, or wasted parts, the goal of lean production is to eliminate waste so that an organization can do its work efficiently. The executives then show you all the "waste" that's in your stores right now—baristas bending over to scoop coffee from a counter below, others waiting for coffee to drain fully before starting a new pot, one worker carrying trays of pastries from storage to the display case, another spending 10 second per drink to read the milk label. They even show you a map showing the winding trail that a barista takes while making a single drink. It looks like a big pile of spaghetti, you think to yourself.

With lean production, the executives tell you, you can reduce the amount of motion that employees spend making drinks, and the amount of time they spend reaching for stuff, reading labels, or moving from here to there. This will make your store more efficient and productive, so that the same number of employees can serve more customers.

You're intrigued by all of this, as nothing would please your supervisors more than increased revenue and lower costs. But you're also worried about how your employees will react. Many of them came to work at Starbucks because it wasn't like other fast-food chains that only focus on speed, speed, and speed. How will they feel once you tell them that they'll have to change the way they work to become faster? What if they feel like you just want them to be coffee making robots, leaving them no time to interact with customers or experiment with new drinks? Consider these issues with three or four other students as you discuss the questions below.

Questions

1. How would an increase in efficiency and production benefit your employees?
2. How would you address employees' concerns that they are being transformed into coffee making robots?

Source: Julie Jargon. "Latest Starbucks Buzzword: 'Lean' Japanese Techniques." *Wall Street Journal.* August 4, 2009. Accessed at http://online.wsj.com/article/SB124933474023402611.html

Practice being a Manager

Balancing Speed and Accuracy

Success in service and manufacturing operations requires managers to maintain high levels of both productivity and quality. High productivity ensures that the company is cost-competitive with rivals; and high quality helps the company to attract customers and grow revenues and profits. Because productivity and quality are basic drivers of company success, managers must be adept at measuring and improving both. This exercise will give you some practice in developing productivity and quality measures.

STEP 1 Form work groups. Your professor will organize your class into small groups of three or four students.

Scenario: Your group is a management team working to improve productivity and quality in a pharmaceutical company. You have been assigned two units of this company as the focus of your improvement efforts. The first is a pill-packaging unit, and the second is a research and development (R&D) laboratory.

Workers in the packaging unit are responsible for checking to ensure that the pills in the box match the packaging and labeling, placing the appropriate labels and packaging information on each box, and then certifying with a stamp that the box of pills is ready for shipping to wholesale customers, for example, chains like Walgreens and Costco. Mistakes in packaging, if undetected by pharmacists, could have serious, even fatal, outcomes. These manufacturing workers are skilled and highly trained. If they detect a problem, they have the authority to halt production.

Workers in the R&D unit are responsible for developing new drugs and for testing their effectiveness and safety. The company relies for its success upon a steady pipeline of promising new products. At the same time, some basic research (e.g., study of progression of a particular type of cancer) is necessary in order to develop new drugs. These workers are mostly Ph.D.s and highly skilled laboratory technicians.

STEP 2 Develop metrics. Working as a team, develop some productivity and quality measures for (a) packaging unit workers and (b) R&D unit workers. Be sure to consider whether productivity and quality should be measured on an individual or unit basis, and why.

STEP 3 Analyze the metrics. Critically examine your team's measures for each unit. What unintended consequences might develop as workers in each unit strive to improve on the measures you have designed? Are you more confident of your measures in one unit versus the other? Why or why not?

STEP 4 Debrief as a class. What are some of the challenges of measuring productivity and quality? Are these challenges greater for particular types of work? Which level of measurement and accountability—individual or unit—is most likely to generate positive results? Why? What impact do productivity and quality systems of measurement and improvement have on workers? How can firms ensure productivity and quality without overloading workers and/or fostering unhealthy levels of stress?

How to Handle Disgruntled Customers

How a company manages its customers is an important indicator of its future success. But managing customers can be as difficult as it is critical. For example, one customer may like to be greeted by an employee and immediately helped upon entering the store. Another might find this approach a bit aggressive. What is your style? If you were responsible for interacting with customers, which approach would you use? The following assessment will evaluate your perspectives on the relationship a company has with its customers. Be candid as you respond to the questions using a scale from 1 to 9, in which 1 means you strongly disagree, 5 means you are neutral, and 9 means you strongly agree (other numbers indicate varying degrees of agreement or disagreement).[62]

1. I try to bring a customer with a problem together with a product/service that helps solve that problem.
   1 2 3 4 5 6 7 8 9

2. I keep alert for weaknesses in a customer's personality so I can use them to put pressure on them to agree with me.
1 2 3 4 5 6 7 8 9

3. I try to influence a customer by information rather than pressure.
1 2 3 4 5 6 7 8 9

4. It is necessary to stretch the truth when describing a product to a customer.
1 2 3 4 5 6 7 8 9

5. I decide what product/service to offer on the basis of what I can convince customers to accept, not on the basis of what will satisfy them in the long run.
1 2 3 4 5 6 7 8 9

6. I paint too rosy a picture of my product/service to make them sound as good as possible.
1 2 3 4 5 6 7 8 9

7. I try to find out what kind of products/services will be most helpful to a customer.
1 2 3 4 5 6 7 8 9

8. I try to sell a customer all I can convince them to buy, even if I think it is more than a wise customer would buy.
1 2 3 4 5 6 7 8 9

9. I begin talking about the product/service before exploring a customer's need with him or her.
1 2 3 4 5 6 7 8 9

10. I try to help customers achieve their goals.
1 2 3 4 5 6 7 8 9

11. I try to figure out what a customer's needs are.
1 2 3 4 5 6 7 8 9

12. A good employee has to have the customer's best interest in mind.
1 2 3 4 5 6 7 8 9

13. I try to sell as much as I can rather than to satisfy a customer.
1 2 3 4 5 6 7 8 9

14. I try to give customers an accurate expectation of what our product/service will do for them.
1 2 3 4 5 6 7 8 9

15. I imply to a customer that something is beyond my control when it is not.
1 2 3 4 5 6 7 8 9

16. I try to achieve my goals by satisfying customers.
1 2 3 4 5 6 7 8 9

17. If I am not sure if our product/service is right for a customer, I will still apply pressure to get him or her to buy.
1 2 3 4 5 6 7 8 9

18. I answer a customer's question about product/services as correctly as I can.
1 2 3 4 5 6 7 8 9

19. I offer the product/service that is best suited to the customer's problem.
1 2 3 4 5 6 7 8 9

20. I treat a customer as a rival.
1 2 3 4 5 6 7 8 9

21. I spend more time trying to persuade a customer to buy than I do trying to discover his or her needs.
1 2 3 4 5 6 7 8 9

22. I am willing to disagree with a customer in order to help him or her make a better decision.
1 2 3 4 5 6 7 8 9

23. I try to get customers to discuss their needs with me.

1	2	3	4	5	6	7	8	9

24. I pretend to agree with customers to please them.

1	2	3	4	5	6	7	8	9

SCORING

Determine your score by entering your response to each survey item below, as follows. Total each column to derive two scores.

Customer Orientation

1. regular score ________
3. regular score ________
7. regular score ________
10. regular score ________
11. regular score ________
12. regular score ________
14. regular score ________
16. regular score ________
18. regular score ________
19. regular score ________
22. regular score ________
23. regular score ________

TOTAL ________

Selling Orientation

2. regular score ________
4. regular score ________
5. regular score ________
6. regular score ________
8. regular score ________
9. regular score ________
13. regular score ________
15. regular score ________
17. regular score ________
20. regular score ________
21. regular score ________
24. regular score ________

TOTAL ________

You can find the interpretation for your score at: login.cengagebrain.com

Reel to Real

Biz Flix

© GREENLIGHT

In Bruges

The tagline for the award-winning 2008 film *In Bruges* was "Shoot first. Sightsee later." That's because it's the story of two hit men—Ray (Colin Farrell) and Ken (Brandan Gleeson)—who tragically botch the job of murdering a priest in a confessional by accidentally killing an innocent young bystander. Ray and Ken are ordered to hide out in the beautiful medieval Flemish city of Bruges, Belgium. They spend their days sightseeing, interacting with the locals, and bickering with each other while awaiting further orders from Harry, their boss (Ralph Fiennes). This video features two scenes that show Ken and Harry interacting with a ticket seller (Rudy Blomme), who makes it more difficult for them to visit a historic bell tower than they'd like.

What to Watch for and Ask Yourself

1. Ken is the customer and the ticket seller responds to him as a customer. Do you perceive the ticket seller as having a customer focus as emphasized in this chapter? Why or why not?
2. As you were watching the ticket seller interact with Ken and Harry in the second part of this video, did you predict that his customer approach could result in negative results for him? Why or why not?
3. These scenes offer a lesson in customer focus. What did the ticket seller fail to understand about his customers? Could he have handled the situations better?

Management Workplace

© CENGAGE

Preserve

When John Lively, director of operations at Preserve, arrived for his first day on the job 10 years ago, there wasn't much to see. The company, which makes housewares and personal care products from recycled plastics, was just getting started. There were about three or four people in one room doing whatever it took to get the company off the ground. In 1999, the idea of an information technology (IT) department and all the organizational tools we now take for granted were still new. Lively says he had a lot to learn—and fast! In this video Lively describes the challenges that Preserve faced when Wal-Mart placed an order and the small company had to scramble to meet demand, manage its inventory, and ensure that products would be delivered on time.

What to watch for and Ask Yourself

1. What is one of the key ways that the company has improved its process control and quality control?
2. What are some of the inventory issues that arose when Wal-Mart decided to carry Preserve's products? What were some of the solutions?
3. As the company has grown, what types of controls did it have to establish in its operations?

Endnotes

Chapter One

[1] "Is the Global Domination of Starbucks Finally on the Wane?" *Belfast Telegraph*, 3 July 2008, 1; J. Adamy, "Schultz's Second Act Jolts of Starbucks; Already Intense, He Faces New Pressure: Peltz Owns a Stake," *Wall Street Journal*, 19 May 2008, A1; M. Barbaro and A. Martin, "Overhaul, Make It a Venti," *New York Times*, 30 January 2008, C1; E. Campbell, E. Ailworth, and A. Jennings, "Average Joe Figured Out the Problem a While Ago," *Boston Globe*, 3 July 2008, E1; P. McNamara and B. Hutchinson, "Not So Grande for Starbucks. Java Giant's Bean Counters to Close 600 Stores," *New York Daily News*, 2 July 2008, 6; D. Mitchell, "Starbucks Faces Existential Crisis in Downturn," *Washington Post*, 22 March 2009, G01.

[2] K. Voigt, "Top Dogs," *Wall Street Journal*, 15 March 2002, W1.

[3] M. Herper and R. Langreth, "Dangerous Devices," *Forbes,* 27 November 2006, 94.

[4] "Business Services: Global Industry Guide," *Data Monitor*, 21 January 2010, available online at http://www.marketresearch.com [accessed 18 April 2009].

[5] T. Peters, "The Leadership Alliance" (Pat Carrigan excerpt), *In Search of Excellence,* Video Arts distributor, 1985, videocassette.

[6] M. Gottfredson, S. Schaubert, and E. Babcock, "Achieving Breakthrough Performance," *Stanford Social Initiative Review* (Summer 2008): 35.

[7] D. A. Wren, A. G. Bedeian, and J. D. Breeze, "The Foundations of Henri Fayol's Administrative Theory," *Management Decision* 40 (2002): 906–918.

[8] H. Fayol, *General and Industrial Management* (London: Pittman & Sons, 1949).

[9] R. Stagner, "Corporate Decision Making," *Journal of Applied Psychology* 53 (1969): 1–13.

[10] D. W. Bray, R. J. Campbell, and D. L. Grant, *Formative Years in Business: A Long-Term AT&T Study of Managerial Lives* (New York: Wiley, 1993).

[11] G. Fowler, "EBay to Unload Skype in IPO, Citing Poor Fit," *The Wall Street Journal*, 15 April 2009, B1; G. Fowler and E. Ramstad, "EBay Looks Abroad for Growth—Online Auctioneer to Buy Korean Site as It Refocuses on E-Commerce, PayPal," *Wall Street Journal*, 16 April 2009, B2.

[12] A. Johnson, "Pfizer Outlines Post-Wyeth R&D Structure—Company Splits Research on Traditional Drugs from Biologics and Strives to Retain Scientists," *Wall Street Journal*, 8 April 2009, B4.

[13] R. J. Grisson, "Probability of the Superior Outcome of One Treatment over Another," *Journal of Applied Psychology* 79 (1994): 314–316; J. E. Hunter and F. L. Schmidt, *Methods of Meta-Analysis: Correcting Error and Bias in Research Findings* (Beverly Hills, CA: Sage, 1990).

[14] B. Morris, "The Accidental CEO," *Fortune*, 28 June 2003, 58.

[15] Ibid.

[16] "Xerox's Chief Copies Good Practice, Not Past Mistakes," *Irish Times*, 21 March 2003, 62.

[17] J. P. Donlon, "The X Factor," *Chief Executive*, June 2008, 26–32.

[18] J. McNish, "Xerox's Success Is a Reflection of Her Dedication; Anne Mulcahy," *Globe and Mail*, 11 September 2008, B1.

[19] J. Lunsford, "Get into Hot Water to Save Fuel," *Wall Street Journal*, 11 June 2008, B1.

[20] H. S. Jonas III, R. E. Fry, and S. Srivastva, "The Office of the CEO: Understanding the Executive Experience," *Academy of Management Executive* 4 (1990): 36–47.

[21] P. Dvorak, "Companies Cut Holes in CEOs Golden Parachutes," *Wall Street Journal*, 15 September 2008, B4; P. Sellers, "Lessons of The Fall," *Fortune*, 9 June 2008, 70–80.

[22] Jonas et al., "The Office of the CEO."

[23] Ibid.

[24] M. Arndt, "Creativity Overflowing," *BusinessWeek*, 8 May 2006, 50.

[25] Jonas et al., "The Office of the CEO."

[26] Q. Huy, "In Praise of Middle Managers," *Harvard Business Review* (September 2001): 72–79.

[27] I. Barat, "Rebuilding After a Catastrophe: How Caterpillar Is Responding to Tornado's Lesson," *Wall Street Journal,* 19 May 2008, B1–2.

[28] C. Hymowitz, "CEOs Work Hard to Maintain the Faith in the Corner Office," *Wall Street Journal*, 9 July 2002, B1; L. Mitchell, "How to Do the Right Thing," *Optimize*, February 2002, http://www.optimizemag.com [accessed 1 February 2003].

[29] "Management & Professional: Regional Manager," *Pharmacy Today*, 18 October 2006, 27.

[30] J. Adamy, "A Menu of Options: Restaurants Have a Host of Ways to Motivate Employees to Provide Good Service," *Wall Street Journal*, 30 October 2006, R1, R6.

[31] C. Hymowitz, "Today's Bosses Find Mentoring Isn't Worth the Time and Risks," *Wall Street Journal*, 13 March 2006, B1.

[32] S. Tully, "What Team Leaders Need to Know," *Fortune*, 20 February 1995, 93.

[33] L. Liu and A. McMurray, "Frontline Leaders: The Entry Point for Leadership Development in the Manufacturing Industry," *Journal of European Industrial Training* 28, no. 2–4 (2004): 339–352.

[34] "What Makes Teams Work?" *Fast Company*, 1 November 2000, 109.

[35] L. Landro, "The Informed Patient: Bringing Surgeons Down to Earth—New Programs Aim to Curb Fear That Prevents Nurses from Flagging Problems," *Wall Street Journal*, 16 November 2005, D1.

[36] Ibid.

[37] N. Steckler and N. Fondas, "Building Team Leader Effectiveness: A Diagnostic Tool," *Organizational Dynamics*, Winter 1995, 20–34.

[38] Tully, "What Team Leaders Need to Know."

[39] H. Mintzberg, *The Nature of Managerial Work* (New York: Harper & Row, 1973).

40 C. P. Hales, "What Do Managers Do? A Critical Review of the Evidence," *Journal of Management Studies* 23, no. 1 (1986): 88–115.

41 "Cessna CEO Joins Mesa Mayor to Open New Jet Center," *Business Wire*, for February 2009, available online at http://www .Reuters.com [accessed 18 April 2009].

42 S. Humphries, "Grapevine Goes High-Tech," *The Courier Mail*, 10 January 2009.

43 C. Arnst, "The Best Medical Care in the U.S.: How Veterans Affairs Transformed Itself," *BusinessWeek*, 17 July 2006, 50.

44 C. Cosh, "In Wal-Mart We Trust," *National Post*, 28 March 2008, A15.

45 J. Scheck, "R&D Spending Holds Steady in Slump—Big Companies Invest to Grab Sales in Recovery; The IPod Lesson," *Wall Street Journal*, 6 April 2009, A1.

46 L. A. Hill, *Becoming a Manager: Mastery of a New Identity* (Boston: Harvard Business School Press, 1992).

47 R. L. Katz, "Skills of an Effective Administrator," *Harvard Business Review* (September–October 1974): 90–102.

48 C. A. Bartlett and S. Ghoshal, "Changing the Role of Top Management: Beyond Systems to People," *Harvard Business Review* (May–June 1995): 132–142.

49 F. L. Schmidt and J. E. Hunter, "Development of a Causal Model of Process Determining Job Performance," *Current Directions in Psychological Science* 1 (1992): 89–92.

50 J. B. Miner, "Sentence Completion Measures in Personnel Research: The Development and Validation of the Miner Sentence Completion Scales," in *Personality Assessment in Organizations*, ed. H. J. Bernardin and D. A. Bownas (New York: Praeger, 1986), 147–146.

51 M. W. McCall, Jr., and M. M. Lombardo, "What Makes a Top Executive?" *Psychology Today*, February 1983, 26–31; E. van Velsor and J. Brittain, "Why Executives Derail: Perspectives across Time and Cultures," *Academy of Management Executive* (November 1995): 62–72.

52 McCall and Lombardo, "What Makes a Top Executive?"

53 J. Sandberg, "Overcontrolling Bosses Aren't Just Annoying; They're Also Inefficient," *Wall Street Journal*, 30 March 2005, B1.

54 Hill, *Becoming a Manager*, p. 17.

55 Ibid., p. 55.

56 Ibid., p. 57.

57 Ibid., p. 64.

58 Ibid., p. 67.

59 Ibid., p. 103.

60 Ibid., p. 161.

61 J. Pfeffer, *The Human Equation: Building Profits by Putting People First* (Boston: Harvard Business School Press, 1996); *Competitive Advantage Through People: Unleashing the Power of the Work Force* (Boston: Harvard Business School Press, 1994).

62 M. A. Huselid, "The Impact of Human Resource Management Practices on Turnover, Productivity, and Corporate Financial Performance," *Academy of Management Journal* 38 (1995): 635–672.

63 D. McDonald and A. Smith, "A Proven Connection: Performance Management and Business Results," *Compensation & Benefits Review* 27, no. 6 (1 January 1995): 59.

64 I. Fulmer, B. Gerhart, and K. Scott, "Are the 100 Best Better? An Empirical Investigation of the Relationship between Being a 'Great Place to Work' and Firm Performance," *Personnel Psychology* (Winter 2003): 965–993.

65 B. Schneider and D. E. Bowen, "Employee and Customer Perceptions of Service in Banks: Replication and Extension," *Journal of Applied Psychology* 70 (1985): 423–433; B. Schneider, J. J. Parkington, and V. M. Buxton, "Employee and Customer Perceptions of Service in Banks," *Administrative Science Quarterly* 25 (1980): 252–267.

66 D. Simon and J. DeVaro, "Do the Best Companies to Work for Provide Better Customer Satisfaction?" *Managerial and Decision Economics*, 27 (2006): 667–683.

67 P. L. Hunsaker, *Management: A Skills Approach* (Upper Saddle River, NJ: Pearson Prentice Hall, 2005), 24–25.

68 D. Simon and J. DeVaro, "Do the Best Companies to Work for Provide Better Customer Satisfaction?" *Managerial and Decision Economics*, 27 (2006): 667–683.

69 P. L. Hunsaker, *Management: A Skills Approach* (Upper Saddle River, NJ: Pearson Prentice Hall, 2005), 24–25.

Chapter Two

1 "Stop Sprawl: How Big Box Stores Like Wal-Mart Affect the Environment and Communities," The Sierra Club, available online at http://www.SierraClub.com [accessed 13 May 2009]; P. Gogoi, "Wal-Mart: A 'Reputation Crisis,'" *BusinessWeek*, 31 October 2006, available online at http://www.businessweek .com [accessed 13 May 2009]; M. Hamstra, " Wal-Mart to Settle Labor Lawsuits," *Supermarket News*, 5 January 2009; S. Kapner, "Changing of the Guard at Wal-Mart," *Fortune*, 2 March 2009, 68–76; C. Palmeri, "For Exiting Wal-Mart, CEO Victory Lap," *BusinessWeek*, 24 November 2008, 11.

2 Y. Kane, "Sony CEO Urges Managers to 'Get Mad'; Conference Told That Company Needs to Be More Innovative, Bold," *Wall Street Journal*, 23 May 2008, B8.

3 E. Romanelli and M. L. Tushman, "Organizational Transformation as Punctuated Equilibrium: An Empirical Test," *Academy of Management Journal* 37 (1994): 1141–1166.

4 H. Banks, "A Sixties Industry in a Nineties Economy," *Forbes*, 9 May 1994, 107–112.

5 L. Cowan, "Cheap Fuel Should Carry Many Airlines to More Record Profits for 1st Quarter," *Wall Street Journal*, 4 April 1998, B17A.

6 "Airlines Still in Upheaval, 5 Years after 9/11," *CNNMoney.com*, 8 September 2006, available online at http://money.cnn .com/2006/09/08/news/companies/airlines_sept11/?postversion =2006090813&eref=yahoo [accessed 25 July 2008].

7 B. Jones, "The Changing Dairy Industry," Department of Agricultural & Applied Economics & Center for Dairy Profitability, available online at http://www.aae.wisc.edu/jones/Presentations/ Wisc &TotalDairyTrends.pdf [accessed 25 July 2008].

8 N. Klym, "Digital Music Distribution," available online at http:// cfp.mit.edu/groups/core-edge/docs/Digital-Music Casestudy.pdf [accessed 25 July 2008]; "30 Products for 30 Years," *MacWorld*, June 2006, 15–16; T. Mennecke, "CD Sales, Shipments Down in 2005," *Slyck News*, 31 March 2006, available online at http://www.slyck .com/news.php?story=1143 [accessed 25 July 2008]; P. Burrows, "Microsoft Singing Its Own iTune," *BusinessWeek Online,* 11 July 2006, available online at http://www.businessweek.com/technology/ content/jul2006/tc20060706_956447.htm [accessed 25 July 2008]; E. Schonfeld, "iTunes Sells 6 Billion Songs, and Other Fun Stats from the Philnote," *TechCrunch*, 6 January 2009, available online at http://www.techcrunch.com [accessed 26 April 2009].

9 "Samsung Invests $2.1B in LCD Line," *Electronic News,* 7 March 2005; "LG Phillips Develops World's Largest LCD Panel Measuring 100 Inches," NewLaunches.com, 7 March 2006, available online at http://www.newlaunches.com/archives/lgphilips_ develops_worlds_ largest_lcd_panel_measuring_100_inches.php [accessed 25 July 2008]; H. Ryoo, "Samsung to Invest $1 Billion in New LCD Production Line," eWeek, 1 April 2003, available

online at http://www.eweek. com/c/a/Past-News/Samsung-to-Invest-1-Billion-in-New-LCDProduction-Line [accessed 25 July 2008]; "Samsung Develops World's Largest (820) Full HDTV TFT-LCD," available online at http://www.samsung. com/us/business/semiconductor/newsView.do?news_id=638 [accessed 25 July 2008]; E. Ramstad, "I Want My Flat TV Now!" *Wall Street Journal,* 27 May 2004, B1; P. Watt, "LCD Factories Expand," *PCWorld*, available online at http://blogs.pcworld.com/staffblog/archives/003369.html [accessed 24 July 2008].

10 R. Norton, "Where Is This Economy Really Heading?" *Fortune*, 7 August 1995, 54–56.

11 "CEO Confidence Survey," *The Conference Board*, 9 April 2009, available online at http://www.conference-board.org [accessed 27 April 2009].

12 "Despite Recession, U.S. Small Business Confidence Index Increases Six Points; Small Business Research Board Study Finds Increase in Key Indicators," *U.S. Business Confidence*, 23 February 2009, available online at http://www.ipasbrb.net [accessed 27 April 2009].

13 A. Weintraub, "It's on the Tip of Your Tongue," *BusinessWeek*, 31 July 2006, 32.

14 J. Fletcher, "Extreme Nesting," *Wall Street Journal*, 7 January 2000, W1.

15 B. Sackett, "A Shopper for All Seasons; The Workplace Concierge Taking Care of Business," *The Washington Times,* 30 November 2007, C08.

16 Ibid.

17 "The Civil Rights Act of 1991," U.S. Equal Employment Opportunity Commission, available online at http://www.eeoc.gov/policy/cra91.html [accessed 25 July 2008].

18 "Compliance Assistance—Family and Medical Leave Act (FMLA)," U.S. Department of Labor: Employment Standards Administration Wage and Hour Division, available online at http://www.dol.give/ [accessed 25 July 2005].

19 R. J. Bies and T. R. Tyler, "The Litigation Mentality in Organizations: A Test of Alternative Psychological Explanations," *Organization Science* 4 (1993): 352–366.

20 M. Orey, "Fear of Firing," *BusinessWeek*, 23 April 2007, 52–62.

21 S. Gardner, G. Gomes, and J. Morgan, "Wrongful Termination and the Expanding Public Policy Exception: Implications and Advice," *SAM Advanced Management Journal* 65 (2000): 38.

22 Orey, "Fear of Firing."

23 Ibid.

24 R. Flandez, "Building a Robust Customer Forum," *Wall Street Journal*, 12 March 2008 [online edition].

25 R. Johnston and S. Mehra, "Best-Practice Complaint Management," *Academy of Management Experience* 16 (November 2002): 145–154.

26 D. Smart and C. Martin, "Manufacturer Responsiveness to Consumer Correspondence: An Empirical Investigation of Consumer Perceptions," *Journal of Consumer Affairs* 26 (1992): 104.

27 S. Morrison, "Companies Have a Treasure Trove of Customer Intelligence; Now They also Have the Tools to Make Sense of It," *Wall Street Journal*, 28 January 2008, R6.

28 S. A. Zahra and S. S. Chaples, "Blind Spots in Competitive Analysis," *Academy of Management Executive* 7 (1993): 7–28.

29 "The Cola Wars: Over a Century of Cola Slogans, Commercials, Blunders, and Coups," http://www.geocities.com/colacentury/ [accessed 13 May 2009].

30 M. Frazier, "You Suck: Dyson, Hoover and Oreck Trade Accusations in Court, on TV as Brit Upstart Leaves Rivals in Dust," *Advertising Age*, 25 July 2005, 1.

31 J. M. Moran, "Getting Closer Together— Videophones Don't Deliver TV Quality Sound, Visuals, but They're Improving," *Seattle Times*, 15 March 1998, C1.

32 A. Lavallee and R. Urken, "For Cellphones, Cheaper Rates on Global Calls; New Software Applications Route Traffic over the Web; What What Echo Echo?" *Wall Street Journal*, 20 August 2008, D1.

33 K. G. Provan, "Embeddedness, Interdependence, and Opportunism in Organizational Supplier-Buyer Networks," *Journal of Management* 19 (1993): 841–856.

34 C. Unninayar and N. P. Sindt, "Diamonds an Industry in Transition: Sometimes the Speed of Change Is Alarming," *Couture International Jeweler,* August–Sept. 2003, 68–75; N. Gaouette, "Israel's Diamond Dealers Tremble: Diamond Colossus DeBeers Today Launches Fundamental Changes to $56 Billion Retail Market," *Christian Science Monitor,* 1 June 2001, available online at http://www.csmonitor.com/2001/0601/p6s1.html [accessed 25 July 2008].

35 M. Dalton, "AB InBev Suppliers Feel Squeeze," *Wall Street Journal*, 17 April 2009, B2.

36 D. Birch, "Staying on Good Terms," *Supply Management*, 12 April 2001, 36.

37 S. Parker and C. Axtell, "Seeing Another Viewpoint: Antecedents and Outcomes of Employee Perspective Taking," *Academy of Management Journal* 44 (2001): 1085–1100; B. K. Pilling, L. A. Crosby, and D. W. Jackson, "Relational Bonds in Industrial Exchange: An Experimental Test of the Transaction Cost Economic Framework," *Journal of Business Research* 30 (1994): 237–251.

38 "Seafood HACCP," U.S. Food and Drug Administration Center for Food Safety & Applied Nutrition, available online at http://www.cfsan.fda.gov/~comm/haccpsea.html [accessed 12 March 2009].

39 N. Casey and M. Trottman, "Toys Containing Banned Plastics Still on Market; Restrictions on Phthalates Don't Take Effect Until '09; Fears of Reproductive Defects," *Wall Street Journal*, 23 October 2008, D1.

40 S. Dudley, "The Coming Shift in Regulation," *Regulation*, 1 October 2002.

41 S. Dudley, "Regulation and Small Business Competitive," *Federal Document Clearing House*, Congressional Testimony, Prepared Remarks for the House Committee on Small Business Subcommittee on Regulatory Reform and Oversight, 20 May 2004.

42 H. Morley, "Bush Orders Cut in Regulations—Change Will Cut Red Tape for Small Businesses," *Knight-Ridder Tribune*, 17 August 2002.

43 "EU's Aggressive Anti-Smoking Campaign," *Creative Bits*, http://creativebits.org/eus_ agressive_anti-smoking_campaign, 17 January 2005 [accessed 13 May 2009].

44 Hughlett, "PETA Targets McDonald's over Slaughter of Chickens," *The Chicago Tribune*, 16 February 2009, available online at http://www.Chicagotribune.com [accessed 10 May 2009].

45 S. Simon and J. Jargon, "PETA Ads to Target McDonald's," *Wall Street Journal*, 1 May 2009, B7.

46 "Ethical Dangers Multiply," *Purchasing*, 17 October 1996; J. Dubinsky, "How to Foster Ethical Conduct: Companies Have a Clear Role in Preventing Conflicts of Interest," *Supplier Selection & Management*, 1 June 2001; "Amerinet Joins Groups Issuing Compliance Documents Based on Code of Conduct," *Hospital Materials Management*, 1 January 2003, 6; M. Lawson, "The Ethical Dilemma of Corporate Generosity," *Australian Financial Review*, 5 December 2002, 16.

47 "Another Ford Trial: Steering around Activists," *Wall Street Journal*, 26 July 2006, A2.

48 "2009 AHA Environmental Scan," *Hospitals and Health Networks* 9 (2008): 35–42.

49 D. F. Jennings and J. R. Lumpkin, "Insights between Environmental Scanning Activities and Porter's Generic Strategies: An Empirical Analysis," *Journal of Management* 4 (1992): 791–803.

50 S. E. Jackson and J. E. Dutton, "Discerning Threats and Opportunities," *Administrative Science Quarterly* 33 (1988): 370–387.

51 B. Thomas, S. M. Clark, and D. A. Gioia, "Strategic Sensemaking and Organizational Performance: Linkages among Scanning, Interpretation, Action, and Outcomes," *Academy of Management Journal* 36 (1993): 239–270.

52 R. Daft, J. Sormunen, and D. Parks, "Chief Executive Scanning, Environmental Characteristics, and Company Performance: An Empirical Study," *Strategic Management Journal* 9 (1988): 123–139; V. Garg, B. Walters, and R. Priem, "Chief Executive Scanning Emphases, Environmental Dynamism, and Manufacturing Firm Performance," *Strategic Management Journal* 24 (2003): 725–744; D. Miller and P. H. Friesen, "Strategy-Making and Environment: The Third Link," *Strategic Management Journal* 4 (1983): 221–235.

53 D. Ionescu, "Update: Apple Hits 1 Billion App Store Downloads," *PC World*, 24 April 2009, available online at http://www.pcworld.com [accessed 10 May 2009].

54 D. M. Boje, "The Storytelling Organization: A Study of Story Performance in an Office-Supply Firm," *Administrative Science Quarterly* 36 (1991): 106–126.

55 S. Walton and J. Huey, *Sam Walton: Made in America* (New York: Doubleday, 1992).

56 D. Rushe, "Wal-Martians," *Sunday Times* (London), 10 June 2001, 5.

57 D. R. Denison and A. K. Mishra, "Toward a Theory of Organizational Culture and Effectiveness," *Organization Science* 6 (1995): 204–223.

58 F. Haley, "Mutual Benefit: How Does Genencor Maintain Its Incredibly Loyal Workforce? By Involving Its Employees in Almost Everything," *Fast Company*, October 2004, 98–100.

59 C. Gallo, "The Napkin Test," *BusinessWeek Online*, 10 December 2007, available online at http://www.businessweek.com [accessed 11 May 2009].

60 S. Yearout, G. Miles, and R. Koonce, "Multi-Level Visioning," *Training & Development*, 1 March 2001, 31.

61 M. A. Salva-Ramirez, "McDonald's: A Prime Example of Corporate Culture," *Public Relations Quarterly* (Winter 1995): 30–32.

62 A. Zuckerman, "Strong Corporate Cultures and Firm Performance: Are There Tradeoffs?" *Academy of Management Executive*, November 2002, 158–160.

63 E. Schein, *Organizational Culture and Leadership*, 2nd ed. (San Francisco: Jossey-Bass, 1992).

64 E. Byron, "'Call Me Mike!'—To Attract and Keep Talent, JCPenney CEO Loosens Up Once-Formal Workplace," *Wall Street Journal*, 27 March 2006, B1.

65 C. Daniels, "Does This Man Need a Shrink? Companies Are Using Psychological Testing to Screen Candidates for Top Jobs," *Fortune*, 5 February 2001, 205.

66 S. Chakravarty, "Hit 'Em Hardest with the Mostest (Southwest Airlines' Management)," *Forbes*, 16 September 1991, 48.

67 R. Suskind, "Humor Has Returned to Southwest Airlines after 9/11 Hiatus," *Wall Street Journal*, 13 January 2003, A1.

68 Ibid.

69 K. Godsey, "Slow Climb to New Heights; Combine Strict Discipline with Goofy Antics and Make Billions," *Success*, 1 October 1996, 20.

70 D. L. McCain, "The MSTAT-I: A New Measure of an Individual's Tolerance for Ambiguity," *Educational and Psychological Measurement*, 53 (1993): 183–190.

Chapter Three

1 "Leagues & Governing Bodies," *Street & Smith's Sports Business Daily*, 25 April 2008, available online at http://www.sportsbusinessdaily.com [accessed 29 November 2009]; "Stallworth Suspended without Pay for a Season," *Washington Post*, 14 August 2009, D07; "The NFL Gets Tougher," *USA Today*, 16 November 2009, 6A; J. Bell & S. Leahy, "Goodell's Power Concerns Union," *USA Today*, 28 July 2009, 7C; H. Karp, "Why the NFL Spies on Its Players," *Wall Street Journal*, 7 November 2008, W1; M. Maske, "NFL Players Are Expected to Agree on Conduct Policy," *Washington Post*, 15 March 2007, available online at http://www.washingtonpost.com [accessed 29 November 2009]; M. Maske, "Teams Can Be Fined Under Conduct Policy," *Washington Post*, 21 May 2008, E03; B. Schrotenboer, "NFL Crime," *San Diego Union-Tribune*, 19 April 2008, available online at http://legacy.signonsandiego.com [accessed 29 November 2009]; M. Seeley, "Strong Safety Net from NFL Security," *ESPN*, 25 January 2006, available online at http://sports.espn.go.com [accessed 29 November 2009].

2 J. Schramm, "Perceptions on Ethics," *HR Magazine* 49 (November 2004): 176.

3 M. Jackson, "Workplace Cheating Rampant, Half of Employees Surveyed Admit They Take Unethical Actions," *Peoria Journal Star*, 5 April 1997.

4 C. Smith, "The Ethical Workplace," *Association Management* 52 (2000): 70–73.

5 D. Jones, "More Workers Do Now Than Before Recent Big Scandals," *USA Today*, 12 February 2003, B7.

6 R. Guha and R. Krishna, "Corporate News: India Charges Satyam's Founder, Eight Others," *Wall Street Journal*, 8 April 2009, B4.

7 M. Bordwin, "Don't Ask Employees to Do Your Dirty Work," *Management Review*, 1 (October 1995).

8 M. Schweitzer, L. Ordonez, and B. Douma, "Goal Setting as a Motivator of Unethical Behavior," *Academy of Management Journal* 47 (2004): 422–432.

9 S. Taub, "Fraud Gets Ex-CFO 70 Months," *CFO*, 8 November 2007, available online at http://www.cfo.com [accessed 27 August 2009].

10 D. Palmer and A. Zakhem, "Bridging the Gap between Theory and Practice: Using the 1991 Federal Sentencing Guidelines as a Paradigm for Ethics Training," *Journal of Business Ethics* 29, no. 1/2 (2001): 77–84.

11 K. Tyler, "Do the Right Thing: Ethics Training Programs Help Employees Deal with Ethical Dilemmas," *HR Magazine*, February 2005, available online at http://moss07.shrm.org/Publications/hrmagazine/EditorialContent/Pages/0205tyler.aspx [accessed 13 March 2009].

12 D. R. Dalton, M. B. Metzger, and J. W. Hill, "The 'New' U.S. Sentencing Commission Guidelines: A Wake-Up Call for Corporate America," *Academy of Management Executive* 8 (1994): 7–16.

13 B. Ettore, "Crime and Punishment: A Hard Look at White-Collar Crime," *Management Review* 83 (1994): 10–16.

14 F. Robinson and C. C. Pauze, "What Is a Board's Liability for Not Adopting a Compliance Program?" *Healthcare Financial Management* 51, no. 9 (1997): 64.

15 D. Murphy, "The Federal Sentencing Guidelines for Organizations: A Decade of Promoting Compliance and Ethics," *Iowa Law Review* 87 (2002): 697–719.

16 Robinson and Pauze, "What Is a Board's Liability?"

17 L. A. Hays, "A Matter of Time: Widow Sues IBM over Death Benefits," *Wall Street Journal*, 6 July 1995, A1.

18 T. M. Jones, "Ethical Decision Making by Individuals in Organizations: An Issue-Contingent Model," *Academy of Management Review* 16 (1991): 366–395.

19 S. Morris and R. McDonald, "The Role of Moral Intensity in Moral Judgments: An Empirical Investigation," *Journal of Business Ethics* 14 (1995): 715–726; B. Flannery and D. May, "Environmental Ethical Decision Making in the U.S. Metal-Finishing Industry," *Academy of Management Journal* 43 (2000): 642–662.

20 L. Chao, "China Court Issues Rare Piracy Penalty to Windows Copycats," *Wall Street Journal*, 22 August 2009, A9.

21 L. Kohlberg, "Stage and Sequence: The Cognitive-Developmental Approach to Socialization," in *Handbook of Socialization Theory and Research*, ed. D. A. Goslin (Chicago: Rand McNally, 1969); L. Trevino, "Moral Reasoning and Business Ethics: Implications for Research, Education, and Management," *Journal of Business Ethics* 11 (1992): 445–459.

22 L. Trevino and M. Brown, "Managing to be Ethical: Debunking Five Business Ethics Myths," *Academy of Management Executive* 18 (May 2004): 69–81.

23 M. R. Cunningham, D. T. Wong, and A. P. Barbee, "Self-Presentation Dynamics on Overt Integrity Tests: Experimental Studies of the Reid Report," *Journal of Applied Psychology* 79 (1994): 643–658; J. Wanek, P. Sackett, and D. Ones, "Toward an Understanding of Integrity Test Similarities and Differences: An Item-Level Analysis of Seven Tests," *Personnel Psychology* 56 (Winter 2003): 873–894.

24 H. J. Bernardin, "Validity of an Honesty Test in Predicting Theft among Convenience Store Employees," *Academy of Management Journal* 36 (1993): 1097–1108.

25 J. M. Collins and F. L. Schmidt, "Personality, Integrity, and White Collar Crime: A Construct Validity Study," *Personnel Psychology* (1993): 295–311.

26 W. C. Borman, M. A. Hanson, and J. W. Hedge, "Personnel Selection," *Annual Review of Psychology* 48 (1997).

27 P. E. Murphy, "Corporate Ethics Statements: Current Status and Future Prospects," *Journal of Business Ethics* 14 (1995): 727–740.

28 S. Nonis and C. Swift, "An Examination of the Relationship between Academic Dishonesty and Workplace Dishonesty: A Multicampus Investigation," *Journal of Education for Business* (November 2001): 69–77.

29 L.W. Andrews, "The Nexus of Ethics," *HR Magazine*, August 2005, available at http://www.shrm.org [accessed 29 November 2009].

30 "More Corporate Boards Involved in Ethics Programs; Ethics Training Becoming Standard Practice," *PR Newswire*, 16 October 2006.

31 S. J. Harrington, "What Corporate America Is Teaching about Ethics," *Academy of Management Executive* 5 (1991): 21–30.

32 L. A. Berger, "Train All Employees to Solve Ethical Dilemmas," *Best's Review—Life-Health Insurance Edition* 95 (1995): 70–80.

33 L. Trevino, G. Weaver, D. Gibson, and B. Toffler, "Managing Ethics and Legal Compliance: What Works and What Hurts," *California Management Review* 41, no. 2 (1999): 131–151.

34 Ibid.

35 E. White, "Theory & Practice: What Would You Do? Ethics Courses Get Context; Beyond Checking Boxes, Some Firms Start Talking About Handling Gray Areas," *The Wall Street Journal*, 12 June 2006, B3.

36 "2007 National Business Ethics Survey," available online at http://www.ethics.org [accessed 17 July 2008].

37 G. Alliger and S. Dwight, "A Meta-Analytic Investigation of the Susceptibility of Integrity Tests to Faking and Coaching," *Educational and Psychological Measurement* 60 (2000): 59–72; D. S. Ones, C. Viswesvaran, and F. L. Schmidt, "Comprehensive Meta-Analysis of Integrity Test Validities: Findings and Implications for Personnel Selection and Theories of Job Performance," *Journal of Applied Psychology* 78 (1993): 679–703; "2008 Report to the Nation on Occupational Fraud and Abuse," Association of Certified Fraud Examiners," available online at http://www.acfe.com/resources/publications.asp?copy=rttn [accessed 15 July 2008]

38 G. Weaver and L. Trevino, "Integrated and Decoupled Corporate Social Performance: Management Commitments, External Pressures, and Corporate Ethics Practices," *Academy of Management Journal* 42 (1999): 539–552; L. Trevino, G. Weaver, D. Gibson, & B. Toffler, "Managing Ethics and Legal Compliance: What Works and What Hurts," *California Management Review* 41, no. 2 (1999): 131–151.

39 J. Salopek, "Do the Right Thing," *Training & Development* 55 (July 2001): 38–44.

40 M. Gundlach, S. Douglas, and M. Martinko, "The Decision to Blow the Whistle: A Social Information Processing Framework," *Academy of Management Executive* 17 (2003): 107–123.

41 M. Schwartz, "Business Ethics: Time to Blow the Whistle?" *Globe & Mail*, 5 March 1998, B2.

42 "More Corporate Boards Involved in Ethics Programs," *PR Newswire*.

43 H. R. Bower, *Social Responsibilities of the Businessman* (New York: Harper & Row, 1953).

44 "Beyond the Green Corporation," *BusinessWeek*, 29 January 2007.

45 Z. Zuno, "Americans Send the Message: Get Down to Business on Corporate Citizenship: Ben & Jerry's, Target, Patagonia, SC Johnson and Gerber Top the 4th GolinHarris Corporate Citizenship Index in Rating of 152 Brands by 5,000 Americans," *Business Wire*, 6 December 2006.

46 B. McKay and S. Vranica, "Firms Use Earth Day to Show Their Green Side; Eco-Friendly Messages Fill the Air, but Are They Being Heard in the Din?" *Wall Street Journal*, 22 April 2008, B7.

47 A. Murray, "Environment (A Special Report); Waste Not: Wal-Mart's H. Lee Scott Jr. on What the Company Is Doing to Reduce its Carbon Footprint—And Those of Its Customers," *Wall Street Journal*, 24 March 2008, R3.

48 S. L. Wartick and P. L. Cochran, "The Evolution of the Corporate Social Performance Model," *Academy of Management Review* 10 (1985): 758–769.

49 S. Waddock, C. Bodwell, and S. Graves, "Responsibility: The New Business Imperative," *Academy of Management Executive* 16 (2002): 132–148.

50 T. Donaldson and L. E. Preston, "The Stakeholder Theory of the Corporation: Concepts, Evidence, and Implications," *Academy of Management Review* 20 (1995): 65–91.

51 M. B. E. Clarkson, "A Stakeholder Framework for Analyzing and Evaluating Corporate Social Performance," *Academy of Management Review* 20 (1995): 92–117.

52 I. M. Jawahar and G. McLaughlin, "Toward a Descriptive Stakeholder Theory: An Organizational Life Cycle Approach," *Academy of Management Review* 26 (2001): 397–414.

53 B. Agle, R. Mitchell, and J. Sonnenfeld, "Who Matters to CEOs? An Investigation of Stakeholder Attributes and Salience, Corporate Performance, and CEO Values," *Academy of Management Journal* 42 (1999): 507–525.

54 B. Steinberg, "Omnicom Lands Bank of America; Account Had Been Sought for Its Size, Concentration; Defeat for WPP, Interpublic," *Wall Street Journal*, 1 September 2005, B5.

55 "Industry Comparison: Interpublic Group of Cos. (IPG)," *Wall Street Journal*, available online at http://online.wsj.com [accessed 30 August 2009].

56 L. E. Preston, "Stakeholder Management and Corporate Performance," *Journal of Behavioral Economics* 19 (1990): 361–375.

57 E. W. Orts, "Beyond Shareholders: Interpreting Corporate Constituency Statutes," *George Washington Law Review* 61 (1992): 14–135.

58 A. B. Carroll, "A Three-Dimensional Conceptual Model of Corporate Performance," *Academy of Management Review* 4 (1979): 497–505.

59 Ibid.

60 C. Lawton and J. Lublin, "Dell's Founder Returns as CEO as Rollins Quits—Computer Firm Expects to Miss Earnings Mark: Stock Rises after Hours," *Wall Street Journal*, 1 February 2007, C1.

61 D. Woodruff, "Europe Shows More CEOs the Door," *Wall Street Journal*, 1 July 2002.

62 C. Bray, "Ex-Monster President Found Guilty in Backdating Case," 13 May 2009, *Wall Street Journal*, C4.

63 J. Bandler, "McKelvey Admits Monster Backdating; Ex-CEO to Repay Millions but Avoids Jail Due to Illness," *Wall Street Journal*, 24 January 2008, B4.

64 "Results—How You're Helping," The Hunger Site, available online at http:// www.thehungersite.com [accessed 30 August 2009].

65 R. Christianson, "'Simplicity' Outrageous," *Wood & Wood Products*, September 2008, 11.

66 K. Scannell, "Witness Says Police-Vest Maker Ignored Safety Concerns," *Wall Street Journal*, 15 November 2004, C1.

67 J. White, "Move by Honda Ups the Ante on Car Safety," *Wall Street Journal*, 30 October 2003, D1.

68 A. McWilliams and D. Siegel, "Corporate Social Responsibility: A Theory of the Firm Perspective," *Academy of Management Review* 26, no.1 (2001): 117–127; H. Haines, "Noah Joins Ranks of Socially Responsible Funds," *Dow Jones News Service*, 13 October 1995. A meta-analysis of 41 different studies also found no relationship between corporate social responsibility and profitability. Though not reported in the meta-analysis, when confidence intervals are placed around its average sample-weighted correlation of .06, the lower confidence interval includes zero, leading to the conclusion that there is no relationship between corporate social responsibility and profitability. See M. Orlitzky, "Does Firm Size Confound the Relationship between Corporate Social Responsibility and Firm Performance?" *Journal of Business Ethics* 33 (2001): 167–180; S. Ambec and P. Lanoie, "Does It Pay to Be Green? A Systematic Overview," *Academy of Management Perspectives*, 22 (2008): 45–62.

69 M. Orlitzky, "Payoffs to Social and Environmental Performance," *Journal of Investing* 14 (2005): 48–51.

70 M. Orlitzky, F. Schmidt, and S. Rynes, "Corporate Social and Financial Performance: A Meta-Analysis," *Organization Studies* 24 (2003): 403–441.

71 Orlitzky, "Payoffs to Social and Environmental Performance."

72 Orlitzky, Schmidt, and Rynes, "Corporate Social and Financial Performance."

73 A. Murray and A. Strassel, "Environment (A Special Report); Ahead of the Pack: GE's Jeffrey Immelt on Why It's Business, Not Personal," *Wall Street Journal*, 24 March 2008, R3.

74 K. Kranhold, "Greener Postures: GE's Environment Push Hits Business Realities; CEO's Quest to Reduce Emissions Irks Clients; The Battle of the Bulbs," *Wall Street Journal*, 14 September 2007, A1.

75 "Ecoimagination is GE," 2008 Ecoimagination Annual Report," available online at http://ge.ecoimagination.com [accessed 30 August 2009].

76 D. Kadlec and B. Van Voorst, "The New World of Giving: Companies Are Doing More Good, and Demanding More Back," *Time*, 5 May 1997, 62.

77 P. Carlin, "Will Rapid Growth Stunt Corporate Do-Gooders?" *Business & Society Review* (Spring 1995), 36–43.

78 K. Brown, "Chilling at Ben & Jerry's: Cleaner, Greener," *Wall Street Journal*, 15 April 2004, B1.

79 J. E. Wanek, P. R. Sackett, and D. S. Ones, "Towards an Understanding of Integrity Test Similarities and Differences: An Item Level Analysis of Seven Tests," *Personnel Psychology* 56 (2003): 873–894.

Chapter Four

1 M. Dolan, J. Stoll, and N. Boudette, "Ford's Stumble Signals Rising Risks; Pickup, SUV Sales Take Surprisingly Steep Fall; Return to Profit in '09 Now 'Unlikely,'" *Wall Street Journal*, 23 May 2008, A1; D. Kiley, "Ford's Savior?" *BusinessWeek*, 16 March 2009, 30; M. Spector, "Ford Eyes More Cuts As Recovery Advances; Earnings Improve, Quality Ratings Up; Volvo Sales Possible," *Wall Street Journal*, 23 April 2008, A1; M. Spector, "Ford Plans a Taurus Redesign," *Wall Street Journal*, 23 January 2008, D7; A. Taylor, "Can This Car Save Ford?" *Fortune*, 5 May 2008, 170; A. Taylor, "Fixing up Ford," *Fortune*, 25 May 2009, 44.

2 L. A. Hill, *Becoming a Manager: Master a New Identity* (Boston: Harvard Business School Press, 1992).

3 J. Jargon, "General Mills Sees Wealth via Health," *Wall Street Journal*, 25 February 2008, A9.

4 E. A. Locke and G. P. Latham, *A Theory of Goal Setting & Task Performance* (Englewood Cliffs, NJ: Prentice Hall, 1990).

5 M. E. Tubbs, "Goal-Setting: A Meta-Analytic Examination of the Empirical Evidence," *Journal of Applied Psychology* 71 (1986): 474–483.

6 J. Bavelas and E. S. Lee, "Effect of Goal Level on Performance: A Trade-Off of Quantity and Quality," *Canadian Journal of Psychology* 32 (1978): 219–240.

7 Harvard Management Update, "Learn by 'Failing Forward,'" *Globe & Mail*, 31 October 2000, B17.

8 C. C. Miller, "Strategic Planning and Firm Performance: A Synthesis of More Than Two Decades of Research," *Academy of Management Performance* 37 (1994): 1649–1665.

9 H. Mintzberg, "Rethinking Strategic Planning: Part I: Pitfalls and Fallacies," *Long Range Planning* 27 (1994): 12–21, and "Part II: New Roles for Planners," 22–30; H. Mintzberg, "The Pitfalls of Strategic Planning," *California Management Review* 36 (1993): 32–47.

10 J. D. Stoll, "GM Sees Brighter Future," *Wall Street Journal*, 18 January 2008, A3; D. Welch, "Live Green or Die," *BusinessWeek*, 26 May 2008, 36–41; L. Greenemeier, "GM's Chevy Volt to Hit the Streets of San Francisco and Washington, D.C.," *60-Second Science Blog*, available online at http://www .scientificamerican.com, 5 February 2009 [accessed 29 May 2009].

11 Mintzberg, "The Pitfalls of Strategic Planning."

12 Locke and Latham, *A Theory of Goal Setting & Task Performance.*

13 A. King, B. Oliver, B. Sloop, and K. Vaverek, *Planning & Goal Setting for Improved Performance: Participant's Guide* (Cincinnati, OH: Thomson Executive Press, 1995).

14 C. Loomis, J. Schlosser, J. Sung, M. Boyle, and P. Neering, "The 15% Delusion: Brash Predictions about Earnings Growth Often Lead to Missed Targets, Battered Stock, and Creative Accounting—And That's When Times Are Good," *Fortune*, 5 February 2001, 102; H. Paster, "Manager's Journal: Be Prepared," *Wall Street Journal*, 24 September 2001, A24; P. Sellers, "The New Breed: The Latest Crop of CEOs Is Disciplined, Deferential, Even a Bit Dull," *Fortune*, 18 November 2002, 66; H. Klein and M. Wesson, "Goal and Commitment and the Goal-Setting Process: Conceptual Clarification and Empirical Synthesis," *Journal of Applied Psychology* 84 (1999): 885–896.

15 Locke and Latham, *A Theory of Goal Setting & Task Performance*.

16 Klein and Wesson, "Goal and Commitment and the Goal-Setting Process: Conceptual Clarification and Empirical Synthesis."

17 A. Pressman, "Ocean Spray's Creative Juices," *BusinessWeek*, 15 May 2006, 88–90.

18 A. Bandura and D. H. Schunk, "Cultivating Competence, Self-Efficacy, and Intrinsic Interest through Proximal Self-Motivation," *Journal of Personality & Social Psychology* 41 (1981): 586–598.

19 Locke and Latham, *A Theory of Goal Setting & Task Performance*.

20 M. J. Neubert, "The Value of Feedback and Goal Setting over Goal Setting Alone and Potential Moderators of This Effect: A Meta-Analysis," *Human Performance* 11 (1998): 321–335.

21 E. H. Bowman and D. Hurry, "Strategy through the Option Lens: An Integrated View of Resource Investments and the Incremental-Choice Process," *Academy of Management Review* 18 (1993): 760–782.

22 M. Lawson, "In Praise of Slack: Time Is of the Essence," *Academy of Management Executive* 15 (2000): 125–135.

23 "Total Paid Circulation," *Newspaper Association of America*, available online at http://www.naa.org [accessed 29 May 2009].

24 D. Lieberman, "Papers Take a Leap Forward, Opening Up to New Ideas," *USA Today*, 30 January 2006, http://www.usatoday.com/tech/news/techinnovations/2006-01-30-newspaper-schange_ x.htm [accessed 29 May 2009].

25 N. A. Wishart, J. J. Elam, and D. Robey, "Redrawing the Portrait of a Learning Organization: Inside Knight-Ridder, Inc.," *Academy of Management Executive* 10 (1996): 7–20.

26 J. McGregor et al., "How Failure Breeds Success: Everyone Fears Failure. But Breakthroughs Depend on It. The Best Companies Embrace Their Mistakes and Learn from Them," *BusinessWeek*, 10 July 2006, 42.

27 J. C. Collins and J. I. Porras, "Organizational Vision and Visionary Organizations," *California Management Review* (Fall 1991): 30–52.

28 Ibid.

29 J. C. Collins and J. I. Porras, "Organizational Vision and Visionary Organizations," *California Management Review* (Fall 1991): 30–52; J. A. Pearce II, "The Company Mission as a Strategic Goal," *Sloan Management Review* (Spring 1982): 15–24. Collins and Porras define an organization's mission: "A mission is a clear and compelling goal that serves to unify an organization's efforts. An effective mission must stretch and challenge the organization, yet be achievable." However, many others define mission as an organization's purpose. In this edition, to be more specific and avoid confusion, we used Collins and Porras's term "purpose statement," meaning a clear statement of an organization's purpose or reason for existence. Furthermore, we continued to use Collins and Porras's definition of a mission (i.e., "a clear and compelling goal . . .,"), but instead call it "the strategic objective."

30 "President Bush Announces New Vision for Space Exploration Program," The White House, available online at http://www.whitehouse.gov/news/releases/2004/01/ 20040114-1.html [accessed 17 April 2005].

31 "NASA's Exploration Systems Mission Directorate," Exploration: NASA's Plans to Explore the Moon, Mars, and Beyond, available online at http://www.nasa.gov [accessed 29 May 2009].

32 R. Van Hoek and K. Pegels, "Growing by Cutting SKUs at Clorox," *Harvard Business Review* (April 2006): 22.

33 L. Lorberf, "Running the Show—An Open Book: When Companies Share Their Financial Data with Employees, the Results Can Be Dramatic," *Wall Street Journal*, 23 February 2009, R8.

34 R. Rodgers and J. E. Hunter, "Impact of Management by Objectives on Organizational Productivity," *Journal of Applied Psychology* 76 (1991): 322–336.

35 "Web MBO Teams with Deloitte & Touche to Deliver Innovative Web-Based 'Management-by-Objectives and Performance Management' Solutions," *PR Newswire*, 19 June 2001.

36 C. S. Covel, "Moving Across Country to Cut Costs," *Wall Street Journal*, 10 January 2008, B4.

37 S. McCartney, "Is Your Boss Spying on Your Upgrades?" *Wall Street Journal*, 12 August 2008, D1.

38 Adapted from quality procedure at G & G Manufacturing, Cincinnati, Ohio.

39 N. Humphrey, "References a Tricky Issue for Both Sides," *Nashville Business Journal* 11 (8 May 1995): 1A.

40 K. R. MacCrimmon, R. N. Taylor, and E. A. Locke, "Decision Making and Problem Solving," in *Handbook of Industrial & Organizational Psychology*, ed. M. D. Dunnette (Chicago: Rand McNally, 1976), 1397–1453.

41 A. Zimmerman, "Cricket Lee Takes on the Fashion Industry," *Wall Street Journal*, 17 March 2008, R1.

42 MacCrimmon, Taylor, and Locke, "Decision Making and Problem Solving."

43 G. Kress, "The Role of Interpretation in the Decision Process," *Industrial Management* 37 (1995): 10–14.

44 J. Jargon, "As Profit Cools, Starbucks Plans Price Campaign," *Wall Street Journal*, 30 April 2009, B3.

45 Zimmerman, "Cricket Lee Takes on the Fashion Industry."

46 Ibid.

47 "Notebook Shipments Surpass Desktops in the U.S. Market for the First Time, According to IDC," IDC, available online at http://www.idc.com, 28 October 2008 [accessed 30 May 2009].

48 *Consumer Reports Buying Guide 2006*, 129–131.

49 "New-Vehicle Ratings Comparison by Car Category," ConsumerReports.org, http://www.consumerreports.org/ cro/cars/index.htm, 19 February 2005 [accessed 29 May 2009].

50 P. Djang, "Selecting Personal Computers," *Journal of Research on Computing in Education* 25 (1993): 327.

51 "European Cities Monitor," Cushman & Wakefield, 2007, available online at http://www.berlin-partner.de/ fileadmin/chefredaktion/documents/pdf_Presse/European_Investment_Monitor_2007.pdf [accessed 29 May 2009].

52 "The PLUS Decision Making Model," Ethics Resource Center, http://www.ethics.org/resources/decision-making-model.asp, 19 February 2005 [accessed 29 May 2009].

53 B. Dumaine, "The Trouble with Teams," *Fortune*, 5 September 1994, 86–92.

54 L. Pelled, K. Eisenhardt, and K. Xin, "Exploring the Black Box: An Analysis of Work Group Diversity, Conflict, and Performance," *Administrative Science Quarterly* 44, no. 1 (1 March 1999): 1.

55 B. Scudamore, "Gather Round! For a Group Interview," *Inc.*, August 2006, 94.

[56] I. L. Janis, *Groupthink* (Boston: Houghton Mifflin, 1983).

[57] C. P. Neck and C. C. Manz, "From Groupthink to Teamthink: Toward the Creation of Constructive Thought Patterns in Self-Managing Work Teams," *Human Relations* 47 (1994): 929–952; J. Schwartz and M. L. Wald, "'Groupthink' Is 30 Years Old, and Still Going Strong," *New York Times*, 9 March 2003, 5.

[58] "Merck Wins Suit on Vioxx Monitoring," *Wall Street Journal*, 5 June 2008, D8.

[59] A. Mason, W. A. Hochwarter, and K. R. Thompson, "Conflict: An Important Dimension in Successful Management Teams," *Organizational Dynamics* 24 (1995): 20.

[60] C. Olofson, "So Many Decisions, So Little Time: What's Your Problem?" *Fast Company*, 1 October 1999, 62.

[61] R. Cosier and C. R. Schwenk, "Agreement and Thinking Alike: Ingredients for Poor Decisions," *Academy of Management Executive* 4 (1990): 69–74.

[62] Ibid.

[63] B. Breen, "BMW: Driven by Design," *Fast Company*, 1 September 2002, 123.

[64] K. Jenn and E. Mannix, "The Dynamic Nature of Conflict: A Longitudinal Study of Intragroup Conflict and Group Performance," *Academy of Management Journal* 44, no. 2 (2001): 238–251; R. L. Priem, D. A. Harrison, and N. K. Muir, "Structured Conflict and Consensus Outcomes in Group Decision Making," *Journal of Management* 21 (1995): 691–710.

[65] A. Van De Ven and A. L. Delbecq, "Nominal versus Interacting Group Processes for Committee Decision Making Effectiveness," *Academy of Management Journal* 14 (1971): 203–212.

[66] A. R. Dennis and J. S. Valicich, "Group, Sub-Group, and Nominal Group Idea Generation: New Rules for a New Media?" *Journal of Management* 20 (1994): 723–736.

[67] C. R. Schwenk, "Effects of Devil's Advocacy and Dialectical Inquiry on Decision Making: A Meta-Analysis," *Organizational Behavior & Human Decision Performance* 47 (1990): 161–176; M. Orlitzky and R. Hirokawa, "To Err Is Human, to Correct for It Divine: A Meta-Analysis of Research Testing the Functional Theory of Group Decision-Making Effectiveness," *Small Group Research* 32, no. 3 (June 2001): 313–341.

[68] S. G. Rogelberg, J. L. Barnes-Farrell, and C. A. Lowe, "The Stepladder Technique: An Alternative Group Structure Facilitating Effective Group Decision Making," *Journal of Applied Psychology* 77 (1992): 730–737; S. G. Rogelberg and M. S. O'Connor, "Extending the Stepladder Technique: An Examination of the Self-Paced Stepladder Groups," *Group Dynamics: Theory, Research, & Practice* 2 (1998): 82–91.

[69] S. Rogelberg, M. O'Connor, and M. Sedergurg, "Using the Stepladder Technique to Facilitate the Performance of Audioconferencing Groups," *Journal of Applied Psychology* 87 (2002): 994–1000.

[70] R. B. Gallupe, W. H. Cooper, M. L. Grise, and L. M. Bastianutti, "Blocking Electronic Brainstorms," *Journal of Applied Psychology* 79 (1994): 77–86.

[71] R. B. Gallupe and W. H. Cooper, "Brainstorming Electronically," *Sloan Management Review*, Fall 1993, 27–36.

[72] Ibid.

[73] G. Kay, "Effective Meetings through Electronic Brainstorming," *Management Quarterly* 35 (1995): 15.

[74] A. LaPlante, "90s Style Brainstorming," *Forbes ASAP*, 25 October 1993, 44.

[75] R.J. Aldag and L. W. Kuzuhara, *Mastering Management Skills: A Manager's Toolkit* (Mason, OH: Thomson South-Western, 2005), 172–173.

Chapter Five

[1] R. Burrows and A. Ricadela, "Cisco Seizes the Moment," *BusinessWeek*, 25 May 2009, 46; E. McGirt, "How Cisco's CEO John Chambers Is Turning the Tech Giant Socialist," *Fast Company*, 25 November 2008, available online at http://www.fastcompany.com [accessed 8 June 2009]; B. White, "Cisco's Homegrown Experiment; Slower Growth Forces Networking Company to Be Its Own Start-Up," *Wall Street Journal*, 23 January 2007, A14; B. White and V. Vara, "Re-Routed: Cisco Changes Tack in Takeover Game," *Wall Street Journal*, 17 April 2008, A1; S. Wildstrom, "Meet Cisco, the Consumer Company," *BusinessWeek*, 4 May 2009, 73.

[2] L. Kahney, "Inside Look at the Birth of the iPod," *Wired*, 21 July 2004, available online at http://www.wired.com/news/culture/0,64286-0.html, http://www.apple-history.com/?page=gallery& model=ipod [accessed 8 June 2009]; K. Hall, "Sony's iPod Assault Is No Threat to Apple," *BusinessWeek*, 13 March 2006, 53; N. Wingfield, "SanDisk Raises Music-Player Stakes," *Wall Street Journal*, 21 August 2006, B4; "Growing Louder: Microsoft Plods after iPod Like a Giant—Powerful, Determined, Untiring," *Winston-Salem Journal*, 15 November 2006, D1–2; A. Athavaley and R. A. Guth, "How the Zune Is Faring So Far with Consumers," *Wall Street Journal*, 12 December 2006, D1, D7; P. Cruz, "US Top Selling Computer Hardware for January 2007," Bloomberg.com, available online at http://www.bloomberg.com/apps/news?pid=conewsstory&refer=conews&tkr=AAPL:US&sid=ap0bqJw2VpwI [accessed 29 July 2008].

[3] J. Barney, "Firm Resources and Sustained Competitive Advantage," *Journal of Management* 17 (1991): 99–120; J. Barney, "Looking Inside for Competitive Advantage," *Academy of Management Executive* 9 (1995): 49–61.

[4] J. Snell, "Apple's Home Run," *Macworld*, November 2006, 7.

[5] K. Boehret, "The Mossberg Solution: IPod to Reach Out and Touch Someone," *Wall Street Journal*, 29 April 2009, B11.

[6] Athavaley and Guth, "How the Zune Is Faring So Far with Consumers," D7.

[7] "iTunes Tops 200 Million TV Episodes Sold, Including over One Million HD Episodes," *Apple*, available online at http://www.apple.com, 16 October 2008 [accessed 4 June 2009]; "Thanks *a* Billion," *Apple*, available online at http://www.apple.com [accessed 4 June 2009]; E. Schonfeld, "iTunes Sells 6 Billion Songs, and Other Fun Stats from the Philnote," *TechCrunch*, available online at http://www.techcrunch.com, 6 January 2009 [accessed 4 June 2009].

[8] S. H. Wildstrom, "ZUNE 2.0: Playing Tomorrow's Tune?," *BusinessWeek*, 10 December 2007, 87.

[9] J. Warren, "At New Web Store, Many Songs Sell for a Few Cents," *Wall Street Journal*, 14 October 2006, P2.

[10] E. Smith and Y. Kane, "Apple Changes Tune on Music Pricing," *Wall Street Journal*, 7 January 2009, B1.

[11] S. Hart and C. Banbury, "How Strategy-Making Processes Can Make a Difference," *Strategic Management Journal* 15 (1994): 251–269.

[12] R. A. Burgelman, "Fading Memories: A Process Theory of Strategic Business Exit in Dynamic Environments," *Administrative Science Quarterly* 39 (1994): 24–56; R. A. Burgelman and A. S. Grove, "Strategic Dissonance," *California Management Review* 38 (Winter 1996): 8–28.

[13] T. Audi, "Last Resort: Ailing Sheraton Shoots for a Room Upgrade; Starwood to Tackle Biggest Hotel Brand; The 'Ugly Stepchild,'" *Wall Street Journal*, 25 March 2008, A1.

[14] Burgelman and Grove, "Strategic Dissonance."

15 E. Smith and M. Peers, "Cost Cutting Is an Uphill Fight at Warner Music," *Wall Street Journal*, 24 May 2004, B1.

16 A. Fiegenbaum, S. Hart, and D. Schendel, "Strategic Reference Point Theory," *Strategic Management Journal* 17 (1996): 219–235.

17 "Most and Least Reliable Brands," *Consumer Reports*, available online at http://www.consumerreports.org/cro/money/resource-center/ most-and-least-reliable- brands-5-07/cars/0507brandscars1.htm [accessed 29 July 2008].

18 S. Segan and E. Griffith, "The Best (and Worst) Tech Support in America," *PC Magazine*, 29 July 2008, available online at http://www.pcmag.com/article2/0,2817, 2326603,00.asp [accessed 29 July 2008].

19 Hart and Banbury, "How Strategy-Making Processes Can Make a Difference"; C. C. Miller and L. B. Cardinal, "Strategic Planning and Firm Performance: A Synthesis of More Than Two Decades of Research," *Academy of Management Journal* 37 (1994): 1649–1665; D. King, D. Dalton, C. Daily, and J. Covin, "Meta-Analyses of Post-Acquisition Performance: Indications of Unidentified Moderators," *Strategic Management Journal* 25 (2004): 187–200; C. R. Schwenk, "Effects of Formal Strategic Planning on Financial Performance in Small Firms: A Meta Analysis," *Entrepreneurship Theory & Practice* (Spring 1993): 53–64.

20 P. Buller and G. McEvoy, "Creating and Sustaining Ethical Capability in the Multi-National Corporation," *Journal of World Business* 34 (1999): 326–343.

21 C. Palmieri, "Inside Tesco's New U.S. Stores," *BusinessWeek Online*, 4 December 2007; "Unique Products, Reasonable Prices Spell Success for Trader Joe's," *The Food Institute Report* 81 (3 March 2008): 4; "Trader Joe's: Why the Hype?," *Bulletin* (Bend, OR), 27 March 2008.

22 D. Carpenter, "SWOT Team Solves Supply Chain Issues," *Materials Management in Health Care* (April 2006): 40–42.

23 A. Fiegenbaum and H. Thomas, "Strategic Groups as Reference Groups: Theory, Modeling and Empirical Examination of Industry and Competitive Strategy," *Strategic Management Journal* 16 (1995): 461–476.

24 "Continued Weaknesses in Housing and the Overall Economy Are Now Foreseen to Result in Three Consecutive Years of Market Declines," *Home Improvement Research Institute*, available online at HTP://www.hiri.org [accessed 5 June 2009].

25 R. K. Reger and A. S. Huff, "Strategic Groups: A Cognitive Perspective," *Strategic Management Journal* 14 (1993): 103–124.

26 M. Hogan, "Big Box Battle: Home Depot vs. Lowe's," *BusinessWeek Online*, 22 August 2006, 7; F. Miller, "Growing Pains," *Kitchen & Bath Business* (September 2006): 53.

27 About Aubuchon Hardware, available online at http://www.hardwarestore.com/about-aubuchon-hardware.aspx [accessed 29 July 2008].

28 84 Lumber, available online at http://www.84lumber.com [accessed 29 July 2008].

29 "Menard, Inc.," *Hoover's Company Profiles*, 8 May 2003.

30 J. Samuelson, "Tough Guy Billionaire," *Forbes*, 24 February 1997, 64–66.

31 S. Bucksot, C. Jensen, and D. Tratensek, "Where Are We Headed?" *2005 Market Measure: The Industry's Annual Report*, http://www.nrha.org/MM2004.pdf, 6 March 2005 [accessed 8 June 2009].

32 H. Murphy, "Menard's Tool in Retail Battle: Gigantic Stores," *Crain's Chicago Business*, 12 August 2002, 3.

33 M. Lubatkin, "Value-Creating Mergers: Fact or Folklore?" *Academy of Management Executive* 2 (1988): 295–302; M. Lubatkin and S. Chatterjee, "Extending Modern Portfolio Theory into the Domain of Corporate Diversification: Does It Apply?" *Academy of Management Journal* 37 (1994): 109–136; M. H. Lubatkin and P. J. Lane, "Psst . . . The Merger Mavens Still Have It Wrong!" *Academy of Management Executive* 10 (1996): 21–39.

34 "Our Company," Johnson & Johnson, available online at http://www.jnj.com/our_company/ index.htm [accessed 17 March 2009].

35 "About Samsung," Samsung, available online at http://www.samsung.com/us/aboutsamsung/index.html [accessed 29 July 2008].

36 B. Henderson, "The Experience Curve—Reviewed: IV. The Growth Share Matrix or the Product Portfolio," *The Boston Consulting Group*, available online at http://www.bcg.com/publications/files/Experience_Curve_IV_ Growth_Share_Matrix_1973.pdf, 1973 [accessed 6 June 2009].

37 "Phonebook Company Yellow Book Enters into Lynchburg, Va.-Area Market," *Lynchburg (VA) News & Advance*, 16 January 2005; "Leading Independents Project Double-Digit Gains in 2004; Plan Aggressive Expansion," *Yellow Pages & Directory Report*, 27 August 2004; G. David, "The Good Book/Unmellow Yellow: A Battle among Business Directories Could Cut Your Ad Costs," *FSB*, 1 November 2003, 85.

38 D. Hambrick, I. MacMillan, and D. Day, "Strategic Attributes and Performance in the BCG Matrix—A PIMS-based Analysis of Industrial Product Businesses," *Academy of Management Journal* 25 (1982): 510–531.

39 J. Armstrong and R. Brodie, "Effects of Portfolio Planning Methods on Decision Making: Experimental Results," *International Journal of Research in Marketing* 11 (1994): 73–84.

40 J. A. Pearce II, "Selecting among Alternative Grand Strategies," *California Management Review* (Spring 1982): 23–31.

41 "About REI," *REI*, available online at http://www.rei.com/aboutrei/about_rei.html [accessed 7 June 2009]; "Recreational Equipment, Inc.," *Hoover*, available online at http://www.hoovers.com [accessed 7 June 2009].

42 J. A. Pearce II, "Retrenchment Remains the Foundation of Business Turnaround," *Strategic Management Journal* 15 (1994): 407–417.

43 S. Hillis, "Microsoft, EA Sign Sports Game Ad Deal," *Reuters*, available online at http://www.reuters.com/, 25 July 2007 [accessed 7 June 2009].

44 B. Charny, "Videogame Makers See Winning Model in China," *Wall Street Journal*, 13 May 2009.

45 E. Ramstad and P. Dvorak, "Off-the-Shelf Parts Create New Order in TVs, Electronics," *Wall Street Journal*, 16 December 2003, A1.

46 M. Mangalindan, "Irked by eBay, Some Sellers Trade Elsewhere; Niche Sites Tout Lower Fees, Tutorials, More Photos; Buyers Still Face Fraud Risks," 12 August 2008, D1.

47 "About Etsy," *Etsy*, available online at http://www.etsy.com [accessed 8 June 2009].

48 R. E. Miles and C. C. Snow, *Organizational Strategy, Structure, & Process* (New York: McGraw-Hill, 1978); S. Zahra and J. A. Pearce, "Research Evidence on the Miles-Snow Typology," *Journal of Management* 16 (1990): 751–768; W. L. James and K. J. Hatten, "Further Evidence on the Validity of the Self Typing Paragraph Approach: Miles and Snow Strategic Archetypes in Banking," *Strategic Management Journal* 16 (1995): 161–168.

49 G. Charles, "KitKat: The Nestlé Brand Has Reversed a Sales Decline by Focusing on Fewer Variants," *Marketing* (4 March 2009): 19.

50 R. Feintzeig, "Amusement Park Is Given a Second Chance to Thrill—With or Without the Hard Rock Name, New Owners Hope to Draw Tourists to the Myrtle Beach, S.C., Attraction," *Wall Street Journal*, 18 March 2009.

51 M. Chen, "Competitor Analysis and Interfirm Rivalry: Toward a Theoretical Integration," *Academy of Management Review* 21 (1996): 100–134; J. C. Baum and H. J. Korn, "Competitive Dynamics of Interfirm Rivalry," *Academy of Management Journal* 39 (1996): 255–291.

52 Ibid.

53 S. Leung, "Wendy's Sees Green in Salad Offerings—More Sophistication, Ethnic Flavors Appeal to Women, Crucial to Building Market Share," *Wall Street Journal*, 24 April 2003, B2.

54 Subway, available online at http://www.subway.com, [accessed 29 July 2008]; N. Torres, "Full Speed Ahead," Entrepreneur.com, available online at http://www.entrepreneur.com/ magazine/ entrepreneur/ 2007/january/172060.html [accessed 29 July 2008].

55 G. Marcial, "How Wendy's Stayed Out of the Fire," *BusinessWeek*, 9 December 2002, 138.

56 R. D'Aveni, "Business Insight (A Special Report); Leaders of the Pack: A Look at Strategies for Securing Market Domination—and Keeping It," *Wall Street Journal*, 3 March 2007, R9.

57 D. Ketchen, Jr., C. Snow, and V. Street, "Improving Firm Performance by Matching Strategic Decision-Making Processes to Competitive Dynamics," *Academy of Management Executive* 18 (2004): 29–43.

58 S. Matthews, "Financial: Salads Help McD Post First U.S. Sales Gain in 14 Months," *Chicago Sun-Times*, 14 May 2003, 69.

59 Y. Kane, "Sony Price Cut Helps Its PS3 Gain Traction; Move Boosts Sales of Game Consoles in Time for Holidays," *Wall Street Journal*, 26 November 2007, B4.

60 D. Wakabayashi, "Hope Fades for PS3 as a Comeback Player—In Battle of the Game Consoles, Nintendo Wii and Microsoft Xbox Widen Leads over Sony's PlayStation," *Wall Street Journal*, 29 December 2008, B1; N. Wingfield, "Microsoft Cuts Xbox to $199," *Wall Street Journal*, 4 September 2008, B9; N. Wingfield, "Microsoft to Cut Xbox 360 Pro Price," *Wall Street Journal*, 11 July 2008, B6.

61 Wakabayashi, "Hope Fades for PS3 as a Comeback Player."

62 J. M. Houston and R. D. Smither, "The Nature of Competitiveness: The Development and Validation of the Competitiveness Index," *Educational and Psychological Measurement* 52 (1992): 407–418.

Chapter Six

1 K. Capwell, "Novartis: Radically Remaking Its Drug Business," *Business Week*, 22 June 2009, 30–35; A. Greil & J. Whalen, "Earn ings Digest: Novartis's Net Drops 45%, Hit by Generics," 18 January 2009, B4; B. Martinez & J. Goldstein, "Big Pharma Faces Grim Prognosis; Industry Fails to Find New Drugs to Replace Wonders Like Lipitor," *Wall Street Journal*, 6 December 2007, A1; J. Whalen, "Novartis Plans Restructuring; CEO Vasella Says Moves Aim to Trim Bureaucracy Layers," *Wall Street Journal*, 11 December 2007, A21; J. Whalen, "Overhaul Spurs Novartis Labs," *Wall Street Journal*, 20 November 2008, B3.

2 T. M. Amabile, R. Conti, H. Coon, J. Lazenby, and M. Herron, "Assessing the Work Environment for Creativity," *Academy of Management Journal* 39 (1996): 1154–1184.

3 Ibid.

4 A. H. Van de Ven and M. S. Poole, "Explaining Development and Change in Organizations," *Academy of Management Review* 20 (1995): 510–540.

5 "Swedes to Use Body Heat to Warm Offices," ABC News, available online at http://abcnews.go.com/International/ wireStory?id=410819 [accessed 17 September 2008]; E. Yerger, "Company in Sweden Uses Body Heat to Warm Office Building," *Unusual Things*, available online at http://www.popfi.com/ 2008/01/14/ company-to-use-body-heat-to-warmoffice-building-2 [accessed 17 September 2008]; D. Chazan, "Office Block Warmed by Body Heat," BBC News, available online at http://news.bbc.co.uk/2/hi/science/nature/7233123.stm [accessed 17 September 2008].

6 Ibid.

7 Amabile et al., "Assessing the Work Environment for Creativity."

8 S. McBride, "Thinking About Tomorrow: How We Watch Movies and TV," *Wall Street Journal*, 28 January 2008, R1.

9 P. Anderson and M. L. Tushman, "Managing Through Cycles of Technological Change," *Research/Technology Management*, May–June 1991, 26–31.

10 R. N. Foster, *Innovation: The Attacker's Advantage* (New York: Summit, 1986).

11 A. Otis, "The Impetus for Vermont Buying Colorado Railcar DMU's," Trainriders Northeast, 1 January 2007, available online at www.railivemont.org [accessed 11 November 2009]; www .usrailcar.com.

12 M. L. Tushman, P. C. Anderson, and C. O'Reilly, "Technology Cycles, Innovation Streams, and Ambidextrous Organizations: Organization Renewal Through Innovation Streams and Strategic Change," in *Managing Strategic Innovation and Change*, ed. M. L. Tushman and P. Anderson (New York: Oxford Press, 1997), 3–23.

13 P. Landers, "Brain Surgery Made Simple—New Less-Invasive Procedures Reduce Pain, Recovery Time; Sending in the Tiny Robots," *Wall Street Journal*, 31 October 2002, D1.

14 "Breakthrough Brain Surgery: Neurosurgeons Can Now Remove Brain Cancer Endoscopically," *ScienceDaily*, 1 August 2005, available at http://www.sciencedaily.com [accessed 8 November 2009].

15 W. Abernathy and J. Utterback, "Patterns of Industrial Innovation," *Technology Review* 2 (1978): 40–47.

16 Chris Tribbey "Blu Capabilities Still Up in the Air," *Home Media Magazine*. Apr 11 2008. http://www.homemediamagazine.com/ news/blu-capabilities-still-air-12504 [accessed 8 November 2009].

17 M. Schilling, "Technological Lockout: An Integrative Model of the Economic and Strategic Factors Driving Technology Success and Failure," *Academy of Management Review* 23 (1998): 267–284; M. Schilling, "Technology Success and Failure in Winner-Take-All Markets: The Impact of Learning Orientation, Timing, and Network Externalities," *Academy of Management Journal* 45 (2002): 387–398.

18 Amabile et al., "Assessing the Work Environment for Creativity."

19 Ibid.

20 M. Csikszentmihalyi, *Flow: The Psychology of Optimal Experience* (New York: Harper & Row, 1990).

21 S. Kirsner, "Adobe Idol," *Fast Company,* May 2007, 95.

22 D. Murphy, "Ways That Managers Can Help Workers—Or Hinder Them," *San Francisco Chronicle*, 26 November 2000, J1; M. Schrage, "Your Idea Is Brilliant; Glad I Thought of It," *Fortune*, 16 October 2000, 412.

23 K. M. Eisenhardt, "Accelerating Adaptive Processes: Product Innovation in the Global Computer Industry," *Administrative Science Quarterly* 40 (1995): 84–110.

24 Ibid.

25 E. Masamitsu, "This Is My Job: Parachute Tester," *Popular Mechanics* 185 (June 2008): 174.

26 L. Hansen, "A High-Flying Career: Testing Parachutes," NPR, 6 July 2008, available online at http://www.npr.org [accessed 8 November 2009].

27 R. Winslow, "Atomic Speed: Utility Cuts Red Tape, Builds Nuclear Plant Almost on Schedule," *Wall Street Journal Interactive*, 22 February 1984.

28 C. Salter, "Ford's Escape Route," *Fast Company*, 1 October 2004, 106.

29 L. Kraar, "25 Who Help the U.S. Win: Innovators Everywhere Are Generating Ideas to Make America a Stronger Competitor. They Range from a Boss Who Demands the Impossible to a Mathematician with a Mop," *Fortune*, 22 March 1991.

30 M. W. Lawless and P. C. Anderson, "Generational Technological Change: Effects of Innovation and Local Rivalry on Performance," *Academy of Management Journal* 39 (1996): 1185–1217.

31 J. Muller, "Chrysler Redesigns the Way It Designs: Karenann Terrell's High-Tech Quest for Change," *BusinessWeek*, 2 September 2002, 26B.

32 B. Warmoth, "'Harry Potter and the Deathly Hallows' Could Still Get a John Williams Score," MTV, 15 July 2009, available online at http://moviesblog.mtv.com [accessed 8 November 2009].

33 K. Kelly, "Older Harry Rates a PG-13: The Awkward, Lovelorn Hero of 'Goblet of Fire' May Lose Kids, Gain Broader Audience," *Wall Street Journal,* 16 November 2005, B1.

34 "From Major to Minor," *The Economist*, 12 January 2008, 55–56.

35 "Sales of Music CDs Sank 20% in 2008," *Wall Street Journal*, 2 January 2009, A12.

36 Ibid.

37 K. Lewin, *Field Theory in Social Science: Selected Theoretical Papers* (New York: Harper & Brothers, 1951).

38 A. Deutschman, "Making Change: Why Is It So Darn Hard to Change Our Ways?" *Fast Company*, May 2005, 52–62.

39 Lewin, *Field Theory in Social Science.*

40 A. B. Fisher, "Making Change Stick," *Fortune*, 17 April 1995, 121.

41 J. P. Kotter and L. A. Schlesinger, "Choosing Strategies for Change," *Harvard Business Review* (March–April 1979): 106–114.

42 S. Giessner, G. Viki, T. Otten, S. Terry, and D. Tauber, "The Challenge of Merging: Merger Patterns, Premerger Status, and Merger Support," *Personality and Social Psychology Bulletin* 32, no. 3 (2006): 339–352.

43 J. Scanlon, "San Diego Zoo's Newest Exhibit: Innovation," *BusinessWeek*, 14 October 2009, available online at http://www.businessweek.com/innovate/content/oct2009/id20091014_325112.htm?chan=innovation_special+report+--+growth+through+innovation_special+report+--+growth+through+innovation [accessed 11 November 2009].

44 D. Haugen, "Welcome to Blue Shirt Nation," *Twin Cities Business*, April 2009, available online at http://www.tcbmag.com [accessed 11 November 2009].

45 B. Orwall, "Disney Decides It Must Draw Artists into Computer Age," *Wall Street Journal*, 23 October 2003, A1.

46 J. P. Kotter, "Leading Change: Why Transformation Efforts Fail," *Harvard Business Review* 73, no. 2 (March–April 1995): 59.

47 G. Pitts, "A Classic Turnaround—With Some Twists," *The Globe and Mail*, 7 July 2008, B1.

48 Ibid.

49 P. Engardio and J. McGregor, "Lean and Mean Gets Extreme," *BusinessWeek*, 23 March 2009, 60.

50 Pitts, "A Classic Turnaround."

51 R. Carrick, "Rising from the Stock Market Rubble," *The Globe and Mail (Canada)*, 21 June 2008, B15; W. Dabrowski. "Celestica Buoyed by Smartphone Market Potential: Electronics Maker's CEO Optimistic about Ability to 'Compete and Win' Despite Fall in Profit, Revenue," *The Toronto Star*, 24 April 2009, B04.

52 Ibid.

53 S. Cramm, "A Change of Hearts," *CIO*, 1 April 2003, available online at http://www.cio.com/archive/ 040103/hs_leadership.html, 20 May 2003.

54 M. Ihlwan, L. Armstrong, and M. Eidam, "Hyundai: Kissing Clunkers Goodbye," *BusinessWeek*, 17 May 2004, 46.

55 "J. D. Power and Associates Initial Quality Study: Top-Rated Manufacturers," Cars.com, 25 June 2009, available online at http://www.cars.com [accessed 12 November 2009].

56 P. Ingrassia, "Why Hyundai Is an American Hit," *Wall Street Journal*, 14 September 2009, A13.

57 R. N. Ashkenas and T. D. Jick, "From Dialogue to Action in GE WorkOut: Developmental Learning in a Change Process," in *Research in Organizational Change and Development*, vol. 6, ed. W. A. Pasmore and R. W. Woodman (Greenwich, CT: JAI Press, 1992), 267–287.

58 T. Stewart, "GE Keeps Those Ideas Coming," *Fortune*, 12 August 1991, 40.

59 J. D. Duck, "Managing Change: The Art of Balancing," *Harvard Business Review on Change* (Boston: Harvard Business School Press, 1998), 55–81.

60 C. Costanzo, "B of A's Six Sigma Teams Begin Work on Integration with Fleet," *American Banker*, 10 March 2004, 1.

61 W. J. Rothwell, R. Sullivan, and G. M. McLean, *Practicing Organizational Development: A Guide for Consultants* (San Diego, CA: Pfeiffer & Co., 1995).

62 N. Shirouzu, "Gadget Inspector: Why Toyota Wins Such High Marks on Quality Surveys—Hajime Oba Is a Key Coach as Japanese Auto Maker Steps Up U.S. Production—Striving to Reach Heijunka," *Wall Street Journal*, 15 March 2001, A1.

63 Ibid.

64 P. J. Robertson, D. R. Roberts, and J. I. Porras, "Dynamics of Planned Organizational Change: Assessing Empirical Support for a Theoretical Model," *Academy of Management Journal* 36 (1993): 619–634.

65 J. E. Ettlie and R. D. O'Keefe, "Innovative Attitudes, Values, and Intentions in Organizations," *Journal of Management Studies* 19 (1982): 163–182.

Chapter Seven

1 I. Brat & B. Grule, "Boss Talk: Global Trade Galvanizes Caterpillar; Maker of Heavy Equipment Thrives Under CEO Owens, Fervent Free-Trade Advocate," *Wall Street Journal*, 26 February 2007, B1; T. Kelly, "Squash the Caterpillar," *Forbes*, 21 April 2008, 136; J. Muller, "Surviving Globalism," *Forbes*, 27 February 2006, 44; J. Owens, "Embrace Globalism," *Wall Street Journal*, 17 April 2006, A17; J. Owens, "*The Realities and Rewards of Globalism*," *Vital Speeches of the Day*, 15 April 2006, 404.

2 T. Friedman, "It's a Flat World, After All," *New York Times*, 3 April 2005, 33.

3 "World Investment Report, 2006," United Nations Conference on Trade & Development, available online at http://www.unctad.org/en/docs/wir2006annexes_en.pdf [accessed 30 January 2007].

4 D. Michaels, "Lufthansa Set to Buy Struggling Austrian Airlines—The Proposal, Valued at Up to $479.5 Million, Continues German Carrier's String of International Acquisitions," *Wall Street Journal*, 4 December 2008, B3.

5 A. Cordeiro, "Hershey to Expand in Asia," *Wall Street Journal*, 12 March 2009, B5.

6 J. Miller, "China's Low Fruit Prices Highlight EU's Vulnerabilities over Trade," *Wall Street Journal,* 26 December 2006, A4.

7 L. Etter, "Can Ethanol Get a Ticket to Ride?," *Wall Street Journal,* 1 February 2007, B1.

8 G. Williams III, "News on the Road Column," *San Antonio Express–News*, 3 March 2006.

9 "Determination of Total Amounts and Quota Period for Tariff-Rate Quotas for Raw Cane Sugar and Certain Imported Sugars, Syrups, and Molasses," *Federal Register*, 15 April 2002, 18162.

10 J. Sparshott, "U.S. Sugar Growers Fear Losses from Free-Trade Push," *Washington Times*, 24 March 2005, C07.

11 "Understanding the WTO," *World Trade Organization,* available online at http://www.wto.org/english/thewto_e/whatis_e/tif_e/agrm9_e.htm [accessed 5 August 2008].

12 C. Hale, "HortFACT—Why Fireblight Shouldn't Be a Market Access Problem," Hortnet, available online at http://www.hortnet.co.nz/publications/ hortfacts/hf205010.htm [accessed 18 March 2009]; "USTR Lists Barriers to U.S. Trade, Focusing on Agriculture—Annual Report Also Emphasizes Intellectual Property, Transparency," U.S. Department Press Releases & Documents, 7 February 2007.

13 "USTR Lists Barriers to U.S. Trade." J. Morgan, "Building Seeds of Case against OZ Apple Ban," *Dominion Post,* 18 January 2007, 7.

14 "GATT/WTO," Duke Law: Library & Technology, available online at http://www.law.duke.edu [accessed 12 June 2009].

15 "The History of the European Union," *Europa—The European Union Online,* available online at http://europa.eu.int/abc/history/index_en.htm; http://europa.eu/abc/european_countries/index_en.htm [accessed 6 August 2008].

16 D. Luhnow, "Crossover Success: How NAFTA Helped Wal-Mart Reshape the Mexican Market," *Wall Street Journal*, 31 August 2001, A1.

17 "Testimony of Under Secretary of Commerce for International Trade Grant D. Aldona: The Impact of NAFTA on the United States Economy," Senate Foreign Relations Committee, Subcommittee on International Economic Policy, Export & Trade Promotion, 7 February 2007.

18 L.H. Teslik, "NAFTA's Economic Impact," Council on Foreign Relations, available online at http://www.cfr.org/publication/15790/naftas_economic_impact.html#4 [accessed 6 August 2008].

19 UNASUR, Union of South American Nations, available online at http://www.comunidadandina.org/ingles/sudamerican.htm [accessed 6 August 2008].

20 "Selected Basic ASEAN Indicators, 2005," Association of Southeast Nations, available online at http://www.aseansec.org/stat/Table1.pdf [accessed 18 March [2009]; "Top Ten ASEAN Trade Partner Countries/Regions, 2005," Association of Southeast Nations, available online at http://www.aseansec.org/Stat/Table20.pdf [accessed 18 March 2009].

21 "Selected Basic ASEAN Indicators, 2005," Association of Southeast Nations, available online at http://www.aseansec.org/stat/Table1.pdf [accessed 6 August 2008]; "Top Ten ASEAN Trade Partner Countries/Regions, 2005," Association of Southeast Nations, available online at http://www.aseansec.org/Stat/Table20.pdf [accessed 6 August 2008]; "ASEAN Free Trade Area (AFTA)," Association of Southeast Nations, available online at http://www.aseansec.org/12021.htm [accessed 6 August 2008].

22 "Member Economies," Asia Pacific Economic Cooperation, available online at http://www.apec.org/apec/member_economies/key_websites.html [accessed 6 August 2008]; "Frequently Asked Questions (FAQs)," Asia-Pacific Economic Cooperation, available online at http://www.apec.org/apec/tools/ faqs.html [accessed 6 August 2008].

23 *PriceCheckTokyo,* available online at http://www.pricechecktokyo.com [accessed 6 August 2008].

24 Z. Greenburg, "World's Most Expensive Cups of Coffee," *Forbes*, 24 July 2008, online at http://www.forbes.com [accessed 13 June 2009].

25 "The Big Mac Index," *The Economist*, available online at http://www.economist.com/markets/indicators/displaystory.cfm?story_id=13055650 [accessed 18 March 2009].

26 Ibid.

27 "The Big Mac Index," *The Economist,* available online at http://www.economist.com/markets/indicators/displaystory.cfm?story_id=8649005 [accessed 10 February 2007].

28 "The Global Competitiveness Report: 2008–2009," World Economic Forum, available online at http://www.weforum.org/documents/GCR0809/index.html [accessed 14 June 2009].

29 "Freer Trade Cuts the Cost of Living," *World Trade Organization,* available online at http://www.wto.org/english/thewto_e/whatis_e/10ben_e/10b04_e.htm [accessed 18 March 2009].

30 T. Agins, "For U.S. Fashion Firms, A Global Makeover—Tommy Hilfiger Finds Assimilating in Europe Requires a New Look," *Wall Street Journal,* 2 February 2007, A1.

31 A. Sundaram and J. S. Black, "The Environment and Internal-Organization of Multinational Enterprises," *Academy of Management Review* 17 (1992): 729–757.

32 H. S. James, Jr., and M. Weidenbaum, *When Businesses Cross International Borders: Strategic Alliances & Their Alternatives* (Westport, CT: Praeger Publishers, 1993).

33 J. T. Areddy, "China's Export Machine Threatened by Rising Costs," *Wall Street Journal,* 30 June 2008, A1.

34 A. Davidson, "TV Boss with the X Factor," *Sunday Times*, 23 September 2007, Business 9; J. Ewing, "From Reality TV to Big-Screen in Dreams," *BusinessWeek*, 11 February 2008, 64.

35 A. Davidson, "TV Boss with the X Factor," *Sunday Times,* 23 September 2007, Business 9.

36 "Workplace Code of Conduct," Fair Labor Association, http://www.fairlabor.org/all/code/index.html, 12 May 2003; A. Bernstein, M. Shari, and E. Malkin, "A World of Sweatshops," *BusinessWeek*, 6 November 2000, 84.

37 "New Restaurants," McDonald's, available online at http://www.mcdonalds.com/corp/franchise/purchasingYourFranchise/newRestaurants.html [accessed 18 March 2009].

38 C. Adler, "How China Eats a Sandwich: Opening Subway Franchises in the People's Republic," *Fortune*, 21 March 2005, F310 [B].

39 D. Hemlock, "World Wise: Strategies That Work around the Corner Don't Always Work in Locales Abroad, Office Depot's Chief Executive Says," *South Florida Sun*, 18 December 2000, 16.

40 Ibid.

41 "Company Profile," Fuji Xerox, available online at http://www.fujixerox.co.jp/eng/company/profile.html [accessed 6 August 2008].

42 "Arrow, Shell Seal a Venture," *Wall Street Journal,* 15 September 2008, available online at http://online.wsj.com/article/SB122144583046434931.html [accessed 18 September 2008].

43 B. R. Schlender, "How Toshiba Makes Alliances Work," *Fortune*, 4 October 1993, 116–120; "Joint Ventures," *Encyclopedia of Business*, 2nd ed., available online at http://www.referenceforbusiness.com/encyclopedia/Int-Jun/Joint-Ventures.html#WHY_JOINT_VENTURES_FAIL [accessed 6 August 2008].

44 M. Dolan and J. Bennett, "Corporate News: Ford Seeks Loans, Guarantees from an Array of Governments," *Wall Street Journal*, 10 June 2009, B3.

45 J. McCracken, "Retail Ventures May Sell Value City Chain," *Wall Street Journal*, 23 January 2008, A2.

46 M. W. Hordes, J. A. Clancy, and J. Baddaley, "A Primer for Global Start-Ups," *Academy of Management Executive*, May 1995, 7–11.

47 D. Pavlos, J. Johnson, J. Slow, and S. Young, "Micromultinationals: New Types of Firms for the Global Competitive Landscape," *European Management Journal* 21, no. 2 (April 2003): 164; B. M. Oviatt and P. P. McDougall, "Toward a Theory of International New Ventures," *Journal of International Business Studies* (Spring 1994): 45–64; S. Zahra, "A Theory of International New Ventures: A Decade of Research," *Journal of International Business Studies* (January 2005): 20–28.

48 M. Copeland, "The Mighty Micro-Multinational," *Business 2.0*, 1 July 2006, 106.

49 "2008 Annual Review," The Coca-Cola Company, available online at http://www.thecoca-colacompany.com/investors/pdfs/2008_annual_review/2008_annual_review.pdf [accessed 14 June 2009].

50 F. Vogelstein, "How Intel Got Inside," *Fortune*, 4 October 2004, 127.

51 "Customer Care in the Netherlands," The Netherlands Foreign Investment Agency, http://www.nfia.com/solutions.php?pageid=11 [accessed 13 February 2007] (content no longer available online).

52 J. Oetzel, R. Bettis, and M. Zenner, "How Risky Are They?" *Journal of World Business* 36, no. 2 (Summer 2001): 128–145.

53 "European Cities Monitor," Cushman & Wakefield, 2008, available online at http://www.cushwake.com/cwglobal/docviewer/2008_ European_Cities_Monitor.pdf [accessed 30 May 2009].

54 K. D. Miller, "A Framework for Integrated Risk Management in International Business," *Journal of International Business Studies*, 2nd Quarter 1992, 311.

55 A. Osborn and D. Gauthier-Villars, "Twisty Road: Renault Deal in Russia Shows Kremlin Tactics," *Wall Street Journal*, 21 March 2008, A1.

56 G. Fowler, "In China's Offices, Foreign Colleagues Might Get an Earful," *Wall Street Journal*, 13 February 2007, B1.

57 G. Hofstede, "The Cultural Relativity of the Quality of Life Concept," *Academy of Management Review* 9 (1984): 389–398; G. Hofstede, "The Cultural Relativity of Organizational Practices and Theories," *Journal of International Business Studies*, Fall 1983, 75–89; G. Hofstede, "The Interaction between National and Organizational Value Systems," *Journal of Management Studies*, July 1985, 347–357; M. Hoppe, "An Interview with Geert Hofstede," *Academy of Management Executive*, February 2004, 75–79.

58 R. Hodgetts, "A Conversation with Geert Hofstede," *Organizational Dynamics*, Spring 1993, 53–61.

59 R. G. Linowes, "The Japanese Manager's Traumatic Entry into the United States: Understanding the American-Japanese Cultural Divide," *Academy of Management Executive* 7 (1993): 21–40.

60 J. S. Black, M. Mendenhall, and G. Oddou, "Toward a Comprehensive Model of International Adjustment: An Integration of Multiple Theoretical Perspectives," *Academy of Management Review* 16 (1991): 291–317; R. L. Tung, "American Expatriates Abroad: From Neophytes to Cosmopolitans," *Columbia Journal of World Business* 33 (1998): 125-144; A. Harzing, "The Persistent Myth of High Expatriate Failure Rates," *International Journal of Human Resource Management* 6 (1995): 457–475; A. Harzing, "Are Our Referencing Errors Undermining Our Scholarship and Credibility? The Case of Expatriate Failure Rates," *Journal of Organizational Behavior* 23 (2002): 127–148; N. Forster, "The Persistent Myth of High Expatriate Failure Rates: A Reappraisal," *International Journal of Human Resource Management* 8 (1997): 414–433.

61 J. Black, "The Right Way to Manage Expats," *Harvard Business Review* 77 (March–April 1999): 52; C. Joinson, "No Returns," *HR Magazine*, 1 November 2002, 70.

62 C. Joinson, "No Returns."

63 J. S. Black and M. Mendenhall, "Cross-Cultural Training Effectiveness: A Review and Theoretical Framework for Future Research," *Academy of Management Review* 15 (1990): 113–136.

64 K. Essick, "Executive Education: Transferees Prep for Life, Work in Far-Flung Lands," *Wall Street Journal*, 12 November 2004, A6.

65 P. W. Tam, "Culture Course—'Awareness Training' Helps U.S. Workers Better Know Their Counterparts in India," *Wall Street Journal*, 25 May 2004, B1.

66 W. Arthur, Jr., and W. Bennett, Jr., "The International Assignee: The Relative Importance of Factors Perceived to Contribute to Success," *Personnel Psychology* 48 (1995): 99–114; B. Cheng, "Home Truths about Foreign Postings; To Make an Overseas Assignment Work, Employers Need More Than an Eager Exec with a Suitcase. They Must Also Motivate the Staffer's Spouse," *BusinessWeek Online*, available online at http://www.businessweek.com/careers/content/jul2002/ca20020715_9110.htm [accessed 20 March 2009].

67 S. P. Deshpande & C. Viswesvaran, "Is Cross-Cultural Training of Expatriate Managers Effective? A Meta-Analysis," *International Journal of Intercultural Relations* 16, no. 3 (1992): 295–310;

68 R. Donkin, "Recruitment: Overseas Gravy Train May Be Running Out of Steam—Preparing Expatriate Packages Is Challenging the Expertise of Human Resource Management," *Financial Times*, 30 November 1994, 10.

69 Eschbach, G. Parker, and P. Stoeberl, "American Repatriate Employees' Retrospective Assessments of the Effects of Cross-Cultural Training on Their Adaptation to International Assignments," *International Journal of Human Resource Management* 12 (2001): 270–287; "Culture Training: How to Prepare Your Expatriate Employees for Cross-Cultural Work Environments," *Managing Training & Development*, 1 February 2005.

70 R. W. Boatler, "Study Abroad: Impact on Student Worldmindedness," *Journal of Teaching in International Business* 2, no. 2 (1990): 13–17; R. W. Boatler, "Worldminded Attitude Change in a Study Abroad Program: Contact and Content Issues," *Journal of Teaching in International Business* 3, no. 4 (1992): 59–68; H. Lancaster, "Learning to Manage in a Global Workplace (You're on Your Own)," *Wall Street Journal*, 2 June 1998, B1; D. L. Sampson & H. P. Smith, "A Scale to Measure Worldminded Attitudes," *Journal of Social Psychology* 45 (1957): 99–106.

Chapter Eight

1 C. Bartz, "A Question of Management: Carol Bartz on How Yahoo's Organizational Structure Got in the Way of Innovation," *Wall Street Journal*, 2 June 2009, R4; K. Delaney, "Spreading Change: As Yahoo Falters, Executive's Memo Calls for Overhaul; 'Peanut Butter Manifesto' Seeking Focus and Cuts Makes Waves at Web Titan; Can It Wring More From Ads?" *Wall Street Journal*, 18 November 2006, A1; J. Fortt, "Yahoo's Taskmaster," *Fortune*, 27 April 2009, 80–84; B. Garlinghouse, "Yahoo Memo: The 'Peanut Butter Manifesto,'" *Wall Street Journal*, 18 November 2006, available online at http://online.wsj.com [accessed 6 December 2009]; R. Hof, "What Yahoo Needs from Bartz Right Now," *BusinessWeek*, 14 January 2009, 7; R. Hof, "Yahoo's Bartz Starts Strong," *BusinessWeek*, 23 April 2009, 24; J. Vascellaro, "Yahoo's Decker Sets a New Reorganization," *Wall Street Journal*, 21 June 2008, A4; J. Vascellaro, "Yahoo CEO Set to Install Top-Down Management," *Wall Street Journal*, 23 February 2009, B1; J. Vascellaro, "Yahoo Posts 78% Profit Drop, Cuts Jobs," *Wall Street* Journal, 22 April 2009, B1.

2 "Sony Corporation of America: Overview," available online at http://www.sony.com/SCA/index.shtml [accessed 8 August 2008].

3 M. Hammer and J. Champy, *Reengineering the Corporation: A Manifesto for Business Revolution* (New York: Harper & Row, 1993).

4 J. G. March and H. A. Simon, *Organizations* (New York: John Wiley & Sons, 1958).

5 "Bayer Group: Profile and Organization," Bayer AG, available online at http://www.bayer.com/bayer-group/profileand-organization/page2351.htm [accessed 20 March 2009].

6 "Fact & Figures: Our Businesses," Fast Facts, available online at http://www.utc.com [accessed 13 November 2009].

7 "Company Overview," UTC 2008 Annual Report, available online at http://www.utc.com [accessed 13 November 2009].

8 "Company Structure," About Swisscom, available online at http://www.swisscom.ch [accessed 14 November 2009].

9 "Our Company: The Best Brands in the World," Coca-Cola Enterprises http://www.cokecce.com/srclib/1.1.1.html [content no longer online, accessed 14 November 2009].

10 "Who We Are," P&G, available online at http://www.pg.com [accessed 14 November 2009].

11 "Corporate Info: Corporate Structure—Four Pillars," Procter & Gamble, available online at http://www.pg.com/jobs/ corporate_structure/four_ pillars.jhtml [accessed 20 March 2009]; "P&G Management," Procter & Gamble, available online at http://www.pg.com/news/management/bios_photos.jhtml [accessed 20 March 2009].

12 L. R. Burns, "Adoption and Abandonment of Matrix Management Programs: Effects of Organizational Characteristics and Interorganizational Networks," *Academy of Management Journal* 36 (1993): 106–138.

13 D. Ball, "Unilever Shakes Up Its Management to Spur Growth," *Wall Street Journal*, 11 February 2005, A2.

14 H. Fayol, *General and Industrial Management*, trans. C. Storrs (London: Pitman Publishing, 1949).

15 M. Weber, *The Theory of Social and Economic Organization*, trans. and ed. A. M. Henderson and T. Parsons (New York: Free Press, 1947).

16 Fayol, *General and Industrial Management*.

17 J. Greene, S. Hamm, and J. Kerstetter, "How CEO Steve Ballmer Is Remaking the Company That Bill Gates Built," *BusinessWeek*, 17 June 2002, 66.

18 E. E. Lawler, S. A. Mohrman, and G. E. Ledford, *Creating High Performance Organizations: Practices and Results of Employee Involvement and Quality Management in Fortune 1000 Companies* (San Francisco: Jossey-Bass, 1995).

19 S. Curry, "Retention Getters," *Incentive*, 1 April 2005.

20 R. W. Griffin, *Task Design* (Glenview, IL: Scott, Foresman, 1982).

21 F. Herzberg, *Work and the Nature of Man* (Cleveland, OH: World Press, 1966).

22 A. Markels, "Team Approach: A Power Producer Is Intent on Giving Power to Its People—Groups of AES Employees Do Complex Tasks Ranging from Hiring to Investing—Making Sure Work Is 'Fun,'" *Wall Street Journal*, 3 July 1995, A1.

23 J. R. Hackman and G. R. Oldham, *Work Redesign* (Reading, MA: Addison-Wesley, 1980).

24 Y. Fried and G. R. Ferris, "The Validity of the Job Characteristics Model: A Review and Meta-Analysis," *Personnel Psychology* 40 (1987): 287–322; B. T. Loher, R. A. Noe, N. L. Moeller, and M. P. Fitzgerald, "A Meta-Analysis of the Relation of Job Characteristics to Job Satisfaction," *Journal of Applied Psychology* 70 (1985): 280–289.

25 T. Burns and G. M. Stalker, *The Management of Innovation* (London: Tavistock, 1961).

26 Hammer and Champy, *Reengineering the Corporation*.

27 Ibid.

28 C. Tuna, "Remembrances: Champion of 'Re-Engineering' Saved Companies, Challenged Thinking," *Wall Street Journal*, 6 September 2008, A12.

29 J. D. Thompson, *Organizations in Action* (New York: McGraw-Hill, 1967).

30 D. Pink, "Who Has the Next Big Idea?" *Fast Company*, 1 September 2001, 108.

31 C. Tuna, "Remembrances: Champion of 'Re-Engineering' Saved Companies, Challenged Thinking," *Wall Street Journal*, 6 September 2008, A12.

32 G. M. Spreitzer, "Individual Empowerment in the Workplace: Dimensions, Measurement, and Validation," *Academy of Management Journal* 38 (1995): 1442–1465.

33 K. W. Thomas and B. A. Velthouse, "Cognitive Elements of Empowerment," *Academy of Management Review* 15 (1990): 666–681.

34 L. Munoz, "The Suit Is Back—Or Is It? As Dot-Coms Die, So Should Business Casual. But the Numbers Don't Lie," *Fortune*, 25 June 2001, 202; F. Swoboda, "Casual Dress Becomes the Rule," *Las Vegas Review-Journal*, 3 March 1996.

35 A. C. Lu-Lien Tan, "Business Attire: The Office Coverup," *Wall Street Journal*, 5 August 2006, P1.

36 "Suits Lose Appeal as Casual Dress Rules in London Offices," *Evening Standard* (London), 19 October 2004.

37 "SHRM Online Poll Results," Society for Human Resource Management, http://www.shrm.org/poll/results.asp?Question#89, 21 May 2003 [accessed 19 November 2009].

38 K. McCullough, "Analysis: More Companies Allowing Employees to Dress Down, Which Makes Productivity Go Up," *Money Club*, 26 March 1996.

39 W. Bounds, "Phone Calls Are Public Affairs for Open-Plan Office Dwellers," *Wall Street Journal*, 10 July 2002, B1.

40 "Designing the Ever-Changing Workplace," *Architectural Record*, September 1995, 32–37.

41 A. Frangos, "Property Report: See You on the Way Up! Office Stairs Get 'Aspirational,'" *Wall Street Journal*, 19 May 2004, B1.

42 J. Sandberg, "Cookies, Gossip, Cubes: It's a Wonder Any Work Gets Done at the Office," *Wall Street Journal*, 28 April 2004, B1.

43 L. Gallagher, "At Work: Get Out of My Face: Open Offices Were Hailed as the Answer to Hierarchical, Rigid Organizations. Employees Would Rather Have Privacy," *Forbes*, 18 October 1999, 105.

44 S. Hwang, "Cubicle Culture: Office Vultures Circle Still-Warm Desks Left Empty by Layoffs," *Wall Street Journal*, 14 August 2002, B1.

45 G. Kahn, "Making Labels for Less—Supply-Chain City Transforms Far-Flung Apparel Industry; Help for 'The Button Guy,'" *Wall Street Journal*, 13 August 2004, B1.

46 G. G. Dess, A. M. A. Rasheed, K. J. McLaughlin, and R. L. Priem, "The New Corporate Architecture," *Academy of Management Executive* 9 (1995): 7–18.

47 G. McWilliams, "Apple Uses Software, Outsourcing to Gain Share As Sony Struggles to Grow," *Wall Street Journal*, 10 March 2005, A1.

48 "About the Independent Carton Group," Independent Carton Group, available online at http://independentcartongroup.com [accessed 15 November 2009].

49 C. C. Snow, R. E. Miles, and H. J. Coleman, Jr., "Managing 21st Century Network Organizations," *Organizational Dynamics*, Winter 1992, 5–20.

50 J. H. Sheridan, "The Agile Web: A Model for the Future?" *Industry Week*, 4 March 1996, 31.

51 G. Bruner, K. James, P. Hensel, *Marketing Scales Handbook* (Chicago: American Marketing Association, 2001), vol. 3, 931–934.

Chapter Nine

1 "About GEAE / History," *GE Aircraft Engines*, available online at http://www.geae.com/aboutgeae/history.html 21 January 2002; "About GEAE / Locations," *GE Aircraft Engines*, available online at http://www.geae.com/aboutgeae/location.html 21 January 2002; C. Fishman, "Engines of Democracy," *Fast Company*, 1 October 1999, 174; C. Fishman, "How Teamwork Took Flight: This Team Built a Commercial Engine—and Self-Managing GE Plant—from Scratch," *Fast Company*, 1 October 1999, 188.

2 B. Dumaine, "The Trouble with Teams," *Fortune*, 5 September 1994, 86–92.

3 K. C. Stag, E. Salas, and S. M. Fiore, "Best Practices in Cross Training Teams," in *Workforce Cross Training Handbook,* ed. D. A. Nembhard (Boca Raton, FL: CRC Press), 156–175.

4 M. Marks, "The Science of Team Effectiveness," *Psychological Science in the Public Interest* (December 2006): pi–i.

5 J. R. Katzenbach and D. K. Smith, *The Wisdom of Teams* (Boston: Harvard Business School Press, 1993).

6 S. G. Cohen and D. E. Bailey, "What Makes Teams Work: Group Effectiveness Research from the Shop Floor to the Executive Suite," *Journal of Management* 23, no. 3 (1997): 239–290.

7 S. E. Gross, *Compensation for Teams* (New York: American Management Association, 1995); B. L. Kirkman and B. Rosen, "Beyond Self-Management: Antecedents and Consequences of Team Empowerment," *Academy of Management Journal* 42 (1999): 58–74; G. Stalk and T. M. Hout, *Competing against Time: How Time-Based Competition Is Reshaping Global Markets* (New York: Free Press, 1990); S. C. Wheelwright and K. B. Clark, *Revolutionizing New Product Development* (New York: Free Press, 1992).

8 J. Marquez, "Hewitt-BP Split May Signal End of "Lift and Shift" Deals," *Workforce Management*, 29 December 2006: 3.

9 R. D. Banker, J. M. Field, R. G. Schroeder, and K. K. Sinha, "Impact of Work Teams on Manufacturing Performance: A Longitudinal Field Study," *Academy of Management Journal* 39 (1996): 867–890.

10 C. Fishman, "The Anarchist's Cookbook: John Mackey's Approach to Management Is Equal Parts Star Trek and 1970s Flashback," *Fast Company*, 1 July 2004, 70.

11 Stalk and Hout, *Competing against Time.*

12 C. Passariello, "Brand-New Bag: Louis Vuitton Tries Modern Methods on Factory Lines; For Craftsmen, Multitasking Replaces Specialization; Inspiration from Japan; 'What Do Our Clients Want?'" *Wall Street Journal*, 9 October 2006, A1.

13 J. L. Cordery, W. S. Mueller, and L. M. Smith, "Attitudinal and Behavioral Effects of Autonomous Group Working: A Longitudinal Field Study," *Academy of Management Journal* 34 (1991): 464–476; T. D. Wall, N. J. Kemp, P. R. Jackson, and C. W. Clegg, "Outcomes of Autonomous Workgroups: A Long-Term Field Experiment," *Academy of Management Journal* 29 (1986): 280–304.

14 "Declaration of Interdependence," Whole Foods Market, available online at http://www.wholefoodsmarket.com/company/declaration.html [accessed 12 August 2008].

15 Fishman, "The Anarchist's Cookbook."

16 R. Lieber, "Leadership Ensemble: How Do the Musicians of Orpheus Get to Carnegie Hall? They Practice—Not Just Their Music, but a Radical Approach to Leadership That Has Become a Compelling Metaphor for Business," *Fast Company*, 1 May 2000, 286.

17 A. Erez, J. Lepine, and H. Elms, "Effects of Rotated Leadership and Peer Evaluation on the Functioning and Effectiveness of Self-Managed Teams: A Quasi-Experiment," *Personnel Psychology* 55, no. 4 (2002): 929.

18 J. Hoerr, "The Payoff from Teamwork—The Gains in Quality Are Substantial—So Why Isn't It Spreading Faster?" *BusinessWeek*, 10 July 1989, 56.

19 T. Aeppel, "Missing the Boss: Not All Workers Find Idea of Empowerment As Neat As It Sounds—Some Hate Fixing Machines, Apologizing for Errors, Disciplining Teammates—Rah-Rah Types Do the Best," *Wall Street Journal*, 8 September 1997, A1.

20 R. Liden, S. Wayne, R. Jaworski, and N. Bennett, "Social Loafing: A Field Investigation," *Journal of Management* 30 (2004): 285–304.

21 J. George, "Extrinsic and Intrinsic Origins of Perceived Social Loafing in Organizations," *Academy of Management Journal* 35 (1992): 191–202.

22 T. T. Baldwin, M. D. Bedell, and J. L. Johnson, "The Social Fabric of a Team-Based M.B.A. Program: Network Effects on Student Satisfaction and Performance," *Academy of Management Journal* 40 (1997): 1369–1397.

23 K. H. Price, D. A. Harrison, and J. H. Gavin, "Withholding Inputs in Team Contexts: Member Composition, Interaction Processes, Evaluation Structure and Social Loafing," *Journal of Applied Psychology* 91(6) (2006): 1375–1384.

24 Hoerr, "The Payoff from Teamwork."

25 C. Joinson, "Teams at Work," *HR Magazine*, 1 May 1999, 30.

26 R. Wageman, "Critical Success Factors for Creating Superb Self-Managing Teams," *Organizational Dynamics* 26, no. 1 (1997): 49–61.

27 R. Karlgaard, "Leadership Lessons from the Tour de France," *Forbes*, 31 July 2009, online at http://www.forbes.com [accessed 16 November 2009].

28 N. Wingfield, "Tech Journal: To Rebuild Windows, Microsoft Razed Walls Three-Year Effort to Create Latest Version Meant Close Collaboration Among Workers to Avoid Vista's Woes," *The Wall Street Journal*, 20 October 2009, B9.

29 Harrison et al., "Time Matters."

30 R. T. King, Jr., "Jeans Therapy: Levi's Factory Workers Are Assigned to Teams, and Morale Takes a Hit—Infighting Rises, Productivity Falls as Employees Miss the Piecework System," *The Wall Street Journal*, 20 May 1998, A1.

31 Ibid.

32 J. Vascellaro, "Google Searches for Ways to Keep Big Ideas at Home—Giant Speeds Access to Bosses in Effort to Transform More Projects Into Products," *Wall Street Journal*, 18 June 2009, B1.

33 G. Bylinsky, "Heroes of U.S. Manufacturing," *Fortune*, 19 March 2001, 177; D. Cadrain, "Put Success in Sight," *HR Magazine*, May 2003, 48(5), 84–92.

34 R. Williams, "Self-Directed Work Teams: A Competitive Advantage," *Quality Digest*, available at http://www.qualitydigest.com [accessed 18 November 2009].

35 Kirkman and Rosen, "Beyond Self-Management: Antecedents and Consequences of Team Empowerment."

36 S. Easton and G. Porter, "Selecting the Right Team Structure to Work in Your Organization," in *Handbook of Best Practices for Teams*, vol. 1, ed. G. M. Parker (Amherst, MA: Irwin, 1996).

37 R. M. Yandrick, "A Team Effort: The Promise of Teams Isn't Achieved without Attention to Skills and Training," *HR Magazine*, June 2001, 46(6), 136–144.

38 R. J. Recardo, D. Wade, C. A. Mention, and J. Jolly, *Teams* (Houston: Gulf Publishing Co., 1996).

39 D. R. Denison, S. L. Hart, and J. A. Kahn, "From Chimneys to Cross-Functional Teams: Developing and Validating a Diagnostic Model," *Academy of Management Journal* 39, no. 4 (1996): 1005–1023.

40 A. M. Townsend, S. M. DeMarie, and A. R. Hendrickson, "Virtual Teams: Technology and the Workplace of the Future," *Academy of Management Executive* 13, no. 3 (1998): 17–29.

41 K. Butler, "Virtual Reality: Most Teams Work Remotely, Increasing Need for Different Processes," *Employee Benefit News*, 1 February 2008.

42 J. Hyatt, "MySQL: Workers in 25 countries with no HQ," *Fortune*, 1 June 2006, available online at http://money.cnn.com/2006/05/31/ magazines/fortune/mysql_greatteams_fortune/index.htm [accessed 12 August 2008].

43 Wellins, Byham, and Dixon, *Inside Teams*.

44 Townsend, DeMarie, and Hendrickson, "Virtual Teams."

45 W. F. Cascio, "Managing a Virtual Workplace," *Academy of Management Executive* 14 (2000): 81–90.

46 R. Katz, "The Effects of Group Longevity on Project Communication and Performance," *Administrative Science Quarterly* 27 (1982): 245–282.

47 D. Mankin, S. G. Cohen, and T. K. Bikson, *Teams and Technology: Fulfilling the Promise of the New Organization* (Boston: Harvard Business School Press, 1996).

48 K. Lovelace, D. Shapiro, and L. Weingart, "Maximizing Cross-Functional New Product Teams' Innovativeness and Constraint Adherence: A Conflict Communications Perspective," *Academy of Management Journal* 44 (2001): 779–793.

49 L. Holpp and H. P. Phillips, "When Is a Team Its Own Worst Enemy?" *Training*, 1 September 1995, 71.

50 S. Asche, "Opinions and Social Pressure," *Scientific American* 193 (1995): 31–35.

51 S. G. Cohen, G. E. Ledford, and G. M. Spreitzer, "A Predictive Model of Self-Managing Work Team Effectiveness," *Human Relations* 49, no. 5 (1996): 643–676.

52 M. Fischetti, "'Team Doctors, Report To ER': Is Your Team Headed for Intensive Care? Our Specialists Offer Prescriptions for the Five Illnesses That Can Afflict Even the Best Teams," *Fast Company*, 1 February 1998, 170.

53 K. Bettenhausen and J. K. Murnighan, "The Emergence of Norms in Competitive Decision-Making Groups," *Administrative Science Quarterly* 30 (1985): 350–372.

54 M. E. Shaw, *Group Dynamics* (New York: McGraw-Hill, 1981).

55 A. M. Isen and R. A. Baron, "Positive Affect as a Factor in Organizational Behavior," in *Research in Organizational Behavior* 13, ed. L. L. Cummings and B. M. Staw (Greenwich, CT: JAI Press, 1991): 1–53.

56 C. R. Evans and K. L. Dion, "Group Cohesion and Performance: A Meta Analysis," *Small Group Research* 22, no. 2 (1991): 175–186.

57 R. Stankiewicsz, "The Effectiveness of Research Groups in Six Countries," in *Scientific Productivity*, ed. F. M. Andrews (Cambridge: Cambridge University Press, 1979), 191–221.

58 F. Rees, *Teamwork from Start to Finish* (San Francisco: Jossey-Bass, 1997).

59 S. M. Gully, D. S. Devine, & D. J. Whitney, "A Meta-Analysis of Cohesion and Performance: Effects of Level of Analysis and Task Interdependence," *Small Group Research* 26, no. 4 (1995): 497–520.

60 Gully, Devine, and Whitney, "A Meta-Analysis of Cohesion and Performance."

61 E. Matson, "Four Rules for Fast Teams," *Fast Company*, August 1996, 87.

62 S. E. Jackson, "The Consequences of Diversity in Multidisciplinary Work Teams," in *Handbook of Work Group Psychology*, ed. M. A. West (Chichester, UK: Wiley, 1996).

63 F. Tschan and M. V. Cranach, "Group Task Structure, Processes and Outcomes," in *Handbook of Work Group Psychology*, ed. M. A. West (Chichester, UK: Wiley, 1996).

64 D. E. Yeatts and C. Hyten, *High Performance Self Managed Teams* (Thousand Oaks, CA: Sage Publications, 1998); H. M. Guttman and R. S. Hawkes, "New Rules for Strategic Development," *Journal of Business Strategy* 25, no. 1 (2004): 34–39.

65 Ibid.; J. Colquitt, R. Noe, and C. Jackson, "Justice in Teams: Antecedents and Consequences of Procedural Justice Climate," *Personnel Psychology*, 1 April 2002, 83.

66 D. S. Kezsbom, "Re-Opening Pandora's Box: Sources of Project Team Conflict in the '90s," *Industrial Engineering* 24, no. 5 (1992): 54–59.

67 A. C. Amason, W. A. Hochwarter, and K. R. Thompson, "Conflict: An Important Dimension in Successful Management Teams," *Organizational Dynamics* 24 (1995): 20.

68 A. C. Amason, "Distinguishing the Effects of Functional and Dysfunctional Conflict on Strategic Decision Making: Resolving a Paradox for Top Management Teams," *Academy of Management Journal* 39, no. 1 (1996): 123–148.

69 K. M. Eisenhardt, J. L. Kahwajy, and L. J. Bourgeois III, "How Management Teams Can Have a Good Fight," *Harvard Business Review* 75, no. 4 (July–August 1997): 77–85.

70 Ibid.

71 C. Nemeth and P. Owens, "Making Work Groups More Effective: The Value of Minority Dissent," in *Handbook of Work Group Psychology*, ed. M. A. West (Chichester, UK: Wiley, 1996).

72 J. M. Levin and R. L. Moreland, "Progress in Small Group Research," *Annual Review of Psychology* 9 (1990): 72–78; S. E. Jackson, "Team Composition in Organizational Settings: Issues in Managing a Diverse Work Force," in *Group Processes and Productivity*, ed. S. Worchel, W. Wood, and J. Simpson (Beverly Hills, CA: Sage, 1992).

73 B. W. Tuckman, "Development Sequence in Small Groups," *Psychological Bulletin* 63, no. 6 (1965): 384–399.

74 Gross, *Compensation for Teams*.

75 J. F. McGrew, J. G. Bilotta, and J. M. Deeney, "Software Team Formation and Decay: Extending the Standard Model for Small Groups," *Small Group Research* 30, no. 2 (1999): 209–234.

76 Ibid.

77 J. Case, "What the Experts Forgot to Mention: Management Teams Create New Difficulties, but Succeed for XEL Communication," *Inc.*, 1 September 1993, 66.

78 J. R. Hackman, "The Psychology of Self-Management in Organizations," in *Psychology and Work: Productivity, Change, and Employment*, ed. M. S. Pallak and R. Perloff (Washington, DC: American Psychological Association, 1986), 85–136.

79 A. O'Leary-Kelly, J. J. Martocchio, and D. D. Frink, "A Review of the Influence of Group Goals on Group Performance," *Academy of Management Journal* 37, no. 5 (1994): 1285–1301.

80 Gregory P. Smith, "How Nucor Steel Rewards Performance and Productivity" Businessknowhow.com. Accessed online at http://www.businessknowhow.com/manage/nucor.htm [accessed 23 March 2009].

[81] A. Zander, "The Origins and Consequences of Group Goals," in *Retrospections on Social Psychology*, ed. L. Festinger (New York: Oxford University Press, 1980), 205–235.

[82] M. Erez and A. Somech, "Is Group Productivity Loss the Rule or the Exception? Effects of Culture and Group-Based Motivation," *Academy of Management Journal* 39, no. 6 (1996): 1513–1537.

[83] S. Sherman, "Stretch Goals: The Dark Side of Asking for Miracles," *Fortune*, 13 November 1995.

[84] B. Kenney, "The Zero Effect: How to Green Your Facility," *Industry Week*, 1 July 2008, 36.

[85] S. Kerr and S. Landauer, "Using Stretch Goals to Promote Organizational Effectiveness and Personal Growth: General Electric and Goldman Sachs," *Academy of Management Executive* (November 2004): 134–138.

[86] K. R. Thompson, W. A. Hochwarter, and N. J. Mathys, "Stretch Targets: What Makes Them Effective?" *Academy of Management Executive* 11, no. 3 (1997): 48–60.

[87] S. Tully, "Why to Go for Stretch Targets," *Fortune*, 14 November 1994, 145.

[88] Sherman, "Stretch Goals."

[89] Dumaine, "The Trouble with Teams."

[90] G. A. Neuman, S. H. Wagner, and N. D. Christiansen, "The Relationship between Work-Team Personality Composition and the Job Performance of Teams," *Group & Organization Management* 24, no. 1 (1999): 28–45.

[91] M. A. Campion, G. J. Medsker, and A. C. Higgs, "Relations between Work Group Characteristics and Effectiveness: Implications for Designing Effective Work Groups," *Personnel Psychology* 46, no. 4 (1993): 823–850.

[92] B. L. Kirkman and D. L. Shapiro, "The Impact of Cultural Values on Employee Resistance to Teams: Toward a Model of Globalized Self-Managing Work Team Effectiveness," *Academy of Management Review* 22, no. 3 (1997): 730–757.

[93] J. Newport, "Golf Journal: Team USA's Management Victory; Ryder Cup Captain Paul Azinger Used a Group-Dynamic Philosophy with Lessons for Golf and Beyond," *Wall Street Journal*, 27 September 2008, W9.

[94] J. Bunderson and K. Sutcliffe, "Comparing Alternative Conceptualizations of Functional Diversity in Management Teams: Process and Performance Effects," *Academy of Management Journal* 45 (2002): 875–893.

[95] J. Barbian, "Getting to Know You," *Training*, June 2001, 60–63.

[96] J. Hackman, "New Rules for Team Building—The Times Are Changing—And So Are the Guidelines for Maximizing Team Performance," *Optimize*, 1 July 2002, 50.

[97] K. Mollica, "Stay Above the Fray: Protect Your Time—and Your Sanity—by Coaching Employees to Deal with Interpersonal Conflicts on Their Own," *HR Magazine*, April 2005, 111.

[98] Wellins, Byham, and Dixon, *Inside Teams.*

[99] E. Salas, D. DiazGranados, C. Klein, C. Burke, K. Stagl, G. Goodwin, & S. Halpin, "Does Team Training Improve Team Performance? A Meta-Analysis," *Human Factors* v50 i6 (2008): 903–933.

[100] S. Caudron, "Tie Individual Pay to Team Success," *Personnel Journal* 73, no. 10 (October 1994): 40.

[101] Ibid.

[102] Gross, *Compensation for Teams.*

[103] G. Ledford, "Three Case Studies on Skill-Based Pay: An Overview," *Compensation & Benefits Review* 23, no. 2 (1991): 11–24.

[104] J. R. Schuster and P. K. Zingheim, *The New Pay: Linking Employee and Organizational Performance* (New York: Lexington Books, 1992).

[105] M. Bolch, "Rewarding the Team," *HR Magazine*, v52 i2 (2007), available online at http://moss07.shrm.org/Publications/hrmagazine/Editorial Content/Pages/Bolch.aspx.

[106] Cohen and Bailey, "What Makes Teams Work."

[107] R. Allen and R. Kilmann, "Aligning Reward Practices in Support of Total Quality Management," *Business Horizons* 44 (May 2001): 77–85.

[108] J. H. Sheridan, "'Yes' to Team Incentives," *Industry Week*, 4 March 1996, 63.

[109] J. A. Wagner, "Studies of Individualism-Collectivism: Effects on Cooperation in Groups," *Academy of Management Journal* 38, no. 1 (1995): 152–172.

Chapter Ten

[1] M. Gottfied, "What a Cause with That?" *Forbes,* 8 January 2007, 83; A. Levin, "Chain Profile: Burgerville," *Food Service Equipment & Supplies,* October 2006, 52–54; C. Lydgate, "Reinventing the Cheeseburger," *Inc. Magazine,* November 2007, 124–125; S. Reda, "Sticky Strategies for Retention: Retailers Take Different Approaches to Keeping Associates in the Field," *Stores,* October 2008, available online at http://www.stores.org [accessed on 13 December 2009]; M. Rogers, "Natual Resources," *Chain Leader,* March 2006, 53–58.

[2] S. Bing, "The Feds Make a Pass at Hooters," *Fortune*, 15 January 1996, 82.

[3] J. Helyar, "Hooters: A Case Study," *Fortune*, 1 September 2003, 140.

[4] A. Samuels, "Pushing Hot Buttons and Wings," *St. Petersburg (FL) Times*, 10 March 2003, 1A.

[5] J. Casale, R. Ceniceros, and M. Hofmann, "Hooters Wannabe Resists Girls-Only Policy," *Business Insurance* 43, no. 4 (2009): 23.

[6] P. S. Greenlaw and J. P. Kohl, "Employer 'Business' and 'Job' Defenses in Civil Rights Actions," *Public Personnel Management* 23, no. 4 (1994): 573.

[7] Associated Press, "Hooters Settles Suit, Won't Hire Waiters," *Denver Post*, 1 October 1997, A11.

[8] D. Lewis, "EEOC: Damage Awards Reach $420m in 2004," *Boston Globe*, 20 February 2005, D2.

[9] J. L. Ledvinka, *Federal Regulation of Personnel and Human Resource Management* (Boston: Kent Publishing Co., 1982), 137–198.

[10] C. Cummins, "BP's Accident Put Its Celebrated CEO on the Hot Seat," *Wall Street Journal*, 16 June 2006, B1.

[11] A. Smith, "BP Faces Disaster Report from Baker Panel," CNNMoney.com, 17 January 2007, available online at http://money.cnn.com/2007/01/ 15/news/companies/bp/index.htm [accessed 23 March 2009].

[12] Greenlaw and Kohl, "Employer 'Business' and 'Job' Defenses in Civil Rights Actions."

[13] "$50 Million, Less Attorneys' Fees and Costs, Paid to Class Members in December 2005 in Abercrombe & Fitch Discrimination Lawsuit Settlement," available online at http://www.afjustice.com [accessed 14 July 2009].

[14] W. Peirce, C. A. Smolinski, and B. Rosen, "Why Sexual Harassment Complaints Fall on Deaf Ears," *Academy of Management Executive* 12, no. 3 (1998): 41–54.

[15] B. Mims, "Suit Claims Costco Forced Woman to Quit After She Complained of Harassment," *Salt Lake Tribune*, 24 February 2005, C14.

[16] "'Reprehensible' Sexual Harassment Ultimately Costs Custom Companies $1.1 Million," *HR Manager's Legal Reporter* (May 2007): 1.

17 "Facts about Sexual Harassment." U.S. Equal Employment Opportunity Commission, available online at http://www.eeoc.gov/facts/fs-sex.html [accessed 23 March 2009].

18 Peirce, Smolinski, and Rosen, "Why Sexual Harassment Complaints Fall on Deaf Ears."

19 Ibid.

20 E. Larson, "The Economic Costs of Sexual Harassment," *The Freeman 46*, August 1996, available online at http://www.fee.org/publications/the-freeman/article.asp?aid= 4114 [accessed 13 August 2008].

21 C. Koons, "Australia's Recovering Mining Industry Struggles to Fill Jobs," *Wall Street Journal*, 21 September 2009, A15.

22 M. Jordan, "Dairy Farms Run Low on Labor—Even in Recession, U.S. Job Candidates Are Scarce; Milk Producers Relying on Immigrants Worry About a Crackdown," *Wall Street Journal*, 30 July 2009, A13; L. Landro, "Staff Shortages in Labs May Put Patients at Risk," *Wall Street Journal*, 13 May 2009, D1.

23 G. Hyland-Savage, "General Management Perspective on Staffing: The Staffing Commandments," in *On Staffing*, ed. N. C. Bukholder, P. J. Edwards, Jr., and L. Sartain (Hoboken, NJ: Wiley, 2004), 280.

24 R. D. Gatewood and H. S. Field, *Human Resource Selection* (Fort Worth, TX: Dryden Press, 1998).

25 Ibid.

26 *Griggs v. Duke Power Co.*, 401 U.S. 424, 436 (1971); *Albemarle Paper Co. v. Moody*, 422 U.S. 405 (1975).

27 J. A. Breaugh, *Recruitment: Science and Practice* (Boston: PWSKent, 1992).

28 J. Breaugh and M. Starke, "Research on Employee Recruitment: So Many Studies, So Many Remaining Questions," *Journal of Management* 26 (2000): 405–434.

29 K. Maher, "Corporations Cut Middlemen and Do Their Own Recruiting," *Wall Street Journal*, 14 January 2003, B10.

30 A. Milkovits, "Survey Shows Methods Vary for Selecting Police Recruits," *Providence Journal*, 19 May 2003, B-01.

31 C. Camden and B. Wallace, "Job Application Forms: A Hazardous Employment Practice," *Personnel Administrator* 28 (1983): 31–32.

32 J. Kennedy, "Europeans Expect Different Type of Résumé," *Chicago Sun-Times*, 3 June 1999, 73.

33 T. Minton-Eversole, "Background Screens Even More Crucial during Economic Slump," Society of Human Resource Management, 30 July 2008, available online at http://www.shrm.org/hrdisciplines/staffingmanagement/articles [accessed on 13 December 2009].

34 K. Maher, "Career Journal: The Jungle," *Wall Street Journal*, 6 May 2003, B8.

35 S. Adler, "Verifying a Job Candidate's Background: The State of Practice in a Vital Human Resources Activity," *Review of Business* 15, no. 2 (1993–1994): 3–8.

36 W. Woska, "Legal Issues for HR Professionals: Reference Checking/Background Investigations," *Public Personnel Management* 36 (Spring 2007): 79–89.

37 "More Than 70 Percent of HR Professionals Say Reference Checking Is Effective in Identifying Poor Performers," Society for Human Resource Management, available online at http://www.shrm.org/press_published/CMS_011240.asp [accessed 3 February 2005].

38 J. Hunter, "Cognitive Ability, Cognitive Aptitudes, Job Knowledge, and Job Performance," *Journal of Vocational Behavior* 29 (1986): 340–362.

39 F. L. Schmidt, "The Role of General Cognitive Ability and Job Performance: Why There Cannot be a Debate," *Human Performance* 15 (2002): 187–210.

40 K. Murphy, "Can Conflicting Perspectives on the Role of *g* in Personnel Selection Be Resolved?" *Human Performance* 15 (2002): 173–186.

41 E. E. Cureton, "Comment," in *Research Conference on the Use of Autobiographical Data as Psychological Predictors*, ed. E. R. Henry (Greensboro, NC: The Richardson Foundation, 1965), 13.

42 J. R. Glennon, L. E. Albright, and W. A. Owens, *A Catalog of Life History Items* (Greensboro, NC: The Richardson Foundation, 1966).

43 Gatewood and Field, *Human Resource Selection*.

44 N. Schmitt, "Beyond the Big Five: Increases in Understanding and Practical Utility," *Human Performance* 17 (2004): 347–357.

45 G. Dean, "The Bottom Line: Effect Size," in *The Write Stuff: Evaluations of Graphology—The Study of Handwriting Analysis*, ed. B. Beyerstein and D. Beyerstein (Buffalo, NY: Prometheus Books, 1992); K. Dunham, "Career Journal: The Jungle, Seeing the Future," *Wall Street Journal*, 15 May 2001, B12; J. Kurtz and W. Wells, "The Employee Polygraph Protection Act: The End of Lie Detector Use in Employment Decisions?" *Journal of Small Business Management* 27, no. 4 (1989): 76–80; B. Leonard, "Reading Employees," *HRMagazine* (April 1999): 67; S. Lilienfeld, J. Wood, and H. Garb, "The Scientific Status of Projective Techniques," *Psychological Science in the Public Interest* 1 (2000): 27–66; E. Neter and G. Ben-Shakhar, "The Predictive Validity of Graphological Inferences: A Meta-Analytic Approach," *Personality & Individual Differences* 10 (1989): 737–745.

46 I. Kotlyar and K. Ades, "HR Technology: Assessment Technology Can Help Match the Best Applicant to the Right Job," *HR Magazine* (1 May 2002): 97.

47 M. S. Taylor and J. A. Sniezek, "The College Recruitment Interview: Topical Content and Applicant Reactions," *Journal of Occupational Psychology* 57 (1984): 157–168.

48 M. Harris, "Reconsidering the Employment Interview: A Review of Recent Literature and Suggestions for Future Research," *Personnel Psychology* (Winter 1989): 691–726.

49 Taylor and Sniezek, "The College Recruitment Interview."

50 R. Burnett, C. Fan, S. J. Motowidlo, and T. DeGroot, "Interview Notes and Validity," *Personnel Psychology* 51, (1998): 375–396; M. A. Campion, D. K. Palmer, and J. E. Campion, "A Review of Structure in the Selection Interview," *Personnel Psychology* 50, no. 3 (1997): 655–702.

51 J. Cortina, N. Goldstein, S. Payne, K. Davison, and S. Gilliland, "The Incremental Validity of Interview Scores Over and Above Cognitive Ability and Conscientiousness Scores," *Personnel Psychology* 53, no. 2 (2000): 325–351; F. L. Schmidt and J. E. Hunter, "The Validity and Utility of Selection Methods in Personnel Psychology: Practical and Theoretical Implications of 85 Years of Research Findings," *Psychological Bulletin* 124, no. 2 (1998): 262–274.

52 T. Judge, "The Employment Interview: A Review of Recent Research and Recommendations for Future Research," *Human Resource Management Review* 10, no. 4 (2000): 383–406.

53 K. Tyler, "Training Revs Up," *HR Magazine* (April 2005), Society for Human Resource Management, available online at http://www.shrm.org [accessed 23 March 2009].

54 Ibid.

55 S. Livingston, T. W. Gerdel, M. Hill, B. Yerak, C. Melvin, and B. Lubinger, "Ohio's Strongest Companies All Agree That Training Is Vital to Their Success," *Cleveland Plain Dealer*, 21 May 1997, 30S.

56 G. Kesler, "Why the Leadership Bench Never Gets Deeper: Ten Insights about Executive Talent Development," *Human Resource Planning*, 1 January 2002, 32.

57 The Oil Spill Training Company, available online at http://oilspilltraining.com/home/index.asp [accessed 14 August 2008].

58 J. Borzo, "Almost Human: Using Avatars for Corporate Training, Advocates Say, Can Combine the Best Parts of Face-to-Face Interaction and Computer-Based Learning," *Wall Street Journal*, 24 May 2004, R4.

59 D. L. Kirkpatrick, "Four Steps to Measuring Training Effectiveness," *Personnel Administrator* 28 (1983): 19–25.

60 L. Bassi, J. Ludwig, D. McMurrer, and M. Van Buren, "Profiting from Learning: Do Firms' Investments in Education and Training Pay Off?" American Society for Training and Development, available online at http://www.astd.org/NR/rdonlyres/91956A5E-6E57-44DDAE5D-FCFFCDC11C3F/0/ASTD_Profiting_From_Learning.pdf [accessed 14 August 2008].

61 J. Stack, "The Curse of the Annual Performance Review," *Inc.*, 1 March 1997, 39.

62 D. Murphy, "Are Performance Appraisals Worse Than a Waste of Time? Book Derides Unintended Consequences," *San Francisco Chronicle*, 9 September 2001, W1.

63 K. R. Murphy and J. N. Cleveland, *Understanding Performance Appraisal: Social, Organizational and Goal-Based Perspectives* (Thousand Oaks, CA: Sage, 1995).

64 D. J. Schleicher, D. V. Day, B. T. Mayes, and R. E. Riggio, "A New Frame for Frame-of-Reference Training: Enhancing the Construct Validity of Assessment Centers," *Journal of Applied Psychology* (August 2002): 735–746.

65 Stack, "The Curse of the Annual Performance Review."

66 J. Sandberg, "Performance Reviews Need Some Work, Don't Meet Potential," *Wall Street Journal*, 20 November 2007, B1.

67 C. Hymowitz, "Do '360' Job Reviews by Colleagues Promote Honesty or Insults?" *Wall Street Journal*, 12 December 2000, B1.

68 D. A. Waldman, L. E. Atwater, and D. Antonioni, "Has 360 Feedback Gone Amok?" *Academy of Management Executive* 12, no. 2 (1998): 86–94.

69 H. H. Meyer, "A Solution to the Performance Appraisal Feedback Enigma," *Academy of Management Executive* 5, no. 1 (1991): 68–76; G. C. Thornton, "Psychometric Properties of Self-Appraisals of Job Performance," *Personnel Psychology* 33 (1980): 263–271.

70 G. C. Thornton, "Psychometric Properties of Self-Appraisals of Job Performance," *Personnel Psychology* 33 (1980): 263–271.

71 J. Smither, M. London, R. Flautt, Y. Vargas, and I. Kucine, "Can Working with an Executive Coach Improve Multisource Feedback Ratings over Time? A Quasi-Experimental Field Study," *Personnel Psychology* (Spring 2003): 21–43.

72 J. Smither, M. London, R. Flautt, Y. Vargas, and I. Kucine, "Can Working with an Executive Coach Improve Multisource Feedback Ratings over Time? A Quasi-Experimental Field Study," *Personnel Psychology* (Spring 2003): 21–43.

73 C. Tuna, "In Some Offices, Keeping Workers Earns a Bonus; More Firms Like Penske Tie Top Managers' Pay to Employee Retention," *Wall Street Journal*, 30 June 2008, B6.

74 Ibid.

75 G. T. Milkovich and J. M. Newman, *Compensation*, 4th ed. (Homewood, IL: Irwin, 1993).

76 J. A. Livingston, "Child Care Wages and Benefits Study," Child Care Resource, 2 August 2006, available online at http://www.childcareresource.org/home_announce/cc%20wages%20and%20benefits%20report.final.augst.2006.pdf [accessed 14 August 2008].

77 "A Worthy Wage?" *American Federation of Teachers*, 1 May 2008, available online at http://www.aft.org/news/ download/AFT-WorthyWage-Day2008-Ad.pdf [accessed 14 August 2008].

78 M. L. Williams and G. F. Dreher, "Compensation System Attributes and Applicant Pool Characteristics," *Academy of Management Journal* 35, no. 3 (1992): 571–595.

79 "Delta Employees Share $158 Million this Valentine's Day," M2 Presswire, 14 February 2008, available online at http://infotrac-college.thomsonlearning.com/ itw/infomark/459/518/38866979w16/purl=rc1_WAD_ 0_A174761438& dyn=8!xrn_19_0_A174761438?sw_aep=olr_wad [accessed 15 August 2008].

80 J. Kaufman, "Sharing the Wealth: At McKay Nursery, Migrant Workers Get a Chance to Own Part of the Company," *Wall Street Journal*, 9 April 1998, R10.

81 M. Bloom, "The Performance Effects of Pay Dispersion on Individuals and Organizations," *Academy of Management Journal* 42, no. 1 (1999): 25–40.

82 "2007 Trends in CEO Pay," AFL-CIO, available online at http://www.aflcio.org/corporatewatch/paywatch/pay/index.cfm [accessed 15 August 2008]; C. Hymowitz, "Pay Gap Fuels Worker Woes," *Wall Street Journal*, 28 April 2008, B8.

83 W. Grossman and R. E. Hoskisson, "CEO Pay at the Crossroads of Wall Street and Main: Toward the Strategic Design of Executive Compensation," *Academy of Management Executive* 12, no. 1 (1998): 43–57.

84 Bloom, "The Performance Effects of Pay Dispersion."

85 J. S. Rosenbloom, "The Environment of Employee Benefit Plans," in *The Handbook of Employee Benefits*, ed. J. S. Rosenbloom (Chicago: Irwin, 1996), 3–13.

86 "Employer Costs for Employee Compensation Summary," Bureau of Labor Statistics, http://www.bls.gov/news.release/ecec.nr0.htm [accessed on 13 December 2009].

87 A. E. Barber, R. B. Dunham, and R. A. Formisano, "The Impact of Flexible Benefits on Employee Satisfaction: A Field Study," *Personnel Psychology* 45 (1992): 55–75; B. Heshizer, "The Impact of Flexible Benefits on Job Satisfaction and Turnover Intentions," *Benefits Quarterly* 4 (1994): 84–90; D. M. Cable and T. A. Judge, "Pay Preferences and Job Search Decisions: A Person-Organization Fit Perspective," *Personnel Psychology* 47 (1994): 317–348.

88 B. T. Beam and J. J. McFadden, *Employee Benefits* (Chicago: Dearborn Financial Publishing, 1996).

89 S. Needleman, "Bad Firings Can Hurt Firm's Reputation," *Wall Street Journal*, 8 July 2008, D4.

90 A. Rupe, "Horrors from the Bad-Firing File," *Workforce Management*, November 2003, 16.

91 P. Michal-Johnson, *Saying Good-Bye: A Manager's Guide to Employee Dismissal* (Glenview, IL: Scott, Foresman & Co., 1985).

92 M. Bordwin, "Employment Law: Beware of Time Bombs and Shark-Infested Waters," *HR Focus*, 1 April 1995, 19; D. Jones, "Fired Workers Fight Back . . . and Win; Laws, Juries Shift Protection to Terminated Employees," *USA Today*, 2 April 1998, 01B.

93 T. Bland, "Fire at Will, Repent at Leisure," *Security Management* 44 (May 2000), 64.

94 "Mass Layoffs in December 2007 and Annual Totals for 2007," Bureau of Labor Statistics News, 24 January 2008, available online at http://www.bls.gov/news.release/archives/mmls_01242008.pdf [accessed 15 August 2008].

95 J. R. Morris, W. F. Cascio, and C. E. Young, "Downsizing after All These Years: Questions and Answers about Who Did It, How Many Did It, and Who Benefited from It," *Organizational Dynamics* 27, no. 3 (1999): 78–87.

96 K. Maher, "Hiring Freezes Cushion New Layoffs," *Wall Street Journal,* 24 January 2008, A13.

97 K. E. Mishra, G. M. Spreitzer, and A. K. Mishra, "Preserving Employee Morale during Downsizing," *Sloan Management Review* 39, no. 2 (1998): 83–95.

98 K. Frieswick, "Until We Meet Again?" *CFO,* 1 October 2001, 41.

99 J. Hilsenrath, "Adventures in Cost Cutting," *Wall Street Journal*, 10 May 2004, R1.

100 M. Jackson, "Downsized, but Still in the Game: Keeping Up Morale Crucial after Job Cuts," The Boston Globe, 11 January 2009, available online at http://www.boston.com/business/articles/2009/01/11/downsized_but_still_in_the_game/?p1=Well_MostPop_Emailed7 [accessed 10 September 2009].

101 D. R. Dalton, W. D. Todor, and D. M. Krackhardt, "Turnover Overstated: The Functional Taxonomy," *Academy of Management Review* 7 (1982): 117–123.

102 J. R. Hollenbeck and C. R. Williams, "Turnover Functionality versus Turnover Frequency: A Note on Work Attitudes and Organizational Effectiveness," *Journal of Applied Psychology* 71 (1986): 606–611.

103 C. R. Williams, "Reward Contingency, Unemployment, and Functional Turnover," *Human Resource Management Review* 9 (1999): 549–576.

104 J. McCarthy and R. Goffin, "Measuring Job Interview Anxiety: Beyond Weak Knees and Sweaty Palms," *Personnel Psychology* 54, no. 3 (2004): 31.

Chapter Eleven

1 J. Farrel, "Every Customer Counts," *Retail Merchandiser*, January/February 2008, 51–52; E. Holmes, "Corporate News: Ann Taylor to Revamp Racks," *Wall Street Journal*, 21 May 2009, B4; A. Merrick, "Ann Taylor's Loftier Goal: A More Upscale Shopper," *Wall Street Journal*, 14 September 2007, B1; D. Moin, "More Cuts at Ann Taylor," *Women's Wear Daily*, 31 July 2009, 5; V. O'Connell, "Retailers Reprogram Workers in Efficiency Push," *Wall Street Journal*, 10 September 2008, A1; A. Pasquarelli, "A Rip in the Fabric: Hit by Downturn, Ann Taylor Cuts Staff, Closes Stores; Is Leader to Blame?" *Crain's New York Business*, 17 November 2008, 3; J. Saranow, "Ann Taylor, Talbots Plan Further Cuts," *Wall Street Journal*, 7 November 2008, B6; A. Steigrad, "Ann Taylor Sees Loss, Ups Store Closings," *Women's Wear Daily*, 9 March 2009, 14.

2 J. P. Campbell and R. D. Pritchard, "Motivation Theory in Industrial and Organizational Psychology," in *Handbook of Industrial and Organizational Psychology*, ed. M. D. Dunnette (Chicago: Rand McNally, 1976).

3 C. Tuna, "Pay, Your Own Way: Firm Lets Workers Pick Salary; Big Bonus? None at All? In Throwback to '80s, Employees Make Call," *Wall Street Journal*, 7 July 2008, B6.

4 C. Tkaczyk, "Offer Affordable (Awesome) Day Care," *Fortune*, 17 August 2009, 26.

5 S. Monson, "Feeling Perky," *Seattle Times*, 24 December 2006, G1.

6 Ibid.

7 E. A. Locke, "The Nature and Causes of Job Satisfaction," in *Handbook of Industrial and Organizational Psychology*, ed. M. D. Dunnette (Chicago: Rand McNally, 1976).

8 A. H. Maslow, "A Theory of Human Motivation," *Psychological Review* 50 (1943): 370–396.

9 C. P. Alderfer, *Existence, Relatedness, and Growth: Human Needs in Organizational Settings* (New York: Free Press, 1972).

10 D. C. McClelland, "Toward a Theory of Motive Acquisition," *American Psychologist* 20 (1965): 321–333; D. C. McClelland and D. H. Burnham, "Power Is the Great Motivator," *Harvard Business Review* 54, no. 2 (1976): 100–110.

11 J. H. Turner, "Entrepreneurial Environments and the Emergence of Achievement Motivation in Adolescent Males," *Sociometry* 33 (1970): 147–165.

12 L. W. Porter, E. E. Lawler III, and J. R. Hackman, *Behavior in Organizations* (New York: McGraw-Hill, 1975).

13 C. Ajila, "Maslow's Hierarchy of Needs Theory: Applicability to the Nigerian Industrial Setting," *IFE Psychology* (1997): 162–174.

14 J. Spencer, "Shirk Ethic: How to Fake a Hard Day at the Office—White-Collar Slackers Get Help from New Gadgets: The Faux 4 A.M. E-Mail," *Wall Street Journal*, 15 May 2003, D1.

15 E. E. Lawler III and L. W. Porter, "The Effect of Performance on Job Satisfaction," *Industrial Relations* 7 (1967): 20–28.

16 Porter, Lawler, and Hackman, *Behavior in Organizations.*

17 Ibid.

18 J. Lublin, "Creative Compensation: A CEO Talks about His Company's Innovative Pay Ideas; Free Ice Cream, Anyone?" *Wall Street Journal*, 10 April 2006, R6.

19 C. Caggiano, "What Do Workers Want?" *Inc.*, November 1992, 101–104; "National Study of the Changing Workforce," Families & Work Institute, available online at http://www.familiesandwork.org/summary/nscw.pdf [accessed 31 May 2005].

20 A. Brooks, "I LOVE my WORK," *American: A Magazine of Ideas* 6 (Sept./Oct. 2007), 20–28.

21 H. Dolezalek, "Good Job! Recognition Training," *Training*, 28 July 2008.

22 S. Ladika, "Rewarding Exempt Employees," *HRMagazine* 51 (September 2006): 117–121.

23 Dolezalek, "Good Job!"

24 J. Laabs, "Satisfy Them with More Than Money," *Personnel Journal* 77, no. 11 (1998): 40.

25 R. Kanfer and P. Ackerman, "Aging, Adult Development, and Work Motivation," *Academy of Management Review* (2004): 440–458.

26 E. White, "The New Recruits: Older Workers," *Wall Street Journal,* 14 January 2008, B3.

27 Tuna, "Pay, Your Own Way."

28 S. J. O'Malley, "Motivate the Middle: How Mid-Level Performance Can Bring Top Growth to the Bottom Line," *Bank Investment Consultant*, February 2007, 39.

29 S. Stecklow, "Fast Finns' Fines Fit Their Finances—Traffic Penalties Are Assessed According to Driver Income," *Wall Street Journal*, 2 January 2001, A1.

30 J. McGregor, "CEO Pay: Schwarzman Tops Corporate Library List," *BusinessWeek,* 17 August 2009, 10.

31 J. S. Adams, "Toward an Understanding of Inequity," *Journal of Abnormal Social Psychology* 67 (1963): 422–436.

32 J. Greenberg, "Employee Theft as a Reaction to Underpayment Inequity: The Hidden Costs of Pay Cuts," *Journal of Applied Psychology* 75 (1990): 561–568.

33 R. A. Cosier and D. R. Dalton, "Equity Theory and Time: A Reformulation," *Academy of Management Review* 8 (1983): 311–319; M. R. Carrell and J. E. Dittrich, "Equity Theory: The Recent Literature, Methodological Considerations, and New Directions," *Academy of Management Review* 3 (1978): 202–209.

34 "Anger at 30,000 Feet," *Fortune,* 10 December 2007, 32.

35 M. Cimini, "Profile of the American Airlines' Pilot Sickout," *Compensation and Working Conditions* (Winter 1999): 21–26.

[36] J. Bendich, "When Is a Temp Not a Temp?" *Trial Magazine*, 1 October 2001, 42.

[37] U.S. Department of Labor, "2002 Statistics Fact Sheet: Back Wages for Fair Labor Standards Act Violations Increased by 29%," available online at http://www.dol.gov/esa/whd/statistics/200212.htm [accessed 25 March 2009]; M. Orey, "Lawsuits Abound from Workers Seeking Overtime Pay," *Wall Street Journal*, 30 May 2002, B1.

[38] K. Maher, "Workers Are Filing More Lawsuits against Employers over Wages," *Wall Street Journal*, 5 June 2006, A2.

[39] A. Zimmerman, "Big Retailers Face Overtime Suits as Bosses Do More 'Hourly' Work," *Wall Street Journal*, 26 May 2004, A1.

[40] C. Chen, J. Choi, and S. Chi, "Making Justice Sense of Local-Expatriate Compensation Disparity: Mitigation by Local Referents, Ideological Explanations, and Interpersonal Sensitivity in China-Foreign Joint Ventures," *Academy of Management Journal* (2002): 807–817.

[41] K. Aquino, R. W. Griffeth, D. G. Allen, and P. W. Hom, "Integrating Justice Constructs into the Turnover Process: A Test of a Referent Cognitions Model," *Academy of Management Journal* 40, no. 5 (1997): 1208–1227.

[42] S. Barr, "While the SEC Watches the Markets, the Job Market Is Draining the SEC," *Washington Post*, 10 March 2002, C3.

[43] S. Needleman, "Burger Chain's Health-Care Recipe—Paying More for Insurance Cuts Turnover, Boosts Sales and Productivity," *Wall Street Journal*, 31 August 2009, B4.

[44] R. Folger and M. A. Konovsky, "Effects of Procedural and Distributive Justice on Reactions to Pay Raise Decisions," *Academy of Management Journal* 32 (1989): 115–130; M. A. Konovsky, "Understanding Procedural Justice and Its Impact on Business Organizations," *Journal of Management* 26 (2000): 489–512.

[45] E. Barret-Howard and T. R. Tyler, "Procedural Justice as a Criterion in Allocation Decisions," *Journal of Personality & Social Psychology* 50 (1986): 296–305; Folger and Konovsky, "Effects of Procedural and Distributive Justice on Reactions to Pay Raise Decisions."

[46] R. Folger and J. Greenberg, "Procedural Justice: An Interpretive Analysis of Personnel Systems," in *Research in Personnel and Human Resources Management*, vol. 3, ed. K. Rowland and G. Ferris (Greenwich, CT: JAI, 1985); R. Folger, D. Rosenfield, J. Grove, and L. Corkran, "Effects of 'Voice' and Peer Opinions on Responses to Inequity," *Journal of Personality & Social Psychology* 37 (1979): 2253–2261; E. A. Lind and T. R. Tyler, *The Social Psychology of Procedural Justice* (New York: Plenum, 1988); Konovsky, "Understanding Procedural Justice and Its Impact on Business Organizations."

[47] K. A. Dolan, "When Money Isn't Enough," *Forbes*, 18 November 1996, 164–170.

[48] V. H. Vroom, *Work and Motivation* (New York: John Wiley & Sons, 1964); L. W. Porter and E. E. Lawler III, *Managerial Attitudes and Performance* (Homewood, IL: Dorsey & Richard D. Irwin, 1968).

[49] P. V. LeBlanc and P. W. Mulvey, "How American Workers See the Rewards of Work," *Compensation & Benefits Review* 30 (February 1998): 24–28.

[50] A. Fox, "Companies Can Benefit When They Disclose Pay Processes to Employees," *HR Magazine*, July 2002, 25.

[51] S. Wellner, "Spoiled Brats—Your HR Policies May Be Contributing to a Sense of Employee Entitlement," *HR Magazine*, November 2004, available online at http://www.shrm.org [accessed 25 March 2009].

[52] K. W. Thomas and B. A. Velthouse, "Cognitive Elements of Empowerment," *Academy of Management Review* 15 (1990): 666–681.

[53] C. Hymowitz, "When Meeting Targets Becomes the Strategy, CEO Is on Wrong Path," *Wall Street Journal*, 8 March 2005, A8.

[54] E. L. Thorndike, *Animal Intelligence* (New York: Macmillan, 1911).

[55] S. Nassauer, "Now at Hotels: The $250 Cigarette; Major Chains Get Tough with Fines for Smoking; Busted for Butts in the Trash," *Wall Street Journal*, 21 February 2008, D1.

[56] B. F. Skinner, *Science and Human Behavior* (New York: Macmillan, 1954); B. F. Skinner, *Beyond Freedom and Dignity* (New York: Bantam, 1971); B. F. Skinner, *A Matter of Consequences* (New York: New York University Press, 1984).

[57] A. M. Dickinson and A. D. Poling, "Schedules of Monetary Reinforcement in Organizational Behavior Management: Latham and Huber Revisited," *Journal of Organizational Behavior Management* 16, no. 1 (1992): 71–91.

[58] R. Ho, "Attending to Attendance," *Wall Street Journal*, 7 December 1998, 6.

[59] D. Grote, "Manager's Journal: Discipline without Punishment," *Wall Street Journal*, 23 May 1994, A14.

[60] J. B. Miner, *Theories of Organizational Behavior* (Hinsdale, IL: Dryden, 1980).

[61] Dickinson and Poling, "Schedules of Monetary Reinforcement in Organizational Behavior Management."

[62] F. Luthans and A. D. Stajkovic, "Reinforce for Performance: The Need to Go beyond Pay and Even Rewards," *Academy of Management Executive* 13, no. 2 (1999): 49–57.

[63] K. D. Butterfield, L. K. Trevino, and G. A. Ball, "Punishment from the Manager's Perspective: A Grounded Investigation and Inductive Model," *Academy of Management Journal* 39 (1996): 1479–1512.

[64] R. D. Arvey and J. M. Ivancevich, "Punishment in Organizations: A Review, Propositions, and Research Suggestions," *Academy of Management Review* 5 (1980): 123–132.

[65] R. D. Arvey, G. A. Davis, and S. M. Nelson, "Use of Discipline in an Organization: A Field Study," *Journal of Applied Psychology* 69 (1984): 448–460; M. E. Schnake, "Vicarious Punishment in a Work Setting," *Journal of Applied Psychology* 71 (1986): 343–345.

[66] A. D. Stajkovic and F. Luthans, "A Meta-Analysis of the Effects of Organizational Behavior Modification on Task Performance, 1975–95," *Academy of Management Journal* 40, no. 5 (1997): 1122–1149; A. D. Stajkovic and F. Luthans, "Behavioral Management and Task Performance in Organizations: Conceptual Background, Meta-Analysis, and Test of Alternative Models," *Personnel Psychology* 56, no. 1 (2003): 155–194.

[67] S. McCartney, "How US Airways Vaulted to First Place; Airline Is Now Tops in On-Time Arrivals; 100 New Mechanics," *Wall Street Journal*, 22 July 2008, D3.

[68] E. A. Locke and G. P. Latham, *Goal Setting: A Motivational Technique That Works* (Englewood Cliffs, NJ: Prentice-Hall, 1984); E. A. Locke and G. P. Latham, *A Theory of Goal Setting and Task Performance* (Englewood Cliffs, NJ: Prentice-Hall, 1990).

[69] "Franchising—In with the New: As More Boomers Retire, Franchisers Set Their Sights on a Much Younger Crowd," *Wall Street Journal*, 28 September 2009, R9.

[70] G. P. Latham and E. A. Locke, "Goal Setting—A Motivational Technique That Works," *Organizational Dynamics* 8, no. 2 (1979): 68.

[71] Ibid.

[72] C. A. Arnolds and C. Boshoff, "Compensation, Esteem Valence, and Job Performance: An Empirical Assessment of Alderfer's ERG Theory," *International Journal of Human Resource Management* 13, no. 4 (2002): 697–719.

[73] Maslow, "A Theory of Human Motivation."

Chapter Twelve

1 K. Brooker and D. Burke, "The Pepsi Machine," *Fortune*, 6 February 2006, 68; B. McKay, "Boss Talk: PepsiCo CEO Adapts to Tough Climate," *Wall Street Journal*, 11 September 2008, B1; B. Morris, "The Pepsi Challenge: Can This Snack and Soda Giant Go Healthy?" *Fortune*, 18 February 2008, 54; M. Useem, "New Ideas for This Pepsi Generation," *U.S. News & World Report*, 1 December 2008, 49; N. Zmuda and R. Parekh, "Pepsi Upends Brands with 1.2 Bil Shake-up," *Advertising Age*, 20 October 2008, available online at http://adage.com [accessed 20 June 2009].

2 W. Bennis, "Why Leaders Can't Lead," *Training & Development Journal* 43, no. 4 (1989).

3 A. Zaleznik, "Managers and Leaders: Are They Different?" *Harvard Business Review* 55 (1977): 76–78; A. Zaleznik, "The Leadership Gap," *Washington Quarterly* 6 (1983): 32–39.

4 Bennis, "Why Leaders Can't Lead."

5 K. Voigt, "Enron, Andersen Scandals Offer Ethical Lessons—Businesspeople Can Strive to Avoid Common Pitfalls through the 'Three Ms,'" *Wall Street Journal Europe*, 3 September 2002, A12.

6 S. Berfield, "The Best of 2006: Leaders," *BusinessWeek*, 18 December 2006, 58.

7 D. Jones, "Not All Successful CEOs Are Extroverts," *USA Today*, 7 June 2006, B.1.

8 Ibid.

9 R. J. House and R. M Aditya, "The Social Scientific Study of Leadership: Quo Vadis?" *Journal of Management* 23 (1997): 409–473; T. Judge, R. Illies, J. Bono, and M. Gerhardt, "Personality and Leadership: A Qualitative and Quantitative Review," *Journal of Applied Psychology* (August 2002): 765–782; S. A. Kirkpatrick and E. A. Locke, "Leadership: Do Traits Matter?" *Academy of Management Executive* 5, no. 2 (1991): 48–60.

10 House and Aditya, "The Social Scientific Study of Leadership"; Kirkpatrick and Locke, "Leadership: Do Traits Matter?"

11 Kirkpatrick and Locke, "Leadership: Do Traits Matter?"

12 E. A. Fleishman, "The Description of Supervisory Behavior," *Journal of Applied Psychology* 37 (1953): 1–6; L. R. Katz, *New Patterns of Management* (New York: McGraw-Hill, 1961).

13 S. Tully and E. Levenson, "In This Corner! The Contender—Jamie Dimon—The New CEO of J.P. Morgan Chase," *Fortune*, 3 April 2006, 54.

14 A. Lashinsky, D. Burke, and S. Kaufman, "The Hurd Way: How a Sales Obsessed CEO Rebooted HP," *Fortune*, 17 April 2006, 92.

15 J. B. Fuller, C. E. P. Patterson, K. Hester, and D. Stringer, "A Quantitative Review of Research on Charismatic Leadership," *Psychological Reports* 78 (1996): 271–287; R. G. Lord, C. L. De Vader, and G. M. Alliger, "A Meta-Analysis of the Relation between Personality Traits and Leadership Perceptions: An Application of Validity Generalization Procedures," *Journal of Applied Psychology* 71, no. 3 (1986): 402–410.

16 P. Weissenberg and M. H. Kavanagh, "The Independence of Initiating Structure and Consideration: A Review of the Evidence," *Personnel Psychology* 25 (1972): 119–130.

17 R. J. House and T. R. Mitchell, "Path-Goal Theory of Leadership," *Journal of Contemporary Business* 3 (1974): 81–97; F. E. Fiedler, "A Contingency Model of Leadership Effectiveness," in *Advances in Experimental Social Psychology*, ed. L. Berkowitz (New York: Academic Press, 1964); V. H. Vroom and P. W. Yetton, *Leadership and Decision Making* (Pittsburgh: University of Pittsburgh Press, 1973); P. Hersey and K. H. Blanchard, The *Management of Organizational Behavior*, 4th ed. (Englewood Cliffs, NJ: Prentice Hall, 1984); Kerr and Jermier, "Substitutes for Leadership."

18 F. E. Fiedler and M. M. Chemers, *Leadership and Effective Management* (Glenview, IL: Scott, Foresman, 1974); F. E. Fiedler and M. M. Chemers, *Improving Leadership Effectiveness: The Leader Match Concept*, 2nd ed. (New York: Wiley, 1984).

19 Fiedler and Chemers, *Improving Leadership Effectiveness*.

20 F. E. Fiedler, "The Effects of Leadership Training and Experience: A Contingency Model Interpretation," *Administrative Science Quarterly* 17, no. 4 (1972): 455; F. E. Fiedler, *A Theory of Leadership Effectiveness* (New York: McGraw-Hill, 1967).

21 J. Helyar, "Why Is This Man Smiling?" *Fortune*, 18 October 2004, 130.

22 L. S. Csoka and F. E. Fiedler, "The Effect of Military Leadership Training: A Test of the Contingency Model," *Organizational Behavior & Human Performance* 8 (1972): 395–407.

23 House and Mitchell, "Path-Goal Theory of Leadership."

24 House and Mitchell, "Path-Goal Theory of Leadership."

25 G. Edmondson, K. Kerwin, and K. Anhalt, "Hot Audi: It's Finally Blasting into the Luxury-Car Pack. Can It Stay There?" *BusinessWeek*, 14 March 2005, 24.

26 B. M. Fisher and J. E. Edwards, "Consideration and Initiating Structure and Their Relationships with Leader Effectiveness: A Meta-Analysis," *Proceedings of the Academy of Management*, August 1988, 201–205.

27 M. Copeland, K. Crawford, J. Davis, S. Hamner, C. Hawn, R. Howe, P. Kaihla, M. Maier, O. Malik, D. McDonald, C. Null, E. Schonfeld, O. Thomas, and G. Zachary, "My Golden Rule," *Business 2.0*, 1 December 2005, 108.

28 J. C. Wofford and L. Z. Liska, "Path-Goal Theories of Leadership: A Meta-Analysis," *Journal of Management* 19 (1993): 857–876.

29 House and Aditya, "The Social Scientific Study of Leadership."

30 P. Hersey and K. Blanchard, *Management of Organizational Behavior: Leading Human Resources*, 8th ed. (Escondido, CA: Center for Leadership Studies, 2001).

31 W. Blank, J. R. Weitzel, and S. G. Green, "A Test of the Situational Leadership Theory," *Personnel Psychology* 43, no. 3 (1990): 579–597; W. R. Norris and R. P. Vecchio, "Situational Leadership Theory: A Replication," *Group & Organization Management* 17, no. 3 (1992): 331–342.

32 Ibid.

33 V. H. Vroom and A. G. Jago, *The New Leadership: Managing Participation in Organizations* (Englewood Cliffs, NJ: Prentice Hall, 1988).

34 C. Fishman, "How Teamwork Took Flight: This Team Built a Commercial Engine—and Self-Managing GE Plant—from Scratch," *Fast Company*, 1 October 1999, 188.

35 Ibid.

36 Ibid.

37 G. A. Yukl, *Leadership in Organizations,* 3rd ed. (Englewood Cliffs, NJ: Prentice Hall, 1995).

38 B. M. Bass, *Bass & Stogdill's Handbook of Leadership: Theory, Research, and Managerial Applications* (New York: Free Press, 1990).

39 R. D. Ireland and M. A. Hitt, "Achieving and Maintaining Strategic Competitiveness in the 21st Century: The Role of Strategic Leadership," *Academy of Management Executive* 13, no. 1 (1999): 43–57.

40 K. Kranhold, "The Immelt Era, Five Years Old, Transforms GE," *Wall Street Journal*, 11 September 2006, B1.

41 G. Colvin, "Lafley and Immelt: Q & A," *Fortune*, 11 December 2006, 75.

42 P. Thoms and D. B. Greenberger, "Training Business Leaders to Create Positive Organizational Visions of the Future: Is It

Successful?" *Academy of Management Journal* (Best Papers & Proceedings 1995): 212–216.

43 M. Weber, *The Theory of Social and Economic Organizations*, trans. R. A. Henderson and T. Parsons (New York: Free Press, 1947).

44 D. A. Waldman and F. J. Yammarino, "CEO Charismatic Leadership: Levels-of-Management and Levels-of-Analysis Effects," *Academy of Management Review* 24, no. 2 (1999): 266–285.

45 K. B. Lowe, K. G. Kroeck, and N. Sivasubramaniam, "Effectiveness Correlates of Transformational and Transactional Leadership: A Meta-Analytic Review of the MLQ Literature," *Leadership Quarterly* 7 (1996): 385–425.

46 J. M. Howell and B. J. Avolio, "The Ethics of Charismatic Leadership: Submission or Liberation?" *Academy of Management Executive* 6, no. 2 (1992): 43–54.

47 A. Deutschman, "Is Your Boss a Psychopath?" *Fast Company*, July 2005, 44.

48 Howell and Avolio, "The Ethics of Charismatic Leadership."

49 J. M. Burns, *Leadership* (New York: Harper & Row, 1978); B. M. Bass, "From Transactional to Transformational Leadership: Learning to Share the Vision," *Organizational Dynamics* 18 (1990): 19–36.

50 Bass, "From Transactional to Transformational Leadership."

51 B. M. Bass, *A New Paradigm of Leadership: An Inquiry into Transformational Leadership* (Alexandra, VA: U.S. Army Research Institute for the Behavioral and Social Sciences, 1996).

52 K. Swisher, "A Question of Management: Carol Bartz on How Yahoo's Organizational Structure Got in the Way of Innovation," *Wall Street Journal*, 2 June 2009, R4.

53 K. Spors, "Small Business (A Special Report); Top Small Workplaces 2007: What Makes a Great Workplace? Among Other Things: Having Employees Who Feel Empowered and Convinced They Have a Future at the Company," *Wall Street Journal*, 1 October 2007, R1.

54 Ibid.

55 Bass, "From Transactional to Transformational Leadership."

56 F. E. Fiedler and M. M. Chemers, *Improving Leadership Effectiveness: The Leader Match Concept* (New York: Wiley, 1984).

Chapter Thirteen

1 M. Chafkin, "Get Happy," *Inc.*, May 2009, 66; J. O'Brien, "Zappos Knows How to Take It," *Fortune*, February 2009, 54; M. Zager, "Zappos Delivers Service . . . With Shoes on the Side," *Apparel Magazine*, January 2009, 10; N. Zmuda, "Surfing for Sales: Zappos Execs Aim To Hit $1 Billion," *Footwear News*, 21 August 2006, 1.

2 E. E. Lawler III, L. W. Porter, and A. Tannenbaum, "Manager's Attitudes toward Interaction Episodes," *Journal of Applied Psychology* 52 (1968): 423–439; H. Mintzberg, *The Nature of Managerial Work* (New York: Harper & Row, 1973).

3 J. D. Maes, T. G. Weldy, and M. L. Icenogle, "A Managerial Perspective: Oral Communication Competency Is Most Important for Business Students in the Workplace," *Journal of Business Communication* 34 (1997): 67–80.

4 R. Lepsinger and A. D. Lucia, *The Art and Science of 360 Degree Feedback* (San Francisco: Pfeiffer, 1997).

5 I. M. Botero, "Good Communication Skills Needed Today," *Business Journal: Serving Phoenix and the Valley of the Sun*, 21 October 1996.

6 E. E. Jones and K. E. Davis, "From Acts to Dispositions: The Attribution Process in Person Perception," in *Advances in Experimental and Social Psychology*, vol. 2, ed. L. Berkowitz (New York: Academic Press, 1965), 219–266; R. G. Lord and J. E. Smith, "Theoretical, Information-Processing, and Situational Factors Affecting Attribution Theory Models of Organizational Behavior," *Academy of Management Review* 8 (1983): 50–60.

7 M. Nicholson and R. Hoye, "Contextual Factors Associated with Poor Sport Spectator Behaviour," *Managing Leisure* 10 (April 2005): 94–105.

8 D. Simons and C. Chabris, "Gorillas in Our Midst: Sustained Inattentional Blindness for Dynamic Events," *Perception* 28 (1999): 1059–1074.

9 A. Taylor, "GM Gets Its Act Together. Finally," *Fortune*, 5 April 2004, 136.

10 H. H. Kelly, *Attribution in Social Interaction* (Morristown, NJ: General Learning Press, 1971).

11 J. M. Burger, "Motivational Biases in the Attribution of Responsibility for an Accident: A Meta-Analysis of the Defensive-Attribution Hypothesis," *Psychological Bulletin* 90 (1981): 496–512.

12 D. A. Hofmann and A. Stetzer, "The Role of Safety Climate and Communication in Accident Interpretation: Implications for Learning from Negative Events," *Academy of Management Journal* 41, no. 6 (1998): 644–657.

13 D. A. Hofmann and A. Stetzer, "The Role of Safety Climate and Communication in Accident Interpretation: Implications for Learning from Negative Events," *Academy of Management Journal* 41, no. 6 (1998): 644–657.

14 C. Perrow, *Normal Accidents: Living with High-Risk Technologies* (New York: Basic Books, 1984).

15 A. G. Miller and T. Lawson, "The Effect of an Informational Opinion on the Fundamental Attribution Error," *Journal of Personality & Social Psychology* 47 (1989): 873–896; J. M. Burger, "Changes in Attribution Errors over Time: The Ephemeral Fundamental Attribution Error," *Social Cognition* 9 (1991): 182–193.

16 F. Heider, *The Psychology of Interpersonal Relations* (New York: Wiley, 1958); D. T. Miller and M. Ross, "Self-Serving Biases in Attribution of Causality: Fact or Fiction?" *Psychological Bulletin* 82 (1975): 213–225.

17 J. R. Larson, Jr., "The Dynamic Interplay between Employees' Feedback-Seeking Strategies and Supervisors' Delivery of Performance Feedback," *Academy of Management Review* 14, no. 3 (1989): 408–422.

18 M. Porter, J. Lorsch, & N.Nohria, "Seven Surprises for New CEOs," *Harvard Business Review* (October 2004): 62–72.

19 M. Reddy, "The Conduit Metaphor—A Case of Frame Conflict in Our Language about Our Language," in *Metaphor and Thought*, ed. A. Ortony (Cambridge: Cambridge University Press, 1979), 284–324.

20 G. L. Kreps, *Organizational Communication: Theory and Practice* (New York: Longman, 1990).

21 Ibid.

22 Y. Kane and P. Dvorak, "Howard Stringer, Japanese CEO—Caught between Two Worlds, the Sony Chief Tightens His Management Grip; Will It Work?" *Wall Street Journal*, 3 March 2007, A1.

23 J. Sandberg, "Ruthless Rumors and the Managers Who Enable Them," *Wall Street Journal*, 29 October 2003, B1.

24 Ibid.

25 G. Hoover, "Maintaining Employee Engagement when Communicating Difficult Issues," *Communication World*, 1 November 2005, 25.

26 W. Davis and O'Connor, "Serial Transmission of Information: A Study of the Grapevine," *Journal of Applied Communication Research* 5 (1977): 61–72; C. Hymowitz, "Managing: Spread the

Word, Gossip Is Good," *Wall Street Journal*, 4 October 1988, [accessed 13 September 1999].

27 D. T. Hall, K. L. Otazo, and G. P. Hollenbeck, "Behind Closed Doors: What Really Happens in Executive Coaching," *Organizational Dynamics* 27, no. 3 (1999): 39–53.

28 J. Kelly, "Blowing the Whistle on the Boss," *PR Newswire*, 15 November 2004, http://www.prnewswire.com [accessed 13 June 2005].

29 R. McGarvey, "Lords of Discipline," *Entrepreneur Magazine*, 1 January 2000, page number not available.

30 S. Needleman, "Career Journal: Tips for Managers on Handling Their Workers' Personal Problems," *Wall Street Journal*, 25 April 2006, B9.

31 C. Hirschman, "Firm Ground: EAP Training for HR and Managers Improves Supervisor-Employee Communication and Helps Organizations Avoid Legal Quagmires," *Employee Benefit News*, 13 June 2005, http://www.benefitnews.com [accessed 1 July 2005].

32 A. Mehrabian, "Communication without Words," *Psychology Today* 3 (1968): 53; A. Mehrabian, *Silent Messages* (Belmont, CA: Wadsworth, 1971); R. Harrison, *Beyond Words: An Introduction to Nonverbal Communication* (Upper Saddle River, NJ: Prentice Hall, 1974); A. Mehrabian, *Non-Verbal Communication* (Chicago: Aldine, 1972).

33 M. L. Knapp, *Nonverbal Communication in Human Interaction*, 2nd ed. (New York: Holt, Rinehart & Winston, 1978).

34 H. M. Rosenfeld, "Instrumental Affiliative Functions of Facial and Gestural Expressions," *Journal of Personality & Social Psychology* 24 (1966): 65–72; P. Ekman, "Differential Communication of Affect by Head and Body Cues," *Journal of Personality & Social Psychology* 23 (1965): 726–735; A. Mehrabian, "Significance of Posture and Position in the Communication of Attitude and Status Relationships," *Psychological Bulletin* 71 (1969): 359–372.

35 J. Saranow, "A Personal Trainer for Your Voice," *Wall Street Journal*, 3 February 2004, D1.

36 C. A. Bartlett and S. Ghoshal, "Changing the Role of Top Management: Beyond Systems to People," *Harvard Business Review*, May–June 1995, 132–142.

37 A. Joyce, "Confidentiality as a Valued Benefit; Loose Lips Can Defeat the Purpose of an Employee Assistance Program," *Washington Post*, 11 May 2003, F05.

38 T. Andrews, "E-Mail Empowers, Voice-Mail Enslaves," *PC Week*, 10 April 1995, E11.

39 "The Joys of Voice Mail," *Inc.*, November 1995, 102.

40 R. G. Nichols, "Do We Know How to Listen? Practical Helps in a Modern Age," in *Communication Concepts and Processes*, ed. J. DeVitor (Englewood Cliffs, NJ: Prentice Hall, 1971); P. V. Lewis, *Organizational Communication: The Essence of Effective Management* (Columbus, OH: Grid Publishing Company, 1975).

41 E. Atwater, *I Hear You*, rev. ed. (New York: Walker, 1992).

42 R. Adler and N. Towne, *Looking Out/Looking In* (San Francisco: Rinehart, 1975).

43 P. LaBaree, "Feargal Quinn: Ireland's 'Pope of Customer Service' Dominates His Market—and Continues to Beat Bigger and Better-Financed Rivals—with a Leadership Philosophy That Is at Once Folksy and Radical," *Fast Company*, 1 November 2001, 88.

44 P. LaBarre, "Leader—Feargal Quinn," *Fast Company*, 19 December 2007, online at http://www.fastcompany.com [accessed 25 June 2009].

45 Atwater, *I Hear You*.

46 J. Sandberg, "Not Communicating with Your Boss? Count Your Blessings," *Wall Street Journal*, 22 May 2007, B1.

47 H. H. Meyer, "A Solution to the Performance Appraisal Feedback Enigma," *Academy of Management Executive* 5, no. 1 (1991): 68–76.

48 T. D. Schellhardt, "Annual Agony: It's Time to Evaluate Your Work, and All Involved Are Groaning," *Wall Street Journal*, 19 November 1996, A1.

49 L. Anguish, N. Cossack, and A. Maingault, "Payroll Cuts, Personal Hygiene, Extra Leave," *HR Magazine*, 1 June 2003, 41.

50 J. S. Black and M. Mendenhall, "Cross-Cultural Training Effectiveness: A Review and Theoretical Framework for Future Research," *Academy of Management Review* 15 (1990): 113–136.

51 F. Trompenaars, *Riding the Waves of Culture: Understanding Diversity in Global Business* (London: Economist Books, 1994).

52 N. Forster, "Expatriates and the Impact of Cross-Cultural Training," *Human Resource Management* 10 (2000): 63–78.

53 N. J. Adler, *From Boston to Beijing: Managing with a World View* (Cincinnati: South-Western, 2002).

54 Ibid.

55 Ibid.

56 R. Mead, *Cross-Cultural Management* (New York: Wiley, 1990).

57 Ibid.

58 Edward T. Hall, *The Dance of Life* (New York: Doubleday, 1983).

59 E. T. Hall and W. F. Whyte, "Intercultural Communication: A Guide to Men of Action," *Human Organization* 19, no. 1 (1961): 5–12.

60 N. Libman, "French Tip: Just Walk the Walk and Talk the Talk, but Not Too Loud," *Chicago Tribune Online*, 17 March 1996.

61 C. Tkaczyk and M. Boyle, "Follow These Leaders," *Fortune*, 12 December 2005, 125.

62 M. Campanelli and N. Friedman, "Welcome to Voice Mail Hell: The New Technology Has Become a Barrier between Salespeople and Customers," *Sales & Marketing Management* 147 (May 1995): 98–101.

63 D. Harbrecht, "CEO Q&A: Baxter's Harry Kraemer: 'I Don't Golf,'" *BusinessWeek Online*, 28 March 2002, available online at http://www.businessweek.com [accessed 13 April 2009].

64 E. Florian and W. Henderson, "Class of '01: Ellen Florian Spotlights Four Retirees—Their Legacies, Their Plans, and What They've Learned That Can Help You Work Better," *Fortune*, 13 August 2001, 185.

65 E. W. Morrison, "Organizational Silence: A Barrier to Change and Development in a Pluralistic World," *Academy of Management Review* 25 (2000): 706–725.

66 L. Landro, "The Informed Patient: Bringing Surgeons Down to Earth—New Programs Aim to Curb Fear That Prevents Nurses from Flagging Problems," *Wall Street Journal*, November 16, 2005, D1.

67 K. Maher, "Global Companies Face Reality of Instituting Ethics Programs," *Wall Street Journal*, 9 November 2004, B8.

68 Ibid.

69 "An Inside Look at Corporate Hotlines," *Security Director's Report*, February 2007, 8.

70 C. Hymowitz, "Sometimes, Moving Up Makes It Harder to See What Goes on Below," *Wall Street Journal*, 15 October 2007, B1.

71 Ibid.

72 D. Kirkpatrick and D. Roth, "Why There's No Escaping the Blog," *Fortune (Europe)*, 24 January 2005, 64.

73 W. Ross, Jr., "What Every Human Resource Manager Should Know about Web Logs," *SAM Advanced Management Journal*, 1 July 2005, 4.

[74] C. G. Pearce, I. W. Johnson, and R. T. Barker, "Assessment of the Listening Styles Inventory: Progress in Establishing Reliability and Validity," *Journal of Business and Technical Communication* 17, no. 1 (2003): 84–113.

Chapter Fourteen

[1] E. Hromadka, "Green Manufacturing: Innovative Design, Improved Processes and Recycling Efforts in Indiana," *Indiana Business*, May 2008, 10; B. Kenney, "The Zero: How to Green," *Industry Week*, June 2007, 36–43; J. McIntosh, "A Solid Program to Reduce Waste," Subaru Factory Sets New Standards for Going Green and Reduces Costs in the Process," *The Toronto Star*, 27 September, 2008, W21; C. Woodyard, "It's Waste Not, Want Not at Super Green Subaru Plant," *USA Today*, 19 February 2009, 1B.

[2] R. Leifer and P. K. Mills, "An Information Processing Approach for Deciding upon Control Strategies and Reducing Control Loss in Emerging Organizations," *Journal of Management* 22 (1996): 113–137.

[3] L. Abboud and J. Biers, "Energy (A Special Report); Business Goes on an Energy Diet," *Wall Street Journal*, 27 August 2007, R1.

[4] Ibid.

[5] R. Grais-Targow, "Big Salmon Exporter Fights Virus—Chile's Share of Global Output Expected to Fall; Pickup Unlikely Until 2011," *Wall Street Journal*, 7 July 2009, B6.

[6] D. Clark, "Boss Talk: Otellini Hopes Everyone Gets an Intel Chip; CEO Oversees Restructuring as Firm Turns to Powering Gadgets for Web," *Wall Street Journal*, 28 April 2008, B1.

[7] Paul Thurrott. "What You Need to Know About Windows 7 Beta 1," *Windows IT Pro Magazine*, 1 February 2009, 7.

[8] Leifer and Mills, "An Information Processing Approach."

[9] C. Conkey and M. Trottman, "S. News: Big Changes Called for at FAA; Top Inspector Sees Too Much Reliance on Airline Reports," *Wall Street Journal*, 11 April 2008, A4.

[10] Cassell Bryon-Low, "Pound for Pound, a Veggie Peddler Takes on the EU—East London's Ms. Devers Snubs the Metric System; Selling by the Bowl Is Alleged," *Wall Street Journal*, 22 January 2008, A1.

[11] R. Crockett and J. McGregor, "Six Sigma Still Pays Off at Motorola," *BusinessWeek*, 4 December 2006, 50.

[12] "Speed Demons Will Meet Their Match on the Piste." *Times Online*, 5 January 2008, available online at http://travel.timesonline.co.uk [accessed 11 August 2009].

[13] Andrea Coombes, Bully for You: Hair-Raising Bad-Bass Stories, and Tips on How to Cope," *MarketWatch*, 17 July 2006, available online at http://wwws.workplacebullying.org [accessed 30 July 2009].

[14] M. Weber, *The Protestant Ethic and the Spirit of Capitalism* (New York: Scribner's, 1958).

[15] L. Criner, "Politicians Come and Go, Bureaucracies Stay and Grow," *Washington Times*, 11 March 1996, 33.

[16] C. Forelle, "On the Road Again, but Now the Boss Is Sitting beside You," *Wall Street Journal*, 14 May 2004, A1.

[17] M. Boyle, "Expensing It: Guilty As Charged—When Times Are Tough, Employees Become Even More Devoted to Mastering the Art of Self-Perking," *Fortune*, 9 July 2001, 179; R. Grugal, "Be Honest and Dependable: Integrity—The Must-Have," *Investor's Business Daily*, 11 April 2003, A03.

[18] J. Lublin, "CEO Bonuses Rose 46.4% at 100 Big Firms in 2004," *Wall Street Journal*, 25 February 2005, A1.

[19] S. Williford, "Nordstrom Sets the Standard for Customer Service," *Memphis Business Journal*, 1 July 1996, 21.

[20] A. DeFelice, "A Century of Customer Love: Nordstrom Is the Gold Standard for Customer Service Excellence," *CRM Magazine*, 1 June 2005, 42.

[21] R. T. Pascale, "Nordstrom: Respond to Unreasonable Customer Requests!" *Planning Review* 2 (May–June 1994): 17.

[22] Ibid.

[23] Ibid.

[24] J. R. Barker, "Tightening the Iron Cage: Concertive Control in Self-Managing Teams," *Administrative Science Quarterly* 38 (1993): 408–437.

[25] N, Byrnes, "The Art of Motivation," *BusinessWeek*, 1 May 2006, 56–62.

[26] Barker, "Tightening the Iron Cage."

[27] C. Manz and H. Sims, "Leading Workers to Lead Themselves: The External Leadership of Self-Managed Work Teams," *Administrative Science Quarterly* 32 (1987): 106–128.

[28] J. Slocum and H. A. Sims, Typology for Integrating Technology, Organization and Job Design," *Human Relations* 33 (1980): 193–212.

[29] C. C. Manz and H. P. Sims, Jr., "Self-Management as a Substitute for Leadership: A Social Learning Perspective," *Academy of Management Review* 5 (1980): 361–367.

[30] C. Manz and C. Neck, *Mastering Self-Leadership*, 3rd ed. (Upper Saddle River, NJ: Pearson, Prentice Hall, 2004).

[31] R. S. Kaplan and D. P. Norton, "Using the Balanced Scorecard as a Strategic Management System," *Harvard Business Review* (January–February 1996): 75–85; R. S. Kaplan and D. P. Norton, "The Balanced Scorecard: Measures That Drive Performance," *Harvard Business Review* (January–February 1992): 71–79.

[32] J. Meliones, "Saving Money, Saving Lives," *Harvard Business Review* (November–December 2000): 57–65.

[33] John Murphy, "Toyota Boss Vows to Change Priorities," *Wall Street Journal*, 26 June 2009, B2.

[34] M. H. Stocks and A. Harrell, "The Impact of an Increase in Accounting Information Level on the Judgment Quality of Individuals and Groups," *Accounting, Organizations & Society* (October–November 1995): 685–700.

[35] B. Morris, "Roberto Goizueta and Jack Welch: The Wealth Builders," *Fortune*, 11 December 1995, 80–94.

[36] B. Birchard, "Metrics for the Masses," *CFO*, 1 May 1999, available online at http://www.cfo.com [accessed 13 April 2009].

[37] E. Varon, "Implementation Is Not for the Meek," *CIO*, 15 November 2002, available online at http://www.cio.com [accessed 5 September 2008].

[38] "Welcome Complaints," Office of Consumer and Business Affairs, Government of South Australia, available online at http://www.ocba.sa.gov.au/businessadvice/complaints/03_welcome.html [accessed 20 June 2005].

[39] C. Bielaszka-DuVernay, "How to Get the Bad News You Need," *Harvard Management Update*, January 2007, 3–5.

[40] C. B. Furlong, "12 Rules for Customer Retention," *Bank Marketing* 5 (January 1993): 14.

[41] Customer retention graphs, available online at http://www.voxinc.com/ customer-experience-graphs/ impact-customer-retention.htm [accessed 1 August 2009].

[42] M. Raphel, "Vanished Customers Are Valuable Customers," *Art Business News*, June 2002, 46.

[43] F. F. Reichheld, "Lead for Loyalty," *Harvard Business Review* 79 (July–August 2001): 76.

[44] C. A. Reeves and D. A. Bednar, "Defining Quality: Alternatives and Implications," *Academy of Management Review* 19 (1994): 419–445.

[45] K. Nirmalya, "Strategies to Fight Low-Cost Rivals," *Harvard Business Review* 84 (December 2006): 104–112.

[46] D. R. May and B. L. Flannery, "Cutting Waste with Employee Involvement Teams," *Business Horizons*, September–October 1995, 28–38.

[47] M. Conlin and P. Raeburn, "Industrial Evolution: Bill McDonough Has the Wild Idea He Can Eliminate Waste. Surprise! Business Is Listening," *BusinessWeek*, 8 April 2002, 70.

[48] Ibid.

[49] J. Sprovieri, "Environmental Management Affects Manufacturing Bottom Line," *Assembly*, 1 July 2001, 24.

[50] B. Byrne, "EU Says Makers Must Destroy Their Own Brand End-of-Life Cars," *Irish Times*, 23 April 2003, 52.

[51] Jennifer L. Schenker. "Cows to Kilowatts: A Bounty from Waste," 3 December 2008, available online at http://www.businessweek.com [accessed 1 August 2009].

[52] "The End of the Road: Schools and Computer Recycling," Intel, available online at http://www.intel.com/education/recycling_computers/recycling.htm [accessed 5 September 2008].

[53] M. Tuckey, N. Brewer, and P. Williamson, "The Influence of Motives and Goal Orientation on Feedback Seeking," *Journal of Occupational and Organizational Psychology* 75, no. 2 (2002): 195.

Chapter Fifteen

[1] "Starbucks VIA Ready Brew; A Breakthrough in Instant Coffee," *BusinessWeek*, 2 March 2009; J. Adamy, "McDonald's to Expand, Posting Strong Results," *Wall Street Journal*, 7 January 2009, B1; J. Adamy, "Handcuffed by Image, Starbucks Brews up Discounts," *Wall Street Journal*, 9 February 2009, B3; M. Barbaro and A. Martin, "Overhaul, Make a Venti," *New York Times*, 30 January 2008, C1; M. Bartiromo, "Howard Shultz on Reinventing Starbucks," *BusinessWeek*, 21 April 2008, 19; E. Campbell, E. Ailworth, and A. Jennings, "Average Joe Figured Out Problem a While Ago," *Boston Globe*, 3 July 2008, E1; N. Gohring, "Starbucks Wants Your Ideas," *IDG News Service*, 26 March 2008, available online at http://www.CIO.com [accessed 1 July 2009]; J. Jarvins, "The Buzz from Starbucks Customers," *BusinessWeek*, 28 April 2008, 104; J. Nocera, "Curing What Ails Starbucks," *New York Times*, 12 January 2008, C1; T. Wailgum, "How IT Systems Can Help Starbucks Fix Itself," *CIO*, 25 January 2008, available online at http://www.CIO.com [accessed 1 July 2009]; T. Wailgum, "Free Wi-Fi: Should Retailers Offer It to Customers?" *CIO*, 8 August 2008, available online at http://www.CIO.com [accessed 1 July 2009]; T. Wailgum, "Starbucks Spikes in Its 'New' Business Strategy with a Double Shot of IT," *CIO*, 20 March 2009, available online at http://www.CIO.com [accessed 1 July 2009].

[2] R. Lenzner, "The Reluctant Entrepreneur," *Forbes*, 11 September 1995, 162–166.

[3] M. Totty, "Who's Going to Win the Living-Room Wars? The Battle to Control Home Entertainment Is Heating Up," *Wall Street Journal*, 25 April 2005, R1.

[4] P. Grant and A. Schatz, "For Cable Giants, AT&T Deal Is One More Reason to Worry," *Wall Street Journal*, 7 March 2006, A1.

[5] P. Grant, "Cable Firms Woo Business in Fight for Telecom Turf," *Wall Street Journal*, 17 January 2007, A1.

[6] R. D. Buzzell and B. T. Gale, *The PIMS Principles: Linking Strategy to Performance* (New York: Free Press, 1987); M. Lambkin, "Order of Entry and Performance in New Markets," *Strategic Management Journal* 9 (1988): 127–140.

[7] G. L. Urban, T. Carter, S. Gaskin, and Z. Mucha, "Market Share Rewards to Pioneering Brands: An Empirical Analysis and Strategic Implications," *Management Science* 32 (1986): 645–659.

[8] M. Garry and S. Mulholland, "Master of Its Supply Chain: To Keep Its Inventory Costs Low and Its Shelves Fully Stocked, Wal-Mart Has Always Invested Extensively—and First—in Technology for the Supply Chain," *Supermarket News*, 2 December 2002, 55.

[9] N. Buckley and S. Voyle, "Can Wal-Mart Conquer Markets outside the US?" *Financial Times*, 8 January 2003.

[10] M. Santosus, "Technology Recycling: Rising Costs of High-Tech Garbage," *CIO*, 15 April 2003, 36.

[11] R. Smith, "Wireless Firms Eye 'Smart Grids'—Cellphone Carriers Cut Prices in Aggressive Push for Deals with Utilities," *Wall Street Journal*, 16 April 2009, B5.

[12] S. Lubar, *Infoculture: The Smithsonian Book of Information Age Inventions* (Boston: Houghton Mifflin, 1993).

[13] Ibid.

[14] A. Lavallee, "Unilever to Test Mobile Coupons—In Trial at Supermarket, Cellphones Will Be the Medium for Discount Offers," *Wall Street Journal*, 29 May 2009, B8.

[15] B. Worthen, "Bar Codes on Steroids," *CIO*, 15 December 2002, 53.

[16] M. Totty, "Technology (A Special Report)—Business Solutions," *Wall Street Journal*, 2 June 2009, R13.

[17] M. Stone, "Scanning for Business," *PC Magazine*, 10 May 2005, 117.

[18] N. Rubenking, "Hidden Messages," *PC Magazine*, 22 May 2001, 86.

[19] J. Hibbard, "How Yahoo! Gave Itself a Face-Lift," *BusinessWeek*, 9 October 2006, 74.

[20] A. Carter and D. Beucke, "A Good Neighbor Gets Better," *BusinessWeek*, 20 June 2005, 16.

[21] Rubenking, "Hidden Messages."

[22] G. Saitz, "Naked Truth—Data Miners, Who Taught Retailers to Stock Beer Near Diapers, Find Hidden Sales Trends, a Science That's Becoming Big Business," *Newark (NJ) Star-Ledger*, 1 August 2002, 041.

[23] M. Overfelt, "A Better Way to Sell Tickets," *Fortune Small Business*, 1 December 2006, 76.

[24] D. Bartholomew, "Software Net Ensnares Medical Claims Cheats," *Baseline*, September 2007, 43.

[25] "Privacy Policy," http://www.drugstore.com [accessed 28 June 2009].

[26] F. J. Derfler, Jr., "Secure Your Network," *PC Magazine*, 27 June 2000, 183–200.

[27] "Authentication," Webopedia, available online at http://www.webopedia.com/TERM/ a/authentication.html [accessed 12 September 2008].

[28] "Authorization," Webopedia, available online at http://www.webopedia.com/TERM/a/ authorization.html [accessed 12 September 2008].

[29] L. Seltzer, "Password Crackers," *PC Magazine*, 12 February 2002, 68.

[30] "Two-Factor Authentication," Information Security Glossary, available online at http://www.rsa.com [accessed 28 June 2009].

[31] B. Grimes, "Biometric Security," *PC Magazine*, 22 April 2003, 74.

[32] K. Karagiannis, "Security Watch: Don't Make It Easy," *PC Magazine*, 8 April 2003, 72; M. Steinhart, "Password Dos and Don'ts,"

PC Magazine, 12 February 2002, 69; L. Seltzer, "Are Pa55.W0rd5 Dead?" *PC Magazine*, 28 December 2004, 86.

33 M. McQueen, "Laptop Lockdown," *Wall Street Journal*, 28 June 2006, D1.

34 S. Patton, "Simply Secure Communications," *CIO*, 15 January 2003, 100.

35 C. Metz, "Total Security," *PC Magazine*, 1 October 2003, 83.

36 J. DeAvila, "Wi-Fi Users, Beware: Hot Spots Are Weak Spots," *Wall Street Journal,* 16 January 2008, D1.

37 J. van den Hoven, "Executive Support Systems & Decision Making," *Journal of Systems Management* 47, no. 8 (March–April 1996): 48.

38 "Business Objects Customers Take Off with Performance Management; Management Dashboards Help Organizations Gain Insight and Optimize Performance," *Business Wire*, 4 April 2005.

39 "Intranet," Webopedia, available online at http://www.webopedia.com/TERM/i/intranet.html [accessed 26 August 2001].

40 S. Holz, "Bring Your Intranet into the 21st Century," *Communication World,* January–February 2008, 14–18.

41 J. Ericson, "The Hillman Group Leverages Consolidated Reporting, Geographic Analysis to Support its Hardware Manufacturing/distribution Leadership," *Business Intelligence Review*, 1 March 2007, 12.

42 "Web Services," Webopedia, available online at http://www.webopedia.com/TERM/W/Web_ Services.html [accessed 16 April 2009].

43 S. Overby, "This Could Be the Start of Something Small," *CIO*, 15 February 2003, 54.

44 "Extranet," Webopedia, available online at http://www.webopedia.com/TERM/E/extranet.html [accessed 12 September 2008].

45 S. Hamm, D. Welch, W. Zellner, F. Keenan, and F. Engardio, "Down but Hardly Out: Downturn Be Damned, Companies Are Still Anxious to Expand Online," *BusinessWeek*, 26 March 2001, 126.

46 Hamm, Welch, Zellner, Keenan, and Engardio, "Down but Hardly Out."

47 K. C. Laudon and J. P. Laudon, *Management Information Systems: Organization and Technology* (Upper Saddle River, NJ: Prentice Hall, 1996).

48 R. Hernandez, "American Express Authorizer's Assistant," *Business Rules Journal*, August 2001, available online at http://www.bizrules.com/page/art_amexaa.htm [accessed 12 September 2008].

49 R. Heinssen, Jr., C. Glass, and L. Knight, "Assessing Computer Anxiety: Development and Validation of the Computer Anxiety Rating Scale," *Computers in Human Behavior* (1987): 49–59.

Chapter Sixteen

1 "About JCPenney," JCPenney, available online at http://www.jcpenney.net [accessed 15 August 2009]; I. Brat, E. Byron, and A. Zimmerman, "Retailers Cut Back on Variety, Once the Spice of Marketing," *The Wall Street Journal*, 26 June 2009, A1; R. Dodes, "Showdown on 34th Street," *The Wall Street Journal*, 1 August 2009, A1; R. Dodes, "JCPenney Nearly Breaks Even," *The Wall Street Journal*, 15 August 2009, B5; Reuters, "Across Low and High Ends, Retails Sales Fell in May," *New York Times*, 4 June 2009, B5; S. Rosenbloom, "Store from Middle America Opens an Outlet in Midtown," *The New York Times*, 25 July 2009, B1; J. Wohl, "U.S. Retailers Miss Lowered Forecasts: Upscale Department Stores including Neiman Marcus Post the Steepest Declines," *Toronto Star*, 5 June 2009, B04.

2 "Ryanair Asks Passengers If They Will Stand on Short Flights," http://www.breakingtravelnews.com/news/articles, 9 July 2009 [accessed 2 August 2009]; "Ryanair Celebrates 20 Years of Operations," Ryanair, 31 May 2005, available online at http://www.ryanair.com [accessed 12 September 2008].

3 B. Baker, "America's Best Drive-Thru 2008 Is?.?.?. Chick-fil-A! (Again)," *QRS Magazine*, http://www.qsrmagazine.com/reports [accessed 2 August 2009].

4 "Historical Income Tables—Families: Table F-23—Families by Total Money Income, Race, and Hispanic Origin of Householder: 1967 to 2007," U.S. Census Bureau, available online at http:// www.census.gov/hhes/www/income/histinc/f23.html [accessed 1 September 2009].

5 M. Baily and M. Slaughter, "What's Behind the Recent Productivity Slowdown," *The Wall Street Journal*, 13 December 2008, A15.

6 "Employment Projections, Table 1: Civilian labor force by sex, age, race, and Hispanic origin, 1986, 1996, 2006, and projected 2016," *U.S. Bureau of Labor Statistics*, 4 December 2007, available online at http://www.bls.gov [accessed 9 September 2009].

7 "Auto Affordability Worsens Slightly Comerica Bank Chief Economist Reports," PRNewsire-FirsCall, 10 November 2008, available online at http://comerica.mediaroom.com [accessed 9 September 2009].

8 Ibid.

9 "Cars' Affordability: Cheapest Since 1980."

10 R. Harbour and M. Hill, "Productivity Gap Narrows across North America and Europe," *The Harbour Report*, available online at http://www.theharbourreport.com/index2.jsp (also see http://www.oliverwyman.com/ow/automotive) [accessed 2 August 2009].

11 "Profiled International' America's Most Productive Companies," *Drug Week*, 15 May 2009, 265; "America's Most Productive Companies," available online at http://www.americasmostproductive.com [accessed 2 August 2009].

12 "Study: Automakers Initial Quality Improves Considerably," *Quality Digest*, available online at http://www.qualitydigest.com [accessed 2 August 2009]; "2008 Initial Quality Study Results," available online at http://www.jdpower.com/autos/articles/2008-Initial- Quality-Study-Results [accessed 2 August 2009].

13 "Embattled U.S. Automakers Make Substantial Gains in Initial Quality, Outpacing Industry-Wide Improvement," J.D. Power and Associates, 22 June 2009, available online at http://www.jdpower.com [accessed 10 September 2009].

14 M. Rechtin "Porsche, Hyundai Score Big Gains in J.D. Power Quality Survey," *Auto Week,* 7 June 2006, available online at http://www.autoweek.com/apps/pbcs.dll/article?AID=/20060608/FREE/60607007/1041&te [accessed 15 September 2008].

15 "Basic Concepts," American Society for Quality, available online at http://www.asq.org/learn-about-quality/basic-concepts.html [accessed 2 August 2009].

16 R. E. Markland, S. K. Vickery, and R. A. Davis, "Managing Quality" (Chapter 7) in *Operations Management: Concepts in Manufacturing and Services* (Cincinnati, OH: South-Western College Publishing, 1998).

17 REVA Electric Car Company, available online at http://www.revaindia.com [accessed 2 August 2009].

18 "New Industrial LCD Panels with 100,000 Hour MTBF LED Backlight Systems from Toshiba America Electronic Components," *Your Industry News*, 26 August 2009, available online at http://www.yourindustrynews.com [accessed 12 September 2009].

19 L. L. Berry and A. Parasuraman, *Marketing Services* (New York: Free Press, 1991).

20 P. Judge, "When a Customer Believes in You . . . They'll Stick with You Almost No Matter What," *Fast Company* 47 (June 2001): 138.

21 Ibid.

22 Ibid.

23 "*Fortune* Names EMC the Only Technology Company among World's 10 Most Admired Companies for Product and Service Quality," *BusinessWeek*, 16 March 2009, available online at http://www.businessweek.com [accessed 2 August 2009]; also available at http://www.emc.com/about/news/press/2009 [accessed 2 August 2009]

24 "FAQs—General Information on ISO," International Organization for Standardization, available online at http://www.iso.org/iso/support/ faqs/faqs_general_ information_on_iso.htm [accessed 12 September 2009].

25 "ISO 9000 Essentials," and "ISO 14000 Essentials," International Organization for Standardization, available online at http://www.iso.org/iso/iso_catalogue/management_ standards/iso_9000_iso_14000.htm [accessed 12 September 2009].

26 J. Briscoe, S. Fawcett, and R. Todd, "The Implementation and Impact of ISO 9000 among Small Manufacturing Enterprises," *Journal of Small Business Management* 43 (1 July 2005): 309.

27 R. Henkoff, "The Hot New Seal of Quality (ISO 9000 Standard of Quality Management)," *Fortune*, 28 June 1993, 116.

28 "Frequently Asked Questions about the Malcolm Baldrige National Quality Award," National Institute of Standards & Technology, available online at http://www.nist.gov/ public_affairs/factsheet/baldfaqs.htm [accessed 12 September 2009].

29 "Baldrige Award Application Forms," National Institute of Standards & Technology, available online at http://www.quality.nist.gov/PDF_files/2009_Award_ Application_Forms.pdf [accessed 12 September 2009].

30 "Frequently Asked Questions and Answers about the Malcolm Baldrige National Quality Award."

31 "Criteria for Performance Excellence," Baldrige National Quality Program 2008, available online at http://www.quality.nist.gov/PDF_files/2008_ Business_Criteria.pdf [accessed 15 September 2008].

32 Ibid.

33 "Baldrige Index Beaten by S&P 500 For Second Year," NIST Tech Beat, available online at http://www.quality.nist.gov/Stock_Studies.htm [accessed 12 September 2009].

34 J. W. Dean, Jr., and J. Evans, *Total Quality: Management, Organization, and Strategy* (St. Paul, MN: West, 1994).

35 J. W. Dean, Jr., and D. E. Bowen, "Management Theory and Total Quality: Improving Research and Practice through Theory Development," *Academy of Management Review* 19 (1994): 392–418.

36 R. Allen and R. Kilmann, "Aligning Reward Practices in Support of Total Quality Management," *Business Horizons*, 1 May 2001, 77. F. Reichheld and P. Rogers, "Motivating Through Metrics," *Harvard Business Review* (September 2005): 20–24.

37 R. Carter, "Best Practices: Freudenberg-NOK/Cleveland, GA: Continuous Kaizens," *Industrial Maintenance & Plant Operations*, 1 June 2004, 10.

38 R. Levering, M. Moskowitz, L. Munoz, and P. Hjelt, "The 100 Best Companies to Work for," *Fortune*, 4 February 2002, 72.

39 "Table 647. Gross Domestic Product in Current and Real (2000) Dollars by Type of Product and Sector; 1990 to 2007," *The 2009 Statistical Abstract*, U.S. Census Bureau, available online at http://www.census.gov [accessed 12 September 2009].

40 R. Hallowell, L. A. Schlesinger, and J. Zornitsky, "Internal Service Quality, Customer and Job Satisfaction: Linkages and Implications for Management," *Human Resource Planning* 19 (1996): 20–31; J. L. Heskett, T. O. Jones, G. W. Loveman, W. E. Sasser, Jr., and L. A. Schlesinger, "Putting the Service-Profit Chain to Work," *Harvard Business Review* (March–April 1994): 164–174.

41 J. Paravantis, N. Bouranta, and L. Chitiris, "The Relationship between Internal and External Service Quality," *International Journal of Contemporary Hospital Management* 21 (2009): 275–293.

42 G. Brewer, "The Ultimate Guide to Winning Customers: The Customer Stops Here," *Sales & Marketing Management* 150 (March 1998): 30; F. F. Reichheld, *The Loyalty Effect: The Hidden Force behind Growth, Profits, and Lasting Value* (Cambridge, MA: Harvard Business School Press, 2001).

43 J. Heskett, T. Jones, G. Loveman, E. Sasser, and L. Schlesinger, "Putting the Service-Profit Chain to Work," *Harvard Business Review* 86 (July–August 2008): 118–129.

44 L. L. Berry and A. Parasuraman, "Listening to the Customer—The Concept of a Service-Quality Information System," *Sloan Management Review* 38, no. 3 (Spring 1997): 65; C. W. L. Hart, J. L. Heskett, and W. E. Sasser, Jr., "The Profitable Art of Service Recovery," *Harvard Business Review* (July–August 1990): 148–156.

45 G. Stoller, "Companies Give Front-Line Employees More Power," *USA Today*, 27 June 2005, A1.

46 S. Hale, "The Customer Is Always Right— Usually—Some Are Just Annoying, but Others Deserve the Boot," *Orlando Sentinel*, 15 April 2002, 54.

47 D. E. Bowen and E. E. Lawler III, "The Empowerment of Service Workers: What, Why, How, and When," *Sloan Management Review* 33 (Spring 1992): 31–39; D. E. Bowen and E. E. Lawler III, "Empowering Service Employees," *Sloan Management Review* 36 (Summer 1995): 73–84.

48 Bowen and Lawler, "The Empowerment of Service Workers: What, Why, How, and When."

49 G. Stoller, "Companies Give Front-Line Employees More Power," *USA Today*, 27 June 2005, A1.

50 S. Silke Carty, "Chrysler Wrestles with High Levels of Inventory as Unsold Vehicles Sit on Lots," *USA Today*, 2 November 2006, available online at http://www.usatoday.com/money/autos/2006-11-02-chrysler-high-inventory_x.htm?loc=interstitialskip [accessed 15 September 2008]; J. D. Stoll, "Chrysler Maintains Plan to Cut Production as Inventory Rises," *The Wall Street Journal*, 24 August 2006, http://www.wsj.com [content no longer available online].

51 Ibid.

52 P. Dumpala, "iPhone 3GS Out-of-Stock in 44 States," *The Business Insider (Silicon Valley Insider)*, 29 June 2009, available online at http://www.businessinsider.com [accessed 13 September 2009].

53 D. Drickhamer, "Reality Check," *Industry Week*, November 2001, 29.

54 D. Drickhamer, "Zeroing In on World-Class," *Industry Week*, November 2001, 36.

55 J. Zeiler, "The Need for Speed," *Operations & Fulfillment*, 1 April 2004, 38.

56 J. R. Henry, "Minimized Setup Will Make Your Packaging Line S.M.I.L.E.," *Packaging Technology & Engineering*, 1 February 1998, 24.

57 J. Donoghue, "The Future Is Now," *Air Transport World*, 1 April 2001, 78; D. Evans, "Aftermarket Outlook," *Aviation Maintenance Magazine*, 1 May 2006, available online at http://www.aviationtoday.com [accessed 13 September 2004].

[58] K. Clark, "An Eagle Eye for Inventory," *Chain Store Age*, May 2005, Supplement, 8A.

[59] N. Shirouzu, "Why Toyota Wins Such High Marks on Quality Surveys," *The Wall Street Journal*, 15 March 2001, A1.

[60] Ibid.

[61] G. Gruman, "Supply on Demand; Manufacturers Need to Know What's Selling before They Can Produce and Deliver Their Wares in the Right Quantities," *Info World*, 18 April 2005, available online at http://www.infoworld.com [accessed 15 April 2009].

[62] J. A. Perriat, S. LeMay, S. Chakrabarty, "The Selling Orientation—Customer Orientation (SOCO) Scale: Cross-Validation of the Revised Version," *Journal of Personal Selling & Sales Management* 24, no. 1 (2004): 49–54.

Glossary

360-degree feedback
a performance appraisal process in which feedback is obtained from the boss, subordinates, peers and coworkers, and the employees themselves

Absolute comparisons
a process in which each decision criterion is compared to a standard or ranked on its own merits

Accommodative strategy
a social responsiveness strategy in which a company accepts responsibility for a problem and does all that society expects to solve that problem

Achievement-oriented leadership
a leadership style in which the leader sets challenging goals, has high expectations of employees, and displays confidence that employees will assume responsibility and put forth extraordinary effort

Acquaintance time
a cultural norm for how much time you must spend getting to know someone before the person is prepared to do business with you

Acquisition
the purchase of a company by another company

Action plan
the specific steps, people, and resources needed to accomplish a goal

Active listening
assuming half the responsibility for successful communication by actively giving the speaker nonjudgmental feedback that shows you've accurately heard what he or she said

Address terms
cultural norms that establish whether you should address business people by their first names, family names, or titles

Adverse impact
unintentional discrimination that occurs when members of a particular race, sex, or ethnic group are unintentionally harmed or disadvantaged because they are hired, promoted, or trained (or any other employment decision) at substantially lower rates than others

Advocacy groups
concerned citizens who band together to try to influence the business practices of specific industries, businesses, and professions

Affective cultures
cultures in which people display emotions and feelings when communicating

Analyzers
companies using an adaptive strategy that seeks to minimize risk and maximize profits by following or imitating the proven successes of prospectors

Appointment time
a cultural norm for how punctual you must be when showing up for scheduled appointments or meetings

Asia-Pacific Economic Cooperation (APEC)
a regional trade agreement between Australia, Canada, Chile, the People's Republic of China, Hong Kong, Japan, Mexico, New Zealand, Papua New Guinea, Peru, Russia, South Korea, Taiwan, the United States, and all the members of ASEAN, except Cambodia, Laos, and Myanmar

Assemble-to-order operation
a manufacturing operation that divides manufacturing processes into separate parts or modules that are combined to create semicustomized products

Association of affinity patterns
when two or more database elements tend to occur together in a significant way

Association of Southeast Asian Nations (ASEAN)
a regional trade agreement between Brunei Darussalam, Cambodia, Indonesia, Laos, Malaysia, Myanmar, the Philippines, Singapore, Thailand, and Vietnam

Attack
a competitive move designed to reduce a rival's market share or profits

Attribution theory
the theory that we all have a basic need to understand and explain the causes of other people's behavior

A-type conflict (affective conflict)
disagreement that focuses on individuals or personal issues

Authentication
making sure potential users are who they claim to be

Authority
the right to give commands, take action, and make decisions to achieve organizational objectives

Authorization
granting authenticated users approved access to data, software, and systems

Autonomy
the degree to which a job gives workers the discretion, freedom, and independence to decide how and when to accomplish the job

Average aggregate inventory
average overall inventory during a particular time period

Background checks
procedures used to verify the truthfulness and accuracy of information that applicants provide about themselves and to uncover negative, job-related background information not provided by applicants

Balanced scorecard
measurement of organizational performance in four equally important areas: finances, customers, internal operations, and innovation and learning

Bar code
a visual pattern that represents numerical data by varying the thickness and pattern of vertical bars

Bargaining power of buyers
a measure of the influence that customers have on a firm's prices

Bargaining power of suppliers
a measure of the influence that suppliers of parts, materials, and services to firms in an industry have on the prices of these inputs

BCG matrix
a portfolio strategy, developed by the Boston Consulting Group, that categorizes a corporation's businesses by growth rate and relative market share, and helps managers decide how to invest corporate funds

Behavior control
the regulation of the behaviors and actions that workers perform on the job

Behavioral addition
the process of having managers and employees perform new behaviors that are central to and symbolic of the new organizational culture that a company wants to create

Behavioral formality
a workplace atmosphere characterized by routine and regimen, specific rules about how to behave, and impersonal detachment

Behavioral informality
a workplace atmosphere characterized by spontaneity, casualness, and interpersonal familiarity

Behavioral substitution
the process of having managers and employees perform new behaviors central to the "new" organizational culture in place of behaviors that were central to the "old" organizational culture

Behavior observation scales (BOSs)
rating scales that indicate the frequency with which workers perform specific behaviors that are representative of the job dimensions critical to successful job performance

Benchmarking
the process of identifying outstanding practices, processes, and standards in other companies and adapting them to your company

Biographical data (biodata)
extensive surveys that ask applicants questions about their personal backgrounds and life experiences

Biometrics
identifying users by unique, measurable body features, such as fingerprint recognition or iris scanning

Blog
a personal website that provides personal opinions or recommendations, news summaries, and reader comments

Bona fide occupational qualification (BFOQ)
an exception in employment law that permits sex, age, religion, and the like to be used when making employment decisions, but only if they are "reasonably necessary to the normal operation of that particular business." BFOQs are strictly monitored by the Equal Employment Opportunity Commission

Bounded rationality
a decision-making process restricted in the real world by limited resources, incomplete and imperfect information, and managers' limited decision-making capabilities

Brainstorming
a decision-making method in which group members build on each others' ideas to generate as many alternative solutions as possible

Budgeting
quantitative planning through which managers decide how to allocate available money to best accomplish company goals

Bureaucratic control
the use of hierarchical authority to influence employee behavior by rewarding or punishing employees for compliance or noncompliance with organizational policies, rules, and procedures

Bureaucratic immunity
the ability to make changes without first getting approval from managers or other parts of an organizaion

Business confidence indices
indices that show managers' level of confidence about future business growth

Buyer dependence
the degree to which a supplier relies on a buyer because of the importance of that buyer to the supplier and the difficulty of finding other buyers for its products

Cash cow
a company with a large share of a slow-growing market

Cafeteria benefit plans (flexible benefit plans)
plans that allow employees to choose which benefits they receive, up to a certain dollar value

Central America Free Trade Agreement (CAFTA-DR)
a regional trade agreement between Costa Rica, the Dominican Republic, El Salvador, Guatemala, Honduras, Nicaragua, and the United States

Centralization of authority
the location of most authority at the upper levels of the organization

Chain of command
the vertical line of authority that clarifies who reports to whom throughout the organization

Change agent
the person formally in charge of guiding a change effort

Change forces
forces that produce differences in the form, quality, or condition of an organization over time

Change intervention
the process used to get workers and managers to change their behavior and work practices

Character of the rivalry
a measure of the intensity of competitive behavior between companies in an industry

Charismatic leadership
the behavioral tendencies and personal characteristics of leaders that create an exceptionally strong relationship between them and their followers

Closure
the tendency to fill in gaps of missing information by assuming that what we don't know is consistent with what we already know

Coaching
communicating with someone for the direct purpose of improving the person's on-the-job performance or behavior

Coercion
the use of formal power and authority to force others to change

Cognitive ability tests
tests that measure the extent to which applicants have abilities in perceptual speed, verbal comprehension, numerical aptitude, general reasoning, and spatial aptitude

Cohesiveness
the extent to which team members are attracted to a team and motivated to remain in it

Commission
a compensation system in which employees earn a percentage of each sale they make

Communication
the process of transmitting information from one person or place to another

Communication medium
the method used to deliver an oral or written message

Company hotlines
phone numbers that anyone in the company can call anonymously to leave information for upper management

Compensation
the financial and nonfinancial rewards that organizations give employees in exchange for their work

Competitive advantage
providing greater value for customers than competitors can

Competitive analysis
a process for monitoring the competition that involves identifying competition, anticipating their moves, and determining their strengths and weaknesses

Competitive inertia
a reluctance to change strategies or competitive practices that have been successful in the past

Competitors
companies in the same industry that sell similar products or services to customers

Complex environment
an environment with many environmental factors

Complex matrix
a form of matrix departmentalization in which managers in different parts of the matrix report to matrix managers, who help them sort out conflicts and problems

Component parts inventories
the basic parts used in manufacturing that are fabricated from raw materials

Compression approach to innovation
an approach to innovation that assumes that incremental innovation can be planned using a series of steps and that compressing those steps can speed up innovation

Concentration of effect
the total harm or benefit that an act produces on the average person

Conceptual skills
the ability to see the organization as a whole, understand how the different parts affect each other, and recognize how the company fits into or is affected by its external environment

Concertive control
the regulation of workers' behavior and decisions through work group values and beliefs

Conduit metaphor
the mistaken assumption that senders can pipe their intended messages directly into the heads of receivers with perfect clarity and without noise or perceptual filters interfering with the receivers' understanding of the message

Consideration
the extent to which a leader is friendly, approachable, and supportive and shows concern for employees

Consistent organizational culture
a company culture in which the company actively defines and teaches organizational values, beliefs, and attitudes

Constructive feedback
feedback intended to be helpful, corrective, and/or encouraging

Contingency theory
a leadership theory that states that in order to maximize work group performance, leaders must be matched to the situation that best fits their leadership style

Continuous improvement
an organization's ongoing commitment to constantly assess and improve the processes and procedures used to create products and services

Continuous reinforcement schedule
a schedule that requires a consequence to be administered following every instance of a behavior

Control
a regulatory process of establishing standards to achieve organizational goals, comparing actual performance against the standards, and taking corrective action, when necessary

Control loss
the situation in which behavior and work procedures do not conform to standards

Controlling
monitoring progress toward goal achievement and taking corrective action when needed

Conventional level of moral development
the second level of moral development, in which people make decisions that conform to societal expectations

Cooperative contract
an agreement in which a foreign business owner pays a company a fee for the right to conduct that business in his or her country

Core capabilities
the internal decision-making routines, problem-solving processes, and organizational cultures that determine how efficiently inputs can be turned into outputs

Core firms
the central companies in a strategic group

Corporate-level strategy
the overall organizational strategy that addresses the question "What business or businesses are we in or should we be in?"

Corporate portal
a hybrid of executive information systems and intranets that allows managers and employees to use a web browser to gain access to customized company information and to complete specialized transactions

Cost leadership
the positioning strategy of producing a product or service of acceptable quality at consistently lower production costs than competitors can, so that the firm can offer the product or service at the lowest price in the industry

Counseling
communicating with someone about non-job-related issues that may be affecting or interfering with the person's performance

Creative work environments
workplace cultures in which workers perceive that new ideas are welcomed, valued, and encouraged

Creativity
the production of novel and useful ideas

Cross-cultural communication
transmitting information from a person in one country or culture to a person from another country or culture

Cross-functional team
a team composed of employees from different functional areas of the organization

Cross-training
training team members to do all or most of the jobs performed by the other team members

C-type conflict (cognitive conflict)
disagreement that focuses on problem- and issue-related differences of opinion

Customer defections
a performance assessment in which companies identify which customers are leaving and measure the rate at which they are leaving

Customer departmentalization
organizing work and workers into separate units responsible for particular kind of customers

Customer focus
an organizational goal to concentrate on meeting customers' needs at all levels of the organization

Customer satisfaction
an organizational goal to provide products or services that meet or exceed customers' expectations

Customs classification
a classification assigned to imported products by government officials that affects the size of the tariff and imposition of import quotas

Cybernetic feasibility
the extent to which it is possible to implement each step in the control process

Data clusters
when three or more database elements occur together (i.e., cluster) in a significant way

Data encryption
the transformation of data into complex, scrambled digital codes that can be unencrypted only by authorized users who possess unique decryption keys

Data mining
the process of discovering unknown patterns and relationships in large amounts of data

Data warehouse
stores huge amounts of data that have been prepared for data mining analysis by being cleaned of errors and redundancy

Decentralization
the location of a significant amount of authority in the lower levels of the organization

Decision criteria
the standards used to guide judgments and decisions

Decision making
the process of choosing a solution from available alternatives

Decision support system (DSS)
an information system that helps managers understand specific kinds of problems and potential solutions and analyze the impact of different decision options using "what if" scenarios

Decoding
the process by which the receiver translates the written, verbal, or symbolic form of a message into an understood message

Defenders
companies using an adaptive strategy aimed at defending strategic positions by seeking moderate, steady growth and by offering a limited range of high-quality products and services to a well-defined set of customer

Defensive bias
the tendency for people to perceive themselves as personally and situationally similar to someone who is having difficulty or trouble

Defensive strategy
a social responsiveness strategy in which a company admits responsibility for a problem but does the least required to meet societal expectations

De-forming
a reversal of the forming stage, in which team members position themselves to control pieces of the team, avoid each other, and isolate themselves from team leaders

Delegation of authority
the assignment of direct authority and responsibility to a subordinate to complete tasks for which the manager is normally responsible

Delphi technique
a decision-making method in which members of a panel of experts respond to questions and to each other until reaching agreement on an issue

De-norming
a reversal of the norming stage, in which team performance begins to decline as the size, scope, goal, or members of the team change

Departmentalization
subdividing work and workers into separate organizational units responsible for completing particular tasks

Dependent demand system
an inventory system in which the level of inventory depends on the number of finished units to be produced

Design competition
competition between old and new technologies to establish a new technological standard or dominant design

Design iteration
a cycle of repetition in which a company tests a prototype of a new product or service, improves on that design, and then builds and tests the improved prototype

Destructive feedback
feedback that disapproves without any intention of being helpful and almost always causes a negative or defensive reaction in the recipient

Devil's advocacy
a decision-making method in which an individual or a subgroup is assigned the role of a critic

Dialectical inquiry
a decision-making method in which decision makers state the assumptions of a proposed solution (a thesis) and generate a solution that is the opposite (antithesis) of that solution

Differentiation
the positioning strategy of providing a product or service that is sufficiently different from competitors' offerings that customers are willing to pay a premium price for it

Direct competition
the rivalry between two companies that offer similar products and services, acknowledge each other as rivals, and act and react to each other's strategic actions

Direct foreign investment
a method of investment in which a company builds a new business or buys an existing business in a foreign country

Directive leadership
a leadership style in which the leader lets employees know precisely what is expected of them, gives them specific guidelines for performing tasks, schedules work, sets standards of performance, and makes sure that people follow standard rules and regulations

Discontinuous change
the phase of a technology cycle characterized by technological substitution and design competition

Discretionary responsibilities
the social roles that a company fulfills beyond its economic, legal, and ethical responsibilities

Discussion time
a cultural norm for how much time should be spent in discussion with others

Disparate treatment
intentional discrimination that occurs when people are purposely not given the same hiring, promotion, or membership opportunities because of their race, color, sex, age, ethnic group, national origin, or religious beliefs

Disseminator role
the informational role managers play when they share information with others in their departments or companies

Distal goals
long-term or primary goals

Distinctive competence
what a company can make, do, or perform better than its competitors

Distributive justice
the perceived degree to which outcomes and rewards are fairly distributed or allocated

Disturbance handler role
the decisional role managers play when they respond to severe problems that demand immediate action

Diversification
a strategy for reducing risk by buying a variety of items (stocks or, in the case of a corporation, types of businesses) so that the failure of one stock or one business does not doom the entire portfolio

Dog
a company with a small share of a slow-growing market

Dominant design
a new technological design or process that becomes the accepted market standard

Downsizing
the planned elimination of jobs in a company

Downward communication
communication that flows from higher to lower levels in an organization

Dynamic environment
an environment in which the rate of change is fast

Dysfunctional turnover
loss of high-performing employees who voluntarily choose to leave a company

E

Economic order quantity (EOQ)
a system of formulas that minimizes ordering and holding costs and helps determine how much and how often inventory should be ordered

Economic responsibility
a company's social responsibility to make a profit by producing a valued product or service

Economic value added (EVA)
the amount by which company profits (revenues, minus expenses, minus taxes) exceed the cost of capital in a given year

Effectiveness
accomplishing tasks that help fulfill organizational objectives

Efficiency
getting work done with a minimum of effort, expense, or waste

Electronic brainstorming
a decision-making method in which group members use computers to build on each others' ideas and generate as many alternative solutions as possible

Electronic data interchange (EDI)
when two companies convert their purchase and ordering information to a standardized format to enable the direct electronic transmission of that information from one company's computer system to the other company's computer system

Electronic scanner
an electronic device that converts printed text and pictures into digital images

Empathetic listening
understanding the speaker's perspective and personal frame of reference and giving feedback that conveys that understanding to the speaker

Employee involvement team
a team that provides advice or makes suggestions to management concerning specific ideas

Employee separation
the voluntary or involuntary loss of an employee

Employee stock ownership plan (ESOP)
a compensation system in which a company pays a percentage of its profits to employees in addition to their regular compensation

Employee turnover
loss of employees who voluntarily choose to leave the company

Employment benefits
a method of rewarding employees that includes virtually any kind of compensation other than wages or salaries

Employment references
sources such as previous employers or coworkers who can provide job-related information about job candidates

Empowering workers
permanently passing decision-making authority and responsibility from managers to workers by giving them the information and resources they need to make and carry out good decisions

Empowerment
feelings of intrinsic motivation, in which workers perceive their work to have impact and meaning and perceive themselves to be competent and capable of self-determination

Encoding
putting a message into a written, verbal, or symbolic form that can be recognized and understood by the receiver

Entrepreneur role
the decisional role managers play when they adapt themselves, their subordinates, and their units to change

Environmental change
the rate at which a company's general and specific environments change

Environmental complexity
the number and the intensity of external factors in the environment that affect organizations

Environmental scanning
searching the environment for important events or issues that might affect an organization

Equity theory
a theory that states that people will be motivated when they perceive that they are being treated fairly

Ethical behavior
behavior that conforms to a society's accepted principles of right and wrong

Ethical charismatics
charismatic leaders who provide developmental opportunities for followers, are open to positive and negative feedback, recognize others' contributions, share information, and have moral

standards that emphasize the larger interests of the group, organization, or society

Ethical intensity
the degree of concern people have about an ethical issue

Ethical responsibility
a company's social responsibility not to violate accepted principles of right and wrong when conducting its business

Ethics
the set of moral principles or values that defines right and wrong for a person or group

Evaluation apprehension
fear of what others will think of your ideas

Executive information system (EIS)
a data processing system that uses internal and external data sources to provide the information needed to monitor and analyze organizational performance

Expatriate
someone who lives and works outside his or her native country

Expectancy
the perceived relationship between effort and performance

Expectancy theory
the theory that people will be motivated to the extent to which they believe that their efforts will lead to good performance, that good performance will be rewarded, and that they will be offered attractive rewards

Experiential approach to innovation
an approach to innovation that assumes a highly uncertain environment and uses intuition, flexible options, and hands-on experience to reduce uncertainty and accelerate learning and understanding

Expert system
an information system that contains the specialized knowledge and decision rules used by experts and experienced decision makers so that nonexperts can draw on this knowledge base to make decisions

Exporting
selling domestically produced products to customers in foreign countries

External environments
all events outside a company that have the potential to influence or affect it

External recruiting
the process of developing a pool of qualified job applicants from outside the company

Extinction
reinforcement in which a positive consequence is no longer allowed to follow a previously reinforced behavior, thus weakening the behavior

Extranets
networks that allow companies to exchange information and conduct transactions with outsiders by providing them direct, web-based access to authorized parts of a company's intranet or information system

Extrinsic reward
a reward that is tangible, visible to others, and given to employees contingent on the performance of specific tasks or behaviors

Feedback
the amount of information the job provides to workers about their work performance

Feedback control
a mechanism for gathering information about performance deficiencies after they occur

Feedback to sender
in the communication process, a return message to the sender that indicates the receiver's understanding of the message

Feedforward control
a mechanism for monitoring performance inputs rather than outputs to prevent or minimize performance deficiencies before they occur

Figurehead role
the interpersonal role managers play when they perform ceremonial duties

Finished goods inventories
the final outputs of manufacturing operations

Firewall
a protective hardware or software device that sits between the computers in an internal organizational network and outside networks, such as the Internet

Firm-level strategy
a corporate strategy that addresses the question "How should we compete against a particular firm?"

First-line managers
train and supervise the performance of nonmanagerial employees who are directly responsible for producing the company's products or services

First-mover advantage
the strategic advantage that companies earn by being the first to use new information technology to substantially lower costs or to make a product or service different from that of competitors

Fixed interval reinforcement schedule
an intermittent schedule in which consequences follow a behavior only after a fixed time has elapsed

Fixed ratio reinforcement schedule
an intermittent schedule in which consequences are delivered following a specific number of behaviors

Flow
a psychological state of effortlessness, in which you become completely absorbed in what you're doing and time seems to pass quickly

Focus strategy
the positioning strategy of using cost leadership or differentiation to produce a specialized product or service for a limited, specially targeted group of customers in a particular geographic region or market segment

Formal communication channel
the system of official channels that carry organizationally approved messages and information

Forming
the first stage of team development, in which team members meet each other, form initial impressions, and begin to establish team norms

Four-fifths (or 80 percent) rule
a rule of thumb used by the courts and the EEOC to determine whether there is evidence of adverse impact. A violation of this rule occurs when the selection rate for a protected group is less than 80 percent or four-fifths of the selection rate for a nonprotected group

Franchise
a collection of networked firms in which the manufacturer or marketer of a product or service, the franchisor, licenses the entire business to another person or organization, the franchisee

Functional departmentalization
organizing work and workers into separate units responsible for particular business functions or areas of expertise

Functional turnover
loss of poor-performing employees who voluntarily choose to leave a company

Fundamental attribution error
the tendency to ignore external causes of behavior and to attribute other people's actions to internal causes

Gainsharing
a compensation system in which companies share the financial value of performance gains, such as productivity, cost savings, or quality, with their workers

General Agreement on Tariffs and Trade (GATT)
a worldwide trade agreement that reduced and eliminated tariffs, limited government subsidies, and established protections for intellectual property

General Electric workout
a three-day meeting in which managers and employees from different levels and parts of an organization quickly generate and act on solutions to specific business problems

General environment
the economic, technological, sociocultural, and political trends that indirectly affect all organizations

Generational change
change based on incremental improvements to a dominant technological design such that the improved technology is fully backward compatible with the older technology

Geographic departmentalization
organizing work and workers into separate units responsible for doing business in particular geographic areas

Global business
the buying and selling of goods and services by people from different countries

Global consistency
when a multinational company has offices, manufacturing plants, and distribution facilities in different countries and runs them using the same rules, guidelines, policies, and procedures

Global new ventures
new companies that are founded with an active global strategy and have sales, employees, and financing in different countries

Goal
a target, objective, or result that someone tries to accomplish

Goal acceptance
the extent to which people consciously understand and agree to goals

Goal commitment
the determination to achieve a goal

Goal difficulty
the extent to which a goal is hard or challenging to accomplish

Goal specificity
the extent to which goals are detailed, exact, and unambiguous

Goal-setting theory
the theory that people will be motivated to the extent to which they accept specific, challenging goals and receive feedback that indicates their progress toward goal achievement

Government import standard
a standard ostensibly established to protect the health and safety of citizens but, in reality, often used to restrict imports

Grand strategy
a broad corporate-level strategic plan used to achieve strategic goals and guide the strategic alternatives that managers of individual businesses or subunits may use

Groupthink
a barrier to good decision making caused by pressure within the group for members to agree with each other

Growth strategy
a strategy that focuses on increasing profits, revenues, market share, or the number of places in which the company does business

Hearing
the act or process of perceiving sounds

Holding cost
the cost of keeping inventory until it is used or sold, including storage, insurance, taxes, obsolescence, and opportunity costs

Horizontal communication
communication that flows among managers and workers who are at the same organizational level

Hostile work environment
a form of sexual harassment in which unwelcome and demeaning sexually related behavior creates an intimidating and offensive work environment

Human resource management (HRM)
the process of finding, developing, and keeping the right people to form a qualified work force

Human skills
the ability to work well with others

Imperfectly imitable resource
a resource that is impossible or extremely costly or difficult for other firms to duplicate

Incremental change
the phase of a technology cycle in which companies innovate by lowering costs and improving the functioning and performance of the dominant technological design

Independent demand system
an inventory system in which the level of one kind of inventory does not depend on another

Individualism-collectivism
the degree to which a person believes that people should be self-sufficient and that loyalty to one's self is more important than loyalty to team or company

Industry regulation
regulations and rules that govern the business practices and procedures of specific industries, businesses, and professions

Industry-level strategy
a corporate strategy that addresses the question "How should we compete in this industry?"

Informal communication channel ("grapevine")
the transmission of messages from employee to employee outside of formal communication channels

Information
useful data that can influence people's choices and behavior

Initiating structure
the degree to which a leader structures the roles of followers by setting goals, giving directions, setting deadlines, and assigning tasks

Innovation streams
patterns of innovation over time that can create sustainable competitive advantage

Inputs
in equity theory, the contributions employees make to the organization

Instrumentality
the perceived relationship between performance and rewards

Intermittent reinforcement schedule
a schedule in which consequences are delivered after a specified or average time has elapsed or after a specified or average number of behaviors has occurred

Internal environment
the events and trends inside an organization that affect management, employees, and organizational culture

Internal motivation
motivation that comes from the job itself rather than from outside rewards

Internal recruiting
the process of developing a pool of qualified job applicants from people who already work in the company

Interorganizational process
a collection of activities that take place among companies to transform inputs into outputs that customers value

Interpersonal skills
skills, such as listening, communicating, questioning, and providing feedback, that enable people to have effective working relationships with others

Interviews
a selection tool in which company representatives ask job applicants job-related questions to determine whether they are qualified for the job

Intranets
private company networks that allow employees to easily access, share, and publish information using Internet software

Intraorganizational process
the collection of activities that take place within an organization to transform inputs into outputs that customers value

Intrinsic reward
a natural reward associated with performing a task or activity for its own sake

Inventory
the amount and number of raw materials, parts, and finished products that a company has in its possession

Inventory turnover
the number of times per year that a company sells or "turns over" its average inventory

ISO 14000
a series of international standards for managing, monitoring, and minimizing an organization's harmful effects on the environment

ISO 9000
a series of five international standards, from ISO 9000 to ISO 9004, for achieving consistency in quality management and quality assurance in companies throughout the world

Job analysis
a purposeful, systematic process for collecting information on the important work-related aspects of a job

Job characteristics model (JCM)
an approach to job redesign that seeks to formulate jobs in ways that motivate workers and lead to positive work outcomes

Job description
a written description of the basic tasks, duties, and responsibilities required of an employee holding a particular job

Job design
the number, kind, and variety of tasks that individual workers perform in doing their jobs

Job enlargement
increasing the number of different tasks that a worker performs within one particular job

Job enrichment
increasing the number of tasks in a particular job and giving workers the authority and control to make meaningful decisions about their work

Job evaluation
a process that determines the worth of each job in a company by evaluating the market value of the knowledge, skills, and requirements needed to perform it

Job rotation
periodically moving workers from one specialized job to another to give them more variety and the opportunity to use different skills

Job specialization
a job composed of a small part of a larger task or process

Job specifications
a written summary of the qualifications needed to successfully perform a particular job

Joint venture
a strategic alliance in which two existing companies collaborate to form a third, independent company

Just-in-time (JIT) inventory system
an inventory system in which component parts arrive from suppliers just as they are needed at each stage of production

Kanban
a ticket-based JIT system that indicates when to reorder inventory

Kinesics
movements of the body and face

Knowledge
the understanding that one gains from information

Leader role
the interpersonal role managers play when they motivate and encourage workers to accomplish organizational objectives

Leader-member relations
the degree to which followers respect, trust, and like their leaders

Leadership
the process of influencing others to achieve group or organizational goals

Leadership style
the way a leader generally behaves toward followers

Leading
inspiring and motivating workers to work hard to achieve organizational goals

Learning-based planning
learning better ways of achieving goals by continually testing, changing, and improving plans and strategies

Legal responsibility
a company's social responsibility to obey society's laws and regulations

Liaison role
the interpersonal role managers play when they deal with people outside their units

Licensing
an agreement in which a domestic company, the licensor, receives royalty payments for allowing another company, the licensee, to produce the licensor's product, sell its service, or use its brand name in a specified foreign market

Line authority
the right to command immediate subordinates in the chain of command

Line function
an activity that contributes directly to creating or selling the company's products

Listening
making a conscious effort to hear

Local adaptation
modifying rules, guidelines, policies, and procedures to adapt to differences in foreign customers, governments, and regulatory agencies

Magnitude of consequences
the total harm or benefit derived from an ethical decision

Make-to-order operation
a manufacturing operation that does not start processing or assembling products until a customer order is received

Make-to-stock operation
a manufacturing operation that orders parts and assembles standardized products before receiving customer orders

Management
getting work done through others

Management by objectives (MBO)
a four-step process in which managers and employees discuss and select goals, develop tactical plans, and meet regularly to review progress toward goal accomplishment

Market commonality
the degree to which two companies have overlapping products, services, or customers in multiple markets

Materials requirement planning (MRP)
a production and inventory system that determines the production schedule, production batch sizes, and inventory needed to complete final products

Matrix departmentalization
a hybrid organizational structure in which two or more forms of departmentalization, most often product and functional, are used together

Maximize
choosing the best alternative

Mechanistic organization
an organization characterized by specialized jobs and responsibilities; precisely defined, unchanging roles; and a rigid chain of command based on centralized authority and vertical communication

Media advocacy
an advocacy group tactic that involves framing issues as public issues; exposing questionable, exploitative, or unethical practices; and forcing media coverage by buying media time or creating controversy that is likely to receive extensive news coverage

Meta-analysis
a study of studies, a statistical approach that provides one of the best scientific estimates of how well management theories and practices work

Middle managers
responsible for setting objectives consistent with top management's goals and for planning and implementing subunit strategies for achieving these objectives

Milestones
formal project review points used to assess progress and performance

Modular organization
an organization that outsources noncore business activities to outside companies, suppliers, specialists, or consultants

Monitor role
the informational role managers play when they scan their environment for information

Monochronic cultures
cultures in which people tend to do one thing at a time and view time as linear

Moore's law
the prediction that about every 2 years, computer processing power would double and its cost would drop by 50 percent

Motivation
the set of forces that initiates, directs, and makes people persist in their efforts to accomplish a goal

Motivation to manage
an assessment of how enthusiastic employees are about managing the work of others

Multifactor productivity
an overall measure of performance that indicates how much labor, capital, materials, and energy it takes to produce an output

Multifunctional teams
work teams composed of people from different departments

Multinational corporation
a corporation that owns businesses in two or more countries

National culture
the set of shared values and beliefs that affects the perceptions, decisions, and behavior of the people from a particular country

Needs
the physical or psychological requirements that must be met to ensure survival and well-being

Negative reinforcement
reinforcement that strengthens behavior by withholding an unpleasant consequence when employees perform a specific behavior

Negotiator role
the decisional role managers play when they negotiate schedules, projects, goals, outcomes, resources, and employee raises

Neutral cultures
cultures in which people do not display emotions and feelings when communicating

Noise
anything that interferes with the transmission of the intended message

Nominal group technique
a decision-making method that begins and ends by having group members quietly write down and evaluate ideas to be shared with the group

Nonsubstitutable resource
a resource that produces value or competitive advantage and has no equivalent substitutes or replacements

Nontariff barriers
nontax methods of increasing the cost or reducing the volume of imported goods

Nonverbal communication
any communication that doesn't involve words

Normative control
the regulation of workers' behavior and decisions through widely shared organizational values and beliefs

Normative decision theory
a theory that suggests how leaders can determine an appropriate amount of employee participation when making decisions

Norming
the third stage of development, in which team members begin to settle into their roles, group cohesion grows, and positive team norms develop

Norms
informally agreed-on standards that regulate team behavior

North American Free Trade Agreement (NAFTA)
a regional trade agreement between the United States, Canada, and Mexico

Objective control
the use of observable measures of worker behavior or outputs to assess performance and influence behavior

Objective performance measures
measures of job performance that are easily and directly counted or quantified

Online discussion forums
the in-house equivalent of Internet newsgroups. By using web- or software-based discussion tools that are available across the company, employees can easily ask questions and share knowledge with each other.

Open office systems
offices in which the physical barriers that separate workers have been removed in order to increase communication and interaction

Operational plans
day-to-day plans, developed and implemented by lower-level managers, for producing or delivering the organization's products and services over a 30-day to six-month period

Operations management
managing the daily production of goods and services

Opportunistic behavior
a transaction in which one party in the relationship benefits at the expense of the other

Optical character recognition
the ability of software to convert digitized documents into ASCII text (American Standard Code for Information Interchange) that can be searched, read, and edited by word processing and other kinds of software

Options-based planning
maintaining planning flexibility by making small, simultaneous investments in many alternative plans

Ordering cost
the costs associated with ordering inventory, including the cost of data entry, phone calls, obtaining bids, correcting mistakes, and determining when and how much inventory to order

Organic organization
an organization characterized by broadly defined jobs and responsibility; loosely defined, frequently changing roles; and decentralized authority and horizontal communication based on task knowledge

Organizational change
a difference in the form, quality, or condition of an organization over time

Organizational culture
the values, beliefs, and attitudes shared by organizational members

Organizational development
a philosophy and collection of planned change interventions designed to improve an organization's long-term health and performance

Organizational heroes
people celebrated for their qualities and achievements within an organization

Organizational innovation
the successful implementation of creative ideas in organizations

Organizational process
the collection of activities that transform inputs into outputs that customers value

Organizational silence
when employees withhold information about organizational problems or issues

Organizational stories
stories told by organizational members to make sense of organizational events and changes and to emphasize culturally consistent assumptions, decisions, and actions

Organizational structure
the vertical and horizontal configuration of departments, authority, and jobs within a company

Organizing
deciding where decisions will be made, who will do what jobs and tasks, and who will work for whom

Outcome/input (O/I) ratio
in equity theory, an employee's perception of how the rewards received from an organization compare with the employee's contributions to that organization

Outcomes
in equity theory, the rewards employees receive for their contributions to the organization

Outplacement services
employment-counseling services offered to employees who are losing their jobs because of downsizing

Output control
the regulation of workers' results or outputs through rewards and incentives

Overreward
a form of inequity in which you are getting more outcomes relative to inputs than your referent

Overt integrity test
a written test that estimates job applicants' honesty by directly asking them what they think or feel about theft or about punishment of unethical behaviors

Paralanguage
the pitch, rate, tone, volume, and speaking pattern (i.e., use of silences, pauses, or hesitations) of one's voice

Partial productivity
a measure of performance that indicates how much of a particular kind of input it takes to produce an output

Participative leadership
a leadership style in which the leader consults employees for their suggestions and input before making decisions

Path-goal theory
a leadership theory that states that leaders can increase subordinate satisfaction and performance by clarifying and clearing the paths to goals and by increasing the number and kinds of rewards available for goal attainment

Perception
the process by which individuals attend to, organize, interpret, and retain information from their environments

Perceptual filters
the personality-, psychology-, or experience-based differences that influence people to ignore or pay attention to particular stimuli

Performance appraisal
the process of assessing how well employees are doing their jobs

Performance feedback
information about the quality or quantity of past performance that indicates whether progress is being made toward the accomplishment of a goal

Performing
the fourth and final stage of team development, in which performance improves because the team has matured into an effective, fully functioning team

Personality-based integrity test
a written test that indirectly estimates job applicants' honesty by measuring psychological traits, such as dependability and conscientiousness

Personality tests
tests that measure the extent to which applicants possess different kinds of job-related personality dimensions

Piecework
a compensation system in which employees are paid a set rate for each item they produce

Planning
choosing a goal and developing a strategy to achieve that goal; determining organizational goals and a means for achieving them

Policies
a standing plan that indicates the general course of action that should be taken in response to a particular event or situation

Policy uncertainty
the risk associated with changes in laws and government policies that directly affect the way foreign companies conduct business

Political uncertainty
the risk of major changes in political regimes that can result from war, revolution, death of political leaders, social unrest, or other influential events

Polychronic cultures
cultures in which people tend to do more than one thing at a time and view time as circular

Pooled interdependence
work completed by having each job or department independently contribute to the whole

Portfolio strategy
a corporate-level strategy that minimizes risk by diversifying investment among various businesses or product lines

Position power
the degree to which leaders are able to hire, fire, reward, and punish workers

Positive reinforcement
reinforcement that strengthens behavior by following behaviors with desirable consequences

Postconventional level of moral development
the third level of moral development, in which people make decisions based on internalized principles

Preconventional level of moral development
the first level of moral development, in which people make decisions based on selfish reasons

Predictive patterns
patterns that help identify database elements that are different

Primary stakeholder
any group on which an organization relies for its long-term survival

Private spaces
spaces used by and open to just one employee

Proactive strategy
a social responsiveness strategy in which a company anticipates responsibility for a problem before it occurs and does more than society expects to address the problem

Probability of effect
the chance that something will happen and then harm others

Problem
a gap between a desired state and an existing state

Procedural justice
the perceived fairness of the process used to make reward allocation decisions

Procedures
a standing plan that indicates the specific steps that should be taken in response to a particular event

Processing information
transforming raw data into meaningful information

Product boycott
an advocacy group tactic that involves protesting a company's actions by persuading consumers not to purchase its product or service

Product departmentalization
organizing work and workers into separate units responsible for producing particular products or services

Product prototype
a full-scale working model that is being tested for design, function, and reliability

Production blocking
a disadvantage of face-to-face brainstorming in which a group member must wait to share an idea because another member is presenting an idea

Productivity
a measure of performance that indicates how many inputs it takes to produce or create an output

Profit sharing
a compensation system in which a company pays a percentage of its profits to employees in addition to their regular compensation

Project team
a team created to complete specific, one-time projects or tasks within a limited time

Prospectors
companies using an adaptive strategy that seeks fast growth by searching for new market opportunities, encouraging risk taking, and being the first to bring innovative new products to market

Protecting information
the process of ensuring that data are reliably and consistently retrievable in a usable format for authorized users, but no one else

Protectionism
a government's use of trade barriers to shield domestic companies and their workers from foreign competition

Proximal goals
short-term goals or subgoals

Proximity of effect
the social, psychological, cultural, or physical distance between a decision maker and those affected by his or her decisions

Public communications
an advocacy group tactic that relies on voluntary participation by the news media and the advertising industry to get the advocacy group's message out

Punctuated equilibrium theory
the theory that companies go through long periods of stability (equilibrium), followed by short periods of dynamic, fundamental change (revolution), and finishing with a return to stability (new equilibrium)

Punishment
reinforcement that weakens behavior by following behaviors with undesirable consequences

Purchasing power
the relative cost of a standard set of goods and services in different countries

Purpose statement
a statement of a company's purpose or reason for existing

Quality
a product or service free of deficiencies, or the characteristics of a product or service that satisfy customer needs

Question mark
a company with a small share of a fast-growing market

Quid pro quo sexual harassment
a form of sexual harassment in which employment outcomes, such as hiring, promotion, or simply keeping one's job, depend on whether an individual submits to sexual harassment

Quota
a limit on the number or volume of imported products

Radio frequency identification (RFID) tags
tags containing minuscule microchips that transmit information via radio waves and can be used to track the number and location for the objects into which the tags have been inserted

Rare resource
a resource that is not controlled or possessed by many competing firms

Rater training
training performance appraisal raters in how to avoid rating errors and increase rating accuracy

Rational decision making
a systematic process of defining problems, evaluating alternatives, and choosing optimal solutions

Raw data
facts and figures

Raw material inventories
the basic inputs in a manufacturing process

Reactive strategy
a social responsiveness strategy in which a company does less than society expects

Reactors
companies using an adaptive strategy of not following a consistent strategy, but instead reacting to changes in the external environment after they occur

Reciprocal interdependence
work completed by different jobs or groups working together in a back-and-forth manner

Recovery
the strategic actions taken after retrenchment to return to a growth strategy

Recruiting
the process of developing a pool of qualified job applicants

Reengineering
fundamental rethinking and radical redesign of business processes to achieve dramatic improvements in critical measures of performance, such as cost, quality, service, and speed

Referents
in equity theory, others with whom people compare themselves to determine if they have been treated fairly

Refreezing
supporting and reinforcing new changes so that they "stick"

Regional trading zones
areas in which tariff and nontariff barriers on trade between countries are reduced or eliminated

Regulation standards
the costs associated with implementing or maintaining control

Reinforcement
the process of changing behavior by changing the consequences that follow behavior

Reinforcement contingencies
cause-and-effect relationships between the performance of specific behaviors and specific consequences

Reinforcement theory
the theory that behavior is a function of its consequences, that behaviors followed by positive consequences will occur more frequently, and that behaviors followed by negative consequences, or not followed by positive consequences, will occur less frequently

Related diversification
creating or acquiring companies that share similar products, manufacturing, marketing, technology, or cultures

Relationship behavior
the establishment of mutually beneficial, long-term exchanges between buyers and suppliers

Relative comparisons
a process in which each decision criterion is compared directly with every other criterion

Resistance forces
forces that support the existing state of conditions in organizations

Resistance to change
opposition to change resulting from self-interest, misunderstanding and distrust, or a general intolerance for change

Resource allocator role
the decisional role managers play when they decide who gets what resources

Resource scarcity
the abundance or shortage of critical organizational resources in an organization's external environment

Resource similarity
the extent to which a competitor has similar amounts and kinds of resources

Resources
the assets, capabilities, processes, employee time, information, and knowledge that an organization uses to improve its effectiveness and efficiency, create and sustain competitive advantage, and fulfill a need or solve a problem

Response
a competitive countermove, prompted by a rival's attack, to defend or improve a company's market share or profit

Results-driven change
change created quickly by focusing on the measurement and improvement of results

Retrenchment strategy
a strategy that focuses on turning around very poor company performance by shrinking the size or scope of the business

Rules and regulations
standing plans that describe how a particular action should be performed, or what must happen or not happen in response to a particular event

S

S.M.A.R.T. goals
goals that are specific, measurable, attainable, realistic, and timely

Satisficing
choosing a "good enough" alternative

Schedule of reinforcement
rules that specify which behaviors will be reinforced, which consequences will follow those behaviors, and the schedule by which those consequences will be delivered

Schedule time
a cultural norm for the time by which scheduled projects or jobs should actually be completed

S-curve pattern of innovation
a pattern of technological innovation characterized by slow initial progress, then rapid progress, and then slow progress again as a technology matures and reaches its limits

Secondary firms
the firms in a strategic group that follow strategies related to but somewhat different from those of the core firms

Secondary stakeholder
any group that can influence or be influenced by a company and can affect public perceptions about the company's socially responsible behavior

Secure sockets layer (SSL) encryption
internet browser-based encryption that provides secure off-site web access to some data and programs

Selection
the process of gathering information about job applicants to decide who should be offered a job

Selective perception
the tendency to notice and accept objects and information consistent with our values, beliefs, and expectations, while ignoring or screening out or not accepting inconsistent information

Self-control (self-management)
a control system in which managers and workers control their own behavior by setting their own goals, monitoring their own progress, and rewarding themselves for goal achievements

Self-designing team
a team that has the characteristics of self-managing teams but also controls team design, work tasks, and team membership

Self-managing team
a team that manages and controls all of the major tasks of producing a product or service

Self-serving bias
the tendency to overestimate our value by attributing successes to ourselves (internal causes) and attributing failures to others or the environment (external causes)

Semiautonomous work group
a group that has the authority to make decisions and solve problems related to the major tasks of producing a product or service

Sequence patterns
when two or more database elements occur together in a significant pattern, but one of the elements precedes the other

Sequential interdependence
work completed in succession, with one group's or job's outputs becoming the inputs for the next group or job

Service recovery
restoring customer satisfaction to strongly dissatisfied customers

Setup cost
the costs of downtime and lost efficiency that occur when a machine is changed or adjusted to produce a different kind of inventory

Sexual harassment
a form of discrimination in which unwelcome sexual advances, requests for sexual favors, or other verbal or physical conduct of a sexual nature occurs while performing one's job

Shared spaces
spaces used by and open to all employees

Shareholder model
a view of social responsibility that holds that an organization's overriding goal should be profit maximization for the benefit of shareholders

Simple environment
an environment with few environmental factors

Simple matrix
a form of matrix departmentalization in which managers in different parts of the matrix negotiate conflicts and resources

Single-use plans
plans that cover unique, one-time-only events

Situational (SWOT) analysis
an assessment of the strengths and weaknesses in an organization's internal environment and the opportunities and threats in its external environment

Situational favorableness
the degree to which a particular situation either permits or denies a leader the chance to influence the behavior of group members

Situational theory
a leadership theory that states that leaders need to adjust their leadership styles to match their followers' readiness

Skill variety
the number of different activities performed in a job

Skill-based pay
compensation system that pays employees for learning additional skills or knowledge

Slack resources
a cushion of extra resources that can be used with options-based planning to adapt to unanticipated change, problems, or opportunities

Social consensus
agreement on whether behavior is bad or good

Social loafing
behavior in which team members withhold their efforts and fail to perform their share of the work

Social responsibility
a business's obligation to pursue policies, make decisions, and take actions that benefit society

Social responsiveness
refers to a company's strategy to respond to stakeholders' economic, legal, ethical, or

discretionary expectations concerning social responsibility

Specificability tests (aptitude tests)
tests that measure the extent to which an applicant possesses the particular kind of ability needed to do a job well

Specific environment
the customers, competitors, suppliers, industry regulations, and advocacy groups that are unique to an industry and directly affect how a company does business

Spokesperson role
the informational role managers play when they share information with people outside their departments or companies

Stability strategy
a strategy that focuses on improving the way in which the company sells the same products or services to the same customers

Stable environment
an environment in which the rate of change is slow

Staff authority
the right to advise, but not command, others who are not subordinates in the chain of command

Staff function
an activity that does not contribute directly to creating or selling the company's products, but instead supports line activities

Stakeholder model
a theory of corporate responsibility that holds that management's most important responsibility, long-term survival, is achieved by satisfying the interests of multiple corporate stakeholders

Stakeholders
persons or groups with a "stake" or legitimate interest in a company's actions

Standardization
solving problems by consistently applying the same rules, procedures, and processes

Standards
a basis of comparison for measuring the extent to which various kinds of organizational performance are satisfactory or unsatisfactory

Standing plans
plans used repeatedly to handle frequently recurring events

Star
a company with a large share of a fast-growing market

Stepladder technique
a decision-making method in which group members are added to a group discussion one at a time (like a stepladder). The existing group members listen to each new member's thoughts, ideas, and recommendations; then the group shares the ideas and suggestions that it had already considered, discusses the new and old ideas, and makes a decision

Stock options
a compensation system that gives employees the right to purchase shares of stock at a set price, even if the value of the stock increases above that rate

Stockout
the point when a company runs out of finished product

Stockout costs
the costs incurred when a company runs out of a product, including transaction costs to replace inventory and the loss of customers' goodwill

Storming
the second stage of development, characterized by conflict and disagreement, in which team members disagree over what the team should do and how it should do it

Strategic alliance
an agreement in which companies combine key resources, costs, risk, technology, and people

Strategic dissonance
a discrepancy between a company's intended strategy and the strategic actions managers take when implementing that strategy

Strategic group
a group of companies within an industry against which top managers compare, evaluate, and benchmark strategic threats and opportunities

Strategic leadership
the ability to anticipate, envision, maintain flexibility, think strategically, and work with others to initiate changes that will create a positive future for an organization

Strategic objective
a more specific goal that unifies company-wide efforts, stretches and challenges the organization, and possesses a finish line and a time frame

Strategic plans
overall company plans that clarify how the company will serve customers and position itself against competitors over the next two to five years

Strategic reference points
the strategic targets managers use to measure whether a firm has developed the core competencies it needs to achieve a sustainable competitive advantage

Structural accommodation
the ability to change organizational structures, policies, and practices in order to meet stretch goals

Structural interviews
interviews in which all applicants are asked the same set of standardized questions, usually including situational, behavioral, background, and job-knowledge questions

Subjective performance measures
measures of job performance that require someone to judge or assess a worker's performance

Suboptimization
performance improvement in one part of an organization but only at the expense of decreased performance in another part

Subsidies
government loans, grants, and tax deferments given to domestic companies to protect them from foreign competition

Supervised data mining
the process when the user tells the data mining software to look and test for specific patterns and relationships in a data set

Supplier dependence
the degree to which a company relies on a supplier because of the importance of the supplier's product to the company and the difficulty of finding other sources of that product

Suppliers
companies that provide material, human, financial, and informational resources to other companies

Supportive leadership
a leadership style in which the leader is friendly to and approachable, shows concern for employees and their welfare, treats them as equals, and creates a friendly climate

Survey feedback
information that is collected by surveys from organizational members and then compiled, disseminated, and used to develop action plans for improvement

Sustainable competitive advantage
a competitive advantage that other companies have tried unsuccessfully to duplicate and have, for the moment, stopped trying to duplicate

Tactical plans
plans created and implemented by middle managers that specify how the company will use resources, budgets, and people over the next six months to two years to accomplish specific goals within its mission

Tariff
a direct tax on imported goods

Task identity
the degree to which a job, from beginning to end, requires the completion of a whole and identifiable piece of work

Task interdependence
the extent to which collective action is required to complete an entire piece of work

Task significance
the degree to which a job is perceived to have a substantial impact on others inside or outside the organization

Task structure
the degree to which the requirements of a subordinate's tasks are clearly specified

Team diversity
the variances or differences in ability, experience, personality, or any other factor on a team

Team leaders
managers responsible for facilitating team activities toward goal accomplishment

Team level
the average level of ability, experience, personality, or any other factor on a team

Teamwork
collaboration between managers and nonmanagers, across business functions, and between companies, customers, and suppliers

Technical skills
the ability to apply the specialized procedures, techniques, and knowledge required to get the job done

Technological discontinuity
the phase of an innovation stream in which a scientific advance or unique combination of existing technologies creates a significant breakthrough in performance or function

Technological lockout
the inability of a company to competitively sell its products because it relied on old technology or a nondominant design

Technological substitution
the purchase of new technologies to replace older ones

Technology
the knowledge, tools, and techniques used to transform input into output

Technology cycle
a cycle that begins with the "birth" of a new technology and ends when that technology reaches its limits and is replaced by a newer, substantially better technology

Televised/videotaped speeches and meetings
speeches and meetings originally made to a smaller audience that are either simultaneously broadcast to other locations in the company or videotaped for subsequent distribution and viewing

Temporal immediacy
the time between an act and the consequences the act produces

Testing
the systematic comparison of different product designs or design iterations

Threat of new entrants
a measure of the degree to which barriers to entry make it easy or difficult for new companies to get started in an industry

Threat of substitute products or services
a measure of the ease with which customers can find substitutes for an industry's products or services

Top managers
executives responsible for the overall direction of the organization

Total quality management (TQM)
an integrated, principle-based, organization-wide strategy for improving product and service quality

Trade barriers
government-imposed regulations that increase the cost and restrict the number of imported goods

Traditional work group
a group composed of two or more people who work together to achieve a shared goal

Training
developing the skills, experience, and knowledge employees need to perform their jobs or improve their performance

Trait theory
a leadership theory that holds that effective leaders possess a similar set of traits or characteristics

Traits
relatively stable characteristics, such as abilities, psychological motives, or consistent patterns of behavior

Transactional leadership
leadership based on an exchange process, in which followers are rewarded for good performance and punished for poor performance

Transformational leadership
leadership that generates awareness and acceptance of a group's purpose and mission and gets employees to see beyond their own needs and self-interests for the good of the group

Transition management team (TMT)
a team of 8 to 12 people whose full-time job is to manage and coordinate a company's change process

Two-factor authentication
authentication based on what users know, such as a password and what they have in their possession, such as a secure ID card or key

Uncertainty
extent to which managers can understand or predict which environmental changes and trends affect their businesses

Underreward
a form of inequity in which you are getting fewer outcomes relative to inputs than your referent is getting

Unethical charismatics
charismatic leaders who control and manipulate followers, do what is best for themselves

instead of their organizations, want to hear only positive feedback, share only information that is beneficial to themselves, and have moral standards that put their interests before everyone else's

Unfreezing
getting the people affected by change to believe that change is needed

Unity of command
a management principle that workers should report to just one boss

Unrelated diversification
creating or acquiring companies in completely unrelated businesses

Unstructured interviews
interviews in which interviewers are free to ask the applicants anything they want

Unsupervised data mining
the process when the user simply tells the data mining software to uncover whatever patterns and relationships it can find in a data set

Upward communication
communication that flows from lower to higher levels in an organization

Valence
the attractiveness or desirability of a reward or outcome

Validation
the process of determining how well a selection test or procedure predicts future job performance. The better or more accurate the prediction of future job performance, the more valid a test is said to be

Valuable resource
a resource that allows companies to improve efficiency and effectiveness

Value
customer perception that the product quality is excellent for the price offered

Variable interval reinforcement schedules
an intermittent schedule in which the time between a behavior and the following consequences varies around a specified average

Variable ratio reinforcement schedule
an intermittent schedule in which consequences are delivered following a different number of behaviors, sometimes more and sometimes less, that vary around a specified average number of behaviors

Variation
a deviation in the form, condition, or appearance of a product from the quality standard for that product

Virtual organization
an organization that is part of a network in which many companies share skills, costs, capabilities, markets, and customers to collectively solve customer problems or provide specific products or services

Virtual private network (VPN)
software that securely encrypts data sent by employees outside the company network, decrypts the data when they arrive within the company computer network, and does the same when data are sent back to employees outside the network

Virtual team
a team composed of geographically and/or organizationally dispersed coworkers who use telecommunication and information technologies to accomplish an organizational task

Virus
a program or piece of code that, without your knowledge, attaches itself to other programs on your computer and can trigger anything from a harmless flashing message to the reformatting of your hard drive to a systemwide network shutdown

Visible artifacts
visible signs of an organization's culture, such as the office design and layout, company dress code, and company benefits and perks, like stock options, personal parking spaces, or the private company dining room

Visionary leadership
leadership that creates a positive image of the future that motivates organizational members and provides direction for future planning and goal setting

Voluntary export restraints
voluntarily imposed limits on the number or volume of products exported to a particular country

Web services
using standardized protocols to describe data from one company in such a way that those data can automatically be read, understood, transcribed, and processed by different computer systems in another company

Whistleblowing
reporting others' ethics violations to management or legal authorities

Wholly owned affiliates
foreign offices, facilities, and manufacturing plants that are 100 percent owned by the parent company

Work sample tests
tests that require applicants to perform tasks that are actually done on the job

Work team
a small number of people with complementary skills who hold themselves mutually accountable for pursuing a common purpose, achieving performance goals, and improving interdependent work processes

Worker readiness
the ability and willingness to take responsibility for directing one's behavior at work

Work-in-process inventories
partially finished goods consisting of assembled component parts

World Trade Organization (WTO)
the successor to GATT; the only international organization dealing with the global rules of trade between nations. Its main function is to ensure that trade flows as smoothly, predictably, and freely as possible

Wrongful discharge
a legal doctrine that requires employers to have a job-related reason to terminate employees

Name Index

C

G

H

M

N

S

X

Y

Z

Subject Index

A

B

C

D

E

F

G

H

I

J

K

L

M

N

O

P

Q

R

S

T

U

V

W